THE OXFORD HANDBOOK OF

ECONOMICS AND HUMAN BIOLOGY

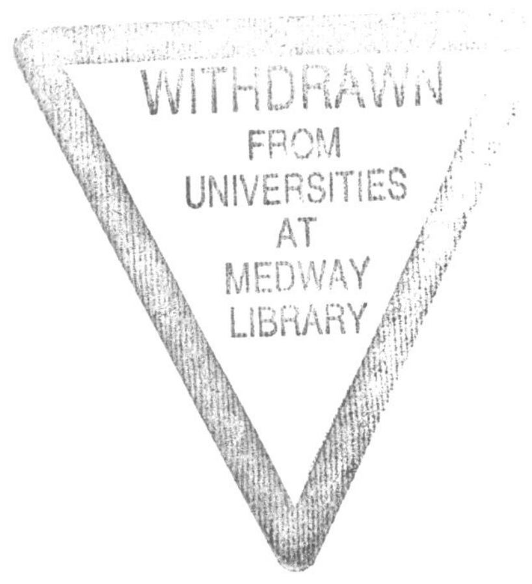
WITHDRAWN
FROM
UNIVERSITIES
AT
MEDWAY
LIBRARY

THE OXFORD HANDBOOK OF

ECONOMICS AND HUMAN BIOLOGY

Edited by

JOHN KOMLOS

and

INAS R. KELLY

OXFORD
UNIVERSITY PRESS

Oxford University Press is a department of the University of Oxford. It furthers the University's objective of excellence in research, scholarship, and education by publishing worldwide. Oxford is a registered trade mark of Oxford University Press in the UK and certain other countries.

Published in the United States of America by Oxford University Press
198 Madison Avenue, New York, NY 10016, United States of America.

Library of Congress Cataloging-in-Publication Data
Names: Komlos, John, 1944— , editor. | Kelly, Inas Rashad, editor.
Title: The Oxford handbook of economics and human biology / edited by John Komlos and Inas R. Kelly.
Other titles: Economics and human biology
Description: Oxford; New York : Oxford University Press, [2016] | Includes bibliographical references and index.
Identifiers: LCCN 2015039703 | ISBN 978-0-19-938929-2 (alk. paper)
Subjects: | MESH: Biological Phenomena. | Body Weights and Measures—economics. | Economics, Medical. | Socioeconomic Factors.
Classification: LCC QH307.2 | NLM QH 307.2 | DDC 338.4/757—dc23
LC record available at http://lccn.loc.gov/2015039703

1 3 5 7 9 8 6 4 2
Printed by Sheridan, USA

CONTENTS

About the Editors ix
List of Contributors xi

PART I INTRODUCTION TO ECONOMICS AND HUMAN BIOLOGY

Introduction 3
INAS R. KELLY AND JOHN KOMLOS

1. Growth Faltering in the First Thousand Days after Conception and Catch-up Growth 9
JERE R. BEHRMAN

2. Biological Measures of Well-Being 32
RICHARD H. STECKEL

3. Crisis and Human Biology 52
PRASHANT BHARADWAJ AND TOM S. VOGL

4. The Biological Standard of Living in Europe from the Late Iron Age to the Little Ice Age 70
NIKOLA KOEPKE

5. Econometrics of Economics and Human Biology 109
GREGORY COLMAN AND DHAVAL DAVE

PART II BIOLOGICAL MEASURES AS AN OUTCOME

6. Body Mass Index Through Time : Explanations, Evidence, and Future Directions 133
SCOTT A. CARSON

7. Health, Body Weight, and Obesity 152
DARIUS N. LAKDAWALLA AND JULIAN REIF

8. Inequality and Heights 179
MATTHIAS BLUM

9. Adult Weight and Height of Native Populations 192
ASHER ROSINGER AND RICARDO GODOY

10. Slave Heights 210
RICHARD H. STECKEL

11. Female Heights and Economic Development: Theory and Evidence 226
DEBORAH OXLEY

12. The Impact of Socioeconomic Inequality on Children's Health and Well-Being 244
BALTICA CABIESES, KATE E. PICKETT, AND RICHARD G. WILKINSON

13. Growth and Maturation of Children and Adolescents: Variability Due to Genetic and Environmental Factors 266
ALAN D. ROGOL

14. Global Perspectives on Economics and Biology 276
NICHOLAS J. MEINZER AND JÖRG BATEN

15. Global BMI Trends 296
KATRIN KROMEYER-HAUSCHILD, ANJA MOSS, AND MARTIN WABITSCH

16. Poverty and Obesity in Developed Countries 317
CHAD D. MEYERHOEFER AND MUZHE YANG

PART III BIOLOGICAL MEASURES AS AN INPUT TO MONETARY OUTCOMES, PRODUCTIVITY, AND WELFARE

17. Biomarkers as Inputs 337
STEPHEN F. LEHRER

18. How Genetics Can Inform Health Economics 366
GEORGE L. WEHBY

19. Twins Studies in Economics 385
JERE R. BEHRMAN

20. Public and Private Returns to Investing in Nutrition 405
HAROLD ALDERMAN AND DAVID E. SAHN

21. The Double Burden of Malnutrition 434
SUSAN L. AVERETT AND YANG WANG

22. Biological Health Risks and Economic Development 454
ELIZABETH FRANKENBERG, JESSICA Y. HO, AND DUNCAN THOMAS

23. Obesity and Income Inequality in OECD Countries 485
DEJUN SU

24. Height and Wages 501
OLAF HÜBLER

25. Why Do People with Higher Body Weight Earn Lower Wages? 521
JANE GREVE

26. Wealth and Weight 543
JAY L. ZAGORSKY

27. Family Economics and Obesity 564
SVEN E. WILSON

28. Obesity and Welfare Regimes 583
AVNER OFFER

29. Children's Anthropometrics and Later Disease Incidence 604
KARRI SILVENTOINEN

30. Birth Weight as an Indicator of Human Welfare 621
W. PETER WARD

31. A Pound of Flesh: The Use of Birthweight as a Measure of Human Capital Endowment in Economics Research 632
FLORENCIA TORCHE AND DALTON CONLEY

32. Neuroeconomics: A Flourishing Field 650
JASON A. AIMONE AND DANIEL HOUSER

PART IV REGIONAL STUDIES

33. The African Enigma: The Mystery of Tall African Adults Despite Low National Incomes Revisited 669
ALEXANDER MORADI AND KALLE HIRVONEN

34. East Asia on the Rise: The Anthropometric History of China, Japan, and Korea 693
DANIEL JONG SCHWEKENDIEK

35. Economics and Human Biology in Latin America 710
MORAMAY LÓPEZ-ALONSO

36. Racial Differences in Health in the United States: A Long-Run Perspective 730
LEAH PLATT BOUSTAN AND ROBERT A. MARGO

37. Antebellum Puzzle: The Decline in Heights at the Onset of Modern Economic Growth 751
LEE A. CRAIG

38. The Anthropometric History of the Mediterranean World 765
BRIAN A'HEARN

Index 797

About the Editors

John Komlos is Professor Emeritus of Economics and Economic History at the University of Munich. He has also taught at Duke University, Harvard University, the University of North Carolina at Chapel Hill, and the University of Vienna. He received PhDs in both history and economics from the University of Chicago. Komlos founded the field of Economics and Human Biology with the journal of the same name in 2003. He is among the very few scholars to publish in major journals of five disciplines: economics, history, biology, statistics, and demography. His work has been cited extensively around the globe.

Inas R. Kelly is Associate Professor of Economics at Queens College and the City University of New York Graduate Center. She is a research associate in the Health Economics program at the National Bureau of Economic Research (NBER) and has been co-editor of the journal *Economics and Human Biology* since January 2013. She has published extensively in the field of health economics.

Contributors

Brian A'Hearn is a Fellow and Tutor in Economics, Pembroke College, University of Oxford.

Jason A. Aimone is an assistant professor of economics at the Hankamer School of Business, Baylor University.

Harold Alderman is Social Protection Advisor, Africa Region at the World Bank.

Susan L. Averett is the Charles A. Dana Professor of Economics in the Department of Economics at Lafayette College in Easton, Pennsylvania.

Jörg Baten is a professor of economic history in the Department of Economics and Social Sciences, University of Tuebingen, and co-editor of *Economics and Human Biology*.

Jere R. Behrman is the William R. Kenan Jr. Professor of Economics at the University of Pennsylvania.

Prashant Bharadwaj is an associate professor of economics at the University of California, San Diego.

Matthias Blum is a lecturer in economics at Queen's University Belfast Management School.

Leah Platt Boustan is an associate professor of economics at the University of California at Los Angeles (UCLA) and a research associate at the National Bureau of Economic Research (NBER).

Baltica Cabieses is a senior lecturer in the faculty of medicine, Universidad del Desarrollo - Clínica Alemana, Chile.

Scott A. Carson is a professor of economics in the College of Business and Engineering, University of Texas, Permian Basin.

Gregory Colman is an associate professor in the Department of Economics, Pace University, and a research economist of the National Bureau of Economic Research (NBER).

Dalton Conley is Dean of Social Sciences and University Professor of the Social Sciences at New York University.

Lee A. Craig is Department Head, Alumni Distinguished Undergraduate Professor in the Department of Economics, North Carolina State University.

Dhaval Dave is the Stanton Research Professor in the Department of Economics, Bentley University, and a research associate at the National Bureau of Economic Research (NBER).

Elizabeth Frankenberg is a professor in the Sanford School of Public Policy, Duke University.

Ricardo Godoy is a professor of International Development, Brandeis University.

Jane Greve is a senior researcher at KORA, the Danish Institute for Local and Regional Governmental Research.

Kalle Hirvonen is an associate research fellow at the International Food Policy Institute.

Jessica Y. Ho is a research scientist in the Sanford School of Public Policy and the Population Research Institute (DuPRI) at Duke University.

Daniel Houser is Chairman and Professor in the Department of Economics and is Director of the Interdisciplinary Center for Economic Science at George Mason University.

Olaf Hübler is Professor Emeritus of Econometrics at the Institute for Empirical Economics at the Leibniz University of Hannover.

Inas R. Kelly is an associate professor of economics at Queens College of the City University of New York, a research associate of the National Bureau of Economic Research (NBER), and co-editor of *Economics and Human Biology*.

Nikola Koepke is a researcher at the University of Barcelona.

John Komlos is Professor Emeritus at the University of Munich, a research associate at the National Bureau of Economic Research (NBER), and the founding editor of *Economics and Human Biology*.

Katrin Kromeyer-Hauschild is the Head of the Anthropology Working Group at the Institute of Human Genetics at the University Hospital of the Friedrich-Schiller-University, Jena.

Darius N. Lakdawalla is Associate Professor in the University of Southern California School of Policy, Planning, and Development, and is Director of Research at the USC Schaeffer Center for Health Policy and Economics.

Stephen F. Lehrer is an associate professor of economics at NYU Shanghai and is Associate Professor, School of Policy Studies and Department of Economics, Queen's University (Canada).

Moramay López-Alonso is an associate professor of history at Rice University.

Robert A. Margo is a professor of economics in the Department of Economics, Boston University, and a research associate of the National Bureau of Economic Research (NBER).

Nicholas J. Meinzer is a research assistant at Eberhard Karls, Universität Tübingen.

Chad D. Meyerhoefer is an associate professor of economics, Lehigh University, and a research associate of the National Bureau of Economic Research (NBER).

Alexander Moradi is a senior lecturer in economics at the University of Sussex.

Anja Moss is a research associate and study coordinator in the Division of Pediatric Endocrinology and Diabetes, Interdisciplinary Obesity Unit, at the Department of Pediatrics and Adolescent Medicine at Ulm University.

Avner Offer is Chichele Professor of Economic History, University of Oxford, and a Fellow of All Souls College, Emeritus.

Deborah Oxley is Professor of Social Science History, a Fellow of All Souls College, Oxford University, and a Leverhulme Major Research Fellow.

Kate E. Pickett is a professor of epidemiology, Department of Health Sciences, University of York, England.

Julian Reif is an assistant professor of finance and economics in the College of Business and the Institute of Government and Public Affairs (IGPA) at the University of Illinois at Urbana-Champaign.

Alan D. Rogol is Professor Emeritus (Pediatrics and Pharmacology) at the University of Virginia.

Asher Rosinger holds a PhD and an MPH from the University of Georgia.

David E. Sahn is the International Professor of Economics and Director, Cornell University Food and Nutrition Policy Program (CFNPP), Division of Nutritional Sciences and Department of Economics, Cornell University, and an IZA Research Fellow.

Daniel Jong Schwekendiek is an associate professor of East Asian Studies, Sungkyunkwan University.

Karri Silventoinen is Senior Lecturer in Demography, Department of Social Research, University of Helsinki.

Richard H. Steckel is SBS Distinguished Professor of Economics, Anthropology, and History at the Ohio State University and a research associate with the National Bureau of Economic Research (NBER).

Dejun Su is an associate professor in the Department of Health Promotion, Social and Behavioral Health and is Director, Center for Reducing Health Disparities College of Public Health, University of Nebraska Medical Center.

Duncan Thomas is the Norb F. Schaefer Professor of International Studies; Professor of Economics, Global Health and Public Policy in the Department of Economics, Duke University; and Development Program Director at the National Bureau of Economic Research (NBER).

Florencia Torche is a professor of sociology at New York University.

Tom S. Vogl is Assistant Professor of Economics and International Affairs, Princeton University; a Faculty Research Fellow, National Bureau of Economic Research (NBER); and a faculty affiliate, Bureau for the Economic Analysis of Development (BREAD).

Martin Wabitsch is the head of the Division of Pediatric Endocrinology and Diabetes, Interdisciplinary Obesity Unit at the Department of Pediatrics and Adolescent Medicine at Ulm University.

Yang Wang is an assistant professor of economics at Lafayette College.

W. Peter Ward is Professor of History Emeritus at the University of British Columbia.

George L. Wehby is an associate professor at the University of Iowa College of Public Health and is a research associate with the National Bureau of Economic Research (NBER).

Richard G. Wilkinson is Emeritus Professor of Social Epidemiology, Division of Epidemiology and Public Health, University of Nottingham, England.

Sven E. Wilson is a professor of political science and an adjunct professor, Department of Economics, Brigham Young University, and Research Economist, National Bureau of Economic Research (NBER).

Muzhe Yang is an associate professor, Department of Economics, Lehigh University.

Jay L. Zagorsky is an economist and a research scientist at Ohio State University.

PART I

INTRODUCTION TO ECONOMICS AND HUMAN BIOLOGY

INTRODUCTION

INAS R. KELLY AND JOHN KOMLOS

The *Oxford Handbook on Economics and Human Biology* explores a relatively new and expanding field of economics that makes use of biological insights and introduces the reader to the main approaches, insights, and results obtained in this area of research over the previous three decades. We ask questions such as: what role does anthropometrics have in determining economic outcomes? In turn, what roles do economic factors play in transforming anthropometrics over time? The primary focus of this interdisciplinary volume is on examining in detail how economic processes affect human biological outcomes—and the other way around: how biological outcomes affect economic processes. By human biology, we mean all aspects of the organism that are measurable and for which data are available. These include such measures as height, weight, the body mass index (BMI, constructed from height and weight), cholesterol levels, blood pressure, and birth weight. This perspective differs from health and health economics insofar as health is usually defined in terms of the absence of disease, whereas the economics and human biology research program is concerned with the functioning of the human biological system and how it is impacted by its socioeconomic environment.

The volume has three main purposes. The first is to introduce the reader to the research on biological outcomes of historical and contemporary populations and to explore the extent to which human biology is affected by economic processes over time and cross-sectionally. The second is to focus on biological markers (such as height and weight) as inputs, highlighting labor market aspects that emphasize how biological markers (such as body composition) affect labor market outcomes including wages, unemployment, and wealth. The extent to which these biological markers affect labor productivity and human capital accumulation will also be explored. The third purpose is to introduce the reader to developmental aspects and policy, particularly correlates of malnutrition and poverty. The policies that have been introduced worldwide to address these deficits are explored in some detail.

The roots of the systematic study of the relationship between human biology and the economy in which it is embedded go as far back as 1829, when Louis R. Villermé, a statistician of public health, recognized that a population's physical stature was influenced by economic factors. In the modern period, the field of anthropometric history was born in the mid-1970s with Richard Steckel's studies on slave heights and those of Robert Fogel on the nutritional factors in the demographic transition. The field really expanded after Fogel received the Nobel Prize in economics in 1993. Since then, the field has taken off substantially.

Analyzing biological and economic measures together enables us to gain valuable and hitherto unknown perspectives on the well-being of populations, both historical and contemporary. Some of the topics explored are the momentous changes associated with economic growth and transformations such as the Industrial Revolution, the onset of modern economic growth, and globalization. A basic premise is that as the economy affects our pocketbook and our lifestyles, its effects actually penetrate deep into our cells, our organs, and our bones. It does so, for instance, through the food we eat which, in turn, is obviously a function of incomes, relative prices, agricultural productivity, the organization of markets, and all the other salient aspects of the economy. These economic variables thus have significant effects on our bodies at the microlevel, affecting weight, comorbidities, and height. These biological measures in turn have effects on labor market outcomes and productivity. The effects of crisis (manmade and natural) can shed light on these effects, and differences across native populations and migrants can also be revealing in this context.

At the macrolevel, population density, urbanization, inequality, social and occupational structure, taxation, government redistribution, poverty, entitlements, the disease environment, and the organization of medical services all play a role. These various aspects of institutional development are shown to have significant effects on structural changes in biological measures over time and across geographic regions, and vice versa. It is not necessarily standard to think of these macroeconomic measures as being linked to overall anthropometric measures in a country, and yet they play an important role, particularly from a policy perspective.

Through the strong linkages between economics and human biology, policy makers may wish to redirect resources to alleviate conditions such as obesity and early-life growth faltering. The advantages to this approach run deep. If the economic returns to investing in nutrition, well-being, infant health, and other biological measures are quantifiable, ignoring the salient role that they play would be a dire omission in the economics literature. From a policy perspective, government intervention is justified in economics if externalities are present, as Averett and Wang argue with malnutrition in their chapter in this handbook. In fact, market failure may be less the exception and more the rule, particularly when you factor in considerations surrounding human biology. Offer argues in his chapter that market-liberal welfare regimes, for example, have contributed to the high prevalence of obesity.

The extent to which human biology plays a role in economic development needs to be better understood. If severe inequities arise with income and wages, for example, due to disparities in height, weight, endowment at birth, and the like, the reasons for this need to be explored in order to better understand the workings of economies. If this is due to discrimination, then optimal matches in the workplace are not occurring, and productivity is lower than optimal. In other words, individuals are not being paid the value of their marginal product of labor. Moreover, the mental health effects in this context cannot be ignored. Differences can arise in health (both physical and mental), in quantity and quality of education, in the labor market, in levels of risk aversion, and they can arise across race, gender, and sexual orientation. An understanding of these disparities can also shed light on the transfer to welfare across generations, as argued by Oxley in her chapter in this handbook. These are all issues that the field of economics and human biology attempts to address, filling a critical gap in the general research in either economics or biology alone.

The use of econometrics for the empirical testing of theories in economics and human biology allows researchers to carefully address issues of self-selection, heterogeneity (both observed and unobserved), endogeneity, and confounding factors. As Colman and Dave argue in their chapter, randomized controlled trials, the gold standard of causal research, are often impossible or unethical in this context. Having alternative tools allows us to establish causal effects using the observational data most often available. The emerging use of biomarkers and twin studies, as shown in this handbook, have also become useful as tools in this field.

The interdisciplinary nature of this handbook is paramount and one of its greatest strengths. Economists, anthropologists, historians, biologists, biochemists, physicians, environmentalists, and researchers in public health and public policy, as well as others often all have similar questions and yet approach them from different perspectives using different methodologies. Often they use terminology specific to their disciplines, thus placing an obstacle to collaboration with researchers from other disciplines. Yet it is this very cross-fertilization that can be very fruitful and allow us to arrive at the answers we seek. The study of economics and human biology also needs to be viewed through the dimension of space and time in order provide an accurate portrait of the variation exhibited both historically and geographically. You will thus find several chapters in this handbook that discuss historical perspectives, as well as some that focus on specific geographical areas.

The handbook is divided into four parts. The first part, the Introduction to Economics and Human Biology, provides the reader with a general background on the topic. Four chapters after the introductory chapter provide a background on anthropometrics: Behrman's chapter on growth faltering and catch-up growth, Steckel's chapter on measuring well-being with biological indicators, Bharadwaj and Vogl's chapter on economic crisis and human biology, and finally Koepke's chapter, which follows the biological standard of living in Europe from the Late Iron Age to the Little Ice Age. Next, the chapter by Colman and Dave explores econometric methods used in empirically identifying relationships in how economics impact the human organism.

The second part of the handbook is on biological measures as outcome variables. Here, measures such as height, weight, body mass, and general biological well-being are analyzed using a number of variables, many reflecting changing economic conditions over time. The first group of papers in this part explores weight, height, and obesity. We begin with Carson's chapter, which explores changes in the body mass index through time. Lakdawalla and Reif's chapter explores economic reasons for why body mass has increased substantially over time. Blum's chapter on inequality and heights explores determinants of inequality in heights in detail. Rosinger and Godoy's chapter on native populations and Steckel's chapter on slave heights add important dimensions regarding subpopulations.

Next, female biological well-being is addressed. The important role of height as an indicator of women's health, productivity, and welfare is examined from an historical perspective in Oxley's chapter.

The next two chapters in this part of the handbook focus on the young: infants, children, and adolescents. Cabieses, Pickett, and Wilkinson's chapter stresses the role of socioeconomic inequality, whereas Rogol's chapter on auxology, the study of growth and development, highlights genetic and environmental factors responsible for the growth and maturation—or lack thereof—of children and adolescents.

The last group of chapters in this part summarize the importance of taking a global perspective for many of the topics explored thus far. Meinzer and Baten's chapter takes a historical perspective and follows global trends and cycles in physical stature from the Neolithic Agricultural Revolution to modern times. Kromeyer-Hauschild, Moss, and Wabitsch provide an overview of trends in BMI across the world and over time, whereas the focus is on the dual burden of poverty and obesity in developed countries in Meyerhoefer and Yang's chapter.

The third part of the handbook introduces biological measures as key independent variables and determinants of economic outcomes. Genetic markers, a new tool available to researchers, are covered in the first two chapters: both Lehrer's and Wehby's chapters provide insights into the burgeoning role of genetic biomarkers and genes as inputs in determining economic outcomes. Behrman's chapter then provides a thorough introduction to the economics of twin studies; it describes the strengths and limitations of various twins methods developed in economics.

The next chapters in this part explore investments in health. Alderman and Sahn's chapter examines the impact of nutrition on productivity and the general economic returns of investing in proper nutrition. The double burden of malnutrition—that both undernutrition and obesity are drivers of adverse health outcomes—is explored in Averett and Wang's chapter on a topic that is increasingly important globally, especially in developing economies. Biological health risks (such as hypertension, cholesterol, high glucose levels, and inflammation) in the context of economic development are explored in Frankenberg, Ho, and Thomas's chapter.

We then turn to monetary outcomes of biological attributes. Su's chapter provides a global perspective—with a focus on countries belonging to the Organization for Economic Cooperation and Development (OECD)—by examining the effect of obesity on income inequality. Hübler's chapter summarizes the literature on the effect of height on wages and provides an extensive theoretical background. The effects of body mass on both wages and wealth are then explored in Greve's and Zagorsky's chapters, respectively, with possible reasons for the prevalent negative relationship found in several studies. Wilson's chapter on family economics and obesity reminds us that the economics of obesity should be studied within the context of the family, especially with childhood obesity on the rise in economically prosperous nations.

Obesity and welfare regimes are then discussed with Offer's chapter on how market-liberal welfare regimes tend to have the highest prevalence of obesity. The welfare regime hypothesis put forth in this chapter argues that obesity may be a response to stress and that stress is generated by market competition; more specifically, by the uncertainty that the market competition generates. Reasons for this uncertainty are explored in detail in this chapter.

We then turn to child and infant anthropometrics. Silventoinen's chapter discusses children's anthropometrics and later disease incidence, highlighting the adverse effects of low birthweight and short stature. Birthweight as a health indicator is discussed in further detail in Ward's chapter. Torche and Conley's chapter extends the discussion on birthweight as a widely used yardstick for welfare by analyzing its use as a measure of human capital endowment in economic research. These two chapters on birthweight highlight its role in medicine, biology, and economics.

The last chapter in this part is on neuroeconomics, a flourishing field that promises new insights into the field of economics and human biology. Aimone and Houser's chapter provides a summary of this burgeoning field, the limitations of standard economic theory, and how neuroeconomics can help explain behaviors such as trust, reciprocity, and betrayal.

The fourth part of the handbook encompasses regional studies in economics and human biology. The focus is on Africa in Hirvonen and Moradi's chapter, which explores the phenomenon of surprisingly tall African men and women in spite of low incomes. The focus then turns to Asia in Schwekendiek's chapter, which highlights the rich history of anthropometric growth over time in China, Japan, and Korea and the role that economic performance plays. We turn to North America in both Boustan and Margo's chapter, which discusses racial differences, and Craig's chapter, which provides reasons for the "antebellum puzzle"—the mysterious finding that the American population became shorter at the onset of modern economic growth in the decades prior to the US Civil War.

This finding dovetails with a literature that is critical of the excessive emphasis on gross domestic product (GDP) growth as the primary if not the sole indicator of living standards (Stiglitz, Sen, & Fitoussi, 2010). In contrast, the anthropometric evidence at the onset of modern economic growth emphasizes that a rising GDP was compatible with a decline in nutritional status of children and youth who had no agency to determine their own destiny. And these are exactly the age groups that are almost always left out of conventional analysis inasmuch as monetary measures pertain exclusively to adults and not to children and youth who are not employed. That is another major distinction between conventional views and anthropometric views of welfare. Methodological individualism is very concerned about agency, but those who were hurt by economic growth in the Antebellum United States had no agency at all, and that is worth emphasizing. Hence, economic growth was by no means a Pareto-optimal process. Instead, there were gainers and losers. That is also a new and useful insight into the dynamics of economic development.

A'Hearn's chapter presents an anthropometric history of the Mediterranean world. These insightful chapters on anthropometrics and economic performance in different regions across the globe conclude this interesting, novel, and interdisciplinary volume that we hope will be a useful resource for researchers in economics and other social sciences. As editors of this handbook, we feel privileged to be able to present the reader with this impressive body of research and hope it will serve as a valuable resource for a long time to come. Finally, we would like to thank David Pervin for his vision, guidance, perseverance, and patience in bringing this volume to fruition.

Reference

Stiglitz, J., Sen, A., & Fitoussi, J.- P. 2010. *Mismeauring Our Lives: Why GDP Doesn't Add Up.* New York: New Press.

CHAPTER 1

GROWTH FALTERING IN THE FIRST THOUSAND DAYS AFTER CONCEPTION AND CATCH-UP GROWTH

JERE R. BEHRMAN

1.1 Background

Early-life growth faltering is of considerable concern for many low- and middle-income countries (LIMICs). Average growth paths for children in undernourished populations typically indicate birth lengths/weights below medians for well-nourished populations, then fairly sharp relative declines until leveling off around 2 years of age, and possibly a slight catch-up with further aging (Figure 1.1). Approximately 170 million children under 5 years old, mostly in LIMICs, suffer growth faltering as measured by being stunted (i.e., heights/lengths <2 standard deviations [SD] below World Health Organization [WHO, 2006] medians for well-nourished populations; de Onis et al. [de Onis, Blössner, & Borghi, 2011]). Growth faltering has prevalences of approximately 40% in a number of South Asian and sub-Saharan African countries (de Onis et al., 2011). Recent surveys indicate that early-life growth faltering is associated with less satisfactory outcomes in education, labor markets, marriage markets, health, and parenting (e.g., Victora et al., 2008, summarized herein).

Prominent studies based on such associations argue for redirecting resources to alleviate early-life growth faltering, particularly during the first thousand days (FTD) after conception (up to 2 years of age). Martorell et al. (Martorell, Khan, & Schroeder, 1994), for example, conclude that catch-up growth after early childhood might occur in some

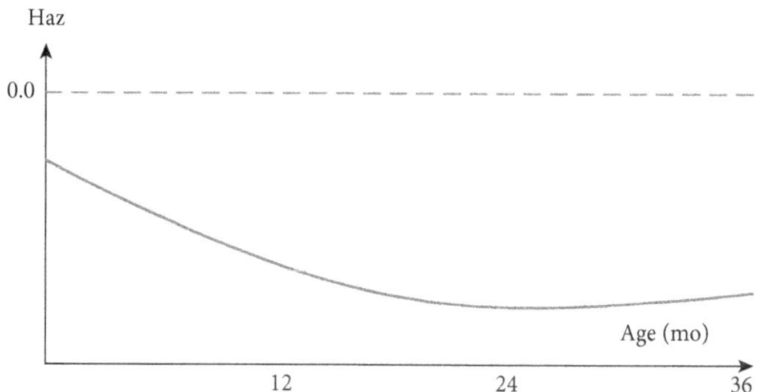

FIGURE 1.1 Stereotypical average HAZ versus age in undernourished population, with median HAZ = 0 for well-nourished population.

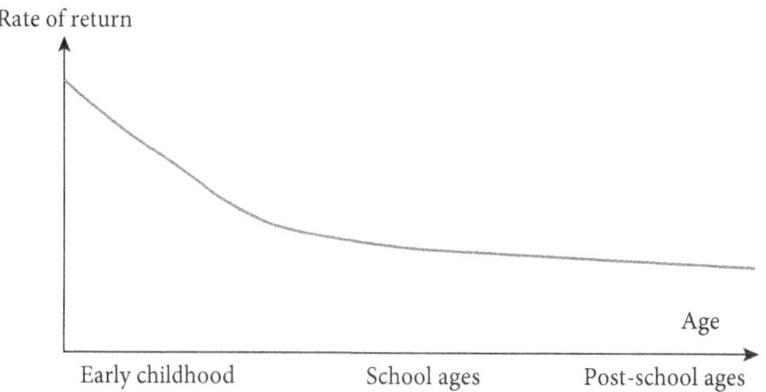

FIGURE 1.2 Rate of return to investments versus child age, as suggested by Heckman (2006).

circumstances but that "subjects who remained in the setting in which they became stunted experience little or no catch-up in growth later in life." Victora et al.'s (2008, p. 340, emphasis added) influential *Lancet* article stated that their first key message is "Poor fetal growth or stunting in the first 2 years of life leads to *irreversible* damage, including shorter adult height, lower attained schooling, reduced adult income, and decreased offspring birthweight." Victora et al.'s (Victora, de Onis, Hallal, Blössner, & Shrimpton, 2010, p. e473) *Pediatrics* article summarized their study of child growth patterns in 54 countries: "Children from low- and middle-income countries are born with weights and lengths below WHO growth standards, and early growth faltering is even faster than currently assumed. The window of opportunity for preventing undernutrition ends at 2 years of age." These conclusions resonate with Heckman's (2006) claim that rates of return are highest for early-life human capital investments and decline as children age (Figure 1.2).

This chapter considers selected empirical evidence on impacts of FTD growth faltering and possible subsequent catch-up growth and addresses those questions that merit further investigation.

1.2 Life Cycle Framework of FTD Growth Faltering and Catch-Up Growth

Figure 1.3 presents a simplified framework with six life-cycle stages: (1) the FTD, (2) subsequent early childhood (i.e., from 2 years to normal school-entry ages), (3) late childhood, (4) adolescence, (5) adulthood (including intergenerational effects through fertility and parenting), and (6) old age. Children start life with endowments, both genetic and otherwise. Conditional on these endowments, FTD development (upper right box) is affected by risk factors (upper left box) including malnutrition, infections, pregnancy and birth complications, and inadequate stimulation/nurturing. These risk factors are mitigated by familial inputs (e.g., family-provided stimulation, nutrition) and community inputs (e.g., accessibility and quality of day care, preschool programs, and health care). The FTD outcomes (upper right box) in turn affect outcomes in subsequent sequential life cycle stages that may be exclusively for the children under consideration and their families or may include spillovers on others. FTD growth faltering (e.g., stunting) is the most common measure of the long-run nutritional status component of the physical status outcome. Familial and community inputs (center left box) may moderate the four FTD risk factors and their impacts on outcomes such as FTD growth faltering and how FTD outcomes produce impacts over the life cycle. These investment inputs occur for each stage within particular contexts and have associated resource costs. Across contexts, the effects of these investments and their resource costs are likely to vary.

Caregivers (mainly parents) make decisions that affect child developmental outcomes, including FTD growth faltering. Outcomes in subsequent life cycle stages are conditional on FTD outcomes (or inputs that determine them), subsequent life cycle familial and public inputs, and stochastic factors (e.g., variations in disease/nutrition/cognitive environments). Production functions give vectors of outcomes for the sth life cycle stage (Y_s) dependent on a matrix of familial production inputs from conception to the sth life cycle stage (F_s), a matrix of community-level production inputs from conception to the sth life cycle stage (C_s), a vector of genetic and other endowments at conception (E_0), and a matrix of stochastic production factors from conception to the sth life cycle stage (U_s):

$$Y_S = Y_S\,(\mathrm{F}_S, \mathrm{C}_S, \mathrm{E}_0, \mathrm{U}_S)\,. \tag{1}$$

Production function features highlight several issues: (1) endowments at conception and the history of familial, public, and stochastic production inputs since conception may matter, so right-side matrices have multiple rows for life cycle stages since conception and multiple columns for inputs in each stage; (2) within life cycle stages, inputs

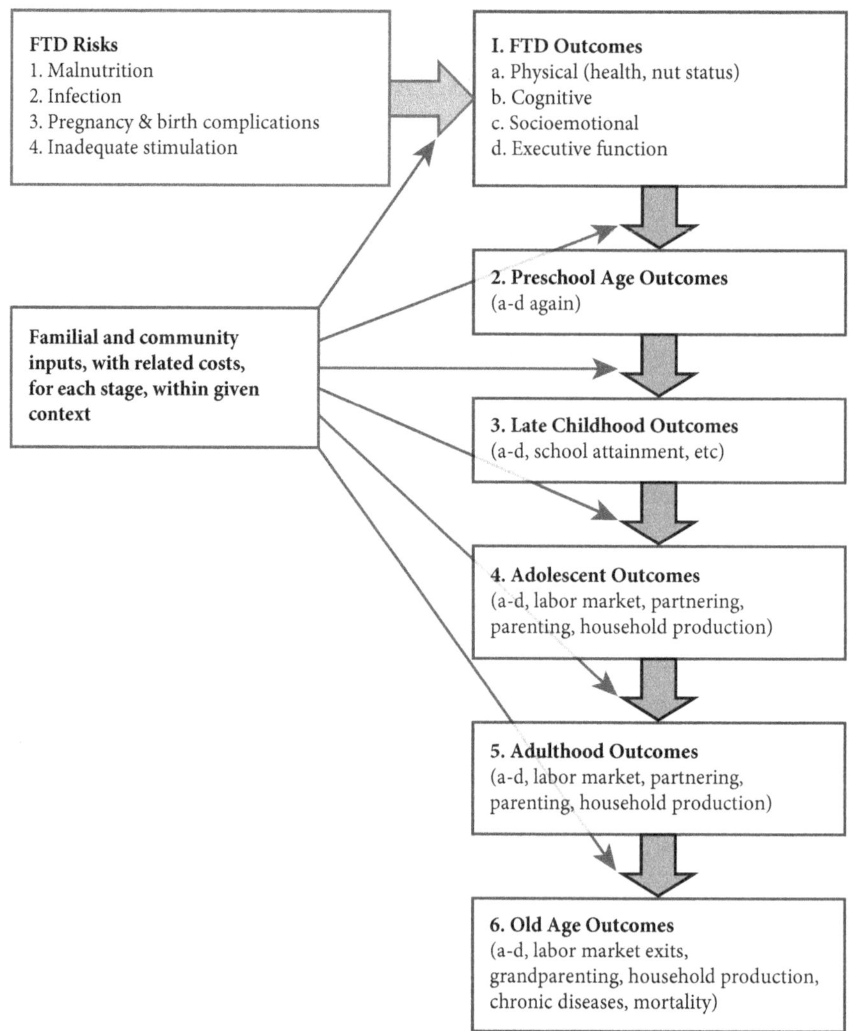

FIGURE 1.3 First thousand days (FTD) growth faltering within life cycle framework.

may compensate or reinforce each other; and (3) across life cycle stages, inputs may compensate or reinforce each other through dynamic complementarities (Cunha & Heckman, 2007). Better FTD nutrition-related inputs, for instance, are hypothesized to improve learning through stimulation at that stage and through preschool or school programs in later life cycle stages.

Production functions are only technical relations, including biological aspects, between inputs up to life cycle stage *s* and child outcomes in life cycle stage *s*. But what determines inputs is critical. Within standard economic models, familial inputs are determined by familial decisions (perhaps with some intrafamilial bargaining) that aim to maximize expected familial welfare (perhaps with different weights on different family members) subject to the production functions in relation (1), a matrix of welfare function preferences (W_s), a matrix of knowledge about technology and markets (K_s), a matrix of prices and policies that the household has faced and expects to face in the future (P_s), a matrix of resources that the household has had and expects to have in the future, including child endowments in Equation (1) (R_s) and a matrix of stochastic shocks, including those in Equation (1), that the household has faced and expects to face in the future (V_s):

$$F_S = F_S\ (\mathrm{W}_S, \mathrm{K}_S, \mathrm{P}_S, \mathrm{R}_S V_S)\,. \tag{2}$$

There are six dimensions to these demand relations:

1. Right-side variables refer not only to periods from conception to the sth stage, but also, if investors are forward-looking, include expected future distributions (or parameters underlying such distributions).
2. If right-side variables vary across child life cycle stages, then relations need to be added to represent how they evolve over time (e.g., preferences may depend on communication campaigns, knowledge may depend on investments in learning, policy-related factors may depend on whether relevant governments allocate public inputs to favor the better-off because of their political influence or the poorer because of anti-poverty concerns).
3. Through substitution into Equation (1), demand relations can be obtained for outcomes in stage s (Y_s).
4. Behavioral decisions are critical in determining outcomes and whether they compensate or reinforce prior differences (e.g., if parents have strong "inequality aversion" [Behrman, Pollak, & Taubman, 1982] regarding outcome distributions among their children, a program that provides nutrients to other than the most malnourished of their children might induce considerable reallocation of parental resources from the target child to other children).
5. To evaluate the total impact of FTD growth faltering or of interventions to reduce such faltering, various individual impacts over the life cycle must be combined (with care not to double count; e.g., if one impact such as schooling attainment is primarily a channel through which growth faltering or interventions affect adult productivities) by using weights (real prices) for individual impacts (some of which, e.g., adverting mortality,[1] pose challenges) and discounting back to the FTD. For example, US$1,000 in 40 years—when some productivity effects may occur—with a 3% discount rate has a present discounted value [PDV] of US$307 (US$252 with adjustment for Indian survival probabilities); with a moderate discount rate of 6%, this is US$97 (US$80).
6. To estimate benefit–cost ratios (or internal rates of return) to interventions to reduce FTD growth faltering, the PDV of total resource costs (including private and public resource costs and distortion costs but not transfers) of the intervention and costs induced by the intervention (e.g., if increased schooling attainment is induced years later, there are likely to be resource costs for this additional schooling) need to be calculated.

Finally, estimation of Equations (1) and (2) is very challenging because of tremendous information requirements (many variables, some of which are difficult to observe, over many years), random and systematic measurement errors in observed variables, and unobserved factors including endowments at conception that may affect both left-side and right-side variables and thus cause spurious correlations. FTD growth faltering is determined, inter alia, by endowments and familial investments (left-center box) and cannot practically—to say nothing of ethically—be distributed randomly (although public investments that affect growth faltering might be explored with randomized designs). The challenges are greater, moreover, if heterogeneous responses are allowed across contexts, families, or individuals. Studies provide estimates, although with considerable simplifications with regard to number of variables, number of periods covered, impacts of unobserved factors, treatment of right-side behavioral relations, functional forms, and homogeneity of parameters.

1.3 FTD Growth and Outcomes in Subsequent Life Cycle Stages

1.3.1 Direct Estimates of FTD Growth and Outcomes in Subsequent Life Cycle Stages

Several empirical approaches relate FTD growth directly to outcomes in subsequent life cycle stages. These can be considered special cases of conditional demand functions derived from Equation (2), in which outcomes at some later life cycle stage are conditional on indicators of FTD growth faltering. Common simplifying assumptions are:

(A1) First-order or main effects in Taylor-series expansions of conditional demand functions capture the essence of the phenomena being investigated. Therefore, these studies provide no illumination about static and dynamic interactions that are emphasized in recent economics literature.

(A2) FTD outcomes other than physical growth can be ignored, consistent with other FTD outcomes being uncorrelated with FTD growth—a strong assumption because all of these outcomes are determined primarily by the same family inputs, community inputs, and genetic and other endowments. This assumption also is consistent with FTD growth serving as a proxy for correlated components of other outcomes, which leads to interpretation problems because *ceteris paribus* coefficient estimates for FTD growth represent not only causal impacts of FTD growth but also of correlated components of other FTD outcomes.[2]

I now summarize selected studies on FTD growth and later-life outcomes that fit into this general simplified framework, some of which depend on further simplifications.

1.3.1.1 *Longitudinal Associations between FTD Growth Faltering and Later Life Outcomes*

Most related studies in the nutritional and public health literatures that cover fairly long life cycle segments are associational. Perhaps the most prominent of these, Victora et al. (2008), is based primarily on the COHORTS data that cover at least 15 years of life cycles for undernourished birth cohorts with sample sizes of 1,000+ for subpopulations defined by specific geographical locations when born in Brazil, Guatemala, India, the Philippines, and South Africa (Richter et al., 2012). Table 1.1 summarizes associations of FTD height/length (cm or height-for-age *z*-scores [HAZ]) and weight (kg or weight-for-age *z*-scores [WAZ]), which are significant for various outcomes. As noted earlier, the authors state that their first key message is that "Poor fetal growth or stunting in the first 2 years of life leads to irreversible damage, including shorter adult height, lower attained schooling, reduced adult income, and decreased offspring birthweight." This conclusion depends on interpreting associations between FRD growth and later-life outcomes as causal, which depends on assumptions (A1) and (A2) and on further assumptions:

(A3) FTD growth indicators are sufficient statistics for everything through the FTD. That is, there are no inputs into FTD growth that have impacts on later-life outcomes that occur through channels other than through FTD growth. For instance, genetic endowments relating to innate health and innate abilities have no *direct* impact on later-life outcomes such as adult health and cognitive skills, but only *indirect* impacts through FTD growth outcomes (or, if A2 is not maintained, through other FTD outcomes).

(A4) Familial and community inputs for life cycle stages subsequent to the FTD that are correlated with those during the FTD do not affect later-life outcomes of interest, or, if they do affect these later-life outcomes, they are not correlated with the FTD growth indicator. That is, persistent familial factors (e.g., parental schooling attainment, long-run wealth or income) and persistent community factors (e.g., disease environments, accessibility and quality of social services) are assumed to not be correlated with FTD growth (even though a priori they would seem to determine FTD growth through Equation (2)), or they are assumed to have no post-FTD impact on any other variables that affect the outcomes of interest (e.g., if adult labor market outcomes are of interest, these persistent familial and community background variables are assumed to not affect any post-FTD learning or any other post-FTD channels that affect adult labor market outcomes).

Thus, the assumptions seem very strong for the Victora et al. (2008) conclusions about longer run effects of FTD growth failure based on their empirical analysis. They also present no evidence about the extent, impacts, and costs of post-FTD growth, which would seem necessary for their conclusion about irreversibility.

Table 1.1 Selected associations between first thousand days (FTD) anthropometric measures and adult outcomes

Schooling Attainment	0.5 Grades for 1 HAZ at Age 2
	0.5 grades for 1 WAZ at age 2
	0.3 grades for 1 kg at birth
Adult height	3.2 cm for 1 HAZ at age 2
	0.7–1.0 cm for 1 cm at birth
Labor income	8% for 1 HAZ at age 2 males
	8–25% for 1 HAZ at age 2 females
Birthweight of offspring	70–80 g for 1 HAZ or 1 of mother at age 2

Source: Constructed by author based on Victora et al. (2008)

1.3.1.2 *Birthweights and Subsequent Outcomes with Control for Endowments Shared by Identical Twins*

Monozygotic (MZ, identical) twin fixed-effects (FE) (or within-MZ twins) estimates control for all factors shared by identical twins including the life cycle stages of their parents and genetic endowments at conception.[3] MZ-FE estimates thus have advantages over the associations just discussed because they do not confound effects of persistent components of familial and community background and genetic endowments with impacts of FTD growth (i.e., they do not require assumptions A3 and A4). A prominent critique of MZ-FE estimates for estimating schooling impacts (the most widespread use of this method) is that between-MZ twins schooling attainment differences are assumed to be random but in fact may be due to other parental responses to differences between twins that may have direct impacts on outcomes of interest (e.g., birthweight differences associated with schooling differences and also with differences in outcomes subsequent to schooling; see Bound & Solon, 1999). This critique holds for FTD growth at 2 years, but not for birthweights because between-MZ twins birthweight differences do not reflect efforts by parents to favor one twin but are merely chance outcomes of placement relative to placentas. For the same reason, MZ-FE estimates of birthweight impacts on later outcomes are not confounded by persistent familial and community background characteristics shared by twins. Table 1.2 summarizes estimated impacts of birthweight (from birth certificates) on selected outcomes with comparisons of ordinary least squares (OLS) and MZ-FE estimates for US twins. Under the assumption that MZ-FE estimates give true causal effects of birthweight, the OLS positive significant associations with body mass index (BMI) and with birthweight in the next generation reflect substantial upward biases due to shared family and community background and genetic endowments that are controlled in MZ-FE estimates. Under the same assumption, on the other hand, the OLS positive associations of birthweight with schooling attainment and particularly ln wages understate considerably the true (MZ-FE) effects. These results may reflect that genetic endowments are multidimensional, and those components associated with physical growth on average are inversely associated with those associated with intellectual development, so that OLS estimates are biased upward for BMI and birthweight and toward zero for schooling and wage rates (Behrman & Rosenzweig, 2004; Behrman et al., 2014). MZ-FE estimates for Chinese women indicate greater birthweight impacts on schooling attainment than for men because of women's comparative advantage in skill-intense occupations, thus illustrating that context matters (Rosenzweig & Zhang, 2013). The relevance of such results for broader populations requires:

(A5) Inferences can be made for broader populations from MZ-FE estimates. Debate is considerable about this assumption because twins are small percentages of populations, and being twins is perceived as being different. However, some of this debate is misplaced (e.g., the "common environment" assumption between MZ and DZ twins is critical for heritability estimates but not for MZ-FE estimates; to a first-order approximation, MZ-FE estimates control for what is different about being twins) or not reflective of recent developments in twins analysis (e.g., showing that if whatever causes differences between twins for right-side variables such as birthweights also has direct impact in the same direction on outcome variables of interest, then the MZ-FE estimates establish upper bounds on absolute magnitudes of true effects) (Kohler, Behrman, & Schnittker, 2011). Of course, one important respect in which twins differ from the general population is that distributions of birthweights for twins are to the left, although considerably overlapping, of those for singletons (Behrman & Rosenzweig, 2004). This means that the Table 1.2 results are more relevant than would be results from singleton populations for low birthweight babies of particular interest for catch-up growth.

Table 1.2 Monozygotic-fixed effects (MZ-FE)/ ordinary least squares (OLS) estimates for impact of birthweight over life cycle

	MZ-FE/OLS (%)
Schooling	210
BMI	28
Ln Wage	706
Child Birthweight	25

Constructed by author based on Behrman and Rosenzweig (2004)

1.3.1.3 *Birthweight and Post-FTD Outcomes for Synthetic Cohorts by Linking Estimates Across Life Cycle Segments*

FTD growth and outcomes in later life can be linked by several approaches,[4] including using longitudinal data that follow cohorts from early life over a number of years (as in the first study reported), linking data on adult life cycle stages with earlier birth records (as in the second study), or linking estimates from different studies across different life cycle stages.[5] The last approach requires an assumption related to (A3):

(A6) Linking variables across life cycle stages provide sufficient statistics for what preceded them. That is, if one study linking birthweight to schooling attainment is combined with another study linking schooling attainment to adult productivities, then schooling attainment is a sufficient statistic for all birthweight impacts up to the end of schooling that may affect adult productivities.

Table 1.3 summarizes estimates of impacts of moving children from low birthweight to normal birthweight status in low-income contexts using the synthetic-cohort approach and the best estimates that the authors could find for each linked life cycle segment (based on randomized controlled trials or econometric methods) to avoid omitted variable biases (e.g., due to unobserved genetic endowments-related innate health and abilities). Other than an illustration of this approach, these estimates illustrate three important points. First, particularly for outcomes later in the life cycle, discount rates matter. Second, even with discounting at the usual rates, outcomes later in the life cycle may be very important in judging impacts of reducing FTD growth faltering, particularly if they persist over long life cycle segments (e.g., persistent productivity effects). Third, whether interventions to reduce low birthweight babies make economic sense depends in part on costs.

1.3.1.4 *Instrumental Variable (IV) Estimates of HAZ or Stunting at 24 Months and Multiple Outcomes into Adult Life Cycle Stages*

Hoddinott et al. (2013*b*) investigated impacts of FTD growth faltering on a more comprehensive set of outcomes than in any other previous prospective study, including human capital (schooling, intelligence, reading), marriage, fertility, adult health (cardiovascular disease risk factors, physical performance), labor markets, and household poverty. They used an IV approach to attempt to control for endogeneity and measurement error in their FTD growth indicators. They use the INCAP Guatemalan data, based on random assignment of more (protein-dense) and less (no-protein) nutritious supplements available free at community centers in four villages in 1969–76, which led to different exposures during the FTD depending on village and birth timing. The sample villages had experienced considerable prior FTD growth faltering by 24 months, with mean HAZs of less than −3 and stunting prevalences of 86%. They use

Table 1.3 Estimates of present discounted values in US dollars of seven major impacts of moving one infant out of low birthweight status in a low-income developing country

	Annual Discount Rate (%)		
Impacts	3	5	10
1. Reduced Infant mortality	$95	$99	$89
2. Reduced neonatal care	$42	$42	$42
3. Reduced costs of infant and child illness	$36	$35	$34
4. Productivity gain from reduced stunting	$152	$85	$25
5. Productivity gain from increased cognitive ability	$367	$205	$60
6. Reduced costs of chronic diseases	$49	$15	$1
7. Intergenerational effects	$92	$35	$257
Total Benefits	$832	$510	$257

Amounts are in US dollars.
Source: Constructed by author based on Alderman and Behrman (2006).

as instruments child-specific FTD exposure to nutritional supplementation, depending on village and birth date, which means that their estimates are not contaminated by family and community background and genetic endowments during the FTD also having post-FTD impacts (and, if successful, avoiding A3).[6] To limit estimation problems related to post-FTD familial and community inputs (and therefore limit A4 to unobservables), they controlled for birth-year dummy variables, maternal schooling, paternal schooling, parental wealth, whether parents had died before participants were 15 years old, school quality at age 7 years, distance to village center, and village of origin. Their preferred IV estimates indicate some important effects: a 1 unit increase in HAZ was significantly associated with 0.8 grades more schooling, approximately 0.25 SD higher test scores for reading and nonverbal cognitive skills, better marriage partners (1.4 years older, 1.0 grades more schooling, 1.0 cm taller), 21% greater household per capita expenditure as adults, and 10 percentage points lower probability of living in poverty as adults. For women, these results included 0.8 years older at first birth, 0.6 fewer pregnancies, and 0.4 fewer children but no significant impacts on adult health. They conclude that attrition is not a major problem because they control for numerous observables that might be associated with attrition, and their results are robust to explorations of impacts of attrition related to observables. They find that, for a number of outcomes, the IV point estimates differ fairly substantially from the OLS estimates, thus suggesting that controlling for endogeneity and measurement error is important and that associational studies that do not may be misleading regarding the magnitudes of effects. Arguably, this is the most persuasive study yet available about the causal effects of FTD growth—or whatever FTD growth is proxying for—on life cycle outcomes in poorly nourished populations. They acknowledge (see note 2) that they do not confidently identify effects of FTD growth from other FTD outcomes unless they accept A2. This leaves open the question of to what extent these results (as the previous studies reviewed) justify interventions directly to increase FTD growth versus other outcomes correlated with FTD growth. The study, finally, is based on a very particular context: children born between 1962 and 1977 in four Guatemalan villages with high growth-faltering prevalence. If the results hold roughly the same for other poorly nourished populations, then they are very important because of high growth-faltering prevalence in South Asia and sub-Saharan Africa. However, the external validity of these results is difficult to assess because of the lack of other data from poorly nourished populations with initial randomized assignment and follow-ups for decades into mid-adulthood.

Hoddinott et al. (Hoddinott, Alderman, Behrman, Haddad, & Horton, 2013*a*) utilize the cost data for reducing growth faltering from 17 different LIMICs with high growth-faltering prevalences from Bhutta et al. (2008) and the estimated relation between stunting at 2 years and household consumption when the children became adults from Hoddinott et al. (2013*b*) to estimate the benefit–cost ratios for interventions to reduce stunting. Their estimates indicate that benefit-cost ratios are generally substantially greater than 1 (median of 18.4) with substantial cross-country variance due to variations in costs and projected wage growth (range 3.8–47.9). These costs are conditional on the same assumptions as the results in Hoddinott et al. (2013*b*) plus:

(A7) The relation between reducing stunting and adult consumption similar to that found in Hoddinott et al. (2013*a*) holds across the 17 countries considered, with adjustments for different projected earnings growth across countries; this is a strong assumption given different skill mixes across labor markets of the sort emphasized by Rosenzweig and Zhang (2013).

1.3.2 Estimates of FTD Growth Determinants on Subsequent Life Cycle Outcomes

Direct estimation of Equation (2) may be informative about the impacts of FTD growth determinants on later outcomes. Such estimates do not require A2 (i.e., there are no FTD growth outcomes correlated with FTD growth) because the question is to elucidate long-run impacts of FTD growth determinants whether or not FTD growth is the sole channel for such impacts. Household and community factors are the major proximate

Table 1.4 Benefit-cost estimates for nutritional interventions for preschool children with discount rates of 3–5%

	Benefit-Cost Ratio
1. Reducing LBW for pregnancies with high probabilities LBW	
1a. Treatments for women with asymptomatic bacterial infections	0.58–4.93
1b. Treatment for women with presumptive STD	1.26–10.71
1c. Drugs for pregnant women with poor obstetric history	4.14–35.20
2. Improving infant and child nutrition in populations with high prevalence of child malnutrition	
2a. Breastfeeding promotion in hospitals in which norm has been promotion of use of infant formula	5.6–67.1
2b. Intergrated child care programs	9.4–16.2
2c. Intensive preschool program with considerable nutrition for poor families	1.4–2.9
3. Reducing micro nutrient deficiencies	
3a. Iodine (per woman of child-bearing age)	15–520
3b. Vitamin A (per child under 6 years)	4.3–43
3c. Iron (pregnant women)	6.1–14

determinants of FTD growth. However, generally, household and community resources are highly correlated across life cycle stages and have impacts across such stages, which makes it challenging to identify their impacts during the FTD alone on subsequent life cycle outcomes; A4 is very strong for these determinants of FTD growth. But some studies, examples of which we now consider, consider marginal determinants that arguably give more credible estimates.

1.3.2.1 *Protein-Dense Nutritional Supplements and Multiple Outcomes into Adulthood*

The Guatemalan INCAP longitudinal data used by Hoddinott et al. (2013*b*) also has been used to investigate the impacts of the *atole* protein-dense supplement relative to the *fresco* no-protein supplement on outcomes over the life cycle. The randomized nature of these data means that estimates using them are likely not to be particularly contaminated by familial, community, and genetic endowment determinants later in the life cycle, so A3 and A4 need not be invoked (or perhaps invoked in weaker forms). Estimates suggest fairly substantial effects decades later when the sample members were 26–42 years old: approximately 40% increased real wage rates for men; approximately 0.25 standard deviation increases in reading skills and cognitive abilities for both men and women; and higher birthweights by approximately 100 g for the children of women who had received the supplements (Behrman et al., 2009; Hoddinott, Maluccio, Behrman, Flores, & Martorell, 2008; Maluccio et al., 2009). These results are consistent with FTD growth being important or an important proxy for other developments, though, as noted, they do not demonstrate that FTD growth itself is the only or even the primary channel through which these effects occur because they refer to the effects of the supplements that may occur through channels other than FTD growth, and they do not compare effects through various channels. For the educational and labor market outcomes, these studies report no significant difference between being exposed to protein-dense nutritional supplements for up to 24 versus up to 36 months of age, but there is no significant impact from being exposed for 36–72 months. For intergenerational effects, by contrast, exposure throughout childhood up to 15 years of age, not just up to 24 or 36 months, produces significantly positive estimates.

1.3.2.2 *Other FTD Nutritional Interventions and Post-FTD Outcomes for Synthetic Cohorts that Link Estimates Across Life Cycle Segments*

As in Table 1.3 for birthweight, there are estimates for FTD nutritional interventions for synthetic cohorts that link estimates across life cycle segments for low-income populations. To provide perspective about the magnitudes of such impacts, it is useful to consider the implied benefit–cost ratios. Table 1.4 gives some illustrative values. Based on these estimates, benefit–cost ratios from selected FTD nutritional interventions in poorly nourished populations appear considerable.

1.4 Catch-Up Growth and Implications

1.4.1 Is There Catch-Up Growth?

1.4.1.1 *Average Patterns Across Ages*

Figure 1.1 gives a stylized characterization of average patterns of HAZ within undernourished populations. Prentice et al. (2013) note that, in terms of HAZ, this pattern implies some slight catch-up that continues into early adulthood based on the COHORTS data. Partially in response, several subsequent studies point out that although there may be some catch-up on average in terms of HAZ, the HAZ for adults in these populations still are considerably below those for well-nourished populations, and the deficit in height on average increases in these populations (Leroy, Ruel & Habicht, 2013; Leroy, Ruel, Habichat & Frongillo, 2014; Lundeen et al., 2014a, 2014b). Height deficits can increase with age even if HAZ deficits decline because height standard deviations that reference well-nourished populations increase with age. Thus, whether these linear growth patterns are consistent on average with some catch-up linear growth (as indicated by increasing HAZ) or increased deficits in linear growth (as indicated by increasing height deficits) depends on the appropriate measure of linear growth deficits. If our interest is not in relative adult height (HAZ) or absolute adult height (height deficits) per se, a natural question is to determine which is more highly associated with the outcomes we are concerned with (i.e., in labor markets, marriage markets, and adult health). Several studies for different economies report significant associations between height and adult outcomes (e.g., Behrman & Deolalikar, 1989; Case & Paxson, 2008; Persico, Postlewaite, & Silverman, 2004).[7] But data on adults alone cannot identify whether HAZ or height deficits are more important because HAZ is just a linear transformation of height—thus, HAZ, height, and height deficits all are perfectly correlated. Some insight about the relative importance of HAZ versus height deficits might be gained by examining empirical associations or, better yet, the causal effects of pre-adult trajectories of HAZ and height on important adult outcomes.

1.4.1.2 *Regression Estimates*

There are several regression estimates pertaining to catch-up growth in the literature. These estimates can be viewed as linear approximations to a version of Equation (2) that has H_s, an indicator of height and one of the elements in the vector of outcomes Y_s, as the dependent variable, and with the history of Y_s for previous life cycle stages substituted into the right side to represent conditional demand functions. For most (but not all) of these studies, the height element in Y_{s-1} is assumed to be a sufficient statistic for all past history, thus involving assumptions A2 and A3 (although not necessarily explicitly).[8]

$$H_s = \alpha_0 + \alpha_1 H_{s-1} + \alpha_2 W_s + \alpha_3 K_s + \alpha_4 P_s + V_s. \qquad (2A)$$

The critical parameter for catch-up growth in this formulation is α_1, under the assumption that the indicator for α_1 controls for age.[9] A value of α_1 that is not significantly different from 1.0 is interpreted to mean no catch-up growth, and a value of α_1 that is not significantly different from 0.0 is interpreted to be complete catch-up growth or path independence. Presumably, a value of α_1 that is significantly less than zero implies regression toward the mean.

One group of estimates of Equation (2A),[10] mostly found in the nutritional literature, uses OLS and generally assumes α_2 is zero (though in some cases controls are included for child age and gender and family background characteristics, particularly those related to parental schooling and family resources). These studies report estimates of α_1 that are not very different from 1.0, suggesting little to modest recovery from childhood stunting on average (Adair, 1999; Stein et al., 2010; Lundeen et al., 2014*b*). The estimates of α_1 are affected by upward omitted-variable bias if, as seems plausible, there is serial correlation over time in unobserved family and community factors (middle box on the left in Figure 1.1) that determine both H_s and H_{s-1}.[11] A second group of studies uses econometric methods such as instrumental variables or dynamic panel estimators to attempt to eliminate such omitted-variable bias, control for measurement error, and find smaller estimates of α_1. These suggest that between one-third and one-fourth of earlier linear growth deficiencies on average are reversed (Alderman, Hoddinott, & Kinsey, 2006; Behrman, Deolalikar, & Lavy, 1994; Georgiadis et al., 2015; Hoddinott & Kinsey,

2001; Mani, 2012; Outes & Porter, 2013). The estimates in all of these studies, whether they use instrumental variables to attempt to control for endogeneity and measurement error or not, probably are biased upward because of A3 (i.e., other outcomes can be ignored) since there probably are positive correlations among child outcomes so that the growth indicator in part proxies for them.

1.4.1.3 *Individual Patterns*

These regression estimates yield average patterns. Even if average growth faltering does not change much, as in Figure 1.1, there may be considerable movement for individual children, with some children experiencing growth recovery and others experiencing growth faltering. If so, and if determinants of these movements can be identified, then there may be significant possibilities for increasing growth recovery and, perhaps equally important, reducing growth faltering after the FTD. One way of exploring whether there is much individual movement around the average growth paths is to explore how much of the variation in HAZ at a later age is predicted by HAZ at an earlier age (basically estimating Equation (2A) without any other right-side variables except for HAZ at the earlier age). Based on longitudinal data on 7,266 children in the Young Lives (YL) study in Ethiopia, India, Peru, and Vietnam, HAZ at about age 1 year predicts much of HAZ variation at age 5 years, but 40–71% is not predicted. Similarly, HAZ at age 5 years does not predict 26–47% of HAZ variation at 8 years (Schott et al., 2013). These data do not yet permit following the same children when they become older, although subsequent rounds of data will become available in the future.

1.4.2 Implications

1.4.2.1 *Associations with Cognitive Achievement*

Crookston et al. (2013) use the YL data to determine whether changes in growth after infancy are associated with schooling and cognitive achievement at age 8 years. They represent growth by HAZ at 1 year and HAZ at 8 years that was not predicted by HAZ at 1 year (or residual HAZ at 8, conditioning on HAZ at 1). They find that HAZ at 1 is inversely associated with overage for grade and positively associated with mathematics achievement, reading comprehension, and receptive vocabulary. Unpredicted growth from 1 to 8 years of age is also inversely associated with overage for grade (odds ratio range across countries: 0.80–0.84) and positively associated with mathematics achievement (effect size range: 0.05–0.10), reading comprehension (0.02–0.10), and receptive vocabulary (0.04–0.08). Children who recovered in linear growth had better outcomes than did children who were persistently stunted but were not generally different from children who experienced no growth faltering. They conclude that improvements in child growth after early faltering might have significant benefits on schooling and cognitive achievement and that, although early interventions remain critical, interventions to improve the nutrition of preprimary and early primary school-aged children also merit consideration. Using the same YL data, Georgiadis et al. (2015) find that, within the FTD, postnatal growth in the first year generally predicts cognitive skills at age 8 in all four countries, but fetal growth and post-infancy growth are at times (but less frequently) significant predictors. They also show that the use of actual HAZ at various ages versus initial HAZ and unpredicted HAZ for older ages are both consistent with the same underlying recursive model even though some of the coefficients of actual versus unpredicted growth differ in their relations to that model. These YL results suggest that there may be some important associations between post-FTD growth and various outcomes, but these results require a strong set of assumptions, including A1–A3, to permit inferences about causality for either FTD growth or post-FTD growth.

1.4.2.2 *Determinants of Growth Patterns*

Controlling for initial HAZ, Schott et al. (2013) characterize child growth up to age 1 year, and from ages 1 to 5 and 5 to 8 years and identify key household and community factors associated with these growth measures using the YL data. Multiple regression analysis suggests that parental schooling, consumption, and mothers' height are key correlates of HAZ at age 1 and also are associated with unpredicted change in HAZ from ages 1 to 5 and 5 to 8 years, given initial HAZ. These results underline the importance of children's starting point in infancy in determining subsequent growth, point to key household and community factors that may determine early growth in early life and subsequent growth recovery and growth failure, and indicate that these factors vary some by country, urban/rural designation, and child sex. That household and community factors are important determinants of both FTD growth and subsequent growth not predicted by HAZ in the FTD suggests possibilities for affecting both early growth and subsequent growth through these determinants.

1.5 Conclusion

Early-life growth failure is widespread in many LIMICs, particularly in South Asia and sub-Saharan Africa. Studies find strong associations between early-life (FTD) growth failure and outcomes over the life cycle and into the next generation. Strong assumptions are needed to interpret these as yielding causal estimates, with the strength of the assumptions differing across studies. MZ-FE estimates suggest that birthweight effects differ substantially from associations when all common endowments that MZ twins share are controlled. Several studies using the Guatemalan INCAP data report evidence of strong impacts of randomly allocated protein-dense nutritional supplements, particularly during the FTD, on adult and intergenerational outcomes, for which lessening FTD growth faltering may have been the channel: about a quarter of a standard deviation on adult cognitive skills and abilities, more than 40% on adult male wage rates, and about 100 g of women's children's birthweights. Another study using different birth cohort exposures to the INCAP alternative supplements finds associations between growth faltering at 2 years and a number of outcomes over the life cycle, arguably without biases due to unobserved determinants but probable biases due to failure to control for other possible channels. Based on such studies, there are very viable claims that growth faltering in the FTD has high costs through reducing schooling attainment, adult height, and adult earnings, among other outcomes (e.g., Table 1.1), and that it is irreversible.

However, there are estimates that suggest that both post-FTD catch-up growth and growth faltering can be considerable, that household and community factors are likely determinants of both FTD growth faltering and post-infancy growth not predicted by growth measures in the FTD, and that such unpredicted growth is almost as significantly associated with cognitive achievements later in childhood as are growth indicators in the FTD. These results certainly raise questions about the claims of irreversibility and the "closing window of opportunity" at age 2. They suggest that, although it may be that the rates of return to investing in early life are relatively high (as suggested in Figure 1.2), given current investments in children, subsequent nutritional investments may have high rates of returns as well.

There are many limitations in the existing literature, mostly related to the assumptions noted explicitly above, and these limitations suggest the need for further research.

1. Most available studies to date rely on strong assumptions to make inferences of causality, particularly in light of probable endogeneity of growth failure. Even studies that plausibly control for unobserved endowments, for example, generally do not control for other channels through which effects may be transmitted. These weaknesses are pervasive in investigations both of the importance of growth faltering in the FTD and of the importance of subsequent nutritional outcomes.
2. There are few datasets with which to assess long-run effects, particularly data with characteristics (e.g., initial randomization, natural experiments including twins) that permit at least some exploration of the robustness of the estimates to weakening some of the assumptions. Much of what appears to be known with relatively great confidence, for example, depends on studies of one dataset in one particular context: the Guatemalan INCAP data. Also there is a basic quandary regarding how to assess longer run effects over the life cycle because longitudinal data, although having some considerable advantages, also means that the early-life experiences being examined occurred in much different contexts that prevailed decades ago.
3. Another limitation of the current literature is that most studies consider only reduced-form linear relations that provide little insight into static or dynamic substitution/complementarities that might arise from production technologies or from parental behaviors, but that would require much more structural approaches to investigate (and that also would allow exploration of counterfactual policies).
4. There is some information on the costs of altering growth faltering either in the FTD or post-FTD, but many studies do not address the cost side even though it is difficult to see how policy inferences can be made without knowledge of the costs as well as the benefits.

5. Empirical investigations in this area tend to focus on undernourished children who tend to be from poor families, and thus they potentially are informative about policies related to pro-poor redistribution. But they make virtually no effort to inform about policies to increase efficiency due to market imperfections, although there should be potential for "win-win" policies to address both anti-poverty and efficiency aims if the poor are particularly subject to market imperfections, as often claimed.
6. There is little attention paid in the literature to the probable diminishing marginal returns to investments in the FTD and post-FTD. This is an important area of research. Even if it is the case that, given current investments, children in poorly nourished LMIC populations may have rates of returns as shown in Figure 1.2, shifting those investments from older to younger children would seem likely to reduce the rates of return for early-life investments and increase those for older ages, thus twisting this curve.

In conclusion, it is quite possible that early-life growth faltering and subsequent catch-up or faltering are very important for the outcomes over their life cycles of hundreds of millions of children. However, there remains much to be learned about the nature of causal effects and interventions at different ages to determine the (possibly high) benefits relative to costs.

Acknowledgments

The writing of this chapter was supported by the Bill and Melinda Gates Foundation (Global Health Grant OPP1032713), Eunice Shriver Kennedy National Institute of Child Health and Development (Grant R01 HD070993), and Grand Challenges Canada (Grant 0072-03 to the Grantee, The Trustees of the University of Pennsylvania). The author thanks various collaborators for useful discussions of the topics covered in this chapter (particularly Harold Alderman, Benjamin Crookston, Kirk Dearden, Anil D. Deolalikar, Andreas Georgiadis, John Hoddinott, Victor Lavy, Elizabeth Lundeen, John Maluccio, Subha Mani, Reynaldo Martorell, Mary Penny, Aryeh D. Stein, and Whitney Schott) and the editor, John Komlos, for useful comments on an earlier draft. Only the author is responsible for the interpretations given in this chapter.

Notes

1. Estimates for valuing averted mortality per child range widely from cheapest alternatives for averting mortality (e.g., ~$1,000 for vaccinations in Pakistan; Summers, 1992) to what compensating differentials that individuals require to assume more risk (e.g., based on wage tradeoffs, ~$10,000,000 for the United States; Viscusi & Aldy 2003).

2. Hoddinott et al. (2013*b*) explicitly recognize this possibility: "We did not consider HAZ or stunting at 2 y to be the causal factor per se. Rather the cause was the cascade of factors at societal, household, and individual levels, such as those depicted in the UNICEF conceptual framework (36), which ultimately determines nutrient availability at the cellular level and directly has an effect on growth and development in the first 1000 [days after conception]." This implies that to remedy problems for which FTD growth failure proxied in their study, the whole "cascade of factors at societal, household, and individual levels" would have to addressed.
3. Dizygotic (DZ, fraternal) twins-FE estimates also control for all factors shared by twins, including parent life cycle stages, but not genetics at conception. Estimates suggest that DZ genetic differences are important for socioeconomic outcomes (e.g., consistent with about a quarter of US adult twins earnings variance: Behrman, Rosenzweig & Taubman, 1994). Siblings-FE estimates control for all factors shared by siblings but not for parent life cycle stages or individual-specific deviations from common family genetics at conception.
4. Actual cohort studies follow a birth cohort over many years of their lives. Synthetic cohort studies link estimates for multiple birth cohorts for different life segments (e.g., one birth cohort for each of the life cycle stages in Figure 1.3).
5. Another possibility starts with an older sample and solicits recall information on early life; this is subject to recall errors but may be useful for salient early-life events for which recall is likely to be relatively accurate. I am not aware of good examples of this approach on this chapter's topics.
6. Being twins and ln mother's height are also in their preferred instrument sets; alternative estimates indicate that these variables are not significant if included in second-stage estimates.
7. Although generally these studies do not control for endogeneity of height, which may be proxying for unobserved genetic endowments. One study using the Guatemalan INCAP data that attempts to control for the endogeneity of height finds that a significant OLS association of height with wages does not remain significant if height is treated as endogenous, with randomized nutritional supplements among the identifying instruments (Behrman, Hoddinott, Maluccio, & Martorell, 2011).
8. Exceptions include lagged height from earlier life cycle stages and thus do not use A3, but do assume, as in A2, that all other outcomes can be ignored. See Lundeen et al. (2014*b*).
9. If not, the coefficient estimate for α_1 presumably will reflect normal age growth between life cycle stage *s-1* and life cycle stage *s*. In this case, comparisons in the rest of this sentence have to be adjusted for the normal age growth.
10. Or of a slight variant in which H_{s-1} is subtracted from both sides so that the coefficient of H_{s-1} in the relations estimated is $\alpha_1 - 1$.
11. Eckhardt et al. (Eckhardt, Suchindran, Gordon-Larsen, & Adair, 2005) report that diets after age 2 years are significantly associated with heights up to age 18.5 years, which seems to suggest catch-up growth.

References

Adair, L. (1999). Filipino children exhibit catch-up growth from age 2 to 12 years. *Journal of Nutrition*, *129*, 1140–1148.

Alderman, H., & Behrman, J. R. (2006). Reducing the incidence of low birth weight in low-income countries has substantial economic benefits. *World Bank Research Observer*, *21*(1), 25–48.

Alderman, H., Hoddinott, J., & Kinsey, B. (2006). Long term consequences of early childhood malnutrition. *Oxford Economic Papers, 58*(3), 450–474.

Behrman, J. R., Calderon, M. C., Preston, S. H., Hoddinott, J. F., Martorell, R., & Stein, A. D. (2009). Nutritional supplementation of girls influences the growth of their children: Prospective study in Guatemala. *American Journal of Clinical Nutrition, 90*(5), 1372–1379.

Behrman, J. R., & Deolalikar, A. B. (1989). Wages and labor supply in rural India: The role of health, nutrition and seasonality. In D. E. Sahn (Ed.), *Causes and implications of seasonal variability in household food security* (pp. 107–118). Baltimore, MD: Johns Hopkins University.

Behrman, J. R., Deolalikar, A. B., & Lavy, V. (1994). Dynamic decision rules for child growth in rural India and the Philippines: Catching up or staying behind? Washington, DC: World Bank Working Paper.

Behrman, J. R., Hoddinott, J. F., Maluccio, J. A., & Martorell, R. (2011). *Brains versus brawn: Labor market returns to intellectual and physical human capital in a poor developing country*. Washington, DC: International Food Policy Research Institute Working Paper.

Behrman, J. R., Hoddinott, J. F., Maluccio, J. A., Soler-Hampejsek, E., Behrman, E. L., Martorell, R., . . . Stein, A. D. (2014). What determines adult cognitive skills? Influences of pre-school, school and post-school experiences in Guatemala. *Latin American Economic Review, 23*(4), 1–32.

Behrman, J. R., Pollak, R. A., & Taubman, P. (1982). Parental preferences and provision for progeny. *Journal of Political Economy, 90*(1), 52–73.

Behrman, J. R., & Rosenzweig, M. R. (2004). Returns to birthweight. *Review of Economics and Statistics, 86*(2), 586–601.

Behrman, J. R., Rosenzweig, M. R., & Taubman, P. (1994). Endowments and the allocation of schooling in the family and in the marriage market: The Twins Experiment. *Journal of Political Economy, 102*(6), 1131–1174.

Bhutta, Z. A., Ahmed, T., Black, R. E., Cousens, S., Dewey, K., Giugliani, E., . . . Maternal and Child Undernutrition Study Group. (2008). What works? Interventions for maternal and child undernutrition and survival. *Lancet, 371*(9610), 417–440.

Bound, J., & Solon, G. (1999). Double trouble: On the value of twins-based estimation of the return to schooling. *Economics of Education Review, 18*(2), 169–182.

Case, A., & Paxson, C. (2008). Stature and status: Height, ability, and labor market outcomes. *Journal of Political Economy, 116*(3), 499–532.

Crookston, B. T., Schott, W., Cueto, S., Dearden, K. A., Engle, P., Georgiadis, A., . . . Behrman, J. R. (2013). Postinfancy growth, schooling, and cognitive achievement: Young lives. *American Journal of Clinical Nutrition, 98*(6), 1555–1563.

Cunha, F., & Heckman, J. (2007). The technology of skill formation. *American Economic Review, 97*(2), 31–47.

de Onis, M., Blössner, M., & Borghi, E. (2011). Prevalence and trends of stunting among preschool children, 1990–2020. *Public Health Nutrition, 1*(1), 1–7.

Eckhardt, C. L., Suchindran, C., Gordon-Larsen, P., & Adair, L. S. (2005). The association between diet and height in the postinfancy period changes with age and socioeconomic status in Filipino youths. *Journal of Nutrition, 135*(9), 2192–2198.

Georgiadis, A., Benny, L., Crookston, B. T., Duc, L. T., Hermida, P., Mani, S., . . . Behrman, J. R. (2015). *Growth trajectories from conception to middle childhood and cognitive skills at age 8 years: Evidence from four low- and middle-income countries*. Oxford, UK: Oxford University.

Heckman, J. J. (2006). Skill formation and the economics of investing in disadvantaged children. *Science, 312*(5782), 1900–1902.

Hoddinott, J., Alderman, H., Behrman, J. R., Haddad, L., & Horton, S. (2013*a*). The economic rationale for investing in stunting reduction. *Maternal and Child Nutrition, 9*(Suppl. 2), 69–82.

Hoddinott, J., Behrman, J. R., Maluccio, J. A., Melgar, P., Quisumbing, A. R., Ramirez-Zea, M., . . . Martorell, R. (2013*b*). Adult consequences of growth failure in early childhood. *American Journal of Clinical Nutrition, 98*(5), 1170–1178.

Hoddinott, J., & Kinsey, B. (2001). Child growth in the time of drought. *Oxford Bulletin of Economics and Statistics, 63*(4), 409–436.

Hoddinott, J. F., Maluccio, J. A., Behrman, J. R., Flores, R., & Martorell, R. (2008). Effect of a nutrition intervention during early childhood on economic productivity in Guatemalan adults. *Lancet, 371*(9610), 411–416.

Kohler, H. -P., Behrman, J. R., & Schnittker, J. (2011). Social science methods for twins data: Integrating causality, endowments, and heritability. *Biodemography and Social Biology, 57*(1), 88–141.

Leroy, J. L., Ruel, M., & Habicht, J. -P. (2013). Critical windows for nutritional interventions against stunting. *American Journal of Clinical Nutrition, 98*(3), 854–855.

Leroy, J. L., Ruel, M., Habicht, J. -P., & Frongillo, E. A. (2014). Linear growth deficit continues to accumulate beyond the first 1000 days in low- and middle-income countries: Global evidence from 51 national surveys. *Journal of Nutrition, 144*, 1460–1466.

Lundeen, E. A, Stein, A. D., Adair, L. A., Behrman, J. R., Bhargava, S. K., Dearden, K. A., . . . Victora, C. G. (2014*a*). Height-for-age z scores increase despite increasing height deficits among children in 5 developing countries. *American Journal of Clinical Nutrition, 100*(3), 821–825.

Lundeen, E. A., Behrman, J. R., Crookston, B. T., Dearden, K. A., Engle, P., Georgiadis, A., . . . Stein, A. D. (2014*b*). Growth faltering and recovery in children aged 1–8 years in four low- and middle-income countries: Young lives. *Public Health Nutrition, 17*(09), 2131–2137.

Maluccio, J. A., Hoddinott, J. F., Behrman, J. R., Quisumbing, A. R., Martorell, R., & Stein, A. D. (2009). The impact of improving nutrition during early childhood on education among Guatemalan adults. *Economic Journal, 119*(537), 734–763.

Mani, S. (2012). Is there complete, partial, or no recovery from childhood malnutrition? Empirical evidence from Indonesia. *Oxford Bulletin of Economics and Statistics, 74*(5), 691–715.

Martorell, R., Khan, K. L., & Schroeder, D. (1994). Reversibility of stunting: Epidemiological findings in children from developing countries. *European Journal of Clinical Nutrition, 48*, S45–S57.

Outes, I., & Porter, C. (2013). Catching up from early nutritional deficits? Evidence from rural Ethiopia. *Economics & Human Biology, 11*(2), 148–163.

Persico, N., Postlewaite, A., & Silverman, D. (2004). The effect of adolescent experience on labor market outcomes: The case of height. *Journal of Political Economy, 112*(5), 1019–1053.

Prentice, A. M., Ward, K. A., Goldberg, G. R., Jarjou, L. M., Moore, S. E., Fulford, A. J., & Prentice, A. (2013). Critical windows for nutritional interventions against stunting. *American Journal of Clinical Nutrition, 97*, 911–918.

Richter, L. M., Victora, C. G., Hallal, P. C., Adair, L. S., Bhargava, S. K., Fall, C. H., . . . COHORTS Group. (2012). Cohort profile: The consortium of health-orientated research in transitioning societies. *International Journal of Epidemiology, 41*(3), 621–626.

Rosenzweig, M. R., & Zhang, J. (2013). Economic growth, comparative advantage, and gender differences in schooling outcomes: Evidence from the birthweight differences of Chinese twins. *Journal of Development Economics*, *104*(0), 245–260.

Schott, W., Crookston, B. T., Lundeen, E. A., Stein, A. D., Behrman, J. R., & Young Lives Determinants and Consequences of Child Growth Project Team. (2013). Child growth from ages 1 to 8 years in Ethiopia, India, Peru and Vietnam: Key distal household and community factors. *Social Science & Medicine*, *97*, 278–287.

Stein, A. D., Wang, M., Martorell, R., Norris, S. A., Adair, L. S., Bas, I., . . . Cohorts Group. (2010). Growth patterns in early childhood and final attained stature: Data from five birth cohorts from low- and middle-income countries. *American Journal of Human Biology*, *22*(3), 353–359.

Summers, L. H. (1992). Investing in all the people. *Pakistan Development Review*, *31*(4), 367–406.

Victora, C. G., Adair, L., Fall, C., Hallal, P. C., Martorell, R., Richter, L., & Sachdev, H. S. (2008). Maternal and child undernutrition: Consequences for adult health and human capital. *Lancet*, *371*(9609), 340–357.

Victora, C. G., de Onis, M., Hallal, P. C., Blössner, M., & Shrimpton, R. (2010). Worldwide timing of growth faltering: Revisiting implications for interventions. *Pediatrics*, *125*, e473–e480.

Viscusi, W. K., & Aldy, J. E. (2003). The value of a statistical life: A critical review of market estimates throughout the world. *Journal of Risk and Uncertainty*, *27*, 15–76.

World Health Organization (WHO). (2006). *WHO child growth standards: Length/height-for-age, weight-for-age, weight-for-length, weight-for-height, and body mass index-for-age: Methods and development*. Geneva: World Health Organization.

CHAPTER 2

BIOLOGICAL MEASURES OF WELL-BEING

RICHARD H. STECKEL

What is well-being, or, more to the point in the social sciences, how can it be measured? The subject is more subtle than it may appear, but people who study the problem agree that it has three important ingredients, shown in Figure 2.1. These components (material, health, and psychological) interact or depend on one another. One may suppose that, ultimately, well-being is a psychological phenomenon—it's all in the mind, a feeling, or sensation. One could even go beyond this, arguing that the processes of the mind are biochemical and, in principle, could be measured as such. Scientists are a long way from this achievement, however, and for now we must be satisfied with preferences or whatever people say, demonstrate, or choose.

These choices exhibit patterns. Except in pathological cases, people prefer good health to bad and more as opposed to fewer material goods or services. Satiation occurs near the tipping point at which too much of a product is dissatisfying. In colonial New England, for example, indentured servants insisted they not be fed lobster more than twice per week. Therefore, people allocate their expenditures across goods and services so as to balance tradeoffs (i.e., marginal utilities in relation to costs).

One can also distinguish individual from aggregate well-being. The individual level is simpler because it's defensible to assume that tastes or preferences do not change, at least in the short run. These preferences often differ across individuals, although there are similarities across subgroups defined by education, age, gender, and so forth. Under the convenient assumption of comparability, it is then possible to consider this year's market basket of consumption to that of last year, or this year's income to that of the previous year. Typically individuals do not worry about externalities of consumption, such as pollution or congestion, in judging their choices on aggregate well-being because they are a very small part of the market. This proposition does not hold for nations or large regions of countries.

What is an economist or psychologist to do in quantifying national well-being? Most would start measuring at the individual level and then aggregate, with the qualification noted earlier about interpersonal comparisons. Still, in considering income (a measure

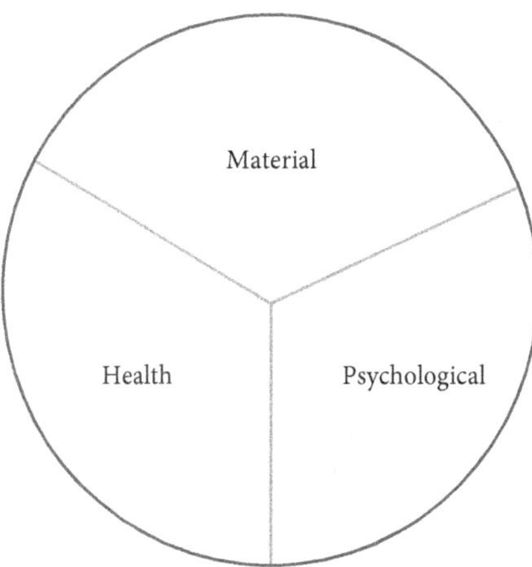

FIGURE 2.1 Components of well-being.

of access to resources or material goods and services) versus health, weighting schemes differ. In gauging health, the process is highly democratic—each person counts the same: a death is a death regardless of the status of the person. However, with respect to income, those people having greater access to resources count more in the aggregate statistics.

Readers can readily understand the existence of a literature or philosophy on measuring well-being. This is a field in itself, but practical people—those charged with analyzing evidence, delivering reports, and developing policy—are aware of these issues but cannot dwell on them. They must make choices or recommendations, and this chapter reviews common ones.

Concepts are most useful if they are readily measurable, if there is an empirical counterpart: numbers such as prices and quantities left by markets, length of life as indicated on death certificates, or even feelings of happiness as recorded on responses to questionnaires.

It should be noted that technology and public purpose heavily determine the cost and availability of evidence related to national well-being. Bills of mortality, for example, were recorded for centuries, especially in cities, but systematic national efforts to record deaths soon after they occurred appeared only in the mid to late 19th century, after the germ theory of disease defined a role for these documents. With regard to technology, one might like to have a time series of blood pressure measurements, but practical blood pressure cuffs did not arrive until the early 20th century.

This chapter emphasizes biological measures of well-being, but it is important to place them in perspective relative to monetary measures commonly used by societies. Gross domestic product (GDP) per capita is essentially universal, and for this reason the concept receives special consideration.

Biological measures have certain advantages over monetary quantities such as income or wealth. For one, they are more comparable across time and space. Life expectancy at birth, for example, means about the same thing in ancient Egypt as in modern America.

The benefits of income, on the other hand, depend on the goods and services available for purchase and their prices. Over long periods of time, it is important to correct prices for inflation or deflation, and price levels may differ across regions or countries. One may speculate what GDP means in a hunter-gathering society, yet numerous biological measures of well-being would be well-defined.

In addition, there are diminishing returns to income but not to health, at least within the current range of possibilities. Income relative to that of others matters for people's well-being in the sense that the very rich may provoke envy. There is even evidence that living near people who are much richer is bad for health, perhaps by creating anxiety to "keep up with the Jones." Health inequalities, however, may also reduce health and well-being through exposure to diseases harbored by the poor or the unwashed.

2.1 Common Biological Measures

The number of biological measures available is nearly limitless, particularly when considering the cellular or molecular level. Imagine white blood cell counts, cortisol (a steroid hormone released in response to stress), cholesterol readings, and temperature, which all help diagnose health. Useful as these may be at the individual level, public health officials have not provided long times series of evidence for social scientists or policy makers to study.

Here, I examine the unique and valuable contributions of four biological measures—life expectancy at birth, morbidity, physical stature, and skeletal remains—to understanding levels and changes in human well-being. People desire far more than material goods and, in fact, they are quite willing to trade material things in return for better physical health. Health is so important to the quality of life for most people that the "biological standard of living" is a useful concept. Biological measures may be especially valuable for historical studies and for other research circumstances where monetary measures are thin or lacking. But note that they are informative also for modern populations because they provide another perspective on well-being. A concluding section ruminates on the future evolution of biological approaches in measuring happiness.

2.1.1 Life Tables

The life table or average length of life is the oldest and most widely used biological measure. The concept and the data required to construct this measure were understood by the early 1800s, but, in most countries, it took many decades to form administrative structures to collect the necessary evidence, which are death certificates and estimates of the size of the population at risk (Swanson, Siegel, & Shryock, 2004, ch. 12–14).

Although there is a cohort life table, which is based on the mortality experience of an entire birth cohort, most life tables are the period variety, which imagines a synthetic or artificial cohort that experiences the probabilities of death of people of different ages and observed in a single year. The probabilities of death are calculated from information on the number of deaths by age, gathered from death certificates, and the number of people alive at each age, usually estimated from census counts of the population. One calculates life expectancy at birth by supposing that an actual birth cohort experiences the mortality rates of people of different ages observed in a single year, say 2000. Thus, a period life table provides a cross-section measure of health that will underestimate the actual life expectancy of people born in 2000 if mortality rates fall over time, as was the case in the 20th century. Likely, those people who were old in 2000, for example, had higher mortality rates than those who will be old in 2050. The actual birth cohort will live longer on average than the cross-sectional evidence would predict. Of course, this is not inevitable because mortality rates may fluctuate over time or rise sharply during an epidemic.

The 20th century witnessed a vast expansion in population studies that were well-grounded in evidence (Caldwell & Caldwell, 2006). By the middle of the 20th century, scholars had formulated an influential generalization called the "demographic transition," which depicted progress from pre-modern regimes of high fertility and high mortality (in the neighborhood of 3.0–3.5%) to the post-modern situation in which both were low (about 1.0–1.5%). Typically, the fertility decline preceded the fall in mortality, and, depending on the country and time period, the difference may have been several decades or longer. The process of change tended to be more rapid in the 20th as opposed to the 19th century, and those of the past half-century occurred even more quickly.

The health side of change is often called the "mortality transition," and recent large compilations of evidence on the topic can be found in Riley (2001) and in Maddison (2001). Both document and discuss possible explanations for change in the world of 1800 with 1 billion people and life expectancy of perhaps 25 years, to the present world of more than 6 billion people and a life expectancy of about 66 years. By 1900, life expectancy across the world had risen slightly, to more than 30 years, but important differences existed by region, with European countries and their colonial offshoots (plus Japan) having a 20-year advantage (46 vs. 26 years) over the rest of the world, which had changed little if at all. Today, there is even more variation across countries, where life expectancy differs by 2:1 (about 40 years to slightly more than 80 years). Even those nations with the lowest life expectancy today, however, are better off in this regard than the healthiest countries of two centuries ago.

There is little doubt that cost-effective public health measures played an important role by reducing exposure to pathogens via cleaner water, waste removal, sewage treatment, personal hygiene, and chemical control of disease vectors. More controversial are explanations for improving health in Europe and its offshoots prior to 1900, before the public health movement flourished and long before antibiotics and other advances in medical technology were available. One school of thought led by McKeown (1976) and by Fogel (2004) emphasizes improving diets that stemmed from the agricultural revolution of the 18th and 19th centuries, which featured new crops and equipment as well as enclosures, transportation improvements, and eventually the rise of free trade. Others claim that rising incomes and/or a decline in the virulence of pathogens were important.

2.1.2 Morbidity

Of course, not all years of life are equal in terms of strength and vigor. For this reason, demographers have proposed ways to adjust length of life in terms of quality. Measuring the quality of health is challenging in part because there are numerous measures of morbidity and illness, and even if one standard is widely accepted, consistent collection of evidence over time and across space is usually difficult and expensive. The point generally holds with greater force for the past because few if any surveys are available, although Section 1.7 on skeletal remains demonstrates how bone lesions reflect chronic morbidity conditions.

A few decades ago, health economists devised the concept of quality-adjusted life years (QALY) to help estimate cost-benefit ratios from various health interventions (Klarman, Francis, & Rosenthal, 1968; Torrance, Thomas, & Sackett, 1972). The method places a weight from 0 to 1 on the time spent in different health states. A year in perfect health is worth 1 and death is assigned a 0. There are intermediate values for states of life like living with a pacemaker implant, undergoing kidney dialysis, and many other conditions. Some painful or agonizing states are considered worse than death and receive negative values. After considering the additional years of life created by various interventions and weighting these additional years for the quality of health, the result is a common measure that is useful for assessing the benefits of health care spending or other interventions. The method has a number of practical and technical difficulties related to measuring the quality of life (assigning numerical values to morbidity), but physical examinations and surveys are ways to gain such information. One popular survey (EQ-D5) asks the extent to which individuals have functional problems in five areas: mobility, pain/discomfort, self-care, anxiety/depression, and pursuit of usual activities (http://www.euroqol.org/).

If such data were available over the entire life span of an individual, one could construct a graph by age that depicts health, measured on a scale from 0 to 1, over the life course. In this situation, the area under the curve is a biological measure of the quality of life measured by length of life adjusted for health while living. There is obviously a tradeoff between duration and health quality that provide the same QALY, or many different curves can have the same area.

In the United States, morbidity surveys began with Hagerstown, Maryland, in 1921–24 but an ongoing program did not begin until 1956 (Perrott, 1949). The National Center for Health Statistics interviews the noninstitutionalized population for information on doctor visits, hospital stays, acute conditions, limits on physical activity, and so forth while other surveys gain data through physical examinations and various psychological and physiological tests. Numerous industrial countries such as Japan, the United Kingdom, and the Netherlands have similar surveillance systems.

Historical Statistics of the United States compiles dozens of morbidity statistics, including the incidence rates of many diseases (Steckel, 2006). For example, immunizations led to abrupt declines in many infectious diseases in the middle of the 20th century. Rates of measles had ranged from 250 to 750 per 100,000 population from 1912 up to about 1960, but, by 1966, the rate sank to about 20 per 100,000 or less. As another example, there is evidence showing little time trend in the average number of restricted activity days per person from 1967 to 1995, based on data from the National Health Interview Survey. Of course, interview data on restricted activity may be subject to cultural norms of what constitutes sickness or disability.

2.1.3 Stature and Nutritional Status

J. M. Tanner's authoritative book on *A History of the Study of Human Growth* recounts the long history of studying body size and proportions (Tanner, 1981). Artists were among the first to study human form quantitatively for purposes of accurately rendering sculptures and paintings. What might be called scientific interest in heights began during the Enlightenment. Early studies of *auxology*—that is, the study of human growth—were sporadic, imprecise attempts made by individuals. However, whereas systematic data on both national income and life expectancy awaited large-scale government action, useful measurements of height and related attributes could be made on a small scale. Thus, auxology made important progress before the end of the 19th century. The results of an explosion of growth studies in the 20th century are contained in *Worldwide Variation in Human Growth* (Eveleth & Tanner, 1976/1990).

Figure 2.2 displays the growth velocity of well-nourished boys taken from the National Health and Nutrition Examination Survey (NHANES) survey (Hamill, Drizd, Johnson, Reed, & Roche, 1977). Even though infants grow rapidly, the rate declines during childhood and reaches a preadolescent minimum around age 11. Nutritional requirements increase substantially during the subsequent adolescent growth spurt. Although the adolescent spurt is somewhat larger for boys, they end up 4.5–5 inches taller primarily because the boys have 2 additional years of growth at preadolescent rates. Several studies confirm the similarity of this pattern across a wide range of well-nourished ethnic groups; children who grow up under good conditions are approximately the same height regardless of ethnic heritage (Steckel, 1995, provides additional discussion and references).

Numerous studies establish the importance of diet, exposure to disease, and physical activity or work for the growth of children (Eveleth & Tanner, 1976/1990). In this context, it is useful to think of the body as a biological machine that operates on food as fuel, which it expends in moderate amounts at idle (resting in bed and replacing

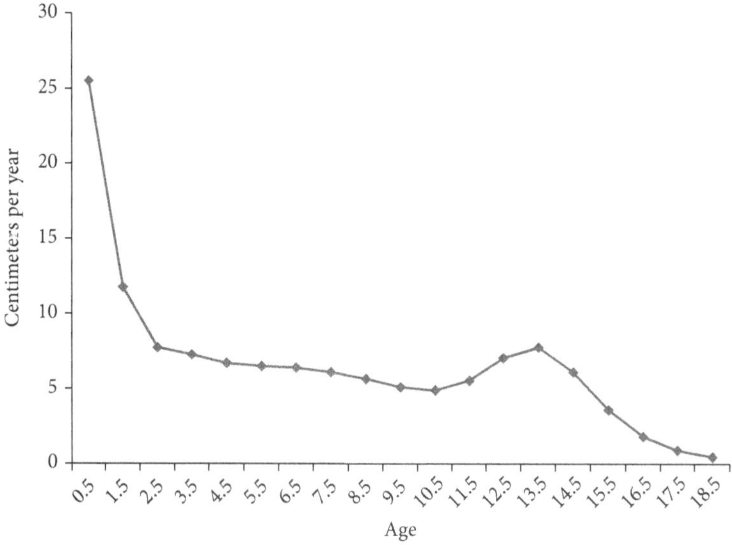

FIGURE 2.2 Growth velocity of boys under good conditions.

Source: Hamill et al., 1977.

worn-out cells) but in larger quantities while working or fighting infection. During World War II, for example, children's heights floundered in Russia and the Netherlands under restricted food intake. Disease may also stunt growth because it can divert nutritional intake to fight infection or result in incomplete absorption of what is consumed. Similarly, physical activity or work places a claim on the diet. For these reasons, average adult height reflects a population's history of *net* nutrition.

If better times follow a period of deprivation, growth may exceed that ordinarily found under good conditions. Catch-up (or compensatory) growth is an adaptive biological mechanism that complicates the study of child health using adult height because it can partially or substantially erase the effects of deprivation. Between birth and maturity, a person could potentially undergo several episodes of deprivation and recovery, thereby obscuring important fluctuations in the quality of life.

Preferably, researchers would have the complete growth history available for study, such as the curve depicted in Figure 2.2. Even these data would be inadequate for a thorough understanding adult height, however, because diet, disease, and physical activity may trade off in combinations that affect growth at each age. Although very useful for analysis, velocity at each age provides only proximate knowledge of why average adult height takes on the value it does (or did). Thus, a thorough understanding requires dozens of pieces of information, and even more if components of diet and varieties of disease are viewed separately. Essentially, such information is never available. In sum, average height is a good measure of welfare or the quality of life during childhood and adolescence but—like any other economic indicator—it can be difficult to analyze or explain because it reflects or captures many conditions over the period of growth.

Income is a potent determinant of stature that operates through diet, disease, and work intensity, but analysis of the relationship must recognize other factors. Personal hygiene, public health measures, and the disease environment affect illness, and work intensity is a function of technology, culture, and methods of labor organization. In addition, the relative price of food, cultural values such as the pattern of food distribution within the family, methods of preparation, and tastes and preferences for foods may also be relevant for net nutrition. Yet, influential policy-makers view higher incomes for the poor as the most effective means of alleviating protein-energy malnutrition in developing countries. Extremely poor families may spend two-thirds or more of their income on food, but even a large share of their very low incomes purchases few calories. Malnutrition associated with extreme poverty has a major impact on height, but expenditures beyond those needed to satisfy caloric requirements purchase largely variety, palatability, and convenience.

Impoverished families can afford little medical care, and additional income improves health through control of infectious diseases. Although tropical climates have a bad reputation for diseases, King (1966) argues that poor health in developing countries is largely a consequence of poverty rather than climate. A group of diseases are spread by vectors that need a warm climate, but poverty is responsible for the lack of doctors, nurses, drugs, and equipment to combat these and other diseases. Poverty, via malnutrition, increases the susceptibility to disease.

At the individual level, extreme poverty results in malnutrition, retarded growth, and stunting. Higher incomes enable individuals to purchase a better diet and height increases correspondingly, but once income is sufficient to satisfy caloric requirements, only modest increases are attainable through change in the diet. Height may continue to rise with income because individuals purchase more or better housing and medical care. As income increases, consumption patterns change to realize a larger share of genetic potential, but environmental variables are powerless after attaining the capacity for growth.[1] The limits to this process are clear from the fact that people who grew up in very wealthy families are not physical giants.

If the relationship between height and income is nonlinear at the individual level, then the relationship at the aggregate level depends on the distribution of income. Average height may differ for a given per capita income depending on the fraction of people with insufficient income to purchase an adequate diet or to afford medical care. Because the gain in height at the individual level increases at a decreasing rate as a function of income, one would expect average height at the aggregate level to rise, for a given per capita income, with the degree of equality of the income distribution (assuming there are people who have not reached their genetic potential).[2] Therefore one should be cautious in estimating and interpreting the relationship between per capita income and average height at the aggregate level without taking into account other factors, such as the distribution of income, entitlements, relative prices, and the organization of medical care.

The aggregate relationship between height and income can be explored by matching the results of 18 national height studies tabulated in Eveleth and Tanner (1976/1990)

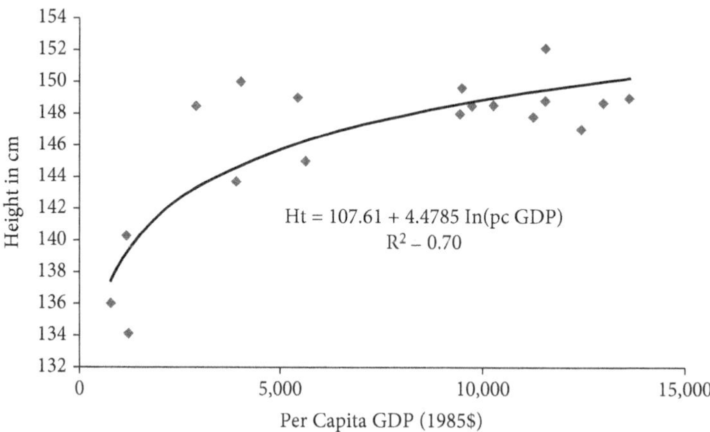

FIGURE 2.3 Per capita gross domestic product and height at age 12 (boys).

Source: Compiled from data in Eveleth & Tanner (1976/1990) and the Penn World Tables: http://pwt.econ.upenn.edu/php_site/pwt_index.php

with per capita income data compiled by Summers and Heston (1991). Despite the large number of factors that may influence the relationship, Figure 2.3 shows that there is a high correlation between a country's average height and the log of its per capita income, which is about 0.82. Although Figure 2.3 illustrates the case of boys, a similar relationship holds for girls and for adults. Figure 2.3 makes clear that income has diminishing returns on average height: once basic necessities are satisfied, higher income has less impact on health and physical growth. Thus, stature is a good measure of deprivation but not of opulence. One should be wary of estimating GDP from height because the curve displayed in Figure 2.3 is a function of health technology and the disease environment. Over time, the curve has shifted upward, receiving, for example, a large boost with the rise of the germ theory of disease, which led to several cost-effective innovations such as water purification.

Regional and national data series exist for heights, but historians have constructed them using data originally collected for other purposes. In the past 30 years, scholars have completed several large historical studies or compilations of evidence on height with an interest in understanding the standard of living. Although there are many data sources, such as slave manifests, muster rolls, convict records, passport applications, and so forth, the most abundant source is military organizations beginning in the middle of the 18th century, which routinely recorded heights for identification purposes, to assess fighting strength, and to make uniforms. Among the country studies are those on Austria-Hungry, England, and Japan (Floud, Wachter, & Gregory, 1990; Komlos, 1989; Mosk, 1996). Steckel and Floud (1997) organized a large effort for a comparative study of England, France, the Netherlands, Sweden, Germany, the United States, Australia, and Japan. John Komlos edited papers compiling evidence for numerous countries around the globe, and Steckel surveyed the state of the field as of the mid-1990s (Komlos, 1994, 1995; Steckel, 1995). Thus, historical perspective is available for numerous countries.

Moreover, the World Bank, the United Nations, and other agencies now regularly collect height data as part of occasional surveillance programs, to evaluate interventions, and to investigate socioeconomic mechanisms that affect physical growth and child health.

Collectively, the existing studies about stature both confirm and contradict certain long-held beliefs about differences and changes in human well-being. Heights substantiate the poor heath in cities relative to rural areas prior to 1900, a pattern long known from historical population studies. In 19th century Sweden, for example, average height was 3–8 cm greater in rural areas compared with Stockholm, depending on the time period and rural area (Sandberg & Steckel, 1988).

Comparing height patterns with traditional monetary measures of social performance across developing and developed countries in the second half of the 20th century revealed a useful role for heights: assessing biological inequality (Steckel, 1983). Steckel found that average height was not only a logarithmic function of average income at the national level, but that holding income constant, average height increased as the degree of income inequality declined. From this insight, researchers began to study occupational and regional differences in stature as a proxy for inequality. In late 18th century England, for example, the average heights at age 14 of poor boys admitted to the Marine Society were 20 cm below those of upper class boys who attended the elite academy at Sandhurst (Floud et al., 1990). During the same era, the difference in average height between the rich and the poor in the United States was roughly 3 cm (Margo & Steckel, 1983).

2.1.4 American Slaves

Anthropometric history has uncovered surprising patterns of evidence that challenged traditional interpretations of the past and sometimes provided new insights for human biology. An example includes the extraordinary growth depression in childhood and substantial later recovery by American slave teenagers, which is based on the heights of approximately 48,000 individuals exported from the cotton states. The children were among the smallest ever measured and would have caused alarm in a modern pediatrician's office. Yet the adults were comparable in height to the contemporary nobility of Europe, about half an inch shorter than Union Army troops, and less than 2 inches below modern height standards (average for males and females). Children adopted from poor into rich countries also show substantial catch-up growth, which proves the pattern is biologically possible. Selectivity cannot explain the pattern because the heights of slaves shipped by traders were little different from those transported by plantation owners, and higher death rates for shorter individuals would explain at most a trivial portion of the growth acceleration by teenagers (Steckel & Ziebarth, 2015).

The extent of deprivation and catch-up was extraordinary and unprecedented in historical or modern populations, which suggests that slavery was somehow responsible. All height studies, whether for the past or the present, show that the height percentiles attained by children and by adults were similar within the same population or community.

The health deficit of young slaves probably began with low birthweights, which were associated with seasonal rhythms in the diet, work, and disease of pregnant slaves, which was followed by attenuated breastfeeding and a low-protein diet until slaves began working around age 10 (Steckel 1986*a*, 1986*b*, 1987). Nonworking slaves were fed little meat, a result commonly achieved through dietary segregation of food prepared in central kitchens whereby children and adults usually ate at separate times and places, with children in the nursery and working adults in the fields. If rations were allocated to families, then owners placed strict limits on the amount of meat given to slaves who did not work in the fields. Owners discovered that the workers could not perform hard labor without meat in their diet, which implies that parents paid a heavy price for sluggish field work (possibly a whipping) if they shared the meat rations with their children. Such feeding practices no doubt stressed the family as a unit in its ability to protect and nurture children.

Remarkably, this pattern of deprivation and catch-up was profitable for slave owners. Dietary studies show that protein is essential for growth. Meat rations limited to workers and protein deficits estimated for poor children in developing countries suggest that the protein deficit was 50% or more. Assuming a protein deficit was the only obstacle to achieving modern height standards, one can calculate the rate of return on feeding children enough meat protein to reach these standards based on the protein content and price of pork, as well as knowledge that slave values increased by 1.37% per inch of height. The rate of return is actually negative if the deficits were as high as 50%, and they remain under 1% if one allows mortality rates to fall in half from better nutrition. Rates of return would have been even lower if well-nourished children were highly active and required more supervision, or if there was a "leaky nutritional bucket"; that is, if these children had parasites, malaria, and other diseases that would have diverted or absorbed some of the better nutrition. It is well-established that poor nutrition in early childhood permanently reduces cognitive ability, which would have limited the capacity of former slaves to compete in the economy following emancipation. It may seem paradoxical, but planters who owned all future labor found that poor nutrition was profitable in their rearing of young children.

2.1.5 Long-Term Trends

Economic historians were surprised to find that heights in America declined during the middle of the 19th century (Figure 2.4), which occurred during the midst of an industrial revolution and rapid economic growth. While per capita incomes grew by 55% from 1830 to 1860, average height declined by 1.2 inches. Hence the term "antebellum puzzle," in which measures of human welfare were moving in opposite directions (Craig, forthcoming). One case see from Figure 2.5 that height declines occurred throughout the country (Zehetmayer, 2011). In additioin, both the United States and England experienced substantial and sustained height declines during industrialization prior to the late

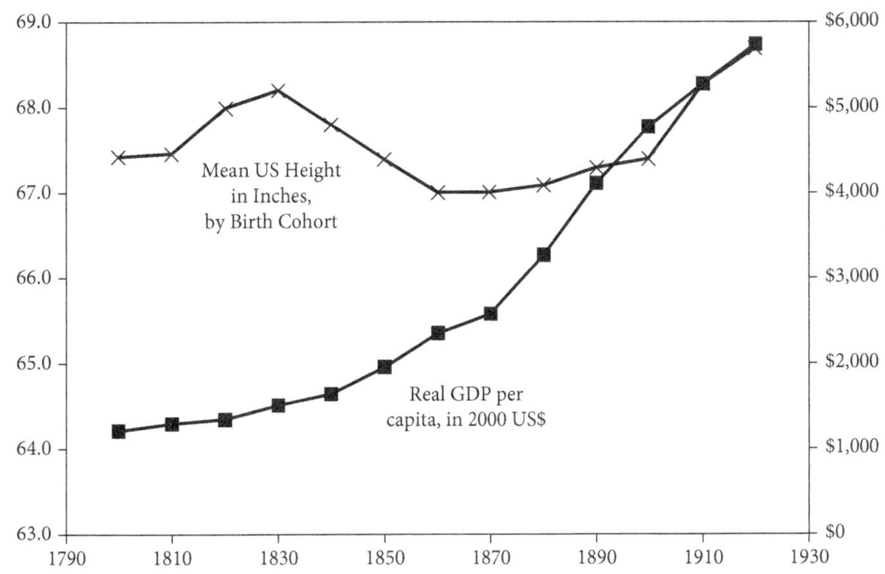

FIGURE 2.4 The trend in height versus real gross domestic product per capita.

Source: Carig, forthcoming

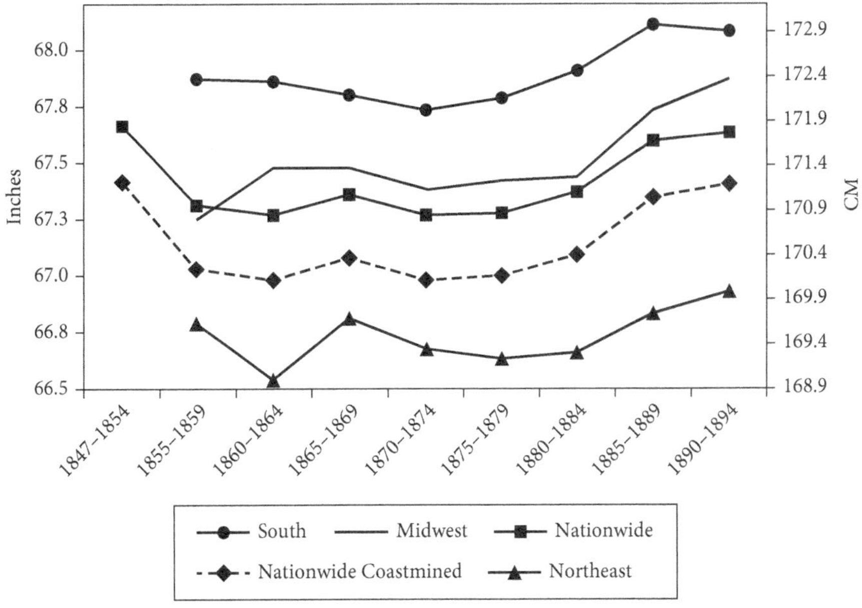

FIGURE 2.5 National and regional estimates of heights for recruits born in the United States.

Source: Zehetmayer, 2011, p. 320.

19th century (Steckel & Floud, 1997), but some European countries experienced shorter term problems during the mid-19th century as well.[3] Numerous explanations for the American case are now under investigation, including urbanization, the rise of public schools that spread diseases among children, higher food prices, growing inequality, and higher rates of interregional trade and migration that spread pathogens (Komlos, 1998; Steckel, 1995).

Notably, the average height of Americans has leveled off in recent decades, while those of Europeans continue to grow. The Dutch are now the tallest, with the men averaging around 183 cm while Americans fall some 5 cm below. Average heights in northern Europe now exceed those in the United States, but explanations have been difficult to quantify and evaluate. Some people point to differences in the health care system, which is heavily subsidized and widely provided or universal in northern Europe as opposed to the United States. Inequality could play a role also, with democratic socialism leveling disposable incomes and raising average heights relative to the United States. Perhaps diets are the culprit, whereby Americans eat more fast food and snacks that crowd out fruits and vegetables that provide essential micronutrients.

2.1.6 Native Americans

With the possible exception of slaves, no group in American history has suffered greater misunderstanding closer to vilification and manipulation than Native Americans. In many Euro-American eyes of the mid-19th century, they were bad Indians who terrorized settlers and stole horses. Near the turn of the century, they became entertainers and caricatures, as illustrated by Buffalo Bill's Wild-West shows. The *Saturday Evening Post* then serialized romantic stories of the Old West, which were followed by Western movies in which Indians were usually the bad guys. By the 1960s, Native Americans were often portrayed as victims, and, by the 1990s, as ecologically sensitive caretakers of the land. It is difficult to sort fact from fiction in this diverse landscape of images.

Fortunately, height data provide some facts about nutritional status and health-related quality of life. Euro-Americans were not the tallest population in the world, at least in the middle of the 19th century. By a small margin, this honor went to native Americans who used horses to hunt and migrate across the Great Plains (Steckel & Prince, 2001). According to data originally collected by Franz Boas, the men in eight of these tribes averaged 172.6 cm (N = 1,123); the Cheyenne topped the list at 176.7 cm (n = 29), and the Arapaho were second at 174.3 cm (N = 57). The average heights follow an inverted U shape with respect to latitude. The shortest tribes occupied the northern (Assiniboin) and the southern plains (Comanche), whereas the Arapahoe and the Cheyenne of Colorado and Wyoming were the tallest. Their achievement is all the more remarkable because the tribes suffered repeated bouts of smallpox and other epidemic diseases that substantially reduced their numbers. It is unlikely that the Plains tribes were tall due to selective editing or removal of short people by disease. They were tall prior to the epidemics of the 1830s, and the selective effect of mortality on average height is quite small.

Several ecological and socioeconomic variables explain much of the height differences. The tribes were taller if they lived in environments with more green vegetation—a source of food for people and animals; did not live close to the major trails leading to the west, which were centers for the spread of diseases and conflict (specifically the Santa Fe and Oregon trails); and had smaller land areas per capita, an effect possibly driven by the costs of policing or defending territory. Boas was able to estimate the birth year of each person, which could be linked with conditions during the growing years. Higher rainfall during the growing years (estimated from tree rings) promoted plant growth and the supply of food that increased adult height. On the other hand, epidemics, as assessed from historical accounts, had no effect on height, and, surprisingly, the initial transition to reservations was beneficial for growth (although reservation living was unhealthy near the turn of the century).

2.1.7 Skeletal Remains

Evidence from skeletons vastly extends the reach of anthropometric history by depicting aspects of well-being over the millennia, from hunter-gatherers to settled agriculture, the rise of cities, global exploration and colonization, and industrialization. Skeletons are widely available for study in many parts of the globe. A group of skeletons can provide age- and source-specific detail on nutrition and biological stress from early childhood through old age; indeed, several indicators of health during childhood are typically measurable from the skeletons of adults. Skeletal remains also exist for women and for children, two groups often excluded from more familiar historical sources such as tax documents, muster rolls, and wage records. The value of skeletons is substantially enhanced when combined with contextual information from archaeology, historical documents, climate history, and geography.

Bones are living tissues that receive blood and adapt to mechanical and physiological stress. If a bone is injured by trauma, infection, or erosion of cartilage such that joint surfaces deteriorate, a scar forms and leaves a mark that is usually permanent or at least identifiable if the person dies many years later (Larsen, 1997). More generally, the skeleton is an incomplete but very useful repository of an individual's history of health and biological stress that often takes the form of chronic morbidity. Physical anthropologists have learned that bones can be used to estimate stature and that various lesions (such as tooth enamel deformities) reflect poor health in early childhood. Other lesions on the skull reveal iron deficiencies in early childhood, and serious skeletal infections leave permanent marks on a bone's surface. The front of the tibia is particularly vulnerable in this regard because it has little soft tissue for protection and even small injuries are compounded by dietary deficiencies, such as a lack of vitamin C. Trauma is readily identified by bone misalignment, skull indentations, or weapon wounds, and degenerative joint disease, caries, and abscesses are signs of aging.

Scholars have completed few large-scale comparative studies of community health using skeletal data. The field is relatively new, and building up a database by analyzing skeletons one at a time is highly time-consuming. In addition, the variables collected by physical anthropologists and the details of measurement tend to vary across sites and schools of thought, so meta-analysis based on evidence from past published studies is generally not an option.

The Backbone of History: Health and Nutrition in the Western Hemisphere is the largest comparative skeletal study undertaken to date, which sought to study not only the Neolithic revolution but health across a broad swath of time, space, and ethnic groups (Steckel & Rose, 2002). Collaborators pooled their evidence on seven skeletal features from 12,520 remains found at 65 localities that were collectively inhabited from 4000 BC to the early 1900s. They distilled the skeletal evidence into a health index, discussed in more detail later, that theoretically could range from 0 (most severe expression in all categories) to 100 (complete absence of lesions or signs of deficiency for every individual at the locality), but in practice averaged 72.8 (standard deviation [*SD*] = 8.0) and varied from 53.5 to 91.8 (Steckel, Sciulli, & Rose, 2002). Surprisingly, Native Americans were among both the healthiest and the least healthy populations, with European Americans and free blacks falling near the middle of the distribution.

The health index was estimated from the 12,520 skeletons of individuals who lived at 65 localities in the Western Hemisphere over the past several thousand years (Steckel & Rose, 2002). Age-specific rates of morbidity pertaining to the health indicators during childhood (stature, linear enamel defects, and anemia) were calculated by assuming that conditions persisted from birth to death, an assumption justified by knowledge that childhood deprivation is correlated with adverse health as an adult (Barker, 1994). The duration of morbidity prior to death is unknown for the infections, trauma, degenerative joint disease, and dental decay (and will be the subject of future research), but was approximated by an assumption of 10 years. Results are grouped into age categories of 0–4, 5–9, 10–14, 15–24, 25–34, 35–44, and 45+. Next, the age-specific rates for each skeletal measure were weighted by the relative number of person-years lived in a reference population that is believed to roughly agree with pre-Columbian mortality conditions in the Western Hemisphere (Model West, level 4), and the results were multiplied by life expectancy in the reference population (26.4 years) and expressed as a percent of the maximum attainable health. The seven components of the index were then weighted equally to obtain the overall index. Of course, numerous assumptions underlying the index can be challenged, modified, and refined. In particular, conditions like dental decay and trauma probably have different effects depending on the social safety net, common production technology, medical technology, and other factors that vary in unknown ways across societies. In addition, the index is an additive measure that ignores interactions.

The most intriguing finding from this project was a long-term decline in the health index in pre-Columbian America. On average, the health index fell by 0.0025 points per year from roughly 7,500 years ago to about 450 years ago, which amounts to 17.5 points over seven millennia. A decline of this magnitude represents a significant deterioration in health; it is larger than the difference between the most and least healthy groups who lived in the Western Hemisphere.

Unfortunately, the observations are concentrated in the two millennia before the arrival of Columbus, when there was clearly a great deal of diversity in health across sites. The highest value for the index did occur at the oldest site, but two sites in the later era also scored above 80. The least healthy sites (scores under 65) were all concentrated within 2,000 years of the present.

Steckel and Rose (2002) estimated a sequence of regressions that examined the statistical connection between health and various ecological categories like climate, size of settlement, diet terrain, and vegetation. Climate—as measured in categories of tropical, subtropical, and temperate—bore no relevance to the health index. This result was unanticipated and bears further study with more refined measures. Living in a larger community was deleterious to health. Groups living in paramount towns or urban settings had a health index nearly 15 points (2 *SD*) below that expressed for mobile hunter-gatherers and others not living in large, permanent communities. Of course, large pre-modern communities faced unsanitary conditions conducive to the spread of infectious disease and other maladies. Diet was also closely related to the change in the health index, with performance being nearly 12 points lower for those subsisting mainly on the triad of corn, beans, and squash, compared with the more diverse diet of hunter-gatherer groups. Because the transition to settled agriculture usually occurred with the rise of large communities, it is difficult to separate their effects on health.

Higher elevations reduced health: people who lived above 300 m scored about 15 points lower in the index. The exact mechanism for this relationship is unknown, but it is likely that a richer array of foods was available (with less work effort) at lower elevations. Vegetation surrounding the site may have affected health via the type and availability of resources for food and shelter. Forests, for example, provide materials for the diet, fuel, and housing and also sheltered animals that could have been used for food. Semi-deserts posed challenges for the food supply relative to more lush forests or grasslands, but the dry climate might have inhibited the transmission of some diseases. Those living in forests and semi-deserts had a health index about 9 points higher than inhabitants of open forests and grasslands. Flood plain or coastal living provided easy access to aquatic sources of food and enabled trade compared with more remote, interior areas, but trade may have promoted the spread of disease. Uneven terrain found in hilly or mountainous areas may have provided advantages for defense but could have led to more accidents and fractures. Apparently, the net benefit to health favored coastal areas, where the health index was about 8 points higher compared with noncoastal regions.

2.2 Frontiers

For more than three centuries scholars have struggled to measure and analyze personal and national well-being. The subject is complicated, and, despite great leaps forward, much remains to be understood. Although some overlap exists, the customary measures of human well-being used by social scientists may be classified into three broad categories: material, psychological, and health.

Over the past century, researchers have made considerable progress in defining and implementing monetary measures such as GDP. Although research continues to expand on monetary measures, the pace has slowed relative to the high point of the mid-20th century and has reached diminishing returns in adding new useful information. There has been a recent resurgence of interest in measuring well-being through survey techniques that ask about "happiness" (for a starting point in this literature, see the papers by Kahneman and Krueger [2006], and Tella and MacCulloch [2006]). But nagging questions remain about whether people's evaluations of what they report as their "happiness" mean the same thing in one country or era as another. Of course, the same thing can be said about monetary measures: a dollar for me is very different from a dollar to my grandfather when he was my age. At least so far, psychologists have come forward with new approaches to the measurement of well-being that have captured the attention of social scientists.

This chapter focuses on biological measures of well-being, where great progress has been made over the past two centuries in measuring life expectancy, morbidity, and nutritional status. In my view, the next great research frontier will use nano-size biosensors to measure brain activity and assay biochemicals in a search for patterns and determinants of well-being and happiness. For example, miniature total analysis systems, commonly called "lab-on-a-chip devices," contain all the necessary elements for analyzing miniscule amounts of bodily fluids, including the intake, transport, mixing, separation, and measuring of results (Focus, 2006; Whitesides, 2006). Nanotechnology presents legitimate risks and concerns, and the public must be educated to judge the benefits and costs, and, if necessary, be prepared to intelligently regulate the development of these remarkable devices. Nanosensory systems, however, do offer the possibility of vastly improved measures of morbidity. Various concentrations of proteins or other chemicals in the blood may signals high stress levels, increased risk of heart attack, various cancers, epileptic seizure, or inflammation in specific organs. One could ultimately imagine monthly or even daily reports on a country's state of health much like we receive on per capita income or jobs, but based on information gathered by and uploaded from nano-scale devices imbedded in the bodies of a national sample of individuals.

The historical pioneers in the measurement of human well-being have been economists on the monetary measures, human biologists and economists on stature and nutritional status, psychologists on the happiness surveys and brain chemistry, and demographers on issues of life expectancy. Anthropologists, economists, human biologists, medical specialists, historians, and others have also begun to examine these issues in studies of skeletons. The disciplinary boundaries are blurring as researchers increasingly seek and recognize the interrelationships among these traditionally distinct ways of thinking about human well-being.

Notes

1. Of course, it is possible that higher incomes could purchase products such as alcohol, tobacco, or drugs that impair health.
2. This argument is reasonable over the range of data used in the empirical analysis discussed herein. However, within an extremely poor country, it might be possible for average height to increase with an increase in inequality if the rich did not approximately attain their genetic potential.
3. Heights in several European countries declined during the late 1830s and the 1840s in connection with harvest failures and/or rising food prices. By the late 19th century, the public health movement noticeably diminished the consequences for health of events associated with industrialization.

References

Barker, D. J. P. (1994). *Mothers, babies and disease in later life*. London: BMJ Publishing Group.

Caldwell, J. C., & Caldwell, B. (2006). *Demographic transition theory*. Dordrecht, DE: Springer.

Craig, L. A. (forthcoming). The Antebellum Puzzle. In J. Komlos & I. R. Kelly (Eds.), *Oxford handbook of economics and human biology*. Oxford: Oxford University Press.

Eveleth, P. B., & Tanner, J. M. (1976/1990). *Worldwide variation in human growth*. Cambridge: Cambridge University Press.

Floud, R., Wachter, K. W., & Gregory, A. (1990). *Height, health and history: Nutritional status in the United Kingdom, 1750–1980*. Cambridge: Cambridge University Press.

Focus. (2006). Labs-on-a-chip: Origin, highlights and future perspectives on the occasion of the 10th µTAS conference. *Lab on a Chip, 6*(10), 1266–1273.

Fogel, R. W. (2004). *The escape from hunger and premature death, 1700–2100*. Cambridge: Cambridge University Press.

Hamill, P. V., Drizd, T. A., Johnson, C. L., Reed, R. B., & Roche, A. F. (1977). NCHS growth curves for children birth-18 years. United States. *Vital and Health Statistics, 11*(165), 1–74.

Kahneman, D., & Krueger, A. B. (2006). Developments in the measurement of subjective well-being. *Journal of Economic Perspectives, 20*(1), 3–24.

King, M. H. (1966). *Medical care in developing countries: A primer on the medicine of poverty and a symposium from Makerere*. Nairobi, KE: Oxford University Press.

Klarman, H. E., Francis, J. O. S., & Rosenthal, G. D. (1968). Cost effectiveness analysis applied to the treatment of chronic renal disease. *Medical Care, 6*(1), 48–54.

Komlos, J. (1989). *Nutrition and economic development in the eighteenth-century Habsburg monarchy: An anthropometric history*. Princeton, NJ: Princeton University Press.

Komlos, J. (1994). *Stature, living standards, and economic development: Essays in anthropometric history*. Chicago: University of Chicago Press.

Komlos, J. (1995). *The biological standard of living on three continents: Further explorations in anthropometric history*. Boulder, CO: Westview Press.

Komlos, J. (1998). Shrinking in a growing economy? The mystery of physical stature during the Industrial Revolution. *Journal of Economic History, 58*(3), 779–802.

Larsen, C. S. (1997). *Bioarchaeology: Interpreting behavior from the human skeleton*. New York: Cambridge University Press.

Maddison, A. (2001). *The world economy: A millennial perspective. Development Centre studies*. Paris: Development Centre of the Organisation for Economic Cooperation and Development.

Margo, R. A., & Steckel, R. H. (1983). Height of native-born Whites during the Antebellum period. *Journal of Economic History, 43*(1), 167–174.

McKeown, T. (1976). *The modern rise of population*. London: Edward Arnold.

Mosk, C. (1996). *Making health work: Human growth in modern Japan*. Berkeley, CA: University of California Press.

Perrott, G. S. J. (1949). The morbidity survey in public health work. *American Journal of Public Health and the Nations Health, 39*(6), 741–742.

Riley, J. C. (2001). *Rising life expectancy: A global history*. New York: Cambridge University Press.

Sandberg, L. G., & Steckel, R. H. (1988). Overpopulation and malnutrition rediscovered: Hard times in 19th-century Sweden. *Explorations in Economic History, 25*(1), 1–19.

Steckel, R. H. (1983). Height and per capita income. *Historical Methods, 16*, 1–7.

Steckel, R. H. (1986*a*). A peculiar population: The nutrition, health, and mortality of American slaves from childhood to maturity. *Journal of Economic History, 46*, 721–741.

Steckel, R. H. (1986*b*). A dreadful childhood: The excess mortality of American slaves. *Social Science History, 10*, 427–465.

Steckel, R. H. (1987). Growth depression and recovery: The remarkable case of American slaves. *Annals of Human Biology, 14*, 111–132.

Steckel, R. H. (1995). Stature and the standard of living. *Journal of Economic Literature. December, 33*(4), 1903–1940.

Steckel, R. H. (2006). Health, nutrition and physical well-being. In S. B. Carger, S. S. Gartner, M. R. Haines, et al. (Eds.), *Historical statistics of the United States, millennial edition* (Vol. 2, pp. 499–620). New York: Cambridge University Press.

Steckel, R. H., & Floud, R. (1997). *Health and welfare during industrialization*. Chicago: University of Chicago Press.

Steckel, R. H., & Prince, J. (2001). Tallest in the world: Native Americans of the Great Plains in the nineteenth century. *American Economic Review, 91*, 287–294.

Steckel, R. H., & Rose, J. C. (2002). *The backbone of history: Health and nutrition in the western hemisphere*. New York: Cambridge University Press.

Steckel, R. H., Sciulli, P. W., & Rose, J. C. (2002). A health index from skeletal remains. In R. H. Steckel & J. C. Rose (Eds.), *The backbone of history: Health and nutrition in the Western hemisphere* (pp. 61–93). New York: Cambridge University Press.

Steckel, R. H., & Ziebarth, N. (2015). *Selectivity and measured catch-up growth of American slaves*. Columbus, OH: Ohio State University.

Summers, R., & Heston, A. (1991). The Penn World Table (Mark 5): An expanded set of international comparisons, 1950–1988. *Quarterly Journal of Economics, 106*(2), 327–368.

Swanson, D. A., Siegel, J. S., & Shryock, H. S. (2004). *The methods and materials of demography*. San Diego, CA: Elsevier Academic.

Tanner, J. M. (1981). *A history of the study of human growth*. Cambridge: Cambridge University Press.

Tella, R. D., & MacCulloch, R. (2006). Some uses of happiness data in economics. *Journal of Economic Perspectives, 20*(1), 25–46.

Torrance, G. W., Thomas, W. H., & Sackett, D. L. (1972). A utility maximization model for evaluation of health care programs. *Health Services Research*, *7*(2), 118–133.

Whitesides, G. M. (2006). The origins and the future of microfluidics. *Nature Reviews Neuroscience*, *442*(27), 368–373.

Zehetmayer, M. (2011). The continuation of the antebellum puzzle: stature in the US, 1847–1894. *European Review of Economic History*, *15*(2), 313–327.

CHAPTER 3

CRISIS AND HUMAN BIOLOGY

PRASHANT BHARADWAJ AND TOM S. VOGL

3.1 Introduction

In modern parlance, the word "crisis" describes a pronounced shock, an adverse event, often economic or financial in nature. But, the word's earliest appearances in English texts refer to human illness, with a "crisis" being the critical juncture in the progression of a disease that determines whether the sufferer recovers or dies.[1] The links between crisis and human biology extend well beyond this point, however, and they are the subject of a burgeoning literature in economics. How do the various manifestations of crisis—from deep recessions to pandemics to natural disasters—affect human health, reproduction, and child development, and how do changes in health endowments, incomes, prices, and behaviors mediate these effects?

This chapter reviews the empirical evidence on the effects of crisis on human biology, assessing the capacity of economic theory and methodology to illuminate this evidence. We define crises as acute (as opposed to chronic), severe, and unexpected negative events, thus helping us focus our discussion by circumscribing a subset of the vast literature linking a variety of acute shocks with human biology.[2] We focus on crises that affect entire populations at once, which are likely to have the gravest consequences. Crises strike at various scales, afflicting individuals, families, communities, or entire populations. But only those in the last category supersede the ability of markets and insurance systems to absorb some of the impact of their effects.

Our focus, then, is on events that most would already perceive as terrible and worth avoiding, even at considerable cost. This insight might lead some to wonder why these events merit further study at all. But government decisions regarding crisis prevention and mediation rely on information on the costs and benefits of such interventions. The evidence we review suggests that the effects of aggregate crises are both longer lasting (felt over the lifecycle) and more extensive (involving nonobvious human biological outcomes) than many might appreciate. Thus, from a policy perspective, our review may lend additional support to arguments in favor of increased disaster preparedness or increased focus on post-disaster adaptation strategies. From a broader scientific perspective, however, the results cast in stark relief the way the human body reacts to a variety of grave insults.

We organize our discussion around five types of aggregate crises: recessions, famines, epidemics, natural and environmental disasters, and wars.[3] Taking a broad view of "human biology"—including health, child development, and reproduction—we detail the effects of each type of crisis on human biological outcomes. Whenever the literature allows, we discuss the roles of health endowments, incomes, prices, and behaviors in mediating the results, and we note how the results may vary between rich and poor settings. Notably, one type of crisis can lead to another crisis—for example, a disease epidemic can cause economic fluctuations, or a war can result in a famine. We note these possibilities as potential pathways where relevant, but, due to space considerations, we focus on the impacts of the crisis that likely occurred first. In the same vein, we do not dwell on the specific pathways through which crises affect human biology. Little existing research sheds light on these mechanisms, so we point to them as a fruitful topic for future research.

3.2 Conceptual Issues

Before reviewing the evidence, we further develop our definitions of the two concepts at the center of this chapter: crisis and human biology. To begin, we set the selection criteria for the crises we study, discussing their theoretical underpinnings and implications. We describe how behavioral responses, price adjustments, and insurance arrangements may mitigate or exacerbate the effects of a crisis, with particular attention paid to how these mechanisms may play out at different levels of aggregation. The research we review does not necessarily shed direct light on these mechanisms, but we draw attention to them as a way to motivate our choice to focus on large-scale crises. After defining crisis, we move on to setting the parameters for the outcomes we consider.

Our definition of crisis narrows the scope of the relevant literature considerably. The *acute* criterion precludes us from focusing on serious, long-lasting problems that many label "crises," such as what the editorial board of *The Lancet* (2013) calls the "global crisis of . . . malnutrition in children." The *severe* criterion leads us to direct our attention to studies of large shocks, rather than marginal changes in rainfall in agricultural areas, for example. And the *unexpected* criterion forces us to exclude important problems that unfold in a gradual and anticipated way, such as the so-called pension crisis. Our restrictive definition does occasionally rule out relevant research that falls slightly outside its boundaries. In these cases, we allow ourselves to deviate. For example, we include research on the HIV/AIDS "crisis," even if the pandemic is by now chronic and expected. We reason that it was once acute and unexpected and that, viewed through a broader lens, its history is still short.

That said, even with the three criteria, our definition includes a very wide range of negative shocks with a wide range of effects. Some crises affect individuals or families in isolation; for instance, when a parent loses his job or dies. Others occur at the local level, such as when a plant closes or an agricultural community experiences a growing season with limited rain. And yet others strike entire populations or economies; these crises, which include famines and sudden epidemics, receive the most attention from policy makers and the media because they are so wide-reaching. Crises at these three levels are likely to have differing effects on human biology depending on the extent of risk sharing, market integration, reserves, and safety nets. Aggregate crises are worse than the sum of many localized crises because they have stronger price effects and are more difficult to insure. If a single agricultural community has a bad crop year, then its members may suffer income losses. If an entire region has a bad crop year, however, these income losses may be compounded by increases in the price of food. More generally, the impact of a crisis is contingent on both the extent of *ex ante* insurance—whether through buffer-stock saving, formal insurance systems, informal risk sharing, or government safety nets—and the extent of *ex post* behavioral responses (see Skoufias, 2003, for more on coping strategies relevant to economic crises and natural disasters). For these reasons, we focus on aggregate crises. The scope of aggregation may vary—a state in one application, a country in the next—but we maintain a focus on crises broad enough to defy many risk mitigation strategies and price adjustment effects.

Apart from the characterization of crisis, our topic also requires us to define human biology. We take a broad view of the concept, including mortality, physical growth, physical morbidity, mental health, cognitive function, and fertility. These domains of human biology have considerable overlap in the literature. In some cases, the impact of crisis in one domain mediates its impact in another. In other cases, the impact in one domain complicates estimation of impacts in another. For example, impacts on mortality or fertility may introduce selection bias in estimates of impacts on morbidity or cognitive function among survivors. This concern arises in all research concerning shocks with potential effects on population composition, but it is especially pertinent for the study of major health crises, such as famines or pandemics.

Much of the research we review follows how the human biology impact of a crisis spills over into social and economic outcomes. We include such analyses in our discussion only when we can confidently attribute the effects of a crisis on social and economic outcomes to a human biology pathway. For example, one can safely trace the human capital effects of disease exposure in utero to a human biology pathway, but the same link is not possible for the lifelong consequences of exposure to war in childhood.

3.3 Recessions

Of all the crises we consider, recessions are the most natural for economists to study. Importantly, recessions typically have other root causes, some of which we consider in subsequent sections. But a large literature considers the effects of recessions per se, perhaps because recessions with varying causes often share common features. This literature pays special attention to the interplay between *income effects* owing to contractions in economic resources and *substitution effects* from reductions in the opportunity cost of time, for example. Much of the literature estimates the relationship between continuous measures of aggregate economic conditions (such as growth rates or employment rates) and human biology, which bundles together booms, mild recessions, and deep recessions. Although we are most interested in the effects of deep recessions, the work on these continuous measures provides important complementary evidence, so we include it in our review.

Perhaps the most striking finding in this literature is that population health improves during economic downturns in wealthy countries. Using both aggregate time-series and state-level panel data from the United States, Ruhm (2000) finds that a percentage point increase in the unemployment rate is associated with a .5% decrease in all-age mortality. Gerdtham and Ruhm (2006) find similar evidence from across the Organization for Economic Cooperation and Development (OECD), as do Granados, Tapia, and Roux (2009) for the historical United States, even in crises so pronounced as the Great Depression.[4] In seeking an explanation for these results, Ruhm (2000) emphasizes that the opportunity costs of leisure and other health inputs decrease during recessions, as do negative externalities from increased economic activity.[5] Evidence for these mechanisms is mixed in contemporary data. On the one hand, he finds that sedentarism, smoking, drinking, and fat consumption are pro-cyclical, consistent with opportunity cost effects from higher wages and job stress. Additionally, mortality from vehicle accidents is strongly pro-cyclical, consistent with externalities from increased activity.

On the other hand, Stevens, Miller, Page, and Filipski (2011) show that pro-cyclical mortality is concentrated among young children, twenty-somethings, and especially the elderly, for whom the opportunity cost of time is small; the pattern is absent among adults of prime working age. These findings are difficult to reconcile with a theory that indicates individuals take worse care of themselves during recessions. Rather, Stevens et al. propose that mortality declines during recessions primarily reflect cyclicality in the quality of health care, perhaps due to staffing costs. They report that staffing in skilled nursing facilities rises during recessions and also that pro-cyclicality is more pronounced for deaths occurring in nursing homes and in states where more elderly live in nursing homes.

Pro-cyclical mortality and counter-cyclical health are also apparent among the very young, but these patterns may have other causes, most importantly because changes in fertility patterns influence the distribution of health among infants. Fertility falls during recessions in the United States (Currie & Schwandt, 2013, in both national time series and state-level panel data. If this pattern varies across different types of women, then it may affect the distribution of child health. Indeed, Dehejia and Lleras-Muney (2004) present evidence that the composition of new mothers changes during recessions in a way that increases the prevalence of maternal characteristics that promote child health. At the same time, holding these characteristics constant, maternal health behavior improves during recessions. Both margins of change—selection and behavioral adjustment—improve the average health of US infants born during recessions, both across the country and within states. A percentage point increase in the unemployment rate is associated with a .25–.5% decline in the prevalence of low birthweight.

In poor countries, the opposite pattern generally holds. Analyzing Demographic and Health Survey data from 59 African, Asian, and Latin American countries, Baird, Friedman, and Schady (2011) find strong counter-cyclicality in infant mortality. Within countries over time, fluctuations in gross domestic product (GDP) per capita are negatively associated with fluctuations in infant mortality, a result robust to the inclusion of flexible country-specific time trends and thus accounting for joint secular trends in economy and health. The result is also robust to mother fixed effects—thus controlling for changes in the composition of mothers. A 1% decrease in GDP per capita adds .25–.5 infant deaths per 1,000 live births. Most country-specific studies in the developing world also find that mortality rises in downturns (Bhalotra, 2010; Cutler, Knaul, Lozano, Méndez, & Zurita, 2002; Paxson & Schady, 2005). Where data exist, they suggest similar results for other health outcomes such as birthweight (Bozzoli & Quintana-Domeque 2014). Nevertheless, counterexamples also exist. In Colombia, sudden drops in the international price of coffee cause infant health to improve in coffee-growing regions, arguably because of falling opportunity costs of maternal time with children (Miller & Urdinola, 2010). In Indonesia, child weight-for-age held steady through the financial crisis because mothers buffered children's caloric intake by eating less themselves (Block et al., 2004). Broadly speaking, however, most results point to pro-cyclical health in developing countries.

The differences in results between rich and poor countries suggest that income effects may dominate when a recession reduces resources to dire levels, as in a crisis. This theory would be compelling if the effects of booms and busts had asymmetric effects, in which busts have stronger negative effects than booms have positive effects. The literature offers some evidence to this effect. In poor countries, deep recessions elevate female infant mortality particularly strongly—far exceeding effects proportional to the impacts of small negative shocks or positive shocks (Baird et al., 2011). But in a twist that remains open to interpretation, the effects of aggregate shocks on male infant mortality are both smaller and more symmetric. Furthermore, infant mortality is neither significantly more counter-cyclical in low-income (compared to middle-income) countries, nor in children born to less-educated (compared to more-educated) women.

Beyond these contemporaneous impacts, research suggests that survivors of early-life exposure to economic crisis may suffer life-long sequelae in developing countries. The most convincing evidence comes from the historical record. In Dutch cohorts from the 19th century, those with birth years coinciding with recessions experienced higher mortality risk through the life cycle (van den Berg, Lindeboom, & Portrait, 2006). Around the same time, men born during the Great French Wine Blight exhibited relative shortfalls in adult height if they were born in wine-growing regions that underwent a deep recession (Banerjee, Duflo, Postel-Vinay, & Watts, 2010). More recent evidence also suggests that exposure to economic shocks in early life can result in mental health impacts in adulthood (Adhvaryu, Fenske, & Nyshadham, 2014). At least for the young, the human biology impacts of deep recessions last far longer than do the direct economic impacts.

3.4 Famines

An extreme manifestation of recession is famine, a phenomenon that has received much attention in the economics literature at least since Amartya Sen's (1981) analysis of the Bengal Famine of 1944 (see also Ó Gráda, 2009). The idea that famines kill is not novel; hence, the literature we summarize in this section addresses the issue of how famines affect the health and human capital of those who *survive*. This relationship is key to the notion that famines can have consequences beyond the loss of life in the short run.

Selection poses a major stumbling block to estimating the effects of famine. If mortality is concentrated among the weakest individuals, then survivors of famine will be positively selected, leading researchers to understate the impact of famine on survivors. Moreover, although the weather plays an important role in triggering famines, the intensity and duration of famines often result from failures of policy and political will. Hence, areas affected by famines might also be areas that otherwise would have received less public transfers, for example. Survivors are therefore likely to be selected in a way that resembles selective sorting into cities or neighborhoods, possibly confounding the analysis.

An influential series of papers examines the long-run impacts of the Dutch famine, which occurred in 1944–45. Reviewing these papers, Roseboom et al. (2001) conclude that prenatal exposure to the Dutch famine resulted in worse adult health along various dimensions, especially coronary heart disease (CHD). The studies focus not only on long-term health as an outcome but also on whether the *timing* of the famine in utero matters in different ways. Cohorts exposed during the first trimester were affected differently than cohorts exposed during the third trimester. For example, cohorts exposed late in gestation tended to have lower weight at birth and increased glucose concentrations (a marker for diabetes) in adulthood. Cohorts affected in the first trimester, in contrast, tended to not have any lower birthweight but had higher tendencies for CHD in adulthood. Perhaps the most interesting conclusion of the Dutch famine studies is that undernutrition during gestation can affect long-term health even if there is no indication of poorer health at birth (as measured by birthweight). Other studies on this particular famine have also found intergenerational birthweight effects, suggesting that the effects of famine last across multiple generations (Stein & Lumey, 2000).[6]

Researchers have examined the long-run health consequences of famines in many other contexts as well. In China, Gørgens, Meng, and Vaithainathan (2012) studied the Great Famine (1959–61) and found that survivors of early-childhood exposure were significantly shorter than people who were not exposed. An important contribution of this study is its idea to use the *children* of survivors to control for selection into survivorship.

Past research on the Chinese famine has struggled to find effects on survivors because famine mortality was apparently linked with potential height. The authors argue that although children inherit the genotype of their parents with regards to height, they do not inherit their phenotype. So they adjust for height differences in the next generation and interpret the residual height deficit in affected cohorts as the effect of famine. Notably, this strategy assumes that the scarring effects of famine do not transcend generations, which seems difficult to defend a priori. Nonetheless, the study makes important progress on dealing with selection effects.[7]

In a different context, Dercon and Porter (2010) highlight similar results stemming from one of Africa's worst famines, which occurred in Ethiopia in 1984. Using a household measure of famine intensity and comparing siblings with different famine exposure, the authors find that early-life famine exposure significantly reduces height in adulthood by at least 3 cm. Comparing exposed and nonexposed siblings is another way to control for selection effects because siblings have similar height potentials.

Although some studies show conflicting results of famine exposure (Luo, Mu, & Zhang, 2006; Stanner et al., 1997), the studies that explicitly account for selection and measurement error seem to consistently show a negative effect on health of famine exposure. A logical next step, then, is to examine how survivors fare in school, on the marriage market, and on the labor market, as recent studies have done.[8] Overall, these studies find that famine exposure at young ages (typically measured in utero or before the age of 2) negatively impacts long-term nonhealth outcomes. Most of these studies use similar strategies of comparing exposed and nonexposed cohorts in areas with differing famine intensity. We highlight two complementary studies that examine the long-run labor market impacts of the Chinese famine.

Almond, Edlund, Li, and Zhang (2010) use multiple sources of variation to study the impacts of the famine. Choosing a narrow window of birth cohorts (1956–64) to reduce confounding, they compare cohort-level changes across provinces with differing famine intensity. They also use residents of Hong Kong, which was under British rule and was thus unaffected by the famine, as a second control group. Among men, they find that in utero exposure to the famine increases illiteracy by 9%, reduces labor force participation by 6%, and reduces the probability of marriage by 6.5%. Women are similarly impacted, albeit with smaller magnitudes.

Meng and Qian (2009) build on this study by using a finer source of variation (county-level rather than province-level) and by using institutional features of the centrally planned procurement system to instrument for famine intensity. To account for positive selection into survival, they estimate the effect of exposure on the upper quantiles of the outcomes of interest. Their findings are consistent with prior studies on the famine (in terms of health and educational attainment), but accounting for measurement error and selection leads to larger magnitudes than those found in prior studies. They find that in utero famine exposure reduces the 90th percentile of adult height by 3 cm, weight by 1.5 kg, and educational attainment by half a year.

3.5 Epidemics

Like famines, epidemics have direct effects on human biology, and hence, economic research has contributed to our understanding of these crises mainly by looking for broad, long-term, or indirect impacts. Here again, changes in patterns of mortality and fertility complicate the estimation of impacts among survivors, but, in this case, they may also have interesting macroeconomic implications. At least since Malthus (1798/1966), economists have noted that widespread disease may increase the ratios of land or capital to labor, thus raising per capita living standards.[9] Along these lines, Voigtländer and Voth (2013) present evidence that the Black Death was a crucial turning point in the emergence of modern economic growth in Europe. A key feature of the bubonic plague in this respect is its rapid progression to death; as a result, it caused widespread mortality without sustained morbidity. More generally, the macroeconomic effects of an epidemic depend on its relative mortality and morbidity burdens. With greater morbidity, the surviving population becomes less productive, pushing back against the Malthusian benefits of epidemic mortality.

A fitting example is HIV/AIDS, which Young (2005) argues may bring increased prosperity to Africa. Incorporating positive wage effects from AIDS mortality, negative fertility responses to HIV, and negative effects of orphanhood on the next generation's human capital, Young calibrates a positive net effect of the epidemic on future living standards. However, the calibration depends heavily on his assumption that morbidity from HIV/AIDS does not meaningfully decrease productivity and on his estimate that fertility falls with rising HIV prevalence.

Subsequent research casts doubt on both of these crucial ingredients to Young's argument. First, HIV has become a chronic disease, and mounting evidence suggests that it has serious productivity consequences (Habyarimana, Mbakile, & Pop-Eleches, 2010; Levinsohn, McLaren, Shisana, & Zuma, 2013; Thirumurthy, Zivin, & Goldstein, 2008). Second, follow-up research has found that increases in regional and community-level HIV prevalence are not associated with falling fertility (Fortson, 2009; Juhn, Kalemli-Ozcan, & Turan, 2013). Using these revised fertility estimates, Kalemli-Ozcan and Turan (2011) recalibrate Young's model and find no macroeconomic benefit from HIV/AIDS.

A further indirect effect of the HIV pandemic on human biology is that it diverts resources and attention away from other important health care goals. Analyzing data from 14 sub-Saharan African countries from 1988 to 2005, Case and Paxson (2011) find that subnational regions with larger increases in HIV prevalence experienced erosions in antenatal care, institutional deliveries, and immunization. In corroborating evidence, Grépin (2012) analyzes country-level panel data to show that expansions in international aid for HIV programs are associated with declines in immunization. Such crowd-out effects are not limited to HIV. In Taiwan, for example, Bennett, Chiang, and Malani (2015) find that the onset of the severe adult respiratory syndrome (SARS) epidemic reduced outpatient medical visits by nearly one-third within a few weeks. Thus, epidemics affect health care access not only through policy makers' resource allocation decisions but also through fear of contagion in health care settings.

At the microeconomic level, studies show lasting effects of early-life morbidity due to epidemics. The 1918 influenza pandemic has attracted particular attention due to its sharp, unexpected, and indiscriminate nature. As with other crises involving significant mortality, positive mortality selection is likely to bias researchers toward finding no long-term effect on survivors. Nevertheless, drawing on both cohort-level variation and state-cohort panel variation in the United States, Almond (2006) estimates that in utero exposure to the flu pandemic reduced educational attainment, reduced adult income, and raised adult disability.[10] Cohorts that were in utero during the pandemic were 4% less likely to finish high school, 3% more likely to be poor, and 8% more likely to have a disability that prevented work in middle age.

Other research examines the lasting consequences of early-life exposure to malaria, a disease known for its widespread toll. Some of this literature studies the consequences of malaria eradication in settings where the disease is endemic (Bleakley, 2010; Cutler, Fung, Kremer, Singhal, & Vogl, 2010; Lucas, 2010), leveraging regional differences in baseline prevalence to isolate variation in the extent of malaria decline due to eradication. Comparing cohorts born before versus after eradication in high- versus low-prevalence areas, these studies find largely positive effects of malaria-free childhood human capital and labor market outcomes. The elimination of an endemic disease has little to do with crisis, but Lucas (2010) notes that Paraguay underwent a pronounced epidemic just before its eradication campaign. In that setting, the elimination of *epidemic* malaria at birth raised schooling by three-quarters of a year in the most infected region. Further evidence on the consequences of in utero exposure to a malaria crisis can be found in Barreca's (2010) analysis of malaria outbreaks in the early-20th-century United States. Drawing on an ordinary least squares (OLS) specification with state and birth cohort fixed effects, as well as an instrumental variables strategy that relies on climatic fluctuations to identify the effects of malaria outbreaks, Barreca finds that early-life exposure to epidemic malaria reduces schooling and adult labor supply while increasing poverty. A standard deviation increase in the malaria death rate in high malaria states during gestation led to a 0.04-year decrease in educational attainment, a 0.35 percentage point decrease in full-year work, and a 0.38 percentage point increase in poverty. These analyses shed much light on how health insults in early life affect the trajectories of social and economic outcomes over the life cycle.

3.6 Natural Disasters and Environmental Crises

Natural disasters like earthquakes and floods often result in loss of life and property, as do environmental crises like nuclear accidents and dramatic increases in air pollution.

Although both are forms of "crisis," one can perhaps distinguish them on the basis of the extent of human involvement in their genesis. This differentiation is rather loose, however, because some natural disasters are at least partly attributable to human action via climate change. Hence, we treat them jointly in this section.

We begin with papers that examine the impact of natural or environmental disasters on fertility. In the case of fertility, the effect of natural or environmental disaster can be positive or negative. Fertility may fall due to a loss of property or income, or it may rise if parents wish to "replace" deceased children. At least in developing countries, the evidence points toward replacement effects. Examining responses to three different earthquakes, Finlay (2009) finds that fertility rises after an earthquake. Similarly, studying the aftermath of the 2004 Indian Ocean Tsunami in Indonesia, Nobles, Frankenberg, and Thomas (2014) find increased fertility in harder-hit areas. The effect reflected both the behavior of women whose children died (thus replacing their *own* lost children) and the behavior of women who did not yet have children (thus replacing the *community*'s lost children). These results stand in contrast to that of Lin (2010), who finds that in Italy and Japan, short-run instability due to natural disasters is associated with decreased fertility.

Many papers have documented the mortality effects of natural disasters and extreme weather events. For example, in a paper examining the effects of natural disasters in more than 141 countries over two decades, Neumayer and Plümper (2007) find that mortality effects of natural disasters tend to be concentrated among women. This is an important study because it suggests relevant inequalities in the impact of natural disasters. Since mortality effects of natural disasters are well-documented in other review articles (see, e.g., Cavallo & Noy, 2010, and Bourque, Siegel, Megumi, & Wood, 2007) we now focus our attention to perhaps less widely studied extreme weather events. For example, Deschenes and Moretti (2009) find that both extreme heat and extreme cold result in short-run mortality increases, with different causes of mortality at different ends of the temperature spectrum. Heat primarily advances the mortality of those who are already weak by a few days or weeks. In response to cold extremes, however, people who might otherwise live a few more years might die; hence, the mortality impact of extreme cold is longer lasting. Given the general pattern of mobility in the United States, with people moving from colder to warmer climates, this finding suggests that migration could be one driving force behind increasing life expectancy. An important addition to this body of work is the recent research of Barreca, Clay, Deschenes, Greenstone, and Shapiro (2013), who find that the heat-mortality relationship in the United States has declined in recent decades. They attribute this decline to the adoption of air conditioning.

Extreme weather also has short-run consequences in the developing country context. In a broad study examining the impacts of early-life weather conditions on infant mortality in 28 African countries, Kudamatsu, Persson, and Strömberg (2012) find that extreme weather fluctuations have a significant impact on infant mortality in Africa via malnutrition and malaria. Analyzing even more extreme weather variation, Anttila-Hughes and Hsiang (2013) study the aftermath of typhoons in the Philippines, finding elevated infant mortality rates that far exceed the direct effects of the storms. Burgess, Deschenes, Donaldson, and Greenstone (2013) also estimate a significant relationship between weather and mortality in India, which is mostly driven by high temperature extremes at the time of crop growth in rural areas. In a related paper that speaks to differences between aggregate crises and local shocks, Burgess and Donaldson (2010) show that the expansion of India's railroad network diminished the mortality impact of agriculturally damaging weather shocks.

The evidence of the impact of pollution crises on health in developing countries is considerably less. Jayachandran (2009) is one of the few researchers to examine the mortality effects of forest fires. Forest fires produce atmospheric pollution that can travel large distances, with the potential of affecting the health of people far away. Using data from Indonesia, she finds that prenatal exposure to particulate matter due to forest fires in 1997 led to around 16,400 fewer surviving infants in Indonesia. Changing focus to urban pollution, Arceo-Gomez, Hanna, and Oliva (2012) use variation due to thermal inversions (which despite their frequency might qualify as crises) to find a similar result that pollution exposure is a significant contributor to infant mortality in Mexico City.[11] Several other recent papers examine the effects of marginal changes in environmental damage in developing countries, which fall outside the purview of our review.

Along similar lines, a large literature considers the long-term effects of early-life exposure to pollution (Bharadwaj, Gibson, Zivin, & Neilson, 2014; Currie, Zivin, Mullins, & Neidell, 2013, but much of this literature considers marginal changes in pollution levels or environmental policies that improve pollution, neither of which qualifies as a crisis. A notable exception is Almond, Edlund, and Palme (2009) analysis of the Chernobyl nuclear disaster's aftermath. Leveraging spatial and temporal variation in exposure to the radiation cloud in Sweden, Almond et al. find that prenatal exposure to radiation decreases cognitive achievement in later life, albeit without observable health impacts.[12]

3.7 Wars

Many of the crises we review in part reflect human action, but nowhere is human responsibility graver than in the case of war. Wars and other conflicts are disruptive along social, political, and economic lines, with significant potential to affect human biology.[13] Most research on this topic has focused on the impact of conflict exposure in early childhood on subsequent physical growth. Analyses of this question must grapple with standard concerns about selective mortality, fertility, and migration, in addition to the fact that wars often accompany other undesirable phenomena: recession, disease, food shortage, and deterioration of health infrastructure, *inter alia*. Although separately identifying each mechanism would be an interesting area for future research, existing research does not concern itself with isolating the underlying mechanism.

The Nigerian Civil War was one of the earliest civil wars in postindependence Africa, making it a suitable context for studying long-run effects of childhood exposure. Akresh, Bhalotra, Leone, and Osili (2012) examine its impact on adult stature, finding that individuals from ethnic groups most heavily exposed to the war attained significantly lower stature as adults. Exposure to conflict during adolescence was more damaging than exposure only in early childhood, which the authors attribute to possible disruptions in the normal growth spurt experienced in adolescence. Adult height is also the primary outcome in Agüero and Deolalikar's (2012) study of the Rwandan genocide of 1994. Whereas they, too, find that exposure to the genocide leads to decreased height (relative to trends in neighboring countries), they find the effects to be greater when exposure occurs at a younger age. Thus, while both Akresh, Lucchetti, and Thirumurthy (2012) and Agüero and Deolalikar (2012) find that childhood and adolescent exposure to wars reduces adult height, they differ on when exposure matters more.

Shifting from adult outcomes to child outcomes, Bundervoet, Verwimp, and Akresh (2009) examine the consequences of exposure to civil war in Burundi on child height-for-age *z*-scores. The authors use variation in the timing and geographic spread of the war to estimate that an additional month of civil war exposure reduced height for age by about 0.05 *z*-scores. The effects are concentrated in children who were exposed to conflict between ages 0 and 2 years, consistent with the idea that the first few years of life are a critical period for physical growth.

When two countries go to war, residents of the winning country might benefit by suffering less destruction or disruptions to economic systems or public health delivery. Hence, when thinking about the impacts of intercountry conflict, a crucial question arises regarding the *net* health impacts of such conflict. Akresh, Caruso, and Thirumurthy (2014) address this issue by examining the health impacts on both sides of the Eritrean-Ethiopian conflict of 1998–2000. Children on both sides suffered equally in terms of the effect on height-for-age *z*-scores, but children in the losing nation suffered more than those in the winning country.

Whereas war-induced migration is a central concern for interpretation of the results so far, the arrival of refugees in large numbers could also pose a health risk to the locals in the areas where they arrive. Baez (2011) examines the health of local children as a function of the refugee influx from the genocides in Burundi and Rwanda. In 1994–95, North-Western Tanzania received hundreds of thousands of refugees; however, topographical characteristics induced geographical variation in refugee inflows. Baez uses this variation to estimate negative effects on the health (as measured by anthropometrics and child mortality) and human capital attainment of local children 1 year after the arrival of refugees. We hope this important study opens the door to further research on the health impacts of conflict for people not directly involved in the conflict.

3.8 Conclusion

A burgeoning economics literature considers the effects of various shocks on human biology. Mixed into this literature are shocks large and small, positive and negative, local and aggregate. In this review, we have homed in on a subset of these shocks—aggregate crises—in the hope of highlighting commonalities in their effects. The literature suggests that these unexpected, pronounced, negative, and population-wide events affect human reproduction, mortality, and morbidity over the life cycle. To shed further light on the roles of prices and insurance arrangements, a fruitful line of future inquiry would compare crises at different scales (Bundervoet et al., 2009 and Caruso, 2015 are recent examples) or those occurring in environments with differing levels of market integration or insurance system development (Kahn, 2005, is an excellent example).

More broadly, however, the literature highlights the lasting effects that social, economic, political, environmental, and pathological crises have on the human body. Children, who are never complicit in creating crisis, carry the burden of exposure for the rest of their lives. Although advances in methodology and data availability have allowed researchers to uncover these nuanced but powerful effects, much work remains in improving crisis response, especially in poor countries. As the findings demonstrate, improvements in this arena would have beneficial effects long after the acute period of a crisis subsides, on outcomes far beyond its most obvious sequelae.

Acknowledgments

We thank Khurram Ali and Terry Moon for research assistance. Richard Akresh, Matthew Gibson, and the Editor John Komlos provided helpful comments on previous versions of this review.

Notes

1. In the *Oxford English Dictionary*, all quotations with the word before the year 1600 used this definition.
2. See Ruhm (2006), Strauss and Thomas (2007), and Currie and Vogl (2013) for reviews.
3. We omit major political crises, for example regime change (as in the Soviet Union) or political partition and reunification (as in the partition of British India or the reunification of Germany).
4. Despite the overall mortality decrease during the Great Depression, relief spending during this era was associated with further decreases in mortality (Fishback, Haines, & Kator, 2007).
5. For additional evidence on these mechanisms, see Ásgeirsdóttir, Corman, Noonan, Ólafsdóttir, and Reichman (2014).
6. For more recent results on the Dutch famine, see Painter et al. (2006); Stein et al. (2007); Rooij, Painter, Holleman, Bossuyt, and Roseboom (2007); and Rooij Wouters, Yonker, Painter, and Roseboom (2010).
7. Mu and Zhang (2011) find that female survivors have a higher incidence of disability, which they attribute to greater selective male mortality during the famine. Two other papers use similar strategies to find that exposed cohorts are shorter in the long run (Chen & Zhou, 2007; Meng & Qian, 2009).

8. See Shi (2011), Almond (2006), Brandt, Siow, and Vogel (2008), and Meng and Qian (2009) on China; Dercon and Porter (2010) on Ethiopia; Scholte, van den Berg, and Lindeboom (2015) on the Netherlands; and Neelsen and Stratmann (2011) on Greece.
9. The same general equilibrium reasoning also applies to famine and war, but it has drawn more interest in the literature on disease.
10. Brown and Thomas (2011) point out that the 1918 pandemic coincided with World War I military deployments that changed the composition of new parents, which they argue can account for much of Almond's estimated flu impact. However, data from countries with less involvement in World War I indicate similar impacts of in utero exposure to the pandemic (Lin & Liu, 2014; Richter & Robling, 2013).
11. A thermal inversion occurs when warm air settles over a layer of cooler air near the ground, trapping the cool air and any pollutants inside it.
12. In a related paper using nuclear weapons testing rather than nuclear disaster as a source of variation, Black, Bütikofer, Devereux, and Kjell (2013) find similar long-run impacts of prenatal exposure.
13. Whereas the term "war" is typically used to denote fighting across borders, and the term "conflict" often denotes within-country fighting (such as civil or ethnic conflicts), we use the terms interchangeably in this chapter.

References

Adhvaryu, A., Fenske, J., & Nyshadham, A. (2014). *Early life circumstance and adult mental health.* Unpublished manuscript.

Agüero, J. M., & Deolalikar, A. (2012). *Late bloomers? Identifying critical periods in human capital accumulation. Evidence from the Rwanda genocide.* Unpublished manuscript.

Akresh, R., Bhalotra, S., Leone, M., & Osili, U. O. (2012). War and stature: Growing up during the Nigerian Civil War. *American Economic Review, 102*(3), 273–277.

Akresh, R., Caruso, G., & Thirumurthy, H. (2014). *Medium-term health impacts of shocks experienced in utero and after birth: Evidence from detailed geographic information on war exposure* (NBER Working Paper No. 20763). Cambridge, Ma: National Bureau of Economic Research.

Akresh, R., Lucchetti, L., & Thirumurthy, H. (2012). Wars and child health: Evidence from the Eritrean–Ethiopian conflict. *Journal of Development Economics, 99*(2), 330–340.

Almond, D. (2006). Is the 1918 influenza pandemic over? Long-term effects of in utero influenza exposure in the post-1940 US population. *Journal of Political Economy, 114*(4), 672–712.

Almond, D., Edlund, L., & Palme, M. (2009). Chernobyl's subclinical legacy: Prenatal exposure to radioactive fallout and school outcomes in Sweden. *Quarterly Journal of Economics, 124*(4), 1729–1772.

Almond, D., Edlund, L., Li, H., & Zhang, J. (2010). Long-term effects of the 1959-1961 China famine: Mainland China and Hong Kong. In T. Ito & A. K. Rose (eds.), *The economic consequences of demographic change in East Asia* (Vol. 19, Chapter 9, pp. 321-350). Chicago: University of Chicago Press.

Anttila-Hughes, J. K., & Hsiang, S. M. (2013). Destruction, disinvestment, and death: Economic and human losses following environmental disaster. *Available at SSRN2220501.*

Arceo-Gomez, E. O., Hanna, R., & Oliva, P. (2012). *Does the effect of pollution on infant mortality differ between developing and developed countries? Evidence from Mexico City* (NBER Working Paper No. 18349). Cambridge, Ma: National Bureau of Economic Research.

Ásgeirsdóttir, T. L., Corman, H., Noonan, K., Ólafsdóttir, Þ., & Reichman, N. E. (2014). Was the economic crisis of 2008 good for Icelanders? Impact on health behaviors. *Economics & Human Biology, 13*, 1–19.

Baez, J. E. (2011). Civil wars beyond their borders: The human capital and health consequences of hosting refugees. *Journal of Development Economics, 96*(2), 391–408.

Baird, S., Friedman, J., & Schady, N. (2011). Aggregate income shocks and infant mortality in the developing world. *Review of Economics and Statistics, 93*(3), 847–856.

Banerjee, A., Duflo, E., Postel-Vinay, G., & Watts, T. (2010). Long-run health impacts of income shocks: Wine and phylloxera in nineteenth-century France. *Review of Economics and Statistics, 92*(4), 714–728.

Barreca, A., Clay, K., Deschenes, O., Greenstone, M., & Shapiro, J. S. (2013). *Adapting to climate change: The remarkable decline in the US temperature-mortality relationship over the 20th century* (NBER Working Paper No. 18692). Cambridge, MA: National Bureau of Economic Research.

Barreca, A. I. (2010). The long-term economic impact of in utero and postnatal exposure to malaria. *Journal of Human Resources, 45*(4), 865–892.

Bennett, D., Chiang, C. F., & Malani, A. (2015). Learning during a crisis: The SARS epidemic in Taiwan. *Journal of Development Economics, 112*, 1–18.

Bhalotra, S. (2010). Fatal fluctuations? Cyclicality in infant mortality in India. *Journal of Development Economics, 93*(1), 7–19.

Bharadwaj, P., Gibson, M., Zivin, J. G., & Neilson, C. (2014). *Grey matters: Fetal pollution exposure and human capital formation.* NBER Working Paper No. 20662. Cambridge, Ma: National Bureau of Economic Research.

Black, S. E., Bütikofer, A., Devereux, P. J., & Kjell, S. G. (2013). This is only a test? Long-run impacts of prenatal exposure to radioactive fallout (NBER Working Paper No.18987). Cambridge, Ma: National Bureau of Economic Research.

Bleakley, H. (2010). Malaria eradication in the Americas: A retrospective analysis of childhood exposure. *American Economic Journal: Applied Economics, 2*(2), 1–45.

Block, S. A., Kiess, L., Webb, P., Kosen, S., Moench-Pfanner, R., Bloem, M. W., & Timme, C. P. (2004). Macro shocks and micro outcomes: Child nutrition during Indonesia's crisis. *Economics & Human Biology, 2*(1), 21–44.

Bozzoli, C., & Quintana-Domeque, C. (2014). The weight of the crisis: Evidence from newborns in Argentina. *Review of Economics and Statistics, 96*(3), 550–562.

Brandt, L., Siow, A., & Vogel, C. (2008). *Large shocks and small changes in the marriage market for famine born cohorts in China.* Working paper, University of Toronto.

Bourque, L. B., Siegel, J. M., Megumi, K., & Wood, M. M. (2007). Morbidity and Mortality Associated with Natural Disasters. *Handbook of Disaster Research, Handbooks of Sociology and Social Research*, 97–112. Springer New York.

Brown, R., & Thomas, D. (2011). On the Long Term Effects of the 1918 US Influenza Pandemic. Working Paper, Duke University, Durham, NC.

Bundervoet, T., Verwimp, P., & Akresh, R. (2009). Health and Civil War in Rural Burundi. *Journal of Human Resources, 44*(2), 536–563.

Burgess, R., Deschenes, O., Donaldson, D., & Greenstone, M. (2013). *The unequal effects of weather and climate change: Evidence from mortality in India.* Working paper, MIT, Cambridge, MA.

Burgess, R., & Donaldson, D. (2010). Can openness mitigate the effects of weather shocks? Evidence from India's Famine Era. *American Economic Review, 100*(2), 449–453.

Caruso, G. D. (2015). The Legacy of Natural Disasters: The Intergenerational Impact of 100 Years of Natural Disasters in Latin America. *Available at SSRN2560891.*

Case, A., & Paxson, C. (2011). The impact of the AIDS pandemic on health services in Africa: Evidence from demographic and health surveys. *Demography, 48*(2), 675–697.

Cavallo, E., & Noy, I. (2010). *The economics of natural disasters.* Working paper, Inter-American Development Bank.

Chen, Y., & Zhou, L. (2007). The long term health and economic consequences of 1959–1961 famine in China. *Journal of Health Economics, 26*(4), 659–681.

Currie, J., & Vogl, T. (2013). Early-life health and adult circumstances in developing countries. *Annual Review of Economics, 5*(1), 1–36.

Currie, J., Zivin, J. G., Mullins, J., & Neidell, M. (2013). What do we know about short—and long-term effects of early-life exposure to pollution? *Annual Review of Resource Economics, 6*, 217–247.

Currie, J., & Schwandt, H. (2013). *Within-mother analysis of seasonal patterns in health at birth. Proceedings of the National Academy of Sciences of the United States of America, 110*(30), 12265–12270.

Cutler, D., Fung, W., Kremer, M., Singhal, M., & Vogl, T. (2010). Early-life malaria exposure and adult outcomes: Evidence from malaria eradication in India. *American Economic Journal: Applied Economics, 2*(2), 72–94.

Cutler, D., Knaul, F., Lozano, R., Méndez, O., & Zurita, B. (2002). Financial crisis, health outcomes and ageing: Mexico in the 1980s and 1990s. *Journal of Public Economics, 84*(2), 279–303.

Dehejia, R. H., & Lleras-Muney, A. (2004). Booms, busts, & babies' health. *Quarterly Journal of Economics, 119*(3), 1091–1130.

Dercon, S., & Porter, C. (2010). *Live aid revisited: Long-term impacts of the 1984 Ethiopian Famine on children.* (Center for the Study of African Economies Working paper WPS/2010-39). Oxford: Department of Economics, University of Oxford.

Deschenes, O., & Moretti, E. (2009). Extreme weather events, mortality, & migration. *Review of Economics and Statistics, 91*(4), 659–681.

Finlay, J. E. (2009). *Fertility response to natural disasters: The case of three high mortality earthquakes* (World Bank Policy Research Working Paper No.4883). Cambridge, MA: Harvard School of Public Health.

Fishback, P. V., Haines, M. R., & Kantor, S. (2007). Births, deaths, & New Deal Relief during the Great Depression. *Review of Economics and Statistics, 89*(1), 1–14.

Fortson, J. G. (2009). HIV/AIDS and fertility. *American Economic Journal: Applied Economics, 1*(3), 170–194.

Gerdtham, U.-G., & Ruhm, C. J. (2006). Deaths rise in good economic times: Evidence from the OECD. *Economics & Human Biology, 4*(3), 298–316.

Gørgens, T., Meng, X., & Vaithianathan, R. (2012). Stunting and selection effects of famine: A case study of the Great Chinese Famine. *Journal of Development Economics, 97*(1), 99–111.

Granados, J. A., Tapia, R., & Roux, A. V. D. (2009). Life and death during the Great Depression. *Proceedings of the National Academy of Sciences, 106*(41), 17290–17295.

Grépin, K. A. (2012). HIV donor funding has both boosted and curbed the delivery of different non-HIV health services in Sub-Saharan Africa. *Health Affairs, 31*(7), 1406–1414.

Habyarimana, J., Mbakile, B., & Pop-Eleches, C. (2010). The impact of HIV/AIDS and ARV treatment on worker absenteeism implications for African Firms. *Journal of Human Resources, 45*(4), 809–839.

Jayachandran, S. (2009). Air quality and early-life mortality evidence from Indonesia's wildfires. *Journal of Human Resources*, *44*(4), 916–954.

Juhn, C., Kalemli-Ozcan, S., & Turan, B. (2013). HIV and fertility in Africa: First evidence from population-based surveys. *Journal of Population Economics*, *26*(3), 835–853.

Kahn, M. E. (2005). The death toll from natural disasters: The role of income, geography, & institutions. *Review of Economics and Statistics*, *87*(2), 271–284.

Kalemli-Ozcan, S., & Turan, B. (2011). HIV and fertility revisited. *Journal of Development Economics*, *96*(1), 61–65.

Kudamatsu, M., Persson, T., & Strömberg, D. (2012). *Weather and infant mortality in Africa* (CEPR Discussion Paper No.9222). London: Center for Economic Policy Research.

Levinsohn, J. A., McLaren, Z., Shisana, O., & Zuma, K. (2013). HIV status and labor market participation in South Africa. *Review of Economics and Statistics*, *95*(1), 98–108.

Lin, C.-Y. C. (2010). Instability, investment, disasters, & demography: Natural disasters and fertility in Italy (1820–1962) and Japan (1671–1965). *Population and Environment*, *31*(4), 255–281.

Lin, M.-J., & Liu, E. M. (2014). Does in utero exposure to illness matter? The 1918 influenza epidemic in Taiwan as a natural experiment. *Journal of Health Economics*, *37*, 152–163.

Lucas, A. M. (2010). Malaria eradication and educational attainment: Evidence from Paraguay and Sri Lanka. *American Economic Journal. Applied Economics*, 2(2), 46.

Luo, Z., Mu, R., & Zhang, X. (2006). Famine and overweight in China. *Applied Economic Perspectives and Policy*, *28*(3), 296–304.

Malthus, T. R. (1798/1966). *First essay on population, 1798* (Vol. 14). London: Macmillan.

Meng, X., & Qian, N. (2009). The long term consequences of famine on survivors: Evidence from a unique natural experiment using China's Great Famine (NBER Working Paper No. 14917). Cambridge, MA: National Bureau of Economic Research.

Miller, G., & Urdinola, B. P. (2010). Cyclicality, mortality, and the value of time: The case of coffee price fluctuations and child survival in Colombia. *Journal of Political Economy*, *118*(1), 113–155.

Mu, R., & Zhang, X. (2011). Why does the Great Chinese Famine affect the male and female survivors differently? Mortality selection versus son preference. *Economics & Human Biology*, 9(1), 92–105.

Neelsen, S., & Stratmann, T. (2011). Effects of prenatal and early life malnutrition: Evidence from the Greek famine. *Journal of Health Economics*, *30*(3), 479–488.

Neumayer, E., & Plümper, T. (2007). The gendered nature of natural disasters: The impact of catastrophic events on the gender gap in life expectancy, 1981–2002. *Annals of the Association of American Geographers*, *97*(3), 551–566.

Nobles, J., Frankenberg, E., & Thomas, D. (2014). The effects of mortality on fertility: Population dynamics after a natural disaster (NBER Working Paper No. w20448). Cambridge, MA: National Bureau of Economic Research.

Ó Gráda, C. (2009). *Famine: A short history*. Princeton, NJ: Princeton University Press.

Painter, R. C., de Rooij, S. R., Bossuyt, P. M., Simmers, T. A., Osmond, C., Barker, D. J., . . . Roseboom, T. J. (2006). Early onset of coronary artery disease after prenatal exposure to the Dutch famine. *American Journal of Clinical Nutrition*, *84*(2), 322–327.

Paxson, C., & Schady, N. (2005). Child health and economic crisis in Peru. *World Bank Economic Review*, *19*(2), 203–223.

Richter, A., & Robling, P. O. (2013). *Transgenerational effects of the 1918–19 influenza pandemic in Sweden*. Working paper, Swedish Institute for Social Research.

Rooij, S. R., Painter, R. C., Holleman, F., Bossuyt, P. M. M., & Roseboom, T. J. (2007). The metabolic syndrome in adults prenatally exposed to the Dutch famine. *American Journal of Clinical Nutrition, 86*(4), 1219–1224.

Rooij, S. R., Wouters, H., Yonker, J. E., Painter, R. C., & Roseboom, T. J. (2010). Prenatal undernutrition and cognitive function in late adulthood. *Proceedings of the National Academy of Sciences, 107*(39), 16881–16886.

Roseboom, T. J., Van Der Meulen, J. H. P., Ravelli, A. C. J., Osmond, C., Barker, D. J. P., & Bleker, O. P. (2001). Effects of prenatal exposure to the Dutch famine on adult disease in later life: An overview. *Molecular and Cellular Endocrinology, 185*(1), 93–98.

Ruhm, C. J. (2000). Arc recessions good for your health? *The Quarterly Journal of Economics, 115*(2), 617–650.

Ruhm, C. J. (2006). A healthy economy can break your heart (NBER Working Paper No. 12102). Cambridge, MA: National Bureau of Economic Research.

Scholte, R., van den Berg, G. J., & Lindeboom, M. (2015). Long-run effects of gestation during the Dutch Hunger Winter famine on labor market and hospitalization outcomes. *Journal of Health Economics, 39*, 17–30.

Sen, A. (1981). *Poverty and famine*. Oxford, England: Clarendon Press.

Shi, X. (2011). Famine, fertility and fortune in China. *China Economic Review, 22*(2), 244–259.

Skoufias, E. (2003). Economic crises and natural disasters: Coping strategies and policy implications. *World Development, 31*(7), 1087–1102.

Stanner, S. A., Bulmer, K., Andres, C., Lantseva, O. E., Borodina, V., Poteen, V., & Yudkin, J. S. (1997). Does malnutrition in utero determine diabetes and coronary heart disease in adulthood? Results from the Leningrad Siege study, a cross sectional study. *British Medical Journal, 315*(7119), 1342–1348.

Stein, A. D., & Lumey, L. H. (2000). The relationship between maternal and offspring birth weights after maternal pre-natal famine exposure: The Dutch Famine birth cohort study. *Human Biology, 72*(4), 641–654.

Stein, A. D., Kahn, H. S., Rundle, A., Zybert, P. A., van der Pal-de Bruin, K. M., & Lumey, L. H. (2007). Anthropometric measures in middle age after exposure to famine during gestation: Evidence from the Dutch Famine. *American Journal of Clinical Nutrition, 85*(3), 869–876.

Stevens, A. H., Miller, D. L., Page, M. E., & Filipski, M. (2011). *The best of times, the worst of times: Understanding pro-cyclical mortality* (NBER Working Paper No.17657). Cambridge, MA: National Bureau of Economic Research.

Strauss, J., & Thomas, D. (2007). Health over the life course. *Handbook of Development Economics, 4*, 3375–3474.

Thirumurthy, H., Zivin, J. G., & Goldstein, M. (2008). The economic impact of AIDS treatment labor supply in Western Kenya. *Journal of Human Resources, 43*(3), 511–552.

Van Den Berg, G. J., Lindeboom, M., & Portrait, F. (2006). Economic conditions early in life and individual mortality. *American Economic Review, 96*(1), 290–302.

Voigtländer, N., & Voth, H.-J. (2013). The three horsemen of riches: Plague, war, & urbanization in early modern Europe. *Review of Economic Studies, 80*(2), 774–811.

Young, A. (2005). The gift of the dying: The tragedy of AIDS and the welfare of future African generations, *Quarterly Journal of Economics, 120*(2), 423–466.

CHAPTER 4

THE BIOLOGICAL STANDARD OF LIVING IN EUROPE FROM THE LATE IRON AGE TO THE LITTLE ICE AGE

NIKOLA KOEPKE

4.1 Introduction

It is generally accepted that human well-being is a multidimensional concept that encompasses much more than command over goods and services (Boarini, Johansson, & Mira d'Ercole, 2006; World Health Organization [WHO], 1995) and that nutrition and health (individually and in synergistic relationship) are fundamental aspects of living standards. Because nutrition and health are not necessarily related to material well-being, the study of the biological standard of living (BLS) is an important complementary dimension of overall well-being.[1]

Anthropometric indicators, especially physical mean height as a proxy of a population's BLS, are advantageous measures of well-being insofar as they capture how well a society is able to provide adequate living conditions for the population (Komlos, 1998). This is the case because about 20% of the variation in height—and the chance of growing to one's full height potential—is determined by environmental factors (McEvoy & Visscher, 2009; Silventoinen, 2003). Moreover, mean height as a measurement of well-being has the advantage of being applicable to the diverse social and economic systems that existed over the course of time, and its use makes it possible to adequately depict the various spheres of inequality in a population.

Using the anthropometric approach is particularly important for pre-modern periods because only a very few and limited written and archaeological sources give information on other measures of well-being in the very long run. Instead, skeletal remains provide information on mean height and thus enable us to investigate BLS much farther back in time. Already, Wing and Brown (1979) argued that height is a useful indicator of long-term changes in well-being in regional comparisons. The first such study of prehistoric populations, though, was conducted for the Americas by Steckel and Rose (2002). For Europe, most studies have focused on narrow osteological-anthropological aspects of small regions and rather short time periods and have generally been based on a small number of observations (e.g., De Beer, 2004; Huber, 1967; Kunitz, 1987). The first long-run study of archaeological periods comparing different European regions and using inferential statistics was conducted by Koepke and Baten (2005a). It is useful to extend their dataset to prehistoric times. A first step in this direction is the study presented here, for which I collected data going back to the Late Iron Age. In this way, I hope, inter alia, to shed further light on the causes of the long-run trajectory of well-being, including the potential effect of the ascendancy of the Roman Empire as well as other ecological and cultural-socioeconomic changes that occurred until the Little Ice Age (LIA), with its suggested culmination in the 17th century CE.

Research on the Neolithic era has found that the transition from foraging to settled agricultural subsistence tended to result in deteriorating human health and height due to an increase in population density, malnutrition, and disease (Cohen & Armelagos, 1984; Mummert, Esche, Robinson, & Armelagos, 2011).[2] Similarly, in later pre- and early historic Europe, the ancient Roman expansion in particular (as well as the later decline of the *imperium Romanum* and the transition to medieval times) caused huge changes—especially economically, politically, and in the social context. These changes presumably affected the BLS; therefore, the question of general well-being during the ascendancy of the Roman Empire is a prominent topic of scholarly interest.

Focusing on traditional economic indicators suggests that the rise of the Roman Empire brought about unprecedented economic growth with a general improvement in living conditions (Bowman and Wilson, 2009; Finley, 1973; Milanovic, Lindert, & Williamson, 2010; Temin, 2006; Ward-Perkins, 2005). Yet economic measures are problematic as indicators of the long-term trajectory of well-being because the existing data, such as information on prices, are only sporadically available (Bowman & Wilson, 2009; Szaivert & Wolters, 2005) and thus do not provide a thorough understanding of the changes before and after the Roman period. Similarly, a food basket can only be reconstructed for short periods (Allen, 2009).[3] Thus, other aspects of living conditions also should be considered, even though the utilization of most alternative measures of well-being (such as infant mortality rate) cannot be applied to archaeological periods due to the missing quantitative information.[4] However, the potential effects on the health-related human capital outcome as fundamental factors of well-being can be studied by investigating the BLS. Turning to mean height as proxy of the European BLS, only studies of smaller regional and temporal extent have been conducted, and scholarly research varies regarding trends in the net nutritional status. As a result, no consensus has emerged concerning the effect of the *imperium Romanum* on well-being: on the one hand, the findings on mean height mostly indicate that living conditions for the common people were not ideal during the *imperium Romanum* and improved after its decline (Angel, 1984; Barbiera & Dalla-Zuanna,

2009; Cardoso & Gomez, 2009; Giannecchini & Moggi-Cecchi, 2008; Koepke & Baten, 2005a; Özer, Sağır & Özer, 2011; Paine et al., 2009; Redfern & DeWitte, 2011; Scheidel, 2012); on the other hand, some researchers have found that Roman health conditions seem to have been comparably favorable (Jongman, 2007; Kron, 2005; Lo Cascio, 2006; Paine & Storey, 2006; Pitts & Griffin, 2012). For the centuries following the period of the Roman Empire, previous studies indicate particularly healthy conditions for the early Middle Ages and a certain decrease in the BLS in the subsequent centuries. These include Cardoso and Gomez (2009) for Portugal and Haidle (1997) for Southern Germany. Maat (2003) and Brothwell (2003) confirmed this finding for the region of today's Netherlands, and, similarly, Steckel (2004) found a comparably high BLS in Northern Europe in (early) medieval times and a considerable decrease in mean height since the Middle Ages.

To place the potential effect of Roman ascendancy and the regional framework of the earlier and later socioeconomic changes in chronological context, I use an expanded set of data: to examine the long-run trend of the European well-being proxied by mean height estimated from skeletal remains, the dataset covers the millennia prior to the beginning of the process of industrialization, 8th cent. BCE to 17th cent. CE.

4.2 Method and Data

4.2.1 Bones as Information on Mean Height as a Proxy of the BLS: General Advantages and Limitations

To proxy the evolution of living conditions in archaeological times, information on mean height as the measure of choice is compiled from human skeletal remains. Although uncertainties are naturally inherent to any study of archaeological periods and the data are generally rather limited in comparison with the systematic information available on modern times, skeletal material is preserved comparably well in the archaeological record and thus is available in comparably large, comprehensive amounts.[5] An additional advantage is that the source also provides information on females (in contrast to most written sources until the 20th century). Therefore bone remains are the ideal data source to create a numéraire to quantitatively determine the long-term history of former living standards prior to the availability of written records in the early 18th century.[6]

However, a number of considerations must be taken in to account when evaluating the data. The femur is best correlated to human height and thus can be used as indicator of the BLS. In addition to femur length providing information on height, the availability of the skull and pelvis are necessary because they enable us to determine an individual's age and sex. It is essential to know the sex because the correlation between bone length and height is sex specific, and only skeletal remains from fully grown adult individuals can be taken into account to depict former living conditions correctly.[7] These aspects limit the amount of useful data. It is also important that the evidence stem from regular cemeteries (i.e., no mass graves or graveyards reserved for the nobility); in this way, one can ensure that one is estimating the height of the average population.[8] As to dating, ascertaining the chronology of burials is generally possible by examining the grave goods and information on the cemetery strata (including carbon dating). However, dating limitations further reduce the amount of analyzable data. Only those observations are useful that can at least enable us to determine the century of the burial as well as the age at death and, correspondingly, the birth cohort. In general, a better temporal resolution than one century is beyond the means of the archaeological evidence. Finally, the comparability of the data has to be assured. The data need to have a homogenous genetic height potential; by large, this seems to be the case for the European continent (Bertranpetit, 2012; Lao et al. 2008), although future research on the genetic modulators of growth might challenge this theory (Grasgruber, Cacek, Kalina, & Sebera, 2014; Lettre, 2011). And because most of the data were not measured personally but by the excavators, who employed different methods for height reconstruction, in order to make the available height data comparable I standardized them (using algorithms developed by Koepke, 2014*a*).

Overall, skeletal remains are a great source with which to study well-being in the very-long-run perspective because, despite their limitations, the data provide an unparalleled record of information on the trajectory of net nutritional status. In contrast to other archaeological data, skeletal remains are available in comparably large amounts and are applicable to comparisons between different economies and societies.[9]

4.2.2 The New Estimates of Physical Stature Based on Archeological Remains

I compiled information on 18,502 individuals from 484 European cemeteries spanning the period from the 8th century BCE to the 18th century CE.[10] One shall analyze the data in 100-year intervals (Koepke, 2008, 2014a).[11] The regional distribution of the height data enables us to differentiate three major European regions: North-Eastern, Central-Western, and Mediterranean Europe.[12] As a basic requirement, in order to make sure that the data are not distorted and I can correctly depict the potential effects of environmental circumstances, I controlled for migration and social status (based on grave goods).[13] For both variables, I found no statistically significant effect on height (Koepke, 2008). I considered only those centuries for which more than 35 individuals per major region are available.[14] Thus, the utilized height series are based on 18,240 individuals (Table 4.1). I used weighted least squares regression (WLS) to adapt for the variation in the sample sizes.

Table 4.1 Regions of Europe Covered by the Height Dataset (in Number of Individuals)

Century	Central-Western	North-Eastern	Mediterranean	Total
8 BCE	**79**	26	**172**	277
7 BCE	8	33	**140**	181
6 BCE	**46**	**96**	**236**	378
5 BCE	3	10	**404**	417
4 BCE	6	23	**158**	187
3 BCE	**39**	**117**	34	190
2 BCE	**82**	**81**		163
1 BCE	**41**	**37**	**114**	192
1 CE	**88**	**217**	**211**	516
2 CE	**1146**	**174**	**445**	1765
3 CE	**407**	**181**	**124**	712
4 CE	**1225**	**318**	**566**	2109
5 CE	**222**	**125**	**468**	815
6 CE	**1387**	**198**	**150**	1735
7 CE	**1477**	**279**	**56**	1812
8 CE	**266**	**787**		1053
9 CE	**327**	**533**	12	872
10 CE	**153**	**287**	20	460
11 CE	**136**	**1423**	**51**	1610
12 CE	**216**	**462**	**130**	808
13 CE	**189**	**358**	4	551
14 CE	**242**	**554**	7	803
15 CE	**55**	17	**61**	133
16 CE	**455**	18	4	477
17 CE	**66**	**80**	5	151
18 CE	**103**	32		135

Highlighted in bold are the observations included in the statistical analysis.

4.2.3 Explanatory Variables in an Archaeological Context

Various direct and indirect multilayered factors interact with one another in explaining the height trajectory. In general, when working with archaeological periods, one must keep in mind that the data on potential explanatory variables are naturally scarce.[15]

I focus on variables that proxy the indicator "diet quality and quantity" as potentially the most important direct determinant of height in pre-industrial times. No significant changes seem to have occurred in the other direct determinants over the centuries: neither in child labor (physical stress during growth) (e.g., Bradley, 1991; Hindman, 2009, esp. p. 33), nor in health conditions (the germ theory was only introduced in the 19th century: Carmichael, 1995; David, Johansson, & Pozzi, 2010; Scheidel, 2012). In general, tuberculosis, typhus, leprosy, malaria, and other diseases were always present to some degree (Arcini, 1999; Sallares, 2002). However, to capture any potentially unobserved specific effects, I control for potential regional differences and documented temporal shocks by using dummy variables for regions and periods in the regression analysis.

Focusing on potential causes of variations in diet as the main direct explanatory variable for the BLS in the study period, a wide range of environmental circumstances might have had a significant influence on the height outcome—both non-anthropogenic, natural endowments as well as anthropogenic, socioeconomic-cultural causes. Based on findings for the late pre-industrial period, I assume that climate change, the consumption of dairy products and beef, population density, urbanization, shock-like occurrences of disease and war, and institutional changes affecting legal conditions and technical progress, as well as gender aspects (potentially affecting entitlement and distribution within a society) might have been relevant in determining the mean height outcome in the very long run.

To start with, natural factors can determine the net nutritional outcome -all the more so in pre-industrial times when adjustment options to the surrounding habitat were still restricted. These factors are primarily geographic and climatic aspects. To account for these, I dissect the final data into the previously mentioned three main European regions (Mediterranean, Central-Western, and North-Eastern Europe), following Koepke and Baten (2005a, 2008), to control for any potential unobserved region-specific conditions. In addition, I proxy possible temporal changes in the basic natural endowments using period dummy variables.

Concerning natural circumstances, ***climate change*** and variation in climate is a factor of particular importance because it can influence harvest and husbandry yields (and thus food prices), the basic metabolic rate, and infection exposure (respiratory diseases and malaria). However, according to current climatological research, climate's impact on long-term BLS conditions only takes effect either when the short-term weather is highly fluctuating or even more so if there is long-term, sustained climate change (>30 years, with an anomaly continuing over a long period: Pei et al., 2013). The Intergovernmental Panel on Climate Change (IPCC, 2013) states that a climate shock becomes crucial if abrupt and/or accelerated changes reach a threshold of a global average temperature increase of 1.5–5.8°C. According to new climatological estimates, however, overall, over the course of the centuries under study, the changes were not as extreme as the current warming period.

During the centuries following the Late Iron Age, the most decisive climatic extreme seems to have been the LIA, with a temperature that was approximately 1–2°C colder than average. As discussed by Koepke (2008), several studies indicate that, in European temperate zones, substantial cooling in the 16th and especially 17th centuries (and the beginning of the 18th century CE) is negatively correlated with nutritional status (e.g., Baten, 2002). However, the discussion remains whether the LIA actually had a significant effect in all over Europe (Büntgen & Hellmann, 2014; Jordan, 1996; contrary to Kelly & Ó Gráda, 2014). When analyzing the potential impact of the LIA, presumably it will be largely region-specific because cooler and wetter conditions in warm and dry regions tend to result in different consequences than in colder regions.[16]

The only other potential temperature variation in the analyzed period was the Medieval Warm Period (or Medieval Climate optimum, from approximately 700 to 1200 CE). However, recent climatological studies found this warming period to be not as extreme as formerly assumed (IPCC, 2007), and it was recently named the "Medieval Climate (A)nomaly" (Werner et al., 2014). And, again, the potential effects of this warmer period on BSL could be different for warm (e.g., Mediterranean) and cold (e.g., Scandinavian) regions.

Moreover, it should be kept in mind that in addition to changes in surface temperature, changes in precipitation are also relevant (Jones & Mann, 2004; Morellòn et al., 2012; Pei et al., 2013). Besides, the severity of climatic changes might not be of strong significance due to compensating factors, such as trade or new farming practices (Tello et al., 2014).

To adequately depict the effect of climate change on the BLS, one needs high-resolution, region-specific data. However, the available data on the very-long-run development of climate change depict only the overall conditions for the Northern Hemisphere (IPCC, 2013) based on temperature curves with large variations. Detailed climatological estimates for the centuries under study are only available for the Alpine area (Büntgen et al., 2011; Esper, Düthorn, Krusic, Timonen, & Büntgen, 2014).[17] Thus, for the moment, I must stick to simplified results by controlling only for Northern Hemispheric temperature changes in the centuries CE, as provided by Koepke and Baten (2005*b*; based on Mann & Jones, 2003): they found no statistically significant impact in the overall long run.[18] Similarly, I also find no statistically significant effect for the centuries CE when utilizing the expanded dataset (not shown). My results provide a certain degree of support for the importance of climate: the tall mean height of North-Eastern Europeans (particularly in the warm 11th–12th century CE) shows a dramatic decline in the 17th century—which presumably is associated with the nadir of the temperature trend during the LIA. The statistically significant negative impact of a colder climate becomes perceptible from the 9th century onward, concomitant with the increase in population.

For the temporal extended analysis presented here, all I can do is consider any possible chronological variations in the natural factors by subsuming them with period dummies and region dummies.

Besides the natural factors, there are a number of potential socioeconomic-cultural determinants of the net nutrition of a population, including the types of food products and the yields from agriculture and animal husbandry, both of which depend on the basic prerequisites of natural endowments and applied technology and methods. For the period studied, the most useful measure for diet quality is the ***cattle share***, which shows the availability/consumption of dairy products and meat products.[19] In general, high quantity is an indicator of a high-quality diet. In particular, fermented milks and blood-based products (Howcroft, Eriksson, & Lidén, 2012) provide a mix of high-quality, amino-acid-rich proteins with vitamins and micronutrients that are essential for height growth (Dror & Allen, 2011). The effect of milk as a concentrated dietary source—and the consequent positive impact of a pastoral economy—was found to play a significant role in otherwise inadequate living conditions for recent centuries and in low-income countries today (e.g., Baten & Blum, 2014; Baten & Murray, 2000; Grasgruber et al., 2014; Hoppe, Mølgaard, & Michaelsen, 2006; Jamison, Leslie, & Musgrove, 2003; Komlos, 1998; Prince & Steckel, 2001; Scott & Duncan, 2002). For the time prior to the invention of refrigeration, various researchers have found a direct effect of geographic proximity on the local supply of fresh milk and easily spoiling dairy products (Komlos, 1989; Woolgar, Serjeantson, & Waldron, 2006).[20] Another implication of not having access to milk is that water was a poor substitute because it bore the danger of being unclean: when not properly boiled, water can represent a particularly severe health threat for weaning toddlers that will negatively affect their growth outcomes.

Moreover, in general during this period, consumption of animal products was rare, and grain was the dominant part of the diet (Adamson, 2004; Hirschfelder, 2005, p. 81; Schofield, 2006; Walter & Schofield, 1989).[21]

Thus, I hypothesize that higher consumption of dairy products and beef made a difference in the quality of diet in the centuries under study. The existing sporadic historic sources indicate that variations in consumption occurred due to culturally induced differences.[22] Was this really the case, and is a potential outcome visible in the height series?

To estimate variation in dairy consumption, the cattle share in comparison to the frequency of other animal bones is used as indicator.[23] I assume that this proxy correctly depicts the availability and consumption in particular of dairy products because various studies indicate that the milk production was the prime focus of husbandry and that the milk produced was always fully utilized (see Koepke & Baten, 2008, for and detailed discussion and references on primary production).[24] One factor discussed in the literature as potentially affecting milk consumption and its positive outcome, including regional variation in mean height, is genetic: namely, primary milk (lactose) intolerance (e.g., Grasgruber et al., 2014). However, for the overall consumption of dairy products in Europe it is irrelevant whether such consumption is due to imposed diet as consequence of availability resulting from environmental reasons or due to diet preferences explained by lactose intolerance. Remarkably, the ability to digest milk correlates with the consumption of dairy products and cattle herding. The distribution differs within Europe, showing an increasing frequency of cattle herding and lactose tolerance from South to North due to gene–culture co-evolution during the Neolithic transition.[25] An additional factor causing this pattern is probably that, for cattle husbandry, a cooler climate and its corresponding vegetation are advantages. Nevertheless, in general, even people with lactose intolerance can digest a cup of fresh milk and use fermented dairy products (which have a much reduced lactose content due to production processes) to obtain an adequate intake of protein, calcium, iron, vitamin D, and other nutrients.[26] Still, in the long run, the potential advantages for North-Easterners were twofold: they could make better use of the benefits of dairy products due to their higher lactose tolerance (Baten & Blum, 2014), and they had more dairy products available due to a higher cattle share (which might also have resulted in higher beef consumption, which provided additional benefits for growth). Moreover, presumably, the additional foodstuff protected them better from bad harvests, and, in general, they could store fresh dairy products for longer due to the colder climate. Therefore, one can conclude that the percentage of cattle bones found in food production related archaeological sites (not sacral or cemetery sites) depicts the consumption of dairy products correctly and thus is a good indicator of the BLS.

Overall, the data suggest that the Mediterranean cattle share was consistently lower than the Central-Western cattle share, with the share in North-Eastern Europe ranking highest. Moreover, the Mediterranean European series in particular depicts an extreme decline occurring during the centuries before the start of the Common Era. Later, the cattle bone share recovered somewhat, but it stagnated at a low level until the 6th century CE. These findings concur with what can be concluded from ancient texts and seem to move in accordance with the height data.[27]

Another factor affecting animal protein availability is ***cattle plague*** (Spinage, 2003), which can cause devastation to livestock and presumably was especially destructive during ancient times when no effective vaccine was available. Because the effect of cattle plague could be independent of the cattle share, I tested its possible impact for each major European region using a dummy variable "cattle plague" based on Barrett and Rossiter (1999).

Improved cultivation methods presumably had a positive influence on the food supply (Grupe, 2003; Wiese & Zils, 1987). For the centuries under study, I assume that the crucial innovation was the ***three-field crop rotation*** system, which enlarged agricultural output and improved net nutrition due to a reduction of risk factors, a diversity of crop types, and soil regeneration. To control for the potential influence of the three-field crop rotation system once regularly in use, I generated a dummy variable that takes the value of 0 for unaffected centuries and 1 for the 11th century CE onward, when with certainty three-field rotation was in use.

Population concentration can also be important for the BLS outcome via effects on health as well as on diet production and/or distribution. In my study, I use the quantity of ***land per capita*** to depict the maximum space that was available for food production and also to depict the environment for health by assuming that higher values should be positive for the BLS due to lower population pressure (Armelagos, 1990; Cohen & Armelagos, 1984; Livi-Bacci, 1991; Steckel & Rose, 2002).[28] To construct the proxy, I compiled data based on estimations of population density (such as those by Allen, 2003; McEvedy & Jones, 1988; for details, see Koepke, 2008; Koepke & Baten, 2005a).[29] In the quantitative analysis, I controlled for land per capita, calculated as square kilometers per inhabitant in logarithmic form, to account for the decreasing marginal product. For the centuries under study, estimates show that the population was not stationary. The series indicate that population was by far densest in the Mediterranean region until the 15th century CE, when North-Eastern and Central-Western Europe finally caught up. Before then, population density increased only gradually in all three European regions—with an intermediate boost during the *imperium Romanum* (especially strong in Mediterranean Europe) and a decline afterward—until a constant amplification set in from the 10th century CE onward. The total European population increased from approximately 22 million to 55 million from the middle of the 10th century to 1300. The only exception was the stagnation in those centuries affected by the Great Plague and the Hundred Years War (around the 14th century), whereas the Thirty Years War is not discernible in the data in terms of an obvious decline in population numbers (see also Cunha & Cunha, 2006; Livi-Bacci, 1991).[30]

In addition to general population numbers, a higher ***urbanization rate*** presumably also had an effect on the BLS. Although I must keep in mind that the degree of potential harm from urbanization depends on the character of the urban settlements in historic times, living in the crowded conditions of dense settlements commonly seems to have yielded a height penalty (see, e.g., Nutton, 2000; Scobie, 1986; contrary Flemming, 2014). Increasing urbanization represented a higher chance of inadequate sanitary conditions, agglomerations of refuse disposals, and cramped housing (with accompanying dampness, parasitism, risk of infection, and violence).[31] Moreover, increasing urbanization could result in an unfavorable food supply because the bulk of urban inhabitants were generally active in nonagricultural work and thus had to be fed by the hinterland (Wilson, 2011); moreover, de facto nontradable goods potentially result in worse urban subsistence possibilities compared with rural settlements (Komlos, 1998). Correspondingly, in archaeological data and in pre- and early historic periods, a higher urbanization rate seems to have meant a higher risk to human well-being (Gowland & Redfern, 2010; Jackson, 1988; Weeber, 1990). However, can this finding be confirmed for the long run, or did a favorable urban infrastructure equalize the potentially negative outcome?

The data that I utilized to construct the variable "urbanization rate" are based on estimations by Allen (2003) and others (for details, see, Koepke, 2008). The development of the urbanization rate is measured by the percentage of the overall number of settlements. In the course of the centuries under study, the urbanization rate moves similarly to the development of population density: in Central-Western Europe and particularly in the Mediterranean region, the urbanization rate increased around the turn of the Eras from the centuries BCE to CE. After a certain decline, from the 10th century CE onward, the urbanization rate increased constantly all over Europe (with the exception of stagnation around the 16th century).

In addition to the basic cultural-social circumstances, shock incidences—namely, ***epidemics*** and ***war/persecution***—influence human well-being and significantly affect environmental living conditions when compared to the basic situation in cases of long durations and supraregional spreading. If the population is affected by an intense war, the short-term impact is normally negative for net nutrition (e.g., Moradi, 2010) due to factors such as fallow fields or scorched-earth tactics that disturb the production and allocation of diet goods. However, the overall effect of war on human height might have been positive in cases in which the demographic shock was so enormous that the consequences resulted in improved circumstances for the survivors. Similarly, the overall long-term effect of a heavy epidemic could be twofold depending on the extremity of the incidence. A prominent example is the outcome of the Great Bubonic Plague in the 14th century CE, which caused a population decimation that directly reduced the breeding grounds for infection and also improved the BLS due to the change in subsistence toward a more pastorally focused diet; in the longer term, this epidemic seems to have caused improved well-being (Allen, 2008). In attempting to capture a possible effect on the BLS in the long run, I generated the dummy variables "war/persecution" and "plague" for those centuries that are known to have been dominated by a major war or epidemic event.[32] Those centuries during which the specific conditions presumably were dominant in Europe as a whole—which included either the large-scale spread of epidemic diseases or large-scale wars—were coded as 1 whereas for the remaining centuries, the dummy was coded as 0.

A further potential explanatory variable for the temporal and regional variation in the trajectory of well-being is the ***Roman impact*** on political, economic, and sociocultural spheres associated with the integration of a region into the ancient Roman Empire. Archaeological and ancient written sources generally indicate that integration substantially changed environmental conditions, both in the heartland as well as in the provinces.[33] Certain factors have often been described as beneficial for living conditions, but they actually might not have been as ideal for the BLS of the population. Recent case studies indicate that, during Roman times, the population seems to have been comparably short (Scheidel, 2012); however, according to some researchers, Roman net nutrition conditions seem to have been good (e.g., Kron, 2005).

Although I cannot differentiate the independent effects of the subfactors in the quantitative analysis, it is nevertheless important to keep in mind that the net effect of Roman ascendency included economic upswings and the innovation of commonly used *thermae*, as well as other aspects that potentially influenced BLS outcome.

The positive aspects of Roman influence presumably included the introduction of a wider variety of vegetables and fruits, in combination with new arable land and/or the widespread consumption of *garum*.[34] Other factors may have included the efficiency of the Roman market (Kessler & Temin, 2007), the integration of food markets, and improved housing quality (a common architecture featuring stone houses with heating systems), all of which possibly positively affected the net nutrition of Roman birth cohorts. The system of organized grain provisions for male Roman citizens might have helped to protect the population from starvation (compare Garnsey, 1998[35]). But, overall, the focus on grain presumably took its toll due to the detrimental effect of the low-quality protein intake from plants and particularly wheat (Grasgruber et al., 2014).

Various other factors could also have had an adverse impact on people's nutritional status, starting with the specific occupation policy applied by the Romans in different regions.[36] In particular, the extreme increase in trade and army movements presumably resulted in an unprecedented introduction of pathogens and infectious diseases (Duncan-Jones, 1996; Stannard, 1993).[37] Likewise, the market integration of formerly remote regions could have been negative due to the subtraction of diet goods that were previously available for the general indigenous population (Komlos, 1989).

The potential effect of medical care and sanitary conditions on well-being is of particular importance. According to Tulchinsky and Varavikova (2014), medical care was comparably better under Roman ascendancy. However, a proper public health structure was missing (Thüry, 2001). The impact of Roman sanitary facilities (public bathes, latrines etc.) on the BLS is debatable, but presumably negative.[38] Also a common awareness of urban pollution and adequate hygiene seems to have been lacking (Lindsay, 2000; Nutton, 2000; Jackson, 1988).[39] In addition, culturally induced potentially negative aspects included high exposure to lead (water pipes, cooking pots, toys, cosmetics (Stuart-Macadam, 1991) and early weaning (e.g., Barbiera & Dalla-Zuanna, 2009).[40]

A further aspect that might have resulted in a BLS decline during the Roman period is the degree of inequality.[41] In addition to basic economic disparities, legal conditions were different for Roman citizens, who had civil privileges, and non-Roman indigenous people, who had no or reduced property and human rights. Moreover, for the first time in European history, many people were no longer working in the subsistence economy, so only a part of the civilian population was working in food production, and a large part had to be fed, which created a class of people (workers) who were dependent on wage income, which probably created the danger of deteriorating net nutrition (Haines, 2004).

Because the net effect of Roman influence is composed of a wide variety of subfactors, it might also be possible that this combination of detrimental and beneficial factors equates to a nil effect on the BLS. The overall outcome could also differ for the heartland and the provinces. Unfortunately, the sources of data do not allow us to control for the various subfactors of the Roman impact. Therefore, to test the effect of becoming or being part of the Roman Empire, I used a dummy variable for "Roman impact" that takes the value of 1 for centuries and regions that belonged to the *imperium Romanum* and 0 for unaffected areas.

Finally, the cultural-socioeconomic circumstances and the effect on the BLS could have been influenced by a socially contrived differentiation of gender roles, which can result in ***gender inequality*** that further determines the entitlements and distribution of the direct determinants of the BLS. In historic Europe, the differentiation of gender roles seems to have mainly resulted in female discrimination due to common, patriarchically oriented structures (see, e.g., Horrell, Meredith, & Oxley, 2009; Oxley, 2004). Female discrimination can result in either immediate feminicide after birth (George, 2006; Klasen & Wink, 2002; Olds, 2006) or in the general neglect of girls on different levels (e.g., public endowments, household allocations) that can result in a diverging nutritional status for the genders during their growth years. This can affect height dimorphism and health disparities (Bogin, 1999; Eveleth & Tanner, 1976; Frongillo & Begin, 1993; Harris, Gálvez, & Machado, 2009; Moradi & Guntupalli, 2009; Sabir & Ebrahim, 1984).[42] In this context, two aspects are of interest for the long-run development of well-being: (1) the variation in gender inequality and its immediate effect on the mean height trajectory and (2) the potential danger of an extended burden affecting the next generation. The fetal growth (height and inner organs) and general future well-being of either sex is affected similarly when both the basic net nutrition of a birth cohort of females is insufficient and the living conditions of expectant and breast-feeding mothers are inadequate (Barker, 1995; Currie & Vogl, 2013; Martin-Gronert & Ozanne, 2006; Osmani & Sen, 2003).[43] However, for the centuries under study, a further aspect of gender inequality must be taken into account: Koepke (2014*b*) indicated that the degree of female discrimination in European regions was so pronounced that unwanted girls were eliminated before reaching adulthood and that those few females reaching adulthood were not treated unequally in comparison with their male contemporaries.[44] Thus, gender inequality did not vary enough in the course of the centuries to have a significant impact on the long-run trajectory of mean height. To control for gender inequality, I used the relative height differences from the dataset as a function of regions and centuries.

4.3 The Current State of Research: 8th Century BCE to 18th Century CE Europe

It is clear that the archaeological data only allow limited generalizations. Nevertheless, the observed mean height trajectory with its temporal and regional differences and the analysis of potential explanations is informative.

4.3.1 Change in Mean Height from the Late Iron Age to the LIA

To attempt to determine how the European BLS evolved over the course of the centuries from the Late Iron Age to the LIA, one first must fix a point in time when to assume that the LIA started. A discussion is ongoing regarding during which century the colder anomalies set in (e.g., IPCC, 2013; Mann, 2003) or even whether any significant shock actually took place (Kelly & Ó Gráda, 2014) depending on region. The coldest phase is often associated with the Maunder Minimum in solar activity (c. 1645–c. 1715); correspondingly, the 17th century CE seems to have been the nadir period of the LIA (IPCC,

2013), followed by some warming in the 18th century. Interestingly, a "draw down" of the height level is particularly visible in the North-Eastern data, regardless of which century from the 14th century CE onward I take as the starting century of the LIA. According to the descriptive statistics, the negative effect is most pronounced in the 17th century.

How did the European BLS evolve over the course of the 26 centuries before the 18th century CE? Considering the European data in total, I find the trajectory of the mean height to increase on average approximately 0.5 cm per 1,000 years in the very long run since the Late Iron Age. This result indicates that the BLS improved, although marginally, even prior to industrialization and its associated secular trend in height. However, looking at the development of mean height by regions for Mediterranean, Central-Western, and North-Eastern Europe from the 8th century BCE to the 18th century CE (Figure 4.1), the upward tendency in the BLS is not steady over time, and it is variable with respect to the three European regions.[45]

The data series indicate remarkable variations between centuries and between the different major European regions. Conventional economic measures point to the Mediterranean as generally having been the richest region. However, the regional comparison of the BLS indicates that, overall, the basic needs of life for North-Eastern Europeans were actually met better: they tended to be taller. Conversely, the

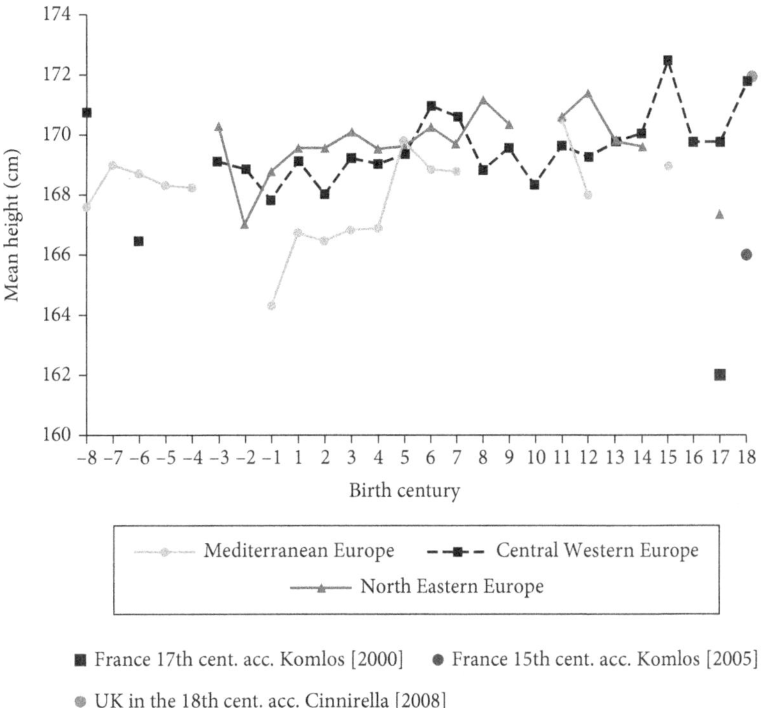

FIGURE 4.1 The mean height trajectory by major European region, 8th century CE to 18th century CE.

Mediterranean population had the smallest mean height on average.[46] Between these two lies the Central-Western height series. This result presumably can be explained by the more favorable environmental living conditions in the North-East, including low population density, lower urbanization rate, and a protein-rich diet.[47]

Assessing the temporal evolution of the data series in more detail shows that more beneficial and detrimental centuries occurred in alternation.[48] In particular, the ancient Roman period seem to have been detrimental to BLS: after the mean height had moved on a similar level from the 8th to the 3rd century BCE, the Mediterranean series shows an extreme deterioration in the 1st century BCE; this birth cohort has a mean height of 164.3 cm, a value of 8 cm below the predicted mean for the Mediterranean series. This worsening BLS could be explained by reduction changes in the proximity to animal protein because, with Roman ascendancy, a shift toward an extremely grain- and cereal-intensive agriculture took place (Garnsey, 1999). Moreover, this century of pronounced decline in mean height coincides with the first large wave of Roman expansion. This could also explain the decline in mean height in Central-Western Europe that occurred for the birth cohort of the 1st century BCE; negative aspects associated with the Roman expansion and the beginning of Roman occupation are, for example, military actions and the arrival of additional inhabitants in unprecedented amounts. The 1st century CE shows some recovery in mean heights in the Mediterranean, as well as in Central-Western Europe—likely due to a considerable stabilization during the early Principate after a long period of unrest. But, according to the data, the subsequent centuries did not show an upward trajectory in mean height (Figure 4.1), indicating rather insufficient welfare conditions: overall, mean height stagnated during the period of the *imperium Romanum*, and there was a downturn in Central-Western mean height in the 2nd century CE cohort. Because this particular century is considered the Roman heyday (Bowman & Wilson, 2009), the decline is striking and rather unexpected at first glance. However, the data suggest the occurrence of another economic growth paradox, one similar to that found in various studies of the early industrial period (e.g., Chanda, Craig, & Treme, 2008; Haines, 2004; Komlos, 1998; Margo & Steckel, 1983). Potentially negatively influencing factors associated with the economic boom on the BLS include, for example, market integration (resulting in a subtraction of vital goods that were formerly available in the indigenous periphery; see Komlos, 1989) and a deteriorating health environment, as discussed earlier. The fact that there is no decisive mean height decline for the unoccupied *Germania Magna* and the other unoccupied parts of North-Eastern Europe confirms the impression of this detrimental Roman impact.

In the 5th and 6th centuries CE, a pronounced increase in Mediterranean mean height occurred, indicating improving BLS conditions in the former Roman heartland after the decline of the *imperium Romanum*. Correspondingly, in contrast to the transition from the Iron Age to the Roman Empire, the transition to the medieval period meant an ameliorated BLS. This result confirms previous case studies (such as Barbiera & Dalla-Zuanna, 2009; Cardoso & Gomez, 2009; Giannecchini & Moggi-Cecchi, 2008; Paine et al., 2009; Steckel, 2004). The data even show a convergence of mean height in the three European regions with the Period of the Migration of Nations starting in the

5th century CE: the Mediterranean series reached the height level of the other regions. This presumably was caused once more by various factors: a return to an emphasis on pastoralism (Giovanni, 2001), the transformation of other cultural aspects (such as changes in breastfeeding customs: see Barbiera & Dalla-Zuanna, 2009; Dittmann & Grupe, 2000), a decline in population density (the 6th century was particularly affected by the Justinian plague), and a steep decline in urbanization. A positive effect on the BLS was presumably also caused by a reduction in socioeconomic inequality due to welfare redistribution from rich to poor strata (see, e.g., Blum, 2013).

During the 11th and 12th centuries CE, mean height increased in Central-Western Europe and in particular in North-Eastern Europe (similar to the findings of, e.g., Brothwell, 2003; Maat, 2003). Notably, no deterioration in mean height occurred in the 14th century, although that century includes the Hundred Years War, the main phase of the late medieval agrarian crisis, the Great Famine, and the main outbreak of the bubonic plague. One potential explanation is the shift to a more pastorally based diet for the surviving population (Allen, 2008; Dyer, 1994); similarly, the archaeo-zoological data show an increase in cattle bones (Koepke & Baten, 2008).

For the 15th to 18th century CE, only a very limited amount of data is available, mainly for North-Eastern Europe. The North-Eastern height series indicates a loss in its, on average, leading position, especially in the 17th century CE; this birth cohort has a mean height of 167.3 cm, a value of 7 cm below the predicted mean for the North-Eastern height series. This development might have been caused by the coldest phase of the LIA, which presumably affected the North-East more than the more southern regions, but it could also have resulted from the Thirty Years War.[49]

The utilized skeletal data indicate a recovery of the BLS in the 18th century because it is also commonly found in studies based on written data from this period. That living conditions improved over the course of the 18th century presumably (at least to a certain extent) was caused by improved climatic conditions (see, e.g., Komlos, 2002).[50]

In summary, I conclude from my dataset that both regional differences and temporal variation in mean height occurred in pre- and early historic Europe, indicating that the BSL experienced neither constant stagnation nor a linearly increasing trend in the very long run from the Iron Age onward. So, what does explain the mean height trajectory in the very long run?

4.3.2 Explanations for the Height Trajectories

To assess which of the potential explanatory variables just discussed had a significant impact on the European height trajectory in the very long run, I applied pseudo-panel WLS regressions on the aggregated level. As commonly conducted, the basic regression model uses the mean height (MH) of a population as the dependent variable, and variations to it are explained by the independent variables EC_i:

$$MH = \beta_0 + \sum_i \beta_i \ EC_i + \varepsilon$$

The extent to which the mean heights of different subgroups vary indicate the degree of the varying independent environmental conditions.

All of the models are WLS estimates (applying the square root of the sample size) to adjust for the nonuniform data distribution available and, thus, to limit the danger of a wrong assessment of centuries with a smaller number of observations (Table 4.1). As a reference group, I chose Central-Western Europeans of the Migration Period/early Middle Ages (following Koepke & Baten, 2005*a*, 2008 for comparison purposes). To control for intertemporal heterogeneity, I included dummies for the periods.[51] In conducting the WLS regressions, I controlled for the major regions to depict potential fixed effects.

Table 4.2 presents several regression models that explore the impact of the potential determinants under discussion. The regressions confirm (especially columns 4 and 7

Table 4.2 Regressions: Explanatory Variables of the Mean Height in Europe, 8th Century BCE to 18th Century CE

1	2	3	4	5	6	7
Constant	167.5	169.6	166.0	168.6	169.0	167.4
	(0.00)	(0.00)	(0.00)	(0.00)	(0.00)	(0.00)
Mediterranean Europe	0.3	**−1.1**		0.3	−1.4	
	(0.79)	(0.02)		(0.82)	(0.16)	
Central-Western Europe	Reference Category					
North -Eastern Europe	−0.1	0.4		0.0	0.0	
	(0.86)	(0.25)		(0.96)	(0.96)	
Early prehistory	−1.6	−0.9		**−1.9**		
	(0.23)	(0.18)		(0.06)		
Late prehistory	**−1.4**	**−1.1**		**−1.6**		
	(0.08)	(0.07)		(0.01)		
Antiquity	**−1.7**	**−1.4**		−0.8		
	(0.01)	(0.01)		(0.21)		
Early Middle Ages	Reference Category					
High Medieval Period	−0.1	−0.8		−0.05		
	(0.91)	(0.37)		(0.96)		
Late Medieval Period	−1.0	−1.1		−12		
	(0.60)	(0.38)		(0.38)		

Table 4.2 Contniued

1	2	3	4	5	6	7
Modern	−3.2 (0.19)	−1.7 (0.19)		−2.9 (0.11)		
Cattle share	0.1 (0.22)		**0.1** (0.01)	0.0 (0.66)	0.0 (0.80)	**0.1** (0.01)
Three-field rotation	0.8 (0.55)	0.7 (0.45)		0.8 (0.46)	0.2 (0.79)	
Cattle plague	−0.1 (0.89)	−0.2 (0.54)		0.3 (0.58)	−0.1 (0.89)	
Land per capita (log)	0.3 (0.82)		0.2 (0.70)		0.1 (0.90)	−0.2 (0.65)
Urbanization rate				**−0.3** (0.01)		
War/persecution	0.1 (0.90)	0.0 (0.92)		0.1 (0.80)	0.2 (0.65)	
Plague	−0.1 (0.88)	−0.1 (0.86)		0.3 (0.59)	0.0 (0.95)	
Gender inequality	1.2 (0.30)	0.5 (0.59)	1.7 (0.15)	1.2 (0.24)	1.5 (0.21)	
Roman impact					**−1.5** (0.02)	**−1.4** (0.00)
Adj. R^2	0.49	0.43	0.30	0.61	0.44	0.43
N	42	52	42	42	42	42

Weighted Least Square Regression: number of cases adjusted for aggregated observation using square roots. P-values in parentheses. Statistically significant coefficients in bold.

in Table 4.2) that, in the very long run, dairy and beef consumption (as proxied by the cattle share) had a significant, positive impact on the height outcome.[52] This finding suggests that the advantage of protein proximity was always crucial to biological well-being.

The multivariate regression analysis also verifies the harmful effect of a higher urbanization rate on the BLS (Table 4.2, column 5): the coefficient is negative and highly statistically significant.[53] As expected, the result rejects assumptions that suppose a preponderance of advantageous infrastructural features in urban settlements and instead supports the various studies that have found a detrimental effect, as discussed in Section 2.3.

Table 4.2, columns 6 and 7 show the model in which I control for the "Roman impact" The coefficient is highly significant and negative, thus confirming the first visual impression from Figure 4.1: the result indicates that the overall net effect of growing up within the *imperium Romanum* and being affected by the associated environmental circumstances was in fact cumulatively detrimental.[54] This finding is interesting because there are contradictory hypotheses concerning the effect of Roman ascendancy (see Section 2.3.). It seems that for the period of the Roman Empire, the concept of growth puzzle conditions is valid, as was found for the early Industrial period (e.g., Komlos, 1998, 2007; Margo & Steckel, 1983).

Concerning the question of potential regional differences, the results support the impression from Figure 4.1 that living conditions in Mediterranean Europe were generally relatively poor.[55]

None of the other independent variables is statistically significant for the very-long-run trajectory of mean height. There are different possible explanations for this result: first, it could be that no significant changes actually took place at all, as seems to have been the case with the gender effect. The data indicate that, for the adult population, no significant change in height dimorphism occurred (for a detailed discussion, see Koepke, 2014*b*). Similarly, the explanation for the finding that land per capita has no significant impact on the very-long-run trajectory of the BLS might be that a change in population density on average was irrelevant due to sufficiently abundant land availability in pre- and early history. Land only became scarce in later preindustrial societies after a certain threshold in population density was reached, and, at some point, this scarcity resulted in changes in the land-to-labor ratio, which caused marginal labor productivity to decline (Dyer, 1998; Woolgar et al., 2006). I find support for this hypothesis because the determinant "land per capita" becomes statistically significant if I run the model for the 10th to 18th centuries only (Koepke & Baten, 2005*a*), thus matching the increasing population pressure, which seems to have become tangible from the 9th century CE onward in the European case (Livi-Bacci, 1991).[56]

Second, the insignificance of the variables might alternatively result partly from the vague archaeological information on the determinants, which can only generate rough proxies—either simplified dummies or insufficient data series. For example, the fact that there are no full records of when cattle plague occurred presumably explains why "cattle plague" does not reach significance. Likewise, it is not possible to depict the human disease environment exactly (although described in detail in contemporary written sources) because of various issues, including the fact that a clear taxonomy did not exist (Cohn, 2010; Siraisi, 1990). For example, in contemporary writings, "plague" could represent any severe disease or epidemic; sources refer to many different occurrences, ranging from the Antoninian plague (smallpox) and the Justinian bubonic plague (Harbeck et al., 2013) to widespread ergotism (especially in medieval texts: Willerding, 1986).

Most likely the low data quality—that is, the inadequate resolution in the available series (temporal and regional)—also partially explains the absence of an effect of variation in climatic temperature. But an additional explanation could be that mean temperature per se has only a limited correlation to harvest yields and other aspects of the BLS, and information on other crucial meteorological quantities (e.g., precipitation) is missing.

Third, counterbalancing effects could also be a potential explanation for the finding of no significant impact by some of the determinants. For example, compensating negative and positive effects might operate in the case of "war/persecution," but these cannot be differentiated due to the low temporal resolution of the available data. Similarly, counterbalancing effects might explain the missing influence of the three-field rotation technique in the very long run. The fact that the dummy variable depicting improved cultivation methods is insignificant could be explained by compensation due to either previous population growth (Boserup, 1983; Cohen, 1989) or immediately subsequent population growth (e.g., Grupe, 2003) and overexploitation (Jordan, 2013).[57]

In addition to environmental determinants explaining (small) regional variations in mean height, a further factor recently put forward for recent decades is the potential effect of a varying distribution of specific haplogroups and associated growth profiles (especially I-M170 and R1b-U106; Grasgruber et al., 2014). It is debatable whether the genetic impact is less important for historic times because, according to Grasgruber et al. (2014), only at present, with the increase of living standards, have genetic factors moved to the foreground.[58] However, research on the genetic underpinnings that regulate growth in height is far from finalized (Lettre, 2011).[59]

One of the already identified genetic traits associated with mean height is primary lactose intolerance (for references, see Leonardi, 2013). However, for the historic context it is important to consider that, for milk consumption to have an effect on mean height, it does not matter whether this consumption results from diet preferences explained by lactose intolerance (i.e., genetics) or from an imposed intake due to dairy product availability caused by environmental factors (see discussion in Section 2.3.). Further research will verify whether genetic factors need to be taken into account when studying the European mean height trajectory in the long term.

In summary, according to the current state of the research, the explanatory variables of significant importance in generating the long-run BLS evolution are (1) dairy products and beef consumption with a positive effect and (2) urbanization and (3) the Roman influence, both with negative influences on mean height.

4.4 Conclusion

Taller mean height results from beneficial growth conditions and indicates a healthier configuration of the whole body, which implies physically and physiologically favorable human capital and thus a better basis for future development (e.g., Ulijaszek, 2006). Studying the development of the biological standard of living in Europe from the early Iron Age onward, including its potential explanatory variables, helps to shed light on the conditions that preceded modern economic development. I employed skeletal material as an indicator of human height for more than 18,000 individuals and other archaeological sources from three major European regions, with material dating from the 8th century BCE to the 18th century CE. The anthropometric approach is particularly important to gathering information on well-being in periods for which no adequate written sources exist.

Naturally, the data do not enable us to make strong causal claims, but the results provide new insights: it is possible to depict living conditions in a cross-regional overview from prehistoric times onward. I find that mean height increased in the very long run, but not following a constant upward trend. The evolution of European mean height shows temporal variations between centuries and regions: for example, it declined from the Iron Age to the period of the Roman Empire (particularly in the Mediterranean region), increased from the centuries of Roman ascendancy to medieval times, and later declined again, especially in the 17th century CE in the North-East (presumably affected by the nadir of the LIA) before increasing to an hitherto unprecedented level in the 18th century.

Regarding possible explanations for the height trajectory in the very long run, my findings indicate that the variation was positively triggered by dairy product availability and its corresponding consumption. This result is as expected. My results also confirm that the urbanization rate was a central driver of the failure to constantly improve the BLS in pre-modern times. Moreover, my study once more challenges the conventional perception that the medieval times were the "Dark Ages" and the Roman period was the "Golden Age": My analysis (based on a much larger dataset than that used in Koepke & Baten, 2005*a*) indicates an overall negative Roman impact and an improving BLS afterward.

One interesting result is that, for the overall background conditions, I found diet quality (as depicted by the cattle share) to be more important in economic significance than the negative Roman impact. Romanization does not result in a persisting legacy of health-related well-being because, according to the data, nutritional status in the three European regions aligned instantly after the decline of the Roman Empire.

In summary, the interdisciplinary approach of combining anthropometry and archaeology helps us to expand economic historic research to an extent that was otherwise impossible: taking our research back to study periods for which written sources are insufficient and thus allowing us to better understand where we came from.

Currently, new research methods are being refined and applied to skeletal material, thus enabling the study of stress indicators, health, nutrition, and more; therefore, extensive additional archaeo-biological material is currently being compiled that awaits future research. Better funding, improved technology (isotope analysis, DNA analysis, age determination in children, etc.) and the joint work of various collaborators will allow us to provide improved depictions of the path that the European BLS took in the very long run and why.

Notes

1. Other terms used instead of BLS are net nutrition or net nutritional status.
2. However, one must keep in mind that the existing studies on pre-sedentariness and its beginning still exhibit several contradictory results due to comparably low numbers of observations, such as five observations for Mesolithic times for Britain (Roberts & Cox, 2003).
3. It is impossible to find information on an everywhere homogenous and at all times consumed good that could be used as a numéraire for a long-term study. Moreover, although rough ratings are possible (Allen, 2009), numbers such as those from Diocletian's price edict are problematic to analyze because the numbers represent inflicted restrictions or are only valid for single, small regions (e.g., the indications on *ostraca*). Furthermore, the adequate consideration of inflation in the course of the first millennium CE is problematic; see, e.g., Temin, 2006.
4. For example, infant mortality rates cannot be estimated correctly because the archaeological data are not representative enough due to the poor preservation conditions of neonatal and infant bones. Similarly, it is also problematic to reconstruct life expectancy based on written sources (as concluded by Parkin, 1992). Likewise, no sufficient data are available to reconstruct the level of schooling in the long run. An exception for the ancient Roman period are *elogii* on tombstones, which provide some information on age-heaping, as analyzed by Duncan-Jones (1990), but these data are likely flawed (see critique by De Moor & van Zanden, 2008, esp. p. 8).
5. Moreover, the effects of low preservation are already taken into account in the height reconstruction methods. Correspondingly, controlling for a potential bias due to varying burial customs (inhumation and cremation) shows no significant differences in mean height.
6. Life expectancy as single indicator for well-being is more problematic because commonly utilized methods for age determination from skeletons are generally not as exact as height determination and the data based on different estimation methods are not properly standardizable. Alternatively, bone material can also provide information on diet or health stress, but the diagnosis and interpretation is less straightforward. In general, paleopathology is limited to conditions with osteological manifestations, but it cannot account for acute soft-tissue infections (van Schaik, Vinichenko, & Rühli, 2014). Moreover, when working with data on infectious diseases, a potential difficulty lies in the fact that paleopathological studies can only detect chronic illnesses that result in bone changes, which means that individuals without markers might have developed an illness and recovered successfully or died beforehand.

   However, the utilization of multiple indicators of diet and health can assist in the interpretation of the health of past populations. Some indicators that have been used in the literature are *cribra orbitalia* (indicating chronic iron-deficiency anemia and other disorders) and enamel hypoplasia (indicating infection, parasitism, or vitamin D deficiency), but these, unfortunately, are also nonspecific stress indicators.

In addition, chemical analyses can provide additional insight, and an increasing amount of bio-archaeological research has provided information on specific health conditions. Currently, however, the amount of perfectly reliable data is still comparably limited because the associated elaborate investigation methods (such as stable isotope analyses) are expensive. Correspondingly, so far, only some pilot studies have been conducted (such as Peck, 2013; Müldner & Richards, 2005); these studies have focused on skeletal lesions as an indicator of morbidity (e.g., Steckel, 2010). Promising future research on Europe will be based on the application of improved methods, such as the new study by van Schaik, Vinichenko, & Rühli (2014) that quantifies past disease burden by utilizing a pre-antibiotic and pre-chemotherapeutic osteological series with modern autopsy records in combination with a modern comorbidity index of disease severity.

In sum, the living statistic that can be estimated with the best accuracy from the skeleton still seems to be height (Brothwell, 1981).

7. Growth in height is finalized when the epiphysis of the claviculae is completed. Contrary to live measures, skeletal data from individuals from the age group *senilis* (>60 years) can also be taken into consideration because shrinking does not affect bone length. Conversely, the consideration of subadult individuals is problematic because they cannot be sex and age-determined with enough detail to allow for the application of height-for-age *z*-scores. In addition, children's remains (*infans* I and II) bear the danger of decomposing after burial. Thus, for children, it is not possible to decide whether a bone length predominantly results from age or living conditions.

The fact that still-growing individuals are excluded results in the advantage that one does not have to be concerned with truncation. However, this also brings about a certain sample deficiency: I cannot screen out a survivor bias in the data because weaker individuals might have already died during childhood. However, adult outcome correlates with early-life health (Currie & Vogl, 2013), and recent studies (e.g., Quaranta, 2013) have found that scarring effects dominate over selection effects. Moreover, in any case, I can obtain insights about the health outcomes of the surviving adults, which is interesting in itself.

8. Although not representing an entire society, of course. Nevertheless, the data are useful if a comparative project based on numerous sites, rural and urban, is conducted and the data are weighted.
9. In general, one must keep in mind, though, that bone material gives estimates not live measures.
10. Naturally, it is not possible to collect data randomly in statistical terms; however, I compiled data from any regular cemetery I could access. Of course, I cannot assume that the data represent the entire population, but I can assume that they present an adequate sample of the average, particularly because I conducted a large comparative study and considered numerous sites.
11. Concerning the chronology, I only included definitely dated observations; in archaeological terms, "accurately dated" means assignable to one century. Individuals of uncertain dating have been excluded. Because the birth century is used as the unit of the analysis, this approach may result in a small degree of uncertainty about the long-run trajectory due to the also sometimes difficult assessment of the exact adult age at death. However, I found the problem of dating vagueness to not be seriously biasing when controlling for the imprecise data with a dummy variable.

12. "Mediterranean Europe" includes Italy, Southern France, Spain, Portugal, and the Balkans. "Central-Western Europe" includes the Benelux, Northern and Eastern France, the UK, Southern and Western Germany, Switzerland, and Austria. "North-Eastern Europe" subsumes Scandinavia, Poland, North and Eastern Germany, and Hungary.
13. I tested for migration because migrants presumably experienced different conditions during upbringing than did the indigenous population (and it is known for the European case that migrant streams moved both from the Mediterranean region into Central and Western Europe and also that North-Eastern European tribes migrated to the South).

    And, to the extent possible, I tested for social status to consider social composition and potential social selectivity (within the context of regular cemeteries) when analyzing height trends in the nonaggregated data. In the individuals under study those of "high/middle status" were only marginally statistically significantly taller for all of Europe (at the 10% level), and the results were insignificant if the data are divided into the three major European regions. I conclude that the economic composition of the observations did not cause the observed height variations.
14. The mean height series presented here are based on separate male and female data, which are adjusted for female height and merged (following Koepke & Baten, 2005*a*, 2008).
15. For example, population estimates are generally rough approximations, and urbanization rates are also sketchy (Zimmermann, 1996; Zorn, 1994). Nevertheless, the available estimates based on the archaeological sources can be used to get a rough idea of potential effects.
16. Even within the North-Ern Hemisphere, the effect of climate change on food production can depend on longitudinal and latitudinal location. Climate change—especially when described only as temperature change—may have different effects on food production for different regions: in a colder region, a temperature increase will be positive, whereas it may be rather negative in an already warm region. The opposite holds for a temperature reduction, which is correlated with increased precipitation and which could even improve food production in the warm Mediterranean region, where precipitation tends to be a limiting factor.
17. However, the attempt to utilize a single regional temperature series in order to measure climate effects in widely distributed European regions, as is often done in studies, is problematic.
18. As already stated by Koepke and Baten (2005*b*), any inference based on this regression result is impaired due to missing data on precipitation and the low temporal and regional resolution of the accessible temperature series. Actually, considering the fact that climate change is ultimately regional/local, the missing impact is not surprising.
19. Future extended research (following the study by Izdebski, Koloch, Słoczyński, & Tycner-Wolicka, 2014, on the agricultural output in Central-Eastern Europe) will also enable us to control for increased agricultural production.
20. Hard cheeses were tradable, but the archaeological findings do not indicate a widespread trade of this type of good across the borders of the three major European regions under study.
21. Legumes seem to have been an important protein and calcium source for the poorer strata (Adamson, 2004). Similarly, eggs (with the advantage of being not only seasonally available, although on a limited basis—see Arcini (1999)—have been presumed to be important, but their remains are rarely found in an archaeological context. The same is the case

for fish bones, which are easily overlooked in archaeological excavations and are therefore likely to be underrepresented in archaeo-zoological assemblages.

22. According to the ancient written sources, there were large variations between the major European regions: the Germanic tribes regularly consumed large amounts of milk and meat—in contrast to their Mediterranean contemporaries. This documentation started with Poseidonius (c. 80 CE) who reported that the Germanic people enjoy "per extremity" grilled meat together with milk in their daily diet (Poseidonius, book 30). Similarly, Tacitus (*Germania* 5,1) and Caesar (*de bello Gallico* 6,35,6) emphasized the importance of cattle for tribes in the Germania Magna (Thüry, 2007). Dairy cattle are also registered in the *leges Barbarorum* (e.g., in the L Bai IX,2; see Weber, 1985) of the Germanic tribes dating from the end of the 5th to the end of the 8th century CE. In contrast, cattle seem to have been mostly used for traction power in the *imperium Romanum* (e.g., Cassiodorus, variae 3,50). Nevertheless, also in Roman times, cattle dairy products (other than cattle meat) were yields of interest: see especially Pliny the Elder (*Naturalis Historia* 8, 179), who stressed that the milk efficiency (and working capacity) of even the autochthonous cow was remarkable despite its smaller size. Correspondingly, studies on archaeo-zoological sources indicate that, where cattle husbandry was conducted, the animals were always also used for their milk yield (see Koepke & Baten, 2008, for references), which were fermented for consumption (see, e.g., Alcock, 2006). However, if cows are intensively used as draft animals, it can affect their milk production.
23. For archaeological centuries, the only source to depict protein-in-diet conditions are animal bones taken from archaeo-zoological assemblages (for details, see Koepke & Baten, 2008) by using the relative share of cattle bones with respect to the total share of domesticated large animal bones as an indicator of dairy product and meat consumption. In other words, cattle share is the percentage of cattle bones in all bones. In contrast to absolute numbers, the relative shares of bones of the large animal types can be used as an indicator because they are not affected by taphonomic biases.
24. The archaeo-zoological data on hand indicates no significant changes in the ovine supply, whereas the pig and cattle share developed more or less antipodally in all three parts of Europe.
25. Recent analyses of prehistoric DNA find the co-expansion of lactase persistence and dairying culture, thus supporting the gene–culture co-evolution hypotheses that the dissemination and frequency of lactose persistence in Europeans increased only after the domestication of dairy animals, diffusion of pastoralism, and milk exploitation from Neolithic times onward (Leonardi, 2013).

    Remarkably, even before the transition, European herders already seem to have realized the importance of dairy as a diet component because they applied methods to reduce lactose concentration (pottery evidence). However, with the North-Ern expansion of the Neolithic husbandry cultures, a selection process seems to have set in that supported an increase in the frequency of the lactase persistence allele and, correspondingly, the spread of pastoralism.
26. Moreover, research indicates that, in general, primary lactose intolerance mainly affects adult. However, it might come into effect already during the adolescent growth spurt because onset can occur from age 2–5 years and continues to develop further through adolescence. Generally, symptoms of lactose intolerance rarely develop in people younger than 6 years.
27. Concerning the written sources, please refer to note 22.

28. In addition, overpopulation bears the danger of permanent settlements in regions that were unsuitable for agricultural production while, at the same time, potentially also affecting local ecosystems due to accompanying changes in the fauna and flora (Grupe, 2003).
29. Other estimates in the literature on prehistoric centuries only discussed the whole world as one research unit. For the centuries CE, different studies exist on single periods and regions. Considering other regions in the world as well, in all cases, the estimates by McEvedy and Jones (1988) resulted in comparably low values, but they fit with UN estimates: see the web page of the US Census Bureau, Population Division. Newer estimates would have been available for the later centuries, but those data were not used here because their combination with the data for earlier centuries could result in some discontinuity.
30. Komlos and Nefedovb (2002) even concluded that there "are indications that population actually started to decline even before the plague".
31. The complexity of the potential effects resulting from crowded conditions in urban settings can be exemplified by parasite exposure, which is primarily caused by unsanitary circumstances and the accumulation of waste, and affects the disease environment directly, as well as the food quality because of inadequate fecal-oral separation (rivers, kitchens, wells, etc.). To better measure the actual contamination interaction, an option to measure vermin or worm infestation would be the analysis of coprolite remains (mineralized or desiccated excrements). But, so far, this kind of study has been conducted only rarely, and data are not adequate for a long-run study. Correspondingly, I cannot create a direct variable on parasite exposure. However, conditions can be assumed to have been more rampant when associated with a higher urbanization rate.
32. "All-encompassing" endemic epidemics are mentioned in the historic accounts. These are, for example, the "Great Plague" under the reign of Marcus Aurelius Antoninus (the so-called Antoninian plague) and the Justinian plague. For these particular cases, various written sources exist, and the effects can also be seen in production breaks in coin minting and in manufacturing (e.g., Duncan-Jones, 1996).
33. However, for example, concerning the new provinces, the BLS outcome depends on the actual occupation policy (whether it was more of an integrative process or was an "extinctional" act) and, similarly, to what extent a subsequent relocation of autochthonous men was undertaken (to prevent rebellion: e.g., Zanier, 2000), which would affect agricultural production. And the province-specific BLS will also differ depending on differences in the increase in population (influx of the army, civil servants, traders, and their families).
34. Unfortunately, it is not testable to what extent the commonly consumed fermented fish paste was a decisive factor in supporting net nutrition during Roman ascendancy, but it might have represented an add-on because the hydrolysis of the high-protein content results in more amino acids (on this process, see Mehta, Kamal-Eldin, & Iwanski, 2012, especially. p. 292).
35. Garnsey (1998) questioned whether the supply of male Roman citizens with grain donations was adequate for the needs of the whole population. Moreover, in medieval times, urban councils took action to supply the population with cereals as a "kind of care policy" (Engel, 1993, especially p. 265), so the Roman conditions might not have made any substantial impact in terms of caloric provision.
36. For the heartland, the occupation of new arable land could have resulted in an additional supply of resources deducted from the new provinces. However, conditions might also have worsened due to military under armament, which could cause additional taxation and the withdrawal of agricultural workers.

37. In combination with the associated road net expansion itself, the settlement structure also densified.
38. According to written sources, for example, baths were often unclean and unhealthy places because ancient doctors advised their patients to visit the *thermae* as a cure for illness, and the water seems to not have been replaced on a regular basis (Scobie, 1986; Thüry, 2001). Drinking water was commonly drawn from public wells, and the danger of contamination was mentioned even in ancient sources (Thüry, 2001).
39. Rivers, which were used to supply drinking water, were also used as garbage dumps. Sewage and latrines were often located near wells and kitchens, which certainly resulted in a wide diffusion of parasites; this became more intensified due to the common use of public latrines, thus presumably resulting in the spread of bowel diseases to vast parts of the population.
40. Moreover, the common custom of engaging wet nurses who mostly originated from poorer strata and had low net nutrition might have affected the quality of milk fed to babies.
41. The inequality extraction ratio estimated by Milanovic et al. (2010) at least indicates improved conditions in medieval times in comparison with the period of the Roman Empire.
42. Two background aspects are important in the context of the variation in height dimorphism as an indicator of gender-specific living conditions: (1) females generally have a smaller mean height than males, but the relative height difference does not increase with mean height (Gustafsson & Lindenfors, 2004). (2) According to various studies in recent decades, females show no stronger biological buffering against stressors than do males (Stinson, 2000). Instead of sex-related differences in robustness, gender-biased parental investment was found to be more essential for height growth. Conditions for females can even aggravate when overall living conditions are worsening (Frongillo & Begin, 1993; Moradi & Guntupalli, 2009).
43. The extent to which the wider transgenerational transmission of maternal phenotypes has an effect on offspring health has also been discussed (Susser et al., 2012).
44. Concerning long-run development and a potential legacy of intergenerational effects for health-related outcomes in the offspring, the comparably good living conditions for females reaching adulthood mean that despite the poor overall socioeconomic status of females, the next generation is not negatively affected. This hypothesis can actually be confirmed by the height series showing no general decline, but instead an overall upward tendency in the average European BLS (Koepke, 2014*b*).
45. The series are based on the coefficients of the birth cohort century variables from the WLS regression on the individual level (controlling for sex, social status, and migration, with at least 35 individuals per century and region). The data given are adjusted for female height and pooled for both genders. Taking all the data into account (including those centuries with less than 35 observations, not shown here), the additional data points fit quite well into the series shown in Figure 4.1.
46. The data show the largest variability in the Mediterranean region; in addition, this region also contains the birth century with the lowest mean height in European development—the 1st century BCE.
47. As described in Section 2.3, according to the data on hand, the food quality (and quantity)—namely, the availability of quality protein and micronutrients that are particularly important for longitudinal body growth—was higher in the North, whereas its production

and consumption was lower in the Mediterranean region. In addition, due to dense urbanization and the generally incomparably high population numbers, it can be assumed that in Mediterranean Europe, the birth cohorts on average experienced a rather inferior biological standard of living.

48. Concerning this finding, it is not possible to speak of cycles because the temporal resolution does not allow us to test for an association with business cycles, as is possible for later decades (e.g., Komlos, 1998).
49. Unfortunately, for comparison purposes concerning this period, I could not compile enough data for Mediterranean Europe, where the effect of both climate and war should have been less pronounced.
50. The written sources on height data are mainly military recruit measurements and thus only depict information on males. Moreover, the skeletal material gives estimates not live measures. Nevertheless, the direction of changes in the height trajectory can be evaluated. In doing so (see Figure 4.1), I find the decline in BLS in the 17th century confirmed by height studies focusing on recent centuries—although in comparison to my data on the wider European regions, for example, the mean height for the 17th century France was much lower (Komlos, Hau, & Bourguinat, 2003). For the 18th century, the different sources indicate improved conditions: e.g., male height was 167–168 cm in France in 1735–50 (Komlos et al., 2003, especially p. 168) and 172 cm in mid-18th century Britain (Cinnirella, 2008). This matches with my Central-Western mean height series that averages both regions and falls at c. 170 cm.
51. Prehistory was separated into an early (8th–5th century BCE) as well as a late part, beginning from the 6th BCE to approximately 500 BCE. In Central-Western Europe (and far into France and Spain), the change of the Early Iron Age to the Latène period took place, and, approximately parallel in the North-East, the Jastorf culture arose, while on the Apennine Peninsula, the Etruscans entered their golden age after centuries of formation. It follows that the ancient period starts at different times in the different regions, but it continues for a similarly long period in the three major European regions until the 5th century CE, when the Migration period/early medieval began, followed in each region by the high and late medieval periods from the 10th and 13th century CE onward, respectively, and the modern period, which starts with the 16th century.
52. The model in column 2 accounts for the widest range of possible testable variables (with an adjusted R^2 of 0.49). Here, only two of the variables are statistically significant for the very-long-term trajectory of mean height: the period dummies standing for late prehistory (at the 10% level) and antiquity (at the 1% level). In both periods, Europeans on average were shorter in height than during the early Middle Ages. None of the other variables has a statistically (or economically) significant impact in this model. In terms of economic significance, however, there is one exception: a higher cattle share results in a 0.59 cm increase in mean height.

    Column 3 depicts a model in which "cattle share" and "land per capita" are excluded from the regression. In this specification, the explanatory power becomes smaller in magnitude (adjusted R^2 is 0.43), and the dummy for Mediterranean Europe becomes significantly negative, indicating that it captures the excluded variables and that the environmental determinants are driving the regional differences.

    In column 4, I focus on the two potential key determinants of "cattle share" and "land per capita" (adjusted R^2 is 0.30). The regression result indicates that only the net effect of living in a cattle-rich setting mattered for the mean height trajectory: it is statistically significant at the 1% level (with a slightly positive coefficient), whereas living in an environment with a higher availability of land per capita is insignificant.

53. In column 5, I test how the mean heights changed with urbanization by adding "urbanization rate" to the base line model (replacing "land per capita" to avoid multicollinearity). The result indicates that the claim of a detrimental effect on net nutrition due to the higher urbanization rate is verified (with an adjusted R^2 of 0.61): this explanatory variable is highly statistically significantly negative. The effect of the remaining variables is negligible, with the exception of the dummies depicting the prehistoric periods that are statistically significant (at the 5% and 1% levels).
54. In column 6, I vary the first model by including the "Roman impact" dummy (excluding the time dummies to avoid multicollinearity; adjusted R^2 is 0.44), and I find the coefficient to be highly significant and negative: −1.46 cm (at the 1% level). In this model, none of the other variables is significant. However, as before, the insignificance of the Mediterranean dummy disappears as soon as I exclude cattle share and land per capita from the model (not shown). Controlling solely for the Roman impact for each affected region (not shown here), the influence for Mediterranean Europe was more extreme than for Central-Western Europe. The Roman impact on Mediterranean Europe remains negatively significant if I exclude the extreme low value of the 1st century BCE.

    In the model in column 7, I focus on the "Roman impact" by also including land per capita and cattle share (adjusted R^2 is 0.43). The coefficient of the "Roman impact" dummy is statistically significantly negative at the 1% level—now decreasing mean height by 1.43 cm on average. Additionally, "cattle share" variable is highly statistically significant in affecting mean height, but with the expected positive sign. In fact, the data indicate that in terms of economic significance (see Koepke, 2014*a*, especially table 4.2 for descriptives), the positive impact of a higher cattle share (+0.6 cm) can outweigh the negative Roman effect (−0.5 cm). Although this regression model has a lower adjusted R^2, it can still explain 43% of the mean height. If I control for the Roman impact for each major European region separately (not shown here), the detrimental effect is not only significant for the Mediterranean but also for Central-Western Europe.
55. The dummy for Mediterranean Europe becomes significantly negative at the 5% level if I do not control for the determinants, which tend to depict the environmental circumstances particularly well: namely, cattle share and land per capita; this result suggests that the Mediterranean dummy subsumes the excluded variables, which indicate that the regional differences are triggered by the environmental determinants: the excluded factors "cattle share" and "land per capita" depict the favorable aspects of proximity to protein and a comparably good epidemiological environment, which are not provided to a similar extent in the Mediterranean region as in the other European regions. If I exclude only cattle share from the model (see column 3), the "Mediterranean Europe" dummy also becomes statistically significant (at the 10% level). This finding demonstrates the importance of different environmental circumstances in explaining the height differences between Mediterranean populations and other European people.
56. The missing significant effect of land per capita could, of course, have also been caused by the so-called Malthusian trap, with the interaction of nutritional status and fertility rate (e.g., Scott & Duncan, 2002). Alternatively, the potential explanation could also be that Boserup (1966) was correct in stating that technological adaptation and investments in land allow a larger population to be fed. Similarly, Garnsey (1990, especially p. 144) stated that food crises were frequent, but not disastrous "in large part because of human

anticipation and adaptability ... vulnerability of populations led to increased agricultural production, emergency imports and food distribution." However, in this study, I cannot ultimately decide what the main cause was for the missing effect of land per capita due to the temporal resolution of the data, which covers approximately three or four generations.

57. Running a model solely controlling for three-field cultivation methods, I found this determinant to have a positive impact on long-run height development, which was statistically significant at the 1% level (not shown). Similarly, the innovation of heavy ploughs seems to have been correlated with increased population density and urbanization during the High Middle Age (Andersen, Jensen, & Skovsgaard, 2013); however, at the current stage of research, it is not clear which factor was the trigger.
58. In this context, the discussion also remains as to whether the exhaustion of the genetic height potential really is the reason for the recent deceleration of the height trend, or whether the stagnation might be also be explained by a change in food preferences away from red meat and other protein-rich foodstuffs (see also Baten & Blum, 2014).
59. Moreover, as indicated by Grasgruber et al. (2014), the significance of the few haplogroups controlled for in their multiple regression might be distorted due to multicollinearity effects.

References

Adamson, M. (2004). *Food in medieval times.* Westport, CT: Greenwood.

Alcock, J. (2006). *Food in the Ancient World.* Westport, CT: Greenwood.

Allen, R. C. (2003). Progress and poverty in early modern Europe. *Economic History Review,* 56(3), 403–443.

Allen, R. C. (2008). The nitrogen hypothesis and the English agricultural revolution: A biological analysis. *Journal of Economic History, 68,* 182–210.

Allen, R. C. (2009). How prosperous were the Romans? Evidence from Diocletioan's price edict (301 AD). In A. Bowman & A. Wilson (Eds.). (2009). *Quantifying the Roman economy* (pp. 327–345). Oxford: Oxford University Press.

Andersen, T. B., Jensen, P. S., & Skovsgaard, C. V. (2013). The heavy plough and the agricultural revolution in Medieval Europe. *Discussion Papers on Business and Economics, University of Southern Denmark,* 6/2013. Available at http://ssrn.com/abstract=2362894 or http://dx.doi.org/10.2139/ssrn.2362894

Angel, J. (1984). Health as a crucial factor in the changes from hunting to developed farming. In M. Cohen & G. Armelagos (Eds.), *Paleopathology at the origins of agriculture* (pp. 51–74). Orlando, FL: Academic Press.

Arcini, C. (1999). *Health and disease in early Lund.* Lund: Medical Faculty Lund University.

Armelagos, G. (1990). Health and disease in prehistoric populations in transition. In A. Swedlund & G. Armelagos (Eds.), *Disease in populations in transition* (pp. 127–144). New York: Bergin and Garvey.

Barbiera, I., & Dalla-Zuanna, G. (2009). Population dynamics in Italy in the Middle Ages: New insights from archaeological findings. *Population and Development Review,* 35(2), 367–389.

Barker, D. J. P. (1995). The fetal and infant origins of disease. *European Journal of Clinical Investigation,* 25(7), 457–463.

Barrett, T., & Rossiter, P. (1999). Rinderpest: The disease and its impact on humans and animals. *Advances in Virus Research,* 53, 89–110.

Baten, J. (2002). Climate, grain production and nutritional status in 18th century southern Germany. *Journal of European Economic History*, 30(1), 9–47.

Baten, J., & Blum, M. (2014). Why are you tall while others are short? Agricultural production and other proximate determinants of global heights. *European Review of Economic History*, 18(2), 144–165.

Baten, J., & Murray, J. (2000). Heights of men and women in nineteenth century Bavaria: Economic, nutritional, and disease influences. *Explorations in Economic History*, *37*, 351–369.

Bertranpetit, J. (2012). Tracing the origins of European populations through the analysis of genomes. *Jornades UPF d'Arqueologia*, un fòrum de debat sobre el fenomen migratori a la prehistòria d'Europa. [Migrations in the prehistory of Europe: Archaeological, linguistic and genetic evidence.] Paper presented at the *Jornades UPF d'Arqueologia* 2014, University Pompeu Fabra, Barcelona, March 2.

Blum, M. (2013). Cultural and genetic influences on the "biological standard of living", historical methods. *Journal of Quantitative and Interdisciplinary History*, 46(1), 19–30.

Boarini, R., Johansson, Å., & Mira d'Ercole, M. (2006). Alternative measures of well-being. OECD Economics Department Working Paper No. 476. Paris: OECD Publishing

Bogin, B., 1999. *Patterns of Human Growth*. Cambridge: Cambridge University Press.

Boserup, E. (1966). *The conditions of agricultural growth: The economics of agrarian change under population pressure*. London: Allen and Unwin.

Boserup, E. (1983). The impact of scarcity and plenty on development. In R. Rotberg & T. Rabb (Eds.), *Hunger and history. The impact of changing food production and consumption patterns in society* (67–94). Cambridge: Cambridge University Press.

Bowman, A., & Wilson, A. (Eds.). (2009). *Quantifying the Roman economy*. Oxford: Oxford University Press.

Bradley, K. (1991). *Discovering the Roman family: Studies in Roman social history*. Oxford: Oxford University Press.

Brothwell, D. (1981). *Digging up bones: The excavation, treatment, and study of human skeletal remains*. Ithaca, NY: Cornell University Press.

Brothwell, D. (2003). Wealth, health and theoretical archaeology. In *Wealth, Health and Human Remains in Archaeology*. Symposium Nederlands Museum Anthrop. Praehist. Amsterdam (pp. 39–55). Amsterdam: W. H. Metz.

Büntgen, U., & Hellmann, L. (2014). The Little Ice Age in scientific perspective: Cold spells and caveats. *Journal of Interdisciplinary History*, 44(3), 353–368.

Büntgen, U., Tegel, W, Nicolussi, K., McCormick, M., Frank, D., Trouet, V., . . . Esper, J. (2011). 2500 Years of European climate variability and human susceptibility. *Science*, *331*, 578–582.

Cardoso, H., & Gomez, J. (2009). Trends in adult stature of peoples who inhabited the modern Portuguese territory from the Mesolithic to the late 20th century. International Journal of Osteoarchaeology, 19, 711–725.

Carmichael, A. (1995). History of public health and sanitation in the West before 1700. In K. Kiple (Ed.), *The Cambridge world history of human disease* (pp. 192–200). Cambridge: Cambridge University Press.

Chanda, A., Craig, L., & Treme, J. (2008). Convergence (and divergence) in the biological standard of living in the USA, 1820–1900. *Cliometrica*, 2(1), 19–48.

Cinnirella, F. (2008). Optimists or pessimists? A reconsideration of nutritional status in Britain. *European Review of Economic History*, 12(3), 325–354.

Cohen, M. (1989). *Health and the rise of civilization*. New Haven, CT: Yale University Press.

Cohen, M., & Armelagos, G. (1984). *Palaeopathology at the origins of agriculture*. Orlando, FL: Academic Press.

Cohn, S. (2010). Changing pathology of plague. In S. Cavaciochi (Ed.), *Economic and biological interactions in pre-industrial Europe, from the 13th to the 18th century* (pp. 33–56). Fondazione Istituto Internazionale di Storia Economica F. Datini, Prato: Ser. 2, Atti delle Settimane di Studi e altri convegni 41. Firenze: Firenze University Press.

Cunha, C., & Cunha, B. (2006). Impact of plague on human history. *Infectious Disease Clinics of North America*, *20*, 253–272.

Currie, J., & Vogl, T. (2013). Early-life health and adult circumstance in developing countries. *Annual Review of Economics*, *5*, 1–36.

David, P. A., Johansson, S. R., & Pozzi, A. (2010). The demography of an early mortality transition: Life expectancy, survival and mortality rates for Britain's royals, 1500–1799. Discussion Papers in Economic and Social History No. 83. Oxford: University of Oxford.

De Beer, H. (2004). Observations on the history of Dutch physical stature from the late-Middle Ages to the present. *Economics and Human Biology*, 2(1), 45–55.

De Moor, T., & van Zanden, J. (2008). "Every woman counts". A gender-analysis of numeracy in the Low Countries during the Early modern period. Working paper for the Third Flemish-Dutch Conference, Antwerp, January 31–February 1.

Dittmann, K., & Grupe, G. (2000). Biochemical and palaeopathological investigations on weaning and infant mortality in the early Middle Ages. *Anthropologischer Anzeiger*, *58*, 345–355.

Dror, D., & Allen, L. (2011). The importance of milk and other animal-source foods for children in low-income countries. *Food & Nutrition Bulletin*, 32(3), 227–243.

Duncan-Jones, R. (1990). *Structure and scale in the Roman economy*. Cambridge: Cambridge University Press.

Duncan-Jones, R. (1996). The impact of the Antonine plague. *Journal of Roman Archaeology*, *9*, 108–136.

Dyer, C. (1994). *Everyday life in medieval England*. London: Hambledon.

Dyer, C. (1998). Did the peasants really starve in medieval England? In M. Carlin & J. Rosenthal (Eds.), *Food and eating in Medieval Europe* (pp. 53–71). London: Hambledon.

Engel, E. (1993). *Die deutsche Stadt des Mittelalters*. Munich: C. H. Beck.

Esper, J., Düthorn, E., Krusic, P., Timonen, M., & Büntgen, U. (2014). Northern European summer temperature variations over the Common Era from integrated tree-ring density records. *Journal of Quaternary Science*, 29(5), 487–494.

Eveleth, P., & Tanner, J. (1976). *Worldwide variation in human growth*. Cambridge: Cambridge University Press.

Finley, M. (1973). *The ancient economy*. London: Chatto & Windus.

Flemming, R. (2014). Medicine and health in Roman cities: The case for the defence. Working paper presented at the 10th European Social Science History Conference, Vienna, April 23–26.

Frongillo, E., & Begin, F. (1993). Gender bias in food intake favors male preschool Guatemalan children. *Journal of Nutrition*, 123(2), 189–196.

Garnsey, P. (1990). Responses to food crisis in the ancient Mediterranean world. In: Newman, L. F. (Ed.), *Hunger in history. Food shortage, poverty, and deprivation* (pp. 126–146). Cambridge: Blackwell.

Garnsey, P. (1998). *Cities, peasants and food in classical antiquity. Essays in social and economic history*. Cambridge: Cambridge University Press.

Garnsey, P. (1999). *Food and Society in Classical Antiquity*. Cambridge: Cambridge University Press.

George, S. (2006). Millions of missing girls: From fetal sexing to high technology sex selection in India. *Prenatal Diagnosis, 26*(7), 604–609.

Giannecchini, M., & Moggi-Cecchi, J. (2008). Stature in archaeological samples from Central Italy: Methodological issues and diachronic changes. *American Journal of Physical Anthropology, 135*, 284–292.

Giovannini, F. (2001). *Natalità, mortalità e demografia dell'Italia medievale sulla base dei dati archeologici*. Oxford: B.A.R. (Int. Ser. 950).

Gowland, R., & Redfern, R. (2010). Childhood health in the Roman world: Perspectives from the centre and margin of the empire. *Childhood in the Past, 3*, 15–42.

Grasgruber, P., Cacek, J., Kalina, T., & Sebera, M. (2014). The role of nutrition and genetics as key determinants of the positive height trend. *Economics and Human Biology, 15*, 81–100.

Grupe, G. (2003). Stable nitrogen isotope analysis of archaeological human bone from medieval times. In R. Noël, I. Paquay, & J. -P. Sosson (Eds.), *Au-Delà de l'Ècrit. Les hommes et leurs vécus matériels au Moyen Âge à la lumière des sciences et des techniques. Nouvelles Perspectives* (pp. 281–294). Actes du Colloque international de Marche-en-Famenne October, 2002. Court-Saint-Étienne: Brepols.

Gustafsson, A., & Lindenfors, P. (2004). Human size evolution: No evolutionary allometric relationship between male and female stature. *Journal of Human Evolution*, 47(4), 253–266.

Haidle, M. (1997). *Mangel—Krisen—Hungersnöte? Ernährungszustände in Süddeutschland und der Nordschweiz vom Neolithikum bis ins, 19. Jh.* Urgeschichtliche Materialh. 11. Tübingen: Mo Vince Verlag.

Haines, M. (2004). Growing incomes, shrinking people—Can economic development be hazardous to your health? Historical evidence from the United States, England, and the Netherlands in the nineteenth century. *Social Science History*, 28(2), 249–270.

Harbeck, M., Seifert, L., Hänsch, S., Wagner, D. M., Birdsell, D., Parise, K. L., . . . Scholz, H. C. (2013). *Yersinia pestis* DNA from skeletal remains from the 6th century AD reveals insights into Justinianic plague. *PLoS Pathogens*, 9(5), e1003349. doi: 10.1371/journal.ppat.1003349

Harris, B., Gálvez, L., & Machado, H. (2009). *Gender and well-being in Europe: Historical and contemporary perspectives*. Burlington, VT: Ashgate.

Hindman, H. (2009). *The world of child labor: An historical and regional survey*. Armonk, NY: M. E. Sharpe.

Hirschfelder, G. (2005). *Europäische* Esskultur. Eine Geschichte der Ernährung von der Steinzeit bis heute. Frankfurt: Campus Verlag.

Hoppe, C., Mølgaard, C., & Michaelsen, K. (2006). Cow's milk and linear growth in industrialised and developing countries. *Annual Review of Nutrition, 26*, 131–173.

Horrell, S., Meredith, D., & Oxley, D. (2009). Measuring misery: Body mass, ageing and gender inequality in Victorian London. *Explorations in Economic History*, 46(1), 93.

Howcroft, R., Eriksson, G., & Lidén, K. (2012). The Milky Way: The implications of using animal milk products in infant feeding. *Anthropozoologica*, 42(2), 31–43.

Huber, N. (1967). *Anthropologische Untersuchungen an den Skeletten aus dem alamannischen Reihengräberfeld von Weingarten, Kr. Ravensburg*. Naturwissenschaftliche Untersuchungen zur Vor- u. Frühgeschichte in Württemberg und Hohenzollern 3. Stuttgart: Müller & Gräff.

IPCC (2007), Jansen, E., Overpeck, J., Briffa, K. R., Duplessy, J.-C., Joos, F, Masson-Delmotte, V., . . . Shang, D. (2007), Palaeoclimate. In: S. Solomon et al. (Eds.). *Climate Change 2007: The physical science basis. Contribution of Working Group I to the fourth assessment report of the Intergovernmental Panel on Climate Change.* Cambridge/New York: Cambridge University Press.

Intergovernmental Panel on Climate Change (IPCC) et al. (2013). Information from paleoclimate archives. In T. F. Stocker et al. (Eds.), *Climate change 2013: The physical science basis. Contribution of Working Group I to the fifth assessment report of the Intergovernmental Panel on Climate Change.* Cambridge/New York: Cambridge University Press.

Izdebski, A., Koloch, G., Słoczyński, T., & Tycner-Wolicka, M. (2014). On the use of palynological data in economic history: New methods and an application to agricultural output in central Europe, 0–2000 AD. *mpra.ub.uni-muenchen.de/54582/*

Jackson, R. (1988). *Doctors and diseases in the Roman Empire.* London: British Museum Publ.

Jamison, D., Leslie, J., & Musgrove, P. (2003). Malnutrition and dietary protein evidence from China and from international comparisons. *Food and Nutrition Bulletin, 24,* 145–154.

Jones, P. D., & Mann, M. E. (2004). Climate over past millennia. *Reviews of Geophysics, 42,* RG2002. doi: 10.1029/2003RG000143.

Jongman, W. (2007). Gibbon was right: The decline and fall of the Roman economy. In O. Hekster, G. de Kleijn, & D. Slootjes (Eds.), *Crises and the Roman Empire. Proceedings of the Seventh Workshop of the International Network Impact of Empire (Nijmegen, June, 20–24, 2006)* (pp. 183–199). Leiden: E. J. Brill.

Jordan, W. (1996). *The Great Famine. Northern Europe in the early fourteenth century.* Princeton, NJ: Princeton University Press.

Jordan, C. (2013). *An Ecosystem Approach to Sustainable Agriculture. Environmental Challenges and Solutions Volume 1.* Dordrecht: Springer, esp. Chapter 2: A history of unsustainability in agriculture, pp. 39–62.

Kelly, M., & Ó Gráda, C. (2014). Debating the Little Ice Age. *Journal of Interdisciplinary History,* 45(1), 57–68.

Kessler, D., & Temin, P. (2007). The organization of the grain trade in the early Roman Empire. *Economic History Review,* 60(2), 313–332.

Klasen, S., & Wink, C. (2002). A turning point in gender bias in mortality? An update on the number of missing women. *Population and Development Review, 28,* 285–312.

Koepke, N. (2008). *Regional differences and temporal development of the nutritional status in Europe from 8th century BCE to 18th century CE.* PhD thesis, Faculty of Economics, University of Tuebingen, Germany.

Koepke, N. (2014*a*). The wider background of the second transition in Europe: Information from skeletal material. In M. Zuckerman (Ed.), *Modern environments and human health: Revisiting the second epidemiological transition* (pp. 55–80). Hoboken, NJ: Wiley.

Koepke, N. (2014*b*). The relative status of females in pre- and early historic Europe. Working paper presented at the 10th European Social Science History Conference (ESSHC), Vienna, April 23–26.

Koepke, N., & Baten, J. (2005*a*). The biological standard of living in Europe during the last two millennia. *European Review of Economic History,* 9(1), 61–95.

Koepke, N., & Baten, J. (2005*b*). Climate and its impact on the biological standard of living in north-east, centre-west and south Europe during the last 2000 years. *History of Meteorology,* 2(1), 147–159.

Koepke, N., & Baten, J. (2008). Agricultural specialization and height in ancient and medieval Europe. *Explorations in Economic History,* 42(2), 127–146.

Komlos, J. (1989). *Nutrition and economic development in the eighteenth century Habsburg monarchy: An anthropometric history.* Princeton, NJ: Princeton University Press.

Komlos, J. (1998). Shrinking in a growing economy? The mystery of physical stature during Industrial Revolution. *Journal of Economic History*, *58*, 779–802.

Komlos, J. (2002). *Global warming and the secular increase in human height*. Economic History working paper. University of Munich. econhist.userweb.mwn.de/globalwarming.pdf

Komlos, J. (2007). Anthropometric evidence on economic growth, biological well-being and regional convergence in the Habsburg Monarchy, c. 1850–1910. *Cliometrica*, 1(3), 211–237.

Komlos, J., & Nefedovb, S. (2002). A compact macromodel of pre-industrial population growth. *Historical Methods*, 35(2), 92–94.

Komlos, J., Hau, M., & Bourguinat, N. (2003). The anthropometric history of early- modern France. *European Review of Economic History*, 7(2), 159–190.

Kron, G. (2005). Anthropometry, physical anthropology, and the reconstruction of ancient health, nutrition, and living standards. *Historia. Zeitschrift für Alte Geschichte*, 54(1), 68–83.

Kunitz, S. (1987). Making a long story short: A note on men's height and mortality in England from the first through the nineteenth centuries. *Medical History*, *31*, 269–280.

Lao, O., Lu, T., Nothnagel, M., Junge, O., Freitag-Wolf, S., Caliebe, A., . . . Kayser, M. (2008). Correlation between genetic and geographic structure in Europe. *Current Biology*, 18(16), 1241–1248.

Leonardi, M. (2013). Lactase persistence and milk consumption in Europe: An interdisciplinary approach involving genetics and archaeology. *Documenta Praehistorica*, *XL*, 85–96.

Lettre, G. (2011). Recent progress in the study of the genetics of height. *Human Genetics*, *129*, 465–472.

Lindsay, H. (2000). Death, pollution and funerals in the city of Rome. In V. M. Hope & E. Marshall (Eds.), *Death and disease in the ancient city* (pp. 152–173). London/New York: Routledge.

Livi-Bacci, M. (1991). *Population and nutrition. An essay on European demographic history*. Cambridge studies in population, economy and society in past time 14. Cambridge: Cambridge University Press.

Lo Cascio, E. (2006). Did the population of Imperial Rome reproduce itself? In G. R. Storey (Ed.) *Urbanism in the preindustrial world: Cross-cultural approaches* (pp. 52–68). Tuscaloosa: University of Alabama Press.

Maat, G. (2003). Male stature. A parameter of health and wealth in the low countries, 50-1997 AD. In H. Metz (Ed.), *Wealth, health and human remains in archaeology* (pp. 57–88). Symposium Vijfentwintigste Kroon-Vooordracht. Amsterdam: Stichting Nederlands Museum.

Mann, M. (2003). Little Ice Age. In M. MacCracken & J. Perry (Eds.), *Encyclopedia of global environmental change, Vol. 1: The Earth system: Physical and chemical dimensions of global environmental change* (pp. 504–509). Hoboken, NJ: Wiley.

Mann, M., & Jones, P. (2003). Global surface temperatures over the past two millennia. *Geophysical Research Letters*, 30(15), 1820.

Margo, R., & Steckel, R. (1983). Heights of native-born whites during the antebellum period. *Journal of Economic History*, *43*, 167–174.

Martin-Gronert, M., & Ozanne, S. (2006). Maternal nutrition during pregnancy and health of the offspring. *Biochemical Society Transactions*, *34*, 779–782.

McEvedy, C., & Jones, R. (1988). *Atlas of world population history*. London: Penguin.

McEvoy, B., & Visscher, P. (2009). Genetics of human height. *Economics and Human Biology*, *7*(3), 294–306.

Mehta, B. M., Kamal-Eldin, A., & Iwanski, R. Z. (2012). *Fermentation: Effects on food properties*. Boca Raton, Florida, USA: CRC Press, Taylor and Francis Group.
Milanovic B., Lindert, P. H., & Williamson, J. G. (2010). Pre-industrial inequality. *Economic Journal, 121*, 255–272.
Moradi, A. (2010). Nutritional status and economic development in sub-Saharan Africa, 1950–1980. *Economics and Human Biology, 8*, 16–29.
Moradi, A., & Guntupalli, A. (2009). Gender dimorphism: Discrimination in rural India, 1930–1975. In M. Pal, P. Bharati, B. Ghosh, & T. S. Vasulu (Eds.), *Gender and discrimination: Health, nutritional status, and the role of women in India* (pp. 258–277). New Delhi: Oxford University Press.
Morellón, M., Pérez-Sanz, A., Corella, J., Büntgen, U., Catalán, J., González Sampériz, P., . . . Valero-Garcés, B. (2012). A multi-proxy perspective on millennium-long climate variability in the Southern Pyrenees. *Climate of the Past, 8*, 683–700.
Mummert, A., Esche, E., Robinson, J., & Armelagos, G. J. (2011). Height and robusticity during the agricultural transition: Evidence from the bioarchaeological record. *Economics and Human Biology*, 9(3), 284–301.
Müldner, G., &Richards, M. P. (2005) Fast or feast: Reconstructing diet in later medieval England by stable isotope analysis. *Journal of Archaeological Science, 32*, 39–48.
Nutton, V. (2000). Medical thoughts on urban pollution. In V. M. Hope & E. Marshall (Eds.), *Death and Disease in the Ancient City* (pp. 65–73). London: Routledge.
Olds, K. (2006). Female productivity and mortality in early-20th-century Taiwan. *Economics and Human Biology*, 4(2), 206–221.
Özer, B. K., Sağır, M., & Özer, İ. (2011). Secular changes in the height of the inhabitants of Anatolia (Turkey) from the 10th millennium B.C. to the, 20th century A.D. *Economics and Human Biology*, 9(2), 211–219.
Osmani, S., & Sen, A. (2003). The hidden penalties of gender inequality: Foetal origins of ill-health. *Economics and Human Biology*, 1(1), 105–121.
Oxley, D. (2004). Living standards of women in Prefamine Ireland. *Social Science History*, 28(2), 271.
Paine, R. R., & Storey, G. R. (2006). Epidemics, age at death, and mortality in ancient Rome. In G. R. Storey (Ed.) *Urbanism in the preindustrial world: Cross-cultural approaches* (pp. 69–85). Tuscaloosa: University of Alabama Press.
Paine, R. R., Vargiu, R., Signoretti, C., & Coppa, A. (2009). A Health Assessment for Imperial Roman Burials Recovered from the Necropolis of San Donato and Bivio CH, Urbino, Italy. *Journal of Anthropological Sciences, 87*, 193–210.
Parkin, T. (1992). *Demography and the Roman society*. Baltimore, MD: Johns Hopkins University Press.
Peck, J. (2013). Status, health, and life style in Middle Iron Age Britain. *International Journal of Paleopathology, 3*, 83–94.
Pei, Q., Zhang, D. D., Li, H. F., & Li, G. (2013). Short- and long-term impacts of climate variations on the agrarian economy in pre-industrial Europe. *Climate Research*, 56(2), 169–180.
Pitts, M., & Griffin, R. (2012). Exploring health and social well-being in late Roman Britain: An intercemetery approach. *American Journal of Archaeology*, 116(2), 253–276.
Prince, J., & Steckel, R. (2001). Tallest in the world: Native Americans of the Great Plains in the nineteenth century. *American Economic Review, 91*, 287–294.

Quaranta, L. (2013). *Scarred for life—How conditions in early life affect socioeconomic status, reproduction and mortality in Southern Sweden, 1813-1968*. Lund Studies in Economic History 59.

Redfern, R. C., & DeWitte, S. N. (2011). A new approach to the study of Romanization in Britain: A regional perspective of cultural change in late Iron Age and Roman Dorset using the Siler and Gompertz-Makeham models of mortality. *American Journal of Physical Anthropology*, 144, 269–285.

Roberts, C., & Cox, M. (2003). *Health and disease in Britain: From prehistory to the present day*. Thrupp, UK: Sutton.

Sabir, N., & Ebrahim, G. (1984). Are daughters more at risk than sons in some societies? Journal of Tropical Pediatrics, 30, 237–239.

Sallares, R. (2002). *Malaria and Rome. A history of malaria in ancient Italy*. Oxford: Oxford University Press.

Scheidel, W. (2012). Physical well-being. In W. Scheidel (Ed.), *The Cambridge companion to the Roman economy* (pp. 321–333). Cambridge: Cambridge University Press.

Schofield, P. (2006). Medieval diet and demography. In C. Woolgar, D. Serjeantson, & T. Waldron (Eds.), *Food in medieval England. Diet and nutrition* (pp. 239–253). Oxford: Oxford University Press.

Scobie, A. (1986). Slums, sanitation, and mortality in the Roman world. *Klio*, 68(2), 399–433.

Scott, S., & Duncan, C. (2002). *Demography and nutrition. Evidence from historical and Contemporary populations*. Oxford: Blackwell.

Silventoinen, K. (2003). Determinants of variation in adult body height. *Journal of Biosocial Science*, 35, 263–285.

Siraisi, N. G. (1990). *Medieval & early Renaissance medicine*. Chicago: University of Chicago Press.

Spinage, C. (2003). *Cattle plague. A history*. New York: Cluver Academic/Plenum.

Stannard, D. (1993). Disease, human migration, and history. In K. Kiple (Ed.), *The Cambridge world history of human disease* (pp. 35–42). Cambridge: Cambridge University Press.

Steckel, R. (2004). New light on the "Dark Ages": The remarkably tall stature of northern European men during the medieval era. *Social Science History*, 28(2), 211–229.

Steckel, R. (2010). The Little Ice Age and health: Europe from the early middle ages to the nineteenth century. Economics Seminar paper. University of Toronto.

Steckel, R., & Rose, J. (2002). *The backbone of history: Health and nutrition in the western hemisphere*. Cambridge: Cambridge University Press.

Stinson, S. (2000). Growth variation: Biological and cultural factors. In S. Stinson, B. Bogin, R. Huss-Ashmore & D. O'Rourke (Eds.), *Human biology. An evolutionary and biocultural perspective* (pp. 425–463). New York: Wiley-Liss.

Stuart-Macadam, P. (1991). Anaemia in Roman Britain: Poundbury Camp. In H. Bush & M. Zvelebil (Eds.), *Health in past societies. Biocultural interpretations of human skeletal remains in archaeological context*. BAR International Series 567. Oxford: Tempvs Reparatvm.

Susser, E., Kirkbride, J., Heijmans, B., Kresovich, J., Lumey, L., & Stein, A. (2012). Maternal prenatal nutrition and health in grandchildren and subsequent generations. *Annual Review of Anthropology*, *41*, 577–610.

Szaivert, W., & Wolters, R. (2005). *Löhne, Preise, Werte. Quellen zur römischen Geldwirtschaft*. Darmstadt: Wissenschaftliche Buchgesellschaft.

Tello, E., Martínez J. L., Jover, J., Olarieta J. R., García-Ruiz, R., González de Molina, M., . . . Koepke, N. (2014). Building on Allen's nitrogen hypothesis: The English agricultural revolution during the climatic Maunder Minimum (1645–1715). Working paper. University of Barcelona.

Temin, P. (2006). The economy of the early Roman empire. *Journal of Economic Perspectives, 20*, 133–151.

Thüry, G. (2001). *Müll und Marmorsäulen. Siedlungshygiene in der römischen Antike.* Mainz: von Zabern.

Thüry, G. (2007). *Kulinarisches aus dem römischen Alpenvorland.* Linzer Archäologische Forschungen XXXIX. Linz: Stadtmuseum/PG Druckerei.

Tulchinsky, T., & Varavikova, E. (2014). *The new public health: An introduction for the 21st century.* New York: Academic Press.

Ulijaszek, S. (2006). The international growth standard for children and adolescents project: Environmental influences on preadolescent and adolescent growth in weight and height. *Food and Nutrition Bulletin, 27*(4:Suppl. Growth Standard), 279–294.

van Schaik, K., Vinichenko, D., & Rühli, F. J. (2014). Health is not always written in bone: Using a modern comorbidity index to assess disease load in paleopathology. *American Journal of Physical Anthropology*, 154(2), 215–221.

Walter, J., & Schofield, R. (1989). *Famine, disease and the social order in early modern society.* Cambridge: Cambridge University Press.

Ward-Perkins, B. (2005). *The fall of Rome and the end of civilization.* Oxford: Oxford University Press.

Weber, S. (1985). Zur Rolle von Haus- und Nutzvieh nach den leges Barbarorum. In F. Horst & B. Krüger (Eds.), *Produktivkräfte und Produktionsverhältnisse in ur- und frühgeschichtlicher Zeit* (pp. 325–330). Berlin: Akademie-Verlag.

Weeber, K. -W. (1990). *Smog über Attika. Umweltverhalten im Altertum.* Frankfurt: Büchergilde Gutenberg.

Werner, J. P., Büntgen, U., Ljungqvist, F. C., Esper, J., Fernández-Donado, L., Gonzalez-Rouco, F. J., . . . Zorita, E. (2014). The medieval climate (a)nomaly over Europe. *Geophysical Research Abstracts, 15*, 2013–9209.

Wiese, B., & Zils, N. (1987). *Deutsche Kulturgeographie: Werden, Wandel und Bewahrung deutscher Kulturlandschaften.* Herford: Busse Seewald.

Willerding, U. (1986). Zur Agrarproduktion von der jüngeren vorrömischen Eisenzeit bis ins frühe Mittelalter. *Historicum*, spring, 10–20.

Wilson, A. (2011). City sizes and urbanization in the Roman Empire. In A. Bowman & A. Wilson (Eds.), *Settlement, urbanization, and population. Oxford Studies in the Roman Economy* 2 (pp. 161–195). Oxford: Oxford University Press.

Wing, E., & Brown, A. (1979). *Paleonutrition. Method and theory in prehistoric foodways.* New York: Academic Press

Woolgar, C., Serjeantson, D., & Waldron, T. (Eds.). (2006). *Food in medieval England. Diet and nutrition.* Oxford: Oxford University Press.

World Health Organization (WHO). (1995). *Physical status:* The use and interpretation of anthropometry. Geneva: Author.

Zanier, W. (2000). Der Alpenfeldzug 15 v.Chr. und die augusteische Okkupation in Süddeutschland. In L. Wamser, C. Flügel, & B. Zieghaus (Eds.), *Die Römer zwischen Alpen und Nordmeer: Zivilisatorisches Erbe einer europäischen Militärmacht* (pp. 11–17). Mainz: von Zabern.

Zimmermann, A. (1996). Zur Bevölkerungsdichte in der Urgeschichte Mitteleuropas. In I. Campen, J. Hahm, & M. Uerpmann (Eds.), *Spuren der Jagd—die Jagd nach Spuren* (pp. 49–61). Tübinger Monographien zur Urgeschichte 11, Festschrift für H. Müller-Beck. Rahden, Germany: VML Verlag Marie Leidorf GmbH.

Zorn, J. R. (1994). Estimating the population size of ancient settlements: Methods, problems, solutions, and a case study. *Bulletin of the American Schools of Oriental Research*, 295, 31–48.

CHAPTER 5

ECONOMETRICS OF ECONOMICS AND HUMAN BIOLOGY

GREGORY COLMAN AND DHAVAL DAVE

5.1 Introduction

Researchers have used a wide variety of econometric techniques to study the causes and consequences of obesity, in large part because the method often described as the gold standard of causal research—the randomized controlled trial (RCT)—is unsuitable to many questions of interest to economists (although not all). Randomized trials can answer some interesting economic questions, such as the effect of TV watching on childhood obesity or of unhealthy diets on healthcare spending. However, randomization would be impractical or unethical, if not impossible, for many of the most important questions in obesity research, such as the long-term effect on obesity of changing relative prices of healthy versus unhealthy foods, the effect of obesity on labor market outcomes, or the effect on obesity of fast-food advertising. For such questions, the only data available are observational, and the researcher must confront the main challenge to causal inference—the nonrandom choice of the independent variable, known as the *self-selection problem*, which we briefly describe. (For a fuller discussion, see Angrist & Pischke, 2009.)

Suppose that a researcher wants to identify the causal effect of obesity on wages. In the language of experiments, obesity is the treatment and wage is the outcome. We will discuss this question using the potential outcomes framework of Rubin (1974) and following the notation of Imbens (2014).

Assume we have n observations randomly drawn from a large population. Let Y_i be the outcome, in this case, wage, of person i. We assume that the treatment, obesity, is binary. Let $W_i = 1$ if the person is obese, and zero otherwise. We assume that there exist two potential outcomes for each person, denoted $Y_i(W_i)$: $Y_i(0)$ is the person's wage if he is not obese, and $Y_i(1)$ represents his wage if he is. It is worth noting that $Y_i(1)$ does not refer to the outcome post-treatment and $Y_i(0)$ to pre-treatment; they both refer to the same time period and represent alternate states of the world. The difference $Y_i(1)-Y_i(0)$ is the (causal) "treatment effect" for person i, denoted T_i. It is possible that the obesity of one person or group of persons affects the wages of others, perhaps because employers are willing to pay a premium for normal weight workers. We rule this out by an assumption known as the stable unit treatment value assumption (SUTVA).

Two features of the distribution of T_i that researchers commonly seek to estimate are $E(T_i)$, the average treatment effect (ATE), and $E(T_i \mid W_i = 1)$, the average treatment effect among the treated (ATT). For example, the ATE may refer to the average effect of obesity on wages if everyone in the population became obese, whereas ATT shows the average effect just among those who are currently obese. The challenge for causal inference is that the treatment effect T_i is never observed. If the person is obese, we observe $Y_i(1)$, his outcome when obese, but not $Y_i(0)$, his outcome when at normal weight. The latter, more fully denoted $[Y_i(0) \mid W_i = 1]$, is known as the "counterfactual" outcome. Similarly, if he is of normal weight, we observe $Y_i(0)$ but not $Y_i(1)$. Thus, we can calculate $E[Y_i(1) \mid W_i = 1]$ and $E[Y_i(0) \mid W_i = 0]$, but not $E[Y_i(1) \mid W_i = 0]$ nor $E[Y_i(0) \mid W_i = 1]$. That is, we cannot observe both potential outcomes for the same individual for the same time period.

One simple solution to the unobservability of T_i is to compare the average wages of those who are currently obese, $E[Y_i \mid W_i = 1]$, with the average wages of those who are normal weight, $E(Y_i \mid W_i = 0)$. Note that among obese persons we only observe their treated outcome. Thus, $E(Y_i \mid W_i = 1) = E[Y_i(1) \mid W_i = 1]$. Similarly, among normal weight persons we only observe their untreated outcome: $E[Y_i \mid W_i = 0] = E[Y_i(0) \mid W_i = 0]$. The observed difference, which we can calculate, therefore, is

$$\textit{Observed difference} = E[Y_i(1) \mid W_i = 1] - E[Y_i(0) \mid W_i = 0].$$

To interpret this difference, subtract and add the counterfactual quantity, $E[Y_i(0) \mid W_i = 1]$.

$$\begin{aligned} &= E[Y_i(1) \mid W_i = 1] - E[Y_i(0) \mid W_i = 1] + E[Y_i(0) \mid W_i = 1] \\ &\quad - E[Y_i(0) \mid W_i = 0] \\ &= E[Y_i(1) - Y_i(0) \mid W_i = 1] + E[Y_i(0) \mid W_i = 1] - E[Y_i(0) \mid W_i = 0] \end{aligned}$$

Therefore,

$$\begin{aligned} &E[Y_i(1) \mid W_i = 1] - E[Y_i(0) \mid W_i = 0] = \\ &E[T_i \mid W_i = 1] + E[Y_i(0) \mid W_i = 1] - E[Y_i(0) \mid W_i = 0] \end{aligned} \tag{1}$$

The left-hand side of Equation (1) is the observed difference in average outcomes between currently obese and currently normal weight individuals. The first term on the right-hand side of Equation (1) is the ATT. Thus, the observed difference is the ATT only if the rest of Equation 1 equals 0, $E[Y_i(0) \mid W_i = 1] - E[Y_i(0) \mid W_i = 0] = 0$; that is, if the wages of normal weight and obese persons would have been the same had the obese workers not become obese. However, this is unlikely to be true. Studies show that obese persons have higher subjective discount rates (Ikeda, Kang, & Ohtake, 2010; Zhang & Rashad, 2008), which may reduce wages independently of body weight. That is, we would expect $E[Y_i(0) \mid W_i = 1] < E[Y_i(0) \mid W_i = 0]$, which implies that $E[Y_i(1) \mid W = 1] < E[Y_i(0) \mid W = 0]$ even if the causal effect of obesity on wages is zero. The empirical challenge, of course, is that individuals "self-select" into obesity, with $E[Y_i(0) \mid W_i = 1] - E[Y_i(0) \mid W_i = 0]$ measuring this "selection bias." Thus, the difference in outcomes that we typically observe in nonexperimental data reflects a potential causal effect plus this selection bias.

It is possible that the selection bias disappears if we compute separate ATEs and ATTs within observable subgroups or strata of the population. For example, perhaps the bias is zero among persons with similar observable characteristics, such as the level of education. Denote these conditioning variables as X. Then, it may be the case that $E[Y_i(0) \mid W_i = 1, X] = E[Y_i(0) \mid W_i = 0, X]$. In this case, there is "selection on observables." More formally, $E[Y_i(0)] \mid W_i, X] = E[Y_i(0) \mid X]$. Thus, controlling for X, $Y_i(0)$ is mean-independent of treatment status, W_i, and the observed difference conditional on X would capture the causal effect of interest.

Often, however, it is not possible to find stratifying variables that completely remove selection bias. That is, selection depends on unobservables as well. Much of the econometrics used to study the causes and consequences of obesity attempt to deal with this challenge. In this chapter, we briefly discuss the econometric methods that economists have in their arsenal to guide causal inference with nonexperimental data, with a particular focus on implementation and the key identifying assumptions underlying each empirical strategy.

5.2 Panel Data and Fixed Effects

One potential solution to bypassing selection bias exploits panel data—repeated observations over time on a given sample of persons (or families, states, countries, or some other panel unit). Thus, potential outcomes are indexed for person, treatment status, and time: $Y_{it}(0)$ denotes the untreated outcome of person i in time period t and $Y_{it}(1)$ denotes the treated outcome for the same person and period. Following Angrist and Pischke (2009), Baum and Ford (2004), and Cawley (2004), we consider a model in which the unobserved factors that influence selection into obesity are fixed over time. Denote these factors G_i (e.g., representing genetic component). In addition, the researcher often has data on observed characteristics that may affect selection, some of which vary over time, such as marital and health status, and some of which do not, such as race and ethnicity. Let the time-constant variables be C_i and the time-varying variables be X_{it}. The treatment indicator may also vary over time, and is denoted W_{it}. Then, conditional on the time-constant G_i, observed characteristics C_i and X_{it}, and the time period, the average untreated outcome (wages if not obese) is the same for obese and normal weight persons: $E[Y_{it}(0) \mid C_i, X_{it}, G_i, t, W_{it}] = E[Y_{it}(0) \mid C_i, X_{it}, G_i, t]$. In other words, controlling for both observed (C_i, X_{it}) and unobserved (G_i) determinants of selection, obesity is essentially random.

To apply fixed-effects methods, researchers generally make three further assumptions: (1) the functional form of the treated and untreated outcomes is linear in G_i, (2) the treatment effect is additive, and (3) the treatment effect is constant for all *i*, in contrast to the preceding discussion. Thus, in the most commonly applied fixed effects models, it is assumed that ATE = ATT = TE, where TE stands for treatment effect. For notational simplicity, define $a_i = a + b * C_i$. Applying these assumptions, $E[Y_{it}(0)] = a_i + g * t + X_{it} * B + G_i$, and $E[Y_{it}(1)] = a_i + g * t + X_{it} * B + G_i + TE$. Under these assumptions, the observed outcome is:

$$Y_{it} = a_i + g * t + W_{it} * TE + X_{it} * B + G_i + v_{it}, \quad (2)$$

where v_{it} is a mean-zero random error term for person *i* in time *t*.

This equation cannot be estimated with ordinary least squares (OLS) because G_i, although constant, is unobserved and correlated with W_{it} and possibly with C_i. Two methods are commonly used to remove the G_i. One is to first-difference the data. Then the regression becomes:

$$Y_{i,t} - Y_{i,t-1} = g + TE * \left(W_{i,t} - W_{i,t-1}\right) + \left(X_{i,t} - X_{i,t-1}\right)B + v_{i,t} - v_{i,t-1}. \quad (3)$$

Note that this eliminates not only G_i but a_i (time-invariant observed determinants of Y) as well. The second and more commonly used method is to mean-difference the data: subtract from each variable its average for each person or unit. The result is:

$$Y_{i,t} - \overline{Y}_1 = g_t - \overline{g} + (W_{i,t} - \overline{W}_1)TE + (X_{i,t} - \overline{X})\beta + v_{i,t} - \overline{v}_1 \quad (4)$$

Known as the fixed-effects method, this mean-differencing also eliminates any time-invariant variables. For criteria for choosing between first-differencing and mean-differencing, see Wooldridge (2010).[1] The key assumption necessary for both fixed-effects and first-differenced models to yield a consistent treatment effect is that of strict exogeneity:

$$E\left[v_{i,t} \mid W_{i,t}, X_{i,t}, G_i\right] = 0, \quad (5)$$

which states that there is no correlation between the observed factors (W, X) and the remaining idiosyncratic error term $v_{i,t}$, for all *i* and *t*. This rules out selection on time-varying unobservable factors and anticipation effects.[2] If strict exogeneity fails, both the fixed effects and first-differenced estimators are inconsistent, and they converge to different probability limits. Hence, comparing these two estimates can be an indirect check of the strict exogeneity assumption, and, for this reason, robustness across both estimators would be validating.

Applying both OLS and fixed-effects methods, Baum and Ford (2004) found that obese workers earned statistically significantly lower wages than did non-obese workers. The absolute size of the effect in the fixed-effects models, however, was much smaller than the OLS estimates. This is a common result of applying fixed-effects methods, for two reasons. One is that perhaps there is negative selection into obesity, with obese persons having lower earning capacity even if they were not obese. Another possible explanation is that the fixed-effects procedure amplifies the measurement error of the independent variables (Griliches & Hausman, 1986). Self-reported body mass index (BMI) is naturally reported with some measurement error. This error is a larger proportion of the *difference* between a person's current and average BMI—the quantity used by the fixed-effect model—than it is of BMI itself, which is used by OLS. The larger the measurement error, the more the independent variable resembles white noise, whose correlation with anything is, of course, zero. Thus, measurement error biases the coefficients toward zero, known as *attenuation bias*. Furthermore, the bias due to measurement error in fixed-effects models increases with the correlation of the independent variable with its own past values, and, of course, a person's BMI is highly correlated over time. To reduce the attenuation bias, researchers have used long-differences in the hopes that the change in the independent variable over a long period will be large relative to the measurement error (Colman & Dave, 2012).[3]

As mentioned earlier, first-differencing or mean-differencing will not remove time-varying factors that influence selection into obesity, which would violate the strict exogeneity assumption. One alternative is to control for both time-varying and time-invariant unobserved factors by including the lagged dependent variable. Since one model is not a special or nested case of the other, one cannot formally test which is appropriate. The choice can only be made by understanding the selection process. If individuals are selecting into obesity because of genetic or other time-invariant influences, then first-differencing or mean-differencing is appropriate. If individuals are selecting into obesity because of their prior level of obesity, then including the lagged dependent variable is appropriate. Unfortunately, both influences may be involved, as when genetic factors induce obesity, which reduces physical activity, which then increases obesity.

Under a special case, estimates from the two models—the fixed-effects model or the model without the fixed effects but which includes the lagged dependent variable—can bound the causal effect of interest. This special case occurs under the assumption that at least one of the two models is correct in specifying the selection process, and selection into treatment is negatively correlated with the lagged outcome. Colman and Dave (2012) exploit this result in their study of the causal effects of physical activity on risk factors for heart disease, where selection into physical activity is hypothesized to be negatively correlated with prior poor health and is supported by the data. They estimate both sets of models, and, under the assumption that at least one of these specifications captures the selection process, are able to bound the causal effect of physical activity on these measures of health.

5.3 Instrumental Variables

If the unobserved heterogeneity across individuals determining selection into obesity varies over time, thus violating strict exogeneity, then fixed-effects or first-differencing will not reveal the causal effect. A different solution, which can be used with cross-sectional or longitudinal data, is to use instrumental variables (IV). We will first consider the traditional constant-effect IV model and then allow the effect to vary over persons.

The observed outcome is:

$$Y_i = a + TE * W_i + u_i, \tag{6}$$

where Y_i denotes wages; W_i is an indicator for obesity; TE is the treatment effect, which is assumed for now to be the same for everyone; and u_i is the error term. Single-equation OLS estimates would be inconsistent because W_i is correlated with u_i. Suppose that W_i depends on another observable variable, Z_i, which is omitted from the structural equation because it has no direct effect on Y_i and is thus uncorrelated with u_i:

$$W_i = c_0 + c_1 * Z_i + v_i \tag{7}$$

Equation (7) is often called the "first-stage" regression equation. The goal is to estimate the TE parameter. Using the properties of covariance:

$$cov(Y_i, Z_i) = TE * cov(W_i, Z_i) + cov(u_i, Z_i) = TE * cov(W_i, Z_i). \tag{8}$$

Equation (8) follows because $\text{cov}(u_i, Z_i) = 0$ by assumption. Therefore:

$$TE = \frac{\text{cov}(Y_i, Z_i)}{\text{cov}(W_i, Z_i)} \tag{9}$$

Note that this result is predicated on two assumptions: (1) $cov(W_i, Z_i) \neq 0$, and (2) $cov(u_i, Z_i) = 0$. If these two assumptions are met, the IV estimate will deliver a consistent and asymptotically normally distributed estimate of the true causal effect of W_i on Y_i.

The first IV assumption can be tested. A weak correlation between the instrument Z_i and the endogenous factor W_i causes two problems. The IV estimator will be badly biased, and inferences based on the standard errors calculated according to IV formulas will be unreliable. Whereas IV estimates in general have a lower degree of precision because not all of the variation in the endogenous variable is being used for identification, overinflation of the standard errors (e.g., beyond a factor of 5–10) for the IV estimate relative to the OLS estimate is usually a tell-tale sign of weak instruments. Based on Staiger and Stock (1997) and Stock, Wright, and Yogo (2002), it is common to judge an instrument as sufficiently strong if the F-test on its significance in the first-stage regression exceeds 10. If not, the results are said to suffer from "weak instruments." The weak instruments problem is compounded in an overidentified system (number of instruments exceeds the number of endogenous variables), and two-stage least squares (2SLS) is biased toward OLS. In this case, Angrist and Pischke (2009) recommend using the limited information maximum likelihood (LIML) estimator because it is "median-unbiased" and recommend limiting the number of instruments. The bias would be smallest in the case of a just-identified system (one instrument in the case of one endogenous variable, for instance).[4] If IV is used, then care should be taken to construct confidence intervals that do not depend on the strength of the instrument, such as those proposed by Anderson and Rubin (1950) and more recent variants. It is also a useful exercise to always estimate and check the reduced-form specification, relating the outcome directly to the IVs. An insignificant reduced-form effect would imply that either the first-stage is weak and/or there is no causal effect of the treatment on the outcome. If the causal relation is not evident in the reduced-form model, it is not there or cannot be identified with the current set of IVs.[5]

The second assumption, commonly known as the *exclusion restriction*, cannot be directly tested because to do so would require observing the structural error term. It is tempting to test whether the residuals from an OLS estimate of the structural equation are correlated with the instrument, but because of the endogeneity of W_i, the residuals are not consistent estimators of the structural errors. In an overidentified system with multiple instruments, one could potentially test for the exclusion restriction, although this test should be interpreted with caution due to several limitations, which we discuss herein.[6]

As a notable application of IV methods, we consider Cawley (2004). Using the National Longitudinal Survey of Youth for 1979, he instruments the respondent's obesity with that of a sibling, on the idea that siblings with the same parents share half of their genes, and there is a large genetic component to obesity. He finds that sibling BMI is a strong instrument for the respondent's BMI, with first-stage F-statistics of 30 for white males and 20 for Hispanic males. The second requirement is that sibling BMI is uncorrelated with any of the unobserved characteristics of the respondent that affect his or her wages. As mentioned earlier, this cannot be tested statistically. Nonetheless, to support the exogeneity of the instrument, often researchers show respondents' observed characteristics averaged separately by the value of the instrument in order to assess whether the IV is systematically correlated with observables. In the same spirit, Cawley regresses the respondents' years of education and IQ scores on the sibling's weight, age, and gender, finding in general no significant relation. Such tests cannot be dispositive because the respondents' unobserved wage-related characteristics are in the error term in such regressions and may bias the coefficients on the siblings' characteristics. Nonetheless, such exercises provide some reassurance that the instruments are properly excluded from the structural equation. For further discussion of sibling BMI as an instrument for respondent BMI, see Gregory and Ruhm (2011). As another example, Wehby et al. (Wehby, Murray, Wilcox, & Lie, 2012) employ genetic markers associated with smoking as IVs to estimate the causal effect of smoking behaviors on obesity.

The preceding discussion assumes that there is a single treatment effect for the whole population or at most within a few subgroups defined by gender or race. Many applications of instrumental variables relax this assumption. More formally, assume that there is a binary instrument, Z_i, a binary treatment, W_i, and a continuous outcome, Y_i. The instrument affects the treatment, and the treatment affects the outcome. Formally, $W_i = W_i(Z_i)$ and $Y_i = Y_i(W_i)$. Note that we assume that Z_i does not affect Y_i except through W_i (i.e., that the exclusion restriction is valid). As an example, the instrument could be equal to 1 if the person lives next door to a fast-food restaurant, the treatment could equal 1 if the person eats fast-food, and the outcome could be BMI. It would seem unlikely that merely living next to a fast-food restaurant would increase BMI unless the person ate more as a result.

Treatment depends on the instrument, $W_i(Z_i)$, but not in a deterministic way. Each person has two potential responses to the instrument. A person may eat fast-food if he lived next to a fast-food restaurant, $W_i(1) = 1$, but chooses not to eat fast-food if he lives far from a fast-food restaurant, $W_i(0) = 0$. Or, he could choose to eat fast-food no matter what: $W_i(1) = 1$ and $W_i(0) = 1$. Or, he could choose never to eat fast-food: $W_i(1) = 0$ and $W_i(0) = 0$. Or he could choose to eat fast-food if he lives far from it, $W_i(0) = 1$, but not eat fast-food if it is next door, $W_i(1) = 0$. These four groups are respectively referred to in the IV literature as: (1) *compliers* (those who are "moved" by the instrument to consume more fast-food only if they live close to a fast-food restaurant), (2) *always-takers* (fast-food consumers regardless of distance to a fast-food restaurant), (3) *never-takers* (non-consumers of fast-food regardless of distance), and (4) *defiers* (those who are also "moved" by the instrument, but in the reverse direction) (Angrist, Imbens, & Rubin, 1996). Thus, each person has two potential outcomes, $Y_i(0)$, the outcome if untreated, and $Y_i(1)$, the outcome if treated, as well as two potential treatments, $W_i(0)$, the treatment if $Z_i = 0$, and $W_i(1)$, the treatment if $Z_i = 1$. Consistent with the exclusion restriction, the maintained assumption is that Z_i is independent of these potential treatments and outcomes. If someone chose to live far from a fast-food restaurant because she knows its likely effect on her BMI, this would violate the assumption of independence.

Imbens and Angrist (1994) and a number of subsequent papers have shown that not all of the enumerated groups actually contribute to the IV estimator. For example, an estimate of the effect of fast-food consumption on BMI based on the given instrument—proximity to a fast-food restaurant—cannot reflect the behavior of the second and third groups because they do not respond to the instrument. If we further assume that there are no defiers (known as the *monotonicity assumption*)[7]; then it becomes clear that IV estimates reveal the behavior only among compliers. That is, IV does not reveal an average population effect (ATE or ATT), but rather the causal effect among a specific part of the population: those who respond to the instrument. In this example, proximity to a fast-food restaurant shows the effect of fast-food on BMI only for those whose consumption of fast-food depends on this proximity. Thus, the causal effect is local to this group and is therefore referred to as the *local average treatment effect* (LATE).

It is not possible to identify which observations in a population or sample are compliers because for this we would have to know both potential responses to the instrument. For example, we may observe the fast-food consumption of someone who lives next to a fast-food restaurant but not his consumption had he lived far from the restaurant. However, assuming that there are no defiers, we can estimate the population share of each of the remaining groups. Persons who eat fast-food while living far from a restaurant [$W_i(0) = 1$] are always-takers, people who do not eat fast-food although they live near it [$W_i(1) = 0$] are never-takers, and compliers are the remainder. It is quite useful to calculate these proportions to see the relevance of the IV estimate. It may be that only a small share of the population are compliers, in which case the IV estimates have very limited external validity (Imbens, 2014).

Several studies have looked at the question of fast-food and obesity using distance to a fast-food restaurant or some similar instrument. For example, Chou, Grossman, and Saffer (2004) find that the per capita number of restaurants in a given state is positively correlated with both the respondent's BMI and his or her probability of being obese. The authors note that they cannot establish that restaurants were distributed randomly with respect to the prospective BMI of the population and that possibly the rise in the number of restaurants reflects changes in the scarcity of households' non-market time. In addition, the correlation may reflect the tendency of fast-food restaurants to locate near potential customers, who may be relatively obese (Meltzer & Chen, 2011). A more recent study using similar methods is Lhila (2011). Zhao, Kaestner, and Xu (2014) take advantage of the random geographic dispersion of families that occurred as a result of the Moving to Opportunity for Fair Housing Demonstration (MTO) to take a fresh look at the effect of proximity of fast-food on obesity, finding that such environmental factors appear not to explain the decline in obesity observed in the MTO study. Anderson and Matsa (2011) exploit the placement of interstate highways in rural areas in an IV context to obtain exogenous variation in proximity to fast-food restaurants and find no significant evidence of a causal effect between such restaurant consumption and obesity.

Often a study will have more than one instrument for a given treatment. For example, both fast-food prices as well as restaurant proximity may be used to predict fast-food consumption. This enables the researcher to calculate two IV effects, one for each instrument. If one assumes that the treatment effect is the same for all persons, then the results should be the same. Conventionally, one would test their equality using the Hausman test (Hausman, 1978). This has been the rationale underlying the test of overidentifying restrictions as a test of the exclusion restriction, that the instrumental variables are orthogonal to the structural error term. A rejection of the equality of the separate IV effects was taken to imply that one of the instruments was invalid.[8] However, once the possibility is allowed that different instruments identify different LATEs, the value of such tests comes into question. Current practice is to perform such tests and caution the reader that rejection may simply imply different although valid LATEs.

5.4 Regression Discontinuity Design

Instruments that are strong and plausibly random with respect to both treatment and outcomes can be challenging to find. Another method, regression discontinuity design (RDD), exploits settings in which a participant is treated if an observed variable, known as the "forcing" or "running" variable, exceeds or falls short of a known threshold (Angrist & Pischke, 2009; Imbens & Lemieux, 2008; Lee & Lemieux, 2010). An example is Schanzenbach (2009), who studies the effect of eligibility for school lunch subsidies on children's weight. According to the rules of the program, students whose family income is below 130% of the federal poverty line (FPL) qualify for free school lunches, those whose family income is between 130% and 185% receive reduced-price lunches, and children from families whose income is above 185% pay full price for a school lunch. Thus, in this case, the running variable is family income, and treatment depends on this variable falling short of the established limits. The basic assumption underlying RDD is that families just below the cutoff are essentially identical to those just above the cutoff yet receive very different treatment. More generally, following the notation established earlier and denoting the running variable by X and the threshold by X^*, the following assumption is made for a small δ:

$$E[Y_i(0) \mid W=1, X < X^* + \delta, X > X^* - \delta]$$
$$= E[Y_i(0) \mid W=0, X < X^* + \delta, X > X^* - \delta]. \quad (10)$$

Thus, in a small neighborhood surrounding the discontinuous threshold (X^*), the observed outcome for those who are not treated $E[Y_i(0) \mid W=0]$ is a valid counterfactual $E[Y_i(0) \mid W=1]$ for those who are treated.

In Schanzenbach (2009), the RDD estimate of the treatment effect is the difference between the obesity of children just below a cutoff with that of children just above it. If every child whose family income fell below the cutoff were required to eat a school lunch, and no child above the cutoff were allowed to buy one, the previous example would be called a "sharp RDD." But, in fact, children who qualify are merely more likely to buy school lunches than are students who do not qualify. Therefore, this example is categorized as a "fuzzy RDD." Just as with an IV, compliance cannot be assumed. Eligibility is in effect an instrument for treatment, and therefore the effect that is being identified is a LATE. It shows the effect of school lunches on the obesity of children whose behavior was changed by the school lunch subsidy.

One challenging aspect of applying RDD is estimating the average outcomes for treated and controls in the neighborhood of the cutoff. In Schanzenbach's study, the question is how to estimate the obesity of children whose family incomes are just below and just above the income limits. If the neighborhood of the cutoff is dense with observations, the researcher can simply take the difference between the average values of the outcomes on either side for a fixed bandwidth δ. This simple nonparametric estimator may not be attractive, however, because it has been shown to be biased, with the bias increasing with δ. Imbens and Lemieux (2008) suggest using local linear regression as an alternate nonparametric method that does not discard all observations beyond the bandwidth. However, datasets may not always have sufficient density of observations across values of the forcing variable. A common solution is to regress obesity on a flexible function of family income separately among families who qualify and among families who do not qualify and take the difference in the predicted values of obesity at the threshold. The danger in this method is that the results may change substantially for different functional forms.[9] Such parametric methods may be more sensitive to outcome values for observations farther away from the discontinuity, and such "global methods" (in contrast to local estimation) also place weight in estimating the regression function in areas that are of limited use to the treatment or setting being studied. In any case, it would be a concern if the results were dependent on using observations farther away from the cutoff or were sensitive to the polynomial order.[10] Schanzenbach (2009) predicts obesity using a fourth-order polynomial in income and states that the results are not sensitive to the order of the polynomial or the inclusion of other covariates. Although this robustness is validating, and researchers commonly control for higher order (cubic or quartic or higher) polynomials of the forcing variable, more recently, Gelman and Imbens (2014) recommend against their use. They suggest that estimators be based instead on local regression methods or on quadratic polynomials.

Graphical analyses are an integral component of RDD. Plots that show strong discontinuities in the outcome and the probability of being treated at the thresholds go a long way in visually presenting and motivating the identification strategy. Credibility of the RD research design should also be assessed by inspecting two additional plots. First, the covariates should not show any significant jumps around the cutoffs. Second, a threat to the identification assumption underlying the RDD is potential manipulation of the forcing variable. That is, estimates would be biased if individuals are endogenously manipulating their labor supply and earnings just to be on a given side of the threshold and control their eligibility for income-tested programs. Thus, the density of the forcing variable should also be inspected for whether there is a discontinuity at the threshold, which would suggest that individuals can manipulate the forcing variable around this cutoff.

5.5 Difference-in-Differences

The fixed-effects method described earlier relies on variation in outcomes and treatments over time at the individual level. However, often interest focuses on the effects of changes in policies at the state or federal level. For such studies, the method used is difference-in-differences (DD). In the simplest version, there is a policy that takes effect at a specific time and involves two groups of persons: one group affected by the policy change—the "treatment" group—and other unaffected—the "control" group. The control group serves as a counterfactual for the difference in outcomes pre- and post-policy for the treatment in the absence of the policy shift.

A recent example is the passage of the Patient Protection and Affordable Care Act (ACA), passed in 2010. One provision in the Act requires insurance companies who cover the children of employed members to continue covering them until the children turn 26. This provision took effect in September 2010. Its greatest effect was on young adults aged 23–25, many of whom had lost their health insurance from college and had not yet obtained health insurance from a full-time job (Antwi, Moriya, & Simon, 2013). Thus, these persons were the treatment group affected by the policy. Persons 26 or older in 2010 were not affected by the change and are thus a natural control group. Researchers have asked whether the law has increased insurance coverage among persons aged 23–25 and if this increased coverage has affected health outcomes such as obesity (Barbaresco, Courtemanche, and Qi, 2015).

To apply DD, assume we have data on the mean BMI among treatment and control groups both before and after the policy change. Let *Treat* = 1 if the person is between 23 and 25, zero otherwise. Let *After* = 1 if the person was interviewed after September 2010, and zero otherwise. Finally, and crucially, assume that the trend in BMI before the policy took effect was the same in both groups. Then, the expected outcomes can be expressed as follows:

$$E(BMI_i) = \alpha + \lambda * Treat + \beta * After + \delta * Treat * After \qquad (11)$$

Table 5.1 shows the average BMI among treatment and control groups both before and after the policy change.

The coefficient λ shows the average difference in BMI between treatment and control groups before the policy took effect, β show the change in average BMI that would have occurred in both treatment and control groups had the policy not changed, and δ shows the change in average BMI among the treatment group beyond what would have happened had the pre-policy trend continued.

Table 5.1 Basic DD Estimation

$E(BMI_i)$	Before	After	Δ
Treated	$\alpha+\lambda$	$\alpha+\lambda+\beta+\delta$	$\beta+\delta$
Control	α	$\alpha+\beta$	β
Δ	λ	$\lambda+\delta$	δ

Denoting Y_{iT} as outcome for individual i in the treatment group and Y_{iC} as outcome for individual i in the control group, Equation (12) encapsulates this key identifying assumption, known as the *parallel trends assumption*. The DD estimate will yield a causal effect and purge the selection bias if the outcome trend for the control group pre- and post-policy is a valid counterfactual to the outcome trend for the treatment group *in the absence of the policy*. Thus, in the absence of policy changes, the following condition is assumed to hold in order for the DD estimator to yield a consistent causal effect:

$$\left[E\left(Y_{iT} \mid After=1\right) - E\left(Y_{iT} \mid After=0\right)\right] = \left[E\left(Y_{iC} \mid After=1\right) - E\left(Y_{iC} \mid After=0\right)\right] \quad (12)$$

A virtue of the DD method is that it does not require treatment and control groups to have the same *level* of the outcome. It does not matter, in this example, that the average BMI among 27- to 29-year-olds is about 1 point greater than among 23- to 25-year-olds (Barbaresco, Courtemanche, & Qi, 2015). It only matters that the average BMI of both groups would have followed the same time *trend* had the policy not changed. Of course, what would have happened to the treatment group had they not been treated cannot be observed. But one can test whether the trends among treatment and control groups differed before the policy change.

As a side note, although similarity in levels is not required, it would add a degree of validation to the control group. Even if trends over the sample period are parallel, significant differences in baseline means would be indicative of nonparallel trends at some point prior to the sample period or prior to the age ranges observed. In addition, if the baseline pre-policy levels are substantially different, then results may also depend in important ways on the particular choice of a functional form for the outcome measure. Specifically, note that if the baseline pre-policy levels of BMI are substantially different, and if trends in BMI between the treatment and control groups are parallel, then trends in the log of BMI are by definition not parallel, and vice versa.

Barbaresco, Courtemanche, and Qi (2015) plot the average BMI from 2001 to 2013 among both persons aged 23–25 and those aged 27–29, showing that the strongly upward trends are almost precisely parallel, which tends to support the assumption that the older age group is a valid control for the younger age group. Ideally for the researcher, although perhaps not for the health of the population, the trend for the older age group would continue rising at the same slope, but, after 2009, the trends in both groups change markedly. To interpret the DD estimate as a causal effect, one must assume that the change in the trend among 27- to 29-year-olds shows what would have happened to 23- to 25-year-olds in the absence of the ACA. The change in the trend among the older ages after 2009, however, raises the question of whether influences on BMI other than the ACA changed at the same time, changes such as the Great Recession, which as the authors discuss affected labor market experiences of younger workers differently from others (Board of Governors of the Federal Reserve System, 2014).

As with an RDD, establishing credibility for a DD research design often takes the form of graphical analyses. For instance, it is recommended that the researcher inspect trends in the outcome measures for both the treatment and control groups prior to policy implementation in order to assess the parallel trends assumption. If there are multiple treatments over time (e.g., staggered state policy changes), then an event study graph may be helpful in establishing similar trends in the baseline periods and a visual break in the trend at the time of policy implementation.

If it is suspected that trends between the treated and nontreated units are not similar, then it may be advisable to introduce an additional control group, which would allow the researcher to difference out this deviation in trends in the context of a difference-in-difference-in-differences (DDD) framework (see, e.g., Corman, Dave, Reichman, & Das, 2013; Dave & Kaestner, 2009). For instance, in the context of studying the effects of the ACA's adult dependent coverage mandate discussed earlier, a third difference might relate to introducing state-level variation. This follows from the fact that certain states, such as Massachusetts, had already implemented similar provisions prior to the ACA. Thus, differences in outcomes between affected younger adults (aged 23–25) and nonaffected older adults (aged 27–29) within these control states would help bypass any differential trends between these groups in the noncontrol states.[11] In addition, explicitly controlling for unit-specific parametric trends (e.g., state-specific linear trends if the policy is varying at the state level) may also help account for any further nonparallel trends between the treatment and control groups.

One often underappreciated point with respect to the construction of appropriate control and treatment groups is to ascertain that the characteristics being used to define these groups are not affected by the policy under study. Such compositional selection would bias the DD or DDD estimates because the effects would conflate both a potential treatment effect as well as potential mechanical differences across the treatment and control groups due to differences in the samples being compared over time. This issue arises, for instance, in studies of welfare reform, wherein researchers have typically defined target and control groups based on the woman's level of education, marital status, and minor children—characteristics that themselves may have been impacted by welfare reform (Dave, Corman, & Reichman, 2012). In such instances, it is recommended to not employ such characteristics in defining the groups, if possible, and to further check that these sample characteristics are not correlated with the policy in question and that membership in the treatment or control group cannot be predicted based on the policy being studied.

A recent innovation in DD analysis involves the construction of a synthetic control group to provide a potentially better counterfactual for the treated unit (Abadie, Diamond, & Hainmueller, 2010). In their study, Abadie et al. (2010) study the effects of Proposition 99, a comprehensive tobacco control program implemented in California in 1989, on California's cigarettes sales. The conventional DD estimator would compare outcomes in California pre- and post-1989 with outcomes over the same period in a control group comprising the 38 other states that had not instituted comprehensive tobacco control. However, as trends show, cigarette consumption in California versus the rest of the United States differed markedly, thus violating the parallel trends assumption and making the other 38 states a poor counterfactual for what would have happened in California in the absence of Proposition 99. Abadie et al. (2010) show that a weighted combination of units can provide a better comparison for the treatment unit than can any single unit alone or than can the whole. They construct a synthetic California as the convex combination of states from the donor pool of the 38 potential control states, choosing weights such that this synthetic control closely resembles California in terms of smoking rates and predictors of smoking prior to policy enactment.[12] Sabia et al. (Sabia, Swigert, & Young, 2015) recently used this method to study the effects of medical marijuana laws on body weight and physical activity. Based on both conventional DD and synthetic control DD methods, they find that these laws are associated with a 2–6% decrease in the probability of being obese, with some of this decrease being driven by an increase in physical mobility among older individuals.

Whereas the synthetic control approach is data-driven in its choice of weights used to construct the counterfactual, it offers a few important advantages. It makes transparent how each potential donor unit contributes to the counterfactual of interest. It also makes explicit any similarities or differences between the treated unit and the synthetic control prior to the intervention, and forcing the counterfactuals to have more similar trends prior to the policy may raise the likelihood of satisfying the critical parallel trends assumption. The choice of a synthetic control does not require access to data post-intervention, and hence it allows researchers to decide on the control group and the study design without knowing how these decisions will impact the study's results or conclusions (Abadie et al., 2010). Furthermore, with multiple treatments, as in Sabia et al. (2015), this approach is more flexible in allowing for heterogeneous treatment effects across the various treated units (e.g., states).

5.6 Heterogeneous Treatment Effects

As mentioned in Section 3 on IVs, allowing a given treatment to have different effects on different people is often essential to evaluating the external validity of IV results, even though the group affected (the compliers) cannot in general be identified. Often, however, the researcher is interested in the effect of a treatment on identifiable subgroups of the population, possibly defined by the level of obesity or of wages. A straightforward approach would be to assess heterogeneous responses through interaction terms or subgroup stratified analyses, with the groups defined based on some sociodemographic factors. However, these typically require ex ante postulation of the observed source of heterogeneity. That is, a study may hypothesize that there may be differential responses to the treatment based on gender or educational attainment and in turn stratify the sample or include relevant interaction terms along these lines. Here, we briefly discuss two models that supplement such stratification analyses and may help to assess heterogeneity in the treatment effects along further dimensions that may be unobserved.

The first is the quantile regression (QR) model, which is particularly useful for assessing differential effects across the outcome distribution. Following the notation given earlier, suppose we are interested in the effects of some treatment W on outcome Y.

$$Y_i = Q\left(\lambda_q W + X_i B + \varepsilon_i\right). \tag{13}$$

In Equation (13), the conditional q^{th} quantile ($0 < q < 1$) of the outcome is represented by Q, and the parameter of interest is λ. Within the qth quantile, λ_q captures the treatment effect, and this effect is allowed to differ across the outcome continuum. Wehby and Courtemanche (2012) apply this model to their study of the effects of cigarette prices on BMI. Although several studies have addressed this question (e.g., Chou et al., 2004; Gruber & Frakes, 2006; Rashad, Chou, & Grossman, 2006), they had estimated an average response that ignores the possibility that this response may be different at different points of the BMI distribution. Wehby and Courtemanche (2012) explore this possibility and estimate QR models; they find that although the long-run effect of cigarette price on BMI is consistently negative, this effect is more than three times as strong at higher levels of BMI (90th quantile) relative to low levels (10th quantile).

Heterogeneity based on observable characteristics can be readily evaluated by stratification. However, much of the heterogeneity in the treatment response may also stem from unobservable factors. Indeed, observable individual-level and area-level factors typically can explain only a small fraction of the variance in body weight (Wehby & Courtemanche, 2012) or most other risky behaviors (Cutler & Glaeser, 2005). Since the outcome is a function of both observables and unobservables, QR methods can help inform heterogeneity across unobservable factors as captured along the distribution of Y. However, quantile regression does not provide any information on the source of the heterogeneity.

This brings us to the next set of models, the finite mixture models (FMM), which are well-suited for this task of framing the observed source of the heterogeneity. Within the FMM, the outcome variable Y is assumed to be drawn from a population that is an additive mixture of C distinct components or subpopulations represented in proportions π_k that add up to 1. The density function for a C-component finite mixture model is given by:

$$g(Y_i \mid X_{i,}; B_1, B_2, \ldots, B_C; \pi_1, \pi_2, \ldots., \pi_C) = \sum_{K=1}^{C} \pi_k f_k(Y_i \mid X_i; B_k) \tag{14}$$

In the case of a normal mixture, it is assumed that the kth density, denoted f_k with its associated set of parameters B_k, follows a normal distribution. Alternate distributions such as Poisson-distributed subpopulations can also be specified. Parameter estimates can then be employed to compute the posterior probability of belonging in each of the latent classes or components. Thus, it can be determined ex post which individual characteristics are predictive of belonging to a high-response or low-response class.

Deb et al. (Deb, Gallo, Ayyagari, Fletcher, & Sindelar, 2011) apply the FMM, using a normal mixture for BMI, to study how job-loss induced by a business closure is associated with body weight. They find that such job loss is associated with a higher BMI, and the FMM estimates indicate that those who exhibit the highest response are already in the problematic range for BMI. Individuals in the high-response group have a higher BMI prior to the business closure and are also found to be relatively younger, have lower net worth, have higher depressive symptoms, are less educated, and are more likely to be female. These results imply that the negative effects of job loss on body weight appear to be concentrated among a vulnerable and at-risk subpopulation. Thus, the FMM was helpful in identifying subpopulations whose behaviors were affected relatively more by their job loss.

Often researchers are interested in knowing how a treatment or policy might affect those most in need of help—for instance, how an anti-obesity measure might affect those who are already obese. And it may be tempting to stratify the sample across normal weight, overweight, and obese individuals in order to explore this question. Researchers should exercise caution, however, when estimating models that assess heterogeneous treatment effects based on the outcome distribution or based on groupings that may differ across unobservable characteristics predictive of the outcome. The issue is apparent in the case of stratifying the sample based on BMI; clearly, this would be a form of endogenous stratification since membership in a given BMI-defined class is not random. The same concern would also apply to quantile regression models: sorting of individuals across the various BMI quantiles is likely correlated with unmeasured factors. If these unobservables across the various quantiles (or outcome-defined groupings) are differentially correlated with the treatment being studied, then this would bias estimates of the heterogeneity in the treatment effects. Similarly, in the FMM models, if the unobservables are differentially correlated with the treatment variable across the components, then the comparison of the treatment effects across groups would be biased. Intuitively, it would be difficult to parse out whether the observed treatment effects differ because of differences in response or differences in bias due to heterogeneity in the unobservables.

Thus, these methods do not eliminate the problem of nonrandom selection into treatment. Addressing selection bias in the treatment variable is of paramount concern because if treatment is endogenous, then these methods would also bias comparisons of the treatment effects across groups of interest. Furthermore, even if treatment is independent of the error term for the average individual, this independence may not hold for the stratified samples or for separate quantiles or components if the unobservables are correlated with membership in a given class. Therefore, these methods should be supplemented with a careful inspection of how observable characteristics differ across the quantiles or components and also with an assessment of how the treatment effects vary across some of these exogenous or predetermined characteristics.

Charles and DeCicca (2008) and Dave and Kelly (2012) study how the economic cycle affects body weight and eating habits, respectively. A key issue in this literature linking economic downturns to health is that most individuals do not experience job loss and therefore may not be impacted by economic recession. Any estimate linking area-level (e.g., state or metropolitan statistical area) measures of the labor market to individual health would be an "intent-to-treat"-type effect, an average population effect that conflates both the treatment effects on those who are impacted (ATT) and null effects for those who are not. Thus, a key question relates to identifying who is being impacted. For the reasons noted earlier, it would not be appropriate to stratify on or interact area-level unemployment with the individual's own unemployment status; in this example, this would be akin to stratifying on the endogenous treatment variable. Both studies therefore exploit the fact that certain sociodemographic groups (such as poorly educated individuals) are more likely to experience job loss as the unemployment rate rises in their state, and these studies predict the propensity of becoming unemployed based on the area unemployment rate, exogenous sociodemographic factors, and interactions between them. This propensity score is exogenous since it is a convex combination of the state's unemployment rate and exogenous/predetermined individual-specific factors. The sample can then be stratified on this propensity score (Charles & DeCicca, 2008), or the treatment variable can be interacted with this score (Dave & Kelly, 2012) in order to assess whether the effects are stronger for those groups at greater risk of becoming unemployed.

Abadie et al. (Abadie, Chingos, & West, 2013) discuss a different type of endogenous stratification in the context of RCTs (although the issue is also relevant when nonexperimental data are used), wherein researchers are interested in understanding how a policy intervention may help those most in need. Thus, a common practice is to predict the values that the outcome variable might take (in the absence of the treatment) based on the control observations and then use this relationship to predict outcomes for all units in the study. The sample is then stratified based on these potential outcomes in order to assess heterogeneity in the treatment effects. Abadie et al. (2013) term this "endogenous stratification" because it uses in-sample data on the outcome to stratify the sample. They show that this procedure leads to substantial bias in the treatment effects and instead recommend alternative estimators based on leave-one-out and split-sample techniques, which have much improved small-sample behaviors.

5.7 Conclusion

This brief survey of the estimation strategies used to identify the causes and consequences of obesity illustrates a number of abiding concerns among researchers. The first is the persistent danger that selection bias will contaminate estimates of the causal effect, whether it be the effect of obesity on health and labor outcomes or the effect of various determinants of obesity. This reflects the infeasibility of conducting RCTs for many of the most important causal relationships. The second is that, nonetheless, many peculiarities of laws as well as variation in the economic and biological environment can provide researchers with enough plausibly exogenous variation in the key independent variables to identify a causal effect. Finally, recent research has highlighted the benefits of allowing the causal effect to vary among persons, either by unobserved characteristics, such as complier status in IV analyses, or among observed characteristics, including different levels of the dependent variable, as in quantile regression. Such flexible estimation methods have liberated research from overreliance on the mean effect in the population and revealed in which subsets of the population the estimable or interesting causal effect applies.

Notes

1. With two time periods, first-differencing and mean-differencing (fixed effects) are equivalent. The fixed-effects model exploits more of the within-panel variation due to the mean-differencing, and when the $v_{i,t}$ are serially uncorrelated, fixed effects is more efficient than first-differencing.
2. Another estimator sometimes applied to panel data is the random-effects model. However, the added assumption required for this model to yield consistent effects is that the unobserved time-invariant factors (G_i) are independent of all of the observed factors (W, X). If this additional assumption holds, then both fixed and random effects are consistent, although the random-effects model is more efficient. If this assumption fails, then only the fixed-effects model is consistent. This independence assumption is unlikely to hold in practice and difficult to justify a priori.
3. Similar to the fixed-effects estimator, first-differencing can also be very sensitive to classical measurement error (the measurement error in the explanatory variable is uncorrelated with the true dependent and independent variables and with the equation error) in one or more of the explanatory variables.
4. In the just-identified case, LIML and 2SLS are equivalent.
5. This assumes that there are no "defiers." If there are defiers, then it may still be possible that the treatment effects are positive for everyone, but the reduced form is zero because the effects on compliers are being cancelled out by the effects on defiers (Angrist & Pischke, 2009). See text for discussion on compliers and defiers.
6. Hahn and Hausman (2002) construct an alternate specification test statistic that compares the conventional 2SLS estimator with the "reverse" 2SLS estimator (based on a reverse regression of W on Y). Rejection of this specification test would suggest that either the exclusion restriction is false (based on overidentifying restrictions) or a weak instruments problem.
7. The monotonicity assumption maintains that whereas the instrument may have no effect on some people (e.g., the always-takers or the never-takers), all those who are affected by the instrument are affected in the same way, in the same direction. This is often a reasonable and justifiable assumption, although if there is concern regarding defiers, then it is

possible to indirectly test for potential differences in the direction of the IV effects in the first stage through nonlinear terms, splines, defining bins for the IVs, and/or testing the first-stage IV effects for separate subsamples.

8. A further limitation of this test is the inherent assumption that at least one of the IVs is valid in terms of the exclusion restriction, and the test can also have poor finite sample properties.
9. Often researchers choose the optimal polynomial order based on some global goodness-of-fit measure, such as the Akaike Information Criterion; but see Gelman and Imbens (2014) for a critique of using higher order polynomials in RDD.
10. Imbens and Lemieux (2008) and Lee and Lemieux (2010) further detail these issues and provide excellent guides to practice for RDD.
11. If the estimates are based on aggregate data, for instance state-year panels, then it may be preferable to estimate the models via generalized least squares (GLS) using state population as a weighting matrix. OLS-based estimates would produce treatment effects that would ignore the differences in population size across states; hence, these estimates would represent a mean across states rather than across individuals. Population weighting would generate an average treatment effect across individuals, with states with a higher population given a greater weight, and may also improve the precision of the estimates.
12. For instance, they find a weighted convex combination of Colorado (weight = 0.164), Connecticut (0.069), Montana (0.199), Nevada (0.234), and Utah (0.334) produces the "best" synthetic California such that smoking outcomes and predictors between real and synthetic California are similar prior to Proposition 99.

References

Abadie, A., Chingos, M., & West, M. (2013). Endogenous stratification in randomized experiments (NBER Working Paper No. 19742). Cambridge, MA: National Bureau of Economic Research.

Abadie, A., Diamond, A., & Hainmueller, J. (2010). Synthetic control methods for comparative case studies: Estimating the effect of California's tobacco control program. *Journal of the American Statistical Association*, *105*(490), 493–505.

Anderson, M., & Matsa, D. (2011). Are restaurants really supersizing America? *American Economic Journal: Applied Economics*, *3*, 152–188.

Anderson, T., & Rubin, H. (1950). The asymptotic properties of estimates of the parameters of a single equation in a complete system of stochastic equations. *Annals of Mathematical Statistics*, 570–582.

Angrist, J., Imbens, G., & Rubin, D. (1996). Identification of causal effects using instrumental variables, *Journal of the American Statistical Association*, *91*(434), 444–455.

Angrist, J., & Pischke, J. S. (2009). *Mostly harmless econometrics: An empiricist's companion*. Princeton, NJ: Princeton University Press.

Antwi, Y., Moriya, A., & Simon, K. (2013). Effects of federal policy to insure young adults: Evidence from the 2010 Affordable Care Act's dependent-coverage mandate. *American Economic Journal: Economic Policy*, *5*(4), 1–28.

Barbaresco, S., Courtemanche, C., & Qi, Y. (2015). Impacts of the Affordable Care Act dependent coverage provision on health-related outcomes of young adults. *Journal of Health Economics*, *40*, 54–68.

Baum, C., & Ford, W. (2004). The wage effects of obesity: A longitudinal study. *Health Economics, 13*(9), 885–899.

Board of Governors of the Federal Reserve System. (2014). *In the shadow of the Great Recession: Experience and perspectives of young workers.* Washington DC: Author.

Cawley, J. (2004). The impact of obesity on wages. *Journal of Human Resources, 39*(2), 451–474.

Charles, K., & DeCicca, P. (2008). Local labor market fluctuations and health: Is there a connection and for whom? *Journal of Health Economics, 27*(6), 1532–1550.

Chou, S., Grossman, M., & Saffer, H. (2004). An economic analysis of adult obesity: Results from the Behavioral Risk Factor Surveillance System. *Journal of Health Economics, 23*(3), 565–587.

Colman, G., & Dave, D. (2012). Physical activity and health. *International Journal of Arts and Sciences, 5*(6), 29–45.

Corman, H., Dave, D., Reichman, N., & Das, D. (2013). Effects of welfare reform on illicit drug use among adult women. *Economic Inquiry, 51*(1), 653–674.

Cutler, D., & Glaeser, E. (2005). What explains differences in smoking, drinking, and other health-related behaviors? *American Economic Review, 95*(2), 238–242.

Dave, D., Corman, H., & Reichman, N. (2012). Effects of welfare reform on educational acquisition of young adult women. *Journal of Labor Research, 33*(2), 251–282.

Dave, D., & Kaestner, R. (2009). Health insurance and ex ante moral hazard: Evidence from Medicare. *International Journal of Health Care Finance and Economics, 9*(4), 367–390.

Dave, D., & Kelly, I. (2012). How does the business cycle affect eating habits? *Social Science and Medicine, 74*, 254–262.

Deb, P., Gallo, W., Ayyagari, P., Fletcher, J., & Sindelar, J. (2011). The effect of job loss on overweight and drinking. *Journal of Health Economics, 30*(2), 317–327.

Gelman, A., & Imbens, G. (2014). Why high-order polynomials should not be used in regression discontinuity designs (NBER Working Paper No. 20405). Cambridge, MA: National Bureau of Economic Research.

Gregory, C., & Ruhm, C. (2011). Where does the wage penalty bite? In Michael Grossman & Naci Mocan (Eds.), *Economic aspects of obesity* (pp. 315–347). Chicago: University of Chicago Press.

Griliches, Z., & Hausman, J. (1986). Errors in variables in panel data. *Journal of Econometrics, 31*(1), 93–118.

Gruber, J., & Frakes, M. (2006). Does falling smoking lead to rising obesity? *Journal of Health Economics, 25*(2), 183–197.

Hahn, J., & Hausman, J. (2002). A new specification test for the validity of instrumental variables. *Econometrica, 70*, 163–189.

Hausman, J. (1978). Specification tests in econometrics. *Econometrica, 46*(6), 1251–1271.

Ikeda, S., Kang, M., & Ohtake, F. (2010). Hyperbolic discounting, the sign effect, and the body mass index. *Journal of Health Economics, 29*(2), 268–284.

Imbens, G. (2014). Instrumental variables: An econometrician's perspective (NBER Working Paper No. 19983). Cambridge, MA: National Bureau of Economic Research.

Imbens, G., & Angrist, J. (1994). Identification and estimation of local average treatment effects. *Econometrica, 62*(2), 462–475.

Imbens, G., & Lemieux, T. (2008). Regression discontinuity designs: A guide to practice. *Journal of Econometrics, 142*, 615–635.

Lee, D., & Lemieux, T. (2010). Regression discontinuity designs in economics. *Journal of Economic Literature, 48*, 281–355.

Lhila, A. (2011). Does access to fast food lead to super-sized pregnant women and whopper babies? *Economics & Human Biology*, *9*(4), 364–380.
Meltzer, D., & Chen, Z. (2011). The impact of minimum wage rates on body weight in the United States. In Michael Grossman & Naci Mocan (Eds.), *Economic aspects of obesity* (pp. 17–34). Chicago: University of Chicago Press.
Rashad, I., Chou, S., & Grossman, M. (2006). The super size of America: An economic estimation of body mass index and obesity in adults. *Eastern Economic Journal*, *32*, 133–148.
Rubin, D. (1974). Estimating causal effects of treatments in randomized and non-randomized Studies. *Journal of Educational Psychology*, *66*, 688–701.
Sabia, J., Swigert, J., & Young, T. (2015). The effect of medical marijuana laws on body weight and physical activity (working paper). San Diego: San Diego State University.
Schanzenbach, D. (2009). Do school lunches contribute to childhood obesity. *Journal of Human Resources*, *44*(3), 684–709.
Staiger, D., & Stock, J. (1997). Instrumental variables regression with weak instruments. *Econometrica*, *65*(3), 557–586.
Stock, J., Wright, J., & Yogo M. (2002). A survey of weak instruments and weak identification in generalized method of moments, *Journal of Business and Economic Statistics*, *20*(4), 518–529.
Wehby, G., & Courtemanche, C. (2012). The heterogeneity of the cigarette price effect on body mass index. *Journal of Health Economics*, *31*(5), 719–729.
Wehby, G., Murray, J., Wilcox, A., & Lie, R. (2012). Smoking and body weight: Evidence using genetic instruments. *Economics and Human Biology*, *10*(2), 113–126.
Wooldridge, J. (2010). *Econometric analysis of cross section and panel data*. Cambridge, MA: MIT Press.
Zhang, L., & Rashad, I. (2008). Obesity and time preference: The health consequences of discounting the future. *Journal of Biosocial Science*, *40*(1), 97–113.
Zhao, Z., Kaestner, R., & Xu, X. (2014). Spatial mobility and environmental effects on obesity. *Economics & Human Biology*, *14*, 128–140.

PART II

BIOLOGICAL MEASURES AS AN OUTCOME

CHAPTER 6

BODY MASS INDEX THROUGH TIME

Explanations, Evidence, and Future Directions

SCOTT A. CARSON

6.1 INTRODUCTION

OBESITY is a well-established risk factor for various health conditions. There are multiple explanations that shed light on the modern obesity epidemic, and long-term studies are instrumental in understanding its development over time. The body mass index (BMI)—weight in kilograms divided by height in meters squared—is the primary means of classifying obesity.[1] However, interpreting BMI variation is more problematic than interpreting stature variation—a measure for cumulative net nutrition—because BMIs increase when weight in the numerator increases or when height in the denominator is low. This implies that BMI must be interpreted with caution because it is the ratio of net current to net cumulative nutrition until about age 20 and does not change thereafter. BMI is also more difficult to interpret than stature because its variation depends on when privation occurs. For example, if an individual receives poor nutrition as a child, she is less likely to reach her genetically predetermined stature. If this short stature persists, and a short person receives abundant calories as an adult, that individual is more likely to be obese because more weight is distributed over smaller physical dimensions (Sorkin, Muller, & Andres, 1999, p. 257). On the other hand, a well-fed child is more likely to reach her genetically determined stature and have lower BMIs in later life because her weight is distributed over larger physical dimensions, *ceteris paribus*.

Although tautological, the traditional explanation for obesity as calories-in versus calories-out treats the source of calories consumed from carbohydrates, proteins, and fats equally, as if the source of calories is irrelevant. However, this explanation was not always the only accepted one for BMI variation, and, prior to the 1980s, a widely held view for changes in obesity was that it varied with the types of calories consumed. For example, it was once believed that obesity resulted from consuming proportionally more calories from sugars and simple carbohydrates relative to proteins and fats (Ebbeling et al., 2012; Taubes, 2010, 2012), and recent obesity studies are re-evaluating this interpretation (Riera-Crichton & Tefft, 2014; Seidell, 1998; van Dam & Seidell, 2007). Part of the modern obesity increase may be related to an increase in the consumption of beverages high in sugar (Lieberman, 2000, p. 1066; Nielsen & Popkin, 2004, pp. 451–452; van Dam & Seidell, 2007, pp. s75, s78–s88). The omitted factor in the calories-in versus calories-out interpretation may be insulin and insulin resistance, which is associated with diets high in sugars and simple carbohydrates. Insulin resistance develops when cells become insensitive to insulin, meaning they cannot use glucose for energy. Insulin resistance is also associated with high triglyceride levels in the bloodstream and develops when high amounts of lipids are stored as fatty acids in adipose tissue, and it is the simultaneous increase in insulin resistance, type 2 diabetes, high blood pressure, and obesity that is associated with metabolic syndrome and poor health (Eckel, Grundy, & Zimmet, 2005).

Another alternative to the calories-in, calories-out explanation is the *thrifty-gene hypothesis*, which holds that certain populations are genetically predisposed to obesity (Neel, 1962, p. 354). The effects of these genes act through hyperinsulinemia, which promotes fat accumulation when calories are abundant to be used for survival later during periods of nutritional and dietary stress. Later life obesity associated with the thrifty gene propagates through gestational diabetes if a genotype modifies metabolic adaptations for survival when malnourished fetuses adapt to dietary stress by storing fat in utero for survival after birth.[2] The hypothesis was first used to explain an increase in modern type 2 diabetes because individuals with this genetic expression were at greater risk of diabetes after nutrition became more abundant and reliable (Joffe & Zimmet, 1998, p. 139; Neel, 1962; Prentice, Hennig, & Fulford, 2008; Prentice, Rayco-Solon, & Moore, 2005). However, as an explanation for adult-onset diabetes, the thrifty-gene hypothesis has been challenged (Speakman, 2006, 2008) and remains controversial (Prentice et al., 2008, p. 160).

Related to the thrifty-gene hypothesis is the *Barker hypothesis*, which postulates that many adult chronic conditions are not always the result of bad genes and unhealthy lifestyles but instead the result of poor intrauterine conditions and early postnatal nutrition (Wells, 2003). For example, a fetus that receives an insufficient amount of iodine during the second trimester of pregnancy is more likely to develop diseases of the nervous system—such as multiple sclerosis—later in life. The Barker hypothesis also suggests that in-utero conditions are related to later-life risks of heart disease and stroke (Barker, 1992, 1997). Obesity, BMI, cardiovascular disease, stroke, and even cognitive function vary with a mother's net nutritional conditions that affect her child both before and shortly after birth (Barker, 1992, 1997, 1998; Ellias, Ellias, Sullivan, Wolf, & D'Agostro, 2003, 2005; Osmond & Barker, 2000; Ost et al., 2014).

Fat accumulation (for sake of simplicity) may also be related to stress and hormones. Stress is related to the proteins associated with the hormones adiponectin, cortisol, ghrelin, and leptin. The adiponectin protein regulates glucose levels and how fatty acids are digested, and adiponectin levels are inversely related to percent body fat. The hormone cortisol is a steroid released under stressful conditions, and women may respond differently than men to increased amounts of cortisol because they consume more fatty acids and simple sugars under stressful conditions (Epel, Lapidus, McEwen, & Brownell, 2001; Newman, O'Connor, & Conner, 2007). Ghrelin is an amino acid that lines the stomach and increases before meals are consumed and decreases after consumption. Leptin is a cell signaling protein released from adipose tissue that regulates hunger, appetite, energy intake, and metabolism (Sills & Crawley, 1996; Teff et al., 2004). Leptin's absence is also associated with obesity and excess food consumption. Adiponectin, ghrelin, and leptin function in the brain where they stimulate glucocorticoids, and elevated glucocorticoids are associated with obesity-related stress (Björntorp, 2001; Offer, Pechey, & Ulijaszek, 2012). Market economies are based on occupational and economic hierarchies, and social stress accrues from occupational subordination; therefore, stress-related hormones may be associated with economic development (Offer et al., 2012).[3] In sum, whereas the modern explanation of an excess of calories consumed above calories expended for work is undeniably true, alternative explanations are important in evaluating how BMI and obesity varied over the long run.

6.2 Body Mass and Health

Measuring obesity is ideally made by examining an individual's percent body fat, fat-free mass, or waist-to-hip ratio. Burkhauser and Cawley (2008) indicate that BMI has limitations in measuring obesity because it does not distinguish between fat and fat-free mass, such as bone and muscle (Baum & Ruhm, 2009, pp. 635–648). However, these measurements are expensive to collect, so the BMI, which is easy and inexpensive to calculate, has become the standard measure for obesity. The World Health Organization developed the current BMI classification system. BMIs of less than 18.5 are classified as underweight, BMIs between 18.5 and 24.9 are normal weight, BMIs between 25.0 and 29.9 are overweight, BMIs greater than 30.0 are obese.

Changes in health are frequently associated with changes in weight, so BMI is an important variable that measures health. In modern populations, Waaler (1984) finds a U-shaped relationship between BMIs and relative mortality risk in a Norwegian population, which led to a number of important follow-up studies (Allebeck & Berg, 1992; Andres, Elahis, Tobin, Mueller, & Brant, 1985; Fogel, 1993, 1994; Fogel & Costa, 1997; Koch, 2011; Stevens et al., 1998). Waaler and subsequent studies also find that relative mortality risk is high for populations with BMIs of less than 19, are low and stable for men with BMIs between 19 and 27, and is high for individuals with BMIs above 27. Costa (1993, p. 442), Murray (1997, p. 599), and Henderson (2005, p. 346) show the U-shaped relationship is stable over time, and Jee et al. (2006) show that the relationship is similar across ethnic groups. For BMIs of less than 19, infectious diseases, malnutrition, and respiratory conditions are common (Calle, Thun, Petrelli, Rodriguez, & Meath, 1999,

p. 1001; Jee et al., 2006, p. 783), and greater rates of heart disease, stroke, diabetes, high blood pressure, and the likelihood of many cancers are common among people with high BMIs (Atlas, 2011, p. 104; Eckel et al., 2005, pp. 1417–1421; Popkin, 2009, p. 113).

BMIs also vary with diets, and, in the 20th century, a distinct nutritional pattern emerged in which rural diets that were rich in proteins and complex carbohydrates transitioned to urban diets high in saturated fats and simple sugars (Popkin, 1993, pp. 145–148; Popkin, 2009). BMIs and obesity also vary with technological change and physical activity (Lakdawalla & Philipson, 2002, 2009; Laudabaum, Mannalithera, Meyer, & Singh, 2014; Sharma, Zaric, Campbell, & Gilliland, 2014), and changing US labor markets may be associated with BMI variation through the effects associated with less physical activity required at work. (Baum & Ruhm, 2009, p. 638; Church et al., 2011).

6.3 The History of US BMIs

Fogel (1994, p. 373) finds that the bottom 10% of the French labor force in 1790 did not receive a sufficient amount of calories to perform any work. Although more calories were available in England, 3% of the English population also did not receive sufficient nutrition to participate in the labor force. Consequently, 18th-century Europeans and the English were shorter and were mostly underweight (Fogel, 2004, pp. 59–66).

Various studies consider 19th- and early 20th-century US BMI variation over time and by characteristics (Table 6.1). The majority of BMIs by observation period indicate that the BMIs of men decreased throughout the late 19th and early 20th centuries. BMIs began their century-long increase after World War I with a hiatus during the Great Depression and World War II; increase resumed in the 1950s (Komlos & Brabec, 2010, 2011). Moreover, all historical BMI studies show a marked BMI advantage for rural agricultural workers and greater BMIs associated with African Americans. Because rural farmers were in close proximity to food supplies rich in protein and complex carbohydrates, farmers received adequate nutrition, were more physically active, and, as a consequence, probably had greater muscle mass and consequently greater BMI values than did workers in other occupations; this situation persisted until the end of the 19th century. Farmers were also in closer proximity to food supplies, which was associated with lower food prices (Komlos, 1987). Hence, the BMIs of rural unskilled workers as well as farmers were .5% and .7% greater, respectively, than workers with no identified occupations (Carson, 2012*a*, pp. 383–384; Carson, 2013b).[4]

Three data sources are used here to consider how BMIs and obesity varied between 1800 and 2010: US prison records, the National Health and Nutrition Examination Survey (NHANES), and the National Health Interview Survey (NHIS). We supplement the NHANES data with NHIS data because the NHANES does not collect valuable economic variables, such as occupations, which are available in the NHIS. This chapter considers obesity patterns using male prison records, NHANES, and NHIS to contrast how obesity varied by demographic and socioeconomic characteristics between 1800

Table 6.1 Comparison of late 19th and early 20th Century BMIs

Study	Observation Period	Sample	ΔBMI over Time	ΔFarmer	Δ Mulatto Compared to Black
Cuff, 1993, White	1860–1885	West Point Cadets	0.8		
Coclanis and Komlos, 1995, White	1860–1930	The Citadel	1.7		
Carson, 2009, Black and White	1870–1920	Texas Prisoners	Blacks, −0.4 Whites, 0.2	0.2 0.1	−0.3
Bodenhorn, 2010, White	1795–1844	New York Legislators	−1.7		
Carson, 2012, Black and White	1850–1929	US Prisons	Black Youth −1.06	0.4	−0.4
			White Youth −1.05	0.5	
Carson, 2012, Black and White	1840–1929	US Prisons	Black Adults −2.3	0.2	−0.4
			White Adults −2.0	0.3	
Carson and Hodges, 2012, Black and White	1870–1910	Philadelphia Prison	Blacks and Whites combined 0.2	0.1	−0.4

Source: Cuff (1993); Coclanis and Komlos (1995); Carson, (2009); Bodenhorn, (2010); Carson (2012a, pp. 383–385 and pp. 389–392); Carson and Hodges (2012).Notes: ΔBMI is the difference between BMIs at the beginning and end of the series presented in each study's observation period. ΔFarmer is the unit farmer BMI difference relative to the no occupation category. Δ Mulatto is the unit mulatto BMI difference relative to darker complexioned blacks.

and 2010. There is concern when comparing the NHIS with NHANES data because the NHIS is self-reported, which may misrepresent height and weight measurements; thus, results should be interpreted with caution (Goodman, Hinden, & Khandelwal, 2000; Kuczmarski, Kuczmarski, & Naijar, 2001; Strauss, 1999). The NHIS also omits height below 59 and above 76 inches (150 and 193 cm) and omits weights below 99 and over 285 pounds (45 and 129 kg). Assessing the degree of these potential biases is addressed in part by comparing the percent of the NHANES and NHIS samples in the combined overweight and obese categories.

Nineteenth-century BMIs of white men were almost all in the normal category, with few adult men in the obese category (Figure 6.1). The average adult black male BMI in the historical sample is 23.9, with 1.3% in the obese category and .7% in the underweight category. The average adult white male BMI in the historical sample is 22.7, with 1.0% in

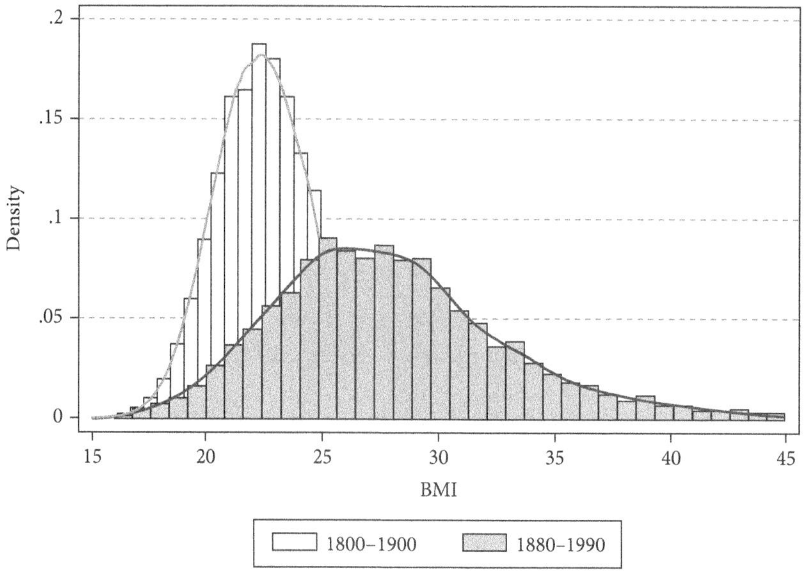

FIGURE 6.1 Nineteenth century and modern White male BMI distributions by year of birth.

Note: Historical represents males from the prison records, born between 1800 and 1900 and observed between 1840 and 1920. Modern represents males from the NHANES III.

Source: Historical: Carson (2012a); Modern: NHANES III.

the obese category and 2.3% in the underweight category. The corresponding values for modern US populations are 27.4 and 27.5 for blacks and whites, respectively, indicating that their BMIs have increased by 15% and 21%, respectively. Greater black compared to white BMIs during the 19th century may reflect greater intrauterine deprivation, thus making these individuals susceptible to obesity if nutrition improved in adulthood (Bodenhorn, 2010 Carson, 2008, 2012*c* 2015*b*; Steckel, 1979).

Comparing historical and modern BMI variance is even more striking. The historical adult standard deviation is 2.4, whereas its modern counterpart is between 6.5 and 5.5, indicating that variances increased by more than a factor of two, respectively. In sum, average BMIs and percentages in the obese categories have increased over time, but their variances have increased even more.

6.4 Factors Associated with US BMIs

6.4.1 Over Time

BMIs increase when the percent change in weight is greater than twice the percent change in height[5]; weight generally contributes more to BMI variation than does height (Carson, 2015*a*; Dawes, 2014, p. 30). There are two ways to measure BMI variation over time: birth and period effects. Birth effects measure how BMIs varied since birth, whereas period effects measure how BMIs vary by observation period. Measured by birth effects, the increase in obesity may have occurred earlier than currently believed (Coclanis & Komlos, 1995; Komlos & Brabec, 2010, p. 631; 2011, p. 235). Measured by birth cohorts, the epidemic began after World War I and accelerated in the 1950s; whereas, using period effects, US obesity began abruptly in the 1970s and 1980s. Although neither measurement provides a definitive answer, considering birth and period effects together provides a richer explanation for when the increase in obesity began.

Komlos and Brabec (2010, 2011) use NHANES data to show that BMIs began to increase among the birth cohorts of the post-World War I era. Between 1900 and 1965, the average BMI of black females increased by 68%, whereas it increased by 39% for white females. BMI increases were most pronounced after the two world wars.

Using data from 19th-century US prisons and the NHANES III, Figure 6.2 presents average adult US male BMIs. Between 1800 and 1900, black and white adult average BMIs decreased moderately. The average black and white male BMI cohort born in 1910 were 25.4 and 25.7, respectively, whereas birth cohorts in the 1950s were 28.4 and 28.7, indicating that BMIs by birth cohort began to increase much earlier than expected.

On the other hand, since BMI is more responsive to weight than height, BMI by period effects are frequently interpreted as reflecting changes in current net nutrition. Cuff (1993, p. 178) finds that West Point military recruit BMIs in the mid-19th century

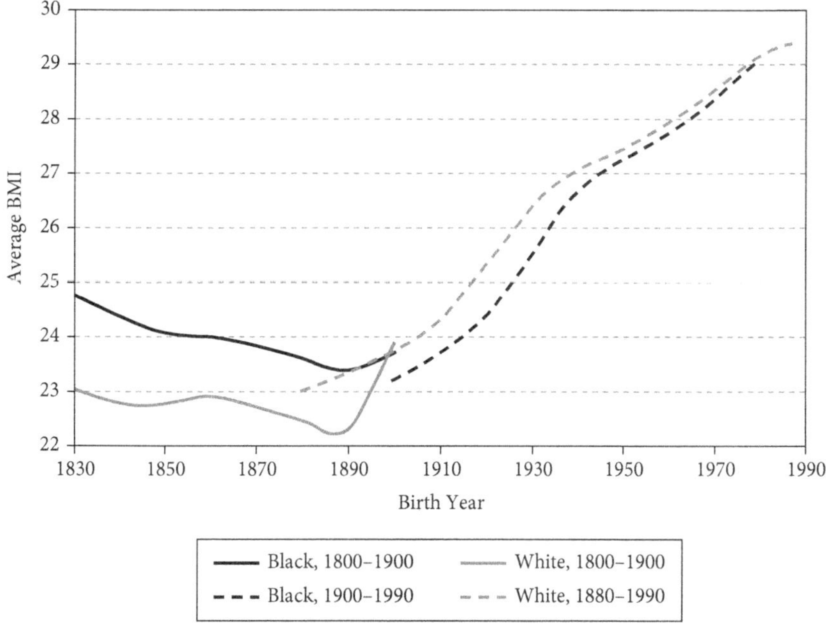

FIGURE 6.2 Average BMI values of Black and White adult men by birth cohort over time.

Note: Average BMIs are adjusted for age.

Source: Historical: Carson (2012a); Modern: Komlos and Brabec (2010).

were sufficiently low that a large proportion of cadets were in the high relative health risk category; 40% of 20- to 21-year-old cadets had BMIs below 19, the threshold at which mortality risk increases (Costa, 1996, pp. 66, 81–86; Costa & Steckel, 1997; Fogel, 1993, p. 15; Murray, 1997, pp. 597–603; Riley, 1994, pp. 486–492; Waaler, 1984, pp. 23–37). Cuff also finds that cadet BMIs increased slightly over time, and BMIs generally decreased in the late 19th century (Carson, 2009, 2012*a*, 2012*b*; Carson & Hodges 2012; Costa & Steckel 1997, pp. 51–54; Cuff, 1993, p. 177; Carson, 2014*a*). Today, the rate of obesity among black and white men is similar.

Using data from 19th-century US state prisons and NHANES measured by observation period between 1840 and 1920 and between 1980 and 2008, Figure 6.3 shows the percentage of black and white adults in the obese category. About 1% of 19th-century blacks and whites were obese, with little change in either average BMIs or the percent of obese men throughout the century. Measured by either birth cohort or period cohorts, these large increases in BMI and obesity indicate that the modern obesity epidemic began earlier than previously believed. Lifestyle changes that began in the 1950s and 1960s, with reduced physical activity associated with transportation technologies and television, deserve additional attention (Komlos & Brabec, 2010, 2011). There is also little evidence that BMIs and obesity have changed since 2000 (Flegal, Carroll, Kit, & Ogden, 2012; Flegal, Carroll, & Ogden, 2010; Flegal, Carroll, Ogden, & Johnson, 2002; Hedley et al., 2004, pp. 2848–2850; Ogden, Carroll, Curtin, Lamb, & Fleagal, 2010; Ogden et al., 2006; Ogden, Carroll, Kit, & Flegal, 2012).

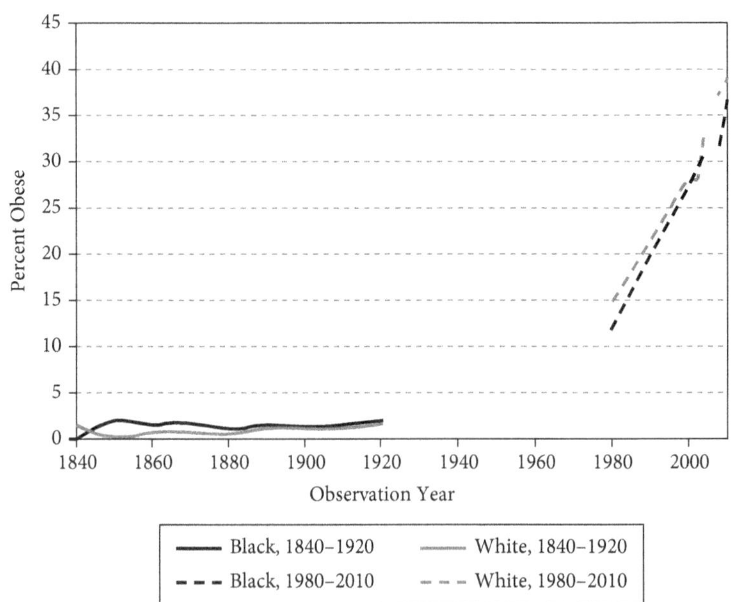

FIGURE 6.3 Percent obese among adult Black and White men by data of measurement.

Source: Historical: Carson (2012a); Modern: Ogden et al. (2006); Flegal et al. (2012).

Less is known about 19th-century women's BMI and obesity variation. Women may have had heavier weights because of evolutionary responses to child-bearing, where more energy is stored in the fat required to fuel the development of large-brain offspring (Dunbar, 2012, p. 55; Pond, 1977). Fat and its distribution may have also played a role in women's sexual attractiveness and mate selection (Anderson, Crawford, Nadeau, & Lindberg, 1992; Pawlowski & Dunbar, 2005; Tovée et al., 1999). Moreover, women accumulate weight during pregnancy that can be difficult to lose after childbirth (Lieberman, 2000). There are other reasons women may be more likely to be obese than men. For example, BMI is inversely related to height, and women reach shorter terminal statures than do men (Carson, 2011, 2013c; Herbert et al., 1993, p. 1438). There is also a psychosocial relationship between gender and obesity; women may be more likely to be depressed and, subsequently, more likely to be obese (BeLue, Francis, & Colaco, 2009; Needham & Crosnoe, 2005).

Women were less likely be imprisoned during the 19th century; because prisons recorded weight, this means fewer records of women's historical weight survive. Like males, average female BMIs by birth cohort were low and declined throughout the 19th century, and average black and white women's BMIs were similar. By the late 20th century, black women were more likely than white women to have high BMIs and be obese (Figure 6.4).

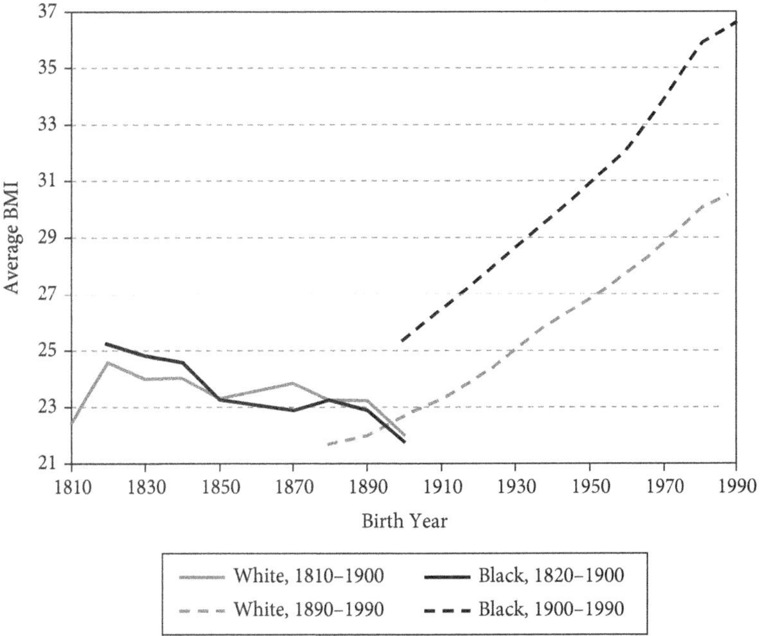

FIGURE 6.4 Black and White average female BMI over time by birth cohort.

Note: Age-adjusted average BMIs.

Source: Carson data set; Komlos and Brabec (2010).

6.4.2 Occupations

Whereas workers in all occupations were more obese compared to farmers, in the 19th century, modern sedentary white-collar and skilled workers have become more overweight and obese (Table 6.2; Church et al., 2011; Laudabaum et al., 2014; Sharma et al., 2014, p. 18). Between the late 19th and early 21st centuries, obesity increased for each occupational category and increased by factors of 2.5 and 3.7 for black and white unskilled workers, respectively. In the past, nonagricultural workers required greater physical activity than today because transportation technology and daily activities required workers to be more physically active. In sum, BMIs and obesity have increased for every occupation.

Table 6.2 Nineteenth and 21st Century Black and White Male Weight Distributions (Percent) by Occupation

	Blacks							
		Historical				Modern		
	Under	Normal	Over	Obese	Under	Normal	Over	Obese
White-Collar	0.8	73.4	24.4	1.5	0.7	26.0	45.1	28.3
Skilled	0.9	70.4	26.9	1.8	0.4	29.9	41.3	28.4
Agricultural	0.6	68.2	29.9	1.3	0.0	37.3	36.1	26.5
Unskilled	0.8	71.3	26.9	1.1	0.4	29.2	40.9	29.5
No Occupation	0.7	67.7	30.5	1.1	1.4	42.3	36.8	19.5
	Whites							
		Historical				Modern		
	Under	Normal	Over	Obese	Under	Normal	Over	Obese
White-Collar	3.6	79.4	15.2	1.9	0.2	29.5	46.8	23.5
Skilled	2.2	82.3	14.6	1.0	0.3	28.7	45.8	25.2
Agricultural	2.0	81.8	15.1	1.1	0.7	27.5	46.2	25.6
Unskilled	2.2	82.8	14.3	0.7	0.4	28.3	44.2	27.2
No Occupation	2.5	83.9	12.9	0.6	1.0	44.1	34.1	20.8

Source: Historical, Carson (2012a); Modern: NHIS.

6.4.3 Residence

BMIs and obesity have also varied by region. Between the late 19th and early 21st centuries, obesity within the Northeast increased by 2,825% for blacks and by 4,350% for white men in the Midwest (Table 6.3; Atlas, 2011, p. 105; Mokdad et al., 1999, 2001, pp. 1196–1198). The percentage in the underweight and normal categories in every region decreased. Modern BMIs and obesity are higher in the southern and central United States and lower in northeastern and western states (Hines, 2011). Southern urban obesity is greater than in other regions (Lieberman, 2000, p. 1065). Regional BMI variation increased because of different socioeconomic status, ethnicities, geographic conditions, access to economic opportunity, education, access to nutrition, and income and inequality differentials (Chang & Lauderdale, 2005; Sobal, 2011, p. 110 Carson, 2013*a*, 2015*d*; Carson & Hodges, 2014*d*). Regional obesity variation may be explained, in part, by diet, and Southern diets were more calorie-dense than elsewhere within the United States (Carson, 2014*b*; Hilliard, 1972; Ransom & Sutch, 1977). Consequently, over time, by occupations, and across the United States, obesity has increased with the transition to a modern economy.

Table 6.3 Nineteenth and 21st Century Black and White Male Obesity Prevelance (Percent) by Residence

	Blacks							
	Historical				Modern			
	Under	Normal	Over	Obese	Under	Normal	Over	Obese
Northeast	0.6	74.2	24.4	0.8	0.4	31.8	44.4	23.4
Midwest	1.3	81.2	16.6	1.0	0.4	29.9	41.5	28.2
South	0.8	68.6	29.4	1.2	0.4	28.6	41.0	30.0
West	0.6	67.9	29.6	2.0	0.8	29.7	41.6	27.9
	Whites							
	Historical				Modern			
	Under	Normal	Over	Obese	Under	Normal	Over	Obese
Northeast	1.9	82.7	14.6	0.8	0.3	29.9	45.7	24.1
Midwest	4.2	86.1	9.1	0.6	0.4	28.5	44.4	26.7
South	2.6	82.5	14.0	0.9	0.3	28.9	44.6	26.1
West	1.4	78.4	18.8	1.4	0.2	29.6	47.0	23.2

Source: Historical, Carson (2012a); Modern: NHIS.

6.5 Discussion and Future Directions

Considerable progress has been made in explaining the rise of the modern obesity epidemic, yet there are important gaps in our understanding of its major causes, and progress in interpreting obesity trends will rely on cross-pollination among medicine, the hard sciences, and the social sciences. New areas for obesity research that have developed for modern populations, but with limited application in historical BMI studies, are public policy, obesity and taxation, insurance, pharmaceuticals, and food marketing (Beydoun, Powell, & Wang, 2008; Brownwell et al., 2009; Chou, Rashad, & Grossmand, 2008). Moreover, many other areas in obesity research provide insight into how modern obesity developed. For example, an important question for historical and future studies is the number of calories consumed per day over those required to maintain healthy body weight. This "energy gap" is the number of calories required to reduce current obesity levels to healthy nutritional intake and has policy applications. Wang et al. (Wang, Orleans, & Gortmaker, 2012) consider the *Healthy People 2010* goals and show that reducing future obesity levels will require an average reduction in consumption of 120 kilocalories per day among youth. Carson (2014*b*) and Carson (2015*c*) use similar calorie extrapolation techniques to show that the average adult calories expended per day during the late 19th and early 20th centuries was around 3,000, and future obesity studies will rely on these relationships to calculate historical and modern calorie intakes.

Health and obesity may also be related to peer effects through selection, in which obese individuals are more likely to associate with individuals of similar weight and physical activity levels. These relationships were first considered by Christakis and Fowler (2007) who demonstrated that the likelihood that a person is obese is 57% higher if the person has an obese friend. These social relationships extend to family members; if one sibling is obese, the other is 40% more likely to be obese as well (Christakis & Fowler, 2007, pp. 370, 375–377; Ozanne, 2015, p. 973). Christakis and Fowler (2007) also find that there are three degrees of separation between individuals before social relationships are no longer significant (Dunbar, 2012, pp. 62–65). Economics also contributes to obesity research through assortative mating studies (Silventoinen, Kaprio, Lahelma, & Viken, 2003). These studies demonstrate that obese individuals are more likely to marry partners with similar attributes.

Farmers and unskilled workers had greater BMIs than workers in other occupations, and men from the Northeast and Middle Atlantic weighed less, whereas Southerners weighed more. The inference is that close proximity to agriculture enabled farmers to consume more calories. Southerners weighed more because their lower population density meant that their disease load was lower (Carson, 2015*a*). Assessment of these historical international trends awaits the collection of new datasets from historical records.

6.6 Conclusion

The 20th-century obesity epidemic is a leading health concern in epidemiology, economics, and human biology studies. Although individuals in the 19th century were mostly in the normal BMI category, overweight and obesity are both now much more common than healthy body weights. Whether obesity is measured by birth or period effects, it is clear that obesity increased in the late 20th century, a trend that may have been well under way by mid-century. This indicates that the average BMI for a man 68 inches (163 cm) tall increased by 25% between the mid-19th century and 2010, whereas the percent in the obese category increased by 400%.

There is considerable debate regarding whether BMIs and obesity have increased as a result of increased consumption of calorie-dense foods or if the modern sedentary lifestyle is the main cause. Regardless of the source of obesity, it is clear that obesity has increased across all ethnic groups, socioeconomic status levels, and residence locations, indicating that the plausible explanation for the obesity epidemic is a combination of consuming more calorie-dense foods relative to energy expended during physical activity. The increase has been greatest among black females. Regional variation also indicates that obesity within the United States has been widespread. Recent studies on the obesity epidemic indicate that proximity to fast food establishments and lack of physical activity are factors in obesity's increase. How BMI and obesity changed over time will also contribute to understanding the policies needed to reduce obesity.

Acknowledgments

I appreciate comments from John Komlos, Gary Taubes, John Cawley, Lee Carson, Doug Henderson, James Eldridge, and Paul Hodges. Shahil Sharma, Chinuedu Akah, Meekam Okeke, Tiffany Grant, Bryce Harper, Greg Davis, Kellye Manning, and Brandon Hayes provided research assistance.

Notes

1. BMIs are generally high for well-nourished populations relative to work effort expended and low for poorly nourished populations.
2. Gestational diabetes occurs when a pregnant women who has never had diabetic symptoms produces high blood sugar levels during pregnancy; this occurs when insulin receptors do not function, likely due to pregnancy-related factors.
3. However, the hormone–market stress hypothesis may not be the primary explanation for obesity because, during their economic development, British, French, and US populations

faced stress from droughts and disease, but there is little evidence that these populations were obese (Carson, 2009, 2012*a*).

4. Using the 1977 Standard Occupational Classification system. Five broad occupational categories are considered here: white-collar, skilled, farmers, unskilled, and without a listed occupation. Managers, professionals, and sales representatives are classified as white-collar workers. Clerks, craftsmen, and operatives are classified as skilled workers. Farm laborers and farmers are classified as farmers. Household laborers, general laborers, service workers, and transportation workers are classified as unskilled workers. Those with no occupations and not in the labor force are classified as workers with no occupations.
5. $BMI = \frac{w(kg)}{(h(m))^2} = wh^{-2} \Rightarrow \ln BMI = \ln w - 2\ln h. \quad \therefore \quad \frac{\%\Delta BMI}{\%\Delta w} = 1$ and $\frac{\%\Delta BMI}{\%\Delta h} = -2$

References

Allebeck, P., & Berg, C. (1992). Height, body mass index, and mortality: Do social factors explain the association? *Public Health, 106*, 375–382.

Anderson, J. L., Crawford, C. W., Nadeau, J., & Lindberg, T. (1992). Was the Duchess of Windsor right? A cross-cultural study of the socioecology of the ideals of female body shape. *Ethnology and Sociobiology, 13*, 197–227.

Andres, R., Elahis, D., Tobin, J., Mueller, M., & Brant, L. (1985). Impact of age of weight goals. *Annals of Internal Medicine, 103*, 1030–1033.

Atlas, S. (2011). *In excellent health: Setting the record straight on America's health care.* Stanford, CA: Hoover Institution Press.

Barker, D. (1992). *Fetal and infant origins of adult disease.* London: British Medical Journal.

Barker, D. (1997). Maternal nutrition, fetal nutrition, and disease in later life. *Nutrition, 13*(9), 807–813.

Barker, D. (1998). In utero programming of chronic disease. *Clinical Science, 95*, 111–128.

Baum, C., & Ruhm, C. (2009). Age, socioeconomic status, and obesity growth. *Journal of Health Economics, 28*, 635–648.

BeLue, R., Francis, L. A., & Colaco, B. (2009). Mental health problems and overweight in nationally representative sample of adolescents: Effects of race and ethnicity. *Pediatrics, 123*, 697–702.

Beydoun, M. A., Powell, L. M., & Wang, Y. (2008). The association of fast food, fruit, and vegetable prices with dietary intakes among US adults: Is there modification by family income? *Social Science and Medicine, 66*, 2218–2229.

Björntorp, P. (2001). Do stress reactions cause abdominal obesity and comorbidities? *Obesity Reviews, 2*, 76–86.

Bodenhorn, H. (2010). Height, weight, and body mass index values of 19th century New York legislative officers. *Economics and Human Biology, 8*, 291–293.

Brownwell, K. D., Farley, T., Willett, W. C., Popkin, B. M. Chaloupka, F. J., Thompson, J. W., & Ludwig, D. S. (2009). The public health and economic benefits of taxing sugar-sweetened beverages. *New England Journal of Medicine, 361*, 1599–1605.

Burkhauser, R. V., & Cawley, J. (2008). Beyond BMI: The value of more accurate measures of fatness and obesity in social science research. *Journal of Health Economics, 27*, 519–529.

Calle, E., Thun, M., Petrelli, J., Rodriguez, C., & Meath, C. W. (1999). Body-mass index and mortality in a prospective cohort of U.S. adults. *New England Journal of Medicine, 341*, 1097–1104.

Carson, S. A. (2008). The effect of geography and vitamin D on African-American stature in the 19th century: Evidence from prison records. *Journal of Economic History, 68*, 812–830.

Carson, S. A. (2009). Racial differences in body-mass indices of men imprisoned in 19th century Texas. *Economics and Human Biology, 7*, 121–127.

Carson, S. A. (2011). Height of female Americans in the 19th century and the Antebellum Puzzle. *Economics and Human Biology, 9*, 157–164.

Carson, S. A. (2012*a*). Nineteenth century race, body mass, and industrialization: Evidence from American prisons. *Journal of Interdisciplinary History, 42*, 371–391.

Carson, S. A. (2012*b*). Demographic, residential, and socioeconomic effects on the distribution of 19th century White body mass index values. *Mathematical Population Studies, 19*(3), 147–157.

Carson, S. A. (2012*c*). A quantile approach to the demographic, residential, and socioeconomic effects on 19th century African-American body mass index values. *Cliometrica, 6*(2), 193–209.

Carson, S. A. (2013*a*). Body mass, wealth, and inequality in 19th century U.S. Joining the debate surrounding equality and health. *Economics and Human Biology, 11*(1), 90–94.

Carson, S. A. (2013*b*). The significance and relative contributions of demographic, residence, and socioeconomic status in 19th century US BMI variation. *Historical Methods, 46*(2), 67–76.

Carson, S. A. (2013*c*). Socioeconomic effects on the stature of nineteenth century U.S. women. *Feminist Economics, 19*, 122–143.

Carson, S. A. (2014*a*). Institutional change and 19th century southern Black and White BMI variation. *Journal of Institutional and Theoretical Economics, 170*(2), 296–316.

Carson, S. A. (2014*b*). Nineteenth century US Black and White working class physical activity and nutritional trends during economic development. *Journal of Economic Issues, 48*(3), 765–786.

Carson, S. A. (2015*a*). A weighty issue: Diminished 19th century net nutrition among the US working class. *Demography, 52*, 945–966.

Carson, S. A. (2015*b*). Biology, complexion, and socioeconomic status: Accounting for 19th century US BMIs by race. *Australian Economic History Review, 55*(3), 238–255.

Carson, S. A. (2015*c*). The Mexican calorie allocation among the working class in the American West, 1870–1920. *Essays in Economic & Business History, 33*, 26–50.

Carson, S. A. (2015*d*). The relationship between 19th century BMIs and family size: Economies of scale and positive externalities. *Journal Homo of Comparative Human Biology, 66*(2), 165–175.

Carson, S. A., & Hodges, P. E. (2012). 'Black, & white body mass index values in 19th century developing Philadelphia County. *Journal of BioSocial Science, 44*(3), 273–288.

Carson, S. A., & Hodges, P. E. (2014*d*). The relationship between body mass, wealth, and inequality across the BMI distribution: Evidence from nineteenth century prison records. *Mathematical Population Studies, 21*, 78–94.

Chang, V., & Lauderdale, D. S. (2005). Income disparities in body mass index and obesity in the United States, 1971–2002. *Archives of Internal Medicine, 165*, 2112–2128.

Chou, S. Y., Rashad, I., & Grossmand, M. (2008). Fast food restaurant advertising on television and its influence on childhood obesity. *Journal of Law and Economics, 51*, 599–618.

Christakis, N., & Fowler, J. (2007). The spread of obesity in a large social network over 32 years. *New England Journal of Medicine*, *357*(4), 370–378.

Church, T., Thomas, D., Tudor-Locke, C., Katzmarzyk, P. T., Earnest, C. P., Rodarte, R. Q., Martin, C. K., . . . Bouchard, C. (2011). Trends over five decades in U.S. occupation-related physical activity and their associations with obesity. *PlosOne*, *6*, 5.

Coclanis, P., & Komlos, J. (1995). Nutrition, & economic development in post-reconstruction South Carolina. *Social Science History*, *19*, 91–115.

Costa, D. (1993). Height, wealth, and disease among the native-born in the rural, antebellum North. *Social Science History*, *17*, 355–383.

Costa, D. (1996). Health and labor force participation of older men, 1900–1991. *Journal of Economic History*, *56*(1), 62–89.

Costa, D., & Steckel, R. (1997). Long-term in health, welfare, and economic growth in the United States. In: D. Costa & R. Steckel (Eds.), *Health and welfare during industrialization* (pp. 47–89). Chicago: University of Chicago Press.

Cuff, T. (1993). The body mass index values of mid-19th century West Point cadets. *Historical Methods*, *26*(4), 171–183.

Dawes, L. (2014). *Childhood obesity in America*. Cambridge, MA: Harvard University Press.

Dunbar, R. I. (2012). Obesity: An evolutionary perspective. In A. Offer, R. Pechey, & S. Ulijaszek (Eds.), *Insecurity, inequality, & obesity* (pp. 55–68). Oxford: Oxford University Press.

Eckel, R., Grundy, S., & Zimmet, P. (2005). The metabolic syndrome. *Lancet*, *365*(9468), 1415–1428.

Ebbeling, C., Swain, J., Feldman, H., Wong, W., Hachey, D., Garcia-Lago, E., & Ludwig, D. (2012). Effects of dietary composition on energy expenditure during weight loss maintenance. *Journal of the American Medical Association*, *307*(24), 2627–2634.

Ellias, M., Ellias, P., Sullivan, L., Wolf, P., & D' Agostro, R. (2003). Lower cognitive function in the presence of obesity, & hypertension: The Framingham Heart Study. *International Journal of Obesity*, *27*, 260–268.

Ellias, M., Ellias, P., Sullivan, L., Wolf, P., & D'Agostro, R. (2005). Obesity, diabetes, & cognitive deficit: The Framingham Heart Study. *Neurology of Aging*, *26*, S11–S16.

Epel, E., Lapidus, R., McEwen, B., & Brownell, K. (2001). Stress may add bite to appetite in women: A laboratory study of stress-induced cortisol and eating behavior. *Psychoneuroendocrinology*, *26*, 37–49.

Flegal, K., Carroll, M., Kit, B., & Ogden, C. (2012). Prevalence of obesity, & trends in the distribution of body mass index among US adults, 1999–2010. *Journal of the American Medical Association*, *307*(5), 491–497.

Flegal, K., Carroll, M., & Ogden, C. (2010). Prevalence and trends in obesity among US adults. *Journal of the American Medical Association*, *303*(3), 235–241.

Flegal, K. Carroll, M., Ogden, C., & Johnson, C. (2002). Prevalence, & trends in obesity among US adults, 1999–2000. *Journal of the American Medical Association*, *288*(14), 1723–1727.

Fogel, R. (1993). New sources and new techniques for the study of secular trends in nutritional status, health, mortality, and the process of aging. *Historical Methods*, *26*(1), 5–38.

Fogel, R. (1994). Economic growth, population theory, and physiology: The bearing of long-term processes on the making of economic policy. *American Economic Review*, *84*(3), 369–395.

Fogel, R. (2004). *The escape from hunger and premature death, 1700–2000*. Cambridge: Cambridge University Press.

Fogel, R., & Costa, D. (1997). A theory of technophysio evolution, with some implications for forecasting population, health care costs, and pension costs. *Demography*, *34*(1), 49–66.

Goodman, E. Hinden, B. P., & Khandelwal, S. (2000). Accuracy of teen and parental reports of obesity and body mass index. *Pediatrics*, *106*, 52–58.

Hedley, A., Ogden, C., Johnson, C., Carroll, M., Curtin, L., & Flegal, K. (2004). Prevalence of overweight and obesity among US children, adolescents, and adults, 1999–2002. *Journal of the American Medical Association*, *291*(23), 2847–2850.

Henderson, R. M. (2005). The bigger the healthier: Are the limits of BMI risk changing over time? *Economics & Human Biology*, *3*, 339–366.

Herbert, P., Richards-Edwards, J., Manson, J. A., Ridker, P., Cook, N., O'Conner, G., ... Hennekens, C. (1993). Height and incidence of cardiovascular disease in male physicians. *Circulation*, *88*, 1437–1443.

Hilliard, S. B. (1972). *Hog, meat and hoecake: Food supply in the Old South, 1840–1860*. Carbondale: Southern Illinois University Press.

Hines, C. (2011). The demography of obesity. In J. Cawley (Ed.), *The Oxford handbook of the social science of obesity* (pp. 35–47). Oxford: Oxford University Press.

Jee, H., Jee, J. W., Sull, P. J., Lee, S. Y., Ohrr, H., Guallar, E., & Samet, J. (2006). Body-mass index, & mortality in Korean men and women. *New England Journal of Medicine*, *355*, 779–787.

Joffe, B., & Zimmet, P. (1998). The thrifty genotype in the type 2 diabetes: An unfinished symphony moving to its finale? *Endocrine*, *9*(2), 139–141.

Koch, D. (2011). Waaler revisited: The anthropometrics of mortality. *Economics and Human Biology*, *9*(1), 106–117.

Komlos, J. (1987). The Height and Weight of West Point Cadets: Dietary Change in Antebellum America. *Journal of Economic History*, *47*, 897–927.

Komlos, J., & Brabec, M. (2010). The trend of mean BMI values of US adults, birth cohorts 1882–1986 indicates that the obesity epidemic began earlier than hitherto thought. *American Journal of Human Biology*, *22*, 631–638.

Komlos, J., & Brabec, M. (2011). The trend of BMI values of US adult by deciles, birth cohorts 1882–1986 stratified by gender and ethnicity. *Economics and Human Biology*, *9*(3), 234–250.

Kuczmarski, M. F., Kuczmarski, R. S., & Naijar, M. (2001). Effects of age on validity of self-reported height, weight, and body mass index: Findings from the third Health and Nutrition Examination Survey, 1988–1994. *Journal of the American Dietetic Association*, *101*, 28–34.

Lakdawalla, D., & Philipson, T. (2002). *The growth of obesity and technological change: A theoretical and empirical examination* (NBER Working Paper 8946). Cambridge, MA: National Bureau of Economic Research.

Lakdawalla, D., & Philipson, T. (2009). The growth of obesity. *Economics and Human Biology*, *7*(3), 283–293.

Laudabaum, U., Mannalithera, A., Meyer, P., & Singh, G. (2014). Obesity, abdominal obesity, physical activity, and caloric intake in U.S. adults: 1988–2010. *American Journal of Medicine*, *127*(8), 717–727.

Lieberman, L. S. (2000). Obesity. In K. Kiple & K. Coneè Ornelas (Eds.), *The Cambridge world history of food* (pp. 1062–1077). Cambridge: Cambridge University Press.

Mokdad, A., Bowman, B., Ford, E., Vinicor, F., Marks, J., & Koplan, J. (2001). The continuing epidemics of obesity and diabetes in the United States. *Journal of the American Medical Association*, *186*, 1195–1200.

Mokdad, A., Serdula, M., Dietz, W., Bowman, B., Marks, J., & Koplan, J. (1999). The spread of the obesity in the United States, 1991–1998. *Journal of the American Medical Association, 282*(16), 1519–1523.

Murray, J. (1997). Standards of the present for people of the past: Height, weight, and mortality among men of Amherst College, 1834–1949. *Journal of Economic History, 57*(3), 585–606.

Needham, B., & Crosnoe, R. (2005). Overweight status and depressive symptoms during adolescence. *Journal of Adolescent Health, 36*, 48–55.

Neel, J. (1962). Diabetes mellitus: A "thrifty" genotype rendered detrimental by "progress"? *American Journal of American Genetics, 14*(4), 353–362.

Newman, E., O'Connor, D., & Conner, M. (2007). Daily hassles and eating behavior: The role of cortisol reactivity status. *Psychoneuroendocrinology, 32*, 125–132.

Nielsen, S. J., & Popkin, B. (2004). Changes in beverage intake between 1977 and 2001. *American Journal of Preventative Medicine, 27*(3), 205–2010.

Offer, A., Pechey, R., & Ulijaszek, S. (2012). *Insecurity, inequality, & obesity in affluent societies.* Oxford: Oxford University Press.

Ogden, C., Carroll, M., Curtin, L., Lamb, M., & Flegal K. (2010). Prevalence of high body mass index in US children and adolescents, 2007–2008. *Journal of the American Medical Association, 303*(3), 242–249.

Ogden, C., Carroll, M., Curtin, L., McDowell, M., Tabak, C., & Flegal, K. (2006). Prevalence of overweight and obesity in the United States, 1999–2004. *Journal of the American Medical Association, 295*(13), 1549–1555.

Ogden, C., Carroll, M., Kit, B., & Flegal, K. (2012). Prevalence of obesity and trends in body mass index among US children and adolescents, 1999–2010. *Journal of the American Medical Association, 307*(5), 483–490.

Osmond, C., & Barker, D. (2000). Fetal infant and childhood growth are predictors of coronary heart disease, diabetes, and hypertension in adult men and women. *Environmental Health Perspective, 108*(3), 545–553.

Ost, A., Lempradl, A., Casas, E., Weigert, M., Timko, T., Deniz, M., . . . Pospisilik, A. (2014). Paternal diet defines offspring chromatin state and intergenerational obesity. *Cell, 159*(6), 1352–1364.

Ozanne, S. (2015). Epigenetic signatures of obesity. *New England Journal of Medicine, 372*(1), 973–974.

Pawlowski, B., & Dunbar, R. I. M. (2005). Waist: Hip ratio vs. BMI as predictors of fitness in women. *Human Nature, 16*, 50–63.

Pond, C. M. (1977). The significance of lactation in the evolution of mammals. *Evolution, 31*, 177–199.

Popkin, B. (1993). Nutritional patterns and transitions. *Population Development and Review, 19*, 138–157.

Popkin, B. (2009). *The world is fat: The fads, trends, policies, & products that are fattening the human race.* New York: Avery Books.

Prentice, A., Hennig, B. J., & Fulford, A. J. (2008). Evolutionary origins of the obesity epidemic: Natural selection of thrifty genes or genetic drift following predation release? *International Journal of Obesity, 32*, 1607–1610.

Prentice, A., Rayco-Solon, P., & Moore, S. (2005). Insights from the developing world: Thrifty genotypes and thrifty phenotypes. *Proceedings of the Nutrition Society, 64*, 153–161.

Ransom, R., & Sutch, R. (1977). *One kind of freedom: The economic consequences of emancipation.* Cambridge: Cambridge University Press.

Riera-Crichton, D., & Tefft, N. (2014). Macronutrients and obesity: Revisiting the calories in, calories out framework. *Economics and Human Biology, 14*, 33–49.

Riley, J. C. (1994). Height, nutrition, and mortality risk reconsidered. *Journal of Interdisciplinary History, 24*(3), 465–492.

Seidell, J. C. (1998). Dietary fat and obesity: An epidemiological perspective. *American Journal of Clinical Nutrition, 67*, 546S–550S.

Sharma, S., Zaric, G., Campbell, K., & Gilliland, J. (2014). The effect of physical activity on obesity: Evidence from the Canadian NPHS panel. *Economics and Human Biology, 14*(1), 1–21.

Sills, T., & Crawley, J. (1996). Individual difference in sugar consumption predict amphetamine-induced dopamine overflow in nucleus accumbens. *European Journal of Pharmacology, 303*, 177–181.

Silventoinen, K., Kaprio, J., Lahelma, E., & Viken, R. (2003). Assortative mating in body height, & BMI: Finnish twins, & their spouses. *American Journal of Human Biology, 15*, 620–627.

Sobal, J. (2011). The sociology of obesity. In John Cawley (Ed.), *The Oxford handbook of the social science of obesity* (pp. 105–119). Oxford: Oxford University Press.

Sorkin, J., Muller, D., & Andres, R. (1999). Longitudinal change in the heights of men and women: Consequential effects on body mass index. *Epidemiologic Reviews, 21*(2), 247–260.

Speakman, J. (2006). Thrifty genes for obesity and the metabolic syndrome—time to call off the search? *Diabetes & Vascular Disease Research, 3*(1), 7–11.

Speakman, J. (2008). Thrifty genes for obesity, an attractive but flawed idea, and an alternative perspective: The 'drifty gene' hypothesis. *International Journal of Obesity, 32*, 1611–1617.

Steckel, R. (1979). Slave height profiles from coastwise manifests. *Explorations in Economic History, 16*, 363–380.

Stevens, J., Cai, J., Pamuk, E., Williamson, D., Thun, M., & Wood, J. (1998). The effect of age on the association between body mass index and mortality. *New England Journal of Medicine, 338*(1), 1–7.

Strauss, R. (1999). Comparison of measures and self-reported weight and height in a cross sectional sample of young adolescents. *International Journal of Obesity, 23*, 904–908.

Taubes, G. (2010). *Why we get fat: And what to do about it.* New York: Anchor Books.

Taubes, G. (2012). World view: Treat obesity as physiology, not physics. *Nature, 492*, 155.

Teff, K., Elliott, S., Tschöp, M., Kieffer, T., Rader, D., Heiman, M., . . . Havel, P. (2004). Dietary fructose reduces circulating insulin and leptin, attenuates postprandial suppression of ghrelin, and increases triglycerides in women. *Journal of Clinical Endocrinology & Metabolism, 89*, 2963–2972.

Tovée M. J., Maisey D. S., Emery, J. L., & Cornelissen, P. L. (1999). Visual cues to female attractiveness. *Proceedings of the Royal Society, 266B*, 211–218.

Van Dam, R. M., & Seidell, J. C. (2007). Carbohydrate intake and obesity. *European Journal of Clinical Nutrition, 61*, S75–S99.

Waaler, H. (1984). Height, weight, and mortality: The Norwegian experience. *Acta Medica Scandinavica, 215*(679), 1–56.

Wang, C., Orleans, T., & Gortmaker, S. (2012). Reaching the Healthy People goals for reducing childhood obesity. *American Journal of Preventive Medicine, 42*, 437–444.

Wells, J. (2003). The thrifty phenotype hypothesis: Thrifty offspring or thrifty mother? *Journal of Theoretical Biology, 221*(1), 143–161.

CHAPTER 7

HEALTH, BODY WEIGHT, AND OBESITY

DARIUS N. LAKDAWALLA AND JULIAN REIF

7.1 Introduction

The recent rise in obesity has generated enormous popular interest and policy concern in developed countries, where it has become a major health problem. Although obesity is most often conceived of as a problem of public health or personal attractiveness, it is very much an economic issue, one of behavior in response to incentives (Cawley, 2011). The stubbornness of obesity's rise owes itself in large part to several incentives promoting weight gain.

The most basic incentives are prices and income, both of which play an important role in the determination of food intake and body weight. Although prices and income vary considerably across the population, they both display clear long-run trends. The relative price of food has declined consistently over time, while incomes have risen. The former trend tends to increase food intake and weight, while the latter trend has a variety of competing effects. Yet there appears to be little doubt that, in developed countries, body weight has been rising consistently and continues to do so (Komlos & Brabec, 2011).

The increase in body weight has triggered considerable concern due to the wealth of evidence that higher than average body weight is positively related to mortality risk. In general, there appears to be a U-shaped relationship between mortality risk and height-adjusted body weight. Patients whose weights fall below a particular threshold or above a particular threshold appear to have higher mortality risks compared to those in the middle. The literature on this subject is voluminous, but a few studies serve as representative and widely cited examples from the United States. For example, Lew and Garfinkel (1979) report on a long-term prospective study of 750,000 nationally representative men and women followed from 1959 to 1972. They find that mortality was lowest among those of average weight and that mortality risk appeared to rise as weight moved further away from average. Their results confirmed an earlier US-based study, known as the *Build and Blood Pressure Study 1959*, conducted by the Society of Actuaries, that found similar results (Society of Actuaries, 1959).

Economists have devoted attention to understanding the causes of the increase in body weight and more generally the determinants of variation in body weight. Various theories of body weight increase have been developed and tested and their implications for welfare analyzed. Not surprisingly, economists have focused in particular on the role of prices—for food and for physical activity—along with the role of income. In addition, the effects of complementary human capital and other health behaviors—for example, smoking—have been analyzed. In this chapter, we review the theoretical and empirical contributions of economists in explaining how body weight is determined and the implications for welfare. We highlight areas in which the evidence is conclusive and map out regions that are still lacking in solid evidence.

It seems clear that price matters. Reductions in the price of food, coupled with increases in the economic cost of physical activity, appear to have played a causal role in weight growth. There is also some evidence that smoking cessation has played a secondary role in driving up weight among a modest segment of the population. In addition, economists have noted how social interactions and cognitive biases have reinforced and magnified these fundamental price effects.

Our chapter is laid out as follows. We begin by characterizing the essential economic theory of body weight, along with appropriate citations to the studies that have developed these ideas. We then turn to the question of what explains the rise in body weight, with a focus on five issues: food prices, exercise, income, social interactions, and cigarette consumption.

7.2 Theory

7.2.1 Factors Affecting Weight

7.2.1.1 *Food Prices*

From a theoretical point of view, the role of food prices is fairly clear. Decreases in the relative price of food will tend to increase food intake and thus body weight. However, the situation becomes more complex when we consider the many different kinds and types of food. For instance, decreases in the relative price of food compared to housing ought to lead to higher food intake. But what if this decline is triggered primarily by reductions in the price of leafy green vegetables? And what if the declines in the price of these goods are much greater than corresponding declines in the price of sugary snacks?

The possibility of non-zero cross-price elasticities creates a number of challenges for researchers. First and most simply, a reduction in the price of one type of food may be accompanied by relative increases in the prices of other types of food. Therefore, the net impact on body weight depends on whether the intake of one food rises by more than the intake of the other falls. This is not just a problem of cross-price elasticities, but also one of the multidimensional nature of food.

The cross-price elasticity problem is thrown into sharpest relief when one thinks about the consumption of specific foods as a set of derived demands. Suppose, for instance, that an individual has a stable demand for calories, fat, sugars, vitamins, and so on. If true, there is a natural compensating mechanism that blunts the impact of food price changes on body weight and health. If the price of ice cream rises, the individual will naturally seek to fill her demand for fat through other types of foods. One can expect unambiguous effects on nutrient intake only when all fatty foods covary in price; however, this is extremely unlikely to be the case.

The general theme of compensating behavior recurs in the study of food price changes and body weight. There is no question that own-price elasticities are negative, sometimes substantially so; it is less clear that price changes happen uniformly across broad enough food groups so as to effect changes in total nutrient intake. The role of compensating behavior adds another layer of complexity atop the usual problems of simultaneity and identification.

7.2.1.2 *Exercise Levels*

All else equal, increases in exercise levels lead to weight loss. People tend to lose weight when the level of energy they expend exceeds the energy they ingest in the form of nutrition. However, changes in body weight are not quite as simple as the difference between energy intake and output because the human body tends to compensate for short-term energy imbalance by adjusting basal metabolic rate. Therefore, short-term energy "surpluses" may not result in weight gain and vice-versa. This ability to compensate has limits because basal metabolic rate cannot fall arbitrarily. When limits are reached, weight change occurs.

Clinically, there is some metabolic cost of living to the next period, even with minimal exercise levels. For example, the average resting metabolic rate for a 150-pound man is about 1,500 calories per day (Wilson et al., 1991). However, it is important to recognize that the precise quantitative relationship between calorie intake, exercise, and weight is not a purely mechanical one. Simple mechanical models of calorie intake related to weight considerably overstate the effect of calories on weight because excess calorie intake can be partially metabolized away before weight rises. According to Wilson et al. (1991), "When normal subjects consume hypercaloric diets, less weight is gained than would be predicted on the basis of the excess calories ingested . . . humans can apparently partially adapt to chronic excessive carbohydrate and protein intake, and this protective effect attenuates the weight gain. Part of this adaptive response is related to an increase in . . . the resting metabolic rate." Nonetheless, although the quantitative relationship may not be a mechanical one that is fully determined by thermodynamics, sustained increases in exercise will typically lead to weight loss, all else equal.

7.2.1.3 *Preferences, Health, and Ideal Body Weight*

From an economic perspective, decisions about body weight depend on more than just health. Individuals each have a concept of "ideal" body weight. Conceptually, economists define "ideal" body weight as the weight an individual would choose if altering body weight were costless. Given that weight change is indeed costly, actual body weight will not generally coincide with ideal body weight. However, all else equal, increases in ideal body weight will tend to raise actual body weight and vice-versa.

Economists have made the point that ideal body weight need not be the same as the optimal body weight for health and longevity. Other considerations like social norms and individual preferences for beauty may play a role as well. From a policy perspective, the key point is that, even in the absence of costless weight change, rational individuals may not choose an optimally healthy body weight (Lakdawalla & Philipson, 2009; Philipson & Posner, 2003).

Although health is not the only factor driving the preference for ideal body weight, it almost surely plays a role in some cases. As such, the "demand for health" manifests as a demand for "closeness" to ideal body weight. To appreciate this point, imagine an individual whose subjectively ideal body weight is exactly equal to the optimally healthy body weight. Moving closer to this ideal body weight increases utility and can be thought of as the "good" associated with body weight. In a standard utility-maximization framework, this "good" is normal, in the sense that richer people will choose to expend more resources to move closer to their ideal body weight. This dynamic also creates a positive relationship between education, which raises permanent income, and closeness to ideal body weight (Lakdawalla & Philipson, 2009).

Economists have not so far devoted attention to the issue of how subjectively ideal body weight is determined, although education provides a useful example of how such analysis might be valuable. Subjectively ideal body weight may itself be a decision that results from individuals weighing the relative importance of appearance, health, and other more fundamental goods that are influenced by body weight. Characteristics that increase the return to good health—such as higher levels of education—may move subjectively ideal body weight closer to the optimally healthy body weight. On the other hand, characteristics that increase the return to attractive appearance—such as being single or living in a market with more desirable mates—may move subjectively ideal body weight toward a more attractive level that may or may not coincide with optimal health.

7.2.1.4 *Social Interactions*

Activities such as eating and exercising are social in the sense that consumer utility depends on the consumption habits of other people in the consumer's social group. Social interactions can arise in these contexts for a number of different reasons. Eating and exercising are often more enjoyable in the company of others. The probability that a consumer decides to go to a restaurant instead of eating at home may depend on whether a friend accompanies her. Deciding how much food to order may depend on what other people order.

The precise effect of social interactions on consumption often depends on the assumed functional relationship between the group and the individual. Two common parametric specifications are *proportional spillovers*, in which individual utility is increasing linearly in the mean consumption of the group, and *conformity*, which greatly penalizes an individual's consumption that deviates far from the mean.

Brock and Durlauf (2001) show that proportional spillovers and conformity result in identical behavior when the individual's consumption choice is discrete. They also prove that multiple equilibria are possible. For example, suppose consumers are deciding whether or not to exercise. Their decisions depend both on their own preferences and on the decisions of the other members in their social groups. In the model derived by Brock and Durlauf, there can exist one equilibrium in which many members of a social group exercise frequently and another equilibrium in which only a few exercise.

Reif (2014) shows that these two types of social interactions generate disparate effects on aggregate consumption when the consumer faces a continuous rather than a discrete choice. Conformity, a desire to consume at the same level as others, reduces the dispersion of consumption within a group by discouraging individual heterogeneity. Thus, it increases the consumption of some individuals and reduces the consumption of others. By contrast, spillovers increase everyone's consumption. This latter model (but not the former) provides a possible explanation for why the recent increase in obesity has been so rapid. Even a moderate amount of social interactions can greatly amplify the effect of changes in factors that affect obesity, such as a reduction in the price of food.

7.2.2 Effect of Income on Weight

Theoretically, there are several channels of causality running from income to body weight. The first is the standard effect that operates on food as a normal good. Richer people have more to spend on food and all other goods. By itself, this would imply that richer people are always heavier than poorer people.

The actual variation in body weight across income groups rarely matches this pattern; additional causal mechanisms are thus required. Another salient mechanism is the demand for health and attractiveness. Just like food, health and appearance are likely to be normal goods. It is interesting to ask how preferences for appearance are formed, but for our purposes, we can take as given the preference for a slender build, at least in Western countries. As a result, richer people might choose to purchase more attractiveness or health in the form of weight control or weight reduction. Coupled with the pure income effects on food intake and weight, the result is a possibly nonmonotonic relationship between income and weight determined by the competing interaction between the demand for food and the demands for health and appearance (Lakdawalla & Philipson, 2009).

A final issue to consider is the manner in which income is earned. The arguments presented earlier fully summarize the impacts of unearned income on weight, but the effect of earned income reflects both the income itself and the nature of the work that was done to earn the income. Earning income through participation in a sedentary job is likely to generate a positive relationship between income and weight, whereas participation in an active job will do the opposite (Lakdawalla & Philipson, 2009).

These different effects help make sense of the differing relationships between income and weight within and between countries. Richer countries tend to be heavier than poorer countries, whereas richer women are often thinner than poorer women in developed countries. The nature of work will tend to vary more across countries than within countries. Therefore, richer countries might be more likely to engage in sedentary jobs than are poorer countries: this may help explain the strength of the relationship between income and weight. On the other hand, it is less clear that a rich American executive has a systematically more sedentary job than a poor American retail clerk. Across these groups, the relevant underlying differences that may lead to differences in weight are the demand for food and the competing demands for health and appearance (Lakdawalla & Philipson, 2009).

7.3 What Explains the Rise in Obesity?

7.3.1 Measuring Obesity

Obesity is defined as a condition of excessive body fat accumulation (World Health Organization, 2000). Most individuals do not know their body fat levels, and measuring it properly requires using clinical instruments, so obesity is a difficult characteristic for surveys to measure. Instead, most social science surveys report an individual's body mass index (BMI), which is calculated as weight in kilograms divided by height in meters squared. This is an appealing measure because most individuals know their weight and height and can self-report them, thus obviating the need and expense associated with hiring a medical professional.

There are two main shortcomings of employing self-reported BMI as a measure of obesity. First, individuals may not report truthfully their height and weight. Ezzati, Martin, et al. (2006) find that women under-report their weight, and both men and women over-report their height. This bias is larger in telephone interviews than in in-person interviews.

A second, larger shortcoming is that BMI is an imperfect proxy for body fat. (Burkhauser & Cawley, 2008) use the National Health and Nutrition Examination Survey (NHANES) to show that BMI does a poor job of measuring obesity defined using more accurate measures such as total body fat and percent body fat. For example, when they define obesity using percent body fat instead of BMI, the calculated prevalence of obesity in the NHANES population more than doubles.

Because most surveys lack an alternative measure to BMI, there is little research available indicating how important this measurement problem is for empirical studies. One exception is Wada and Tekin (2010), who argue that the mixed findings on the effect of obesity on labor market outcomes is attributable to using BMI as a measure of obesity. Using data from NHANES, they obtain two separate measures of obesity: excess body fat, which is associated with poor health, and fat-free mass, which is associated with good health. They go on to show that excess body fat is correlated with decreased wages, but fat-free mass is correlated with increased wages. BMI, by contrast, cannot distinguish between these two types of body fat, and thus the authors argue that it is fundamentally ill-suited to the task of determining the effect of obesity on wages.

Unfortunately, it is difficult to avoid this measurement error problem because few surveys contain measures of obesity other than BMI. This problem is likely greatest when employing BMI to estimate the effects of obesity on different outcomes of interest because measurement error in independent variables causes attenuation bias. Employing BMI may be less of a problem when estimating the determinants of obesity because measurement error in the dependent variable often only causes reduced precision.

7.3.2 Food Prices

7.3.2.1 *Endogeneity and Measurement Issues*

Typically, researchers are interested in recovering the demand for food and, by extension, the demand for body weight. This requires identifying the impact of movement along the demand curve (how quantity demanded varies with price). The exogeneity of food prices is an important identification challenge faced by such an approach. Food prices might be higher in areas with higher demand for food and during periods with higher demand for food. Both these examples would result in the classic form of simultaneity bias that exerts downward pressure on estimated coefficients; shifts in the demand curve become entangled with movements along it. Naturally, these biases presume that part of the observed variation in price is driven by demand. Pure supply-driven price variation results in clean identification using standard regression methods. Unfortunately, demand for food and body weight are unlikely to be homogeneous. Variation might occur due to differences in socioeconomic status or the underlying demand for health.

The most common approach to identification is to control for area and time fixed-effects in panel data (Greene, 2011). This approach presumes fixed differences in demand across regions or fixed aggregate differences in demand across time periods. This strategy is threatened by differing local time trends in demand. For instance, if demand is rising faster in southern states than northern states, then the differences between regions are not fixed over time; this invalidates the area fixed-effects approach. Moreover, the trends over time are not common across all areas; this invalidates the period fixed-effect approach. In principle, one could address these concerns by including local time trends within the empirical model, but this approach is sensitive to the specification used.

A more robust but much more difficult approach is to instrument for food prices. This requires identifying a factor that influences the supply of food, but not the demand for food. One seemingly natural candidate is the cost of transporting food across areas, but this candidate illustrates one of the difficulties with this approach: the cost of transporting food may be correlated with the cost of exercise (e.g., areas with extensive roads might attract populations more inclined to commute from outlying suburbs than to walk to work).

In spite of the difficulties, several instruments have been proposed in the literature. One candidate is the proximity of interstate highways, which is argued to affect the distribution of fast food and other restaurants (Anderson & Matsa, 2011). The local average treatment effect in this case is specific to the impact of restaurants, although this in itself is an important policy question. This instrument has been shown to pass a variety of validity tests. The weakness is the relatively small size of the effect of interstate location on restaurant utilization. Alternatively, Lakdawalla and Philipson (2002) propose the use of relative food taxes as an instrument for the relative price of food. Specifically, this approach exploits differences across states in the decision to exempt food from sales taxation. Tax exemption lowers the relative price of food to consumers, compared to nonexempt states. The drawback to using this approach is the absence of significant changes over time in tax-exemption policies within states. As a result, relative taxes fail to vary much over time within a state. This precludes the use of state fixed-effects in combination with the instrument and sacrifices the ability to test for the possibility that tax-exempt states have systematically different demands for food and body weight compared to nonexempt states.

A final approach, suitable for panel data, exploits dynamic panel data analysis methods (Greene, 2011). These models can partially address the simultaneity issue by controlling for lagged dependent variables. The identifying assumption here is that heterogeneity across individuals (or areas) is well captured by variation in the last period's weight or food intake. Although this is a fairly easy solution to implement, it is only a partial solution to the problem of unobserved heterogeneity because it does not address the deeper problem of identifying exogenous, supply-driven variation in prices. For this reason, an instrumental variable (or plausible fixed-effects) approach is required.

In sum, there are a number of possible approaches to identification, but all suffer from one or more key weaknesses. Nonetheless, the collage of evidence pieced together from different identification strategies can still be informative, as we will argue.

7.3.2.2 *Measurement Challenges*

On top of the identification issues, the measurement of food prices is not straightforward. The first challenge is posed by the multidimensional nature of food. There are hundreds of food items that vary in taste, nutrition values, and energy density. Moreover, variation in the nutritional composition of foods may significantly alter their influence on body weight (Riera-Crichton & Tefft, 2014). It is not feasible to include the prices of each food item in an analysis. The common strategy is to construct a composite food price index that represents a group of food items. Such price indices include prices for all food items, prices for fast food, prices for full-service restaurants, and prices for food at home. But using such food indices assumes that the price effects on body weight are the same across different food items, which is not true for a number of reasons.

First, different food items might have different effects on weight. Even if lettuce and butter make up equal expenditure shares in a consumer's food basket, it is hard to argue that a fixed change in the price of lettuce has the same impact as a similarly sized change in the price of butter. One way to overcome this issue is to place more weight on foods that have larger impacts on body weight by constructing an index of price per calorie. This approach implicitly places more weight on calorie-dense foods, for which a given change in intake should have a larger impact on body weight (Goldman, Lakdawalla, & Zheng, 2009).

However, any approach to aggregation suffers from the need to make uniform assumptions about the composition of consumption. Individuals vary in their food intake, and this variation is systematically related to weight. If heavier people eat more calorically dense foods, any index approach will tend to understate the effect of a change in the price of such foods on the heavy and overstate the effects on the light. An alternative approach is to split the index into components and avoid the problems associated with constructing an index. One way of implementing this approach is to include prices for a few key foods—for example, fruits and vegetables, milk, and meats. Forming price indices within these more homogeneous groups may pose less of a problem because prices within these groups tend to co-vary and the effects on weight may be similar. Various studies have implemented this by focusing on "high-calorie" versus "low-calorie foods" or "healthy" versus "unhealthy" food groups (Gelbach, Klick, & Stratmann, 2007; Miljkovic, Nganje, & de Chastenet, 2008; Powell, 2009; Powell & Bao, 2009; Powell & Chaloupka, 2009; Sturm & Datar, 2005, 2008). A key validity issue is whether or not these groups are in fact homogeneous in terms of price changes and effects on weight. In addition, omitted prices for other types of food might be correlated both with prices for the included food groups and with body weight.

The second issue is measurement error in food prices themselves. The most frequently used food price data is the American Chamber of Commerce Researchers Association (ACCRA) Cost of Living Index reports, which provide quarterly information on prices in approximately 300 U. cities (Auld & Powell, 2009; Beydoun, Powell, & Wang, 2008; Chou, Grossman, & Saffer, 2004; Goldman et al., 2009; Lakdawalla & Philipson, 2002; Powell, 2009; Powell & Bao, 2009; Powell & Chaloupka, 2009; Powell, Zhao, & Wang, 2009; Sturm & Datar, 2005, 2008). Some studies used regional food prices provided by Bureau of Labor Statistics (Gelbach et al., 2007). The US Department of Agriculture (USDA) provides prices for agricultural products at the state level (Miljkovic et al., 2008). Regardless of the source, measured prices almost always diverge from the prices that particular individuals face in their community. The result is downward bias in the estimated effects of food prices; this reinforces the typical simultaneity bias caused by poor identification.

A recent attempt to overcome the measurement issue is a USDA-sponsored project to link the NHANES to local food prices. The idea is to link NHANES data at a disaggregated geographic level to supermarket scanner data on food prices in a local community.

One advantage of the NHANES-USDA project is the availability of dietary recall data, laboratory measures of nutrient availability, and objective measures of body mass. This makes for an exceptionally rich database that allows researchers to link prices to food intake, nutrient intake, and body weight. However, the limitations of the NHANES illustrate the inherent tradeoffs of doing research on body weight and food prices. Due in part to the extremely burdensome nature of the survey, NHANES respondents are not followed longitudinally nor are the samples as large as one finds in studies like the National Health Interview Survey (NHIS), which relies entirely on self-reported data on health-related variables.

7.3.2.3 *Empirical Findings*

There is a substantial literature linking food prices and body weight. Here, we review 14 important examples drawn from this literature.

7.3.2.3.1 *Effects in Children*

We surveyed six studies examining the association between food prices and body weight among children and adolescents (Auld & Powell, 2009; Powell, 2009, Powell & Bao, 2009; Powell & Chaloupka, 2009; Sturm & Datar 2005, 2008). All of these studies relied on food price data from the same source: the ACCRA Cost of Living Index, discussed earlier. As a result, all are subject to the typical measurement concerns surrounding the ACCRA data, and indeed, all geographical food price data.

Apart from the similarity in the measurement of prices, however, these studies took a number of different empirical approaches. In particular, these studies run the gamut of fixed-effects, random effects, and repeated cross-section methods. A generic concern in the analysis of body weight data is unobserved heterogeneity across individuals in the propensity to gain weight. Unfortunately, all three approaches are imperfect solutions to the problem. Repeated cross-section methods impose the least general assumptions by presuming that all individual-specific unobservables are uncorrelated with the model's variables of interest. The random effects method weakens these slightly, but imposes distributional assumptions on how the unobserved heterogeneity varies. The fixed-effect approach involves the most general assumption by allowing each individual to have a unique and idiosyncratic level of weight; however, in most applications, the fixed-effects approaches used cannot cope with heterogeneity in the propensity to gain weight. This would amount to a fixed-effects model in first-differences of body weight.

Auld and Powell used repeated cross-sectional data of the Monitoring the Future Survey to examine how fast food price and price of fruits and vegetables are associated with adolescent BMI and overweight status (Auld & Powell, 2009). Although the repeated cross-sectional nature of the data limited them in some respects, the use of quantile regression methods was an important contribution to this literature. The study demonstrated that fast food price was negatively related to BMI and overweight status, whereas fruit and vegetable prices were positively related to BMI but not statistically significantly associated with overweight status. The quantile regressions demonstrated that the effects were much larger in the top quintile of the conditional distribution of BMI. This latter effect suggests the most price-sensitivity in the portion of the distribution that policy makers often seek to target.

The fixed-effects studies relied on several different panel datasets. One study analyzed four waves of the National Longitudinal Survey of Youth (NLSY; 1997–2000) using individual fixed-effects models and found that, among adolescents aged 12–17, the price of fast food was negatively associated with BMI (elasticity of −0.078), whereas the relationship between price of food at home and BMI was statistically insignificant (Powell, 2009). A second study analyzed two waves of the Child Development Supplement of the Panel Study of Income Dynamics (1997 and 2002–2003), using ordinary least squares (OLS) and individual fixed-effects models. Price of fruits and vegetables was found to be positively correlated with higher BMI percentile in both OLS and fixed-effects estimations. Price of fast food, however, was not statistically significantly related to children's BMI (Powell & Chaloupka, 2009). Finally, two studies used the Childhood Longitudinal Survey to examine the effects of prices for fruits and vegetables, and meats, on the change in child BMI. Fruit and vegetable prices were found to be positively associated with 1-year, 3-year, or 5-year BMI change among children, whereas meat prices exhibited statistically insignificant effects (Sturm & Datar, 2005, 2008).

Finally, the one study employing random effects found qualitatively similar results to an analogous fixed-effects study. Powell and Bao analyzed three waves of the child–mother merged files from the 1979 cohort of the NLSY (Powell & Bao, 2009). Their findings resemble the earlier results of (Powell & Chaloupka, 2009).

Overall, the literature finds evidence that higher prices of fast food depress body weight, but higher prices for fruits and vegetables may have the opposite effect. There is also some evidence that price effects are most pronounced in the upper reaches of the BMI distribution. However, simultaneity is a problem in nearly all of these studies: if changes in body weight cause changes in food demand and prices, the estimates in this literature are not causal. Moreover, heterogeneity in the propensity to gain weight is also a concern.

7.3.2.3.2 *Effects in Adults*

We also surveyed seven studies examining food price effects for adults. Three of these attempted instrumental variables approaches to the simultaneity problem, while the remainder employed a mix of panel data and OLS approaches.

Chou, Grossman, and Saffer (2004) authored perhaps the earliest peer-reviewed study in this area. They relied on repeated cross-sectional data from the 1984–1999 Behavioral Risk Factor Surveillance System (BRFSS) combined with ACCRA price data aggregated at the state level. They find that fast food prices, prices at full-service restaurants, and prices for food at home were all negatively related to adult BMI and obesity status, with price elasticities for BMI equal to −0.048, −0.021, and −0.039, respectively. The Chou et al. study allowed for fixed-effects at the geographic level, but individual fixed-effects were not possible with the data used.

Another study used the cross-sectional data of the Continuing Survey of Food Intakes by adults aged 20–65 and found that BMI was negatively associated with price of fruits and vegetables, but the effect of fast food prices on BMI was statistically insignificant. Neither price index was statistically significantly associated with obesity status (Beydoun et al., 2008). This paper is largely in agreement, or at least fails to reject, the earlier work of Chou et al.

The last study in this vein investigated how the prices of three representative food items—sugar, potatoes, and milk—were related to BMI using repeated cross-sectional data of the BRFSS (1991, 1997, and 2002). The authors found that the obesity status of adults was positively associated with the price of potatoes, but negatively associated with the prices of sugar and of milk (Miljkovic et al., 2008). Although this study is somewhat hard to interpret, it represents a nice example of the difficulties associated with analyzing the prices of individual foods. Results may vary with the particular foods that are included and excluded. For example, what basket of foods does the price of potatoes most faithfully represent?

One study in this genre to use both individual fixed-effects and dynamic panel data methods is that of Goldman et al. (2009). They apply dynamic panel data methods to panel data from the 1992–2004 Health and Retirement Study (HRS) linked to ACCRA price data. Moreover, Goldman et al. also constructed indices of price per calorie, using representative baskets of food consumption. They found that increases in price per calorie were negatively associated with BMI among Americans aged 50 and older (the sample frame of the HRS). Moreover, the effects differed over the time horizon studied: price elasticity was −0.06 in the short term and −0.42 in the long term, where the long term spanned more than 30 years. This dataset allowed for heterogeneity across individuals in their propensity to gain weight but not for the endogeneity in food prices changes. Moreover, it is also limited to older adults.

At least three other studies used instrumental variables approaches to address the simultaneity problem in food prices and body weight. One recent study used the proximity of interstate highways as the instrument for effective food price at restaurants and found no causal relationship between restaurant price and obesity (Anderson & Matsa, 2011). The validity argument presented in favor of this instrument is quite compelling, but the first-stage treatment effect is relatively modest. Proximity to interstate highways has a relatively small impact on restaurant patronage; it is thus hard to know whether restaurant availability has no effect or whether the effects are not large enough to be detectable, given the size of the first-stage effect.

A second study used regional price of unleaded gasoline as the instrument for the regional relative price of healthy food (Gelbach et al., 2007). Both BMI and obesity status were positively related to relative price of healthy food, with a price elasticity of 0.01. This study is subject to concerns about validity because gasoline prices might also affect the cost of transportation and of exercise.

Finally, Lakdawalla and Philipson (2002) used state-level relative food taxes as an instrument for the relative price of food and found a negative and large effect of relative food price on BMI (elasticity of −0.6) among young adults. However, the lack of time-series variation in the relative taxes imposed on food prevents the use of any fixed-effect design; as a result, this study is vulnerable to area-specific or individual-specific heterogeneity that persists in the local average treatment effect.

A final, somewhat unique study estimated how the minimum wage affected adult BMI using the repeated cross-sectional data of the BRFSS 1984–2006 and historical federal and state minimum wage data from the Bureau of Labor Statistics (Meltzer & Chen, 2011). The authors hypothesized that minimum wage would be associated with body weight because minimum-wage labor is a major input into the production of restaurant food and fast food. The authors conclude that a $1 decrease in the real minimum wage is associated with a 0.06 unit increase in BMI. This study is both intriguing and compelling, but it is somewhat hard to translate into the context of the larger discussion about food prices without further information about how much the minimum wage affects food prices.

The literature on adults somewhat clouds the issue of whether and to what extent changes in the price of restaurant food and fast food affect body weight. Anderson and Matsa (2011) is a well-conceived instrumental variables study arguing for no effect, but this may be due to a modest treatment effect. Most of the other studies in this literature seem to agree that high restaurant prices reduce body weight, although none has a design robust to the simultaneity issues that Anderson and Matsa emphasize.

However, most of the literature does seem to agree that broad-based increases in food prices tend to reduce body weight, as we would expect. The effects of prices for specific foods, however, remain much less certain. This is likely due to the intractable empirical problem of omitted variables because it is fundamentally impossible to measure every dimension along which food prices vary.

7.3.2.3.3 *Effects by Body Weight Status*

One question that arises is whether or not the effects of prices vary across particular subpopulations. For example, Auld and Powell applied quantile regression methods to examine how food price effects vary across the body weight distribution (Auld & Powell, 2009). Meltzer and Chen used similar methods to investigate how the effects of the minimum wage on body weight vary by weight distribution (Meltzer & Chen, 2011). Both studies show that the effects, in terms of units of BMI, are larger at the upper tail of the BMI distribution. Because BMI is detrimental to health only when it is extremely low or high, such results would indicate that food price policies (either tax or subsidy) could be most effective among those who are obese.

However, identification issues remain to be addressed. Although useful, both studies rely on cross-sectional methods. Using quantile regression in fixed-effects models or combining quantile regression with instrumental variable approach is both more robust and more challenging because the corresponding methodologies are not well-developed yet.

7.3.2.3.4 *Effects by Socioeconomic Status*

An additional issue is whether the effects of food price on body weight vary by socioeconomic status. At least five studies have attempted to address this question (Averett & Smith, 2014; Beydoun et al., 2008; Powell, 2009; Powell & Bao, 2009; Powell & Chaloupka, 2009). One study (Beydoun et al., 2008) conducted separate analyses for adults grouped by Poverty Income Ratio (PIR). The effects of the price of fruits and vegetables on BMI or obesity status were the largest among those near poor (PIR between 131 and 299) relative to those who were poor (PIR between 0 and 130) or nonpoor (PIR 300 or more). However, it is unknown whether these effects were statistically different from each other. The fifth study examines whether financial hardship affects obesity risk and finds little evidence to support a causal relationship from financial hardship to obesity (Averett & Smith, 2014).

The other three studies, examining food price effects among children or adolescents, stratified analyses by mother's education or family income level. It was found that the food price effects were greatest for the group with mother's education of high school or less relative to the group with mother's education of some college and above (Powell, 2009; Powell & Bao, 2009). In addition, the low- or middle- income group was more price sensitive than the high-income group (Powell, 2009; Powell & Bao, 2009; Powell & Chaloupka, 2009). However, again, there was no statistical test of whether the estimates from stratified analysis were different from each other. Nonetheless, taking the results at face value suggests that the poorest groups are most price responsive.

7.3.3 Technologies that Subvert Self-Control

Some researchers have noted that a substantial share of Americans' caloric intake has come from snacks consumed between meals. The cause of this increase is hypothesized to be increases in the availability of prepared foods. In particular, Cutler, Glaeser, and Shapiro (2003) argue that improvements in food processing technology have led to substantial increases in the availability of ready-made foods. The resulting decrease in the cost of meal production at home has thus led to an increase in the number of meals (most notably snacks) but not necessarily an increase in the number of calories consumed per meal. In particular, Cutler et al. interpret this phenomenon as the result of decreased fixed costs of preparing meals. Furthermore, they note that the types of foods with the biggest increases in consumption are those that have enjoyed the greatest rate of technological progress in processing.

In principle, the decline in the cost of preparing meals will lead to weight gain for rational, utility-maximizing individuals. Cutler et al. emphasize an additional explanation beyond the pricing effect. Specifically, they argue that high fixed costs of food preparation serve as a commitment device for individuals who lack self-control, in the sense of making time-inconsistent decisions. They argue that this additional feature explains why the biggest increases in weight appear in the right tail of the body weight distribution—specifically, the argument is that those who are the heaviest must also have the least self-control and are thus the most susceptible to innovations that subvert commitment devices.

It is difficult to test the self-control theory directly because many of its implications cannot be easily disentangled from neoclassical theory. Indeed, standard price theory suggests that the heaviest consumers of a product might also respond the most to a given reduction in price because the income effect will be stronger. Thus, even the distributional effects may not unambiguously document the presence of a self-control explanation.

The difficulties of testing it notwithstanding, if one accepts the self-control explanation, several striking welfare implications emerge. In the neoclassical framework, reductions in the fixed cost of food preparation lead to weight gain but unambiguous improvements in welfare. In other words, it is optimal to weigh more when fixed costs are lower. On the other hand, reductions in fixed costs in the presence of self-control problems can worsen welfare. An individual with a self-control problem will pay for a device that imposes external controls (e.g., a time lock on a refrigerator). Thus, the reduction in the cost of food preparation is like leaving the refrigerator unlocked for longer periods of time; this is costly to the individual with self-control problems. This cost must then be offset against the standard welfare benefits of price declines. The net effect on welfare may be either positive or negative.

7.3.4 Exercise

7.3.4.1 *Endogeneity and Measurement*

Measuring the causal effect of exercise on body weight faces several challenges. The first is the lack of precise measures of exercise in many databases. To deal with this issue, people have relied on categorical measures of strenuousness, including physical demands of jobs and the physical strenuousness of typical exercise.

Endogeneity issues also appear because overweight people are less likely to exercise. The solutions proposed to this problem have included analysis of longitudinal data that demonstrates people with greater exercise levels gain less weight over time and randomized trials of exercise participation programs.

7.3.4.2 *Empirical Findings*

Economists have demonstrated that variation in the costs and levels of exercise tends to produce the predicted effect on weight. For example, Lakdawalla and Philipson (2007) demonstrate that time spent in more strenuous jobs leads to weight loss, relative to the same amount of time spent in more sedentary jobs. These differences are quantitatively quite significant—perhaps not surprising, given the amount of time that full-time workers spend at their jobs. Using the NLSY, they conclude that after 18 years on the job, men in the most physically demanding occupations are about 25 pounds (or 14%) lighter than men in the least physically demanding occupations.

Rashad (2006) tackles the fundamental question of whether exercise and food intake effects can be identified in real-world data. Using structural estimation methods and the NHANES, she shows that increases in net caloric intake—that is, caloric intake adjusted for exercise—increase body weight. This effect is deceptively difficult to recover in real-world data because thin, highly active people will tend to consume more calories and thus confound a simple regression analysis of calories and body weight.

A related question central to the economics literature on body weight is whether and to what extent manipulating financial incentives can change exercise patterns. Charness and Gneezy show that, at least in the short-term, financial incentives to exercise lead both to an increase in the incentivized exercise activity and a net overall increase in exercise activity (Charness & Gneezy, 2009). However, the generalized and long-term effects of financial incentives for exercise are mixed at best. For example, Cawley and Price find evidence of very modest effects associated with employer-based incentives for weight loss, which includes both effects on exercise and calorie intake (Cawley & Price, 2013). The latter result is particularly instructive because even modest increases in physical activity—about 100 kilocalories per day, equivalent to a 15-minute walk—would be enough to reverse the rapid growth in US obesity (Hill, Wyatt, Reed, & Peters, 2003). Indeed, this suggests that changing behavior by means of targeted financial incentives is quite difficult.

7.3.5 Income

7.3.5.1 *Endogeneity and Measurement Issues*

The effects of income on weight are theoretically ambiguous because both food and closeness to ideal body weight are normal goods. The former generates a positive relationship between income and body weight, whereas the latter generates a negative relationship for the overweight.

Adding to the theoretical complexity are the empirical challenges of identifying the causal impact of income on body weight. Clearly, there are a number of unobserved third factors that could influence both income and body weight: unobserved human capital, rate of time preference, or baseline energy and metabolism. All these factors create problems of interpretation for simple correlations between income and weight. Although these issues are fairly well understood, there are few obvious candidates for valid identification strategies. As a result, identification of the causal impact of income on weight remains a somewhat open question. In the following discussion, we summarize what is known, given the limits of current methods, and attempt to draw some conclusions in light of the uncertainty. Moreover, as we discuss, the potentially nonmonotonic income–weight effect imposes additional identification challenges. Conclusions could depend on the functional form of income: linear, log, quadratic, categorical, or splines.

The analysis of income and body weight faces fairly typical measurement challenges that afflict many areas of economics. Self-reported income is subject to a variety of reporting errors both classical and nonclassical, even in surveys that focus heavily on the accuracy of these measures (Moore, Stinson, & Welniak, 2000).

In the particular context of body weight, this problem is exacerbated by the crudeness with which income tends to be elicited in health surveys like the NHIS, NHANES, and BRFSS. In NHIS and NHANES, two categorical family income variables are provided; one is the combined total family income based on separate questions on different sources of income, while the other is the PIR. In both NHIS 2004 and NHANES 2003–2004, there were 11 family income levels, with the lowest level of $0–4,999 and the highest of $75,000 or more. In addition, those who did not provide a specific income amount were asked whether their family income was more than $20,000. The PIR variable includes 14 levels, ranging from under 0.50 to 5.00 and over. In BRFSS 2004, one question was asked about annual household income from all sources, and the value items included eight levels, with the lowest level of $0–9,999, and the highest level of $75,000 and over.

There are some surveys, such as the HRS, specifically designed to measure income and wealth as accurately as possible, which also collect information on body weight. The HRS, for example, collects self-reported income on height and weight, although it will soon begin to collect objectively measured height and weight, thus further enhancing its value to this literature. Of course, it should be noted that the HRS samples the population over the age of 50 and thus prevents the analysis of effects on children and young adults who could, in principle, exhibit quite a different level of responsiveness to income.

7.3.5.2 *Empirical Findings*

The evidence on income also encompasses both adults and children. The literature on children can be seen as part of the larger literature on how household income affects child health. The literature on adults, in contrast, has aligned itself more closely with the particularities of body weight.

7.3.5.2.1 *Income and Child Weight*

Using pooled data from the 1997–2002 Health Surveys of England, Currie et al. (2007) found that the log of family income was not statistically associated with measured obesity status for children in England. In slight contrast, another study analyzed wave 2 (1996) and wave 3 (2001–2002) of the National Longitudinal Study of Adolescent Health, which surveyed a nationally representative sample of adolescents in the United States and found that, when controlling for age, family poverty status was positively associated with becoming obese or staying obese from wave 2 to wave 3 among females. However, the effect was not present for males, and even the female effect disappeared once parental education, family structure, and neighborhood poverty measures were included as additional control variables (Lee, Harris, & Gordon-Larsen, 2009). Hofferth and Curtin (2005) examined how family income was associated with overweight status among children aged 6–11. Using the data of 1997 Panel Study of Income Dynamics Child Development Supplement, the authors found that, relative to children of moderate household income (185–<300% poverty line), children of poor households (<100% poverty line) were less likely to be overweight and had lower BMI. Childhood overweight status and BMI of near-poor households (100–<130% poverty line), households of working-class (130–<185% poverty line), and high-income households (300% or higher poverty line) were not statistically different from those of children from moderate-income households (Hofferth & Curtin, 2005).

As a whole, the evidence suggests that income may not play an independent causal role in childhood weight above and beyond the usual suite of socioeconomic characteristics. From the latter perspective, however, low socioeconomic status seems to be associated with less healthy body weight outcomes for children.

7.3.5.2.2 *Income–Weight Patterns Among Adult Populations*

Several studies have found that income is negatively associated with body weight for women but not for men. One example is Garcia Villar and Quintana-Domeque's work; this paper examined how the log of household income was associated with BMI and obesity status for Europeans using the European Community Household Panel, a survey based on a standardized questionnaire that involves annual interviewing of a representative panel of households and individuals in member states of the European Union during 1994–2001 (García Villar & Quintana-Domeque, 2009). OLS and Probit model results showed that log of household income was negatively associated with women's BMI or obesity status in six out of nine countries and that the effects operated primarily through earned individual income. The associations between household income and men's BMI were not statistically significant for six out of the nine countries, positive for one country, and negative for the other two.

Another study on both US and European data examined how various measures of energy intake and expenditure, as well as socioeconomic status, affect obesity rates in the United States and Europe using cross-sectional data from the Survey of Health, Aging and Retirement in Europe, and the HRS in the United States (Michaud, van Soest, & Andreyeva, 2007). The study found that, controlling for wealth, income quintiles were negatively associated with obesity among females but the relationship for males was indefinite.

The differences across gender may point to a larger issue identified by a number of other studies: the nonlinearity of the body weight–income effect, as discussed earlier. Lakdawalla and Philipson (2009) examined how body weight varied with income quartiles in the United States using NHIS 1976–1994 data. An inverted U-shaped BMI–income relationship was found among American males; individuals in the bottom and the top quartiles of the income distribution had lower BMI than did those in the 2nd quartile, and average BMI peaked at the 3rd income quartile. Within females, however, the relationship was uniformly negative.

A number of other studies have focused on the nonlinearities in the relationship between income and body weight. One finds a U-shaped relationship between household income and BMI or obesity status for male and female combined using the BRFSS 1984–1999 (Chou, Grossman et al., 2004). However, within the observed income range, the relationship was negative, with an income–BMI elasticity of −0.02. The pooling across genders, however, makes it hard to directly compare this result to other examples in the literature.

Another study that stratified by sex finds an inverted U-shaped relationship between BMI and income for both males and females (Jolliffe, 2011). This study employed three cross-sections of the NHANES 1999–2004. At lower income levels, there was a positive association between income and BMI, but at higher income levels the association turned negative. The study also pointed out that the association turns negative at a lower income threshold among women. This would make it more likely to observe the negative relationship among women when estimating linear effects.

Finally, a study using the 2002 wave of HRS and the first wave of England Longitudinal Survey of Aging found that household income, measured in three categories, was negatively associated with obesity status in both the United States and England, with a steeper gradient for the United States (Banks, Marmot, Oldfield, & Smith, 2006).

A final strand of the literature examines the relationship between income and weight gain. Using the 1986–2002 data of the BRFSS, Truong and Sturm found no statistically significant association between relative income position and weight gain during the period 1986–2002 (Truong & Sturm, 2005). Another study, using the NHANES (1971–2002), found similar results (Chang & Lauderdale, 2005). Both studies correlate a household's contemporaneous position in the income distribution with body weight. This creates a difficulty of interpretation because households can switch over from the low-income to high-income groups in the data. Contemporaneous income is clearly a noisy measure of permanent income; therefore, the finding of no effect may have more to do with measurement error than with the size of the underlying parameters.

These studies do not claim to identify causal effects (nor should they). All are focused on describing the patterns in body weight across income groups. The preponderance of evidence suggests that nonlinearity is a frequent characteristic of this relationship but that, among women, the relationship is typically more negative. From a theoretical perspective, this would suggest that the demand for healthy body weight is a stronger force than the income effect on food consumption.

7.3.5.2.3 *Causal Effects of Income*

One of the very few studies to search for the causal impact of income on weight is Cawley, Moran, and Simon (2010), who exploit the "Social Security Benefit Notch" to examine the effects of Social Security income on body weight. Relative to birth cohorts born before 1915 or after 1917, Americans born from 1915 to 1917 received extra Social Security benefits due to a quirk in the benefit calculation formula. There is thus a discrete break in benefit amounts across cohorts visible in the time series. The validity of the instrument seems quite plausible, although questions have been raised in other contexts about coincidental differences in health across these cohorts: the 1918 influenza pandemic has been argued to have affected the health of cohorts that were in utero at the time (Almond, 2006). Nonetheless, this is likely to be a fairly indirect source of bias. Similar to the Anderson and Matsa paper, this is a reasonably compelling instrumental variable design (concerns about the 1918 influenza epidemic notwithstanding). The variation in retirement income due to the benefits notch was found to be statistically significantly related to total Social Security income but had no statistically significant effect on measures of body weight.

The generalizability of this style of approach is unclear. The bump in Social Security income or similar exogenous bumps in income transfer programs (e.g., the Earned Income Tax Credit) represent fairly small changes to permanent income. And, they typically target particular subpopulations—for example, the elderly or the poor—thus leaving open the question of whether and how the results generalize. It is also unclear whether the Social Security notch generates enough movement in lifetime income to generate an economically meaningful test of whether income matters.

How a person earns her income also matters for body weight. For example, an individual whose job requires her to remain seated for the entire day is more likely to gain weight than a worker whose job involves walking. Because high-paying jobs are often more sedentary than low-paying jobs, residents of developing countries may experience less daily exercise and begin gaining weight as their income levels rise.

One study that examines this channel is that by Lakdawalla and Philipson (2007), who estimate the effect of on-the-job exercise on body weight later in life. They measure job-related exercise using Department of Labor data that detail the characteristics of different occupations. These comprehensive data include measures of the strength and fitness demands for all occupations in the United States. The authors link these data to the NLSY, a panel survey that contains data on respondents' body weight over time. They estimate that spending 18 years in the most fitness-demanding occupation reduces a man's weight by 25 pounds (14%) relative to the least demanding occupation. Conversely, spending 18 years in the most strength-demanding occupation *increases* a man's weight by 28 pounds (15%) relative to the least demanding occupation. These weight gains occur years after the men choose their occupations, thus suggesting a causal relationship between on-the-job exercise and weight gain. By contrast, the authors find that female body weight already differs systematically across occupations at the commencement of the job, thus suggesting that selection is a significant factor for women. Consequently, the authors conclude that they cannot identify a causal effect for women with these data.

7.3.6 Social Interactions

7.3.6.1 *Measurement and Identification Challenges*

The main goal of a social interactions study is to identify the effect of a group's or an individual's behavior on another individual. This effect is often termed "endogenous social interactions" because it is caused by the individuals in the model rather than by outside factors. For example, a researcher may be interested in estimating whether a student's weight is affected by the average weight of her classmates. Defining an individual's social group is difficult, however, because it could in principle include anybody. An individual's eating behavior can be influenced by her best friend, classmates, family, coworkers, or even television personalities. Moreover, the source of the influence may differ drastically across individuals. Thus, any variable that is intended to capture the effect of social interactions on the individual is likely to suffer from measurement error, which will cause bias in estimation (Conley & Topa, 2003).

Even putting aside the measurement issues, researchers face many challenges when trying to identify endogenous social interactions (Manski, 1993). There are two main reasons why an individual's weight may be correlated with the weight of her social group other than endogenous social interactions. First, individuals are likely to form social groups with other people similar to themselves. This endogenous selection would lead to a positive relationship between the individual's weight and her group's weight, but the relationship would not be causal.

Second, the individual and the group may simultaneously react to a common unobservable. For example, a reduction in the price of fast food that causes everyone to eat more will increase everybody's weight at the same time. This is a significant problem because the econometrician rarely observes all the determinants of an individual's weight, and it is likely that at least some of those unobserved determinants are correlated across members of the individual's social group.

In theory, one can resolve this identification problem by finding an appropriate instrument. In practice, however, it is usually difficult to justify a proposed instrument because factors that affect a group's consumption generally also affect the individual's consumption and thus do not satisfy the exclusion restriction. An alternative approach proposed in at least one recent study is to rely on agent-based simulation methods (Trogdon & Allaire, 2014). Such models suggest, intuitively, that obesity can "spread" if obese individuals are particularly popular and vice-versa.

7.3.6.2 *Empirical Findings*

Christakis and Fowler (2007) analyzed data from the Framingham Heart Study, a survey of several thousand individuals who underwent repeated physical examinations, including measurements of height and weight, over a period of 30 years. One of the unique aspects of this survey is the inclusion of social network information that identifies a respondent's close friends, many of whom were also respondents in the same survey.

The researchers estimated a logistic model in which the individual's obesity status is a function of the obesity status of the friend. In addition to controlling for age, sex, and education, they also controlled for the individual's obesity status in the previous time period in order to account for any possible predisposition to obesity. They also attempted to control for the endogenous selection of friends by including a lagged indicator variable for the friend's obesity status.

In order to address the possibility of bias resulting from common unobservables, Christakis and Fowler made use of data on the directionality of the friend relationship.

For example, in their data, they observe whether individual A indicates individual B as a friend and vice versa. The researchers find that social interactions are strongest when the relationship is mutual. In the case of one-sided friendships, they find a social interactions effect only for the individual that perceived a relationship. That is, if individual A indicates individual B as a friend, but not vice versa, then there was a social interactions effect for A but not for B. Christakis and Fowler argue that if common unobservables were driving their results then they would not observe these asymmetric effects.

Cohen-Cole and Fletcher (2008) criticize the Christakis and Fowler study for not sufficiently controlling for environmental factors and for estimating a dynamic specification that is prone to bias. They argue that employing the directionality of the relationship cannot conclusively rule out the possibility that common unobservables are driving the results. Cohen-Cole and Fletcher replicate the Christakis and Fowler results using the Add Health dataset, which has a structure similar to the Framingham Heart Study. They then show that incorporating individual fixed effects and group trends into the econometric specification nullifies the result. They conclude that the results in Christakis and Fowler are driven by environmental factors rather than endogenous social interactions.

7.3.7 Decline in Cigarette Consumption

Although obesity has increased over the past 50 years, cigarette consumption has decreased dramatically. This decline has been attributed to a large increase in the real cost of cigarettes, an increase in the knowledge of the dangers of smoking, and the enactment of national and state-level policies that discourage smoking (Chaloupka & Warner, 2000; De Walque 2007; Gruber & Zinman, 2001; Reif, 2014). Because the medical literature has documented a link between smoking cessation and weight gain (Pinkowish, 1999), some researchers have hypothesized that the historical decline in smoking may have contributed to the recent rise in obesity.

7.3.7.1 Identification Challenges

It is difficult to identify the causal effect of cigarette consumption on obesity because a number of different factors affect both of these behaviors. For example, health-conscious individuals are both less likely to smoke and less likely to be overweight. A common solution to this endogeneity problem is to instrument for smoking behavior using cigarette prices or taxes.

Employing cigarette prices as an instrument for smoking behavior is problematic, however, because prices may be endogenously set by cigarette companies. For example, cigarette companies may change the price they charge in a particular state in response to a demographic shift. If this demographic shift also results in changes in eating behavior, then this will lead to a spurious correlation between cigarette prices and obesity.

Because of these endogeneity concerns, it may be preferable to employ cigarette taxes as an instrument instead of cigarette prices. Cigarette taxes are levied at the city, county, state, and federal levels and vary substantially across both geographic areas and time. Although using taxes instead of prices discards potentially useful variation due to regional differences in transportation costs, retailing costs, and local competition, the loss is not substantial. Gruber and Koszegi (2001) estimate that 80% of the variation in cigarette prices within states over time is driven by tax changes, suggesting that instrumenting with taxes rather than prices may not sacrifice much statistical power.

Like cigarette prices, however, cigarette taxes also suffer from validity concerns when employed as an instrument for cigarette consumption. They are set by local and state legislatures, which may be responding to the demands of consumers. For example, states where cigarette smoking is particularly unpopular may be more likely to increase cigarette taxes, and these states may also be more likely to harbor health-conscious consumers.

An alternative instrument to cigarette prices and taxes is local and state antismoking laws. Many states have enacted policies that, among other things, restrict the location of cigarette vending machines and ban smoking in restaurants, bars, and workplaces. Most of these laws, however, were not enacted until the 1990s or later, which limits their use to later time periods. Moreover, these laws are subject to the same endogeneity critiques as cigarette taxes.

7.3.7.2 *Empirical Findings*

Chou et al. (2004) estimate the effect of cigarette prices on BMI and an indicator for obesity status using repeated cross-section data from the BRFSS. They control for state fixed effects, quadratic time trends, the per capita number of restaurants, food prices, clean indoor air laws, and a large set of individual-level controls. They find that cigarette prices have a positive effect on both BMI and the probability of being obese.

Gruber and Frakes (2006) investigate this topic using the same BRFSS data as Chou et al, but they arrive at a different conclusion. They include cigarette taxes instead of cigarette prices in their specification and account for changes over time using year fixed effects instead of a quadratic time trend. This results in a negative relationship between cigarette taxes and body weight, implying that the historical decrease in smoking behavior reduced rather than increased obesity.

The main estimates presented in Chou et al. and Gruber and Frakes correspond to reduced form specifications that examine the effect of cigarette prices or taxes on body weight. Gruber and Frakes additionally estimate a first-stage regression of smoking participation on cigarette taxes. The authors then proceed to show that these first-stage results imply implausibly large effects of smoking on obesity in both their own paper and Chou et al.'s paper. For example, Gruber and Frakes' estimates imply that quitting smoking reduces the probability of being obese by more than 50%. A result of similar magnitude obtains when applied to Chou et al.'s results, albeit with an opposite sign. Gruber and Frakes conclude that neither their study nor that of Chou et al. produces plausible estimates of the effect of smoking on body weight.

Courtemanche (2009) estimates the effect of cigarette prices and taxes on body weight using the NLSY. These panel data allow him to include individual fixed effects. Identification thus comes from variation in an individual's body weight and smoking status over time. A key innovation in this study is the inclusion of lagged prices and taxes. This is motivated by the dynamic rational addiction model of (Becker & Murphy, 1988), which predicts that the effects of cigarette prices on consumption are larger in the long run than in the short run.

Consistent with Gruber and Frakes, Courtemanche finds that cigarette prices and taxes have a negative effect on body weight, but the effect only appears after 4 years. He also estimates that a rise in cigarette prices is associated with an increase in the level of exercise and a reduction in the grams of fat consumed. The majority of the effect on exercise is delayed for about 4 years, similar to the effect on body weight. Courtemanche concludes that the negative relationship between cigarette prices and body weight may be explained by people's decisions to exercise more and eat healthier following an increase in cigarette prices.

7.4 Conclusion

There is a significant and growing literature on how food prices, exercise, and income affect body weight. Nonetheless, all of it suffers from substantial empirical challenges of causal inference that have not yet been satisfactorily overcome. Regardless, the literature consistently finds that broad-based increases in food prices lead to lower body weight, as the simplest economic model would predict. It is much harder to identify the effects of changes in the prices of specific foods.

Evidence suggests that the amount and type of physical activity required by one's occupation matters for body weight and that providing individuals with incentives to exercise reduces body weight, at least in the short run. Research in this area is likely to continue due to the increasing popularity of workplace wellness programs, which often provide financial incentives for participating in healthy activities.

For income, it has also been difficult to recover causal effects. However, the literature has established with reasonable confidence the nonlinearity of the relationship between income and body weight. This is a theoretical prediction of the competition between the demand for healthy body weight, which rises with income, and the demand for food, which also rises with income.

Some recent studies have found that the presence of social interactions and the decline in cigarette consumption may have contributed to the observed increase in body weight over the past decades. As with other studies on body weight, however, causal inference remains a significant challenge.

The future advance of this literature requires continued refinement in the measurement of body weight, food prices, exercise, and income, all of which suffer from serious inaccuracy. Moreover, methods of causal inference must improve if we are to progress toward the estimation of causal parameters. Although a variety of causal inference methods have been proposed, none has so far been demonstrated as compelling in both validity and power.

References

Almond, D. (2006). Is the 1918 influenza pandemic over? Long-term effects of in utero influenza exposure in the post-1940 US population. *Journal of Political Economy, 114*(4), 672–712.

Anderson, M. L., & Matsa, D. A. (2011). Are restaurants really supersizing America? *American Economic Journal: Applied Economics, 3*(1), 152–188.

Auld, M. C., & Powell, L. M. (2009). Economics of food energy density and adolescent body weight. *Economica, 76*(304), 719–740.

Averett, S. L., & Smith, J. K. (2014). Financial hardship and obesity. *Economics and Human Biology, 15*, 201–212.

Banks, J., Marmot, M., Oldfield, Z., & Smith, J. P. (2006). Disease and disadvantage in the United States and in England. *Journal of the American Medical Association, 295*(17), 2037–2045.

Becker, G. S., & Murphy, K. M. (1988). A theory of rational addiction. *Journal of Political Economy, 96*(4), 675–700.

Beydoun, M. A., Powell, L. M., & Wang, Y. (2008). The association of fast food, fruit and vegetable prices with dietary intakes among US adults: Is there modification by family income? *Social Science & Medicine, 66*(11), 2218–2229.

Brock, W. A., & Durlauf, S. N. (2001). Discrete choice with social interactions. *The Review of Economic Studies, 68*(2), 235–260.

Burkhauser, R. V., & Cawley, J. (2008). Beyond BMI: The value of more accurate measures of fatness and obesity in social science research. *Journal of Health Economics, 27*(2), 519–529.

Cawley, J. (2011). *The Oxford handbook of the social science of obesity*. New York: Oxford University Press.

Cawley, J., Moran, J., & Simon, K. (2010). The impact of income on the weight of elderly Americans. *Health Economics, 19*(8), 979–993.

Cawley, J., & Price, J. A. (2013). A case study of a workplace wellness program that offers financial incentives for weight loss. *Journal of Health Economics, 32*(5), 794–803.

Chaloupka, F. J., & Warner, K. E. (2000). The economics of smoking. *Handbook of Health Economics, 1*, 1539–1627.

Chang, V. W., & Lauderdale, D. S. (2005). Income disparities in body mass index and obesity in the United States, 1971-2002. *Archives of Internal Medicine, 165*(18), 2122–2128.

Charness, G., & Gneezy, U. (2009). Incentives to exercise. *Econometrica, 77*(3), 909–931.

Chou, S. -Y., Grossman, M., & Saffer, H. (2004). An economic analysis of adult obesity: Results from the Behavioral Risk Factor Surveillance System. *Journal of Health Economics, 23*(3), 565–587.

Christakis, N. A., & Fowler, J. H. (2007). The spread of obesity in a large social network over 32 years. *New England Journal of Medicine, 357*(4), 370–379.

Cohen-Cole, E., & Fletcher, J. M. (2008). Is obesity contagious? Social networks vs. environmental factors in the obesity epidemic. *Journal of Health Economics, 27*(5), 1382–1387.

Conley, T. G., & Topa, G. (2003). Identification of local interaction models with imperfect location data. *Journal of Applied Econometrics, 18*(5), 605–618.

Courtemanche, C. (2009). Rising cigarette prices and rising obesity: Coincidence or unintended consequence? *Journal of Health Economics, 28*(4), 781–798.

Currie, A., Shields, M. A., & Price, S. W. (2007). The child health/family income gradient: Evidence from England. *Journal of Health Economics, 26*(2), 213–232.

Cutler, D. M., Glaeser, E. L., & Shapiro, J. M. (2003). Why have Americans become more obese? *The Journal of Economic Perspectives, 17*(3), 93–118.

De Walque, D. (2007). Does education affect smoking behaviors? Evidence using the Vietnam draft as an instrument for college education. *Journal of Health Economics, 26*(5), 877–895.

Ezzati, M., Martin, H., Skjold, S., Vander Hoorn, S., & Murray, C. J. (2006). Trends in national and state-level obesity in the USA after correction for self-report bias: Analysis of health surveys. *Journal of the Royal Society of Medicine, 99*(5), 250–257.

García Villar, J., & Quintana-Domeque, C. (2009). Income and body mass index in Europe. *Economics & Human Biology, 7*(1), 73–83.

Gelbach, J. B., Klick, J., & Stratmann, T. (2007). Cheap donuts and expensive broccoli: The effect of relative prices on obesity. *Social Science Research Network.* Available at: http://papers.ssrn.com/sol3/papers.cfm?abstract_id=976484

Goldman, D., Lakdawalla, D., & Zheng, Y. (2009). *Food prices and the dynamics of body weight.* Cambridge, MA: National Bureau of Economic Research.

Greene, W. H. (2011). *Econometric analysis.* New York: Prentice Hall.

Gruber, J., & Frakes, M. (2006). Does falling smoking lead to rising obesity? *Journal of Health Economics, 25*(2), 183–197.

Gruber, J., & Koszegi, B. (2001). Is addiction "rational"? Theory and evidence. *The Quarterly Journal of Economics, 116*(4), 1261–1303.

Gruber, J., & Zinman, J. (2001). Youth smoking in the United States: Evidence and implications. In J. Gruber (Ed.), *Risky behavior among youths: An economic analysis* (pp. 69–120). Chicago: University of Chicago Press.

Hill, J. O., Wyatt, H. R., Reed, G. W., & Peters, J. C. (2003). Obesity and the environment: Where do we go from here? *Science, 299*(5608), 853–855.

Hofferth, S. L., & Curtin, S. (2005). Poverty, food programs, and childhood obesity. *Journal of Policy Analysis and Management, 24*(4), 703–726.

Jolliffe, D. (2011). Overweight and poor? On the relationship between income and the body mass index. *Economics & Human Biology, 9*(4), 342–355.

Komlos, J., & Brabec, M. (2011). The trend of BMI values of US adults by deciles, birth cohorts 1882–1986 stratified by gender and ethnicity. *Economics & Human Biology, 9*(3), 234–250.

Lakdawalla, D., & Philipson, T. (2002). The growth of obesity and technological change: A theoretical and empirical examination. Cambridge, MA: National Bureau of Economic Research.

Lakdawalla, D., & Philipson, T. (2007). Labor supply and weight. *Journal of Human Resources, 42*(1), 85–116.

Lakdawalla, D., & Philipson, T. (2009). The growth of obesity and technological change. *Economics & Human Biology, 7*(3), 283–293.

Lee, H., Harris, K. M., & Gordon-Larsen, P. (2009). Life course perspectives on the links between poverty and obesity during the transition to young adulthood. *Population research and policy review, 28*(4), 505–532.

Lew, E. A., & Garfinkel, L. (1979). Variations in mortality by weight among 750,000 men and women. *Journal of Chronic Diseases, 32*(8), 563–576.

Manski, C. F. (1993). Identification of endogenous social effects: The reflection problem. *The Review of Economic Studies, 60*(3), 531–542.

Meltzer, D. O., & Chen, Z. (2011). The impact of minimum wage rates on body weight in the United States. In M. Grossman & N. Mocan (Eds.), *Economic aspects of obesity* (pp. 17–34). Chicago: University of Chicago Press.

Michaud, P.-C., van Soest, A. H., & Andreyeva, T. (2007). Cross-country variation in obesity patterns among older Americans and Europeans. *Forum for Health Economics & Policy, 10*(2), 1558–9544.

Miljkovic, D., Nganje, W., & de Chastenet, H. (2008). Economic factors affecting the increase in obesity in the United States: Differential response to price. *Food Policy, 33*(1), 48–60.

Moore, J. C., Stinson, L. L., & Welniak, E. J. (2000). Income measurement error in surveys: A review. *Journal of Official Statistics-Stockholm, 16*(4), 331–362.

Philipson, T., & Posner, R. (2003). The long-run growth in obesity as a function of technological change. *Perspectives in Biology and Medicine, 46*(3), 87–108.

Pinkowish, M. (1999). Hand in glove: Smoking cessation and weight gain. *Patient Care, 33*(2), 134.

Powell, L. M. (2009). Fast food costs and adolescent body mass index: Evidence from panel data. *Journal of Health Economics, 28*(5), 963–970.

Powell, L. M., & Bao, Y. (2009). Food prices, access to food outlets and child weight. *Economics & Human Biology, 7*(1), 64–72.

Powell, L. M., & Chaloupka, F. J. (2009). *Economic contextual factors and child body mass index.* Cambridge, MA: National Bureau of Economic Research.

Powell, L. M., Zhao, Z., & Wang, Y. (2009). Food prices and fruit and vegetable consumption among young American adults. *Health & Place, 15*(4), 1064–1070.

Rashad, I. (2006). Structural estimation of caloric intake, exercise, smoking, and obesity. *Quarterly Review of Economics and Finance, 46*(2), 268–283.

Reif, J. (2014). Addiction and social interactions: Theory and evidence. *Social Science Research Network.* Available from: http://papers.ssrn.com/sol3/papers.cfm?abstract_id=2331654

Riera-Crichton, D., & Tefft, N. (2014). Macronutrients and obesity: Revisiting the calories in, calories out framework. *Economics and Human Biology, 14*, 33–49.

Society of Actuaries. (1959). *Build and blood pressure study, 1959.* Chicago: Society of Actuaries.

Sturm, R., & Datar, A. (2005). Body mass index in elementary school children, metropolitan area food prices and food outlet density. *Public Health, 119*(12), 1059–1068.

Sturm, R., & Datar, A. (2008). Food prices and weight gain during elementary school: 5-year update. *Public Health, 122*(11), 1140.

Trogdon, J. G., & Allaire, B. T. (2014). The effect of friend selection on social influences in obesity. *Economics and Human Biology, 15*, 153–164.

Truong, K. D., & Sturm, R. (2005). Weight gain trends across sociodemographic groups in the United States. *American Journal of Public Health, 95*(9), 1602.

Wada, R., & Tekin, E. (2010). Body composition and wages. *Economics & Human Biology, 8*(2), 242–254.

Wilson, J. D., Braunwald, E., Isselbacher, K. J., Petersdorf, R. G., Martin, J. B., Fauci, A. S., & Root, R. K. (Eds.). (1991). Harrison's Principles of Internal Medicine. McGraw-Hill, New York.

World Health Organization. (2000). *Obesity: Preventing and managing the global epidemic.* Geneva: World Health Organization.

CHAPTER 8

INEQUALITY AND HEIGHTS

MATTHIAS BLUM

8.1 Introduction

This chapter provides an overview of using physical stature as an indicator of inequality in society; it introduces opportunities and limitations of height inequality and presents an overview of the literature. The limitations of height inequality are similar to other anthropometric indicators in that height reflects the outcome of all socioeconomic influences on it, such as social status, income, and education. Height inequality may be affected also by the provision of public goods, such as social insurance or a clean and safe environment. Inequality in purchasing power and height inequality are related but not identical, and both of these metrics are important in their own right (Komlos, 2007*a*; Moradi & Baten, 2005; Pradhan, Sahn, & Younger, 2003). Height inequality within a birth cohort is determined during the main growth periods of the human body; the time around birth is considered to be important, but, in cases of suboptimal nutrition and health conditions during early childhood, catch-up growth can be substantial. Therefore, a birth cohort's height distribution provides information about inequality in terms of nutritional and health conditions between birth and adulthood (Howe et al., 2012).

A series of studies emphasize the importance of height inequality as a valuable proxy for inequality in human and health capital. There is considerable evidence that taller individuals tend to attain higher levels of education and that height is also positively associated with better economic, health, and cognitive outcomes (Case & Paxson, 2010; Cinnirella, Piopiunik, & Winter, 2011). Baten and Mumme (2010) compare the number of school years of tall and short individuals born between 1945 and 1984 in a panel of 42 developing countries. They find that—without exception—the upper 50% of a country's

The author can be contacted at Queen's University Belfast, Queen's University Management School, 185 Stranmillis Road, Belfast BT9 5EE, United Kingdom. Email: matthias.blum@qub.ac.uk; Phone: +44 28 9097 4428.

height distribution is characterized by up to 1.9 more years of school attendance. Height also tends to increase productivity in adulthood and is found to be associated with success in marriage markets (Gao & Smyth, 2010; Manfredini, Breschi, Fornasin, & Seghieri, 2013).

In this chapter, two basic aspects of height inequality are discussed: height inequality within a population and height gaps between various social groups. For example, average height between social groups is used as an indicator of differences in their living standards. Similarly, differences in height between urban and rural dwellers or between ethnic groups may help shed light on nutritional advantages of one group compared to the other. Another branch of the literature utilizes the fact that height potentials in a population are normally distributed (Quetelet, 1835). Any deviation of the actual height distribution from the "natural" distribution of height potentials is assumed to be caused by factors associated with unequal distribution of resources reflecting the degree of inequality in a population around its time of birth.

However, we need to keep in mind selection mechanisms that might have biased the sample of interest. For example, height distributions of students, migrants, soldiers, and conscripts are substantially narrower due to selection into these groups. For example, samples consisting of students tend to be positively selected with regard to their socioeconomic status because lower classes tend to be underrepresented, and upper classes tend to be overrepresented among them. As a consequence, students tend to be taller than average in all societies and at all times. A similar issue arises with conscript samples, with a truncated left tail due to minimum height requirements. Truncated regression techniques can identify a sample's true mean and true height inequality within a group of soldiers who have undergone a minimum-height selection (A'Hearn, 2004; Komlos, 2004; Komlos & Kim, 1990). Any selection leading to an underrepresentation of upper classes, such as in cases of low-skilled workers, may lead to downward-biased average heights and downward-biased height inequality (see Figure 8.1).

8.2 The Nature of Height Distributions

The normal distribution of heights is illustrated using the records of approximately 4,000 German soldiers born during the period 1900–1920. Individuals in this dataset have been separated by socioeconomic background using their father's profession as the relevant indicator (Armstrong, 1972). Upper-class individuals are identified by professional occupations; individuals with middle-lower-class backgrounds are identified by unskilled and skilled professions. The mean height value of the upper social strata is 172.1 cm; the mean height value of the middle-lower class is 170.4 cm. These values indicate that these groups experienced differences in biological well-being driven by differences in nutrition, health, and other factors influencing the determination of adult average height. Differences between these groups ought not be attributed to differences in genes because the sample at hand was drawn from a homogenous population (Blum, 2013*a*). Height inequality within each of these groups is not identical but is of similar magnitude. The distributions have a standard deviation of 6.30 and 6.35 cm (Figure 8.1, Table 8.1).

Although mean average height values illustrate general differences between social classes, there is a considerable overlap of the corresponding height distributions that suggests that a great deal of variation in height is not driven by socioeconomic factors but by individual genetic disposition or by individual height potentials. Therefore, it is important to distinguish the distribution of height potentials, which is determined by nature, and the distribution of actual heights. In a scenario in which every single

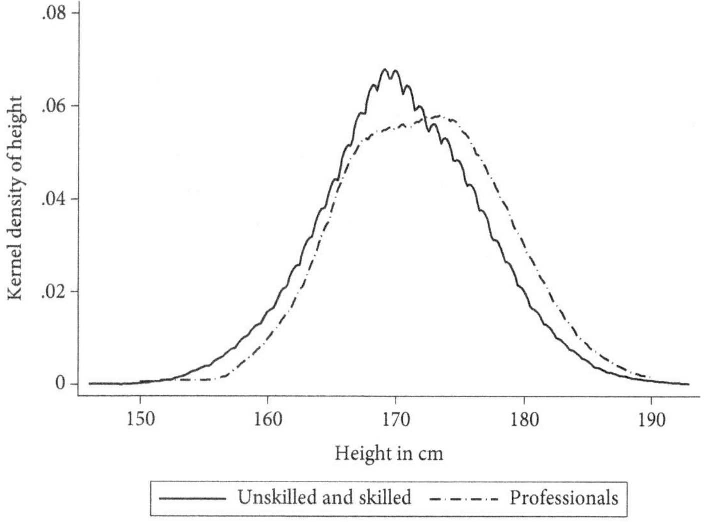

FIGURE 8.1 Height distribution of German soldiers (by class), birth cohorts 1900–1920.

Data source: Blum (2011, 2013*c*)

Table 8.1 Descriptive statistics of male German heights, birth cohorts 1900–1920

	N	Mean	Standard deviation	Minimum	Maximum
Lower-middle class	3324	170.4	6.30	146	191
Upper class	712	172.1	6.35	148	190

Note: Differences in average height between the two groups are statistically significant at the 0.01 level.

Source: See Figure 8.1.

individual obtains the optimal amount and quality of nutrition and experiences no health (or any other) burden that decelerates the growth process, these two distributions would be identical (Blum & Baten, 2011). Height gaps between social classes in the German case, as shown in Figure 8.1, are relatively modest compared to other studies. Komlos (2007*b*) finds that during the late 18th and early 19th centuries, the height gap between the rich and the poor in England reached 22 cm at age 16 (Figure 8.2).

Boix and Rosenbluth (2014) report that estimated height differences in ancient Egypt between pharaohs and common males were more than 9 cm, and height differences between Mycenae royals and commoners were more than 6 cm. In late 18th-century Germany, Komlos (1989) finds height differences of more than 4 cm for 17-year-olds in the upper versus middle classes; height difference between the upper class and peasants exceeded 13 cm.

The extreme values in this German sample are 191 cm and 146 cm—a difference of 45 cm or approximately 31% of the shorter individual's stature. Imagine for the sake of this argument that these individual heights are solely a function of net nutrition (or more broadly, income). Does this height gap suggest that the monetary income gap between these two individuals during their respective growth processes was also 31%? This is highly unlikely because there is no one-to-one relationship between anthropometric and monetary income metrics. A key to understanding and interpreting the differences between these two measures is diminishing returns to nutrition and health with regard to height. Individuals from rich families tend to have lower marginal returns to income with respect to their future adult height, whereas for poor individuals the converse is true. In other words, the latter individual is expected to benefit more from the same additional unit of consumption; individuals at the upper end of the social ladder

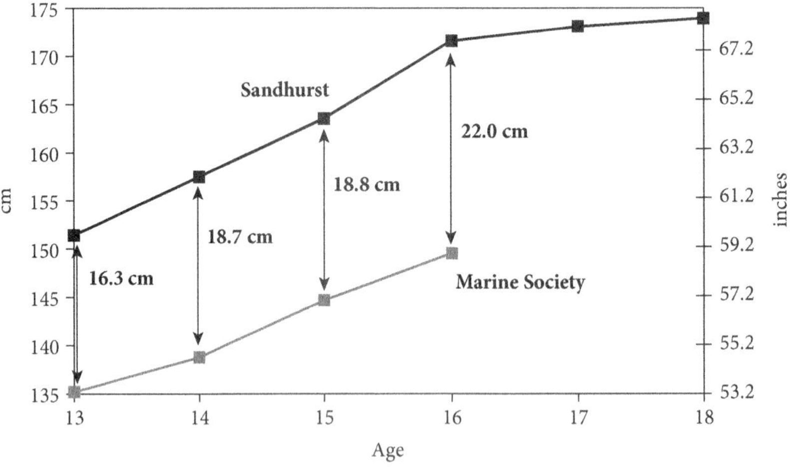

FIGURE 8.2 Height profile of Sandhurst and Marine Society boys.

Note: Children from the upper and lower classes are represented, respectively, by students at the prestigious Royal Military Academy at Sandhurst and children from poor London neighborhoods who entered the Marine Society.

Source: Komlos (2007*b*).

may experience little to no height increase with additional consumption (Blum, 2013*b*). The rationale behind this is that human growth occurs within naturally given boundaries; these limits cannot be overcome, and, within these boundaries, height is a function of decreasing marginal returns to net nutrition.

8.3 Height Inequality from a Macroeconomic Perspective

In contrast to individual height, which is commonly used in microeconomic studies, some authors use aggregated height data to investigate height inequality at a population level. Here, the most commonly used indicator for height inequality is the coefficient of height variation (henceforth CV) defined as $CV=\frac{\sigma}{\mu}100$, where σ is the standard deviation of heights and μ represents the mean height in the sample.

In Figure 8.3, characteristics of height inequality values from 714 male populations taken from all world regions during the 19th and 20th centuries are illustrated. Although

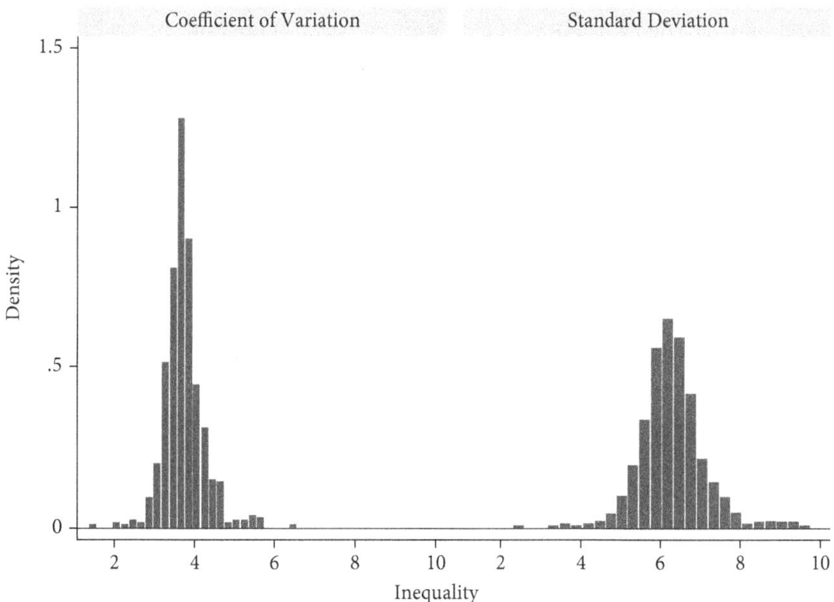

FIGURE 8.3 Male height inequality at a macroeconomic level in 123 countries, 19th and 20th centuries.

Note: Standard deviation is measured in cm whereas the coefficient of variation is a dimensionless metric. On their own, standard deviation values have little to say about the level of inequality; only a comparison of two or more observations allows for a meaningful interpretation. Each data point used in this figure is computed on a decadal basis and represents inequality of a birth cohort's adult height.

Data source: Blum (2013*b*)

these height inequality distributions look approximately normal, a skew test suggests that they are positively skewed, and normality is rejected at the 1% level.

It is important to mention that most of the empirical evidence is based on male height distributions. However, Blum (2013*d*) shows that the relationship between male and female height distributions is statistically significant and characterized by an R^2 value of 0.39, indicating that it is reasonable to assume that conclusions based on male height inequality data are also valid for the entire population.

Macroeconomic height inequality (CV) has been used in a series of studies to assess facets of socioeconomic inequality from a different perspective or to investigate inequality for periods and places for which conventional indicators are unavailable. Credibility for this methodology is partly based on empirical studies that provide evidence of a link between different metrics of inequality. For example, Moradi and Baten (2005) show a positive relationship between Gini coefficients of monetary income and height inequality (CV) in sub-Saharan Africa. They suggest the following formula to estimate a Gini coefficient on the basis of height inequality: Gini = 20.5 * CV – 33.5.

Similarly, Blum and Baten (2011) report that height inequality is correlated with skill-premia of skilled workers relative to unskilled workers. They find a positive and statistically significant relationship between wage differentials and inequality in biological living standards and use this correlation to introduce an additional tool to the inequality literature; namely, the estimation of skill premia based on height inequality. The rationale behind this skill–height link is straightforward: both cognitive and physiological developments are partly a function of resources invested, and if resources constitute a limit to human development, then the result could be an advantage afforded to well-fed children.

A number of studies are based on height inequality. In a recent study, Van Zanden, Baten, Foldvari, and van Leeuwen (2013) use average height in combination with height inequality at a population level to trace global inequality over the 19th and 20th centuries. They find that between 1820 and 1950, increasing per capita income corresponds with increasing global inequality. They also report that the global income distribution was unimodal in the 19th century but became increasingly bimodal between 1910 and 1970 and transformed back into a unimodal distribution between 1980 and 2000.

Baten and Fraunholz (2004) investigate the interactions of globalization and inequality in Latin America by using height CVs as a proxy for socioeconomic inequality. They find that within-country inequality of initially closed economies increased with openness, whereas closed economies had lower inequality; under full economic integration, inequality is expected to fall again. On the other hand, the presence of height inequality seems to encourage countries to restrict openness in order to limit the negative impact of international competition (Baltzer & Baten, 2008). In their study of sub-Saharan Africa, Moradi and Baten (2005) find that specialized cash cropping increases within-country inequality, measured by height CVs. Diversified cash cropping, however, has the opposite effect. Baten and Mumme (2010) use height inequality as a proxy for relative deprivation and find that height inequality had a strong negative propensity to start civil wars in the period 1816 to 1999.

8.4 Social Differences and Height Inequality

The aforementioned mechanisms determining differences in height of social groups are commonly used to identify differences in living standards of social strata. The driving force of height differences between social classes are differences in purchasing power, education, physical workload, and epidemiological environment, enabling some individuals to enjoy beneficial nutritional and health conditions while other individuals tend to achieve less of their height potential due to suboptimal living conditions. In a modern setting, access to health care and a social safety net also have substantial influence.

For example, in Switzerland, social class was found to be the most important determinant of height differences between those born between 1875 and the 1940s, accounting for up to a 7 cm height gap between the upper and lower class in the city of Bern; the corresponding height difference between rural dwellers was less than 3 cm (Kues, 2010; Schoch, Staub, & Pfister, 2012). During the 19th century, the US population was becoming shorter in general, but average height of the elite did not decline and, in some cases, even increased. Upper-class families were wealthy enough to shield their children from rising prices of nutrients (Sunder, 2011, 2013). This pattern does not hold for historical settings only; for modern-day India, Perkins, Khan, Smith, and Subramanian (2011) examine differences in height by wealth, education, and caste and find that these factors determine differences in health outcomes which, in turn, may be reflected in inequalities in height. Similar evidence exists for Sri Lanka, where differences in education and household incomes were driving forces of height inequality (Ranasinghe et al., 2011). Evidence from Germany suggests that differences in labor market success, in addition to the associated psychological effects of unemployment, net out-migration, and fertility, affect height inequality (Baten & Böhm, 2010). Similarly, in a large sample of English children, maternal education was the most important explanatory variable; children whose mothers had attained the highest education levels, compared to those with no education or only basic levels, were 0.39 cm taller at birth and 1.4 cm taller at the age of 11.5 (Galobardes et al., 2012).

8.5 Height Differences Between Ethnic Groups

Anthropometric indicators have served as an alternative to conventional metrics when it comes to investigating living standards of members of different ethnic groups. The advantage of average height and height inequality arises from the fact that even though ethnic groups may live in close proximity, their economic experiences differ; for example, US slaves did not receive conventional income but were provided with food, clothing, and housing, whereas freed slaves and whites received income but had to spend their income on the aforementioned items. Pioneer studies revealed that African Americans were shorter compared to white Americans. On the other hand, slaves were taller than whites born in Europe, whereas heights of free men declined in the antebellum period (Margo & Steckel, 1982; Steckel, 1979). Slaves fared better in terms of average heights, and the birth cohorts of the 1840s were almost as tall as their white counterparts.

Anthropometric indicators are also used to investigate inequality during more recent periods. Komlos (2010) investigates height trends by ethnicity in the United States during the second half of the 20th century. He reports that between white and black men born between 1975 and 1986, the height gap increased by 0.43 cm, reaching 1.0 cm. Black women experienced a decline in stature, resulting in a considerable height gap between black and white women of 1.95 cm. Similarly, evidence from pre-World War I Hungary indicates that—contrary to widespread belief—Jews were not richer than non-Jews, according to average height measurements (Bolgar, 2013). In fact, income distribution among Jewish men was more unequal than among Christians. A comparison of New Zealanders and Maori reveals that stature varied by social class, with professionals and men in rural occupations substantially taller than their peers (Inwood, Oxley, & Roberts, 2010).

8.6 Regional Differences in Height

In the absence of detailed regional per capita income statistics, economic historians often resort to regional physical stature as a proxy for nutritional standards or economic development in general. Accordingly, Baten and Blum (2014) and Hatton and Bray (2010) discuss height trends by world regions and among European nations during the 19th and 20th centuries, respectively. On a subnational level, Steckel (2010) explains differences in physical stature between Native American tribes living in the Great Plains, finding that food scarcity, rainfall, and tribal area, as well as proximity to trails used by Western settlers explain a substantial share of these differences between tribes. Using a similar strategy, Köpke and Baten (2005) trace height inequality in Europe during the past two millennia. They find that heights in Central, Western, and Southern Europe developed similarly during the period under observation. Komlos (1985) analyzes conscript data from the Habsburg Empire between the 1740s and the 1830s and finds significant differences in stature. He concludes that early industrializing regions could improve their income levels due to increasing productivity of labor. However, industrialization in these regions was associated with decreasing average heights. A study on modern-day Russia reveals substantial height differences between regions affected by civil war and regions that were unaffected by war (Fedorov & Sahn, 2005). Using a modern household panel survey for Spain, Quintana-Domeque, Bozzoli, and Bosch (2012) trace Spanish regional heights throughout the second half of the 20th century.

8.7 Urban Versus Rural Differences

In investigating differences in average height between urban and rural areas, researchers often refer to the existence (or absence) of an "urban penalty." It is assumed that both urban and rural life come with benefits and disadvantages with respect to living standards, and these differences may be reflected in the physical stature of their respective populations. In the past, rural life offered nutritional advantages due to proximity to agriculture. Urban dwellers may have enjoyed higher wages through higher economic activity; the existence of schools and libraries; and perhaps more opportunities for personal professional development. On the other hand, for most of history, cities were characterized by insufficient sanitary systems, overpopulation, and high transaction costs of acquiring nutrients, which created an adverse health environment. Therefore, height differences are not necessarily identical to differences in (conventional) incomes; in fact, there is evidence of shrinking heights in growing economies (Komlos, 1997, 1998). During the late 19th century, as a consequence of medical and sanitary innovations and also improved transportation, urban nutritional supply and disease environments tended to improve relative to those in rural areas (Szreter & Mooney, 1998). Some empirical evidence on this matter is provided by Martínez-Carrión and Moreno-Lázaro (2007) who find that in Castile-Leon, urban and rural heights were about the same during the mid-19th century, but urban heights were intermittently above rural ones thereafter. Similarly, rural residents in late 19th-century Scotland still had a distinct height advantage over their urban counterparts (Riggs & Cuff, 2013); Zehetmayer's (2013) study of US Army recruits suggests an urban height penalty of up to 1.5 cm. Interestingly, during the 19th century, the nutritional status in Bavaria, Prussia, and France was relatively low near towns because peasants sold their products in market towns, which simultaneously deprived local areas of food supply (Baten, 2009). In modern-day China, Treiman (2012) reports that rural–urban disparities in schooling, health care, housing, and retirement benefits remain large and perhaps have become larger in recent decades because the urban sector has benefited from China's transition to a market economy more than the rural sector. Research on the North Korean famine during the 1990s revealed that children born in the capital city of Pyongyang had higher height-for-age z scores, indicating that they enjoyed comparative advantages in food supply (Schwekendiek, 2010).

8.8 Institutional and Political Differences

The strategy in illuminating the effect of institutional differences on heights can be seen, for example, in the case of the Korean peninsula. The division of a once relatively homogenous population into a communist North and a capitalist South offers of a natural experiment. Schwekendiek and Pak (2009) investigate the differences of children's height and find that South Korean preschool children in 1997 were 6–7 cm taller than their Northern counterparts. In a subsequent survey from 2002, the average height gap was approximately 8 cm. North Korean boys and girls escaping to South Korea were also found to be on average about 3–4 cm shorter than their Southern peers. Ironically, the stature of North Koreans born before the division of Korea exceeded that of their South Korean peers, but all North Korean cohorts born thereafter were shorter than their South Korean counterparts, indicating that South Korea was better at providing nutrition and health resources (Pak, 2004; Pak, Schwekendiek, & Kim, 2011). Similarly, Komlos and Kriwy (2003) observe that West Germans tended to be taller than East Germans. After unification, there was a tendency for East German males (but not females) to catch up with their West German counterparts.

8.9 Conclusion

This chapter provides an introduction to two concepts based on height inequality as an indicator of socioeconomic inequality. Height differences between social groups, such as upper and lower classes, urban and rural dwellers, or between members of different ethnic groups, are discussed. Moreover, inequality in the biological standard of living is explored using either the standard deviation of individual heights or their coefficient of variation as indicators.

There are several lessons to be learned from studying height inequality. Contrary to monetary income values, height and height inequality values range within natural boundaries, and the height of a healthy person cannot be below or above these boundaries. Between these boundaries, heights do not increase with nutritional and health inputs in a linear fashion; in fact, height is a function of decreasing marginal returns to inputs, resulting in lower returns to net nutrition (i.e., smaller height gains, at higher nutritional levels for a given number of inputs).

This chapter also provides a brief introduction into the literature in order to illustrate the opportunities this methodology has to offer. Essentially, the main driving forces of height inequality are differences in purchasing power, education, physical workload, and epidemiological environment, enabling wealthy individuals, self-sufficient peasants and farmers, or those living in low population densities to enjoy beneficial nutritional and health conditions. In a modern setting, access to health care and a social safety net also have substantial influence. In sum, analysis of height inequality enables us to improve our understanding of the dynamics of economic development.

References

A'Hearn, B. (2004). A restricted maximum likelihood estimator for truncated height samples. *Economics and Human Biology*, *2*(1), 5–19.

Armstrong, W. A. (1972). The use of information about occupation. In E. A. Wrigley (Ed.), *Nineteenth-century society: Essays in the use of quantitative methods for the study of social data* (pp. 191–310). Cambridge, UK: Cambridge University Press.

Baltzer, M., & Baten, J. (2008). Heights, inequality, and trade in the Latin American periphery, 1950-2004. *Economics and Human Biology*, *6*(2), 191–203.

Baten, J. (2009). Protein supply and nutritional status in nineteenth century Bavaria, Prussia and France. *Economics and Human Biology*, *7*(2), 165–180.

Baten, J., & Blum, M. (2014). Why are you tall while others are short? Agricultural production and other proximate determinants of global heights. *European Review of Economic History*, *18*(2), 144–165.

Baten, J., & Böhm, A. (2010). Children's height and parental unemployment: A large-scale anthropometric study on Eastern Germany, 1994-2006. *German Economic Review*, *11*(1), 1–24.

Baten, J., & Fraunholz, U. (2004). Did partial globalization increase inequality? The case of the Latin American periphery, 1950–2000. *CESifo Economic Studies*, *50*(1), 45–84.

Baten, J., & Mumme, C. (2010). Globalization and educational inequality during the 18th to 20th centuries: Latin America in global comparison. *Revista de Historia Económica*, *28*(2), 279–305.

Blum, M. (2011). Government decisions before and during the First World War and the living standards in Germany during a drastic natural experiment. *Explorations in Economic History*, *48*(4), 556–567.

Blum, M. (2013*a*). Culture and genetic influences on the "biological standard of living." *Historical Methods*, *46*(1), 19–30.

Blum, M. (2013*b*). The influence of inequality on the standard of living: Worldwide anthropometric from the 19th and 20th centuries. *Economics and Human Biology*, *11*(4), 436–452.

Blum, M. (2013*c*). War, food rationing, and socioeconomic inequality in Germany during the First World War. *Economic History Review*, *66*(4), 1063–1083.

Blum, M. (2013*d*). Estimating male and female height inequality. *Economics and Human Biology*, *14*(1), 103–108.

Blum, M., & Baten, J. (2011). Anthropometric within-country inequality and the estimation of skill premia with anthropometric indicators. *Review of Economics*, *62*(2), 107–138.

Boix, C., & Rosenbluth, F. (2014). Bones of contention: The political economy of height inequality. *American Political Science Review*, *108*(1), 1–22.

Bolgar, D. (2013). Wealthier Jews, taller Gentiles: Inequality of income and physical stature in fin-de-siecle Hungary. *Economics and Human Biology*, *11*(4), 433–435.

Case, A., & Paxson, C. (2010). Causes and consequences of early-life health. *Demography*, *47*(Suppl.), S65–S85.

Cinnirella, F., Piopiunik, M., & Winter, J. (2011). Why does height matter for educational attainment? Evidence from German children. *Economics and Human Biology, 9*(4), 407–418.

Fedorov, L., & Sahn, D. E. (2005). Socioeconomic determinants of children's health in Russia: A longitudinal study. *Economic Development and Cultural Change, 53*(2), 479–500.

Galobardes, B., McCormack, V. A., McCarron, P., Howe, L. D., Lynch, J., Lawlor, D. A., & Smith, G. D. (2012). Social inequalities in height: Persisting differences today depend upon height of the parents. *PLoS One, 7*(1), e29118.

Gao, W., & Smyth, R. (2010). Health human capital, height and wages in China. *Journal of Development Studies, 46*(3), 466–484.

Hatton, T. J., & Bray, B. E. (2010). Long run trends in the heights of European men, 19th-20th centuries. *Economics and Human Biology, 8*(3), 405–413.

Howe, L. D., Tilling, K., Galobardes, B., Smith, G. D., Gunnell, D., & Lawlor, D. A. (2012). Socioeconomic differences in childhood growth trajectories: At what age do height inequalities emerge? *Journal of Epidemiology and Community Health, 66*(2), 143–148.

Inwood, K., Oxley, L., & Roberts, E. (2010). Physical stature in 19th-century New Zealand: A preliminary interpretation. *Australian Economic History Review, 50*(3), 262–283.

Komlos, J. (1985). Stature and nutrition in the Habsburg monarchy, the standard-of-living and economic-development in the 18th-century. *American Historical Review, 90*(5), 1149–1161.

Komlos, J. (1989). *Nutrition and economic development in the eighteenth-century Habsburg monarchy: An anthropometric history*. Princeton, NJ: Princeton University Press.

Komlos, J. (1997). On the puzzling cycle in the biological standard of living: The case of antebellum Georgia. *Explorations in Economic History, 34*(4), 433–459.

Komlos, J. (1998). Shrinking in a growing economy? The mystery of physical stature during the Industrial Revolution. *Journal of Economic History, 58*(3), 779–802.

Komlos, J. (2004). How to (and how not to) analyze deficient height samples: An introduction. *Historical Methods, 37*(4), 160–173.

Komlos, J. (2007*a*). Anthropometric evidence on economic growth, biological well-being and regional convergence in the Habsburg monarchy, c. 1850–1910. *Cliometrica, 1*(3), 211–237.

Komlos, J. (2007*b*). On English pygmies and giants: The physical stature of English youth in the late-18th and early-19th centuries. *Research in Economic History, 25*, 149–168.

Komlos, J. (2010). The recent decline in the height of African-American women. *Economics and Human Biology, 8*(1), 58–66.

Komlos, J., & Kim, J. H. (1990). Estimating trends in historical heights. *Historical Methods, 23*(3), 116–120.

Komlos, J., & Kriwy, P. (2003). The biological standard of living in the two Germanies. *German Economic Review, 4*(4), 459–473.

Köpke, N., & Baten, J. (2005). The biological standard of living in Europe during the last two millennia. *European Review of Economic History, 9*(1), 61–95.

Kues, A. B. (2010). Taller—healthier—more equal? The biological standard of living in Switzerland in the second half of the 20th century. *Economics and Human Biology, 8*(1), 67–79.

Manfredini, M., Breschi, M., Fornasin, A., & Seghieri, C. (2013). Height, socioeconomic status and marriage in Italy around 1900. *Economics and Human Biology, 11*(4), 465–473.

Margo, R. A., & Steckel, R. H. (1982). The heights of American slaves: New evidence on slave nutrition and health. *Social Science History, 6*(4), 516–538.

Martínez-Carrión, J. -M., & Moreno-Lázaro, J. (2007). Was there an urban height penalty in Spain, 1840–1913? *Economics and Human Biology, 5*(1), 144–164.

Moradi, A., & Baten, J. (2005). Inequality in sub-Saharan Africa 1950–80: New estimates and new result. *World Development*, *33*, 1233–1265.

Pak, S. (2004). The biological standard of living in the two Koreas. *Economics and Human Biology*, *2*(3), 511–521.

Pak, S., Schwekendiek, D., & Kim, H. K. (2011). Height and living standards in North Korea, 1930s–1980s. *Economic History Review*, *64*(S1), 142–158.

Perkins, J. M., Khan, K. T., Smith, G. D., & Subramanian, S. V. (2011). Patterns and trends of adult height in India in 2005–2006. *Economics and Human Biology*, *9*(2), 184–193.

Pradhan, M., Sahn, D. E., & Younger, S. D. (2003). Decomposing world health inequality. *Journal of Health Economics*, *22*(2), 271–293.

Quetelet, L. A. J. (1835). *Sur l'homme el le developpement de ses facultes*. Paris: Bachelier.

Quintana-Domeque, C., Bozzoli, C., & Bosch, M. (2012). The evolution of adult height across Spanish regions, 1950–1980: A new source of data. *Economics and Human Biology*, *10*(3), 264–275.

Ranasinghe, P., Jayawardana, M. A., Constantine, G. R., Sheriff, M. H., Matthews, D. R., & Katulanda, P. (2011). Patterns and correlates of adult height in Sri Lanka. *Economics and Human Biology*, *9*(1), 23–29.

Riggs, P., & Cuff, T. (2013). Ladies from hell, Aberdeen free gardeners, and the Russian influenza: An anthropometric analysis of WWI-era Scottish soldiers and civilians. *Economics and Human Biology*, *11*(1), 69–77.

Schoch, T., Staub, K., & Pfister, C. (2012). Social inequality and the biological standard of living: An anthropometric analysis of Swiss conscription data, 1875–1950. *Economics and Human Biology*, *10*(2), 154–173.

Schwekendiek, D. (2010). Regional variations in living conditions during the North Korean food crisis of the 1990s. *Asia Pacific Journal of Public Health*, *22*(4), 460–476.

Schwekendiek, D., & Pak, S. (2009). Recent growth of children in the two Koreas: A meta-analysis. *Economics and Human Biology*, *7*(1), 109–112.

Steckel, R. H. (1979). Slave height profiles from coastwise manifests. *Explorations in Economic History*, *16*(4), 363–380.

Steckel, R. H. (2010). Inequality amidst nutritional abundance: Native Americans on the Great Plains. *Journal of Economic History*, *70*(2), 265–286.

Sunder, M. (2011). Upward and onward: High-society American women eluded the antebellum puzzle. *Economics and Human Biology*, *9*(2), 165–171.

Sunder, M. (2013). The height gap in 19th-century America: Net-nutritional advantage of the elite increased at the onset of modern economic growth. *Economics and Human Biology*, *11*(3), 245–258.

Szreter, S., & Mooney, G. (1998). Urbanization, mortality, and the standard of living debate: New estimates of the expectation of life at birth in nineteenth-century British cities. *Economic History Review*, *51*(1), 84–112.

Treiman, D. J. (2012). The "difference between heaven and earth": Urban–rural disparities in well-being in China. *Research in Social Stratification and Mobility*, *30*(1), 33–47.

Van Zanden, J. L., Baten, J., Foldvari, P., & van Leeuwen, B. (2013). The changing shape of global inequality 1820–2000: Exploring a new dataset. *Review of Income and Wealth*, *60*(2), 279–297.

Zehetmayer, M. (2013). Health, market integration, and the urban height penalty in the US, 1847–1894. *Cliometrica*, *7*(2), 161–187.

CHAPTER 9

ADULT WEIGHT AND HEIGHT OF NATIVE POPULATIONS

ASHER ROSINGER AND RICARDO GODOY

9.1 INTRODUCTION

WEIGHT and height are critical indicators of short- and long-term human nutrition and health. Secular changes in weight and height can reflect shifts in energetic availability or disease load within and between populations (Ulijaszek, 2003). Such changes in nutritional status have been documented in the history of species *Homo* and have been associated with milestones, such as cooking with fire, the adoption of agriculture, and the Industrial Revolution (Aiello & Wheeler, 1995; Bogin & Keep, 1999; Floud, Fogel, Harris, & Hong, 2011; Komlos, 1994; Leonard & Robertson, 1994; Luca, Perry, & Di Rienzo, 2010).

Most recently, the social sciences have used the nutrition transition to understand the health effects of shifts from traditional, nutrient-rich foods to fatty, sugary, and highly processed foods and drinks (Popkin, 1994). The transition is associated with changes in dietary availability and physical activity, which, in turn, affect body composition and risks of chronic disease (Popkin, 2011). Evidence documenting the nutrition transition has accumulated worldwide in the past 20 years (Lourenco, Santos, Orellana, & Coimbra, 2008; Popkin, Adair, & Ng 2012; Sibai et al., 2010; Ulijaszek & Koziel, 2007; Zhai et al., 2009) and suggests that the nutrition transition takes many forms (Himmelgreen, Cantor, Arias, & Romero Daza, 2014). Globalization and development interact with local economic, cultural, and lifestyle profiles to produce different nutritional phenotypes and genotypes.

Here, we examine whether positive secular trends in weight and height in native populations are a function only of economic modernization that led to changes in energetic balance and food availability or whether they also appear for other reasons. Given the fast rate of modernization of native groups, accurate measures of weight and height matter for current and future generations of researchers who may want to assess baseline conditions before structural transformations took place in rural economies.

We limit the review to studies of the covariates of secular trends (Ulijaszek, 1998) of weight, height, and body mass index (BMI; weight in kg/standing height in m^2) that relied on primary data of living adult men and nonpregnant women from small-scale, native, tribal, or ethnic minorities in rural areas of developing nations and to studies that compare cross-sectional studies of these populations with national averages (Ng et al., 2014). Studies of native populations in industrial countries were excluded (e.g., First Nations populations in the Americas). We follow Stoddard et al.'s (2011, p. 1637) definition of "native" as a term that describes people who occupy ancestral lands; who differ in language, culture, and ethnic identification from colonizers; and who view themselves as part of a group.

We focus mainly on studies published since 2000 in peer-reviewed journals. Sometimes we draw on a newly minted 9-year annual panel study (2002–2010, inclusive) among the Tsimane', a horticultural-foraging society of native Amazonians in Bolivia (the Tsimane' Amazonian Panel Study [TAPS]). The sample includes 769 adults (>21 years of age) from 172 households in 13 villages and is freely available to the public (http://heller.brandeis.edu/sustainable-international-development/tsimane/index.html).

9.2 Weight

9.2.1 Weight and BMI Data

Weight changes, measured in kilograms among adults who have stopped linear growth, are an important indicator of nutritional status that reflects energy balance because weight is the sum of energy inputs (food intake) minus energy outputs (physical activity and metabolic demands) (Snodgrass, 2012). BMI is the most widely used indicator of body composition due to its simplicity and general comparability across populations. BMI has been critiqued because it overestimates body fat among heavily muscled individuals and can be an unreliable predictor of adiposity among native populations where stunting is common (Du et al., 2013; Shaw & Braverman, 2012; Wilson et al., 2011). For example, 10.6% of Malaysian aborigines were classified as overweight (BMI: 25–29.9) or obese (BMI: 30+) when using BMI as a classification tool, but only 0.8% were classified as overweight or obese when using percent body fat (Yusof, Ching, Ibrahim, & Lola, 2007). Many studies assessing the nutrition transition among native populations use weight, BMI, and the percent of the population that is overweight and obese as evidence for the transition.

9.2.2 Nutrition Transition Among Native Populations

Although studies of the nutrition transition highlight gains in weight and BMI in relation to changes in economy and diet, considerable variation exists among native populations depending on the timing and level of their integration with the global and national economy. Here, we discuss several examples of a general trend of native populations who have had rapid rises in weight gain and the prevalence of overweight and obesity followed by more ambiguous results (see Table 9.1).

Between 1989 and 2004, economic reforms in China led to an increase in BMI and the share of overweight and obese people in rural areas (Du et al., 2013; Zhai et al., 2009). Only approximately 7% of rural Chinese were classified as overweight or obese in 1989, and this increased to just under 25% by 2004, nearly matching the prevalence rate of overweight or obese people in urban areas (Zhai et al., 2009). In a different analysis examining ethnic minorities in China between 1989 and 2006, only approximately 10% of the minority groups were overweight or obese in 1989 and 1997, yet the prevalence increased rapidly in the following 10 years to approximately 20% by 2006 (Ouyang & Pinstrup-Andersen, 2012). In comparison, the majority Han ethnicity had a steady rise in prevalence of overweight and obesity, going from 14% in 1989 to 29% in 2006. The economic reforms during this time led to increased consumption of animal products and lower consumption of carbohydrates, which the authors suggest drove the increase in weight (Ouyang & Pinstrup-Andersen, 2012; Zhai et al., 2009).

Similarly to the trend in China, we found examples of weight gain following dietary change accompanying modernization in populations ranging from the Pacific Islands to South America (Lourenco et al., 2008; Ulijaszek, 2003). From 1952 to 1996, the mean weight of women of three age classes in the Cook Islands increased from 66–74 kg to 89–94 kg while the range of mean BMI increased from 26–28 kg/m^2 to 33–34.5 kg/m^2 (Ulijaszek, 2003). Ulijaszek explains the increases in average weight and BMI of women by excess energy availability in the diet through a decline of traditional staples and increased consumption of sugars, oils, and meat, rather than by a decrease in energy expenditure.

Studies among Suruí in Brazil found that an increase in monetary income between 1988 and 2005 was associated with socioeconomic stratification and the emergence of higher rates of overweight and obesity (Lourenco et al. 2008; Santos & Coimbra, 1996). During this period, men and women gained an average of 11.3 kg and 8.6 kg, respectively, which shifted mean BMI from the normal to the overweight category. Lourenco and colleagues (2008) explain the increase in weight through lifestyle and dietary shifts that included eating rice, noodles, and deep-fried foods and consuming soft drinks. Similarly, the Xavante of Brazil experienced a swift increase in weight and BMI (8.9 kg and 4 kg/m^2 for men; 13.8 kg and 5.9 kg/m^2 for women) between 1962 and 2006 (Welch et al., 2009).

As the previous examples indicate, modernization or contact with Western civilization often leads to weight gain. A final example of rapid weight gain comes from the Toba of northern Argentina. A 2004–05 study with 331 adults found that 35% of women and 25% of men were overweight, and 23% of women and 12% of men were obese (Valeggia, Burke, & Fernandez-Duque, 2010). A related cross-sectional study approximately 6 years later (2010) among a sample of 275 Toba, found markedly higher rates of overweight (31.3%) and obesity (45.1%) (Lagranja, Phojanakong, Navarro, & Valeggia, 2014).

Table 9.1 Trends in weight, body mass index (BMI), and height changes among native populations with adult longitudinal data or multiple cross-sectional surveys

Country	Population	Sex	Δ weight; Δ BMI over time	% Δ overweight/ obese	Δ height	Years	Reference(s)
Argentina	Toba	M F	3.9 kg/m²; 4.3 kg/m²	25.5%; 19%	nr	2004–2010	Valeggia et al., 2010; Lagranja et al., 2014
Australia	Aborigines	MF	nr	nr	No Δ	1924–1996	Pretty et al., 1998
Bolivia	Tsimane'	M F	3.8 kg, 1.9 kg/m²; 4.8 kg, 2.7 kg/m²	12.6%; 16.6%	No Δ No Δ	2002–2010	TAPS panel data & Godoy et al., 2006
Brazil	Ribeirinhos	M F	0.5 kg, 0.17 kg/m²; 2.5 kg, 1.1 kg/m²	−12%; No Δ	1 cm; 1.5 cm	2002–2009	Piperata et al., 2011
Brazil	Surui	M F	11 kg, 3.9 kg/m²; 8.4 kg, 3.7 kg/m²	nr	1.4 cm; 1.7 cm	1988–2005	Santos & Coimbra, 1996; Lourenco et al., 2008
Brazil	Xavante	M F	8.9 kg, 4 kg/m²; 13.8 kg, 5.9 kg/m²;	nr	−2.8 cm; −0.2 cm	1962–2006	Welch et al., 2009
Brazil	Xingu	MF			No Δ	1924–1954	Eveleth, 1974
Brazil	Khisêdjê	M F	0.4 kg/m²; 1.2 kg/m²	nr	nr	1999–2011	Mazzucchetti et al., 2014
China	All eastern ethnic minorities	MF	0.75 kg/m²	10%	nr	1989–2006	Ouyang & Pinstrup-Andersen, 2012; Zhai et al., 2009
Colombia	Rural	MF	nr	nr	No Δ	1977	Himes & Mueller, 1977
Cook Islands	Rarotonga	F	20.3 kg, 6.6 kg/m²	nr	3.9 cm	1952–1996	Ulijaszek, 2003

(*Continued*)

Table 9.1 Contniued

Country	Population	Sex	Δ weight; Δ BMI over time	% Δ overweight/ obese	Δ height	Years	Reference(s)
Guyana	Wapishana & Patamona	F	nr	nr	−1 cm	1946–1966	Dangour, 2003
		M			−1.4 cm		
India	Sikh	F	nr	nr	0.05cm/yr	1975–1976	Singal et al., 1981
India	Great Andamanese	F	nr	nr	−1.8/c	1879–1927	Stock & Migliano, 2009 [Estimates are per century, c]
		M			−4.7/c		
	Onge	F	nr	nr	2.8/c	1927–1962	
		M			3.6/c		
Indonesia	Javanese	F	nr	nr	nr	1944–2005	Ashizawa et al., 2009
		M			3.6 cm		
Mexico	Triqui	M	9.1 kg, 3.5 kg/m^2	34.7%	1 cm	1940–2002	Rodríguez & Mendoza, 2007
Mexico	Zapotec	M	nr	nr	No Δ	1890–1975	Himes et al., 1975
Mexico	Oaxaca	F	nr	nr	1.6 cm	1968–2000	Malina et al., 2004
		M			2.7 cm		
Mexico	Maya	M	nr	nr	No Δ	1890–1980	McCullough, 1982
PNG	Telefolmin	M	nr	nr	No Δ	1983–2008	Adhikari et al., 2011
		F			No Δ		
Peru	Matsigenka	M	−2.9 kg, 0.6 kg/m^2;	nr	−5.8 cm;	1977–1999	Izquiredo, 2005
		F	3.1 kg, 1.5 kg/m^2	nr	−0.1 cm		
Solomon Islands	6 groups	MF	nr	nr	Unclear		Page et al., 1977
South Africa	North/Central Bushmen	M	nr	nr	3.5 cm	1910–1960	Tobias, 1962
		F			1.9 cm	1924–1958	
	South Bushmen	M			2.2 cm		
		F			1.4 cm		

Δ change; M, male; F, female; MF, values from sexes combined in article; % overweight and obese: BMI ≥ 25.0. nr: not reported even though measures were taken.

Despite the data coming from two different cross-sectional samples, within the span of 5–6 years, the prevalence of obesity and overweight for Toba increased from 47.5% to 76.4%. Socioeconomic status (SES) and community leadership positions along with store-bought versus foraged food were associated with obesity. SES was also positively, linearly related with BMI among both men and women (Valeggia et al., 2010). Although these examples of rapid weight gain provide evidence of the nutrition transition among native populations, we now discuss other examples that do not support the transition.

9.2.3 Ambiguous Results

Results from separate cross-sectional and longitudinal data among four native populations in Bolivia, Brazil, and Peru fail to indicate the same dramatic rise of obesity as those just described. Among the Tsimane', small increases in mean population weight have been seen in the past 10 years. Comparing results from two cross-sectional studies in 2001–2002 and 2008 in 37 and 40 communities, we find that women's weight and BMI increased from 51.9 kg to 53.8 kg and 22.9 kg/m^2 to 23.7 kg/m^2. For men, weight and BMI remained fairly constant, with means of 62.4 kg to 62.2 kg and 23.3 kg/m^2 to 23.5 kg/m^2 (Godoy et al., 2005; Rosinger, Tanner, Leonard, & TAPS Study Team, 2013). This finding is similar to the TAPS longitudinal sample of 13 Tsimane' villages, which indicated a small secular increase in mean BMI among men and women of 0.37% and 0.64% per year, respectively, from 2002 to 2006 (inclusive) (Zeng et al., 2013). The new TAPS panel data from 2002 to 2010 indicate the trend of increasing BMI is continuing because Tsimane' women's BMI increased from 21.6 kg/m^2 in 2002 to 24.3 in 2010 and men's increased from 21.8 kg/m^2 to 23.7 during that time.

Similarly, in Brazil, Piperata and colleagues (2011) found that rural Ribeirinhas (mixed-ethnicity native Amerindians) women between 2002 and 2009 gained on average 2.5 kg and 1.1 kg/m^2 BMI units while men's weight and BMI stayed stable. The increase was negatively associated with changes in household income from wage labor and government conditional cash transfer programs. These trends are similar to the Khisêdjê population in central Brazil whose BMI remained fairly stable between 1999 and 2011, with women's BMI increasing 1.2 kg/m^2 while men's increased 0.4 kg/m^2 (Mazzucchetti et al., 2014). These two examples stand in contrast with other native Brazilian populations (Lourenco et al., 2008; Welch et al., 2009), and, despite the modest increase in weight for women, Piperata et al. (2011) found low rates of overweight or obesity in the longitudinal sample, with the overall prevalence dropping from 31% in 2002 to 25% in 2009.

None of the studies we found showed strong evidence of decline; however, an intriguing example provides evidence of differences in the direction of trends for women and men. Between 1977 and 1999, Izquierdo (2005) found that Matsigenkan women of Peru gained 3.1 kg in weight and 1.5 kg/m^2 in BMI. However, men lost 2.9 kg in weight, although BMI increased slightly from 23.6 kg/m^2 to 24.2 kg/m^2 due to a significant height decrease (Izquierdo, 2005). Lifestyle changes among the Matsigenka, including intrusion by oil companies, are credited with disrupting traditional food systems but do not explain why the direction of trends in weight for women and men differed.

In sum, the examples from the Tsimane', Ribeirinhas, and Matsigenka illustrate that native Amazonian women may be more sensitive to weight changes than are men. Moreover, there is a tendency for weight and BMI values to increase. Although the populations reviewed here are not exhaustive, the average change in weight we found for women was 8.8 kg over an average study period of 19.4 years, or 0.38 kg/year. Men experienced a smaller change in average weight gain of 5.1 kg for men over 21 years, or 0.19 kg/year. Similarly, the average change for women in BMI was 3.1 kg/m^2, an average increase of 0.16 kg/m^2 per year. On average, men gained 2.1 kg/m^2, an increase of 0.1 kg/m^2 per year.

9.2.4 Comparison of Body Weight of Native Populations with the rest of the Population

Despite the evidence accumulated so far indicating a pattern of weight gain, several studies suggest that native populations remain lighter and less likely to be obese or overweight compared with non-native populations, likely due to dietary traditions and activity patterns or isolation from industrial food sources. Cross-sectional and longitudinal studies from Mexico (Stoddard et al., 2011), Malaysia (Yusof et al., 2007), India (Bisai & Bose, 2009; Mungreiphy & Kapoor, 2010), Bolivia (Pérez-Cueto & Kolsteren, 2004), Brazil (Coimbra et al., 2013), Peru (Romero, Zavaleta, Cabrera, Gilman, & Miranda, 2014), and China (Ouyang & Pinstrup-Andersen, 2012) suggest that native rural populations weigh less and have a lower prevalence of being overweight and obese than do people from the rest of their nations (Ng et al., 2014) or from their peers living in cities (Table 9.2). For example, in China, ethnic minorities weighed significantly less and had lower prevalence of overweight (16%) and obesity (3%) than the majority Han ethnicity (25% and 4%, respectively) for the nine regions sampled (Ouyang & Pinstrup-Andersen, 2012). Stoddard et al. (2011) found that Mexicans who self-identified as Indians had 10–30% lower odds of being obese than those who did not identify as being Indian.

Between 1994 and 1998, Pérez-Cueto and Kolsteren (2004) found that rural Bolivian women who spoke Quechua or Aymara were, respectively, 34% and 57% less likely to be obese than their Spanish-speaking peers. Bolivia is an interesting case study because about half of the population identifies as native; yet, between 1994 and 1998, the number of people who reported speaking the native Quechua and Aymara languages decreased by 6% and 3%, respectively. This decrease in spoken native language coincided with a secular increase of overweight between 1994 and 1998 of all rural women, signaling that broad changes in national culture and assimilation may lead to the adoption of "industrial food consumption habits" that, in turn, lead to increased weight among native women.

Table 9.2 Comparison of most recent data available of select native populations adult body mass index (BMI) and overweight and obesity prevalence with national or majority ethnicity population average

Country	Populations	Sex	BMI Δ	% overweight/ obese Δ	Year	Reference(s)
Argentina	Toba vs. general population.	M F		18% 29%	2010	Lagranja et al., 2014
Bolivia	Tsimane' vs. general population	M F		–31.7% –34%	2008	Rosinger et al., 2013
Brazil	Amerindian vs. general population	M F	– 1.3 kg/m^2 –0.4 kg/m^2	– –	2004	de Oliveira Alvim et al., 2014
Brazil	All indigenous vs. general population	F	–	– 13.1%	2009	Coimbra et al., 2013
Chile	Pehuenche	M F		–2.8% 15.7%	2013	Velásquez & Briones, 2012
China	All eastern ethnic minorities vs. Han	MF	–0.89 kg/m^2	– 10%	2006	Ouyang & Pinstrup-Andersen, 2012
China	Deng (Tibet) vs. Han	MF	–2.40 kg/m^2	–22.7%		Zhao, Li, & Zheng., 2014
China	Lhoba (Tibet) vs. Han	MF	– 1.22 kg/m^2	– 10.6%		Zhao et al., 2014
China	Monba (Tibet) vs. Han	MF	– 1.00 kg/m^2	– 11.4%		Zhao et al., 2014
Honduras	Miskito vs. general population	F	4.5 kg/m^2	21.6%	2005	Arps, 2011
India	Tangkhul Naga vs. general population	F	–	– 10.9%	2006	Mungreiphy & Kapoor, 2010
Malaysia	Orang Asli	MF	–	–36.1%	2002	Yusof et al., 2007
Mexico	Indigenous vs. nonindigenous population	MF	–0.9	– 10.1%	2002	Stoddard et al., 2011
Peru	Ashaninkas vs. general population	M F	–	–9.3% –24%	2008	Romero et al., 2014

Comparison national population data come from article cited or from Ng et al. (2014) that lists national overweight and obesity prevalence in 2013. Δ indicates difference between latest year of data available for native population and national average (author's calculation). Negative values indicate that the native population has values less than the national average. % overweight and obese: BMI ≥ 25.0. Year: year data were collected among native population compared against 2013 data.

Coimbra et al. (2013) conducted the first National Survey of Indigenous People's Health and Nutrition in Brazil in 2008–2009 and found that the prevalence of obesity (15.8%) among native women (aged 14–49) was comparable to the obesity rate of non-native women, but the rate of overweight was lower among native women (30.3%) than non-native women (43%). This study suggests that although a high proportion of women from Brazilian native populations are at risk of being overweight and obese, their risk is slightly lower than non-native women.

However, some native populations have seen their weights and BMIs increase past the point of national averages. For example, in a descriptive, cross-sectional examination of the native Pehuenche Indians of Chile living around 1,500 m above sea level, Cartes Velásquez and Navarrete Briones (2012) found higher rates of overweight and obesity among women, but not men, than among the general Chilean populations (Ng et al., 2014). Eighty percent of women and 65% of men in the sample were overweight or obese. Similarly, Arps (2011) found that native Miskito women in Northeastern Honduras had an average weight and BMI of 69.0 kg and 29.6 kg/m^2, higher than the mean BMI for women in Honduras (25.1 kg/m^2).

Overall, 10 of 13 native populations reviewed in Table 9.2 had a recent overweight and obesity prevalence of at least 10 percentage points lower than the national averages for men and women combined.

9.2.5 Possible Determinants of Weight

In this section, we discuss some of the most common determinants identified with weight changes of native populations. The causes of changes in weight are hard to untangle owing to endogeneity biases. Only one study (Colchero & Sosa-Rubi, 2012) tried to correct for endogeneity by using instrumental variables, and we found no study that tried to exploit natural experiments to identify causality.

9.2.5.1 *Wealth, Human Capital, and SES*

Weight and body composition have long been associated with wealth, human capital, and SES (Ulijaszek & Koziel, 2007). However, many studies attempting to link economic factors with weight suffer from endogeneity due to omitted variable biases, whereby economic factors may be correlated with other unmeasured factors like access to foods, which may be partly responsible for the relation between economic factors and weight gain. For example, in both the 2001–2002 and 2008 Tsimane' studies, modern human capital and wealth were associated with higher BMI (Godoy et al., 2005; Rosinger et al., 2013). A separate cross-sectional study of Tsimane' social status and hierarchy found that an increase in rank among men was associated with an increase in BMI by 3.2% (Reyes-García et al., 2008). The authors suggested that social obligations among the elite are more likely to be lifted, thus reducing energy outputs while allowing more access to marketed or processed foods. However, when using the longitudinal sample from 2002–2006, we found mixed and weak evidence about the effects of wealth on weight and BMI (Godoy et al., 2009).

We found two studies that were useful examples of attempting to solve the issues of endogeneity and selection bias through the use of instrumental variables and Heckman correction, respectively. For example, Colchero and Sosa-Rubi (2012) found that a 1,000 pesos increase in income (representing 79% of monthly mean income) was associated with a 4.1% increase in body weight among rural Mexican women, and the results remained even once they instrumented household income with the number of rooms in the household and household expenditures on clothes and footwear.

Many studies are not designed at the outset to test differences between subpopulations and, as a result, may suffer from selection bias. A longitudinal study comparing health inequalities of ethnic Chinese minorities to Han Chinese illustrated that level of economic development in the home province was a major contributor to the difference in BMI. However, the difference in BMI between the minorities and Han was no longer significant after adjusting for the Heckman correction method (Ouyang & Pinstrup-Andersen, 2012).

9.2.5.2 *Integration into the Market and Dietary Change*

Many studies point to differences in market participation, wage labor, access to market foods, and government cash transfers when attempting to explain changes in weight among native populations (Arps, 2011; Godoy et al., 2005; Lourenco et al., 2008; Piperata et al., 2011; Ulijaszek, 2003; Valeggia et al., 2010). Cross-sectional studies often use community-to-city distance to proxy for participation in the market economy (Hidalgo et al., 2014; Lindegarde, Widen, Gebb, & Ahren, 2004; Romero et al., 2014; Rosinger et al., 2013; Valeggia et al., 2010). A common finding from these studies is that weight increases when people shift from producing their own food to purchasing it in the market (Lindegarde et al., 2004; Rosinger et al., 2013; Valeggia et al., 2010). Overall, in regions where secular trends of weight gain are most obvious, increases in income, SES, and wealth are often translated into dietary shifts that provide greater access to calorically dense food products.

9.2.5.2.1 *Community Attributes*

Community attributes, such as demographic composition of the community and stigma associated with being a minority may also affect vulnerability to weight gain. Stoddard et al. (2011) found that living in a Mexican community where 30% or more of the population identified as native was associated with lower risk of obesity. Likewise, Colchero and Sosa-Rubi (2012) found that people who identified as native in rural Mexico weighed less and had lower odds of being obese and overweight. A potential reason for the effect of community composition on risk of obesity is less stress, stigma, and/or discrimination on account of being native when most people in a community identify as natives.

9.3 Height

Standing height captures an adult's history of nutrition and health while the subject was growing, typically until the early 20s (Lohman, Roche, & Martorell, 1988).

9.3.1 Errors in Reported and Measured Height

Patel et al. (2007) reviewed the literature from industrial nations comparing (1) reported own and parental height with (2) measured own and parental height and found evidence of substantial errors. They found that adults tended to overestimate their own height. Using the TAPS survey data for 2005, they found that in a sample of 555 Tsimane' adults (>20 years of age), more than half the sample reported inaccurately the height of their same-sex living parent, with a tendency to report no difference when, in fact, large differences existed. To our knowledge, researchers have yet to use reported own or parental height in native populations in developing countries. Ulijaszek et al. (1998, p. 28) and Ulijaszek and Kerr (1999) present a typology of measurement errors of height.

9.3.2 Age Estimates

In addition to height, the analysis of secular trends of adult height requires accurate measures of age. Obtaining accurate or consistent age estimates in remote native societies is difficult because people lack birth certificates and are rarely asked about their age. Thus, people do not know their age. The TAPS annual panel suggests that 17% of adults older than 21 years of age admitted not knowing their age and guessed or provided their best estimate when asked about their age. If one restricts the sample to those who reported knowing their age, 54.1% of the observations showed an increase or a decrease of more than 1 year from one annual survey to the next; these were clearly errors or inconsistencies because surveyors noted the survey date so they could estimate the exact elapsed time between surveys in relation to the age reported by the subject.

Because age and birth period both enter the analysis of secular trends of height on the right side of the equation, classical measurement error of age could be one methodological reason why researchers have found no change in the secular trend of height in native societies.

9.3.3 Analysis

Formal methods to establish secular trends come in two forms. The first method consists of comparing changes in mean adult height between different cross-sectional samples collected at different times (e.g., Malina, Selby, Buschang, Aronson, & Wilkinson, 1983; McCullough, 1982; Stock & Migliano, 2009; Tobias, 1962; Ulijaszek, 1993). For instance, using surveys from 1879 until 1927, Stock and Migliano (2009) concluded that the Great Andamanese experienced a secular decline in height, compared with the Onge and Jarawa in the Andaman Islands who were measured only during 1927–1962 or 1927–1986 and who saw a positive secular trend in height. If selective mortality of shorter adults was more prevalent in 1879 than in 1927, then this alone could explain the differential secular trends between groups without needing to invoke the history of colonialism, as these researchers do.

The analysis by Malina et al. (2004), although simple, stands out as a model of the first method. Their careful attention and discussion of interobserver reliability in measures of height (but not of age) and their comparison of standing and sitting height of young adults (aged 19–29) from the same rural community in Oaxaca, Mexico, by the same researchers in two studies spanning 32 years allows them to show that the height for women and for men increased by 1.6 cm and 2.7 cm, respectively (Malina et al., 2004). With the findings empirically well established, they test and rule out the role of gene flow as a cause (Little et al., 2006), leaving open the specifics of what drove the increase in height.

The second method for estimating secular trends consists of using cross-sectional data to regress adult height (outcome), in some cases corrected for age-related shrinkage (Godoy et al., 2006; Himes & Malina, 1975; Himes & Mueller, 1977; Pretty, Henneberg, Lambert, & Prokopec, 1998), against age and dummy variables for birth periods. The coefficient of the age variable captures the annual change in height from the life cycle, whereas the coefficients for the dummy variables for birth periods capture the effect of having been born in particular birth periods relative to a benchmark time period excluded from the regression. If the regression pools different cross-sectional surveys, then n–1 dummy variables for the different cross-sectional surveys should be included. The coefficients for the birth-period dummies allow one to assess the direction of the secular trend. Although technically more sophisticated than the first method, econometric estimates might suffer from inflated standard errors owing to random measurement error of height, an attenuation bias from age guessing and from selective mortality in relation to birth period, and omitted-variable bias from failure to control for environmental and economic conditions while the subject was growing. Studies that include age-adjusted height as an outcome introduce further random error into the height measure owing to the possible mismeasure of age.

9.3.4 Findings

It has become standard practice going back to the work of Tobias (1962) to say that in native populations the secular increase in height found in developed countries need not appear; to point out cases of increases, decreases, or no change in secular trends; and then to go on to discuss how the depth and form of modernization in the rural economy, access to improved health and nutrition, adverse shocks to health, or changes in gene flows between populations might explain the heterogeneity of results (Little, Peña Reyes, & Malina, 2006; Malina et al., 1983; Pretty et al., 1998, p. 507; Stock & Migliano, 2009; Ulijaszek, 1993). The studies reviewed confirm the standard reading of the evidence. Methodological shortcomings aside, the studies reviewed hint at a positive secular trend in height in South Africa, Indonesia and India, the Pacific, the Andaman Islands, and Latin America (Ashizawa, Rahmawati, & Hastuti, 2009; Malina et al., 2004; Singal &

Sidhu, 1981; Stock & Migliano, 2009; Tobias, 1962; Ulijaszek, 1993, 2001). The nine studies showing a positive secular trend of height suggest that the height of women increased by 0.076 cm/year and the height of men increased by 0.069 cm/year. The four studies showing a negative secular trend of height suggest that height declined by 0.02 cm/year among women and 0.11 cm/year among men (Dangour, 2003; Izquierdo, 2005; Stock & Migliano, 2009; Welch et al., 2009). Eight studies found no change in the secular trend of height (Adhikari et al., 2011; Eveleth, Salzano, & de Lima 1974; Godoy et al., 2006; Himes & Malina, 1975; Himes & Mueller, 1977; McCullough, 1982; Page, Friedlaender, & Moellering, 1977; Pretty et al., 1998).

Two noteworthy findings seem to emerge. First, these estimates suggest that with a positive secular trend, the gain is about the same for women and men, but when the secular trend is negative, then men seem to experience much more negative trends (−0.11 cm/year) than women (−0.02 cm/year). Second, we find heterogeneity in secular trends in height within the same geographical area. For instance, among native Amazonians, the secular trend in height increased for the Surui; declined for the Xavante, Wapishana, and Matsigenka; and remained unchanged among the Tsimane' and Xingu. Page et al. (1977) also found a great deal of heterogeneity in the secular trend in height among ethnic groups in the Solomon Islands.

One should consider these results tentative and subject to interpretation. Of the 13 studies that relied on primary data collected by researchers, the median sample size was 275 for women and 217 for men, with minimum values of 46 for women and 52 for men. What is worrisome is not the modest sample size, which authors routinely acknowledge as a limitation, but the failure ex ante to do a power analysis to evaluate if they could have detected meaningful effect sizes at conventional statistical levels from their samples. Not one study mentions power analysis. Or, consider endogeneity. Issues of endogeneity are sometimes acknowledged but never resolved. Adhikari et al. (2011) and Friedlaender and Rhoads (1982) in the Pacific Islands and Piperata et al. (2011) in the Brazilian Amazon mention the construction of large-scale mines in the Pacific and government policies in Brazil as exogenous shocks that could have affected secular trends in adult height, but they do not isolate and estimate the effect of the shocks. Combined, all these limitations make it difficult to draw convincing conclusions about secular changes in height in preliterate, small-scale rural societies. Until researchers address the concerns discussed here and are confident that they have something to explain, it might be premature to engage in discussions of the causes of secular trends in height in native societies, intellectually stimulating as those discussions might be.

9.4 Conclusion

Our analysis of longitudinal studies of native populations provides evidence of an average increase of 5.1 and 8.8 kg in weight for men and women over an average of 20 years studied and evidence that 10 of 13 native populations reviewed have an overweight and obesity prevalence of at least 10 percentage points lower than non-native populations. In contrast to weight, 12 out of 21 studies found no change ($n = 8$) or a decline ($n = 4$) in height. What we know should be considered tentative about the determinants of weight and height changes owing to inconsistent attention to sample size, random sampling, and causal identification.

Although studies discussing changes in weight have increased significantly in the past 15 years thanks to the growing interest in the nutrition transition, secular trend analysis of height in native populations seems to have fallen out of favor. Of the 21 studies reviewed, only five took place in the past decade. This is a pity because, when well done, secular trends of height could tell us a great deal about vulnerability, cultural adaptation, and the plasticity of human growth to socioeconomic and environmental stresses. It is not that height data are not being collected, but rather that researchers are dedicating more time to studies of secular weight changes because weight fluctuates more rapidly than height.

Longitudinal analyses in native societies present an opportunity to assess trends in weight and height as the economy and diet of these societies change. The simple setting offered by rural, native populations allows one to remove the confounding noise of urbanization, income inequality, immigration, government policies, and ethnic heterogeneity plaguing secular trend analysis of body size in industrial nations. These studies will further our understanding of how different economic systems in different environments are embodied into human biology.

References

Adhikari, A., Sen, A., Brumbaugh, R. C., & Schwartz, J. 2011. Altered growth patterns of a mountain Ok population of Papua New Guinea over 25 years of change. *American Journal of Human Biology, 23*, 325–332.

Aiello, L. C., & Wheeler, P. (1995). The Expensive Tissue Hypothesis, The brain and the digestive system in human evolution. *Current Anthropology, 36*, 199–221.

Arps, S. (2011). Socioeconomic status and body size among women in Honduran Miskito communities. *Annals of Human Biology, 38*(4), 508–519.

Ashizawa, K., Rahmawati, N. T., & Hastuti, J. (2009). Body size and shape, and its secular change in Javanese-Indonesian adults. *Anthropological Science, 117*(3), 165–170.

Bisai, S., & Bose, K. (2009). Undernutrition in the Kora Mudi tribal population, West Bengal, India: A comparison of body mass index and mid-upper-arm circumference. *Food & Nutrition Bulletin, 30*(1), 63–67.

Bogin, B., & Keep, R. (1999). Eight thousand years of economic and political history in Latin America revealed by anthropometry. *Annals of Human Biology, 26*(4), 333–351.

Cartes Velásquez, R., & Navarrete Briones, C. (2012). Caracterización antropométrica de población pehuenche adulta, consideraciones nutricionales. Alto Biobio, Chile. *Memorias del Instituto de Investigaciones en Ciencias de la Salud, 10*(2), 30–37.

Coimbra, C. E. A., Santos, R. V., Welch, J. R., Cardoso, A. M., de Souza, M. C., Garnelo, L., . . . Horta, B. L. (2013). The First National Survey of Indigenous People's Health and Nutrition in Brazil: Rationale, methodology, and overview of results. *BMC Public Health, 13*(1), 52.

Colchero, M., & Sosa-Rubi, S. (2012). Heterogeneity of income and lifestyle determinants of body weight among adult women in Mexico, 2006. *Social Science & Medicine, 75*(1), 120–128.

Dangour, A. D. (2003). Cross-sectional changes in anthropometric variables among Wapishana and Patamona Amerindian adults. *Human Biology, 75*(2), 227–240.

de Oliveira Alvim, R., Mourao-Junior, C. A., de Oliveira, C. M., Krieger, J. E., Mill, J. G., & Pereira, A. C. (2014). Body mass index, waist circumference, body adiposity index, and risk for type 2 diabetes in two populations in Brazil: General and Amerindian.

Du, T., Sun, X., Yin, P., Huo, R., Ni, C., & Yu, X. (2013). Increasing trends in central obesity among Chinese adults with normal body mass index, 1993–2009. *BMC Public Health, 13*(1), 327.

Eveleth, P. B. Salzano, F. M, & de Lima, P. E. (1974). Child growth and adult physique in Brazilian Xingu Indians. *American Journal of Physical Anthropology, 41*, 95–102.

Floud, R., Fogel, R. W., Harris, B., & Hong, S. C. (2011). *The changing body: Health, nutrition, and human development in the western world since 1700*. Cambridge, UK: Cambridge University Press.

Friedlaender, J. S., & Rhoads, J. G. (1982). Patterns of adult weight and fat change in six Solomon Islands societies: A semi-longitudinal study. *Social Science & Medicine, 16*(2), 205–215.

Godoy, R., Leonard, W. R., Reyes-García, V., Goodman, E., McDade, T., Huanca, T., . . . Vadez, V. (2006). Physical stature of adult Tsimane' Amerindians, Bolivian Amazon in the 20th century. *Economics & Human Biology, 4*, 184–205.

Godoy, R., Reyes-García, V., Gravelee, C., Huanca, T., Leonard, W., McDade, T., . . . TAPS Bolivia Study Team. (2009). Moving beyond a snapshot to understand changes in the well-being of native Amazonians. *Current Anthropology, 50*(4), 563–573.

Godoy, R., Reyes-García, V., Vadez, V., Leonard, W. R., Huanca, T., & Bauchet, J. (2005). Human capital, wealth, and nutrition in the Bolivian Amazon. *Economics & Human Biology, 3*(1), 139–162.

Hidalgo, G., Marini, E. Sanchez, W., Contreras, M., Estrada, I., Comandini, O., . . . Dominguez-Bello MG. (2014). The nutrition transition in the Venezuelan Amazonia: Increased overweight and obesity with transculturation. *American Journal of Human Biology, 26*(5), 710–712.

Himes, J. H., & Malina, R. M. (1975). Age and secular factors in the stature of adult Zapotec males. *American Journal of Physical Anthropology, 43*, 367–369.

Himes, J. H., & Mueller, W. H. (1977). Aging and secular change in adult stature in rural Colombia. *American Journal of Physical Anthropology, 46*, 275–280.

Himmelgreen, D. A., Cantor, A., Arias, S., & Romero Daza, N. (2014). Using a biocultural approach to examine migration/globalization, diet quality, and energy balance. *Physiology & Behavior, 134*, 76–85.

Komlos, J. (Ed.). (1994). *Stature, living standards, and economic development: Essays in anthropometric history*. Chicago: University of Chicago Press.

Izquierdo, C. (2005). When "health" is not enough: Societal, individual and biomedical assessments of well-being among the Matsigenka of the Peruvian Amazon. *Social Science & Medicine, 61*(4), 767–783.

Lagranja, E. S., Phojanakong, P., Navarro, A., & Valeggia, C. R. (2014). Indigenous populations in transition: An evaluation of metabolic syndrome and its associated factors among the Toba of northern Argentina. *Annals of Human Biology, 42*(1), 84–90.

Leonard, W. R., & Robertson, M. L. (1994). Evolutionary perspectives on human nutrition: The influence of brain and body size on diet and metabolism. *American Journal of Human Biology, 6*, 77–88.

Lindegarde, F., Widen, I., Gebb, M., & Ahren, B. (2004). Traditional versus agricultural lifestyle among Shuar women of the Ecuadorian Amazon: Effects on leptin levels. *Metabolism, 53*(10), 1355–1358.

Little, B. B., Peña Reyes, M., & Malina, R. M. (2006). Opportunity for natural selection and gene flow in an isolated Zapotec-speaking community in southern Mexico in the throes of a secular increase in size. *Human Biology, 78*(3), 295–305.

Lohman, T., Roche, A., & Martorell, M. (1988). *Anthropometric standardization reference manual.* Champaign, IL: Human Kinetics.

Lourenco, A., Santos, R., Orellana, J., & Coimbra, C., Jr. (2008). Nutrition transition in Amazonia: Obesity and socioeconomic change in the Suruí Indians from Brazil. *American Journal of Human Biology, 20*(5), 564–571.

Luca, F., Perry, G. H., & Di Rienzo, A. (2010). Evolutionary adaptations to dietary changes. *Annual Review of Nutrition, 30*, 291–314.

Malina, R. M., Reyes, M. E. P, Tan, S. K., Buschang, P. H., Little, B. B., & Koziel, S. (2004). Secular change in height, sitting height, and leg length in rural Oaxaca, southern Mexico: 1968–2000. *Annals of Human Biology, 31*(6), 615–633.

Malina, R. M., Selby, H. A., Buschang, P. H., Aronson, W. L., & Wilkinson, R. G. (1983). Adult stature and age at menarche in Zapotec-speaking communities in the valley of Oaxaca, Mexico, in a secular perspective. *American Journal of Physical Anthropology, 60*, 437–449.

Mazzucchetti, L., Galvão, P. P. D. O., Tsutsui, M. L. D. S., Santos, K. M. D., Rodrigues, D. A., Mendonça, S. B., & Gimeno, S. G. A. (2014). Incidence of metabolic syndrome and related diseases in the Khisêdjê indigenous people of the Xingu, Central Brazil, from 1999--2000 to 2010-2011. *Cadernos de saude publica, 30*(11), 2357–2367.

McCullough, J. M. (1982). Secular trend for stature in adult male Yucatec Maya to 1968. *American Journal of Physical Anthropology, 58*, 221–225.

Mungreiphy, N. K., & Kapoor, S. (2010). Socioeconomic changes as covariates of overweight and obesity among Tangkhul Naga tribal women of Manipur, north-east India. *Journal of Biosocial Science, 42*(3), 289–305.

Ng, M., Fleming, T., Robinson, M., Thomson, B., Graetz, N., Margono, C., . . . Gupta, R (2014). Global, regional, and national prevalence of overweight and obesity in children and adults during 1980–2013: A systematic analysis for the Global Burden of Disease Study 2013. *Lancet, 384*(9945), 766–781.

Ouyang, Y., & Pinstrup-Andersen, P. (2012). Health inequality between ethnic minority and Han populations in China. *World Development, 40*(7), 1452–1468.

Page, L. B., Friedlaender, J., & Moellering, R. C., Jr. (1977). Culture, human biology and disease in the Solomon Islands. In G. A. Harrison (Ed.), *Population structure and human variation* (pp. 143–163). Cambridge, UK: Cambridge University Press.

Patel, A. M., Godoy, R. A., Seyfried, C., Reyes-García, V., Huanca, T., Leonard, W. R., . . . Tanner, S (2007). On the accuracy of perceived parental height in a native Amazonian society. *Economics and Human Biology, 5*, 165–178.

Pérez-Cueto, F. J. A., & Kolsteren, P. W. V. J. (2004). Changes in the nutritional status of Bolivian women 1994–*1998*: Demographic and social predictors. *European Journal of Clinical Nutrition, 58*(4), 660–666.

Piperata, B., Spence, J., Da-Gloria, P., & Hubbe, M. (2011). The nutrition transition in Amazonia: Rapid economic change and its impact on growth and development in Ribeirinhos. *American Journal of Physical Anthropology, 146*, 1–13.

Popkin, B. (1994). The nutrition transition in low-income countries: An emerging crisis. *Nutrition Reviews, 52*(9), 285–298.

Popkin, B. (2011). Contemporary nutritional transition: Determinants of diet and its impact on body composition. *Proceedings of the Nutrition Society, 70*(1), 82–91.

Popkin, B., Adair, L., & Ng, S. (2012). Global nutrition transition and the pandemic of obesity in developing countries. *Nutrition Reviews, 70*(1), 3–21.

Pretty, G. L., Henneberg, M., Lambert, K. M., & Prokopec, M. (1998). Trends in stature in the South Australian aboriginal Murraylands. *American Journal of Physical Anthropology, 106*, 505–514.

Reyes-García, V., McDade, T., Molina, J., Leonard, W., Tanner, S., Huanca, T., & Godoy, R. (2008). Social rank and adult male nutritional status: Evidence of the social gradient in health from a foraging-farming society. *Social Science & Medicine, 67*, 2107–2115.

Rodríguez, R. M. R., & Mendoza, K. S. (2007). Estado nutricional en la marginación y la pobreza de adultos triquis del estado de Oaxaca, México. *Revista Panamericana Salud Pública, 22*(4), 261.

Romero, C., Zavaleta, C., Cabrera, L., Gilman, R. H., & Miranda, J. J. (2014). Hipertensión arterial y obesidad en indígenas asháninkas de la región Junín, Perú. *Revista Peruana de Medicina Experimental y Salud Publica, 31*(1), 78–83.

Rosinger, A., Tanner, S., Leonard, W. R., & TAPS Study Team. (2013). Precursors to over-nutrition: The effects of household market food expenditures on measures of body composition among Tsimane' adults in lowland Bolivia. *Social Science & Medicine, 92*, 53–60.

Santos, R. V., & Coimbra, C. E. A., Carlos, E. A., Jr. (1996). Socioeconomic differentiation and body morphology in the Suruí of Southwestern Amazonia. *Current Anthropology, 37* (5), 851–856.

Shaw, N., & Braverman, E. (2012). Measuring adiposity in patients: The utility of body mass index (BMI), percent body fat, and leptin. *PLoS One, 7*(4), E33308.

Sibai, A., Nasreddine, L., Mokdad, A., Adra, N., Tabet, M., & Hwalla, N. (2010). Nutrition transition and cardiovascular disease risk factors in Middle East and North African countries: Reviewing the evidence. *Annals of Nutrition and Metabolism, 57*, 193–203.

Singal, P., & Sidhu, L. S. (1981). Ageing and secular changes in adult stature of Jat-Sikh and Bania females of Punjab (India). *Anthropologischer Anzeiger, 39*(4), 313–320.

Snodgrass, J. J. (2012). Human energetics. In S. Stinson & B. Bogin (Eds.), *Human biology: An evolutionary and biocultural perspective* (2nd ed., pp. 325–384). New York: Wiley.

Stock, J. T., & Migliano, A. B. (2009). Stature, mortality, and life history among indigenous populations of the Andaman Islands. *Current Anthropology, 50*(5), 713–725.

Stoddard, P., Handley, M. A., Vargas Bustamante, A., & Schillinger, D. (2011). The influence of indigenous status and community indigenous composition on obesity and diabetes among Mexican adults. *Social Science & Medicine, 73*(11), 1635–1643.

Tobias, P. V. (1962). On the increasing stature of the Bushmen. *Anthropos, 57*(3–6), 801–810.

Ulijaszek, S. J. (1993). Evidence for a secular trend in heights and weights of adults in Papua New Guinea. *Annals of Human Biology, 20*(4), 349–355.

Ulijaszek, S. J. (1998). The secular trend. In S. J. Ulijaszek, F. E. Johnston, & M. A. Preece (Eds.), *The Cambridge encyclopedia of human growth and development* (pp. 395–398). Cambridge, UK: Cambridge University Press.

Ulijaszek, S. J. (2001). Increasing body size among adult Cook Islanders between 1966 and 1996. *Annals of Human Biology, 28*(4), 363–373.

Ulijaszek, S. J. (2003). Trends in body size, diet and food availability in the Cook Islands in the second half of the 20th century. *Economics & Human Biology, 1*(1), 123–137.

Ulijaszek, S. J., Johnston, F. E., & Preece, M. A. (Eds.). (1998). *The Cambridge encyclopedia of human growth and development*. Cambridge, UK: Cambridge University Press.

Ulijaszek, S. J., & Kerr, D. A. (1999). Anthropometric measurement error and the assessment of nutritional status. *British Journal of Nutrition, 82*, 165–177.

Ulijaszek, S., & Koziel, S. (2007). Nutrition transition and dietary energy availability in Eastern Europe after the collapse of communism. *Economics and Human Biology, 5*, 359–369.

Valeggia, C., Burke, K., & Fernandez-Duque, E. (2010). The impact of socioeconomic change on nutritional status among Toba and Wichi populations of Argentina. *Economics and Human Biology, 8*(1), 100–110.

Welch, J., Ferreira, A., Santos, R., Gugelmin, S., Werneck, G., & Coimbra, C. (2009). Nutrition transition, socioeconomic differentiation, and gender among adult Xavante Indians, Brazilian Amazon. *Human Ecology, 37*(1), 13–26.

Wilson, H. J., Dickinson, F., Griffiths, P. L., Azcorra, H., Bogin, B., & Varela-Silva, I. M. (2011). How useful is BMI in predicting adiposity indicators in a sample of Maya children and women with high levels of stunting? *American Journal of Human Biology, 23*(6), 780–789.

Yusof, H. M., Ching, T. S., Ibrahim, R., & Lola, S. (2007). Anthropometric indices and life style practices of the indigenous Orang Asli adults in Lembah Belum, Grik of Peninsular Malaysia. *Asia Pacific Journal of Clinical Nutrition, 16*(1), 49–55.

Zeng, W., Eisenberg, D., Jovel, K., Undurraga, E., Nyberg, C., Tanner, S., . . . TAPS Bolivia Study Team. (2013). Adult obesity: Panel study from native Amazonians. *Economics and Human Biology, 11*(2), 227–235.

Zhai, F., Wang, H., Du, S., He, Y., Wang, Z., Ge, K., & Popkin, B. (2009). Prospective study on nutrition transition in China. *Nutrition Reviews, 67*(S1), S56–S61.

Zhao, D., Li, Y., & Zheng, L. (2014). Ethnic inequalities and sex differences in body mass index among Tibet minorities in China: Implication for overweight and obesity risks. *American Journal of Human Biology, 26*(6), 856–858.

CHAPTER 10

SLAVE HEIGHTS

RICHARD H. STECKEL

In the past several decades, journals have published hundreds of articles using heights as a measure of health or biological aspects of the standard of living (Steckel, 1995, 2009). Economists, historians, human biologists, and other scientists find this measure useful in part because there are millions of such records collected in numerous countries over the past three centuries. Most were taken for purposes of identification, such as for soldiers or convicts, but, by the second quarter of the 19th century, some efforts targeted welfare considerations, including whether children were fit for factory work (Tanner, 1981).

In pondering what can be learned from heights, it is useful to imagine the body as a biological machine that consumes fuel (protein, fat, micronutrients, and so forth), much like a diesel engine that consumes a blend of hydrocarbons. The biological machine is always running, and, at idle, the fuel supports breathing, blood circulation, and cell replacement. If attacked by a disease, the fuel mobilizes the immune system. Physical activity or work also requires fuel and, under very strenuous conditions, may require up to 10,000 calories per day.

Physical growth requires fuel; if it is lacking, the growth of children will be retarded or delayed because the biological machine's highest priority is survival. Whatever energy is available will go to maintenance, support of the immune system, and perhaps light physical activity. If good times return, the body will grow at an expedited rate through a process called *catch-up growth*. Chronic and severe malnutrition, however, causes stunting and may be expressed by a delay in achieving final adult height.

Genes are crucial determinants of growth for individuals, but, in the aggregate or at the population level, these differences approximately cancel so that average height accurately reflects a population's history of net nutrition (fuel minus claims on that fuel). Of course, there are genetic differences between men and women, and men end up about 4.5 inches (11.43 cm) taller than women primarily because they mature later (i.e., grow an additional 2 years at preadolescent rates). The genetic potential for growth might differ slightly for people of various continental or ethnic origins, but various studies show that most people who grow up under good environmental conditions are approximately the same height (Malcolm, 1974; Martorell & Habicht, 1986).

Heights are particularly useful for understanding the living standards of American slaves because traditional records of socioeconomic achievement are generally lacking for this population. Few slaves received schooling (it was illegal in the slave states), and they did not earn wages or accumulate wealth. True, a few slaves had monetary accounts kept by their owners, which they earned by selling eggs and garden produce or for Sunday work, but these are not sufficiently common or well-documented to provide a useful picture of living standards. In this regard, heights are useful monitors of other populations that did not engage in market activity, such as native tribes, women, and children.

10.1 Data Sources

The height records studied in this chapter come from one major source. These were generated by the 1807 American law abolishing the Atlantic slave trade and its requirement that ship captains prove that slaves arriving at the port of destination were not smuggled from Africa. These manifests provide a wealth of demographic information about the slaves on board including name, age, sex, height, port of origin, port of destination, and the name and residence of the owner or shipper (Wesley, 1942). I have coded the slave heights from all manifests readily available at the National Archives in Record Group 36, including some 24,500 documents involving approximately 135,000 slaves who were transported in the coastwise trade from 1811 to 1861.

Other sources used for comparative purposes include muster rolls of U.S. Colored Troops (USCT) who fought or otherwise supported the Union effort in the Civil War (Margo & Steckel, 1992). Following the Emancipation Proclamation on January 1, 1863, the Union actively recruited colored regiments. In May of that year, the War Department established the Bureau of Colored Troops to facilitate recruitment, and, in the next 2 years, formed 175 regiments composed of roughly 180,000 free blacks and former slaves. The muster rolls do not distinguish blacks who were already free from newly freed slaves, but the individuals enlisting in the Deep South were far more likely to have been slaves emancipated by the Proclamation of January 1863.

Three additional sources used for comparative purposes are given in Table 10.1. They are ads for runaway slaves, certificates of good character drawn from the New Orleans slave market, and descriptions of slave contraband obtained by Union troops during the Civil War.

Some have questioned whether the heights on the manifests were distorted by professional traders who preferred working slaves who were tall for their age (Pritchett &

Table 10.1 Average Heights of Adult Black Men and Women from Alternative Sources

Group	Location	Height (M)	Height (F)	Source
Slave manifests	Atlantic and Gulf coasts	67.2[a]	62.7[a]	Steckel and Ziebarth (2016)
U.S. Colored Troops[b]	Southern states[a]	67.1		Margo and Steckel (1982)
Runaway slaves	Mainland colonies	67.2	62.7	Komlos (1994)
Certificates of good character	New Orleans, 1830	67.1	62.9	Pritchett and Freudenberger (1992)
Slave contraband	Mississippi, 1863	67.4		Margo and Steckel (1982)

[a] After deleting extreme outliers using a 1% trim of the sample.

[b] The majority were born in Border States and South Carolina

Freudenberger, 1992). If so, perhaps the amount of measured catch-up growth was exaggerated. Komlos and Alecke (1996) disputed this conclusion, and my own work (Steckel & Ziebarth, 2016) has been able to identify professional traders, finding no systematic differences of practical importance in the heights of slaves shipped by traders versus nontraders.

The average heights obtained from various sources are almost identical (Table 10.1). These comparisons do not prove the absence of selectivity, but they do place the burden of proof on those who would claim that it existed and was an important distortion in the manifests. It is conceivable but unlikely that the heights in all these independent sources were biased in approximately offsetting ways, such that the average heights appear to show no bias.

10.2 Height-by-Age Patterns

Tables 10.2 and 10.3 show average height-by-age for males and females listed on the manifests. Several interesting patterns emerge. One is that the children were extraordinarily short, falling below the first percentile of modern height standards as tabulated by the National Center for Health Statistics. The young children were among the smallest ever measured and would have been cause for alarm in a modern pediatrician's office.

Yet the slaves had a healthy adolescent growth spurt (more on this below) and recovered to roughly the 20th percentile of modern height standards (average for males and

Table 10.2 Height by Age of Male Slaves

Age[a]	Mean	*SD*	*N*	Mean Percentile[b]	Fitted Height[c]	Point Velocity[d]	Fitted Percentile[b]
4	36.71	3.35	581	0.29	36.54	2.70	0.29
5	39.25	3.41	500	0.37	39.13	2.49	0.37
6	41.30	4.05	573	0.32	41.52	2.30	0.32
7	43.53	4.10	555	0.50	43.74	2.14	0.50
8	45.18	4.34	766	0.39	45.81	2.01	0.39
9	48.35	3.58	791	2.22	47.78	1.93	2.22
10	49.84	3.99	1,336	1.75	49.68	1.89	1.75
11	52.00	3.85	1,061	2.37	51.58	1.91	2.37
12	53.47	4.13	1,914	1.72	53.53	2.00	1.72
13	55.22	4.10	1,418	1.21	55.60	2.13	1.21
14	57.53	4.02	2,046	0.97	57.56	2.23	0.97
15	60.04	3.74	1,587	0.71	60.04	2.22	0.71
16	62.24	3.11	1,888	0.64	62.16	1.99	0.64
17	64.14	2.91	1,904	1.61	63.96	1.58	1.61
18	65.18	2.87	3,240	4.10	65.30	1.10	4.10
19	66.23	2.78	2,619	9.22	66.19	0.70	9.22
20	66.49	2.77	3,929	11.07	66.73	0.41	11.07
21	67.20	2.76	2,581	17.21	67.04	0.23	17.21
22	67.14	2.72	3,265	16.61	67.04		17.21

[a] At last birthday; average age = age + 0.5.

[b] Calculated from Steckel (1996).

[c] From Preece-Baines model 1.

[d] First derivative of model 1 curve at average age.

Source: Slave manifests (see text).

females). About 5.5 inches (14 cm) below modern height standards as young children, they gained about 4 inches (10.2 cm) relative to those standards as adults.

This pattern of human growth is very unusual relative to those in historical times and to populations now living in poor developing countries (Steckel, 1986b). Developing countries that had relatively small children also had relatively small teenagers and adults. In other words, it was unusual, if not unique, to achieve the catch-up growth of

Table 10.3 Height by Age of Slave Females

Age[a]	Mean	*SD*	*N*	Mean Percentile[b]	Fitted Height[c]	Point Velocity[d]	Fitted Percentile[b]
4	36.66	3.40	577	0.44	36.44	2.75	0.31
5	39.06	3.40	556	0.61	39.06	2.50	0.61
6	41.28	4.05	692	0.94	41.45	2.28	1.17
7	43.33	4.08	650	1.21	43.65	2.11	1.72
8	45.23	4.48	918	1.33	45.70	2.00	2.09
9	48.39	3.75	919	3.90	47.66	1.95	2.13
10	49.75	4.23	1,288	1.81	49.62	1.98	1.62
11	51.98	4.09	1,143	1.28	51.65	2.10	0.94
12	53.36	4.30	1,836	0.33	53.83	2.24	0.54
13	55.94	4.12	1,544	0.65	56.10	2.27	0.77
14	58.22	3.72	2,179	2.44	58.06	2.06	2.12
15	60.07	3.28	2,213	7.90	60.05	1.52	7.80
16	61.34	2.71	3,105	14.38	61.29	0.97	13.90
17	62.15	2.60	2,486	18.04	62.03	0.55	16.73
18	62.36	2.68	3,676	18.26	62.44	0.28	19.11
19	62.75	2.79	1,578	23.07	62.64	0.14	21.62
20	62.55	2.88	2,885	20.45	62.74	0.07	22.92
21	62.78	2.83	797	23.43	62.79	0.03	23.55
22	62.74	2.87	1,538	22.87	62.79		23.55

[a] Age at last birthday; average age = age + 0.5.

[b] Calculated from Steckel (1996).

[c] From Preece-Baines model 1.

[d] First derivative of model 1 curve at average age.

Source: Slave manifests (see text).

slaves. A regression of height relative to modern standards at older ages on height relative to modern British standards at young ages gives a sense of the extent to which slaves were different. The following equation was estimated:

$$LRHTA = -0.0138 + 0.8575\ LRHTC;\ N = 39,\ R^2 = .46$$
$$(-1.17) \qquad (5.61)$$

where *LRHTA* is the natural log of relative height as adults or older teenagers (aged 16–18) and *LRHTC* is the natural log of relative height as children (aged 3–8); t-statistics are given in parentheses.

The extent to which slaves fit the pattern for developing countries can be assessed by substituting the relative height of slave children into the equation. At age 4, slaves attained 87.4% of modern height standards (average for males and females), which implies an estimated relative height as adults of 87.9% of modern standards. An 80% confidence interval for the predicted value of relative adult height is [81.7%, 94.5%]. Yet slaves reached 95.1% of standard height at age 17.5 and 96.2% of standard height at age 18.5. In contrast with American slaves, the conditions that produced low heights for children in developing countries tended to persist throughout the growing years.

Populations that were contemporary or approximately contemporary with slaves are a second source for comparisons. Table 10.3 (Steckel, 1986b) displays the centiles of modern height standards attained from childhood to maturity for a variety of American, European, and Caribbean slave populations who lived during the 19th and the late 18th centuries. This table confirms that American slaves had an unusual growth pattern. As young children, American slaves were smaller than any of the populations. However, the advantages of Caribbean slaves and German peasants were slight (or nonexistent, as in the case of Trinidad males ages 6.5 and beyond). Yet, by age 16.5, American male slaves were taller than factory workers and laboring classes in England, the poor of Italy, students in Habsburg military schools, the middle class of Stuttgart, German peasants, and factory workers in Russia. As adults, they also exceeded the aristocrats of Stuttgart and Moscow middle school pupils, were about ½ inch (1.25 cm) below the Swedish schoolchildren, and less than 1 inch (2.5 cm) below the nonlaboring classes in England. At age 17.5, American female slaves exceeded Boston women of American or Irish parents, factory workers in England or Russia, and the upper class in Italy and were slightly more than 1 inch (2.5 cm) below the tallest group (schoolchildren in Sweden). In contrast with slaves, the centiles for free populations followed a more pronounced U-shaped pattern, ultimately attaining levels near those of childhood. Exceptions to the symmetric pattern, such as the nonlaboring classes in England, had catch-up growth considerably below that for American slaves. Caribbean slaves also had much less catch-up growth.

One may ask why the growth patterns of slaves were different. First, however, it is useful to ponder whether such a pattern of growth was biologically plausible. This chapter's introduction and Section 1 on sources indicated that selectivity bias was unlikely to have been the cause of this pattern. Tanner reports that poor children adopted into an orphanage in Germany during the 18th century had a similar pattern of growth depression and recovery (Tanner, 1981). Additional evidence comes from children today who were adopted from poor countries into rich industrial ones. Barry Bogin has studied this phenomenon and notes that children adopted from Guatemala into the United States are several inches taller than those who remained behind (Bogin, 2001). Therefore humans have an extensive capacity for catch-up growth provided good environmental conditions appear prior to adolescence.

If the height data are credible, then why were young slave children so small? The origins of poor health can be traced to difficult periods of fetal and infant growth. Slave newborns probably weighed on average less than 5.5 pounds or 2,500 g compared with modem standards of 3,450 g (Steckel, 1986a). Conditions may have improved temporarily for those infants who survived the early neonatal period. Although direct information from instructions to overseers and other sources is scanty, breast milk was probably the most important, if not the only, source of nutrition early in infancy. Breast milk is nutritionally ideal, provides some immunity, and is clean, but this source is ordinarily insufficient for normal growth by age 4–6 months. The number of pounds of cotton picked per day by mothers attained normal levels within 3 months after delivery, which suggests that supplementation began earlier. The transition away from breast milk and toward solid foods and manual feeding must have been a difficult adjustment accompanied by elevated rates of illness and mortality. Manual feeding introduced unsanitary implements and contaminated food or liquid, and the diet emphasized starchy products such as pap and gruel. This diet lacked sufficient protein and was probably deficient in iron and calcium. It is not surprising that the post-neonatal infant mortality rate was as high as 162 per 1,000 in a sample of plantation records. Moreover, the average rate of loss was nearly 50% higher in months 1–4 compared with months 5–8, which agrees with other evidence that breastfeeding may have been attenuated in early infancy.

Why was catch-up growth so slow from early childhood to early adolescence? Earlier discussion noted that heights are a measure of net nutrition: that is, actual diet minus claims on the diet made by illness, physical effort, and maintenance. Although the incidence of illness is difficult to measure, the mortality data in Table 10.4 suggest that

Table 10.4 Mortality Rates per Thousand by Age for Slaves and the Antebellum Population

Age	Slaves	United States
0	350	179
1–4	201	93
5–9	54	28
10–14	37	19
15–19	35	28
20–24	40	39

Sources: Age 0 (slaves): Steckel (1986*a*, fn 5 and 7); Steckel (1979, p. 92); United States: Haines and Avery (1980, p. 88; average for the Model West and the logit tables.

sickness decreased during childhood. Slave mortality rates declined sharply after age 5, and fell below 10 per 1,000 after age 6 (based on data for individual years of age). The excess mortality of slaves compared with the entire U.S. population was concentrated before age 5, and the excess infant mortality was nearly as large as the infant mortality rate for the U.S. population.

It is also unlikely that work effort made an important claim on the diet before late childhood. Interviews of ex-slaves suggest that the transition to the adult labor force was gradual and may have begun in some instances as early as age 6 or 7 (Crawford, 1988). Slave children, however, did not produce enough, on average, to more than cover their maintenance costs until about age 10 (Fogel & Engerman, 1974). If the judgments about the decline in sickness and lack of work effort are correct, the conclusion that the diet remained poor is inescapable.

There is independent evidence that the childhood diet was poor. Slave owners frequently discussed the care and feeding of slaves among themselves and within southern agricultural journals. It is clear that deliberations focused on working slaves. One planter stated that "a negro deprived of a meat diet is not able to endure the labor that those can perform who are liberally supplied with it." Others usually stated allowances of meat, corn, and other foods in terms of working or laboring hands. If children were mentioned at all, they usually received "proportionally less." Proportional to what? The emphasis in these recommendations on the labor force suggests that "proportional to work effort" was the operative assumption. In addition, the allocations were frequently made to families, and the vagueness or lack of specifics about nonworkers conveys no information about actual consumption by children. Meat was scarce—a half a pound (.23 kg) of pork per day was a typical recommended ration for a worker—and was probably regarded as a luxury. Parents and other workers in the family may have claimed meat and other nutritional foods at the expense of children. This behavior has occurred repeatedly during hard times within developing countries. Children suffered during a mild subsistence crisis in Sweden at the middle of the 19th century. The emphasis by owners on the labor force could have given legitimacy to reallocation within the family, especially during hard times.

Slave mortality rates changed little after age 7. If the mortality rates are accepted as an index of illness, then variations in the incidence of disease by age had little influence on the course of net nutrition during the remaining years of growth. What was the interplay of diet and physical exertion on growth during these years? Tables 10.2 and 10.3 make clear that most of the absolute difference between slave heights and modern standards was made up during the late adolescent and postadolescent period. Although the upward climb through the centiles is dramatic at these ages, the foundations of this achievement should be sought in earlier years.

The modest decline through the centiles that occurred for slaves after age 13.5 in males and after age 11.5 in females does not signify a decline in net nutrition. Heights accelerated at these ages in the standard population due to an earlier growth spurt. Indeed, the facts that the ages of the peaks of the adolescent growth spurts were only about 1–1.5 years behind the standard population and that the peak velocities were nearly as high among slaves are strong evidence of a good diet that continued during adolescence.

Although the rapid rise through the centiles after adolescence and the emphasis on protein for laborers suggest that the diet remained good during these years, it is also possible that improvement occurred in part through learning to be more efficient at field work. Slaves in their early teens who were expected to keep up with adults faced two disadvantages: one was energy requirements for growth, and the other was inexperience. If slaves gradually accumulated skills that reduced energy requirements for a particular task, then more energy from a given diet would have been available for growth.

10.3 Rates of Return

Standard practice excluded meat from children's diets. How was this decision reached? Even though slave owners lacked the rudiments of scientific understanding of nutrition and health, knowledge about profitable feeding practices could have accumulated through a long process of trial, error, and adjustment. By the late antebellum period, planters had considerable experience with the institution of slavery. Is it possible that slave owners had discovered through trial and error that feeding meat to children was unprofitable? The fact that the growth profile of slaves was so different from those of free populations enhances the prospects for this line of reasoning. Moreover, planters had considerable experience with the feeding of livestock and had reasons to suspect a connection between diet and growth.

Feeding meat to slave children can be considered as an investment. The net income was negative during the early years of the investment period because meat was costly and children did not work. However, children fed nutritionally adequate amounts of meat emerged taller and stronger once they entered the labor force. What was the rate of return on this type of investment? Some assumptions, however, are necessary to make the problem tractable. The growth profile was the outcome of an investment strategy that excluded meat from the diet before age 10, at which time children entered the labor force and received one-half pound (.23 kg) of pork per day. It is assumed that this ration was sufficient to maintain modern height standards. In other words, the growth spurt was delayed, and slaves failed to achieve modern standards as adolescents and adults because they were underfed as children. An alternative strategy, the one for which the rate of return is sought, was to feed children adequate amounts of meat beginning at age 1. Suppose the second strategy would have produced workers who first entered the work force and who attained modern height standards at exactly age 10 and maintained them thereafter. The amounts of meat necessary to achieve this are a function of the protein deficits of children. The actual deficits are unknown, but height data, dietary studies for developing countries, and animal experiments suggest that a 50% deficit is a reasonable first approximation. Based on the protein content of pork and the price of pork during the late antebellum period, annual outlays per child sufficient to cover the deficit would have ranged from about $3.80 at age 1 to $5.90 at age 9 (Steckel, 1986b).

Data assembled by the Union Army on contraband and runaway slaves during the Civil War show that the value of slaves—and presumably their net earnings (the difference between value of output and the cost of maintenance)—increased by approximately 1.4% (relative to the mean) per inch of height (Margo & Steckel, 1992). Table 10.2 gives the increment from actual height to modern standards, and net earnings estimates by age are available from Fogel and Engerman (1974). For the purpose of these calculations, the investment period ended when final adult height was reached; the present value of the additional net earnings at and beyond this age was estimated from the higher price implied by the increase in the slave's height at this age. Probabilities of survival were calculated from the source reported in Table 10.4 and from the closest-fitting model life table (Model West, level 4), and these were reduced by 50% to accommodate lower mortality rates resulting from a better diet. Based on studies of height in relation to diet in developing countries, it is plausible to assume that the protein deficit was in the neighborhood of 50%. If correct, these sources and methods produce a rate of return close to zero (average for males and females), even after allowing for a fall in mortality rates (see Table 10.5). In other words, the present value of expected outlays exceeded the present value of expected returns. Therefore, it was profitable to exclude meat from the diet of slave children.

The findings of this chapter have implications for research on the postbellum southern economy. Work in this area has generally recognized the effects of slavery on factors such as literacy and occupations and has incorporated economic, social, political, and educational discrimination after the war, but the poor nutrition of slaves as children may also have been relevant. Recent studies establish that moderate but chronic nutritional deprivation during early childhood temporarily retards the acquisition of motor skills and permanently stunts mental development.

Evidence on wealth accumulation is consistent with a nutritional legacy of slavery that impeded cognitive development and socioeconomic achievement. By matching census manuscript schedules of households in Georgia in 1870 and 1880, one can conclude that the survival rates of young children were approximately the same for blacks and whites. This finding is consistent with a decline in field work by black women after the war (Ransom & Sutch, 1977) and with parental control over the diets of their children, which would have allowed regular amounts of meat. It is believable to report, then, that the wealth of black men in Georgia in 1900 and 1910 was about four times higher for those born after as opposed to before 1865 (Steckel, 2015).

The nature and determinants of the slave personality have been widely debated in the literature on slavery. One view portrays the typical plantation bondsman as Sambo, who was "docile," "humble," and "childlike" (Elkins, 1959). The extent and form of slave resistance to bondage have also been debated. This literature generally ignores the possible role of nutrition on behavior, possibly because perceptions of the typical diet were reasonably favorable. Yet there is considerable evidence that nutrition influences personality development. Moderately malnourished children are apathetic, emotionally

Table 10.5 Calculated Rates of Return on Feeding Meat to Slave Children

Assumed Protein Deficiency (%)	Mortality Rate	
	Plantation Records	West, level 4
10	14.845	14.366
15	10.829	10.372
20	8.133	7.690
25	6.123	5.690
30	4.530	4.106
35	3.217	2.800
40	2.104	1.691
45	1.139	0.731
50	0.290	-0.114
55	-0.468	-0.869
60	-1.151	-1.549
65	-1.773	-2.168
70	-2.343	-2.735
75	-2.868	-3.258
80	-3.355	-3.743

Source: See text. Modern protein standards are 16 g, ages 1–3; 20 g, ages 4–6; 25 g ages 7–9 as given in Passmore, Nicol, and Rao (1974, table 1).

withdrawn, less aggressive, and more dependent. The finding that children were poorly nourished should be integrated into research on the slave personality.

Investments in good nutrition for slave children would have had low rates of return, yet free populations tended to invest relatively more in the growth of young children. Why is this so? One possible explanation hinges on the crucial nature of nutrition in early childhood to cognitive skills; planters may have valued only the physical development of raw labor, whereas free populations also valued (or valued relatively more) mental development because it promoted success in a competitive market environment. Another is altruism. It is possible that slave owners cared relatively little for slave children, whereas free parents were willing to transfer resources toward young children.

Whatever the reasons for the relatively poor health of slave children, the height data imply that certain conceptions of slave childhood should be redrawn. Eugene Genovese, for example, portrays these ages as "protected years" that provided a "foundation of physical health" and that it was a "time to grow physically" and to "parry the most brutal features of [their] bondage" (Genovese, 1974). Instead, poor nutrition restricted exploration and play and retarded growth. Actually, children may have sought to escape childhood and to join the labor force because of the nutritional rewards.

If slave owners used food to promote the work ethic, it may have been done partly at the expense of the slave family, at least as it influenced interaction between children and working-age slaves. Slave workers generally had breakfast and lunch in the fields and may well have eaten after the children during the evening. Discussions by slave owners suggest that children were often fed separately. Working adults may have had relatively little time to spend with young children on a regular basis. Under these conditions, grandparents or other older slaves may have played the most important role in socializing young slave children. After emancipation, parents in nuclear families may have been poorly equipped, through lack of experience, to train young children.

10.4 Age at Menarche and Childbearing

The extent to which slave owners may have intruded into the sexual lives of their slaves has been a source of controversy since the abolitionist era of the mid-19th century. At that time, some anti-slavery forces charged that slave owners manipulated reproductive behavior such that young slave women had babies early and often (Hinks, McKivigan, & Williams, 2007).

One can test this hypothesis by comparing the average age at menarche with the average age at first birth. Unfortunately, registration of slave births, and indeed of births in general, was nonexistent in the mid-19th century South. Therefore, some other method must be employed for finding the mean of the first-birth distribution. Many years ago, Hajnal set out to compare the mean age at first marriage of various populations. Wishing to avoid the impact of the age distribution, he used the mean of the first-marriage schedule as his measure of location. He interpreted the first-marriage schedule as the schedule of first marriages that would be observed in an artificial cohort that experienced no mortality or migration, and he called the mean age at first marriage of such a cohort the *singulate* mean (Hajnal, 1953). The singulate mean (or mean of the nuptiality schedule) is now widely used by demographers both as a summary measure and as a parameter entering models designed to estimate other demographic parameters from incomplete or inaccurate data.

Hajnal showed that the singulate mean could be estimated from just the marital status distribution of the population. Specifically, from a classification of the population by standard 5-year age groups into single, married, widowed, and divorced, one can construct the proportion of women (or men) in each age group who are ever-married

(married and widowed and divorced/total) or its complement (which is easier to compute), the proportion never married (single/total). By integrating by parts the familiar formula for the calculation of the singulate mean age of marriage, Hajnal devised a formula involving only the proportions never-married by 5-year age groups.

The extension of the methodology of computing the singulate mean to fertility is immediate. All one needs is a breakdown of the proportion of women with no children ever born by 5-year age groups. Unfortunately, the data on slaves in plantation records and in the probate listings only provide us with a breakdown of women with no *surviving* children by 5-year age groups. Biases introduced by this fact, however, are negligible.

Data from probate records are used here to calculate the observed proportion of women with no children by standard age groups. The plantation record sample consists of 34 large plantations in which children could be matched with mothers through birth histories or an enumeration of the slaves by families. The probate data sample has 540 plantations of various sizes in which slave women are listed with their surviving children. The singulate mean age at first birth is 21.0 years from plantation records and 20.6 years from probate records (Trussell & Steckel, 1978; Table 10.5). Since the probate data are more representative of the antebellum slave population, one may conclude that the better estimate of mean age at first birth is the probate data figure of 20.6 years.

Whether the singulate mean age of first childbearing of slaves is early or late can only be judged in relation to its closeness to the mean age at which childbearing is physiologically or biologically possible. An observed mean age of 20 would be late if childbearing could begin at 12 but early if childbearing could only commence at 20. Among samples of populations around the world, a large variation exists in the ages of menarche reported in the literature, from a low of 12.4 years among Chinese to a high of 18.4 and 18.6 among girls of the Lumi and Bundi peoples in New Guinea (Eveleth & Tanner, 1976/1990).

Many factors have been found to be associated with age of menarche, such as fatness in adolescence, physique, health status, and month of the year, but the best-established factor is nutrition. Severe malnutrition unquestionably delays menarche (Tanner, 1978). Fortunately, a body of data confirms that menarche in slaves occurred at an age that must be considered early by the historical standards listed by Tanner. Growth is a process marked by the passage of events that occur in a well-defined order: the development of teeth, the appearance of pubic hair, and the spurt in growth, measured by height or weight gain, during adolescence. Particularly important is the observation that menarche occurs soon after the peak of the adolescent growth spurt. The length of time between the age of peak growth spurt and menarche differs among populations. Data cited by Eveleth and Tanner (1976/1990) show mean delays of 1.0 and 1.5 years for surveyed populations, and it is safe to assume that the delay does not exceed 2 years.

The data in Table 10.3 show that point velocity peaks between 12.5 and 13.5 years. A more precise estimate is available from the Preece-Baines model (1) curve and this is 13.1 years, which implies conservatively that menarche occurred by age 15.1 years (Preece & Baines, 1978). Assuming conservatively a waiting time to conception of 2 years, and 9 months to birth, slave women could have had a first child by age 18. Since the observed mean is in fact 20.6 or some 2.6 years later, one must conclude that slave women did not bear children at the earliest possible age. More reasonable estimates of the mean ages of menarche and waiting time until the first birth indicate that successful manipulation would have led to an observed mean age of first childbearing of from 16.5 to 17 years.

Therefore, young slave women typically were not forced to have children as early as possible, which raises the question of why. Two reasons come to mind. One is that births to women of young ages are more likely to result in infant or maternal mortality, the latter being far more costly than the value of an infant child to the owner. Second, if reproduction was not manipulated and slaves were allowed to choose their own partners, marriage at young ages could have been costly in terms of labor force harmony. Modern studies establish that partners going through divorce or other discord are less productive. It is quite likely, then, that owners promoted a culture of delayed cohabitation, which is consistent with reports that slaves required the owner's permission to marry.

10.5 Conclusion and Suggestions for Research

The extraordinary height-by-age profile of American slaves is one of the most striking findings of the new anthropometric history, a field that analyzes stature and weight to understand biological aspects of living standards in the past. Although anthropometric studies extend back at least to the 19th century, the new approach departs from earlier traditions by investigating specific historical questions and by explaining the methodology in terms readily understood by economists, historians, and other social scientists. Concepts of net nutrition and of the body as a biological machine have been keys to conveying the meaning of anthropometric data for historical research.

The field thrives for several reasons: height measurements are super abundant, particularly for men; data are easy to collect; small samples can provide valuable insights; and the evidence portrays the individual experience, which can be aggregated to any suitable level of analysis, such as time period, region, or socioeconomic status.

Like many new fields, the research raises as many questions as it answers. In the case of American slaves, to what extent was their growth profile the outcome of an optimization process, a topic taken up by Rees and colleagues (Rees, Komlos, Long, & Woitek, 2003)? What levers of net nutrition, such as diet and work, did owners manipulate to achieve their goals? To what extent did severe early childhood deprivation affect learning and socioeconomic achievement following emancipation? Were there intergenerational consequences of their nutritional experience? Did cognitive deficits sustained by slaves confirm southern views of racism? To what extent did nutritional recovery occur for children born following 1865, and, if vigorous for this generation, did it create a political backlash of Jim Crow and lynching? What was the relationship of net nutrition to slave personalities? How does the American experience compare with that of other slave societies? What might have been the economic and health consequences of a "Marshall Plan" for the South following the Civil War? If the nation made such an investment, what would have been the rate of return? These and related questions could occupy a generation of scholars.

In sum, the new anthropometric history has successfully addressed questions that have occupied the study of slavery since the 19th century. Although there were no doubt exceptions, owners generally did not manipulate fertility so that slave women were forced to have children soon after they were physically capable. Young children were extraordinarily malnourished, but adolescent slaves had diets adequate to support substantial catch-up growth despite the claims on the diet made by work. This pattern of net nutrition, creating physical growth depression and recovery, was profitable under generous assumptions about protein deficits in childhood. Given the sensitivity of cognitive development to early childhood nutrition, the generation born under slavery accumulated less wealth at the turn of the century than the cohort born following emancipation.

References

Bogin, B. (2001). *The growth of humanity*. New York, Wiley-Liss.

Crawford, S. (1988). *Quantified memory: A study of the WPA and Fisk University slave narrative collections*. Chicago: University of Chicago Press.

Elkins, S. M. (1959). *Slavery: A problem in American institutional and intellectual life*. Chicago: University of Chicago Press.

Eveleth, P. B., & Tanner, J. M. (1976/1990). *Worldwide variation in human growth*. Cambridge: Cambridge University Press.

Fogel, R. W., & Engerman, S. L. (1974). *Time on the cross: The economics of American Negro slavery*. New York: W.W. Norton.

Genovese, E. D. (1974). *Roll, Jordan, roll: The world the slaves made*. New York: Pantheon Books.

Haines, M. R., & Avery, R. C. (1980). The American life table of 1830–1860: An evaluation. *Journal of Interdisciplinary History, 11*(1), 73–95.

Hajnal, J. (1953). Age at marriage and proportions marrying. *Population Studies, 7*, 111–132.

Hinks, P. P., McKivigan, J. R., & Williams, R. O. (2007). *Encyclopedia of antislavery and abolition*. Westport, CT: Greenwood Press.

Komlos, J. (1994). The height of runaway slaves in colonial America, 1720–1770. In J. Komlos (Ed.), *Stature, living standards, and economic development: Essays in anthropometric history* (pp. 93–116). Chicago: University of Chicago Press.

Komlos, J., & Alecke, B. (1996). The economics of antebellum slave heights reconsidered. *Journal of Interdisciplinary History, 26*(3), 437–457.

Malcolm, L. A. (1974). Ecological factors relating to child growth and nutritional status. In A. F. Roche & F. Falkner (Eds.), *Nutrition and malnutrition: Identification and measurement* (pp. 329–352). New York: Plenum Press.

Margo, R. A., & Steckel, R. H. (1982). The heights of American slaves: New evidence on slave nutrition and health. *Social Science History, 6*, 516–538.

Margo, R. A., & Steckel, R. H. (1992). The nutrition and health of slaves and antebellum southern Whites. In R. W. Fogel & S. L. Engerman (Eds.), *Without consent or contract: Conditions of slave life and the transition to freedom (Vol. 2, pp. 508–521)*. New York: W. W. Norton.

Martorell, R., & Habicht. J.-P. (1986). Human growth: A comprehensive treatise. In F. Falkner & J. M. Tanner (Eds.), *Methodology and ecological, genetic, and nutritional effects on growth* (pp. 241–262). New York: Plenum Press.

Passmore, R., Nicol, B. M., & Rao, M. N. (1974). *Handbook on human nutritional requirements.* Geneva: World Health Organization.

Preece, M. A., & Baines, M. J. (1978). A new family of mathematical models describing the human growth curve. *Annals of Human Biology, 5*(1), 1–24.

Pritchett, J. B., & Freudenberger, H. (1992). A peculiar sample: The selection of slaves for the New Orleans market. *Journal of Economic History, 52*(1), 109–127.

Ransom, R. L., & Sutch, R. (1977). *One kind of freedom: The economic consequences of emancipation*. Cambridge: Cambridge University Press.

Rees, R., Komlos, J., Long, N. V., & Woitek, U. (2003). Optimal food allocation in a slave economy. *Journal of Population Economics, 16*(1), 21–36.

Steckel, R. H. (1979). Slave mortality: Analysis of evidence from plantation records. *Social Science History, 3*(3/4), 86–114.

Steckel, R. H. (1986*a*). A dreadful childhood: The excess mortality of American slaves. *Social Science History, 10*(4), 427–465.

Steckel, R. H. (1986*b*). A peculiar population: The nutrition, health, and mortality of American slaves from childhood to maturity. *Journal of Economic History, 46*(3), 721–741.

Steckel, R. H. (1995). New perspectives on the standard of living. *Challenge, 38*(5), 12–18.

Steckel, R. H. (1996). Percentiles of modern height standards for use in historical research. *Historical Methods, 29*, 157–166.

Steckel, R. H. (2009). Heights and human welfare: Recent developments and new directions. *Explorations in Economic History, 46*(1), 1–23.

Steckel, R. H. (2015). *A dreadful childhood: The long shadow of American slavery.* Columbus: Ohio State University Press.

Steckel, R. H., & Ziebarth, N. (2016). *Selectivity and measured catch-up growth of American slaves*. Columbus: Ohio State University Press.

Tanner, J. M. (1978). *Fetus into man: Physical growth from conception to maturity*. Cambridge, MA: Harvard University Press.

Tanner, J. M. (1981). *A history of the study of human growth*. Cambridge: Cambridge University Press.

Trussell, J., & Steckel, R. H. (1978). The age of slaves at menarche and their first birth. *Journal of Interdisciplinary History, 8*, 477–505.

Wesley, C. H. (1942). Manifests of slave shipments along the waterways, 1808–1864. *Journal of Negro History, 27*(2), 155–174.

CHAPTER 11

FEMALE HEIGHTS AND ECONOMIC DEVELOPMENT

Theory and Evidence

DEBORAH OXLEY

11.1 Introduction

Female physical stature matters, not only for individual welfare, nor mainly for what it means in terms of the economic power women and girls deliver as workers—both highly important concerns in their own right. It is not even just of interest because the experience of girls and women in society may be at odds with that of boys and men, intriguing though this is speaking at once to biological differences but more to social discriminations. There is also an additional fourth dimension that places female stature in a league of its own in terms of its importance to human society, and that is women's role as mothers (Osmani & Sen, 2003). Tall or short, these bodies conceive, protect, deliver, feed, and shape the fortunes of every generation, of every class, of every country, at every time. Women are both productive and reproductive, thus placing them at the center of economic development in the past, present, and future.

11.2 Early Studies

What is great about stature is that it captures a number of factors to which gross domestic product (GDP) is not sensitive: urban disamenities and the disease environment, non-market production and distribution, and intrahousehold resource allocation with its connection to local labor market opportunities. Many of these concern women in particular. Adding gender to anthropometrics leads to different periodization and trends. It makes us rethink the dynamics of history. Take one example. Good nutrition leads to tall women, early menarche, and high potential fertility (Komlos, 1989). As such, it may be implicated in the population growth that preceded the British industrial revolution (Komlos, 1990), itself anticipated by unprecedented gains in calories available per capita (Meredith & Oxley, 2014). Did nutritional gains and population growth cause economic revolution? Gender and anthropometrics make a provocative combination.

Some of the early classics in anthropometric history tended to focus on men because the preeminent source of microdata for the 19th century was military recruits, leaving women out of the picture until they were also militarized in the 20th century. When they were added, female stature suggested different trends (Komlos & Kriwy, 2003; Whitwell, Nicholas, & de Souza, 1997). Other sources were more conducive for studying female stature. The market in kidnapped Africans and their children afforded early insight into African living standards, human growth, and conditions under US slavery (Steckel, 1979, 1986). Steckel also went on to pioneer the use of other sources that reflected on women, such as skeletons (Steckel & Rose, 2005). Other exciting sources have now been found, such as passport applications (Sunder, 2011). But what initially modified the 19th-century British landscape were the records of prisoners.

Criminal women changed the anthropometric scene. Increasing criminalization led to many ordinary working women and men being transported to Australia or incarcerated in modern prisons, in the process being recorded and measured. Convict stature told a tale of declining living standards during British industrialization. These records also opened up a new line of enquiry into the status of women. Hitherto, the working assumption was that men and women, boys and girls, shared equally within households: the neoclassical model. Juxtaposing the sexes traced out something more complicated. During economic change, rural female stature fell more rapidly than did others, suggesting that marginalization within the agricultural labor market nudged out women's claim on family resources, chiming with findings from household budgets (Horrell & Humphries, 1992; Johnson & Nicholas, 1995; Nicholas & Oxley, 1993; cf. Harris, 1998). Convict data also cast light on Ireland (Nicholas & Steckel, 1997) and on disparate trends in women's living standards in the four provinces in the run-up to the Great Famine, pointing toward population growth and family size as a hazard to welfare (Hatton & Martin, 2010; Oxley, 2004). Prison records are now widely used in such research (Carson, 2011; Horrell & Oxley, 2012; Riggs, 1994).

What about the actual numbers in the story of female stature? Koepke and Baten (2005) used skeletal remains to describe European stature over the course of two millennia. Male stature averaged around 67 inches. Female stature centered around 63.4 inches. Both sexes exhibited some volatility. Across the centuries, average female heights fluctuated between 62.7 and 64.3 inches, reaching peaks in the 6th century and again in the 15th and 16th centuries. In between—during the "Dark Ages" (especially the 10th–12th centuries)—women lost ground relative to men. No height data are reported for the 17th century or later.

By the 19th century, some women were being measured and recorded. Convict women in England at the start of the 19th century appear short, at around 61.2 inches (taller if rural, Irish, or especially Scottish; shorter if from London), and stature was falling (Johnson & Nicholas, 1995; Nicholas & Oxley, 1993). There was little improvement until later in the century. By its close, more affluent women—the mothers of college students—recorded a median stature of 62.5 inches, their daughters taller at 63.9 inches, thus exceeding today's average (63.7 inches) (Pearson & Lee, 1903). This speaks not only to an upward trend, but to the diversity of stature by class.

In the colonies, the descendants of Britain's convicts grew tall, with criminal women in New South Wales in the 1890s averaging 62.8 inches (Powys, 1901). Americans were taller still. Black women incarcerated in America at the same time were 63.3 inches, white women a quarter inch taller again (Carson, 2011). This was part of an upswing after a decline in the first part of the century, when African-American women registered above 62 inches, in some studies as high as 63 inches (Komlos, 1992). As would be expected, economic status earned biological reward: American women holding passports registered an impressive average of 64.3 inches and rising to over 65 inches, bucking an otherwise downward trend (Sunder, 2011). As with the English college families, this exceeded today's average for non-Hispanic white American women at 64.9 inches.

Interestingly, women in Dutch penitentiaries in the mid-19th century cannot be regarded as exceptional compared with other criminal women cited earlier, at 61.9 inches (de Beer, 2010). Yet, at present, Dutch women are about the tallest in the world, with an average of 67.2 inches. This demonstrates the pace at which change can occur. It also begs the question of why other countries have not followed suit. The empirical works on stature offer rankings, suggest comparative living standards, and highlight that female and male trajectories frequently diverge, most notably in the timing of trends, and that class matters for the distribution of heights around a mean.

New metrics are today emerging to quantify gender disparity or gender differences in physical stature (Cámara, 2015; Guntupalli & Baten, 2009), and these are used to think about gender discrimination (Guntupalli & Moradi, 2009). Opening up the household via anthropometrics led to penetrating work into the impact of fatherlessness on families (Horrell, Humphries, & Voth, 1998, 2001). Within families lay another key source for anthropometrics and gender: children (Harris, 1994, 2009).

11.3 The Growth of Children

Understanding the stature of girls as opposed to adult females poses particular issues. These are to do with the tempo of growth, the age of puberty, and how deprivation impacts both. Although girls and boys grow in a roughly similar way, they end up at different sizes, and the pathways of growth that lead them there differ. Figure 11.1 depicts the classic "instantaneous" individual growth velocity curves that established British standards in the 1960s (Tanner, Whitehouse, & Takaishi, 1966*a*, 1966*b*). These are based on aggregated data, but with each individual curve arranged so that the adolescent peaks coincide with each other; consequently, the horizontal axis represents biological and not actual chronological age.

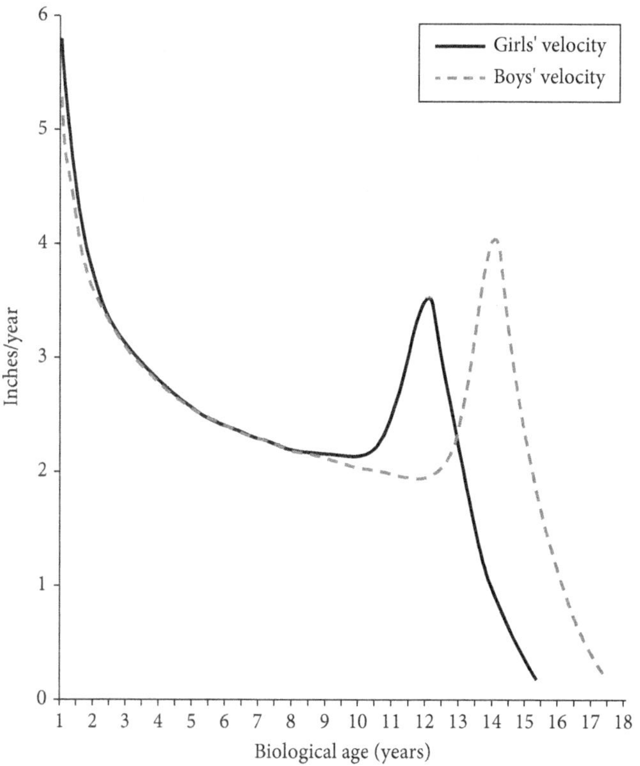

FIGURE 11.1 Individual velocity curves for 1960s Britain.

Note: These curves represent velocity at any given instant for the typical child. They are peak-velocity centered, meaning that they capture biological, not chronological, age.

Source: Drawn from Tanner, Whitehouse, & Takaishi (1966*b*), appendix table 1, p. 625.

Both sexes exhibit extremely rapid growth in the first 2 years of life (even faster in utero). This drops precipitously, falling to one-quarter or less of the initial rate by age 2 years. Velocity continues to gradually slow until the adolescent growth spurt that precedes puberty kicks in. Notably, girls' prepubertal growth spurt (which precedes menarche by about a year) anticipates boys by about 2 years. Peak growth rates rise markedly to around 3.5 inches per year for girls and just over 4 inches per year for boys. In both cases, the spurt is followed by a dramatic slowdown over the remaining 3 or so years of growth. Girls exceed the growth rate of boys by 10% or more at around age 1 year and again, in a more sustained manner, from 10.5 to nearly 13 years of age (girls being taller than boys around then). Boys grow a little more rapidly than girls in the first 4 months of life, and most clearly after age 13. Later maturity—2 or more extra years of growth—makes men on average taller than women.

Differential timing thus complicates the comparison of boys and girls. The solution has been to develop age- and sex-specific standards for the well-nourished boy and girl, a type of biological ideal achievable under propitious circumstances. The widely used measuring rod is provided by the World Health Organization (WHO), most comprehensively in 2007 (henceforth WHO_{2007}). This has evolved from a study of American children by the National Center for Health Statistics in 1977, into a carefully structured study representing children from across the world nurtured in "environments supportive of unconstrained growth" (World Health Organization [WHO] 2006*a*, p. 56, 2006*b*, p. 7). It is part of a larger project that includes the WHO Multicenter Growth Reference Study comprising anthropometric measurements of children aged 0–5 years and, most recently, the International Fetal and Newborn Growth Consortium for the 21st Century (Intergrowth-21st), which now provides international standards for fetal growth (Papageorghiou et al., 2014) as well as newborn weight, length, and head circumference (Villar et al., 2014*a*).

Standards now exist for healthy growth from conception to maturity. Unlike Figure 11.1, WHO_{2007} is cross-sectional data arranged by chronological (not biological) age and thus combines individuals reaching puberty at different ages (the phase-difference effect), yielding somewhat flatter, more elongated velocity curves. Originally, we identified historical samples by their location at a given percentile of a modern standard (Steckel, 1995). So many clustered at the very bottom of the range that it became desirable to develop a more graduated measure. We now use height-for-age *z*-scores (HAZ) to measure where an individual, sample, or population sits in terms of the modern WHO_{2007} distribution. The *z*-score measures the relative distance of an individual value away from a median height (μ) with standard deviation (σ), both of which are specific to each age-sex combination[1]: $z = \frac{X_i - \mu}{\sigma}$.

Because *z*-scores are measured in standard deviations, they are sometimes referred to as *standard deviation scores* (SDS). Following the rules of a normal distribution, a *z*-score in excess of ±1.98 is statistically significant at the 5% level ($p<0.05$). Positive scores indicate values above the WHO_{2007} median, whereas significant negative *z*-scores indicate deprivation. Impressive use of this technique has recently been made in studies of German children during the hunger blockade of World War I (Cox, 2015) and in reassessing growth among American slaves within an adaptive framework (Schneider, 2014).

A major advantage of *z*-scores is that "as standardized quantities, they are comparable across ages, sexes, and [anthropometric] measure (as a measure of 'dimensionless quantity')" (Wang & Chen, 2012, pp. 32–33). Horrell and Oxley have, however, cautioned against the temptation to pool HAZ for boys and girls from deprived populations, arguing that *z*-scores are not constant but vary by age and sex because of inherent gender differences in the pattern of human growth (Horrell & Oxley, 2015). Similar concerns have been raised regarding body mass index (BMI; Silverwood, Leon, & De Stavola, 2009). This is because deprivation slows the tempo of growth, pushing puberty and the adolescent growth spurt later and, depending upon the degree of nutritional disadvantage, lower. These patterns are gender specific.

Let us imagine what growth might look like for girls and boys under three different degrees of deprivation, at 1, 2, and 3 standard deviations below the WHO_{2007} median. In the model, growth must start and end on the same *z*-score (that is to say, the child who starts in the −1 *z*-score will end in the −1 z-score), but, in between, the growth rate is free to move in accordance with the proposed velocity curves presented in Figure 11.2. This family of hypothetical growth curves is designed to impose lower-later-longer growth

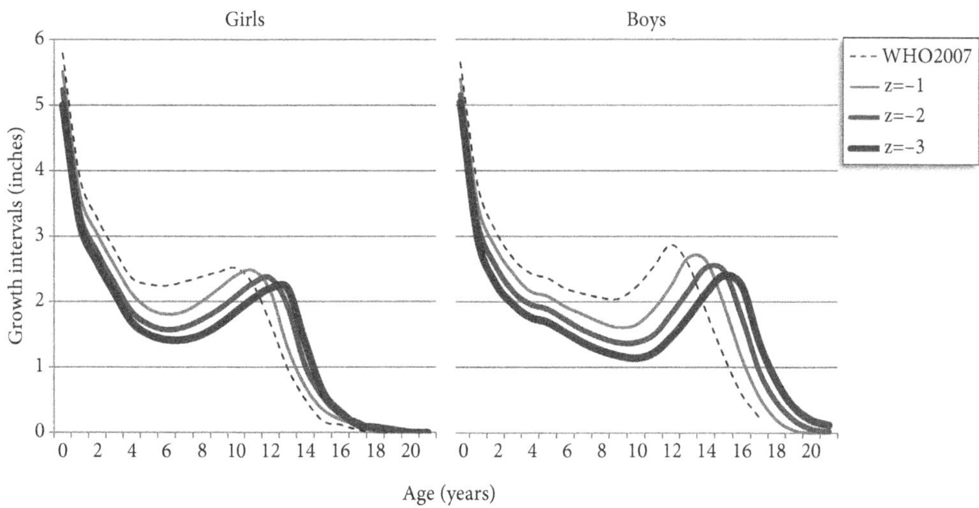

FIGURE 11.2 Family of theoretical velocity growth curves for deprived girls and boys.

within known boundaries. WHO_{2007} cross-sectional standards are the dotted black lines in Figure 11.2. From birth, growth rates slow; then, as each population approaches puberty, its growth accelerates to a peak, followed by steep decline. This process is delayed for the disadvantaged groups, who continue to experience declining rates of growth before a later, more muted pubertal spurt and delayed maturity.

Lower-later-longer growth of the disadvantaged means that they temporarily fall even further behind the modern benchmark before catching up. The distance below WHO_{2007} is described by the *z*-curves for each of the three scenarios given in Figure 11.3. WHO_{2007} girls arrest the declining rate of growth by about age 5, then commence a gradual upward swing in anticipation of the pubertal growth spurt. At the same time, growth rates are still falling for deprived girls. Thus, a gap opens up. It will keep getting bigger even when growth accelerates for the undernourished as they finally enter their delayed growth spurt (from around 7 years) because the well-nourished girls are still growing faster. This gap will only start to close when growth slows for the well-nourished WHO_{2007} population post-peak (after about age 10). The *z*-curves thus trace a U-shape, first dipping, then recovering, all because of the timing of puberty.

A similar patterns pertains for boys, but later. Girls reach puberty around 2 years earlier than boys. For deprived girls, their HAZ curve will naturally dip then rise about 2 years before that of boys. Furthermore, because peak growth for girls is a little less than for boys (by about half an inch), the trough for girls should be shallower than for boys. For each scenario ($z = -1, -2, -3$), this suggests a distinctive double-U shape, with males dipping deeper and later than females. The more nutritionally challenged, the more pronounced the two troughs.

Differences between deprived girls and modern girls, deprived boys and modern boys, and between deprived girls and boys complicate the interpretation of HAZ against the modern standard. It therefore matters from which part of the age distribution a

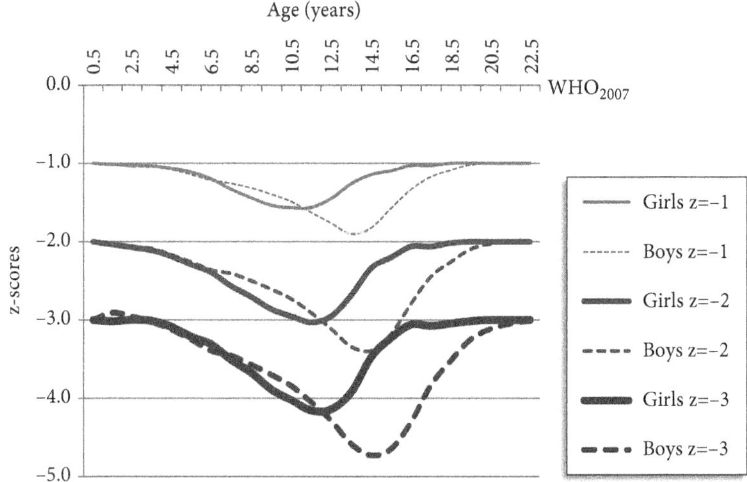

FIGURE 11.3 Associated suite of HAZ-curves for deprived girls and boys.

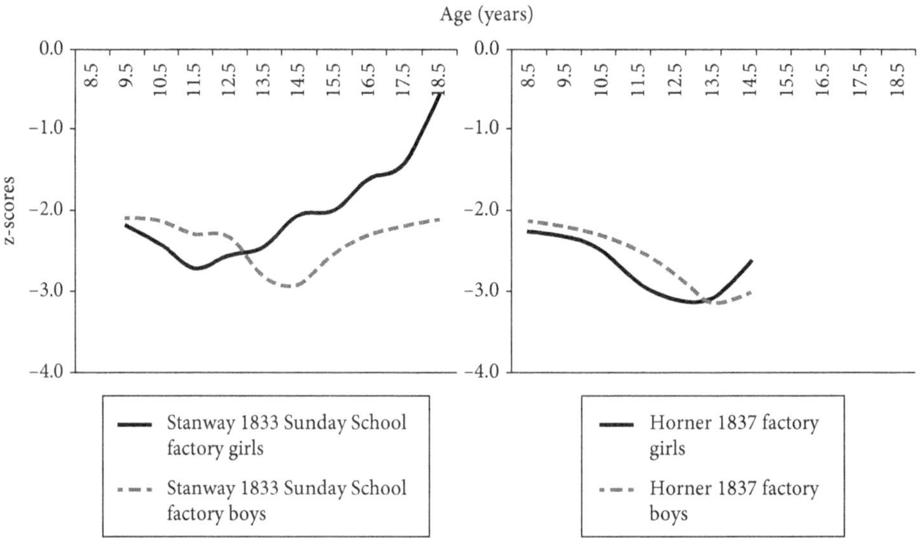

FIGURE 11.4 HAZ-curves for 19th-century factory children.

Source: Stanway (1833); Horner (1837).

sample is drawn when comparing girls with boys because, for no reason other than biology, there are moments when girls should have greater HAZ than boys, and vice versa.

Horrell and Oxley went on to argue on the basis of these considerations that deviations from this double-U form point to gender discrimination in the treatment of children. Figure 11.4 illustrates this, reporting on boys and girls working in factories in the North of England. Factory children from more affluent families sending their children to Sunday School in Manchester conform to the predicted pattern of HAZ curve: girls dip and recover first, followed by a lower later dip for boys (based on 1,062 children measured by Samuel Stanway in 1833). This was not the case for the factory children recorded by Inspector Leonard Horner in 1837, some 16,402 children drawn more widely from the North of England. Girls' HAZ fell much more appreciably, dipping as low as boys, and their upswing only anticipated boys' by about 6 months. At age 14, Stanway's girls had an average stature of 57.75 inches; Horner's of just 56 inches. This was a difference of 1.75 inches, twice that between the boys (56.6 and 55.75 inches, respectively, in the Stanway and Horner samples). Stature clearly demonstrated lower net nutritional status among Horner's girls in spite of equal wages. This was not an earner bias, but a gender bias within the family. The likely source was not parental decisions to underfeed girls, but to allocate the bulk of additional household labors to their daughters rather than their sons, thus training them for motherhood. But without compensating nutrition, this double-burden imposed significant biological cost.

11.4 Height and Health

There are problems with growing up stunted. As discussed elsewhere in this volume, there is evidence that shortness affects productivity, earning capacity, success in the marriage market, and probably cognition. One particular area of concern is the connection with health and longevity.

Epidemiologist Hans Th Waaler presented the scientific community with a set of relationships among height, weight, morbidity, and mortality that fundamentally advanced our understanding (Waaler, 1984). These were based on 18 million observations from 1.8 million Norwegians measured repeatedly by the National Mass Radiography Service between 1963 and 1975. The central finding was that health risk—morbidity and mortality—related to both height and weight. Risk curves took on a "bathtub" shape when graphed against body mass (weight adjusted for height, kg/m^2): there was a range of body mass at which risk was invariant, but at the lower and upper ends of the BMI distribution, risks were elevated: see Figure 11.5. Two particularly pertinent results were (1) that female risk was felt most acutely at the bottom end of the body mass spectrum and (2) that height was more important than weight in predicting ill-health and mortality: stunting was hazardous. Being below attainable height proxied for a level of disadvantage—in the uterus and/or in growing up—that bespoke broader damage: a nutritional shortfall that adversely affected not only stature, but the vital organs, epigenetic effects, and, consequently, lifetime health and linked to the Barker Hypothesis as discussed below. Waaler's study has since been updated with additional longitudinal observations, strengthening the negative relationship between height and mortality and amplifying that optimal health outcomes were achieved at different body masses for males and females by age (Engeland, Bjorge, Selmer, & Tverdal, 2003). Findings have largely been robust to checks for socioeconomic status (Koch, 2011).

The application to historical data has been profound, giving rise to arguments that humans are now in control of their own "technophysio evolution" (Fogel, 1993, 2004;

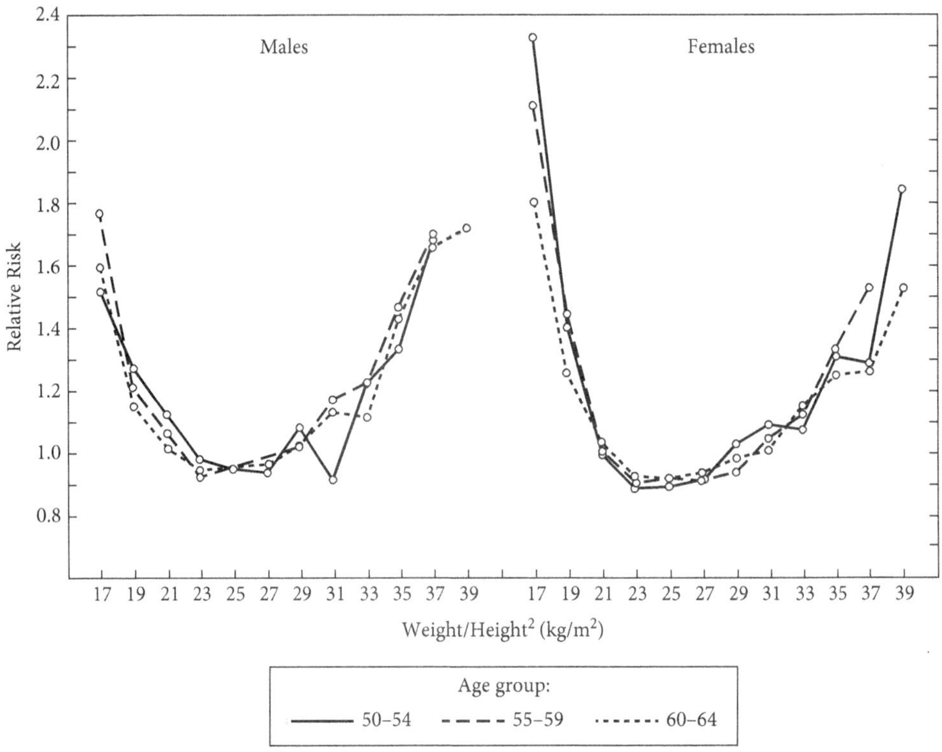

FIGURE 11.5 Relative mortality for three age groups according to body mass.

Source: Figure 15 in Waaler (1984), p. 23. Reproduced with kind permission from John Wiley and Sons, License 3625270832197.

Fogel & Costa, 1997). Economic welfare shaped bodies and lives. In turn, the strength of bodies and the duration of productive lives influence a society's economic capacity, as well as individual and public decisions about investment in human capital (Floud, Fogel, Harris, & Sok, 2011). Economic growth has now led to a secular rise in both stature and weight, to a point where public health is more concerned with over- than undernutrition (Komlos & Baur, 2004, Komlos & Brabec, 2011).

Height, weight, and body mass have been extensively studied for the 19th-century American Union Army, with Fogel and collaborators proving the powerhouse in this new endeavor (e.g., Costa, 1993, 2004; Fogel, Cain, Burton, & Bettenhausen, 2013; Kim, 1996; Linares & Su, 2005). As with studies of stature, the military nature of the historical evidence initially led to a concentration on men. This soon changed. Children were being weighed and measured by the early 20th century (Jackson & Thomas, 1995), and anthropological expeditions in Australia's past yielded height and weight data for both males and females, thus helping to measure the welfare gap between invaders and the indigenous people (Nicholas et al., 1998). Floud offered early insight into body mass in England by utilizing published summary data, often for the middle and upper classes (Floud, 1998). Individual data for prison populations offered up a new source. In the

United States, it shed light on racial differences (e.g., Carson, 2012); in the United Kingdom, on gender. Records for prisoners held in Wandsworth and Paisley Houses of Correction have now been used to examine gender and health inequality by considering the distribution of household consumption, its relationship to local labor market conditions, and its likely health consequences. Although women and children working in industrializing Paisley did very well in the body mass and stature stakes, for women in London, conditions were particularly bleak, with body mass declining consistently more or less from when they married to a level where even the average middle-aged woman faced elevated mortality risk levels of nearly 30% (Horrell, Meredith, & Oxley, 2009; Meredith & Oxley, 2015). It was short stature, even more than weight, that heralded this bleak prospect. Undersized mothers point to a further problem: the intergenerational transmission of health inequality.

11.5 Man That Is Born of a Woman: Height and Reproduction

Intergrowth-21st has now established that healthy, well-nourished mothers support the same level of fetal growth and newborn length the world over (Villar et al., 2014*b*). The large differences that do exist across the globe in birthweight and fetal development thus appear to arise from deficient nutrition, inadequate unsanitary environments, disease burden, and poor maternal health. It is through new developments in biological science linking conditions in utero to later-life ill-health and death, and a fresh focus on issues of gender discrimination and economic development, that a spotlight has been shone on the significance of female stature as a determinant of maternal and child well-being.

Female heights and weights were a source of some considerable interest in 19th-century Britain, where anthropometrics had a strong foothold (see Anthropometric Committee, 1884). It was recognized early on that the future health and strength of the nation depended in large measure on the welfare of its mothers. Maternal health, nurturing practices (especially breastfeeding), and babies' weights filled many of the 843 pages in the report of the Inter-Departmental Committee on Physical Deterioration (1904) and preoccupied anthropometricians (Karn & Pearson, 1922). The theme has not been entirely neglected in the historiography (Costa, 1998; Goldin & Margo, 1989; McCalman & Morley, 2003; Ward, 1993). In England, reductions in infant mortality from the 1870s have been tied to improvements in maternal health (Millward & Bell, 2001).

In a pivotal paper, Osmani and Sen took the case further by linking reproductive trajectories to questions of discrimination. They argued that in developing countries there were unrecognized "hidden penalties" imposed by gender inequality. Maternal deprivation (specifically undernourishment) hurt girls *and* boys, and consequently damaged all of society. Motherhood was implicated as a vector for the transmission of intergenerational inequality and ill-health.

Gender discrimination imposed particularly high costs on developing countries and "Undertaking social reforms aimed at eliminating gender inequality may turn out to be the most cost-effective method of preventing this double jeopardy" (Osmani & Sen, 2003, p. 119). The double jeopardy arose from an "overlapping health transition." The Western shift to small families (the demographic transition) was dialectically connected with an evolving disease environment (the epidemiological transition). In the first health regime, illness and death stalked the very young. Infectious diseases inflicted high rates of infant and child mortality, especially on those living in overcrowded conditions whose hunger increased their susceptibility to then-prevalent, contagious, nutrition-sensitive illnesses like measles, diarrhea, tuberculosis, cholera, and most respiratory diseases (Fogel, 1986, p. 481). Over time, this was replaced by a second epidemiological regime dominated by chronic illness and death at older ages. (The cause of this shift is widely debated; for the state of the debate, see Harris, 2004). Sometimes characterized as a move from poverty to affluence, health risk shifted from undernutrition to overnutrition (e.g., diabetes, coronary heart disease). For Osmani and Sen, developing countries "telescope" this process through rapid fertility decline and growing incomes teamed with persisting inequalities that permit both health regimes to co-exist and simultaneously wreak havoc (2003, p. 107).

The important connection here is that maternal deprivation exacerbates both health regimes. Underfed mothers have smaller babies with fewer life chances and greater health risks before and after their birth (regime one). Deprived fetuses adapt to poor intrauterine conditions—the "thrifty-phenotype"—in ways that improve immediate survival, but that adversely affect later-life health through susceptibility to chronic disease (regime two). Higher incomes, better infant nutrition, infrastructure provision (sanitation, housing), and reduced infection brought improved survival and longer lives, but the penalty of fetal stress was still felt in adult ill-health: in short stature and being underweight with attendant risks, chronic morbidity, and older-age mortality (Godfrey & Barker, 2001). Here, Osmani and Sen were making use of the *Barker Hypothesis* on the fetal origins of adult disease (first enunciated by Barker in 1993). This connected low birthweight with elevated adult health risks: listed as hypertension, type 2 diabetes, cardiovascular disease, obstructive lung disease, renal damage, and some cancers (Osmani & Sen, 2003, p. 117). As they note, and which more current research confirms (e.g., Wells, 2013), risks were greatest for individuals experiencing a "mismatch" between intrauterine undernutrition and later childhood overnutrition. The fetus that learned to cope with shortage becomes the adult prone to weight gain and obesity-related illnesses. This may connect directly to the problem of the "thin-fat Indian" whose frame is slight, central adiposity high, and diabetes rates astronomical (for a meta-analysis, see Kurpad, Varadharajan, & Aeberli, 2011).

Maternal height and child health have now been directly examined. Low birthweight mothers have low birthweight children, and both are connected with socioeconomic status (Currie & Moretti, 2007). Bhalotra and Rawlings (2011) have recently made a powerful contribution quantifying the hidden penalties of gender inequality and deepening our understanding of intergenerational effects. They use microdata on 600,000 mothers and their (more than 2 million) children born between 1970 and 2000, across 38 developing countries, to test how welfare crossed the generations. Maternal health was operationalized as adult stature, body mass, and incidence of anemia; child health was measured through neonatal, infant, and under-5 years mortality risk, low birthweight, stunting, and gender-specific HAZ; and the model examined within-country variation across individual families (Bhalotra & Rawlings, 2011, pp. 287–288). Their findings reveal strong connections between maternal and child health, felt most strongly at the lower end of the stature distribution: "Indicators of both the contemporary health of the mother and of her health stock are significant predictors of the survival and growth of her births in most countries in the sample" (p. 287). A single standard deviation decrease in maternal height raised children's health risk by 5–10%. Short mothers recorded lower birthweights, and their offspring suffered greater mortality at all age levels and were more prone to stunting; all results were statistically significant and the product of regression controlling for selected individual characteristics such as mother's education and age. As noted, the results were nonlinear: there were not continued gains for the children of mothers of above-average height, but there were very material costs to the children of mothers who were short. Persisting intergenerational health inequalities were thus most likely among groups and in countries with notable female disadvantage. This is where returns to investment in women's health would be greatest. Prenatal conditions, like female stature itself, are key (Coffey, 2014).

Female stature is thus placed center stage in the pageant of economic and human development. Female height is both a measure of accumulated welfare across the growing years (nutrition, health) and an input into the health of the next generation. It is the stock of maternal health—not just the conditions prevailing during pregnancy—that influence fetal development with its attendant long-run impacts (Barker, 1997). This is because the fetal environment is quite literally shaped by the size of the uterus and its efficiency in the transmission of oxygen via the placenta, as well as by the mother's consumption of both good and bad intake (nutrition vs. alcohol), exertion in work, disease exposure, stress levels, and more. The mother's stature and size—and, indeed, her eggs—are the product of her own conception and childhood; if she herself was subject to fetal adaptations, she may be predisposed to hypertension and restricted weight gain during pregnancy and thus deliver low birthweight babies. As noted earlier, such babies face elevated risks of mortality and stunting and have a restricted ability for catch-up growth. In addition, their own fetal adaptations will produce adverse consequences in later life, including (for females) hypertension during their own pregnancies and their own small babies. So, accumulated maternal health exerts a profound influence on her offspring; through them, she will shape her grandchildren and later generations. Thus, welfare is correlated across generations, establishing "health dynasties." It is possible that seemingly inherited genomic traits are in fact recurring epigenetic environmental responses (Bhalotra & Rawlings, 2011, p. 288). Perhaps we do not yet even know just how tall women should be vis-à-vis men.

11.6 Conclusion

More than for males, female stature provides the bridge to welfare across generations. Boys and girls share the same interuterine conditions, but from birth girls and women do not necessarily share the same welfare as boys and men, and anthropometrics has provided a special avenue into quantifying this disparity. But whatever the divergence in experience, male welfare is inextricably connected to that of women. Secular rises may be steep, but they progress subject to a maternal constraint, and, to some extent, the two sexes must move in broadly similar step. The heights of girls and boys, men and especially women, measure economic activity, but they also cause it. Economic development, moderated by levels of inequality, disamenities, public health, population growth, family size, nonmarket factors, and the treatment of women, is largely responsible for the size and shape of the human form. But it is the size, shape, and brilliance of humans that is central to economic development. How numerous we are, how strong, how clever, how long-lived—the sum of our individual health and welfare—these are the factors that shape the economy and in turn shape us—and so the cycle continues. At the fulcrum, the lynchpin of this complex yet powerful motor is female stature: a record of past, and determinant of future, performance.

Note

1. Technically, HAZ are calculated with a more complicated formula that includes a term correcting for skewness (the power of the Box-Cox transformation); because this is unity for the WHO_{2007} height data, the equation resolves itself into the simple form cited here.

References

Anthropometric Committee. (1884). Final report of the Anthropometric Committee, 1883. In *Report of the Fifty-Third Meeting of the British Association for the Advancement of Science* (pp. 253–307).

Barker, D. J. P. (1993). Intrauterine growth retardation and adult disease. *Current Obstetrics Gynaecology*, 3, 200–206.

Barker, D. J. P. (1997). Maternal nutrition, fetal nutrition and diseases in later life. *Nutrition*, *13*, 807–813.

Bhalotra, S., & Rawlings, S. B. (2011). Intergenerational persistence in health in developing countries: The penalty of gender inequality? *Journal of Public Economics*, 95, 286–299.

Cámara, A. D. (2015). A biosocial approach to living conditions: Inter-generational changes of stature dimorphism in 20th-century Spain. *Annals of Human Biology*, 42(2), 167–177.

Carson, S. A. (2011). Height of female Americans in the 19th century and the antebellum puzzle. *Economics and Human Biology*, 9(2), 157–164.

Carson, S. A. (2012). The body mass index of blacks and whites in the United States during the nineteenth century. *Journal of Interdisciplinary History*, *XLII*(3), 371–391.

Coffey, D. (2014). Early life mortality and height in Indian states. *Economics and Human Biology*.

Costa, D. (1993). Height, weight, wartime stress and older age mortality. Evidence from the Union Army Records. *Explorations in Economic History*, *30*, 424–449.

Costa, D. (1998). Unequal at birth: A long-term comparison of income and birth weight. *Journal of Economic History*, *58*(4), 987–1009.

Costa, D. L. (2004). The measure of man and older age mortality: Evidence from the Gould sample. *Journal of Economic History*, *64*, 1–23.

Cox, M. E. (2015). Hunger games: Or how the Allied blockade in the First World War deprived German children of nutrition, and Allied food aid subsequently saved them. *Economic History Review*, *68*(2), 600–631.

Currie, J., & Moretti, E. (2007). Biology as destiny? Short- and long-run determinants of intergenerational transmission of birth weight. *Journal of Labor Economics*, *25*(2), 231–263.

de Beer, H. (2010). Physical stature and biological living standards of girls and young women in the Netherlands, born between 1815 and 1865. *History of the Family*, *15*(1), 60–75.

Engeland, A., Bjorge, T., Selmer R. M., & Tverdal, A. (2003). Height and body mass index in relation to total mortality. *Epidemiology*, *14*, 293–299.

Floud, R. (1998). *Height, weight and body mass of the British population since 1820* (NBER Historical Working Paper No. 108). Cambridge, MA: National Bureau of Economic Research.

Floud, R., Fogel, R. W., Harris, B., & Sok, C. H. (2011). *The changing body: Health, nutrition, and human development in the Western World since 1700*. Cambridge, UK: Cambridge University Press.

Fogel, R. W. (1986). Nutrition and the decline in mortality since 1700: Some preliminary findings. In S. L. Engerman & R. E. Gallman (Eds.), *Long-term factors in American economic growth* (pp. 439–556). Chicago: University of Chicago.

Fogel, R. W. (1993). New sources and new techniques for the study of secular trends in nutritional status, health, mortality, and the process of aging. *Historical Methods*, *26*, 5–43.

Fogel, R. W. (2004). *The escape from hunger and premature death, 1700-2100*. Cambridge, UK: Cambridge University.

Fogel, R. W., Cain, L., Burton, J., & Bettenhausen, B. (2013). Was what ail'd ya what kill'd ya? *Economics and Human Biology*, *11*, 269–280.

Fogel, R. W., & Costa, D. L. (1997). A theory of technophysio evolution, with some implications for forecasting population, health care costs, and pension costs. *Demography*, *34*, 49–66.

Godfrey, K. M., & Barker, D. J. P. (2001). Fetal programming and adult health. *Public Health Nutrition*, *4*, 611–624.

Goldin, C., & Margo, R. A. (1989). The poor at birth: Birth weights and infant mortality at Philadelphia's Almshouse Hospital, 1848-1873. *Explorations in Economic History*, *26*, 360–379.

Guntupalli, A., & Baten, J. (2009). Measuring gender well-being with biological welfare indicators. In B. Harris, L. Gálvez, & H. Machado (Eds.), *Gender and well-being in Europe: Historical and contemporary perspectives* (pp. 43–58). Farnham, UK: Ashgate.

Guntupalli, A. M., & Moradi, A. (2009). What does gender dimorphism in stature tell us about discrimination in rural India, 1930-1975? In M. Pal, P. Bharati, B. Ghosh & T. Vasulu (Eds.), *Gender and discrimination: Health, nutritional status, and role of women in India* (pp. 258–277). New Delhi: Oxford University Press.

Harris, B. (1994). The height of schoolchildren in Britain, 1900–50. In J. Komlos (Ed.), *Stature, living standards and economic development: Essays in anthropometric history* (pp. 25–38). Chicago: University of Chicago.

Harris, B. (1998). Gender, height and mortality in nineteenth- and twentieth-century Britain: Some preliminary reflections. In J. Komlos & J. Baten (Eds.), *The biological standard of living in comparative perspective* (pp. 413–448). Stuttgart, DE: Franz Steiner Verlag.

Harris, B. (2004). Public health, nutrition, and the decline of mortality: The McKeown Thesis revisited. *Social History of Medicine*, *17*(3), 379–407.

Harris, B. (2009). Anthropometric history, gender and the measurement of well-being. In B. Harris, L. Gálvez, & H. Machado (Eds.), *Gender and well-being in Europe: Historical and contemporary perspectives* (pp. 59–83). Farnham, UK: Ashgate.

Hatton, T. J., & Martin, R. M. (2010). The effects on stature of poverty, family size, and birth order: British children in the 1930s. *Oxford Economic Papers*, *62*, 157–184.

Horner, Leonard in British Parliamentary Paper. (1837). (99) *Factory Children. A return of the number and names of the surgeons who have furnished the inspectors of factories with tables containing the stature of children measured by them, etc.* (pp. 171–181).

Horrell, S., & Humphries, J. (1992). Old questions, new data and alternative perspectives: Families' living standards in British industrial revolution. *Journal of Economic History*, 52(4), 849–880.

Horrell, S., Humphries, J., & Voth, H. -J. (1998). Stature and relative deprivation: Fatherless children in early industrial Britain. *Continuity and Change*, *13*, 73–115.

Horrell, S., Humphries, J., & Voth, H. -J. (2001). Destined for deprivation: Human capital formation and intergenerational poverty in nineteenth-century England. *Explorations in Economic History*, *38*, 339–365.

Horrell, S., Meredith, D., & Oxley, D. (2009). Measuring misery: Body mass, ageing and gender inequality in Victorian London. *Explorations in Economic History*, *46*, 93–119.

Horrell, S., & Oxley, D. (2012). Bringing home the bacon? Regional nutrition, stature and gender in the Industrial Revolution. *Economic History Review*, *65*, 1354–1379.

Horrell, S., & Oxley, D. (2015). Gender discrimination in nineteenth-century England: Evidence from factory children. *University of Oxford Discussion Papers in Economic and Social History*, *133*, 1–50.

Inter-Departmental Committee on Physical Deterioration. (1904). British Parliamentary Paper [Cd.2175] Vol. I Report and appendix [Cd.2210] Vol. II List of witnesses and minutes of evidence [Cd.2186] Vol. III Appendix and general index.

Jackson, R., & Thomas, M. (1995). Height, weight and well-being. *Australian Economic History Review*, *35*, 39–65.

Johnson, P., & Nicholas, S. (1995). Male and female living standards in England and Wales, 1812-1857: Evidence from criminal height records. *Economic History Review*, *XLVIII*(3), 470–481.

Karn, M. N., & Pearson, K. (1922). Study of the data provided by a baby clinic in a large manufacturing town. In *Studies in national deterioration* 10. Cambridge, UK: Cambridge University.

Kim, J. M. (1996). *The economics of nutrition, body build, and health: Waaler surfaces and physical human capital.* Doctoral dissertation, University of Chicago.

Koch, D. (2011). Waaler revisited: The anthropometrics of mortality. *Economics & Human Biology*, *9*(1), 106–117.

Koepke, N., & Baten, J. (2005). The biological standard of living in Europe during the last two millennia. *European Review of Economic History*, *9*(1), 61–95.

Komlos, J. (1989). The age at menarche in Vienna: The relationship between nutrition and fertility. *Historical Methods, 22*(4), 158–163.

Komlos, J. (1990). Nutrition, population growth, and the Industrial Revolution in England. *Social Science History, 14*(1), 69–91.

Komlos, J. (1992). Toward an anthropometric history of African-Americans: The case of the Free Blacks in Antebellum Maryland. In C. Goldin & H. Rockoff (Eds.), *Strategic factors in nineteenth century American economic history: A volume in honor of Robert W. Fogel* (pp. 297–329). Chicago: University of Chicago.

Komlos, J., & Baur, M. (2004). From the tallest to (one of) the fattest: The enigmatic fate of the American population in the twentieth century. *Economics and Human Biology, 2*, 57–74.

Komlos, J., & Brabec, M. (2011). The trend of BMI values of US adults by deciles, birth cohorts 1882-1986 stratified by gender and ethnicity *Economics and Human Biology, 9*, 234–250.

Komlos, J., & Kriwy, P. (2003). The biological standard of living in the two Germanies. *German Economic Review, 4*(4), 459–473.

Kurpad, A. V., Varadharajan, K. S., & Aeberli, I. (2011). The thin-fat phenotype and global metabolic disease risk. *Current Opinion in Clinical Nutrition and Metabolic Care, 14*(6), 542–547.

Linares, C., & Su, D. (2005). Body mass index and health among Union Army veterans: 1891–1905. *Economics and Human Biology, 3*, 367–387.

McCalman, J., & Morley, R. (2003). Mothers' health and babies' weights: The biology of poverty at the Melbourne Lying-in Hospital, 1857-83. *Journal of the Society for the Social History of Medicine, 16*(1), 39–56.

Meredith, D., & Oxley, D. (2014). Food and fodder: Feeding England, 1700–1900. *Past and Present, 222*(1), 163–214.

Meredith, D., & Oxley, D. (2015). Blood and bone: Body mass, gender and health inequality in 19th century British families. *History of the Family, 20*(2), 204–230.

Millward, R., & Bell, F. (2001). Infant mortality in Victorian Britain: The mother as medium. *Economic History Review, 54*, 699–733.

Nicholas, S., Gregory, R., & Kimberley, S. (1998). The welfare of indigenous and white Australians 1890–1940. In J. Komlos & J. Baten (Eds.), *The biological standard of living in comparative perspective* (pp. 35–54). Stuttgart, DE: Franz Steiner Verlag.

Nicholas, S., & Oxley, D. (1993). Living standards of women during the industrial revolution. *Economic History Review, 46*, 723–749.

Nicholas, S., & Steckel, R. H. (1997). Tall but poor: Living standards of men and women in pre-famine Ireland. *Journal of European Economic History, 26*, 105–134.

Osmani, S., & Sen, A. (2003). The hidden penalties of gender inequality: Fetal origins of ill-health. *Economics and Human Biology, 1*, 105–121.

Oxley, D. (2004). Living standards of women in prefamine Ireland. *Social Science History, 28*, 271–295.

Papageorghiou, A. T., Ohuma, E. O., Altman, D. G., Todros, T., Ismail, L. G., Lambert, A., . . . Villar, J. (2014). International standards for fetal growth based on serial ultrasound measurements: The Fetal Growth Longitudinal Study of the INTERGROWTH-21st project. *Lancet, 384*, 869–879.

Pearson, K., & Lee, A. (1903). On the laws of inheritance in man. Part I. Inheritance of physical characters. *Biometrika, 2*(4), 357–462.

Powys, A. O. (1901). Data for the problem of evolution in man. Anthropometric data from Australia. *Biometrika, 1*(1), 30–49.

Riggs, P. (1994). The standard of living in Scotland, 1800–1850. In J. Komlos (Ed.), *Stature, living standards, and economic development: Essays in anthropometric history* (pp. 60–75). Chicago: University of Chicago Press.

Schneider, E. B. (2014). Children's growth in an adaptive framework: Explaining the growth patterns of American slaves and other historical populations. *University of Oxford Discussion Papers in Economic and Social History, 130*, 1–30.

Silverwood, R. J., Leon, D. A., & De Stavola, B. L. (2009). Long-term trends in BMI: Are contemporary childhood BMI growth references appropriate when looking at historical datasets? *Longitudinal and Life Course Studies, 1*(1), 27–44.

Stanway, Samuel in British Parliamentary Paper [450]. (1833). *Factory Inquiry Commission*. D1. p.88 f.698.

Steckel, R. H. (1979). Slave height profiles from coastwise manifests. *Explorations in Economic History, 16*, 363–380.

Steckel, R. H. (1986). A peculiar population: The nutrition, health, and mortality of American slaves from childhood to maturity. *Journal of Economic History, 46*(3), 721–741.

Steckel, R. H. (1995). Percentiles of modern height standards for use in historical research. *NBER Working Paper Series on Historical Factors in Long Run Growth, Historical Paper 75*, 1–29.

Steckel, R. H., & Rose, J. C. (eds.). (2005). *The backbone of history: Health and nutrition in the western hemisphere*. Cambridge, UK: Cambridge University.

Sunder, M. (2011). Upward and onward: High-society American women eluded the antebellum puzzle. *Economics and Human Biology, 9*(2), 165–171.

Tanner, J. M., Whitehouse, R. H., & Takaishi, M. (1966*a*). Standards from birth to maturity for height, weight, height velocity, and weight velocity: British children, 1965. Part 1. *Archive of Disease and Childhood, 41*, 454–471.

Tanner, J. M., Whitehouse, R. H., & Takaishi, M. (1966*b*). Standards from birth to maturity for height, weight, height velocity, and weight velocity: British children, 1965. Part 2. *Archive of Disease and Childhood, 41*, 613–635.

Villar, J., et al. (2014*a*). International standards for newborn weight, length, and head circumference by gestational age and sex: The Newborn Cross-Sectional Study of the INTERGROWTH-21st project. *Lancet, 384*, 857–868.

Villar, J., et al. (2014*b*). The likeness of fetal growth and newborn size across non-isolated populations in the INTERGROWTH-21st project: The Fetal Growth Longitudinal Study and Newborn Cross-Sectional Study. *Lancet Diabetes & Endocrinology, 2*(10), 781–792.

Waaler, H. T. (1984). Height, weight and mortality: The Norwegian experience. *Acta Medica Scandinavica, 679*(Suppl), 1–56.

Wang, Y., & Chen, H. J. (2012). Use of percentiles and Z-scores in anthropometry. In V. R. Preedy (Ed.), *Handbook of anthropometry: Physical measures of human form in health and disease* (pp. 29–48). New York: Springer.

Ward, P. W. (1993). *Birth weight and economic growth: Women's living standards in the industrializing West*. Chicago: University of Chicago.

Wells, J. C. K. (2013). Famine and the thrifty phenotype: Implications for long-term health. In L. H. Lumey & A. Vaiserman (Eds.), *Early life nutrition and adult health and development* (pp. 29–55). Hauppauge, NY: Nova Science.

Whitwell, G., Nicholas, S., & de Souza, C. (1997). Height, health and economic growth in Australia, 1860–1940. In R. H. Steckel & R. H. Floud (Eds.), *Health and welfare during industrialization* (pp. 379–421). Chicago and London: National Bureau of Economic Research.

World Health Organization (WHO) Multicentre Growth Reference Study Group. (2006*a*). Assessment of differences in linear growth among populations in the WHO Multicentre Growth Reference Study. *Acta Paediatrica* (Suppl. 450), 56–65.

World Health Organization (WHO) Multicentre Growth Reference Study Group. (2006*b*). Enrolment and baseline characteristics in the WHO Multicentre Growth Reference Study. *Acta Paediatrica* (Suppl. 450), 7–15.

World Health Organization (WHO) Reference. (2007). *Growth reference data for 5–19 year olds*. Retrieved from http://www.who.int/growthref/en/

CHAPTER 12

THE IMPACT OF SOCIOECONOMIC INEQUALITY ON CHILDREN'S HEALTH AND WELL-BEING

BALTICA CABIESES, KATE E. PICKETT, AND RICHARD G. WILKINSON

12.1 Introduction

The foundations of almost every aspect of human development are laid throughout fetal life and early childhood. What happens during these years, starting in the womb, has lifelong effects on many aspects of health and well-being (Marmot, 2010). In a global context of profound social inquality between and within countries, attention to childhood health and well-being has long been seen as a key indicator of progress in human and economic development, equality, and human rights. In order to have an impact on inequalities in health and other outcomes, we need to address social gradients in children's access to fair, positive, and systematic opportunities to develop their best selves (Hajizadeh, Nandi, & Heymann, 2014). Because infants and children have no agency, adult society must protect their rights and destinies.

The 2005 United Nations Convention on the Rights of Children (UNCRC) demanded that children should have the *first call* on societies' concerns and capacities in order to protect their vital, vulnerable years of growth from "the mistakes, misfortunes and vicissitudes of the adult world" (UNICEF, 2005, p. 31). Their right to grow up with a level of material resources sufficient to protect their physical and mental development is a right to be protected in good times and in bad. As this Convention stated, "Guaranteeing that right should not depend on whether economies are in growth or recession, or on whether interest rates are rising or falling, or on whether a particular government is in power or a particular policy in fashion" (UNICEF, 2005, p. 31).

The large body of evidence from both developed high-income and developing low- and middle-income countries (LMICs) demonstrating the devastating effect of poverty on children (Autor, 2014; Chin & Culotta, 2014) is well-known. Children and youth who live in poor material and social conditions (e.g., with insufficient food, inadequate housing, low quality of care, etc.) are at greater risk of impairments to healthy development (Ravallion, 2014). Consequently, they are less likely to achieve their optimal educational capabilities and as adults are more likely to suffer from job insecurity, underemployment, and poor working conditions, and more likely to participate in illegal activities and end up being incarcerated (Bellamy, 2004; UNICEF, 2005). However, it is not only these well-known consequences of material poverty that affect population levels of child well-being—another strand of scientific evidence shows that inequality and relative socioeconomic position are also key for childhood well-being and for the intergenerational transmission of deprivation and disadvantage (Aizer & Currie, 2014). Societies with a wide gap between rich and poor consistently do worse than do more equal societies on a range of health and social indicators (Muntaner, Rai, Ng, & Chung, 2012; Wilkinson & Pickett, 2009*b*). This affects children, too, as they experience early in life the physical, emotional, and social disadvantages of growing up in an unequal world.

Policy reports in many high-income countries such as Canada (Smythe, 2007) and the United Kingdom (Rough, Goldblatt, Marmot, & Nathanson, 2014), as well as the worldwide Millennium Developmental Goals have advocated that the life of every child counts (Ibekwe, Ugboma, Onyire, & Muonke, 2011). Unfair and preventable (i.e., inequitable) differences between and within countries in, for example, infant death rates, life expectancy at birth, immunization coverage, and children living in material poverty are seen as unacceptable. There is a global concern about absolute poverty, but only more recently has there been a full recognition of the need to tackle inequality. Reducing childhood socioeconomic inequality could improve child mortality and life expectancy rates, as well as contribute to the goal of reducing health inequalities in the general population (Department of Health, 2007).

This chapter introduces global evidence on the impact of socioeconomic inequality on children's health and well-being. It also describes the underlying pathways leading from socioeconomic inequality to child well-being.

12.2 Global Evidence on the Impact of Inequality on Children's Well-Being

12.2.1 Defining Key Concepts

Before presenting some evidence, we first briefly define the core concepts that are discussed in this chapter. *Childhood* is widely defined as the period of human life that goes from birth through 13 years of age. *Early childhood* is defined in most countries as the period before entry into formal schooling. The UNCRC defines a child as anyone younger than 8 years, unless national laws recognize the age of majority as earlier; this overlaps with the UN definition of young people—between the ages of 15 and 24 years (often split into teenagers aged 13–19 and young adults aged 20–24). Childhood is a very dynamic and extended period in a person's life; young people are constantly developing, and their experience, including the duration of "being young," varies widely between and within countries and different communities. Despite the fact that all of childhood shapes later health and well-being, it is generally accepted that the antenatal period and the first 3 years of life are especially sensitive and critical periods that affect lifetime trajectories of human development and capabilities (Shonkoff, Boyce, & McEwen, 2009).

Health has been defined by the World Health Organization (WHO) (1948) as a state of complete physical, mental, and social well-being and not merely the absence of disease or infirmity. *Well-being* is a multidimensional concept. According to the WHO, it refers to a state in which an individual realizes his or her own potential, can cope with the normal stresses of life, can work productively and fruitfully, and is able to make a contribution to her or his community (Primack, 2003). For children, well-being is directly related to their emotional environment and the social circumstances into which they are born and continue to grow, live, work, and develop (Rough et al., 2014). Hence, children's well-being cannot be assessed by any single factor and a socioecological perspective has been proposed. This perspective locates the child's well-being in the context of family, friendship networks, school, and community, rather than solely in the context of household material living standards (Bradshaw, 2011).

Inequality has been defined as the systematic and structural differences between social groups (Sergeant & Firth, 2006; Wilkinson & Pickett, 2008). Such structural differences include dimensions of socioeconomic position like material housing conditions, income, education, type of occupation, and social class (Marmot, 2009). When these differences are considered preventable and unfair, they are often defined as inequities (Marmot, 2010). Since the Black Report on inequalities in health in the United Kingdom was published in 1978 (Black, Morris, & Smith 1980; Smith, Bartley, & Blane 1990), an extensive body of scientific literature on socioeconomic inequalities in health has been produced. This includes evidence from developing, emerging, and developed economies; however, there is much less evidence that health-related policies are effective in reducing health inequalities (Fosu, 2010; Jen, Jones, & Johnston, 2009).

12.2.2 An Overview of the Impact of Socioeconomic Inequality on Children's Well-Being

How strong is the effect of social inequality on child health and well-being? There are at least 1,800 studies exploring this effect in the scientific literature (see Figure 12.1), and interest in the subject continues to grow. Most studies have been conducted in high-income countries, but there is a significant body of work from LMICs. Despite

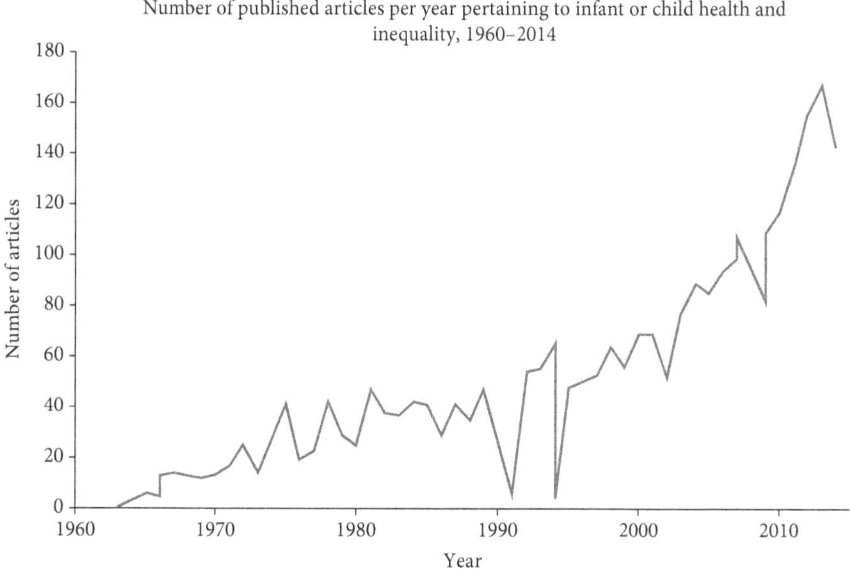

FIGURE 12.1 Number of published articles per year pertaining to infant or child health and inequality, 1960–2014.

occasional controversies around the measures of both inequality and health used in such studies, there is a very strong and consistent association between household socioeconomic position and child health and well-being in almost every country in the world. Notably, in 2011, Edwards reported (Edwards, 2011) life span inequality in a comprehensive panel of 180 countries observed in 1970 and 2000. He found that a convergence in infant mortality rates has reduced global inequality in life expectancy at birth over this period, but also found very large between-country variation, especially across developed countries. Clark (2011) analyzed data from 195 countries between 1955 and 2005 and similarly found that average life expectancy converged during this time but that infant mortality rates had continuously diverged. He explained that this discrepancy arose from the inability of poor countries to improve infant mortality as much as they have improved life expectancy. The positive effect of gross domestic product per capita (GDP PC) on life expectancy weakens and, indeed, eventually disappears completely at higher levels of economic development, whereas the effect of GDP PC on infant mortality grows stronger. Thus, with increasing GDP, global disparities in life expectancy are reduced, but inequalities in infant mortality increase. Overall, evidence suggests significant differences between countries related to their economic development and demographic and epidemiological variations, as well as to the effect of social and health policies, in protecting the life of the most vulnerable, including children. Therefore, developed and developing countries deserve to be considered separately because they face complex yet different challenges in promoting human development and social well-being for all and preventing inequalities.

Nevertheless, the associations between societal levels of income inequality, individual socioeconomic position, and children's health and well-being display some general patterns. First, there is an *inverse or negative relationship* between income inequality and health and well-being; that is, the wider the gap (the more unequal or hierarchical the society), the worse health outcomes are for children. In the language of epidemiological causality (Greenland, Pearl, & Robins, 1999; Rothman & Greenland, 2005), there is a dose–response effect of the degree of inequality on child health and well-being (Marshall, 2005). Second, there is a *finely graded social gradient* in children's health and well-being, right across society. This means that not only poor children (i.e., those living below the poverty line and suffering from absolute material poverty) are affected by socioeconomic position and inequality, but the entire population of children. This implies that *relative poverty* and relative socioeconomic position are relevant for all (Genovese, Rezzonico, & Gualzata, 2004; Hillemeier, Lynch, Harper, Raghunathan, & Kaplan, 2003; Wilkinson & Pickett, 2009*b*) individuals, children, and families who are not at the very apex of the societal socioeconomic pyramid (Genovese et al., 2004; Starfield, Riley, Witt, & Robertson, 2002; Starfield, Robertson, & Riley, 2002). They might not be suffering from inadequate housing standards or lack of food, but they nevertheless experience worse health and a shorter life expectancy, lower life satisfaction and well-being, and more social problems than the most well-off (Pueyo, Serra-Sutton, Alonso, Starfield, & Rajmil, 2007). Third, socioeconomic inequality for children *interacts with other factors*, such as poverty rates, unemployment rates, social policies, and health policies, among others, in its impact on child well-being (Hillemeier et al., 2003). These interactions can produce complex effects for children and their families. Generally, they affect children indirectly through their impact on parental capacity to meet their own and their children's emotional, developmental, and physical needs.

12.2.3 Income Inequality and Child Health and Well-Being in High-Income Countries

There are many studies of the relationship between socioeconomic inequality and children's well-being in the scientific literature. Among high-income countries, the United Kingdom, Canada, the Netherlands, and the Nordic countries have led research in this area. Researchers have looked at inequality between and within developed countries, examining links between inequality and several measures of health status and well-being, including accident rates (Black et al., 1980), infant mortality (Collison, Dey, Hannah, & Stevenson, 2007; Macinko, Shi, & Starfield, 2004; Oakley, Maconochie, Doyle, Dattani, & Moser, 2009;), low birthweight (Lima, de Oliveira, Lyra Cde, Roncalli, & Ferreira, 2013; Nkansah-Amankra, Dhawain, Hussey, & Luchok, 2010), prematurity (Kolodziej, Lopuszanska, Bielicki, & Jankowska, 2007; Regidor et al., 2014; Ronzio 2003), teenage pregnancy (Wilkinson & Pickett 2009*b*), poverty rates (Szwarcwald, Andrade, & Bastos, 2002), IQ (Marmot, 2010), child well-being (Pickett & Wilkinson 2007*b*), and others. In 2007, for example, Pickett and Wilkinson (2007*b*) used the first UNICEF index of child well-being in rich countries to examine the associations between child well-being and material living standards (as measured by average income), the scale of differentiation in social status (income inequality), and social exclusion (children living in relative poverty) in 23 high-income countries. The UNICEF index of child well-being encompassed 39 indicators related to dimensions such as material well-being, health and safety, and educational well-being (UNICEF Innocenti Research Centre, 2007). They found that the overall index of child well-being was closely and negatively correlated with income inequality and the proportion of children living in relative poverty, but not with average income (Figure 12.2).

Recently, Pickett and Wilkinson (2015) analyzed the updated 2013 UNICEF index of child well-being in rich countries. The 2013 index was somewhat different from the 2007 index, most notably in the exclusion of subjective well-being and the addition of measures related to housing and environment. Once again, the overall index of child well-being was closely and negatively correlated with income inequality ($r = -0.60$, $P = .004$, $N = 21$) but not with average income ($r = -0.346$, $P = .12$). The lack of association with average income for both the 2007 and 2013 indices is similar to the lack of association between average income and life expectancy, as well as other health and social outcomes among adults

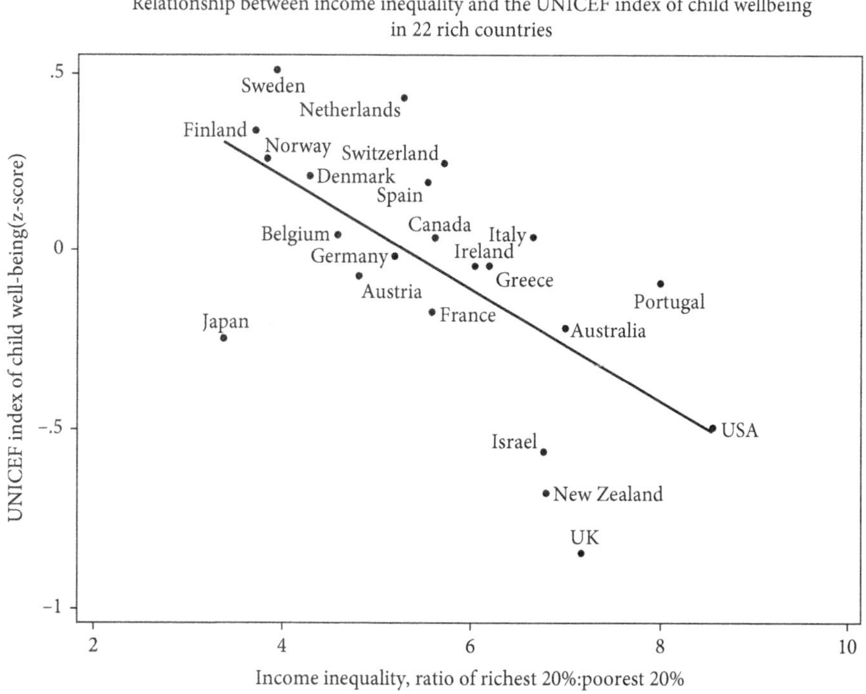

FIGURE 12.2 Relationship between income inequality and the UNICEF index of the child well-being in 22 rich countries.

Redrawn from Pickett and Wilkinson 2007*a*

that have been widely reported (Wilkinson & Pickett, 2010). In rich developed countries, relative or rank income matters more than absolute income. Adjustment for income inequality, children in relative poverty, and the child poverty gap did not change the lack of association between average income and child well-being. Twenty indicators of child well-being (excluding child poverty) were defined consistently in both the 2007 and 2013 UNICEF reports, and the authors used these variables to create an indicator of change in child well-being over the approximate decade 2000–10. Between 2000 and 2010, child well-being scores improved most in Italy, Norway, Portugal, the United Kingdom, and Germany. The biggest declines were seen in Sweden, Canada, Japan, Switzerland, and France. Countries that experienced the largest increases in income inequality (measured as the change in the Organization of Economic Cooperation and Development [OECD] Gini coefficient between 2000 and 2009) had significantly greater declines in child well-being ($r = -0.51$, $P = .02$; see Figure 12.3).

Similar correlations between income inequality and measures of child well-being have been reported for the fifty US states. Higher state-level income inequality has been associated with higher rates of teenage births, juvenile homicides, infant mortality, low birthweight, child overweight, mental health problems, and high school dropouts, as well as with worse educational scores (Pickett & Wilkinson 2007*a*). States with higher

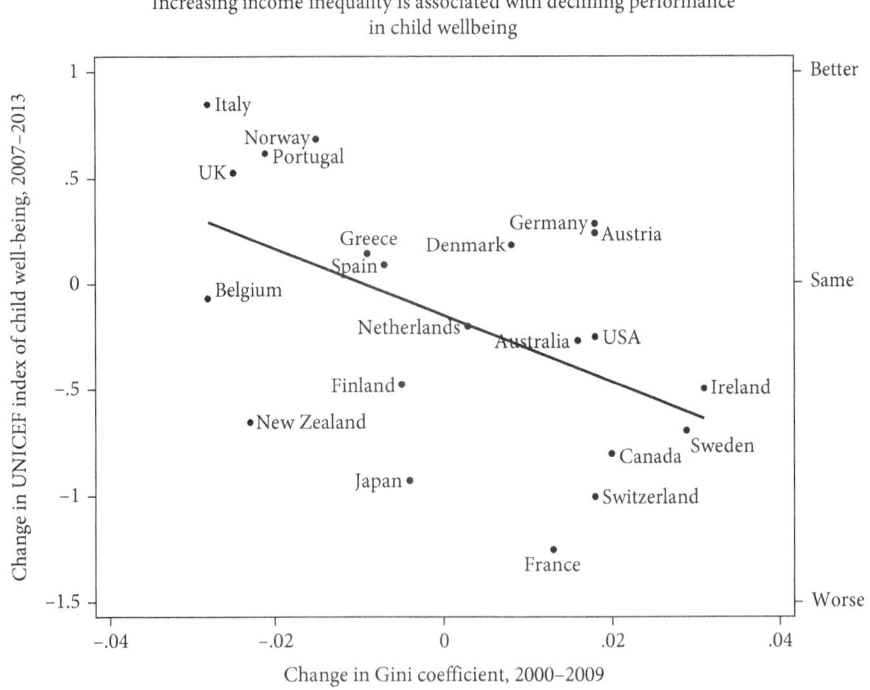

FIGURE 12.3 Increasing income inequality is associated with declining performance in child well-being.

Redrawn from Pickett and Wilkinson 2007*b*

average incomes have significantly fewer teenage births and fewer children dropping out of high school, but they fare no better than poorer states on other measures of child well-being. Social gradients in these outcomes are, of course, present within states, but nevertheless the inequality impact is statistically significant. Among US states, better performance on the 2013 Kids Count Index of child well-being (published by the Annie E. Casey Foundation; Kids Count Data Center, 2013)) was significantly associated with lower levels of income inequality ($r = -0.36$, $P = .01$) (Pickett & Wilkinson, 2015*a*).

The magnitude of the effect of income inequality on child well-being in the studies just described is substantial. Infant mortality rates, rates of childhood overweight, and rates of bullying and victimization from bullying are 2–3 times higher in the more equal of the developed countries compared to the less equal; teenage birth rates are 6–8 times higher. In the United States, twice as many children drop out of high school in the most unequal states.

12.2.4 Income Inequality and Child Health and Well-Being in LMICs

The earliest paper on income inequality and health, published some 35 years ago, showed a cross-sectional association between Gini coefficients of income inequality and both infant mortality and life expectancy at age 5 among a group of 56 developed and developing countries (Rodgers, 1979). There have continued to be studies of income inequality in relation to child well-being (in particular infant, e.g., Babones, 2008; Flegg, 1982; Hales, Howden-Chapman, Salmond, Woodward, & Mackenbach, 1999) in LMICs, although in these countries the need for economic development and growth to raise average standards of living is often seen as obviating any need to focus on the distribution of income and wealth. For example, a review of socioeconomic inequality in malnutrition in developing countries conducted in 2008 (Van de Poel, Hosseinpoor, Speybroeck, Van Ourti, & Vega, 2008) concluded that in all 47 countries assessed, stunting and wasting disproportionately affected those living in poor housing conditions and that income inequality was not relevant in the poorest third of countries, whereas poverty rates were significantly related to malnutrition. However, the belief that "wealthier is healthier" in terms of both population health and economic health is coming under increasing scrutiny, particularly following the global financial crisis. Biggs and colleagues studied 22 Latin American countries from 1960 to 2007, finding a substantial relationship between income inequality and infant mortality rates, and they also reported that when inequality was rising, economic growth was related to only a modest improvement in health, whereas during periods of decreasing inequality, there was a very strong effect of rising GDP (Biggs, King, Basu, & Stuckler, 2013). This perhaps mirrors what happened to child well-being historically in the United States and United Kingdom during another period of rapid structural change (Komlos, 1998). During the Industrial Revolution, childhood height declined among the working class as income inequality increased, showing that economic development, even in its early stages, does not necessarily benefit population well-being.

There are also studies looking at the effects of inequality on children's well-being within LMICs. Income inequality at subnational levels (e.g., regions, cities) has been linked to health within Argentina, Brazil, Chile, China, Ecuador, and India (Pickett & Wilkinson, 2015*b*). A review conducted in 2010 (Houweling & Kunst, 2010) found that childhood mortality is systematically and considerably higher among lower socioeconomic groups within LMICs. Most proximate mortality determinants, including malnutrition, exposure to infections, maternal characteristics, and health care are worse among more deprived groups. A study in India found that, at the state level, literacy levels were more important than average income levels for infant mortality (Rajan, Kennedy, & King, 2013) and that income inequality is closely related to poor use of antenatal care, childbirth within hospitals, underuse of vaccination schemes, infant underweight, and infant deaths. A study in Brazil found similar significant associations between municipality-level income inequality and infant mortality (Ramalho, Sardinha, Rodrigues, & Duarte, 2013). In summary, studies across and within LMICs show a robust association between income inequality and child health, often after adjusting for average income and poverty rates. The link between relative socioeconomic inequality and absolute poverty is intricate and requires further exploration in LMICs; however, it is clear that the distribution as well as the level of development is relevant to improving the population level of well-being in children. In 2008, the Countdown Equity Analysis group analyzed household survey data from 54 countries and found that coverage gaps for family planning, maternal and newborn care, immunization, and treatment of sick children were closely related to socioeconomic inequality (Countdown Equity Analysis et al., 2008).

12.2.5 Social Gradients in Child Health and Well-Being in Relation to Inequality

Researchers have noted that adverse effects of income inequality may be specific to health and social problems that have inverse social gradients (Pickett & Wilkinson, 2015*b*), and similar results have been found for child health (Bird, 2014). In 29 OECD countries, greater income inequality was related to higher post-neonatal mortality rates and teenage overweight, both of which have steep social gradients, whereas there was no association for child suicide, which did not have clear evidence of a social gradient in some countries. There was no association between income inequality and child asthma or adolescent smoking, both of which have some evidence of social gradients; however, other studies have linked inequality to asthma in developed and developing countries (Uphoff, Cabieses, Wright, & Pickett, 2015), and to adolescent smoking in LMICs (Li & Guindon, 2013). An interpretation of this specificity is that income inequality intensifies the health effects of social hierarchy and social comparisons, thus increasing socioeconomic disparities in health.

There is some evidence that social gradients in adult health vary in relation to income inequality, such that people in all socioeconomic circumstances experience better health in more equal countries, including those at the top of the social scale. However, these studies are limited in number, and there is some inconsistency in results (Pickett & Wilkinson, 2015*b*); even less is known about such patterns in child health and well-being. One study showed that infant mortality rates were higher for all social classes and the social gradient was steeper in less-equal England and Wales than in more-equal Sweden, with the greatest difference among lower social class groups (Leon, Vagero, & Olausson, 1992). There is a similar pattern in the literacy scores of young people when arranged by their parent's level of education, showing a steeper social gradient and lower average score in more unequal countries (Willms, 2003). In an international analysis, social gradients in child health by parent's education varied between cohorts from countries with different levels of income inequality (Bird, 2014). Children in more equal countries were taller at all levels of parental education, with the greatest difference among the children of the least educated parents. For parent-reported health and chronic illness, the findings were more variable, with gradients often steepest among children from the cohorts from the most unequal countries, but the level of the gradient had a less consistent relationship with income inequality.

Between 2002 and 2010, Elgar and colleagues found increasing socioeconomic inequalities in adolescent health, including levels of physical activity, body mass index (BMI), and psychological and physical symptoms, although gaps in life satisfaction fell. Higher income inequality was related to lower physical activity, higher BMI, more psychological and physical symptoms, and steeper social gradients in psychological and physical symptoms and life satisfaction (Elgar et al., 2015).

12.3 Pathways Linking Socioeconomic Inequality to Children's Health and Well-Being

12.3.1 Material and Psychosocial Pathways

The relative importance of material and psychosocial factors in the causal pathways linking income inequality to health has been debated over many years and is too large a topic to be addressed in detail here (Marmot & Wilkinson, 2001). It is probably sufficient to say that lack of material resources plays a larger role in LMICs and among the very poor in rich developed countries (and perhaps increasingly so within regimes adopting austerity economics) but that psychosocial factors play an important role in all societies and for people at all socioeconomic levels. The moral, economic, and social justice arguments for poverty alleviation are clear, and the lifelong impact of poverty on trajectories of health and social well-being add to those imperatives. The psychosocial pathway from income inequality to compromised health and well-being is less well known.

Studies showing that relative differences in socioeconomic position impact health and well-being more than do absolute measures support a central role for psychosocial mechanisms. Although most studies are of adults, one study found that self-reported psychosomatic symptoms in adolescents were more closely related to relative affluence (i.e., relative deprivation or rank affluence within regions or schools) than to absolute affluence in 48,523 adolescents in eight developed and middle-income countries (Elgar et al., 2013).

What, then, are the psychosocial processes through which children are affected by inequality and relative socioeconomic status? Three kinds of processes are likely to play important roles. First, inequality may affect children indirectly through its impact on the quality of family life and relationships; in other words, through its impact on their parents' quality of life, health, and well-being. Second, children may be directly aware of increased status differentiation in the wider society and make invidious social comparisons themselves, consciously or subconsciously. Third, epigenetic processes may be involved, whereby the psychosocial environment affects gene expression, and this can occur during fetal development, early childhood or later.

12.3.2 Indirect Effects of Income Inequality Acting on Family Life and Relationships

Income inequality has been consistently linked to factors that are known to be strongly associated with the quality of family life and relationships. These include the prevalence of mental illness and levels of illicit drug use, both of which may compromise parenting and the capability of parents to provide a stable home environment and consistent attachment. Even mild to moderate depression and anxiety can have adverse effects on family life. There is a very strong correlation between income inequality and mental illness, and, in some of the most unequal developed countries, such as the United Kingdom and United States, between a fifth and a quarter of the adult population, many of whom will of course be parents, have experienced mental illness within a 12-month period (Pickett & Wilkinson, 2010).

Because income inequality heightens the importance of status and consequently income and status competition, people work longer hours and accumulate more household debt in more unequal societies (Bowles & Park, 2005; Iacoviello, 2008). Lack of time for family life and the stress of debt must be significant problems in the lives of families in unequal societies. UNICEF UK commissioned a qualitative study of family life in three countries to explore relationships among inequality, consumerism, and family life and the lived experiences of children. They did ethnographic and focus group studies in Sweden, which has low inequality and high child well-being; Spain, with midrange inequality and high well-being; and the United Kingdom, with high inequality and low well-being (Ipsos-Mori & Nairn, 2011, pp. 2–4). In their summary findings, they reported that:

> British families [were] struggling, pushed to find the time their children want, something exacerbated by the uncertainty about the rules and roles operating within the family household. And we found less participation in outdoor and creative activities amongst older and more deprived children.

> Many UK children do not refer to material goods when talking about what makes them happy, and also understand the principles of moderation in consumption, but many have parents who feel compelled to purchase, often against their better judgement.
>
> Children [have a] growing awareness of inequality as they approach secondary school and the role of consumer goods in identifying and creating status groups within peer groups . . . Whilst many UK parents are complicit in purchasing status goods to hide social insecurities this behaviour is almost totally absent in Spain and Sweden. Inequality also has its part to play in access to sporting and creative activities in the UK.

A sad consequence of the impact of inequality on family life is demonstrated in a US study showing an association between income inequality and child maltreatment rates (Eckenrode, Smith, McCarthy, & Dineen, 2014). This effect was independent of child poverty rates and other demographic and economic factors. It is important to note here that associations between income inequality and compromised well-being for children cannot be explained by family breakdown, as is frequently asserted by right-wing politicians and media. Although children raised in single-parent households in some of the more unequal developed countries are indeed at a disadvantage, there is no international association between child well-being and the prevalence of single-parent households. In the more equal developed countries, such as the Scandinavian countries, the links between single parenthood and poverty found within countries are broken through universal and welfare provision of family support and services.

Higher levels of social cohesion and women's status in more equal countries must also support the quality of family life and indirectly enhance child well-being (Wilkinson & Pickett, 2009*a*). Parents can raise children to fit into a society based on trust, reciprocity, collectivism, and cooperation, rather than prepare them to compete in an individualistic, materialistic, and adversarial world.

12.3.3 Direct Effects of Income Inequality Acting on Children Through Status Differentiation

Recent studies clarify that greater income inequality leads to increased status anxiety among adults across the socioeconomic spectrum (Layte, 2012), to reduced solidarity (Paskov & Dewilde, 2012), to lower levels of agreeableness (de Vries, Gosling, & Potter 2011), and a greater tendency to "self enhance" (i.e., consider oneself to be better than average; Loughnan et al., 2011). It is therefore natural to expect that children will also become aware of status differences within their own society and of the psychosocial context in which they are maturing. The age at which children become consciously aware of class and status differences may vary, but research has found that children are fully conscious of differences before they leave primary school and that they can rank occupations hierarchically and place people into social classes by indicators such as clothing, houses, and cars (Simmons & Rosenberg, 1971; Tudor, 1971).

Status differentiation, or one's awareness of how other people perceive your status, affects physiology, cognitive performance, and emotions. A meta-analysis of 208 laboratory studies of acute psychological stressors and cortisol responses, many of which were conducted with students and young people, showed that stronger cortisol responses were elicited if tasks were uncontrollable or characterized by "social-evaluative threat" (threats to self-esteem or social status; Dickerson & Kemeny, 2004). Children's cognitive performance was shown to be affected by status differentiation in a study of 11- to 12-year-old Indian boys. Boys from high and low castes could solve mazes equally well before they knew each other's caste, lower caste children did much less well as soon as caste was publically declared (Hoff & Pandey, 2004). Similar processes were evident when black and white American school children and college students were given cognitive tests (Steele & Aronson, 1995). When told the tests were to measure intelligence, the black students did much less well because this provoked their awareness of stereotyped perceptions of African Americans. Such "stereotype threat" can lead to worse performance when gender or class differences are invoked as well as ethnic differences. Other experiments have shown how the creation of artificial differences in status can lead to differences in behavior and performance (Peters, 1987).

Income inequality seems to have powerful effects on relationships between children. Pickett and Wilkinson have found that the proportion of children finding their peers kind and helpful is lower in more unequal rich countries (Pickett & Wilkinson, 2007*a*). Elgar and colleagues looked at income inequality and school bullying in 117 nationally representative samples of adolescents between 1994 and 2006, finding that inequality was significantly related to bullying others and being a victim of bullying, and the relationship was partially mediated by country differences in homicides, suggesting that a social milieu of interpersonal violence affects children as well as adults (Elgar et al., 2013). Similarly, juvenile homicides rates are, like adult homicide rates, correlated with income inequality (Pickett, Mookherjee, & Wilkinson, 2005). The researchers interpret these associations as reflecting the importance of loss of face and people's sensitivity to feeling disrespected and looked down on in societies where status is more salient.

Studies of socioeconomically mixed neighborhoods find that poor children gain no advantage in well-being from living in affluent neighborhoods. In a UK study, poor boys living in well-off neighborhoods were the most likely, and poor boys in poor areas the least likely, to have behavioral problems, whereas rich children living in poor neighborhoods were more likely to engage in antisocial behavior (Odgers, Donley, Caspi, Bates, & Moffitt, 2015). In the US "Moving to Opportunity" program, started in the 1990s, in which poor families were randomized to receive help to move to more affluent neighborhoods, children whose families had moved before the age of 13 had better long-term socioeconomic outcomes than did control children, whereas those who moved when they were 13 years or older did worse, perhaps because disruption of friendship networks is more likely to result in social exclusion for older children (Chetty, Hendren, & Katz, 2015). Living in more unequal communities seems to enhance awareness of status differences and differences in opportunities and social inclusion, consistent with the literature that shows health benefits for ethnic minorities of living in communities with higher proportions of people of the same ethnicity (Pickett & Wilkinson, 2008).

12.3.4 Epigenetics and Biological Impact of Chronic Stress

As well as direct and indirect psychosocial effects of income inequality on children's health and well-being, understanding of epigenetic processes has led to a new appreciation of the interactions between the social environment and human genetics. A wide range of the social determinants of health, such as mother's health and education, housing conditions, poverty, and parenting affect gene expression and lifelong and intergenerational trajectories of health and well-being.

Researchers have found differences in genetic expression related to early life parenting programs 25 years after the interventions took place (Zhang & Meaney, 2010). Adverse early life experiences can affect the developing brain and increase risk of depression in later life. The developing brain is highly plastic in the first few years of life, and this means that the environment can change the trajectories of rapidly developing neurological and other biological circuits that shape emotional functions and stress responsivity throughout life (Murgatroyd & Spengler, 2011). Early childhood experiences of trauma and maltreatment lead to long-lasting epigenetic changes, including changes associated with risk of depression, diabetes, and some cancers (Yang et al., 2013).

Telomere length is a biological marker of chronic stress, sometimes described as accelerated cellular aging. In an American birth cohort study, children who had been exposed to early social disadvantage (measured as maternal depression, socioeconomic deprivation, family instability, and poor parenting) had shorter telomere length by age 9. There was an interaction between exposure to social disadvantage and genetic variation associated with the dopamine and serotonin (both are powerful neurotransmitters) systems, such that children with genetic vulnerability had the shortest telomere length when exposed (Mitchell et al., 2014). In a Romanian study, children with greater randomized exposure to institutional care (vs. foster care) also had shorter telomere length (Drury et al., 2012).

The idea that children's genes are plastic and open to social intervention and influence and that even young children demonstrate the physiological consequences of chronic stress provides additional impetus for policy solutions to improve childrens's' well-being and life chances through reductions in inequality.

12.4 Policy Implications of Research on Inequality and Children's Health and Well-Being

Income inequality has a robust and consistent association with worse child health and well-being in developed, emerging, and developed countries, and psychosocial pathways offer the best explanation of how inequality affects children across the socioeconomic spectrum, directly and through its impact on their parents and adult society. Of course, other factors also affect child well-being to varying degrees in different societies, including absolute poverty levels and other measures of social differentiation, such as ethnicity (McLeod, Nonnemaker, & Call, 2004), although multilevel analyses show that inequality effects are independent of family socioeconomic position. There are also interactions between inequality and social cohesion and social capital and their effects on children's health and well-being (Lindstrom, Lindstrom, Moghaddassi, & Merlo, 2006; Lindstrom & Malmo Shoulder-Neck Study, 2006). Welfare regimes can offer protection against the adverse effects of inequality, poverty, and deprivation, and the positive effect of strong health and social policies to protect the lives of children cannot be overestimated. Regidor and colleagues (Regidor et al., 2011) analyzed changes in infant mortality from the late 19th century in 17 wealthy countries, classified according to political traditions, family policy models, and period of infant mortality transition. They found that Social Democratic and Scandinavian countries lowered infant mortality rates first, whereas the Southern European countries were the last in Europe (outside of Eastern Europe). Similar patterns were reported in a separate analysis of old and new members of the European Union in 2007 (Matkovic, Sucur, & Zrinscak, 2007). Direct causal links between family supportive policies and child health cannot be inferred from these studies, but they clearly display a relationship between policy and child health over extensive periods. There is a need for high-quality longitudinal research to explore this further and to expand our understanding of the links between income inequality, effective policies, and children's well-being. Houweling and Kunst (2010) have suggested that the increasing political focus on addressing child health inequalities needs to be accompanied by more evidence on the contribution of specific determinants like national policies and on ways to ensure that interventions reach those in the most vulnerable socioeconomic groups.

12.5 Conclusion

The importance of childhood experiences for health and well-being throughout adult life has been established over recent decades. This chapter describes evidence of a strong, consistent association between socioeconomic inequality and children's health and well-being within and between countries globally. Attention to childhood health and well-being is a key indicator of progress in human and economic development, equality, and human rights. Hence, countries worldwide need to address the social gradient in children's access to fair, positive, and systematic opportunities to develop their capabilities. Childhood is crucial in capacity development, the formation of human capital, and social mobility, and there is increasing evidence that returns on investment in early childhood are much greater than investment in education and well-being at later ages (Heckman, 2013; Pickett & Wilkinson, 2014). As advocates for children, clinicians, policy makers, and public health professionals can use the research evidence to tackle the root causes of poor childhood health and well-being.

Acknowledgments

Dr. Cabieses is supported by the Fondecyt Fund, Number 11130042, from National Commission for Science and Technology, Conicyt, Chile. Professor Pickett is supported by the UK National Institute for Health Research Collaboration for Leadership in Applied Health Research and Care (CLAHRC) for Yorkshire and Humber.

References

Aizer, A., & Currie, J. (2014). The intergenerational transmission of inequality: maternal disadvantage and health at birth. *Science, 344*(6186), 856–861. doi:10.1126/science.1251872.

Autor, D. H. (2014). Skills, education, and the rise of earnings inequality among the other 99 percent. *Science, 344*(6186), 843–851. doi:10.1126/science.1251868.

Babones, S. J. (2008). Income inequality and population health: Correlation and causality. *Social Science Medicine, 66*(7), 1614–1626.

Bellamy, N. (2004). The state of the world's children 2005. Childhood under threat. In *UNICEF*, edited by UNICEF. New York: UNICEF.

Biggs, B., King, L., Basu, S., & Stuckler, D. (2013). Is wealthier always healthier? The impact of national income level, inequality, and poverty on public health in Latin America. *Social Science Medicine, 71*(2), 266–273.

Bird, P. K. (2014). *Social gradients in child health and development in relation to income inequality. Who benefits from greater income equality?* York, UK: University of York Health Sciences.

Black, D., Morris, J., & Smith, C. (1980). *Inequalities in health: Report of a research working group*. London: Department of Health and Social Security.

Bowles, S., & Park, Y. (2005). Emulation, inequality, and work hours: Was Thorsten Veblen right? *Economic Journal, 115*, F397–F412.

Bradshaw, J. (2011). Introduction. In J. Bradshaw (Ed.), *The well-being of children in the UK*. Bristol: Polity Press.

Chetty, R., Hendren, N., & Katz, L. F. (2015). *The effects of exposure to better neighborhoods on children: New evidence from the moving to opportunity experiment.* Cambridge, USA: National Bureau of Economic Research.

Chin, G., & Culotta, E. (2014). The science of inequality. What the numbers tell us. Introduction. *Science, 344*(6186), 818–821. doi:10.1126/science.344.6186.818.

Clark, R. (2011). World health inequality: Convergence, divergence, and development. *Social Science Medicine, 72*(4), 617–624. doi:10.1016/j.socscimed.2010.12.008.

Collison, D., Dey, C., Hannah, G., & Stevenson, L. (2007). Income inequality and child mortality in wealthy nations. *Journal of Public Health (Oxford), 29*(2), 114–117.

Countdown Equity Analysis Group, Boerma, J. T., Bryce, J., Kinfu, Y., Axelson, H., & Victora, C. G. (2008). Mind the gap: Equity and trends in coverage of maternal, newborn, and child health services in 54 Countdown countries. *Lancet, 371*(9620), 1259–1267. doi:10.1016/S0140-6736(08)60560-7.

Department of Health. (2007). *Implementation plan for reducing health inequalities in infant mortality: A good practice guide.* London: National Health Service.

de Vries, R., Gosling, S., & Potter, J. (2011). Income inequality and personality: Are less equal U.S. states less agreeable? *Social Science Medicine, 72*(12), 1978–1985. doi:10.1016/j.socscimed.2011.03.046.

Dickerson, S. S., & Kemeny, M. E. (2004). Acute stressors and cortisol responses: A theoretical integration and synthesis of laboratory research. *Psychological Bulletin, 130*(3), 355–391.

Drury, S. S., Theall, K., Gleason, M. M. Smyke, A. T. De Vivo, I., Wong, J. Y., . . . Nelson, C. A. (2012). Telomere length and early severe social deprivation: Linking early adversity and cellular aging. *Molecular Psychiatry 17*(7), 719–727. doi:10.1038/mp.2011.53.

Eckenrode, J., Smith, E. G., McCarthy, M. E., &. Dineen, M. (2014). Income inequality and child maltreatment in the United States. *Pediatrics, 133*(3), 454–461. doi:10.1542/peds.2013-1707.

Edwards, R. D. (2011). Changes in world inequality in length of life: 1970–2000. *Population and Development Review, 37*(3), 499–528.

Elgar, F. J., De Clercq, B., Schnohr, C. W. Bird, P., Pickett, K. E., Torsheim, T., Hofmann, F., & Currie C. (2013). Absolute and relative family affluence and psychosomatic symptoms in adolescents. *Social Science & Medicine, 91*(0), 25–31. doi:http://dx.doi.org/10.1016/j.socscimed.2013.04.030.

Elgar, F. J., Pfortner, T. K., Moor, I., De Clercq, B., Stevens, G. W., & Currie, C. (2015). Socioeconomic inequalities in adolescent health 2002-2010: A time-series analysis of 34 countries participating in the Health Behaviour in School-aged Children study. *Lancet, 385*(9982), 2088–2095. doi:10.1016/S0140-6736(14)61460-4.

Elgar, F. J., Pickett, K. E., Pickett, W., Craig, W., Molcho, M., Hurrelmann, K., & Lenzi, M. (2013). School bullying, homicide and income inequality: A cross-national pooled time series analysis. *International Journal of Public Health, 58*(2), 237–245. doi:10.1007/s00038-012-0380-y.

Flegg, A. T. (1982). Inequality of income, illiteracy and medical-care as determinants of infant-mortality in underdeveloped-countries. *Population Studies-A Journal of Demography, 36*(3), 441–458.

Fosu, A. K. (2010). Inequality, income, and poverty: comparative global evidence. *Social Science Quarterly, 91*(5), 1432–1446.

Genovese, C., Rezzonico, A., & Gualzata, R. (2004). Absolute poverty and relative poverty. *Krankenpfl Soins Infirm, 97*(11), 65–66.

Greenland, S., Pearl, J., & Robins, J. M. (1999). Causal diagrams for epidemiologic research. *Epidemiology, 10*(1), 37–48.

Hajizadeh, M., Nandi, A., & Heymann, J. (2014). Social inequality in infant mortality: What explains variation across low and middle income countries? *Social Science Medicine, 101*, 36–46. doi:10.1016/j.socscimed.2013.11.019.

Hales, S., Howden-Chapman, P., Salmond, C., Woodward, A., & Mackenbach, J. (1999). National infant mortality rates in relation to gross national product and distribution of income. *Lancet, 354*(9195), 2047.

Heckman, J. J. (2013). *Giving kids a fair chance*. Boston: MIT Press.

Hillemeier, M. M., Lynch, J., Harper, S., Raghunathan, T., & Kaplan, G. A. (2003). Relative or absolute standards for child poverty: A state-level analysis of infant and child mortality. *American Journal of Public Health, 93*(4), 652–657.

Hoff, K., & Pandey, P. (2004). Belief systems and durable inequalities: An experimental investigation of Indian caste. *A policy research working paper.* Washington, DC: World Bank.

Houweling, T. A., & Kunst, A. E. (2010). Socio-economic inequalities in childhood mortality in low- and middle-income countries: A review of the international evidence. *British Medical Bulletin, 93*, 7–26. doi:10.1093/bmb/ldp048.

Iacoviello, M. (2008). Household debt and income inequality, 1963–2003. *Journal of Money, Credit and Banking, 40*(5), 929–965.

Ibekwe, P., Ugboma, H., Onyire, N., & Muoneke, U. (2011). Perinatal mortality in Southern Nigeria: Less than half a decade to the Millennium Developmental Goals. *Annals of Medicine and Health Sciences Research, 1*(2), 215–222.

Ipsos-Mori, & Nairn, A. (2011). *Children's well-being in UK, Sweden and Spain: The role of inequality and materialism*. London: UNICEF UK.

Jen, M. H., Jones, K., & Johnston, R. (2009). Global variations in health: Evaluating Wilkinson's income inequality hypothesis using the World Values Survey. *Social Science Medicine, 68*(4), 643–653.

Kids Count Data Center. (2013). *Kids Count overall rank*. Baltimore, USA: Annie E. Casey Foundation.

Kolodziej, H., Lopuszanska, M., Bielicki, T., & Jankowska, E. A. (2007). Social inequality in premature mortality among Polish urban adults during economic transition. *American Journal of Human Biology, 19*(6), 878–885. doi:10.1002/ajhb.20665.

Komlos, J. (1998). Shrinking in a growing economy? The mystery of physical stature during the industrial revolution. *Journal of Economic History, 58*(03), 779–802.

Layte, R. (2012). The association between income inequality and mental health: Testing status anxiety, social capital, and neo-materialist explanations. *European Sociological Review, 28*(4), 498–511.

Leon, D. A., Vagero, D., & Olausson, P. O. (1992). Social class differences in infant mortality in Sweden: Comparison with England and Wales. *British Medical Journal, 305*(6855), 687–691.

Li, D. X., & Guindon, E. G. (2013). Income, income inequality and youth smoking in low- and middle-income countries. *Addiction*. doi:10.1111/add.12075.

Lima, M. C., de Oliveira, G. S., Lyra Cde, O., Roncalli, A. G., & Ferreira, M. A. (2013). [The spatial inequality of low birth weight in Brazil]. *Cien Saude Colet, 18*(8), 2443–2452.

Lindstrom, M., & Group Malmo Shoulder-Neck Study. (2006). Psychosocial work conditions, social participation and social capital: A causal pathway investigated in a longitudinal study. *Social Science Medicine, 62*(2), 280–291. doi:10.1016/j.socscimed.2005.06.005.

Lindstrom, M., Lindstrom, C., Moghaddassi, M., & Merlo, J. (2006). Social capital and neo-materialist contextual determinants of sense of insecurity in the neighbourhood: A multilevel analysis in Southern Sweden. *Health Place, 12*(4), 479–489. doi:10.1016/j.healthplace.2005.08.001.

Loughnan, S., Kuppens, P., Allik, J., Balazs, K, de Lemus, S., Dumont, K., . . . Haslam, N. (2011). Economic inequality is linked to biased self-perception. *Psychological Science, 22*(10), 1254–1258. doi:10.1177/0956797611417003.

Macinko, J. A., Shi, L., & Starfield, B. (2004). Wage inequality, the health system, and infant mortality in wealthy industrialized countries, 1970–1996. *Social Science Medicine, 58*(2), 279–292.

Marmot, M. (2009). Closing the health gap in a generation: The work of the Commission on Social Determinants of Health and its recommendations. *Global Health Promotion,* Suppl 1, 23–27. doi:16/1_suppl/23 [pii] 10.1177/1757975909103742.

Marmot, M. (2010). *Fair society, healthy lives.* London: Marmot Review.

Marmot, M., & Wilkinson, R. G. (2001). Psychosocial and material pathways in the relation between income and health: A response to Lynch et al. *British Medical Journal, 322*(7296), 1233–1236.

Marshall, T. (2005). Bradford-Hill criteria provide the way ahead for controversial theory. *International Journal of Surgery, 3*(4), 287–288. doi:10.1016/j.ijsu.2005.10.006.

Matkovic, T., Sucur, Z., & Zrinscak, S. (2007). Inequality, poverty, and material deprivation in new and old members of the European Union. *Croatian Medical Journal, 48*(5), 636–652.

McLeod, J. D., Nonnemaker, J. M., & Call, K. T. (2004). Income inequality, race, and child well-being: An aggregate analysis in the 50 United States. *Journal of Health and Social Behavior, 45*(3), 249–264.

Mitchell, C., Hobcraft, J., McLanahan, S. S., Siegel, S. R., Berg, A., Brooks-Gunn, J., . . . Notterman, D. (2014). Social disadvantage, genetic sensitivity, and children's telomere length. *Proceedings of the National Academy of Science of the USA, 111*(16), 5944–5999. doi:10.1073/pnas.1404293111.

Muntaner, C., Rai, N., Ng, E., & Chung, H. (2012). Social class, politics, and the spirit level: Why income inequality remains unexplained and unsolved. *International Journal of Health Services, 42*(3), 369–381.

Murgatroyd, C., & Spengler, D. (2011). Epigenetics of early child development. *Frontiers of Psychiatry, 2*(16). doi:10.3389/fpsyt.2011.00016.

Nkansah-Amankra, S., Dhawain, A., Hussey, J. R., & Luchok, K. J. (2010). Maternal social support and neighborhood income inequality as predictors of low birth weight and preterm birth outcome disparities: Analysis of South Carolina Pregnancy Risk Assessment and Monitoring System survey, 2000–2003. *Maternal and Child Health* Journal, *14*(5), 774–785. doi:10.1007/s10995-009-0508-8.

Oakley, L., Maconochie, N., Doyle, P., Dattani, N., & Moser, K. (2009). Multivariate analysis of infant death in England and Wales in 2005–06, with focus on socio-economic status and deprivation. *Health Statistics Quarterly,* (42), 22–39.

Odgers, C. L., Donley, S., Caspi, A., Bates, C. J., & Moffitt, T. E. (2015). Living alongside more affluent neighbors predicts greater involvement in antisocial behavior among low-income boys. *Journal of Child Psychology and Psychiatry, 56*(10), 1055–1064. doi:10.1111/jcpp.12380.

Paskov, M., & Dewilde, C. (2012). Income inequality and solidarity in Europe. *Research in Social Stratification and Mobility, 30*(4), 415–432.

Peters, W. (1987). *A class divided: Then and now.* New Haven, CT: Yale University Press.

Pickett, K. E., Mookherjee, J., & Wilkinson, R. G. (2005). Adolescent birth rates, total homicides, and income inequality in rich countries. *American Journal of Public Health, 95*(7), 1181–1183.

Pickett, K. E., & Wilkinson, R. G. (2007*a*). Child wellbeing and income inequality in rich societies: Ecological cross sectional study. *British Medical Journal, 335*, 1080.

Pickett, K. E., & Wilkinson, R. G. (2007*b*). Child wellbeing and income inequality in rich societies: Ecological cross sectional study. *British Medical Journal, 335*(7629), 1080.

Pickett, K. E., & Wilkinson, R. G. (2008). People like us: Ethnic group density effects on health. *Ethnicity and Health, 13*(4), 321–334.

Pickett, K. E., & Wilkinson, R. G. (2010). Inequality: An underacknowledged source of mental illness and distress. *British Journal of Psychiatry, 197*, 426–428.

Pickett, K. E., & Wilkinson, R. (2015). Income inequality and child wellbeing: An update and ethical discussion. *Journal of Pediatrics*, 135(2), S39–S47. (in press).

Pickett, K. E., & Wilkinson, R. G. (2015*a*). The ethical and policy implications of research on income inequality and child well-being. *Pediatrics, 135*(Suppl 2, S39–S47). doi:10.1542/peds.2014-3549E.

Pickett, K. E., & Wilkinson, R. G. (2015*b*). Income inequality and health: A causal review. *Social Science Medicine, 128*, 316–326. doi:10.1016/j.socscimed.2014.12.031.

Primack, B. A. (2003). The WHO-5 Wellbeing Index performed the best in screening for depression in primary care. *ACP Journal Club, 139*(2), 48.

Pueyo, M. J., Serra-Sutton, V., Alonso, J., Starfield, B., & Rajmil, L. (2007). Self-reported social class in adolescents: Validity and relationship with gradients in self-reported health. *BMC Health Service Research, 7*, 151. doi:10.1186/1472-6963-7-151.

Rajan, K., Kennedy, J., & King, L. (2013). Is wealthier always healthier in poor countries? The health implications of income, inequality, poverty, and literacy in India. *Social Science Medicine, 88*, 98–107. doi:10.1016/j.socscimed.2013.04.004.

Ramalho, W. M., Sardinha, L. M., Rodrigues, I. P., & Duarte, E. C. (2013). Inequalities in infant mortality among municipalities in Brazil according to the Family Development Index, 2006–2008. *Rev Panam Salud Publica, 33*(3), 205–212.

Ravallion, M. (2014). Income inequality in the developing world. *Science, 344*(6186), 851–855. doi:10.1126/science.1251875.

Regidor, E., Pascual, C., Martinez, D., Calle, M. E., Ortega, P., & Astasio, P. (2011). The role of political and welfare state characteristics in infant mortality: A comparative study in wealthy countries since the late 19th century. *International Journal of Epidemiology, 40*(5), 1187–1195. doi:10.1093/ije/dyr092.

Regidor, E., Santos, J. M., Ortega, P., Calle, M. E., Astasio, P., & Martinez, D. (2014). Decreasing income inequality and emergence of the association between income and premature mortality: Spain, 1970–2010. *Health Place, 27*, 30–37. doi:10.1016/j.healthplace.2014.01.010.

Rodgers, G. B. (1979). Income and inequality as determinants of mortality: An international cross-section analysis. *Population Studies, 33*, 343–351.

Ronzio, C. R. (2003). Urban premature mortality in the U.S. between 1980 and 1990: changing roles of income inequality and social spending. *Journal of Public Health Policy, 24*(3–4), 386–400.

Rothman, K. J., & Greenland, S. (2005). Causation and causal inference in epidemiology. *American Journal of Public Health, 95* Suppl 1, S144–S150. doi:10.2105/AJPH.2004.059204.

Rough, E., Goldblatt, P., Marmot, M., & Nathanson, V. (2014). Inequalities in child health. In BMA Board of Science (Eds.), *Growing up in the UK—Ensuring a healthy future for our children*. London: BMA Board of Science.

Sergeant, J. C., & Firth, D. (2006). Relative index of inequality: Definition, estimation, and inference. *Biostatistics, 7*(2), 213–224. doi:10.1093/biostatistics/kxj002.

Shonkoff, J. P., Boyce, W. T., & McEwen, B. S. (2009). Neuroscience, molecular biology, and the childhood roots of health disparities: Building a new framework for health promotion and disease prevention. *Journal of the American Medical Association, 301*(21), 2252–2259. doi:10.1001/jama.2009.754.

Simmons, R. G., & Rosenberg, M. (1971). Functions of children's perceptions of the stratification system. *American Sociological Review, 36*, 235–249.

Smith, G. D., Bartley, M., & Blane, D. (1990). The Black report on socioeconomic inequalities in health 10 years on. *British Medical Journal, 301*(6748), 373–377.

Smythe, S. (2007). *Child and youth development and income inequality: A review of selected literature*. Vancouver: Canada´s Social Development Partnership Program.

Starfield, B., Riley, A. W., Witt, W. P., &. Robertson, J. (2002). Social class gradients in health during adolescence. *Journal of Epidemiology and Community Health, 56*(5), 354-361.

Starfield, B., Robertson, J., & Riley, A. W. (2002). Social class gradients and health in childhood. *Ambulatory Pediatrics, 2*(4), 238–246.

Steele, C. M., & Aronson, J. (1995). Stereotype threat and the intellectual test performance of African-Americans. *Journal of Personality and Social Psychology, 69*, 797–811.

Szwarcwald, C. L., Andrade, C. L., & Bastos, F. I. (2002). Income inequality, residential poverty clustering and infant mortality: A study in Rio de Janeiro, Brazil. *Social Science Medicine, 55*(12), 2083–2092.

Tudor, J. F. (1971). The development of class awareness in children. *Social Forces, 49*, 470–476.

UNICEF. (2005). Child poverty in rich countries 2005. In *UNICEF Innocenti Research Centre* (Eds.), Innocenti Report Card and 6. Florence: UNICEF.

UNICEF Innocenti Research Centre. (2007). Child poverty in perspective: An overview of child well-being in rich countries. In *Innocenti Report Card*. Florence: UNICEF

Uphoff, E. P., Cabieses, B., Wright, J., & Pickett, K. E. (2015). International prevalence rates of asthma and allergy are associated with income inequality. *Journal of Allergy and Clinical Immunology, 136*(1), 189–190. doi:10.1016/j.jaci.2015.01.037.

Van de Poel, E., Hosseinpoor, A. R., Speybroeck, N., Van Ourti, T., & Vega, J. (2008). Socioeconomic inequality in malnutrition in developing countries. *Bulletin of the World Health Organization, 86*(4), 282–291.

Wilkinson, R. G., & Pickett, K. (2010). *The spirit level: Why equality is better for everyone*. London: Penguin.

Wilkinson, R. G., & Pickett, K. E. (2008). Income inequality and socioeconomic gradients in mortality. *American Journal of Public Health, 98*(4), 699–704.

Wilkinson, R. G., & Pickett, K. E. (2009*a*). Income inequality and social dysfunction. *Annual Review of Sociology, 35*, 493–512.

Wilkinson, R. G., & Pickett, K. E. (2009*b*). *The spirit level: Why more equal societies almost always do better.* London: Penguin.

Willms, J. D. (2003). Literacy proficiency of youth: Evidence of converging socioeconomic gradients. *International Journal of Educational Research, 39*, 247–252.

World Health Organization. (1948). *Definition of Health*. www.who.org.

Yang, B. Z., Zhang, H., Ge, W., Weder, N., Douglas-Palumberi, H., Perepletchikova, P., Gelernter, J., & Kaufman, J. (2013). Child abuse and epigenetic mechanisms of disease risk. *American Journal of Preventive Medicine, 44*(2), 101–107. doi:10.1016/j.amepre.2012.10.012.

Zhang, T. Y., & Meaney, M. J. (2010). Epigenetics and the environmental regulation of the genome and its function. *Annual Review of Psychology, 61*, 439–466, C1–C3. doi:10.1146/annurev.psych.60.110707.163625.

CHAPTER 13

GROWTH AND MATURATION OF CHILDREN AND ADOLESCENTS

Variability Due to Genetic and Environmental Factors

ALAN D. ROGOL

13.1 Introduction

Auxology is the study of growth and development (maturation). In the context of this chapter, I apply it to the evaluation and measurement of growth—both to define the broad range of normal for a population and to identify deviations from normal, whether physiological or pathological. Measuring length or height in infants and children is a fundamental component of medical visits for infants, children, and adolescents. Just like the temperature and heart rate, length should be considered a "vital sign." Serial measurements of growth as plotted on standard growth charts are important in monitoring the overall health and well-being of an infant, child, or adolescent. Charts that depict expected ranges and trajectories of anthropometric measurements and indicators are among the principal tools used by researchers, clinicians, and policy makers to assist in assessing the health and nutritional well-being of individuals at nearly all life stages and/or the general well-being of communities and broader populations (Garza & de Onis, 2007). In general, a normal pattern of growth suggests good general health and well-being, but growth slower than the lower limit of normal raises the possibility of an underlying subacute or chronic illness. Deviations from "normal" or, more importantly, from previously obtained measurements may alert the health care provider to abnormalities potentially associated with concomitant treatable conditions or genetic disorders. The greater the deviation from normal (shorter, lighter), the more likely that the child has had a period of abnormally slow growth. A derived metric, the relative weight-for-height, is designated the body mass index (BMI). It is calculated as

$$\text{BMI} = \text{Weight (Kg)/height}^2(\text{m}^2).$$

Normal curves for these parameters are available and widely used, particularly those from the World Health Organization (WHO) (Centers for Disease Control and Prevention [CDC], 2012; Rogol & Hayden, 2014) and the CDC (Grummer-Strawn, Reinhold, & Krebs, 2010; Rogol & Hayden, 2014). The import of these is not so much the precise spot where one plots on these graphs (percentile), but the progress made over time. For normally growing children, the relative position on the growth chart at any one time is greatly dependent on the child's genetic background for height. The key element in the interpretation of growth curves (height, weight, and BMI) is the progress made over time, or, stated in another way, what is important is the growth trajectory. Thus, during childhood, to stay the same (e.g., in height) is to fall behind.

Precisely how one measures the various parameters of growth is beyond the scope of this chapter, but the interested reader is directed to work by Rogol and Hayden (2014), Cox and Savage (1998), Rogol and Lawton (1991), and Rogol (2015), especially the graphics displayed at the end of the article by Rogol (2015) that display the various charts. The differences between these two sets of charts reflect their origins and the not inconsequential difference between a growth *standard* (how one "should" grow, everything else being ideal; the WHO chart) and a growth *reference*, which depicts how children of a specific population grew during a specific epoch (the CDC chart). Although both depend on the specific population studied, it is the latter (a growth reference) that may mimic or, in fact, may deviate greatly from the standard (ideal). Factors that may be important come mainly from the environment and include food (and protein) availability, stress (e.g., conflict-induced displacement and migration), and environmental toxins (e.g., lead, among a host of others).

The use of a growth standard presents a tool that can be used effectively for *comparative* purposes and to assess both interventions and health policies (Garza & deOnis, 2007; Garza, Frongillo, & Dewey, 1994). This approach broadens the definition of health beyond the absence of disease to the adoption of practices and behaviors associated with good health outcomes (e.g., breastfeeding and complementary feeding, access to preventative and curative health care and healthful environments; Garza & de Onis, 2007).

Growth may be proportionate (physiologic, also in many pathologic conditions) or disproportionate, which may lead the physician to consider and then evaluate the child for various pathologic causes of growth abnormalities.

13.2 Genetic Potential for Adult Height

Many methods are available to estimate the adult height of children and adolescents. One of the more popular is the target height (TH), which is an estimate (with a wide confidence interval) of a child's adult height based on the heights of his or her biological parents. It is commonly determined by calculating the mid-parental height (MPH) using the following formulae (Rogol, 2015; Rogol & Hayden, 2014; Tanner, Goldstein, & Whitehouse, 1970):

$$\textbf{Target height (MPH) for girls}: \\ \left(\left[\textbf{Father's height cm} - \textbf{13 cm}\right] + \textbf{Mother's height cm}\right) / 2 \\ \left(\textbf{to determine average}\right).$$

$$\textbf{Target height (MPH) for boys}: \\ \left(\left[\textbf{Father's height cm}\right] + \left[\textbf{Mother's height cm} + \textbf{13 cm}\right]\right) / 2 \\ \left(\textbf{to determine average}\right).$$

This formula is based on the mean difference in height between women and men of approximately 13 cm. Children will, on average, grow to their mid-parental percentile. The confidence intervals are large. For girls and boys, 8.5 cm on either side of the calculated target height equates to the 3rd and 97th percentiles of mature adult height. As an example, 95% of the males of biological parents whose target height is 180 cm will have adult heights ranging from 171.5 to 188.5 cm, spanning approximately the 25th and 95th percentiles for normal males on a CDC chart! These estimates are for "any" child of the same biological parents, but what about the more clinically relevant question: "what is the estimated adult height of the individual child being evaluated"? This common question (at least for a pediatrician or pediatric endocrinologist) introduces an additional concept, that of *biological age*. One grows until one's biological age is "adult," that is, until the ends (epiphyses) of the long bones (e.g., the tibia and femur of the leg) close at maturity. The timing of biological events such as this one is, on average, that of the calendar (chronological) age for the vast majority of children. Females reach their adult height at approximately 18 years and boys several years later. After the age of approximately 2–3 years, one "hits one's stride" (at least on the growth chart) and continues to grow along one of the height trajectories (percentiles) noted. This phenomenon is likely due to the infant being further away from the constraints or excesses of the intrauterine environment and, other things being equal, will grow along the trajectory of his or her genetic potential. This phenomenon is also the same for some of the other growth parameters, for example, the weight and BMI standard deviation score (BMI SDS). Thus, the growth trajectory runs along a certain percentile or at least a very narrow band of percentiles (Butler, McKie, & Ratcliffe, 1990). If that is true, then one can predict the adult height of such a child/adolescent by marching along that percentile line until mature height is reached. That does not always occur, and a surrogate for the biological age becomes necessary. The most commonly used at all ages is bone age, but in adolescents, the maturation of secondary sexual characteristics (breast and pubic hair development in girls and the genitalia, testes, and pubic hair in boys) can be used.

The bone age is usually determined from the interpretation of a single radiograph of the hand and wrist, which is a surrogate for the maturation of the epiphyses of the long bones. The technical aspects are described in the monograph by Rogol and Hayden (2014). The auxologic precept is that one reaches adult height at epiphyseal maturity and that, at any biological age, one is a specific fraction of his or her adult height. For example, a 13-year-old with a bone age of 10 years would have 3 "extra" years of growth compared to a 13-year-old with a biological age (bone age) of 13 years. That translates to approximately 17 cm at adult height, even if both attain the same adult height. The path (trajectory) of how these subjects reached their adult height describes some of the wide range of normal physiology for growth and maturation. The 13-year-old with the delayed bone age is a prepubertal boy (as would be most boys of 10 years), but the 13-year-old with the average bone age for 13 years is a maturing adolescent who would have significant external signs of puberty. This scenario, commonly called *constitutional delay of growth and puberty* (CDGP) is one of the most prevalent variants of physiologic growth and does not necessarily indicate a pathologic process. Evaluation and perhaps transient treatment with a puberty-promoting agent to get the adolescent through the difficult psychosocial aspects of this condition may be prudent.

Perhaps half of the variation in the timing (and perhaps *tempo)* of puberty is genetically determined (Bordini & Rosenfield, 2011). However, sex hormones, hormonally active environmental chemicals ("environmental disruptors"), and diverse somatic stimuli (e.g., nutrition) can affect the pubertal process. Suboptimal nutrition may be an important factor in the later onset of puberty, and overnutrition accelerates its onset (Biro et al., 2001; Bordini & Rosenfield, 2011).

13.3 Monitoring Growth in Infants, Children, and Adolescents

From the preceding section, it seems obvious that growth parameters should be monitored periodically and more frequently in young infants given their much greater degree of growth. Normal growth can be defined as a Gaussian phenomenon (Rogol & Hayden, 2014). Values for continuous variables such as height and weight are distributed along a bell-shaped (normal distribution) curve. The percentile of either parameter may be directly read from the curves or interpreted from summary tables. The standard deviation score (SDS) or *z*-score may be calculated by subtracting the mean value of the reference (or standard) of the population from the observed value and dividing by the SD value of the reference population. In equation form this would be:

Height SDS = (child's height — normal population mean for children of same age and sex) / SD of the height of children of same age and sex.

Similar parameters may be derived for the various components of body composition, fat mass, fat-free (lean) mass, and bone mass (Rogol & Hayden, 2014; Wells et al., 2012). Body composition measurement techniques used may vary according to the clinical situation. Body composition is affected by genetic, but more importantly, environmental conditions. As a general rule, most undernourished children are underweight for height. On the other hand, both height and weight are affected as more serious malnutrition occurs. Although short for age, the weight is often more affected than the height, denoted by a weight SDS lower than the height SDS and likely a BMI SDS below the lowest percentile of normal.

13.4 Variants of Normal Growth

From a public health point of view the environment—stress, caloric deprivation, and infectious disease—overwhelmingly outpace the pathological variants noted herein. It is from these variants, including those caused by pathological conditions and processes, that one can learn the mechanisms of growth alterations and perhaps remediate them. That is clear in malnutrition whether caused by energy (calorie), protein-energy, or micronutrient deficiencies. Even in the physiologic sense, appetite may clearly affect later growth. Van Jaarsveld and colleagues studied a large number of twin pairs to test the hypothesis that sibling differences in infant appetite predicted differential weight gain (growth) during childhood. Appetite during the first 3 months of life was assessed with tools (inventories) that measured food responsiveness and satiety responsiveness. The results indicated that a more robust appetite (higher food responsiveness or lower satiety responsiveness) in early infancy was prospectively associated with more rapid growth up to age 15 months. Their goal was to predict future obesity, and they limited their data to weight determinations (Johnson, van Jaarsveld, Llewellyn, Cole, & Wardle, 2014; Van Jaarsveld, Boniface, Llewellyn, & Wardle, 2014).

I shall not delve into individual conditions and their mechanisms here, nor discuss the clinical evaluation or treatments for specific conditions. For an overview of the approach to such individuals and their individual conditions, see Rogol (2015). However, I shall discuss some general concepts associated with pathological conditions.

Several of the more common variants, for example, the CDGP and the notion of target height, have been briefly discussed already. These conditions clearly contribute to the variability in normal growth (and adult height) and have been partially described in a series of genome-wide association (GWA) studies of large numbers of subjects; however, the combined explanation of the variance found in height has been low and disappointing.

Aside from single-gene conditions that affect height by hormonal deficits or some significant malabsorption syndromes, the genetic basis for height determination is unclear. One of the more directed studies has been done by Guo and co-workers (2014) who performed whole-exome sequencing in 14 children with severe short stature and some affected family members. They identified a specific genetic cause in 5 of the 14; however, it should be noted that each had the phenotype of severe short stature and do not represent the usual subject from a "normal" population. Large-scale pooled next-generation sequencing of more than 1,000 (targeted) genes to identify genetic causes of short stature has been done (Wang et al., 2013). However, even those targeted genetic studies are unable to account for a majority of the variation in human height.

GWA studies are a powerful method to understand variations in an unbiased manner in humans (as well as plant and animal variability). The numbers of subjects screened and the variants identified are now more than 250,000 and 697, respectively, and these numbers are increasing rapidly. These variants together explain approximately 20% of the heritability for adult height (Wood et al., 2014). The almost 700 variants were clustered in 423 loci that were enriched for genes, pathways, and tissue types known to affect growth. Many fewer genes are involved in the size (and many other characteristics) of canine breeds. The IGF-I gene seemingly has a major role in the relative sizes of individual canine breeds, which vary over a 40-fold range as opposed to perhaps a 1.5-fold in the human (Sutter et al., 2007).

Similar GWA studies have been undertaken to try to disentangle the timing of pubertal maturation in children (Dauber & Hirschhorn, 2011; Lango Allen et al., 2010). A few new genes have been found; for example, one is very near the LIN28B gene, but its presence (individual single nucleotide polymorphisms [SNPs]) explains less than 1% (approximately 1 month) of the variation in the timing of puberty (Ong et al., 2009). Using an alternative approach, Costa-Barbosa and colleagues detected a series of individual genes that lead to pituitary gonadotropin failure (Kallmann syndrome; Costa-Barbosa et al., 2013), but none appears to be prominent in the physiologic timing of pubertal maturation in children.

13.4.1 Familial (Genetic) Short Stature

Children with this condition are short, with a height of less than the 2.3 percentile and with a biologic age (bone age) that is concordant with their chronological age. This latter equivalence sets the timing of pubertal maturation to be within the normal range. Their parents' heights are usually less than the 10th centile. Thus, as children and adolescents and continuing to adulthood, children with familial short stature are short and relatively slow growing (to maintain that low percentile [channel] on the growth chart). However, they should be normal in other aspects of growth (e.g., body composition and the regional distribution of body fat). These children undergo puberty within the usual time frame. The genetic "factors" are likely based on the polygenic interaction of growth-associated genes, as noted earlier (Cooke, Divall, & Radovick, 2011).

13.4.2 CDGP

As noted earlier, subjects with CDGP are growing and maturing normally for their bone age. Hence, they are quite normal for their biological age. As late adolescents/emerging adults, they will "catch-up" in height and pubertal maturation and have an adult height within the specified target height range of their parents. Characteristics of children with CDGP include normal size at birth, height velocity that slows within the first 3–5 years of life and then normalizes, height and height velocity concordant with bone age (not chronologic age), significant slowing of height velocity just before pubertal maturation and growth spurt, and delayed but normal puberty. There is a significant familial incidence.

13.4.3 Intrauterine Growth Restriction (IUGR)

Small size for the duration of gestation babies may reflect maternal (illness, nutrition, drugs, and placental insufficiency) or fetal issues (genetics, placental insufficiency, and infection). IUGR is usually defined as length or birthweight (or both) below the 2.3 percentile, although some authors choose the 10th centile for gestational age as the dividing point between a normal gestation and one in which the fetus is growth restricted. The vast majority of these infants will achieve a normal length and weight within the first 2 years, often within the first 3–6 months. Ten to fifteen percent will not and are then considered to no longer have a growth variant but a pathological cause for their diminished weight and/or length. For those infants who have a complete catch-up growth pattern, no further specific evaluation is required.

It should be noted that these three variants of normal are common (counted as a few percent of a population) compared to many of the rare single-gene defects that may greatly affect growth. Thus, it is not uncommon for a single individual to fulfill criteria for two of the normal variants (and rarely all three). Those with combinations are often the smallest and tend to seek medical opinion about growth at an earlier age than some of the others.

13.5 Examples of Genetic Causes of Diminished Growth

Genetics, outside of the normal variability, clearly also plays a role in the evolution of growth and body composition. Children with *Down syndrome* (trisomy 21) are disproportionately small and have abnormalities in body composition (Van Gameren et al., 2012), and those with *Prader-Willi syndrome* (abnormality on chromosome 15) have a markedly abnormal body composition, characterized by obesity and markedly reduced lean body mass (Hauffa, Hirohara, Roos, Gillessen Kaesbach, & Gasser, 2000). Children with this condition, which may cause extreme obesity due to hyperphagia beyond the age of 1 or 2 years, may be very weak, feed poorly, and fail to thrive (underweight for height) during the first year of life. Even at that time, despite being malnourished, their underweight body is characterized by an excess of fat and a diminished lean body mass. Thus, there are genetic underpinnings for growth (height and weight) as well as for body composition—fat, fat-free (lean) mass, and bone—but also a less well-known phenomenon, such as the regional distribution of body fat (Heymsfield et al., 2015) in the upper and lower body, in the trunk versus extremities, and as subcutaneous versus visceral fat. It is the visceral (intra-abdominal) component of fat that has the implications for cardiovascular disease morbidity and mortality (Manson & Bassuk, 2015).

Specific examples of single-gene abnormalities are common endocrine causes of short stature/growth failure. Multiple disorders of growth hormone synthesis and secretion, as well as diminished production of IGF-I (Laron syndrome) have been described (Dauber, Rosenfeld, & Hirschhorn, 2014).

13.6 Overview of Growth in Children/Adolescents with Medical Conditions or Environmental Issues

Are there features that suggest pathological growth? A variety of systemic conditions (diseases) are associated with growth slowed enough to keep the child/adolescent from maintaining his or her relative position (channel) on the growth curve. In well-nourished populations, these are likely below 5–10% of all slowly growing children. The more severe have *growth failure* as a hallmark. Often, the biological age is delayed as well; thus, the normal adult height potential is preserved if the pathological process is attenuated or "cured." Key elements in the structured evaluation of such children by a health care professional include the gastrointestinal tract (e.g., pain, decreased appetite, diarrhea) and the pulmonary system (severe asthma and recurrent pulmonary infections). There are many other signs and symptoms that might direct attention to a specific organ system, but I present those noted only as examples. One key element is to note all medications and over-the-counter (OTC) agents and possible environmental exposures that may be toxic per se or lead to severe pulmonary symptoms of asthma, recurrent infections, or gastrointestinal symptoms of severe diarrhea. Common medications that may affect growth are glucocorticoids and those used to treat attention-deficit hyperactivity disorder (ADHD), a very prevalent condition that is treated with amphetamine-like agents in the United States.

The key arbiter in the overall evaluation of growth over time is the growth chart. That is why I emphasized at the beginning of this chapter that the accuracy of measurements and the proper plotting and interpretation of growth trajectories are critical. Weight loss, poor weight gain, underweight-for-height, and/or delayed pubertal maturation are consistent with many pathological processes and must be distinguished from the more prevalent variations in normal growth distinguished earlier. As causes of short stature, endocrine and single-gene or chromosomal disorders are many times less common than simple variations on the theme of normal growth. The endocrine/genetic causes for short stature are often characterized by delay in bone age. However, they may be important to diagnose because some of them (e.g., hypothyroidism) are amenable to specific therapy.

References

Biro, F. M., McMahon, R. P., Striegel-Moore, R., Crawford, P. B., Obarzanek, E., Morrison, J. A., . . . Falkner, F. (2001). Impact of timing of pubertal maturation on growth in black and white female adolescents: The National Heart, Lung, and Blood Institute Growth and Health Study. *Journal of Pediatrics, 138*, 636–643.

Bordini, B., & Rosenfield, R. L. (2011). Normal pubertal development: Part 1: The endocrine basis of puberty. *Pediatrics in Review, 33*, 223–229.

Butler, G. E., McKie, M., & Ratcliffe, S. G. (1990). The cyclic nature of prepubertal growth. *Annals of Human Biology, 17*, 177–198.

Centers for Disease Control and Prevention (CDC). (2012). CDC growth standards. https://www.cdc.gov/growthcharts/cdc_charts.htm.

Cooke, D. W., Divall, S. A., & Radovick, S. (2011). Normal and aberrant growth. In S. Melmed, K. S. Polonsky, P. R. Larsen, & H. M. Kronenberg (Eds.), *Williams textbook of endocrinology*, 12th ed. (pp. 935–1053). Philadelphia: Saunders Elsevier.

Costa-Barbosa, F. A., Balasubramanian, R., Keefe, K. W., Shaw, N. D., Al-Tassan, N., Plummer, L., . . . Crowley, W. F. Jr. (2013). Prioritizing genetic testing in patients with Kallmann syndrome using clinical phenotypes. *Journal of Clinical Endocrinology and Metabolism, 98*, E943–E953.

Cox, L. A., & Savage, M. O. (1998). Practical auxology: Techniques of measurement and assessment of skeletal maturity. In C. J. Kelnar, M. O. Savage, H. E. Stirling, & P. Saenger (Eds.), *Growth disorders: Pathophysiology and treatment* (p. 225). Cambridge: Chapman and Hall.

Dauber, A., & Hirschhorn, J. N. (2011). Genome-wide association studies in pediatric endocrinology. *Hormone Research in Paediatrics, 75*, 322–328.

Dauber, A., Rosenfeld, R. G., & Hirschhorn, J. N. (2014). Genetic evaluation of short stature. *Journal of Clinical Endocrinology and Metabolism, 99*, 3080–3092.

Garza, C., & de Onis, M. (2007). Introduction to a symposium: A new 21st-century international growth standard for infants and young children. *Journal of Nutrition, 137*, 142–143.

Garza, C., Frongillo, E., & Dewey, K. G. (1994). Implications of growth patterns of breast-fed infants for growth references. *Acta Paediatrica Supplement, 1994*(404), 4–10.

Guo, M. H., Shen, Y., Walvoord, E. C., Miller, T. C., Moon, J. E., Hirschhorn, J. N., & Dauber, A. (2014). Whole exome sequencing to identify genetic causes of short stature. *Hormone Research in Paediatrics, 82*, 44–52.

Grummer-Strawn, L. M., Reinhold, C., & Krebs, N. F. (2010). Use of the World Health Organization and CDC charts for children aged 0–59 months in the USMMWR. *Recommendations and Reports, 59*(RR–9), 1–15.

Hauffa, B. P., Hirohara, G., Roos, M., Gillessen Kaesbach, G., & Gasser, T. (2000). Spontaneous growth in German children and adolescents with genetically confirmed Prader-Willi syndrome. *Acta Paediatrica, 89*, 1302–1311.

Heymsfield, S. B., Ebbeling, C. B., Zheng, J., Pietrobelli, A., Strauss, B. J., Silva, A. M., & Ludwig, D. S. (2015). Multi-component molecular-level body composition reference methods: Evolving concepts and future directions. *Obesity Reviews, 16*, 282–294.

Johnson, L., van Jaarsveld, C. H., Llewellyn, C. H., Cole, T. J., & Wardle, J. (2014). Associations between infant feeding and the size, tempo and velocity of infant weight gain: SITAR analysis of the Gemini twin birth cohort. *International Journal of Obesity (London), 38*, 980–987.

Lango, A., Estrada, K., Lettre, G., Berndt, S. I., Weedon, M. N., Rivadeneira, F., . . . Hirschhorn, J. N. (2010). Hundreds of variants clustered in genomic loci and biological pathways affect human height. *Nature, 467*(7317), 832–838.

Manson, J. E., & Bassuk, S. S. (2015). Biomarkers of cardiovascular disease risk in women. *Metabolism, 64*(3 Suppl 1), S33–S39.

Ong, K. K., Elks, C. E., Li, S., Zhao, J. H., Luan, J., Andersen, L. B., . . . Wareham, N. J. (2009). Genetic variation in LIN28B is associated with the timing of puberty. *Nature Genetics, 41*(6), 729–733.

Rogol, A. D. (2015) Diagnostic approach to short stature. http://www.uptodate.com/contents/diagnostic-approach-to-short-stature2015.

Rogol, A. D., & Hayden, G. F. (2014). Etiologies and early diagnosis of short stature and growth failure in children and adolescents. *Journal of Pediatrics, 164*(Suppl. May), S1–S14.

Rogol, A., & Lawton, E. L. (1991). Body measurements. In J. A. Lohr (Ed.), *Pediatric procedures* (pp. 1–9). Philadelphia: Lippincott.

Sutter, N. B., Bustamante, C. D., Chase, K., Gray, M. M., Zhao, K., Zhu, L., . . . Ostrander, E. A. (2007). A single IGF1 allele is a major determinant of small size in dogs. *Science, 316*(5821), 112–115.

Tanner, J. M., Goldstein, H., & Whitehouse, R. H. (1970). Standards for children's height at ages 2–9 years allowing for heights of parents. *Archives of Disease in Childhood, 45*, 755–762.

Van Gameren-Oosterom, F. B., Van Dommelen, P., Oudesluys-Murphy, A. M., Buttendijk, S. E., Van Buuren, S., & Van Woowe, J. P. (2012). Healthy growth in children with Down syndrome. *PLoS One, 7*, e31079.

Van Jaarsveld, C. H. M., Boniface, D., Llewellyn, C. H., & Wardle, J. (2014). Appetite and growth: A longitudinal sibling analysis. *JAMA Pediatrics, 168*, 345–350.

Wang, S. R., Carmichael, H., Andrew, S. F., Miller, T. C., Moon, J. E., Derr, M. A., . . . Dauber, A. (2013). Large-scale pooled next-generation sequencing of 1077 genes to identify genetic causes of short stature. *Journal of Clinical Endocrinology and Metabolism, 98*, e-1428–1437.

Wells, J. C., Williams, J. E., Chomtho, S., Darch, T., Grijalva-Eternod, C., Kennedy, K., . . . Fewtrell, M. S. (2012). Body-composition reference data for simple and reference techniques and a 4-component model: A new UK reference child. *American Journal of Clinical Nutrition, 96*, 1316–1326.

Wood, A. R., Esko, T., Yang, J., Vedantam, S., Pers, T. H., Gustafsson, S., . . . Frayling, T. M. (2014). Defining the role of common variation in genomic and biological architecture of adult human height. *Nature Genetics, 46*, 1176–1186.

CHAPTER 14

GLOBAL PERSPECTIVES ON ECONOMICS AND BIOLOGY

NICHOLAS J. MEINZER AND JÖRG BATEN

COMPARING the biological well-being of populations from all over the world using average heights as a proxy for nutritional status or the biological standard of living, reveals several common trends.[1] Over time, the most important structural breaks in human history were the introduction of agriculture in the Neolithic and the Industrial Revolution. Both these transitions initially reduced the biological standard of living of most of the affected populations before additional innovations resulted in an increase in height, most notably in the rich countries after the late 19th century.

In Section 1, we discuss evidence of the initially negative impact of agriculture in general and of differences between agricultural specializations in particular. Easier access to more abundant high-quality protein, for example, improved the biological well-being of cattle herding populations over those relying predominantly on cereal cultivation.

Some of the sources containing height data are not representative for the whole population from which the measured people have been selected. In Section 2, we discuss how sample selectivity is addressed and taken into account in historical height studies. Following a brief note on genetic factors and the paramount importance of environmental factors in explaining differences in average height between populations, the surprisingly high biological living standard of slaves in the United States is presented as a reminder that well-being also has nonbiological dimensions.

Section 3 reviews studies of the negative impact of urbanization and early industrialization on average heights in a number of countries in the late 18th and early 19th centuries before key innovations in transportation, sanitation, and health care were invented.

Once balanced and diverse diets were available to urban populations and sewerage and modern medicine proved to be effective against most negative aspects of high population density, average heights began to increase, as we describe in Section 4.

Section 5 discusses migration effects and the impact of a sudden change of the living environment that allows for a substantially higher biological standard of living on the average heights of immigrants' descendants, who tend to grow substantially taller than their parents from the first generation onward.

Section 6 reviews research that uses the variation of heights in a population to gain insights on inequality. Where inequality is high, especially regarding access to health care and nutritionally valuable foods, the better-off tend to be taller than the rest of the population. This increases the variation of heights at the population level. This is used to assess inequality in cases in which income data are unavailable or of questionable quality. For example, in low-income countries such as those of Africa in the early 20th century, anthropometric evidence is available, whereas conventional monetary indicators are often lacking.

14.1 Early Global Developments

In the early 1980s, studies using bone samples from all over the world found that switching from a hunter-gatherer lifestyle to agriculture—the Neolithic agricultural and demographic transition—was associated with deteriorating biological well-being along many dimensions. The decline of average stature was only one of the indicators used in the studies on paleopathology at the origins of agriculture (Cohen & Armelagos, 1984). Where long-term changes in average heights in pre-Neolithic populations may have been driven mainly by environmental and ecological factors (Gallagher, 2013), the main nutritional problems facing farmers' health were micronutrient deficiencies arising from a less diverse diet based on one or another staple cereal and recurring food shortages when stores were depleted before harvest or at a time of harvest failure.

Mummert et al. (Mummert, Esche, Robinson, & Armelagos, 2011) recently reviewed the literature that emerged as results of the Cohen and Armelagos volume and found that the early results have generally been corroborated for many other samples of prehistoric skeletal remains. However, the effects of transition to agriculture on stature were not the same everywhere because some main cereal crops were more favorable than others, and the diet could be diversified using different resources. For example, two of the five studies that found heights to increase when agriculture was introduced pertain to rice farmers in Thailand, where this specific kind of agriculture provided better nutrition than pre-agricultural subsistence. Moreover, two studies of the southeastern United States found that heights were constant during the transition. Fourteen studies of samples from Africa, the Americas, Asia, Europe, and the Middle East all report that farming populations were on average shorter than their horticulturist or hunter-gatherer predecessors. In Northern China, the average male height from the samples dating back to the period before the beginning of intensive agriculture (Peiligang period, 7000–5000 BCE), was 174 cm, several centimeters taller than people living there in the late 20th century. Samples from the region dating to the Han dynasty (206 BCE–220 CE) have male average heights of about 166 cm (Figure 14.1). On the other side of the globe, skeletal samples of Mesoamerican Maya display heights decreasing by more than 5 cm during the pre-classic period (2000 BCE–250 CE), when a sedentary lifestyle and agriculture were adopted. In Anatolia, heights also clearly declined during the transition, whereas in Britain the introduction of dairy farming resulted in increasing stature in the second millennium BC (Figure 14.1). Other early populations more or less stagnated, either at a low level (Southern China, Coastal Peru) or on a somewhat higher level (Bahrain on the Arabian Peninsula).

Boix and Rosenbluth (2014) address long-run developments of the biological standard of living and inequality for societies from a number of regions using human

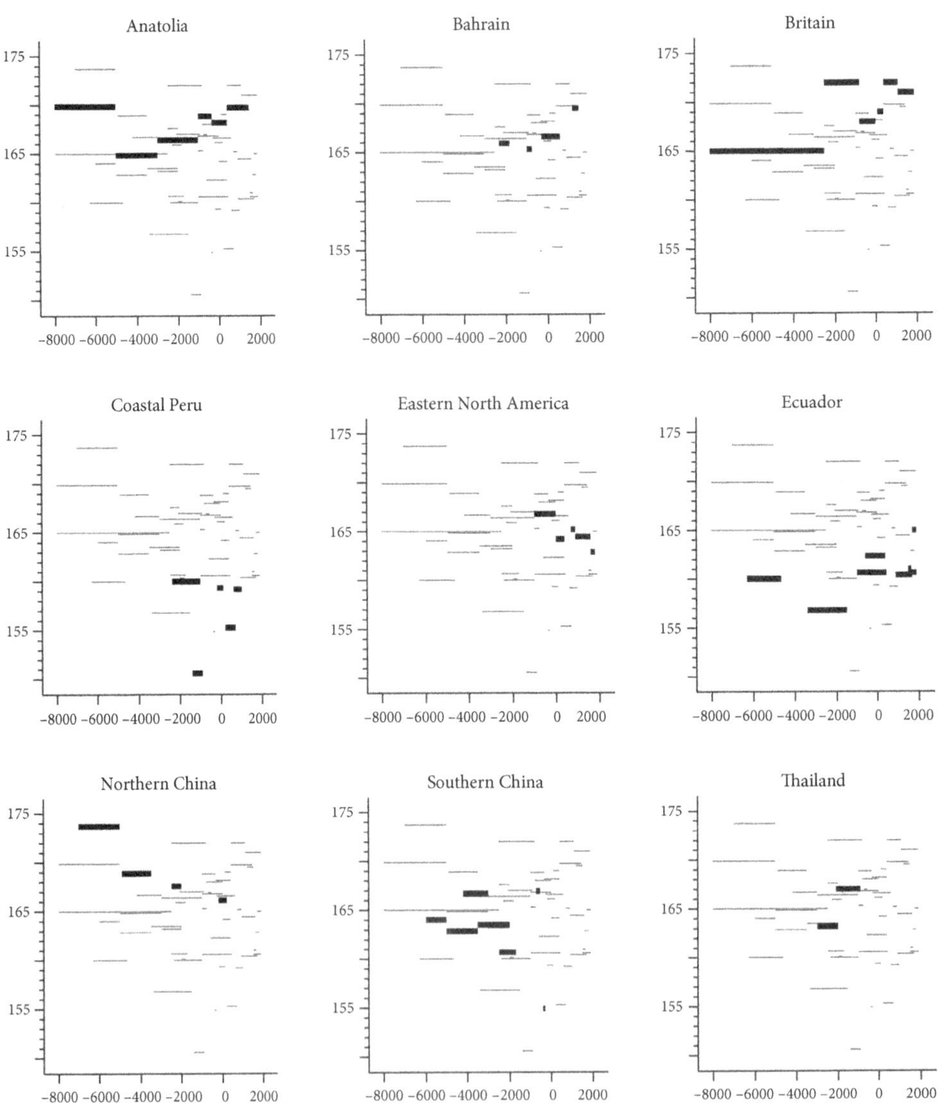

FIGURE 14.1 Heights during the agricultural transition.

Sources: Mummert et al. (2011, 290–292) for Bahrain, Britain, Ecuador, Eastern North America, Coastal Peru, Northern China, and Thailand; Őzer et al. (2011, 2014) for Anatolia; various sources for Southern China. Average male heights [cm], estimated from longbone measurements.

osteological data. They report that the Neolithic demographic transition, with its introduction of agriculture and a sedentary lifestyle, led to declining average heights and increasing inequality in the biological standard of living. In simple hunter-gatherer communities, consumption was distributed more or less equitably, and low population density ensured surprisingly high biological well-being for people in many different regions. A sedentary agricultural lifestyle, with substantial stockpiles that could be easily expropriated by people specializing not in production but in interpersonal violence and theft, had several important effects on living standards and inequality. Continuing innovation in military technology tended to increase the opportunity costs of producers and thus make it more attractive for them to come to terms with a "stationary bandit" (Olsen, 1993) protecting them against the uncertainties of dealing with mobile predators. Height differentials between the elite and the ordinary people in the resulting hierarchical societies also led to increased coefficients of variation of height, highlighting differences between societies with otherwise similar average living standards.

Regional patterns of agricultural specialization determined biological well-being during the following millennia in agricultural societies. Koepke and Baten (2008) show that "proximity to protein production" explains a substantial share of the differences in height between populations of several large European regions over the period from the beginning of the Common Era until 1800 (Figure 14.2). They find that a higher share of cattle bones among the found animal bones can serve as a proxy for specialization on the production of milk (and beef). Using a sample of more than 2 million animal bones and about 9,500 individual human heights, mostly estimated from measurements

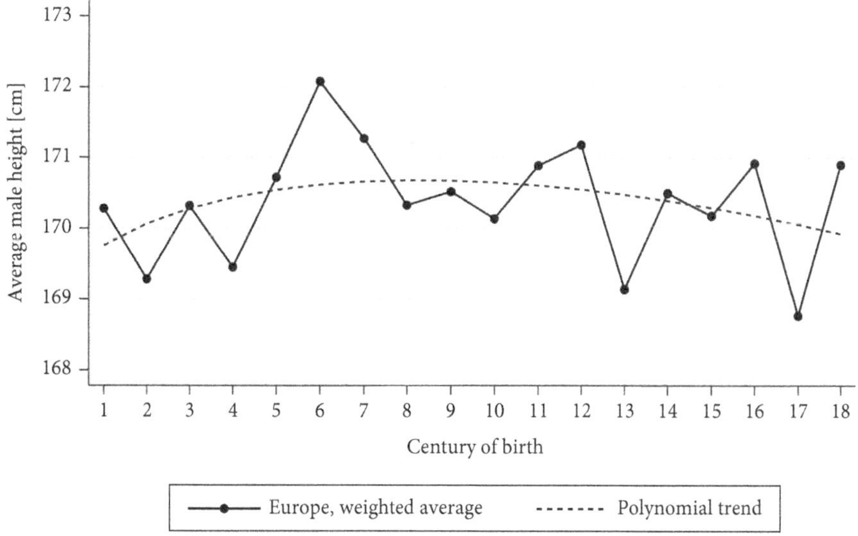

FIGURE 14.2 European height trend 1st to 8th century.

Sources: Koepke and Baten (2005, 2008), The level of heights was adjusted to male heights of average Europeans using the regional coefficients and weighting them with sample weights.

The smoothed European height trend was estimated with a second-degree fractional polynomial regression.

of excavated long bones, Koepke and Baten report a correlation between cattle share and stature. Lower population density is also associated with taller people. In their model, an additional standard deviation of the cattle-bone share among the animal bone remains implies an increasing height by 1 cm, whereas an additional standard deviation of (the logarithm of) land per capita (i.e., an increase from the mean of 0.13 km^2 to 0.23 km^2 per person) raises heights by 7 mm. By using their osteological database, they show in another study that average stature within three large European regions (Mediterranean, Central/Western Europe, and Northeastern Europe) decreased over time when population density or inequality increased, whereas people grew taller when the climate was warmer (Koepke & Baten, 2005). The Medieval Warm Period, for example, shows up in their data as a temporary reversal of the general (slight) downward trend in heights over the Middle Ages.

14.2 Sample Selectivity and Genetic Factors

In general, archaeological data are scarcer compared to data from more recent written sources. Similar to archival evidence, it is filtered by selection processes: some burial grounds from which skeletal remains have been obtained may have been reserved to members of specific social strata, others to people who died at a certain age or succumbed to disease. All of this might imply that they are not representative of the members of their wider community regarding their physical well-being. The sample drawn by mortuary customs is further reduced by natural forces that determine the preservation of the archaeological material and by the contingencies of discovery and excavation.

Selectivity of the samples introduces biases in the case that not every human remains of the population had the same chance to be included in a given study. Especially where individuals are included in the sample based on criteria related to their biological well-being, results may not be representative for a larger population (such as grenadier soldiers who were selected based on stature). Not surprisingly, discussions of sample selectivity biases have always been an important part of the anthropometric literature in economic history (Fogel et al., 1983). When studying heights using data from recruits of professional armies, for example, we have to consider self-selection of people aiming at a career in the armed forces as well as minimum height requirements (Komlos, 2004). Selectivity is not an issue with military data of conscripts if all young men (or a subsample drawn by lot) were measured before selection[2] Deviations from normality can provide hints to selection biases, but normality of height distributions alone should not be taken as an indication of representativeness because sampling strategies targeting specific heights can also result in populations with normally distributed heights, with means deviating substantially from the population average. As an example, consider basketball players. Since the height of players in various positions follows a normal distribution with a different mean for each position, the mixed distribution deviates from the normal Gaussian one. Therefore, the deviation of the mixed distribution from a normal one can at least be a sign that the sample was drawn with more than one target height or is composed of markedly different subsamples. Special samples, such as university students, or other samples of substantial height selectivity should not be included in studies that strive for national representativeness of samples, but, of course, they yield valuable results for more specialized types of questions such as the distribution of nutritional status by social class.

Apart from social selectivity biases, regional biases also often play a role. Anthropometricians take such biases into account to the extent possible (see the review in Baten & Blum, 2014). It needs to be considered whether heights were perhaps drawn from one region of an exceptionally tall or short population.

A potential selectivity issue is changing labor market bias: with volunteer armies, the propensity to join the military might vary inversely with labor market conditions such as the rate of unemployment or the wage level. Aware of this issue, anthropometricians have employed several strategies to avoid allowing it to bias the estimated height trends significantly. First, several scholars used a variety of different samples to assess sample-specific biases. It is unlikely that samples of different institutional contexts have identical tendencies to select the height in exactly the same manner (Komlos, 2004). Second, cross-sectional samples at a particular year of recruitment will not be affected by labor market conditions yet can be analyzed by birth cohorts to obtain estimates of trends in nutritional status. In addition, including the year of recruitment in a regression picks up the effect of labor market conditions on the supply of recruits. Third, a large proportion of the global height evidence stems from general conscription or systematically recorded anthropological samples that usually do not include this kind of labor market bias or other social selectivity biases. Fourth, secondary characteristics of samples that might underlie a selection process can be explored. Heights tend to be correlated with occupational status or education (i.e., more educated individuals and those with higher status occupations are often taller). If occupational composition of a sample or the educational status (measured with age-heaping methods, for example) can be compared with census information that is normally representative by definition, the potential selectivity can be studied in detail (Stegl & Baten, 2009).

Which role does the genetic factor play? Analyses of the physical stature of immigrants indicates that migration into societies enjoying a higher standard of living enables the children of these immigrants to become taller than they would have been in their original less-developed regions. Among other factors, regional differences in average heights can be explained by differences in market integration, agricultural techniques, and dietary customs that regulate the access to high-quality food, especially animal protein, well into the recent past.

As it turns out, height differences between distant populations, with a few potential exceptions, are not determined primarily by genetic factors. Whereas earlier literature often assumed significant hereditary contributions to height differences between many groups of people, modern textbooks emphasize that environmental influences are the leading factors (Bogin, 2001). On average, children of migrant parents from countries with lower living standards often grow up to be taller than both their parents, but they remain shorter than the population average in the host country. This can be understood without invoking genetic factors insofar as undernourished women's smaller bodies are unable to nurture and give birth to large babies. The next generation, having taller and healthier mothers, can grow even taller, converging to the level of biological well-being supported by the environment, which is reflected in the average physique of the domestic population. Although an often-mentioned number puts the heritability of individual adult height (but not population averages) at around 80%, a review of McEnvoy and Visscher (2009) reports that the genes known to be associated with height can so far account for only 5% of the variation in heights.

14.3 Industrialization and Early Market Integration

The Industrial Revolution, with its impact on farming and food production, initially had negative effects on stature and health in a number of countries (Komlos & Baten, 2004). People who moved from agriculture to manufacturing jobs in the cities consumed a less diverse diet and reduced the consumption of fresh produce and dairy products that could not be provided in large quantities to the growing urban centers. Urbanization also aggravated the detrimental effects of poor hygiene due to high population density and increased mobility before the germ theory of disease induced major investments in public sanitation. As a consequence, urban heights in the early industrial period were uniformly less than rural heights.

The unexpected decrease in heights in the United States during a time when real incomes were increasing after the onset of modern economic growth became known as the "antebellum puzzle" discussed extensively in Chapter 12 of this volume (Komlos, 1996). This basic pattern has since been found in many different sources of height data and shows, as Komlos concludes, "that during the early stages of modern economic growth, progress was not uniform in all dimensions of human existence."

Heights declined during the first Industrial Revolution everywhere in Europe due to rapid population growth and to the increasing share of labor in the industrial sector. Komlos (1985) documents that heights declined beginning in the second half of the 18th century in the Habsburg Empire. Stature in this region stabilized and even increased again only in the first decades of the 19th century. With increasing market integration, the people from agriculturally dominated peripheral regions lost their nutritional advantage. Food was exported to the Austrian core, and average heights converged toward the lower levels of the more urbanized proto-industrial regions. In Lower Austria and Bohemia, recruits born in the 1740s were only about 165 cm tall, of similar size as their contemporaries in the British military. Recruits from Hungary, at the periphery of the empire, were 170 cm tall in the 1740s before the downward convergence began.

Komlos (2007) showed also that heights continued to increase in the Habsburg Empire over the course of the 19th century and into the 20th century. The secular improvement of biological living standards was led by the Austrian core regions, but the economically backward regions in Eastern Europe and the Balkans exhibited even faster growth, converging toward higher levels. Whereas Austrian recruits born in the late 1840s still averaged around 165 cm, those born at the end of the 19th century stood 3 cm taller. Recruits from areas in modern-day Ukraine and Poland averaged just short of 163 cm in the late 1840s but had almost reached 167 cm by the end of the century.[3]

Agricultural techniques continued to be one of the main factors driving height differences between regions well into the 19th century and were still a relevant factor where technologies such as refrigerated transportation were not yet introduced. Baten (2009) finds that the number of cattle per person as a proxy for milk consumption at the place of birth of the recruits is associated with a large share of the regional variation in average heights of German and French conscripts. He uses individual conscript lists and broadens the database using published conscription statistics on the district level for birth cohorts of the early 19th century. Differentiating agricultural districts in Bavaria (southern Germany) into milk- and beef-producing regions, potato-growing regions, and the remainder, in which rye and wheat cultivation were prevalent, confirms the result that districts with access to animal protein had lower rates of conscripts rejected for being too short. The results also hold for the neighboring kingdom of Prussia (northern Germany), where almost a third of the variation in districts' rejection rates of conscripts (for small stature) can be explained by different levels of milk production. In late 19th-century France, a similar amount of the variation in the share of tall conscripts (those taller than 167 cm) can be explained by milk production in their département. This proximity-to-protein effect is a global one because it could be observed in Africa (Moradi & Baten, 2005), the Middle East (Stegl & Baten, 2009), and other world regions.

The relationship between consumption of dairy products and taller stature is indeed likely to be causal, as a systematic review and meta-analysis of modern experimental studies of the effects of increased dairy product intake and linear growth shows (De Beer, 2012). Overall, children ingesting an additional 245 mL of milk every day grew 4 mm taller every year, implying an adult height difference of several centimeters.

Zehetmayer (2013) recently reported an "urban height penalty" of about 1.5 cm for US soldiers born in the second half of the 19th century in one of the 10 most populous cities and 0.9 cm for those from the 90 next-largest cities, compared to rural-born recruits. The size of the urban penalty found in studies of other American samples, he reports, ranges from 0.5 to 3.6 cm; this is the amount by which urban dwellers were shorter than their compatriots from rural counties. Average heights of recruits born in rural areas during that time fluctuated between 171 and 172 cm. As for specific characteristics of those cities that were detrimental to the well-being of children and adolescents, the study identifies the size of the manufacturing sector, death rates, and lagging integration into the railroad network. On the one hand, railroads improved the access of city dwellers to high-quality foods, particularly sources of protein, but, on the other hand, facilitated spreading diseases to the countryside (see Komlos, 1998, for further review of the urban penalty).

A study of Frenchmen born in 1848 revealed an urban height penalty of similar magnitude for Paris and other large cities in individual-level regressions once the socioeconomic backgrounds of the recruits, their occupations, and education levels were controlled for (Heyberger, 2014).

Educational attainment of German conscripts measured at the turn of the 21st century correlates with their height and weight. By analyzing records of 230,000 men born between 1979 and 1982, Hiermeyer (2009) finds that those with advanced secondary schooling stood 1.1 cm taller than their peers with only rudimentary secondary schooling and had a lower body mass index (BMI) of 1 kg/m^2. Cinnirella, Piopiunik, and Winter (2011) report a similar finding of a height advantage among German pupils attending advanced secondary schools, and Baten and Böhm (2010) find that children entering school in the German state of Brandenburg are shorter if their parents are unemployed or have not finished high school. They explain this as the result of primary school teachers recommending taller boys more often for advanced secondary schooling than their shorter counterparts with similar grades. Recruits from the Netherlands, though not directly comparable to the Germans due to differences in the educational system and reporting, exhibit an even larger height differential between the extremes of secondary school attainment. Huang, van Poppel, and Lumey (2015) report that this differential is largely independent of parental occupation and the available indicators of familial background, lending support to hypotheses that link height and cognitive abilities.

14.4 The Secular Change in Body Size

A temporary decline in average heights during early industrialization, discussed in the literature as the "early industrial growth puzzle," was followed by an unprecedented surge of biological well-being, reaching perhaps a plateau only recently, after about 150 years, as Cole (2003) hypothesized.

In samples from 15 European countries, the average height of young men increased between 8 and 14 mm per decade after the 1860s (Hatton & Bray, 2010). The increase was slowest in the period before World War I but seems to have been fastest during the period from 1911/15 to 1951/55 and slowed down again afterward, except for the southern European samples (Figure 14.3). Correlations between average heights of samples from the same European countries but different periods imply that heights started to converge only in the postwar period.

Grasgruber et al. (Grasgruber, Cacek, Kalina, & Sebera, 2014) correlate heights of samples of young adult males from 45 European and neighboring countries with various indicators of health, nutrition, wealth, and the prevalence of certain genetic traits. They find the tallest Europeans in the Netherlands and in Montenegro in the Balkans, where

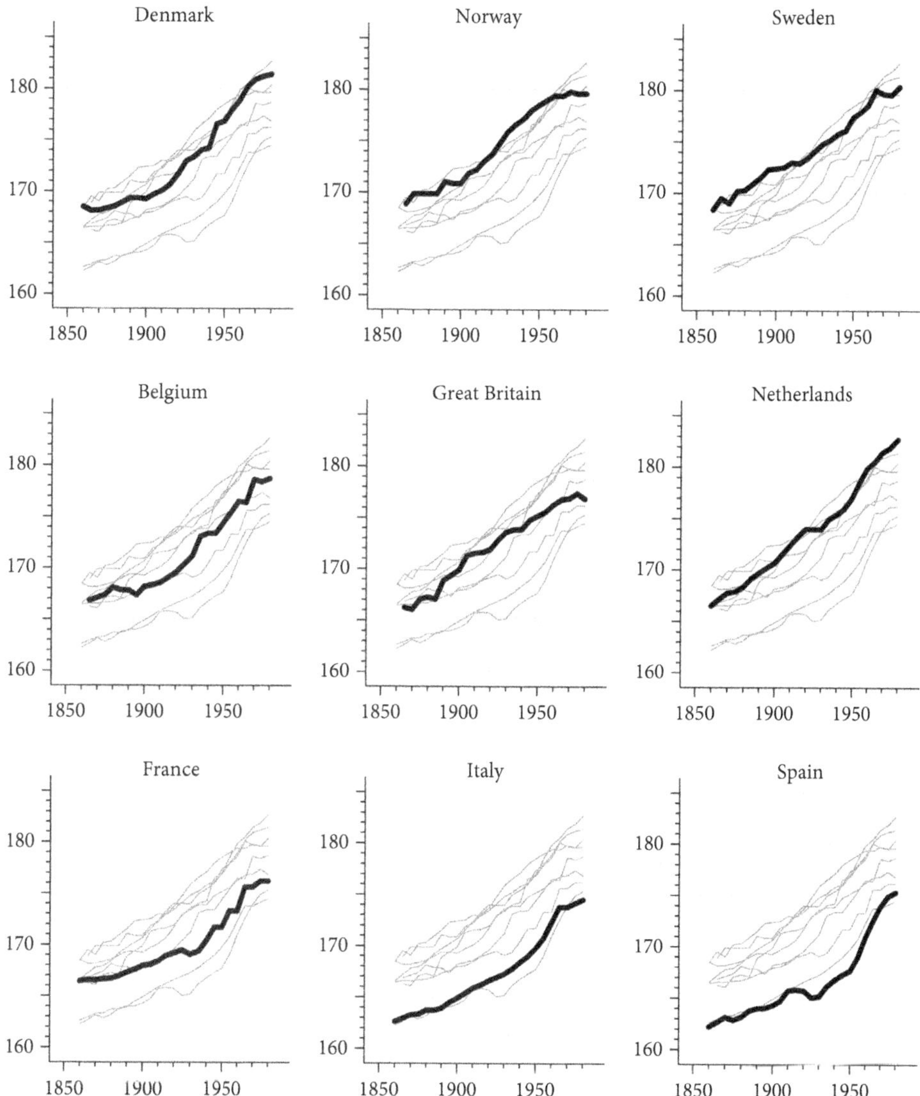

FIGURE 14.3 Trends in the heights of European men.

Sources: Hatton & Bra (2010, 411). Average heights [cm] of young adults in 5-year birth cohorts.

the average male is taller than 183 cm, whereas the shortest Europeans, living in Turkey and Portugal, barely reach an average size of 174 cm. Emphasizing the importance of nutritional factors for linear growth, Grasgruber et al. argue that the height trend may have leveled off because people in the tallest nations today tend to consume more low-quality wheat protein, thus reducing the intake of high-quality protein from milk, pork, and fish relative to the time when average heights increased. They expect further growth if nutrition improves again. Apart from that, they suggest that the importance of genetic factors for height differences between populations may increase with rising living standards. Differences in the frequency of genetic lineages, which they find to be correlated with height, are likely to persist when living standards have converged.

Elsewhere, average heights are still far below European levels. Ranasinghe et al. (2011), for example, report that contemporary Sri Lankan mean height of men is 164 cm, but the shortest men in his sample are from Indonesia, with an average height of only 158 cm for males, more than 25 cm shorter than the tallest contemporary populations—the Dutch—and even shorter than Dutch conscripts were in the mid-19th century.

Baten and Blum (2012*a*, 2012*b*, 2014) conducted the most comprehensive study comparing heights of men from 156 countries, reaching back into the early 19th century for most European countries and the Western offshoots, many Latin American and East Asian countries, and a few individual countries from other regions.

Various sources were included in the study, such as on African slave lists in the 19th century, and compared to early military sources from the same time in which colonial powers such as the Dutch measured African recruits because they needed military personnel for the colonies in Indonesia. Therefore, the potential bias arising from slavery or from voluntary armies could be estimated by comparing the different sources. Because most of the samples relied on conscript armies in which all the male inhabitants of a country of a given age had to serve (or a random sample drawn by the lot was taken), the sample selectivity issues of this sample were small.

The general trends showed that the Western offshoots started with a relatively tall height that declined slightly over time with increasing population density, as countries such as the United States, Canada, Argentina, and Australia were increasingly populated by Europeans (Figure 14.4). Their relatively abundant protein-rich diet of the early 19th century was slightly less abundant around the 1880s, but the Western offshoots had the tallest people in the world during the whole period under consideration when examined at the continental level. This is the case even though Northern and Western European countries had taller populations by World War II than did North America (Komlos & Baur, 2004). The decline in Argentina and the United States was particularly marked in the mid-19th century, whereas in Canada the decline was slightly less pronounced. Men in Western and also Eastern Europe had a dramatic increase in height starting in the late 19th century, which moved them from average heights in the 19th century to be among the tallest, jointly with the men in the overseas offshoots of Great Britain. Men in East Asia experienced a temporary decline in heights in the late 19th and early 20th centuries, which moved them from a medium rank to one of the lowest rankings in the world. After World War II, average heights in East Asia increased at similar rates as heights increased in Europe, with the exception of North Korea, where heights stagnated during six decades of communist rule (Pak, Schwekendiek, & Kim, 2011). Recently, East Asia moved back to an average position relative to the global scale. The only two regions that always had short populations were South and Southeast Asia, although stature increased slowly in Southeast Asia over the second half of the 20th century. Latin America and the Caribbean, as well as sub-Saharan Africa, remained relatively close to the average height level. The rank of Middle Eastern heights started relatively high in the mid-19th century, with substantially taller men than in Europe, for example, but then fell back to an average position.

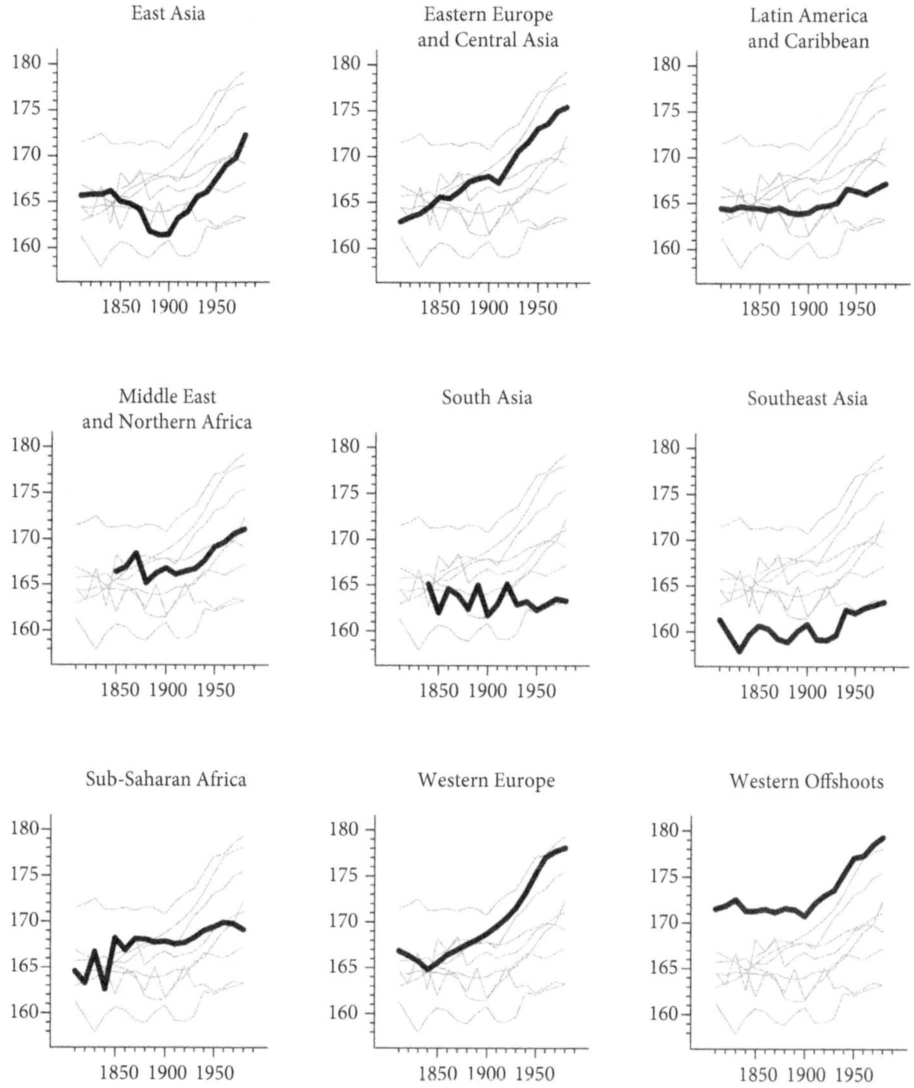

FIGURE 14.4 Global height trends.

Source: Modified from Baten and Blum (2014). Average male heights [cm] in birth-decade cohorts.

14.5 MIGRATION

Mass migration during the first era of globalization introduced many people to new environments. Franz Boas found in his 1911 landmark study on immigrants and their descendants in the United States that children of people from many European regions who grew up in the United States became taller than their parents, although not as tall as their American-born siblings. Reporting to a commission on immigration, the research focused on the malleability of cranial measurements, which were then perceived to be markers of "racial identity," showing that the "bodily form" of humans was responding much faster to a changing environment than previously thought.

As mentioned earlier, catch-up growth of migrant populations in countries with higher living standards is still observed today. Smith et al. (Smith, Bogin, Varela-Silva, & Loucky, 2003) noticed that the offspring of Guatemalan Maya who migrated to the United States in the 1980s were not only 10 cm taller than Maya children in Guatemala in 2000, but also taller than a cohort of Maya children in the United States who were measured a decade earlier.[4] However, more than 40% of the Maya immigrant children in the sample were overweight or obese, up from roughly 25% in 1992, compared to less than 5% in the Guatemalan sample.

14.6 Height Inequality

Height research also enables the study of global patterns of inequality. Traditionally, anthropometric historians measured height inequality by comparing the centimeter difference between occupational groups. For example, children of farmers who had large estates in 19th-century Bavaria were around 3 cm taller than were laborers in the same region (Baten, 2000). In India, Guntupalli and Baten (2006) find substantial differences between caste groups.

However, the usage of these occupational groups also provides a number of problems. Some of these sources only report the occupation of the recruits, but not the occupation of the parents; however, the latter is a much more important determinant of height of the recruit insofar as the parents' occupation and income is the main determinant of their child's nutritional status. Furthermore, when the occupation was recorded, the recruits might have reported a transient occupation. Farmers' sons, for example, were often recorded as agricultural laborers in conscript rolls because they had not yet inherited the farm. Finally, some occupational titles remain poorly defined, and many people had multiple occupations (i.e., artisans often farmed a small plot of land).

Because of these issues, Baten (2000) suggests an alternative method, one that takes the coefficient of variation (CV)[5] of height as a measure of height inequality. Studying Bavarian conscript registers, in which almost all of the young men were recorded at a clearly defined age, he compared the height CVs with the height differences among various occupational groups. The unit of observation was district and birth cohort. The high correlation between these differences by occupational affiliation and the height CV imply that it is a reasonable measure of height inequality. Moradi and Baten (2005) discuss, for example, the case of Togo and Uganda. Although average heights are similar in samples including 800 individuals aged 30–34 years from both countries, the distributions are quite different. Most of the men from Togo were quite close to the mean of 160 cm, which is close to average height, whereas the heights of Ugandan men were more dispersed (i.e., there were both more slightly shorter and more slightly taller men measured in Uganda than in Togo), even though both samples were representative of the general population.

Because individual height is not only determined by nutrition, but also has a very strong genetic component, height inequality never equals zero using this measure, although it is still unclear at which value the minimum is situated. According to the available empirical evidence, the CVs of height have a minimum value of 3–3.2% and can be as high as 4–5%.

A major potential problem with the CV of height method of measuring inequality is immigration of individuals who have been raised in a very different environment and are on average taller or shorter than the rest of the population. Fortunately, the country of birth is recorded in most height datasets, and studies always excluded first-generation immigrants from their studies. Nevertheless, immigration, and in some cases also emigration if selected groups of extreme height emigrated in large numbers, have to be considered when using the CV measure of inequality. To avoid problems with regional variation, height inequality should be used primarily for regions of similar size, so that existing economic differences between regions have roughly the same probability of increasing height inequality.

Finally, a certain degree of height inequality could arise from the fact that only a certain number of individuals survived up to the age of 20 (i.e., only the inequality of survivors is measured). However, this bias exists in almost all inequality measures. In most societies, mortality between age 20 and 50 is not high enough to introduce a substantial bias if retrospective evidence is used that arranges individuals according to their birth cohorts. Nevertheless, populations with very high mortality rates might already experience a certain degree of survivor bias among individuals younger than 50, even though Guntupalli and Baten (2006) studied this for the Indian case of the early 20th century and found no significant survivor bias by testing average heights.

A number of studies compare income and wealth inequality with height inequality based on the CV of height. Moradi and Baten (2005), for instance, regress income inequality on height inequality and a number of control variables. They find that the height CV for African regions systematically explains income inequality in this relatively large sample. A comparison of time series of the height CV and the Gini coefficient of taxation in Kenya based on Bigsten (1986) also reveals a general correlation.

More recently, Baten and Mumme (2013) compared the height CV, transformed into a Gini coefficient of height,[6] and the Gini coefficient of income inequality for a number of world regions (Figure 14.5) and found a strong correlation between the two measures. It has been argued that the height–Gini result may vary more than the income–Gini in Africa because human beings originally came from this continent and there is more genetic variation in Africa as a consequence; because only smaller groups of individuals spread out to the rest of the world, genetic variability was reduced at every stage of their journey. Therefore, the proponents of this view suggested that height inequality might be larger in Africa. Contrary to expectations, however, one of the outliers in Figure 14.5 (upper left) is sub-Saharan Africa (ssa1900), in which the income–Gini is actually higher than the height–Gini.

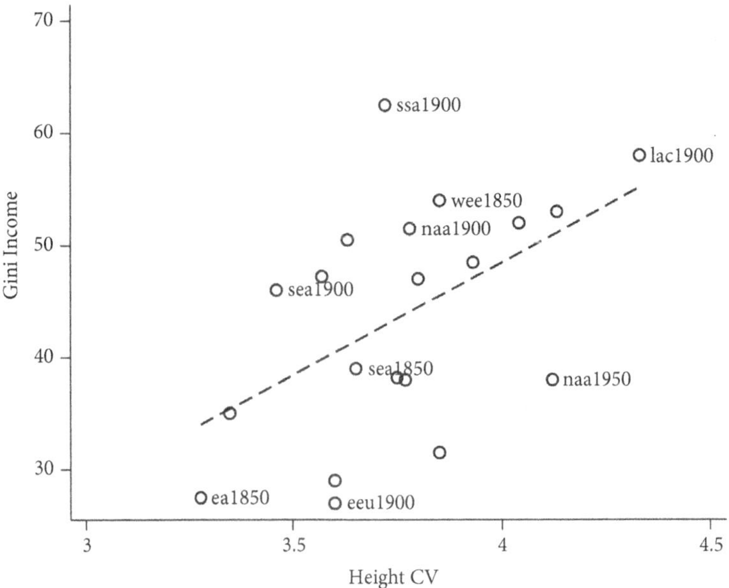

FIGURE 14.5 Height coefficient of variation (CV).

Notes: The abbreviations refer to the world region and the half century (beginning in 1850). Abbrevations of world regions: ea, East Asia; eeu, Eastern Europe; lac, Latin America and Caribbean; men, Middle East/North Africa; naa, North Americal, Australia, New Zealan; wee, Western Europe; sa, South Asia; sea, Southeast Asia; ssa, sub-Saharan Africa. The correlation coefficient between the two variables above is 0.51 ($p = 0.023$).

Sources: Baten and Mumme (2014) for height CV; van Zanden et al. (2014) for Gini coefficients.

By implementing the same method, Van Zanden, Baten, Foldvari, and van Leeuwen (2014) take a novel approach to measure global inequality. In addition to Gini coefficients of income inequality from the literature, which are available mainly for developed countries in Western Europe and North America, they estimate many Gini coefficients from the consumption inequality reflected in height CVs.[7] They find that although within-country inequality has increased over the last few decades in all regions of the world, levels in most regions are still lower than they were in the 19th century, a time when even the wealthy were worse off than the poor are today. Combining these estimates of within-country inequality with between-country inequality, they show that global inequality has strongly increased until the 1950 and mostly stagnated thereafter on a high level, as Table 14.1 shows.

In their previously mentioned study of inequality in Africa, Moradi and Baten (2005) investigate the influence of cash-crop production and various other factors deemed to be determinants of income and wealth inequality on height-based inequality measures. If large-scale cash crop production replaces subsistence farming, imported food has to be bought in markets, which, in case of food price increases, could aggravate inequality. Apart from the cash crop factor, the authors also studied the influence of cattle farming, which might have reduced inequality within a region because of proximity effects, as discussed earlier. In the African context, the offal and other cheap cuts of meat were

Table 14.1 Gini Coefficients in Various World Regions

	Western Europe	Eastern Europe and Former Soviet Union	South and Southeast Asia	East Asia	Middle East and North Africa	Sub-Saharan Africa	Latin America and Caribbean	Western Offshoots	Within-Country Inequality	Between-Country Inequality	World Gini
1820	54	51	35	45		53	45	56	45	16	49
1850	45	49	38	34	46	46	37	42	38	23	46
1870	50	48	42	41	52	50	48	51	45	32	55
1890	41	36	34	32	35	36	41	45	36	38	52
1910	46	39	35	40	40	42	45	50	40	44	58
1929	48	40	36	44	48	48	55	52	44	49	63
1950	42	35	39	33	43	43	47	39	38	55	65
1960	40	30	39	32	49	53	54	37	38	54	64
1970	38	26	40	29	47	49	53	36	37	56	65
1980	36	27	35	31	47	46	52	37	36	56	65
1990	38	27	41	34	46	47	52	39	39	56	66
2000	40	36	48	43	49	49	54	44	45	54	66

Estimated based on height inequality and income inequality.*Sources*: www.clio-infra.eu; for data quality see table 11.2; combines tables 11.5 and 11.4 from Moatsos, Baten, Foldvari, van Leeuwen, and van Zanden (2014) based on van Zanden et al. (2014).*Note*: Unweighted average of income inequality of individual countries within each regions.

probably more important than milk for the protein supply of the poorest members of society. Moreover, Moradi and Baten find that intraregional inequality was substantially lower in regions of higher education. Heavy industry production centers had higher inequality in the biological standard of living.

The height inequality measurement concept is also used in civil war research. A number of studies have hypothesized that inequality could be an important determinant of civil war because it is most likely easier to recruit an army to fight against the government when a substantial part of the population is highly dissatisfied and would welcome regime change. Baten and Mumme (2014) are the first to approach the problem of civil wars empirically from an anthropometric perspective. They use 700 height inequality observations (from Baten & Blum, 2012*a*) for birth-decade cohorts from different countries over a period from 1820 to 2000 and test this inequality measure as a determinant of civil wars. In about 5% of their 3,400 observations, civil war outbreaks, defined as initiation of hostilities with at least 1,000 annual civilian casualties, occurred. In the main regression, height inequality is always significantly and positively correlated with civil war outbreak, whereas average height has a negative effect and is not significantly correlated.

14.7 Conclusion

In sum, the literature on economics and human biology reviewed here concentrated on studying "human stature" as a proxy of health and the quality of nutrition. This approach enables us to trace global trends from the Neolithic Agricultural Revolution through the Industrial Revolution until the present. No other indicator can be used over such a long time period. Heights decreased substantially during both revolutions as nutrition became less diversified and less protein- and calcium-rich, inequality rose, and both were accompanied by an acceleration in population growth and rising inequality. Only after the 1870s did a rapid increase in stature begin. It was most pronounced in Europe, where refrigeration technology allowed the transport of perishable foodstuffs, and the urban environment and sanitation facilities were slowly improved. In addition, Bismarckian social insurance systems—and later social democratic and socialist policies—reduced inequality. Finally, we reviewed global studies on height inequality that showed a long-run U-shaped trend indicating that within-country inequality first declined during the late 19th and early 20th centuries and then began to increase again by the turn of the 21st century.

Notes

1. The biological standard of living as a concept was first suggested by Komlos (1985).
2. At times, the details of those obviously physically unfit for military service or parts of the population that were exempt have been omitted and have to be accounted for.

3. The average heights mentioned in the text are adjusted adult values from Baten and Blum (2014), accessible under clio-infra.eu (Version December 2014); the original publication reported heights of 18-year-olds who had not reached their final stature. Qualitatively, the trends do not change.
4. Slower growth of the legs, which is more sensitive to the quality of the environment, of the children in Guatemala accounts for as much as 60% of the height difference, demonstrating again that a higher biological standard of living can be achieved more easily in the United States than in rural Guatemala.
5. The coefficient of variation (CV) is the ratio of the standard deviation σ to the mean μ. In the context of height inequality, it is multiplied by 100.
6. Gini equivalents are calculated from height inequality using results from linear regressions of income inequality on height CVs as Gini = 9.25 + 10.46 * CV. See van Zanden et al. (2014, 10 Online Data Appendix) for details.
7. Height inequality measures alone account for 306 of their 1,082 country-decade observations, and 68 observations are based on an average of height Ginis and inequality measures derived from the gross domestic product-to-wage ratio.

References

Baten, J. (2000). Economic development and the distribution of nutritional resources in Bavaria, 1797–1839. *Journal of Income Distribution*, *9*, 89–106.

Baten, J. (2009). Protein supply and nutritional status in 19th century Bavaria, Prussia and France. *Economics and Human Biology*, *7*(2), 165–180.

Baten J., & Böhm, A. (2010). Children's height and parental unemployment: A large scale anthropometric study on eastern Germany, 1994–2006. *German Economic Review*, *11*(1), 1–24.

Baten, J., & Blum, M. (2012*a*). Growing tall but unequal: New findings and new background evidence on anthropometric welfare in 156 countries, 1810–1989. *Economic History and Developing Regions*, *27*(1), S66–S85.

Baten, J., & Blum, M. (2012*b*). An anthropometric history of the world, 1810–1980: Did migration and globalization influence country trends? *Journal of Anthropological Sciences*, *90*, 1–4.

Baten, J., & Blum, M. (2014). Human height since 1820. In J. L. van Zanden et al. (Eds.), *How was life? Global well-being since 1820* (pp. 117–137). Paris: OECD.

Baten, J., & Mumme, C. (2013). Does inequality lead to civil wars? A global long-term study using anthropometric indicators (1816–1999). *European Review of Political Economy*, *32*, 56–79.

Bigsten, A. (1986). Welfare and economic growth in Kenya, 1914–76. *World Development*, *14*(9), 1151–1160.

Boas, F. (1911). *Changes in bodily form of descendants of immigrants.* Washington, DC: Government Printing Office.

Bogin, B. (2001). *The growth of humanity*. New York, NY: Wiley-Liss.

Boix, C., & Rosenbluth, F. (2014). Bones of contention: The political economy of height inequality. *American Political Science Review*, *108*(1), 1–22.

Cohen, M. N., & Armelagos, G. J. (Eds.). (1984). *Paleopathology at the origins of agriculture.* New York, NY: Academic Press.

Cole, T. J. (2003). The secular trend in human physical growth: A biological view. *Economics and Human Biology*, *1*(2), 161–168.

Cinnirella, F., Piopiunik, M., & Winter, J. (2011). Why does height matter for educational attainment? Evidence from German children. *Economics and Human Biology*, *9*(4), 407-418.

De Beer, H. (2012). Dairy products and physical stature: A systematic review and meta-analysis of controlled trials. *Economics and Human Biology*, *10*(2), 299–309.

Fogel, R. W., Engerman, S. J., Floud, R., Friedman, G., Margo, R. A., Sokoloff, K., . . . Wachter, K. W. (1983). Secular changes in American and British stature and nutrition. *Journal of Interdisciplinary History*, *14*(2), 445–481.

Gallagher, A. (2013). Stature, body mass, and brain size: A two-million-year odyssey. *Economics and Human Biology*, *11*(4), 551–562.

Grasgruber, P., Cacek, J., Kalina, T., & Sebera, M. (2014). The role of nutrition and genetics as key determinants of the positive height trend. *Economics and Human Biology*, *15*, 81–100.

Guntupalli, A. M., & Baten, J. (2006). The development and inequality of heights in North, West and East India, 1915–44. *Explorations in Economic History*, *43*(4), 578–608.

Hatton, T. J., & Bray, B. E. (2010). Long run trends in the heights of European men, 19th–20th centuries. *Economics and Human Biology*, *8*(3), 405–413.

Heyberger, L. (2014). Received wisdom versus reality: Height, nutrition, and urbanization in mid-19th-century France. *Cliometrica*, *8*(1), 115–140.

Hiermeyer, M. (2009). Height and BMI values of German conscripts in 2000, 2001 and 1906. *Economics and Human Biology*, *7*(3), 366–375.

Huang, Y., van Poppel, F., & Lumey, L. H. (2015). Differences in height by education among 371,105 Dutch military conscripts. *Economics and Human Biology*, *17*, 202-207.

Koepke, N., & Baten, J. (2005). The biological standard of living in Europe during the last two millennia. *European Review of Economic History*, *9*(1), 61–95.

Koepke, N., & Baten, J. (2008). Agricultural specialization and height in ancient and medieval Europe. *Explorations in Economic History*, *45*(2), 127–146.

Komlos, J. (1985). Stature and nutrition in the Habsburg monarchy: The standard of living and economic development in the 18th century. *American Historical Review*, *90*(5), 1149–1161.

Komlos, J. (1996). Anomalies in economic history: Toward a resolution of the Antebellum Puzzle. *Journal of Economic History*, *56*(1), 202–214.

Komlos, J. (1998). Shrinking in a growing economy? The mystery of physical stature during the Industrial Revolution. *Journal of Economic History*, *58*(3), 779–802.

Komlos, J. (2004). How to (and how not to) analyze deficient height samples. *Historical Methods*, *37*(4), 160–173.

Komlos, J. (2007). Anthropometric evidence on economic growth, biological well-being and regional convergence in the Habsburg monarchy, c. 1850–1910. *Cliometrica*, *1*(3), 211–237.

Komlos, J., & Baten, J. (2004). Looking backward and looking forward: Anthropometric research and the development of Social Science History. *Social Science History*, *28*(2), 1-24.

Komlos, J., & Baur, M. (2004). From the tallest to (one of) the fattest: The enigmatic fate of the American population in the 20th century. *Economics and Human Biology*, 2, 57–74.

McEnvoy, B. P., & Visscher, P. M. (2009). Genetics of human height. *Economics and Human Biology*, *7*(3), 294–306.

Moatsos, M., Baten, J., Foldvari, P., van Leeuwen, B., & van Zanden, J. L. (2014). Income inequality since 1820. In J. L. van Zanden et al. (Eds.), *How was life? Global well-being since 1820* (pp. 199–215). Paris: OECD.

Moradi, A., & Baten, J. (2005). Inequality in sub-Saharan Africa 1950–80: New estimates and new results. *World Development*, *33*(8), 1233–1265.

Mummert, A., Esche, E., Robinson, J., & Armelagos, G. J. (2011). Stature and robusticity during the agricultural transition: Evidence from the bioarchaeological record. *Economics and Human Biology*, *9*(3), 284–301.

Olsen, M. (1993). Dictatorship, democracy, and development. *American Political Science Review* 87–3, 567–576.

Pak, S., Schwekendiek, D., & Kim, H. (2011). Height and living standards in North Korea, 1930s–1980s. *Economic History Review* *64*(s1), 142–158.

Ranasinghe, P., Jayawardana, M. A. N. A. A. D., Constantine, G. R., Sheriff, M. H. R., Matthews, D. R., & Katalunda, P. (2011). Patterns and correlates of adult height in Sri Lanka. *Economics and Human Biology*, 9(1), 23–29.

Smith, P. K., Bogin, B., Varela-Silva, M. I., & Loucky, J. (2003). Economic and anthropological assessments of the health of children in Maya immigrant families in the US. *Economics and Human Biology*, *1*(2), 145–160.

Stegl, M., & Baten, J. (2009). Tall and shrinking Muslims, short and growing Europeans: The long-run welfare development of the Middle East, 1850–1980. *Explorations in Economic History*, *46*(1), 132–148.

Van Zanden, J. L., Baten, J., Foldvari, P., & van Leeuwen, B. (2014). The changing shape of global inequality 1820–2000: Exploring a new dataset. *Review of Income and Wealth*, *60*(2), 279–297.

Zehetmayer, M. (2013). Health, market integration, and the urban height penalty in the US, 1847–1894. *Cliometrica*, *7*(2), 161–187.

CHAPTER 15

GLOBAL BMI TRENDS

KATRIN KROMEYER-HAUSCHILD,
ANJA MOSS, AND MARTIN WABITSCH

15.1 Introduction

The body mass index (BMI; calculated as weight in kilograms/height in meters squared) is an important indicator in monitoring a population's nutritional status and health and for studying trends or investigating differences between populations. The BMI is the most common population-level measure of overweight and obesity, as well as of underweight. Analyzing trends in BMI in children and adults helps to increase our understanding of possible causal and regulating factors, particularly through examining when increases began, the velocity of increase, and rates in different environments. Whereas children's anthropometric status improved in developing countries, and underweight rates are falling, the number of overweight and obese children and adults is increasing at an alarming rate throughout the world. In 2013, the numbers are now more than 2.1 billion (36.9% and 38.0% in men and women, respectively), up from 857 million (28.8% and 29.8% in men and women, respectively) in 1980 (Ng et al., 2014). The World Health Organization (WHO) classifies overweight and obesity as the fifth leading global risk for mortality in the world (WHO, 2009). A high BMI is one of the eight risk factors that account for 61% of cardiovascular deaths (http://www.who.int/healthinfo/global_burden_disease/GlobalHealthRisks_report_part3.pdf). Numerous studies have shown that the risk of illness from high blood pressure, high blood cholesterol, heart disease, stroke, diabetes, certain types of cancer, arthritis, and breathing problems increases as BMI increases. The relationship between BMI and morbidity and mortality risk is U- or J-shaped, with an increased morbidity and mortality risk due to infectious diseases at the lower end of the BMI distribution (Campbell & Ulijaszek, 1994) and with chronic disease risk and mortality at the upper end of the distribution (Flegal, Graubard, Williamson, & Gail, 2005; Lewis et al., 2009). On the basis of morbidity and mortality risk, universal thresholds for classifying adults according to their BMI were proposed by WHO expert reports (WHO, 1995, 2000).[1]

For children and adolescents up to the age of 18 years, the classification of the nutritional status needs to consider the different growth patterns among boys and girls at each age. Therefore, in children and adolescents, the individual BMI is compared with the distribution of BMI in a reference population of the same age and sex. Conventionally, the BMI reference distribution is expressed as percentiles, and BMI values above selected cutoffs are used to define overweight or obesity. For instance, these cutoffs vary from the 85th to the 97th percentile. Such BMI reference percentiles for children and adolescents have been developed for several countries on the basis of national or local data. These different reference populations, as well as differences in cutoff points, lead to discrepancies in estimating overweight and obesity.

Currently, two approaches from the WHO and the International Obesity Task Force (IOTF) to define childhood overweight and obesity exist, and these enhance the validity of international comparisons. The WHO reference is a reconstruction of the 1977 National Center for Health Statistics (NCHS)/WHO reference, supplemented with data from the WHO Child Growth Standards in pre-school ages (de Onis et al., 2007; WHO Multicentre Growth Reference Study Group, 2006). The BMI-for-age curves given in the WHO reference were recommended to define overweight and obesity in children and adolescents aged 5–19 years using thresholds of + 1SD and + 2SD, respectively. At 19 years of age, these thresholds closely coincide with the cutoffs used in adults. The cutoff point of less than −2 standard deviations (SD) is used to classify thinness (this equates to moderately underweight), and less than −3 SD is used to define severe thinness (this equates to severe underweight). As mentioned earlier, the WHO Child Growth Standards provide a tool to assess the nutritional status of infants and children less than 5 years of age. These WHO standards are based on a multicenter study involving breastfed infants and young children from six geographically distinct sites (Brazil, Ghana, India, Norway, Oman, and the United States). Overweight and obesity are defined as the proportion of preschool children with values of greater than + 2 SDs and greater than + 3 SDs, respectively, from the weight-for-length/height medians or the BMI-for-age medians provided by the WHO standards. The cutoff point of less than −2 SD is used to define underweight.

For the IOTF reference, data obtained from six different countries (more than 190,000 subjects in total, aged 0–25 from the UK, Brazil, Hong Kong, the Netherlands, Singapore, and the United States) were pooled (Cole, Bellizzi, Flegal, & Dietz, 2000). This reference defines overweight and obesity by a BMI above the age- and sex-specific percentiles that pass through a BMI of 25 kg/m^2 and 30 kg/m^2 at age 18, respectively. For each dataset, the percentile curves that pass through these cutoffs used in adults were smoothed and then averaged to develop the IOTF reference percentiles. For the definition of thinness grades 1, 2, and 3, cutoffs were derived based on BMI of 16, 17, and 18.5 at 18 years, similar to the approach used for overweight and obesity (Cole, Flegal, Nicholls, & Jackson, 2007).

This chapter provides a brief overview of current prevalence of overweight and obesity worldwide and trends over time. Furthermore, trends over time in BMI and in the BMI distribution are assessed. Although the central interest in this chapter is on BMI, trends in changes in waist circumference and subcutaneous fat mass as determined by skinfold measurements are also reviewed because adiposity studies have shown that the distribution and content of body fat are crucial determinants of obesity-related health risks. A summary of the health outcomes associated with unhealthy BMI values, especially in children, complements this chapter.

15.2 Data Sources

In numerous studies, overweight and obesity prevalence or BMI levels were presented worldwide or for specific regions based on national health surveys, multicenter studies, or reviews. However, comparisons between these studies are difficult due to the use of different data collection methods (e.g., the use of reported rather than measured data, participation rates, age ranges, years of collection, and definitions of overweight and obesity). In the past few years, efforts have been made to define international standards and to collect reliable anthropometric data based on studies using these standardized methods. Several global databases were established to provide comprehensive data. The WHO established two different surveillance tools, the Global Database on Child Growth and Malnutrition and the Global Database on Body Mass Index, for monitoring nutrition transition in preschool children and in adults, respectively. The World Obesity Federation provides comprehensive current obesity prevalence data for children and adults on the *World Maps of Obesity* on their web site (www.worldobesity.org/aboutobesity/world-map-obesity/).

These above-mentioned databases are continually being updated as new information becomes available, and they provide the opportunity to systematically and comprehensively access interactive tools to obtain reliable nationally representative or subnational data in a standardized format.

15.3 Current Prevalence of Malnutrition in Preschool Children

Although the main focus in this chapter is on overweight and obesity, for children up to 5 years, prevalence rates for underweight are also presented because, in this age group, being underweight is especially associated with a higher chance of infectious diseases and for premature death. For the first time in 2011, a data harmonization effort was made from the United Nations Children's Fund (UNICEF), WHO, and the World Bank who jointly report estimates of child malnutrition and trends since 1990 (United Nations Children's Fund et al., 2012). The reported prevalence rates, which were estimated according to the WHO Child Growth Standards, are based on data from the

Global Database on Child Growth and Malnutrition and a UNICEF global database populated in part through its annual data collection exercise that draws on submissions from more than 150 country offices. The most recent report "Levels and Trends in Child Malnutrition: UNICEF/WHO/The World Bank Joint Child Malnutrition Estimates," compiling estimates for 2013, shows that 99 million children under 5 years old worldwide are underweight, and 42 million are overweight (www.who.int/nutgrowthdb/estimates2013/en/). In 2013, while the prevalence rates of overweight are highest in Southern and Northern Africa (19.3% and 12.4%, respectively), Central Asia (11.6%), and South America (7.3%), two-thirds of all underweight children live in Asia and about one third in Africa. Prevalence rates of underweight are higher in low and lower middle income groups than in the upper middle income group. The proportion of children under 5 who are underweight decreased from 25% to 15% between 1990 and 2013. The largest relative decrease occurred in Asia, where the underweight prevalence declined from 32% to 18% in this period, followed by Latin America and the Caribbean, with decreases from 8% to 3%. The smallest relative change is observed in Africa, with a decrease from 23% in 1990 to 17% in 2003. Asia, Latin America, and the Caribbean will most likely achieve the Millennium Goal of halving the 1990 underweight prevalence by 2015.

In contrast, the number of children under 5 who are overweight has increased from 31 million (5.0%) in 1990 to 32 million (5.2%) in 2000 and 42 million (6.3%) in 2013, suggesting that the rate of increase has accelerated (www.who.int/nutgrowthdb/summary_jme_2013.pdf?ua=1). Developed countries have a higher prevalence of overweight (8%) compared with developing countries (4%), but the vast majority of affected children under 5 live in developing countries. Although the increase followed a similar pattern worldwide, the increase has been higher in developing countries than in developed countries in the past two decades. Globally, low-income countries are currently catching up with the lower middle income group.

These data show that underweight is paradoxically coexisting with overweight and obesity in developing countries, referred to as the "double burden of malnutrition." This development seems to be associated with economic changes in these countries and the phenomenon of globalization, which is characterized by a worldwide integration of culture, trade, and foreign investment. These changes are having a major impact on food systems and have transformed the supply and demand of food by altering trade and employment patterns (Popkin, Adair, & Ng, 2012). In both the developed and developing countries, we face an oversupply of calories and of the amenities of modern life that hamper physical activity (Drewnowski & Popkin, 1997; Shetty, 2013). The increase in the prevalence of overweight and obesity developed in parallel to the far-reaching changes in eating habits and life style. As a consequence, populations are increasingly facing modern health risks from chronic and noncommunicable disease, such as cardiovascular diseases and cancers. Many developing countries now face a double burden of disease while still fighting against infectious diseases, such as diarrhea and pneumonia, thus demonstrating a shift from these primarily traditional risks to modern health risks.

15.4 Current Prevalence of Overweight and Obesity in Children and Adults

The Global Burden of Disease Studies (GBD) 2010 and 2013 (Murray & Lopez, 2013; Ng et al., 2014) can be used to describe current prevalence rates in children and adults. These studies are large systematic efforts to describe the global distribution and causes of major diseases, injuries, and health risk factors. The GBD Study 2013 presents up-to-date and comparable information about levels and trends (between 1980 and 2013) in overweight and obesity for 188 countries, 21 regions, and development status (developed or developing) from age 2–4 years to 80 years. Although the WHO definition was used to define overweight and obesity in adults, the IOTF definition was used in children.

The GBD Study 2013 shows that 2.1 billion individuals worldwide were overweight or obese in 2013. Among children and adolescents, 23.8% of boys and 22.6% of girls are overweight and obese in developed countries, compared with 12.9% of boys and 8.4% of girls in developing countries. In children and adolescents, sex differences in the prevalence rates are small in both developed and developing countries. By contrast, adult men in developed countries had higher rates of overweight and obesity than did women, whereas the opposite is true in developing countries.

In 2013, 36.9% of men and 38.0% of women were found to be overweight and obese in contrast to 28.8% of men and 29.8% of women in 1980. In 2013, high proportions of obesity were found in Tonga, where levels of obesity in men and women exceeded 50%, and in Kuwait, Libya, Qatar, and the Pacific Islands of Samoa, Micronesia, and Kiribati, where more than 50% of women were obese. The prevalence of overweight and obesity in children and adolescents was highest (>30%) in the United States and in some countries in the Middle East and Oceania and lowest in African countries (<5%). High prevalence rates of overweight in boys were also found in Australia (>25%) and India (>20%). The respective data for girls were greater than 20% in Australia and greater than 10% in India. The highest obesity rates were estimated in girls in Kuwait (23%), Samoa, Micronesia, and Kiribati (>30%) and in boys in Samoa and Kiribati (>20%). In most Western European countries, more than 20% of boys and girls were overweight and obese, with obesity rates ranging in boys from 14% in Israel and 13% in Malta to 4% in the Netherlands and Sweden. In girls, levels of obesity varied between 13% in Luxemburg and 4% in the Netherlands, Norway, and Sweden.

Half of the world's 671 million obese people are living in just 10 countries: the United States (more than 13%), China and India (15% combined), Russia, Brazil, Mexico, Germany, Pakistan, and Indonesia.

15.5 Time Trends in Overweight and Obesity

The GBD Study 2013 indicated that the prevalence of overweight and obesity has increased worldwide by 47.1% for children and 27.5% for adults between 1980 and 2013 (Ng et al., 2014). Although increases were found in both developed countries and developing countries, the levels and trends have varied substantially. Among women, the highest increase in the prevalence of adult obesity was found in Egypt, Saudi Arabia, Oman, Honduras, and Bahrain, and, among men, the highest prevalence rates were observed in New Zealand, Bahrain, Kuwait, Saudi Arabia, and the United States. In developed countries, the increase was highest in the United States, Australia, and the UK. Globally, the gain in overweight and obesity in adults has accelerated from 1992 to 2002 and has slowed in developed countries since 2006, whereas increases are likely to continue in developing countries. Various surveys of children have even shown a stabilization or decline in prevalence rates of overweight and obesity in different developed countries in the past 10–15 years. This development was more marked in girls and in preschool children (aged 2–6) than in boys and older age groups, respectively (Wabitsch, Moss, & Kromeyer-Hauschild, 2014). Despite this decline, the same countries also reported increasing rates of extreme obesity in children and adolescents. Furthermore, the prevalence rates in these countries are still at a high level and significantly higher than in 1980.

The onset of the obesity epidemic has to be identified convincingly. In most studies, it was commonly assumed that it began in the 1980s. For example, surveys in the United States had indicated only slight increases before 1980 (Flegal, Carroll, Kuczmarski, & Johnson, 1998; Kuczmarski, Flegal, Campbell, & Johnson, 1994; Troiano & Flegal, 1998). The National Health Examination Surveys (NHANES) data show that the fraction of the population that was obese for both children and adults was fairly stable between 1971–1974 and 1976–1980. This observation of a rather slow increase or steady state of obesity and overweight rates in children and adults before 1980 was also confirmed in other countries. However, from historical data, it becomes obvious that the increase in BMI began considerable earlier than generally supposed (Komlos & Brabec, 2011). Analyses by Komlos and Brabec (2010, 2011) using birth cohorts to examine BMI trends in US adults indicate that the BMI values were increasing already among those born at the beginning of the 20th century, with considerable variation over time. The general upward trend was accelerated in the 1920s, as well as in the 1950s, the time after each of the two world wars. The long-term persistence of this trend suggests that the BMI increases are related to the transition to a postindustrial lifestyle, which is characterized, for example, by major labor-saving technological changes, the industrial processing of food, the rise of an automobile-based way of life, the introduction of radio and television broadcasting, and cultural transformations (e.g., eating outside of the home more frequently). This hypothesis is also supported by findings that the decline in income during the Great Depression of the 1930s and World War II, which slowed the adoption of the labor-saving technologies, was accompanied by a decline in the BMI increase.

15.6 General Pattern of Overweight and Obesity

The rise in overweight and obesity has affected all population groups but to varying degrees. It has become apparent that a number of patterns have been linked to the prevalence rates and trends over time, including socioeconomic status (SES), residential area, age, sex, and ethnicity.

In the past few decades, overweight and obesity have affected the socially deprived parts of society, which were characterized by lower income, education levels, and access to care more frequently than other groups. In developed countries, people with lower SES have been found to be far more at risk for becoming overweight and obese than the middle and upper classes, with smaller differences between groups for men than for women (Sobal & Stunkard, 1989). Conversely, in developing countries, high SES shows a positive relationship to overweight and obesity, but more recent research has found that the burden of overweight and obesity tends to shift from groups with higher SES toward the groups with lower SES as the country's gross national product (GNP) increases. In women, this shift apparently occurs at an earlier stage of economic development than in men (Monteiro, Moura, Conde, & Popkin, 2004).

In developing countries, children and adults in the relatively affluent urban areas were more likely to be overweight than persons in rural areas. With the growing rural–urban migration in these countries, overweight will be an increasing problem in developing countries. The rural-to-urban migration was found to be associated with increased inactivity and unfavorable eating patterns, such as a high consumption of fats and sugars (Ebrahim et al., 2010).

The prevalence of obesity increases with aging in both developing and developed countries, but in developing countries, peak rates of obesity tend to be reached at a much earlier age (e.g., at approximately 40 years of age) than in developed countries, where increases occurred at least until the age of 50–60.

As mentioned earlier, women are more likely to be obese, whereas the reverse is true for overweight. In many developed countries, obesity is also more common in minority ethnic groups than in the general population. This difference could be due to a genetic predisposition to obesity in these groups. However, this may only explain a small proportion of the risk because there is increased evidence that environmental determinants such migration, cultural variations in diet, SES, local area characteristics, and physical activity levels accounted for much of this difference (Caprio et al., 2008; Kumanyika, 2008).

The reasons for the above-mentioned patterns linked to obesity are not clearly understood because of their complex nature, involving genetics, physiology, culture, environment, and interactions among these factors. These great variations in prevalence rates within countries or regions indicate that caution is warranted in interpreting the country- or region-specific average trends, especially in low- to middle-income countries with considerable heterogeneity in weight status.

15.7 Trends in Mean BMI and BMI Distribution

A systematic review that estimated worldwide long-term trends of mean BMI for adults 20 years and older in 199 countries and territories between 1980 and 2008 found that the mean BMI increased by 0.4 kg/m^2 per decade for men and by 0.5 kg/m^2 per decade for women (Finucane et al., 2011). There was an increase in all but eight countries among men, with the highest increase of more than 2 kg/m^2 per decade in Nauru and the Cook Islands. In men, regions with almost flat trends were central Africa and south Asia. In high-income countries, the rise was largest in the United States, reaching 1.0 kg/m^2 per decade, and lowest in Brunei, Switzerland, Italy, and France, with increases ranging from 0.3 to 0.4 kg/m^2 per decade. In women, mean BMI increased in 180 of the 199 countries. Whereas the highest increase occurred in women in some countries in Oceania, with more than 2.0 kg/m^2 per decade, in Central and Eastern Europe and Central Asia, the trend was estimated to be nearly flat, with increases of less than 0.2 kg/m^2 per decade. In high-income countries, the increase ranged from 1.2 kg/m^2 per decade for women in the United States, New Zealand, and Australia to 0.1–0.2 kg/m^2 per decade for women in Italy and Singapore. In 2008, the highest mean BMI for men and women was found in some Oceanic countries, similar to the above-mentioned prevalence rates. The lowest rates in men occurred in a few countries in sub-Saharan Africa, and East, South, and Southeast Asia. In high-income countries, the United States had the highest BMI. The sex differences in the mean BMI followed the same pattern as in the prevalence rates, with a higher mean BMI in men than women in high-income subregions compared with a higher BMI in women than men in most low- and middle-income regions.

A study to identify long-run BMI trends of US-born black and white children and adolescents born 1941–2004 shows that BMI values increased substantially with some fluctuation in the rate of changes during this period. Whereas the increase in BMI among black girls started already in the 1940s, the rate of change experienced acceleration among all children and adolescents born in the mid-1950s to early 1960s. After peaks in the BMI values in the mid-1960s and the mid-1980s, the rate of change began to decrease until the mid-1990s, when it began to increase again slightly. During the whole period considered, the BMI values increased by 2.4 units in white girls, 5.6 units in black girls, 1.5 units in white boys, and 3.3 units in black boys (Komlos, Breitfelder, & Sunder, 2009).

The investigation of BMI distribution changes over time gives a more complex picture of weight changes in a population and also offers the possibility of identifying subgroups at high risk for overweight and obesity. A relatively small increase in the average weight of a population can lead to a significant increase in the incidence of obesity. A BMI increase from 26.7 to 28.1 kg/m^2 in the US population between 1991 and 2000 has led to a marked increase in the obesity prevalence (Friedman, 2003). However, the NHANES data also show that BMI has become more unequally distributed in the US population because not everyone has gained 10% of his or her body weight compared with people in earlier decades. Several studies in children and adults have confirmed that increases in mean BMI over time were associated with an increasing variation of BMI values in a population and a shift upward of the BMI values in the entire population, indicating weight gains in the whole population. However, due to a more marked increase in the upper BMI range than in the lower BMI range, a rightward shift of BMI distribution has occurred, suggesting that the heaviest people have become heavier (Flegal & Troiano, 2000; Kromeyer-Hauschild & Zellner, 2007). Some studies have even found that the lower part of the BMI distribution has remained unchanged, whereas an increase in the upper BMI range occurred mainly in younger children (Hulens et al., 2001; Troiano & Flegal, 1998). In an analysis of long-term changes (between 1991 and 2008) in the BMI distribution of women in 37 low- and middle-income countries, the BMI at the 95th percentile has been found to increase 2.5 times faster than the BMI at the 5th percentile (Razak, Corsi, & Subramanian, 2013).

In developing countries, the pattern of changes in the BMI distribution has brought about the double burden of disease in the population because the prevalence of overweight and obesity was rising at a much faster rate than the decline in the prevalence of underweight. In developed countries with already high baseline BMI levels, large shifts at the upper end of the BMI distribution can cause a large increase in the rates of extreme obesity. Thus, Wang et al. (2011) showed that the age-standardized prevalence of extreme obesity increased significantly from 1.1%/1.3% (boys/girls) in NHANES II, to 2.9%/3.1% in NHANES III and 5.1%/4.7% in NHANES 1999–2006. According to the results of the NHANES studies, the rates of severe obesity have tripled in the past 25 years, and more than 400,000 adolescents in the United States might meet criteria for bariatric surgery (Skelton, Cook, Auinger, Klein, & Barlow, 2009). A growing body of studies, especially in adolescents and adults, has shown a trend to an increase of extremely obese individuals, and this increase is more pronounced than the increase in other moderate obesity categories or at younger ages (Skelton et al., 2009; Wang et al., 2011). Higher SES seems to protect against severe obesity. Explanations for this association may include the easy availability and low cost of energy-dense snacks in poor, inner-city neighborhoods. In contrast, fresh fruits and vegetables are often unavailable, and adequate amounts are expensive (Skelton et al., 2009). Recent reports confirm the seemingly paradoxical connection of poverty, food insecurity, and extreme obesity (Casey et al., 2006).

These above-mentioned patterns of changes in the BMI distribution suggest that the causes for the increase in obesity should be sought in part at the population level; however, the causes of obesity appear to have much in common with other diseases in that everyone may be exposed to a given change in the environment, but only those with a susceptibility to the given disease will experience it. For those with a susceptibility to obesity, the conditions appear to be right for their disease to flourish.

15.8 Trends in Waist Circumference and Subcutaneous Fat Mass

Despite BMI being accepted as a proxy for adiposity, it cannot distinguish between body fat and lean tissue and could therefore mask health consequences directly associated with body fat. In addition, BMI gives no indication of body fat distribution. Epidemiological studies in adults as well as in children have clearly shown that the waist circumference (WC), as a simple measure of abdominal obesity, is a stronger marker of health risk than BMI (Bigaard et al., 2005; McCarthy, 2006; Wang, Rimm, Stampfer, Willett, & Hu, 2005). In addition to this, health risk classification based on BMI is complicated because body fat varies by a given BMI between populations. South Asian populations have been found to have a smaller lean body mass but larger fat stores at equivalent BMI levels compared with other ethnic groups, and, consequently, health risks for these groups are higher at lower BMI levels (Banerji, Faridi, Atluri, Chaiken, & Lebovitz, 1999; McKeigue, Shah, & Marmot, 1991; Wang et al., 1994). In children and adolescents, interpretation of BMI values is complicated by different changes of lean body mass and fat mass during growth and development. Measurements of the WC or the assessment of the extent of body fat by measures such as skinfold thickness can help to more precisely quantify the health risk because BMI-based assessment of overweight and obesity may be underestimating the number of persons with enhanced levels of (intra-abdominal) body fat.

International comparisons of WC or prevalence rates of abdominal obesity are complicated by a number of factors similar to the above-mentioned factors for overweight and obesity. For example, no general consensus defining abdominal obesity in children and adolescents exists to date. Although the numerical results are often not comparable, several studies in children and adults have consistently reported increases in WC or abdominal obesity over time, which were usually stronger than those reported for BMI or general obesity (Garnett, Baur, & Cowell, 2011; Janssen, Shields, Craig, & Tremblay, 2011; Li, Ford, McGuire, & Mokdad, 2007).

A recent study in US children and adolescents has shown that the WC and the prevalence of abdominal obesity have remained stable between 2003–2004 and 2011–2012 at high levels after increases that occurred between 1988–1994 and 2003–2004. Among children aged 2–5 years, a slight decrease was even observed in this period (Xi et al., 2014).

Although skinfold thickness measurements were rarely performed in clinical settings, a significant increase in subcutaneous fat mass over time can be noted, which resulted in significant increases in body fat as estimated by skinfold thickness (Nagel et al., 2009). A meta-analysis of 154 studies of 0- to 18-year-olds in developed countries found that triceps skinfold thickness increased at a rate of 0.49 mm per decade from 1951 to 2003 (Olds, 2009). Subscapular skinfold thickness increased at 0.38 mm per decade over this period. This meta-analysis also showed that the rate of increase was greatest in 10- to 14-year-olds and became markedly steeper after approximately 1980.

In school children from Germany, the skinfold thickness at the triceps and the subscapular site was shown to increase not only in overweight children but also in normal and underweight children over a period of 30 years between 1975 and 2005/06. Therefore, the long-term increase in body fatness seems to be a characteristic feature of a great proportion of the population. Moreover, a higher increase in skinfold-SDS than in BMI-SDS in normal-weight children over time suggests greater body fatness for a given BMI. These results indicate that the body composition in children has changed over time, with an increase in fat mass and a decrease in lean body or muscle mass (Kromeyer-Hauschild, Glasser, & Zellner, 2012).

In the light of these findings, reports of a recent break in the obesity epidemic need to be interpreted with caution. The results should be revised and verified with studies focusing on WC or skinfold thickness rather than BMI. In the NHANES in US adults, the use of skinfolds to define obesity indicates a rise in obesity since the beginning of the data series (NHES I, 1959–1962), whereas the rise in BMI-based obesity began later at least in these surveys, namely in 1976–1980 (NHANES II). With the skinfold-based definition of obesity, the rise in the prevalence of obesity was detectable 10 to 20 years earlier than with the BMI-based definition (Burkhauser, Cawley, & Schmeiser, 2009). This corroborates Komlos and Brabec's finding (2010) that the obesity epidemic began earlier than hitherto thought.

Increases in fatness among people who remained in healthy weight categories of BMI could have a significant impact on the incidence of overweight and obesity, with associated comorbidities, and therefore measurements of body composition and further research in this field are important.

15.9 Health Impact of Overweight and Obesity in Adults

Numerous studies have shown that both overweight and obesity are related to a broad range of health issues ranging from specific diseases such as type-2 diabetes and hypertension, to impaired quality of life and psychosocial disturbances. A comprehensive review found statistically significant associations between overweight and the incidence of type-2 diabetes; all cancers except esophageal (female), pancreatic, and prostate cancers; all cardiovascular diseases (except congestive heart failure); asthma; gallbladder disease; osteoarthritis; and chronic back pain. Overweight had the strongest impact on the incidence of type-2 diabetes (Guh et al., 2009). These health risks start to increase at a BMI of 23 kg/m^2 (Emberson, Whincup, Morris, Wannamethee, & Shaper, 2005; Renehan, Tyson, Egger, Heller, & Zwahlen, 2008). Men and women with BMIs of more than 30 had a sevenfold and 12-fold higher risk of type-2 diabetes, respectively, compared with men and women in the normal weight range (Guh et al., 2009). However, there are considerable ethnic differences in the relationship between measures of obesity and health outcomes, which are most likely related to variations in body composition and fat distribution between populations. As mentioned earlier, Asian people have more visceral fat for the same BMI than do other populations, and therefore, the BMI thresholds recommended by the WHO underestimate diabetes and cardiovascular risk for Asian populations (Deurenberg, Deurenberg-Yap, & Guricci, 2002).

Obesity-related disorders cluster in most susceptible individuals (Berenson et al., 1998; Freedman, Dietz, Srinivasan, & Berenson, 1999; Koziel, 2003). Quality of life is impaired most among persons with multiple disorders. Obesity has been generally found to lead to social disadvantages in key areas of life (e.g., education, employment, health care, and social interaction) and to psychological problems, such as depression, body image distress, and low self-esteem, especially among women (Dixon, Dixon, & O'Brien, 2003; Wadden et al., 2006).

The association of obesity with many diseases can affect life expectancy adversely, with cardiovascular deaths as the most common cause of death attributed to obesity (Lim et al., 2012). In adults and already in adolescents, a U-shaped effect of BMI on relative risk of dying exists, indicating an elevated relative risk for both underweight and overweight persons. Belonging to the 75th–85th percentile group doubles the mortality risk in adolescents (Koch, 2011), and, in adults, mortality risk rises with BMI increases within a BMI of more than 25 kg/m^2 (Calle, Thun, Petrelli, Rodriguez, & Heath, 1999; Gu, Paulose-Ram, Yoon, Burt, & Gillum, 2006; Jee et al., 2006). A BMI of greater than 30 reduces life expectancy by an average of 3 years, whereas morbid obesity (BMI >40) reduces life expectancy by 8–10 years (Prospective Studies Collaboration, 2009).

15.10 Cross-Generational Health Impact of Obesity

There is increasing evidence that overweight and obesity in adult life and related health risks are influenced by the intrauterine and early postnatal environment. In recent years, emerging data from animal and human studies suggest that the nutritional status of women before conception and nutrition (excess and deficient), stress (e.g., glucocorticoids), or environmental toxins, among others, during pregnancy and in the early postnatal life of the offspring are risk factors for developing obesity and related diseases throughout life in the offspring (Godfrey & Barker, 2001; Godfrey, Gluckman, & Hanson, 2010; Koletzko et al., 2012).

To explain these associations, the concept of fetal or developmental programming of metabolism and body weight has been proposed (Budge et al., 2005; Plagemann, 2008; Sarr, Yang, & Regnault, 2012). In general, this concept describes the process by which an environmental stimulus during a critical time window in early development can permanently alter the phenotype of an organism. In addition, in epidemiological studies, a transmission of the programming to the next generation was shown, whereby a woman's own fetal growth plays a major role in programming the future health of her children (Rogvi, Forman, Damm, & Greisen, 2012). Although the genotype of programmed offspring does not change, altered gene expression may be the result of exposure-mediated epigenetic changes. Evidence from both epidemiological and animal studies suggests that the programming of obesity could occur by permanently altering pathways involved in the energy balance, such as appetite regulation and energy expenditure (Taylor & Poston, 2007).

Therefore, women of childbearing age with a suboptimal weight status are a high-risk group. Both underweight and overweight/obesity before and during pregnancy are linked to a range of health risks for the mothers but also for their offspring. For example, maternal obesity combined with gestational diabetes is usually associated with a higher risk of preeclampsia and an increased risk of congenital malformations and macrosomy (high birth weight). High birth weight increases the risk of obesity and related diseases in later life. In contrast, maternal undernutrition, which is common in many developing countries, affects a woman's chances of surviving pregnancy, as well as it does her child's health. Usually linked with poor nutrition during pregnancy, maternal undernutrition is associated with impaired fetal growth resulting in low birth weight and other adverse effects like diminished cognitive and physical development, conditions that disadvantage children for the rest of their lives (Osmani & Sen 2003). The nutrient restriction in utero can also program adipocyte metabolism and fat mass to give rise to later obesity and related illnesses, such as heart disease and diabetes in adulthood, especially when infants born at low birth weight experience rapid weight gain during early childhood (Dalziel, Parag, Rodgers, & Harding, 2007; Ong & Dunger, 2004). Interestingly, the association of both prenatal undernutrition and overnutrition with obesity and related chronic diseases seem to share similar mechanisms. These mechanisms involve overfeeding in the postnatal period in low birth weight infants and overfeeding in the prenatal and postnatal period in the high birth weight infants.

The programming theory could offer additional mechanisms that may contribute to the impressive increase in overweight and obesity in adults and children in both developed and developing countries. Accordingly, the origins of obesity and related medical disorders lie not only in the interactions between (susceptibility) genes and lifestyle risk factors, such as unbalanced diet and physical inactivity, but also in the interactions between genes and the embryonic, fetal, and early postnatal environments. In developing countries, girls with low birth weight and/or underweight during early childhood may deliver babies with low birth weight. These infants in turn may retain their early disadvantage, and, as adults, they may face a higher risk of chronic diseases. Thus, a vicious cycle repeats itself, generation after generation. On the other hand, with the worldwide rise of obesity, the prevalence of obesity among pregnant women is increasing (Fisher, Kim, Sharma, Rochat, & Morrow, 2013; Heslehurst, Rankin, Wilkinson, & Summerbell, 2010; Tsoi, Shaikh, Robinson, & Teoh, 2010), contributing to a self-perpetuating cycle of increasing obesity rates and related health risks whereby maternal obesity is linked to high birth weight, especially if the mothers have gestational diabetes or a high gestational weight gain. This high birth weight in turn leads to obesity and related diseases in later life. Data from the Swedish birth registry have shown that a 25–36% increase in maternal BMI over the past decade was associated with a 25% increase in the incidence of large-for-gestational-age babies (Surkan, Hsieh, Johansson, Dickman, & Cnattingius, 2004).

15.11 Health Outcomes of Malnutrition in Childhood

Both forms of malnutrition, underweight and overweight, have potential health impacts in children and adolescents. The highly prevalent undernutrition in children younger than 5 years in developing countries results in severe short- and long-term health outcomes. Underweight children suffer and die more often from serious infectious diseases such as diarrhea, measles, pneumonia, and malaria, as well as from HIV and AIDS than do children who are not underweight (Black et al., 2008). Children who are moderately or mildly underweight may appear to be healthy even when they face adverse consequences like growth impediment, impaired learning ability, and, later in life, low work productivity. In developing countries, there is a greater heterogeneity in nutrition-related problems due to the fact that, in addition to underweight, overweight has emerged among both children and adults in many of these countries.

Although the health consequences of overweight and obesity for children are less clear than in adults, numerous studies suggest that childhood obesity is associated with an increased risk of obesity, morbidity, disability, and premature mortality in adulthood. The risk of obesity in adulthood has been shown to be 2- to 6.5-fold higher for obese children as for non-obese children, with a greater risk for children with higher levels of obesity and for obese children at older ages (Freedman et al., 2005; Serdula et al., 1993). However, in addition to increased long-term health risks, a growing body of evidence suggests that, in developed countries, diseases that were once only observed in obese adults are also occurring in obese children (Cote, Harris, Panagiotopoulos, Sandor, & Devlin, 2013). Almost 50% of obese children exhibit pre- or grade 1 or 2 high blood pressure hypertension, another 29% exhibit high cholesterol levels, 44% exhibit more than 5% fat in their livers, and 74% exhibit more than 5% fat in their muscles (easo.org/obesity-facts-figure). Furthermore, obesity in childhood is associated with endocrine comorbidities (including impaired glucose tolerance, diabetes mellitus, hyperandrogenism in females, and abnormalities in growth and puberty), orthopedic comorbidities (including fractures, genu valgum, musculoskeletal pain, and impaired mobility), and psychological problems such as alienation, distorted peer relationships, poor self-esteem, distorted body image, anxiety, and depression (www.uptodate.com/contents/comorbidities-and-complications-of-obesity-in-children-and-adolescents). These psychosocial risks rise with increasing age and are greater among girls than boys.

The epidemic of obesity in children and its related health risks reduces the average age at which noncommunicable diseases become apparent and therefore contributes to rising economic costs, especially in the health care system. In developing countries, these economic costs are escalating because of the double burden of malnutrition with decreasing but still high prevalence rates of maternal and child undernutrition on one hand and rising prevalence rates of overweight and obesity on the other. The GBD study 2013 has shown that now fewer children are dying from infectious diseases and malnutrition, but, as in developed countries, more young and middle-aged adults are exhibiting noncommunicable diseases and dying from them. The more traditional heath concerns, such as undernutrition and infectious diseases, are replaced by noncommunicable diseases, which become the dominant causes of disability and death worldwide.

Overweight and obesity, with their great number of negative health and social consequences, have been shown to escalate costs from medical treatment and productivity losses due to sick leave and premature pensions. The costs are also escalating because the number of years that patients may be affected by obesity-related diseases and disability increases with the rise in obesity and longevity (Visscher & Seidell, 2001).

15.12 Conclusion

Overweight and obesity have reached pandemic proportions worldwide but tend to show a stabilization or decline in developed countries in recent years. However, there is a rapid rise in developing countries that have undergone demographic, epidemiological, and nutritional transitions. The increasingly "obesogenic environments" defined as "the sum of influences that the surroundings, opportunities or conditions of life have on promoting obesity in individuals or populations" (Swinburn, Egger, & Raza, 1999) are most likely the main driving forces for the obesity epidemic. Because of their associated comorbidities, overweight and obesity, especially, are major contributors to the global burden of disease resulting in enormous economic, social, and human costs. To counter this increase in overweight and obesity and the related health effects, concerted actions by national governments, international organizations, and academic institutions are urgently needed. The primary target should be to reverse the obesogenity of environments in addition to supporting individuals to counteract these obesogenic environments. In developing countries that often simultaneously face rising overweight and a high prevalence of underweight, nutrition supplementation programs should meet the energy and nutrient needs for underweight people while simultaneously ensuring healthful diets to prevent chronic diseases.

Note

1. The WHO classifies a healthy BMI for adults as between 18.5 and 24.9 kg/m^2. A BMI of 18.5 kg/m^2 or below defines underweight, and a BMI of 25.0–29.9 kg/m^2 represents pre-obesity, whereas the term "overweight" is usually used for a BMI in this range. Last, a BMI of 30 kg/m^2 or higher defines obesity.

References

Banerji, M. A., Faridi, N., Atluri, R., Chaiken, R. L., & Lebovitz, H. E. (1999). Body composition, visceral fat, leptin, and insulin resistance in Asian Indian men. *Journal of Clinical Endocrinology and Metabolism, 84*(1), 137–144.

Berenson, G. S., Srinivasan, S. R., Bao, W., III, Newman, W. P., Tracy, R. E., & Wattigney, W. A. (1998). Association between multiple cardiovascular risk factors and atherosclerosis in children and young adults. The Bogalusa Heart Study. *New England Journal of Medicine, 338*(23), 1650–1656.

Bigaard, J., Frederiksen, K., Tjonneland, A., Thomsen, B. L., Overvad, K., Heitmann, B. L., & Sorensen, T. I. (2005). Waist circumference and body composition in relation to all-cause mortality in middle-aged men and women. *International Journal of Obesity, 29*(7), 778–784.

Black, R. E., Allen, L. H., Bhutta, Z. A., Caulfield, L. E., de Onis, M., Ezzati, M., . . . Maternal Child Undernutrition Study Group. (2008). Maternal and child undernutrition: Global and regional exposures and health consequences. *Lancet, 371*(9608), 243–260.

Budge, H., Gnanalingham, M. G., Gardner, D. S., Mostyn, A., Stephenson, T., & Symonds, M. E. (2005). Maternal nutritional programming of fetal adipose tissue development: Long-term consequences for later obesity. *Birth Defects Research. Part C, Embryo Today, 75*(3), 193–199.

Burkhauser, R. V., Cawley, J., & Schmeiser, M. D. (2009). The timing of the rise in US obesity varies with measure of fatness. *Economics and Human Biology, 7*(3), 307–318.

Calle, E. E., Thun, M. J., Petrelli, J. M., Rodriguez, C., & Heath, C. W. (1999). Body-mass index and mortality in a prospective cohort of US adults. *New England Journal of Medicine, 341*(15), 1097–1105.

Campbell, P., & Ulijaszek, S. J. (1994). Relationships between anthropometry and retrospective morbidity in poor men in Calcutta, India. *European Journal of Clinical Nutrition, 48*(7), 507–512.

Caprio, S., Daniels, S. R., Drewnowski, A., Kaufman, F. R., Palinkas, L. A., Rosenbloom, A. L., & Schwimmer, J. B. (2008). Influence of race, ethnicity, and culture on childhood obesity: Implications for prevention and treatment: A consensus statement of shaping America's health and the obesity society. *Diabetes Care, 31*(11), 2211–2221.

Casey, P. H., Simpson, P. M., Gossett, J. M., Bogle, M. L., Champagne, C. M., Connell, C., . . . Weber, J. (2006). The association of child and household food insecurity with childhood overweight status. *Pediatrics, 118*(5), E1406–E1413.

Cole, T. J., Bellizzi, M. C., Flegal, K. M., & Dietz, W. H. (2000). Establishing a standard definition for child overweight and obesity worldwide: International survey. *British Medical Journal (Clinical Research Ed.), 320*(7244), 1240–1243.

Cole, T. J., Flegal, K. M., Nicholls, D., & Jackson, A. A. (2007). Body mass index cut offs to define thinness in children and adolescents: International survey. *British Medical Journal (Clinical Research Ed.), 335*(7612), 194.

Cote, A. T., Harris, K. C., Panagiotopoulos, C., Sandor, G. G., & Devlin, A. M. (2013). Childhood obesity and cardiovascular dysfunction. *Journal of the American College of Cardiology, 62*(15), 1309–1319.

Dalziel, S. R., Parag, V., Rodgers, A., & Harding, J. E. (2007). Cardiovascular risk factors at age 30 following pre-term birth. *International Journal of Epidemiology, 36*(4), 907–915.

de Onis, M., Onyango, A. W., Borghi, E., Siyam, A., Nishida, C., & Siekmann, J. (2007). Development of a WHO growth reference for school-aged children and adolescents. *Bulletin of the World Health Organization, 85*(9), 660–667.

Deurenberg, P., Deurenberg-Yap, M., & Guricci, S. (2002). Asians are different from Caucasians and from each other in their body mass index/body fat per cent relationship. *Obesity Reviews, 3*(3), 141–146.

Dixon, J. B., Dixon, M. E., & O'Brien, P. E. (2003). Depression in association with severe obesity: Changes with weight loss. *Archives of Internal Medicine, 163*(17), 2058–2065.

Drewnowski, A., & Popkin, B. M. (1997). The nutrition transition: New trends in the global diet. *Nutrition Reviews, 55*(2), 31–43.

Ebrahim, S., Kinra, S. Bowen, S. L., Andersen, E., Ben-Shlomo, Y., Lyngdoh, T., . . . Indian Migration Study Group (2010). The effect of rural-to-urban migration on obesity and diabetes in India: A cross-sectional study. *PLoS Medicine, 7*(4), E1000268.

Emberson, J. R., Whincup, P. H., Morris, R. W., Wannamethee, S. G., & Shaper, A. G. (2005). Lifestyle and cardiovascular disease in middle-aged British men: The effect of adjusting for within-person variation. *European Heart Journal, 26*(17), 1774–1782.

Finucane, M. M., Stevens, G. A., Cowan, M. J., Danaei, G., Lin, J. K., Paciorek, C. J., . . . Global Burden of Metabolic Risk Factors of Chronic Diseases Collaborating Group. (2011). National, regional, and global trends in body-mass index since 1980: Systematic analysis of health examination surveys and epidemiological studies with 960 country-years and 9.1 million participants. *Lancet, 377*(9765), 557–567.

Fisher, S. C., Kim, S. Y., Sharma, A. J., Rochat, R., & Morrow, B. (2013). Is obesity still increasing among pregnant women? Prepregnancy obesity trends in 20 states, 2003–2009. *Preventive Medicine, 56*(6), 372–378.

Flegal, K. M., Carroll, M. D., Kuczmarski, R. J., & Johnson, C. L. (1998). Overweight and obesity in the United States: Prevalence and trends, 1960–1994. *International Journal of Obesity and Related Metabolic Disorders, 22*(1), 39–47.

Flegal, K. M., Graubard, B. I., Williamson, D. F., & Gail, M. H. (2005). Excess deaths associated with underweight, overweight, and obesity. *Journal of the American Medical Association, 293*(15), 1861–1867.

Flegal, K. M., & Troiano, R. P. (2000). Changes in the distribution of body mass index of adults and children in the US population. *International Journal of Obesity and Related Metabolic Disorders, 24*(7), 807–818.

Freedman, D. S., Dietz, W. H., Srinivasan, S. R., & Berenson, G. S. (1999). The relation of overweight to cardiovascular risk factors among children and adolescents: The Bogalusa Heart Study. *Pediatrics, 103*(6 Pt. 1), 1175–1182.

Freedman, D. S., Khan, L. K., Serdula, M. K., Dietz, W. H., Srinivasan, S. R., & Berenson, G. S. (2005). The relation of childhood BMI to adult adiposity: The Bogalusa Heart Study. *Pediatrics, 115*(1), 22–27.

Friedman, J. M. (2003). A war on obesity, not the obese. *Science, 299*(5608), 856–858.

Garnett, S. P., Baur, L. A., & Cowell, C. T. (2011). The prevalence of increased central adiposity in Australian school children 1985 to 2007. *Obesity Reviews, 12*(11), 887–896.

Godfrey, K. M., & Barker, D. J. (2001). Fetal programming and adult health. *Public Health Nutrition, 4*(2B), 611–624.

Godfrey, K. M., Gluckman, P. D., & Hanson, M. A. (2010). Developmental origins of metabolic disease: Life course and intergenerational perspectives. *Trends in Endocrinology & Metabolism, 21*(4), 199–205.

Gu, Q., Paulose-Ram, R., Yoon, S., Burt, V., & Gillum, R. F. (2006). Hypertension and risk of cardiovascular disease mortality among the US adults. *Circulation, 114*(18), 897–897.

Guh, D. P., Zhang, W., Bansback, N., Amarsi, Z., Birmingham, C. L., & Anis, A. H. (2009). The incidence of co-morbidities related to obesity and overweight: A systematic review and meta-analysis. *BioMed Central (BMC) Public Health, 9*, 88.

Heslehurst, N., Rankin, J., Wilkinson, J. R., & Summerbell, C. D. (2010). A nationally representative study of maternal obesity in England, UK: Trends in incidence and demographic inequalities in 619 323 births, 1989–2007. *International Journal of Obesity, 34*(3), 420–428.

Hulens, M., Beunen, G., Claessens, A. L., Lefevre, J., Thomis, M., Philippaerts, R., . . . Vansant, G. (2001). Trends in BMI among Belgian children, adolescents and adults from 1969 to 1996. *International Journal of Obesity and Related Metabolic Disorders, 25*(3), 395–399.

Janssen, I., Shields, M., Craig, C. L., & Tremblay, M. S. (2011). Prevalence and secular changes in abdominal obesity in Canadian adolescents and adults, 1981 to 2007–2009. *Obesity Reviews, 12*(6), 397–405.

Jee, S. H., Sull, J. W., Park, J., Lee, S., Ohrr, H., Guallar, E., & Samet, J. M. (2006). Body-mass index and mortality in Korean men and women. *New England Journal of Medicine, 355*(8), 779–787.

Koch, D. (2011). Waaler revisited: The anthropometrics of mortality. *Economics and Human Biology, 9*(1), 106–117.

Koletzko, B., Brands, B., Poston, L., Godfrey, K., Demmelmair, H., & Early Nutrition Project. (2012). Early nutrition programming of long-term health. *Proceedings of the Nutrition Society, 71*(3), 371–378.

Komlos, J., & Brabec, M. (2010). The trend of mean BMI values of US adults, birth cohorts 1882–1986 indicates that the obesity epidemic began earlier than hitherto thought. *American Journal of Human Biology, 22*(5), 631–638.

Komlos, J., & Brabec, M. (2011). The trend of BMI values of US adults by deciles, birth cohorts 1882–1986 stratified by gender and ethnicity. *Economics and Human Biology, 9*(3), 234–250.

Komlos, J., Breitfelder, A., & Sunder, M. (2009). The transition to post-industrial BMI values among US children. *American Journal of Human Biology, 21*(2), 151–160.

Koziel, S. (2003). Obesity and the clustering of cardiovascular disease risk factors in 14-year-old children. *International Journal of Anthropology, 18*(3), 153–160.

Kromeyer-Hauschild, K., Glasser, N., & Zellner, K. (2012). Percentile curves for skinfold thickness in 7- to 14-year-old children and adolescents from Jena, Germany. *European Journal of Clinical Nutrition, 66*(5), 613–621.

Kromeyer-Hauschild, K., & Zellner, K. (2007). Trends in overweight and obesity and changes in the distribution of body mass index in schoolchildren of Jena, East Germany. *European Journal of Clinical Nutrition, 61*(3), 404–411.

Kuczmarski, R. J., Flegal, K. M., Campbell, S. M., & Johnson, C. L. (1994). Increasing prevalence of overweight among US adults. The National Health and Nutrition Examination Surveys, 1960 to 1991. *Journal of the American Medical Association, 272*(3), 205–211.

Kumanyika, S. K. (2008). Environmental influences on childhood obesity: Ethnic and cultural influences in context. *Physiology and Behavior, 94*(1), 61–70.

Lewis, C. E., McTigue, K. M., Burke, L. E., Poirier, P., Eckel, R. H., Howard, B. V., . . . Sunyer, P. (2009). Mortality, health outcomes, and body mass index in the overweight range: A science advisory from the American Heart Association. *Circulation, 119*(25), 3263–3271.

Li, C., Ford, E. S., McGuire, L. C., & Mokdad, A. H. (2007). Increasing trends in waist circumference and abdominal obesity among US adults. *Obesity (Silver Spring), 15*(1), 216–224.

Lim, S. S., Vos, T., Flaxman, A. D., Danaei, G., Shibuya, K., Adair-Rohani, H., . . . Memish, Z. A. (2012). A Comparative Risk Assessment of Burden of Disease and Injury Attributable to 67 Risk Factors and Risk Factor Clusters in 21 Regions, 1990-2010: A Systematic Analysis for the Global Burden of Disease Study 2010. *Lancet 380*(9859), 2224–2260.

McCarthy, H. D. (2006). Body fat measurements in children as predictors for the metabolic syndrome: Focus on waist circumference. *Proceedings of the Nutrition Society, 65*(4), 385–392.

McKeigue, P. M., Shah, B., & Marmot, M. G. (1991). Relation of central obesity and insulin resistance with high diabetes prevalence and cardiovascular risk in South Asians. *Lancet, 337*(8738), 382–386.

Monteiro, C. A., Moura, E. C., Conde, W. L., & Popkin, B. M. (2004). Socioeconomic status and obesity in adult populations of developing countries: A review. *Bulletin of the World Health Organization, 82*(12), 940–946.

Murray, C. J., & Lopez, A. D. (2013). Measuring the global burden of disease. *New England Journal of Medicine, 369*(5), 448–457.

Nagel, G., Wabitsch, M., Galm, C., Berg, S., Brandstetter, S., Fritz, M., Klenk, J., . . . Steinacker, J. (2009). Secular changes of anthropometric measures for the past 30 years in South-West Germany. *European Journal of Clinical Nutrition, 63*(12), 1440–1443.

Ng, M., Fleming, T., Robinson, M., Thomson, B., Graetz, N., Margono, C., . . . Gakidou, E. (2014). Global, regional, and national prevalence of overweight and obesity in children and adults during 1980–2013: A systematic analysis for the Global Burden of Disease Study 2013. *Lancet, 384*(9945), 766–781.

Olds, T. S. (2009). One million skinfolds: Secular trends in the fatness of young people 1951–2004. *European Journal of Clinical Nutrition, 63*(8), 934–946.

Ong, K. K., & Dunger, D. B. (2004). Birth weight, infant growth and insulin resistance. *European Journal of Endocrinology, 151*(Suppl. 3), U131–U139.

Osmani, S., & Sen, A. (2003). The hidden penalties of gender inequality: Fetal origins of ill-health. *Economics and Human Biology, 1*(1), 105–121.

Plagemann, A. (2008). A matter of insulin: Developmental programming of body weight regulation. *Journal of Maternal-Fetal and Neonatal Medicine, 21*(3), 143–148.

Popkin, B. M., Adair, L. S., & Ng, S. W. (2012). Global nutrition transition and the pandemic of obesity in developing countries. *Nutrition Reviews, 70*(1), 3–21.

Prospective Studies Collaboration, Whitlock, G., Lewington, S., Sherliker, P., Clarke, R., Emberson, J., . . . Peto, R. (2009). Body-mass index and cause-specific mortality in 900,000 adults: Collaborative analyses of 57 prospective studies. *Lancet, 373*(9669), 1083–1096.

Razak, F., Corsi, D. J., & Subramanian, S. V. (2013). Change in the body mass index distribution for women: Analysis of surveys from 37 low- and middle-income countries. *PLoS Medicine, 10*(1), E1001367.

Renehan, A. G., Tyson, M., Egger, M., Heller, R. F., & Zwahlen, M. (2008). Body-mass index and incidence of cancer: A systematic review and meta-analysis of prospective observational studies. *Lancet, 371*(9612), 569–578.

Rogvi, R. A., Forman, J. L., Damm, P., & Greisen, G. (2012). Women born preterm or with inappropriate weight for gestational age are at risk of subsequent gestational diabetes and preeclampsia. *PLoS ONE, 7*(3), E34001.

Sarr, O., Yang, K., & Regnault, T. R. (2012). In utero programming of later adiposity: The role of fetal growth restriction. *Journal of Pregnancy.* doi: 10.1155/2012/134758

Serdula, M. K., Ivery, D., Coates, R. J., Freedman, D. S., Williamson, D. F., & Byers, T. (1993). Do obese children become obese adults? A review of the literature. *Preventive Medicine, 22*(2), 167–177.

Shetty, P. 2013. Nutrition transition and its health outcomes. *Indian Journal of Pediatrics, 80*(Suppl. 1), 21–27.

Skelton, J. A., Cook, S. R., Auinger, P., Klein, J. D., & Barlow, S. E. (2009). Prevalence and trends of severe obesity among US children and adolescents. *Academic Pediatrics, 9*(5), 322–329.

Sobal, J., & Stunkard, A. J. (1989). Socioeconomic status and obesity: A review of the literature. *Psychological Bulletin, 105*(2), 260–275.

Surkan, P. J., Hsieh, C. C., Johansson, A. L., Dickman, P. W., & Cnattingius, S. (2004). Reasons for increasing trends in large for gestational age births. *Obstetrics and Gynecology, 104*(4), 720–726.

Swinburn, B., Egger, G., & Raza, F. (1999). Dissecting obesogenic environments: The development and application of a framework for identifying and prioritizing environmental interventions for obesity. *Preventive Medicine, 29*(6 Pt. 1), 563–570.

Taylor, P. D., & Poston, L. (2007). Developmental programming of obesity in mammals. *Experimental Physiology, 92*(2), 287–298.

Troiano, R. P., & Flegal, K. M. (1998). Overweight children and adolescents: Description, epidemiology, and demographics. *Pediatrics, 101*(3 Pt. 2), 497–504.

Tsoi, E., Shaikh, H., Robinson, S., & Teoh, T. G. (2010). Obesity in pregnancy: A major healthcare issue. *Postgraduate Medical Journal, 86*(1020), 617–623.

United Nations Children's Fund, World Health Organization, & The World Bank. (2012). *UNICEF-WHO-World Bank joint child malnutrition estimates.* New York/Geneva/Washington, DC: Authors.

Visscher, T. L., & Seidell, J. C. (2001). The public health impact of obesity. *Annual Review of Public Health, 22*: 355–375.

Wabitsch, M., Moss, A., & Kromeyer-Hauschild, K. (2014). Unexpected plateauing of childhood obesity rates in developed countries. *BioMed Central (BMC) Medicine, 12*: 17.

Wadden, T. A., Butryn, M. L., Sarwer, D. B., Fabricatore, A. N., Crerand, C. E., Lipschutz, P. E., . . . Williams, N. N. (2006). Comparison of psychosocial status in treatment-seeking women with Class III vs. Class I-II obesity. *Surgery for Obesity and Related Diseases, 2*(2), 138–145.

Wang, J., Thornton, J. C., Russell, M., Burastero, S., Heymsfield, S., & Pierson, R. N., Jr. (1994). Asians have lower body mass index (BMI) but higher percent body fat than do whites: Comparisons of anthropometric measurements. *American Journal of Clinical Nutrition, 60*(1), 23–28.

Wang, Y., Rimm, E. B., Stampfer, M. J., Willett, W. C., & Hu, F. B. (2005). Comparison of abdominal adiposity and overall obesity in predicting risk of Type 2 diabetes among men. *American Journal of Clinical Nutrition, 81*(3), 555–563.

Wang, Y. C., Gortmaker, S. L., & Taveras, E. M. (2011). Trends and racial/ethnic disparities in severe obesity among US children and adolescents, 1976–2006. *International Journal of Pediatric Obesity, 6*(1), 12–20.

WHO Multicentre Growth Reference Study Group. (2006). WHO child growth standards based on length/height, weight and age. *Acta Paediatrica, 95*(Suppl. 450), 76–85.

World Health Organization. (1995). *Physical status: The use and interpretation of anthropometry* (WHO Technical Report Series No. 854). Geneva: Author.

World Health Organization. (2000). *Obesity: Preventing and managing the global epidemic* (WHO Technical Report Series No. 894. Geneva: Author.

World Health Organization. (2009). *Global health risks: Mortality and burden of disease attributable to selected major risks.* Geneva: Author.

Xi, B., Mi, J., Zhao, M., Zhang, T., Jia, C., Li, J., . . . Public Health Youth Collaborative and Innovative Study Group of Shandong University. (2014). Trends in abdominal obesity among U.S. children and adolescents. *Pediatrics, 134*(2), E334–E339.

CHAPTER 16

POVERTY AND OBESITY IN DEVELOPED COUNTRIES

CHAD D. MEYERHOEFER AND MUZHE YANG

16.1 Introduction

RATES of overweight and obesity have risen steadily in the past several decades across all regions of the globe. Estimates of overweight and obesity prevalence based on data from 183 countries collected between 1980 and 2013 indicate that the proportion of adults with a body mass index (BMI) of 25 kg/m^2 or higher has grown from 28.8% to 36.9% in men and from 29.8% to 38.0% in women. These prevalence rates are highest in developed countries, with initial levels in excess of 40% among women and nearly 50% among men that rise approximately 10 percentage points over the intervening three decades. Likewise, rates of overweight and obesity in children and adolescents are highest in developed countries, climbing from 16.9% to 23.8% in boys and from 16.2% to 22.6% in girls (Ng et al., 2014).

The worldwide growth of obesity has contributed significantly to the global burden of chronic disease, with obesity becoming one of the leading causes of premature death and disability (Field et al., 2001; Lim et al., 2012). Due to evolving preferences for thinness in modern societies, individuals perceived as overweight or obese also face social stigma, marginalization, and outright discrimination (Sobal, 1991). As evidence of the negative consequences of obesity grows, so do concerns that the poor are disproportionately affected. In the first comprehensive review of the relationship between socioeconomic status (SES) and obesity, Sobal and Stunkard (1989) find a strong inverse association among women in developed societies but inconsistent relationships among men and children. Interestingly, a consistent direct relationship is found among all ages and both genders in developing societies, thus suggesting that the mechanisms that moderate the relationship between SES and obesity are context-specific. These relationships persist in a recent update of Sobal and Stunkard's (1989) initial review conducted by McLaren (2007), although she finds the reversal of the association between low SES and obesity among women to be somewhat less pronounced across the development gradient, possibly due to globalization.

Although these reviews contain a paucity of studies that provide evidence of a causal relationship between poverty and obesity, they clearly indicate the potential for causation in both directions. Not only is it likely that obesity restricts the ability of individuals to raise their SES, but the economic and social conditions that characterize low SES may cause obesity. We seek to identify the mechanisms generating bidirectional causation between obesity and poverty in developed societies. There have been some recent advancements in causal inference, but the majority of studies identify associations. This is not particularly surprising given the difficulty of generating random variation in either body weight or poverty status. Nonetheless, we focus our review on studies that make use of longitudinal surveys and quasi-experimental research designs to mitigate the influence of confounding factors in observational data.

Despite the fact that low SES and poverty are not the same, we treat them interchangeably in our review. SES is a multidimensional rank, generated largely by income, educational attainment, and occupation, whereas poverty status in developed countries is typically determined by relative family income adjusted for household size. Nonetheless, the majority of the literature on this topic references SES, even when income is the sole factor used to identify low-SES individuals, and we follow this convention.

16.2 The Effect of Obesity on Poverty

16.2.1 Obesity and Labor Market Earnings

First, we consider how obesity can limit earning potential or access to financial resources and increase the likelihood that an individual lives below the poverty line. McLean and Moon (1980) describe three labor market mechanisms that could lower the wages of workers with obesity. First, employers may simply have a distaste for workers with obesity (i.e., *cosmetic discrimination*). This would be the case if, for example, employers believe obese workers are perceived negatively by customers or other employees. Second, employers may view obesity as a proxy for low productivity or higher operational costs that are otherwise difficult to quantify, and they may only be willing to hire obese workers at a reduced wage rate (i.e., *statistical discrimination*). Third, employers may provide fewer opportunities for on-the-job training to workers with obesity, resulting in depressed wages over time (i.e., *job promotion discrimination*).

Irrespective of the mechanism, identifying the impact of obesity on wages is challenging because of unobservable characteristics of workers that are correlated with both variables. In particular, research in behavioral genetics indicates that approximately

45–75% of the variation in body weight is due to genetic factors, while the rest is due to individual choices and environment (Comuzzie & Allison, 1998; Farooqi & O'Rahilly, 2007; Pietiläinen, 2014). Neither genes nor environmental attributes are fully observed in survey data, so researchers have used various methods to remove or control for their influence. Early work in this area exploited the fact that siblings share approximately half of their genes and that monozygotic twins share all of their genes to either partially or fully difference away genetic influences using datasets containing wage and BMI information on siblings (Averett & Korenman, 1996; Behrman & Rosenzweig, 2004). Limitations of this approach include small sample sizes that limit statistical power and the inability to account for individual choices and environment.

Baum II and Ford (2004), Cawley (2004), and Han, Norton, and Stearns (2009) all make use of the US National Longitudinal Survey of Youth (NLSY) to estimate individual fixed-effects models that control for the influence of both genetics and time invariant aspects of individual environment in the wage equation. All three studies find that obesity reduces wages for women from 2.3% for all women combined (Baum II & Ford, 2004) to 8.7% for just white women (Cawley, 2004). Han, Norton, and Stearns (2009) also find a reduction in the wages of 4.9% for black women with obesity. The variation in point estimates across the studies is likely due to the fact that Cawley (2004) uses correction equations to account for measurement error in self-reported BMI, whereas the other two studies use uncorrected BMI values. Neither study finds an economically important effect of obesity on the wages of men.[1]

Cawley (2004) additionally uses sibling BMI as an instrumental variable (IV) to identify the effect of the BMI of the focal individual on wages under the more general situation where unobservable environmental influences are time varying. Conceptual validity of the instrument is based on the consistent finding in adoption and other behavioral genetic studies that there is no detectible effect of shared household environment on weight (Grilo & Pogue-Geile, 1991; Wardle, Carnell, Haworth, & Plomin, 2008). In this IV model, the effect of obesity on wages is only statistically significant in the sample of white women, and it indicates that an increase in BMI of 2 standard deviations lowers wages by 9%. Sabia and Rees (2012) apply Cawley's (2004) identification strategy to data from the third wave of the US National Longitudinal Study of Adolescent Health and likewise find that increases in BMI only lower the wages of white women.

Brunello and D'Hombres (2007) also use the average BMI of the focal individual's biological relatives to identify the effect of BMI on wages using data from the European Community Household Panel Survey. They find that increases in BMI reduce the wages of women in southern European countries (Spain, Greece, Italy, and Portugal) by the same magnitude as Cawley (2004) finds for white women in the United States but fail to identify a causal relationship between BMI and wages in northern Europe (Austria, Belgium, Denmark, Finland, and Ireland). In contrast to Cawley (2004), they find a slightly larger impact of BMI on the wages of men than women, but again, only in southern Europe. Using a sample drawn from the same dataset that disproportionately includes households from southern Europe, Atella, Pace, and Vuri (2008) find that, using IV quantile regression, the wage penalty associated with obesity is concentrated in the highest quartile of the wage distribution. Overall, economic studies on the relationship between wages and obesity from Europe and the United States provide evidence that is consistent with the aforementioned inverse relationship between SES and female obesity and the lack of a clear relationship among men.

Because the estimating equations used to identify the causal link between obesity and wages are reduced form, further analysis is required to infer the specific channels through which the effect operates (i.e., potential mediators) and which groups of obese workers face the strongest discrimination (i.e., potential moderators). Brunello and D'Hombres (2007), and Han, Norton, and Stearns (2009) both find evidence that the wages of obese workers are reduced because of cosmetic discrimination by including interactions in their models to moderate the effect of obesity. The moderator used in the former study is an indicator for whether the individual lives in a region where the gender-specific obesity rate is above the national average. They interpret the negative sign on the BMI-region interaction in the wage equation for men as evidence of reduced stigma in regions where a higher percentage of men are obese. The latter study finds that wage reductions are concentrated among white and black women with obesity who work in occupations requiring more interpersonal skills and social interactions with customers. This is also consistent with cosmetic discrimination based on employers' assumption that consumers will react negatively to employees who are obese. Using data from Denmark, Greve (2008) finds that obesity lowers the wages of private-sector employees, but not those employed in the public sector. This result may reflect an enhanced ability of private firms to practice cosmetic discrimination relative to governments due to greater managerial discretion over wage levels in the private sector.

Han, Norton, and Powell (2011) use the NLSY to investigate the role of education and occupation as moderators in the relationship between body weight and wages. In models that control for education and occupation, they identify a negative relationship between BMI and wages for women only, which is consistent with cosmetic discrimination. In addition, high body weight is associated with fewer years of schooling and selection into lower paying occupations for both men and women. This indirect wage penalty is concentrated in the upper tail of the BMI distribution and lowers wages by 3.5%, which is almost twice as large as the direct BMI wage penalty among women. Although the overall wage penalty for women is moderated mostly by education and selection into lower paying occupations as a result of lower education, the wage penalty for men is moderated mostly by occupational choice.

Evidence of statistical discrimination is provided by Bhattacharya and Bundorf (2009), who find that firms offering employer-sponsored coverage pass the incremental medical care costs of obesity back to obese workers through lower cash wages. This wage offset is not observed in firms that do not offer health insurance to their employees. Brunello and D'Hombres (2007) find that the interaction of BMI with an indicator for higher regional obesity rates is positive in their wage equation for women. Rather than interpreting this as a reflection of stigma, they reason that the higher labor supply of women with obesity may reduce wages if there is sorting into occupations by weight status. Such sorting is consistent with statistical discrimination because it implies that employers do not view obese and nonobese workers as perfect substitutes.

Finally, evidence of discrimination in job promotion is provided by Baum II and Ford (2004), who include an interaction term of obesity with a measure of experience to determine that obese workers have flatter earning profiles over time, even though obese workers with little experience do not suffer a wage penalty relative to nonobese workers.[2] The exclusion of obese workers from training opportunities and lower rates of promotion could explain their flat earning profiles. However, the authors point out that obese workers may invest less in training if they are economically myopic, in which case their flatter earning profiles are due to variation in time preferences rather than discrimination. Although they are unable to distinguish between these explanations, research by Komlos, Smith, and Bogin (2004) support the hypothesis of higher rates of time preference among individuals with obesity.

One limitation of most studies on the relationship between labor market earnings and obesity is their reliance on BMI as a measure of fatness. Because BMI does not distinguish between weight associated with muscle mass and weight associated with body fat, it has the potential to misclassify individuals with a healthy body composition as overweight or obese. The few studies that investigate the sensitivity of the obesity–wage relationship to different measures of fatness do find that the estimated impacts of BMI and body fat mass (or its complement, fat-free mass) on wages differ, but the effects are qualitatively similar (Bozoyan & Wolbring, 2011; Johansson, Böckerman, Kiiskinen, & Heliövaara, 2009; Wada & Tekin, 2010). Interestingly, Johansson et al. (2009) identify some cases where BMI is not statistically significant, but measures of waist circumference and fat mass are significantly and negatively associated with labor market success. Clearly, if wage differentials are the results of discrimination as opposed to inherent productivity differences, fatness must be observable to employers, and measures such as waist circumference, rather than BMI, are likely to be more strongly associated with employers' ability to observe high body weight.

16.2.2 Obesity and Employment, Education, and Marriage

Although the literature on obesity and wage discrimination provides consistent evidence of one mechanism through which individuals with obesity—and women in particular—are more likely to be in poverty, there are other potential pathways. If the opportunity cost of employment in terms of home production is the same for individuals with and without obesity, lower earning potential for the former will result in fewer individuals seeking employment. It is also possible that employers will practice discrimination in hiring by favoring nonobese applicants. If wage offers are constrained due to standardization within a firm or because of employment rules, this behavior is consistent with either cosmetic or statistical discrimination, but it would be due to the former if the employer has the ability to adjust the wage offer to match expected productivity.

Using a standard logit model, Han, Norton, and Stearns (2009) find that obesity is negatively associated with the likelihood of employment in the United States for white and Hispanic women, but positively associated with the likelihood of employment among black men (a group with no obesity-related wage penalty). For younger individuals in the United States, Norton and Han (2008) find no association between BMI and employment. Based on data from the United Kingdom, Morris (2006) likewise finds a positive association between BMI and occupational attainment (i.e., average occupational earnings) for men, but a negative association between BMI and occupational attainment for women. In a similar study using the same data, he identifies a negative association between obesity and the likelihood of employment for men, but an imprecisely estimated effect for women (Morris, 2007). By analyzing retrospective data on unemployment collected in the 2003 French Decennial Health Survey, Paraponaris, Saliba, and Ventelou (2005) find that the percentage of time spent unemployed is higher, and the probability of regaining employment is lower, as BMI deviates from the mean level attained at age 20. Providing more direct evidence of discrimination in hiring, Caliendo and Lee (2013) find that obese women, but not obese men, are less likely to regain employment in Germany despite participating in more job training programs and applying to more jobs.

These models, which fail to account for endogeneity, produce somewhat mixed results for men but suggest that there is a weak negative association between obesity and employment for women. To address the endogeneity problem, Morris uses either obesity prevalence in the individual's geographic area of residence, or this variable and the mean BMI in the residence area, as instruments for individual obesity conditional on other area-level factors. The ordinary least squares (OLS) results on the impact of obesity on occupational attainment become imprecisely estimated after instrumenting in his 2006 study (Morris, 2006), but Morris continues to find that obesity reduces the likelihood of employment among men when using IV methods in his 2007 study. Moreover, the IV estimate for women is large, negative, and precisely estimated (Morris, 2007). Overall, obesity lowers the probability of employment by 11% among men and 34% among women relative to the mean level of employment in the gender-specific obese group.

Norton and Han (2008) also use IV methods to estimate the effect of BMI on employment among young adults in the United States. Their instruments are genes related to the neurotransmitters dopamine and serotonin, which affect mood and concentration, how people perceive pleasure and rewards, and behavioral traits like impulsivity and addiction. Norton and Han (2008) cite evidence from the genetics literature linking these genes, through their influence on dopamine and serotonin levels, to food regulation and obesity (see, e.g., Guo, North, & Choi, 2006). The instruments meet conventional standards for statistical power only on the sample of women, but their IV estimates are imprecise for both genders. Although this finding differs substantially from Morris (2007), comparability is made difficult owing to the differences in location (United Kingdom vs. United States) and age (all adults vs. young adults). Nonetheless, Lindeboom, Lundborg, and van der Klaauw (2010) fail to find a statistically significant impact of obesity on the probability of employment at ages 33 and 42 in the United Kingdom, using instruments similar to those proposed by Cawley (2004).

Over time, the proportion of adults with obesity who became obese during childhood or adolescence has grown (Ogden, Carroll, Kit, & Flegal, 2012) and so, too, has the potential for obesity to impact lifetime wealth and SES starting at an earlier age. As demonstrated by Han, Norton, and Powell (2011), poor labor market outcomes among individuals with obesity may be moderated by low educational attainment.

Whereas studies on the impact of obesity on labor market outcomes control for educational attainment, the quality of educational investments generally is not fully observable to researchers, and lower educational quality among obese individuals could lead to sorting into lower paying jobs within broader categories of employment. Educational attainment or quality could be limited if obese children have less physical energy and, as a result, have more limited ability to concentrate; are more likely to miss school; are treated differently by teachers, parents, and peers (Fletcher and Lehrer, 2011); or have higher rates of time preference, thus limiting their willingness to invest in higher education (Komlos et al., 2004).

Because BMI is likely endogenous in an education production function due to unobserved genetic and environmental influences, researchers have made use of IVs to identify causal effects of childhood obesity on educational attainment. Using the same dataset as Norton and Han (2008) to investigate labor supply, Ding et al. (Ding, Lehrer, Rosenquist, & Audrain-McGovern, 2009) and Fletcher and Lehrer (2009, 2011) use genes related to the neurotransmitters dopamine and serotonin as IVs for obesity, in some specifications in conjunction with sibling fixed effects. Estimates of the impact of obesity on grade point average (GPA) found by Ding et al. (2009) are large and statistically significant for high school girls, but are small and imprecisely estimated for high school boys. Obesity reduces girls' GPA by approximately 16%, or half a letter grade, relative to the overall mean. Fletcher and Lehrer pool girls and boys into one group and focus on years of schooling in their 2009 study and performance on a standardized verbal test in their 2011 study. In both cases, they find a negative association between overweight and obesity and educational outcomes in OLS models, but the estimates from the family fixed-effect and genetic IV models are imprecise. Despite the popularity of identification strategies based on genetic traits, there is some disagreement in the field over whether using genes related to dopamine and serotonin regulation as IVs is appropriate. Cawley, Han, and Norton (2011) argue that such instruments violate the exclusion restriction because they impact a large number of illnesses and behaviors that likely have a direct impact on educational attainment.

Given that labor force participation rates for women have historically been lower than for men, the earning potential of husbands is an important determinant of SES for married women. This means that outcomes in the marriage market could serve as another channel through which obesity could lead to poverty in women. In particular, research suggests that women with obesity tend to marry men of lower SES (i.e., "marry down") (Lipowicz, 2003; Sobal & Stunkard, 1989). This is consistent with the selection of thinner women into marriage because they make better marriage partners (Becker, 1981) and the subsequent weight gain of married men and women identified in empirical studies (Averett, Sikora, & Argys, 2008; Sobal, Rauschenbach, & Frongillo, 2003). If obesity is in fact penalized in the marriage market, women with obesity will have lower lifetime family wealth.

Overall, the findings from empirical studies support an association between poverty and obesity in women. There is evidence for several underlying mechanisms, including depressed wages, lower likelihood of employment through different types of discrimination and lower rates of job training, lower educational attainment, and lower family income through marriage. Although some of these disadvantages are experienced by men with obesity, the evidence is much less consistent. A normative evaluation of the various causal pathways from obesity to low SES in women supports the characterization of the observed relationship as one manifestation of gender discrimination.

16.3 The Effect of Poverty on Obesity

16.3.1 Income Shocks, Variation in SES, and Obesity

We now consider how poverty, or low SES, may lead to weight gain and cause obesity. As with studies that investigate the impact of obesity on earnings, the econometric models used to estimate this relationship are reduced form rather than structural. We first review the identification strategies and results of these models, and then we draw on other analyses to infer the underlying mechanisms responsible for the reduced-form estimates. Identification of the causal effect of poverty on obesity requires the random assignment of poverty in order to generate exogenous variation in poverty status. In reality, such random assignment may occur for a particular population at a specific time: for example, individuals could be forced into poverty because of an unexpected catastrophic event, such as a natural disaster. We are not aware of any existing study that uses such a strategy to infer causality between poverty and obesity, but both Simeonova (2011) and Currie and Rossin-Slater (2013) identify the impact of exposure to natural disasters (such as hurricanes) during pregnancy on adverse birth outcomes. Nevertheless, studies by Akee et al. (Akee, Simeonova, Copeland, Angold, & Costello, 2013) and Cawley, Moran, and Simon (2010) present compelling evidence of exogenous changes in transfer income that can be used to estimate the causal effect of income on the obesity status of young adults in poverty and weight gain by the elderly, respectively.

Akee et al. (2013) focus on Native American Indian households in North Carolina, specifically, the children from the Eastern Band of Cherokee Indians. They use data from the longitudinal Great Smoky Mountains Study of Youth, which encompasses the time period prior to and after the opening of a casino at the Eastern Cherokee reservation. The casino is operated by the tribal government, which transfers a portion of the casino profits back to adult tribal members on an annual basis. Two important aspects of the transfer are its size (equal to 20–40% of the annual household income of recipients) and the fact that it is made equally, on a per capita basis, to all adult tribal members regardless of their income levels. This distinguishes it from other types of government assistance programs that rely on voluntary participation, resulting in nonrandom payment receipt.

Akee et al. (2013) use a difference-in-differences method combined with individual fixed effects to compare the changes in BMI and obesity of Native American Indians to non-Indians from the pre-casino period (during childhood) to the post-casino period (during young adulthood). Although the tribal members have no control over the transfer, the difference-in-differences model is necessary in order to account for changes in other macroeconomic factors during the study period that could impact both household income and BMI. They find that receiving the casino disbursement increased the probability of obesity by about 8 percentage points. Moreover, the effect of the transfer is nonlinear, with children from poorer American Indian households gaining more weight. Thus, raising the income of poor households, even by a moderate amount, does not reduce obesity in the short run. This highlights the importance of other characteristics and behaviors of poor households in driving the relationship between poverty and obesity. Another possibility is that income gains take many years, and possibly even a generation, to change some of the underlying factors causing obesity in initially poor households.

Cawley, Moran, and Simon (2010) also utilize a unique social transfer—the US Social Security Benefits Notch—to exploit exogenous variation in social security income received by the elderly. The Social Security Benefits Notch was caused by a legislative error in 1972, when the Congress erroneously invoked double indexation of workers' credited earnings. Although the double indexation was subsequently eliminated in 1977, retirees born prior to 1917 were not affected by this elimination under a grandfather clause. Because of the high inflation that occurred soon after 1972, the retirees born between 1915 and 1917 received significantly higher social security benefits (due to the double indexation). Cawley, Moran, and Simon (2010) define these workers as the treatment group and two adjacent birth cohorts (1901–14 and 1918–30) as the control group.[3] The difference in social security benefits between these two groups is plausibly exogenous after conditioning on age and other explanatory variables.

Using the National Health Interview Survey, Cawley, Moran, and Simon (2010) estimate the effect of income on BMI using the Notch status (equal to one for the treatment group and equal to zero for the control group) as an IV for income. The first-stage results demonstrate that the treatment group received much higher social security benefits than the control group, in the amount of $1,122 for men and $695 for women, on average (in 2006 dollars). However, the IV estimates of the effect of income on body weight are not precisely estimated. Based on the range of values included in the confidence interval around the point estimates, they conclude that the magnitude of the income elasticity of BMI is at most 0.06 for men and 0.14 for women.

The Social Security Benefits Notch provides a rare opportunity to exploit a natural experiment resulting from an administrative error, but this identification strategy is complicated by the fact that the Notch allowed the retirees in the treatment group to receive the extra social security benefit payments for the rest of their lives. As a result, the effect of income on BMI estimated in this study could be a composite effect of individuals' responses to both a contemporaneous increase in income and the expectation of a stream of higher income payments.

One group of studies that attempts to identify the impact of SES on obesity in a more general way, rather than the impact of additional income, makes use of data on adopted children and their rearing parents. These studies have three advantages. First, parents' SES can be considered predetermined relative to the children's obesity status, thus eliminating the potential for reverse causality in a model measuring the impact of parental SES on child obesity. Second, adoptees do not choose their rearing parents, so adoptees' SES (represented by the SES of their adoptive parents) is effectively randomly assigned in the post-adoption period. Third, in nonfamilial adoption cases, rearing parents are genetically unrelated to the adoptees, which provides the opportunity to disentangle the impact of rearing parents' SES on obesity from the genetic influence of biological parents.

Fontaine et al. (2011) use data from two adoption studies and provide compelling evidence on the effect of SES on BMI. Despite the fact that these datasets differ in time periods, countries, and ethnicities, they produce remarkably similar results. The first dataset is the Copenhagen Adoption Study of Obesity (CASO), which includes nonfamilial adoptions that occurred in Copenhagen, Denmark, between 1924 and 1947. Data on the height and weight of adoptees were collected around 1980. The second dataset is the Survey of Holt Adoptees and Their Families (HOLT), which surveyed in 2004–06 those parents who adopted Korean-American children between 1970 and 1980, as well as their offspring.

There are important differences in the survey designs of CASO and HOLT. CASO focuses on adopted offspring but also surveys their adoptive parents and biological parents, whereas HOLT focuses on rearing parents but also surveys their adopted children and biological children (if any). These differences offer a rare opportunity to disentangle the effect of rearing parents' SES on their children's body weight from the effect of genetic factors. The nonfamilial adoption data from CASO allow Fontaine et al. (2011) to use the correlation between rearing parents' SES and their adoptees' BMI to suggest the presence of a causal effect of SES on body weight. In the absence of other factors contributing to this correlation, they argue that the same magnitude should be found in the correlation between rearing parents' SES and their biological children. Then, using the HOLT data, they find that the magnitude of the negative correlation between rearing parents' SES and their biological children's BMI is larger than the magnitude of the negative correlation between rearing parents' SES and their adoptees' BMI, which suggests the presence of a genetic influence. They then further use the CASO data to confirm the presence of the genetic influence by finding a statistically significant negative correlation between biological parents' SES and their adopted-away children. Finally, they estimate regressions of child BMI on parental SES controlling for the BMI of rearing parents (both biological and adoptive), and they find that the SES coefficients estimated using the CASO (HOLT) data, although still significant, are reduced by 44% (47%) for biological parents (biological children) and by 1% (12%) for adoptive parents (adopted children). They conclude that the magnitude of the effect of rearing parents' SES on offspring's BMI may be as large as the genetic effect of BMI.

Rather than using natural adoption experiments to address reverse causality in the relationship between low SES and obesity, some studies make use of longitudinal data collected over long periods of time. Pudrovska, Logan, and Richman (2014) use the Wisconsin Longitudinal Study, which spans the period of 1957–2004. They find that lower SES measured at age 18 is associated with higher body weight at age 65, with the association being stronger for women than for men. Using data from the NLSY, Baum II and Ruhm (2009) find that body weight during young adulthood is negatively associated with SES during childhood, even after controlling for contemporaneous SES. The findings from the United States are consistent with those from European countries such as the United Kingdom and Sweden. Hardy, Wadsworth, and Kuh (2000) use longitudinal data of a British cohort born in 1946 and followed for 43 years through 19 survey waves. They also find that lower SES at age 14 is associated with higher body weight at age 43, and the effect of childhood SES appears to be independent of the effect of adulthood SES. Gustafsson, Persson, and Hammarström (2012) use longitudinal data of a 27-year prospective study from Sweden that tracks a cohort of individuals from age 16 through age 43. They find that lower SES at age 16 is associated with higher body weight for women but not for men.

Several studies also focus on the short- and long-term implications of very low SES during early childhood. Lee et al. (Lee, Andrew, Gebremariam, Lumeng, & Lee, 2014) find that experiencing poverty prior to age 2 is associated with elevated risk of obesity around age 15 for both genders, based on the data from the Study of Early Child Care and Youth Development (1991–2007). Demment, Haas, and Olson (2014), using longitudinal data from a birth cohort in New York state, find that children who grow up in families with persistent low incomes are likely to be overweight during adolescence, but children whose families fall into the low-income category during childhood are likely to become obese during adolescence. Also using data from New York state, Wells et al. (Wells, Evans, Beavis, & Ong, 2010) find that early childhood poverty (birth to 9 years old) is associated with accelerated weight gain from childhood to early adulthood (ages 9–17 years). Furthermore, they find that much of this association can be explained by their constructed "cumulative risk exposure" faced by children during childhood, which includes poor living conditions, family turmoil, separation from parents, and exposure to violence. Wells et al.'s (2010) study highlights the importance of studying the pathways between low SES during childhood and obesity during adulthood. Next, we discuss several potential mediators of the impact of poverty on obesity investigated in the literature.

16.3.2 Mediators between Poverty and Obesity

Three categories of factors have been found in the literature, which could mediate the influence of poverty on obesity: (1) dietary patterns and body weight perceptions, (2) maternal factors, and (3) household environment.

Among research in the first category, several studies find that low-income households consume more energy-dense foods and less healthy foods (such as fruits and vegetables) than do other households. For example, Blisard, Stewart, and Jolliffe (2004) find that among poor households in the United States, weekly expenditures on fruits and vegetables are much lower (by about 28%) than those of higher income households. McLaren (2007) finds the same pattern in other countries, such as Canada, Australia, and several European countries. One hypothesis is that low-income households substitute energy-dense foods for fruits and vegetables in order to meet their calorie requirements because the former are relatively inexpensive.[4]

Nonetheless, there is some debate in the literature over whether healthy foods are affordable to the poor. Drewnowski and Specter (2004) demonstrate that there is a negative correlation between energy density and energy cost, which is consistent with the fact that energy-dense food is typically made from relatively low-cost and affordable ingredients, such as refined grain, fat, and corn sweetener or sugar. However, households do not purchase foods based on their energy density, and it is not clear that the same cost gradient persists under different measures of cost. For example, when Meyerhoefer and Leibtag (2010) calculate the price per ounce of foods stratified by their carbohydrate content, they find that high-carbohydrate foods, which tend to be more energy-dense, are more expensive than medium- or low-carbohydrate foods. Whereas Stewart et al. (Stewart, Hyman, Buzby, Frazão, & Carlson, 2011) estimate that adults on a 2,000 calorie diet can satisfy the 2010 Dietary Guidelines for fruit and vegetable consumption for $2.00–$2.50 per day (in 2008 dollars), Wilde and Llobrera (2009) find that the food budget used to determine food stamp benefits in the United States is not fully consistent with the observed food choices of most low-income Americans.[5]

Economic models provide predictions that are similarly contradictory. Auld and Powell (2009) construct a model that suggests decreases in the price of energy-dense food lead to weight gain, but Schroeter, Lusk, and Tyner (2008) demonstrate using their model that a tax on food away from home, which is generally considered less healthy, could lead to an increase in body weight. Such discrepancies across studies are indicative of the difficulty in identifying the mechanisms underlying food choices, which are driven by not only food costs, but also preferences and social norms.

In addition to research on the consumption behaviors of low-income households, several studies find evidence that lower SES adolescents (Wardle et al., 2004) and adults (Johnston & Lordan, 2014; Wardle & Griffith, 2001) are relatively less aware of their body image. As a result, they exert less effort in attaining slimness. These studies argue that the difference in weight perception between high- and low-SES individuals could be a contributing factor to the SES–obesity gradient.

The second category of research on the mechanisms that drive the poverty–obesity relationship considers maternal attributes that increase the likelihood of obesity among low-income children. Using data from the Longitudinal Study of Australian Children, Khanam, Nghiem, and Connelly (2009) find that mothers' physical and mental health is a key determinant of the child health–income gradient. Drawing on evidence from Sweden, Koupil and Toivanen (2008) find that maternal smoking during pregnancy and mothers' BMI are the main contributors to the overweight and obesity status of their children at age 18. Finally, Costa-Font and Gil (2013) demonstrate that maternal labor market participation is an important mediator for the child obesity–parental SES gradient observed in Spain. Although the specific maternal factors identified by Koupil and Toivanen (2008) and Costa-Font and Gil (2013) are different, possibly due to the differences in countries and populations, both studies find that the body weight of boys and young men is more sensitive to maternal characteristics than is the body weight of girls and young women.

Studies in the third category of mediating factors consider how the environment of poor households, and aspects of the environment related to food access in particular, promotes obesity. A systematic review by Wang and Beydoun (2007) reveals that low-SES households often live in neighborhoods with few, if any, supermarkets or large grocery stores, which limits their access to healthy, low-cost foods. Likewise, Baker et al. (Baker, Schootman, Barnidge, & Kelly, 2006) find two factors—race and income—are strong predictors of the locations of food outlets and their selection of healthy and unhealthy foods: food outlets in wealthy areas carry more fruits; vegetables; and low-fat (or fat-free) meat, poultry, and dairy products than do those in lower income areas (Baker et al., 2006). By implication, poor households may have to travel longer distances than the non-poor to purchase healthy foods. These extra travel costs effectively raise the price of healthy foods, giving poor households economic incentives to substitute less healthy foods that are more likely to result in weight gain. In support of the connection between relatively high costs for certain foods and obesity, Powell and Bao (2009) show that a 10% increase in the price of fruits and vegetables is associated with a 1.4% increase in the BMI of children of low-income families.

16.4 Conclusion

We find a consensus in the literature that obesity contributes to low SES, particularly among women. This effect occurs through labor market discrimination against women in the form of lower wages, as well as through more limited employment opportunities. Lower educational quality and more limited educational attainment by girls with obesity partially mediate these labor market outcomes. It is also possible that some of the discrepancies in outcomes are due to higher discount rates among obese individuals and more limited opportunities for women with obesity in the marriage market.

We also find evidence in the literature, albeit more limited, that poverty causes obesity, but most studies consider the impact of poverty during childhood on child and adult obesity, rather than the impact of persistent poverty throughout the life cycle. In this case, the mechanisms appear more multifaceted and include lower quality diets among low-SES individuals, more limited access to healthy food, and various maternal characteristics, such as maternal health status, smoking, and labor market participation that affect children's body weight.

Although there are some immediate policy recommendations that follow from our review, there is also more work to be done to identify the underlying mechanisms of the poverty–obesity relationship in order to inform future policy. With regard to immediate recommendations, the enforcement of gender discrimination laws by judicial systems and regulatory authorities should target discrimination among women with obesity. In addition, steps should be taken to educate employers about compliance with fair labor standards and to reduce bias and stigma against those with obesity. While there also appears to be a role for anti-poverty policies to reduce the incidence of obesity, more work on the specific mechanisms through which poverty causes obesity is necessary. For example, the findings of Akee et al. (2013) suggest that unconditional cash transfers alone could increase rates of obesity among poor children. It is possible that educational programs related to healthy diets and behaviors or modifications to the living environment are also necessary for anti-poverty policies to be effective in this regard. Our review highlights the need to conduct additional analyses to identify the mechanisms through which poverty causes obesity and to characterize their importance.

Acknowledgment

We thank Jie Peng for her able research assistance.

Notes

1. Baum IIand Ford's (2004) fixed-effects estimator is unconventional in that they only difference the data across two survey waves, but include time period fixed effects. They initially find a statistically significant 0.7% reduction in wages for obese men, but this effect becomes imprecisely estimated when they further difference the data across siblings.
2. Norton and Han (2008) examine the wages of young adults between the ages of 21 and 26. These workers likely have very little, if any, experience, and they also fail to find a wage penalty for obesity among this group.
3. Cawley, Moran, and Simon (2010) use those who benefited most from the Notch (i.e., the portion of retirees who benefited from the Notch and who were born between 1915 and 1917) as the treatment group.
4. For example, Murasko (2009) finds that the negative association between SES and obesity is stronger for household with taller children, thus suggesting that low-income households may substitute more energy-dense food for fruits and vegetables when their children become taller in order to meet the extra calories needed for height growth.
5. Food assistance programs, such as the Supplemental Nutrition Assistance Program, are an important part of the social safety net for the low-income population. There is a large and growing literature on the health impacts of food assistance programs, including numerous studies that investigate the relationship between program participation and obesity. For a detailed summary of this literature and empirical strategies commonly

used for identifying the impact of food assistance program participation on health, see Meyerhoefer and Yang (2011).

References

Akee, R., Simeonova, E., Copeland, W., Angold, W., & Costello, E. J. (2013). Young adult obesity and household income: Effects of unconditional cash transfers. *American Economic Journal: Applied Economics*, 5(2), 1–28.

Atella, V., Pace, N., & Vuri, D. (2008). Are employers discriminating with respect to weight? European evidence using quantile regression. *Economics and Human Biology*, 6(3), 305–329.

Auld, M. C., & Powell, L. M. (2009). Economics of food energy density and adolescent body weight. *Economica*, 76(304), 719–740.

Averett, S., & Korenman, S. (1996). The economic reality of the beauty myth. *Journal of Human Resources*, 31(2), 304–330.

Averett, S. L., Sikora, A., & Argys, L. M. (2008). For better or worse: Relationship status and body mass index. *Economics and Human Biology*, 6(3), 330–349.

Baker, E. A., Schootman, M., Barnidge, E., & Kelly, C. (2006). The role of race and poverty in access to foods that enable individuals to adhere to dietary guidelines. *Preventing Chronic Disease*, 3(3). Retrieved from http://www.cdc.gov/pcd/issues/2006/jul/05_0217.htm

Baum, C. L.,II & Ford, W. F. (2004). The wage effects of obesity: A longitudinal study. *Health Economics*, 13(9), 885–899.

Baum, C. L., II & Ruhm, C. J. (2009). Age, socioeconomic status and obesity growth. *Journal of Health Economics*, 28(3), 635–648.

Becker, G. S. (1981). *A treatise on the family*: Cambridge, MA: Harvard University Press.

Behrman, J. R., & Rosenzweig, M. R. (2004). Returns to birthweight. *Review of Economics and Statistics*, 86(2), 586–601.

Bhattacharya, J., & Bundorf, M. K. (2009). The incidence of the healthcare costs of obesity. *Journal of Health Economics*, 28(3), 649–658.

Blisard, N., Stewart, H., & Jolliffe, D. (2004). *Low-income households' expenditures on fruits and vegetables* (Electronic report May, 2004). Washington, DC: US Department of Agriculture, Economic Research Service.

Bozoyan, C., & Wolbring, T. (2011). Fat, muscles, & wages. *Economics and Human Biology*, 9(4), 356–363.

Brunello, G., & D'Hombres, B. (2007). Does body weight affect Wages? Evidence from Europe. *Economics and Human Biology*, 5(1), 1–19.

Caliendo, M., & Lee, W.-S. (2013). Fat chance! Obesity and the transition from unemployment to employment. *Economics and Human Biology*, 11(2), 121–133.

Cawley, J. (2004). The impact of obesity on wages. *Journal of Human Resources*, 39(2), 451–474.

Cawley, J., Han, E., & Norton, E. C. (2011). The validity of genes related to neurotransmitters as instrumental variables. *Health Economics*, 20(8), 884–888.

Cawley, J., Moran, J., & Simon, K. (2010). The impact of income on the weight of elderly Americans. *Health Economics*, 19(8), 979–993.

Comuzzie, A. G., & Allison, D. B. (1998). The search for human obesity genes. *Science*, 280(5368), 1374–1377.

Costa-Font, J., & Gil, J. (2013). Intergenerational and socioeconomic gradients of child obesity. *Social Science & Medicine*, 93, 29–37.

Currie, J., & Rossin-Slater, M. (2013). Weathering the storm: Hurricanes and birth outcomes. *Journal of Health Economics*, *32*(3), 487–503.

Demment, M. M., Haas, J. D., & Olson, C. M. (2014). Changes in family income status and the development of overweight and obesity from 2 to 15 years: A longitudinal study. *BMC Public Health*, *14*(May), 417.

Ding, W., Lehrer, S. F., Rosenquist, J. N., & Audrain-McGovern, J. (2009). The impact of poor health on academic performance: New evidence using genetic markers. *Journal of Health Economics*, *28*(3), 578–597.

Drewnowski, A., & Specter, S. E. (2004). Poverty and obesity: The role of energy density and energy costs. *American Journal of Clinical Nutrition*, *79*(1), 6–16.

Farooqi, I. S., & S. O'Rahilly. (2007). Genetic factors in human obesity. *Obesity Reviews*, *8*(Suppl. s1), 37–40.

Field, A. E., Coakley, E. H., Must, A., Spadano, J. L., Laird, N., Dietz, W. H., . . . Colditz, G. A. (2001). Impact of overweight on the risk of developing common chronic diseases during a 10-year period. *Archives of Internal Medicine*, *161*(13), 1581–1586.

Fletcher, J. M., & Lehrer, S. F. (2009). The effects of adolescent health on educational outcomes: Causal evidence using genetic lotteries between siblings. *Forum for Health Economics & Policy*, *12*(2). Retrieved December, 2014, from doi:10.2202/1558-9544.1180.

Fletcher, J. M., & Lehrer, S. F. (2011). Genetic lotteries within families. *Journal of Health Economics*, *30*(4), 647–659.

Fontaine, K. R., Robertson, H. T., Holst, C., Desmond, R., Stunkard, A. J., Sørensen, T. I. A., & Allison, D. B. (2011). Is socioeconomic status of the rearing environment causally related to obesity in the offspring? *PLoS One*, *6*(11), E27692.

Greve, J. (2008). Obesity and labor market outcomes in Denmark. *Economics and Human Biology*, *6*(3), 350–362.

Grilo, C. M., & Pogue-Geile, M. F. (1991). The nature of environmental influences on weight and obesity: A behavior genetic analysis. *Psychological Bulletin*, *110*(3), 520–537.

Guo, G., North, K., & Choi, S. (2006). DRD4 gene variant associated with body mass: The National Longitudinal Study of Adolescent Health. *Human Mutation*, *27*(3), 236–241.

Gustafsson, P. E., Persson, M., & Hammarström, A. (2012). Socio-economic disadvantage and body mass over the life course in women and men: Results from the Northern Swedish Cohort. *European Journal of Public Health*, 22(3), 322–327.

Han, E., Norton, E. C., & Powell, L. M. (2011). Direct and indirect effects of body weight on adult wages. *Economics and Human Biology*, 9(4), 381–392.

Han, E., Norton, E. C., & Stearns, S. C. (2009). Weight and wages: Fat versus lean paychecks. *Health Economics*, *18*(5), 535–548.

Hardy, R., Wadsworth, M., & Kuh, D. (2000). The influence of childhood weight and socioeconomic status on change in adult body mass index in a British national birth cohort. *International Journal of Obesity*, *24*(6), 725–734.

Johansson, E., Böckerman, P., Kiiskinen, U., & Heliövaara, M. (2009). Obesity and labour market success in Finland: The difference between having a high BMI and being fat. *Economics and Human Biology*, *7*(1), 36–45.

Johnston, D. W., & Lordan, G. (2014). Weight perceptions, weight control and income: An analysis using British data. *Economics and Human Biology*, *12*, 132–139.

Khanam, R., Nghiem, H. S., & Connelly, L. B. (2009). Child health and the income gradient: Evidence from Australia. *Journal of Health Economics*, *28*(4), 805–817.

Komlos, J., Smith, P. K., & Bogin, B. (2004). Obesity and the rate of time preference: Is there a connection? *Journal of Biosocial Science, 36*(2), 209–219.

Koupil, I., & Toivanen, P. (2008). Social and early-life determinants of overweight and obesity in 18-year-old Swedish men. *International Journal of Obesity, 32*(1), 73–81.

Lee, H., Andrew, M., Gebremariam, A., Lumeng, J. C., & Lee, J. M. (2014). Longitudinal associations between poverty and obesity from birth through adolescence. *American Journal of Public Health, 104*(5), E70–E76.

Lim, S. S., Vos, T., Flaxman, A. D., Danaei, G., Shibuya, K., Adair-Rohani, H., . . . Ezzati, M. (2012). A comparative risk assessment of burden of disease and injury attributable to 67 risk factors and risk factor clusters in 21 regions, 1990–2010: A systematic analysis for the Global Burden of Disease Study (2010). *Lancet, 380*(9859), 2224–2260.

Lindeboom, M., Lundborg, P., & van der Klaauw, B. (2010). Assessing the impact of obesity on labor market outcomes. *Economics and Human Biology, 8*(3), 309–319.

Lipowicz, A. (2003). Effect of husbands' education on fatness of wives. *American Journal of Human Biology, 15*(1), 1–7.

McLaren, L. (2007). Socioeconomic status and obesity. *Epidemiologic Reviews, 29*(1), 29–48.

McLean, R. A., & Moon, M. (1980). Health, obesity, and earnings. *American Journal of Public Health, 70*(9), 1006–1009.

Meyerhoefer, C. D., & Leibtag, C. S. (2010). A spoonful of sugar helps the medicine go down: The relationship between food prices and medical expenditures on diabetes. *American Journal of Agricultural Economics, 92*(5), 1271–1282.

Meyerhoefer, C. D., & Yang, M. (2011). The relationship between food assistance and health: A review of the literature and empirical strategies for identifying program effects. *Applied Economic Perspectives and Policy, 33*(3), 304–344.

Morris, S. (2006). Body mass index and occupational attainment. *Journal of Health Economics, 25*(2), 347–364.

Morris, S. (2007). The impact of obesity on employment. *Labour Economics, 14*(3), 413–433.

Murasko, J. E. (2009). Socioeconomic status, height, and obesity in children. *Economics and Human Biology, 7*(3), 376–386.

Ng, M., Fleming, T., Robinson, M., Thomson, B., Graetz, N., Margono, C., . . . Gakidou, E. (2014). Global, regional, and national prevalence of overweight and obesity in children and adults during 1980–2013: A systematic analysis for the Global Burden of Disease Study 2013. *Lancet, 384*(9945), 766–781.

Norton, E. C., & Han, E. (2008). Genetic information, obesity, and labor market outcomes. *Health Economics, 17*(9), 1089–1104.

Ogden, C. L., Carroll, M. D., Kit, B. K., & Flegal, K. M. (2012). Prevalence of obesity and trends in body mass index among US children and adolescents, 1999–2010. *Journal of the American Medical Association, 307*(5), 483–490.

Paraponaris, A., Saliba, B., & Ventelou, B. (2005). Obesity, weight status and employability: Empirical evidence from a French national survey. *Economics and Human Biology, 3*(2), 241–258.

Pietiläinen, K. H. (2014). Genetics and epigenetics: Myths or facts? In D. W. Haslam, A. M. Sharma, & C. W. le Roux (Eds.), *Controversies in obesity* (pp. 103–108). London, UK: Springer-Verlag.

Powell, L. M., & Bao, Y. (2009). Food prices, access to food outlets and child weight. *Economics and Human Biology, 7*(1), 64–72.

Pudrovska, T., Logan, E. S., & Richman, A. (2014). Early-life social origins of later-life body weight: The role of socioeconomic status and health behaviors over the life course. *Social Science Research, 46*, 59–71.

Sabia, J. J., & Rees, D. I. (2012). Body weight and wages: Evidence from Add Health. *Economics and Human Biology, 10*(1), 14–19.

Schroeter, C., Lusk, J., & Tyner, W. (2008). Determining the impact of food price and income changes on body weight. *Journal of Health Economics, 27*(1), 45–68.

Simeonova, E. (2011). Out of sight, out of mind? Natural disasters and pregnancy outcomes in the USA. *CESifo Economic Studies, 57*(3), 403–431.

Sobal, J. (1991). Obesity and socioeconomic status: A framework for examining relationships between physical and social variables. *Medical Anthropology: Cross-Cultural Studies in Health and Illness, 13*(3), 231–247.

Sobal, J., Rauschenbach, B., & Frongillo, E. A. (2003). Marital status changes and body weight changes: A US longitudinal analysis. *Social Science & Medicine, 56*(7), 1543–1555.

Sobal, J., & Stunkard, A. J. (1989). Socioeconomic status and obesity: A review of the literature. *Psychological Bulletin, 105*(2), 260–275.

Stewart, H., Hyman, J., Buzby, J. C., Frazão, E., & Carlson, A. (2011). *How much do fruits and vegetables cost?* (*USDA* Economic Information Bulletin No. 71). Washington, DC: US Department of Agriculture. Retrieved from http://www.ers.usda.gov/publications/eib-economic-information-bulletin/eib71.aspx

Wada, R., & Tekin, E. (2010). Body composition and wages. *Economics and Human Biology, 8*(2), 242–254.

Wang, Y., & Beydoun, M. A. (2007). The obesity epidemic in the United States—gender, age, socioeconomic, racial/ethnic, and geographic characteristics: A systematic review and meta-regression analysis. *Epidemiologic Reviews, 29*(1), 6–28.

Wardle, J., Carnell, S., Haworth, C. M. A., & Plomin, R. (2008). Evidence for a strong genetic influence on childhood adiposity despite the force of the obesogenic environment. *American Journal of Clinical Nutrition, 87*(2), 398–404.

Wardle, J., & Griffith, J. (2001). Socioeconomic status and weight control practices in British adults. *Journal of Epidemiology and Community Health, 55*(3), 185–190.

Wardle, J., Robb, K. A., Johnson, F., Griffith, J., Brunner, E., Power, C., & Tovée, M. (2004). Socioeconomic variation in attitudes to eating and weight in female adolescents. *Health Psychology, 23*(3), 275–282.

Wells, N. M., Evans, G. W., Beavis, A., & Ong, A. D. (2010). Early childhood poverty, cumulative risk exposure, and body mass index trajectories through young adulthood. *American Journal of Public Health, 100*(12), 2507–2512.

Wilde, P. E., & Llobrera, J. (2009). Using the Thrifty Food Plan to assess the cost of a nutritious diet. *Journal of Consumer Affairs, 43*(2), 274–304.

PART III

BIOLOGICAL MEASURES AS AN INPUT TO MONETARY OUTCOMES, PRODUCTIVITY, AND WELFARE

CHAPTER 17

BIOMARKERS AS INPUTS

STEPHEN F. LEHRER

17.1 Introduction

In this chapter, we follow the US National Institutes of Health Biomarkers Definitions Working Group that, in 1998, defined a biomarker as "a characteristic that is objectively measured and evaluated as an indicator of normal biological processes, pathogenic processes, or pharmacologic responses to a therapeutic intervention." Biomarkers are studied in many scientific fields, and research using data on specific biomarkers to develop tools that either monitor and classify a disease, identify the best treatment, and/or catch early signs of a recurrence receive substantial attention in the popular press. Biomarkers are quite new to the discipline of economics and the social sciences more generally. However, a growing number of datasets now contain various objective measures of genetic, functional, and hormonal biomarkers that researchers are beginning to integrate within their economic analyses.

This chapter presents a selective survey of studies that are primarily within the discipline of economics and that examine how biomarker data influence specific health, social, political, and economic outcomes. Because biomarkers can be classified based on different characteristics, we organize the chapter by first making a distinction between two separate categories of biomarkers: *biological time-varying measures* such as hormones and *biological time-invariant measures* including DNA. This distinction can more intuitively be thought of as the role that the biomarkers fill when entered as an explanatory variable in an estimating equation. What we term "time-varying measures" can be viewed as objective measures for some underlying biological process.[1] Thus, time-varying biomarkers, irrespective of the source by which they are objectively measured, should be viewed as being simply proxies for some underlying process. Although generally they are improvements over other objective measures of a specific biological process, many time-varying biomarker measures contain measurement error.[2]

In contrast, what we term "biological time-invariant measures" are measures that empirical researchers historically treated as a component of individual, specific unobserved heterogeneity that was captured in a fixed effect. Much like the skill development literature in which factor analysis methods are now used to measure cognitive skills (an item previously thought to be a component of innate ability that was captured as permanent unobserved heterogeneity), we can now accurately measure biomarkers in our genetic code (DNA) that capture our heritable predispositions to certain socioeconomic activities and outcomes.

In addition, we discuss an emerging literature that focuses on the interactions between time-varying environmental conditions and time-invariant genetic factors that we believe holds substantial promise for further study and methodological contributions. This chapter concludes by discussing how using biomarker data in empirical studies has informed subsequent research in behavioral genetics and in multiple disciplines including the field of health economics by shedding light on the complex processes through which socioeconomic outcomes emerge. We believe that as more large-scale databases collect and integrate data on biomarkers, researchers will be able to consider richer models to improve our understanding of why specific policy interventions have heterogeneous effects. This knowledge, we argue, may be useful within nascent industries such as personalized medicine and can perhaps shed light on effective directions to target public policy.

17.2 Biological Time-Varying Markers

Time-varying biomarkers, broadly defined, are markers of a contemporaneous biological process or state, and a large list has been shown to be useful in clinical practice. Only a subset of these biomarkers has been investigated in research studies within economics, in the context of providing information about current status or a current biological process. Within this list, biomarkers associated with the endocrine system receive a disproportionate amount of attention because many of these play a role in regulating mood, growth, metabolism, sexual function, and reproductive processes. To affect processes within this system, endocrine glands can release more than 20 major hormones directly into the bloodstream, where they can be transported to certain cells in other parts of the body.

Research in the field of behavioral endocrinology has focused on both levels and changes in specific hormones such as testosterone, cortisol, and cotinine, among others. Many of these hormones regulate behavior by translating differential experiences into variability in gene expression, which in turn affects protein synthesis and changes in physiology and behavior. There is a small but increasing literature studying the relationship between biological time-varying markers such as hormones and economic behavior both in the laboratory and in the field. Generally, studies in the literature use either (1) indirect measures of hormones such as the menstrual cycle, (2) indirect measures of prenatal exposure to hormones like the digit ratio, or (3) direct measurements of hormones in saliva or blood plasma, including experiments with placebo-controlled administration of hormones. In summary, this review suggests that although placebo-controlled studies appear to presently provide the best research design to improve our understanding of the role of some specific time-varying biomarkers, we are still at the early stages and rely crucially on an assumption that exogenously administered hormones act identically within the system to endogenous hormones.

17.2.1 The Menstrual Cycle

There are well-known gender differences in circulating levels of certain hormones, and a number of researchers have turned their attention to variation in hormones such as estradiol, progesterone, and others that change across the menstrual cycle. Initial evidence from Bröder and Hohmann (2003) indicates that this variation is correlated with individual decision making. Specifically, a women's willingness to take financial risk has been found to vary over the menstrual cycle. More convincing evidence using a larger dataset is provided by Ichino and Morretti (2009) who present that these biological differences due to the menstrual cycle may be economically important. Specifically, using data from a large Italian bank, their analysis suggests that menstrual cycles could explain one-third of the gender gap in absenteeism and 14% of the gender gap in wages. However, Herrmann and Rockoff (2012) call these findings into question and demonstrate that the results are not robust to changes in specification.

A highly influential newspaper editorial by Nicholas Kristof published in the *New York Times* on September 4, 2009, postulated that "one of the reasons that girls in Africa and Asia miss school is that they have difficulty managing their menstrual periods."[3] Empirical researchers have now conducted two small-scale randomized studies to test this hypothesis, and they reach somewhat conflicting results. Montgomery et al. (Montgomery, Ryus, Dolan, Dopson, & Scott, 2012) randomly assign female students in Ghana to three groups: a group who received menstrual pads plus puberty education, only puberty education, and controls receiving no intervention. After 3 months, pads plus education was found to improve school attendance by 9%. Pubertal education on its own was also found to improve attendance after 5 months. Oster and Thornton (2011) conducted a randomized trial in Nepal where some randomly chosen students were provided with menstrual cups to see if the availability of these devices increased school attendance. Their impact analysis uncovered no significant effects of access to menstrual cups, and factors such as cultural beliefs, taboos, menstrual cramps, limitations of underwear and water for hygiene, and bullying were suggested to be confounding factors. Taken together, the results from these two randomized evaluations mimic other findings in the health economics literature that demonstrate the importance of health knowledge in using health care services.

Turning to the laboratory setting, Chen et al. (Chen, Katuščak, & Ozdenoren, 2013) and Pearson and Schipper (2013) each find that in independent first-price private value auctions women bid significantly higher than men and earn significantly lower profits than men in many phases of the menstrual cycle.[4] Since understanding gender differences in competitiveness is an important and active area of research,[5] how biomarkers influence measures of competitiveness may suggest policy interventions. For example, Pearson and Schipper (2013) present evidence that women who choose to take hormonal contraceptives (aka the Pill) are more aggressive bidders.

17.2.2 Proxies for Biomarkers, Biomarkers as Proxies, and Imaging Biomarkers

Since Barker (1998), the idea that testosterone and other hormones circulating in utero can have lasting impacts on health by influencing the womb environment during the critical phases of fetal development has attracted substantial attention. To explore whether there are causal links in the long-term consequences from what is now popularly referred to as "fetal programming," researchers—in the absence of long-term panel datasets that also contain parental measures of hormones in utero—use as a proxy the ratio of the length of the second finger (index) to the length of the fourth finger (ring finger), a measure also known as the "2D:4D" ratio. This proxy is motivated by the findings in Manning et al. (Manning, Scutt, Wilson, & Lewis-Jones, 1998) that provide suggestive evidence that the 2D:4D ratio is a marker for the permanent effects of prenatal hormones on the organizational structure of the brain. The evidence in this study indicates that the 2D:4D ratio is negatively correlated with prenatal testosterone exposure and is fixed very early in life.

Using the 2D:4D ratio as a proxy for prenatal testosterone,[6] Dreber and Hoffman (2007) report that it associates with more risk aversion in financial decision making among Swedish university students. This correlation exists for both men and women. However, using a sample of only students with master of business administration (MBA) degrees, Maestripieri et al. (Maestripieri, Hoffman, Anderson, Carter, & Higley, 2009) were unable to replicate this result for their sample of males. However, that study and Coates et al. (Coates, Gurnell, & Rustichini, 2009), who used a sample of financial traders based in London, both found that the 2D:4D ratio associates with career choices and trajectories. Specifically, higher testosterone levels or their proxies of in utero levels are shown to correlate with the long-term profitability of a trader, the number of years a trader remains active, and the odds that an MBA student pursues a career in finance. Although that result is unsurprising at first, this line of research also shows that the gender gap in those with MBAs who enter a financial career is reduced when one accounts for hormones and their proxies. Thus, these studies suggest that there may be a long-term role for in utero biomarkers as proxied by the 2D:4D ratio in explaining gender differences in preferences and career outcomes.

Biomarkers often can reduce measurement error generated by proxy variables. For example, body mass index (BMI) is a common diagnostic for obesity but is heavily critiqued on numerous grounds, including that it does not differentiate between fat and fat-free mass. That is, an additional 5 pounds of muscle will lead to an identical increase in BMI as an additional 5 pounds of fat. Burkhauser and Cawley (2008) argue with

National Health and Nutrition Examination Survey (NHANES) data that there are benefits from using alternative measures of fatness, such as total body fat, percent body fat, and waist circumference, in place of BMI.[7] A growing number of datasets contain information on biomarkers for obesity that are collected using imaging technology. Imaging biomarkers are usually noninvasive, and they produce intuitive, multidimensional results that consist of both qualitative and quantitative data.

For instance, many works in the burgeoning field of neuroeconomics use imaging biomarkers as inputs in their analyses. In these studies, general neural biomarkers are often collected via magnetic resonance imaging (MRI), and subsequent analysis generally finds correlations between these biomarkers and a number of economic outcomes.[8] For example, Gilaie-Dotan et al. (2014) placed participants in an MRI scanner and had them choose between lotteries with monetary outcomes and probabilities explicitly specified in graphical form. Their econometric analysis of the data from two sets of experiments presents evidence of a significant correlation between gray matter volume in the posterior parietal cortex and individual risk attitudes.

17.2.3 Hormones

Perhaps the largest volume of research using time-varying biomarkers within economics involves the use of hormones. Cortisol, testosterone, and cotinine are the hormones that have received the most attention in economics research. These measures are often collected by blood and saliva in both the laboratory and also during home visits in several longitudinal surveys. These hormones have been speculated to be involved in topics ranging from risky behavior to bidding patterns in auctions to the persistence of the cycle of poverty. On the latter, Haushofer and Fehr (2014) summarize evidence indicating that poverty causes stress and negative affective states that in turn may lead to short-sighted and poor decision making. They conclude that more research is needed to understand the mechanisms involved, and they are careful to make a distinction between studies that report associations versus those that use pharmacological treatments to exogenously change hormone levels.

Using survey data from Canada, Lehrer et al. (Lehrer, Tremblay, Vitaro, & Schaal, 2007), citing evidence from behavioral endocrinology literature, point out that hormones levels such as testosterone and cortisol vary during the day as well as in response to environmental stimuli. Using simple regression models that control for time since wake-up (up to a quadratic), the authors find that, in boys, testosterone is highly correlated with adolescent height. The authors postulate that this may be proxying for noncognitive skills that are rewarded in the labor market. Consistent with this speculative finding, a large body of research reports a positive association between testosterone levels and career choices. However, Dreber and Hoffman (2007) and Apicella et al. (2008) each find that circulating testosterone levels are not predictive of risk aversion among male MBA students. Yet, among female MBAs, those with higher circulating testosterone display lower levels of risk aversion. Maestripieri et al. (2009) find that female MBAs are much less likely to enter a financial career than are male MBAs. In men, Apicella et al. (2008) report an association between levels of circulating testosterone and their risk attitudes. Many of the reported findings are simply correlations, and the authors often try to make the case for a proposed mechanism by linking their findings to evidence from rodent studies, where the variation in hormones is more plausibly exogenous.

Researchers have not only examined circulating hormone levels but also hormone levels in utero. For example, Aizer et al. (Aizer, Stroud, & Buka, 2012) examine sibling differences in in-utero exposure to short-term elevated levels of the stress hormone cortisol. Their maternal fixed-effects estimates indicate that elevated cortisol in utero negatively affects offspring cognition, health, and educational attainment later in life. These findings are consistent with randomized experiments using animal subjects in several neurobiological fields, as well as in association studies such as those by Yu et al. (Yu, Lee, Lee, & Son, 2004) and Huizink et al. (Huizink, Robles de Medina, Mulder, Visser, & Buitelaar, 2003) who show significant links between cortisol in utero and respectively impaired development of the brain and spinal cord and lower mental and motor development early in life (at 3 and 8 months).

Turning to risky behaviors, Adda and Cornaglia (2006) use information on the ratio of cotinine concentration in saliva per cigarette smoked to understand how this levels varies as state-level tobacco taxes change over time.[9] Smokers are found to engage in compensatory behavior and increase the intensity of smoking in response to increases in taxes.[10] This finding of compensatory behaviors has important implications for how researchers estimate models of smoking behavior, including the Becker, Grossman and Murphy (1994) rational addiction model.

Abrevaya and Puzzello (2012) and Adda and Cornaglia (2013) have replicated this analysis with alternative datasets and come to differing conclusions that may be due to differences in the amount of within-state variation in taxes. With limited within-state tax variation, precise cigarettes and cotinine tax elasticity estimates are difficult to obtain. Interestingly, in the latter study, cotinine levels are found to be a strong predictor of smoking cessation, conditional on the number of cigarettes smoked. That is, a 1 standard deviation increase in cotinine levels at baseline decreases the likelihood to quit smoking up to 15 years later by 49%. These authors report significant gender differences in the effects of cotinine on quitting, and the effect is much more pronounced for men.[11]

The most convincing research on the influence of hormones on outcomes of interest to economists comes from experiments with placebo-controlled administration of hormones. Zethraeus et al. (2009) present evidence from a series of experiments designed to measure economic behaviors such as altruism, reciprocal fairness, and risk attitudes in which some subjects were randomly administered estrogen and testosterone. They do not find support for the idea that either sex hormone has any significant effect on these dimensions of behavior. Eisenegger, Naef, Snozzi, Heinrichs and Fehr (2010) also randomly assign subjects in the economics laboratory to either be administered testosterone or a placebo. Administration was double-blinded so that no actor in the laboratory had any knowledge of which subjects received the hormone treatment. The experiment was designed in part to sort between two hypotheses in the behavioral endocrinology literature on how testosterone influences behavior: between antisocial and status-seeking behavior.[12] An additional interesting aspect of this study is that the authors asked whether the subject believed if he or she were administered hormones. Those who report that they believed they received testosterone made lower offers than those who believed that they were treated with a placebo. These findings suggest that the experimental economics approach is sensitive for detecting neurobiological effects as subtle as those achieved by the administration of hormones; thus, the role of subjective expectations of treatment is nearly as large as the direct effect of the hormone itself. Last, testosterone administration significantly increased fair bargaining offers compared to placebo, suggesting that testosterone is primarily involved in status-related behavior.

In a more recent study, Kandasamy et al. (2014) provided subjects cortisol tablets over the course of 8 days that significantly increased salivary cortisol. The subjects were then given a choice between playing two lotteries: one with a higher expected value but a small chance of winning and a safer one with a lower expected value but a guarantee of winning something. Cortisol tablets were found to significantly shift economic preferences toward risk aversion as subjects increasingly chose the safe option. This paper shows that risk preferences are not a stable trait, and chronic stress leads to more risk aversion and overweighting of small probability events, particularly for male subjects.

As a whole, the findings of these three studies using random placebo-controlled administration of hormones provide stronger causal evidence on the importance of both psychosocial as well as neuroendocrine factors in determining the influence of testosterone and cortisol on both human social behavior and economic decision making. Yet it is worth stressing that in interpreting this batch of evidence we assumed that an exogenously administered hormone acts similarly to an endogenous hormone. At present, we have no knowledge on whether, and if so how, the doses administered in placebo-controlled studies interact with the suite of pre-existing endogenous hormone levels in the body.[13] Thus, further developments may also require a parallel literature to develop that compares the performance of subjects in correlational studies with those in placebo-controlled experiments to help shed light on whether there is true potential in conducting these experiments.

17.3 Biological Time-Invariant Measures

Although the 2D:4D ratio described earlier is fixed throughout the life cycle and used to proxy prenatal hormone levels, we now turn to discussing studies that use individual biomarkers as inputs to understand how one's own characteristics affect socioeconomic outcomes. The literature exploring biological time-invariant measures has undergone a phenomenal transformation from simply contrasting variance in outcomes between dizygotic and monozygotic twins to looking at portions of the genetic code itself, as well as examining whether there are differential responses to environmental stimuli by genetic code. This literature seeks to shed more light on exactly how biology influences one's destiny.

17.3.1 Genetic Markers

A large literature in economics uses data on twins to control for genetic similarities among individuals. Taubman (1976) is often considered the economics pioneer in using this approach, and Goldberger (1979) may be the first to question what can truly be learned from this source of variation.[14] Earlier research focused on genetic similarity to measure the heritability of income using survey data; this research has shifted to using data from either incentivized experiments or surveys to explore heritability in different measures of economic preferences (e.g., Benjamin et al., 2012b; Cesarini et al., 2008, 2009, 2010, 2012; Wallace, Cesarini, Lichtenstein, & Johannesson, 2007).[15] Research using genetic data has recently moved beyond variance decompositions between twins of different zygosity; now, with the decoding of the human genome, one can go further in analyzing the impacts of specific portions of the genetic code as well as their interactions with environmental influences. Finally, a number of researchers have also aimed to increase the rigor by which genetic information is analyzed both by economists and scientists.

The sequencing of the human genome in 2001 (Venter et al., 2001) provided a means to, in an increasingly affordable manner, measure genetic variation across individuals at approximately 2 million sites on the genome. These points on the human DNA sequences are called *genetic polymorphisms*, of which *single nucleotide polymorphisms* (SNPs) are locations that have received the most attention. At most of these locations, one's genotype can be denoted by the number of risky alleles. That is, an individuals can have the common allele, one risky allele, or two risky alleles. Research has moved from using data collected on a few candidate genotypes to those measuring variation across the full genome.[16]

Much of the early research was limited by the genetic information collected within the dataset being investigated. These data were generally not primarily designed for use by social scientists. The first large-scale longitudinal study that collected information on specific genetic markers was the National Longitudinal Study of Adolescent Health study, commonly referred to as Add Health. Studies used in behavioral genetics to conduct genome-wide association studies (GWAS) lack details on a rich set of conditioning demographic and socioeconomic covariates. Thus, before describing this literature much further, it is worth pointing out that many of the decisions on what biomarker variables were used, resulted from the constraints faced by the researcher of what was available in the data. Generally, the initial biomarkers collected were those hypothesized to be of main importance based on studies that had little replicability.

One set of research has tried to see if candidate genes can predict heterogeneity in economic primitives such as risk aversion and delay discounting parameters. This can provide a biological microfoundation. The burgeoning literature exploring time preferences builds off of Cesarini et al. (2009), who suggest that approximately one-fifth of the variation in these measures is due to genetic factors. These initial results did not consider measurement error and are likely an underestimate. Advances in genetics have led researchers to investigate whether genes that are involved in the dopamine and serotonin systems in the brain's reward pathways represent primitives of behavior (e.g., Dreber et al., 2009; Kuhnen & Chiao, 2009).[17] Although these early studies found some statistically significant associations, they were not found in samples of adolescents (Gee, 2014) and other samples, including those of Carpenter et al. (Carpenter, Garcia, & Lum, 2011) and Dreber et al. (2011).

Several papers used survey data to examine associations between candidate genes and non-health outcomes. For instance, DeNeve and Fowler (2014) explore links between a specific genetic marker and credit card debt, whereas, in a small sample, Kuhnen et al. (Kuhnen, Samanez-Larkin, & Knutson, 2013) find a significant association between a functional polymorphism in the serotonin system and the number of credit lines opened. Numerous behaviors and decisions are linked to the amount of credit card debt one holds, and this includes decisions made by lenders that are beyond the control of the individual himself. Thus, it will be difficult to determine the biological plausibility of the mechanism underlying this association. This approach is often based on convenience, and many of the results are not replicated and are often fairly critiqued because they tend to have insufficient statistical power. Intuitively, if well-powered studies that search the entire genome for associations find only tiny effects, then the large effects found in many of these candidate gene studies, with their much smaller sample sizes, are likely false positives.[18] We believe that, despite the ease with which this research can be undertaken, candidate gene studies are unlikely to convince many in the research community.[19]

A second set of research has begun to explore using genetic data directly as a source of exogenous variation to identify the impact of specific health conditions on socioeconomic outcomes. Ding et al. (Ding, Lehrer, Rosenquist, & Audrain-McGovern, 2009) were the first to propose this source of identifying variation, but this concept was actually subsequently found to be first proposed in the epidemiological literature of Katan (1986).[20] Although using genes as instruments is controversial and subject to criticism,[21] the use of genetic markers has helped elucidate several important findings that extend to other studies within health economics. For example, Ding et al.'s (2009) analysis underscores the challenge researchers face when measuring health as an input. Traditionally, economists used a single measure or proxy of an individual's health, but the concept of comorbidity is well-known in the medical sciences, and these proxies likely introduce significant amounts of measurement error. The authors show that using richer vectors of health conditions is important to understand the effects of a specific condition because poor physical and mental health conditions are positively correlated. By omitting comorbid conditions, different estimates may arise when using different estimators, and specific instruments may no longer be valid. Thus, comorbidity not only adds to the challenge of finding a proper instrument but is also likely present in many health economics applications.[22]

As with all studies that use instrumental variables to identify causal parameters, the plausibility of the (genetic) instrument comes into question. To a large extent, one will never know whether a specific candidate gene is a valid instrumental variable because one cannot randomly assign genes to humans or create human equivalents to knock-out mice.[23] In addition, the role of individual genetic markers in many socioeconomic outcomes is likely quite small and likely explains less than 1% of the variation in that phenotype. This suggests that individual markers are likely weakly correlated.[24] Furthermore, these are dynastic effects, and, without more detailed data on parental outcomes and family environments (as well as parental genes), we cannot separate out the portion of the impact that is uniquely brought on by the child's poor health outcome.[25] Turning to the genetic marker itself, one may worry about *population stratification*—that there are subtle, unaccounted-for genetic differences between groups of individuals and that the gene being investigated is correlated with a missing genetic marker that is driving the results. Similarly, this may happen when genes located close together on the same chromosome are inherited as a group: one may not be attributing the effect to the correct polymorphism. Given these potential threats, Ding et al. (2009) advise researchers using genes as instrumental variables to use Conley et al.'s (Conley, Hansen, & Rossi, 2012) local-to-zero approximation sensitivity analysis.[26] These exercises should also be considered for studies utilizing Mendelian randomization.

There is another trend within this identification approach that may have its antecedents in GWAS and that is worth some discussion. A handful of papers using genetic information as a source of exogenous variation treat the variable as a count of the number of risk alleles. This may sidestep the many instrument problem (Hausman, Newey, Woutersen, Chao, & Swanson, 2012) when using discrete indicators for different genetic variants, but using the count not only makes it difficult to interpret the first-stage estimate, but it also makes a strong functional form assumption that outcomes are linear in the number of risk alleles. By allowing for nonlinear relationships through perhaps discrete indicator variables, one can easily test whether the linearity restriction is supported by the data. Second, discrete variables truly shed more light on what features are driving the estimated effect, and one can then get a better handle on whether the relationships mimic those hypothesized in the scientific literature.

Fletcher and Lehrer (2009*a*, 2009*b*, 2011) also consider a variant of this strategy that exploits genetic inheritance within full biological siblings. This may be truly what is meant by Mendelian randomization, and these authors dubbed this strategy the "genetic lottery." Most importantly, the authors demonstrate how using the genetic lottery can allow one to test whether the family fixed-effects model fully solves the endogeneity problem. That is, they can modify the traditional Hausman test to compare a family fixed estimator to estimates from a family fixed-effects instrumental variable. Their results suggest that the family fixed-effects estimator does not fully solve the endogeneity problem in health when estimating its effects on socioeconomic outcome. An additional advantage of this approach is that the family fixed effect controls for all dynastic effects within the family if the researcher assumes that the effects of the unobserved to the econometrician family factors do not vary between full biological siblings. Thus, with the introduction of genetic data, this empirical strategy demonstrated an easy to implement way that a key identifying assumption in one of workhorse research designs used in family and population economics that has been applied in almost every branch of empirical economics can be tested and also relaxes the assumptions required when interpreting estimates that used an IV estimator with genetic instruments.

To select instruments in many of these papers, researchers have relied on results from published candidate gene studies. Given the prevalence of conflicting findings in the candidate gene literature, the journal *Behavior Genetics* adopted strict standards for publication of candidate gene studies (Hewitt, 2012). To be considered for publication, candidate gene studies must be well-powered and must account for all sources of multiple hypothesis testing; any new finding must be accompanied by a replication. Chabris et al. (2013) illustrate this point—that there are limits to examining candidate genes—by using datasets from three independent longitudinal studies to investigate previously identified candidate genes, and they find fewer significant associations than a traditionally powered analysis would predict. Many early candidate genes failed to replicate because, initially, researchers did not adjust for population stratification in their studies. As discussed earlier, many studies in the literature suffer from low statistical power and this, coupled with potential publication bias as well as undisclosed pretesting, could have led to too many false positives in the literature. Thus, when searching for a plausible genetic instrument by reviewing the literature, researchers need to consider the statistical power of the study. As we discuss next, economists are conducting research in this direction, and only once a credible main genetic effect has been established should researchers begin to explore gene-by-environment (G*E) interactions.

The third major strand of research involves what we term "best practices for GWAS" in an effort to obtain a credible estimate of a main genetic effect. In several scientific fields, GWAS became the fashion starting roughly in 2005, in part as a response to the increasingly well-documented limitations of candidate gene studies.[27] GWAS are not motivated by any theory: they simply examine for an outcome of interest, whether it is associated with one or more of the (typically millions) measured SNPs. Because there are more hypotheses of significant association than data points,[28] one must make corrections for multiple testing. Current requirements recommend that any effect must be replicated in an independent sample. To deal with population stratification in these studies, one generally measures the principal components off the gene chip (i.e., the correlation matrix of all the assayed SNPs) and includes the first four of these to identify the geographic ancestry of individuals in the sample.[29]

Not only do economists focus on different sets of outcomes than those in medical and scientific fields, but they have also established a Social Science Genetic Association Consortium (SSGAC). The consortium works to pool datasets to reduce the costs associated with replicating findings in a GWAS. The work by the consortium has been very ambitious and may have been motivated by The Wellcome Trust

Case Control Consortium's attempts to improve the understanding of the etiological basis of several major causes of global disease by pooling databases collected by individual research teams. An early paper by SSGAC, Rietveld et al. (2013*a*), combined data on 42 cohorts. This provided more than 100,000 individuals to study which of approximately 2 million SNPs influence measures of educational attainment, such as college completion and years of education. This research suggested three specific genetic variants. More recently, Rietveld et al. (2014b) verified the robustness of these findings using data from three new sources, as well as only genetic variation within families. As a whole, this literature presents some convincing estimates of specific genetic effects and the benefits of using larger sample sizes in genetic research focusing on behavioral traits.

Research by the SSGAC has also been used to determine to what extent genetic data are needed to either serve as a control variable or have predictive power to serve as an instrument for specific outcomes. Rietveld et al. (2013*b*) point out that although twin studies suggest that genetic factors may account for as much as 30–40% of the variance in subjective well-being measures, additive effects of genetic polymorphisms that are common in the population can only explain between 5% and 10% of the variation in these measures. Although subjective well-being measures are not accurately measured, if one accounts for measurement error in this analysis, it was found to only increase the amount of explained variation of additive genetic effects from 12% to 18%. That said, this main finding of the limited power of additive effects also suggests that, for many complex socioeconomic phenomena, one may need to consider interactions with various factors,[30] a subset of which are discussed in the next subsection.

From a policy perspective, one may conclude that accounting for genetic factors is unimportant because the effects of individual genetic variants in Rietveld et al. (2013*a*, 2014b) are small in magnitude and explain a very small fraction of variation in outcomes. However, this research suggests that examining polygenic scores is an important future research direction. A polygenic score is used to detect shared genetic etiology among traits and is measured as a linear combination of SNPs. In one of its simplest forms, a polygenic score for a trait could be constructed by adding up the individual alleles, where each allele is weighted by effect sizes estimated from a GWAS (Dudbridge, 2013). The idea is that, using the GWAS results, we can give weights of relative importance to each SNP. Then, with a polygenic score, a researcher could exploit the joint predictive power of many SNPs when used as an input in an estimating equation. As an explanatory variable, these polygenic scores will explain more variation than will individual SNPs and can provide a clearer view on some combined genetic influences. This approach is still in its infancy, and there will be numerous methods developed to construct polygenic scores. The odds that a specific approach is adopted is increasing thanks to canned software routines such as PRSice being jointly developed. We believe future work will also need to account for estimation error in the GWAS and also should consider a partial identification approach for a given polygenic score. After all, for policy applications, these polygenic scores may provide an easier way to identify individuals at high risk for certain outcomes.

17.3.2 Gene–Environment Interactions

Across a host of disciplines, the importance of G*E interactions has been given substantial attention. For example, in a series of papers that argue for the importance for public policy to invest early in child development, Nobel Prize winner James Heckman makes a compelling case that there may be large societal returns to changing early life environments due to G*E effects. Specifically, Heckman (2007) writes,

> Third, the nature versus nurture distinction, although traditional, is obsolete. The modern literature on epigenetic expression and gene environment interactions teaches us that the sharp distinction between acquired skills and ability featured in the early human capital literature is not tenable (Rutter, 2006; Gluckman & Hanson, 2005; Rutter et al., 2006). Additive nature" and "nurture" models, although traditional and still used in many studies of heritability and family influence, mischaracterize gene-environment interactions. Recent analyses in economics that break the "causes" of birthweight into environmental and genetic components ignore the lessons of the recent literature. Genes and environment cannot be meaningfully parsed by traditional linear models that assign unique variances to each component. Abilities are produced, and gene expression is governed by environmental conditions (Rutter, 2006; Rutter et al., 2006). Behaviors and abilities have both a genetic and an acquired character. Measured abilities are the outcome of environmental influences, including in utero experiences, and also have genetic components (p. 13251).

In this section, we summarize how economists have begun to explore G*E effects and what has been learned from these studies. We conclude by suggesting that developing new frameworks and strategies to measure and estimate these G*E effects may hold substantial promise to better understand how biomarkers influence human development.

Much like the prior section, where we focused on direct measures of genetic influences rather than twin studies, studies that focus on adoptees and other segments of the population defined on kinship will not be discussed.[31] G*E effects have received little attention in the literature, despite the fact that many researchers speculate that they are important. For example, Rosenquist et al. (2015) speculate that data limitations may have prevented earlier work in this area, and Eisenberg et al. (Eisenberg, Duckworth, Spinrad, & Valiente, 2014) postulate that the scientific literature on genetic factors has focused heavily on understanding main effects and not considered methods that can explore the sources of heterogeneity in these effects by using environmental conditions or behaviors, as in Kochanska et al. (Kochanska, Kim, Barry, & Philibert, 2011) or suggested in Moffitt, Caspi and Rutter (2005).

One of the first challenges that social scientists face in this area is dealing with selection because the environmental circumstances one faces are often based on choices leading to selection bias.[32] Thus, whereas an individual's DNA sequences is fixed at conception, genetic characteristics may only matter by influencing outcomes if the gene expression only alters due to specific environmental circumstances.[33] In the current literature, a subset of these interactions leading to changes in gene expression may be random and not driven by choice, and, as such, there is no bias in the estimated coefficient. These types of G*E interactions, reported in a number of social science papers including Ding et al. (2009), are grouped under the term epigenetics. More formally, the term "epigenetics" in the sciences refers to nonheritable modifications of genetic material in somatic cells that persist through the process of mitotic cell division. The extent that epigenetic modifications are due to random versus endogenous environmental factors is unknown.

A second main challenges in this area is modeling G*E effects. Rosenquist et al. (2015) conduct a fascinating study that sidesteps this issue by using an estimate-augmented version of a linear age-period cohort model to understand the source of G*E; these researchers used longitudinal data collected between 1971 and 2008 from the offspring cohort of the Framingham Heart Study. Specifically, they tested whether the well-documented association between the rs993609 variant of the FTO gene and BMI varies across birth cohorts, time period, and life cycle. These models partition the time-related variation in obesity to these three distinct sources but cannot identify the specific environmental channel within the source.[34] A key feature of the analysis is using the threshold regression estimator by Hansen (1999) to test for a structural break of unknown timing across cohorts. The selected breakpoint is based on the model that best fits the data using a grid search algorithm. This breakpoint does not necessarily mark the spot where the relationship is most different, but rather it marks the point where the difference between birth cohorts explains the most variation in the data.

Rosenquist et al. (2015) find a robust relationship between birth cohort and the FTO risk allele with BMI, with an observed inflection point for those born after 1942. These findings raise the possibility that genetic associations may differ across birth cohorts due to variations in prevailing environmental contexts. Thus, the low replication rates of many GWAS may also be due to differences in the time period when study subjects were born and the historical moment when researchers conduct their investigations. From an economics perspective, this is not terribly surprising because these studies simply report associations, but the interpretation of the results of such analyses often suggest that the estimated associations are either causal or structural parameters.

Although the differential genetic effect based on the time of birth dimension has attracted substantial attention in the popular press, the more interesting finding from Rosenquist et al. (2015) for the research community relates to testing different G*E effects. Specifically, in specifications that control for gene*cohort effects, gene*age effects, and gene*contemporaneous period effects are statistically insignificant. Only if one ignores gene*cohort effects do we find that the G*E effects are due to contemporaneous events for FTO and BMI. It is not surprising that environments are correlated over the life cycle, and this suggests that changing the cumulative environmental conditions experienced does affect the penetrance of genetic influences.

To model G*E effects, Biroli (2015) integrates genetic factors inside the canonical model of health production developed by Grossman (1972). By doing so, he assumes that genetic variants affect the accumulation of health and human capital by both changing productivity and changing preferences. That is, genetic factors change the parameters of the model, shaping the production possibility frontier and the incentives to investment faced by the agent. Using data from both the Framingham Heart Study and the Avon Longitudinal Study of Parents and Children, he finds evidence that genetic factors do change both the production function of BMI and the level of healthy investment. That is, adolescents carrying the riskier allele in the FTO genotype are at greater risk of obesity even when consuming the same calories and performing the same physical activities as those adolescents with the other genotype. Furthermore, similar to Rosenquist et al. (2015), he finds that the estimated interaction between the FTO genotype and caloric intake is stronger for individuals born in later cohorts. Although this work provides an important economic framework, it does assume that caloric intake is not a behavioral choice and can be treated as exogenous. Thus, future research is needed to consider the endogeneity of the environmental variables selected by individuals.

The idea that environmental factors are exogenous also appears in much of the earlier work on G*E effects. This work did not consider alternative timing of environmental influences, and it takes a similar approach to candidate gene studies in allowing candidate gene*environment interactions. This literature was spawned by a highly cited paper by Caspi et al. (2002) who found that the effects of self-reported childhood maltreatment on adolescent antisocial behavior varied based on one's MAOA gene. More recently, Guo, Roettger, and Cai (2008) report significant interactions between genetic markers and factors like eating regular family meals and repeating a grade on juvenile delinquency. Settle et al. (Settle, Dawes, Christakis, & Fowler, 2010) find a significant interaction between a dopamine receptor gene and social networks in the formation of political ideologies. Shanahan et al. (Shanahan, Vaisey, Erickson, & Smolen, 2008) reports that, in explaining educational outcome, there is a significant interaction between a variant of the dopamine receptor gene DRD2 with environmental factors such as having a parent who belongs to the PTA and how often parents discuss school-related issues with the student. As with candidate gene studies, concerns related to low statistical power due to a combination of potential pre-testing and publication bias likely hold some validity in certain cases.

Studies that have tried to exploit genetic variation within families have the potential to provide more compelling evidence of candidate G*E effects. Similar to Fletcher and Lehrer (2011), the idea is to exploit within-family differences in genetic code to remove biases from dynastic effects. For example, Thompson (2014) exploits within-family variation in genetic inheritance to see if there are differential responses to household income on child education outcomes by variants of the MAOA genes. The results indicate that the gradient is steeper for those with rarer variants. However,[35] one must be cautious in interpreting any evidence from studies estimating G*E effects exploiting within-family variation; this is the lesson that emerges from Conley and Rauscher's (2013) complementary study. These authors explore within twin-pair birthweight differences to study how genetic traits moderate the relationship between birthweight and several outcomes including high school grade point average (GPA). The sole statistically significant G*E effect found has a sign that is the opposite of what had been suggested by prior scientific research. This result also highlights that when using biomarkers there could be significant benefits from using an interdisciplinary research team in which some members are well-equipped to assess whether the estimated effects are plausible in sign and magnitude.[36]

The idea that there is variation in genetic effects across the life cycle as one ages is an element of Rosenquist et al.'s study (2015) and is also found in Hatemi's (2013) analysis of political attitudes.[37] Specifically, using several sources of longitudinal data from the Mid Atlantic Twin Registry,[38] Hatemi (2013) finds that proximate events such as losing one's job, suffering a major financial loss, or getting a divorce can lead to a short-term change in one's economic policy attitudes that is consistent with maximizing self-interest. Specifically, job loss and financial struggles increased the likelihood one would support socialism, unions, and other organizations or policies that may alleviate these financial problems. Not surprisingly, individuals who lost a job are more likely to oppose policies that may have caused their change in economic situations, such as immigration and capitalism. This analysis also suggests that policies can manipulate the effects that a gene has on behavior, but similar to work (described earlier) implicitly assumes that the changes in personal circumstances are exogenous. Furthermore, this work does not decompose the variations in the sources of G*E effects between proximate and global distal environmental factors since birth and simply focuses on short- and medium-run responses by genetic marker to broad changes in individual circumstances.[39]

Taken together, unlike the gene-as-instrumental-variable studies that inherently and implicitly assume that there is a certain "fixed" genetic disposition, the effects of specific genetic markers may certainly vary across the life cycle. This does complicate any critique of a gene as an instrument because that gene may truly only have an effect in specific samples of subjects of certain ages who experienced certain environmental stimuli but not others. As Manski (2013) notes in his view of the incredible certitude taken by many in the public policy community, it may be that embracing our uncertainty about how genetic effects operate given the potential of environment interplay is something that should be emphasized more strongly in the literature. To an extent, the work of the SSGAC in evaluating genome associations is striving to reduce the degrees of certitude represented in any given study. Future research, if well-powered, can also be used to understand why, across the databanks collected by the SSGAC, divergent main effects are observed. That is, if genes influence one's behavior, can one's behavior also influence genetic expression? Indeed, if the genetic mechanisms are not activated or repressed by certain stimuli, then genotype at that given moment may not be relevant. However, specific life events may alter the magnitude of genetic variance on a given trait, or it may in fact instigate different genetic processes altogether.

Although these findings are quite important, much work remains, and it may be necessary to move beyond linear models to study G*E effects. In this vein, Conti and Heckman (2010) provide a more general framework to operationalize and interpret gene–environment interactions. As noted earlier, dealing with selection of environments provides an important empirical hurdle for researchers to overcome to present credible evidence in this area. Van IJzendoorn and Bakermans-Kranenburg (2012) advocate using randomized controlled trials to study how changing environmental interventions have differential effects as a function of genetic endowments.

At present, some of the most compelling evidence on difference in response by genetic marker does not isolate the mechanism to shed light on why treatment effect heterogeneity is observed. To a large extent, researchers in empirical microeconomics already have sets of tools to explore whether interventions have different effects for subgroups defined on the basis of more aggregated predetermined characteristics such as gender and race. For example, Lee and Shaikh (2014) and Lehrer et al. (Lehrer, Pohl, & Song, 2015) provide a set of methodological tools to analyze heterogeneity in causal effects that can additionally incorporate corrections for multiple testing. As a whole, there is tremendous scope in this stream for both empiricists and econometricians to collaborate and develop methodological tools for G*E analyses. These methods can be used to evaluate personalized medicine as well as help guide policy makers in targeting interventions to those individuals who are more likely to benefit from them.

We argue that, in empirical practice, researchers should consider working with more aggregated environmental factors and perhaps exploit regional environmental changes. Indeed, there is a large history in empirical microeconomics of exploring differences in environmental conditions or policies across regions (as in natural experiments), and exploring genetic heterogeneity in the estimated effects seems to be a simple extension. Rosenquist et al. (2015) propose examining estimates of genetic augmented age-period cohort models with samples defined on the basis of geographic regions. If there are difference in structural breakpoints across regions, then this can shed light on the source of G*E effects by potentially exploring if the different cut-points correspond to a geographic pattern in the evolution of a specific environmental change. As a whole, evidence from rigorous G*E studies can help reshape theories as they improve our understanding of the different mechanisms and complex pathways that lead to various health and socioeconomic outcomes.

Although used interchangeably in this chapter, we should also point out that future work will need to more formally define what is meant by G*E effects. This term can be used to refer to situations in which the effect of exposure to an environmental factor on a behavior is conditional upon a person's genotype, as well as to situations in which the genotype's effect is moderated by some environmental effect. Statistically, G*E interactions do have these multiple meanings, but, for policy purposes, it is important to clarify the different statistical applications of gene–environment interaction and which method is the focus of the current exploration. We suggest that researchers use *G*E responses* to refer to situations in which the effect of exposure to an environmental factor on a behavior is conditional upon a person's genotype and *G*E modifications* to refer to differential genetic responses to environment. Personalized medicine and many policies that would target by genotype may be interested in *G*E modifications*, whereas *G*E responses* may be more interesting for researchers to study if they are interested in understanding the heterogeneity in environmental effects on outcomes across the population.

Last, as the literature moves beyond only considering main genetic effects, it is worth pointing out that gene–gene interactions almost certainly do exist.[40] Indeed, both Ding et al. (2006, 2009) and Fletcher and Lehrer (2009*b*, 2011) consider such two-way interactions in their instrument set, but there is not much information even in the behavioral genetics literature on how and why these interactions operate. Thus, future research will also be needed to understand the interactive effects between genes themselves, as well as with environmental interactions.

17.4 Conclusion and Directions for Future Research

With a growing number of longitudinal studies integrating direct biological measures of study participants, we predict that the volume of research exploring biomarkers as inputs, as well their interactions with environmental variables, will grow exponentially. To a large extent, one can view many of these measures as either proxies for some underlying process or components of individual, specific, unobserved heterogeneity that used to be contained in an individual, specific fixed effect. That said, it is reasonable and scientifically plausible to assume that any biomarker measure will have a differential impact as individuals age and that these variable responses may interact with observed covariates or other biomarkers. Furthermore, several measures of biomarkers permit us to enter into the black box of what was assumed to be contained in a fixed effect, as well as help in providing direction in to how to best integrate findings from several scientific fields into empirical research in the social sciences.

This suggested general trajectory for future research that incorporates data on biomarkers is consistent with other recent developments within the discipline of economics. Consider, for example, the unquestioned success of behavioral economics, which primarily integrates findings from psychology, neuroscience, and the decision sciences into economic models. These models and subsequent analyses have played a large role in reshaping public policy in numerous areas (including pension policy), and they introduced the term *nudge* into the vocabulary of policy analysts. That said, in the short to medium term, the evidence surveyed within this chapter suggests that there may be benefits from using slight levels of aggregation as the next step in entering the black box. That is, when trying to investigate gene-by-environment interactions, one could either look at polygenic risk scores with specific environmental shocks or explore specific genes with an aggregate environment indicator. Furthermore, as discussed in preceding sections, the econometric tools used to both analyze gene–environment interactions as well as to construct polygenic risk scores are still in their infancy. By combing improved tools with the newer data sources that will soon become available to the general research community, there is tremendous potential for using biomarkers to fill large gaps in knowledge in multiple areas within economics.

As several of the studies reviewed have indicated, data on biological markers have already proved particularly valuable in the field of health economics. For example, the inclusion of cotinine in smoking demand equations provided new estimates of tax elasticities. Using biomarkers elucidated the importance of constructing an accurate measure of individual health and of the resulting biases in estimating the impact of separate health conditions when ignoring comorbidities. In addition, economists have begun to explore treatment effect heterogeneity along biomarker lines, and this may have significant policy relevance. In conclusion, we believe that using biomarkers as explanatory variables is just another natural progression of research in economic science: because of data limitations, one may begin with a simple model and then, as more information on biomarkers becomes available, develop more complex models that are empirically tractable to test biologically plausible, theoretically justified, and increasingly complex hypotheses.

Acknowledgments

I am extremely grateful to David Cesarini, Weili Ding, and James Niels Rosenquist for often heated conversations over the past 10 years that have helped me to think critically on how researchers should use biomarker data within their analysis. Similar to an Academy Awards acceptance speech, I do not have the space to list others with whom I have had less heated debates, including anonymous reviewers. I also would like to thank SSHRC for research support. I am responsible for all errors, glaring omissions, and interpretations of evidence in the literature.

Notes

1. Although a subset of these measures is well-characterized and has been repeatedly shown to correctly predict relevant clinical outcomes across a variety of treatments and populations, in many cases, the "validity" of biomarkers is assumed in clinical and empirical practice and needs to be continuously re-evaluated.
2. For example, to capture individual obesity, it is likely that measures taken on adipose tissue distribution from either computed tomography (CT) or MRI scans are more accurate than BMI, but there is substantial disagreement of the ideal location to take the scan if only conducting a single-slice acquisition. See Shen et al. (2004) and Liu et al. (2005) for early discussions on this issue, which also documents gender differences in ideal locations.
3. This is one of a variety of appearances of such a hypothesis in the popular press but, because, to the best of our knowledge it has garnered the most attention, it is mentioned here as a motivating example.
4. An important difference between these papers is that Pearson and Schipper (2013) do not observe this finding during the midcycle, when fecundity is highest, and they propose an evolutionary explanation for this distinction.
5. See Niederle and Vesterlund (2011) for a recent survey of this research.
6. To be explicit, the literature generally finds that there is association between 2D:4D to postnatal testosterone levels, and this is a proxy for maternal testosterone while in utero.

There still remains some debate as to the validity of this conjecture, which leads the 2D:4D to serve as a specific proxy for maternal testosterone in utero.

7. That said, because biomarkers associated with obesity may also be associated with a host of other factors, there may be situations in which they exacerbate measurement error relative to traditional proxies. We are grateful to a co-editor (Rashad) for pointing this out.
8. A survey of neuroeconomics is well-beyond the scope for this chapter, and the interested reader is directed to Camerer et al. (Camerer, Cohen, Fehr, Glimcher, & Laibson, forthcoming) for an accessible survey of research that uses imaging biomarkers as inputs.
9. Cotinine is a metabolite of nicotine, and Jarvis et al. (Jarvis, Tunstall-Pedoe, Feyerabend, Vesey, & Saloojee, 1984) point out that the amount of cotinine in the blood is a good marker of exposure to environmental smoke.
10. Such compensatory behavior has also been shown in studies that did not have access to data on biomarkers, such as Evans and Farrelly (1998) and Farrelly et al. (Farrelly, Nimsch, Hyland, & Cummings, 2004), which show that smokers switch to cigarettes with a higher tar and nicotine yield in response to tax changes.
11. It is also worth mentioning that Adda and Cornaglia (2010) use information on cotinine levels in nonsmokers as an outcome to examine how changes in excise taxes and introductions of smoking bans affects environmental smoke. Increasing taxes on cigarettes reduces average exposure to cigarette smoke by nonsmokers, and a larger effect is found for young children living with smokers. Interestingly, smoking bans are found to have increased the exposure to smoking by nonsmokers. In evaluating public policies on tobacco, many analysts have debated how large these indirect benefits from raising taxes and smoking bans can truly be. Data on cotinine can quickly provide a direct measure of some of these benefits, thus demonstrating true societal benefits from using data on biomarkers.
12. An earlier study by Zak et al. (2009) concluded that elevated testosterone causes men to behave antisocially in the ultimatum game, but the researchers did not consider the status-seeking hypothesis.
13. Exogenously changing a specific hormone does not only influence the effect of that endogenous hormone, but it also causes a different response to other hormones in the body. In terminology familiar to many economists, are there unintended consequences.
14. A simple description of the strategy is that if we assume that unobserved genetic and unobserved environmental factors are orthogonal, then comparing within-family regression estimates of the same equation on subsamples of monozygotic and dizygotic twins allows us to identify the net hereditary effect. To be explicit, Goldberger's (1979) opposition was toward variance decompositions and did not object to exploring associations with specific markers. Goldberger pointed out that the estimands in variance decompositions are effectively R^2s which are of limited value for assessing policy impact. He famously remarked that even if it were true that variation in eyesight in a population was explained entirely by genetic factors, introducing eyeglasses could still have a large impact on welfare.
15. See Kohler et al. (Kohler, Behrman, & Schnittker, 2011), who provide an excellent discussion on how to leverage twin studies to model unobserved genetic endowments and causal pathways.
16. See Benjamin et al. (2007, 2012) for more comprehensive reviews of research in this area. Benjamin et al. (2007) coined the term "genoeconomics" for this field.
17. See also Knafo et al. (2008), Mertins et al. (Mertens, Schote, Hoffeld, Griessmair, & Meyer, 2011), and Zhong et al. (Zhong, Israel, Xue, Ebstein, & Chew, 2009) for studies that link specific genetic variants to outcomes measured in the laboratory.

18. For example, Chabris et al. (2012) demonstrate that a series of published genetic associations for general intelligence failed to replicate with a sample of approximately 10,000 individuals. Furthermore, as the work summarized on candidate genes in the preceding paragraph indicates, replication of results from these studies is needed to verify that these associations are not false positives (Chabris et al., 2012 Rietveld et al., 2014a).
19. For completeness, we note that, within the discipline of political science, Fowler and Dawes (2008), Dawes and Fowler (2009), Dawes et al. (2014), and others have conducted candidate gene studies on voter turnout. Charney and English (2012) criticize this style of research, arguing that the specific genes investigated are associated with innumerable behaviors and traits. This undermines the apparent importance of evidence linking a gene to any particular outcome and points out the more significant concern related to statistical power described in this paragraph.
20. The initial draft of this paper was presented at a conference in 2003, and an earlier draft came out as an NBER working paper (Ding et al., 2006). Norton and Han (2008) used genetic data that only became available in 2006. Note that the first applications of what is referred to as *Mendelian randomization* in the epidemiological literature is by Davey Smith (2003), who also uses the same source of identification.
21. See Cawley et al. (Cawley, Han, & Norton, 2011) and Fang (2013), among others.
22. The modeling in Ding et al. (2009) also makes a clear separation between health outcomes (a state variable) and health behaviors (a control variable) that are often treated as equivalent in the health economics literature. Because health behaviors only explain a limited amount of the variation in health status, they are poor proxies for health status, and they may also proxy for non-health preferences such as peer group composition. Further health behaviors could result from, as well as cause, certain particular health states, which has important policy implications. For example, adolescents may decide to smoke because the nicotine in cigarettes may help self-medicate against cravings for food or mediate in some mental illnesses.
23. In addition, Conley (2009) points out that the phenomenon of pleiotropy presents a related challenge. Because many genes code for proteins that may have multiple functions and effects, it is hard to know for certain that the instrument only affects outcomes through the endogenous regressor. Naturally, without random assignment, one may never be certain about the role of any specific genotype.
24. For example, evidence in Wehby et al. (2011), who conduct separate instrumental variable analysis using two independent samples from Norway and the United States, finds that in both samples with different genetic variant instrument sets, each set is weakly correlated with the endogenous regressor of interest: maternal smoking.
25. Studies using Mendelian randomization implicitly assume that there are no dynastic effects to invoke the term randomization. However, by design, genes are inherited from one's parents, who also transmit environments and numerous behaviors across generations.
26. This analysis involves making an adjustment to the asymptotic variance matrix, thereby directly affecting the standard errors. That is, a term that measures the extent to which the exogeneity assumption is erroneous, constructed from prior information regarding plausible values of the impact of genetic factors on second-stage outcomes, is added to the variance matrix.
27. The declining cost of genotyping and technological advances and the availability of canned software packages to do the analyses also likely played a large role in their growth.

See McCarthy et al. (2008), among others, for early examples of work in this area. Other work involves using what is termed *genomic-relatedness-matrix restricted maximum likelihood* (GREML), which, for a sample of unrelated individual pairs, estimates what portion of the total fraction of variance in a trait is attributable to the average effects of SNPs. Thus it determines of genetic similarity predicts phenotypic similarity.

28. See Benjamin et al. (2012a) for a clear discussion and calculation of at what levels one can be confident that an estimated association is statistically significant in genome studies.
29. Researchers also frequently drop observations that are deemed genetic outliers. To the best of our knowledge, there is no discussion of selection bias due to this sampling criteria (possibly since many samples analyzed in this literature are not drawn using random sampling). Future work will likely need to consider reweighting schemes when selection is due to observables, and this would increase the external validity of GWAS.
30. This lower percentage of variation in the outcome explained in Rietveld et al. (2013*b*) is not surprising since Zuk et al. (Zuk, Hechter, Sunyaev, & Lander, 2012) suggested that heritability estimates from traditional biometrical studies of families will overstate those from GWAS results if genes interact nonadditively.
31. Interested readers may read Plug and Vijverberg (2003), Björklund, Lindahl, and Plug (2006), or Sacerdote (2007), among other studies in the economics literature, that focus on samples of adoptees to understand the importance of environment relative to genetic effects and their interactions.
32. Eaves et al. (Eaves, Last, Martin, & Jinks, 1977) and Saudino (1997) postulate that an individual's genes may directly influence his or her exposure to certain environments. Kendler et al. (2008) also point out that there may be indirect channels within families, because one may inherit an environment that arises from one's parent's genes. This can affect the child, even if the child did not inherit the identical risky genes.
33. Equivalently, we could say that the relationship between environmental circumstances and health conditions are modified by an individual's genetic code. We will use this phrasing later when we look at more macroeconomic environmental influences that cannot separate out the exact pathways. Although this may seem unsatisfying, there is a tradition of doing so in the health economics literature, where a number of papers turn their attention to broad environmental shocks such as famines and nuclear disasters. See also Purcell (2002), Rutter and Silberg (2002), and Rutter (2006) for additional discussion of what those in the sciences interpret as G*E correlation.
34. In other words, they are considering the aggregate macroenvironmental conditions and not person-specific conditions as their environmental influences. Due to the data being collected in one small geographic area, biases caused by sorting across regions based on environmental conditions due to unobservables is reduced.
35. Thompson (2014) also point out that parents may make "compensating" investments in which more resources are allocated to the less-able sibling to promote equality. Thus, one cannot rule out with the data that MAOA variants are correlated with the environmental conditions children receive from their parents after conception. Future research is need to see if a child's MAOA status induces differential treatment through the parents' investments in their children's human capital and, if so, to what signals of MAOA status parents respond, given that they are unlikely to have genotyped their children.
36. There are numerous examples of successful interdisciplinary collaborations reviewed in this chapter, including the multiple papers produced by the SSGAC; this work was lauded in an editorial in *Nature* (Hayden, 2013) and by Rosenquist et al. (2015), among others.

37. The 28-item Wilson-Patterson (1968) inventory of contemporary political and social attitudes was used.
38. The sample combined data obtained from records of multiple births from the Virginia Vital Records Office; the North Carolina Department of Environment, Health, and Natural Resources; and the South Carolina Department of Health and Environmental Control.
39. Smith et al. (2012) suggest that distal factors have little effect on genetic or environmental variance components estimates of political attitudes, but note that the evidence base is very weak.
40. See Lazopoulou et al. (2015) and Huang et al. (Huang, Sun, & Sun, 2011), among others, for evidence of significant gene–gene interactions in obesity.

REFERENCES

Abrevaya, J., & Puzzello, L. (2012). Taxes, cigarette consumption, and smoking intensity: Comment. *American Economic Review, 102*(4), 1751–1763.

Adda, J., & Cornaglia, F. (2006). Taxes, cigarette consumption, & smoking intensity. *American Economic Review, 96*(4), 1013–1028.

Adda, J., & Cornaglia, F. (2010). The effect of bans and taxes on passive smoking. *American Economic Journal: Applied Economics*, 2(1), 1–32.

Adda, J., & Cornaglia, F. (2013). Taxes, cigarette consumption, & smoking intensity: Reply. *American Economic Review, 103*(7), 3102–3114.

Aizer, A., Stroud, L., & Buka, S. (2012). *Maternal stress and child outcomes: Evidence from siblings* (NBER Working Paper No. 18422). Cambridge, MA: National Bureau of Economic Research.

Apicella, C. L., Dreber, A., Campbell, B., Gray, P. B., Hoffman, M., & Little, A. C. (2008). Testosterone and financial risk preference. *Evolution and Human Behavior, 29*, 384–390.

Barker D. J. P. (1998). *Mothers, babies and health in later life*. Edinburgh: Churchill Livingstone.

Becker, G. S., Grossman, M., & Murphy, K. (1994). An empirical analysis of cigarette addiction. *American Economic Review, 84*(3), 396–418.

Benjamin, D. J., Cesarini, D., Chabris, C. F., Glaeser, E. L., Laibson, D. I., Guðnason, V., . . . Lichtenstein, P. (2012a). The promises and pitfalls of genoeconomics. *Annual Review of Economics, 4*, 627–662.

Benjamin, D. J., Cesarini, D., van der Loos, M. J. H. M., Dawes, C. T., Koellinger, P. D., Magnusson, D. K. E., . . . Visscher, P. M. (2012b). The genetic architecture of economic and political preferences. *Proceedings of the National Academy of Sciences, 109*(21), 8026–8031.

Benjamin, D. J., Chabris, C. F., Glaeser, E. L., Gudnason, V., Harris, T. B., Laibson, D. I., . . . Purcell, S. (2007). Genoeconomics. In M. Weinstein, J. W. Vaupel, & K. W. Wachter (Eds.), *Biosocial surveys*. Washington, DC: National Academies, 304–335.

Biroli, P. (2015). *Genetic and economic interaction in the formation of human capital: The case of obesity*. Mimeo. Chicago: University of Chicago. Available at https://769262cf-a-62cb3a1a-s-sites.googlegroups.com/ site/pietrobiroli/files/ PietroBiroli_JMP.pdf?attachauth= ANoY7codDH29ZJ Msk3cRXi IghBoHyj2jfqRvequXbwMGIGMcofioKL J7iEo6IYvHKyKqzIN5X4_6-UsqmPXSneqB71iOJPsI_FMiGrMWl6WnpnieYQeCc2WEd_ JAYoRA301RmSozRkV3ICQElwV_ udo3MG19HxMGFDoi-y7uIAXEzo lQ9PbLYHq26zqG6h3j7XXyHLi SWoy501wNciuYSHsqQFs-GJqoLg2XsihT9cj1zn M4run4dipw%3D&attredirects=0

Björklund, A., Lindahl, M., & Plug, E. (2006). The origins of intergenerational associations: Lessons from Swedish adoption data. *Quarterly Journal of Economics, 121*, 999–1028.

Bröder, A., & Hohmann, N. (2003). Variations in risk taking behavior over the menstrual cycle: An improved replication. *Evolution and Human Behavior, 24*(6), 391–398.

Burkhauser, R., & Cawley, J. (2008). Beyond BMI: The value of more accurate measures of fatness and obesity in social science research. *Journal of Health Economics, 2*(2), 519–529.

Camerer, C., Cohen, J., Fehr, E., Glimcher, P., & Laibson, D. (forthcoming). Neuroeconomics. In J. H. Kagel and A. E. Roth (Eds.). *Handbook of experimental economics Volume 2*. Princeton University Press.

Carpenter, J., Garcia, J., & Lum, J. (2011). Dopamine receptor genes predict risk preferences, time preferences, and related economic choices. *Journal of Risk and Uncertainty, 42*, 233–261.

Caspi, A., McClay, J., Moffitt, T. E., Mill, J., Martin, J., Craig, I. W., Taylor, A., & Poulton, R. (2002). Role of genotype in the cycle of violence in maltreated children. *Science, 297*(5582), 851–854.

Cawley, J., Han, E., & Norton, E. (2011). The validity of genes related to neurotransmitters as instrumental variables. *Health Economics, 20*(3), 884–888.

Cesarini D., Dawes, C. T., Fowler, J., Johannesson, M., Lichtenstein, P., & Wallace, B. (2008). Heritability of cooperative behavior in the trust game. *Proceedings of the National Academy of Sciences, 105*, 3271–3276.

Cesarini, D., Dawes, C. T., Johannesson, M., Lichtenstein, P., & Wallace, B. (2009). Genetic variation in preferences for giving and risk-taking. *Quarterly Journal of Economics, 124*, 809–842.

Cesarini D., Johannesson, M., Lichtenstein, P., Sandewall, O., & Wallace, B. (2010). Genetic variation in financial decision-making. *Journal of Finance, 65*, 1725–1754.

Cesarini D., Johannesson, M., Magnusson, P., & Wallace, B. (2012). The behavioral genetics of behavioral anomalies. *Management Science, 58*(1), 21–34.

Chabris, C. F., Lee, J. J., Benjamin, D. J., Beauchamp, J. P., Glaeser, E. L., Borst, G., . . . Laibson, D. I. (2013). Why is it hard to find genes that are associated with social science traits? Theoretical and empirical considerations. *American Journal of Public Health, 103*(S1), S152–S166.

Chabris, C. F., Hebert, B. M., Benjamin, D. J., Beauchamp, J., Cesarini, D., van der Loos, M., . . . Laibson, D. (2012). Most reported genetic associations with general intelligence are probably false positives. *Psychological Science, 23*(11), 1314–1323.

Charney, E., & English, W. (2012). Candidate genes and political behavior. *American Political Science Review, 106*(1), 1–34.

Chen, Y., Katušcak, P., & Ozdenoren, E. (2013). Why can't a woman bid more like a man? *Games and Economic Behavior, 77*, 181–213.

Coates J. M., Gurnell, M., & Rustichini, A. (2009). Second-to-fourth digit ratio predicts success among high-frequency financial traders. *Proceedings of the National Academy of Sciences, 106*(2), 623–628.

Conley, D. (2009). The promise and challenges of incorporating genetic data into longitudinal social science surveys and research, *Biodemography and Social Biology, 55*(2), 238–251.

Conley, D., & Rauscher, E. (2013). Genetic interactions with prenatal social environment: Effects on academic and behavioral outcomes. *Journal of Health and Social Behavior, 54*(1), 109–127.

Conley, T. G., Hansen, C. B., & Rossi, P. E. (2012). Plausibly exogenous. *Review of Economics and Statistics, 94*, 260–272.

Conti, G., & Heckman, J. J. (2010). Understanding the early origins of the education- health gradient: A framework that can also be applied to analyze gene- environment interactions. *Perspectives on Psychological Science*, 5, 585–605.

Davey Smith, G. (2003). Mendelian randomization: Can genetic epidemiology contribute to understanding environmental determinants of disease? *International Journal of Epidemiology*, 32(1), 1–22.

Dawes, C. T., & Fowler, J. H. (2009). Partisanship, voting, and the dopamine D2 receptor gene. *Journal of Politics*, 71(3), 1157–1171.

DeNeve, J. -E., & Fowler, J. (2014). Credit card borrowing and the monoamine oxidase A (MAOA) gene. *Journal of Economic Behavior and Organization*, 107(B), 428–439.

Ding, W., Lehrer, S. F., Rosenquist, N. J., & Audrain-McGovern, J. (2006). *The impact of poor health on education: New evidence using genetic markers* (NBER Working Paper No. 12304). Cambridge, MA: National Bureau of Economic Research.

Ding, W., Lehrer, S. F., Rosenquist, J. N., & Audrain-McGovern, J. (2009). The impact of poor health on academic performance: New evidence using genetic markers. *Journal of Health Economics*, 28(3), 578–597.

Dreber, A., Apicella, C. L., Eisenberg, D. T. A., Garcia, J. R., Zamore, R. S., Lum, J. K., & Campbell, B. (2009). The 7R polymorphism in the dopamine receptor D4 gene (DRD4) is associated with financial risk taking in men. *Evolution and Human Behavior*, 30(2), 85–92.

Dreber, A., & Hoffman, M. (2007). *Risk preferences are partly predetermined.* Mimeo. Stockholm School of Economics.

Dreber, A., Rand, D. G., Wernerfelt, N., Garcia, J. R., Vilar, M. G., Lum, J. K., Zeckhauser, R., (2011). Dopamine and risk choices in different domains: findings among serious tournament bridge players. *Journal of Risk and Uncertainty*, 43(1), 19–38.

Dudbridge, F. (2013). Power and predictive accuracy of polygenic risk scores. *PLoS Genetics*, 9, e1003348.

Eaves, L. J., Last, K. A., Martin, N. G., & Jinks, J. L. (1977). A progressive approach to non-additivity and genotype-environmental covariance in the analysis of human differences. *British Journal of Mathematical and Statistical Psychology*, 30(1), 1–42.

Eisenberg, N., Duckworth, A. L., Spinrad, T. L., & Valiente, C. (2014). Conscientiousness: Origins in childhood. *Developmental Psychology*, 50, 1331–1349.

Eisenegger, C., Naef, M., Snozzi, R., Heinrichs, M. & Fehr, E. (2010). Prejudice and truth about the effect of testosterone on human bargaining behaviour. *Nature* 463(7279), 356–359.

Evans, W. N., & Farrelly, M. C. (1998). The compensating behavior of smokers: Taxes, tar, and nicotine. *RAND Journal of Economics*, 29, 578–595.

Fang, M. Z. (2013). Violating the monotonicity condition for instrumental variable dimorphic patterns of gene-behavior association. *Economics Letters*, 122(1), 59–63.

Farrelly, M. C., Nimsch, C. T., Hyland, A., & Cummings, M. (2004). The effects of higher cigarette prices on tar and nicotine consumption in a cohort of adult smokers. *Health Economics*, 13(1), 49–58.

Fletcher, J. M., & Lehrer, S. F. (2009*a*). *Using genetic lotteries within families to examine the causal impact of poor health on academic achievement* (NBER Working Paper No. 15148). Cambridge, MA: National Bureau of Economic Research.

Fletcher, J. M., & Lehrer, S. F. (2009*b*). The effects of adolescent health on educational outcomes: Causal evidence using genetic lotteries between siblings, *Forum for Health Economics & Policy*, 12(2), Article 8.

Fletcher, J. M., & Lehrer, S. F. (2011). Genetic lotteries within families. *Journal of Health Economics, 30*, 647–659.

Fowler, J. H., & Dawes, C. T. (2008). Two genes predict voter turnout. *Journal of Politics, 70*(3), 579–594.

Gee. S. K. (2014). *All the time in the world: An examination of time preferences using monetary delay discount rates.* MA Research paper, Queen's University, Kingston, Ontario, Canada.

Gilaie-Dotan, S., Tymula, A., Cooper, N., Kable, J., Glimcher, P., & Levy, I. (2014). Neuroanatomy predicts individual risk attitudes. *Journal of Neuroscience, 34*(37), 12394–12401.

Gluckman, P. D., & Hanson, M. (2005). *The fetal matrix: Evolution, development, & disease.* Cambridge: Cambridge University.

Goldberger, A. S. (1979). Heritability. *Economica, 46*(184), 327–247.

Grossman, M. (1972). On the concept of health capital and the demand for health. *Journal of Political Economy, 80*(2), 223–255.

Guo, G., Roettger, M., & Cai, T. (2008). The integration of genetic propensities into social control models of delinquency and violence among male youths. *American Sociological Review, 73*, 543–568.

Hansen, B. E. (1999). Threshold effects in non-dynamic panels: Estimation, testing, & inference. *Journal of Econometrics, 93*, 345–368.

Hatemi, P. K. (2013). The influence of major life events on economic attitudes in a world of gene- environment interplay. *American Journal of Political Science, 57*(4), 987–1000.

Haushofer, J. &Fehr, E. (2014), On the psychology of poverty. *Science, 344*, 862–867.

Hausman, J. A., Newey, W. K., Woutersen, T., Chao, J. C., & Swanson, N. R. (2012). Instrumental variables estimation with heteroskedasticity and many instruments. *Quantitative Economics, 3*(2), 211–255.

Hayden, E. C. (2013). Dangerous Work. *Nature, 502*, 5–6.

Heckman, J. J. (2007). The economics, technology and neuroscience of human capability formation. *Proceedings of the National Academy of Sciences, 104*, 13250–13255.

Herrmann, M., & Rockoff, J. (2012). Does menstruation explain gender gaps in work absenteeism? *Journal of Human Resources, 47*, 493–508.

Hewitt, J. K. (2012). Editorial policy on candidate gene association and candidate gene-by-environment interaction studies of complex traits. *Behavior Genetics, 42*(1), 1–2.

Huizink, A., Robles de Medina, P., Mulder, E., Visser, G., & Buitelaar, J. (2003). Stress during pregnancy is associated with developmental outcome in infancy. *Journal of Child Psychology and Psychiatry, 44*, 810–818.

Huang, W., Sun, Y., & Sun, J. (2011). Combined effects of FTO rs9939609 and MC4R rs17782313 on obesity and BMI in Chinese Han populations. *Endocrine, 39*(1), 69–74.

Ichino, A., & Moretti, E. (2009). Biological gender differences, absenteeism and the earning gap. *American Economic Journal—Applied Economics, 1*(1), 183–218.

Jarvis, M. J., Tunstall-Pedoe, H., Feyerabend, C., Vesey, C., & Saloojee, Y. (1984). Biochemical markers of smoke absorption and self-reported exposure to passive smoking. *Journal of Epidemiology and Community Health, 38*, 335–339.

Kandasamy, N., Hardy, B., Page, L., Schaffner, M., Graggaber, J., Powlson, A. S., . . . Coates, J. (2014). Cortisol shifts financial risk preferences. *Proceedings of the National Academy of Sciences, 111*(9), 3608–3613.

Katan, M. B. (1986). Apolipoprotein E isoforms, serum cholesterol and cancer. *Lancet, 327*, 507–508.

Kendler K. S., Aggen S. H., Czajkowski, N., Roysamb, E., Tambs, K., Torgersen, S., ... Reichborn-Kjennerud, T. (2008). The structure of genetic and environmental risk factors for DSM-IV personality disorders: A multivariate twin study. *Archives of General Psychiatry*, *65*, 1438–1446.

Knafo, A., Israel, S., Darvasi, A., Bachner-Melman, R., Uzefovsky, F., Cohen, L., ... Ebstein, R. P. (2008). Individual differences in allocation of funds in the dictator game associated with length of the arginine vasopressin 1 a receptor RS 3 promoter region and correlation between RS 3 length and hippocampal mRNA. *Genes, Brain and Behavior*, *7*(3), 266–275.

Kochanska, G., Kim, S., Barry, R. A., & Philibert, R. A. (2011). Children's genotypes interact with maternal responsive care in predicting children's competence: Diathesis-stress or differential susceptibility? *Development and Psychopathology*, *23*, 605–616.

Kohler, H. -P., Behrman, J. R., & Schnittker, J. (2011). Social science methods for twins data: Integrating causality, endowments, and heritability. *Biodemography and Social Biology*, *57*(1), 88–141.

Kuhnen C. M., & Chiao, J. Y. (2009). Genetic determinants of financial risk taking. *PLoS One*, *4*(2), e4362. Available at http://journals.plos.org/plosone/article?id=10.1371/journal.pone.0004362

Kuhnen, C. M., Samanez-Larkin, G. R., & Knutson, B. (2013). Serotonergic genotypes, neuroticism, & financial choices. *PLoS One*, *8*, e54632.

Lazopoulou, N., Gkioka, E., Ntalla, I., Pervanidou, P., Magiakou, A. M., Roma-Giannikou, E., ... Kanaka-Gantenbein, C. (2015). The combined effect of MC4R and FTO risk alleles on childhood obesity in Greece. *Hormones* (Athens), *14*(1), 126–133.

Lee, S., & Shaikh, A. (2014). Multiple testing and heterogeneous treatment effects: Re-evaluating the effect of PROGRESA on school enrollment. *Journal of Applied Econometrics*, *29*, 612–626.

Lehrer, S. F., Pohl, V. R., & Song, K. (2015). *Reinvestigating how welfare reform influences labor supply: A multiple testing approach*. Mimeo. Queen's University, Kingston, Ontario, Canada. Available at https://vincentpohl.files.wordpress.com/2014/11/lps_paper_v1.pdf

Lehrer, S. F., Tremblay, R. E., Vitaro, F., & Schaal, B. (2007). *Raging hormones in puberty: Do they influence adolescent risky behavior?* Mimeo. Queen's University, Kingston, Ontario, Canada. Available at http://post.queensu.ca/~lehrers/hormones.pdf

Liu K. H., Chan, Y. L., Chan, J. C., Chan, W. B., Kong, M. O., & Poon, M. Y. (2005). The preferred magnetic resonance imaging planes in quantifying visceral adipose tissue and evaluating cardiovascular risk. *Diabetes and Obesity Metabolism*, *7*, 547–554.

Maestripieri, D., Hoffman, C. L., Anderson, G. M., Carter, S., & Higley, J. D. (2009). Mother–infant interactions in free-ranging rhesus macaques: Relationships between physiological and behavioral variables. *Physiology & Behavior*, *96*(4–5), 613–619.

Manning J. T, Scutt, D., Wilson, J., & Lewis-Jones, D. I. (1998). The ratio of second to fourth digit length: A predictor of sperm numbers and concentrations of testosterone, luteinizing hormone and oestrogen. *Human Reproduction*, *13*, 3000–3004.

Manski, C. (2013). *Public policy in an uncertain world*. Cambridge, MA: Harvard University.

McCarthy, M. I., Abecasis, G. R., Cardon, L. R., Goldstein, D. B., Little, J., Ioannidis, J. P. A. & Hirschhorn, J. N. (2008). Genome-wide association studies for complex traits: Consensus, uncertainty and challenges. *Nature Reviews Genetics*, *9*, 356–369.

Mertins, V., Schote, A. B., Hoffeld, W., Griessmair, M., & Meyer, J. (2011). Genetic susceptibility for individual cooperation preferences: The role of monoamine oxidase a gene (MAOA) in the voluntary provision of public goods. *PLoS One*, *6*(6), 16.

Moffitt, T. E., Caspi, A., & Rutter, M. (2005). Strategy for investigating interactions between measured genes and measured environments. *Archives of General Psychiatry, 62*(5), 473–481.

Montgomery, P., Ryus, C. R., Dolan, C. S., Dopson, S., & Scott, L. M. (2012). Sanitary pad interventions for girls' education in Ghana: A pilot study. *PLoS One, 7*(10), e48274.

Niederle, M., & Vesterlund, L. (2011). Gender and competition. *Annual Review of Economics, 3*, 601–630.

Norton, E. & Han, C. E. (2008). Genetic information, obesity, and labor market outcomes. *Health Economics, 17*(9), 1089–1104.

Oster, E., & Thornton, R. (2011). Menstruation, sanitary products, and school attendance: Evidence from a randomized evaluation. *American Economic Journal: Applied Economics, 3*(1), 91–100.

Pearson, M., & Schipper, B. C. (2013). Menstrual cycle and competitive bidding. *Games and Economic Behavior, 78*(1), 1–20.

Plug, E., & Vijverberg, W. (2003). Schooling, family background, and adoption: Is it nature or is it nurture? *Journal of Political Economy, 111*, 611–641.

Purcell, S. (2002). Variance components models for gene environment interaction in twin analysis. *Twin Research and Human Genetics*, 5(06), 554–571.

Rietveld, C. A., Conley, D., Eriksson, N., Esko, T., Medland, S. E., Vinkhuyzen, A. A. E., . . . Koellinger, P. D. (2014*a*). Replicability and robustness of GWAS for behavioral traits. *Psychological Science, 25*(11), 1975–1986.

Rietveld, C. A., Esko, T., Davies, G., Pers, T. H., Turley, P. A., Benyamin, B., . . . Koellinger, P. D. (2014*b*). Common genetic variants associated with cognitive performance identified using proxy-phenotype method. *Proceedings of the National Academy of Sciences, 111*(38), 13790–4.

Rietveld, C. A., Medland, S. E., Derringer, J., Yang, J., Esko, T., Martin, N. W., . . . Koellinger, P. D. (2013*a*). GWAS of 126,559 individuals identifies genetic variants associated with educational attainment. *Science, 340*(6139), 1467–1471.

Rietveld, C. A., Cesarini, D., Benjamin, D. J., Koellinger, P. D., De Neve, J. -E., Tiemeier, H., . . . Bartels, M. (2013*b*). Molecular genetics and subjective well-being. *Proceedings of the National Academy of Sciences, 110*(24), 9692–9697.

Rosenquist, J. N., Lehrer, S. F., Malley, A. J. O., Zaslavsky, A. M., Smoller, J. W., & Christakis, N. A. (2015). Cohort of birth modifies the association between FTO genotype and BMI. *Proceedings of the National Academy of Sciences, 112*(2), 354–359.

Rutter, M. (2006). *Genes and behavior: Nature-nurture interplay explained.* Oxford: Blackwell.

Rutter, M., Moffitt, T. E., & Caspi, A. (2006). Gene-environment interplay and psychopathology: Multiple varieties but real effects. *Journal of Child Psychology and Psychiatry, 47*(3–4), 226–261.

Rutter, M., & Silberg, J. (2002). Gene–environment interplay in relation to emotional and behavioral disturbance. *Annual Review of Psychology*, 53, 463–490.

Sacerdote, B. (2007). How large are the effects from changes in family environment? A study of Korean American adoptees. *Quarterly Journal of Economics, 122*, 119–157.

Saudino, K. J. (1997). Moving beyond the heritability question: New directions in behavioral genetic studies of personality. *Current Directions in Psychological Science, 6*, 86–90.

Settle, J. E., Dawes, C. T., Christakis, N. A., & Fowler, J. H. (2010). Friendships moderate an association between a dopamine gene variant and political ideology. *Journal of Politics*, 72(04), 1189–1198.

Shanahan, M. J., Vaisey, S., Erickson, L. D., & Smolen, A. (2008). Environmental contingencies and genetic propensities: Social capital, educational continuation, & dopamine receptor gene DRD2. *American Journal of Semiotics, 114* (86), S260–S286.

Shen, W., Punyanitya, M., Wang, Z., Gallagher, D., St-Onge, M. P., Albu J., Heymsfield, S. B., & Heshka, S. (2004). Total body skeletal muscle and adipose tissue volumes: Estimation from a single abdominal cross-sectional image. *Journal of Applied Physiology, 97*, 2333–2338.

Smith, K., Alford, J. R., Hatemi, P. K., Eaves, L. J., Funk, C., & Hibbing, J. R. (2012). Biology, ideology, & epistemology: How do we know political attitudes are inherited and why should we care. *American Journal of Political Science, 56*(1), 17–33.

Taubman, P. (1976). The determinants of earnings: Genetics, family, and other environments: A study of white male twins. *American Economic Review, 66*, 858–870.

Thompson, O. (2014). Economic background and educational attainment: The role of gene-environment interactions. *Journal of Human Resources, 49*(2), 263–294.

Van IJzendoorn, M. H., & Bakermans-Kranenburg, M. J. (2012). A sniff of trust: Meta-analysis of the effects of intranasal oxytocin administration on face recognition, trust to in-group, and trust to out-group. *Psychoneuroendocrinology, 37*, 438–443.

Venter, J. C., Adams, M. D., Myers, E. W., Li, P. W., Mural, R. J., & Sutton, G. G. (2001). The sequence of the human genome. *Science, 291*, 1304–1351.

Wallace, B., Cesarini, D., Lichtenstein, P., & Johannesson, M. (2007). Heritability of ultimatum game responder behavior. *Proceedings of the National Academy of Sciences, 104*, 15631–15634.

Wehby, G., Fletcher, J. M., Lehrer, S. F., Moreno, L. M., Murray, J. C., Wilcox, A., & Lie, R. T. (2011). A genetic instrumental variables analysis of the effects of prenatal smoking on birth weight: Evidence from two samples. *Biodemography and Social Biology, 57*(1), 3–32.

Wilson, G. D., & Patterson, J. R. (1968). A new measure of conservatism, *British Journal of Social and Clinical Psychology, 8*, 264–269.

Yu, I. T., Lee, S. -H., Lee, Y. -S., & Son, H. (2004). Differential effects of corticosterone and dexamethasone on hippocampal neurogenesis in vitro. *Biochemical and Biophysical Research Communications, 317*(2), 484–490.

Zak, P. J., Kurzban, R., Ahmadi, S., Swerdloff, R. S., Park, J., Efremidze, L., . . . Matzner, W. (2009). Testosterone administration decreases generosity in the ultimatum game. *PLoS One, 4*(12), E8330.

Zethraeus, N., Kocoska-Maras, L., Ellingsen, T., von Schoultz, B., Hirschberg, A., & Johannessen, M. (2009). A randomized trial of the effect of estrogen and testosterone on economic behavior. *Proceeding of the National Academy of Sciences, 106*, 6535–6538.

Zhong, S., Israel, S., Xue, H., Ebstein, R. P., & Chew, S. H. (2009), Monoamine oxidase a gene (MAOA) associated with attitude towards longshot risks. *PLoS One, 4*(12), e8516.

Zuk, O., Hechter, E., Sunyaev, S. R., & Lander, E. S. (2012). The mystery of missing heritability: Genetic interactions create phantom heritability. *Proceedings of the National Academy of Sciences, 109*, 1193–1198.

CHAPTER 18

HOW GENETICS CAN INFORM HEALTH ECONOMICS

GEORGE L. WEHBY

GENETIC variation has been well-characterized with the completion of the Human Genome Project in 2003 (HGP, 2015) and several other projects that investigated the human genome over the past decade. Advances in genetic assays that can measure the different aspects of DNA variation and statistical methodologies to analyze large datasets containing millions of genetic variants per individual have enabled the study of association of genetic variation with multiple outcomes, including many diseases but also outcomes of particular interest to social scientists such as personality traits, education, and mental health conditions.

Ample research evidence has indicated that genes influence preferences, health, and health care use, all of which are important variables in conceptual and empirical work in health economics. This evidence has mostly come from twin studies comparing identical and nonidentical twins, although analyses of molecular data have begun to also provide new evidence by comparing genetic variation and outcomes of unrelated individuals. Whereas in reality researchers have only begun to scratch the surface of understanding genetic influences on such outcomes and much work remains to characterize involved genes and understand their functional pathways, this evidence already points to multiple ways in which genetics can inform health economics studies.

This chapter provides a conceptual overview of the pathways through which genes may relate to preferences, health, and health care use and summarizes related empirical research. Next, it discusses some of the main implications of genetics for health economics research, including main research areas and methodological considerations. Finally, it briefly highlights how incorporating genetics in health economics studies can be of interest to policy-making.

18.1 Links Between Genes, Preferences, Human Capital, and Health

Several direct and indirect channels link genes to health. Wehby et al. (Wehby, Domingue, & Boardman, 2015) provide a conceptual framework that illustrates how genes can affect health and health services use. In addition to directly impacting health status, genes can also indirectly affect health by modifying preferences for risk-taking, prevention, and human capital, which can directly affect personal investments in health (e.g., through the effort a person dedicates to preventing disease, as well as his or her use of health care services, which, in turn, affects health status).

18.1.1 Genetic Effects on Health

Genes impact health status directly by modifying disease risk and severity. Multiple chronic conditions such as diabetes, cardiovascular disease, and mental health conditions (e.g., major depression disorder) have been shown to have a strong genetic component. Evidence on the magnitude of overall genetic effects from twin studies indicates that an important fraction of the variance of multiple health conditions—sometimes referred to as the "heritability" parameter in the literature—can be explained by genetic differences, such as 30% of variance in hypertension, 30% for strokes, 50% or more for type-2 diabetes, 30–40% for major depression, approximately 80% for schizophrenia and 40–90% for asthma (Agarwal, Williams, & Fisher, 2005; Cardno & Gottesman, 2000; Carlsson, Ahlbom, Lichtenstein, & Andersson, 2013; Kendler, Gatz, Gardner, & Pedersen, 2006; Thomsen, van der Sluis, Kyvik, Skytthe, & Backer, 2010). There is also evidence that genetic differences explain an important fraction (approximately 50%) of the variance in the number of chronic conditions an individual has (Wehby et al., 2015).

Other health outcomes that are commonly studied in health economics, including self-reported health and body weight, have also been shown through twin studies to be influenced by genes. Twin studies indicate that at least a quarter of the variation in self-reported health status can be explained by genes. For example, Romeis et al. (2000), using data on US male twins from the 1987 Vietnam Era Twin (VET) study, reported that as much as 40% of self-reported health variation can be explained by genetic differences. Wehby et al. (2015), using data from the 1995–1996 National Survey of Midlife Development in the United States (MIDUS), reported that 29% of variation in self-reported health status can be due to genes. A wider range of 25–64% for the effect of genes on variation in self-reported health status has been reported across twin studies (summarized in Mosing et al., 2010).

Recent work that estimates genetic influence using molecular genetic variation between unrelated individuals from the Health and Retirement Study (HRS) (using a method known as genome-wide complex trait analysis (GCTA; Yang, Lee, Goddard,

& Visscher, 2011; explained later) reports that genetic differences can explain close to 18% of the variation in self-reported health (Boardman et al., 2015). Although less than the range reported in twin studies, estimating genetic influences using molecular genetic data, as in Boardman et al.'s work, captures only additive genetic effects and may be sensitive to correlation between genetic variants within a population (Boardman et al., 2015). Therefore, such analyses may (and empirically tend to) produce lower estimates of outcome variance explained by genes than do twin studies—as noted here for self-reported health status, but also found in other traits such as height (e.g., Yang et al., 2010). Nonetheless, this work corroborates the evidence from twin studies that genes may at least moderately explain some of the variation in health status within a population.

Body weight measured by body mass index (BMI; weight in kilograms divided by height in meters squared) has also been well-evaluated in twin studies of genetic influence. Using a large sample of more than 23,000 twins from Sweden, Carlsson et al. (2013) report that as much as 65% of the variance in BMI can be explained by genes. However, estimates of BMI heritability across twin studies has ranged from close to 50% to as much as 90%, and nearly half of that variability is suggested to be due to differences in analytical approaches (Elks et al., 2012). Combining data from several published studies for a total sample of close to 18,000 twin pairs, Nan et al. (2012) estimate heritability of BMI at 61% among older adults, 80% among young adults, and 75% among children. Evidence of a strong genetic influence on BMI also emerges from analyzing genome-wide genetic variation between unrelated individuals; Boardman et al. (2015) report that close to 43% of BMI variation in the HRS sample can be due to genetic effects, consistent with the lower twin-based heritability estimate for older adults (Nan et al., 2012).

It is important to further clarify what these heritability measures mean, especially for BMI given the substantial rise in BMI and obesity over the past three decades in the United States. These estimates indicate that a sizeable fraction of the variation in BMI within a population can be explained by genetic differences between individuals. The genetic influence obviously does not explain the obesity epidemic, which is driven by environmental factors. For example, Courtemanche et al. (Courtemanche, Pinkston, Ruhm, & Wehby, 2015) investigated the effects of several economic factors and found that changes in these factors jointly explain 37% of the rise in BMI, 43% of the obesity rise, and close to 60% of the rise in class II+ obesity (BMI ≥ 35) between 1990 and 2010. Despite the BMI rise in the population, genetic factors would still explain a sizeable proportion of the variation in BMI within the population. Of course, it is possible that changes in environmental factors have moderated genetic effects, and these can be investigated in gene-environment (G×E) interaction studies, as described in Section 2.2.

Even though most of the genetic mechanisms that account for the share of gene-explained variance in such health outcomes are yet to be identified, the evidence on moderate to strong genetic heritability for several health outcomes (including general measures such as self-reported health, number of chronic conditions, and BMI) indicate that genetic differences between individuals in a population can be an important source of heterogeneity when studying the determinants or consequences of these outcomes in health economic research. As discussed later, this heterogeneity can cause bias—specifically a form of omitted variables bias—if the genes that impact these health outcomes are also related (independently from their impact on health outcomes) to factors that influence these outcomes or are influenced by them. For example, as discussed later, genes can also explain variation in educational attainment, and there is evidence that some of the genetic variation between self-reported health status and education is shared (Boardman et al., 2015). Therefore, recognizing the role of genes as an important source of variation not only in health but also in health determinants can be important for interpreting empirical findings and guiding study designs.

18.1.2 Genetic Effects on Economic Preferences

Economic preferences, including those related to risk-taking and future discounting, are important determinants of health. Individuals who are less risk-averse and more present-oriented can invest much less in their health, may engage less in prevention, and may be more prone to adopt risky behaviors such as smoking, binge drinking, or avoiding physical activity (e.g., Fuchs, 1982). Preferences can be shaped by several aspects of the environment where an individual is reared, as well as by social interactions such as peer effects, but they can also be partly modified by genes.

Evidence from twin studies also suggests that genes can explain some of the variation in these preferences. Cesarini et al. (Cesarini, Dawes, Johannesson, Lichtenstein, & Wallace, 2009) find that around 20% of the variation in risk aversion can be due to genetic differences in a twin comparison model. This finding is supported; heritability of risk aversion using genome-wide genetic variation and GCTA is estimated to be around 14% (Benjamin et al., 2012). Based on twin studies, stronger genetic influence is reported on future discounting, with up to 30–50% of the variation in discounting potentially due to genes (Anokhin, Golosheykin, Grant, & Heath, 2011).

These findings for these preferences are supported by research showing strong genetic influences on several risky behaviors such as smoking and excessive alcohol consumption, as well as on preventive behaviors. Based on twin studies, as much as 50% of the variation—with higher estimates reported in some studies—in consistent smoking and alcohol addiction may be explained by genes (Boardman, Blalock, & Pampel, 2010; Maes et al., 2004; McGue et al., 2013; Stacey, Clarke, & Schumann, 2009). Since economic preferences such as risk aversion and future discounting are important determinants of risky behaviors, the evidence of moderate heritability for such preferences and risky behaviors indicates that genes can contribute to a broad range of health behaviors that can in turn affect health. Indeed, there is evidence of genetic influence on certain health behaviors. For example, twin comparisons suggest that a large fraction of variation (40–70%) in engaging in physical activity (exercise) may be explained by genes (Moor et al., 2011; Stubbe et al., 2006). Similarly, there is evidence that use of preventive care and overall personal effort in preventing disease are influenced by genes, as discussed later in Section 1.3 (Wehby et al., 2015).

Another dimension of economic preferences that is relevant for health is the extent to which a person trusts others. This is especially relevant when studying the use of health services, adherence to treatment, and selection of providers, which can be influenced by how much patients trust health care personnel (Mainous et al., 2001). Twin studies suggest a wide range of heritability estimates for trust, between 10% and 60% (Cesarini et al., 2008; Oskarsson, Dawes, Johannesson, & Magnusson, 2012; Sturgis et al., 2010). However, GCTA analysis of genome-wide data suggests heritability of trust at around 24% (Benjamin et al., 2012). Because GCTA estimates again may not capture genetic effects as fully as do twin studies, the evidence from both twin comparisons and GCTA analysis suggests that genes may explain at least a moderate fraction of the variation in trust.

No studies have directly investigated the heritability of trust in health care providers. Wehby et al. (2015), using the MIDUS data on twins, examined the extent to which genes can explain variation in personal beliefs about the effectiveness of health care in case of illness. The specific question was: "When I am sick, getting better is in the doctor's hands," answered on a 7-category scale from strongly agree to strongly disagree. Although this question may not only represent a measure of trust, it does reflect the extent to which a person believes that health care providers can be effective in restoring health. That study finds no evidence of a genetic influence on a person expressing strong beliefs in health care effectiveness (a dichotomous measure for strongly agreeing with the question), with a null heritability estimate (Wehby et al., 2015). Again, this finding could be a reflection of the measure not fully capturing trust in providers versus a general belief about the effectiveness of health care, but it raises the possibility that genetic influence on trust may be context-specific.

18.1.3 Genetic Effects on Preferences for Prevention

The just-summarized research indicates that genes may contribute to determining health status and to shaping several health-related preferences and behaviors. Another set of preferences recently shown to be related to genes are one's preferences for activities to prevent disease or "prevention preferences." Using the MIDUS data and a twin comparison model, Wehby et al. (2015) report that more than one-third of the variation in reporting strong beliefs that personal actions can reduce the risk of heart disease and cancer can be explained by genes. When aggregating these two measures with another measure about beliefs that personal actions influence health status into an index of prevention preferences, Wehby et al. (2015) find that about one-third of the variation in that index is related to genes. These preference measures are unlikely to be reflecting self-efficacy; the study finds no evidence of significant genetic influence on a measure of how much control an individual reports having over his or her health.

Consistent with the effects on prevention preferences, Wehby et al. (2015) find that genetic variation explains an important fraction of the variation in prevention effort. The first measure is an indicator for whether someone works hard to stay healthy; the heritability estimate for that measure is greater than 50%. Another indicator is how much thought and effort the person puts to his or her health; this has a heritability estimate of about 30%. Furthermore, that study finds an important genetic component (about 40% heritability) for whether a preventive check-up was obtained in the past 12 months (Wehby et al., 2015). This finding is consistent with another twin study that reports that genes may explain 37–66% of the variation in women's participation in different programs for cancer screening (Treloar, McDonald, & Martin, 1999).

These results are of particular relevance for research that investigates the demand for and effectiveness of preventive care. Since prevention is considered to be an integral pathway for health production, the potential for genetic effects to modify prevention preferences and activity creates a source of latent heterogeneity that, if ignored, may result in serious bias. For example, studying a preventive behavior as an input for health can be potentially biased by shared genetic effects on both prevention and health if some of the genes that influence prevention preferences and activity impact health in other ways (in which case these genes could cause omitted variables bias). The empirical work on this point, however, is very sparse. Wehby et al. (2015) find very weak evidence that part of the correlation between prevention preferences and health status may be due to some shared genetic influence.

18.1.4 Genetic Effects on Use of Health Care Treatments

In contrast to the findings of a strong genetic influence on prevention preferences and use of prevention services, the evidence on genetic effects on use of curative health services is more mixed. In their twin study using the MIDUS data, Wehby et al. (2015) find that genes seem to influence use of prescription drug use: more than 40% of the variation in that outcome can be explained by genetic differences in their sample. This finding is consistent with the large genetic influence reported for the number of chronic conditions a person has, which is the main driver for use of prescription drugs.

In contrast, Wehby et al. (2015) find no significant genetic influence on any use of outpatient services for physical health problems, inpatient treatments, or urgent care in the past 12 months. The heritability estimate for outpatient care is 17% but is insignificant; the heritability estimates for hospitalizations and urgent care are close to null. Although they find no statistically significant heritability for use of mental health services, they estimate heritability at around 27%, indicating that genes can still play a role in the use of mental health treatments (Wehby et al., 2015). Finding that genes influence the use of mental health services would be consistent with the evidence of genetic effects on mental health conditions (as noted earlier).

Two other studies examine genetic effects on the use of health care treatments. Using the 1987 VET study data, True et al. (1997) report that seeking health treatments for mental health, joint problems, and hearing problems is tied to genes that can explain 42–56% of the variation in use of services. The heritability estimates for seeking treatment for these conditions exceed those for the conditions themselves (heritability estimates of 24–52%). Using 1992 VET data, True et al. (1996) report that genes can explain 41% of the variation in seeking treatment for alcoholism, consistent with the estimates of treatment-seeking for other conditions.

One potential reason for the mixed evidence regarding use of curative health services can be due to differences in samples and measures between studies. The measures used in Wehby et al. (2015) for any use of outpatient care for physical illnesses, any hospitalization, and urgent care use are more generic and general in capturing use of health services than are those used by True et al. (1996, 1997), which are specific to certain conditions. It is worth noting, though, that the heritability estimates for seeking treatment for mental health problems is twice as large in True et al. (1997) than in Wehby et al. (2015). Together, these studies again suggest that genes can play an important role in use of mental health services. Furthermore, as mentioned earlier, Wehby et al. (2015) find no genetic influence on personal beliefs in the effectiveness of curative health services, which could partly explain why the heritability estimates for these conditions are much less than those found for prevention. However, as the authors note, further work is needed using more precise measures and more generalizable samples to examine genetic influences on use of curative health services.

18.1.5 Genetic Effects on Human Capital and Education

The role of human capital in health production has received great attention in health economics. There are both causal and noncausal ways through which human capital can relate to health. Causally, human capital can be considered a technological factor that improves the productivity of household investments and health care inputs for health (Grossman, 1972). Related to that is the person's efficiency in gathering and processing health-related information. For example, individuals who have greater cognitive skills may be more efficient in surveying the Internet to obtain useful information about preventive behaviors or finding higher quality providers; similarly, stronger noncognitive skills may increase a person's benefit from a visit with a provider, such as through improved communication and a subsequently greater flow of information.

Education is the main proxy measure for human capital used in the empirical health economics literature. A wide literature documents education gradients in health and health behaviors (Conti, Heckman, & Urzua, 2010; Cutler & Lleras-Muney, 2010). There is strong evidence from twin and family-based studies that part of the variation in educational attainment is related to genetic differences, with a heritability estimate range of between 40% and 70% (Branigan, McCallum, & Freese, 2013). A recent GCTA analysis of heritability of educational attainment using genome-wide molecular data from the HRS suggests that close to 33% of the variation can be due to genetic differences (Boardman et al., 2015). However, a lower GCTA-based estimate of about 16% has been reported for a Swedish sample (Benjamin et al., 2012). As noted earlier, however, GCTA estimates may not fully capture genetic influences in the heritability estimate and can be specific to the estimation sample.

Genome-wide association studies (GWAS), which investigate the association of a phenotype with a large number of single nucleotide polymorphisms (SNPs; DNA base-pair variants), are beginning to be employed for outcomes of particular interest to social scientists (e.g., educational attainment). Because these studies include a large number of tests, the significance threshold has to be corrected for multiple testing, with $p < 5 \times 10^{-8}$ (or 1×10^{-8}) being commonly used. Because each SNP is likely to have a very small effect on the phenotype, very large samples are needed.

A recent GWAS of educational attainment based on an international consortium of more than 100,000 individuals and a collection of more than 1 million SNPs found three significant SNPs at the GWAS significance threshold (Rietveld et al., 2013). However, collectively, these SNPs explain an extremely small part of variation in education attainment (Rietveld et al., 2013). Building on this work, another study found significant associations of SNPs related to educational attainment (at more relaxed significance thresholds than formal GWAS levels) with measures of cognitive performance and health, thus highlighting potential common pathways, but still explaining a very small fraction (<0.5%) of the variation in the cognitive outcomes (Rietveld et al., 2014). Some of the genes associated with educational attainment and implicated in cognitive performance may be involved in synaptic plasticity, a main neurological process for learning and memory (Rietveld et al., 2014). Much remains to be understood, however, about the genetic architecture of educational attainment and its relationship to related outcomes such as cognitive performance, both in terms of involved genes and their functions.

As a whole, the evidence for genetic influences on educational attainment suggests another potential pathway through which genes can influence health and health behaviors. This is of great relevance for the health economics research on educational gradients because it suggests another link to consider between education and health. It is unclear, however, whether some of these genes can independently affect both education and health (commonly referred to as a gene having "pleiotropic" effects on two outcomes—in which case they would cause omitted variables bias if ignored) or whether part of the causal impact of education is rooted in genetic influences on educational attainment. In other words, this latter scenario reflects genes that influence education but that only indirectly affect health through their effects on education.

Whether two phenotypes are partly correlated because of shared genetic effects can be evaluated in twin analysis—commonly referred to as "bivariate" analysis in contrast to the "univariate" estimation of heritability for a certain phenotype—or, more recently, using the GCTA method applied to genome-wide data. In both cases, the question is whether the correlation between these phenotypes is partly explained by genetic similarity. In the case of education and health, the question is whether individuals who have stronger correlation between education and health are also more genetically similar. Some evidence from twin studies indicates that part of the correlations between education and certain health indicators such as physical health (Johnson et al., 2010) or metabolic markers (Vermeiren et al., 2012) can be due to shared genetic influences.

Recently, Boardman et al. (2015) investigate this question using genome-wide data and GCTA in the HRS and find that some of the association between education and depression can be explained by genes that affect both outcomes; the same is found for education and self-rated health but not for education and BMI. The authors clearly note, however, that this finding does not distinguish between whether the same genes have independent influence these outcomes (i.e., by having pleiotropic effects on education and self-rated health/depression) and whether education mediates such genetic effects on health. The first scenario would be a cause for omitted variable bias, but the second would not (Boardman et al., 2015).

Although such work is important in shedding light on whether education and health are partly connected via genetic pathways, it clearly highlights the need for much further research to elucidate the various ways in which genes can connect education and health. Until that is revealed, one may need to seriously consider the possibility of omitted variable bias due to genes when attempting to identify the causal effects of education on health using individual-level sources of variation in education. Examining the heritability of health literacy (i.e., the extent of individual knowledge about health) can shed some light on the genetic correlation between education and health.

In their twin analysis of the MIDUS data, Wehby et al. (2015) include an indicator for knowledge about own health derived from the following question answered on a 4-category scale from "not at all true" to "extremely true": "I am often aware of various things happening within my body." The authors estimate heritability of a dichotomous indicator for answering this question as "extremely true" or "not at all true" at around 14%, although the estimate is far from being statistically significant. Observing some heritability, however (admittedly without statistical significance), is consistent with the theory that some of the genetic association between education and health can be through better health-related knowledge from education, in contrast to pleiotropic effects.

18.2 Research Implications and Methodologies

Several research areas in health economics can potentially benefit from incorporating genetic information and methods. Among these are examining genetic influences on health and inputs, G×E interactions, controlling for latent biological effects in health production functions and demand functions for health behaviors, and use of genes as instruments to identify causal effects of health on economic and social outcomes. The next sections briefly discuss these areas and the methodologies that may be considered.

18.2.1 Understanding Genetic Influences

Quantifying genetic influences on health status and economic and behavioral determinants of health and whether genes play a role in connecting these inputs with health can further our understanding of the various health production mechanisms and guide empirical models to account for the possibilities of genetic confounders. Such work can examine the overall magnitude of genetic estimates by estimating heritability of health phenotypes as well as the various determinants discussed earlier, such as economic preferences, prevention preferences and effort, use of health services, and human capital and related measures including education and income. In addition to quantifying the magnitude of genetic influences on each of these measures alone, one can examine the extent to which they can be correlated due to genes. We briefly discuss two methodologies to achieve this: twin studies and GCTA using genome-wide data on a large sample of SNPs.

18.2.1.1 *Twin Studies*

As indicated previously, twin studies have been extremely useful for quantifying the overall contribution of genes to a certain trait. Twin analysis and, more broadly, family-based methods (such as those that include biological and adopted children) are based on knowledge about the extent to which family members share DNA on average and certain assumptions about environmental effects. Twin analysis is based on comparing the outcome correlation between identical twins who share all of their genes to that between nonidentical twins who share half of their genes (on average). In the basic model, the difference in these correlations in the studied trait is shown to be half of the variance explained by genetic variation or the "heritability."

The basic model requires certain assumptions, the main one being that identical twins do not share a more similar environment than nonidentical twins. Other assumptions include lack of G×E interactions, no genetic relatedness between parents, and additive genetic effects, although some of these can be relaxed in variations of the basic model. Several methods have been developed to estimate twin models, including regression based methods (e.g., DeFries & Fulker, 1985), structural equation models (Boker et al., 2011), and generalized linear mixed models (Rabe-Hesketh, Skrondal, & Gjessing, 2008).

In addition to estimating the heritability for a single trait—commonly referred to as a univariate analysis—the twin model can be extended to study the extent to which two traits or outcomes are correlated because of shared genetic influences. This analysis—commonly referred to as a bivariate analysis—estimates the "genetic correlation" between two traits. This cross-twin cross-trait analysis assesses how much one trait in one twin can be predicted by the other trait in the co-twin and how this prediction varies between identical and nonidentical twins. Finding stronger prediction among identical twins indicates genetic correlation between the two traits because the traits are more strongly related among more genetically similar individuals. Additional details can be found elsewhere (e.g., Boardman et al., 2015; Wehby et al., 2015).

As mentioned earlier, bivariate analysis does not indicate whether the two variables are related because they are independently influenced by the same genes or because genes affect one indirectly by affecting the other. However, such work could provide useful information for health economics studies by identifying the potential for genes to complicate the specification of health production and demand functions, such as when studying the effects of education or income on health or risky behaviors (e.g., smoking or alcohol consumption). Therefore, more research is needed on the existence and magnitude of genetic correlations between health outcomes (including health-related behaviors) and individual-level economic measures such as income, education, and labor supply.

18.2.1.2 GCTA

Unlike models based on differences in genetic similarity between family relatives (such as twins), which use genetic similarity, GCTA is based on quantifying genetic similarity between unrelated individuals based on a genome-wide set of SNPs and the extent to which that similarity explains outcome variance (Yang et al., 2011). This method was first developed to estimate heritability for height (Yang et al., 2010). Genetic similarity between two individuals is essentially estimated as a weighted correlation of their genotypes on the included SNPs. Restricting the analysis to unrelated individuals is essential to remove confounding from environmental similarity because individuals who are more genetically related may have shared a more similar environment than unrelated individuals. The outcome regression function can then be estimated via restricted maximum likelihood to estimate the outcome variance due to genetic effects and variance due to environmental effects.

GCTA provides estimates of "narrow" heritability, compared to twin comparisons that can more completely capture the full genetic influence on the outcomes. Nonetheless, this method is extremely useful for national samples that have GWAS data (e.g., the HRS) because it opens the door to quantifying genetic influences on several traits and outcomes of interest to social scientists. In addition to evaluating genetic influences on single traits, GTCA can also be employed to estimate genetic correlation between two traits. Examples of applications to outcomes of particular relevance to health economics include Benjamin et al. (2012), who explain heritability of economic preferences, and Boardman et al. (2015), who explain heritability of education, self-reported health, BMI, and depression, as well as the genetic correlation between education and each of these health measures.

18.2.2 G×E Interactions

Another area of research that can benefit from incorporating genetic information is investigating whether the effects of nongenetic or "environmental" health determinants vary by genetic risks, which is broadly described as G×E interactions. This is especially attractive for health economists who wish understand the heterogeneity in impacts of main variables of interest in models of health production or demand for health inputs. These variables can conceptually include individual-level variables such as education or area-level or policy indicators such as cigarette taxes or alcohol prices.

G×E interactions are most meaningful when they are based on exogenous environmental measures that are not themselves a function of genes (Fletcher & Conley, 2013). Otherwise, if the environmental measures are potentially influenced by genes, any observed interactions could be due to gene ×gene interactions, which complicates the interpretations and implications of these analyses. This concern is especially relevant when examining the interactions of individual-level factors such as education or personality traits which themselves may have a genetic component. From this perspective, policy indicators are of particular interest for these analyses since they are plausibly exogenous to genetic variation, especially in a broad sense. One of the few examples of studies investigating interactions between policy effects and genes is Fletcher (2012), which investigated whether cigarette tax effects on smoking differ between individuals who carry a certain genetic risk variant that predicts smoking versus those who do not. That study finds that carrying the risk factor was associated with no effect from taxes on smoking, in contrast to those who did not have that variant and experienced reduced smoking.

When using molecular genetic data, G×E interactions can be directly estimated in regression models of the outcome (e.g., health status or health behavior) on the environmental variable(s) of interest, genetic variable, and interactions between the environmental variable(s) and the genetic variable, controlling for any conceptually relevant covariates. The genetic variables can be specific variants (e.g., SNPs) or *polygenic scores* (described later) that combine multiple SNPs that can potentially modify the impact of such variables on health or health behavior outcomes. One disadvantage of G×E analysis based on individual SNPs is limited power because each SNP likely has a very small impact on the outcome and on modifying the environmental variable effect.

Using polygenic scores can enhance power in G×E because these scores explain greater variation in the outcome than can an individual SNP. However, constructing the polygenic score is guided by the theory for testing a specific G×E interaction. For example, smoking is likely influenced by multiple genes that may operate through different pathways, but perhaps some of these pathways (e.g., those related to addiction) are more relevant when examining interactions with cigarette taxes. If so, then generating polygenic scores specific for genes that are involved in such pathways may be worth considering instead of generating a polygenic score based on a larger set of genes. This streamlining of the polygenic score may not be feasible, however, in many cases because it requires good knowledge about the genetic functions, and this may not be readily available. In such cases or when there is no strong justification a priori to focus on specific pathways, generating an overall polygenic score for the outcome can serve as a reasonable starting point for G×E analysis.

G×E estimation can also be performed using GCTA and genome-wide molecular data from unrelated individuals to examine if heritability estimates are modified by differences in environmental effects. Unlike regression-based models of G×E based on specific SNPs or polygenic scores, these address the general question of whether genetic influence is generally modified by environmental effects without identifying specific mechanisms for interactions. To detect interaction, power is also a consideration in these analyses. Social science applications of this approach to G×E interactions have been relatively sparse to date.

Family-based analyses of overall genetic influence (e.g., twin studies) can also incorporate G×E estimation. The regression-based analyses of heritability, such as the DeFries-Fulker model, have been extended to incorporate G×E interactions (e.g., Rowe, Almeida, & Jacobson, 1999). One example of such work is Boardman (2009), which examined the heritability of different smoking measures among adolescents across state characteristics including cigarette taxes and restrictions on access to cigarettes through vending machines and cigarette advertising. The study finds that higher taxes and restrictions are associated with reduced genetic influence on daily smoking but not on any smoking participation.

18.2.3 Controlling for Latent Genetic Effects

When considering genetic data in health economics studies that use national datasets such as the HRS, which provides genome-wide molecular data on at least a subset of the participants, it is important to control for latent genetic effects by incorporating measurable genetic factors that are relevant to the outcomes or measures of interest (e.g., health outcomes, health behaviors, economic preferences, and education). This can help reduce heterogeneity in these variables and, in certain cases, allow for better control of genetic factors that may result in an omitted variable bias.

One way to do this is to add indicators for specific SNPs that are confirmed through GWAS to be associated with the outcome of interest. However, adding indicators for each SNP may not be practical when several SNPs/genes have been identified for certain traits (e.g., height) because each would explain only a small fraction of the outcome. A similar limitation applies to traits/outcomes for which only a few SNPs have been confirmed so far (e.g., smoking or education). In such cases, based on current knowledge, including a polygenic score may be useful to control as much as possible for genetic effects on a certain outcome.

The polygenic scores accumulate genetic risk from different SNPs. To generate a polygenic score for an outcome in a certain sample, one would use results on effects of SNPs from GWAS (that did not include that specific sample) that investigated that outcome to a generate a weighted sum of SNPs (number of allele copies), where the weights are the coefficients/effects of the SNPs on the outcome as estimated in the GWAS analysis. One could limit the polygenic score to those SNPs that have the strongest evidence of being relevant (e.g., based on significance level and/or magnitude of the coefficient) or include all SNPs from the GWAS that map to the genome-wide dataset available for the sample at hand. One challenge with polygenic scores is that their prediction power may still be very limited in certain cases (e.g., Purcell et al., 2009), although growing evidence indicates their potential usefulness for certain health outcomes and behaviors of interest to social scientists, such as smoking (Belsky et al., 2013) and obesity (Belsky et al., 2012).

18.2.4 Genes as Instruments

Using genes as exogenous sources of variation to identify the causal effects of genetically influenced health conditions and behaviors on outcomes of interest to social scientists and health economists has been an area of some interest over the past few years. Genetic variants are randomly assigned from parents to children within families. Since each SNP (generally) includes two alleles, a parent who carries both alleles has an equal chance of passing either of these two alleles to his or her child. This form of randomization, referred to as *Mendelian randomization* in epidemiology (Lawlor, Harbord, Sterne, Timpson, & Davey Smith, 2008), indicates that genes can be considered instrumental variables in certain cases (Wehby, Ohsfeldt, & Murray, 2008). Example of some applications on questions of interest to health economists include studying effects of health conditions on educational achievement (Fletcher & Lehrer, 2009), effects of maternal smoking on birth outcomes (Wehby, Fletcher et al., 2011; Wehby, Jugessur et al., 2011), effects of maternal alcohol consumption on child's education achievement (von Hinke Kessler Scholder, Wehby, Zuccolo, & Lewis, 2014), impact of smoking on body weight (Wehby, Murray, Wilcox, & Lie, 2012), and impact of smoking cessation during pregnancy on prenatal behaviors (Wehby, Wilcox, & Lie, 2013).

Researchers should carefully consider several concerns, however, about using genes as instruments for their specific research questions (Cawley, Han, & Norton, 2011; Lawlor et al., 2008; von Hinke Kessler Scholder et al., 2014). First, genes can have pleiotropic effects on different outcomes and traits, which could result in a bias if the genetic variant used as the instrument for an endogenous variable is also related to the outcome through an omitted variable; this would violate the independence condition of instrumental variables. For example, if a genetic variant used as an instrument for maternal smoking in a birthweight regression also predicts maternal nutrition, which is unobserved and omitted from the model, then that would result in an invalid instrument. Genetic instruments also need to be strongly related to the endogenous variable not only statistically, but also, ideally, supported by knowledge about functional pathways. Another concern is that genes and SNPs in physical proximity on the same chromosome can be correlated with each other (formally known as *linkage disequilibrium*), which can result in spurious correlations between the genetic instrument and unobservable confounders in certain cases. Another concern is that the frequencies of certain SNPs can differ by ancestry (known as *population stratification*). Therefore, potential instruments should be carefully vetted for each research question.

18.3 Policy Implications

Understanding genetic influences on health outcomes and their determinants that are commonly targeted by policy interventions such as use of health services, prevention activity, risky behaviors (e.g., smoking), and education, as well as their interactions with environmental factors, can be generally useful for informing policy-making in several ways. A few cases are briefly discussed here in relation to important research areas.

Quantifying the contributions of genes to these variables provides information on the sources of variation or disparities within the population and the extent to which these are driven by genetic versus contextual (social) mechanisms. Finding moderate to strong genetic influences would indicate that interventions that do not effectively address the behavioral channels through which unwarranted variation in health and health-related behaviors occur or compensate for biological risks may not necessarily be effective in reducing health disparities within a population. For example, the strong to moderate influence on prevention preferences and use of preventive care reported in Wehby et al. (2015) in a US sample (most of whom had health insurance) suggests that subtle changes in insurance coverage or access to care may not dramatically reduce disparities in use of preventive services. Furthermore, such assessments could provide benchmarks to evaluate changes in genetic influences over time after major public health policies have been enacted.

Although heritability estimates can be generally informative of the potential of genetic variation to interact with policy effects, studying G×E interactions can be useful for understanding how contextual factors and policies impact population health. Such work can also inform whether policies may exacerbate disparities and unintendedly penalize individuals who carry genetic risks for certain conditions. An example of such a question is whether individuals who carry more genetic risk for obesity may be disadvantaged from expansions in employer wellness initiatives under the Affordable Care Act that provide insurance premium rebates in return for achieving weight loss (Downey, 2014). The same question can be considered for interventions to promote physical activity or reduce smoking. In those cases, one can investigate if a policy may mute or exacerbate genetic effects on health or a health-related behavior.

As knowledge of the genetic architecture of outcomes and traits of interest to health economics expands, incorporating genetic data in health economics research is likely to increase and become more fruitful, including providing policy-relevant findings. However, it is important to keep in mind that several challenges remain that will possibly require much time and effort before genetic information can be useful at a broad level. Identifying genetic variants and mechanisms that explain a substantial fraction of the heritability of complex human traits will take time. Meanwhile, research can continue to achieve piecewise advances in knowledge on the interplay between genes and the environment in shaping health, preferences, and human capital.

References

Agarwal, A., Williams, G. H., & Fisher, N. D. (2005). Genetics of human hypertension. *Trends in Endocrinology and Metabolism, 16*, 127–133.

Anokhin, A. P., Golosheykin, S., Grant, J. D., & Heath, A. C. (2011). Heritability of delay discounting in adolescence: A longitudinal twin study. *Behavior Genetics, 41*, 175–183.

Belsky, D. W., Moffitt, T. E., Baker, T. B., Biddle, A. K., Evans, J. P., Harrington, H., . . . Caspi, A. (2013). Polygenic risk and the developmental progression to heavy, persistent smoking and nicotine dependence: Evidence from a 4-decade longitudinal study. *JAMA Psychiatry, 70*, 534–542.

Belsky, D. W., Moffitt, T. E., Houts, R., Bennett, G. G., Biddle, A. K., Blumenthal, J. A., . . . Caspi, A. (2012). Polygenic risk, rapid childhood growth, and the development of obesity: Evidence from a 4-decade longitudinal study. *Archives of Pediatrics & Adolescent Medicine, 166*, 515–521.

Benjamin, D. J., Cesarini, D., Chabriset, C. F., Glaeser, E. L., Laibson, D. I., Guðnason, V., . . . Lichtenstein, P. (2012). The promises and pitfalls of genoeconomics. *Annual Review of Economics, 4*, 627–662.

Boardman, J. D. (2009). State-level moderation of genetic tendencies to smoke. *American Journal of Public Health, 99*, 480–486.

Boardman, J. D., Blalock, C. L., & Pampel, F. C. (2010). Trends in the genetic influences on smoking. *Journal of Health and Social Behavior, 51*, 108–123.

Boardman, J. D., Domingue, B. W., & Daw, J. (2015). What can genes tell us about the relationship between education and health? *Social Science & Medicine, 127*, 171–180.

Boker, S., Neale, M., Maes, H., Wilde, M., Spiegel, M., Brick, T., . . . Fox, J. (2011). OpenMx: An open source extended structural equation modeling framework. *Psychometrika, 76*, 306–317.

Branigan, A. R., McCallum, K. J., & Freese, J. (2013). Variation in the heritability of educational attainment: An international meta-analysis. *Social Forces, 92*, 109–140.

Cardno, A. G., & Gottesman, I. I. (2000). Twin studies of schizophrenia: From bow-and-arrow concordances to star wars Mx and functional genomics. *Americal Journal of Medical Genetics, 97*, 12–17.

Carlsson, S., Ahlbom, A., Lichtenstein, P., & Andersson, T. (2013). Shared genetic influence of BMI, physical activity and type 2 diabetes: A twin study. *Diabetologia, 56*, 1031–1035.

Cawley, J., Han, E., & Norton, E. (2011). The validity of genes related to neurotransmitters as instrumental variables. *Health Economics, 20*, 884–888.

Cesarini, D., Dawes, C. T., Fowler, J. H., Johannesson, M., Lichtenstein, P., & Wallace, B. (2008). Heritability of cooperative behavior in the trust game. *Proceedings of the National Academy of Sciences, USA, 105*, 3721–3726.

Cesarini, D., Dawes, C. T., Johannesson, M., Lichtenstein, P., & Wallace, B. (2009). Genetic variation in preferences for giving and risk taking. *Quarterly Journal of Economics, 124*, 809–842.

Conti, G., Heckman, J., & Urzua, S. (2010). The education-health gradient. *American Economic Review, 100*, 234–238.

Courtemanche, C. J., Pinkston, J. C., Ruhm, C. J., & Wehby, G. L. (2015). *Can changing economic factors explain the rise in obesity?* (NBER Working Paper No. 20892). Cambridge, MA: National Bureau of Economic Research.

Cutler, D. M., & Lleras-Muney, A. (2010). Understanding differences in health behaviors by education. *Journal of Health Economics, 29*, 1–28.

DeFries, J. C., & Fulker, D. W. (1985). Multiple regression analysis of twin data. *Behavior Genetics, 15*(5), 467–473.

Downey, M. (2014). Response to Dr. Cawley. *Journal of Policy Analysis and Management, 33*, 832–834.

Elks, C. E., den Hoed, M., Zhao, J. H., Sharp, S. J., Wareham, N. J., Loos, R. J., & Ong, K. K. (2012). Variability in the heritability of body mass index: A systematic review and meta-regression. *Frontiers in Endocrinology (Lausanne), 3*, 29. doi: 10.3389/fendo.2012.00029. eCollection.

Fletcher, J. M. (2012). Why have tobacco control policies stalled? Using genetic moderation to examine policy impacts. *PLOS One*, *7*, e50576.

Fletcher, J. M., & Conley, D. (2013). The challenge of causal inference in gene-environment interaction research: Leveraging research designs from the social sciences. *American Journal of Public Health*, *103*(Suppl. 1), S42–S45.

Fletcher, J. M., & Lehrer, S. F. (2009). The effects of adolescent health on educational outcomes: Causal evidence using genetic lotteries between siblings. *Forum for Health Economics & Policy*, *12*(2). Article 8.

Fuchs, V. R. (1982). Time preference and health: An exploratory study. In Victor R. Fuchs (Ed.), *Economic aspects of health* (pp. 93–120). Chicago: University of Chicago Press.

Grossman, M. (1972). On the concept of health capital and the demand for health. *Journal of Political Economy*, *80*, 223–255.

Human Genome Project (HGP). (2015). Retrieved April 8, 2015, from http://www.genome.gov/10001772

Johnson, W., Kyvik, K. O., Mortensen, E. L., Skytthe, A., Batty, G. D., & Deary, I. J. (2010). Education the effects of genetic susceptibilities to poor physical health. *International Journal of Epidemiology*, *39*, 406–414.

Kendler, K. S., Gatz, M., Gardner, C. O., & Pedersen, N. L. (2006). A Swedish national twin study of lifetime major depression. *American Journal of Psychiatry*, *163*, 109–114.

Lawlor, D. A., Harbord, R. M., Sterne, J. A., Timpson, N., & Davey Smith, G. (2008). Mendelian randomization: Using genes as instruments for making causal inferences in epidemiology. *Statistics in Medicine*, *27*, 1133–1163.

Maes, H. H., Sullivan, P. F., Bulik, C. M., Neale, M. C., Prescott, C. A., Eaves, L. J., & Kendler, K. S. (2004). A twin study of genetic and environmental influences on tobacco initiation, regular tobacco use and nicotine dependence. *Psychological Medicine*, *34*, 1251–1261.

McGue, M., Zhang, Y., Miller, M. B., Basu, S., Vrieze, S., Hicks, B., . . . Iacono, W. G. (2013). A genome-wide association study of behavioral disinhibition. *Behavior Genetics*, *43*, 363–373.

Mainous, A. G. III, Baker, R., Love, M. M., Gray, D. P., & Gill, J. M. (2001). Continuity of care and trust in one's physician: Evidence from primary care in the United States and the United Kingdom. *Family Medicine*, *33*, 22–27.

Moor, M. M., Willemsen, G., Rebollo-Mesa, I., Stubbe, J., Geus, E. C., & Boomsma, D. (2011). Exercise participation in adolescents and their parents: Evidence for genetic and generation specific environmental effects. *Behavior Genetics*, *41*, 211–222.

Mosing, M. A., Verweij, K. J. G., Medland, S. E., Painter, J., Gordon, S. D., Heath, A. C., . . . Martin, N. G. (2010). A genome-wide association study of self-rated health. *Twin Research and Human Genetics*, *13*, 398–403.

Nan, C., Guo, B., Warner, C., Fowler, T., Barrett, T., Boomsma, D., . . . Zeegers, M. (2012). Heritability of body mass index in pre-adolescence, young adulthood and late adulthood. *European Journal of Epidemiology*, *27*, 247–253.

Oskarsson, S., Dawes, C., Johannesson, M., & Magnusson, P. K. (2012). The genetic origins of the relationship between psychological traits and social trust. *Twin Research and Human Genetics*, *15*, 21–33.

Purcell, S. M., Wray, N. R., Stone, J. L., Visscher, P. M., O'Donovan, M. C., Sullivan, P. F., . . . Fraser, G. (2009). Common polygenic variation contributes to risk of schizophrenia and bipolar disorder. *Nature*, *460*(7256), 748–752.

Rabe-Hesketh, S., Skrondal, A., & Gjessing, H. K. (2008). Biometrical modeling of twin and family data using standard mixed model software. *Biometrics*, *64*, 280–288.

Rietveld, C. A., Medland, S. E., Derringer, J., Yang, J., Esko, T., Martin, N. W., . . . Koellinger, P. D. (2013). GWAS of 126,559 individuals identifies genetic variants associated with educational attainment. *Science*, *340*, 1467–1471.

Rietveld, C. A., Esko, T., Davies, G., Pers, T. H., Turley, P., Benyamin, B., . . . Koellinger, P. D. (2014). Common genetic variants associated with cognitive performance identified using the proxy-phenotype method. *Proceedings of the National Academy of Science USA*, *111*, 13790–13794.

Romeis, J., Scherrer, J., Xian, H., Eisen, S., Bucholz, K., Heath, A., . . . True, W. R. (2000). Heritability of self-reported health status. *Health Services Research*, *35*, 995–1010.

Rowe, D. C., Almeida, D. M., & Jacobson, K. C. (1999). School context and genetic influences on aggression in adolescence. *Psychological Science*, *10*, 277–280.

Stacey, D., Clarke, T. K., & Schumann, G. (2009). The genetics of alcoholism. *Current Psychiatry Reports*, *11*, 364–369.

Stubbe, J. H., Boomsma, D. I., Vink, J. M., Cornes, B. K., Martin, N. G., Skytthe, A., . . . de Geus, E. J. (2006). Genetic influences on exercise participation in 37,051 twin pairs from seven countries. *PLOS One*, *1*, e22.

Sturgis, P., Read, S., Hatemi, P. K., Zhu, G., Trull, T., Wright, M. J., & Martin, N. G. (2010). A genetic basis for social trust? *Political Behavior*, *32*, 205–230.

Thomsen, S. F., van der Sluis, S., Kyvik, K. O., Skytthe, A., & Backer, V. (2010). Estimates of asthma heritability in a large twin sample. *Clinical and Experimental Allergy*, *40*, 1054–1061.

Treloar, S. A., McDonald, C. A., & Martin, N. G. (1999). Genetics of early cancer detection behaviours in Australian female twins. *Twin Research*, *2*, 33–42.

True, W. R., Heath, A. C., Bucholz, K., Slutske, W., Romeis, J. C., Scherrer, J. F., . . . Tsuang, M. T. (1996). Models of treatment seeking for alcoholism: The role of genes and environment. *Alcoholism, Clinical and Experimental Research*, *20*, 1577–1581.

True, W. R., Romeis, J. C., Heath, A. C., Flick, L. H., Shaw, L., Eisen, S. A., . . . Lyons, M. J. (1997). Genetic and environmental contributions to healthcare need and utilization: A twin analysis. *Health Services Research*, *32*, 37–53.

Vermeiren, A. P. A., Bosma, H., Gielen, M., Lindsey, P. J., Derom, C., Vlietinck, R., . . . Zeegers, M. P. (2012). Do genetic factors contribute to the relation between education and metabolic risk factors in young adults? A twin study. *European Journal of Public Health*, *23*, 986–991.

von Hinke Kessler Scholder, S., Wehby, G. L., Zuccolo, L., & Lewis, S. (2014). Alcohol exposure in utero and child academic achievement. *Economic Journal*, *124*, 634–667.

Wehby, G. L., Fletcher. J. M., Lehrer, S. F., Moreno, L. M., Murray, J. C., Wilcox, A., & Lie, R. T. (2011). A genetic instrumental variables analysis of the effects of maternal smoking during pregnancy on birth weight. *Biodemography and Social Biology*, *57*, 3–32.

Wehby, G. L., Jugessur, A., Moreno, L. M., Murray, J. C., Wilcox, A., & Lie, R. T. (2011). Genes as instruments for studying risk behavior effects: An application to maternal smoking and orofacial clefts. *Health Services and Outcomes Research Methodology*, *11*, 54–78.

Wehby, G. L., Murray, J. C., Wilcox, A., & Lie, R. T. (2012). Smoking and body weight: Evidence using genetic instruments. *Economics and Human Biology*, *10*, 113–126.

Wehby, G. L., Ohsfeldt, R. L., & Murray, J. C. (2008). Mendelian randomization' equals instrumental variable analysis with genetic instruments. *Statistics in Medicine*, *27*, 2745–2749.

Wehby, G. L., Wilcox, A., & Lie, R. T. (2013). The impact of cigarette quitting during pregnancy on other prenatal health behaviors. *Review of Economics of Household*, *11*, 211–233.

Wehby, G. L., Domingue, B. W., & Boardman, J. D. (2015). Prevention, use of health services, and genes: Implications of genetics for policy formation. *Journal of Policy Analysis and Management*. doi: 10.1002/pam.21835

Yang, J., Benyamin, B., McEvoy, B. P., Gordon, S., Henders, A. K., Nyholt, D. R., . . . Visscher, P. M. (2010). Common SNPs explain a large proportion of the heritability for human height. *Nature Genetics*, *42*(7), 565–569.

Yang, J., Lee, S. H., Goddard, M. E., & Visscher, P. M. (2011). GCTA: A tool for genome-wide complex trait analysis. *American Journal of Human Genetics*, *88*(1), 76–82.

CHAPTER 19

TWINS STUDIES IN ECONOMICS

JERE R. BEHRMAN

19.1 Introduction

Twins methods have been developed in economics: (1) to control for biological and other endowments in estimates of the impacts of some investments and other behaviors—particularly attending school—on a range of socioeconomic outcomes (labor market outcomes, marriage market and parenting outcomes, health) through monozygotic/ identical (MZ) twins fixed-effects (FE) estimates; (2) to investigate whether parental investments reinforce or compensate for endowment differentials in allocations among children using both MZ and dizygotic/fraternal (DZ) twins; and (3) to investigate impacts of shocks on household behaviors related to the quantity-quality (Q-Q) fertility model using MZs and DZs. A fourth twins method is used widely outside of economics, but relatively less in economics to describe the role of genetic components of biology in socioeconomic outcomes through additive genetics, common environment and unique environment (ACE) model estimates and variance decompositions (heritability). Twins studies share in common the use of special properties of twins but use a range of approaches with different assumptions for the four different types of studies just noted.

The first approach exploits MZ twins to control for identical endowments (genetics at conception, environment). MZ twins are genetically identical at conception, emerging from a single sperm and egg from which two separate embryos later emerge. MZ twinning occurs at roughly constant rates in different populations (Kiely & Kiely, 2001). MZs are rarer than DZs. In most pre–fertility-drug populations, about 1 in 85 births were twins (Plomin, DeFries, McClearn, & McGuffin, 2005), of which about a third were MZs, a third same-sex DZs, and a third opposite-sex DZs (Keith, Papiemik, Keith, & Luke, 1995).

The second, third, and fourth approaches use both MZs and DZs. DZs are ordinary siblings in that they are products of two different eggs and two different sperms. DZs have individual-specific genetics that differ from family average genetics to the same degree as do other siblings, but DZs tend to experience more similar home and neighborhood environments than do other siblings because they are born into the same environment (in part because of being born into the same life cycle stage of their parents). The DZ twinning rate is affected *inter alia* by maternal age and fertility drugs, and therefore differs over time, across women, and among populations. Some women tend to produce more than one egg at each menstrual period and therefore are more likely to have DZs, a tendency that may run across generations. Women older than 35 years are more likely to produce two eggs. Women who have more than two children are also more likely to have DZs. Artificial induction of ovulation and in vitro fertilization-embryo replacement also can give rise to DZs and MZs. The second and fourth twins study approaches noted earlier exploit differences between MZs and DZs to identify constructs of interest. The third approach utilizes primarily only the fact of multiple births, not whether they are MZs or DZs.

There are some datasets of twins raised apart (e.g., Minnesota Study of Twins Raised Apart, Swedish Adoption/Twin Study on Aging), but most twins datasets include twins who were raised together. Examples of US twins datasets are the Midlife Development in the United States Study, the Minnesota Twins Registry data, the National Academy of Science-National Research Council (NAS-NRC) Twin Registry of World War II Veterans, the National Longitudinal Study of Adolescent Health Twin Data, the University of Washington Twins Registry data, and the Vietnam Veterans Twin Registry Data. Register-based twins datasets exist for Australia, Chile, Denmark, Norway, and Sweden, and at least one survey-based twins dataset exists for developing countries (e.g., China). Because twins raised together share genetic factors—with the genetic overlap at conception being 50% for DZ twins (or more if there is positive parental assortative mating) and 100% for MZ twins—and important contexts during childhood and adolescence, twins datasets permit better understanding of how control for genetic and social endowments affects estimated impacts of important behaviors such as schooling attainment, whether intrahousehold allocations compensate or reinforce for individual endowment differences, how quantity shocks in the form of unanticipated multiple births affect household behaviors, and how genetic and social endowments contribute to the variance decomposition of various outcomes.

Twins are not random samples of the population. They differ in their prenatal developmental environments and tend to have inferior endowments at birth: lower APGAR scores,[1] increased incidence of breathing difficulties, and lower birthweights, which has been shown to significantly affect not only infant survival but also adult outcomes (Almond, Chay, & Lee, 2005; Behrman & Rosenzweig, 2004; Black, Devereux, & Salvanes, 2005). Rosenzweig and Zhang (2009) summarize birthweight distributions from US white populations for twins and non-twins based on the Minnesota Twins Registry and the US National Longitudinal Survey 1979, and birthweight distributions for twins and non-twins born in China based on their survey data. In both countries, the average birthweight of singletons is almost 30% higher than that of twins, an approximately 0.7 kg difference.

However, with respect to a number of observed characteristics, twins differ very little from singletons. Studies on the personality and intelligence of twins, for example, suggest that they have traits very similar to those of non-twins (e.g., Deary, Spinath, & Bates, 2006). Comparisons of adult twins datasets with socioeconomic variables from larger populations, moreover, often find no significant or substantial differences (Behrman, Hrubec, Taubman, & Wales, 1980; Behrman, Rosenzweig, & Taubman, 1994, 1996; Kohler, Knudsen, Skytthe, & Christensen, 2002). Moreover, the first twins method described (MZ-FE) controls for any unobserved characteristics shared by twins, including having an identical sibling. So, for this approach, the first-order respects in which twins are different from singletons are controlled. The second twins method described (investigating reinforcing versus compensating behavior for investments in children), exploits MZ-FE and DZ-FE, so, again, the first-order respects in which twins are different from singletons are controlled. The third and fourth approaches, however, do not control for twins FEs.

Then next four sections each consider in turn the four twins methods introduced earlier, followed by a conclusion.

19.1.1 Method 1: MZ-FE Estimates of Impacts of Behavioral Outcomes on Other Outcomes

The first method, using MZ twins to control for genetic and other background unobserved endowments so that they do not cause unobserved variable biases, probably is the common use of twins in economics. Economists and other social scientists long have used sibling comparisons for this purpose (Griliches & Mason, 1972, is an early study). MZs and DZs are more useful for this purpose than other siblings because they share birth dates and, therefore, as noted earlier, differences between them are not confounded by family life cycle differences. DZ-FE estimates do not control for individual-specific differences in genetic endowments from family averages, which may be important (see Method 2). MZ-FE twins estimates control completely for genes at conception because there are not individual-specific deviations from the MZ average genetic endowments at conception (for early studies, see Behrman & Taubman, 1976; Behrman et al., 1980).

MZ-FE studies, conditional on the assumptions under which they are made, estimate causal effects of one variable (e.g., own schooling, birthweight, parental schooling), which may be partly determined directly by unobserved endowments on other variables (e.g., labor market outcomes, marriage market outcomes, health and nutritional input demands and outcomes, parenting outcomes, social support, happiness) that are themselves partly determined directly by endowments. Consider the following representation of a Mincer (1974)-like reduced-form equation relating ln wage rates W_{ij} for the *ith* member of paternal family j to his or her schooling S_{ij} and to three sets of unobserved variables that, for simplicity, are presented as scalars (but which may be vectors) representing (1) endowments f_j common among all children of the paternal family j (e.g., exogenous features of paternal family environments in childhood, including family income, parents' human capital, average genetic endowments among siblings, local schooling and health-related options); (2) endowments specific to child i in family j, represented by c_{ij} (e.g., child-specific deviations from average family genetic endowments); and (3) random wage rate shocks specific to i in j, inclusive of measurement errors in wage rates, represented by u_{ij}:

$$W_{ij} = r_S S_{ij} + f_j + c_{ij} + u_{ij}, \tag{1}$$

where r_S is the effect of schooling on ln wage rates or the Mincerian rate of return to the opportunity costs of time spent in schooling instead of in the labor market, and the three unobserved variables (f_j, c_{ij}, u_{ij}) are defined in units so that their coefficients are all 1. S_{ij} is a function of variables that pertain to parental families and to individual children in parental families:

$$S_{ij} = \alpha_f f_j + \alpha_c c_{ij} + \alpha_s c_{kj} + v_{ij}, \tag{2}$$

where α_f is the effect of the family endowment f_j on schooling investment in child i, α_c is the effect of the child-specific endowment c_{ij} of child i on schooling investment in that child, α_s is the effect of the child-specific endowment c_{kj} of sib k (which is a vector if there are multiple siblings) on schooling investment in child i, and v_{ij} is a disturbance that affects S_{ij} but not W_{ij} except indirectly through S_{ij} (a critical assumption that is discussed later). The sibling endowment c_{kj} affects S_{ij}, the schooling investment in child i, because parents may invest in their different children in ways that reinforce ($\alpha_s < 0$), compensate ($\alpha_s > 0$), or, in the razor-edge case between reinforcment and compensation, are neutral ($\alpha_s = 0$),) with respect to child endowment differentials (Becker, 1991; Becker & Tomes, 1976; Behrman, Pollak, & Taubman, 1982, 1995). The stochastic term reflects chance events experienced by one but not the other twin (e.g., one twin encountering more inspiring role models among teachers, which affects schooling attainment but not wage rates except through schooling attainment).

The parameter of central interest r_S is not identified in Equation (1) if α_a or α_f is not zero. r_S is estimated with bias if Equation (1) is estimated across individuals with different values of f_j and c_{ij}. The regression coefficient for an ordinary least squares (OLS) estimate of relation (1) is $cov\left(W_{ij}, S_{ij}\right) / \sigma 2\left(S_{ij}\right) = \left[r_S(\sigma 2\left(S_{ij}\right) + cov\left(S_{ij}, f_j\right) + cov\left(S_{ij}, c_{ij}\right)\right] / \sigma 2\left(S_{ij}\right)$, which is a biased estimate of r_S unless $cov\left(S_{ij}, f_j\right) + cov\left(S_{ij}, a_{ij}\right) = 0$. Unless schooling is determined independently of f_i and c_{ij} (i.e., if $\alpha_f = \alpha_c = 0$ in relation (2) due to random assignment of schooling), generally, cross-sectional estimates of associations between S

and *W* are biased estimates of the causal impacts of *S* on *W* because *S* is partially proxying for genetic, family background, childhood neighborhood, and other endowments.

With no further assumptions, it is clear that r_S is not identified even if sibling data, including DZs, are used to control in the estimation of r_S for common components of endowments f_j because of the child-specific components of endowments c_{ij}. As long as families or individual children respond to child-specific differences in endowments, sibling estimators do not provide unbiased estimates. Therefore, researchers have used MZs, between whom there are as minimal as possible endowment differences, to identify r_S in estimates of models such as relations (1) and (2), which can be rewritten for MZs as:

$$W_{ij}{}^{MZ} = r_S S_{ij}{}^{MZ} + f_j{}^{MZ} + u_{ij}{}^{MZ} \tag{1A}$$

$$S_{ij}{}^{MZ} = \alpha_f f_j{}^{MZ} + v_{ij}{}^{MZ}, \tag{2A}$$

where superscripts *MZ* refer to MZs. MZ-FE estimators control for all right-side variables in these relations that are common to both members of MZ twinships (including all characteristics of non-twin siblings and whatever is distinctive about being MZs). What is and is not controlled in such relations can be seen in equivalent within-MZ twin relations, in which all factors common to the twins are eliminated. Within-MZ twin estimators are obtained by subtracting relations (1A) and (2A) for the *kth* MZ twin in the *jth* family from relations (2A) and (2A) for the *ith* MZ twin in the same family. With a within-MZ twin estimator (or MZ-FE), all of the unobserved endowment components in (1A) and (2A) are controlled so that consistent estimates of r_S are obtained under the maintained assumption that cov (u, v) is zero:

$$W_{ij}{}^{MZ} - W_{kj}{}^{MZ} = r_S\left(S_{ij}{}^{MZ} - S_{kj}{}^{MZ}\right) + u_{ij}{}^{MZ} - u_{ij}{}^{MZ} \tag{3}$$

Thus, MZ-FE estimators identify true reduced-form impacts of *S* on *W* (and thus the Mincerian rate of return to time spent in school, r_S) under the assumptions noted earlier. Comparisons can be made with estimates of relation (1) for the same *W* dependent variable to estimate to what extent estimates of r_S are biased in cross-sectional estimates that fail to control for unobserved endowments f_j and c_{ij}. Comparisons also can be made between MZ-FE estimates for females and males, among racial and ethnic groups, among parental socioeconomic status (SES) levels, among birth cohorts, and across countries. Comparisons can also be made between MZ-FE and DZ-FE estimators to see if unobserved child-specific endowments c_{ij} are important so that within-sibling estimates that control only for common family endowments f_j are misleading. Finally, comparisons can be made between DZ-FE and ordinary sibling FE estimators to investigate the impact of changes in the timing of births and birth order in the estimated impacts.

A major strength of MZ-FE estimates, in comparison with ACE estimates (discussed in Method 4; but see Kohler, Behrman, & Schnittker, 2011, for an effort to integrate the two approaches), is that, under their maintained assumptions, MZ-FE estimators permit estimation of the causal impact of one behavioral variable such as schooling on other behavorial variables such as those related to labor market, mariage market, parenting, health and nutrition input demands, and outcomes. Such estimates often are of considerable interest in terms of prediction or policy assessments. Moreover MZ-FE estimates do not require assumptions about MZs and DZs having equal shared environments *C* or the absence of genetic-environmental interactions, as do the variance decomposition estimates discussed in Method 4.

Instrumental variables (IV) or two-stage least squares (2SLS) are alternative approaches to eliminating bias in estimated impacts of schooling or other variables, but the indentifying instruments used to date for such estimates (such as changes in minimum schooling requirements or ages for leaving schooling) have the limitation of being local average treatment estimates (LATE) relevant only for those affected by such changes and not for those over the whole distribution of schooling. Differences in schooling for MZs, in contrast, tend to occur for many different schooling levels, not just at the minimum required schooling levels or ages, and thus tend to be more like average treatment effects (ATE) estimators (Amin & Behrman, 2014; Amin, Behrman, & Spector, 2013; Amin, Behrman, Kohler, Xiong, & Zhang, 2015; Behrman et al., 2011, 2015; Kohler et al., 2011; Lundborg, 2013).

MZ-FE estimates have been utilized to investigate schooling impacts on many economic and related outcomes—wage rates, labor force participation, hours worked, earnings, occupation, marital status, spouse characteristics, fertility, mortality, own and others' health/disease/nutritional conditions and behaviors, happiness, and social support—and, to a lesser degree, the impacts of other variables such as fertility and health and nutritional status on some of these outcomes (examples include Amin & Behrman, 2014; Amin et al., 2013; Amin, Behrman, & Kohler, 2015; Amin, Lundborg, & Rooth, 2011; Ashenfelter & Krueger, 1994; Ashenfelter & Rouse, 1998; Behrman et al., 1980, Behrman, Rosenzweig, & Taubman, 1994, 1996; Behrman & Rosenzweig, 1999, 2002, 2004; Behrman & Taubman, 1976; Conley, Strully, & Bennett, 2006; Kohler, Behrman, & Skytthe, 2005; Li, Zhang, & Zhu, 2008; Lundborg, 2013; Miller, Mulvey, & Martin, 1995, 1997, 2001; Rosenzweig & Zhang, 2009; Schnittker, 2008; Schnittker & Behrman, 2012).

A common but not universal result is that MZ-FE estimated impacts of schooling are considerably smaller in absolute magnitudes and often more insignificant than OLS estimates, consistent with relations (1) and (2) and with *d* biases away from zero in OLS estimates because, in OLS estimates, *S* proxies in part for unobserved endowments f_i and c_{ij} in relation (1). This is the pattern for most estimates of impacts of *S* on labor market, marriage market, parenting, social interactions, and health outcomes, although it is somewhat less common for health-related behaviors such as smoking, drinking, and physical activity. An interesting example is that the coefficient estimate for maternal schooling in relations determining child schooling is significantly positive in OLS estimates but significantly negative in MZ-FE estimates using the Minnesota Twins Registry data for twins born between 1936 and 1955, consistent with the possibility that increasing S and holding endowments constant increases mothers' labor force participation and reduces their time with their children, which in turn reduces children's schooling attainment (Behrman & Rosenzweig, 2002). In this case, the OLS estimate is that child schooling is associated with a significant additional 0.3 grades for every additional grade of maternal schooling, but the MZ-FE estimate is a significant reduction of −0.3 grades. Of course, the signs of OLS biases due to unobserved endowments need not be the same for all outcomes but may be positive in some cases and negative in others. Comparison of OLS and MZ-FE estimates of schooling impacts on health outcomes and health-related behaviors for Chinese adults provide an example, with OLS estimates overestimating schooling impacts in comparison with MZ-FE estimates in most cases but underestimating schooling impacts in a number of cases (Behrman et al., 2015). This is possible, as elaborated on in the Behrman study, if there are multiple dimensions to genetic endowments that have different weights in relations similar to Equation (1) for different outcomes.

Most of the MZ-FE literature in economics and the social sciences focuses on estimating schooling impacts on various outcomes, but there are some studies that use MZ-FE estimates to investigate other relations. One example is the estimate of the impacts of fertility and partnerhsip on happiness, in which case controlling for unobserved endowments substantially affects a number of the estimated effects, thus suggesting that standard analyses of contributions of partnerships and children to well-being are subject to biases—often substantial—in both directions (Kohler et al., 2005).

Another example is the estimation of the impacts of birthweight over the life cycle, in which case MZ-FE estimates of causal effects are larger for schooling and earnings outcomes but smaller for adult height, body mass index (BMI), and birthweight for the next generation than are OLS estimates. For example, the MZ-FE estimates of birthweight impacts in comparison with the OLS estimates are twice as large for schooling and about six times as large for earnings, but only about 30% as large for adult BMI. These results are consistent with there being multiple dimensions of unobserved endowments that are controlled in MZ-FE estimates and negative correlations between underlying intellectual endowments and physical endowments (Behrman & Rosenzweig, 2004).

Criticisms of the MZ-FE approach and brief reactions to these criticisms include the following (see Kohler et al., 2011, for more extensive and more formal discussions of the first three:

1. *The disturbance terms in relations (1) and (2) may be correlated* (Bound & Solon, 1999): If between-twin differences in S reflect unobserved factors that also directly determine W so that $cov\left(u_{ij}, v_{ij}\right) \neq 0$, the MZ-FE estimated r_s is still biased, with the sign of the bias determined by the sign of the correlation. For example, if an accident or illness limits schooling and has persistent negative direct effects on adult wage rates in addition to indirect effects through schooling, the MZ-FE estimated r_s is overestimated (as is the OLS estimate for this reason, in addition to any effects of f_i and c_{if}). If, as often seems to be assumed when the independence

between the stochastic terms in equations (1) and (2) is questioned, then the MZ-FE estimator, *certis paribus*, gives an upper-bound estimate of r_S. In this case, that the MZ-FE estimates of schooling impacts often are smaller in absolute magnitude than OLS estimates (as noted earlier) would seem to be more compelling evidence that the OLS estimates are biased upward in absolute magnitudes. On the other hand, if $cov\left(u_{ij}, v_{ij}\right) < 0$ (e.g., the persistent effect of an illness during school ages, beyond any effects through S, also increases life expectancy through directly reducing participation in risky activities), then the MZ-FE estimates, *ceteris paribus*, give lower bound estimates of r_S. One empirical approach for exploring the possibility that $cov\left(u_{ij}, v_{ij}\right) \neq 0$ is to include additional variables that might have persistent effects on both schooling and the outcome of interest, such as measures of birthweight (Amin et al., 2011) or of cognitive ability (Behrman et al., 1980). In these two studies, the estimated r_S is not changed much with these additional controls, but, of course, other applications could have different results.

2. *Measurement error*: FE estimates in general, including MZ-FE, filter out much of the true signal of *S* without also reducing measurement error, so there is a tendency for more measurement error bias toward zero than in simple cross-sectional estimates. MZ-FE studies with reports from other respondents (i.e., the other member of a twin pair, the twins' adult children), so that they can estimate measurement error models, report estimated noise-to-signal ratios of 0.04–0.12 (Amin et al., 2013; Ashenfelter & Krueger, 1994; Ashenfelter & Rouse, 1998; Behrman et al., 1994). The mid-point of this range of a noise-to-signal ratio of about 0.08 implies attenuation biases of about 8% for individual estimates and 26% for MZ-FE estimates, a fairly substantial effect in the latter. Behrman et al. (1980) observe that estimates of noise-to-signal ratios from other studies could account for up to half of the difference between their MZ-FE and OLS estimates. Ashenfelter and Krueger (1994) and Behrman et al. (1994) introduced the use of another report on the twin's schooling to instrument schooling and therefore eliminate the measurement error bias under the assumption that the measurement error in the other report is independent of the measurement error of one's own report. Both studies find that this method for controlling for measurement error increases the estimated returns to schooling in comparison with estimates that do not correct for measurement error. Many, but not all, subsequent studies (including many of those summarized earlier) use reports from other respondents to control for measurement error.
3. *Twins react to each other*: Whether twins reacting to each other causes biases depends on the nature of the interaction. If there is imitation with respect to the right-side determinant, such as *S* in relation (1), there is no resulting bias in either direction for the MZ-FE estimator. But if there is imitation with regard to the dependent variable, such as *W* in relation (1), the estimated r_S is a lower bound if there is positive imitation and an upper bound if there is negative

imitation. If there is positive imitation on the outcome, the maximum downward bias is 50%, but the actual bias is likely to be considerably less because the maximum represents the unlikely situation in which the other twin's outcome (e.g., wage rate) is weighted as much as the direct determinants of one's own outcome.

4. *Epigenetic expression due to genetic–environmental interactions limit the effectiveness of the MZ-FE control for unobserved endowments* (Boardman & Fletcher, 2015): If epigenetic–environmental interactions only affect the right-side variable of interest (S in relation 1) or only affect the dependent variable of interest (W in relation 1), then they do not cause correlated disturbance terms and cause no biases. If they affect both, then they cause the disturbance terms to be correlated between relations (1) and (2), with the same implications for useful upper or lower bound estimates due to $cov\left(u_{ij}, v_{ij}\right) \neq 0$ that are discussed in point 1.
5. *Twins are not representative of larger populations*: As noted in the introduction, this is true for birth-related outcomes although not for many adult outcomes; however, the MZ-FE approach, by controlling for unobserved FEs common to the twins, arguably controls for respects in which such twins differ from the overall population.

19.1.2 Method 2: Compensation Versus Reinforcement of Children's Endowment Differentials Through Parental Intrafamilial Investments

Economic models of intrafamilial investments in children indicate that relative investments in the children depend *inter alia* on relative child-specific endowments as well as on the nature of preferences, the amount of resources the parents use for the children, and the wage production technology.

The Becker and Tomes (1976) "wealth model" posits that parents allocate resources they devote to their children to maximize their children's wealth by investing in each child's human capital until the marginal rate of return to human capital investments equals the market rate of interest, and then they transfer any additional resources to the children in the form of financial transfers. The marginal rate of return to human capital investments is assumed to diminish with increasing human capital investment in each child due to fixed family- and child-specific endowments $f_i + c_{ij}$. These endowments in general differ across children. Because of complementarities between endowments and human capital, for a given level of human capital investment, the marginal rate of return is higher for higher child endowments. If parents devote sufficient resources to their children so that, for each child, the marginal rate of return on human capital investments equals the market rate of interest, and if parents have "equal concern" in the sense that their subwelfare function related to their children's expected wealth is symmetrical in terms of the wealth of each child (and therefore around the 45-degree ray from the origin), then the parents invest more in the human capital of the child with greater endowments but compensate by giving greater financial transfers to the child with less endowments. As a result, the children have equal wealth, and the human capital investments are efficiently equal to market rates of interest. If capital markets are imperfect, so that parents cannot borrow at the market rate of interest to obtain enough resources to invest in their children so that the marginal productivities of human capital of all the children equal the market rate of interest, and if parents devote less than sufficient resources to their children to drive the marginal rate of return to human capital investments for each child to the market rate of interest, then human capital investments are not efficient in that, for at least one child, the marginal rate of return to human capital exceeds the market rate of interest; generally, the parents will invest in their children so that the expected wealth is greater for better endowed children (with the exception of the limiting case in which parents' subwelfare function defined over children's expected wealth is Leontieff or Rawlsian) (Behrman et al., 1995). Whether parents devote sufficient resources to their children to drive the marginal rate of return to human capital investments for each child to the market rate of interest or not, parents reinforce children's endowment differences by investing more in children with greater endowments.

The Behrman, Pollak, and Taubman (1982) *separable earnings and transfers* (SET) model posits that parents are interested in the distribution of earnings per se among their children, not only in the distribution of expected wealth, perhaps because they are interested in their children's capabilities for "earning their own way," and income from earnings are viewed as different from income from returns on intergenerationally transferred financial assets. Labor market earnings, as in the wealth model, are generated by human capital investments and child endowments, with diminishing marginal returns to human capital investments because of the fixed child endowments and complementaries between endowments and human capital in the production of earnings. Parental preferences for the subwelfare function defined over child earnings range from being linear (i.e., only the sum of their children's earnings count, so there is considerable reinforcement of endowment differentials to maximize this sum) to L-shaped Rawlsian or Leontieff curves for which only the earnings of the lowest earning child counts. Parental preferences also can be symmetrical (indicating equal concern) or asymmetrical. By assuming a constant elasticity of substitution subwelfare function and a log linear earnings production function, they derive an expression very similar to the MX-FE relation (3) except that S is in ln form, from which the elasticity of substitution in parental subwelfare function preferences can be estimated. Using the NAS-NRC Twins sample, they obtain estimates that indicate that parents significantly care about inequality aversion (i.e., the curvature is significantly different from the linear case) but still significantly reinforce child endowment differences.

Behrman et al. (1994) show how comparisons between the within-twin correlations of human capital outcomes across MZs and DZs can be used to identify the child-specific endowments c_{ij} in relations (1) and (2) and the responsiveness of schooling to child-specific endowments in the family and in the marriage market. The basic idea is to obtain the "correct" estimates of the impact of schooling on labor market earnings outcomes using relation (3), with MZ earnings as the outcome; then, conditional on that estimate of r_S, use relations (1) and (2) for DZs to estimate child-specific endowments c_{ij} and c_{kj} and how schooling investments respond to those endowments. Estimates from two US twins samples indicate that 27% (42%) percent of the variance in ln earnings (obesity) is due to variability in child-specific endowments (which suggests that they should not be ignored as in DZ-FE or sibling FE analyses); allocations of schooling reinforce rather than compensate for specific child endowments, so that the family acts to increase inequality among its children; and child-specific earnings endowments of men and their wives' schooling are negatively associated.

19.1.3 Method 3: Q-Q Fertility Model

The third approach for using twins for economics analysis is to use unanticipated multiple births (usually twins) as exogenous increases in child quantity to explore the Q-Q fertility model (Becker & Lewis, 1973; Willis, 1973). Rosenzweig and Wolpin (1980*a*, 1980*b*) first proposed and implemented this approach, which basically is to estimate effects of an extra birth at parity *P* due to twins on child quality at previous parities for all women who had at least *P* births. The incidence of twins at *P* is used as an instrument to predict the total number of children born in IV (or 2SLS) estimates. Early studies found evidence that sibship size and children's schooling are negatively related (Hanushek, 1992; Rosenzweig & Wolpin, 1980*b*). But some recent studies (Angrist, Lavy, & Schlosser, 2010; Black et al., 2005; Li et al., 2008) using twin births to assess the impact of an exogenous increase in child quantity on child quality of non-twins in the same families have found little or no evidence of a Q-Q tradeoff with the exception of rural (but not urban) areas of China in the last of these.

Rosenzweig and Zhang (2009) note that these studies do not really examine the impacts of total sibship size on children of parity *P* (or higher) because impacts on the quality of the twins themselves are ignored, perhaps because twins are not comparable to multiple singleton births for two reasons noted in the introduction: (1) twins are more closely spaced, and (2) twins have inferior birth endowments. They argue that a key issue for assessing whether existing evidence from twin studies rejects Q-Q tradeoffs is thus whether these two features affect investments in non-twins within families. If closer spacing of twins affects relative costs of investing in them versus in singleton children, and the endowments of twins are lower than those of singleton births, then twinning not only may lower average resources per child due to increases in sibship size, but also may lead to reallocation of resources differentially across children of different birth orders and thus affect inferences about Q-Q tradeoffs based on estimates of the effects of twinning on non-twins siblings.

Rosenzweig and Zhang (2009) show that estimates of higher parity twinning on older non-twin siblings may underestimate Q-Q tradeoffs; thus, the weak findings in the more recent literature may be consistent with the Q-Q model. Given reinforcing behavior, estimates of the effects of twinning on twins and their older non-twin siblings bound the Q-Q tradeoffs as long as any economies of scale from twinning are not too large, with estimated effects of twinning on older non-twins providing lower bounds. They also explore additional considerations not incorporated in simple Q-Q models such as public goods and birth spacing. They use the modified Q-Q model with survey data on families with twins and with singletons in China, where the "one-child" policy that was strictly enforced in urban areas meant that twinning on the first birth resulted in one exogenous extra birth (and likewise for parity 2 in rural areas where two children were permitted). They find that twin quality is lower than for singleton siblings at *P* and that declines in quality for parity-*P* births are significant so that the basic prediction of the Q-Q model that child quantity increases reduce average quality is not rejected.

19.1.4 Method 4: ACE Model Estimates and Variance Decomposition

This approach, used to estimate heritability and related variance decompositions with ACE or closely related behavioral genetics models, is probably less common than MZ-FE estimates in economics but is the most common use of twin studies outside of economics. Indeed, the Wikipedia article on "Twin Study" (http://en.wikipedia.org/wiki/Twin_study; accessed June 12, 2015) only includes this approach and not the other three covered in this chapter.

These analyses generally have been concerned with decomposing the variance of an observed outcome *Y* ("phenotype"), such as wage rates or health indicator, into the contributions of additive genetic effects (*A*), common environment shared by both twins (*C*), and unique environments that affect each twin differently (*E*). The simplest univariate behavioral genetics approach assumes additive genetic models with no assortative mating and with equal environmental influences across MZs and DZs so that for the *ith* child in the *jth* family:

$$Y_{ij} = aA_{ij} + cC_{ij} + eE_{ij}, \tag{4}$$

a is the association of Y_{ij} with genetic endowments *Aij*, *c* is the association of Y_{ij} with common environments *Cij*, and *e* is the association of Y_{ij} with unique environments *Eij*. MZs are assumed to share 100% of their genes (*A*) and common environment (*C*) so that any differences between members of a MZ twinship are due to unique environments (*E*). The correlation between outcomes for MZs (r_{MZ}) is an estimate of $A + C$. DZs, like ordinary siblings, are assumed also to share the same *C* and, on average, 50% of their genes if there is no assortative mating (in which case the correlation between outcomes for DZ twins (r_{DZ}) is $0.5A + C$). Therefore, the additive genetic effect *A* is twice the difference between the MZ and DZ correlations $A = 2(r_{MZ} - r_{DZ})$, and heritability (h^2)

in the simplest univariate ACE model is defined to be the variance in aA relative to the variance in Y:

$$h2 = a2\ Var(A)\ /\ Var(Y). \tag{5}$$

More recent multivariate behavioral genetics analyses investigate the associations of genes and the environment with correlations among multiple outcomes (Plomin et al., 2005). For example, the simplest bivariate ACE model is an extension to two outcomes, say schooling (S) and wage rates (W), and allows for cross-effects so that, for instance, the determinants of schooling (A^S, C^S, E^S) also affect wage rates in addition to factors that only affect wage rates (A^W, C^W, E^W):

$$S_{ij} = a_{SS}A^S_{ij} + c_{SS}C^S_{ij} + e_{SS}E^S_{ij}. \tag{6}$$

$$W_{ij} = a_{sw}A^s_{ij} + c_{sw}C^s_{ij} + e_{sw}E^s_{ij} + a_{WW}A^W_{ij} + c_{WW}C^W_{ij} + e_{WW}E^W_{ij} \tag{7}$$

The first three terms in Equation (7) indicate associations of the three determinants of S (A^S, C^S, E^S) with W, and the last three terms indicate associations of the three factors (A^W, C^W, E^W) that only affect W but not S. Estimation of this bivariate ACE model permits estimation of heritabilities of S and W and the extent to which ACE factors associated with S in relation (6) also are associated with W in relation (7). Estimation of this model, however, does not identify whether the ACE factors associated with S are associated with W indirectly through S or directly. Nevertheless some limited inferences about the possible impacts of S on W might be made. In the extreme case in which $a_{SW} = c_{SW} = e_{SW} = 0$, there could not be any impact of S on W. On the other hand, if all the associations of (A^S, C^S, E^S) with W are through S, then $a_{SW}a_{ss} = c_{SW}c_{ss} = e_{SW}e_{ss}$, which can be tested and—whether or not satisfied—used to establish the maximum possible impact of S on W.

Note that these relations are related but not identical to the earlier expressions given for the first twins approach, the MZ-FE estimates. However relation (1) differs from the ACE relations because another outcome S is included among the right-side variables, which indicates a direct effect of one outcome on another that is of central interest in the MZ-FE approach. Also both relations (1) and (2) differ from the ACE relations in that (1) the family endowments f_j include both the average family (or twinship) component of A and C because there is no need to distinquish between them in this approach and (2) the child-specific endowment c_{ij}—the individual-specific component of A—is distinguished from the average family component of A. Moreover, relation (2) differs from the ACE relations because the child-specific component of the other twin c_{kj} (or, more generally, of all other siblings) is included because in family models of investment in children, the endowments of all siblings in the family affect the investments in any particular child, and parents may allocate resources to their children so as to reinforce or compensate for endowment differentials (see the discussion in Section 1.2).

Many estimates of heritabilities of outcomes are of interest to economists, particularly those pertaining to health and nutrition, although these do not often appear in the economics literature per se. Wehby (2015) summarizes a number of these and gives citations to relevant studies elsewhere in this *Handbook*, to which interested readers are referred.

A number of questions have been raised or limitations noted about the simple ACE models and, in some cases, extensions developed or empirical evidence presented to attempt to speak to these questions or limitations. Some examples include:

- The assumption of no assortative mating seems violated by many studies, particularly on schooling, although most such studies probably overstate the actual assortative mating on schooling because of unobserved endowment biases. MZ-FE estimates indicate much less assortative mating on schooling than do OLS associations, but still show significantly positive assortative mating (Behrman & Rozenzweig, 2002). Assuming no assortative mating when there is positive assortative mating overstates the genetic contribution (i.e., $A = (1 / s)(r_{MZ} - r_{DZ})$), where s is the proportion of shared genes among DZs; so, if s is assumed to be 0.5 when s actually is greater than 0.5 due to assortative mating, then A is overestimated); if DZ twins share more than 50% of their genes owing to assortative mating, however, the correlation between the A components across DZs can be increased accordingly by using the actual value of s.
- The assumption of equal common environments for MZ and DZ twins has been questioned. If environments are not common but instead more similar for MZ than for DZ twins (e.g, $C^{DZ} < C^{MZ}$), as a number of scholars conjecture, then $A = 2(r_{MZ} - r_{DZ})$ becomes $A + 2(CMZ - CDZ) = 2(r_{MZ} - r_{DZ})$. So, in the standard calculation, the differences in shared environments between MZs and DZs are attributed to genetic differences.
- Epigenetics implies that the expression of genes may differ even for MZ twins; this implies that typical estimates of heritability are lower bound estimates for heritability at conception because, in the simplest ACE model, the unique environment E proxies for the part of A altered by epigenetics.
- There may be nonadditive genetics effects (often denoted **D** for dominance); these can be examined in an ADE model.
- The standard ACE twin design does not permit considering both C and nonadditive genetic effects simultaneously; this limitation can be addressed by expanding the design to include additional relatives such as siblings.
- Gene–environment correlations are not detectable as distinct effects; incorporating adoption models or children-of-twins designs may assess family influences uncorrelated with shared genetic effects.
- The implications of standard models of investments in children—that endowments of all children in families affect investments in any particular child—are ignored (see relation (2) in the MZ-FE twins study approach; Section 1.1).

- These approaches provide only limited and indirect inferences on some questions of great interest in economics, such as the impact of behavioral outcomes such as human capital investments (e.g., schooling) on other behavioral outcomes (although Kohler et al., 2011, is a recent effort to integrate such concerns into the bivariate ACE framework).

As noted, some of these limitations can be dealt with by extending the ACE model or bringing additional information to the analysis. However, even if these limitations are dealt with, a fundamental question is why heritability, a major concern of the ACE literature, is of interest. To illustrate this point, consider Figure 19.1 (also see Behrman et al., 1980; Feldman & Lewontin, 1975; Layzer, 1974). In this figure, reaction functions for some outcome (phenotype, such as wage rates *W*) are plotted against the environment (*N*, combining both *C* and *E*). Suppose that genes come only in two forms (*1*, *2*), and reactions of *W* to changes in *N* differ for the two gene types, as in the figure. The dashed line is the average reaction function for the population. The variance of *W* and the proportion of this variance due to genetics are greater for given environmental changes the greater the vertical distance between the reaction functions for genetic types *1* and *2* over the range of the change in *N*. The relative genetic contribution of a small change around N_0, for example, is much smaller than the genetic contribution of an equal change around N_1. Therefore, heritability estimates are much different around N_0 than around N_1 even though the reaction functions have the same slopes (and thus indicate the same impacts of changing *N* on *W*) around N_0 as around N_1. Within this framework,

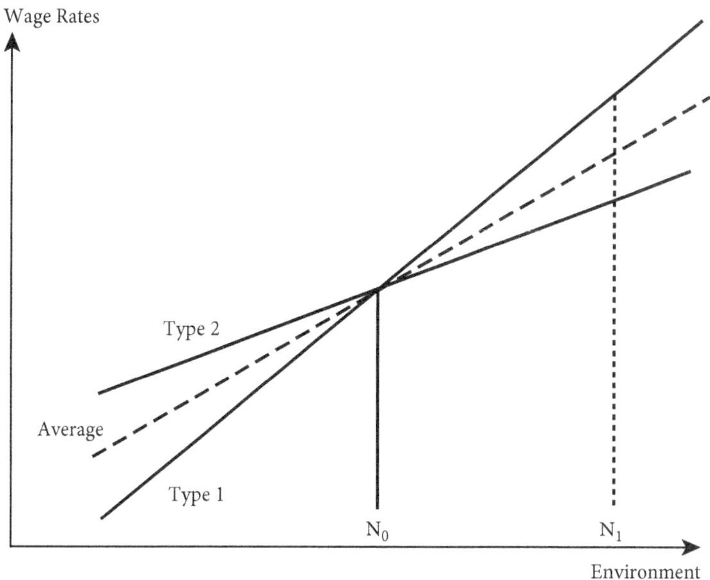

FIGURE 19.1 Wage rate reaction functions for two genetic types, 1 and 2, and average reaction function (drawn by author).

estimates of heritability are not a good guide to what happens to W if N is changed. To explore what happens to W if N is changed, the reaction function slopes are needed, not the variance decomposition for W. Obtaining such estimates for changes in such factors as schooling attainment S is the focus of the MZ-FE method discussed earlier.

19.2 Conclusion

Three twins methods have been developed and implemented in economics to obtain better estimates of the impact of one behavior variable (such as schooling) on other behaviors. These are used to estimate key parameters of intrafamilial allocations and whether parents reinforce or compensate endowment differentials among children and to investigate the Q-Q fertility model. Studies using these methods have found important empirical results; for example, that controlling for endowments affects substantially (generally reducing) the estimated impacts of schooling, that birthweight effects are larger for intellectually related outcomes (schooling, earnings) and less for physical outcomes (own and child anthropometrics) than in standard estimates, that parents significantly reinforce innate endowment differences and therefore inequality, and that child-specific endowments are important and account for about a quarter of earnings variance and a higher share of BMI variance in the United States. Thus, these three twins methods have contributed importantly to empirical knowledge in economics. Although there are many estimates of heritabilities and of related ACE models, particularly in other disciplines but somewhat in economics, the contribution of the variance decompositions from this fourth twins method to answering questions of interest in economics has been much less than the contributions of the three twins methods developed in economics. Variance decompositions are not very informative regarding, for example, magnitudes of the impacts of schooling and other behavioral choices on a range of outcomes in the presence of unobserved endowments, or regarding the nature of intrafamilial allocations of human resource investments among children, or about fertility and related decisions within the Q-Q fertility model.

Technological developments may seem to have made twins methods less relevant by permitting alternative ways of obtaining relevant estimates due to new information. Recent developments and cost reductions in genetic sequencing, for example, have made possible the incorporation of genetic markers in sociodemographic datasets, which clearly enhances the possibilities of incorporating genetics into economic analyses. A special issue of the *American Journal of Public Health* edited by Kaplan et al. (Kaplan, Spittel, & Spotts, 2013) includes a number of papers that discuss the implications and limitations of these developments for the social sciences more broadly, and Wehby (2015, in this handbook) summarizes some relevant studies pertaining to genetics and health economics and how they pertain to the fourth twins approach described in this chapter. These developments may permit an identification of the roles of particular genetic markers in various outcomes and otherwise enhance some dimensions of analyses using twins, probably with particular emphasis on the implications of epigenetics for gene–environment interactions. But these developments do not eliminate the value of twins studies. For example, they permit easy characterization of specific genetic markers but not of the entire set of genes shared by MZ twins (as used in the first twins method); they do not control for average family genetics and other shared dimensions of childhood family and neighborhood background experienced at the same life cycle stage (as in the first and second methods); nor do they use twining as an increase in child quantity (which is the essence of the third method). Thus, twins studies have been and are likely to continue to be valuable for economic analysis, primarily through the MZ-FE approach for controlling for endowments but also through helping to better understand intrafamilial allocations and, to a lesser extent (because of the spread of new technologies that may result in multiple births), to test the implications of the Q-Q fertility model in populations in which multiple births do not reflect conscious fertility-related behaviors.

Acknowledgments

The author thanks the editor, John Komlos, for useful comments on an earlier draft and the following collaborators for useful discussions of topics covered in this chapter: Vikesh Amin, Hans-Peter Kohler, Mark R. Rosenzweig, Jason Schnittker, Paul Taubman, and Junsen Zhang. Only the author is responsible for the interpretations given in this chapter.

Note

1. The APGAR score is a subjective evaluation of the viability of a newborn human baby based on *a*ppearance, *p*ulse, *g*rimace, *a*ctivity, and *r*espiration.

References

Almond, D., Chay, K. Y., & Lee, D. S. (2005). The costs of low birth weight. *Quarterly Journal of Economics, 1203*, 1031–1083.

Amin, V., & Behrman, J. R. (2014). Do more schooled women have fewer children and delay childbearing? Evidence from a sample of U.S. twins. *Journal of Population Economics*, 27(1), 1–31.

Amin, V., Behrman, J. R., & Kohler, H.- P. (2015). Schooling has smaller or insignificant effects on adult health in the US than suggested by cross-sectional associations: New estimates using relatively large samples of identical twins. *Social Science & Medicine, 127*, 181–189.

Amin, V., Behrman, J. R, Kohler, H.- P., Xiong, Y., & Zhang, J. (2015). Causal inferences: Identical twins help and clarity about necessary assumptions is critical. *Social Science & Medicine, 127*, 201–202.

Amin, V., Behrman, J. R., & Spector, T. D. (2013). Does more schooling improve health outcomes and health related behaviors? Evidence from U.K. twins. *Economics of Education Review, 35*, 134–148.

Amin, V., Lundborg, P., & Rooth, D.- O. (2011). Mothers do matter: New evidence on the effect of parents' schooling on children's schooling using Swedish twin data. Discussion paper series//Forschungsinstitut zur Zukunft der Arbeit, 2011.

Angrist, J., Lavy, V., & Schlosser, A. (2010). Multiple experiments for the causal link between the quantity and quality of children. *Journal of Labor Economics, 28*(4), 773–824.

Ashenfelter, O., & Krueger, A. (1994, December). Estimates of the economic return to schooling from a new sample of twins. *American Economic Review, 84* (5), 1157–1174.

Ashenfelter, O., & Rouse, C. (1998, February). Income, schooling, and ability: Evidence from a new sample of identical twins. *Quarterly Journal of Economics, 113*(1), 253–284.

Becker, G. (1991). *A treatise on the family*, 2nd ed. Cambridge, MA: Harvard University.

Becker, G., & Tomes, N. (1976). Child endowments and the quantity and quality of children. *Journal of Political Economy, 84*, S143–S162.

Becker, G. S., & Lewis, H. G. (1973). On the interaction between the quantity and quality of children. *Journal of Political Economy, 81*(2), S279–S88.

Behrman, J. R., Hrubec, Z., Taubman, P., & Wales, T. J. (1980). *Socioeconomic success: A study of the effects of genetic endowments, family environment and schooling*. Contributions to Economic Analysis. Amsterdam: North-Holland Publishing.

Behrman, J. R., Kohler, H.- P., Jensen, V., Pedersen, D., Petersen, I., Bingley, P., & Christensen, K. (2011). Does more schooling reduce hospitalization and delay mortality? New evidence based on Danish twins. *Demography, 48*(4), 1347–1375.

Behrman, J. R., Pollak, R. A., & Taubman, P. (1982, February). Parental preferences and provision for progeny. *Journal of Political Economy, 90*(1), 52–73.

Behrman, J. R., Pollak, R. A., & Taubman, P. (1995). The wealth model: Efficiency in education and equity in the family. In J. R. Behrman, R. A. Pollack, & P. Taubman (Eds.), *From parent to child: Intrahousehold allocations and intergenerational relations in the United States* (pp. 138–182). Chicago: University of Chicago Press.

Behrman, J. R., & Rosenzweig, M. R. (1999). Ability biases in schooling returns and twins: A test and new estimates. *Economics of Education Review, 18*, 159–167.

Behrman, J. R., & Rosenzweig, M. R. (2002). Does increasing women's schooling raise the schooling of the next generation? *American Economic Review, 92*(1), 323–334.

Behrman, J. R., & Rosenzweig, M. R. (2004). Returns to birthweight. *Review of Economics and Statistics, 86*(2), 586–601.

Behrman, J. R., Rosenzweig, M. R., & Taubman, P. (1994, December). Endowments and the allocation of schooling in the family and in the marriage market: The twins experiment. *Journal of Political Economy, 102*(6), 1131–1174.

Behrman, J. R., Rosenzweig, M. R., & Taubman, P. (1996, November). College choice and wages: Estimates using data on female twins. *Review of Economics and Statistics, 73*(4), 672–685.

Behrman, J. R., & Taubman, P. (1976, May). Intergenerational transmission of income and wealth. *American Economic Review, 66*(3), 436–440.

Behrman, J. R., Xiong, Y. & Zhang, J. (2015). Cross-sectional schooling-health associations misrepresented causal schooling effects on adult health and health-related behaviors: Evidence from the Chinese Adults Twins Survey. *Social Science and Medicine, 127*, 190–197.

Black, S. E., Devereux, P. J., & Salvanes, K. G. (2005). The more the merrier? The effect of family size and birth order on children's education. *Quarterly Journal of Economics, 120*(2), 669–700.

Boardman, J. D., & Fletcher, J. M. (2015). To cause or not to cause? That is the question, but identical twins might not have all of the answers. *Social Science & Medicine, 127*, 198–200.

Bound, J., & Solon, G. (1999, April). Double trouble: On the value of twins-based estimation of the return to schooling. *Economics of Education Review, 18*(2), 169–182.

Conley, D., Strully, K., & Bennett, N. G. (2006). Twin differences in birth weight: The effects of genotype and parental environment on neonatal and post-neonatal mortality. *Economics and Human Biology, 4*, 151–183.

Deary, I. J., Spinath, F. M., & Bates, T. C. (2006). Genetics of intelligence. *European Journal of Human Genetics, 14*, 690–700.

Feldman, M. W., & Lewontin, R. C. (1975). The heritability hang-up. *Science, 190*(4220), 1163–1168.

Griliches, Z., & Mason, W. M. M. (1972). Education, income, and ability. *Journal of Political Economy, 80*(Part II), S75–S103.

Hanushek, E. A. (1992, February). The trade-off between child quantity and quality. *Journal of Political Economy, 100*(1), 84–117.

Kaplan, R. M., Spittel, M. L., & Spotts, E. L. (2013). Advancing scientific inquiry by blurring research boundaries. *American Journal of Public Health, 103*(S1), S4.

Keith, L. G., Papiernik E., Keith, D. M., & Luke, B., eds. (1995). *Multiple pregnancy: Epidemiology, gestation, and perinatal outcome*. New York: Parthenon.

Kiely, J. L., & Kiely, M. (2001). Epidemiological trends in multiple births in the United States, 1971–1998. *Twin Research, 4*, 131–133.

Kohler, H. P., Behrman, J. R. & Schnittker, J. (2011). Social science methods for twins data: Integrating causality, endowments, and heritability. *Biodemography and Social Biology, 57*(1), 88–141.

Kohler, H.- P., Behrman, J. R., & Skytthe, A. (2005). Partner + children = happiness? The effects of partnerships and fertility on well-being. *Population and Development Review, 31*(3), 407–445.

Kohler, H.- P., Knudsen, L. B., Skytthe, A., & Christensen, K. (2002). The fertility pattern of twins and the general population compared: Evidence from Danish cohorts 1945–64. *Demographic Research, 6*(14), 383–408.

Layzer, D. (1974). Heritability analyses of IQ scores: Science or numerology? *Science, 183*(4131), 1259–1266.

Li, H., Zhang, J., & Zhu, Y. (2008). The quantity-quality trade-off of children in a developing country: Identification using Chinese twins. *Demography, 45*(1), 223–243.

Lundborg, P. (2013). The health returns to schooling—What can we learn from twins? *Journal of Population Economics, 26*(2), 673–701.

Miller, P., Mulvey, C., & Martin, N. (1995). What do twins studies tell us about the economic returns to education? A comparison of US and Australian findings. *American Economic Review, 85*(3), 586–599.

Miller, P., Mulvey, C., & Martin, N. (1997, February). Family characteristics and the returns to schooling: Evidence on gender differences from a sample of Australian twins. *Economica, 64*(253), 119–136.

Miller, P., Mulvey, C., & Martin, N. (2001, June). Genetic and environmental contributions to educational attainment in Australia. *Economics of Education Review, 20*(3), 211–224.

Mincer, J. B. (1974). *Schooling, experience, and earnings*. New York: NBER.

Plomin, R., DeFries, J. C., McClearn, G. E., & McGuffin, P. (2005). *Behavioral genetics*, 4th ed. New York: Worth.

Rosenzweig, M. R., & Wolpin, K. I. (1980*a*, January). Testing the quantity-quality model of fertility: Results of a natural experiment twins. *Econometrica, 48*(1), 227–240.

Rosenzweig, M. R., & Wolpin, K. I. (1980*b*, April). Life-cycle labor supply and fertility: Causal inferences from household models. *Journal of Political Economy, 88*, 328–348.

Rosenzweig, M. R., & Zhang, J. (2009). Do population control policies induce more human capital investment? Twins, Birth weight and China's 'one-child' policy. *Review of Economic Studies, 76*(3), 1149–1174.

Schnittker, J. (2008). Happiness and success: Genes, families, and the psychological effects of socioeconomic position and social support. *American Journal of Sociology, 114S*, S233–S259.

Schnittker, J., & Behrman, J. R. (2012). Learning to do well or learning to do good? Estimating the effects of schooling on civic engagement, social cohesion, and labor market outcomes in the presence of endowments. *Social Science Research, 41*(2), 306–320.

Wehby, G. L. (2015). How genetics can inform health economics. In J. Komlos, *Handbook of economics and human biology*. New York: Oxford University Press.

Willis, R. J. (1973). A new approach to the economic theory of fertility behavior. *Journal of Political Economy, 81*(2; Part 2), S14–S64.

CHAPTER 20

PUBLIC AND PRIVATE RETURNS TO INVESTING IN NUTRITION

HAROLD ALDERMAN AND DAVID E. SAHN

20.1 Introduction

ALTHOUGH nutrition contributes to welfare in and of itself, it also contributes to individual economic productivity as well as national income growth. The argument that improving nutrition is an investment on par with other productivity-enhancing expenditures rather than simply a form of government social spending designed to improve welfare and equity is hardly new (Berg & Muscat, 1972; Leibenstein, 1957). There are now extensive data to substantiate this point. This review recapitulates some recent evidence brought to this argument by economists.

To elucidate how productivity—generally of adults—is enhanced by investments in sensitive periods for nutrition—generally for young children—it is useful to employ a model that views adult labor outcomes as a cumulative function of investments in various periods of an individual's life, including child development in early childhood, schooling, and adulthood.[1] In the first period, the foundations for an individual's human capital, including his or her health and nutrition, (H_{i1}), are established as a function of investments (I_{i1}) in that period, as well as the individual's own genetic makeup (X_i), family characteristics (F_1), and community infrastructure (V_1). These latter two categories can be time-varying:

$$H_{i1} = h(I_{i1}, X_i, F_1, V_1) \qquad (1)$$

In the following period, the child accumulates other forms of human capital (S_{i2}), which can be considered as schooling or learning (Hanushek & Woessmann, 2008) and which reflect health accumulated earlier as well as current inputs and individual, family, and community characteristics:

$$S_{i2} = s(h(H_{i1}), I_{i2}, X_i, F_2, V_2) \quad (2)$$

When the individual enters employment, his or her wages or earnings reflect both health and learning, along with other individual characteristics, as well as local market conditions:

$$W_{i3} = w(h(H_{i1}), s(Si2), X_i, V_3) \quad (3)$$

This allows for the fade-out of impacts of early inputs or, alternatively, their cumulative effects. Cunha and Heckman (2007) introduce the concept of self-productivity in which higher stocks of health (skills) in one period create even higher levels of health (skills) later. The concept of self-productivity, which is generally applied to cognitive skills, can also be applied to health and nutrition as well. For example, the debate on the degree that a stunted child can catch up to his or her peers (Behrman, this volume; Lundeen et al., 2014; Martorell, Khan, & Schroeder, 1994) can be viewed as a subset of the larger concept of self-productivity. Similarly, cross-productivities address the possibility that better health in one period increases cognitive skills in the same or subsequent periods or vice versa.

A related concept, *dynamic complementarities*, addresses the returns to investments in one period as a function of health accumulated earlier. If, for example, $\delta^2 S_{i2}/\delta I_{i2}\delta H_{i1} > 0$, then higher health (skills) in childhood period lead to greater returns to investments in schooling. As economic efficiency implies larger investments where the returns are highest, complementarity implies allocating more resources to the higher performing students. Thus, from an economic efficiency perspective—abstracting from equity concerns—if there are dynamic complementarities (and this is an empirical question), then investments should be targeted to those with better initial health and greater skills, although this would widen disparities in the population as children age. Of course, if governments want to reduce poverty, even with efficiency costs, they may direct investments toward children with poorer health to compensate for limited prior investments, even if other investments have greater direct efficiency value. Moreover, the presence of dynamic complementarity is an empirical question; for some investments, it may be that $\delta^2 S_{i2}/\delta I_{i2}\delta H_{i1} < 0$, and thus dynamic substitution holds; in which case, returns to some investments in health or schooling are greatest where there is relatively low initial levels of health or skills.

Our goal in this chapter is to present some of the empirical literature on nutrition in the context of this framework of skills and productivity. We note that Bhutta et al. (2013) reported on some of the most effective investments in nutrition, summarizing a range of meta-analyses that provided the span of nutritional outcomes from a set of nutrition-specific interventions. Similarly, Ruel and Alderman (2013) presented a related review of nutrition-sensitive interventions. Such investments address the underlying determinants of fetal and child nutrition—food security; adequate caregiving resources at the maternal, household, and community levels; and access to health services and a safe and hygienic environment—and incorporate specific nutrition goals and actions. The former review even ventured an estimate of the effect of scaling up key interventions and the aggregate cost for achieving that effect. Neither of these reviews, however, focused on how the gains in nutrition translate into economic terms.

One reason that such a conversion from biological measures to economic ones is not undertaken is that a key outcome—the reduction of infant and child mortality stemming from improved nutrition[2]—cannot easily be expressed in an economic metric. This inherent limitation is discussed further later in this chapter. However, improved nutrition can also contribute to economic development by reducing the costs of illness and by enhancing productivity. The former may be achieved either by a decrease of the frequency or duration of illness associated with undernutrition in childhood or by the prevention or delay of adult chronic, noncommunicative diseases associated with malnutrition. Higher adult productivity may be directly attributed to increased stature or to reductions in iron deficiency anemia. Productivity may also be influenced by nutrition indirectly through enhanced cognitive skills, which influence both the timing and amount of schooling invested and the learning per year of schooling. Moreover, cognitive skills as well as noncognitive skills,[3] both of which may be influenced by investments in nutrition, have an impact on productivity independent of any contribution to learning (Doyle, Harmon, Heckman, & Tremblay, 2009; Osmani & Sen, 2003).

Alderman and Behrman (2006) offered a series of estimates of the economic value of avoiding low birthweight. The study converted evidence on the association of low birthweight and outcomes in terms of mortality, as well as the health and cognitive development of the survivors into a money metric to compare the benefits to the costs of a hypothetical intervention that might reduce the risk of low birthweight. Although some of the evidence employed came from randomized trials and could be considered causal, the study was not actually a review of program efficacy. However, it raised a number of methodological points on the economic benefits of nutrition interventions. This section uses evidence presented in Alderman and Behrman (2006) to illustrate these issues and then returns to the broader evidence based on prenatal nutrition. Alderman and Behrman's work indicates the gains achieved from the prevention of a single incident of low birthweight. This is stylized, based on an economy similar to Bangladesh, and indicates the breakeven point per beneficiary—at various discount rates that the government faces—that would make a government investment in preventing low birthweight profitable.

First, although there is little doubt that a child born with low birthweight has a high relative risk of dying during infancy, integrating the cost of this mortality with other outcomes such as improved development for survivors is particularly problematic. Most other outcomes can be assessed in terms of their financial value or cost. However, there is no consensus on how to make such an assessment for mortality. To be sure, a wide range of estimates of the value of averted mortality have been proposed. Three approaches, in particular, have common application. For example, one can evaluate the loss of life in terms of the expected earnings over the individual's lifetime. Another approach—referred to as the value of a statistical life (VSL)—is based on the differences in wages for risky occupations compared to wages elsewhere at similar levels of education and experience (Viscusi & Aldy, 2003). Both of these methodologies generally place more value on a life in higher income countries than in low-income settings (Hammit & Robinson, 2011).[4] A third approach uses the "revealed" behavior of governments: how much do they spend to reduce mortality? There are, however, relatively few estimates that employ this approach, and these estimates on revealed behavior give answers that are lower by orders of magnitude than those derived using either of the previous two approaches (Summers, 1992).

Second, under the revealed behavior assumption for the cost of mortality, neither that cost nor the cost of addressing illness contribute the majority of the estimated cost of low birthweight. This is in contrast with the relative impact of low birthweight on survivors. For example, Alderman and Behrman (2006) estimate that stunting and cognitive impairment associated with low birthweight accounts for 57% of the total costs of low birthweight—or, from another perspective, 57% of the benefits from averting such an outcome—when evaluated at a 5% discount rate, discounting from the period of pregnancy when a nutrition intervention might be effective. Thus, these two categories of benefits provide $290 of the total benefits amounting to $510 (Table 20.1).

Third, as is commonly observed in economics, the amount as well as the proportion of the total benefits attributed to future productivity is sensitive to the assumed discount rate. Because any productivity increase achieved from the higher skills of a child does

Table 20.1 Estimates of present discounted values in U.S. dollars of seven major impacts of moving one infant out of low birthweight status in a low-income developing country

	Annual discount rate (%)		
Impacts	3	5	10
1. Reduced infant mortality	$95	$99	$89
2. Reduced neonatal care	$42	$42	$42
3. Reduced costs of infant and child illness	$36	$35	$34
4. Productivity gain from reduced stunting	$152	$85	$25
5. Productivity gain from increased cognitive ability	$367	$205	$60
6. Reduced costs of chronic diseases	$49	$15	$1
7. Intergenerational effects	$92	$35	$6
Total Benefits	$832	$510	$257

Source: Constructed by authors based on Alderman & Behrman (2006).

not accrue until maturity, the estimated value of this increase is 79% higher (69% lower) when the discount rate is 3% (10%) instead of 5%. As the value of averted mortality and of reduced healthcare for a surviving low-birthweight infant occurs at a different time frame than labor productivity, the share of the estimated total benefits attributed to productivity is 62% at the lower discount rate and only 33% at the higher one (Table 20.1).

Fourth, many of the estimates of the productivity benefits from improved nutrition are synthetic in that they translate an effect size in one period to productivity in another using inference from a general literature. For example, Alderman and Behrman (2006) applied estimates of the association of low birthweight and cognitive capacity in childhood to a different literature on the association of cognitive measures to wages, or to schooling achieved, or both. In other contexts, the impact of stunting on earnings is derived from the relation of stature and schooling, as well as the relation of wages and schooling as commonly estimated. For example, Alderman, Hoddinott, and Kinsey (2006) and related investigations used instrumental variables to control for the fact that both nutrition and schooling reflect household decisions. It is rare, however, to be able to study adult outcomes that are directly and causally linked to an intervention in childhood. One study, by Hoddinott, Behrman et al. (2013), did show that tracking an intervention over decades—in this case, supplementation in childhood—indicated that observed outcomes are in keeping in general with extrapolating from the effect size of the early intervention. However, this may not always be the case; Alderman, Hawkesworth et al. (2014) found no significant difference between the treatment and control group of a trial whose mothers received supplements during pregnancy and whose infants showed an observed significant improvement in birthweight attributed to the intervention[5] (Ceesay et al., 1997) when the individuals of the two groups were revisited at ages 16 to 22.

What is the current evidence base on maternal and prenatal nutrition? There is little doubt that low birthweight is a risk factor for both neonatal mortality and subsequent stunting (Black et al., 2013; Christian et al., 2013). The risk is nuanced, however, with the risk of either neonatal or post-neonatal mortality higher for preterm babies than for small for gestation age (SGA) babies, although it is elevated in either category; the joint risk is higher than for either category alone (Katz et al., 2013). Moreover, fetal and child undernutrition is also a risk factor for subsequent obesity and noncommunicable diseases (NCDs). Because obesity is a risk factor for preterm birth and infant mortality (Black et al., 2013), this brings malnutrition full circle.

It is less clear, however, what, if any, interventions might reduce these risks. One approach, albeit one that can only make a difference over a moderate time horizon, is to improve birth outcomes by increasing the stature of women (Özaltin, Hill, & Subraminian, 2010; Toh-Adam, Srisupundit, & Tongsong, 2012). This, of course, begs the question of what measures can improve stature, an issue addressed in the next section. Other promising interventions to influence birth outcomes include balanced energy and protein supplementation, as well as the provision of calcium and multiple micronutrient supplementation. Other approaches, such as preventive strategies for malaria in pregnancy, also improve birth outcomes (Bhutta et al., 2013) but are not strictly considered nutrition interventions.

The endorsement by Bhutta et al. (2013) of balanced energy and protein supplements can be superficially contrasted with the comment of Prentice et al. (2013) that there are little grounds for optimism with regard to growth enhancement. Both studies cited the same meta-analysis (Kramer & Kukuma, 2003), but Bhutta et al. (2013) noted the reduction in stillbirths as well as the lower proportion of SGA children, whereas Prentice et al. (2013) also acknowledged the differences in SGA yet pointed out that there were no differences in birthweight or birth length. This partial contrast reflects the limitation of meta-analyses for assessing multiple outcomes. To state this somewhat differently, it raises the issue of determining the goal of nutritional interventions and how investments in nutrition are valued, a theme we return to in the next section.

Similar to evidence on the association of low birthweight and prematurity with survival, the relative risk of childhood stunting for low-birthweight children also depends on gestational age; the risk of stunting is somewhat higher for preterm births, even if the baby is of normal size, and is higher still for children born SGA. Moreover, the relative risk is higher for children who are both small and preterm than for the other categories. A study that tracked children from five birth cohorts also found that the size at birth was strongly associated with adult height (Stein et al., 2010). However, despite these associations, it is not clear the degree to which any improvements in birth outcomes attributable to an intervention carry over to subsequent child anthropometry (Lanou et al., 2014) or cognitive development (Alderman, Hawkesworth et al., 2014; Stein, 2014; Walker et al., 2011) without continued interventions over other periods in a child's life in low-income settings.

Studies of twins in the United States did, however, find that the consequences of low birthweight persisted into adulthood; the larger twin at birth earned more as an adult (Behrman & Rosenzweig, 2004; Black, Devereaux, & Salvanes, 2007). Kouropoulos, Stabile, Walld, & Roos (2008) found a similar pattern in Canadian twins.[6] Because these examples indicated a short-term shock in a relatively high-resource environment, it is not clear why families had not made compensatory investments. Torche and Echevarrıa (2011) assumed that such subsequent investments in children explained the fact that low birthweights among twins affected math and Spanish test scores for children from low-income families in Chile but not for those from higher income households. However, that households can compensate individuals does not mean that they always prefer to invest in household equity; in some circumstances, households make greater investments in schooling for children with higher cognitive abilities or skills (Akresh, Bagby, de Walque, & Kazianga, 2012; Behrman, Rosenzweig, & Taubman, 1994).

Low birthweight, however, may manifest in other ways than childhood mortality, stunting, or even cognitive development. A seminal paper by David Barker and Clive Osmond (1986), in which they traced adult illness in England and Wales to birthweight records, has led to a hypothesis of the etiology of diseases termed the *fetal origin hypothesis*. The original epidemiological results, as well as studies of survivors of famines (Hult et al., 2010), showed plausible associations. Since the initial hypothesis was promoted, however, a range of laboratory studies using animals has explored the underlying structural biological model (Harding et al., 2011), bolstering, if not necessarily proving, a causal interpretation. Gluckman et al. (2009) presented the underlying model in terms of epigenetics and argued that this model raises questions regarding the benefit-to-cost ratio of early interventions.[7]

A simulation based on Alderman and Behrman (2006) is germane to this question. The benefits of reducing NCDs attributable to a reduction of low birthweight in that study were based on an assumption that the costs of treatment were centered on age 60. If this assumption is varied by assuming that they are centered at age 49, the contribution to total estimated benefits—based on the odds ratio of chronic disease for low-birthweight children and an assumed cost equivalent to 10 years earnings from lost income plus medical care for those with NCDs—is still small. Indeed, because future benefits are discounted relative to current benefits, benefits from averting one case of low birthweight increase from $15 in the initial paper to $32 under the new assumption (Alderman, 2013). The increase would only bring the present discounted benefits of reduced NCDs to 6% of the new total package of benefits. The proportional increase is larger at higher discount rates than the 5% used in this simulation but from a smaller base. Thus, the potential for influencing adult health by investing in prenatal nutrition adds little to the motivation, which comes from the value of improved cognitive and noncognitive skills.

Low birthweight is not the only concern for prenatal nutrition. For example, to prevent neural tube defects, folate deficiency needs to be addressed *prior* to conception. Supplementation or fortification with folate during pregnancy will also reduce low birthweight (Bhutta et al., 2013). Folate supplementation is generally combined with iron supplements. The evidence that iron supplementation will reduce infant and maternal mortality is extensive; newer evidence also points to increased cognitive function of children aged 7–9 whose mothers received iron supplements during pregnancy (Christian et al., 2010). Similarly, iodine fortification is a highly cost-effective means to prevent cognitive impairment; Horton, Alderman, & Rivera (2009) estimated a benefit-to-cost ratio of 30:1 at a 3% discount rate and 12:1 at 6%. Although iodine fortification of salt is particularly cost effective relative to maternal supplementation, the latter is nevertheless effective (Field, Robles, & Torero, 2009), with promising benefit-to-cost ratios (Behrman, Alderman, & Hoddinott, 2004). However, even though there is some evidence that mild iodine deficiency can be alleviated during school years (Zimmermann et al., 2006), prevention of severe deficiency may be considered a critical intervention for prenatal nutrition, with far less effective interventions available after that period. Thus, there is a well-delineated path from maternal nutrition to cognitive capacity and, by inference, to productivity.

Postpartum depression provides a bridge between the risks of poor health in pregnancy and of risks in infancy. Indeed, not only is maternal depression associated with malnutrition (Patel, Rahman, Jacob, & Hughes, 2004; Stewart, 2007), it is also considered a factor in child cognitive and socioemotional development (Wachs, Black, & Engle, 2009; Walker et al., 2011). The association is equally strong in high-income countries as it is in low-income Asia, likely reflecting reduced maternal sensitivity to her child's needs, an issue more about care than food access. Although there are few interventions that focus on reversing the pernicious effect of this risk on child growth per se, a few trials show that there are effective means to improve birth outcomes through community mobilization (Tripathy et al., 2010). The main outcome tracked in this particular study was neonatal mortality. However, depression was also significantly reduced. Thus, although it is hard to quantify in an economic metric, there are distinct benefits that come from addressing women as individuals, as well as in terms of their reproductive roles.

20.2 Childhood Nutrition and Subsequent Human Capital

Bhutta et al. (2013) used a series of meta-analyses and reviews of best practices in nutrition to estimate the expected impact and cost of scaling up 10 nutrition-specific interventions proven effective in covering 90% of the relevant population in 34 countries with the highest rates of malnutrition in the world. They concluded that this scaling up effort *from present levels of coverage* would cost $9.6 billion annually and would reduce stunting globally by 20% and prevent 15% of all deaths of children under 5.[8] That is, the scaling up would save 1 million lives annually. Without parsing and debating the details of this particular state-of-the-art review of efficacy and, occasionally, effectiveness trials, one limitation of the study illustrates the challenges in determining the economic outcomes from investment in nutrition.

In particular, the intervention that contributed the most to the total cost was treatment for severe acute malnutrition. This intervention also had the lowest cost per life saved. But this intervention contributes little to human capital over the lifetime. The authors acknowledge that even though the model estimates reductions in stunting, it provides only a partial indication of what investments in nutrition can achieve.

The same investments that can achieve these results will also lead to other improvements in cognitive and socioemotional development. Although these outcomes are not included in the model (Bhutta et al., 2013, p. 60), if it is correct that the same investments achieve these additional ends, then it may not matter for the prioritization of investments. If the optimal strategy for addressing child mortality and stunting does not necessarily coincide with the best approach for promoting other aspects of development, however, there are some possible impacts for the timing of interventions and the choice of the platform for effective delivery.[9]

There is little question on the timing of interventions aimed at preventing early mortality. Two-thirds of all deaths of children under 5 in Africa occur in the first year; the corresponding figure for South Asia is 78%.[10] Because many nutrition programs focus on the first 2 years of life, they coincide with the overwhelming majority of any opportunities to prevent early mortality.

The rationale for focusing on the first 2 years of a child's life along with the time from conception, however, comes not only from the opportunity to save lives but also from the evidence that stunting occurs early in a child's life. Using Demographic Health Surveys and Maternal Infant Child surveys conducted in a large number of low- and middle-income countries, Victora, de Onis, Curi Hallal, Blössner, and Shrimpton (2010) confirmed that nutritional status in children deteriorates as early as the first 6 months after birth in all developing regions of the world and continues to decline until about 24 months, after which it appear to level off or be very slightly reversed. This age pattern is supported by prospective cohort studies from the five Consortium of Health-Orientated Research in Transitioning Societies (COHORTS) countries (Brazil, Guatemala, India, the Philippines, and South Africa) that showed similar growth patterns to those shown using the cross-sectional surveys (Stein et al., 2010).

There is little debate that this pattern of stunting by age is widespread, but the implicit view that there is little potential to improve stunting after age 2 is increasingly under challenge (Behrman, this volume; Prentice et al., 2013). A cornerstone of this challenge is the growing body of longitudinal studies that allow a dynamic approach to determining the degree to which stunting is reversible. As mentioned, that evidence is reviewed elsewhere in this volume; thus, we will take up related issues instead. For example, even if catch-up growth beyond the first 2 years is common, from a policy standpoint, it is necessary to determine if there are cost-effective programs to promote this growth. Even before that, it is useful to raise the somewhat eccentric question of whether we are really interested in height per se.

There is substantial evidence that height affects schooling (Alderman et al., 2006; Glewwe & Jacoby, 1995; Yamauchi, 2008) and even more analyses that show that taller individuals earn more than shorter individuals with a similar education level (Schultz, 2003; Thomas & Strauss, 1997; Vogl, 2014). As discussed in section 3, researchers have attempted to indicate the degree to which the wage premium for height is due to greater cognitive skills among taller individuals as opposed to physical stamina. Such research also addresses whether height is a proxy for cognitive skills that may be acquired through other means, perhaps in a more cost effective manner.

This research indicates that height does indeed contribute to labor choices as well as to returns to labor, both indirectly, through schooling in many settings, and directly, where brawn is important. This confirms that estimates of the economic benefits from prevention of stunting, such as reported in Behrman et al. (2004) and Hoddinott, Alderman et al. (2013), focus on real productivity effects and are not merely a proxy for concurrent human capital investments. However, the underlying evidence base is not without limitations, as is almost always the case with programs at scale. Only a handful of studies look at the impact of a change in nutrition on changes in schooling and employ a valid counterfactual let alone track to labor market outcomes.[11] It is possible that, given the complex etiology of nutrition, reducing stunting by affecting food intake may have different impacts on productivity than, say, changing care practices or improving sanitation, even if all of these reduce stunting. That is, the measurement of the long-term impact of an intervention only gives a local average treatment effect for those whose nutrition status was changed by that intervention (Angrist & Krueger, 1994). The impact, then, is not necessarily identical to the impact of height in all circumstances. This issue, however, is generic and not unique to investigations of nutrition.

Two of the most common interventions to prevent stunting—supplementation with complementary foods at the time of weaning and enhancement of caregiving during breastfeeding and weaning—are clearly targeted at children under 2, an age period that, along with growth in utero, is referred to as the 1,000 days from conception. Some programmatic evidence from studies of responses to interventions is supportive of the 1,000 days focus. For example, an analysis of a supplementation trial in Guatemala that had been shown to affect education achievement and adult earnings (Hoddinott, Behrman et al., 2013) found that supplements from age 6 to 36 months contributed to increased growth but at decreasing rates. After 36 months, no impact was observed (Schroeder, Martorell, Rivera, Ruel, & Habicht, 1995). Similarly, Lutter et al. (1990) found that peak responsiveness of weight and length to supplementation in Colombia was between 9 and 12 months. In a study of community-based growth promotion—one that did not include supplementation—Linnemayr and Alderman (2011) noted that only children younger than 18 months benefited. They speculated that this was because breastfeeding promotion was necessarily age-specific, but the study was not designed to explore the contribution of the different elements of the package of services. Indeed, there are concerns about obesity and adult chronic disease associated with weight gain on small frames (Monteiro & Victora, 2005; Uauy & Kain, 2002; Yajnik, 2004). Because, as of yet, relatively few programs have assessed the age-specific risk of obesity and chronic disease, this remains an area for investigation. It is not, however, just the risks of attempting to reverse early stunting outside the 1,000-day window that remains a research priority; there is relatively little evidence on what works on a programmatic scale during prepuberty or adolescence (Prentice et al., 2013).

If the greater concern, however, is the larger development consequences attendant to stunting, then concern about height may be secondary. For example, evidence on this question comes from a comprehensive long-term study of interventions with food supplementation, as well as of child stimulation, provided to stunted children aged 9–24 months for 2 years through weekly home visits by community workers in Jamaica. In that trial, food supplementation had only a modest impact on physical growth, which was no longer apparent by age 7 years, although some recovery from stunting was evident in all children regardless of intervention group (Walker, Grantham-McGregor, Himes, Powell, & Chang, 1996). In contrast, both supplementation and stimulation led to improved cognitive skills in early childhood (Grantham-McGregor, Powell, Walker, & Himes, 1991), and long-term follow-up studies showed that stimulation yielded sustained cognitive benefits and improvements in educational attainment, social behavior, and income in young adulthood (Gertler et al., 2014). The stimulation intervention resulted in a 25% increase in earnings. In contrast, the nutritional arm of the intervention did not close the earnings gap. Gertler et al. (2014) contended that this increase due to stimulation was larger than that reported in the few similar interventions from the United States. A combined strategy of stimulation and micronutrient supplementation was recently delivered in Colombia to children 12–24 months at initiation. After 18 moinths stimulation improved cognitive scores but supplementation has no signnifcant impact (Attanasio et al., 2014).

Similarly, in Bangladesh, psychosocial stimulation, with or without modest-sized food supplements (150–300 kcal/d), among severely underweight children aged 6–24 months upon discharge from the hospital had an impact on mental development and a small impact on weight for age, but there were no synergistic effects (Nahar et al., 2012). That is, any advantage of having programs provide both nutritional supplements and stimulation is likely to come from administrative savings in joint service delivery and not from the interaction of the forms of assistance. Benefits from stimulation to the development of undernourished children is a highly consistent finding, and its inclusion in programs that respond to undernutrition could yield improvements in children's development and longer term returns to education. Furthermore, integrating nutrition and stimulation interventions does not compromise the impact of the individual program components (Grantham-McGregor, Fernald, Kagawa, & Walker, 2014).

This last observation may be critical. Even in the absence of reinforcing benefits, there may be gains to using integrated programs as a means of service delivery if they are cost saving from joint implementation (Alderman, Behrman et al., 2014; Yousafzai, Rasheed, Rizvi, Armstrong, & Bhutta, 2014). It is noteworthy that both the Jamaican trial and the Bangladeshi study cited earlier prioritized children who were malnourished. This seems reasonable because these programs are fairly resource-intensive; it is quite plausible that this subpopulation is particularly responsive to these investments. At this time, however, the body of evidence on integrating stimulation and nutrition comes from small-scale trials, and there is little documentation for programs at scale.

20.3 Contemporaneous Impact of Nutrition on Productivity: The Role of Height, Weight, and Intake

Beyond the impact of nutrition for women and children on cognitive and economic prospects over the life course, there is considerable microeconomic evidence that worker productivity is directly affected by nutritional well-being. The recent empirical studies have their foundation in earlier theoretical work, dating as far back as Adam Smith's *Wealth of Nations* (1776/1960) and the early work of Chadwick (1842/1965) that asserted that important economic losses were due to poor health and sanitary conditions. The efficiency wage theory, initially formulated by Leibenstein (1957) and Mazumdar (1959), and subsequently expanded upon by Mirrlees (1976), Bliss and Stern (1978*a*, 1978*b*), and others, forms the theoretical foundation of the relationship between nutritional well-being and labor market outcomes and has motivated the research on whether wages respond to the nutritional intake of workers.

The impact of nutrition on productivity is expected to differ depending on the structure of the economy and the nature of the nutrition problem. For example, there is emergent evidence that obesity and overweight reduce productivity and wages in developed countries (Cawley, 2004). However, our main concern is with undernutrition in resource-poor countries, where the productivity consequences are expected to be most serious for two reasons: first, the incidence and severity of malnutrition is greatest, and, second, a greater share of jobs involve physical labor where strength and stamina are directly compromised by malnutrition and thus affect returns to work.

Empirical support for the relationship between undernutrition and productivity is found in the observed correlation between nutrition and wages, which has been well established with household survey data (Strauss & Thomas, 1998). And although the preponderance of the microeconomic literature does suggest that nutrition is an important determinant of economic productivity (Thomas & Frankenberg 2002), it is difficult to make a causal argument because numerous confounding influences may intervene. For example, healthier workers may also be better educated or have parents who confer other opportunities and have preferences that contribute to the greater labor market success of their children.

The literature is replete with efforts to test the hypothesized impact of nutrition on productivity (Strauss & Thomas, 1998). Much of the nonexperimental work regresses economic outcomes on height, which, as we discussed earlier in this chapter, in part captures health conditions and investments earlier in life. So although there is considerable evidence that taller workers are indeed more productive and have higher earnings (Deolalikar, 1988; Glick & Sahn, 1997; Haddad & Bouis, 1991; Schultz & Tansel, 1997; Thomas & Strauss, 1997), there remains concern that the contemporaneous benefits of height on the ability to perform work—especially physical work—is in fact the causal pathway to higher productivity. For example, height may be correlated with unmeasured cognitive skills, which, like height, were affected by the types of early childhood conditions we discussed earlier in this chapter.

The formidable challenge of separating the impact of height from other pathways has been studied in some more recent literature. One notable effort is the paper by LaFave and Thomas (2013). Using a longitudinal survey from Central Java, they were able to control for cognitive and noncognitive skills to examine the role of stature in affecting wages in a model that incorporated sectoral choice, occupation, and family background. They found that there were indeed earning-related returns to height that were not captured by controlling for other measures of human capital, and, more specifically, a 1% increase in height is related to a 1.9% increase in hourly earnings when controlling for both cognition and education. Bossavie, Alderman, Giles, and Mete (2014) have a similar conclusion for a study of workers in Pakistan that includes both Raven's scores as well as an index of noncognitive skills.

Complementing this work is a recent paper by Vogl (2014) that addressed the role of height in various labor market outcomes in Mexico. Vogl's estimates indicated that an individual's probability of working in a "brawn"-intensive occupation was increased by 0.63 percentage points for each additional centimeter of height and that this falls to

0.26 when childhood covariates and Raven's score is added to the regression. Similarly, earnings increased by 2.3% for each additional centimeter of height, but inclusion of cognitive test scores reduced this impact by 13%. Adding information on childhood conditions as well as education, which affects sorting into different jobs, further reduced the returns in terms of hourly gains to height to 1.3% for each additional centimeter of height.

The work by Vogl was in part motivated by an earlier paper by Case and Paxson (2008) that also explored the impact of stature on labor market outcomes, but in the United Kingdom and the United States. They observed a smaller height premium than Vogl did in Mexico. More importantly, though, they found that a large share of the association between wages and stature was explained by workers' scores on cognitive tests taken when they were children. And, like the findings for Mexico (Vogl, 2014), height impacted wages through the selection process whereby adults with greater stature sort into occupations that require greater cognitive rather than physical skills. The core of the story, however, that taller people earn more because they are smarter rests on the notion that these outcomes are jointly determined by a set of common factors. These factors include the circumstances in utero and other early childhood experiences, which we highlighted earlier. The challenge remains, however, to better understand the specific influences on early childhood experiences, including maternal behaviors such as smoking, genetics, and pollution, and even malnutrition caused by lack of access to clean water and sanitation.

Another approach to examining the link between nutrition and productivity employs body mass index (BMI) as a more current health indicator and finds that underweight contributes to lower productivity (Glick & Sahn, 1997; Schultz & Tansel, 1997). A more recent study (Pitt, Rosenzweig, & Hassan, 2013) that focused on the role of BMI on labor market outcomes indicated that returns to "brawn," like schooling, differ by occupation, and thus it comes as no surprise that these researchers found that brawn affects occupational choice. Specifically, it tends to sort men more so than women into activities with lower returns to skills. While tending to reduce incentives for schooling among men, this situation in fact increases the importance of nutritional investments because these investments positively and directly affect wages. Thus, in economies where strength is more central to various work activities, the consequence is that not only will occupational differences be greater by gender, but returns to education are likely to be higher for women who inherently are less physical than men; thus, women will tend to concentrate on skill-intensive activities.

Yet a third strain of the literature focuses on nutrient intake: Strauss (1986) estimated a farm production function for Sierra Leone and found that calorie intake had a significant positive effect on the marginal product of agricultural labor. Sahn and Alderman (1988) instrumented per capita household calories using prices, and the results from Sri Lanka indicated that there was a positive effect on market wages for rural men but not women. Behrman and Deolalikar (1989) found that calories impact productivity in the peak season for men. However, the positive effect of intake on productivity is not a universal finding, as shown in studies by Haddad and Bouis (1991) and Deolalikar (1988).

Yet another type of observational data that suggests a productivity impact of nutrition comes from the economic history literature. One example is the work of Margo and Steckel (1982) that found that the value of slaves was associated with their height.

Relying on observational data to prove causation is challenging, and thus there will inevitably be concerns about identifying and actually determining a causal relationship between nutrition and productivity. Quite simply, no matter how well these studies are designed, to the extent that a range of human capital inputs are jointly determined and models do not capture feedbacks among indicators such as health, nutrition, and mobility, microstudies will potentially overstate aggregate productivity effects. This potential can be mitigated by using well-designed randomized control trials. Fortunately, there is a body of experimental studies designed to isolate causal impacts despite the challenges in designing and implementing randomized control trials to examine productivity effects of nutrition. One example is the work of Wolgemuth et al. (Wolgemuth, Latham, Hall, Chesher, & Crompton, 1982) who reported that road workers in Kenya witnessed small productivity gains as a result of energy supplementation.

Iron deficiency is perhaps the aspect of malnutrition that has been most widely researched in terms of impact on productivity. This makes sense given that, physiologically, aerobic capacity declines with decreasing levels of hemoglobin. Depletion of iron stores also contributes to reductions in the amount of oxygen available to muscles. Endurance suffers, and there are greater demands made on the heart in order to achieve the same level of activity. Iron deficiency also raises susceptibility to disease and is associated with fatigue and impaired cognitive development (Haas & Brownlie, 2001). Noteworthy among the many studies that examined causal effects of iron supplementation were the impact on the output of rubber workers in Indonesia (Basta, Soekirman, Karyadi, & Scrimshaw, 1979), cotton mill workers in China (Li et al., 1994), and tea plantation workers in Sri Lanka (Edgerton, Gardner, Ohira, Gunawardena, & Senewiratne, 1979) Additionally, several studies have demonstrated how the cognitive development of children was impaired by iron deficiency (Pollitt, 2001). Another interesting field experiment was the Work and Iron Status Evaluation (WISE) study that provided iron supplements to adults in Central Java, Indonesia, and demonstrated that iron deficiency had a causal impact on time allocation and economic productivity (Thomas et al., 2006).

One other observation study by Knaul (2000) relied on age of menarche as an indicator of early nutrition inputs, thus capturing inputs that are similar to attained height. Beyond reviewing the evidence of the appropriateness of using age of menarche to capture nutritional status, her empirical results indicated that among Mexican women wages increased by 26% for each year that age of menarche was reduced.

Experimental evidence on other nutrition interventions is more mixed in terms of the findings. Randomized food supplementation of sugarcane cutters in Guatemala indicated that those living in treatment villages were not more productive than the control villages (Imminck & Viteri, 1981), and another study in Kenya found a limited impact of food supplementation on the productivity of road workers (Wolgemuth et al., 1982).

20.4 Macroeconomic and Cross-Country Evidence

Complementary to the evidence of the impact of nutrition on productivity at the level of the household or individual, there is literature showing that nutrition and health have contributed in an important way to increases in productivity and economic growth. One strain of that work, primarily done by economic historians, is perhaps best captured by the seminal work of Robert Fogel (1994) that found that inadequacies in diet contributed to disease and early mortality and greatly limited the possibility for productive work in the 18th century in England and France. Large numbers of potential workers were unable to participate in the labor force due to nutrient deficits, and the output of those able to work was significantly reduced. Fogel estimated that 50% of Britain's growth since 1800 was attributable to the increases in dietary energy available for work and to improvements in the efficiency of the transformation of nutrients, particularly calories, into work (Fogel, 2004).[12] Similar estimates indicated that between 1780 and the middle of the 20th century, 30% of the per capita growth in the UK was attributable to improvements in nutrition (World Health Organization [WHO], 2002).

Corroborating the work of historians has been the examination of the impact of health (although not explicitly nutritional status) on economic growth and productivity gains using a range of techniques including cross-country regression models, general equilibrium, and what we refer to as *macrosimulation models* using microestimation techniques. Of these techniques, perhaps the most widely used are the cross-country models that basically relate aggregate outcomes such as gross domestic product (GDP) growth to measures of health such as life expectancy or infant mortality rates. Looking at the more general body of work on the impacts of health on economic outcomes, one finds generally large effects.[13] For example, Barro (1997) estimated that an increase in life expectancy of 10% would lead to an increase in economic growth of 0.4% per year. This finding was broadly consistent with the results of other studies that also showed health-induced increases in productivity (Arora, 1999; Bloom, Canning, & Sevilla, 2004; Bloom & Sachs, 1998; Gallup & Sachs, 2001; Gallup, Sachs, & Mellinger, 1999). Despite the insights gained from these studies, this body of literature has drawn considerable criticism, and caution is warranted in terms of ascribing causal effects. For example, because specifications were often ad hoc, endogeneneity issues were manifold and instruments were often questionable. Similarly, there have been problems of omitted variables and unobservables that may jointly affect health status and income. Moreover, data sources were unreliable, especially from Africa, where there is an acute paucity of time-series statistics (Weil, 2007). Additionally, this literature has rarely used nutrition as the health measure of choice (in contrast to the economic history literature cited earlier). One important reason is that the indicator of nutritional status that offers the greatest promise is height. The problem for cross-country work is that the height of adults is a lagged indicator, capturing the health status of adults when they were infants and young children. Thus, it does not capture the contemporaneous health environment that would be desirable for cross-county models of how nutrition investments in childhood impact subsequent economic growth and poverty.[14]

Some more recent studies attempt to rigorously tackle the identification problem including Acemoglu and Johnson (2007).[15] They used predicted change in mortality based on information on global interventions to reduce disease as an instrument for changes in life expectancy, relying on long-term differences as their source of identification to avoid the problem of other cross-country modeling exercises. Despite health improvements, general equilibrium effects, in part through the impact on labor supply, resulted in there being no positive impact on GDP.[16]

Studies that use macrosimulation built on microsimulation is perhaps best illustrated by the work of Weil (2007), Young (2007), and Ashraf et al. (Ashraf, Lester, & Weil, 2008). Only very modest impacts for health and growth were reported by Weil (2007) and by Ashraf et al. (2008), who used a macroeconomic accounting model in combination with microeconomic estimates of the productivity effects of health improvements. Weil found that closing health gaps accounted for only small differences in economic performance, far smaller than would be implied by the traditional cross-country regressions discussed earlier. Moreover, Young, whose work was focused on the impact of HIV/AIDS in Africa, arrived at the counterintuitive result that living standards, in fact, would rise as a consequence of the scourge of HIV/AIDS. This effect was largely driven by endogenizing fertility, education, and labor market participation, with results driven by feedbacks such as HIV to fertility reduction and parental death leading to orphanhood and ending education that affected future labor supply.

In its totality, the challenges of identification and causal inference in the cross-country and macro research of the impact of nutrition on productivity and economic outcomes are made even more compelling when one considers the role of general equilibrium effects, including diminishing returns to labor inputs, the inelasticity of land and physical capital, and the population growth that results from improved nutrition and health. Likewise, there are other pathways, such as the indirect effect on schooling or investment decisions of households that follow from expectations for a healthier and longer life.

Thus, the ambiguity of the macroeconomic studies suggests that—at least at the level of policy—an important area of future research should focus on how to expand the links between nutrition and economic impacts. This requires paying attention to a range of considerations including labor market policies and conditions; the nature of health spending and how it can be optimized to improve nutrition; the role of other institutions, such as schools and credit and insurance markets; policies that impact access to and productivity of agricultural land, all of which affect the impact of nutrition on productivity and economic performance.

20.4.1 Nutrition and Health Inequality

In previous sections of this chapter, we focused on the role of nutritional well-being as an absolute measure, relying on thresholds or norms such as low birthweight or low height-for-age z-scores that define malnutrition. In this section, we briefly explore the issue of relative well-being and address whether disparities of health and nutritional status warrant attention from policy makers concerned with the general well-being of society and related issues of productivity. We are interested in whether there are any functional consequences that may follow from inequity in nutritional and health outcomes. Given the fact that inequality is a relative rather than absolute indicator, should we concern ourselves with the distribution of health and "relative" health status, above and beyond our primary focus on the absolute level of health?

A number of policy statements and academic papers have vigorously emphasized the need to reduce the differences in health status between countries and between socioeconomic groups within countries (e.g., Whitehead, 2000; WHO, 1985, 1986). This focus on disparities in health outcomes is clearly an aspect of inequality as a public policy concern. One obvious reason is that of social justice, but the paramount importance of reducing health inequalities in the pursuit of social justice does not relate directly to the topic of our chapter on productivity. So what links exist, if any, between health inequalities and productivity?

One foundational although somewhat theoretical idea that supports an indirect pathway from inequalities in health to the productivity of individuals and society is based on Sen's (1979, 1985, 1987) argument that poverty is the deprivation of basic capabilities, not just low levels of income. Low incomes are only *instrumentally significant*, whereas deprivation of capabilities, such as poor health and nutritional status, are *intrinsically important*. Health is thus a more direct measure of capability deprivation than is income or expenditures. And, to the extent that measures of health are appropriate arguments in the social welfare function, there are legitimate reasons to be concerned about health inequality directly affecting society, just as there are for income.

It is also the case that inequalities in the distribution of health may affect other outcomes, such as political stability and social cohesion, which may in turn have implications for productivity and economic prosperity. This is perhaps best illustrated by acute and unaddressed episodes of disease leading to despair and a breakdown of the social contract between a government and its citizens or even social order across borders. The fact that the burdens of disease are unequally shared may also lead to neglect in addressing a public health crisis and, consequently, to suffering and turmoil within affected areas.

The more widespread concern is that inequalities in health and nutrition contribute to differences in preferences and thus reduce political support for investments in public goods that have higher returns. As an example, take the case of malaria and other tropical and communicable diseases that are well known to have broader productivity and economic consequences in affected areas and for infected individuals and households. The level of investment in these diseases is often disproportionately low relative to the burden of disease criteria, which takes into account premature death and disability.[17] But it is not just communicable tropical diseases that are neglected. Indeed, large productivity losses are seen across the life course from maternal and child malnutrition. Unequal disease burdens may thus lead to the neglect of malnutrition and communicable disease by private enterprise (e.g., pharmaceutical companies) as well as public health institutions if the political consensus required to promote spending on health-related public goods or services with large positive externalities (e.g., vaccinations, water and sanitation, nutrition programs) is lacking. This inefficiency—where budgets of the state, international organizations, and even private resources are not allocated to coping with the needs of those at the bottom of the health distribution—is perhaps best illustrated on a global scale by the recent Ebola epidemic, which has high disease burdens in affected countries but, because of the inequality of the burden, accounts for low shares of global as well as within-country health spending.

Another link between inequalities and productivity results from the likely concavity of work output as a function of nutritional status; to the extent that this is the case, productivity will be lower in a population with the same level of average health but with great inequality in health. It is also likely that where a person is positioned in terms of rank, including in terms of the health distribution, will affect discount rates and risk preferences, although how this will impact productivity is not necessarily clear. Lower rank may also influence market conditions and increase the interest rates these individuals face (if they are able to find lenders at all) and may thus have an adverse effect on economic outcomes.

Another argument for paying attention to the distribution of health and nutrition in a population emanates from the assertion that there are inherent health risks associated with disparities in socioeconomic circumstances (Wilkinson, 1997). More recently, Wilkinson (2000), Bruner and Marmot (1999), and Pickett and Cabieses Valdes (this volume) have discussed in great detail how relative deprivation contributes to stress and, subsequently, to compromised health status. Indeed, these two links—between relative deprivation and stress and between stress and health status—are well-documented in the psychological and biomedical literature. In regard to the former, lack of equality can contribute to a loss of dignity, to shame, and to stigmatization of those at the bottom end of the distribution, thereby increasing stress. And there is evidence that stress leads to choices, such as increases in time discounting, that can reduce the potential long-term productivity and economic well-being of individuals (Mani, Mullainathan, Shafir, & Zhao, 2013; Shah, Mullainathan, & Shafir, 2012). The scientific and empirical evidence, especially for the "neuroendocrine" pathways through which psychosocial risk factors link health to inequality, however, is limited. Yet we would agree that it is a provocative concept, one deserving of more careful scrutiny. While such pathways may be difficult to test empirically, what does seem quite convincing are two propositions: (1) inequalities in material well-being give rise to inequality in health outcomes, and (2) inequality in material well-being makes those at the bottom end of the distribution more vulnerable to shocks, with reduced access to basic health services and diminished likelihood of access to and participation in formal and informal forms of mutual assistance, safety nets, and social networks—all of which will have adverse effects on the well-being of individuals but also will result in social costs in terms of poor health and related stress leading to lower productivity.

The most worrisome aspect is the prospect of the emergence of *inequality traps*, analogous to what we find in the literature about poverty traps, in which unequal outcomes persist in health over the life course and even across generations. This can apply to the role of inequality in health in contributing to the perpetuation of poor health outcomes across generations but also to worse outcomes in terms of the ability to improve one's material well-being. This is consistent with the earlier discussion in which those at the lower end of the health distribution are likely to have functional impairments that lead to lower earnings. Likewise, another largely hypothesized modality for a health-related poverty trap operates within mental health, where being low in rank in terms of material well-being creates stress, and this in turn contributes to economic behaviors such as increased discounting (Haushofer & Fehr, 2014).

Given the arguments for public policy to consider equity in health and nutrition, an important distinction derives from Sen's (1985, 1987) work on defining well-being, in which he makes the distinction between equity in health achievements and equity in the capability to achieve good health. Beyond this distinction is a third domain in defining health inequality—that of the equality of access to health services. Indeed, all three concepts are related to social justice, and, likewise, equality in all these three areas is expected to affect outcomes such as economic growth and productivity.

Ideally, we would give priority to examining inequality in terms of the capability to achieve health. However, there is no good metric of health capabilities because genetic diversity, as well as individual preferences, may thwart equalizing health outcomes. Thus, we are left with the objective of reducing disparities in health outcomes. This will inevitably result in orienting public priorities to ensure that critical preventative and curative care will be provided, particularly of those interventions that promote better nutrition in women and children.

There is some empirical evidence and inferential reasoning to suggest that developing countries have greater inequalities in nutrition that may be affecting productivity and incomes. When we examine standardized heights as a general measure of child health, we find little inequality in this indicator of well-being among developed countries. However, in countries with lower living standards and overall worse mean health status, there are correlations with greater levels of inequality in health outcomes (Pradhan, Sahn, & Younger, 2003). There is also reason to expect that other indicators, such as life expectancy at birth, are characterized by greater inequality in poor countries. In part, this may be explained by the availability of basic health and nutrition knowledge and services that is nearly universal in developed countries—including access to water and sanitation or access to oral rehydration as required—but is often inaccessible to large segments of the population in poorer countries, thus exacerbating existing inequalities. It may also be the case that new public health practices and access to primary health care technologies tend to be introduced initially to a small segment of the population and subsequently are rolled out or made available to the wider population, often at a slower pace in more resource-constrained developing countries.[18]

A related issue is that economic and natural shocks that give rise to health and nutrition inequalities may have more deleterious impacts on outcomes such as schooling and labor market outcomes in developing countries because insurance and credit markets are less accessible and safety net programs are less established. This will tend to exacerbate ex ante inequalities. One important implication is the expectation that the introduction of basic public health measures, whether they are fortification of foods with micronutrients, malaria eradication, or breaking the nutrition–infection interaction by improving water and sanitation facilities, will not only improve health and nutrition, but also will reduce inequalities in income through greater impacts on the productivity of low-income earners.

20.5 Conclusion

In this chapter, we examined the evidence regarding the impact of nutrition on productivity at both the micro and macro levels. The clear conclusion is that there are large economic returns to investing in nutrition that can be measured in terms of outcomes at the individual and household level (e.g., higher wages) and at the economy-wide level (e.g., growth in aggregate incomes and GDP). Likewise, the evidence comes from a range of methodologies and disciplines, including the work of economic historians, cross-country models, and microsimulation, as well as from experimental and structural and reduced-form micromodeling. That nutritional improvement can spur economic development, contribute to higher productivity, increase wages, and contribute to the alleviation of poverty are certainly powerful reasons to invest in nutrition. However, we do want to interject a word of caution in terms of how policy makers should consider the role of nutrition and prioritize nutritional investments in the hierarchy of competing needs and objectives. Specifically, the value of improved nutrition is intrinsically, not merely instrumentally, important. This reflects nutrition's importance in improving the quality and duration of life. Although economists have spent considerable time valuing life, for example, employing the concepts of full income or inclusive wealth where health capital enters into the calculations, ultimately, we would argue that improved nutrition is, in and of itself, a policy objective of the highest order. The right to food and good nutritional well-being is a basic human need and requires no further justification.

Notes

1. For different purposes, variations of this approach consider other temporal breakdowns. For example, Almond and Currie (2011) focused on prenatal and postnatal periods, and Cunha and Heckman (2007) conceptualized preschool as a series of investments. See also Behrman (2015; this volume). Also note that these early childhood investments that affect later life outcomes are made by parents and/or the community, and thus the direct returns accrue well into the future to the next generation. However, the parents do not reap the benefits in terms of the nonpecuniary consumption good of having healthy children, as well as the potential for transfers from their children later in life. Nonetheless, there is the potential for insufficient investment by parents since they may undervalue potential returns.

2. Black et al. (2013) maintained that 45% of all child deaths in 2011 were caused by undernutrition, although the scaling up of programs considered in Bhutta et al. (2013) is not expected to prevent the total of these early deaths.
3. Noncognitive skills are often referred to as *socioemotional skills* in literature outside of economics.
4. For example, León and Miguel (2013) estimate a VSL for African users of the airport in Freetown Sierra Leone of US$577,000 compared to US$924,000 for non-African travelers. By extension, the VSL of Africans too poor to travel by air would be far less.
5. The treatment increased birthweight on average by 136 g, which was 4.6 times the standard deviation; in the hungry season, the impact was an increase of 201 g (T = 5.7). This intervention also reduced low birthweight (odds ratio 0.61, 5% confidence interval [CI] 0.47–0.79) and perinatal mortality (odds ratio 0.47, CI 0.23–0.99).
6. Almond et al. (Almond, Clay, & Lee, 2005) showed that in some circumstances twin effects can be misleading, because sets of twins include a high number of very low birthweights—many of which would not survive in less-developed countries. However, their study focused on the cost of in-hospital care rather than subsequent cognitive development or schooling. Using regression discontinuity analysis, Bharadwaj et al. (Bharadwaj, Vellesen Løken, & Neilson, 2013) showed that health interventions for children with very low weights (<1,500 g) had a favorable impact on later academic achievement.
7. See also Almond and Currie (2011).
8. Black et al. (2013) estimate that 45% of all deaths in this age group are caused by undernutrition, but not all can be prevented with the programs reviewed.
9. For example, treatment of acute malnutrition or the provision of vitamin A undoubtedly saves lives but may have little impact on stunting; nor do these particular programs use the same delivery platform as, say, promotion of exclusive breastfeeding during a child's first 6 months or encouragement of diet diversity during weaning.
10. These figures are based on the ratio of infant and child mortality for 2012 reported in WHO (2014). This is an approximation due to the lag structure of data pertaining to a single year and data reflecting 5 years.
11. Moreover, given the time frame to track such outcomes, it is plausible that the initial conditions when the intervention took place are no longer representative of the environment in which one is currently proposing an intervention.
12. Fogel (2004) argued that nutrient intake was so constrained that 20% of the labor force was unable to engage in productive work, and it was increases in agricultural productivity in the 19th century that improved the health and productivity of workers and led to more rapid economic growth.
13. Bloom et al. (2004) provided a good summary of this literature.
14. One other potentially interesting indicator of nutrition, used by Weil (2007), is the age of menarche, which followed from the microstudy of Knaul (2000), discussed earlier. It, too, suffered from the problems of lags in measurement as well as limitations in terms of available data. Nonetheless, Weil (2007) did create an impressive dataset that included age of menarche, finding that a one standard deviation decline in age of menarche contributed to a 24.5% increase in labor input per female worker, which was certainly of considerable importance.
15. See also Acemoglu and Robinson (2008).
16. Despite the rigorous work and compelling nature of this paper, it has been criticized for many underlying assumptions, particularly that lagged health has no effect on economic

outcomes (Bleakley, 2006 and, likewise, that it did not address possibilities such as whether reductions in fertility can offset the population increases that accompany lower mortality (Ashraf et al., 2008; Bloom Canning & Fink 2014), as well as a more robust response in terms of increases in capital stock and land productivity. Another similar paper by Young (2005) focused on the impact of HIV/AIDS using a neoclassical growth model and, similarly, did not find any negative impact on economic growth.

17. This remains the case despite the relatively recent initiatives of institutions such as the Gates Foundation, which is spending large sums to address this imbalance between sources of death and disability and how global health care expenditures are allocated.
18. The speed of diffusion, of course, will vary greatly and, in large part, be a consequence of the strength of the health care institutions that are present in the country of interest.

References

Acemoglu, D., & Johnson, S. (2007). Disease and development: The effect of life expectancy on economic growth. *Journal of Political Economy, 115*(6), 925–985.

Acemoglu, D., & Robinson, J. A. (2008). Persistence of power, elites, and institutions. *American Economic Review, 98*(1), 267–293.

Akresh, R., Bagby, E., de Walque, D., & Kazianga, H. (2012). Child ability and household human capital investment decisions in Burkina Faso. *Economic Development and Cultural Change, 61*(1), 157–186.

Alderman, H. (2013). Economic drivers and consequences of stunting. In M. Gillman, P. Gluckman, & R. Rosenfeld (Eds.), *Recent advances in growth research: Nutritional, molecular and endocrine perspectives* (pp. 131–142). 71st Nestlé Nutrition Institute Workshop, Vienna, October, 2011. Vevey, Switzerland: Karger.

Alderman, H., & Behrman, J. (2006). Reducing the incidence of low birth weight in low-income countries has substantial economic benefits. *World Bank Research Observer, 21*(1), 25–48.

Alderman, H., Behrman, J. R., Grantham-McGregor, S., Lopez-Boo, F., & Urzua, S. (2014). Economic perspectives on integrating early child stimulation with nutritional interventions. *Annals of the New York Academy of Sciences 1308*, 129–138.

Alderman, H., Hawkesworth, S., Lundberg, M., Tasneem, A., Mark, H., & Moore, S. E. (2014). Supplemental feeding during pregnancy compared to maternal supplementation during lactation does not affect schooling and cognitive development through late adolescence. *American Journal of Clinical Nutrition, 99*(1), 122–129.

Alderman, H., Hoddinott, J., & Kinsey, W. (2006). Long term consequences of early childhood malnutrition. *Oxford Economic Papers, 58*(3), 450–474.

Almond, D., Chay, K., & Lee, D. (2005). The costs of low birth weight. *Quarterly Journal of Economics, 120* (3), 1031–1083.

Almond, D., & Currie, J. (2011). Killing me softly. *Journal of Economic Perspectives, 25*(3), 153–172.

Angrist, J., & Krueger, A. (1994). Identification and estimation of local average treatment effects. *Econometrica, 62*(2), 467–476.

Arora, S. (1999). *Health and long-term economic growth: A multi-country study.* PhD dissertation. Ohio State University.

Ashraf, Q. H., Lester, A., & Weil, D. N. (2008). When does improving health raise GDP? In D. Acemoglu, K. Rogoff, & M. Woodford (Eds.), *NBER macroeconomics annual 2008* (vol. 23, pp. 157–204). Cambridge, MA: National Bureau of Economic Research.

Attanasio, O. P., Fernández, C., Emla O. A. Fitzsimons, Sally M. Grantham-McGregor, Costas Meghir, & Marta Rubio-Codina. 2014. "Using the infrastructure of a conditional cash transfer program to deliver a scalable integrated early child development program in Colombia: cluster randomized controlled trial." *British Medical Journal 349*: g5785.

Barker, D. J., & Osmond, C. (1986). Infant mortality, childhood nutrition, and ischaemic heart disease in England and Wales. *Lancet, 327*(8489), 1077–1081.

Barro, R. (1997). *Determinants of economic growth: A cross-country empirical study*. Cambridge, MA: MIT Press.

Basta, S. S., Soekirman, D., Karyadi, D., & Scrimshaw, N. S. (1979). Iron deficiency anemia and the productivity of adult males in Indonesia. *American Journal of Clinical Nutrition, 32*(4), 916–925.

Behrman, J., & Rosenzweig, M. (2004). Returns to birthweight. *Economics and Statistics, 86*(2), 586–601.

Behrman, J. R. (2015). Growth Faltering in the First Thousand Days after Conception and Catch-up Growth. In J. Komlos & I. R. Kelly (Eds.), *The Oxford handbook of economics and human biology*. New York: Oxford University Press.

Behrman, J. R., Alderman, H., & Hoddinott, J. (2004). Malnutrition and hunger. In Bjørn Lomborg (Ed.), *Global crises, global solutions* (pp. 363–420). Cambridge: Cambridge University Press.

Behrman, J. R., & Deolalikar, A. B. (1989). Seasonal demands for nutrient intakes and health status in rural South India. In D. E. Sahn (Ed.), *Seasonal variability in third world agriculture: The consequences for food security*. Baltimore, MD: Johns Hopkins University Press.

Behrman, J. R., Rosenzweig, M. R., & Taubman, P. (1994). Endowments and the allocation of schooling in the family and in the marriage market: The Twins Experiment. *Journal of Political Economy, 102*(6), 1131–1174.

Berg, A., & Muscat, R. (1972). Nutrition and development: the view of the planner. *American Journal of Clinical Nutrition, 25*(2), 186–209.

Bharadwaj, P., Vellesen Løken, K., & Neilson, C. (2013). Early life health interventions and academic achievement. *American Economic Review, 103*(5), 1862–1891.

Bhutta, Z. A., Das, J. K., Rizvi, A., Gaffey, M. F., Walker, N., Horton, S., . . . The Lancet Nutrition Interventions Review Group and the Maternal and Child Nutrition Study Group. (2013). Evidence-based interventions for improvement of maternal and child nutrition: What can be done and at what cost? *Lancet, 382*(9890), 452–477.

Black, R. E., Victora, C. G., Walker, S. P., Bhutta, Z. A., Christian, P., de Onis, M., . . . the Maternal and Child Nutrition Study Group. (2013). Maternal and child undernutrition and overweight in low-income and middle-income countries. *Lancet, 382*(9890), 427–451.

Black, S., Devereaux, P., & Salvanes, K. (2007). From the cradle to the labor market? The effect of birth weight on adult outcomes. *Quarterly Journal of Economics, 122*(1), 409–439.

Bleakley, H. (2006). Disease and development: Comments on Acemoglu and Johnson (2006). Remarks delivered at the NBER Summer Institute on Economic Fluctuations and Growth, July 16. www-personal.umich.edu/~hoytb/Bleakley_Comments_Acemoglu_Johnson.pdf

Bliss, C., & Stern, N. (1978*a*). Production, wages, nutrition: Part I: The theory. *Journal of Development Economics, 5*(4), 331–362.

Bliss, C., & Stern, N. (1978*b*). Production, wages, nutrition: Part II: Some observations. *Journal of Development Economics, 5*(4), 362–398.

Bloom, D., & Sachs, J. (1998). Geography, demography, and economic growth in Africa. *Brookings Papers on Economic Activity, 2*, 207–295.

Bloom, D. E., Canning, D., & Fink, G. (2014). Disease and development revisited. *Journal of Political Economy, 122*(6), 1355–1366.

Bloom, D. E., Canning, D., & Sevilla, J. (2004). The effect of health on economic growth: A production function approach. *World Development, 32*(1), 1–13.

Bossavie, L., Alderman, H., Giles, J., & Mete, C. (2014). *The effect of height on earnings: Is stature just a proxy for cognitive and non-cognitive skills?* Draft. Washington, DC: World Bank.

Bruner, E., & Marmot, M. (1999). Social organization, stress, and health. In M. Marmot & R. G. Wilkinson (Eds.), *Social determinants of health* (pp. 17–43). Oxford: Oxford University Press.

Case, A., & Paxson, C. (2008). Stature and status: Height, ability and labor market outcomes. *Journal of Political Economy, 116*(3), 499–532.

Cawley, J. (2004). The impact of obesity on wages. *Journal of Human Resources, 39*(2), 451–474.

Ceesay, S. M., Prentice, A. M., Cole, T. J., Foord, F., Weaver, L. T., Poskitt, E. M., & Whitehead, R. G. (1997). Effects on birth weight and perinatal mortality of maternal dietary supplements in rural Gambia: 5 year randomised controlled trial. *British Medical Journal, 315*(7111), 786–790.

Chadwick, E. (1842/1965). *Report on the sanitary conditions of the laboring population of Great Britain, 1842*. Edited with an introduction by M. W. Flinn. Edinburgh: Edinburgh University Press.

Christian, P., Lee, S. E., Angel, M. D., Adair, L. S., Arifeen, S. E., Ashorn, P., . . . Black, R. E. (2013). Risk of childhood undernutrition related to small-for-gestational age and preterm birth in low- and middle-income countries. *International Journal of Epidemiology, 42*(5), 1340–1355.

Christian, P., Murray-Kolb, L. E., Khatry, S. K., Katz, J., Schaefer, B. A., Cole, P. M., . . . Tielsch, J. M. (2010). Prenatal micronutrient supplementation and intellectual and motor function in early school-aged children in Nepal. *Journal of the American Medical Association, 304*(24), 2716–2723.

Cunha, F., & Heckman, J. (2007). The technology of skills formation. *American Economic Review, 97*(2), 31–47.

Deolalikar, A. B. (1988). Nutrition and labour productivity in agriculture: Estimates for rural South India. *Review of Economics and Statistics, 70*(3), 406–413.

Doyle, O., Harmon, C., Heckman, J. J., & Tremblay, R. E. (2009). Investing in early human development: Timing and economic efficiency. *Economics and Human Biology, 7*(1), 1–6.

Edgerton, V. R., Gardner, G. W., Ohira, Y., Gunawardena, K. A., & Senewiratne, B. (1979). Iron-deficiency anemia and its effect on worker productivity and activity patterns. *British Medical Journal, 2*(6204), 1546–1549.

Field, E., Robles, O., & Torero, M. (2009). Iodine deficiency and schooling attainment in Tanzania. *American Economic Journal: Applied Economics, 1*(4), 140–169.

Fogel, R. W. (1994). Economic growth, population theory, and physiology: The bearing of the long-term processes on making of economic policy. *American Economic Review, 84*(3), 369–395.

Fogel, R. W. (2004). Health, nutrition, and economic growth. *Economic Development and Cultural Change, 52*(3), 643–658.

Gallup, J. L., & Sachs, J. D. (2001). The economic burden of malaria. *American Journal of Tropical Medicine and Hygiene, 64*(1–2 Suppl.), 85–96.

Gallup, J. L., Sachs, J. D., & Mellinger, A. D. (1999). Geography and economic development. *International Regional Science Review, 22*(2): 179–232.

Gertler, P., Heckman, J., Pinto, R., Zanolini, A., Vermeerch, C., Walker, S., . . . Grantham-McGregor, S. (2014). Labor market returns to an early childhood stimulation intervention in Jamaica. *Science, 344*(6187), 998–1001.

Glewwe, P., & Jacoby, H. (1995). An economic analysis of delayed primary school enrollment and childhood malnutrition in a low income country. *Review of Economics and Statistics, 77*(1), 156–169.

Glick, P., & Sahn, D. E. (1997). Gender and education impacts on employment and earnings in West Africa: Evidence from Guinea. *Economic Development and Cultural Change, 45*(4), 793–823.

Gluckman, P., Hanson, M., Bateson, P., Beedle, A. S., Law, C. M., Bhutta, Z. A., . . . West-Eberhard, M. J. (2009). Towards a new development synthesis: Adaptive developmental plasticity and human disease. *Lancet, 373*(9675), 1654–1657.

Grantham-McGregor, S., Powell, C. A., Walker, S. P., & Himes, J. H. (1991). Nutritional supplementation, psychosocial stimulation, and mental development of stunted children: the Jamaican Study. *Lancet, 338*, 1–5.

Grantham-McGregor, S. M., Fernald, L. C. H., Kagawa, R. M. C., & Walker, S. (2014). Effects of integrated child development and nutrition interventions on child development and nutritional status. *Annals of the New York Academy of Sciences, 1308*(1), 11–32.

Haas, J. D., & Brownlie, T. IV (2001). Iron deficiency and reduced work capacity: A critical review of the research to determine a causal relationship. *Journal of Nutrition, 131*(Supplement), 676S–690S.

Haddad, L. J., & Bouis, H. E. (1991). The impact of nutritional status on agricultural productivity: Wage evidence from the Philippines. *Oxford Bulletin of Economics and Statistics, 53*(1), 45–68.

Hammitt, J., & Robinson, L. (2011). The income elasticity of the value per statistical life: Transferring estimates between high and low income populations. *Journal of Benefit-Cost Analysis, 2*(1): 1–17.

Hanushek, E., & Woessmann, L. (2008). The role of cognitive skills in economic development. *Journal of Economic Literature, 46*(3), 607–668.

Harding, J., Jaquiery, A. L., Hernandez, C. E., Oliver, M. H., Derraik, J. G., & Bloomfield, F. H. (2011). Animal studies of the effects of early nutrition on long-term health. *Nestlé Nutrition Workshop Series: Pediatric Program, 68*, 1–11.

Haushofer, J., & Fehr, E. (2014). On the psychology of poverty. *Science, 344*(6186), 862–867.

Hoddinott, J., Alderman, H., Behrman, J. R., Haddad, L., & Horton, S. (2013). The economic rationale for investing in stunting reduction. *Maternal and Child Nutrition, 9*(Suppl. 2), 69–82.

Hoddinott, J., Behrman, J. R., Maluccio, J. A., Melgar, P., Quisumbing, A. R., Ramirez-Zea, M., . . . Martorell, R. Adult consequences of growth failure in early childhood. (2013). *American Journal of Clinical Nutrition, 98*(5), 1170–1178.

Horton, S., Alderman, H., & Rivera, J. A. (2009). Hunger and malnutrition. In B. Lomborg (Ed.), *Global crises, global solutions: Costs and benefits* (pp. 305–354). Cambridge: Cambridge University Press.

Hult, M., Tornhammar, P., Ueda, P., Chima, C., Bonamy, A. K., Ozumba, B., & Norman, M. (2010). Hypertension, diabetes and overweight: Looming legacies of the Biafran Famine. *PLOS One, 5*(10), e13582.

Imminck, M., & Viteri, F. (1981). Energy intake and productivity of Guatemalan sugarcane cutters: An empirical test of the Efficiency Wage Hypothesis—Part 2. *Journal of Development Economics, 9*(2), 273–287.

Katz, J., Lee, A. C., Kozuki, N., Lawn, J. E., Cousens, S., Biencowe, H., . . . CHERG Small-for Gestational-Age-Preterm Birth Working Group. (2013). Mortality risk in preterm and small-for-gestational-age infants in low-income and middle-income countries: A pooled country analysis. *Lancet, 382*(9890), 417–425.

Knaul, F. M. (2000). Health, nutrition and wages at menarche and earnings in Mexico. In W. D. Savedoff & T. P. Schultz (Eds.), *Wealth from health: Linking social investments to earnings in Latin America*. Washington, DC: Inter-American Development Bank.

Kramer, M., & Kakuma, R. (2003). Energy and protein intake in pregnancy. *Cochrane Database Systematic Review, 2003*(4): CD000032.

LaFave, D., & Thomas, D. (2013). Height and cognition at work: Labor market performance in a low income setting. Draft, Colby College, Waterville, ME. www.bates.edu/economics/files/2013/04/Health-and-Cognition-at-Work-Labor-Market-Performance-in-a-Low-Income-Setting.pdf

Lanou, H., Huybregts, L., Roberfroid, D., Nikièma, L., Kouanda, S., Van Camp, J., & Kolsteren, P. (2014). Prenatal nutrient supplementation and postnatal growth in a developing nation: An RCT. *Pediatrics, 133*(4), 1001–1008.

Leibenstein, H. A. (1957). *Economic backwardness and economic growth*. New York: Wiley.

Li, R., Chen, X., Yan, H., Deurenberg, P., Garby, L., & Hautvast, J. G. (1994). Functional consequences of iron supplementation in iron-deficient female cotton workers in Beijing, China. *American Journal of Clinical Nutrition, 59*(4), 908–913.

Linnemayr, S., & Alderman, H. (2011). Almost random: Evaluating a large-scale randomized nutrition program in the presence of crossover. *Journal of Development Economics, 96*(1), 106–114.

Lundeen, E. A., Behrman, J. R., Crookston, B. T., Dearden, K. A., Engle, P., Georgiadis, A., . . . Stein, A. D. (2014). Growth faltering and recovery in children aged 1–8 years in four low- and middle-income countries: Young lives. *Public Health Nutrition, 17*(9), 2131–2137.

Lutter, C. K., Mora, J. O., Habicht, J. -P., Rasmussen, K. M., Robson, D. S., & Herrera, M. G. (1990). Age-specific responsiveness of weight and length to nutritional supplementation. *American Journal of Clinical Nutrition, 51*(3), 359–364.

Mani, A., Mullainathan, S., Shafir, E., & Zhao, J. (2013). Poverty impedes cognitive function. *Science, 341*(6149), 976–980.

Margo, R. A., & Steckel, R. H. (1982). The height of American slaves: New evidence on slave nutrition and health. *Social Science History, 6*(4), 516–538.

Martorell, R., Khan, L., & Schroeder, D. G. (1994). Reversibility of stunting: epidemiologic findings from children in developing countries. *European Journal of Clinical Nutrition, 48*(Suppl), S45–S47.

Mazumdar, D. (1959). The marginal productivity theory of wages and disguised unemployment. *Review of Economic Studies, 26*(3), 190–197.

Mirrlees, J. A. (1976). A pure theory of underdeveloped economies. In L. Reynolds (Ed.), *Agriculture in development theory* (pp. 84–108). New Haven, CT: Yale University Press.

Monteiro, P., & Victora, C. (2005). Rapid growth in infancy and childhood and obesity in later life—a systematic review. *Obesity Review, 6*(2), 143–154.
Nahar B., Hossain, M. I., Hamadani, J. D., Ahmed, T., Huda, S. N., Grantham-McGregor, S. M., & Persson, L. A. (2012). Effects of a community-based approach of food and psychosocial stimulation on growth and development of severely malnourished children in Bangladesh: A randomised trial. *European Journal of Clinical Nutrition, 66*(6), 701–709.
Oreopoulos, P., Stabile, M., Walld, R., & Roos, L. L. (2008). Short-, medium-, and long-term consequences of poor infant health: An analysis using siblings and twins. *Journal of Human Resources, 43*(1), 88–138.
Osmani, S., & Sen, A. (2003). Investing in maternal nutrition and neonatal outcomes: The hidden penalties of gender inequality: Fetal origins of ill-health. *Economics and Human Biology, 1*(1), 105–121.
Özaltin, E., Hill, K., & Subraminian, S. V. (2010). Association of maternal stature with offspring mortality, underweight, and stunting in low-to middle-income countries. *Journal of the American Medical Association, 303*(15), 1507–1516.
Patel, V., Rahman, A., Jacob, K., & Hughes, M. (2004). Effect of maternal mental health on infant growth in low income countries: New evidence from South Asia. *British Medical Journal, 328*(7443), 820–823.
Pickett, K., & Cabieses Valdes, B. (2015). The impact of socioeconomic inequality on children's health and wellbeing. In J. Komlos & I. R. Kelly (Eds.), *The Oxford handbook of economics and human biology*. New York: Oxford University Press.
Pitt, M., Rosenzweig, M., & Hassan, M. N. (2013). Human capital investment and the gender division of labor in a brawn-based economy. *American Economic Review, 102*(7), 3531–3560.
Pollitt, E. (2001). The developmental and probabilistic nature of the functional consequences of iron-deficiency anemia in children. *Journal of Nutrition, 131*(2), 669S–675S.
Pradhan, M., Sahn, D. E., & Younger, S. D. (2003). Decomposing world health inequality. *Journal of Health Economics, 22*(2), 271–293.
Prentice, A. M., Ward, K. A., Goldberg, G. R., Jarjou, L. M., Moore, S. E., Fulford, A. J., & Prentice, A. (2013). Critical windows for nutritional interventions against stunting. *American Journal of Clinical Nutrition, 97*(5), 911–918.
Ruel, M., & Alderman, H. (2013). Nutrition-sensitive interventions and programs: How Can they help accelerate progress in improving maternal and child nutrition? *Lancet, 382*(9891), 536–551.
Sahn, D. E., & Alderman, H. (1988). The effects of human capital on wages, and the determinants of labor supply in a developing country. *Journal of Development Economics, 29*(2), 157–183.
Schroeder, D., Martorell, R., Rivera, J., Ruel, M. T., & Habicht, J. -P. (1995). Age differences in the impact of nutritional supplementation on growth. *Journal of Nutrition, 125*(4 Suppl), 1051S–1059S.
Schultz, P. (2003). Wage rentals for reproductive human capital: Evidence from Ghana and the Ivory Coast. *Economics and Human Biology, 1*(3), 331–336.
Schultz, T. P., & Tansel, A. (1997). Wage and labor supply effects of illness in Côte d'Ivoire and Ghana: Instrumental variable estimates for days disabled. *Journal of Development Economics, 53*(2), 251–286.
Sen, A. (1979). Personal utilities and public judgment: Or what's wrong with welfare economics? *Economic Journal, 89*(355), 537–558.
Sen, A. (1985). *Commodities and capabilities*. Amsterdam: North-Holland.

Sen, A. (1987). The standard of living: Lecture II: Lives and capabilities. In G. Hawthorn (Ed.), *The standard of living* (pp. 20–38). Cambridge: Cambridge University Press.

Shah, A. K., Mullainathan, S., & Shafir, E. (2012). Some consequences of having too little. *Science, 338*(6107), 682–685.

Smith, A. (1776/1960). *The wealth of nations*. New York: Modern Library.

Stein, A. D. (2014). Nutrition in early life and cognitive functioning. *American Journal of Clinical Nutrition, 99*(1), 1–2.

Stein, A. D., Wang, M., Martorell, R., Norris, S. A., Adair, L. S., Bas, I., . . . the Cohorts Group. (2010). Growth patterns in early childhood and final attained stature: Data from five birth cohorts from low- and middle-income countries. *American Journal of Human Biology, 22*(3), 353–359.

Stewart, R. (2007). Maternal depression and infant growth: A review of recent evidence. *Maternal and Child Nutrition, 3*(2), 94–107.

Strauss, J. (1986). Does better nutrition raise farm productivity? *Journal of Political Economy, 94*(2), 297–320.

Strauss, J., & Thomas, D. (1998). Health, nutrition, and economic development. *Journal of Economic Literature, 36*(2), 766–817.

Summers, L. (1992). Investing in all the people. *Pakistan Development Review, 31*(4), 367–393.

Thomas, D., & Frankenberg, E. (2002). Health, nutrition, and prosperity: A microeconomic perspective. *Bulletin of the World Health Organization, 80*(2), 106–113.

Thomas, D., Frankenberg, E., Friedman, J., Habicht, J. -P., Hakimi, M., Ingwersen, N., . . . Wilopo, S. (2006). Causal effect of health on labor market outcomes: Experimental evidence. California Center for Population Research On-Line Working Paper Series CCPR-070-06, University of California, Los Angeles.

Thomas, D., & Strauss, J. (1997). Health and wages: Evidence on men and women in urban Brazil. *Journal of Econometrics, 77*(1), 159–187.

Toh-Adam, R., Srisupundit, K., & Tongsong, T. (2012). Short stature as an independent risk factor for cephalopelvic disproportion in a country of relatively small-sized mothers. *Archives of Gynecology and Obstetrics, 285*(6), 1513–1516.

Torche, F., & Echevarrıa, G. (2011). The effect of birthweight on childhood cognitive development in a middle-income country. *International Journal of Epidemiology, 40*(4), 1008–1018.

Tripathy, P., Nair, N., Barnett, S., Mahapatra, R., Borghi, J., Rath, S., . . . Costello, A. (2010). Effect of a participatory intervention with women's groups on birth outcomes and maternal depression in Jharkhand and Orissa, India: A cluster-randomised controlled trial. *Lancet, 375*(9721), 1182–1192.

Uauy, R., & Kain, J. (2002). The epidemiological transition: Need to incorporate obesity prevention into nutrition programmes. *Public Health Nutrition, 5*(1A), 223–229.

Victora, C. G., de Onis, M., Curi Hallal, P., Blössner, M., & Shrimpton, R. (2010). Worldwide timing of growth faltering: Revisiting implications for interventions. *Pediatrics, 125*(3), 473–480.

Viscusi, W. K., & Aldy, J. E. (2003). The value of a statistical life: A critical review of market estimates throughout the world. *Journal of Risk and Uncertainty, 27*(1), 5–76.

Vogl, T. (2014). Height, skills, and labor market outcomes in Mexico. *Journal of Development Economics, 107*(1), 84–96.

Wachs, T., Black, M., & Engle, P. (2009). Maternal depression: A global threat to children's health, development, and behavior and to human rights. *Child Development Perspectives, 3*(1), 51–59.

Walker, S. P., Grantham-McGregor, S. M., Himes, J. H., Powell, C. A., & Chang, S. M. (1996). Early childhood supplementation does not benefit the long-term growth of stunted children in Jamaica. *Journal of Nutrition, 126*(12), 3017–3024.

Walker, S. P., Wachs, T. D., Grantham-McGregor, S., Black, M., Nelson, C., Huffman, S., ... Richter, L. (2011). Inequality in early childhood: risk and protective factors for early child development. *Lancet, 378*(9799), 1325–1338.

Weil, D. N. (2007). Accounting for the effect of health on economic growth. *Quarterly Journal of Economics, 122*(3), 1265–1306.

Whitehead, M. (2000). The concepts and principles of equity and health. Programme on Health Policies Discussion Paper, World Health Organization Regional Office for Europe, Copenhagen.

World Health Organization (WHO). (1985). *Targets for health for all.* European Health for All Series No. 1. Geneva: WHO, Regional Office for Europe.

World Health Organization (WHO). (1986). *Social justice and equity in health.* Report on a WHO Meeting; Leeds, UK, 1985. Regional Office for Europe. (ICP/HSR 804/m02), Copenhagen.

World Health Organization (WHO). (2002). *Health, economic growth, and poverty reduction.* Report of the Working Group 1 of the Commission on Macroeconomics and Health. Geneva: WHO.

World Health Organization (WHO). (2014). Global health observatory data repository: Under five mortality data by WHO Region. http://apps.who.int/gho/data/view.main.172?lang=en.

Wilkinson, R. G. (1997). Socioeconomic determinants of health: Health inequalities: Relative or absolute material standards? *British Medical Journal, 314*(7080), 591–595.

Wilkinson, R. G. (2000). The need for an interdisciplinary perspective on the social determinants of health. *Health Economics, 9*(7), 581–583.

Wolgemuth, J. C., Latham, M. C., Hall, A., Chesher, A., & Crompton, D. W. (1982). Worker productivity and the nutritional status of Kenyan road construction laborers. *American Journal of Clinical Nutrition, 36*(1), 68–78.

Yajnik, C. (2004). Early life origins of insulin resistance and type 2 diabetes in India and other Asian countries. *Journal of Nutrition, 134*(1), 205–210.

Yamauchi, F. (2008). Early childhood nutrition, schooling, and sibling inequality in a dynamic context: Evidence from South Africa. *Economic Development and Cultural Change, 56*(3), 657–682.

Young, A. (2005). The gift of dying: The tragedy of AIDS and the welfare of future African generations. *Quarterly Journal of Economics, 120*(2), 423–466.

Young, A. (2007). In sorrow to bring forth children: Fertility amidst the plague of HIV. *Journal of Economic Growth, 12*(4), 283–327.

Yousafzai, A. K., Rasheed, M. A., Rizvi, A., Armstrong, R., & Bhutta, Z. A. (2014). Effect of integrated responsive stimulation and nutrition interventions in the Lady Health Worker programme in Pakistan on child development, growth, and health outcomes: A cluster-randomised factorial effectiveness trial. *Lancet, 384*(9950), 1282–1293.

Zimmermann, M. B., Connolly, K. J., Bozo, M., Bridson, J., Rohner, F., & Grimci, L. (2006). Iodine supplementation improves cognition in iodine-deficient schoolchildren in Albania: A randomized, controlled, double-blind study. *American Journal of Clinical Nutrition, 83*(1), 108–114.

CHAPTER 21

THE DOUBLE BURDEN OF MALNUTRITION

SUSAN L. AVERETT AND YANG WANG

21.1 Introduction

For many developing nations, obesity rates are rising, and obesity is emerging as a significant driver of adverse health outcomes displacing more traditional concerns of malnutrition and infectious disease (Doytch, Dave, & Kelly, 2014; Goryakin & Suhrcke, 2014; Tzioumis & Adair, 2014). The advent of economic development and increased urbanization as well as an increasingly global food supply and falling food prices have created the perfect environment for obesity rates to rise as individuals are incentivized to both consume more calories and lead more sedentary lifestyles. These rising obesity rates coexist along with underweight, which still poses a significant challenge for developing countries (Dieffenbach & Stein, 2012). For the first time in human history, the number of overweight people rivals the number of underweight people (Gardner & Halweil, 2000). This relatively new phenomenon has been called the *double burden of malnutrition* and is defined by the co-occurrence of over- and undernutrition at multiple levels (Doak, Adair, Bentley, Monteiro, & Popkin, 2004).

This double burden is seen mainly in developing countries (Varela-Silva et al., 2012; World Health Organization [WHO], 2015) and is also referred to as the *dual burden of malnutrition* (Roemling & Qaim, 2013), the *phenomenon of under- and overnutrition* (Subramanian, Kawachi, & Smith, 2007), the *short-and-plump syndrome* (Martorell, Mendoza, Castillo, Pawson, & Budge, 1987), and *paradoxical malnutrition* (Jehn & Brewis, 2009). It has only been relatively recently that the dual burden was recognized as a problem (Varela-Silva et al., 2012). Adrianzen et al. were among the first to document this phenomenon. They examined poor families living in the slums of Lima, Peru and found "underdevelopment in height, starting in infancy, but relatively the opposite for weight. Most of these children actually look short and chubby, leading casual observers to think them healthy and well-nourished" (Adrianzen, Baertl, & Graham, 1973, p. 928).

The double burden of malnutrition can occur at the population/group level, the household/family level, and the individual level (Varela-Silva et al., 2012). At the population/group level, a high prevalence of stunting and/or underweight may coexist with a high prevalence of overweight and/or obesity within the same population or group (Jehn & Brewis, 2009).[1]

At the household/family level, the double burden of malnutrition features at least one undernourished member who is stunted or underweight and one overnourished member who is overweight or obese within the same household (Varela-Silva et al., 2012). The most typical presentation is an overweight mother and an underweight or stunted child (Khor, 2008).

The double burden of malnutrition at the individual level can be seen among both adults and children. Double-burdened adults with very short stature were typically once undernourished infants and children, and double-burdened children tend to gain too much weight for their height.[2]

Although observed mainly in developing countries, the phenomenon has also been reported in the United States. For example, Martorell et al. (1987) described the short-and-plump syndrome of Mexican American children, and Smith, Bogin, Varela-Silva, Orden, and Loucky (2002) and Markowitz and Cosminsky (2005) reported the problem of short stature combined with overweight among certain migrant groups in the United States.

Although seemingly dealing with two opposite weight outcomes resulting from either a lack of or an excess of energy, people at either extreme (overweight or underweight) may lack important dietary nutrients (such as iron and vitamin A) and therefore suffer from a wide range of adverse health conditions. For example, underweight is associated with poor maternal and infant health, as well as with childhood growth problems and compromised mental development (Food and Agriculture Organization [FAO], 2005), whereas obesity is associated with such chronic diseases as stroke, hypertension, cardiovascular disease, type-2 diabetes, and certain forms of cancer (WHO, 2015). Childhood obesity may also lead to a higher risk for the adult onset of these chronic diseases (de Onis & Blossner, 2000). And recent research indicates that undernutrition during early life can later lead to overweight or obesity by prompting energy conservation mechanisms in the body that can persist into adulthood and thus also lead to all the obesity-related conditions (Caballero, 2005). In other words, both those who are underweight and those who are overweight or obese share high levels of illness and disability, shorter life expectancies, and lower levels of productivity and this negatively impacts a country's development (Gardner & Halweil, 2000).

The existence of the double burden of malnutrition poses important and interesting questions to researchers across different fields. For example, it is difficult to understand why the double burden of malnutrition can happen among children because if there is enough energy for a child to gain extra weight, then there should be enough energy for him or her to grow taller. In the general population, the causes of the phenomenon of low height-for-weight (i.e., stunting) are usually associated with a total reduction in food intake, often combined with infectious disease and heavy physical labor (Bogin,

1999). This combination should, in principle, result in a deficiency of energy and a reduced body size in both height and weight, which makes the coincident existence of low height-for-weight (stunting) and high weight-for-age (overweight) in communities, families, and individuals quite surprising.

Because under- and overnutrition typically lead to two extreme outcomes in body weight, they might be thought to be associated with very different environmental, behavioral, and individual risk factors and with different adverse consequences, although they may not really be opposite expressions of distinct behavioral, socioeconomic, and environmental conditions. If under- and overweight can occur in the same society or the same household, there might exist some common underlying causes.

While governments in many developing countries continue to struggle with undernutrition, which remains a devastating problem in these countries and affects hundreds of millions of people and causes more than one-half of all child deaths (FAO, 2005), they tend to neglect the growing rate of overweight and obesity. Yet rising obesity rates mean that health systems in these developing countries face increasing pressure to simultaneously confront under- and overweight.

The double burden of malnutrition poses a significant challenge for policy makers because programs targeted at groups, households, or individuals with one extreme weight outcome may conflict with programs targeted at groups, households, or individuals with the other extreme weight outcome. Researchers have noted that to be fully effective, interventions should promote, among other things, changes in dietary and activity patterns that improve health outcomes at both ends of the nutrition spectrum (Doak et al., 2004). Given this, public health programs and government interventions have been called for to play a critical role in educating people about healthy lifestyle choices and improving access to healthy foods (Khan, 2006).

The purpose of this chapter is to document the existence of the double burden of malnutrition and to examine factors leading to its rise. We end the chapter with a discussion of potential policy responses, along with an economic rationale for such intervention.

21.2 Measuring the Double Burden

Anthropometric measures of weight and height are the most practical ways of assessing nutrition, in part because they are easy to collect in survey data. Using these measures, overnutrition has typically been termed "overweight" and/or "obesity," whereas undernutrition has been termed "stunted," "wasted," or "underweight."

For adults, underweight, overweight, and obesity are often defined using the body mass index (BMI).[3] The WHO gives guides for BMI cutoffs (e.g., those with BMI under 18.5 are underweight, equal or greater than 30 are obese, and between 25 and 30 are overweight). For children, defining overweight and obesity is more complicated and involves different classifications using different reference databases and growth standards that are gender- and age-specific to reflect growth throughout childhood. According to the

U.S. Centers for Disease Control and Prevention (CDC), a child is classified as "overweight or obese" if his or her BMI-for-age falls between the 85th and the 94.9th percentile and "obese" if his or her BMI-for-age is equal or greater than the 95th percentile. However, the definitions of child overweight and obesity used by the International Obesity Task Force (IOTF) come from the reference values proposed by Cole et al. (2000) based on cutoff points that are also age- and sex-specific and are developed from longitudinal growth studies and hence are slightly different from the CDC cutoffs.

Similarly, the criteria to define underweight among children are based on the indicators of weight for height. Whereas the WHO uses the cutoff point of –2 z-scores, the CDC uses the 5th percentile (equivalent to –1.65 z-scores), and, again, these are age- and gender-adjusted. Wasting, another form of undernutrition, indicates that the individual has a low weight for her height and is measured by a BMI for age z score less than −2. Stunting, yet another metric for assessing undernutrition, implies that the individual has a low height for her age (a measure of long-term nutritional status) and is measured by a height for age z score less than −2.

For stunted adult women, researchers working in Latin America have repeatedly used 150 cm (59.05 inches) as the cutoff point (Lara-Esqueda et al., 2004; López-Alvarenga, Montesinos-Cabrera, Velázquez-Alva, & González-Barranco, 2003), whereas in more well-nourished populations, such as in Europe, 157 cm (61.81 inches) has been used (Bosy-Westphal, Plachta-Danielzik, Dörhöfer, & Müller, 2009). Stunting in adult men has received less attention in the literature because short stature physically limits a woman's child-bearing ability (Kramer, 2003).

The double burden can also occur at the individual level, as noted in the introduction. This level of double burden can be subdivided in two types: type 1 is a nutritional double burden among adults, and type 2 is a nutritional dual-burden among children. Type 1 double-burdened adults were undernourished infants and children with impaired linear growth resulting in adults with very short stature (Varela-Silva et al., 2012).

The use of differing reference databases and growth standards complicates the classification of the double burden of malnutrition, the comparison of results between studies, and the understanding of its health implications (Varela-Silva et al., 2012). For example, if the CDC criteria are used to define stunting (below the 5th percentile of height for age), then more children will be classified as stunted than would be the case if the WHO criteria (below –2 z-scores of height for age) are used. In a well-nourished population, the differences in number of individuals classified using z-scores versus percentiles may be negligible, but in a population transitioning from being undernourished to overweight, this difference may be very large (Varela-Silva et al., 2012).

21.3 Prevalence

As noted earlier, the double burden can be measured at several different levels including the community, the household, and the individual. Here, we start by showing the

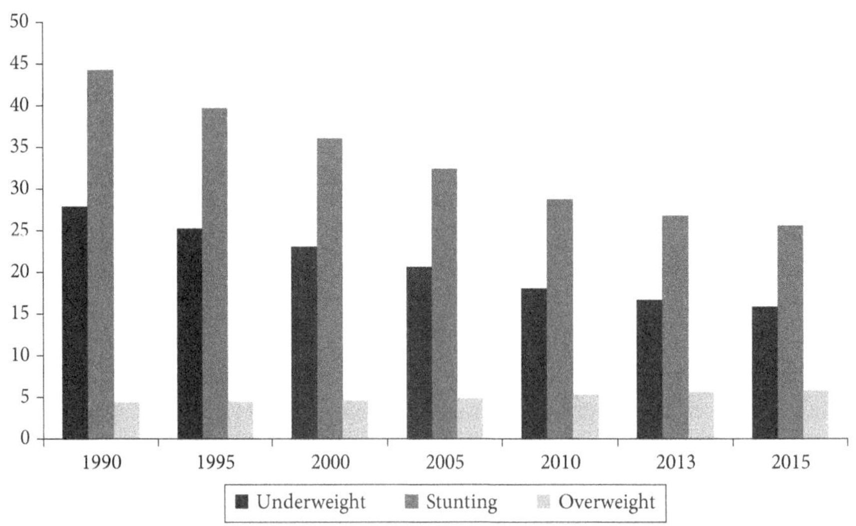

FIGURE 21.1 Malnutrition in children under age 5 in developing countries.

Source: World Health Organization. Figures for 2015 are projections.

prevalence of underweight, stunting, and overweight in children under age 5 in developing countries.

As seen in Figure 21.1, the prevalence of stunting and underweight in children age 5 and under has declined dramatically since 1990, whereas the prevalence of obesity has risen from 4.4% to 5.8%, nearly a 32% increase for this same age group. Yet Figure 21.1 masks some significant heterogeneity across developing countries. For example, stunting rates are lower in South America (10.8% of children under age 5 in 2013) compared to Africa, where the stunting rate of children under age 5 is 34.2% in 2013. Globally, in 2013, 24.5% of children under age 5 were stunted.[4]

In Figures 21.2 and 21.3, we show the prevalence of obesity for adults by gender both globally and for selected countries.[5] Several observations can be made from this figure. First, obesity rates are increasing across the globe. Second, prevalence rates vary across countries, with countries such as India and Kenya experiencing far lower prevalence rates compared to Mexico or Guatemala. Finally, gender differences in prevalence rates are apparent for several countries including South Africa and Mexico. The data in Figures 21.1, 21.2, and 21.3 confirm the existence of the double burden at the country and regional level.

Within countries, several scholars have documented the presence of the double burden. For example, data from Egypt showed a high proportion of overweight and obesity among women, despite a high prevalence of stunting and underweight among children (Khorshid et al., 1998). A smaller survey in Bahrain showed a similar prevalence of underweight (16–26%) and overweight (29–31%) among adults (Al-Mannai, Dickerson, Morgan, & Khalfan, 1996). Additionally, a number of scholars have shown rising obesity despite high undernutrition within the same city (Al-Nuaim, 1997; Delpeuch & Maire,

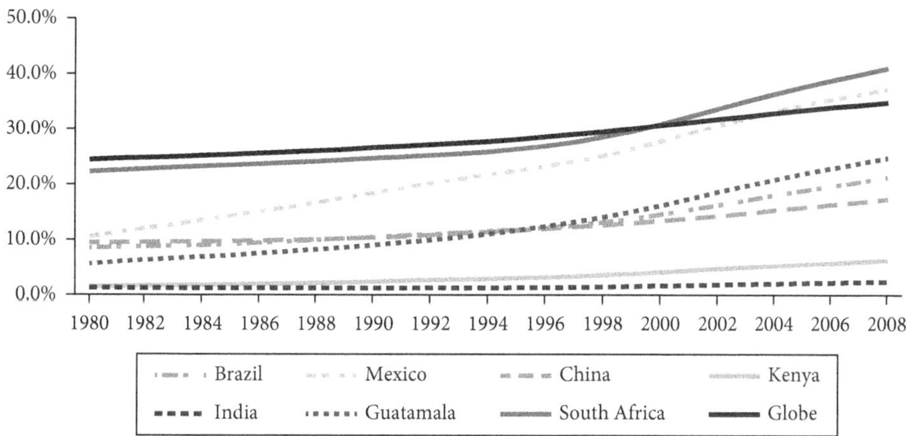

FIGURE 21.2 Obesity prevalence: adult women.

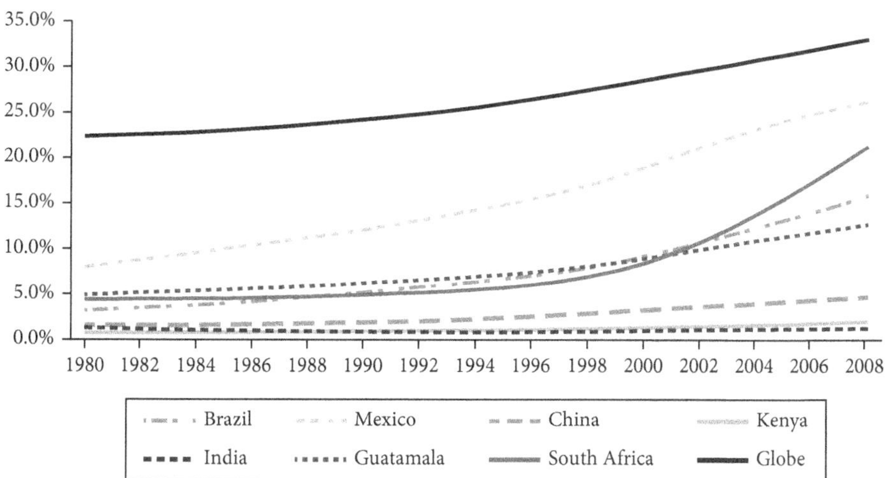

FIGURE 21.3 Obesity prevalence: adult males.

1996). High or rising overweight and obesity prevalence has been found in India, South Africa, and Brazil among disadvantaged communities with highly prevalent underweight and undernutrition (Monteiro, Benicio, Conde, & Popkin, 2000; Steyn et al. 1998). Several studies focusing on the association between growth retardation early in life and adult obesity have found coexisting overweight and stunting, which is related to a history of undernutrition (Black et al., 2013; Popkin, Richards, & Montiero, 1996; Victora et al., 2007).

Doak, Adai, Monteiro, and Popkin (2000) analyzed data from Brazil, China, and Russia. They find that, in Brazil, the prevalence of overweight and underweight are, respectively, 31.8% and 10.6% for adults and 11.9% and 4.7% for children; in China, they are 13.1% and 9.7% for adults and 9.5% and 21.2% for children; whereas in Russia, they are 45.4% and 3%

for adults and 12.8% and 11.1% for children. The proportion of double-burdened households ranged from 6% in Russia to 11% in Brazil. Furthermore, 23%, 45%, and 58% of households with an underweight member also had an overweight member in China, Brazil, and Russia, respectively.

To assess the double burden at the household level, it is necessary to have household-level survey data. A number of researchers have reported these data for several countries. Various combinations of under- and overweight household members have been studied, with perhaps the most common being the overweight/obese mother and her underweight or stunted child (Dieffenbach & Stein, 2012). All the available evidence points to an increase in double-burdened households, although some researchers caution that it is a transitory phenomenon and that overweight even in children will take over (Roemling & Qaim, 2013). Others caution that the presence of the double burden within households is not a distinct phenomenon but one whose presence is driven by maternal overweight (Dieffenbach & Stein, 2012).

Garrett and Ruel (2003) note that of the four countries in the world that had a prevalence of overweight mothers and underweight children coexisting in the same household that exceeded 10%, three of them were in Latin America: Nicaragua 10%, Bolivia 11%, and Guatemala 13%. Lee et al. (2010) report that the prevalence of the double burden increased from 13% to 16% between 1995 and 2000 in Guatemala, and it is expected to continue to rise.

Dieffenbach and Stein (2012) use data from the Demographic and Health Surveys (DHS) of 54 countries to examine the prevalence of the intrahousehold double burden, defined as an overweight mother and a stunted child, for the years 1991 to 2009. They document an increased prevalence in all countries primarily due to increased overweight of mothers. In the countries they studied, the median occurrence of stunted child/overweight mother ranged from 0.5% to 16% of households. Roemling and Qaim (2013) report that 16% of Indonesian households are classified as dual-burdened, meaning that an overweight mother and an underweight child coexist in the same household.

Finally, although the double burden can be present in a single individual, in published research there is little mention of the dual burden at the individual level, and statistics on the prevalence of this type of double burden are not readily available. In the next section, we turn to a discussion of the determinants of the double burden.

21.4 Determinants

To understand the nature of the double burden of malnutrition and to design effective public policies to deal with this issue, it is essential to comprehend its determinants. In this section, we provide a detailed overview of the factors implicated in the existence of the double burden.

21.4.1 Determinants of Undernutrition

Although concerns about undernutrition occur for both adults and children, currently, childhood undernutrition remains one of the most pressing issues in developing economies (Outes & Porter, 2014), with preschool-aged children in developing countries at particular risk (Bhagowalia, Chen, & Masters, 2011). We therefore pay more attention to children while reviewing the determinants of undernutrition, which are, of course, not unique to children.

21.4.1.1 *Food Insecurity*

Broadly speaking, food insecurity indicates that a family/individual lacks consistent access to adequate food due to monetary or other resource constraints. In a developing country, lack of food resources and hunger are common situations for a significant share of the population. Most food security indicators measured at the household level are related to diet quantity and/or diet quality. Numerous studies have documented that food insecurity is predictive of child underweight (e.g., Reis, 2012).

21.4.1.2 *Low Birthweight*

Defined as a birthweight of less than 2500 g, some estimates indicate that 50% of the underweight children in Asia were low birthweight (Gillespie & Haddad, 2003).

21.4.1.3 *Poor Hygiene/Infectious Diseases in Early Childhood*

Diseases such as measles, diarrhea, pneumonia, meningitis, and malaria can all have long-term effects on child growth and development, and numerous studies have consistently shown that diarrhea is the most important infectious disease determinant of stunting (e.g., Black et al., 2013; Spears, 2012).

21.4.1.4 *Women's Educational and Social Status*

With increased education of women comes both more income for the family and also more knowledge about a healthy diet. Scholars have consistently documented a link between underweight or stunted children and lack of education in women (e.g., Behrman & Skoufias, 2004; Bhagowalia et al., 2011; Leroy, Habicht, de Cossio, & Ruel, 2014).

21.4.1.5 *Residential Area*

Living in an urban area has been found to be an important predictor of childhood undernutrition. Caballero (2005) reports that in many developing countries, as families migrate to cities, they lose the ability to grow their own food, and the mothers often join the labor force. This makes the family dependent on cheap nutrient-deficient food, and hence the growth of the children in the family may be adversely affected. In contrast, Liu et al. (2013) report that urban-dwelling Chinese children who tend to come from higher income families and enjoy better health care have higher BMI and are less likely to be underweight than are rural Chinese children, but that urban/rural differences in childhood nutrition have diminished over time in China.

21.4.1.6 *Poverty*

Underlying all of these reasons is poverty. The poor are more likely to be food insecure, and are more prone to live in areas without clean running water or proper sanitation and hence are more likely to suffer the infectious diseases that can lead to underweight or stunting. For example, in Brazil, there is strong evidence for a child nutrition income gradient (Reis, 2012). Many children in developing countries have multiple anthropometric deficits that are suggestive of an early environment characterized by harsh deprivation (McDonald et al., 2013).

21.4.2 Determinants of Overnutrition

Globally, obesity is on the rise. In the past 30 years, obesity rates have grown rapidly, and the speed with which obesity has increased indicates that its growth is likely a result of individual choices in light of changing economic environments rather than a shift in genetic endowments (6Doytch et al., 2014; Kelly, Yang, Chen, Reynolds, & He, 2008; Prentice, 2006).

A large literature in economics has sought to understand the factors that underlie the growth of obesity, and much of this work has been focused on developed countries (e.g., Chou, Grossman, & Saffer, 2004; Lakdawalla & Philipson, 2009). These studies have implicated the following changes as being important explanations for rising obesity rates: increased women's labor force participation and the corresponding reduced time for food preparation, higher levels of income, more sedentary lifestyles, technological progress in food production, time and market production and the increasing prevalence of low cost, calorie-dense fast foods, declining smoking rates, changes in health insurance, and changing prevalence of major depression. From an economic perspective, these shifts in time and income constraints, relative food prices, and changes in the market for health care have all changed individuals' incentives in ways that cause them to ingest more calories and expend less energy.

Developing countries have not been spared the obesity epidemic, and the reasons for the increase are largely the same for these countries as for more developed countries. There are also some factors that are more specific to developing countries that merit further discussion, and we detail these below.

21.4.2.1 *Nutrition Transition*

In the developing world, there increasingly is a shift away from traditional diets high in fiber and carbohydrates toward more Western diets. This is often termed the "nutrition transition" (Kapoor & Anand, 2002; Popkin, 1994). This nutrition transition is associated with the availability of cheaper, energy-dense foods, in particular, the globalization of food markets, which has meant that individuals in developing countries have access to more mass-produced, low-cost foods (Kelly et al., 2008). The low cost of highly refined oils and carbohydrates and the additional sweetness of foods, as well as an increased intake of animal products, mean that people are ingesting far more calories than they used to (Prentice, 2006), and cheaper food is usually less healthy than more expensive fresh fruits and vegetables (Caballero, 2005). This has spillover effects on child nutrition as these nutrient-poor foods may contribute to child malnutrition and lead to obese mothers but malnourished children (Caballero, 2005). And lack of essential micronutrients has been directly linked to obesity in mothers (Asfaw, 2007). People are spending less time in food preparation and eating more meals away from home, which typically means that they ingest more calories (Prentice, 2006).

21.4.2.2 *Sedentary Lifestyle*

Similar to the developed world, lifestyles in the developing world are becoming more sedentary. The increasing use of motorized transportation and energy-sparing devices coupled with increasingly sedentary employment and leisure pastimes (TV and video games) means that less energy is being expended (Kelly et al., 2008), and changes in diet may be further compounded (Popkin & Doak 1998).

21.4.2.3 *Cultural Norms*

In some developing countries, obesity, especially among women, is regarded as a sign of affluence. Thus, it is not unusual to see women being more likely to be obese as compared to men (Case & Menendez, 2009; Ramachandran & Snehalatha, 2010). Out of 300 anthropological societies, 81% considered a "plump" or "filled out" woman as desirable and attractive (Brown & Konner, 1987). Even today in some developing countries, fatness in women and children is viewed positively as a sign of health and prosperity (Hazuda, Haffner, Stern, & Eifler, 1988; Pawson, Martorell, & Mendoza, 1991; Ritenbaugh, 1982).

21.4.2.4 *Remittances*

As individuals in developing countries migrate to higher income countries in search of economic opportunities, they send home remittances. Remittances create an income effect that changes the types of goods that are sold in village stores, and much of this change is to stock more mass-produced foods (Prentice, 2006).

21.4.2.5 *Urbanization*

In addition, as economic development unfolds, people migrate to the cities. This rural-to-urban migration means that people usually lose the ability to grow their own food and hence become reliant on processed foods available in the marketplace (Caballero, 2005).

21.4.2.6 *Fetal Origins Hypothesis*

The fetal origins of disease hypothesis discussed earlier as a factor in undernutrition has been advanced as a factor in rising obesity rates in the developing world. According to this hypothesis, early (intrauterine or early postnatal) undernutrition may increase obesity because of its effects on metabolism, resting energy expenditure, and insulin-like growth factor; given that those in developing countries are more at risk for early undernutrition, this may well be a factor in explaining rising obesity rates (Caballero, 2005). Furthermore, research has found that undereating due to exposure to undernutrition predisposes humans to binge eating, conceivably through a compensatory adaptation to uncertain food supply that is likely to occur under conditions of poverty (Dingemans, Bruna, & Van Furth, 2002; Frisancho, 2003), and binge eating correlates with weight gain and obesity (Hays et al., 2002; Yanovski, 2003).

21.4.2.7 *Education*

Those who are more educated may have a better understanding of the links between body weight and health and therefore make better selections of healthy food and exercise patterns that would lead to lower likelihood of obesity. Because of the high correlation between education and income, educated individuals are more likely to have the higher incomes that would allow them to purchase food of higher quantity and quality. For example, there is empirical evidence that education plays a role in obesity in South Africa (e.g., Averett, Stacey, & Wang, 2014; Goedecke, Jennings, & Lambert, 2006).

21.4.2.8 *Income*

One reason for the increased prevalence of overweight is changes associated with economic development. Some developing nations, such as Brazil and China, have experienced dramatic shifts in their economies and thus in social welfare, with large proportions of the populations benefiting from improved economic and social conditions. One consequence of this improved economic status is a more secure food supply and increased dietary intake derived from nutrient- and energy-dense food (China National Bureau of Statistics, 1999; Mroz & Popkin, 1995; Wang, Monteiro, & Popkin, 2002; Shekar, Heaver, & Lee, 2006). Another consequence is that the energy expenditure in travel from home to place of work decreased markedly while inactive leisure time increased dramatically (Popkin, 1998, 1999; World Bank, 1999). These changes lead to the interesting phenomenon that in the developing countries such as Brazil and China the prevalence of overweight is greater in high-income rather than in low-income groups, whereas in the United States, it is the opposite. On the other hand, the poor are more constrained in their choices, and they are less able to substitute away from the cheaper, less nutritious foods and hence more likely to become obese (Monteiro, Moura, Conde, & Popkin, 2004).

21.4.3 The Rise of the Double Burden

Researchers who have been examining the coexistence of the double burden have determined that it is largely due to the fact that obesity has been rising in developing countries for the reasons outlined in the preceding sections, but poverty and hence child underweight remain relatively constant. The coexistence of over- and underweight within one society, household, or even individual could be explained by the nonuniform transition that developing countries experience. For example, changes in physical activity may not be uniform. Certain groups of a society or certain members of a household may differentially experience changes in physical activity with the introduction of technologies and lifestyles that involve a shift from an active to a sedentary lifestyle. Additionally, in many countries, the transition to a more Western diet may not be experienced uniformly by different groups of a society or different members of a household who may eat differently both in terms of quantity and quality. This may occur as a result of within- or intrahousehold food distribution or cohort differences in the acceptability and desirability of specific foods. Changes in physical activity or diet normally occur first among urban high-income households and last among rural low-income households, possibly contributing to an association between urban residence and the coexistence of underweight and overweight (ACC/SCN, 2000).

Given the globalization of the food supply and increased sedentary lifestyles, the rise in obesity across the globe is perhaps not surprising. What is puzzling is why, with more food, there are still so many underweight children. In particular, how is it that, within the same households, overweight and underweight can coexist? Several studies shed light on this issue. These studies tend to focus on mother and child pairs because underweight (stunted) children and overweight mothers are the most common combination observed in dual-burdened households (Dieffenbach & Stein, 2012; Varela-Silva et al., 2012).

The findings from these studies tend to implicate the same factors even across the quite diverse countries studied by the researchers. These factors include poverty, urbanization, inequality, maternal education, and a lack of nutritious food that provides excess calories to mothers but lacks micronutrients essential for childhood growth. For example, the diets of the poor are often lacking in diversity. Diets that are lacking in diversity are not likely to meet requirements for essential nutrients. Additionally, women with closely placed births find it difficult to shed excess body fat accumulated during pregnancy. In countries undergoing the nutrition transition, the quantity of food available may not be the problem because increasing incomes allow families to buy more food. However, families may still not have enough money to buy nutrient-dense food, thus leading to a situation in which an adult consumes enough energy to gain weight, but a child cannot get enough nutrients to grow appropriately.

Perhaps the WHO says it best when it notes that "Children in low- and middle-income countries are more vulnerable to inadequate pre-natal, infant and young child nutrition. At the same time, they are exposed to high-fat, high-sugar, high-salt, energy-dense, micro-nutrient-poor foods, which tend to be lower in cost. These dietary patterns in conjunction with low levels of physical activity result in sharp increases in childhood obesity while undernutrition issues remain unsolved" (WHO, 2015).

21.5 Policy Implications and Conclusion

From an economics point of view, government intervention is justified if the double burden of malnutrition imposes externalities on the rest of society. It has been well-established that child malnutrition is an important indicator of poor child health status, which is strongly associated with high mortality risk and poor health outcomes, educational performance, and labor market outcomes in later life. Because of these links among early childhood malnutrition, child health, and later economic outcomes, reducing child malnutrition has been listed as one of the United Nations Millennium Development Goals (MDGs).[6]

Shekar, M., Heaver, R., & Lee, Y. K. (2006) make a compelling case for fighting malnutrition, particularly underweight in children, by noting that malnutrition undermines economic growth and perpetuates poverty. It provides three specific rationales for investing in policies aimed at reducing malnutrition: (1) the returns from such investment are high relative to other policies that encourage development, such as reducing barriers to migration or government policies that lower the costs of opening new businesses; (2) the scope of the problem is large, with nearly one-third of children in the developing world being underweight or stunted; and (3) information asymmetries exists because people do not always know what foods or feeding practices are best for their children, and it is not easy to tell when a child is malnourished because micronutrient deficiencies are not usually visible to the untrained eye. Nobel Prize-winning economist Robert Fogel noted that those who are nutritionally deprived and hence cannot work hamper a country's economic growth (Fogel, 1994). Fortunately, evidence suggests that adverse nutrition shocks during critical developmental periods can be reversed to some extent, and children can catch up (Outes & Porter, 2014), thus indicating that policies implemented during childhood are likely to be helpful.

Experts report that direct intervention for undernutrition starts with good pregnancy nutrition, encouragement of breastfeeding, and supplemental feeding when necessary (Gillespie & Haddad, 2003). Other scholars believe that eradicating undernutrition hinges on economic development. Indeed, the reduction of child malnutrition is certainly one of the most desirable components of economic development (Tarozzi & Mahajan, 2007). However, in the development economics literature, there is a debate over whether economic development will improve food security and/or nutritional status (e.g., Subramanian & Deaton, 1996). And we have already seen that the process of economic development and the associated nutrition transition have had an adverse effect in terms of growing rates of obesity, an effect manifested in part through a calorically rich but nutrient-poor diet. This is particularly the case when economic development exacerbates income inequality.

Observational and experimental studies by economists generally suggest that income provided to women benefits children's health and nutritional status more than that provided to men because women are generally the primary caregivers and thus can influence child nutrition directly through better food choices and overall childcare practices, as well as indirectly through their own nutrition. There is considerable empirical evidence to support this point (e.g. Duflo, 2003, 2012; Imai, Annim, Gaiha, & Kulkarni, 2012; Lépine & Strobl, 2013; Cunningham et al., 2015).

Others have suggested that microcredit, particularly aimed at women, could be an effective approach, especially in an area where both poverty and inequality prevail: borrowing households become wealthier and less credit-constrained, so they are more able to afford a nutrient-rich diet (You, 2013). There is some evidence that this can improve nutrition status (Hazarika & Guha-Khasnobis, 2008; Hennink & McFarland, 2013).

A myriad of programs have been implemented to specifically attempt to reduce early childhood malnutrition—they are likely as numerous as the countries into which they have been introduced, and hence a complete accounting of these programs is beyond the scope of this chapter. Here, we highlight several that have been found to be effective. First, international animal donation programs have become an increasingly popular way for people living in developed countries to transfer resources to families living in developing countries, and there is evidence that such programs are effective in improving children's nutritional status (Rawlins, Pimkina, Barrett, Pedersen, & Wydick, 2014). Second, the Mexican PROGRESA program is a large anti-poverty program that originally focused on small, poor, rural communities and had an evaluation sample in which overall treatment was randomly assigned to some communities but not others. Children living in treated communities were found to have improved nutritional status, scored higher on cognitive measures of development, and had increased schooling. These findings suggest that PROGRESA may be having a fairly substantial impact on the potential earnings of currently young children in poor households (Behrman & Hoddinott, 2005). In India, the Integrated Child Development Services (ICDS) program has been in place since 1975. The purpose of ICDS is to improve the health, nutrition, and development of children. Evidence indicates that the program has been effective (Kandpal, 2011). In Bangladesh, the Bangladesh Rural Advancement Committee (BRAC) program has been linked to improvements in children's nutritional status (Chowdhury et al., 2013).

Perhaps the more difficult issue for those developing countries facing the double burden is how to combat rising obesity rates. Even developed countries have not fully grappled with this issue. Making the case that government intervention is warranted to reduce obesity rates is also more difficult. Cawley (2004) makes the argument that if individuals were perfectly rational, their decisions about food and weight imposed no costs on others in society, accurate information about the consequences of obesity were readily and freely available, and markets were perfectly competitive, there would be no market failure and no reason for government intervention. In poorer countries, individuals are less likely to have health insurance, and thus the burden of paying for treatment for diabetes and other comorbidities associated with obesity falls on those least likely to be able to afford it, which further exacerbates poverty and income inequality (Yach, Stuckler, & Brownell, 2006).

Rising rates of overweight and obesity are a product of the changing incentives that people face, and these have essentially conditioned unhealthy choices to be the economically better choices. Thus, thinking about how to realign incentives so that individuals make healthier choices is an important part of any obesity reduction program.

Many researchers emphasize that programs targeting the reduction of underweight must be capable of addressing overweight as well and must be designed carefully to avoid contributing to overweight (Asfaw, 2007). Otherwise, public health policies aiming to address undernutrition for one group of society or one member in a household by improving either the energy density of the food supply or securing the food supply may have the undesired consequence of increasing the likelihood of overweight and obesity for other members (Popkin, Adair, & Ng, 2012). This is particularly the case when maternal schooling is low; thus, policies aimed at reducing poverty and increasing child nutrition must be accompanied by effective behavior change communication to prevent child stunting and to protect women from unhealthy weight gain (Leroy et al., 2014). Similarly, programs designed to reverse overweight may be detrimental to groups vulnerable to underweight.

Clearly understanding the nature, prevalence, and causes of the double burden of malnutrition is essential to designing effective policies. The double burden will require policies that alleviate both obesity in adults and undernutrition in children, so it is not solely a matter of providing more calories. Furthermore, policy makers might find it a more efficient use of their limited resources if, instead of addressing under- and overweight separately, developing countries were to fight both conditions simultaneously.

Notes

1. "High prevalence" here is often defined in the literature as any value greater than the expected prevalence of 15% for overweight and/or obesity and 5% for stunting based on the range of heights and BMIs in the reference or standard populations (Varela-Silva et al., 2012).
2. Note that we need to use different indicators and criteria to identify double-burdened adults and children. The identification is sometimes even subject to researchers' own judgment (Kemkes-Grottenthaler, 2005; Song & Sung, 2008).
3. BMI is calculated by dividing an individual's weight in kilograms by her height in meters squared.
4. Data for Figure 1 is from http://apps.who.int/gho/data/view.main.NUTUNSTUNTINGv?lang=en accessed 12/3/2014.
5. Prevalence rates are from Stevens et al. (2012).
6. See www.unmillenniumproject.org/goals/ for a list of these goals. Last accessed December 4, 2014.

References

ACC/SCN. (2000). United Nations Administrative Committee on Coordination/Sub-Committee on Nutrition. *Fourth report on the world nutrition situation: Nutrition throughout the life cycle.* Geneva: UN Administrative Committee on Coordination/Sub-Committee on Nutrition.

Adrianzen, B., Baertl, J. M., & Graham, G. G. (1973). Growth of children from extremely poor families. *American Journal of Clinical Nutrition, 26*(9), 926–930.

Al-Mannai, A., Dickerson, J. W. T., Morgan, J. B., & Khalfan, H. (1996). Obesity in Bahraini adults. *Journal of the Royal Society for the Promotion of Health, 116*(1), 30–40.

Al-Nuaim, A. R. (1997). Prevalence of glucose intolerance in urban and rural communities in Saudi Arabia. *Diabetic Medicine, 14*(7), 595–602.

Asfaw, A. (2007). Micronutrient deficiency and the prevalence of mothers' overweight/obesity in Egypt. *Economics & Human Biology*, 5(3), 471–483.

Averett, S. L., Stacey, N., & Wang, Y. (2014). Decomposing race and gender differences in underweight and obesity in South Africa. *Economics & Human Biology*. 15, 23–40.

Behrman, J. R., & Hoddinott, J. (2005). Programme evaluation with unobserved heterogeneity and selective implementation: The Mexican PROGRESA impact on child nutrition. *Oxford bulletin of economics and statistics*, 67(4), 547–569.

Behrman, J. R., & Skoufias, E. (2004). Correlates and determinants of child anthropometrics in Latin America: Background and overview of the symposium. *Economics & Human Biology*, 2(3), 335–351.

Bhagowalia, P., Chen, S. E., & Masters, W. A. (2011). Effects and determinants of mild underweight among preschool children across countries and over time. *Economics & Human Biology*, 9(1), 66–77.

Black, R. E., Victora, C. G., Walker, S. P., Bhutta, Z. A., Christian, P., De Onis, M., . . . Uauy, R. (2013). Maternal and child undernutrition and overweight in low-income and middle-income countries. *Lancet*, 382(9890), 427–451.

Bogin, B. (1999). *Patterns of human growth*. Vol. 23. Cambridge: Cambridge University Press.

Bosy-Westphal, A., Plachta-Danielzik, S., Dörhöfer, R. P., & Müller, M. J. (2009). Short stature and obesity: Positive association in adults but inverse association in children and adolescents. *British Journal of Nutrition*, 102(03), 453–461.

Brown, P. J., & Konner, M. (1987). An anthropological perspective on obesity. *Annals of the New York Academy of Sciences*, 499(1), 29–46.

Caballero, B. (2005). A nutrition paradox—underweight and obesity in developing countries. *New England Journal of Medicine*, 352(15), 1514–1516.

Case, A., & Menendez, A. (2009). Sex differences in obesity rates in poor countries: evidence from South Africa. *Economics & Human Biology*, 7(3), 271–282.

Cawley J. (2004). An economic framework for understanding physical activity and eating behaviours. *American Journal of Preventive Medicine*, 27, 115–125.

China National Bureau of Statistics. (1999). China statistical yearbook 1999. Beijing: China Statistical Publishing House.

Chou, S. Y., Grossman, M., & Saffer, H. (2004). An economic analysis of adult obesity: Results from the Behavioral Risk Factor Surveillance System. *Journal of Health Economics*, 23(3), 565–587.

Chowdhury, A. M. R., Bhuiya, A., Chowdhury, M. E., Rasheed, S., Hussain, Z., & Chen, L. C. (2013). The Bangladesh paradox: Exceptional health achievement despite economic poverty. *Lancet*, 382(9906), 1734–1745.

Cole, T. J., Bellizzi, M. C., Flegal, K. M., & Dietz, W. H. (2000). Establishing a standard definition for child overweight and obesity worldwide: international survey. *British Medical Journal*, 320(7244), 1240.

Cunningham, K., Ruel, M., Ferguson, E., & Uauy, R. (2015). Women's empowerment and child nutritional status in South Asia: a synthesis of the literature. *Maternal & child nutrition*, 11(1), 1–19.

Delpeuch, F., & Maire, B. (1996). [Obesity and developing countries of the south]. *Medecine tropicale: revue du Corps de sante colonial*, 57(4), 380–388.

de Onis, M.,& Blossner, M. (2000). Prevalence and trends of overweight among preschool children in developing countries. *American Journal of Clinical Nutrition* 72(4), 1032–1039.

Dieffenbach, S., & Stein, A. D. (2012). Stunted child/overweight mother pairs represent a statistical artifact, not a distinct entity. *Journal of Nutrition, 142*(4), 771–773.
Dingemans, A. E., Bruna, M. J., & Van Furth, E. F. (2002). Binge eating disorder: A review. *International Journal of Obesity, 26*(3), 299–307.
Doak, C. M., Adair, L. S., Bentley, M., Monteiro, C., & Popkin, B. M. (2004). The dual burden household and the nutrition transition paradox. *International Journal of Obesity, 29*(1), 129–136.
Doak, C. M., Adair, L. S., Monteiro, C., & Popkin, B. M. (2000). Overweight and underweight coexist within households in Brazil, China and Russia. *Journal of Nutrition, 130*(12), 2965–2971.
Doytch, N., Dave, D. M., & Kelly, I. R. (2014). Global evidence on obesity and related outcomes: An overview of prevalence, trends, and determinants. *Eastern Economic Journal.* doi: 10.1057/eej.2014.37
Duflo, E. (2003). Grandmothers and granddaughters: Old age pension and intra-household allocation in South Africa. *World Bank Economic Review, 17*(1), 1–25.
Duflo, E. (2012). Women's empowerment and economic development. *Journal of Economic Literature, 50*(4), 1051–1079.
Fogel, R. W. (1994). Economic growth, population theory, and physiology: The bearing of long-term processes on the making of economic policy. *American Economic Review, 84*(3), 369–395.
Food and Agriculture Organization (FAO). (2005). *The state of food insecurity in the world 2005: Eradicating world hunger—key to achieving the millennium development goals.* Rome:. Food and Agriculture Organization of the United Nations. Available at: ftp://ftp.fao.org/docrep/fao/008/a0200e/a0200e00.pdf. Last accessed June 22, 2015.
Frisancho, A. R. (2003). Reduced rate of fat oxidation: A metabolic pathway to obesity in the developing nations. *American Journal of Human Biology, 15*(4), 522–532.
Gardner, G., & Halweil, B. (2000). Underfed and overfed: The global epidemic of malnutrition. Worldwatch Institute report. www.worldwatch.org/node/840. Last accessed November 13, 2014.
Garrett, J. L., & Ruel, M. T. (2003). Stunted child-overweight mother pairs: An emerging policy concern. *Washington, DC: International Food Policy Research Institute.*
Gillespie, S., & Haddad, L. (2003). *The double burden of malnutrition in Asia: Causes, consequences, and solutions.* New Delhi: Sage.
Goedecke, J., Jennings, C. L., Lambert, E. V. (2006). Obesity in South Africa. In: Steyn, K., Fourie, J., Temple, N., eds. *Chronic Diseases of Lifestyle in South Africa: 1995-2005.* MRC Technical Report (pp. 65–79). Cape Town: Medical Reseach Council.
Goryakin, Y., & Suhrcke, M. (2014). Economic development, urbanization, technological change and overweight: What do we learn from 244 Demographic and Health Surveys? *Economics & Human Biology, 14*(3), 109–127.
Hays, N. P., Bathalon, G. P., McCrory, M. A., Roubenoff, R., Lipman, R., & Roberts, S. B. (2002). Eating behavior correlates of adult weight gain and obesity in healthy women aged 55–65 y. *The American journal of clinical nutrition, 75*(3), 476–483.
Hazarika, G., & Guha-Khasnobis, B. (2008). *Household access to microcredit and children's food security in rural Malawi: A gender perspective* (no. 3793). IZA discussion papers. IZA: Bonn.
Hazuda, H. P., Haffner, S. M., Stern, M. P., & Eifler, C. W. (1988). Effects of acculturation and socioeconomic status on obesity and diabetes in Mexican Americans: The San Antonio heart study. *American Journal of Epidemiology, 128*(6), 1289–1301.

Hennink, M., & McFarland, D. A. (2013). A delicate web: Household changes in health behaviour enabled by microcredit in Burkina Faso. *Global Public Health*, *8*(2), 144–158.

Imai, K. S., Annim, S. K., Gaiha, R., & Kulkarni, V. S. (2012). Does women's empowerment reduce prevalence of stunted and underweight children in rural India? DP2012-11, Kobe University: Kobe Japan.

Jehn, M., & Brewis, A. (2009). Paradoxical malnutrition in mother-child pairs: Untangling the phenomenon of over-and undernutrition in underdeveloped economies. *Economics & Human Biology*, *7*(1), 28–35.

Kandpal, E. (2011). Beyond average treatment effects: Distribution of child nutrition outcomes and program placement in India's ICSD. *World Development*, *39*(8), 1410–1421.

Kapoor, S. K., & Anand, K. (2002). Nutritional transition: A public health challenge in developing countries. *Journal of Epidemiology and Community Health*, *56*(11), 804–805.

Kelly, T., Yang, W., Chen, C. S., Reynolds, K., & He, J. (2008). Global burden of obesity in 2005 and projections to 2030. *International Journal of Obesity*, *32*(9), 1431–1437.

Kemkes-Grottenthaler, A. (2005). The short die young: The interrelationship between stature and longevity—Evidence from skeletal remains. *American Journal of Physical Anthropology, 128(2)*, 340–347.

Khan, M. (2006). The dual burden of overweight and underweight in developing countries. *Population Reference Bureau*. Last accessed June 18, 2015 at: http://www.prb.org/Publications/Articles/2006/TheDualBurdenofOverweightandUnderweightinDevelopingCountries.aspx

Khor, G. L. (2008). Food-based approaches to combat the double burden among the poor: Challenges in the Asian context. *Asia Pacific Journal of Clinical Nutrition*, *17*(S1), 111–115.

Khorshid, A., Ibrahim, N., Galal, O., Harrison, G. (1998). Development of food consumption monitoring system in Egypt. *Advances in Agricultural Research in Egypt*, *1*(3), 163–217.

Kramer, M. S. (2003). The epidemiology of adverse pregnancy outcomes: An overview. *Journal of Nutrition, 133(5)*, 1592S–1596S.

Lakdawalla, D., & Philipson, T. (2009). The growth of obesity and technological change. *Economics & Human Biology*, *7*(3), 283–293.

Lara-Esqueda, A., Aguilar-Salinas, C. A., Velazquez-Monroy, O., Gómez-Pérez, F. J., Rosas-Peralta, M., Mehta, R., & Tapia-Conyer, R. (2004). The body mass index is a less-sensitive tool for detecting cases with obesity-associated co-morbidities in short stature subjects. *International Journal of Obesity*, *28*(11), 1443–1450.

Lee, J., Houser, R. F., Must, A., de Fulladolsa, P. P., & Bermudez, O. I. (2010). Disentangling nutritional factors and household characteristics related to child stunting and maternal overweight in Guatemala. *Economics & Human Biology*, *8*(2), 188–196.

Lépine, A., & Strobl, E. (2013). The effect of women's bargaining power on child nutrition in rural Senegal. *World Development*, *45*, 17–30.

Leroy, J. L., Habicht, J. P., de Cossío, T. G., & Ruel, M. T. (2014). Maternal education mitigates the negative effects of higher income on the double burden of child stunting and maternal overweight in rural Mexico. *Journal of Nutrition*, *144*(5), 765–770.

Liu, H., Fang, H., & Zhao Z. (2013). Urban-rural disparities of child health and nutritional status in China from 1989 to 2006. *Economics and Human Biology, 11*(3), 294–309.

López-Alvarenga, J. C., Montesinos-Cabrera, R. A., Velázquez-Alva, C., & González-Barranco, J. (2003). Short stature is related to high body fat composition despite body mass index in a Mexican population. *Archives of Medical Research*, *34*(2), 137–140.

Martorell, R., Mendoza, F. S., Castillo, R. O., Pawson, I. G., & Budge, C. C. (1987). Short and plump physique of Mexican-American children. *American Journal of Physical Anthropology*, *73*(4), 475–487.

Markowitz, D. L., & Cosminsky, S. (2005). Overweight and stunting in migrant Hispanic children in the USA. *Economics & Human Biology*, *3*(2), 215–240.

McDonald, C. M., Olofin, I., Flaxman, S., Fawzi, W. W., Spiegelman, D., Caulfield, L. E., & Danaei, G. (2013). The effect of multiple anthropometric deficits on child mortality: Meta-analysis of individual data in 10 prospective studies from developing countries. *American Journal of Clinical Nutrition*, *97*(4), 896–901.

Monteiro, C. A., Benicio, M. H. D'A, Conde, W. L., & Popkin, B. M. (2000). Shifting obesity trends in Brazil. *European Journal of Clinical Nutrition*, *54*(4), 342–346.

Monteiro, C. A., Moura, E. C., Conde, W. L., & Popkin, B. M. (2004). Socioeconomic status and obesity in adult populations of developing countries: A review. *Bulletin of the World Health Organization*, *82*(12), 940–946.

Mroz, Thomas A., & Barry M. Popkin (1995). "Poverty and the economic transition in the Russian Federation." *Economic Development and Cultural Change*, 1–31.

Outes, I., & Porter, C. (2014). Catching up from early nutritional deficits? Evidence from rural Ethiopia. *Economics & Human Biology*, *11*(2), 148–163.

Pawson, I. G., Martorell, R., & Mendoza, F. E. (1991). Prevalence of overweight and obesity in US Hispanic populations. *American Journal of Clinical Nutrition*, *53*(6), 1522S–1528S.

Popkin, B. M. (1994). The nutrition transition in low-income countries: An emerging crisis. *Nutrition Reviews*, *52*(9), 285–298.

Popkin, B. M. (1998). The nutrition transition and its health implications in lower-income countries. *Public Health Nutrition*, *1*(01), 5–21.

Popkin, B. M. (1999). Urbanization, lifestyle changes and the nutrition transition. *World Development*, *27*(11), 1905–1916.

Popkin, B. M., Adair, L. S., & Ng, S. W. (2012). Global nutrition transition and the pandemic of obesity in developing countries. *Nutrition Reviews*, *70*(1), 3–21.

Popkin, B. M., & Doak, C. M. (1998). The obesity epidemic is a worldwide phenomenon. *Nutrition Reviews*, *56*(4), 106–114.

Popkin, B. M., Richards, M. K., & Montiero, C. A. (1996). Stunting is associated with overweight in children of four nations that are undergoing the nutrition transition. *Journal of Nutrition*, *126*(12), 3009–3016.

Prentice, A. M. (2006). The emerging epidemic of obesity in developing countries. *International Journal of Epidemiology*, *35*(1), 93–99.

Ramachandran, A., & Snehalatha, C. (2010). Rising burden of obesity in Asia. *Journal of Obesity*, *2010*, 8. doi: 10.1155/2010/868573

Rawlins, R., Pimkina, S., Barrett, C. B., Pedersen, S., & Wydick, B. (2014). Got milk? The impact of Heifer International's livestock donation programs in Rwanda on nutritional outcomes. *Food Policy*, *44*, 202–213.

Reis, M. (2012). Food insecurity and the relationship between household income and children's health and nutrition in Brazil. *Health Economics*, *21*(4), 405–427.

Roemling, C., & Qaim, M. (2013). Dual burden households and intra-household nutritional inequality in Indonesia. *Economics & Human Biology*, *11*(4), 563–573.

Ritenbaugh, C. (1982). Obesity as a culture-bound syndrome. *Culture, Medicine and Psychiatry*, *6*(4), 347–361.

Shekar, M., Heaver, R., & Lee, Y. K. (2006). *Repositioning nutrition as central to development: A strategy for large scale action*. World Bank Publications.

Smith, P. K., Bogin, B., Varela-Silva, M. I., Orden, B., & Loucky, J. (2002). Does immigration help or harm children's health? The Mayan case. *Social Science Quarterly, 83*(4), 994–1002.

Song, Y. -M., & Joohon, S. (2008). Adult height and the risk of mortality in South Korean women. *American Journal of Epidemiology, 168(5)*, 497–505.

Spears, D. (2012). Height and cognitive achievement among Indian children. *Economics & Human Biology, 10*(2), 210–219.

Stevens, G. A., Singh, G. M., Lu, Y., Danaei, G., Lin, J. K., Finucane, M. M., . . . Ezzati, M. (2012). National, regional, and global trends in adult overweight and obesity prevalences. *Population Health Metrics, 10*(1), 22.

Steyn, K., Bourne, L., Jooste, P., Fourie, J. M., Rossouw, K., & Lombard, C. (1998). Anthropometric profile of a black population of the Cape Peninsula in South Africa. *East African Medical Journal, 75*(1), 35–40.

Subramanian, S., & Deaton, A. (1996). The demand for food and calories. *Journal of Political Economy, 104*(1), 133–162.

Subramanian, S. V., Kawachi, I., & Smith, G. D. (2007). Income inequality and the double burden of under-and overnutrition in India. *Journal of Epidemiology and Community Health, 61*(9), 802–809.

Tarozzi, A., & Mahajan, A. (2007). Child nutrition in India in the nineties. *Economic Development and Cultural Change, 55*(3), 441–486.

Tzioumis, E., & Adair, L. S. (2014). Childhood dual burden of under-and over-nutrition in low- and middle-income countries: a critical review. *Food and Nutrition Bulletin, 35*(2), 230.

Varela-Silva, M. I., Dickinson, F., Wilson, H., Azcorra, H., Griffiths, P. L., & Bogin, B. (2012). The nutritional dual-burden in developing countries: How is it assessed and what are the health implications? *Collegium Antropologicum, 36*(1), 39–45.

Victora, C. G., Sibbritt, D., Horta, B. L., Lima, R. C., & Wells, J. (2007). Weight gain in childhood and body composition at 18 years of age in Brazilian males. *Acta Pædiatrica, 96*(2), 296–300.

Wang, Y., Monteiro, C., & Popkin, B. M. (2002). Trends of obesity and underweight in older children and adolescents in the United States, Brazil, China, and Russia. *American Journal of Clinical Nutrition, 75*, 971–977.

World Bank. (1999). *World development indicators*. Washington, DC: World Bank (CD-ROM).

World Health Organization (WHO). (2015). Obesity and overweight. Fact sheet no. 311. Geneva: World Health Organization. Last accessed June 18, 2015: http://www.who.int/mediacentre/factsheets/fs311/en/

Yach, D., Stuckler, D., & Brownell, K. D. (2006). Epidemiologic and economic consequences of the global epidemics of obesity and diabetes. *Nature Medicine, 12*(1), 62–66.

Yanovski, S. Z. (2003), Binge eating disorder and obesity in 2003: Could treating an eating disorder have a positive effect on the obesity epidemic? *International Journal of Eating Disorders, 34*, S117–S120. doi: 10.1002/eat.10211

You, J. (2013). The role of microcredit in older children's nutrition: Quasi-experimental evidence from rural China. *Food Policy, 43*, 167–179.

CHAPTER 22

BIOLOGICAL HEALTH RISKS AND ECONOMIC DEVELOPMENT

ELIZABETH FRANKENBERG, JESSICA Y. HO, AND DUNCAN THOMAS

22.1 Introduction

Recent innovations in the measurement and interpretation of biological health risks in population-representative surveys provide unparalleled opportunities to substantially advance understanding of the relationships between economic development and the biological underpinnings of population health, health disparities, and health transitions. With the epidemic of obesity spreading rapidly across the globe and no longer a major concern only in advanced countries, the pressing need for this improved understanding cannot be overstated. Increases in obesity are often accompanied by increases in the prevalence of a broad array of noncommunicable diseases (NCDs), many of which can be controlled, albeit with high-cost treatments. At the same time, as life expectancy increases and fertility declines, populations are aging worldwide. The combination of increasing NCDs and greater shares of older adults is potentially a ticking time bomb that has critical implications for future economic development, the allocation of resources between generations, and population well-being in the years ahead. In short, there is a compelling need from both a scientific and policy perspective for investment in innovative research that provides a fuller understanding of the complex interplay that occurs among biology, behavior, resources, and the health of populations, and, thereby, the implications for poverty, inequality, and public finances.

Because the most prevalent global health risks are shifting from infectious diseases and inadequate nutrition to NCDs, we focus on how metabolic-related biological health risks vary across developing and advanced countries, drawing out the implications for health and economic development. After laying the foundation with anthropometry and hypertension, about which a good deal is known at the population level, we examine blood-based health markers for which population-representative data are more scarce. Specifically, we examine biomarkers for cholesterol, blood sugar, and inflammation, all of which have been implicated in major NCDs including cardiovascular disease, strokes, and cancers. These biological risk markers are selected because, first, they are likely to play a key role in understanding the evolution of global health in the years ahead, and, second, they underscore the value-added of integrating insights from biology with the behavioral sciences to understand that evolution.

In recent years, the population health literature has shifted from relying primarily on self-reported health status and anthropometrics to incorporate a broad array of physical health measures. Self-reports contain valuable information about one's own health status. Overall general health status is arguably the best predictor of subsequent mortality. In part, this is because self-reports summarize an individual's entire health history, health behaviors, and family health history. However, these advantages also complicate interpretation of self-reports because they reflect not only underlying health but also expectations about health, norms regarding health, and information about health. The latter is often related to use of health care; for example, randomized controlled studies have shown that individuals who are randomly assigned to a group that receives more health care are more likely to report themselves as being in poorer health. Interpersonal comparisons of health based on self-reported measures are, therefore, not straightforward (Dow, Gertler, Schoeni, Strauss, & Thomas, 2010; Thomas and Frankenberg, 2002; Idler & Benyamini, 1997).

Biomarkers, in contrast, are quantified measures of general health and nutrition or measures of physiological states that represent the functioning of specific organ systems and physiological processes. In combination with self-reported health, biomarkers are valuable tools for understanding the current and likely future trajectory of population health across the globe. There are several important features of biomarkers. First, they are collected using standardized protocols, at least within a study, and do not rely on the respondent's knowledge of or willingness to report a health condition. Second, they provide evidence on the prevalence of specific risk factors and the underlying physiological mechanisms that affect population health as well as exposures to environmental challenges and genetic predispositions to disease. Third, biomarkers support estimation of subclinical risks in populations (i.e., levels below cutoffs used to define diseases), which provides a rich picture of the distribution of risks at the population level. This is important for health policy planning and the design of forward-looking health programs. Fourth, in many low-income settings, biomarker measures have identified high levels of undiagnosed, untreated, and uncontrolled health conditions, a situation that significantly impacts understanding the state of global health and NCD prevalence, particularly in settings with limited health care access.

For all these advantages, it is important to underscore that much remains unknown about the optimal tradeoff between the costs and benefits of collecting data on biological health risks in population studies. Biomarker measurement can be expensive and is not straightforward, particularly in the context of complex population-based field studies that use different methods to collect, store, and assay biological samples. Standardization of the resulting biomarker values so that they are comparable across studies remains a significant challenge. The development and validation of protocols to harmonize methods and assure that results from different studies are comparable is an active area of ongoing research. Biomarkers for several important domains of health, such as pain, are not fully developed, and combining different biomarkers to construct a picture of overall health taking into account interactions within and across biological systems remains a challenge (McEwen & Stellar, 1993).

Anthropometric measures, such as height, weight, and arm circumference, have been extensively used in the nutrition, health, and economics literatures along with measures of nutrient intake and, in some studies, energy output. Physical performance measures, such as lung capacity assessments and grip strength, have been included in some population surveys. Many studies have measured blood pressure. Until recently, the collection of biological samples in population-based field studies was rare because of costs, feasibility, and perceived value of the markers. In recent years, however, there has been a revolution in the technology of collection and measurement of biomarkers, costs have fallen, and a growing literature indicates that biomarkers are likely to be a powerful tool for health research. In short, information about biological health risks in population-based studies has the potential to dramatically transform the field and yield important new insights into the links between health and economic development.

22.2 Data

The relationship between life expectancy, one measure of overall population health, and per capita gross domestic product (GDP) is displayed in Figure 22.1 for eight countries. We use individual-level measures of health collected in population-representative surveys conducted recently in each of these countries to illustrate key points in the rapidly growing literature on the links between health and development. In the figure, GDP is measured in 2010 in purchasing power parity in US dollars, and life expectancy at birth is estimated for 2005–10 by the United Nations Population Division. Three lower middle income countries (Ghana, India, and Indonesia) are displayed in red; three upper middle income countries (China, South Africa, and Mexico), are in green; and two upper income countries (Russia and the United States) are in blue. GDP per capita ranges between $2,300 (Ghana) and $47,000 (US) and life expectancy generally rises with per capita GDP except for the cases of South Africa (where HIV-related mortality is high) and Russia (where life expectancy is more than 10 years lower for males than females) (Strauss & Thomas, 2008).

The surveys were selected because they include multiple metabolic-related biomarkers for male and female adults of all ages. For the United States, we use the 2009/10

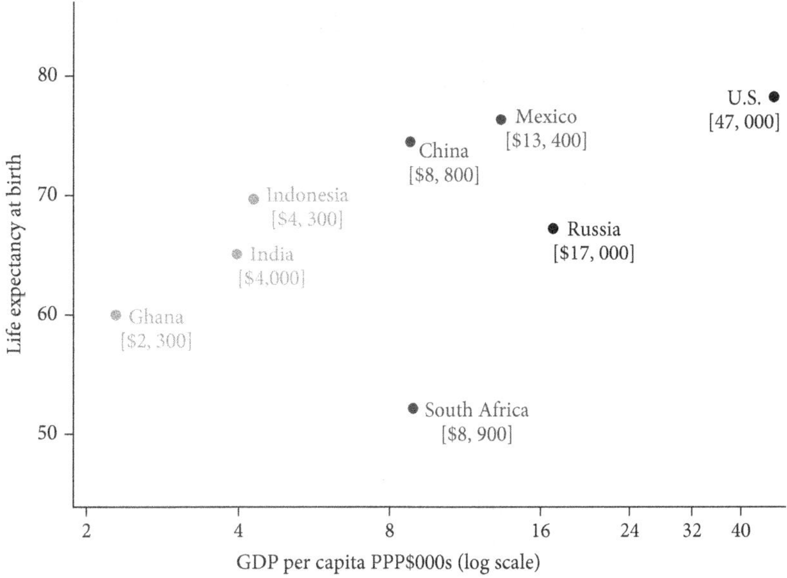

FIGURE 22.1 GDP per capita and life expectancy at birth.

Note: GDP per capita is measured in 2010 purchasing power parity dollars (which are in brackets below each country name) from the Penn World Tables, version 6.3. Life expectancy at birth estimates are for 2005–2010 from the United Nations Population Division.

wave of the National Health and Nutrition Examination Survey (NHANES), a repeated cross-sectional survey that collects an extensive battery of health measures including bio-specimens for hundreds of assays. Data for Russia, Ghana, and India are drawn from the first wave of the Study on Global Ageing and Adult Health (SAGE) surveys collected by the World Health Organization between 2007 and 2010. The surveys are designed to be representative of the adult population with an oversample of adults age 50 and older (Kowal et al., 2012). The Mexican Family Life Survey is a nationally representative longitudinal survey of Mexicans, including those who move to the United States; we use those who were living in Mexico at the time of the third wave, and interviewed between 2007 and 2012 (Rubalcava & Teruel, 2014). The National Income Dynamics Survey (NIDS) is a nationally representative longitudinal sample of South Africans; we use the baseline survey collected in 2008 (Leibbrandt, Woolard, & de Villiers, 2009). Data on the health of Chinese is drawn from the 2009 and 2010 waves of the China Health and Nutrition Survey (CHNS), a longitudinal survey of respondents living in nine provinces in China. The Indonesia Family Life Survey is a longitudinal survey that was representative of 83% of the Indonesian population at baseline (in 1993); we use the fourth wave collected in 2007 (Strauss, Witoelar, Sikoki, & Wattie, 2009). All samples of adults are restricted to those age 30 through 79 in each country. (For reviews of related literatures from different perspectives, see, e.g., Crimmins, 2014; Crimmins, Kim, & Vasunilashorn, 2010; Popkin, Adair, & Ng, 2012; Ng et al., 2014; Roth et al., 2015.)

22.3 Height, Weight, and Body Mass Index

Height and weight have been widely used as markers of health and well-being in the nutrition, history, and economic development literatures. Adult stature, an indicator of the "biological standard of living" (Komlos, 1985), is predictive of morbidity, mortality, and economic prosperity, reaching back over time (in pioneering work by Fogel, 1994; Floud, Fogel, Harris, & Hong, 2011; Komlos & Baten, 1998; Steckel & Floud, 1997), as well as in contemporary societies, particularly in lower income settings (Baten & Blum, 2014; Strauss & Thomas, 1998). Although part of height is inherited, attained adult stature also depends on phenotype influences, with nutrition and disease insults during the first few years of life being pivotal (Martorell & Habicht, 1986). Adult stature is largely determined in the first 24–36 months of life in the absence of large nutrition or health shocks, and so linear growth of young children has been a focus of a very large and rich literature in the health and social sciences. A key advantage of attained adult height is that it is fixed until older ages and so can be used to infer variation in health, nutrition, and well-being across cohorts. Among older adults, for whom shrinkage is important, leg length and arm length have been shown to be good proxies for attained adult stature (McDade & Hayward, 2009).

Weight is difficult to interpret without adjusting for height. Body mass index (BMI), which is weight (in kilograms) divided by the square of height (in meters), has also been linked with mortality; Waaler (1984) documented that, among Norwegian adults, low BMI (below 18.5) and high BMI (above 28) are associated with elevated mortality risks. Similar patterns have been described for mortality and morbidity risks in populations around the globe with those who are overweight (BMI ≥ 25) and, especially, those who are obese (BMI ≥ 30) being at elevated risk of, *inter alia*, cardiovascular diseases, stroke, diabetes, cancers, muscular-skeletal problems, and mortality (Dey, Rothenberg, Sundh, Bosaeus, & Steen, 2002; Must et al., 1999; World Health Organization [WHO], 1999). Studies have shown that BMI affects economic prosperity after controlling height and other human capital characteristics (Strauss & Thomas, 1998). BMI reflects the combination of energy expenditure (including types of physical activity), energy intake (taking into account diet composition), genetic factors, and other lifestyle factors (such as stress exposures and smoking); for some, elevated BMI is indicative of greater muscle mass and may not indicate poor health. BMI is not indicative of a specific health risk but is a portmanteau proxy that may point to elevated risks and, on this score, has proved to provide valuable information about the evolution of population health.

Height and weight, which can be measured quickly and accurately in a field setting using a portable stadiometer and scale, respectively, have been included in population-based surveys for many decades. Although measurement is straightforward, interpretation of BMI is complicated since it reflects the combination of fat, muscle, and body type. Several alternative anthropometric indicators have been shown to provide useful additional information about health status including waist circumference (an indicator of central adiposity), the waist to hip ratio, arm circumference, leg and arm length, and skinfold thickness. Recent technological innovations suggest that body composition may be estimated with bioelectric impedance analysis in field surveys.

One useful summary indicator for our cross-country comparisons is the percentage of the population that is overweight (BMI ≥ 25). It is displayed in Figure 22.2 by age and gender (in panel A) and by education and gender (adjusting for age, in panel B). Similar comparisons of average BMI and the fraction obese yield essentially the same overarching conclusions. The countries are arrayed by level of per capita GDP as in Figure 22.1. The figures by age are nonparametric estimates using locally weighted smoothed scatterplots (Cleveland, 1979). The estimates of the association with education are predicted values from regression models that include linear splines in education, with knots at 6 and 12 years of completed schooling, as well as indicator variables for 10-year age groups. All models are estimated separately by gender for each country.

Generally, the fraction of adults who are overweight rises with GDP until countries enter into middle income and is essentially constant at higher levels of GDP. For example, among adults aged 45–54, about 20% are overweight in India, 30% in Ghana and Indonesia, 40% in China, 60% in South Africa, and more than three-quarters are overweight in Mexico, Russia, and the United States, the three highest income countries. The fraction overweight is higher in the two African countries, given their GDP, particularly for females. Rates for females in Ghana are slightly higher than the rates in Indonesia and China (where GDP is two to four times higher), and rates for females in South Africa are close to those in the three high-income countries (where GDP is two to five times higher).

In every country, the fraction overweight tends to rise with age to around 50 years and then declines, reflecting both life course and cohort effects, with the latter being more important in middle-income countries like China that have enjoyed faster economic growth in recent decades. In all but the most advanced countries, females are more likely to be overweight than males. Figure 2a highlights two striking facts about gender differences. First, the female–male gap is very large in the African countries, with females being almost twice as likely to be overweight as males, which, along with the particularly high rates of BMI given GDP for females, suggests that factors over and above resources may affect BMI in these and other African societies, as well as among African Americans in the United States (Flegal, Carroll, Ogden, & Curtis, 2010; Prentice, 2006). Second, the gender gap is small and possibly reversed among younger adults in the three highest GDP countries where BMI is high and does not rise with GDP.

Figure 22.2b displays the relationship between being overweight and education, a marker of longer run socioeconomic status (SES), so that the figure provides evidence on how biological health risks varies across the SES distribution within each country, controlling age and gender. In every country other than the United States, the best-educated males are far more likely to be overweight than those with little

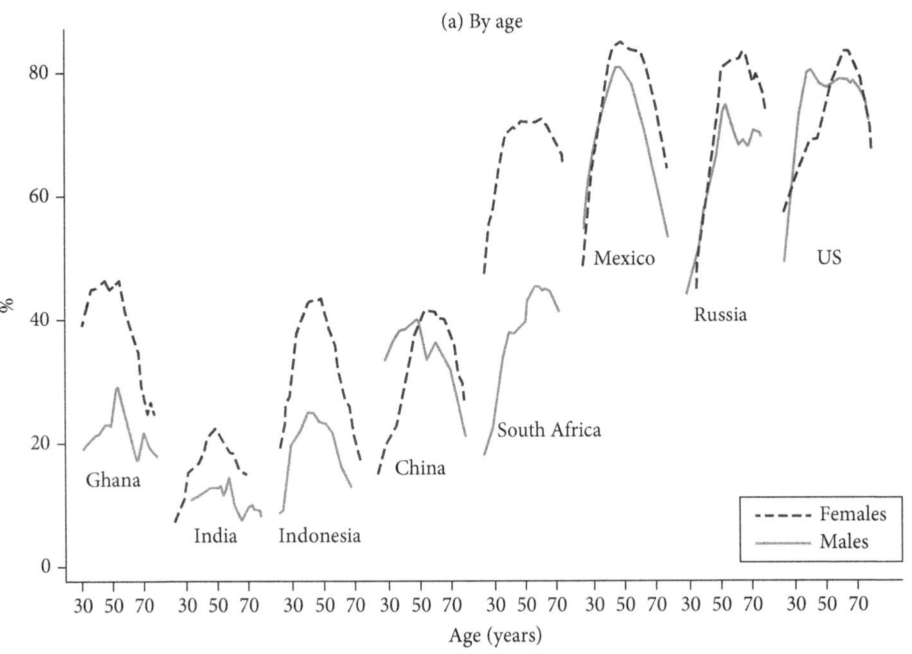

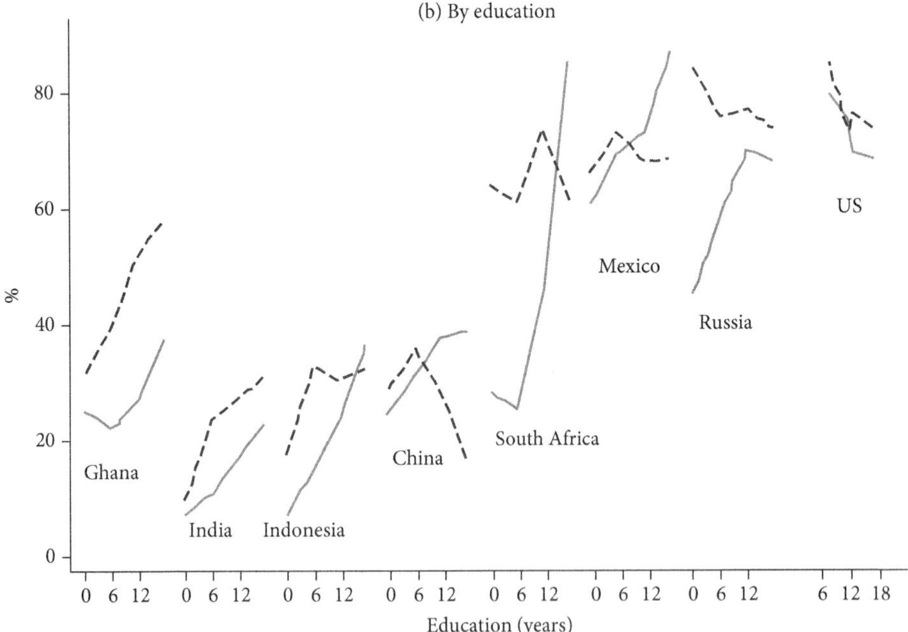

FIGURE 22.2 Percent overweight (BMI > 25) by gender, age and education.

education, even in countries where BMI is high. In South Africa and Mexico, more than 80% of those with the most education are likely to be overweight. In the United States and most advanced countries, it is the less educated who are more likely to be overweight, as is the case for Russian females. In the upper middle income countries—South Africa, Mexico, and China—the fraction of overweight females first rises with education and then falls. In the poorest three countries, better educated females are more likely to be overweight than those with little education, as is the case for males. The pattern (across levels of GDP) of BMI and obesity first rising with education, then an inverted V shape, and then declining, and the pattern of females leading males in this transition in a country are well-documented (Popkin, 2001; Popkin & Gordon-Larsen, 2004). Although these comparisons of the shapes of the relationships are informative, comparisons of the fraction overweight for specific levels of education across countries is complicated because education levels do not have the same relative significance in every country.

Taking Figures 22.2a and 22.2b together, BMI and the fraction overweight tends to rise with overall economic prosperity but tapers off at high levels of BMI and GDP. Within the poorest countries, the fraction overweight rises with education for both males and females. In the richest countries, better educated females are more likely to adopt behaviors that limit BMI, and the BMI-education profile is reversed. In the middle income countries, this transition is evident among females but not among males: better educated females are on the vanguard of changing behavior in response to risks of being overweight. This, in conjunction with the fact that very large fractions of well-educated males in middle income countries are overweight, suggests that there is both considerable scope and arguably an urgent need for programs that will stem the apparently inexorable march toward populations with high rates of overweight and the attendant metabolic disease burdens.

22.4 Hypertension

High blood pressure or *hypertension* is associated with several lifestyle factors including elevated BMI, greater stress, inadequate exercise, excess sodium in the diet, and tobacco consumption. High blood pressure usually develops over many years, and prolonged exposure to elevated blood pressure can damage the inner lining of the arteries, leading to arteriosclerosis (hardening of the arteries) and atherosclerosis (narrowing of the arteries). Moreover, biological mechanisms underlying elevated blood pressure vary over the life course, with stiffness in the arteries playing an increasing role with age. Elevated blood pressure is a major risk factor for heart disease, stroke, and kidney disease, and it has been implicated in later life cognitive decline (Kannel, 2000; Levy, Larson, Vasan, Kannel, & Ho, 1996).

Blood pressure is straightforward to measure in a field setting.[1] Stage 2 hypertension is indicated when systolic pressure is 160 mm Hg or higher or diastolic pressure is 100 mm

Hg or higher; stage 1 hypertension is indicated when systolic or diastolic pressure are 140 and 90 mm Hg or higher, respectively. Figure 22.3 displays the percentage of males (in Figure 3a) and females (in Figure 3b) who are considered stage 2 hypertensive for each of three age groups in each country. The percentage whose blood pressure as measured in the survey exceeds at least one of the cutoffs for stage 2 hypertension is displayed by the solid dark bar for each age group. The percentage whose blood pressure is below the cutoff but report using medication to keep blood pressure low is displayed by the white bar. The sum of the heights of the solid and white bars indicates the percentage who are measured as hypertensive (i.e., uncontrolled hypertension) or on medication to lower blood pressure (i.e., controlled hypertension). This distinction between controlled and uncontrolled hypertension is important. In order to avoid long-term damage to the body system, clinical guidelines recommend that hypertension be controlled through lifestyle changes, medication, or both. As is evident from the heights of the solid bars in Figure 22.3, for many people, hypertension is not controlled, particularly in lower income countries. This may reflect that hypertension is not diagnosed or not treated, or that treatment is ineffective.

Taking controlled and uncontrolled hypertension together, prevalence rises with age in every country. At younger ages, rates of hypertension are generally higher among males relative to females, but because the rate of increase with age tends to be faster for females, older adult females are somewhat more likely to be hypertensive than older adult males. These general patterns by age and gender are well-established for both developed and developing countries.

There are two striking additional features of Figures 22.3a and 22.3b. First, the variation across countries in the rates of hypertension, particularly rates of uncontrolled hypertension, is stunning. Second, levels of uncontrolled hypertension are extremely high in many developing countries, and the vast majority of these cases are undiagnosed. This is profoundly troubling, given the likely future impact on the lives of these people and their families, as well as the impact on the public health sector.

Moreover, South Africa stands apart from all other countries in the figure. In each age group, rates of uncontrolled hypertension are the highest among South Africans by a substantial margin: around 60% of South Africans aged 60–79 are hypertensive (based on field-measurement), and another 10% report controlling hypertension with medication so that more than 70% of this age group suffers from stage 2 hypertension: this is a staggering rate in the population. Even among adults aged 30–44, almost 30% are hypertensive, and fewer than 5% report taking medication. Since the impacts of hypertension cumulate over time, these high rates of hypertension and low rates of control raise serious concerns about the future health of the population; taken in combination with the high rates of obesity, this has powerful implications for the future burden of NCDs in South Africa and the concomitant demands on the health system and public finances supporting that system. This burden is exacerbated by the high rates of infectious disease, weak infrastructure, and high rates of

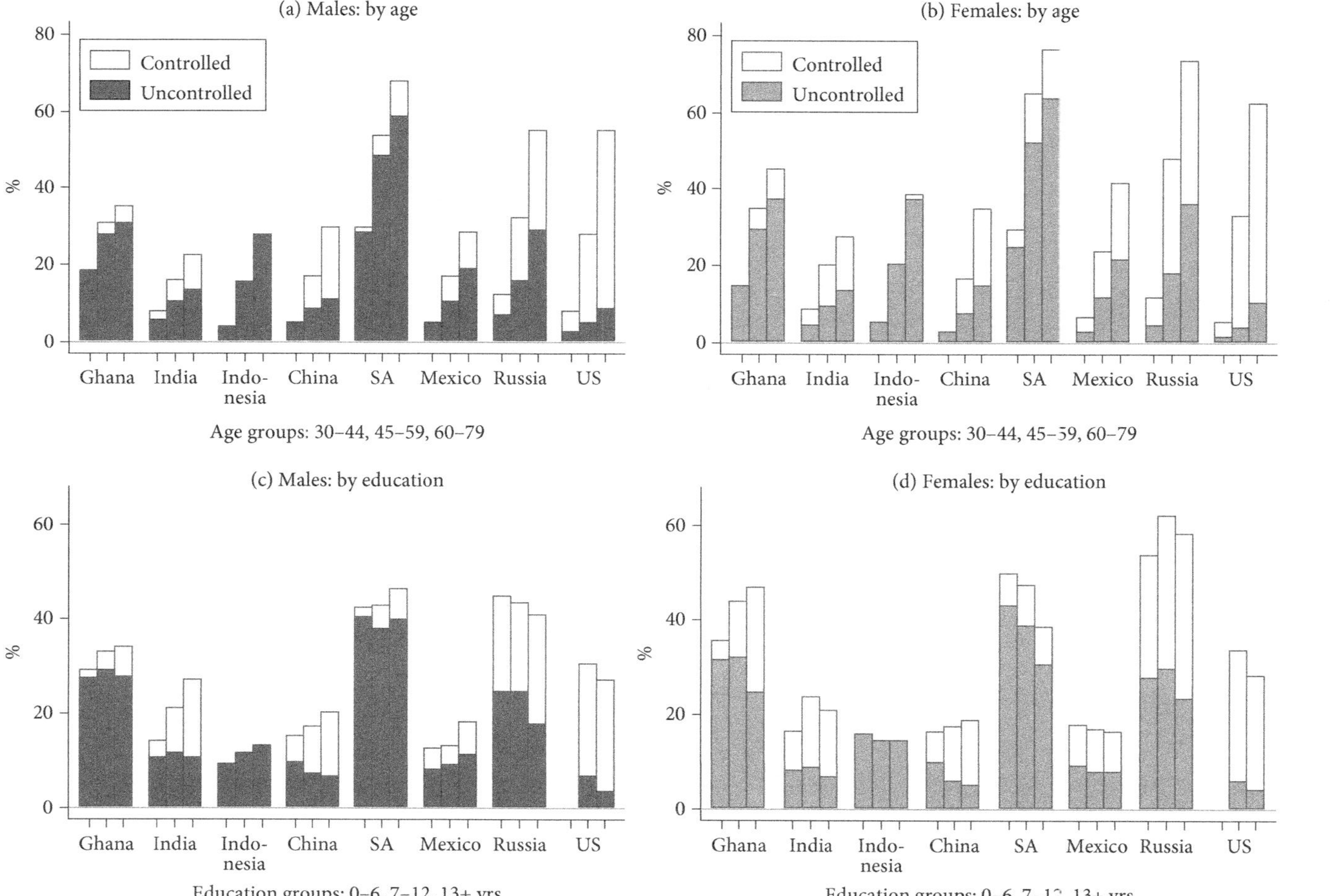

FIGURE 22.3 Percent hypertensive or on medication by gender, age and education.

Note: Hypertensive is stage 2 hypertensive, defined as systolic blood pressure > 160 mmHg and/or diastolic blood pressure > 100 mmHg.

poverty in South Africa. Although the figures are not as dramatic, similar concerns arise in the other African country, Ghana, where about 40% in the 60–79 age group are hypertensive, and fewer than 10% are controlling their blood pressure. The data suggest that without significant changes in health care and lifestyles, the epidemic of obesity and hypertension that is sweeping through Africa will likely impose a heavy burden on future generations.

In Russia and the United States, about 60% of the 60–79 age group are hypertensive, but more than 80% of the Americans and more than 50% of the Russians control hypertension with medication (Ikeda et al., 2014). Approximately 30% of the 60–79 age group are hypertensive in India, China, and Mexico, where about half of those people control blood pressure with medication. In Indonesia, the overall percentage of 60- to 79-year-olds who are hypertensive is also about 30%, but those who are not controlling blood pressure (the solid bar) is overwhelming relative to those who are controlling blood pressure (the white bar). This reflects two factors. First, diagnosis rates in Indonesia are exceptionally low. Only 5% of all males and females aged 60–79 report having been diagnosed as hypertensive. Second, of that 5%, only one in three is actually keeping blood pressure below the cutoffs with medication; for the other two-thirds, either the medication is ineffective or the reports of using medication are wrong (Blacher et al., 2000; Franklin, Khan, Wong, Larson, & Levy, 1999; Izzo, Levy, & Black, 2000; Kannel, 2000; Stevenson, 1999).

The lower panels of the figure display the percentage of males (in Figure 22.3c) and females (in Figure 22.3d) who are hypertensive by three education groups. For males in all but the two highest income countries, the fraction controlling hypertension tends to rise with education, whereas the fraction that is measured hypertensive does not vary much with education and so, overall, total hypertension rates rise slightly with education. For females in the same countries, the fraction measured hypertensive is lowest among those with the most education, but there is no consistent association between education and the fraction controlling hypertension or with total hypertension rates. In the United States, better educated males and females are more likely to be taking medication and less likely to be measured hypertensive, and so total hypertension rates decline with education. In contrast with the striking patterns linking education and being overweight in Figure 22.2, variation in hypertension with education is very modest. Public health programs that result in improved control of blood pressure will likely benefit populations across the entire spectrum of SES in many low-income countries (Addo, Smeeth, & Leon, 2007; Busingye et al., 2014; Colhoun, Hemingway, & Poulter, 1998; Ibrahim et al., 1995; Lee et al., 2012; Lloyd-Sherlock, Beard, Minicuci, Ebrahim, & Chatterji, 2014; Steyn, Bradshaw, Norman, & Laubscher, 2008; Witoelar, Strauss, & Sikoki, 2012; Wu et al., 2008).

In sum, in middle- and low-income countries, the payoffs are likely to be substantial for policies that are effective in improving diagnosis and, when indicated, treatment of hypertension among adults across the entire age spectrum. The returns to programs and policies that result in lifestyle changes and medication use where appropriate are likely to be very high for individuals, their families, and society.

22.5 Other Noninvasive Measures of Health and Nutrition

Some field surveys have included noninvasive activity-related measures in addition to anthropometry and blood pressure. Measures that are also simple, accurate, and inexpensive to field include, for example, heart rate variability, lung capacity, grip strength, timed walks, timed repeated stands from a sitting position, observing a respondent perform specific activities such as walking in a straight line or standing on one leg, and tests of fine motor skills. Accelerometers and pedometers are increasingly being adopted in population-based studies to measure energy expenditure over extended periods of time. Although the link between many of these measures and underlying biology is indirect, the measures do contribute to a fuller representation of the physical health of an individual and, in many cases, provide a valuable complement to self-reported activities of daily living (ADLs) and instrumental ADLs. However, interpretation of activity-based measures can be complicated when they reflect both the capacity to perform the activity and the respondent's desire to perform. For example, the speed with which a respondent stands from a sitting position reflects not only musculo-skeletal difficulties but also exuberance, energy, and other related traits. Similarly, converting accelerometer counts to energy expenditure is complicated by differences in body composition and variation in basal metabolic rates (Steptoe & Wikman, 2011).

There is a long history of measurement of nutrient intake in field surveys. These studies have used individual food intake recalls, food consumption at the household level, or measurement of food prepared and eaten in the home and converted food consumption to calories and nutrients using standardized food composition tables. Each of these approaches to measurement is thought to be subject to substantial error, albeit from different sources. Food recalls are usually asked of an individual respondent and typically span the preceding 24 hours. They miss day-to-day variation in diets, which will be more important in higher income settings. Since extending the recall period is thought to result in a greater understatement of food intake, studies have suggested making daily visits to the same respondent for multiple days or asking respondents to complete food diaries over several days. An alternative that is less demanding of respondent time is the collection of food frequency diaries that typically focus on a specific set of food items (Wiehl & Reed, 1960). In general, these approaches tend to be associated with underreporting of food intakes (Black, Welch, & Bingham, 2000; Hill & Davies, 2001).

A key advantage of food recalls and food diaries is that it is possible, in principle, to obtain individual-specific measures of intakes. Because food consumption is typically measured at the household level, it is difficult to attribute consumption to an individual. The same concern arises with food that is weighed and measured because this is also typically conducted at the household level. Consumption data usually cover at least a week (in some cases, longer periods of time) and include food consumed at home and away from home. Respondents report the quantity of each specific item purchased or consumed out of own production. Converting consumption data to nutrient intakes relies on conversion tables that are not adjusted for quality (which tends to rise with income), wastage (which tends to increase with income), or food purchased but not yet consumed (which also tends to rise with income). The more aggregate the consumption data and the more diversity in foods within the aggregate, the greater the conversion error. Few surveys collect a roster of every person at each meal, including household members and guests, which complicates even per capita measurement of intakes.

Some studies have weighed and measured food by either visiting the household daily for up to a week or by providing scales and asking the respondent to measure all foods consumed. Food that is prepared and all leftovers are weighed, and, in some cases, food consumed by each individual is also weighed. This method is considered the most accurate method to measure intakes and addresses concerns with errors in recall and conversion to nutrients. However, it is extremely demanding of respondents and survey enumerators; in addition, it is difficult to measure food eaten out of the home, which imparts a systematic bias.

The central issue for our purposes is that all these approaches taken to measure food intakes are subject to substantial error. An alternative approach measures energy expenditure using doubly labeled water[2] or indirect calorimetry. However, measurement of specific nutrient intakes requires reliance on biochemical analyses of biological samples such as blood and urine.

22.6 Blood-Based Markers of Health and Health Risks

In contrast with the markers discussed thus far, there has been a revolution in the collection and analysis of biological health risk markers in recent years. Whereas 30 years ago, very few large-scale household surveys collected any biomarkers over and above anthropometry, today, biomarkers are routinely collected in many surveys across the globe. This reflects the combination of two complementary forces. First, understanding of health outcomes has been substantially enriched by the integration of insights from the health and social sciences with biologically plausible models of causal mechanisms (Crimmins & Finch, 2006; Crimmins & Seeman, 2004; McEwen, 1998). These models have elucidated the complex biologic and socioeconomic underpinnings of health inequalities, provided the foundation for models of health and health transitions over the life course, and highlighted how, for some, the impact of health insults cumulate over the life course and may present as physiological deterioration at older ages. These insights have powerful implications for understanding the links between health and development.

The second force underlying this revolution in health measurement is the dramatic decline in the costs of collecting biomarkers in household surveys because of new technologies. There are four primary approaches to collecting and analyzing biological specimens to measure biomarkers. First, respondents are asked to visit a designated site where specimens are collected. A key challenge with this design is that the health of those who participate in the study may not be representative of the health of the entire target population. Of particular concern is that those in worst health may not be willing or able to travel to the site, and those with the highest value of time (who are also likely to be in good health) may be unwilling to travel to the site and participate. The distribution of health of those included in the sample is likely to be sparse in both the lower and upper extremes. Several studies have adopted this approach, although few have described the likely implications of sample selectivity for population estimates of prevalence and associations with individual- and community-level characteristics.

The second approach essentially takes the clinic to the respondent. NHANES, a pioneer of this approach, has been fielded since the early 1960s in the United States by the National Center for Health Statistics. A mobile examination center (MEC), comprising several large trailers equipped with state-of-the-art medical equipment, is parked in a neighborhood and respondents undergo a complete physical examination in the MEC. Some biomarkers are assayed immediately; for others, specimens are stored for later analyses in a laboratory. All assays are conducted using best practices and, where necessary, are validated against an established reference laboratory. It is argued that NHANES provides the best estimates of population health in the United States, although participant nonresponse is an ongoing challenge. A small number of studies have replicated the NHANES approach, but a key impediment to widespread adoption of the model is the cost of the MEC.

The third approach collects specimens in the home and conducts assays at a later time. Collection, storage, and analysis of urine and venous blood samples are relatively complicated. For some biomarkers, samples need to be assayed within a brief window after collection, samples needs to be fractionated with protocols depending on the target biomarkers, and, in some cases, bio-specimens need to be collected over an extended period of time and thus involve multiple visits with the respondent. However, for several bio-specimens, such as saliva, hair, and nail clippings, collection and transportation to a laboratory for analysis is inexpensive and straightforward in complex field studies (protocols have been established to measure many biomarkers with these specimens including, e.g., endocrine and inflammatory responses, infections, exposures to toxins, markers associated with cancers, and genetic material such as DNA and RNA).

In this vein, dried bloods spots (DBS) are potentially powerful bio-specimens which have been collected in the home in several complex field studies in recent years and are being used to measure a rapidly growing number of biomarkers. Collection of DBS is simple: drops of whole blood are collected from a finger (or heel) prick onto absorbent filter paper, which is then dried and stored. The cards are easy to transport to a laboratory where a disc is typically punched out and an assay is conducted. DBS have been used to screen for diseases among newborn babies since the early 1960s (Guthrie & Susi, 1963), have been used in many epidemiological studies, and are increasingly adopted in population surveys (McDade, Williams, & Snodgrass, 2007). A wide array of analytes have been measured using DBS, including, for example, metabolic and nutrition-related markers, HIV, hepatitis and infectious diseases, inflammation markers, cortisol, testosterone, DNA, and RNA. For some assays, the fact that each spot yields a relatively small volume of blood can be a challenge. In addition, widely used protocols for cross-validation of assay implementation across different laboratories have not been fully established, and comparisons of assay results across studies are not straightforward (Crimmins et al., 2013; Crimmins, 2014). However, progress is being made on both these fronts.

The fourth approach to biomarker measurement exploits recent advances in the technology of point-of-care monitors. These portable monitors are usually battery-powered and typically use capillary blood from a finger prick—thereby exploiting the advantages of the third approach to biomarker measurement. They also provide information to the respondent at the time of the assessment—a key advantage of the second approach, essentially bringing the clinic to the home. This is a significant and important advantage during a lengthy interview and is especially valuable in settings where health service use is constrained by price, access, quality, or respondents' resources. Regular measurement of known levels of the biomarker using quality control strips provided by the manufacturer assures that the monitor is accurate and that measures do not drift during the field period. The key limitation is that there are relatively few portable point-of-care monitors that are robust enough and have been validated for complex field settings (as opposed to in a clinic or doctor's office).

The HemoCue photometer is a point-of-care monitor that has been successfully used in numerous studies to measure hemoglobin (Hb) in the home. It is one of the earliest point-of-care monitors developed and has been used since the late 1980s (Bridges, Parvin, & van Assendorf, 1987). It requires only a small sample of blood from a finger stick; it is inexpensive, very robust and portable; does not require electricity or refrigeration; displays the measure within seconds; and has been shown to have high levels of specificity and sensitivity in very diverse settings. Indeed, the HemoCue photometer has provided important population-representative evidence on the prevalence of this indicator of iron deficiency in populations across the globe.

We examine three biological risk factors that have been implicated in cardiovascular disease, stroke, and premature mortality: total cholesterol and glycosylated hemoglobin (HbA1c) are indicative of metabolic functioning, whereas C-reactive protein (CRP) is a marker of inflammation that has broader implications for health and well-being. All three are measured using blood samples, although the measurement strategy varies across countries and biomarkers.

22.6.1 Total Cholesterol

High levels of cholesterol put individuals at risk for cardiovascular disease. Total serum cholesterol levels are related to coronary heart disease and, at some age, tend to increase the risk of cardiovascular and all-cause mortality (Anderson, Castelli, & Levy, 1987; Weverling-Rijnsburger, Jonkers, van Exel, Gussekloo, & Westerndorp, 2003). The three components of cholesterol are low-density lipoprotein (LDL), very-low-density lipoprotein (VLDL), and high-density lipoprotein (HDL) cholesterol. HDL cholesterol has antioxidant and anti-inflammatory functions, and its benefits include the removal of excess cholesterol from blood vessels, prevention of blood vessel blockages, promotion of blood flow, and improved innate immunity (Feingold & Grunfled, 2011; Toth, 2005). Low levels of HDL cholesterol are associated with an increased risk of cardiovascular disease incidence and mortality, including coronary heart disease, coronary artery disease, and stroke (Barter & Rye, 1996; Castelli et al., 1986; Gordon et al., 1989; Weverling-Rijnsburger et al., 2003). In contrast, LDL cholesterol deposits on the inside of blood vessels and creates plaque. Whereas HDL and total cholesterol are not affected by whether an individual has fasted prior to measurement, this is not the case for LDL. Because requiring study participants to fast, and monitoring their fasting behavior, substantially complicates field work, many studies have measured only HDL and total cholesterol.

We focus on total cholesterol, which has been measured in four of the studies we examine using three of the different methods described earlier. In the United States, NHANES brought the clinic to the respondent. In China, after an overnight fast, blood was drawn in the home, frozen, and transported to a national central lab in Beijing. In Indonesia and Mexico, a point-of-care monitor, the CardioChek Analyzer, was used to measure total cholesterol in the home. Recent advances have established that total cholesterol can be measured in DBS.

Results are presented for the percentage of the adult population aged 30 through 80 years for whom measured total cholesterol indicates a high risk of heart disease (240 mg/dL or higher; Jellinger et al., 2012). Because cholesterol levels can be controlled with medication, this percentage is adjusted to include the percentage of the population who report themselves as being on such medication and whose measured total cholesterol indicates successful control (<240 mg/dL). This adjustment is made for the United States and Indonesia; medication use to control cholesterol is not reported in the China or Mexico studies. The fraction of the population on medication is tiny in Indonesia (<0.5%), and the adjustment makes no difference in the figures. It is, however, an important adjustment in the United States, as explained herein.

Percentages with high total cholesterol (or on medication) are displayed by age in Figure 22.4a and by education in Figure 22.4c, estimated separately for males and females. Among females, the levels and variation with age are remarkably similar in Indonesia, China, and Mexico. The percentage rises steeply with age from age 30 to around 50. Among females aged 50 and older, about 1 in 5 have high total cholesterol, and, among these older females, the percentage does not vary with age. Among males, only about 1 in 10 has high total cholesterol or is on medication, and the link with age is muted, rising slightly to around age 50 in China and Mexico and not varying much with age in Indonesia. In the United States, the patterns are completely different in two key dimensions. First, the percentage with high total cholesterol or on medication rises dramatically with age from about 1 in 10 among younger adults (aged 30–39 years) to more than half of older adults (aged 70–79 years). The majority of this age gradient reflects higher rates of medication use among older adults: among those who either have high total cholesterol or are on medication, 15% of those in their thirties and 80% of those in their seventies are controlling cholesterol with medication. Second, the female disadvantage in total cholesterol in Indonesia, China, and Mexico is not apparent in the United States.

The optimal cutoff to identify elevated health risks is not clear, and it is not obvious that a single cutoff is appropriate across all settings included in the figure. We present estimates using a cutoff rather than levels of measured total cholesterol because methods for adjusting measured levels for medication use have not been established. Selecting a lower cutoff (≥200 mg/dL) increases the percentage of the population with elevated risks to between 35% and 40% in Indonesia, China, and Mexico and to about 60% in the United States (including those on medication) but has little impact on the comparisons across countries and demographic groups.

The relationships between high total cholesterol and education, adjusted for age, are displayed in Figure 22.4c. For males and females in China and the United States, the education gradients are not significantly different from zero. In Indonesia, for both males and females, the percentage of the population with high total cholesterol rises with education (by 0.7 percentage points for each year of education). In Mexico, the percentage rises at lower levels of education for females but rises very dramatically at higher levels of education among males. Controlling for age, one-quarter of Mexican males has high levels of total cholesterol[3] (Perova et al., 2001; Witeolar et al., 2012; Yan et al., 2012).

22.6.2 Glycosylated Hemoglobin (HbA1c)

The prevalence of diabetes mellitus, which is indicated by poor control of blood glucose levels, is thought to be growing rapidly in both developed and developing countries. This reflects, in part, aging of populations (since the prevalence of type 2 diabetes rises with age) and the worldwide epidemic of obesity (a powerful diabetes risk factor). The majority of population-based estimates of glucose metabolism have relied on fasting blood samples, which are complicated to collect in a field setting. Several recent studies have relied on glycosylated hemoglobin (HbA1c), which can be assessed without fasting. HbA1c is a measure of plasma glucose concentration which, in turn, is indicative of average blood glucose levels over the previous 3 months. HbA1c levels are elevated when

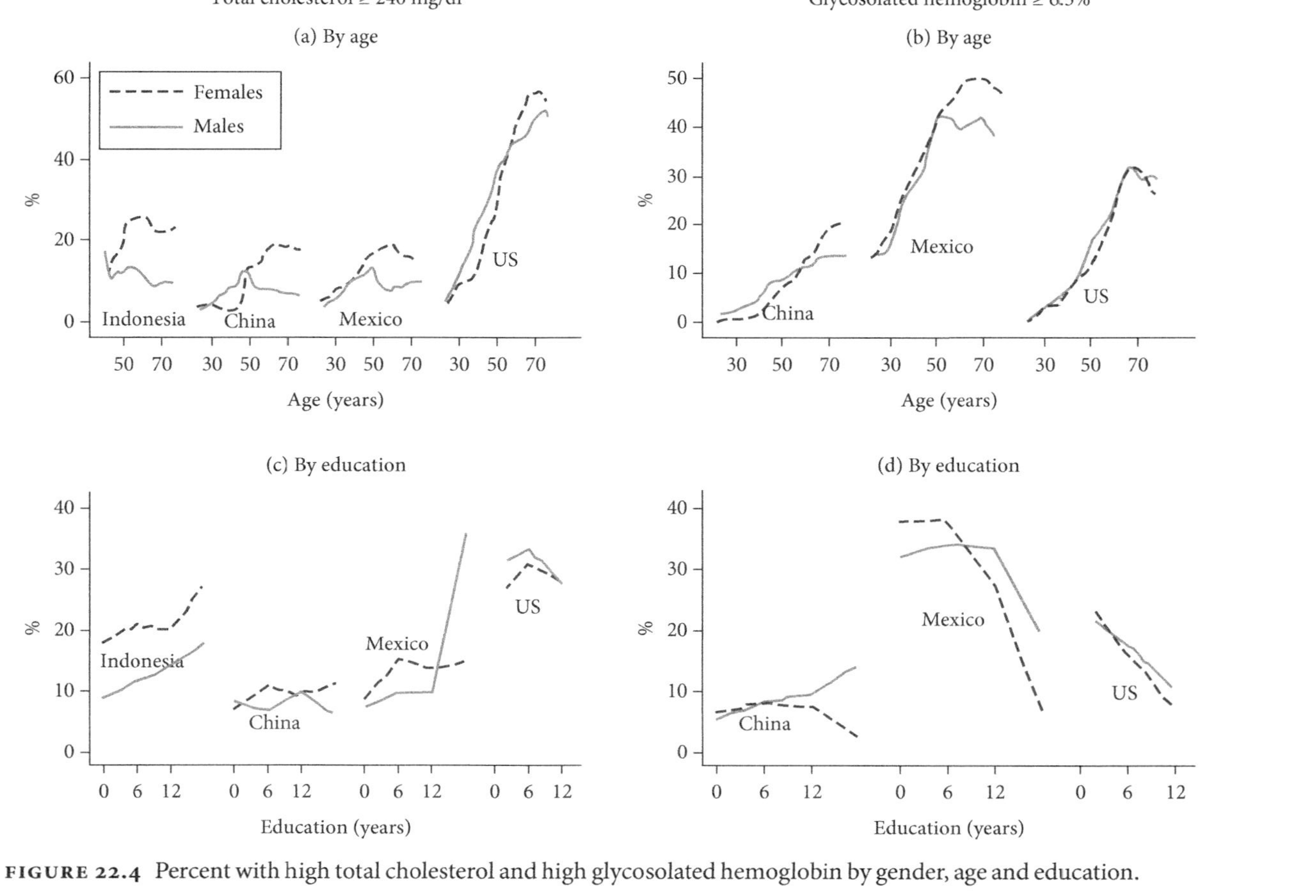

FIGURE 22.4 Percent with high total cholesterol and high glycosolated hemoglobin by gender, age and education.

blood glucose levels are not controlled and are used to indicate diabetes mellitus, which is associated with cardiovascular disease, kidney disease, and retinopathy (Khaw et al., 2004; Rohlfing et al., 2000; Selvin et al., 2010).

Figures 22.4b and 22.4d display the percentages of the population with measured HbA1c that is elevated (≥6.5%) or who report being on medication to control blood sugar in China, Mexico, and the United States. Assays were conducted immediately after collection of blood in China and the United States using high-performance liquid chromatography (HPLC) and were conducted in the home using the in2it A1c Analyzer in Mexico. Measures using the in2it A1c Analyzer have been shown to correlate well with HPLC assessments (Martin, Leroy, Sulmont, & Gillery, 2010).

Diabetes is usually indicated when two recordings of HbA1c are at least 6.5%; however, the data used here are based on a single measure for each respondent. Nonetheless, the first and most striking fact is that rates of elevated HbA1c are extremely high in Mexico: fully one-third of adults aged 30 through 79 are likely to suffer from diabetes. This is about twice the rate in the United States, which, in turn, is about twice the rate in China. In all three countries, elevated HbA1c rises with age, although the rates decline at older ages among Mexican and American males. Other than for older Mexicans, there are no differences between males and females. Only a small fraction of adults who report themselves as controlling blood sugar with medication do not have elevated HbA1c: 1% in China, 2% in Mexico, and only 4% in the United States. In fact, more than 70% of the people who have elevated HbA1c in the United States also report taking medication, and they account for more than two-thirds of those who are on medication. Clearly, rates of elevated blood sugar levels are very high in Mexico and the United States, even in the presence of diagnoses and medication. Moreover, clinical trials have not demonstrated clear benefits to lowering glycosylated hemoglobin using diabetes medications among diabetic patients (Action to Control Cardiovascular Risk in Diabetes Study Group, 2008; Selvin et al., 2008).

As shown in Figure 22.4d, conditional on age, uncontrolled blood sugar or being on medication tends to decline with education among females, particularly in the United States and among Mexican females with at least primary schooling. Among males, the rates rise with education among Chinese, are unrelated to education among Mexicans with high school education or less and then decline, and decline with education among Americans. These patterns are similar to those observed for BMI. Specifically, elevated health risks switch from rising with education to declining with education as levels of development increase, and females tend to be on the vanguard of this switch (Barquera et al., 2013; Yan et al., 2012).

The extremely high levels of elevated HbA1c among Mexicans adults, particularly those in their forties and fifties and among those with less education, is profoundly troubling. Diabetes ranks among the top three causes of death in Mexico (Sistema Nacional de Información en Salud, 2007). Given the close link between diabetes and both age and obesity, as developing countries like Mexico age and as obesity levels also rise in other countries that are aging, diabetes is likely to become a very serious burden on individuals, their families, the health system, and the public sector budget. It is not too early to experiment with and evaluate policies that have the potential to affect these patterns.

22.6.3 C-Reactive Protein

Our final biological risk factor is a marker of inflammation, CRP. Inflammation arises whenever there is an infection or injury and is a defensive response to a potentially harmful challenge. Acute inflammation occurs when increased blood and leukocytes are transported to the tissues that are under assault, and the biological system returns to its normal state within a few days. Prolonged or chronic inflammation occurs when acute inflammation persists rather than resolving, which typically results in tissue damage or destruction. Acute inflammatory processes have been implicated in atherosclerosis and the pathogenesis of cardiovascular disease. Chronic inflammation reflects disease history and risks for future disease, because chronic activation of inflammatory pathways may be set off by early exposure to infectious diseases (Crimmins & Finch, 2006). Inflammation is also elevated among those who are overweight and obese, as well as in those who are currently exposed to an infection or injury. Inflammation is, therefore, a general marker of health and may be a valuable complement to BMI and self-reported health status to indicate overall population health.

CRP is one of many potential markers of inflammation. It is an acute phase protein that reflects general systemic inflammatory response. Part of the immune response to infection, tissue damage, and injury involves increases in circulating levels of CRP. Elevated levels of CRP have been found to be positively associated with cardiovascular disease incidence including myocardial infarction, stroke and peripheral arterial disease; diabetes; metabolic syndrome; and mortality in adults (Alley et al., 2006; Jenny et al., 2007; Kuller, Tracy, Shaten, & Meilahn, 1996; Pradhan, Manson, Rifai, Buring, & Ridker, 2001; Ridker, Buring, Cook, & Rifai, 2003; Ridker, Hennekens, Buring, & Rifai, 2000).

Because chronic inflammation occurs over the entire life course, we present CRP levels for all ages for the countries with CRP measures—Indonesia, China, and the United States—in Figure 22.5a. The percentage of the population with CRP equal to or greater than 3 mg/L, a cutoff indicating chronic inflammation, is displayed. In each country, elevated CRP rates decline during the first few years of life and then rise after around age 10. In China, the rise is steep throughout the life course, and, in the United States, the increase tapers off in early middle age but remains elevated. In Indonesia, there is much less variation with age. At each age, the probability of elevated CRP is similar in China and America but is substantially lower in Indonesia. Overall, only 10% of the Indonesian population has elevated CRP, whereas in China and the United States, the rates exceed 25% and peak for American females around age 65, when half suffer from elevated inflammation.[4]

Gender differences in CRP are relatively small in Indonesia and China, but high levels of CRP are much more common among female adults relative to males in the United States. Patterns by education are displayed in Figure 22.5b, controlling age and gender and restricting the sample to adults aged 30 through 79 (to assure education has been completed). Elevated inflammation declines substantially with education in the United

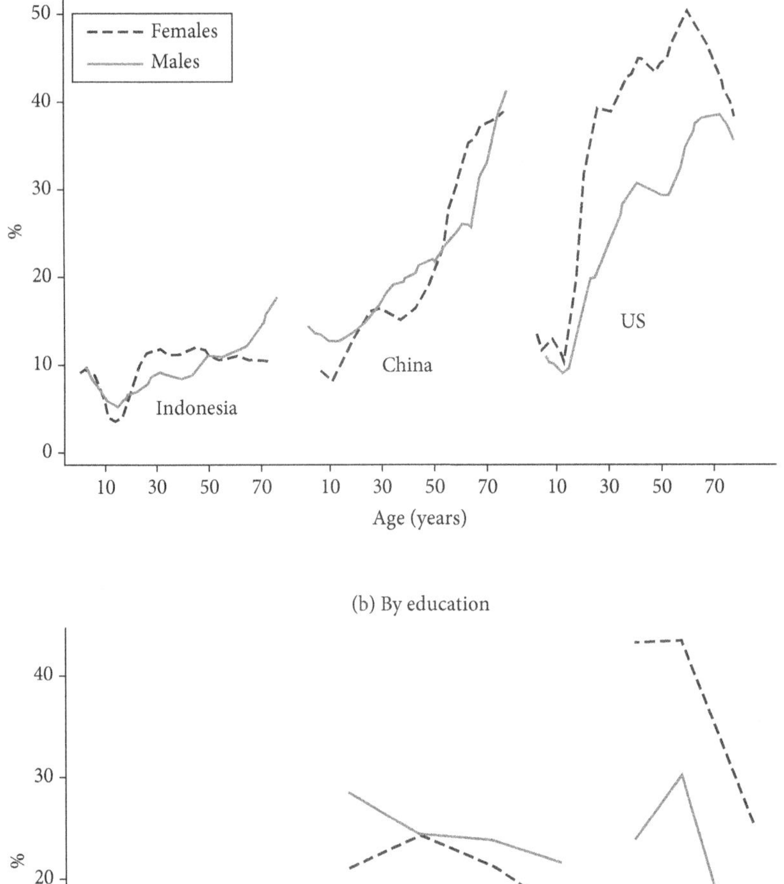

FIGURE 22.5 Percent with high levels of inflammation by gender, age and education (C-reactive protein > 3 mg/dl).

States, modestly in China, and is essentially unrelated to education in Indonesia (Nazmi & Victora, 2007; Yan et al., 2012).

22.7 BMI AND THE OTHER BIOMARKERS

As the epidemic of obesity spreads across the globe, increases in BMI will likely be accompanied by higher rates of NCDs. It is, therefore, of substantial interest to compare the associations between BMI and the other biomarkers across countries. Nonparametric estimates of the associations for each country are presented for hypertension in Figure 22.6 and for elevated HbA1c, total cholesterol, and CRP in Figure 22.7. The estimates, which adjust for age and gender, are displayed for adults aged 30 through 79. For hypertension, total cholesterol, and HbA1c, the percentages include those who report being on medication to control the risk factor. Generally speaking, as BMI increases, the fraction of the population with elevated levels of each of the four biological risks also increases for every country. Consequently, the global epidemic of obesity is likely to be accompanied by elevated rates of hypertension, metabolic health problems, and inflammation.

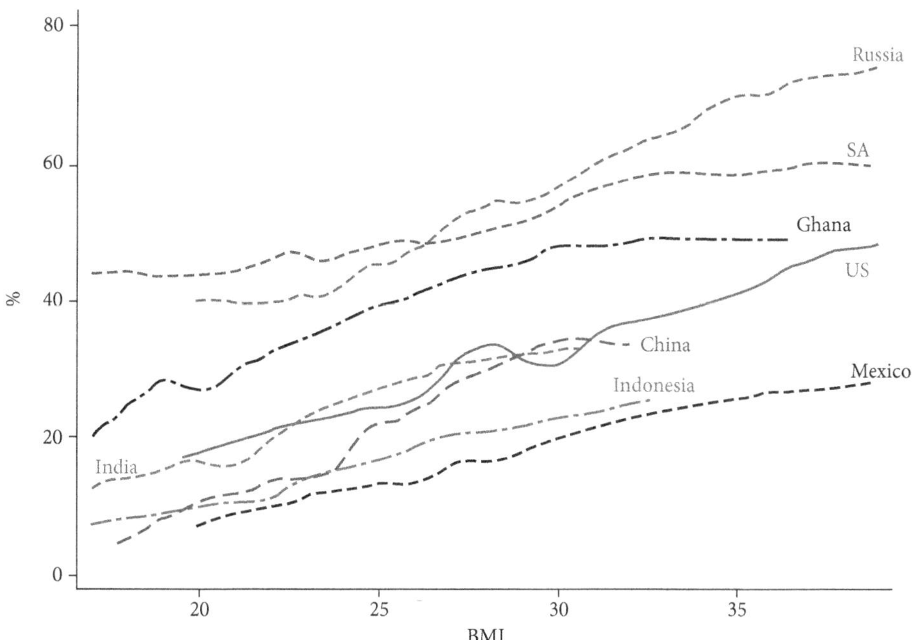

FIGURE 22.6 Relationship between percent hypertensive and BMI.

Note: Hypertensive is stage 2 hypertensive, defined as systolic blood pressure > 160 mmHg and/or diastolic blood pressure > 100 mmHg.

As shown in Figure 22.6, as BMI increases, hypertension rates rise at roughly the same rate in each country so that, for example, if average BMI for a country increases from 25 to 30, it will be accompanied by a 10 percentage point increase in the share of the population that is hypertensive. In part, the slopes reflect biological links between BMI and hypertension.

Another striking feature of the figure is the tremendous heterogeneity across countries in the level of hypertension for any particular BMI. There are three main groups of countries. First, for any BMI, adults in Indonesia and Mexico are the least likely to be hypertensive: as an example, among those whose BMI is 30 kg/m^2, about 20% are hypertensive. Second, in the United States, India, and China, hypertension rates are higher, with the risk rising to 30% for those with BMI of 30 kg/m^2. Third, in Ghana, Russia, and South Africa, hypertension rates are very high, with the risk being around 50% at this BMI level. These very large gaps across countries likely reflect variation in lifestyle such as diet, exercise, and stress; use of health care; and possibly genetic differences. Patterns in China suggest that lifestyle differences are central. At low levels of BMI, hypertension rates in China are very similar to those in the lowest group, Mexico and Indonesia, but at high levels of BMI, hypertension rates are as high as in the second group, the United States and India. The rapid rise in hypertension among heavier Chinese is a serious concern and presumably reflects the impact of lifestyle differences among those who are overweight and obese relative to those who are not. Moreover, the dual burden of elevated BMI and hypertension in the third and possibly second group of countries will elicit a heavy price in terms of population well-being, health care costs, and, possibly, economic productivity in the years to come.

As shown in Figure 22.7a, HbA1c also rises with BMI. The rate of increase is essentially identical for all three countries—Mexico, China, and the United States—except, perhaps, at very high levels of BMI in Mexico, where the curve is much flatter. A 1 unit increase in average BMI for a country is associated with a 1 percentage point increase in the share of the population with elevated HbA1c. Conditional on BMI, rates of elevated HbA1c are the same in China and the United States but about twice as high in Mexico. This is not likely to be driven by genetic differences because, controlling BMI, there are only small differences in the incidence of elevated HbA1c among white Americans and Mexican-origin Americans in NHANES. To the extent that the gap is not due to differences in measurement, it is likely that diet, behavior, and lifestyle factors play a role. As BMI rises in Mexico, this evidence suggests that it will be accompanied by high rates of diabetes, which will likely impose a very large burden on the society.

The relationship between elevated total cholesterol and BMI is displayed in Figure 22.7b. As BMI increases, elevated cholesterol rates rise and then decline; the point of inflection is at lower levels of BMI in China, Indonesia, and Mexico (between 25 and 30 kg/m^2) than in the United States (30 kg/m^2). At every level of BMI, cholesterol rates are much higher in the United States and lowest in China and Mexico, with Indonesia lying between these extremes.

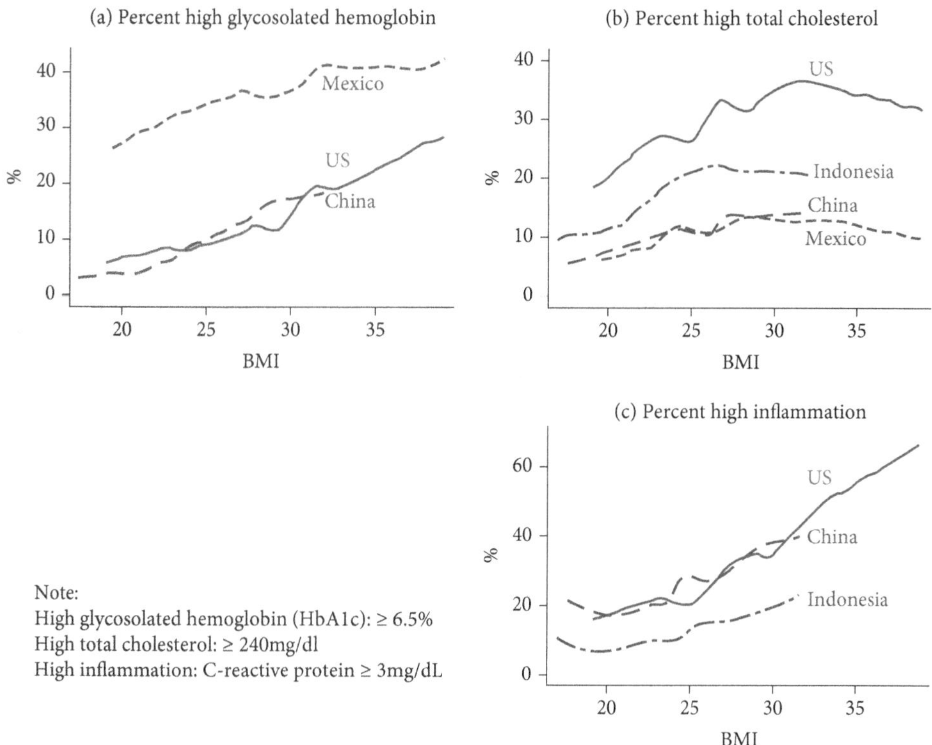

FIGURE 22.7 Relationship between blood-based biomarkers and BMI.

Finally, Figure 7c displays the relationship between BMI and inflammation. In all three countries, the relationship is flat until BMI reaches 25 and then rises. Given BMI, the rates of inflammation are essentially identical in the United States and China but much lower in Indonesia. It is not clear what explains this difference, and it is possible that it reflects differences in measurement.

22.8 Conclusion

The evidence summarized in the figures suggests three main conclusions. First, as the epidemic of obesity reaches more and more parts of the globe and as levels of BMI rise in lower income countries, the burden of NCDs will also rise in roughly predictable ways. The costs to individual, families, and society are likely to be very large indeed. There is an urgent need for a coordinated global effort to design, implement, and evaluate programs and policies that will forestall those costs.

Second, there are important cross-country differences in the relationships among these biomarkers, which likely reflect differences in health conditions, the costs and organization of health care services, and possibly socioeconomic, demographic, and genetic heterogeneity. Understanding the factors that underlie these differences remains an important open question, and new insights into these factors and mechanisms have the potential to yield powerful scientific and policy conclusions regarding population health.

Third, the technology exists to measure major biological markers of health and well-being in even complex field studies, but there is only limited evidence on these risk factors in population-based studies. To be sure, there are significant measurement challenges, and there is considerable work to be done to cross-validate different measures in different settings. Such investments are likely to have a major impact on scientific understanding of the complex interplay among biology, health, and development.

Acknowledgments

Ho is grateful for financial support from the National Institute on Aging (grant T32AG000139 awarded to the Duke Population Research Institute). The comments of Eileen Crimmins, Arun Hendi, Sam Harper, John Komlos, and Teresa Seeman have been very helpful.

Notes

1. Although measurement with a stethoscope and sphygmomanometer is considered the gold standard, the method requires considerable training. It is used in NHANES. In field settings, blood pressure has been measured using automated home monitors with an inflatable cuff placed around the bicep. The monitors are inexpensive, robust, well-validated, and straightforward to use. In the Indonesian, Mexican, South African, and SAGE surveys, blood pressure was measured using an Omron monitor with multisize cuffs to allow for variation in bicep size in the study populations.
2. Doubly labeled water contains a known concentration of stable isotypes of hydrogen and oxygen. As energy is expended, the body produces carbon dioxide and water, and the differences in the isotype elimination rates provide an estimate of total energy expenditure.
3. Using data from the same four countries, we have also explored levels of HDL cholesterol, the "good" cholesterol, low levels of which are risk factors for poor health outcomes. Using 40 g/dL as a cutoff, about one-quarter of Chinese and one-half of Americans have low levels of HDL (or cholesterol is controlled with medication). In Indonesia and Mexico, more than two-thirds of the population is estimated to have low levels of HDL. Although it is possible that this reflects high levels of infection in Indonesia and Mexico, the estimate for Mexico is higher than other estimates from that country. The fact that both the Mexican and Indonesian studies used the CardioChek Analyzer and blood was analyzed in the lab in the Chinese and American studies suggests the differences may reflect differences in measurement protocols. This underscores the importance of future research that validates

biomarker measurement protocols in field settings, taking account of variation in temperature, humidity, and handling of materials.

4. The substantially lower rates of elevated inflammation in Indonesia relative to China and the United States are surprising given that overall infection rates are higher in Indonesia. They may reflect collection and assay differences; while the reported estimates are designed to be translated into comparable units, CRP is measured from plasma in China and the United States but from DBS in Indonesia.

References

Action to Control Cardiovascular Risk in Diabetes Study Group. (2008). Effects of intensive glucose lowering in type 2 diabetes. *New England Journal of Medicine, 358*, 2545–2559.

Addo, J., Smeeth, L., & Leon. D. A. (2007). Hypertension in sub-Saharan Africa: A systematic review. *Hypertension, 50*, 1012–1018.

Alley, D. E., Seeman, T. E., Kim, J. K., Karlamangla, A., Hu, P., & Crimmins, E. M. (2006). Socioeconomic status and C-reactive protein levels in the US population: NHANES IV. *Brain, Behavior, and Immunity, 20*, 498–504.

Anderson, K. M., Castelli, W. P., & Levy, D. (1987). Cholesterol and mortality: 30 years of follow-up from the Framingham Study. *Journal of the American Medical Association, 257*(16), 2176–2180.

Barquera, S., Campos-Nonato, I., Aguilar-Salinas, C., Lopez-Riadaura, R., Arredondo, A., & Rivera-Dommarco, J. (2013). Diabetes in Mexico: Cost and management of diabetes and its complications and challenges for health policy. *Globalization and Health, 9*, 3.

Barter, P. J., & Rye, K. A. (1996). High density lipoproteins and coronary heart disease. *Atherosclerosis, 121*(1), 1–12.

Baten, J., & Blum, M. (2014). Why are you tall while others are short? Agricultural production and other proximate determinants of global heights. *European Review of Economic History, 18*(2), 144–165.

Blacher, J., Staessen, J. A., Girer, X., Gasowski, J., Thijs, L., Liu, L., . . . Safer. M. E. (2000). Pulse pressure not mean pressure determines cardiovascular risk in older hypertensive patients. *Archives of Internal Medicine, 160*(8), 1085–1089.

Black, A. E., Welch, A. A., & Bingham, S. A. (2000). Validation of dietary intakes measured by diet history against 24 h urinary nitrogen excretion and energy expenditure measured by the doubly-labelled water method in middle-aged women. *British Journal of Nutrition, 83*(4), 341–354.

Bridges, N., Parvin, R. M., & Van Assendelft, O. W. (1987). Evaluation of a new system for hemoglobin measurement. *American Clinical Products Review, 6*(4), 22–25.

Busingye, D., Arabshahi, S., Subasinghe, A. K., Evans, R. G., Riddell, M. A., & Thrift, A. G. (2014). Do the socioeconomic and hypertension gradients in rural populations of low- and middle-income countries differ by geographical region? A systematic review and meta-analysis. *International Journal of Epidemiology, 43*(5), 1563–1577.

Castelli, W. P., Garrison, R. J., Wilson, P. W. F., Abbott, R. D., Kalousdian, S., & Kannel, W. B. (1986). Incidence of coronary heart disease and lipoprotein cholesterol levels. *Journal of the American Medical Association, 256*(20), 2835–2838.

Cleveland, W. S. (1979). Robust locally weighted regression and smoothing scatterplots. *Journal of the American Statistical Association, 74*(368), 829–836.

Colhoun, H. M., Hemingway, H., & Poulter, N. R. (1998). Socio-economic status and blood pressure: An overview analysis. *Journal of Human Hypertension, 12*, 91–110.

Crimmins, E. (2014). Physiological differences across populations reflecting early life and later life nutritional status and later life risk for chronic disease. *Population Ageing, 8*, 51–69.

Crimmins, E., Kim, J. K., & Vasunilashorn, S. (2010). Biodemography: New approaches to understanding trends and differences in population health and mortality. *Demography, 47*, S41–S64.

Crimmins, E., & Seeman, T. (2004). Integrating biology into the study of health disparities. *Population and Development Review, 30*, 89–107.

Crimmins, E., Wheaton, F., Vasunilashorn, S., Beltram-Sanchez, H., Zhang, L., & Kim, J. K. (2013). A global perspective on physiological change with age. In S. McDaniel & Z. Zimmer (Eds.), *Global ageing in the twenty first century*. Farnham: Ashgate.

Crimmins, E. M., & Finch, C. E. (2006). Infection, inflammation, height, and longevity. *Proceedings of the National Academy of Sciences, 103*(2), 498–503.

Dey, D. K., Rothenberg, E., Sundh, V., Bosaeus, I., & Steen, B. (2002). Waist circumference, body mass index, and risk for stroke in older people. *Journal of the American Geriatric Society, 50*, 1510–1518.

Dow, W., Gertler, P., Schoeni, R., Strauss, J., & Thomas, D. (2010). *Health prices, health outcomes and labor outcomes: Experimental evidence*. Mimeo, UCLA.

Feingold, K. R., & Grunfeld, C. (2011). The role of HDL in innate immunity. *Journal of Lipid Research, 52*(1), 1–3.

Flegal, K. M., Carroll, M. D., Ogden, C. L., & Curtis, L. R. (2010). Prevalence and trends in obesity among U.S. adults, 1999–2008. *Journal of the American Medical Association, 303*, 234–241.

Floud, R., Fogel, R., Harris, B., & Hong, S. C. (2011). The changing body: Health, nutrition and human development in the Western World since 1700. Cambridge: Cambridge University Press.

Fogel, R. (1994). Economic growth, population theory and physiology: The bearing of long-term processes on the making of economic policy. *American Economic Review, 84*(3), 369–395.

Franklin, S. S., Khan, S. A., Wong, N. D., Larson, M. G., & Levy, D. (1999). Is pulse pressure useful in predicting risk for coronary heart disease? The Framingham heart study. *Circulation, 100*(4), 354–360.

Gordon, D. J., Probstfield, J. L., Garrison, R. J., Neaton, J. D., Castelli, W. P., Knoke, J. D., ... Tyroler, H. A. (1989). High-density lipoprotein cholesterol and cardiovascular disease. *Circulation, 79*, 8–15.

Guthrie, R., & Susi, A. (1963). A simple phenylalanine method for detecting phenylketonuria in large populations of newborn infants. *Pediatrics, 32*, 338–343.

Hill, R. J., & Davies, P. S. W. (2001). The validity of self-reported energy intake as determined using the doubly labelled water technique. *British Journal of Nutrition, 85*(4), 415–430.

Ibrahim, M. M., Rizk, H., Appel, L. J., El Aroussy, W., Helmy, S., Sharaf, Y., ... Whelton, P. K. (1995). Hypertension prevalence, awareness, treatment, and control in Egypt. *Hypertension, 26*, 886–890.

Idler, E. L., & Benyamini, Y. (1997). Self-rated health and mortality: A review of twenty-seven community studies. *Journal of Health and Social Behavior, 38*, 21–37.

Ikeda, N., Sapienza, D., Guerrero, R., Aekplakorn, W., Naghavi, M., Mokdad, A. H., et al. (2014). Control of hypertension with medication: A comparative analysis of national surveys in 20 countries. *Bulletin of the World Health Organization*, *92*, 10–19C.

Izzo, J. L., Levy, D., & Black, H. R. (2000). Importance of systolic blood pressure in older Americans. *Hypertension*, *35*, 1021–1024.

Jellinger, P. S., Smith, D. A., Mehta, A., Ganda, O., Handelsman, Y., Rodbard, H. W., . . . the AACE Task Force for Management of Dyslipidemia and Prevention of Atherosclerosis. (2012). American Association of Clinical Endocrinologists' guidelines for management of dyslipidemia and prevention of atherosclerosis. *Endocrine Practice*, *18*(Suppl 1), 1–78.

Jenny, N. S., Yanez, N. D., Psaty, B. M., Kuller, L. H., Hirsch, C. H., & Tracy, R. P. (2007). Inflammation biomarkers and near-term death in older men. *American Journal of Epidemiology*, *165*(6), 684–695.

Kannel, W. B. (2000). Fifty years of Framingham Study contributions to understanding hypertension. *Journal of Human Hypertension*, *14*, 83–90.

Khaw, K. -T., Wareham, N., Bingham, S., Luben, R., Welch, A., & Day, N. (2004). Association of hemoglobin A1c with cardiovascular disease and mortality in adults: The European prospective investigation into cancer in Norfolk. *Annals of Internal Medicine*, *141*, 413–420.

Komlos, J. (1985). Stature and nutrition in the Habsburg Monarchy: The standard of living and economic development in the eighteenth century. *American Historical Review*, *90*(5), 1149–1161.

Komlos, J., & Baten, J. (1998). *The biological standard of living in comparative perspective*. Stuttgart, DE: Franz Steiner Verlag.

Kowal, P., Chatterji, S., Naidoo, N., Biritwum, R., Fan, W., Lopez Ridaura, R., . . . the SAGE Collaborators. (2012). Data resource profile: The World Health Organization Study on global AGEing and adult health (SAGE). *International Journal of Epidemiology*, *41*, 1639–1649.

Kuller, L. H., Tracy, R. P., Shaten, J., & Meilahn, E. N. (1996). Relation of C-reactive protein and coronary heart disease in the MRFIT nested case-control study. *American Journal of Epidemiology*, *144*(6), 537–547.

Lee, J., Arokiasamy, P., Chandra, A., Hu, P., Liu, J., & Feeney, K. (2012). Markers and drivers: Cardiovascular health of middle-aged and older Indians. In J. P. Smith & M. Majmundar (Eds.), *Aging in Asia: Findings from new and emerging data initiatives* (pp. 387–414). Washington, DC: The National Academies Press.

Leibbrandt, M., Woolard, I., & de Villiers, L. (2009). National Income Dynamics Study Technical Papers No. 1–6. Retrieved from http://www.nids.uct.ac.za/publications/technical-papers, South African Labor and Development Research Unit, University of Cape Town.

Levy, D., Larson, M. G., Vasan, R. S., Kannel, W. B., & Ho, K. K. L. (1996). The progression from hypertension to congestive heart failure. *Journal of the American Medical Association*, *275*(20), 1557–1562.

Lloyd-Sherlock, P., Beard, J., Minicuci, N., Ebrahim, S., & Chatterji, S. (2014). Hypertension among older adults in low- and middle-income countries: Prevalence, awareness and control. *International Journal of Epidemiology*, *43*, 116–128.

Martin, M., Leroy, N., Sulmont, V., & Gillery, P. (2010). Evaluation of the In2it analyzer for HbA1c determination. *Diabetes Metabolism*, *36*(2), 158–164.

Martorell, R., & Habicht, J. -P. (1986). Growth in early childhood in developing countries. In F. Falkner & J. Tanner (Eds.), *Human growth: A comprehensive treatise* (2nd ed., pp. 241–262). New York: Plenum.

McDade, T. W., & Hayward, M. D. (2009). Rational and methodological options for assessing infectious disease and related measures in social science surveys. *Biodemography and Social Biology*, *55*(2), 159–177.

McDade, T. W., Williams, S., & Snodgrass, J. J. (2007). What a drop can do: Dried blood spots as a minimally-invasive method for integration biomarkers into population-based research. *Demography*, *44*, 899–925.

McEwen, B. (1998). Protective and damaging effects of stress mediators. *New England Journal of Medicine*, *338*(3), 171–179.

McEwen, B., & Stellar, E. (1993). Stress and the individual: Mechanisms leading to disease. *Archives of Internal Medicine*, *153*(18), 2093–2101.

Must, A., Spadano, J., Coakley, E. H., Field, A. E., Colditz, G., & Dietz, W. H. (1999). The disease burden associated with overweight and obesity. *Journal of the American Medical Association*, *282*(16), 1523–1529.

Nazmi, A., & Victora, C. G. (2007). Socioeconomic and racial/ethnic differentials of C-reactive protein levels: A systematic review of population-based studies. *BMC Public Health*, *7*, 212.

Ng, M., Fleming, T., Robinson, M., Thomson, B., Graetz, N., Margono, C., . . . Gakidou, E. (2014). Global, regional and national prevalence of overweight and obesity in children and adults during 1980–2013: A systematic analysis for the Global Burden of Disease Study, 2013. *Lancet*, *384*(9945), 766–781.

Perova, N. V., Davis, C. E., Tao, S., Pajak, A., Stein, Y., Broda, G. B., Li, Y., & Tyroler, H. A. (2001). Multi-country comparison of plasma lipid relationship to years of schooling in men and women. *International Journal of Epidemiology*, *30*, 371–379.

Popkin, B. M. (2001). The nutrition transition and obesity in the developing world. *Journal of Nutrition*, *131*, 871S–873S.

Popkin, B. M., Adair, L., & Ng, S. (2012). Global nutrition transition and the pandemic of obesity in developing countries. *Nutrition Reviews*, *70*, 3–21.

Popkin, B. M., & Gordon-Larsen, P. (2004). The nutrition transition: Worldwide obesity dynamics and their determinants. *International Journal of Obesity*, *28*(3), S2–S9.

Pradhan, A. D., Manson, J. E., Rifai, N., Buring, J. E., & Ridker, P. M. (2001). C-reactive protein, interleukin 6, and risk of developing type 2 diabetes mellitus. *Journal of the American Medical Association*, *286*, 327–334.

Prentice, A. M. (2006). The emerging epidemic of obesity in developing countries. *International Journal of Epidemiology*, *35*(1), 93–99.

Ridker, P. M., Buring, J. E., Cook, N. R., & Rifai, N. (2003). C-reactive protein, the metabolic syndrome, and risk of incident cardiovascular events. *Circulation*, *107*, 391–397.

Ridker, P. M., Hennekens, C. H., Buring, J. E., & Rifai, N. (2000). C-reactive protein and other markers of inflammation in the prediction of cardiovascular disease in women. *New England Journal of Medicine*, *342*, 836–843.

Rohlfing, C. L., Little, R. R., Wiedmeyer, H. -M., England, J. D., Madsen, R., Harris, M. I., . . . Goldstein, D. E. (2000). Use of GHb (HbA1c) in screening for undiagnosed diabetes in the U.S. population. *Diabetes Care*, *23*(2), 187–191.

Roth, G. A., Forouzanafar, M. H., Moran, A. E., Barber, R., Nguyen. G., Feigin, V. L., . . . Murray C. J. L. (2015). Demographic and epidemiologic drivers of global cardiovascular mortality. *New England Journal of Medicine*, *372*, 1333–1341.

Rubalcava, L., & Teruel, G. (2014). Mexican family life survey: Third round. Working paper. ENNVIH-MxFLS. Retrieved from www.ennvih-mxfls.org.

Selvin, E., Bolen, S., Yeh, H. -C., Wiley, C., Wilson, L. M., Marinopoulos, S. S., . . . Brancati, F. L. (2008). Cardiovascular outcomes in trials of oral diabetes medications: A systematic review. *Archives of Internal Medicine, 168*(19), 2070–2080.

Selvin, E., Steffes, M. W., Zhu, H., Matsushita, K., Wagenknecht, L., Pankow, J., . . . Brancati, F. L. (2010). Glycated hemoglobin, diabetes, and cardiovascular risk in nondiabetic adults. *New England Journal of Medicine, 362*(9), 800–811.

Sistema Nacional de Información en Salud. (2007). Secretaría de Salud. Mexico City: SSA; National Death Registry 2007. Retrieved from http://dgis.salud.gob.mx/descargas/xls/diez-princausasmort2007_CNEGySR.xls.

Steckel, R. H., & Floud, R. (Eds.). (1997). *Health and welfare during industrialization.* Chicago: University of Chicago Press.

Steptoe, A., & Wikman, A. (2011). The contribution of physical activity to divergent trends in longevity. In E. M. Crimmins, S. H. Preston, & B. Cohen. *International differences in mortality at older ages: Dimensions and sources* (pp. 193–216). Washington D.C.: National Academies Press.

Stevenson, D. R. (1999). Blood pressure and age in cross-cultural perspective. *Human Biology, 71*(4), 529–551.

Steyn, K., Bradshaw, D., Norman, R., & Laubscher, R. (2008). Determinants and treatment of hypertension in South Africans: The first demographic and health surveys. *South African Medical Journal, 98*(5), 376–380.

Strauss, J., & Thomas, D. (1998). Health, nutrition and economic development. *Journal of Economic Literature, 36*, 737–782.

Strauss, J., & Thomas, D. (2008). Health over the life course. In T. P. Schultz and J. Strauss (eds.), *Handbook of Development Economics* (vol. 4, pp. 3375–3474). Amsterdam: Elsevier.

Strauss, J., Witoelar, F., Sikoki, B., & Wattie, A. M. (2009). *The fourth wave of the Indonesian Family Life Survey (IFLS4): Overview and field report.* Working paper WR675/1. Santa Monica, CA: RAND.

Thomas, D., & Frankenberg, E. (2002). The measurement and interpretation of health in social surveys. In C. Murray, J. Salomon, C. Mathers, & A. Lopez (Eds.) *Summary measures of population health: Concepts, ethics, measurement and applications* (pp. 387–420). Geneva: World Health Organization.

Thomas, D., & Strauss, J. (1997). Health and wages: Evidence on men and women in urban Brazil. *Journal of Econometrics, 77*(1), 159–185.

Toth, P. P. (2005). The "good cholesterol": High-density lipoprotein. *Circulation, 111*, E89–E91.

Waaler, H. T. (1984). Height, weight and mortality. *Acta Medica Scandinavica, 215*, 1–56.

Weverling-Rijnsburger, A. W. E., Jonkers, I. J. A. M., van Exel, E., Gussekloo, J., & Westendorp, R. G. J. (2003). High-density vs low-density lipoprotein cholesterol as the risk factor for coronary artery disease and stroke in old age. *Archives of Internal Medicine, 163*, 1549–1554.

Wiehl, D. G., & Reed, R. (1960). Development of new or improved dietary methods for epidemiological investigations. *American Journal of Public Health, 50*, 824–828.

Witoelar, F., Strauss, J., & Sikoki, B. (2012). Socioeconomic success and health in later life: Evidence from the Indonesia Family Life Survey. In J. P. Smith & M. Majmundar (Eds.), *Aging in Asia: Findings from new and emerging data initiatives* (pp. 309–341). Washington, DC: The National Academies Press.

World Health Organization (WHO). (1999). *Obesity: Preventing and managing the global epidemic: Report of a WHO consultation.* WHO Technical Report No. 894. Geneva, Switzerland: Author.

Wu, Y., Huxley, R., Li, L., Anna, V., Xie, G., Yao, C., . . . Yang, X. (2008). Prevalence, awareness, treatment, and control of hypertension in China. *Circulation*, *118*, 2679–2686.

Yan, S., Li, J., Li, S., Zhang, B., Du, S., Gordon-Larsen, P., Adair, L., & Popkin, B. (2012). The expanding burden of cardiometabolic risk in China: The China Health and Nutrition Survey. *Obesity Reviews*, *13*, 810–821.

CHAPTER 23

OBESITY AND INCOME INEQUALITY IN OECD COUNTRIES

DEJUN SU

THE twentieth century witnessed a substantial improvement in nutritional status in developed countries. Among white American males, average adult body mass index (BMI) increased from 22.6 in the late nineteenth century to 28.0 at the end of the twentieth century (Su, 2005). With threats from malnutrition gradually fading, overnutrition, as indicated by an unprecedented prevalence of obesity, arouses serious concerns. It has been estimated that the overall costs incurred by obesity in the United States now amount to about US$150 billion, more than 1% of annual gross national product (GDP; Sassi, 2010). Despite numerous studies on factors contributing to obesity, little research has assessed if and the extent to which obesity might be related to income distribution (Volland, 2012). Such a topic is of particular relevance in consideration of growing income inequality since the 1970s (Frank, 2009; Stone, Trisi, Sherman, & DeBot, 2014) and the concurrent increase in obesity throughout member nations of the Organization for Economic Cooperation and Development (OECD). This chapter starts with an overview of theoretical frameworks relating income inequality to obesity, followed by a review of relevant empirical findings in the United States and other OECD countries.

23.1 Potential Pathways Through Which Income Inequality Impacts Obesity

Previous studies have documented an ecological association between income distribution and population health and mortality (e.g., Kahn, Wise, Kennedy, & Kawachi, 2000; Kaplan, Pamuk, Lynch, Cohen, & Balfour, 1996; Kawachi, Kennedy, Lochner, &

Prothrow-Stith, 1997; Lynch & Kaplan, 1997; Rodgers, 2002; Subramanian, Blakely, & Kawachi, 2003; Wilkinson, 1992). Based on a review of 168 analyses on this topic, Wilkinson and Pickett (2006) found that a large majority (78%) of these studies were wholly or partially supportive of the observation that, after adjusting for differences in per capita income across countries or regions within the same country, health was worse in countries or regions where income differences were larger. This body of literature also offers insights into the potential impact of income distribution on obesity, as detailed herein.

23.1.1 Stress as a Mediator Between Income Inequality and Obesity

The *relative income hypothesis* postulated by Wilkinson (1997) maintains that in developed countries, where most people's living standard has already surpassed a minimum threshold level required to meet the basic needs of decent living, it is the relative rather than absolute income that is more relevant in explaining disparities in health and mortality. Given any average absolute income level, a higher level of income inequality tends to result in a greater prevalence of psychosocial distress and can pose a threat to health. According to this hypothesis, people's sense of achievement and happiness is usually derived from a relative context, from comparisons with other people. It follows that in societies with severe income inequality, except for those on the top of the income and wealth ladder, most others will develop a sense of relative deprivation or even chronic stress. Williams (1990) highlighted the importance of health behaviors, stress, social ties, and attitudinal orientations as critical links between social structure and health status. It was also argued that these psychosocial factors are linked more strongly to health status than is medical care and are related systematically to socioeconomic status (SES). House (2002) identified four psychosocial risk factors for health: (1) social relationships and support, (2) acute or event-based stress, (3) chronic stress in work and life, and (4) psychological dispositions such as anger and hostility, lack of self-efficacy and control, and hopelessness and pessimism. Income inequality and its severity can impact exposure to each of these four psychosocial risk factors. Furthermore, the relative price of medical care and organic food could be positively correlated with income inequality because the rich will pursue these superior goods virtually regardless of how expensive they are (Waldmann, 1992). In a market-driven economy, nutritious and scarce food, such as certain kinds of seafood, can be so expensive that they are usually out of the reach of those in poverty.

Stress happens when "environmental demands tax or exceed the adaptive capacity of an organism, resulting in psychological and biological changes that may place persons at risk for diseases" (Cohen, Kessler, & Gordon, 1998). Sociological studies of stress presume the negative effects of stress on health as a given and are mainly concerned about the social distribution of stress and its determinants. The prevailing paradigm of sociological study of the stress process consists of three components: stressors (exposure), mediators (coping and support), and outcome (psychosocial distress and negative health behavior) (Lennon, 1989; Pearlin, 1989). By contrast, biomedical studies of stress treat the existence of stress as a given and focus more on the biomarkers and health consequences of stress.

Chronic stress can increase the risk for obesity, especially upper body obesity, and other metabolic diseases through alterations in the hypothalamic–pituitary–adrenal (HPA) axis (Bose, Oliván, & Laferrère, 2009). Rising levels of psychological distress have been suggested as a cause of the ongoing rise in obesity prevalence within wealthy societies (Dallman et al., 2004). The importance of SES and relative income in obesity is illustrated in Figure 23.1, where the effect of SES and relative income on obesity is primarily mediated through perceived stress, which in turn impacts social capital and support, utilization of health services, and lifestyle factors such as diet and exercise that are directly related to risk of obesity. After all, obesity is not simply caused by having a high-calorie diet, a sedentary life style, or a combination of both. Underlying these symptoms or behaviors is usually something more fundamental—anxieties, psychological distresses, limited health literacy, lack of self-esteem or efficacy, low educational attainment, low income, dysfunctional family, lack of social support—that is intrinsically linked to individual-level SES. At the same time, obesity can also impact stress through feedback effects, SES and relative income, utilization of health services, social capital and support, and lifestyle (including difficulties finding partners). Evidence from psychological experiments indicates that stress can result in overeating, and obese individuals are more likely to resort to eating in time of anxiety (Greeno & Wing, 1994). Distressed individuals have repeatedly been found to alter their eating habits and behavior in favor of easily digestible, calorie-dense foods (Berridge, Ho, Richard, & DiFeliceantonio, 2010; Dallman, 2010; Volland, 2012). These findings are consistent with obesity trends in the United States, where it was revealed that obesity was more prevalent among low-SES and minority groups (Drewnowski & Darmon, 2005; Komlos & Brabec, 2011; Stunkard, 2007; Zhang & Wang, 2004). There is evidence that the

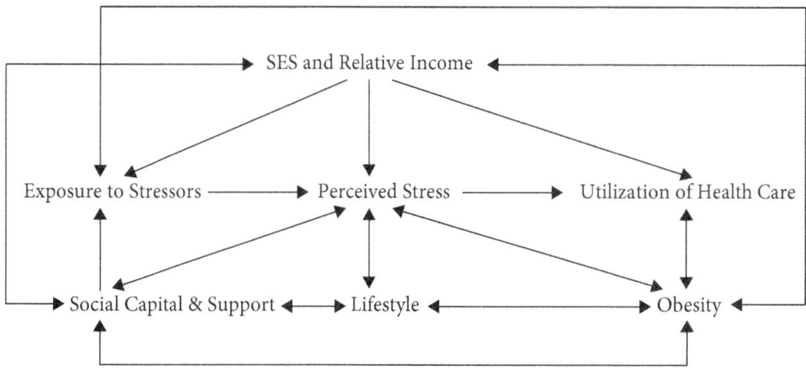

FIGURE 23.1 The interrelationships among socioeconomic status (relative income), stress, and obesity.

severity of overweight has been higher for the poor than for the rest of society throughout the past 35 years (Jolliffe, 2011). A plausible explanation for this association is that individuals with low SES might have restricted access to sports facilities and might opt for low-cost, processed food, or a higher rate of time preference (Komlos, Smith, & Bogin, 2004). McLaren (2007) surveys the literature on SES and obesity and finds that the association between the two variables varies by level of country development and gender. Moreover, Zhang and Wang (2004) suggest that the negative association between SES and obesity is stronger for women and that the association differs across ethnic groups as well.

23.1.2 Ecological Effect of Income Inequality on Obesity

Although stress constitutes an important mediator between income distribution and obesity at the individual level, extant literature also suggests an independent, ecological effect of income distribution on obesity. Subramanian and Kawachi (2004) conceptualized three pathways linking income inequality to health. Each of these can shed light on the association between income inequality and obesity prevalence.

The first is a *structural pathway* that points to a causal effect of income inequality on residential segregation and spatial concentrations of poverty in economically disadvantaged communities. Residents from these deprived communities face elevated risks of obesity due to a host of factors such as an inadequate supply of affordable, nutritional food (Lopez, 2007); poor street or sidewalk conditions that discourage walking; higher crime rates that deter outdoor activities; and lack of adequate facilities for exercise (Gordon-Larsen, Nelson, Page, & Popkin, 2006). Dysfunctional schools mean lack of education, inadequate socialization, and chronic unemployment and underemployment. Using data collected by the Wise-Woman program of the Centers for Disease Control and Prevention, Mobley et al. (2006) examined the relation between characteristics of the built environment and risks for obesity and cardiovascular disease among uninsured, low-income women aged 40–64 years who participated in the US National Breast and Cervical Cancer Early Detection Program. Their findings suggest that, holding other factors constant, an additional fitness facility per 1,000 residents was on average associated with a reduction of 1.39 BMI units. Local crime rates were also found to be positively associated with obesity risk.

The second pathway concerns *social cohesion* or *social capital*. This pathway is based on the observation that higher levels of income inequality are associated with disinvestment in social capital, which in turn can contribute to a series of negative health outcomes as indicated by total mortality as well as rates of deaths from coronary health disease, cancer, and infant mortality (Kawachi et al., 1997). In their study, social capital was defined as "features of social organization such as civic participation, norms of reciprocity, and trust in others that facilitate cooperation for mutual benefit" (p. 1491).

The social capital pathway has implications for the association between income inequality and obesity. According to this pathway, when societies become more unequal and polarized, mistrust and lack of reciprocity will become more commonplace. This in turn will create more psychological stress at the individual level, which can contribute to an increase in behaviors that are detrimental to health, such as smoking, alcohol abuse, the use of illicit drugs, and lack of participation in health promoting activities. In this sense, the "social capital" pathway can be viewed as a component of the psychosocial pathway that has been documented in the literature (e.g., Lynch & Kaplan, 1997; Marmot, 2004; Marmot & Wilkinson, 2001; Wilkinson, 2005). Presumably, an individual who has experienced emotional or psychological stress will become less attentive to issues related to diet, exercise, and weight gain.

The third pathway is the *policy pathway*, whereby the adverse influence of income inequality on health may operate through the formulation and implementation of general social policies as well as through health-related policies. Usually, the more polarized a society is, the more difficult it will be to implement policy initiatives that can effectively address health or health care challenges faced by economically disadvantaged segments of the population. Excessive levels of income inequality are related to underinvestment in human resources such as education, health care, and other social infrastructure (Lynch & Kaplan, 1997; Smith, 1996). In addition, the wealthy can manipulate the political process in such a way as to diminish existing services. In the United States, those states with higher levels of income inequality are also those that invest less in education and medical care (Kaplan et al., 1996). Among the major developed countries, the United States is the only country that does not provide universal health insurance coverage for its citizens. It is also the country with the highest level of income inequality. Are these two related to each other? If so, how are they related? Answers to these questions should also help elucidate why the United States currently has the highest rates of obesity as well as the most rapid increase in obesity prevalence among OECD countries (Su, Esqueda, Li, & Pagan, 2012).

The relevance of the policy pathway also pertains to the extent to which welfare or redistributive policies in a society can alleviate the consequences of poverty on health outcomes including obesity. This concerns the so-called *concavity-induced income inequality effect* (Subramanian & Kawachi, 2004). It rests on the premise that the relation between individual income and health status is concave, such that each additional dollar of income improves individual health by a decreasing amount. This means that the health impact of one additional dollar of income should be more important for the poor than for the rich. Correspondingly, a transfer of income from the rich to the poor should help improve the average health status of the whole society as long as the transfer does not go too far to disincentivize investments, innovations, and economic growth.

23.2 Empirical Findings on the Relationship Between Income Inequality and Obesity

Despite a growing body of research documenting the association between income inequality and health outcomes, so far, few studies have examined how income distribution is related to obesity. Here, I review empirical findings on this topic in two sections, with one focusing on relevant findings based on data from the United States and the other on findings from OECD countries.

23.2.1 Income Inequality and Obesity in the United States

Based on data from the 1990 Behavioral Risk Factor Surveillance System (BRFSS) and 1990 US Census data, Diez-Roux and colleagues (Diez-Roux, Link, & Northridge, 2000) investigated whether income inequality across US states is related to the prevalence of four cardiovascular disease risk factors (BMI, history of hypertension, sedentarism, and smoking). After exploratory analyses, regression models were used to investigate associations of state inequality with risk factor levels before and after adjustment for individual-level income, as well as the interactions between state inequality and individual-level income. It was found that higher BMI and sedentarism were both associated with income inequality, particularly at low income levels (annual household incomes <\$25,000), with associations persisting after adjustment for individual-level income. The associations were also more pronounced among women than among men. This gender difference was also confirmed in a study by Robert and Reither (2004) in which it was reported that income inequality at the census-tract level was positively associated with BMI among women but not among men.

Opposite findings were reported in the study by Kahn et al. (Kahn, Tatham, Pamuk, & Heath, 1998) where it was found that men's abdominal weight gain was positively associated with income inequality at the state level, yet the corresponding association was not observed among women. This study used a US mail survey of 34,158 male and 42,741 female healthy adult volunteers to test the association between residence in geographic regions with relative income inequality and the likelihood of weight gain at the waist. Respondents came from 21 states identified by the household income inequality (HII) index, a measure reflecting the proportion of total income received by the better-off 50% of households in the state. The main outcome measure was self-reported weight gain mainly at the waist as opposed to weight gain at other anatomic sites. After controlling for age and other individual-level factors, men from states with higher income inequality described weight gain at the waist more often than did men from states with less inequality (odds ratio = 1.12, 95% confidence interval [1.03–1.22]).

The significant associations between income inequality and obesity as revealed by these three studies, however, were not confirmed in another similar study by Chang and Christakis (2005) who used data from the 1996–98 BRFSS and the 1990 Census to examine the relationship between individual weight status and income inequality in US metropolitan areas. Based on multilevel analyses stratified by race–sex groups, the study did not find a positive association between income inequality and weight outcomes such as BMI, the odds of being overweight, and the odds of being obese. One limitation of the study is a lag of more than 6 years between measuring income inequality in 1990 and weight status in the 1996–98 BRFSS.

More recently, linking data from 12 consecutive waves of the BRFSS (1994–2005) with a recently published dataset on state-level income inequality based on tax payments, Volland (2012) analyzed whether changes in income inequality can be considered a determinant of variations in body mass and obesity across the United States. The study revealed a significant positive effect of changes in income inequality on BMI and obesity. In particular, the results suggest that one percentage point increase in the state's Gini coefficient (an index of income inequality) increases average BMI by 0.014 unit and the probability of being obese by 0.09%, thus indicating that the overall contribution of income inequality in explaining the growth in obesity prevalence between 1994 and 2005 is limited. Nonetheless, Volland concluded that although these effects were arguably small, they were comparable in size and significance to other state-level factors reported, thus suggesting that income inequality was one of the factors contributing to the increase in obesity prevalence. It was argued that some form of redistributive policy may help containing the spread of unfavorable weight outcomes.

23.2.2 Income Inequality and Obesity in OECD Countries

Based on their ecological analysis of data from 21 developed countries,[1] Pickett et al. (Pickett, Kelly, Brunner, Lobstein, & Wilkinson, 2005) assessed if obesity, deaths from diabetes, and daily calorie intake were associated with income inequality. The findings indicate that, adjusting for gross national per capita income, income inequality was positively correlated with the percentage of obese men ($r = .48$, $p = .03$), the percentage of obese women ($r = .62$, $p = .003$), diabetes mortality rates per 1 million people ($r = .46$, $p = .04$), and average calories consumed per capita per day ($r = .50$, $p = .02$). Correlations were even stronger if analyses were weighted for population size.

Su et al. (2012) extended the analysis by Pickett et al. by incorporating more OECD countries and variables in the analysis. Using data from both the World Health Organization (WHO) and the World Factbook released by the US Central Intelligence Agency (CIA, 2010), this study examined the association between income inequality and gender-specific obesity rates among 31 OECD countries. The WHO Global Infobase provides estimates of obesity rates by country in 2002, 2005, and 2010. This has made it possible to calculate changes in obesity rates among OECD countries between 2002 and 2010.

The data on obesity prevalence were then merged with the CIA World Factbook data that contain information on per capita income, income distribution, urbanization, literacy level, and a whole range of economic indicators for all OECD countries. Among the 34 OECD countries, 31 have estimates of Gini coefficients in or after 2005, whereas three countries—Japan, New Zealand, and Chile—do not have updated Gini estimates after 2005. Because the WHO obesity prevalence estimates were for 2010, this study restricted analysis to the 31 OECD countries that had Gini coefficient estimates in or after 2005 in an effort to synchronize data from the two sources.

Obesity prevalence is defined as the percentage of the population aged between 15 and 100 that have a BMI of 30 or greater. Based on reported statistics and survey data from its member countries, the WHO Global Infobase conducted a series of adjustments to make sure that the finally estimated prevalence rates of obesity for each country are comparable to each other. These changes include adjustments for definitions, adjustments to a standard set of age groups, adjustments of nonrepresentative data to the national population, and adjustments to a standard reporting year using available trend information (World Health Organization [WHO], 2010). The key explanatory variable used in the analysis of obesity prevalence is the Gini index.

There is substantial variation in obesity prevalence and its changes over time among OECD countries (Table 23.1). The average prevalence rate of male obesity is 17.7%, ranging from 8.3% (South Korea) to 44.2% (United States), with a standard deviation (*SD*) of 7.9%. The corresponding range for the female obesity rate is from 7.6% (France) to 48.3% (United States), with a mean of 20.5% and an *SD* of 9.4%. Thus, the United States has the highest obesity prevalence among OECD countries. In terms of changes in obesity prevalence from 2002 to 2010, the ranges of increases are from 0% (Poland and Hungary) to 12.2% (United States) for male obesity and from 0% (Poland and Hungary) to 10.5% (United States) for female obesity.

The OECD countries in the sample also differ considerably in terms of income distribution and socioeconomic development. The Gini index ranges from 23.0 (Sweden) to 48.2 (Mexico), with an *SD* of 5.8. As for the percentage share in household income or consumption of those in the lowest 10% in the national household income distribution, the average is 3.1% across OECD countries in the sample, ranging from 1.7% in Mexico to 7.5% in Switzerland.

The results reveal a weak, positive correlation between income inequality and male obesity rates (Figure 23.2). Countries with higher Gini indexes tend to have a higher prevalence of male obesity. However, this relationship is primarily driven by United States and Mexico, the two countries that lead the OECD countries in terms of both Gini indexes and male obesity prevalence. For the rest of the sample, the association between income inequality and obesity rates is virtually nonexistent. The R^2 for the whole sample is .16, suggesting that the Gini index helps explain only 16% of the variation in male obesity rates across OECD countries.

The positive correlation between income inequality and obesity prevalence becomes more salient when applied to female obesity rates (Figure 23.3). Again, the United States and Mexico are on the top in terms of both the Gini index and the obesity rate. About 35% of the variation in female obesity rates across the OECD countries can be explained by differences in the Gini index across these countries.

Table 23.1 A description of OECD data used in the sample

Variables	Mean	Min	Max	*SD*	*N*
Male obesity rate (%)	17.68	8.30	44.20	7.90	31
Female obesity rate (%)	20.52	7.60	48.30	9.40	31
% Changes in male obesity rate: 2002–2010	3.14	.00	12.20	2.63	31
% Changes in female obesity rate: 2002–2010	3.08	.00	10.50	2.50	31
Gini index in the 2005–2010 period	31.73	23.00	48.20	5.79	31
GDP per capita (thousands of US$)	33.45	11.20	78.00	13.10	31
Ln GDP per capita	10.34	9.32	11.26	0.40	31
% Who can read and write	98.11	87.40	100.00	2.76	31
Urbanization rate	74.74	48.00	97.00	11.93	31
Share of household income in lowest 10%	3.05	1.70	7.50	1.09	30[a]

Sources: World Health Organization Global Infobase and CIA World Factbook.[a] Among the 31 OECD countries in the sample, information on the share of household income by the lowest 10 is missing for Iceland.

In terms of the relation between the Gini index in the 2005–2010 period and changes in obesity prevalence from 2002 to 2010, higher Gini indexes are in general associated with more substantial increases in male obesity rates ($R^2 = .2$) (Figure 23.4). Among all countries, the United States and Mexico experienced the largest increase in male obesity rates from 2002 to 2010, followed by Australia, South Korea, and the United Kingdom. Similarly, Figure 23.5 also reveals a positive correlation between the current Gini index and increases in female obesity rates from 2002 to 2010. About 22% of the variation in the changing female obesity rates can be explained by differences in the current Gini index across OECD countries.

Results based on multivariate linear regression (Table 23.2), reveal a significant association between the Gini index and obesity prevalence for both males and females. After adjusting for the effects of GDP per capita, literacy, urbanization, and the percentage share of household income by the poorest 10% households, on average, each unit of increase in the Gini index corresponds to an increase of .82 percentage points in male obesity rates ($p < .05$). The corresponding effect becomes one percentage point in the case of female obesity rates ($p < .01$). Thus, consistent with findings from the bivariate analysis, higher income inequality is associated with a higher level of obesity prevalence. This

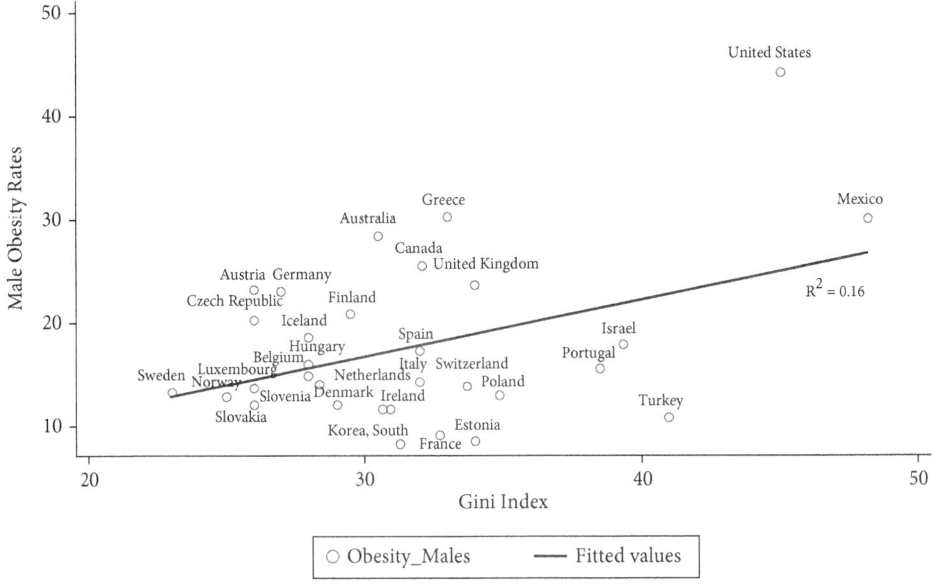

FIGURE 23.2 Gini Index and Male Obesity Rate: OECD countries, 2010

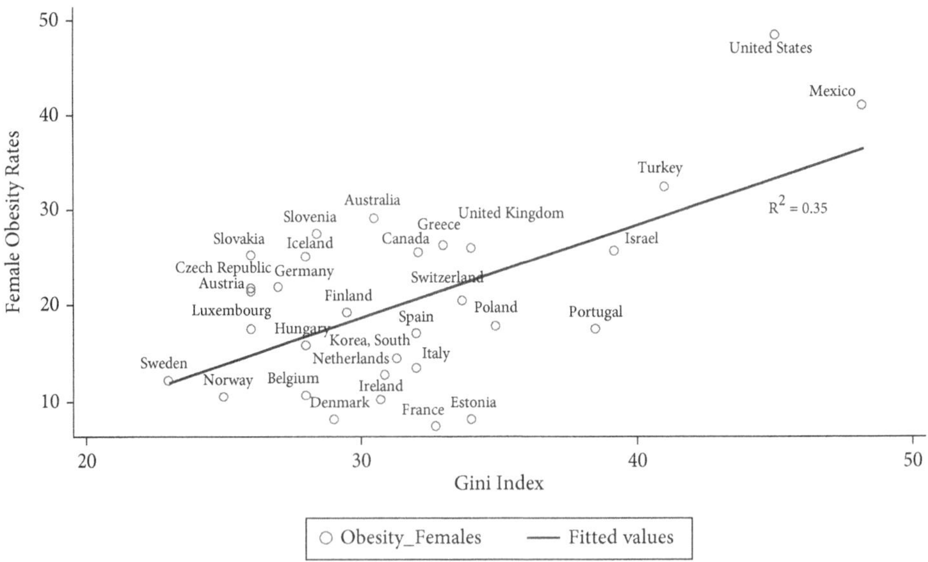

FIGURE 23.3 Gini Index and Female Obesity Rate: OECD countries, 2010

association is stronger in the case of female obesity prevalence. Among all the covariates in the base models, the Gini index turns out to be the only variable that shows a significant association with obesity prevalence. However, Panel b of Table 23.2 shows that the significant association between obesity and the Gini index disappears for both genders when the United States and Mexico are excluded from the analysis.

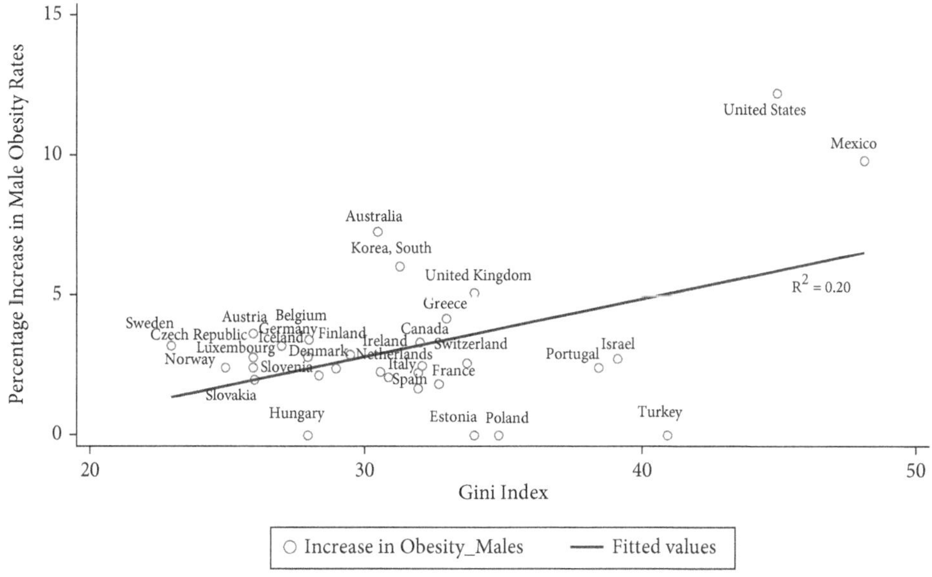

FIGURE 23.4 Current Gini Index and Increases in Male Obesity Rates from 2002 to 2010

FIGURE 23.5 Current Gini Index and Increases in Female Obesity Rates from 2002 to 2010

Income inequality also shows a significant association with changes in obesity prevalence over time. A higher degree of income inequality is associated with more rapid increases in both male and female obesity rates from 2002 to 2010 (Table 23.3). After adjusting for the effects of other covariates in the models, each unit of increase in the Gini index corresponds to a .28 percentage point increase in the male obesity rate and a .29 percentage point increase in the female obesity rate ($p < .01$ in both cases). Again, these effects are only significant when both the United States and Mexico have been

Table 23.2 Linear regressions of obesity rates by gender

Regression Model	a) With US & Mexico		b) Without US & Mexico	
	Males	Females	Males	Females
Gini index in the 2005–2010 period	.82*	1.00**	.01	.07
	(.32)	(.35)	(.38)	(.43)
Ln GDP per capita	8.36	4.48	4.94	.16
	(4.72)	(5.27)	(4.41)	(4.89)
% Who can read and write	.22	−.43	−.25	−1.03
	(.72)	(.80)	(.66)	(.74)
Urbanization rate	−.04	−.10	−.02	−.08
	(.13)	(.15)	(.12)	(.13)
Share of household income by lowest 10%	−1.07	−.27	−.70	.19
	(1.42)	(1.58)	(1.25)	(1.38)
Number of countries	30	30	28	28
R^2	.32	.40	.07	.18

Sources: World Health Organization Global Infobase and CIA World Factbook.* $p < .05$, ** $p < .01$, *** $p < .001$.

Standard errors are included in parentheses.

included in the analysis. Panel b of Table 23.3 illustrates a diminution in the association between increases in estimated rates of obesity and the Gini index when the United States and Mexico are not included.

Conclusion

There are substantial variations in obesity prevalence across OECD countries. These countries also differ considerably from each other when it comes to changes in obesity prevalence in the period from 2002 to 2010. The United States and Mexico are of particular importance insofar as these countries are outliers in terms of both obesity rates and the pace of increases in obesity prevalence over time.

One of the major findings is that when both the United States and Mexico are included in the analysis, differences in obesity prevalence and its changes over time

Table 23.3 Linear regressions of changes in obesity rates from 2002 to 2010 by gender

Regression Model	a) With US & Mexico		b) Without US & Mexico Model	
	Males	Females	Males	Females
Gini index in the 2005–2010 period	.28**	.29**	−.04	.05
	(.10)	(.10)	(.09)	(.11)
Ln GDP per capita	2.80	2.33	1.81	1.72
	(1.43)	(1.43)	(1.05)	(1.28)
% Who can read and write	.04	.07	−.09	−.01
	(.22)	(.22)	(.16)	(.19)
Urbanization rate	.03	.01	.03	.01
	(.04)	(.04)	(.03)	(.03)
Share of household income by lowest 10%	−.32	−.14	−.20	−.07
	(.43)	(.43)	(.30)	(.36)
Number of countries	30	30	28	28
R^2	.44	.37	.31	.12

Sources: World Health Organization Global Infobase and CIA World Factbook.* $p < .05$, ** $p < .01$, *** $p < .001$.
Standard errors are included in parentheses.

across OECD countries are more related to differences in income inequality than to differences in absolute income across these countries. The lack of salience of GDP per capita in explaining obesity prevalence tends to suggest that absolute income is no longer a powerful predictor of obesity prevalence across OECD countries. Presumably, GDP per capita is more relevant in predicting obesity prevalence in less-developed countries where many people are still suffering from malnutrition, and manual labor is still quite prevalent. A similar lack of explanatory power of GDP per capita has also been observed when it comes to disparities in life expectancy across OECD countries (Marmot & Wilkinson, 2001).

These associations between income inequality and obesity prevalence virtually disappear when the United States and Mexico, the two extreme cases in both Gini index and obesity, are excluded from the analysis. This suggests that the revealed association between income inequality and obesity prevalence in both the bivariate and multivariate analyses is essentially driven by the high levels of income inequality and obesity in these two countries. The association is rather weak among the rest of the OECD countries in the sample. These findings underscore the importance of assessing the impact of outliers on the relationship between income inequality and health outcomes. For example, based on their ecological analysis of data from 21 developed countries, Pickett et al. (2005) reported that, adjusting for gross national per capita income, income inequality was positively correlated with obesity. Mexico was not included as one of the 21 countries in the study; meanwhile, because the United States leads the group in both obesity and income inequality, it would be valuable to test the robustness of the conclusion with and without inclusion of the United States.

These findings highlight the exception of the United States and Mexico in obesity prevalence as well as the importance of evaluating the impact of extreme cases or outliers when it comes to assessing the relation between income inequality and health outcomes using aggregated country-level data. In addition to inconclusiveness of findings, none of the studies reviewed herein has addressed the issue of causality—that is, the mechanisms through which income inequality results in obesity. This would be an important step for future research in the sense that if it could be convincingly established that income inequality can contribute to obesity prevalence, then redistributive policies and other measures aiming to reduce income inequality would presumably be an effective weapon in our fight against the ongoing obesity epidemic.

Note

1. The 21 countries are Australia, Austria, Belgium, Canada, Denmark, Finland, France, Germany, Greece, Ireland, Italy, Japan, Netherlands, New Zealand, Norway, Portugal, Spain, Sweden, Switzerland, the United Kingdom, and the United States.

References

Berridge, K.C., Ho, C.-Y., Richard, J. M., & DiFeliceantonio, A. G. (2010). The tempted brain eats: Pleasure and desire circuits in obesity and eating disorders. Brain Research, 1350, 43–64.

Bose, M., Oliván, B., & Laferrère, B. (2009). Stress and obesity: The role of the hypothalamic-pituitary-adrenal axis in metabolic disease. *Current Opinion in Endocrinology, Diabetes and Obesity*, 16, 340–346.

Central Intelligence Agency (CIA). (2010). The world factbook. https://www.cia.gov/library/publications/the-world-factbook/geos/xx.html

Chang, V. W., & Christakis, N. A. (2005). Income inequality and weight status in US metropolitan areas. *Social Science and Medicine, 61*, 83–96.

Cohen, S., Kessler, R. C., & Gordon, L. U. (1998). *Measuring stress: A guide for health and social scientists.* New York: Oxford University Press.

Dallman, M. F. (2010). Stress-induced obesity and the emotional nervous system. *Trends in Endocrinology and Metabolism*, *21*, 159–165.

Dallman, M. F., La Fleur, S. E., Pecoraro, N. C., Gomez, F., Houshyar, H., & Akana, S. F. (2004). Minireview: Glucocorticoids—food intake, abdominal obesity, and wealthy nations in 2004. *Endocrinology, 145*, 2633–2638.

Diez-Roux, A. V., Link, B. G., & Northridge, M. E. (2000). A multilevel analysis of income inequality and cardiovascular disease risk factors. *Social Science & Medicine, 50*, 673–687.

Drewnowski, A., & Darmon, N. (2005). The economics of obesity: Dietary energy density and energy cost. *American Journal of Clinical Nutrition, 82*(1), 265S–273S.

Frank, M. W. (2009). Inequality and growth in the United States: Evidence from a new state-level panel of income inequality measures. *Economic Inquiry, 47*, 55–68.

Gordon-Larsen, P., Nelson, M. C., Page, P., & Popkin, B. M. (2006). Inequality in the built environment underlies key health disparities in physical activity and obesity. *Pediatrics, 117*, 417–424.

Greeno, C. G., & Wing, R. R. (1994). Stress-induced eating. *Psychological Bulletin, 115*(3), 444–464.

House, J. S. (2002). Understanding social factors and inequalities in health: 20th Century progress and 21st century prospects. *Journal of Health and Social Behavior, 43*, 125–142.

Jolliffe, D. (2011). Overweight and poor? On the relationship between income and the body mass index. *Economics and Human Biology, 9*(4), 342–355.

Kahn, H. S., Tatham, L. M., Pamuk, E. R., & Heath, C. W., Jr. (1998). Are geographic regions with high income inequality associated with risk of abdominal weight gain? *Social Science & Medicine, 47*(1), 1–6.

Kahn, R. S., Wise, P. H., Kennedy, B. P., & Kawachi, I. (2000). State income inequality, household income, and maternal mental and physical health: Cross sectional national survey. *British Medical Journal, 321*, 1311–1315.

Kaplan, G. A., Pamuk, E. R., Lynch, J. W., Cohen, R. D., & Balfour, J. L. (1996). Inequality in income and mortality in the United States: Analysis of mortality and potential pathways. *British Medical Journal, 312*, 999–1003.

Kawachi, I., Kennedy, B. P., Lochner, K., & Prothrow-Stith, D. (1997). Social capital, income inequality, and mortality. *American Journal of Public Health, 87*, 1491–1498.

Komlos, J., & Brabec, M. (2011).The trend of BMI values of US adults by deciles, birth cohorts 1882–1986 stratified by gender and ethnicity. *Economics and Human Biology, 9*(3), 234–250.

Komlos, J., Smith, P. K., & Bogin, B. (2004). Obesity and the rate of time preference: Is there a connection? *Journal of Biosocial Science, 36*(2), 209–219.

Lennon, M. C. (1989). The structural contexts of stress. An invited response to Pearlin. *Journal of Health and Social Behavior, 30*(3), 261–268.

Lopez, R. P. (2007). Neighborhood risk factors for obesity. *Obesity (Silver Spring), 15*, 2111–2119.

Lynch, J. W., & Kaplan, G. A. (1997). Understanding how inequality in the distribution of income affects health. *Journal of Health Psychology, 2*, 297–314.

Marmot, M. (2004). Commentary: Risk factors or social causes? *International Journal of Epidemiology, 33*, 297–298.

Marmot, M., & Wilkinson, R. G. (2001). Psychosocial and material pathways in the relation between income and health: A response to Lynch et al. *British Medical Journal, 322*, 1233–1236.

McLaren, L. (2007). Socioeconomic status and obesity. *Epidemiologic Reviews, 29*(1), 29–48.

Mobley, L. R., Root, E. D., Finkelstein, E. A., Khavjou, O., Farris, R. P., & Will, J. C. (2006). Environment, obesity, and cardiovascular disease risk in low-income women. *American Journal of Preventive Medicine, 30*, 327–332.

Pearlin, L. I. (1989). The sociological study of stress. *Journal of Health and Social Behavior, 30*(3), 241–256.

Pickett, K. E., Kelly, S., Brunner, E., Lobstein, T., & Wilkinson, R. G. (2005). Wider income gaps, wider waistbands? An ecological study of obesity and income inequality. *Journal of Epidemiology and Community Health, 59*, 670–674.

Robert, S. A., & Reither, E. N. (2004). A multilevel analysis of race, community disadvantage, and body mass index among adults in the US. *Social Science and Medicine, 59*, 2421–2434.

Rodgers, G. B. (2002). Income and inequality as determinants of mortality: An international cross-section analysis. *International Journal of Epidemiology, 31*, 533–538.

Sassi, F. (2010). *Obesity and the economics of prevention: Fit not fat.* Paris, OECD Publishing.

Smith, G. D. (1996). Income inequality and mortality: Why are they related? *British Medical Journal, 312*, 987–988.

Stone, C., Trisi, D., Sherman, A., & DeBot, B. (2014). A guide to statistics on historical trends in income inequality. Center for Budget and Policy Priorities. http://www.cbpp.org/cms/?fa=view&id=3629

Stunkard, A. J. (2007). *Socioeconomic status and obesity.* New York: Wiley.

Su, D. (2005). Body mass index and old-age survival: A comparative study between the Union Army Records and the NHANES-I Epidemiological Follow-Up Sample. *American Journal of Human Biology, 17*, 341–354.

Su, D., Esqueda, O. A., Li, L., & Pagan, J. A. (2012). Income inequality and obesity prevalence among OECD countries. *Journal of Biosocial Science, 44*(4), 417–432.

Subramanian, S. V., Blakely, T., & Kawachi, I. (2003). Income inequality as a public health concern: Where do we stand? Commentary on "Is exposure to income inequality a public health concern?" *Health Services Research, 38*, 153–167.

Subramanian, S. V., & Kawachi, I. (2004). Income inequality and health: What have we learned so far? *Epidemiologic Reviews, 26*, 78–91.

Volland, B. (2012). The effects of income inequality on BMI and obesity: Evidence from the BRFSS, Papers on Economics and Evolution, Philipps University Marburg, Department of Geography. http://EconPapers.repec.org/RePEc:esi:evopap:2012-10

Waldmann, R. J. (1992). Income distribution and infant mortality. *Quarterly Journal of Economics, 107*(4), 1283–1302.

World Health Organization (WHO). (2010). WHO global infobase. https://apps.who.int/infobase/Comparisons.aspx

Wilkinson, R. G. (1992). Income distribution and life expectancy. *British Medical Journal, 304*, 165–168.

Wilkinson, R. G. (1997). Health inequalities: Relative or absolute material standards? *British Medical Journal, 314*, 591–595.

Wilkinson, R. G. (2005). *The impact of inequality: How to make sick societies healthier.* New York: New Press.

Wilkinson, R. G., & Pickett, K. E. (2006). Income inequality and population health: A review and explanation of the evidence. *Social Science & Medicine, 62*, 1768–1784.

Williams, D. R. (1990). Socioeconomic differentials in health: A review and redirection. *Social Psychology Quarterly, 53*(2), 81–99.

Zhang, Q., & Wang, Y. (2004). Socioeconomic inequality of obesity in the United States: Do gender, age, and ethnicity matter? *Social Science & Medicine, 58*(6), 1171–1180.

CHAPTER 24

HEIGHT AND WAGES

OLAF HÜBLER

23.1 Introduction

In the past, the importance of height was considered only from a biological or medical perspective. However, since the late 1970s, there has been an increasing realization that there is an economic dimension to human growth. One important aspect of this burgeoning literature is the analysis of the relationship between height and wages. The major finding is that the relationship is positively stable in all societies and at all times.

Earnings increase with height for several reasons: tall people have physical advantages, are more disease-resistant, possess greater authority, and have better verbal and nonverbal abilities than their shorter counterparts. Epidemiological studies interpret height as a proxy for nutritional advantages. Economists extend this argument: good health and nutrition are a precondition of high performance and productivity. High income on average is a consequence. The chain of arguments is still longer. Height and wealth can be inherited. When tall people are favored to earn more money, we can expect that their children are also as tall as their parents and start their life with good preconditions of high income. Furthermore, school performance may be affected by height, and schooling is an important determinant of future individual wages. Risk behavior correlates with height, and the former is relevant for returns and wages in many situations. Height does not have a direct causal influence on risk behavior, but an indirect relationship is likely. There exist determinants that have independent effects on height and risk attitudes, or else height produces personal characteristics that are relevant to risk behavior (Hübler, 2013). For example, environmental and family conditions during early adolescence may jointly determine both height and risk tolerance. Hryshko et al. (2011) describe different childhood determinants of risk aversion. Tall people, with their high authority, are more risk-tolerant. Hopfensitz and Wranik (2008) argue that

For helpful comments I thank John Komlos. All errors are my responsibility.

self-efficacy is related to a personal profile characterized by confidence in decision making, competence, optimism, and lack of anxiety. These qualities contribute to a person's ascent of the "corporate ladder" and allow him to earn more money.

It should also be mentioned that employers can discriminate in the sense that they have a preference for tall employees in many occupations for aesthetic reasons. This is independent of the authority issue but is tied to customer's preferences. Finally, life and job satisfaction, on the one hand, and income, on the other hand, show a clear link to height in which the causality can go in both directions.

23.2 Modeling and Theoretical Considerations

In an influential paper exploring the relationship between height and wages, Case and Paxson (2008) argued that the link between these two variables is indirect via abilities. If variables measuring ability are neglected, a positive correlation between height (H) and wages results. In the wage-height equation given here, a capital letter signifies an exogenous variable, whereas a complete word indicates an endogenous variable (i.e., variables that are determined by other influences). The authors present two versions of their theory. On the one hand (Case & Paxson, 2006), the wage equation is modeled as

$$wage = \theta * H + \varepsilon \qquad (1)$$

where θ is a coefficient, and the error term ε depends on abilities (A). Under the assumptions that corr(H, A)>0 and A is unobserved, θ is positive as corr(wage, A)>0. On the other hand (Case & Paxson, 2008) cognitive ability (ability(c)) is modeled as being dependent on individual's endowment (E). The latter variable refers to unobserved characteristics that also determines height:

$$height = \alpha * E + u, \qquad (2a)$$

where α is a coefficient and u is an error term. Because wage is described by a linear relationship with cognitive ability,

$$wage = \beta * ability(c) + v, \qquad (2b)$$

where β is a coefficient and v is an error term. Here, we write ability(c) instead of A(c) because a linear dependence with respect to E is assumed

$$ability(c) = \gamma * E + w, \qquad (2c)$$

where γ is a coefficient and w an error term.

The estimation of the wage equation is similar to (1) if ability in (2b) is substituted by (2c) and E by (2a)

$$wage = \delta * height + e, \tag{2}$$

where $\delta = (\beta\gamma) / \alpha$ and $e = -((\beta\gamma) / \alpha) u + v + \beta * w$. Because $\alpha > 0$, $\beta > 0$, and $\gamma > 0$ are assumed, then $\delta > 0$ follows. The only difference to (1) is expressed by the endogenous character of height.

Vogl (2014) extends this approach. He distinguishes between cognitive ability and physical ability (ability(c), ability(p)) that are determined by childhood nutrition (N), childhood environment (B), and childhood diseases (C). B and N as well as C also have an impact on adult height. The child's wages once he or she enters the labor force is modeled as

$$wage(i) = f[ability(c), ability(p), S, X, \varepsilon(i)], \tag{3}$$

where $i = 1, \ldots, I$ is the industry in which he or she is working, f is a function, S is schooling, X incorporate further income determinants like tenure and experience following the Mincer equation, and $\varepsilon(i)$ is the industry-specific error term in the wage equation. Thomas and Strauss (1997) extend the wage equation by a health indicator. The link to wages is explained via productivity. The worker nutritional input occurs when the worker is still a child and is not yet maximizing anything while his parents maximize their utility with respect to N and B under the restriction of parental income. If ability(c), ability(p), N, and B are unobserved, but height is incorporated into the wage equation, a positive correlation corr(height, wage) follows if, in all industries, the partial derivatives of wages with respect to ability(c), ability(p), and S are positive. In this approach, schooling and industry allocation are included as further wage determinants. The modeling with respect to the industry makes sense because the required abilities vary among industries. Following the positive correlation between abilities and height, we can expect that height also varies between sectors. In the construction sector, physical strength is necessary, whereas industries like research and education are focused on cognitive abilities. These are not the only reasons that industries are wage-relevant. The ability to pay varies among industries due to market power.

Sohn (2015) and Hübler (2009) suggest a modification of Vogl's model by adding discrimination (D) as a determinant of wages insofar as both customers and employers have preferences for tall people. For example, taller private attorneys are better able to attract and retain clients than are their shorter colleagues, as Biddle and Hamermesh (1998) have shown. It is also possible that employers have a preference for tall employees beyond worker productivity. Sohn also analyzes the influences of physical (p), cognitive (c), and other noncognitive (nc) ability (ability(p), ability(c) and ability(nc)) on schooling and wages. This model has similarities to those of Lundborg et al. (2014), Vogl (2014), Case and Paxson (2008), and Persico et al. (2004). The latter emphasize the role of height through the teen years because this component essentially determines the returns to height. They explain this finding by the social consequences of being short during adolescence but do not pay sufficient attention to the fact that height in adolescence is highly correlated with height in adulthood.

Kuhn and Weinberger (2005) stress leadership skills as an important source of high wages. Tall high school teenagers think of themselves as leaders, and this tendency is reinforced by their peers; thus, they gain experience in leadership roles that continue after they enter the labor force. Teenagers who are short may have problems developing a positive self-image. They tend to be less easy-going and more introverted. Tall people are more willing to take risks (Dohmen et al., 2011). Of course, height cannot have a direct causal influence on risk behavior, but a statistical relationship is possible. Either there exist characteristics (Z1) that have independent effects on height and risk attitude or height produces personal characteristics (Z2) that are relevant to risk behavior (Hübler, 2013). The former characteristics are inherited or formed early in life before height is fixed. The influence of parents on their children and conflicts between parents and children are examples. The factors Z2 are developed later if height is nearly fixed. Taking responsibility, decisiveness, and experience with high-risk situations should be mentioned. These considerations lead to a four-equation model extension of the Case-Paxson-Vogl-Sohn approach:

$$ability(k) = f(k)[height, N, B, C, Z1, Z2] \tag{4}$$

$$height = f[N, B, C, Z1] \tag{5}$$

$$risk = f[height, Z1, Z2] \tag{6}$$

$$wage(i) = f[ability(p), ability(c), ability\ (nc), risk, schooling, X, i], \tag{7}$$

where $i = 1, \ldots, I$ is the industry; and k = physical (p), cognitive (c), or noncognitive (nc). These types of abilities are analyzed in the context of height by Schick and Steckel (2015). Equations (4)–(7) represent a recursive econometric system. An interdependent consideration should allow feedback effects; namely, that abilities and risk behavior can be affected by wages. The higher the wage, the more profitable it is to improve the individual's abilities by, for instance, further training. An extended version of model (4)–(7) yields when health and schooling are incorporated as additional equations. Here, we can follow Heckman et al. (2014), who analyze the system of a schooling, health, and wage equation but do not consider the relationship to height:

$$ability(k) = f(k)[height, N, B, C, Z1, Z2] \tag{8}$$

$$height = f[N, B, C, Z1] \tag{9}$$

$$schooling = f[height, Z3] \tag{10}$$

$$health = f[height, schooling, Z4] \tag{11}$$

$$risk = f[height, Z1, Z2]. \tag{12}$$

$$wage(i) = f[ability(k), risk, schooling, X, i], \tag{13}$$

where $Z3$ includes schooling of parents, nationality, and number and age of siblings. Cinnirella et al. (2011) explain why taller children are more likely to enroll in a gymnasium in Germany. They argue that an association between height and noncognitive abilities is responsible, although they do not rule out the possibility of discrimination: teachers reward higher social skills, and taller students possess this characteristic.

Components of $Z4$ are smoking, consumption of alcohol, low or high body mass index (BMI), age, and sex. In this approach, feedback effects can be incorporated in a dynamic system, high income may contribute to better health, and schooling is a possible additional health component. The better an individual is informed about the positive effects of balanced and healthful nutrition and the negative effects of smoking and alcohol, the more likely is good health.

Finally, a life satisfaction equation should be added to the model. A positive correlation between height and satisfaction can be expected because tall people are usually more successful, enjoy more mutual recognition than shorter people. The link to the remaining system is created by wages. The higher the income, the higher is life or workplace satisfaction. The satisfaction function can be written as

$$satisfaction = f(height, health, wage, Z5), \tag{14}$$

where Z5 include components like gender and age. A reverse causality is also possible insofar as happiness and satisfaction contribute to higher performance and higher productivity with the consequence of higher wages. Systems (8)–(14) demonstrate that the simple height–wage relationship is only a reduced form approach under which neglecting relevant influences yields biased estimates. Further possible feedback effects are presented in Figure 24.1. Problems with estimating the relationships depicted in Figure 24.1 and the estimation of (8)–(14) include the following challenges:

- Not all influences can be observed.
- It is unclear whether all feedback effects are considered or whether all feedback influences are effective.
- Additional factors affect wage that are omitted.

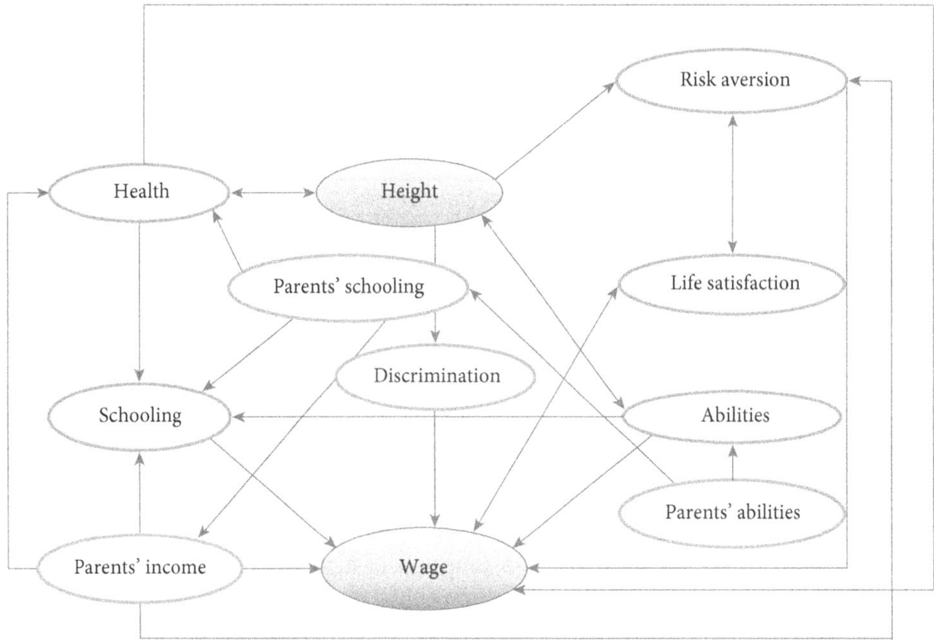

FIGURE 24.1 Relationships between height and wages.

23.3 Methodological Aspects

The available datasets do not contain all variables in (8)–(14). Thus, only a segment of this system is usually estimated in empirical investigations. As a consequence, the results are not fully convincing because biased estimates are likely. If the recursive character of the model is not given, an interdependent or instrumental variables approach should be estimated. The assumptions of a classical linear model are often not fulfilled. The problem is finding good instruments that are highly correlated with the endogenous regressors but uncorrelated with error term in the interesting equation. In a complex system, such as those in (8)–(14), several interdependent relationships are likely. Then it is even more difficult to choose appropriate instruments.

A similar problem arises with measurement errors. Height is often misreported when self-reported. In this case, instrumental variables are also a possible solution. In Hübler (2006) following Schultz (2002), a health indicator—education of the parents—and a regional dummy are used as instruments. From a theoretical and empirical viewpoint, health is preferred compared to the other instruments. Gao and Smyth (2010) apply two instruments: namely, the average number of health institutions in the region where the respondent was born and an index of the location where the respondent lived as an adolescent. In all these cases, only a height and wage equation is analyzed. If, however, the complete system is considered, then health is also problematic as an appropriate instrument.

Additionally, height measurement errors are not always random. Heineck (2006) shows that male and female respondents to the German Socio-Economic Panel tend to overestimate their height. Other studies (Cawley, 2004) emphasize that height in contrast to weight seems not to be affected by low accuracy. An alternative to an instrumental variable estimator is presented by Huang et al. (2012) who use upper arm and lower leg length as an instrument of height. It is unclear whether these instruments are more accurate.

Unobserved heterogeneity can be considered by panel estimates if the individual effects are time-invariant. Problems arise in this context if regressions are estimated with time-invariant or quasi time-invariant regressors like sex, schooling, industry affiliation, or age. For example, sex is eliminated by a fixed-effects estimator. Random-effects estimators mostly fail because the individual effects correlate with regressors, and thus inconsistent estimates follow. An alternative is the Hausman-Taylor estimator. This approach requires specification of which regressors are either correlated or not correlated with the individual effect. This is a priori often difficult to decide. Under this constellation, subgroup estimation (e.g., separate for men and women) might be helpful.

In most empirical studies, wage is regressed on height by a linear model. But such an assumption is too restrictive because there is good reason to think that the relationship is nonlinear (Hübler, 2006). Wages increase initially with height, reach an optimum, and then begin to decline because extremely tall individuals do not match our ideal aesthetic. Or, more generally, people have often less sympathy with those who are far from the statistical norm. This means that very short and very tall individuals tend to be objects of discrimination. This behavior helps to explain the inverse U-shaped relationship between height and wages. The nonlinear pattern is also reinforced by the fact that health problems are associated with both ends of the height spectrum. Some studies report that people who are too tall are not healthy and that short people live longer than taller people (Samaras, Elrick & Storms, 2004). Others have found that short people are less disease-resistant (Waaler, 1984). Hamermesh (2012, p. 12) also finds curvilinear height effects on wages using 1995 microeconomic data from the Netherlands. However, the results are less obvious during the period 2006–2010.

23.4 Empirical Investigations

23.4.1 Regional Differences and Long-Run Developments

In the empirical literature, we find a lot of suggestions that height and wages differ among people from different regions and countries. Average height differences between European countries are documented in Garcia and Quintana-Domeque (2007). The measured means for women vary during the period 1976–1980 between 162.5 cm in Portugal and 168.6 cm in Denmark. The corresponding values for men are 172.9 and 183.7 cm, respectively. Another study (Cinnirella & Winter, 2009) compares the height premium among 13 European countries. Except for Poland, all these premiums are positive, although the positive wage difference between tall and short people is negligible in Belgium and is small in Spain and the Czech Republic. The largest wage differences were found in Italy. Quintana-Domeque et al. (2012) investigate height differences between Spanish regions and height differences between East and West Germany can be found in Komlos and Kriwy (2003). East Germans are shorter than West Germans: 19-year-old West German military recruits measured in 1992 were still 1.5 cm taller than East German recruits. Two years later, the difference was only 0.6 cm. The West–East difference was particularly large among men born in the 1960s. Among women, the West's advantage was larger than among men. The height premium of West Germans exceeds that of East Germans by far after the unification (Hübler, 2009). We find also comparisons between regions outside Europe. For example, Ranasinghe et al. (2011) present differences between rural and urban areas in Sri Lanka.

Height has increased in recent decades. At the same time, per capita national income has increased, and public health expenditures have also grown. The trend since World War II in the United States is described by Komlos (2009) and Komlos and Lauderdale (2007). After a stagnation of height in the US population for about a generation, the height of adults increased among birth cohorts from 1975 to 1986 due to improvements in the quality of life. Nevertheless, the height of black women decreased on average relative to white women, in particular among low- and middle-income strata but not among the high-income group. The black–white height gap has not increased among men. The heights of US white adults continued to be shorter than that of northern and western European populations. Native Americans born between 1825 and 1875 were tall compared to Europeans (Komlos & Carson, 2012). The heights of the American economic elites were not affected by the increase of food prices because they had enough income to compensate for this. The census of 1791/92 shows that Mexicans were shorter than Europeans and North Americans (Grajales-Porras & Lopez-Alonso, 2011). Those from higher income groups were taller, the same phenomenon as observed in the United States and other countries.

Using data from 13 countries, Hatton (2014) and Hatton and Bray (2010) show that, in Europe, the average height of adult men increased by 11 cm from the 19th century to 1980. From their view, improvement in health was the major reason, while rising income and education levels and falling family size had only modest effects. Steckel (1995) argues that the decline of income inequality has contributed to the improvement of average health for a given average income. Gains in height for northern and middle European countries were largest in the period 1911–15 and 1951–55. In southern European countries, the increase follows later, in 1951–55 and 1976–80.

23.4.2 Basic Estimates of Height Premium

The basic estimates of the relationship between height and wages use ordinary least squares (OLS) regressions, often without any other covariates. Table 24.1 lists the results of several studies. Differences are observed in sample size, age range, period considered, accuracy of the dependent variable, and considered covariates. Height premiums are presented in Table 24.1, usually based on the simple two variables regression model between log wages and height.

The estimates show a wide range of height premiums. The coefficients cannot directly be compared because in some studies height is measured in inches, in others in centimeters, and in others in log height. Therefore, a column in Table 24.1 is added to display wage gains due to an increase of 10 cm in height. Except for some outliers, the normal range lies between 2% and 11% for men and between 1% and 14% for women. The median wage gain including outliers is 7% for men and 5% for women. However, in nearly all approaches, the influence of height on income is positively significant. Usually, it is argued that height affects income, but parents' income also has an influence on children's height (Buser, Oosterbeek, Plug, Ponce, & Rosero, 2014). Furthermore, the more covariates are incorporated, the smaller the wage premium. In most cases, self-reported height in adulthood is employed in the estimates. In the investigations of Persico et al. (2004), the effect of height in adulthood on wages becomes insignificant if it is controlled for teen height. Multicollinearity is most likely the reason for this because there is obviously a significant correlation between height attained as a teenager and height in adulthood. The authors show that two adults of the same age and height do not earn the same if one was taller as a teen than the other.

23.4.3 Age Effects

Table 24.1 demonstrates that empirical investigations on height effects on wages focus on different age groups. It seems that prime-age workers (30–40 years old) achieve higher height premiums than do others. Based on the studies listed in Table 24.1, the wage gain for this age group is roughly 12% for men and women. The analogous figure for younger men is 10% and that for older workers is 7%. For younger and older women, we have calculated 5%. However, a systematic analysis on the impact of age is unavailable and presents its own challenges. Differences between younger and older workers may mask some influences that impact on the wage premium of height, and it is difficult to disentangle them. For example, older workers have higher incomes and more experience than younger ones. On average, the education level of older workers is lower than that of the younger generation, their health lags behind, they are more risk averse, and they are shorter. In panel estimates, it is difficult to split age, time, and cohort effects—see Baetschmann (2014).

23.4.4 Differences Between Men and Women

Although many empirical studies find that the height premium is larger for men than for women—see Table 24.1 and Figure 24.2—this result is not always observed. Based

Table 24.1 Empirical studies of the relationship between height and wages

Source	Dataset	Country	Period	Restriction	Gender	Sample Size	Height	Wage Gains Coefficient in Percent
Böckerman et al., 2010	Health 2000	Finland	2000	age: 30–64	men	N = 1,247	0.007***	7
	in Finland				women	N = 1,259	0.005***	5
Böckerman & Vainomäki, 2013	Finnish Twin	Finland	1990	age: 17–45	men	N = 5,060	0.033***	33
	Cohort Study		2004	twins	women	N = 4,680	0.014**	14
Lundborg et al., 2014	SCB	Sweden	1984–1997	age: 28–38	men	N = 145,210	0.006***	6
			1999, 2003					
Hübler, 2009	SOEP	Germany	1985	age: 25–55	men	N = 22,836	0.003***	3
			2004		women	N = 13,918	0.001	1
Case & Paxson, 2008	BCS	UK	1958	age: 42	men	N = 2,253	0.010***	3
			1970	age: 30	women	N = 2,127	0.015***	6
Case, Paxson, & Islam, 2009	BHPS	UK	1997	age: 21–60	men	N = 2,360	0.008**	3
			2005		women	N = 2,618	0.012***	4
Heineck, 2008	BHPS	UK	2004	age: 21–50	men	N = 2,253	0.006*	2
					women	N = 2,397	0.014***	6
Cinnirella & Winter, 2009	SHARE	13 European	2004/05	age<65	men	N = 3,058	0.082***	8
		countries	2006/07					
Persico et al., 2004	NCDS	UK	1958–1965	age: 31–38	men	N = 1,772	0.027***	11
	NLSY	USA	1979, 1994		men	N = 1,577	0.025***	10

Case & Paxson, 2008	PSID	USA	1988–1997	age: 25–60	men	N = 23,465	0.019***	7
					women	N = 21,271	0.012***	5
Vogl, 2014	MxFLS	Mexico	2002	age: 25–65	men	N = 3,860	0.023***	2
			2005					
Gao & Smyth, 2010	CULS	China	2005	age> = 16	men	N = 5,026	0.010***	10
						N = 3,893	0.009***	9
Tao, 2014	TIPED	Taiwan	2004	age: 19–24	women	N = 2,510	0.140	1
			2006	full time				
Sohn, 2015	IFLS	Indonesia	2007		men	N = 8,432	0.036***	36
					women	N = 4,811	0.044***	55
LaFave & Thomas, 2013	WISE	Indonesia	2002q	age: 25–65	men	N = 38,430	3.636***	23
			2009q	log height				
Dinda et al., 2006	ICMR	India	1986	age: 21–50	men	N = 3,567	0.085***	85
			1993	coalminers				

Notes: The last column displays the wage gains in percent if height increases 10 cm. Most studies are based on OLS. Hübler (2006), Gao & Smyth (2010), or Böckerman & Vainomäki (2013) apply an IV estimator and Tao (2014) a sample selection approach. The dependent variable is usually the log of hourly wages. Sometimes, the log of monthly earnings (Dinda et al., 2006), log of annual earnings (Böckerman & Vainomäki, 2013; Lundborg et al., 2014; Sohn, 2015) and entry earnings per month (Tao, 2014) are used.

* $p<0.10$, ** $p<0.05$, *** $p<0.01$.

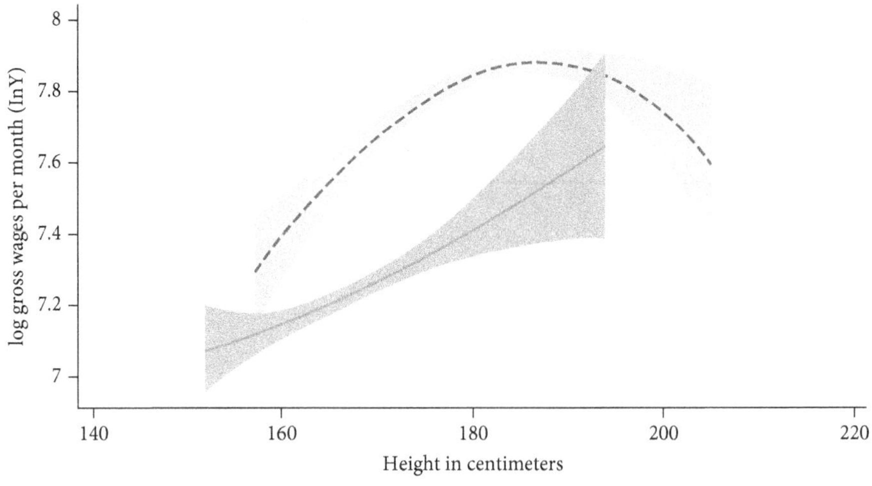

FIGURE 24.2 Height effects on (log) gross wages per month represented by fractional-polynomial prediction plots with confidence intervals.

Source: German Socio-Economic Panel 2012 (Wagner et al. 2007)

on the studies in Table 24.1, we find that men achieve a roughly 15% wage gain due to a 10 cm increase in height. The analogous figure for women is 10%.

Böckerman and Vainiomäki (2013) investigate the differences between Finnish men and women in more detail using twin data. They demonstrate that the gender differences of the height premium depend on the specification and estimation method, whether an OLS or IV estimate is applied, and whether only monozygotic (MZ) or also dizygotic (DZ) twins are considered. In the case of DZ twins, they find the usual result: namely, a significant height premium for both men and women, although the premium is higher for men than for women. Under IV estimates restricted to an MZ sample, the height premium for men is insignificant and is additionally smaller than that for women when social skills are incorporated as further regressors. It should be stressed that taller Finnish women have better social skills than do taller Finnish men. For men, there exists only a weak correlation between social skills and height. These results are in contrast to that of Persico et al. (2004), in which the social skills' effects are strongly significant Böckerman and Vainiomäki (2013) conclude that social skills are not the relevant explanation for the existence of a height premium, as Persico et al. (2004) have maintained. Furthermore, it should be stressed that the course of the wage function with respect to height differs between men and women. As Figure 24.2 demonstrates for Germany, the male course is concave whereas that for women is less clear.

23.4.5 The Importance of Nutrition, Health, Education, and Physical Capacity

Case and Paxson (2008) find a strong correlation between height at age 3 and height in adulthood. Therefore, they argue that the latter provides a marker for the nutrition and health environment that an adult experienced in early life. The strong empirical correlation between height in adulthood and wages might be of an indirect nature. Strauss and Thomas (1998) model the relationships among health, nutrition, and economic development, whereas Thomas and Strauss (1997) review links to wages. Using data from Brazil, they find that among four health indicators—height, BMI, per capita calorie intake, and per capita protein intake—all of them are significantly related to the wage levels of both men and women who work in the market sector.

In Germany, teachers provide more favorable educational track decisions to taller students (Cinnirella et al., 2011), and Spears (2012) shows that, in India, taller children perform better on average on tests of cognitive achievement due to differences in early-life health and net nutrition. Better schooling is the consequence, and better education improves the chances of higher earnings.

Lundborg et al. (2014) argue that the correlation between height and wages can be explained mainly by the positive association between height and physical capacity. They find that 80% of the height premium in Sweden is due to physical capacity. Similarly, Cornelissen and Pfeifer (2010) find that individuals who participate in sport activities in their leisure time earn more than those who do not. However, this does not mean that this premium is due to specific physically demanding job tasks or that the height premium systematically differs in accord with the physical strenuousness of work. In Finland, the height premium is not larger for those with a lot of muscle mass, but the effects are somewhat larger for sedentary work (Böckerman, Johansson, Kiiskinen, & Heliövaara, 2010). It is interesting to note that this investigation finds that the probability of being employed in sedentary work increases with the height. The causality chain of this observation is that tall people have a tendency toward leadership connected with having good interpersonal skills since early adolescence, and these characteristics are required in managerial positions, which typically tend to be sedentary and pay higher wages.

23.4.6 Ambiguous Causality

Most of these studies demonstrate that causality is not always obvious. On the one hand, good nutrition contributes to good health, and this improves the chances of attaining greater height. On the other hand, we find medical and epidemiological studies demonstrating that tall people are more disease-resistant. For example, short people have a greater risk of osteoarthritis. However, studies indicating that taller people are healthier than shorter ones have ignored a wide range of evidence that shorter people can be highly creative, productive, long-lived, athletic, and better for the environment

(Samaras, Elrick, & Storms, 1999). Taller individuals have a higher risk of certain cancers (McEvoy & Visscher, 2009). Genetic as well as environmental influences determine the statistical correlation between height and health.

A similar problem exists between education and height. Is the effect chain "parents' education determines children's education and height" decisive or should we focus on the direct impact of height on success in schooling? Both strands of explanation make sense. Using OLS estimates, von Hinke Kessler Scholder et al. (2012) find a positive correlation between children's height and academic performance and fewer behavioral problems in taller children. IV results differ. In this case, only taller girls have better academic performance, and being taller appears to increase behavioral problems. Finally, we should stress that the importance of risk aversion in the height–wage association is also ambiguous. Tall individuals are less risk-averse due to their higher self-confidence, and risky behavior is rewarded. Height can also produce characteristics that are relevant for risky behavior. The leadership roles preferred by tall individuals require a willingness for decision making and a relatively high degree of risk tolerance. Independent of all these causal links, height and wages are linked via health, abilities, education, and the degree of risk aversion.

23.4.7 Height, Happiness, and Wages

There is evidence for both the height–satisfaction link and the satisfaction–wage relationship. Brewer and Riley (2009) as well as Rietveld et al. (2014) find that tall men report a higher degree of satisfaction than do short men. Deaton and Arora (2009) also report that taller people evaluate their lives more favorably and are more likely to report a range of positive emotions, such as enjoyment and happiness. Denny (2010) finds that height is a protective against depression. However, when controlling for health, the reverse effect is observed, and the relationship disappears completely when health and education are both controlled for. Carrieri and de Paola (2012) argue that happiness is driven by the correlation between height and economic and health conditions. Other empirical studies demonstrate a positive correlation between happiness and wages (Mohanty & Ullah, 2012; Pischke, 2011; Pouwels, Siegers, & Vlasblom, 2008), in which causality goes in both directions. An indirect relationship between height and wage via satisfaction or between height and satisfaction via income is possible.

23.4.8 Should Weight Also Be Considered?

A further critical point of empirical height–wage investigations is the incorporation of weight into the analysis. Although most studies neglect this covariate, some do include weight or BMI. The motivation for including them is that height is a proxy for weight. However, Persico et al. (2004) find that the incorporation of weight leaves the relationship between adult and teen height, on the one hand, and wages, on the other hand, nearly unchanged. Another result is presented by Tao (2014): without controlling for weight, the coefficient of log height on log wages for females is only about a fourth of that in any model that includes the log weight. The log height effect also increases if BMI instead of log weight is incorporated as an additional regressor. In this specification, the BMI effect is insignificant. By contrast, Sohn (2014) detects that the height coefficient reduces to a third for males when weight is added as a wage determinant. For females, this coefficient decreases from 0.444 to 0.315, implying that height and weight are more strongly correlated for men than for women. Or, in other words, it is more important to incorporate weight into the male wage function. However, we should note that in both cases the height and weight effects are significant. Lee (2014) finds that weight or BMI controlling for height is not significantly related to wages. His analysis suggests the existence of a height premium over a broad weight range.

23.4.9 Interpersonal Dominance of Tall People

Arguably, interpersonal dominance is positively correlated with height. Tall people are more readily noticed by their peers and project greater authority. We "look-up" to those who are tall, and we admire them (Frieze, Olson, & Good, 1990). Self-confidence and leadership are the consequence, characteristics that are advantageous in management positions. It is more likely that older than younger employees are in management positions. Several studies have indicated that, at least for men, the advantage of being tall is translated into higher salaries. As in most other effects on height, the relationship is nonlinear: there is an optimal height—usually around 188 cm (6 feet 2 inches) for men and 170 cm (5 feet 7 inches) for women—beyond which the effect disappears and eventually turns negative.

23.4.10 Discrimination Against Short People

Some support has been found for the discrimination hypothesis, although it is not obvious whether employers, customers, or both are responsible for discrimination against short men and women. A problem with all studies is that income differences can be due to unobserved productivity differences and to outright discrimination based on preferences, but only the unexplained income differences are evident. Using Blinder's decomposition procedure, the analysis of log wage differences in Germany between height groups shows significant income differentials by height that can be due either to productivity differences or to discrimination. Roughly 15% of the height-induced wage difference for men and less than 10% for women can be denoted as discrimination (Hübler, 2006, 2009). In the private sector, men within a range of 10 cm around the height with the strongest wage effects earn 5–6% more than other men. The analogous effect for women is negative (0.5%) and insignificant. The discrimination against short and very tall men only takes place in the private sector, not in the public sector. This result could speak in favor of customers' preferences to interact with moderately tall salesmen. Assuming that these favored employees generate higher profits, then we can expect that they earn higher wages. It is also possible that employers prefer tall workers independently of customers' preferences, that employers make systematic mistakes in their evaluation of tall and short people, or that they believe that their customers prefer tall workers when they really do not. In the long run, the wrong evaluation and belief explanations do not seem to hold, because otherwise competitors would have cost advantages and would eventually force employers with misconceptions out of the market. In the public sector, where the profit motive is absent, this reasoning is irrelevant or illegal.

Based on their estimates of Finnish twin data, Böckerman and Vainiomäki (2013) also believe that discrimination against short people may play a role at wage differences. For women, the height premium prevails for MZ in comparison to DZ twins. Therefore, the authors see a hint for possible discrimination against short workers as an explanation for the height premium for women. Further evidence of discrimination due to customer preference is presented by Sohn (2015). He investigated discrimination against short people in Indonesia, and his estimates show significant height premiums for both men and women in the private sector but not in the public sector. Cinnirella and Winter (2009) do not analyze discrimination via earnings but via occupational sorting. They find that height has a significant effect on occupational sorting of employees but not for the self-employed. They interpret their result as employer discrimination against short workers. This study is based on cross-sectional data from 13 European countries.

23.4.11 Differences Among Industries

In addition to occupational sorting, some empirical studies investigate whether heterogeneity of height effects on earnings can be found between industries. For Germany, estimations reveal that impressive height–wage premiums are paid in such sectors as agriculture, stone quarrying, the sand-and-clay industry, recycling, and computing, whereas extremely low premiums are recorded in the service sector. Because a positive correlation between the average height coefficient in the wage function and height based on private-industry data exists, the height premiums can be interpreted as an incentive for self-selection (Hübler, 2009). Another explanation for why the impact of height on wages varies from industry to industry is due to physical abilities. In some economic sectors, the work is focused on sedentary activities, while in others physical strength is required. Research into individual industries and occupations can deliver insights into the reasons that height premiums vary between working activities. There is ample evidence that CEOs are substantially taller than average; for example, Lindqvist (2012), using a representative sample of Swedish men, documents that tall men are significantly more likely to attain managerial positions. An increase in height of 10 cm is associated with a 2.2 percentage point increase in the probability of holding a managerial position. In future, we should also investigate whether height premiums differ between workplace activities and between job tasks (see, e.g., Spitz-Oener, 2006).

23.5 Open Questions and Future Studies

Empirical studies show a wide range of height–wage premiums, as Section 4.2 revealed, depending on the specification of the regression model. Because, in general, a direct relationship between height and wages does not exist except between physical productivity and wages, even though different indirect channels are effective, we need a clear theoretical basis. Simple wage functions with height as the only determinant (e.g., as presented in Figure 24.2) do not reveal the channel that contributes to the relationship.

Ideally, a structural system should be estimated that includes health, education, risk aversion, discrimination, and life satisfaction as major influences with feedback and dynamic effects over the different stages of life. This is seldom possible, insofar as not all necessary information is available, thus making it challenging to identify these influences. However, such an approach would be especially useful if policy implications are the objective of the analysis.

Future investigations should focus on comparisons between countries and on subgroups. Wage effects of height within a firm would also be useful: insider econometrics is the key word here. Moreover, studying heterogeneity in the relationship between height and wages is an important topic that has been neglected. This means that the baseline model should be applied to different subgroups, as Heckman et al. (2014) have demonstrated in another context. From a methodological perspective, we need to decompose the effects into important and unimportant influences that can also identify the joint effect of different variables; for example, principal component analysis, LASSO, and LARS all point in this direction.

From a policy perspective, the following questions should be answered: Does it make sense to subsidize short and very tall people? Can we really say that short and very tall individuals are discriminated against? Evidence is pretty clear that some discrimination is going on, especially in managerial positions and higher up the corporate ladder because height is one aspect of the beauty premium (Hamermesh, 2012). Is it possible to eliminate discrimination? (The answer is that we should try, but a complete removal is very difficult.) Should programs be instituted during adolescence to strengthen the self-esteem of short boys and girls, or is supportive therapy and psychological care in later life for adults more effective in reducing possible discrimination or the negative individual consequences of discrimination?

References

Baetschmann, G. (2014). Heterogeneity in the relationship between happiness and age: Evidence from the German Socio-Economic Panel. *German Economic Review, 15*, 393–410.

Biddle, J. E., & Hamermesh, D. S. (1998). Beauty, productivity, and discrimination: Lawyers' looks and lucre. *Journal of Labor Economics, 16*, 172–201.

Böckerman, P., Johansson, E., Kiiskinen, U., & Heliövaara, M. (2010). The relationship between physical work and the height premium. *Economics and Human Biology, 8*, 414–420.

Böckerman, P., & Vainiomäki, J. (2013). Stature and life-time labor market outcomes: Accounting for unobserved differences. *Labour Economics, 24*, 86–96.

Brewer, G., & Riley, C. (2009). Height, relationship satisfaction, jealousy, and mate retention. *Evolutionary Psychology, 7*(3) 477–489.

Buser, T., Oosterbeek, H., Plug, E., Ponce, J., & Rosero, J. (2014). The impact of positive and negative income changes on the height and weight on young children. IZA Discussion Paper No. 8130.

Carrieri, V., & de Paola, M. (2012). Height and subjective well-being in Italy, *Economics and Human Biology, 10*, 289–298.

Case, A., & Paxson, C. (2006). Stature and status: Height, ability, and labor market outcome. NBER Discussion Paper No. w12466.

Case, A., & Paxson, C. (2008). Stature and status: Height, ability, and labor market outcome. *Journal of Political Economy, 116*, 491–532.

Case, A., Paxson, C., & Islam, M. (2009). Making sense of the labor market premium: Evidence from the British Household Panel Survey. *Economics Letters, 102*, 174–176.

Cawley, J. (2004). The impact of obesity on wages. *Journal of Human Resources, 39*, 451–474.

Cinnirella, F., Piopiunik, M., & Winter, J. (2011). Why does height matter for educational attainment? Evidence from German children. *Economics and Human Biology, 9*, 407–418.

Cinnirella, F., & Winter, J. (2009). Size matters! Body height and labor market discrimination: A cross-European analysis. CESifo Discussion Paper No. 2733.

Cornelissen, T., & Pfeifer, C. (2010). The impact of participation in sports on educational attainment: New evidence from Germany. *Economics of Education Review, 29*(1), 94–103.

Deaton, A., & Arora, R. (2009). Life at the top: The benefits of height. *Economics and Human Biology, 7*, 133–136.

Denny, K. (2010). Height and well-being amongst older Europeans. University College Dublin, UCD Centre for Economic Research, Working Paper Series WP10/36.

Dinda, S., Gangopadhyay, P. K., Chattopadhyay, B. P., Saiyed, H. N., Pal, M., & Bharati, P. (2006). Height, weight and earnings among coalminers in India. *Economics and Human Biology, 4*, 342–350.

Dohmen, T., Falk, A., Huffman, D., Sunde, U., Schupp, J., & Wagner, G. G. (2011). Individual risk attitude: Measurement, determinants and behavioral consequences. *Journal of the European Economic Association, 9*(3), 522–560.

Frieze, I. H., Olson, J. E., & Good, H. N. (1990). Perceived and actual discrimination in the salaries of male and female managers. *Journal of Applied Social Psychology, 20*(1), 46–67.

Gao, W., & Smyth, R. (2010). Health human capital, height and wages in China. *Journal of Development Studies, 46*(3), 466–484.

Garcia, J., & Quintana-Domeque, C. (2007). The evolution of adult height in Europe: A brief note. *Economics & Human Biology, 5*(2), 340–349.

Grajales-Porras, A., & Lopez-Alonso, M. (2011). Physical stature of men in eighteenth century Mexico: Evidence from Puebla. *Economics and Human Biology, 9*, 265–271.

Hamermesh, D. S. (2012). Tall or taller, pretty or prettier: Is discrimination absolute or relative? *IZA Journal of Labor Economics, 1*(2), 1–17.

Hatton, T. J. (2014). How have Europeans grown so tall? *Oxford Economic Papers, 66*, 349–372.

Hatton, T. J., & Bray, B. E. (2010). Long run trends in the heights of European men, 19th-20th centuries. *Economics and Human Biology, 8*, 405–413.

Heckman, J. J., Humphries, J. E. Veramendi, G., & Urzua, S. (2014). Education, health and wages. NBER Working Paper No. w19971.
Heineck, G. (2006). Height and weight in Germany: Evidence from the German Socio-Economic Panel, 2002. *Economics and Human Biology, 4*, 359–382.
Heineck, G. (2008). A note on the height-wage differential in the UK: Cross sectional evidence from BHPS. *Economics Letters, 98*, 288–293.
Hopfensitz, A., & Wranik, T. (2008). Psychological and environmental myopic loss aversion. Toulouse School of Economics, MPRA Paper No. 9305.
Hryshko, D., Luengo-Prado, M. J. & Sorensen, B. E. (2011). Childhood determinants of risk aversion: The long shadow of compulsory education. *Quantitative Economics, 2*, 37–72.
Huang, W., Lei, X., Ridder, G., Strauss, J., & Zhao, Y. (2012). Health, height, height shrinkage and SES at older ages: Evidence from China. IZA Discussion Paper No. 6489.
Hübler, O. (2006). The nonlinear link between height and wages: An empirical investigation. IZA Discussion Paper No. 2394.
Hübler, O. (2009). The nonlinear link between height and wages in Germany, 1985-2004. *Economics and Human Biology, 7*(2), 191–199.
Hübler, O. (2013). Are tall people less risk averse than others? *Journal of Applied Social Science Studies, 133*, 23–42.
Komlos, J. (2009). Recent trends in height by gender and ethnicity in the US in relation to levels of income. NBER Working Paper No. 14653.
Komlos, J., & Carson, L. (2012). The anthropometric history of native Americans, c. 1820-1890. CESifo Working Paper No. 3740.
Komlos, J., & Kriwy, P. (2003). The biological standard of living in the two Germanies. *German Economic Review, 4*(4), 459–473.
Komlos, J., & Lauderdale, B. E. (2007). The mysterious trend in the American heights in the 20th century. *Annals of Human Biology, 34*(2), 206–215.
Kuhn, P., & Weinberger, C. (2005). Leadership skills and wages. *Journal of Labor Economics, 23*(3), 395–436.
LaFave, D., & Thomas, D. (2013). Height and cognition at work: Labor market performance in a low income setting. Working Paper, Department of Economics, Colby College, Waterville, ME.
Lee, W. S. (2014). Big and tall: Is there a height premium or obesity penalty in the labor market? IZA Discussion Paper No. 8606.
Lindqvist, E. (2012). Height and leadership. *Review of Economics and Statistics, 94*(4), 1191–1196.
Lundborg, P., Nystedt, P., & Rooth, D. -O. (2014). Height and earnings: The role cognitive and noncognitive skills. *Journal of Human Resources, 49*(1), 141–166.
McEvoy, B. P., & Visscher, P. M. (2009). Genetics of human height. *Economics and Human Biology, 7*, 294–306.
Mohanty, M. S., & Ullah, A. (2012). Direct and indirect effects of happiness on wages: A simultaneous equations approach. *The Journal of Socio-Economics, 41*, 143–152.
Persico, N., Postlewaite, A., & Silverman, D. (2004). The effect of adolescent experience on labor market outcomes: The case of height. *Journal of Political Economy, 112*, 1019–1053.
Pischke, J. -S. (2011). Money and happiness: Evidence from the industry wage structure. NBER Working Paper 17056.
Pouwels, B., Siegers, J., & Vlasblom, J. D. (2008). Income, working hours, and happiness. *Economics Letters, 99*, 72–74.

Quintana-Domeque, C., Bozzoli, C., & Bosch, M. (2012). The evolution of adult height across Spanish regions, 1950–1980. *Economics and Human Biology, 10*, 264–275.

Ranasinghe, P., Naveen, M. A., Jayawardana, A. A. D., Constantine, G. R., Rezvi Sheriff, M. H., Matthews, D. R., & Katulanda, P. (2011). Patterns and correlates of adult height in Sri Lanka. *Economics and Human Biology, 9*, 23–29.

Rietveld, C. A., Hessels, J., & van der Zwan, P. (2014). The stature of the self-employed and its premium. Tinbergen Institute Discussion Paper TI 2014-109/VII.

Samaras, T. T., Elrick, H., & Storms, D. R. (1999). Height, health and growth hormone. *Acta Paediatrica, 88*, 602–609.

Samaras, T. T., Elrick, H., & Storms, L. H. (2004). Is short height really a risk factor for coronary heart decease and stroke mortality? A review. *Medical Science Monitor, 10*, 63–76.

Schick, A., & Steckel, R. H. (2015). Height, human capital, and earnings: The contributions of cognitive and non-cognitive ability. *Journal of Human Capital, 9*(1), 94–115.

Spears, D. (2012). Height and cognitive achievement among Indian children. *Economics and Human Biology, 10*, 210–219.

Spitz-Oener, A. (2006). Technical change, job tasks and rising educational demands: Looking outside the wage structure. *Journal of Labor Economics, 24*(2), 235–270.

Schultz, T. P. (2002). Wage gains associated with height as a form of health human capital. *American Economic Review, 92*, 349–353.

Sohn, K. (2015). The height premium in Indonesia. *Economics and Human Biology, 16*, 1–15.

Steckel, R. H. (1995). Stature and the standard of living. *Journal of Economic Literature, 33*, 1903–1940.

Strauss, J., & Thomas, D. (1998). Health, nutrition, and economic development. *Journal of Economic Literature, 36*, 766–817.

Tao, H. -L. (2014). Height, weight, and entry earnings of female graduates in Taiwan. *Economics and Human Biology, 13*, 85–98.

Thomas, D., & Strauss, J. (1997). Health and wages: Evidence on men and women in urban Brazil. *Journal of Econometrics, 77*, 159–185.

Vogl, T. S. (2014). Height, skills, and labor market outcomes in Mexico. *Journal of Development Economics, 107*, 84–96.

von Hinke Kessler Scholder, S., Smith, G. D., Lawlor, D. A., Propper, C., & Windmeijer, F. (2012). Child height, health and human capital: Evidence using genetic markers. CMPO Working Papers No. 10/245.

Waaler, H. T. (1984). Height, weight, and mortality: The Norwegian experience. *Acta Medica Scandinavica, 215*, 1–56.

Wagner, G. G., Frick, J., & Schupp, J. (2007). The German Socio-Economic Panel Study—scope, evaluation and enhancement, *Journal of Applied Social Science Studies, 127*, 139–169.

CHAPTER 25

WHY DO PEOPLE WITH HIGHER BODY WEIGHT EARN LOWER WAGES?

JANE GREVE

25.1 Introduction

In recent years, obesity has become one of the most debated health issues in the public sphere. Through the media's increasing focus and often sensation-mongering approach to this subject, the rapid increase in overweight and obesity rates in almost all Western countries has become known in all aspects of society: from government to households. A recent publication in *The Lancet* confirms that the prevalence of overweight and obesity is increasing among children and adults and among both men and women in developing and developed countries (Ng, Fleming, Robinson, Thomson, & Graetz, 2014). As obesity continues to increase in most countries of the world, so do the direct and indirect costs related to obesity. Generally speaking, direct costs include health care costs related to diagnostic and treatment services, whereas indirect costs are related to the value of wages lost due to inability to work because of illness, as well as earnings lost due to discrimination.

Several hypotheses have been posed to explain the impact of body weight on wages (i.e., that obesity leads to changes in productivity or labor supply, taste-based discrimination, and statistical discrimination). In this chapter, I present different hypotheses and empirical evidence on why people with higher body weight tend to earn lower wages. Furthermore, I present an overview of the tendencies in the recent literature on body weight and wages. I mainly discuss the relationship between body weight and wages in Western countries. Although this relationship is also truly relevant in non-Western countries, labor market conditions and the demand for and supply of labor differ significantly from Western countries and consequently produce slightly different results and explanations for the relationship between body weight and wages. Moreover, the majority of the literature on body weight and wages comes from the United States and Europe.[1]

25.2 Is the Group of People Earning a Positive Wage a Selected Group?

Before I examine the question of why we generally see a wage penalty with higher body weight, I will examine the empirical results on *whom* the wage penalty affects. First, the results from an estimation of the relationship between body weight and wages might depend on who is active on the labor market. If the selection into the labor market depends on body weight, this might have an impact on the relationship between body weight and wages.

A review of the existing literature on the relationship between obesity and employment (Burkhauser & Cawley, 2008; Garcia & Quintana-Domeque, 2007; Greve, 2008; Johansson, Böckerman, Kiiskinen, & Heliövaara, 2009; Lindeboom, Lundborg, & van der Klaauw, 2010; Lundborg, Bolin, Höjgård, & Lindgren, 2007; Tunceli, Li, & Williams, 2006) yields quite similar conclusions regarding employment of women: higher body weight is negatively related to the probability of being employed, although the relationship is not significantly different from zero in all countries (Garcia & Quintana-Domeque, 2007).[2] Detecting a consistent relationship between body weight and employment for men appears to be slightly more difficult. Several studies find that obesity is negatively associated with employment for men (Greve, 2008; Lundborg et al., 2007; Han, 2006; Morris, 2007), but some studies find that men in the overweight category tend to be just as likely to be employed as men of a healthy weight (Greve, 2008; Johansson et al., 2009).

An experimental study (Rooth, 2009) found strong evidence of employment discrimination against obese workers in Sweden. In this study, fictitious job applicants with photos included, some obese and some nonobese, were sent to real job openings. The job applicants with photos of obese people received significantly fewer callback responses for interviews, and employers in occupations with more customer contact discriminated more than did those with less customer contact. Thus, when analyzing the effect of obesity on wages, it is important to bear in mind that the sample of wage earners might be a selected group and that the effect could be an underestimation of the true effect.

25.3 Explanations on the Relationship Between Body Weight and Wages

The relationship between body weight and wages can reflect three possible relations: obesity may affect wages, wages may affect obesity, and there may be a third factor that affects both body weight and wages (Cawley, 2004). This third factor could be, for example, that obese people are generally more myopic (i.e., they are less concerned about health effects and less concerned about the future and less likely to invest in education). Thus, an empirical relationship between body weight and wages does not necessarily reflect a causal relationship from increased body weight to lower wages.

Two central hypotheses can explain the causal impact of body weight on wages: supply of and demand for labor. First, increasing body weight may affect labor supply if derived health problems limit both the individual's ability to work and the individual's preferences for work. Second, discrimination against obese people in the labor market can be a consequence of prejudice or of preferences (for nonobese workers) on the part of employers, employees, or customers (Becker, 1971). Determining when differences in employment should be categorized as discrimination is not easy because employment differences are often justified by actual or expected productivity differences or additional costs associated with employing a specific individual. Due to the link between obesity and various diseases, an obese person may have more sick days than a person of a healthy weight. If obese people have a significantly higher rate of absenteeism on average, thereby creating higher costs for the employer, then more sick days may lead to statistical discrimination.

Although several explanations for the association between body mass index (BMI) and wages exist, labor market discrimination against obese people has received increasing attention partly because of increasing concern about both health- and beauty-related productivity loss related to obesity, partly because of an empirically validated increase in the prevalence of weight discrimination (Andreyeva, Puhl, & Brownell, 2008).

25.4 Empirical Model and Results

The relationship between body weight and wages is often estimated using a Mincer-type wage model such as the following:

$$w_i = \propto + \beta BW_i + X_i'\gamma + \varepsilon_i. \qquad (1)$$

In this type of model, individual earnings (or log of hourly wage), w_i, is regressed on a body weight measure (e.g., BMI or classifications into underweight, overweight, and obese), BW_i, and a set of characteristics through which the relationship between body weight and wages could be mediated, X_i. These characteristics could be, for example, years of schooling or work experience, but also individual characteristics such as race, marital status, union membership status, self-reported health status, cognitive skills, and noncognitive skills.

Under the assumption that $cov(BW_i, \varepsilon_i) = 0$, β captures the returns to body weight as measured through preferential or discriminatory treatment in the labor market. However, it is reasonable to believe that important variables that are related to body weight and difficult to measure are missing in this regression, thus violating that $cov(BW_i, \varepsilon_i) = 0$. These variables could, for instance, be measures of attractiveness, self-esteem, self-control, or preferences for current time (current consumption) as opposed to preferences for the future (later consumption).

A number of studies have analyzed the relationship between BMI and "difficult to measure" characteristics, and they generally find that there is a significant relationship between the two factors, although very few studies are able to document that the relationship is causal. For example, Mocan and Tekin (2011) find that being overweight or obese has a negative impact on the self-esteem of females and black males and that, when including self-esteem in the wage equation, the impact of body weight on wage is reduced among white females. Several studies have examined the relationship between body weight and preferences for time (Borghans & Golsteyn, 2006; Cutler & Glaeser, 2005; Komlos, Smith, & Bogin, 2004; Smith, Bogin, & Bishai, 2005) and find some evidence of the relationship between BMI and the ways in which people discount the future. However, the results on the relationship between BMI and time preferences both depend on the proxy for the discount rate and vary between subgroups in the population.

Finally, a growing literature has found evidence of a negative association between body weight and cognitive and noncognitive skills (Cawley & Spiess, 2008; Lundborg, Nystedt, & Rooth, 2014; Sabia, 2007), although the relationship between obesity and cognitive skills are not verified in other studies (Fletcher & Lehrer, 2009).

When estimating the relationship between body weight and wages, previous studies have dealt with the problem of unobserved heterogeneity and simultaneity using different econometric methods. These include a measure of previous body weight (Averett & Korenman, 1996; Conley & Glauber, 2007; Sargent & Blanchflower, 1994; Wada & Tekin, 2010), using twin studies (Averett & Korenman, 1996; Behrman & Rosenzweig, 2001), using sibling or individual fixed effects (Averett & Korenman, 1996; Baum & Ford, 2004; Bozoyan & Wolbring, 2011; Cawley, 2004; Conley & Glauber, 2007; Fahr, 2006; Han, 2006; Han, Norton, & Powell, 2011; Han, Norton, & Stearns, 2009; Härkönen, Räsänen, & Näsi, 2011; Lundborg et al., 2014; Majumder, 2013; Sabia & Rees, 2012; Shimokawa, 2008; Wada & Tekin, 2010), or using instrumental variables (Brunello & D'Hombres, 2007; Cawley, 2004; Cawley, Grabka, & Lillard, 2005; Han, 2006; Johar & Katayama, 2012; Kortt & Leigh, 2010; Lundborg et al., 2007; Morris, 2006; Norton & Han, 2008; Sabia & Rees, 2012; Shimokawa, 2008; Wada & Tekin, 2010).

Table 25.1 provides an overview of the existing literature on the relationship between BMI and wages. Most of the studies on body weight and wages are based on data from the United States (Averett & Korenman, 1996; Baum & Ford, 2004; Behrman & Rosenzweig, 2001; Cawley, 2003; Cawley, 2004; Conley & Glauber, 2007; Gregory & Ruhm, 2009; Han, 2006; Han et al., 2009, 2011; Johar & Katayama, 2012; McLean & Moon, 1980; Mocan & Tekin, 2011; Norton & Han, 2008; Pagan & Davila, 1997; Sabia & Rees, 2012; Wada & Tekin, 2010), but there are also studies from Europe (Atella, Pace, & Vuri 2008; Bozoyan & Wolbring 2011; Brunello & D'Hombres 2007; Cawley et al., 2005; Fahr, 2006; Garcia & Quintana-Domeque, 2007; Greve, 2008; Lundborg et al., 2007, 2014; Morris, 2007; one study from China (Shimokawa, 2008), one study from Australia (Kortt & Leigh, 2010), and one study from the Philippines (Colchero & Bishai, 2012).

Most of the studies find a negative relationship between BMI and wages among women (Atella, Pace, & Vuri, 2008; Averett & Korenman, 1996; Baum & Ford, 2004; Brunello & D'Hombres, 2007; Cawley, 2003, 2004; Cawley et al., 2005; Conley & Glauber, 2007; Garcia & Quintana-Domeque, 2007; Gregory & Ruhm, 2009; Greve, 2008; Han, 2006; Han et al., 2009, 2011; Härkönen et al., 2011; Johansson et al., 2009; Johar & Katayama, 2012; Lundborg et al., 2007; Mocan & Tekin, 2011; Morris, 2006; Register & Williams, 1990; Sargent &

Table 25.1 Overview of the literature on body weight and wages

Author (year of publication)	Data [country; number of observations; age group]	Body weight measure	Method	Effect (men and women)	Notes
Atella, Pace, & Vuri (2008)	European Community Household Panel (ECHP) 1998–2001 [Denmark, Belgium, Ireland, Italy, Greece, Spain, Portugal, Austria and Finland; 10,792 women, 19,308 men; age: 25–64]	Indicators for obesity, overweight, underweight based on BMI	Quantile regression, IV-quantile regression	In pooled data, the relationship is negative and significant all over the distribution for women and negative and significant only in the bottom part of the distribution for men.	Heterogeneous effects across the wage distribution and across countries. Cultural, environmental, or institutional settings do not seem to explain differences among countries.
Averett & Korenman (1996)	National Longitudinal Surveys of Youth (NLSY) 1979–94 [USA; 5,090 women, 4,951 men, age: 23–31 in 1988]	Lagged indicators for obesity, overweight, underweight	Lagged BMI, individual and same-sex-sibling fixed effects (FE)	OLS: Obese men and women earn a significantly lower wage. Sibling FE: Magnitude is reduced for both men and women	
Baum & Ford (2004)	National Longitudinal Surveys of Youth (NLSY) 1979–94 [USA; 12,686; age: 14–21 in 1979]	Lagged indicator for being obese (ref. not obese)	Individual fixed-effects models and a hybrid individual and sibling fixed-effects (FE)	OLS: Wage penalty for obesity for women and men ranges from 0.7% to 6.3%. The wage penalty is larger for women than for men. FE: Results become insignificant for men	Obese people have a flatter wage profile. Supports that they are more myopic or that they meet discrimination in training opportunities.
Behrman & Rosenzweig (2001)	Minnesota Twins Registry (USA; 710 men, 808 women)	BMI	Twin fixed effects	No effect	

(*Continued*)

Table 25.1 Contniued

Author (year of publication)	Data [country; number of observations; age group]	Body weight measure	Method	Effect (men and women)	Notes
Bozoyan & Wolbring (2011)	BIA data Base Project and the German Socio-Economic Pane [Germany; 1,169 women, 1,592 males; age: 22 (in the year 2002) to 60 (in the year 2008)],	BMI, fat free mass (FFM), body fat (BF)	Fixed-effects models (FE)	No significant relationship between BMI and wages. Lagged BF is negatively associated with wages among women. FE: No significant effect of BMI/BF or FFM and wages.	BF is negatively associated with wages among job changers
Brunello & D'Hombres (2007)	European Community Household Panel (ECHP) [9 European countries; 17,767 women, 34,379 men; age: 15–65 in 1998–2001]	BMI	OLS and IV	In the pooled data, a 10% increase in the average BMI reduces the real earnings of males and females by 3.27% and 1.86%, respectively.	Different effects in northern and southern Europe. Only significant effects in southern Europe.
Cawley (2003)	National Longitudinal Surveys of Youth (NLSY) 1981–2000 [USA; 25,843 white women, 11,742 black women, 7,533 Hispanic women, 29,410 white men, 13,414 black men, 9,070 Hispanic men]	BMI, indicators for obesity, overweight, underweight	OLS	Being obese is negatively associated with wages for (black, white, and Hispanic) women and (white and Hispanic) men. For black men there is a positive relationship.	Results differ depending on gender and race. The relationship between weight and wages is more than twice as strong for white females as for black females. Weight affects physical health and disability in a manner that varies by gender and race/ethnicity
Cawley (2004)	National Longitudinal Surveys of Youth (NLSY) 1981–2000 [USA; 45,120 women, 51,899 men; age: 16–44]	BMI, indicators for obesity, overweight, underweight	OLS, individual fixed effects, IV	OLS: Among white, black, and Hispanic females, and Hispanic obese males earn less than healthy-weight males. Obese black men earn more than healthy-weight black men. IV: Only significant results among white women	Results differ depending on race and gender.

Cawley, Grabka, & Lillard (2005)	Panel Study of Income Dynamics (PSID) 1986, 1999, and 2001 and German Socio-Economic Panel (GSOEP) 2002 [USA and Germany; 1,716 US men, 1,698 US women, 6,649 German men, 5,410 German women; age: 25–65]	BMI, indicators for obesity, overweight, underweight	OLS and IV.	Among women, being obese is associated with 20% lower earning in both US and Germany. IV: Higher BMI reduces earnings for women in the US but not for men in both countries and for German women.	Results differ for gender and countries (US and Germany)
Cawley, Han, & Norton (2011)	New Immigrant Survey 2003 [USA; 2,321 women and 2,171 men; Legal immigrants to the US age 18–62]	BMI, indicators for obesity, overweight, underweight	OLS	No significant relationships between BMI and wages	
Colchero & Bishai (2012)	Cebu Longitudinal Health and Nutrition Surveys [Philippines; 9,174 women]	BMI, indicators for obesity, overweight, healthy weight, underweight	OLS. Heckman two-step procedure correcting for selection into the labor market	Overall, obese women do not earn less than healthy weight women	The results differ depending on job type: Women with a higher BMI earn more when self-employed
Conley & Glauber (2007)	Panel Study of Income Dynamics (PSID) 1986, 1999, 2001 [USA; 623 women, 712 men; age: 25+ in 1986, 1999, and 2001]	BMI, indicators for obesity, overweight, underweight	OLS, lagged BMI, and sibling fixed effects	Compared with healthy weight women, obese women earn 18% less	The results differ by gender, age, and race. Only black men earn less when BMI increases. Younger women earn less when they have a higher BMI, whereas there is no difference in wages when BMI increases among older women.
Fahr (2006)	European Community Household Panel (ECHP) 1998–2001 [Denmark, Belgium, Ireland, Italy, Greece, Spain, Portugal, Austria, and Finland; age: 19–44]	Deviations from the mean from optimal BMI	OLS, fixed effects	Social norms vary between countries, and wage penalties for being above the social norm is found for men.	

(*Continued*)

Table 25.1 Contniued

Author (year of publication)	Data [country; number of observations; age group]	Body weight measure	Method	Effect (men and women)	Notes
Garcia & Quintana-Domeque (2007)	European Community Household Panel (ECHP) 1998–2001 [Denmark, Belgium, Ireland, Italy, Greece, Spain, Portugal, Austria, and Finland; 17,971 women, 29,424 men; age: 25–54]	BMI, weight (controlled for height), indicator for being obese	OLS	Significant negative association between obesity and wages among women in Denmark, Finland, and Portugal. Significant and positive association between obesity and wages among men in Belgium.	Differences in labor market institutions, such as collective bargaining coverage and employer-provided health insurance, may explain the different results
Gregory & Ruhm (2009)	Panel Study of Income Dynamics (PSID) 1986, 1999, 2001, 2003, and 2005 [USA; 7,251 women and 5,775 men; age: 25–55]	BMI	Quantile regression and IV quantile	Increased BMI is associated with wage reductions for white females, beginning at low levels of weight. The evidence for black females is more ambiguous. The results for men are dependent on the estimation technique. Among men, earnings increase through a BMI of around 27 and then fall modestly. IV: Among women wages decrease with BMI throughout virtually the entire range of the latter.	The results differ by gender and race over the wage distribution
Greve (2008)	Danish Work Environment Cohort Study 1995, 2000 (Denmark; 3,666 women, 3,618 men; age: 18–60)	BMI, BMI^2, indicator for obesity, overweight, underweight	OLS	Increased BMI reduces wages in the private sector among women. Among men, overweight men earn more than normal weight men in the private sector.	The results differ by gender and age and sector. Significant results in the private sector. No effects are found in the public sector.

Han (2006)	National Longitudinal Surveys of Youth (NLSY) [USA; 12,686; age: 14–21 in 1979]	Indicators for obesity, overweight, underweight based on BMI	OLS, IV, Fixed effects	An increase in BMI results in a statistically significant decrease in hourly wages for women. The results are rather ambiguous for men.	The results differ depending on age and job specification. Among women, the wage penalty for gaining weight remains in all age groups, and the size of the wage penalty increases as the age group becomes older until age of 34 years old. For men, the effect is negative only for individuals younger than 35 years. Among men, the wage penalty for gaining body weight within individuals appears only for occupations requiring social interactions.
Han, Norton, & Stearns (2009)	National Longitudinal Surveys of Youth (NLSY) 1981–2000 [USA; 12,686; age: 14–21 in 1979]	Indicator for overweight and obese	OLS, fixed effects (FE)	OLS: Among women there is a negative relationship between obesity and wages. Among men, there is a positive relationship when overweight, but a negative relationship when obese for white. Negative relationship for being overweight for Hispanic FE: Negative effect of obesity for white and black women. No significant results among men	Differences in results depending on job specification: Being overweight or obese is costly in terms of wages in jobs involving interpersonal skills for white and black women.

(*Continued*)

Table 25.1 Contniued

Author (year of publication)	Data [country; number of observations; age group]	Body weight measure	Method	Effect (men and women)	Notes
Han, Norton, & Powell (2011)	National Longitudinal Surveys of Youth (NLSY) 1981–98 [USA; 12,686; age: 14–22 in 1979]	BMI, indicator for obesity (in late teenage years)	OLS, lagged BMI, sibling fixed-effects models	Late-teen obesity is indirectly associated with 3.5% lower wages for both women and men.	The indirect BMI wage penalty mainly comes through education for women and from occupation classification for men.
Häekönen, Räsänen, & Näsi (2011)	Finnish part of European Community Household Panel (ECHP) 1998–2001 [Finland; 4,159; age: 25–54]	Indicator for obesity	OLS, random effects (RE)	RE: No significant effect on men's earnings, negative effect on women. Obese women earn 5% lower wages	The lower wages among women is partly explained by occupational sorting and tenure.
Johansson et al. (2009)	Finish Health 2000 [Finland; 1,170 women, 1,163 men; age: 30–54]	BMI and classifications, fat mass, waist circumference	OLS	Among women: Overweight relative to normal weight earn significantly less. Among men: Overweight earn significantly more than normal weight. High fat mass is associated with lower wages. But, controlling for general health, this relationship is no longer significant.	The results differ depending on body weight measure (BMI, fat mass, and waist circumference)
Johar & Katayama (2012)	National Longitudinal Surveys of Youth (NLSY) [USA; 8,787; age: 16–41]	BMI	Quantile regression, IV quantile regression	Women: BMI and wages are negatively correlated at all points in the wage distribution. The relationship is larger at higher wage levels. Controlling for endogeneity, these effects are mainly significant for white females..	Job type (social/nonsocial interaction) play an important role in the body weight–wage relationship. These finding are mainly for whites.

				Men: A negative relationship between BMI and wages for white males over all the wage distribution. A positive relationship between BMI and wages for black men (driven by men in nonsocial jobs)	
Kortt & Leigh (2010)	The Household, Income, and Labour Dynamics in Australia (HILDA) 2006–07 [Australia; 3,357 women, 3,465 men; age: 25–54]	BMI and classifications	OLS, IV	OLS: No significant relationship. IV: No significant effect	
Lundborg et al. (2007)	Survey of Health, Ageing and Retirement in Europe (SHARE) 2004 [Europe; 4,189; age: 50+]	BMI and classifications	OLS, IV	Negative effects for men and women, but only statistically significant for women in central Europe (obesity reduces wages by 15%).	The parameter estimate did not change for women when health variables were included.
Lundborg, Nystedt, & Rooth (2014)	Registers from Statistics Sweden and the Swedish National Service Administration register of enlistment. [Sweden; 150,000 men; Enlisted between 1984 and 1997 and lived in Sweden in 1999]	BMI and classifications, lagged BMI	OLS, sibling fixed effects	Negative effects of teenage overweight and obesity on adult wages for men	A large part of the estimated body–wage penalty reflects lower skill acquisition among overweight and obese teenagers.
McLean & Moon (1980)	National Longitudinal Survey for Mature Men [USA; 2,356 men; age: 51–65]	Weight measure based on insurance industry tables of desired weights for men of varying heights	OLS	A small positive relationship between obesity and earning among men	

(Continued)

Table 25.1 Contniued

Author (year of publication)	Data [country; number of observations; age group]	Body weight measure	Method	Effect (men and women)	Notes
Majumder (2013)	National Longitudinal Surveys of Youth (NLSY) [USA; 8,984; age: 18–30)]	BMI and classifications	OLS, fixed effects (FE)	OLS: No effect for women. Underweight white males earn less than normal weight. Overweight and obese black males earn more than normal weight. FE with lagged body weight: No effect for women. Overweight white men earn more than normal weight men.	"Portly banker" effect: Being overweight among white males is a nonverbal signal of power, strength, and capability.
Mocan & Tekin (2011)	National Longitudinal Study of Adolescent Health–Add Health [USA; N = 15,197; age: 20–26]	BMI and classifications	OLS	Negative relationship between BMI (both current and lagged) and wages among women. No significant relationship for men.	Part of the relationship between obesity and wages among women can be explained by self-esteem.
Morris (2006)	Health Survey for England 1997–98 [England; N = 12,137; age: 18–60 for women, 18–65 for men]	BMI and indicator for obesity	OLS/IV	OLS: BMI measures have a positive direct effect on occupational attainment for males (not significant for obesity) and a negative impact for females. IV: The IV coefficients on the BMI measures are insignificant in all models. Hausman test suggests to rely on OLS.	Subsequent analyses of indirect effects using OLS show considerable variation in the results for males depending on the BMI measure and covariates.
Norton & Han (2008)	The National Longitudinal Study of Adolescent Health –Add Health 2002 [USA; N = 2,574; age: 18–26]	Lagged BMI and indicators for overweight and obesity	OLS, IV	No association or effect between BMI and wages for either men or women	

Pagan & Davila (1997)	National Longitudinal Surveys of Youth (NLSY) [USA; 3,486 women, 3,806 men]	BMI and indicator for being obese	Hausman specification test	Women: BMI reduces earnings. Men: BMI increases earning	Overweight men sort themselves into jobs to offset the wage penalty. For women, the obesity–wage penalty varies little across occupations.
Register & Williams (1990)	National Longitudinal Surveys of Youth (NLSY) [USA; 2,469 and 2,646 men women; age: 18–25]	Indicator for being obese	OLS, Heckman selection model	OLS: Obese women earn 12% less than healthy weight women. Men: No effect.	
Sabia & Rees (2012)	The National Longitudinal Study of Adolescent Health–Add Health [USA; 6,234 women, 6,211 men; age: 24–32]	BMI and classifications	OLS, lagged BMI, fixed effects, IV	For women, an increase in BMI reduces wages. For men, overweight earn more than normal weight men. IV: Significant negative effect of higher BMI on wages for white and black women. A positive significant effect of higher BMI on wages among black men.	Results differ by gender and race.
Sargent & Blanchflower (1994)	England, National Child Development Study [England; 12,537; age: 23]	BMI indicators for overweight (85th percentile) and obese (90th percentile) at age 16	OLS, lagged BMI indicators	Obese women earn less than healthy-weight. No significant relationship between obesity and earnings among men.	

(Continued)

Table 25.1 Contniued

Author (year of publication)	Data [country; number of observations; age group]	Body weight measure	Method	Effect (men and women)	Notes
Shimokawa (2008)	China Health and Nutrition Survey (CHNS) 1989, 1991, 1993, 1997, 2000. [China; 1,937 men and 1,413 women; age: 18–60]	BMI and classifications	OLS, individual fixed effects with lagged weight, IV, semi-parametric model	Semi-parametric model: Wage penalty for being underweight and obese among both men and women.	The wage penalty is larger for men than women. As men are more likely to have more strenuous jobs than women, body weight might be more important for men than women.
Wada & Tekin (2010)	National Health and Nutrition Examination Surveys (NHANES) III 1981–2004 [USA; 6,730 white males, 22,479 white females, 9,919 black males, 8,802 black females; age: 18–49]	BMI and indicators for overweight and obesity, body fat (BF) and fat free mass (FFM)	OLS, IV, individual fixed effects	OLS: An increase in BF is associated with decreases in the wages of both white males and white and black females. IV: Increase in BF reduces wages for white men. Increase in FFM is associated with an increase in the wages of both groups.	

(OLS, ordinary least squares method; IV, instrumental variable method)

Blanchflower, 1994; Shimokawa, 2008), although there are race-dependent differences. Studies from the United States estimated by race show that the negative relationship between BMI and wages mainly applies for white women. In a number of studies, this result holds true when tested for causality using lagged BMI, fixed effects or instrumental variables (Averett & Korenman, 1996; Baum & Ford, 2004; Cawley, 2004; Cawley et al., 2005; Gregory & Ruhm, 2009; Han, 2006; Johar & Katayama, 2012; Sabia & Rees, 2012).

The negative relationship between BMI and wages among (white) women seems to differ according to age. At least when studying a young sample, Norton and Han (2008) and Majumder (2013) find no effect of BMI on wages among women. Han (2006) finds that there is a wage penalty for all age groups among women but that the size of the wage penalty increases as the age group becomes older until the age of 34. Moreover, in Greve (2008) there seems to be a higher wage penalty for increasing weight among women aged 31–60 compared to women aged 18–30 working in the private sector, and Lundborg et al. (2007) find that there is a negative wage penalty among women older than 50 years of age, although this result is significant only in central European countries. Johar and Katayama (2012) find that, among women, a higher BMI reduces wages at all points in their wage distribution. However, the strength of the relationship is greater at higher wage levels. In Greve (2008), it is clear that the younger age groups operate at much lower wage levels. Thus, the differences in the relationship between BMI and wages for young and older women might be explained by the fact that these groups operate at different wage levels. However, Conley and Glauber (2007) find that the negative relationship between a lagged BMI and wages is only significant among women aged 25–34 and not among women aged 35–44, when controlling for educational attainment, labor market experience, age of youngest child, ages, and race.

The relationship between BMI and wages among men is more ambiguous than the results among women. Some studies find a negative relationship between BMI and wages (Atella et al., 2008; Averett & Korenman, 1996; Baum & Ford, 2004; Brunello & D'Hombres, 2007; Cawley, 2004; Fahr, 2006; Lundborg et al., 2014; Sabia & Rees, 2012; Shimokawa, 2008), but the results depend on race and often also on the covariates included in the estimations. For white men, Cawley (2004) finds a negative relationship, but when he controls for unobserved heterogeneity, the negative relationship between BMI and wages is no longer significant. Other studies find a positive (Morris, 2006) or an inverted U-shaped (Greve, 2008; Han, 2006; Johansson et al., 2009) relationship between BMI and wages among men. Sabia and Rees (2012) and Cawley (2004) find a positive effect among black males, whereas Majumder (2013) finds positive effects for white men in his sample of 18- to 30-year-old men.

25.5 Explanations for Gender Differences

The differences in the results depending on gender can be explained to a certain extent by the use of BMI as a body weight measure because BMI does not distinguish between fat and fat-free mass. Thus, the inverted U-shaped relationship between BMI and wages for men may be due to men who are muscular with little body fat being classified as overweight. We do not see the same effect among women, mainly because there is less variation in muscle mass for women.

Another reason may be that being overweight is associated with different characteristics for men and women. When McLean and Moon in 1980 found a positive relationship between body weight and wages among men, they suggested that this relationship was explained by the existence of a "portly banker" effect. Thus, whereas being overweight might be associated with negative characteristics, such as sickness and laziness among women, being overweight might be associated with a nonverbal signal of power, strength, and capability among men.

Yet another reason for the gender difference in results might be that men and women select into different jobs with different weight–wage penalties or that they experience different barriers when moving across occupations and different levels of wage discrimination in the jobs they hold. With regards to selection into occupations, Pagan and Davila (1997) argue that men select themselves into jobs to offset the wage penalty, whereas this selection is less prevalent among women because the obesity–wage penalty varies little across occupations for women.

25.6 The Growing Literature on Body Weight and Wages: Body Weight Measures, Identification, and Functional Form

Since the mid-1990s, there has been an increase in economic literature examining the relationship between body weight and wages, and, over the years, contributions have been made in three areas particularly: refinements of body weight measures, identification of the causal impact of body weight on wages using instrumental variables, and estimation of the functional form.

The BMI, which is defined as weight in kilograms over height in meters squared, (kg/m^2), is the standard measure of fatness in epidemiology and medicine and is also used in most of the studies of social consequences of body weight because it is relatively easily measured and available in several data sets (Kelly, 2011). However, BMI may not always be a good predictor of excess of body fat because it does not distinguish between fat and muscles. In adults, it has been shown that body fat percentage, or other measures of body composition, are far more accurate measures of adiposity than BMI (Burkhauser & Cawley, 2008). Still, both Burkhauser and Cawley (2008) and Wada and Tekin (2010) conclude that BMI seems to perform well as a measure for excessive fatness for white women. A number of studies have included other measures of body weight than BMI when analyzing the relationship between body weight and wages (Bozoyan & Wolbring, 2011; Johansson et al., 2009; Wada

& Tekin, 2010). Johansson et al. (2009) find no significant relationship between measures such as high fat mass and waist measurement and wages in Finland. Bozoyan and Wolbring (2011) find a significant negative relationship between high body fat and wages in Germany, although this relationship becomes insignificant in their fixed-effects models. Using different predicted body fat measures, Wada and Tekin (2010) find that measures on body fat are significantly negative related to wages for both men and women in the United States.

Starting with Cawley's pioneering work (Cawley, 2004), variables based on the body weight of biological family members have been heavily used to estimate the causal effect of BMI on wages. These variables seem to be good instruments because they are both correlated with BMI (the relevance restriction) and unrelated to wages (exclusion restriction). The argument for using the body weight of biological family members as an instrument relies on the fact that, on average, biological family members share a significant amount of genes related to weight and that the similarity in weight between biological family members is not due to their common environment.

Norton and Han (2008) took a step further in this direction and used genetic information to estimate the causal effect of lagged BMI on wages. In their paper, they use genes that they find to be empirically correlated with BMI and argue that this genetic information constitutes good instruments because the genes are exogenous, determined at conception, and not correlated with other behavioral factors. However, because the relationship between BMI and the relevant genes is based on an empirical observation, it is difficult to verify that the same genes are not correlated with other (unobserved) behavioral factors and therefore unrelated to wages. This means that one of the main conditions necessary for using it as instrument, namely the exclusion restriction, is violated. Some of the genes that are related to BMI might also be related to, for example, mental health problems that might be correlated with wages (Cawley, Han, & Norton, 2011).

One advantage of using body weight of a biological family member or genes as an instrument is that the compliers—the group for whom we identify the effect—are people who would increase their BMI if they are genetically disposed to being overweight but would not increase weight if they are not so disposed. Thus, we would expect that the group of compliers consists of people with average characteristics and not people belonging to certain ethnic or socioeconomic groups.

However, one drawback of using instrumental variables to deal with the problems of endogeneity is that it is most useful when examining the effect of a continuous variable, such as BMI, on wages and is less well-suited for estimating the effect of, for instance, BMI indicators (being underweight, overweight, or obese relative to being of a healthy weight) on wages. Imposing linearity between BMI and wages seems restrictive because this relationship might be driven by very high or low weight levels. For example, Gregory and Ruhm (2009) estimate semi-parametric wage models (and also use instrumental variables) and find a negative impact of increasing BMI on wages among white men and women beginning at low levels of weight. The results for black women also indicate a negative impact of BMI on wages, with earnings peaking at a low value of BMI. The results for black men are more ambiguous.

In a recent study by Johar and Katayama (2012), the wage penalty is estimated in different parts of the wage distribution. Thus, Johar and Katayama (2012) show that there might be a larger weight–wage penalty in the higher end of the wage distribution, particularly among women.

25.7 Do Obese People Earn Lower Wages Because They Are Discriminated?

Although much of the literature points to discrimination of obese people on the labor market, it has been difficult to provide sufficient evidence that a lower wage is actually due to discrimination against obese people.

Johar and Katayama (2012) and Han et al. (2009) endeavor to get a little closer to estimating a discriminating effect by examining different weight–wage ratios depending on the type of job. In Johar and Katayama (2012), white men and women employed in jobs that require extensive social skills (i.e., jobs involving management or supervision of other workers) earn significantly lower wages when BMI increases compared to men and women not working in these kinds of jobs. In Han et al. (2009), the overall conclusion for men is that overweight or obesity status does not affect wages, regardless of the level of interpersonal skills required in the occupational field. Among white and black women, there is a significant wage penalty for obesity in occupations requiring interpersonal skills of "speak-signal" and "serve." In contrast to this result, among Hispanic women, there is a significant wage increase for obese women in occupations requiring interpersonal skills of "supervise," "speak-signal," and "serve." However, because obesity may be a real parameter of productivity (e.g., in occupations with physical labor or customer contact), the results found in Han et al. (2009) and Johar and Katayama (2012) may not necessarily reflect discrimination but could also indicate that people in healthy weight categories are more productive in certain jobs.

Differences in culture or labor market institutions may be relevant for understanding the relationship between body weight and wages. Existing evidence shows that a high share of union memberships and bargaining coverage reduce wage inequality, indicating that the level of wage discrimination against obese people is low in this institutional setting (Garcia & Quintana-Domeque, 2007). In Greve (2008), the analysis on BMI and wages is divided into the private and public sector, where the wage setting in the public sector compared to the private sector is fairly fixed. The results in Greve (2008) show significant results in the private sector only (a negative relationship between BMI and wages for women and an inverted U-shaped relationship among men), whereas there is no significant relationship between BMI and wages in the public sector.

Differences in cultural norms for slim body types might also give an indication of discrimination against obese people. While Garcia and Quintana-Domeque (2007) find some evidence for this among women, Fahr (2006), arguing that social norms vary between countries, finds wage penalties for being above the social norm for men.

Lower wages among people with higher BMI can also reflect that employers who provide health insurance penalize obese workers and pay lower wages because they fear that they will have to provide more health care to obese workers. Bhattacharya and Bundorf (2009) show that obese workers with employer-sponsored health insurance pay for their higher expected medical expenditures through lower wages, whereas obese workers with insurance coverage through an alternative employer do not experience these types of wage offsets.

Baum and Ford (2004) hypothesize that obese workers receive lower wages because obese workers are more economically myopic and consequently less likely to invest in training. Due to this hypothesis, obese people are less concerned about health effects, less concerned about the future, and therefore less likely to invest in education. Baum and Ford (2004) claim that they find some evidence for this argument because they find a flatter earnings profile among obese workers. However, as also noted by Baum and Ford (2004), a flatter earnings profile could also be due to discrimination in training opportunities.

A significant weight–wage penalty might indicate that obese people encounter barriers in training and skill acquisition in childhood and adolescence. In Conley and Glauber (2007) a BMI lagged 13–15 years is significantly associated with a reduction in women's earnings. Lundborg et al. (2014) find a significant weight-related wage penalty among men, but only for those who were already overweight or obese in adolescence. Using a rich dataset based on military enlistment and registers from Statistics Sweden, Lundborg et al. (2014) employ sibling differences on a sample of approximately 150,000 men and find that a large part of this body weight–wage penalty that overweight and obese people face is explained by lower skill acquisition when they were teenagers. This skill acquisition includes both cognitive and noncognitive skills and indicates the importance of bullying, lower self-esteem, and discrimination by peers and teachers for the later outcomes of overweight and obese children.

25.8 Conclusion

Overall, the literature on body weight and wages seems to agree that, at least for white women, there is a wage penalty for being overweight or obese. However, the results depend on, for instance, the way excessive body weight is measured and the type of job. The question of *why* people with higher body weight tend to earn lower wages is difficult to answer, but, in the literature, there is substantial evidence of weight-based discrimination (Andreyeva et al., 2008; Puhl, Andreyeva, & Brownell, 2008; Rooth, 2009).

From an economic point of view, both individual discrimination and statistical discrimination entail some inefficiency cost for society. Still, to change this state of affairs—to correct the market failure resulting from discriminatory preferences or lack of information and to reduce discrimination—is difficult. Adopting restrictive political measures could lead to a number of drawbacks. First, obesity and the physiological appearance of obese people may indeed—with or without our general consent—be a real parameter of productivity (e.g., in occupations requiring physical labor or customer contact). Second, although the relationship between obesity and illness has been validated by a large number of medical studies, not all obese individuals have health problems. In the case of statistical discrimination against obese people, obesity, as generally related to several health problems that entail costs for the employer, becomes a motive for employers not to employ obese people in order to maximize profit.

Overweight and obesity involve significant costs for both society and the individual. In spite of these costs, we, as a society, have to accept that some people among the adult population indirectly choose to be or become obese. However, we may nonetheless wish to intervene and try to reverse the increasing trend in child obesity—especially because children seldom think about future consequences of an unhealthy lifestyle and are not expected to be rational decision makers. The suggested relationship between body size and cognitive and noncognitive skills during childhood and its significant effects on later wage outcomes (Lundborg, Nystedt, & Rooth, 2014) justifies and necessitates a public intervention affecting habit formation from an early age.

Notes

1. Particularly relevant for this chapter is a virtual special issue devoted to obesity and the labor market published in *Economics and Human Biology* (http://www.journals.elsevier.com/economics-and-human-biology/virtual-special-issues/obesity-and-the-labor-market/).
2. When Han (2006) uses instrumental variable and fixed effects method, he finds that compared to health weight, overweight and obese women are more likely to be employed.

References

Andreyeva, T., Puhl, R. M., & Brownell, K. D. (2008). Changes in perceived weight discrimination among Americans, 1995–1996 through 2004–2006. *Obesity (Silver Spring, MD)*, *16*(5), 1129.

Atella, V., Pace, N., & Vuri, D. (2008). Are employers discriminating with respect to weight?: European evidence using quantile regression. *Economics and Human Biology*, *6*(3), 305–329.

Averett, S., & Korenman, S. (1996). The economic reality of 'The Beauty Myth.' (economic differentials by body mass). *Journal of Human Resources*, *31*(2), 304.

Baum, C. L., & Ford, W. F. (2004). The wage effects of obesity: A longitudinal study. *Health Economics*, *13*(9), 885–899.

Becker, G. S. (1971). *The economics of discrimination* (2nd ed.). Chicago: University of Chicago.

Behrman, J. R., & Rosenzweig, M. R. (2001). *The returns to increasing body weight* (PIER Working Paper No. 01-052). Philadelphia: Penn Institute for Economic Research.

Bhattacharya, J., & Bundorf, M. K. (2009). The incidence of the healthcare costs of obesity. *Journal of Health Economics*. *28*(3), 649–658.

Borghans, L., & Golsteyn, B. H. H. (2006). Time discounting and the body mass index: Evidence from the Netherlands. *Economics and Human Biology*, *4*(1), 39–61.

Bozoyan, C., & Wolbring, T. (2011). Fat, muscles, and wages. *Economics and Human Biology*, *9*(4), 356–363.

Brunello, G., & D'Hombres, B. (2007). Does body weight affect wages?: Evidence from Europe. *Economics and Human Biology*, *5*(1), 1–19.

Burkhauser, R. V., & Cawley, J. (2008). Beyond BMI: The value of more accurate measures of fatness and obesity in social science research. *Journal of Health Economics*, *27*(2), 519–529.

Cawley, J. (2003). What explains race and gender differences in the relationship between obesity and wages? *Gender Issues*, *21*(3), 30–49.

Cawley, J. (2004). The impact of obesity on wages. *Journal of Human Resources, 39*(2), 451–474.

Cawley, J., Grabka, M. M., & Lillard, D. R. (2005). A comparison of the relationship between obesity and earnings in the U.S and Germany. *Journal of Applied Social Science Studies (Schmollers Jahrbuch), 125*(1), 119–129.

Cawley, J., Han, E., & Norton, E. C. (2011). The validity of genes related to neurotransmitters as instrumental variables. *Health Economics, 20*(8), 884–888.

Cawley, J., & Spiess, C. K. (2008). Obesity and skill attainment in early childhood. *Economics and Human Biology, 6*(3), 388–397.

Colchero, M. A., & Bishai, D. (2012). Weight and earnings among childbearing women in Metropolitan Cebu, Philippines (1983–2002). *Economics and Human Biology, 10*(3), 256–263.

Conley, D., & Glauber, R. (2007). Gender, body mass, and socioeconomic status: New evidence from the PSID. *Advances in Health Economics and Health Services Research, 17*, 253.

Cutler, D. M., & Glaeser, E. (2005). What explains differences in smoking, drinking, and other health- related behaviors? *American Economic Review, 95*(2), 238–242.

Fahr, R. (2006). *The wage effects of social norms: Evidence of deviations from peers' body-mass in Europe* (IZA Discussion Paper No. 2323). Bonn, DE: Instituted for the Study of Labor.

Fletcher, J. M., & Lehrer, S. F. (2009). The effects of adolescent health on educational outcomes: Causal evidence using genetic lotteries between siblings. *Forum for Health Economics & Policy, 12*(2), Article 8.

Garcia, J., & Quintana-Domeque, C. (2007). Obesity, employment and wages in Europe. *Advances in Health Economics and Health Services Research, 17*, 187.

Gregory, C., & Ruhm, C. J. (2009). *Where does the wage penalty bite?* (NBER Working Paper No. 14984). Cambridge, MA: National Bureau of Economic Research.

Greve, J. (2008). Obesity and labor market outcomes in Denmark. *Economics and Human Biology, 6*(3), 350–362.

Han, E. (2006). *The effect of obesity on labor market outcomes.* Dissertation, University of North Carolina at Chapel Hill. Retrieved from https://cdr.lib.unc.edu/indexablecontent/uuid:373117ad-f2f4-471d-b356-89f7b4db1a40

Han, E., Norton, E. C., & Powell, L. M. (2011). Direct and indirect effects of body weight on adult wages. *Economics and Human Biology, 9*(4), 381–392.

Han, E., Norton, E. C., & Stearns, S. C. (2009). Weight and wages: Fat versus lean paychecks. *Health Economics, 18*(5), 535–548.

Härkönen, J., Räsänen, P., & Näsi, M. (2011). Obesity, unemployment, and earnings. *Nordic Journal of Working Life Studies, 1*(2), 23–38.

Johansson, E., Böckerman, P., Kiiskinen, U., & Heliövaara, M. (2009). Obesity and labour market success in Finland: The difference between having a high BMI and being fat. *Economics and Human Biology, 7*(1), 36–45.

Johar, M., & Katayama, H. (2012). Quantile regression analysis of body mass and wages. *Health Economics, 21*(5), 597–611.

Kelly, I. R. (2011). *Publicly available data useful for social science research on obesity.* In J. Cawley (Ed.), *The Oxford handbook of the social science of Obesity* (pp. 187–207). Oxford University Press.

Komlos, K., Smith, P. K., & Bogin, B. (2004). Obesity and the rate of time preferences: Is there a connection? *Journal of Biosocial Science, 36*(2), 209–219.

Kortt, M., & Leigh, A. (2010). Does size matter in Australia? *Economic Record, 86*(272), 71–83.

Lindeboom, M., Lundborg, P., & van der Klaauw, B. (2010). Assessing the impact of obesity on labor market outcomes. *Economics and Human Biology, 8*(3), 309–319.

Lundborg, P., Bolin, K., Höjgård, S., & Lindgren, B. (2007). Obesity and occupational attainment among the 50+ of Europe. *Advances in Health Economics and Health Services Research, 17*, 219.

Lundborg, P., Nystedt, P., & Rooth, D. (2014). Body size, skills, and income: Evidence from 150,000 teenage siblings. *Demography, 51*(5), 1573–1596.

Majumder, A. (2013). Does obesity matter for wages? Evidence from the United States. *Economic Papers, 32*(2), 200–217.

McLean, R. A., & Moon, M. (1980). Health, obesity, and earnings. *American Journal of Public Health, 70*(9), 1006.

Mocan, N. H., & Tekin, E. (2011). *Obesity, self-esteem and wages*. In M. Grossman & N. H. Mocan (Ed.), *NBER Chapters, in Economic Aspects of Obesity* (pp. 349–380). University of Chicago Press.

Morris, S. (2006). Body mass index and occupational attainment. *Journal of Health Economics, 25*(2), 347–364.

Morris, S. (2007). The impact of obesity on employment. *Labour Economics, 14*(3), 413–433.

Ng, M., Fleming, T., Robinson, M., Thomson, B., & Graetz, N. (2014). Global, regional, and national prevalence of overweight and obesity in children and adults during 1980–2013: A systematic analysis for the Global Burden of Disease Study 2013. *Lancet, 384*(9945), 766–781.

Norton, E. C., & Han, E. (2008). Genetic information, obesity, and labor market outcomes. *Health Economics, 17*(9), 1089–1104.

Pagan, J. A., & Davila, A. (1997). Obesity, occupational attainment, and earnings. *Social Science Quarterly, 78*(3), 756.

Puhl, R. M., Andreyeva, T., & Brownell, K. D. (2008). Perceptions of weight discrimination: Prevalence and comparison to race and gender discrimination in America. *International Journal of Obesity, 32*(6), 992.

Register, C. A., & Williams, D. R. (1990). Wage effects of obesity among young workers. *Social Science Quarterly, 71*(1), 130.

Rooth, D. (2009). Obesity, attractiveness, and differential treatment in hiring: A field experiment. (Report.) *Journal of Human Resources, 44*(3), 710–735.

Sabia, J. J. (2007). The effect of body weight on adolescent academic performance. *Southern Economic Journal, 73*(4), 871–900.

Sabia, J. J., & Rees, D. I. (2012). Body weight and wages: Evidence from Add Health. *Economics and Human Biology, 10*, 14–19.

Sargent, J. D., & Blanchflower, D. G. (1994). Obesity and stature in adolescence and earnings in young adulthood. Analysis of a British birth cohort. *Archives of Pediatrics & Adolescent Medicine, 148*(7), 681.

Shimokawa, S. (2008). The labour market impact of body weight in China: A semiparametric analysis. *Applied Economics, 40*(8), 949–968.

Smith, P. K., Bogin, B., & Bishai, D. (2005). Are time preference and body mass index associated? Evidence from the National Longitudinal Survey of Youth. *Economics and Human Biology, 3*(2), 259.

Tunceli, K., Li, K., & Williams, L. K. (2006). Long-term effects of obesity on employment and work limitations among U.S. Adults, 1986 to 1999. *Obesity (Silver Spring, Md.), 14*(9), 1637.

Wada, R., & Tekin, E. (2010). Body composition and wages. *Economics and Human Biology, 8*(2), 242–254.

CHAPTER 26

WEALTH AND WEIGHT

JAY L. ZAGORSKY

26.1 Introduction

A common toast used in many societies is to wish the recipient first health and then wealth. One key aspect of health is a person's weight, with low weight often indicating malnourishment and high weight indicating a person at risk for obesity-related illnesses such as diabetes. While toasts and good wishes typically separate health and wealth, this chapter investigates if and how weight and wealth are related.

Neither weight nor wealth has been static in the post-World War II period. Average weight has been climbing rapidly over the past few decades across all countries in the world (Figure 26.1). Whereas in 1980 the average person's body mass index[1] (BMI) was slightly more than 22, which is in the middle of the normal weight range, by 2009, it increased to almost 24, near the top-end of the normal weight range, a growth of almost 10% in just three decades. If weight continues to rise at the same rate as it has over the past three decades then, by 2030, the average individual in the world will be classified as overweight, which is a BMI of 25 or more.

Many researchers have focused on economic reasons to explain why weight has increased over time (Rosin, 2008). One potential reason is that the inflation-adjusted cost of food has been falling over time (Grossman, Tekin, & Wada, 2014; Philipson & Posner, 2003). As food becomes cheaper, more of it is consumed (Courtemanche, Heutel, & McAlvanah, 2015). Another reason for the increase in weight is that jobs are becoming more sedentary (Lakdawalla & Philipson, 2009; Lakdawalla, Philipson, & Bhattacharya, 2005) resulting in people expending fewer calories each day because more time is spent sitting at a desk. There are also noneconomic reasons that explain why weight has increased over time, such as changes in time preferences (Komlos, Smith, & Bogin, 2004), changes in the ideal of beauty (Hamermesh, 2013), and the impact of advertising (Harris, Bargh, & Brownell, 2009; Hoek & Gendall, 2006; Shin-Yi, Rashad, & Grossman, 2008).

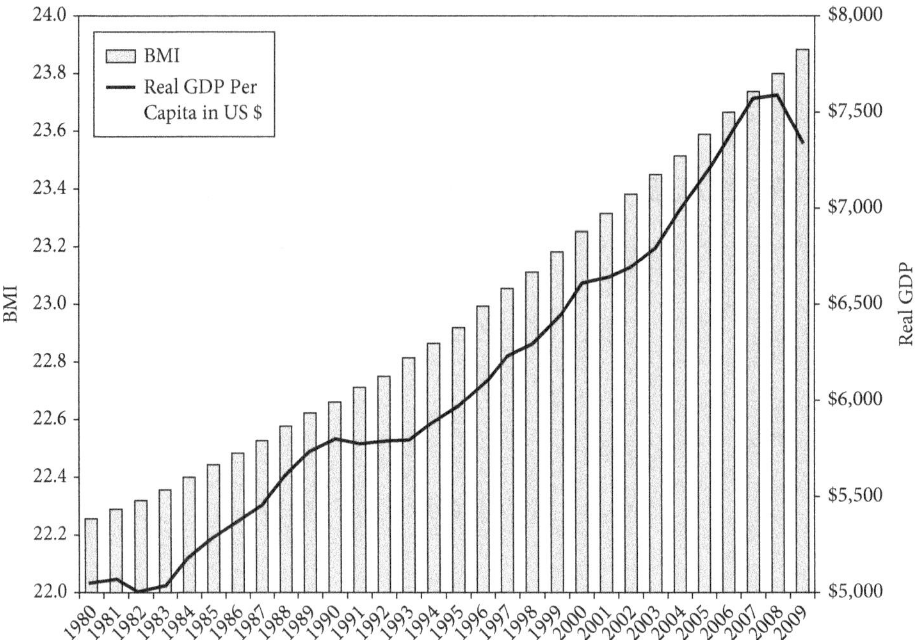

FIGURE 26.1 World average body mass index (BMI) of individuals and world real gross domestic product (GDP) per capita in inflation-adjusted US dollars.

Note: BMI data are from the Global Health Observatory of the World Health Organization located online at http://apps.who.int/gho/data/node.main. The country data have been adjusted by the author for age, gender. and population size to generate the world's averages. Real world GDP per capita data are from the World Bank's World Development Indicators database and are inflation-adjusted to 2005 US dollars.

At the same time that weight has been increasing, the world has become much richer (Figure 26.1). In 1980, if the world's gross domestic product (GDP) were divided evenly, the average person would have received slightly more than $5,000 worth of output. By 2009, when much of the world was still in a deep recession, the inflation-adjusted GDP per capita figure was almost $7,400, a gain of 45% over the three decades.

In this chapter, I analyze the impact of these dramatic changes using both macro data from international agencies and micro data from a longitudinal US survey. Because the causation, direction, and magnitude are so uncertain, the goal of this chapter is not to "prove" causation, but instead to explore the size and direction of the wealth–weight relationship.

26.2 Theoretical Issues for Person Level Data

Income and wealth are both key financial measures. *Income* measures the flow within a specific time period to a family or individual of financial resources such as wages, salaries, government transfer payments, interest, and dividends. *Wealth*, or *net worth*, is the value of a person's assets, such as their car, home, savings accounts, and jewelry, minus liabilities such as credit card balances, student loans, and home mortgages. Whereas income is a flow, wealth is a stock measure showing the amount of financial resources a family or individual has at its disposal to spend beyond income at a single point in time.

Wealth serves as a protector of living standards if, during periods of prosperity, families build up savings or pay off past debts and, during hard economic times, they spend down their savings. Wealth also enables people to set aside resources for important future events such as paying for education, weddings, and retirement.

Although there is a positive relationship between income and wealth, it is not ironclad. For example, some of the wealthy do not work because they live by selling off their assets; conversely, not all people with high incomes have saved up much money. Inheritances and large gifts also break down the relationship between income and wealth because they transfer substantial financial resources between generations. Data from the National Longitudinal Survey of Youth 1979 cohort (NLSY79), the US micro data analyzed in this chapter, show a correlation of just 0.6 between income and wealth reported in 2012.

Theoretically, the relationship between wealth and weight is not obvious. The relationship could be positive because the wealthier a person is, the more food he or she could purchase and consume. Consuming more food means increasing calories and hence a higher likelihood—holding all other factors constant—that a person will gain weight. Another connection is through time preferences: the more impatient people are, the less they will save and the less they will consider the future consequences of their current behavior.

However, increasing wealth typically means that people are able to consume better tasting and more nutritious food, such as fresh fruits and vegetables, instead of heavily processed foods that are designed to have long shelf lives. Hence, greater wealth might enable a person to shift to more expensive but healthier foods, which could reduce a person's weight, even with rising food expenditures. Moreover, greater wealth also means that food consumption can be maintained during economic downturns, which prevents cycles of starvation followed by binges that lead to increased weight gain (Yanovski & Walsh, 2003).

Wealth has implications beyond a person's food consumption. Being richer enables one to afford gym membership, health clubs, and the ability to take time off from work to exercise, all of which enable a person to lose weight. Conversely, being wealthier means a person can afford to drive or take a taxi instead of walking, which leads to less exercise and a boost in weight. These possible explanations all suggest that there should be an association between weight and wealth but that the overall direction of the association is uncertain.

It is entirely possible that wealth does not influence weight because causality could go in either direction, and a more appropriate model is one in which changes in weight influence wealth. Overweight and obese people might be discriminated against in the workforce, resulting in a decreased ability to earn money and build wealth. In addition, obese people might spend much more on medical care, and this increased expenditure could lower their wealth by depleting savings.

Obese and overweight individuals might be more sedentary because it takes more effort to move. However, this increased effort to move might result in higher wealth because being active is expensive. Active people spend more time shopping, going out to restaurants, and doing other expensive activities. Being sedentary is often cheaper than being active because cooking at home is a simple way to save money and build wealth compared to always eating out. Watching television at home instead of attending concerts, movies, or plays is another simple way to save money and build wealth. If spending money is positively related to the number of activities people do, then heavier sedentary people might have more wealth than lighter active people. Because there are no clear outcomes from the theoretical analysis, this chapter uses real-world data to determine what actual relationship exists.

26.3 Theoretical Issues for Country-Level Data

This chapter also uses country-level data to investigate the relationship between wealth and weight at the cross-national level. National-level wealth is calculated differently than individual-level wealth because it consists of items like mineral wealth, land, farms, forests, and educational attainment, and it does not include household wealth because that would double-count numerous categories (e.g., land holdings). Whether a country has diamond mines or large amounts of oil and natural gas within its borders is a matter of luck and completely outside of an individual's control. This means that weight cannot influence national wealth because changes in the average person's weight should have no impact on the amount of endowed natural resources held by a country. Hence, national wealth can affect weight but not the other way around.

The cross-national direction of the wealth–weight relationship is difficult to determine theoretically because societal perceptions of weight are not constant throughout the world. In poor places, rich people are often fat, whereas in wealthy countries, rich people are often of normal weight, defined as a BMI of between 18.5 and 24.9. Thus, in a poor society, it is possible to improve your social status by increasing your weight. People in very poor countries who look big are considered rich and healthy, so, by weighing more, a person can improve his or her social status and take advantage of more economic opportunities.

Conversely, in a rich society, many people attempt to improve their social status by decreasing their weight. Especially for women, looking like a skinny or anorexic model is the ideal. Taken together, this means that as a country changes from poor to rich, the relationship between wealth and weight flips from positive to negative. Whereas in very rich and very poor societies weight often matters as an economic indicator, many countries are neither rich nor poor, and the optimal size of a person for maximum social status is often ambiguous. The next section reviews the literature to understand what previous researchers found when investigating weight and wealth.

26.4 Literature Review

The relationship between wealth and health is important to study (Pollack et al., 2007) because previous research shows that wealth is significantly associated with decreased mortality (Bond Huie, Krueger, Rogers, & Hummer, 2003; Menchik, 1993), better self-rated health (Meer, Miller, & Rosen, 2003), and fewer chronic diseases (Kington & Smith, 1997). Because wealth data are relatively scarce, earlier research first considered the general relationship between health and socioeconomic status (Feinstein, 1993), where socioeconomic status was often proxied by income. Research using income (Cawley, Moran, & Simon, 2010; Han, Norton, & Stearns, 2009; Johar & Katayama, 2012) found a negative relationship between weight and wages for women, but little or no relationship between weight and wages for men.

As wealth data became available, research began investigating the specific relationship between wealth and weight. Au and Johnston (2014) found that wealth shocks from inheritances and lottery wins in Australia had no impact on men, but did have small effects for women, with increased wealth primarily increasing weight among initially poor and obese women.

Hajat et al. (Hajat, Kaufman, Rose, Siddiqi, & Thomas, 2010), using the Panel Study of Income Dynamics (PSID), found a 40–89% higher risk of becoming obese among the less wealthy relative to the wealthiest 20% of the population in the United States. In subsequent research, they found a strong inverse relationship between wealth and mortality and also found an inverse relationship between wealth and having a poor health status (Hajat, Kaufman, Rose, Siddiqi, & Thomas, 2011).

Mazzocchi and Traill (2008) estimated a model that examined the relationships among wealth, weight, and final health outcomes using data from the UK's National Diet and Nutrition Survey. They found that higher wealth was associated with lower weight and better health, and they determined that this was due to the rich eating a better diet rather than participating in more exercise or consuming fewer calories.

Zagorsky (2004) found a large and statistically significant negative relationship between BMI and net worth and suggested that part of the reason for the inverse wealth–BMI relationship was because lighter people received more inheritances than did heavier individuals. One possibility for the inheritance–BMI relationship is that lighter people have lighter parents who were able to accumulate more money during their lifetime. Follow-up research (Zagorsky, 2005) showed that the wealth–BMI relationship was stronger for females than for males and stronger for whites than for blacks. Using longitudinal data, his research also found that weight changes and net worth were related. Individuals who lost or gained a large amount of weight had corresponding large changes in their net worth, but slight weight changes were not associated with any significant changes in wealth.

Fonda et al. (Fonda, Fultz, Rahrig Jenkins, Wheeler, & Wray, 2004) investigated US retirees and those near retirement and found overweight or obese women had lower net worth than did normal women, whereas overweight and obese men had higher net worth. Later research using the same Health and Retirement Survey data (Chung, Domino, & Stearns, 2009) found the most weight gain during retirement happened to people who started off with lower wealth and previously had more physically demanding occupations. Overall, the research reviewed in this section suggests that a negative relationship exists between wealth and weight; however, the relationship does not exist for all groups of people and appears stronger for women than for men.

26.5 Cross-National Relationship

Previous research on the wealth–weight relationship has focused only on individual-level data and excluded any cross-national comparisons. Understanding if there is a relationship between wealth and weight at the country level is important because some countries, like China, are facing rapidly improving economic conditions, while other countries, like Ukraine, are facing rapidly declining economic conditions, and still others, like Liberia, are mired in poverty. Overall, Figure 26.1 shows that the average person in the world has improving economic conditions, but this overall improvement masks substantial heterogeneity. Understanding the relationship between wealth and weight at the country level provides researchers and policy-makers with some ability to forecast the impact of changes in national economic conditions on one aspect of a nation's overall health.

Prior research has not analyzed wealth and weight at the cross-national level because country-level wealth data for much of the world is even rarer than individual-level surveys that contain both wealth and weight information. Although wealth data are rare, cross-national income data do exist for most countries and are typically based on National Income and Product Account (NIPA) information such as GDP, gross national product (GNP), and gross national income (GNI). NIPA information can be used to show the relationship between countries' annual production and weight; unfortunately, NIPA data do not provide a clear indication of wealth nor of the amounts countries have saved for future consumption.

One of the only sources of global wealth information was produced by a World Bank (2006) research project that estimated total wealth for 125 countries in 1995, 149 countries in 2000, and 152 countries in 2005. The World Bank used a very inclusive definition of wealth and calculated three different indicators—produced wealth, natural wealth, and intangible wealth—before inflation adjusting the results to 2000 US dollars.

Produced wealth is the value of a country's factories, buildings, roads, and other investments. Natural wealth is the expected value of a country's oil reserves, minerals, forests, and other endowed resources. Intangible wealth comprises human and institutional capital, where human capital is the value of education, on-the-job training, and learning received by the average citizen. Institutional capital is the hardest of all factors to measure and tracks the rule of law, control of corruption, political stability, and government effectiveness. The World Bank estimates show that in low-income countries, natural capital such as farm and grazing lands comprise the most important share of a country's wealth; however, in high-income countries of the Organization for Economic Cooperation and Development (OECD), intangible human and institutional capital comprise the largest share of wealth (World Bank, 2006; table 1.1).

Not only are country-level wealth data scarce, but country-level weight data also are scarce. What are available are country-level BMI data by gender (Figure 26.1) from the Global Health Observatory (GHO), which is part of the World Health Organization (WHO). Countries where individuals have the highest BMIs are in the Middle East or Pacific Island nations (Table 26.1). Countries with the lowest BMI are either in Southeast Asia or in sub-Saharan Africa. The top five wealthiest countries are all Western European countries, whereas the five lowest wealth countries are all African, showing no overlap between wealth and weight for the 20 countries in the table.

Although there is a positive relationship between wealth and weight using all country-level data (correlation coefficient of +0.40), this is a biased view because countries with small populations in the thousands or low millions like Saint Lucia, Vanuatu, and Namibia appear as the same sized dot in the graph as places with more than a billion people, like China and India (Figure 26.2). To eliminate this bias, the remainder of the

Table 26.1 Top and Bottom Five Countries Based on Average per Capita Body Mass Index (BMI) and Wealth in 2000

	Largest BMI	Smallest BMI	Highest Wealth	Lowest Wealth
1.	Tonga (31.1)	Bangladesh (19.8)	Denmark ($687,959)	Burundi ($2,152)
2.	Kuwait (29.0)	Ethiopia (19.8)	Switzerland ($715,610)	Dem. Rep. Congo ($2,194)
3.	United Arab Emirates (27.9)	Nepal (20.4)	Iceland ($787,113)	Ethiopia ($2,656)
4.	Jordan (27.9)	Dem. Rep. Congo (20.4)	Luxembourg ($827,661)	Sierra Leone ($3,327)
5.	Saudi Arabia (27.7)	Burkina Faso (20.8)	Norway ($832,478)	Liberia ($3,431)

Note: Covers only countries having both World Bank wealth data and BMI data for 2000 in the World Health Organization's Global Health Observatory. BMI is the average of male and female values.

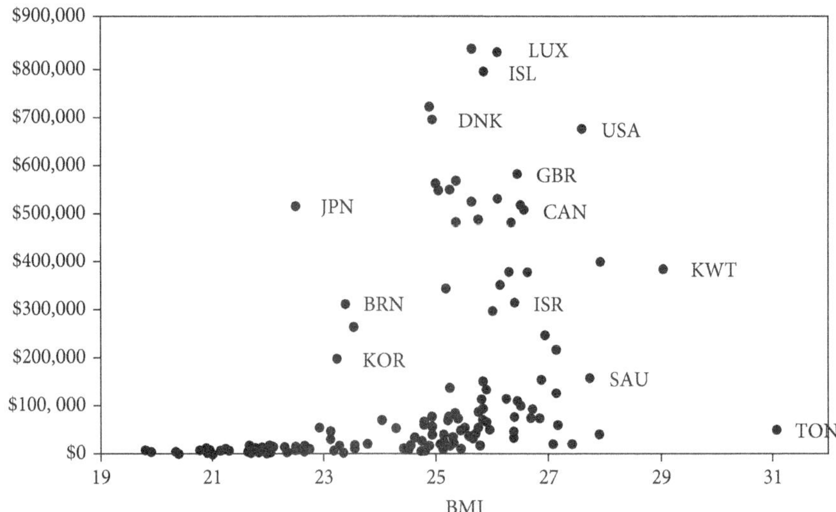

FIGURE 26.2 Average wealth and body mass index (BMI) by country in 2000.

Note: Three-letter country codes from the World Bank's World Development Indicators.

cross-national comparisons in this chapter use population weights to adjust the analysis and ensure that large countries have more influence on the results than do small ones.

Table 26.2 provides summary statistics, after adjusting for population, of the average country's wealth and BMI. The table shows that the average country had approximately $140,000 of wealth per person, $9,000 in GDP, and a citizen with a BMI of 24.5. Over the two 5-year periods of 1995–2000 and 2000–05, the average country experienced roughly a 10% growth in wealth, a 14% growth in GDP, and a 1.7% growth in BMI.

Although the table shows wealth and BMI are increasing for the average country, it does not hold other factors, like changes in GDP, constant. To adjust for these other factors, regressions were run to estimate Equation (1), which seeks to understand how the change in BMI is impacted by the change in wealth after holding GDP, population, and geography constant. The change is measured for the two 5-year periods (1995–2000 and 2000–05) because wealth data are presently only available for these time periods.

$$\text{BMI Change} = f(\text{Wealth Change, GDP Change, Population Change, Geography}) \quad (1)$$

The results of the cross-national wealth–weight regressions are found in Table 26.3, where regressions (1) to (3) examine the relationship between wealth and the absolute change in BMI over 5 years, and regressions (4) to (6) examine the relationship using the percentage change in BMI. Although BMI is the left-hand side or dependent variable in all regressions, the estimations should not be viewed as implying wealth causes changes in weight.

The coefficients at the top of Table 26.3 suggest that the absolute change in wealth and real GDP is not an important factor because the coefficients are small in magnitude,

Table 26.2 Average Amount and Change in Wealth, Gross Domestic Product (GDP), and Body Mass Index (BMI) in Typical Country; 1995–2005 (in 2005 US$)

	Real Wealth	Real GDP	BMI
Average per capita values in 1995	$138,800	$8,092	24.02
Average per capita values in 2000	$136,200	$9,173	24.41
Average per capita values in 2005	$143,900	$10,017	24.85
Percent change 1995–2000	−1.9%	13.3%	1.6%
Percent change 2000–05	5.7%	9.2%	1.8%

Note: Data from 1995, 2000, and 2005 are based on data from 125, 149, and 152 countries, respectively. BMI data are the average of each country's male and female BMI. Yearly averages are weighted by each country's share of the total world's population.

and none is statistically distinct from zero. The coefficients on the percentage change in wealth in the fourth row, however, are all statistically significant. The 0.33 coefficient in column (2) and the 0.29 in column (3) suggest that a 10 percentage point increase in a country's wealth is associated with an absolute BMI increase of roughly 0.03 points over a 5-year period and that a wealth increase of 50 percentage points is associated with an absolute BMI increase of roughly 0.15 points. The 0.014 coefficient in column (5) and the 0.012 in column (6) suggest that a 10 percentage point increase in wealth is associated with a 0.13% percent BMI increase over a 5-year period, while a 50 percentage point increase in wealth is associated with a 0.65% percent BMI increase.

Overall, this section shows that the magnitude of the country-level relationship between wealth and BMI is not large. However, wealth appears to have a small, positive, statistically significant relationship with BMI in cross-national regressions, which means that, as a country becomes richer, we can expect that, on average, the weight of the population will increase as well. One likely reason why wealth does not have a larger relationship to weight is that wealth is generally unevenly distributed. Because of this uneven distribution, the regression results are potentially biased because they are based on mean wealth and would likely be improved by using less biased figures, such as median wealth, which are not presently available.

26.6 Individual Level Relationship

Since 1970, the average global age of individuals has also been steadily rising. As people age, they typically increase both their wealth and weight. How much of the increase in

Table 26.3 Cross-National Regressions Explaining Absolute and Percent Change in Body Mass Index (BMI)

Explanatory Variable	BMI Abs Change (1)	BMI Abs Change (2)	BMI Abs Change (3)	BMI Pct Change (4)	BMI Pct Change (5)	BMI Pct Change (6)
Intercept	0.20 (4.6)	0.25 (8.13)	0.18 (4.35)	0.01 (4.98)	0.01 (8.03)	0.01 (4.72)
$ Change in wealth in millions	1.70 (1.47)		1.11 (0.9)	0.06 (1.31)		0.05 (0.88)
$ Change in real GDP in millions	20.59 (1.42)		11.6 (0.71)	0.71 (1.17)		1.29 (0.19)
Percent change in wealth		0.33 (3.78)	0.29 (3.18)		0.014 (3.8)	0.012 (3.22)
Percent change in real GDP		0.13 (1.57)	0.08 (0.84)		0.006 (1.93)	0.005 (1.45)
Female BMI data	0.03 (2.01)	0.03 (2.04)	0.03 (2.05)	0.001 (2.03)	0.001 (2.08)	0.001 (2.09)
Income-poor country	0.04 (0.81)	–0.19 (4.8)	–0.10 (1.87)	0.003 (1.84)	–0.006 (3.42)	–0.003 (1.36)
Lower middle-income country	0.19 (5.03)	0.01 (0.47)	0.10 (2.24)	0.01 (5.31)	0.001 (1.21)	0.004 (2.15)
Upper middle-income country	0.24 (5.96)	0.07 (2.67)	0.16 (3.65)	0.01 (5.8)	0.003 (3.09)	0.006 (3.26)
Country in Africa	0.03 (1.05)	0.10 (3.21)	0.08 (2.6)	0.002 (1.24)	0.004 (3.43)	0.004 (2.96)
Country in Americas	0.10 (3.27)	0.18 (6.38)	0.14 (4.54)	0.003 (2.3)	0.006 (5.2)	0.005 (3.84)
Country in Europe	–0.04 (1.35)	–0.01 (0.47)	–0.03 (0.93)	–0.002 (1.86)	–0.001 (1.09)	–0.002 (1.37)
Country in Southeast Asia	0.03 (1.33)	0.11 (4.37)	0.09 (3.61)	0.002 (2.47)	0.006 (5.6)	0.005 (5.02)
Change in population	–3.2E-09 (9.59)	–4.4E-09 (10.85)	–4.2E-09 (10.08)	–1.3E-10 (9.42)	–1.9E-10 (11.08)	–1.8E-10 (10.48)
Percent change in population	0.53 (2.26)	1.07 (4.16)	1.07 (4.13)	0.02 (1.61)	0.04 (3.88)	0.04 (3.89)
Data from 2000 to 2005	–0.03 (2.11)	–0.04 (2.55)	–0.03 (2.08)	–0.02 (2.96)	–0.002 (3.43)	–0.002 (3.12)

Note: Dummy variable reference cases are high-income countries and countries outside the Americas whose coastline borders the Pacific Ocean. T statistics in ( ).

weight is attributable to increased age after adjusting for wealth? Most of the published research into the relationship between weight and wealth has been done at the individual level and covers only a relatively narrow age range (Au & Johnston, 2014; Zagorsky, 2005, 2004), and, of the ages covered, the majority has focused on the elderly (Chung et al., 2009; Fonda et al., 2004). To broaden the understanding of the wealth–weight relationship, we investigate the relationship for people in their 20s, 30s, 40s, and 50s using the NLSY79, a nationally representative, randomly selected large panel study (Zagorsky, 1997).

The NLSY79 questioned the same representative group of people, born between 1957 and 1964 (commonly referred to as young Baby Boomers), annually from 1979 to 1994 and every other year since. This research uses the 15 surveys fielded between 1985 and 2012 that contain both wealth and weight information. All data used are publicly available at http://www.bls.gov/nls/nlsy79.htm. NLSY79 respondents self-reported their weight 19 times from 1981 until 2012. Response rates to weight questions asked in surveys when wealth questions were fielded were very high, with 86.2% of respondents providing the information. In 1981, 1982, and 1985, survey respondents were asked to self-report their height. For the vast majority of respondents who reported growing over time, the tallest height was used in the BMI calculations. For the small number of people who reported shrinking, the middle height value was used to calculate BMI.

NLSY79 wealth data are taken from the dataset and adjusted for inflation so that all values are reported in 2012 US dollars. The dataset contains created variables that measure each respondent's total net family worth. These variables were created by summing all asset values and subtracting all debts in each year the wealth module was fielded for the respondent and their spouse, if one exists. Missing assets and debt values were imputed by the survey staff before the total net worth was calculated. To protect respondent privacy, the top 2% of all values in each year were top coded. The top code is the average value of the richest 2%. All results exclude these exceptionally rich people to prevent individuals with extreme wealth from dominating the results. Graphical and regression results that included all top-coded individuals were qualitatively similar to the results given here but are not included due to space limitations.

Figure 26.3 graphs all young Baby Boomers' median net worth and BMI. Using the median eliminates the impact of wealth outliers and shows the amount of money at which half of all people have more than and half less than this amount. Mean graphs, which show the typical value by including both the very rich and very poor in the computations, are not shown since they provide similar images.

In Figure 26.3, wealth typically increases as people age. For example, the typical person with a BMI of 24 had low wealth in their 20s (mean $44,487; median $12,503), moderate amounts of wealth in their 30s (mean $142,808; median $55,053), increasing wealth in their 40s (mean $345,238; median $163,110), and relatively large amounts of wealth in their 50s (mean $601,315; median $194,000).

The graphs of net worth compared to weight and BMI also show a roughly inverted U shape. Peak net worth happens around a BMI of 19 or 20, which is the bottom range of the normal (BMI 18.5–24.9) range; after this point, wealth falls steadily for all ages.

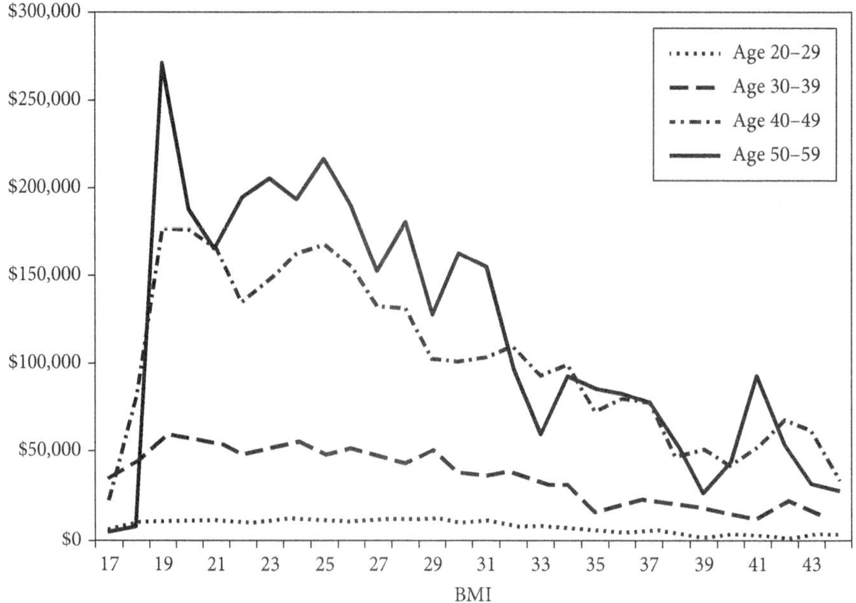

FIGURE 26.3 Median US young Baby Boomers' net worth and body mass index (BMI) by 10-year age groups.

Note: Wealth is inflation-adjusted in 2012 US dollars.

Finally, the graphs show that the relationship between wealth and weight becomes steeper over time. The graph of those in their 20s is a relatively straight line. However, the graph of those in their 50s is sharply peaked and shows dramatic differences in median wealth as BMI changes.

Figure 26.4 repeats the graphical analysis based on gender. The top figure, labeled (A), shows the pattern of BMI for males, and the bottom figure, labeled (B), shows the pattern for females. In general, breaking the data down by gender shows the same inverted U-shaped pattern, with the pattern being more pronounced and the peak happening at a lower BMI for females than for males.

To estimate the specific relationships among an individual's weight, BMI, and age, this chapter uses stacked ordinary least squares (OLS) regressions. In time-series regressions, there is usually just one dependent variable and a set of explanatory independent variables. The NLSY79, however, has a series of wealth and weight variables for each respondent at multiple points in time, as well as a series of independent explanatory variables, some of which are time-dependent. The regression strategy in this section creates multiple inflation-adjusted observations for each respondent, one for each year of wealth and weight data, following Allison (1995) who showed that this technique does not result in biased estimates or inflated test statistics.

It is unlikely that the graphs, descriptive statistics, and regressions in this section are biased because of small sample size issues because the responses come from a nationally representative survey of 9,956 young Baby Boomers. Nonresponse is also not likely a

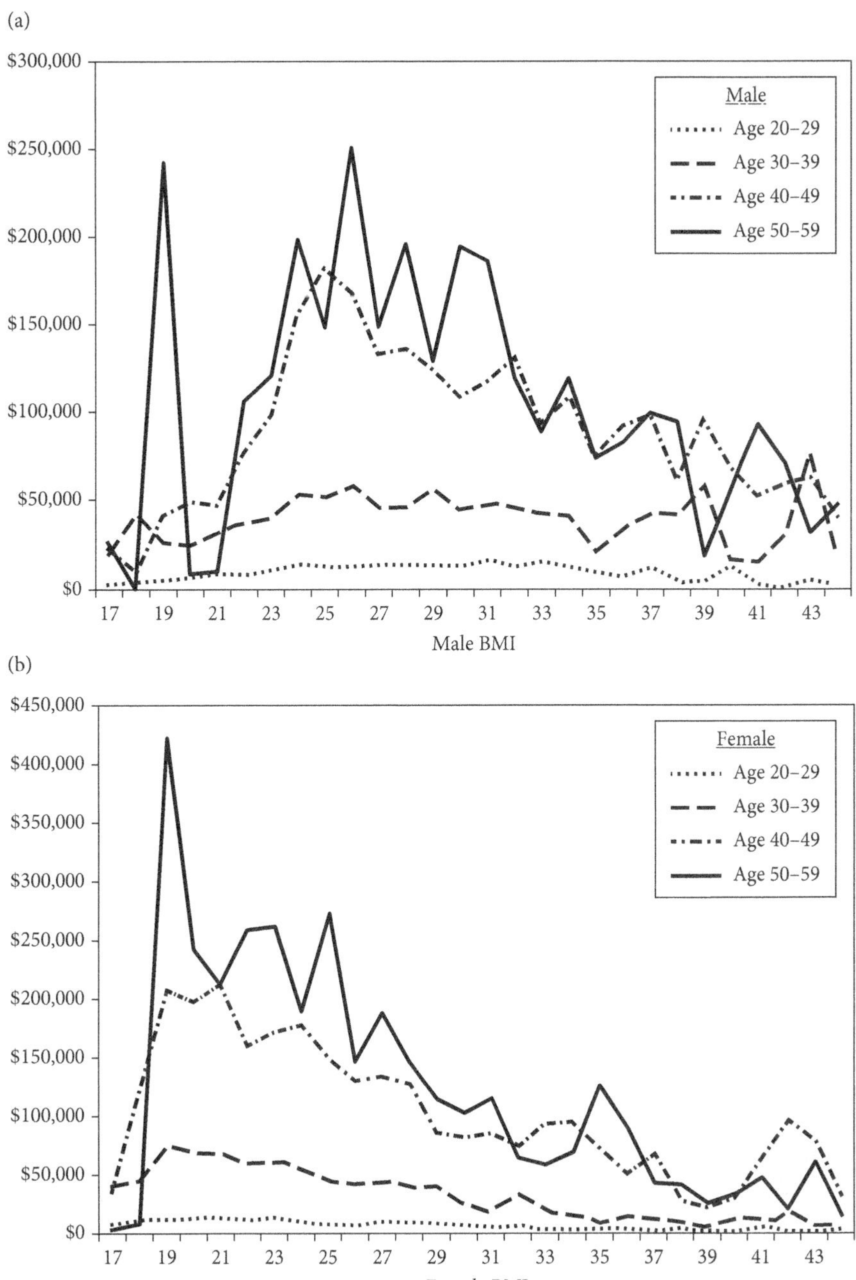

FIGURE 26.4 Median US young Baby Boomers' net worth and body mass index (BMI) by male (A) and female (B).

problem because wealth questions were asked in 15 NLSY79 surveys, and the majority of respondents (57.7%) either answered all 15 possible surveys (41.3%) or missed one survey (16.4%), and only 4.5% answered fewer than five surveys.

Table 26.4 contains four columns of descriptive statistics for the variables used in the person-level regressions. All money values are adjusted into 2012 dollars. The first column of numbers shows the values in 1985, which was the year of the first NLSY79 survey that included both wealth and weight data. The second column shows the values in 2012, which is the latest available NLSY79 survey that contains wealth and weight data. The final two columns show the overall mean across all 15 surveys and the overall standard deviation.

The typical NLSY79 respondent had less than $20,000 of wealth in 1985, at about 23 years of age; the average respondent's wealth grew over time, and, by 2012, net worth was almost a quarter of a million dollars, when the typical respondent was about 51 years old. Total family income also rose from slightly more than $50,000 per young Baby Boomer in 1985 to more than $82,000 in 2012. At the same time that the typical NLYS79 respondent grew richer, they also grew physically heavier, with the average respondent weighing 153.6 pounds in 1985, but more than 185 pounds by 2012; BMI also increased from 23.5 in 1985 to 28.6 in 2012.

The remainder of Table 26.4 shows that the sample is roughly evenly split between men and women. About 15% of the sample is black, slightly more than 6% is Hispanic; about half the respondents are married, and the average respondent has fewer than two children. Most respondents have completed high school (12 years schooling) and have spent some time in college. Respondents have slightly more than three siblings, and the vast majority were born in the United States (>95%), although many grew up speaking a language other than English at home.

Table 26.5 reports regressions with net worth as the dependent variable and weight and BMI values as the independent variables, whereas Table 26.6 reverses the regressions and puts weight and BMI on the left side and net worth on the right side. Since weight and BMI do not follow a true linear relationship, the stacked regression coefficients shown here have very different values and interpretations depending on which variable is used as the explanatory factor on the right-hand side of the regression.

Two numbers are important to highlight in the "overall" columns in Table 26.5. First is the −226 coefficient value in the row marked "Weight" in column (7), which shows for the typical adult that each extra pound of weight is associated with a loss of $226 of wealth. Second is the −1,891 in column (10) along the row marked "BMI," which shows that gaining one additional point of BMI is associated with a reduction of about $1,900 of wealth. Both of these statistically significant coefficients suggest that the heavier a person is, the more likely he or she is to have lower wealth. Although the other regressions clearly show that the relationship between wealth and weight is not linear, regressions in column (7) and (10) provide a rough and simple estimate of the relationship.

Table 26.4 Descriptive Statistics for NLSY79 Variables Used in Individual-Level Regressions

Variable	1985 Survey Mean	2012 Survey Mean	Overall Mean Across 15 Surveys	Overall Std. Dev.
Net worth (in 2012 US$)	$17,625	$249,159	$94,146	$188,932
Family income (in 2012 US$)	$51,802	$82,682	$72,306	$115,331
Weight	153.6	185.5	168.36	39.35
Body mass index (BMI)	23.5	28.6	25.73	5.11
Female share of sample	49.7%	51.5%	50.2%	0.50
Black share of sample	14.2%	15.7%	14.8%	0.35
Hispanic share of sample	6.4%	6.8%	6.5%	0.25
Married share of sample	43.6%	67.8%	61.0%	0.49
Number of children	0.5	1.9	1.27	1.29
Highest grade completed	12.7	13.9	13.14	2.60
Born speaking foreign language	13.8%	13.6%	13.6%	0.34
Number of siblings	3.4	3.4	3.36	2.31
Born in US	95.5%	96.1%	95.8%	0.20
Age	23.6	50.6	32.7	8.00
Year of survey	1985	2012	1994	7.66

The columns marked "Male" and "Female" show that the relationship between wealth and weight is much larger for women than for men. For example, multiplying the coefficients in the "weight" (208) and "weight^2" (−0.85) rows in column (8) by 150 and 160 pounds shows that an increase of 10 pounds for a man is associated with a loss of wealth of $555, whereas the change in wealth for a woman using the coefficients in column (9) (91; −1.12) is a reduction of $3,010 in wealth for the same 10-pound weight gain.

The BMI–wealth relationship is also larger for a woman than for a man. The coefficients in column (11) show that changing from a BMI of 25 to a BMI of 27, a 2-point increase, is associated with a drop in wealth of $2,000 for a man, whereas the same 2-point BMI increase for a woman, using the coefficients in column (12), is associated with a $3,114 decrease.

The positive and statistically significant coefficients on age and survey year show that being older is associated with more wealth, holding weight and BMI constant. The

Table 26.5 Net Worth as the Dependent Variable in Regressions Using Individual-Level Data

	Whole Sample (7)	Male (8)	Female (9)	Whole Sample (10)	Male (11)	Female (12)
Intercept (in millions)	−15,262,884 (113.72)	−13,554,747 (73.41)	−13,447,749 (75.89)	−15,343,848 (121.84)	−13,655,778 (77.89)	−13,465,064 (81.36)
Age	4,019 (18.86)	3,105 (10.76)	3,693 (13.18)	3,893 (19.80)	2,994 (11.13)	3,572 (13.89)
Weight	−226 (16.02)	208 (1.58)	91 (0.79)			
Weight^2		−0.85 (2.68)	−1.12 (3.40)			
Body mass index (BMI)				−1,891 (21.24)	1,288 (1.23)	1,303 (1.87)
BMI^2					−44 (2.49)	−55 (4.65)
Family income	0.32 (68.02)	1.45 (93.17)	1.45 (90.81)	0.32 (71.36)	1.39 (95.40)	1.40 (93.65)
Family income^2		−7.73E-07 (78.74)	−7.68E-07 (77.87)		−7.43E-07 (79.98)	−7.37E-07 (79.75)
Black	−48,085 (40.01)	−36,064 (22.10)	−34,677 (21.71)	−43,810 (39.41)	−33,702 (22.13)	−31,903 (21.68)
Hispanic	−24,002 (12.36)	−18,137 (7)	−24,618 (9.49)	−20,755 (11.59)	−16,185 (6.69)	−21,708 (9.14)
Married	39,727 (38.21)	12,356 (8.44)	11,041 (7.84)	37,800 (39.50)	12,705 (9.35)	11,232 (8.71)
Number of children	−893 (2.23)	17 (0.03)	−134 (0.26)	−721 (1.93)	227 (0.43)	94 (0.19)
Highest grade completed	9,533 (48.35)	4,811 (17.61)	2,998 (10.97)	8,714 (47.73)	4,454 (17.51)	2,720 (10.79)
Born speaking foreign language	−2,797 (1.55)	−4,914 (2.04)	3,877 (1.61)	−1,757 (1.06)	−3,865 (1.72)	3,924 (1.78)
Number of siblings	−1,860 (9.63)	−870 (3.27)	−789 (3.15)	−1,746 (9.80)	−878 (3.54)	−691 (3.0)
Born in US	−11,208 (5.37)	−8,810 (3.12)	−4,606 (1.68)	−10,023 (5.21)	−7,937 (3.02)	−3,698 (1.46)
Year of survey	7,614 (112.38)	6,742 (72.46)	6,704 (74.81)	7,664 (120.50)	6,800 (76.82)	6,711 (80.09)
Female	−11,787 (10.99)			−5,424 (6.14)		
Number observations	98,998	49,098	49,900	108,101	53,191	54,910
R^2	0.262	0.349	0.339	0.265	0.347	0.339

Table 26.6 Weight and Body Mass Index (BMI) as the Dependent Variable in Regressions Using Individual-Level Data

	Weight Whole Sample (13)	Weight Male (14)	Weight Female (15)	BMI Whole Sample (16)	BMI Male (17)	BMI Female (18)
Intercept	−2569.54 (82.69)	−2300.37 (52.07)	−2872.50 (66.16)	−417.60 (94.95)	−342.99 (62.99)	−493.71 (72.55)
Age	0.67 (13.90)	0.62 (9.27)	0.68 (10.07)	0.10 (14.76)	0.06 (7.68)	0.13 (12.77)
Net worth (in 2012 US$)	−1.15E-05 (16.02)	−1.75E-06 (0.97)	−1.96E-05 (11.31)	−2.20E-06 (21.24)	−5.41E-07 (2.39)	−3.83E-06 (13.82)
Net worth^2 (in 2012 US$)		−5.83E-12 (3.95)	2.67E-12 (1.81)		−6.47E-13 (3.50)	7.66E-13 (3.23)
Family income (in 2012 US$)	6.17E-08 (0.06)	3.90E-05 (9.92)	−2.25E-05 (5.39)	−3.58E-07 (2.29)	3.47E-06 (7.21)	−5.20E-06 (7.97)
Family income^2 (in 2012 US$)		−2.29E-11 (9.46)	1.14E-11 (4.53)		−2.08E-12 (6.94)	2.66E-12 (6.72)
Black	8.26 (30.42)	2.71 (7.10)	13.74 (35.90)	1.55 (40.88)	0.56 (11.95)	2.49 (42.33)
Hispanic	1.81 (4.13)	2.00 (3.33)	1.85 (2.96)	1.23 (20.11)	1.33 (18.12)	1.15 (11.92)
Married	2.53 (10.71)	4.89 (14.34)	0.36 (1.04)	0.27 (8.17)	0.52 (12.51)	0.16 (3.14)
Number of children	0.42 (4.66)	0.52 (4.07)	−0.14 (1.10)	0.09 (7.33)	0.10 (6.41)	0.03 (1.29)
Highest grade completed	−0.07 (1.51)	0.02 (0.34)	−0.44 (6.70)	−0.09 (14.98)	−0.08 (10.00)	−0.14 (13.26)
Born speaking foreign language	−2.50 (6.16)	−2.98 (5.33)	−2.01 (3.46)	0.12 (2.05)	0.08 (1 23)	0.16 (1.76)
Number of siblings	−0.48 (11.07)	−0.93 (15.08)	−0.02 (0.35)	−0.04 (6.66)	−0.09 (11.32)	0.001 (0.12)
Born in US	5.27 (11.20)	6.19 (9.43)	4.95 (7.49)	0.60 (9.08)	0.55 (6.87)	0.75 (7.33)
Year of survey	1.37 (88.04)	1.24 (55.82)	1.51 (69.26)	0.22 (100.48)	0.18 (67.59	0.26 (75.93)
Female	−34.77 (161.87)			−0.79 (26.24)		
Number observations	98,998	49,098	49,900	108,101	53,191	54,910
R^2	0.277	0.105	0.139	0.135	0.130	0.159

coefficients also show that marriage, higher income, and more education are all associated with having a higher level of wealth. Having more siblings, being native born, or being black or Hispanic are all associated with lower wealth levels.

To check the robustness of the results, a variety of tests were conducted: for example, additional variables were included, such as labor force and unemployment status. Additional squared terms, such as Age^2 were included and tests were done by including people whose wealth values were and were not top coded. These and other experiments resulted in no qualitative changes to the results.

Regressions were then run that put weight and BMI as the dependent or left-hand variable in the regressions and included net worth in the right-hand list of explanatory variables. The results from these regressions are found in Table 26.6, and, like the results in Table 26.5, the regressions suggest that wealth and weight are negatively related. However, the magnitude of the relationships in Table 26.6 is very different from those found in Table 26.5.

In Table 26.6, relatively large changes in wealth have only a small impact on weight or BMI. For example, the −1.15E-05 coefficient value in the row marked "Net Worth" in column (13) suggests that an increase of $100,000 in wealth is associated only with a 1.15-pound reduction in weight. The −2.20E-06 coefficient in column (16) suggests that an increase of $100,000 in wealth is associated only with a 0.22-point reduction in BMI.

Again, as in Table 26.5, the relationship between wealth and weight is stronger for females than for males. Using the coefficients in columns (14) and (15) shows that a $100,000 increase in wealth is associated with a 0.2-pound gain for men, but almost a 2-pound (1.93) gain for women. The coefficients in columns (17) and (18) suggest that a $100,000 increase in wealth is associated with a 0.06-point BMI decrease for men and a 0.375-point decrease for women.

One drawback of using these net worth figures is that for married respondents net worth is a family-level measure whereas body mass pertains to individuals. Because the NLSY79 does not ask respondents about their spouse's height or weight, there is the potential that the results are influenced by the spouse's BMI instead of the respondent's. Zagorsky (2005), using the same dataset, checked this by separately tracking married and unmarried respondents and adjusting net worth for the number of adults in the household. These adjustments did not change the results. He also removed pregnant women from the regressions since pregnancy temporarily changes BMI, and he applied Cawley's (2004) adjustment factors, which account for people systematically under-reporting their weight and found that neither adjustment qualitatively impacted the results.

26.7 Conclusion

This chapter explored the relationship between wealth and weight and showed that the world is getting both richer and heavier. The cross-national analysis using macro data indicates a small but positive statistically significant relationship between BMI and wealth. This means that as a country becomes richer we expect to find the average citizen becomes heavier. Conversely, individual-level analysis using US micro data shows a negative statistically significant relationship between BMI and wealth and between weight and wealth. The difference in Figure 26.3 between a person in his or her 50s with a BMI in the low 20s and a BMI in the low 30s is more than $100,000 in wealth. This means that as individuals in the United States become richer, we expect to find that they (on average) weigh less.

The positive relationship seen in macro data and the negative relationship seen in micro data is puzzling because the macro data suggest that increased wealth means heavier people, whereas the micro data suggest that increased wealth means lighter people. Either the United States is not representative of other countries in the world, or, if it is representative for the wealth–weight relationship, either the macro or micro results must be wrong.

If the results are not an ecological fallacy, one potential explanation for this seeming contradiction is that the macro data are heavily weighted toward poorer developing countries, such as India, China, Nigeria, and Brazil, which make up a majority of the world's population. The micro data represent the experiences of just one rich, developed country and, within this country, only middle-aged young Baby Boomers. Societal perceptions are not constant throughout the world. In poor places, richer people are typically fatter, whereas in wealthy countries, richer people often strive to be very thin. The results in this chapter might be separately capturing the poor and rich cases in the macro and micro sections, respectively. If this explanation is true, then as the world experiences continued economic development, the macro wealth–weight relationship should change from positive to negative over time. Nevertheless, whatever the true explanation, more research is needed in the future to untangle this conundrum and provide a consistent and unified answer.

Note

1. The BMI formula is equal to (weight in pounds ÷ (height in inches ÷ height in inches)) × 703. The 703 scale factor converts pounds and inches into metric measurements. The Center for Disease Control provides an online BMI calculator at http://www.cdc.gov/healthyweight/assessing/bmi/index.html.

References

Allison, P. D. (1995). *Survival analysis using the SAS system: A practical guide.* Cary, NC: SAS Institute.

Au, N., & Johnston, D. W. (2014). Too much of a good thing? Exploring the impact of wealth on weight. *Health Economics*, doi: 10.1002/hec.3094.

Bond Huie, S. A., Krueger, P. M., Rogers, R. G., & Hummer, R. A. (2003). Wealth, race, and mortality. *Social Science Quarterly*, 84(3), 667–684.

Cawley, J. (2004). The impact of obesity on wages. *Journal of Human Resources*, 39(2), 451–474.

Cawley, J., Moran, J., & Simon, K. (2010). The impact of income on the weight of elderly Americans. *Health Economics*, 19(8), 979–993.
Chung, S., Domino, M. E., & Stearns, S. C. (2009). The effect of retirement on weight. *Journal of Gerontology B*, 64(5), 656–665.
Courtemanche, C., Heutel, G., & McAlvanah, P. (2015). Impatience, incentives, and obesity. *Economic Journal*, 125, 1–31. doi: 10.1111/ecoj.12124
Feinstein, J. S. (1993). The relationship between socioeconomic status and health: A review of the literature. *Milbank Quarterly*, 71(2), 279–322.
Fonda, S. J., Fultz, N. H., Rahrig Jenkins, K., Wheeler, L. M., & Wray, L. A. (2004). Relationship of body mass and net worth for retirement-aged men and women. *Research on Aging*, 26(1), 153–176.
Grossman, M., Tekin, E., & Wada, R. (2014). Food prices and body fatness among youths. *Economics & Human Biology*, 12, 4–19.
Hajat, A., Kaufman, J. S., Rose, K. M., Siddiqi, A., & Thomas, J. C. (2010). Do the wealthy have a health advantage? Cardiovascular disease risk factors and wealth. *Social Science & Medicine*, 71(11), 1935–1942.
Hajat, A., Kaufman, J. S., Rose, K. M., Siddiqi, A., & Thomas, J. C. (2011). Long-term effects of wealth on mortality and self-rated health status. *American Journal of Epidemiology*, 173(2), 192–200.
Hamermesh, D. (2013). *Beauty pays: Why attractive people are more successful*. Princeton, NJ: Princeton University Press.
Han, E., Norton, E. C., & Stearns, S. C. (2009). Weight and wages: Fat versus lean paychecks. *Health Economics*, 18(5), 535–548.
Harris, J. L., Bargh, J. A., & Brownell, K. D. (2009). Priming effects of television food advertising on eating behavior. *Health Psychology*, 28(4), 404–413.
Hoek, J., & Gendall, P. (2006). Advertising and obesity: A behavioral perspective. *Journal of Health Communication*, 11(4), 409–423.
Johar, M., & Katayama, H. (2012). Quantile regression analysis of body mass and wages. *Health Economics*, 21(5), 597–611.
Kington, R. S., & Smith, J. P. (1997). Socioeconomic status and racial and ethnic differences in functional status associated with chronic diseases. *American Journal of Public Health*, 87(5), 805–810.
Komlos, J., Smith, P., & Bogin, B. (2004). Obesity and the rate of time preference: Is there a connection? *Journal Biosocial Science*, 36(2), 209–219.
Lakdawalla, D., & Philipson, T. (2009). The growth of obesity and technological change. *Economics & Human Biology*, 7(3), 283–293.
Lakdawalla, D., Philipson, T., & Bhattacharya, J. (2005). Welfare-enhancing technological change and the growth of obesity. *American Economic Review*, 95(2), 253–257.
Mazzocchi, M., & Traill W. B. (2008). *A structural model of wealth, obesity and health in the UK*. 12th Congress of the European Association of Agricultural Economists. Ghent, Belgium.
Meer, J., Miller, D. L., & Rosen, H. S. (2003). Exploring the health-wealth nexus. *Journal of Health Economics*, 22(5), 713–730.
Menchik, P. (1993). Economic-status as a determinant of mortality among black-and-white older men—Does poverty kill. *Population Studies*, 47(3), 427–436.
Philipson, T., & Posner, R. (2003). The long-run growth in obesity as a function of technological change. *Perspectives in Biological Medicine*, 46(3 Suppl), S87–107.

Pollack, C. E., Chideya, S., Cubbin, C., Williams, B., Dekker, M., & Braveman, P. (2007). Should health studies measure wealth? A systematic review. *American Journal of Prevention Medicine*, 33(3), 250–264.

Rosin, O. (2008). The economic causes of obesity: A survey. *Journal of Economic Surveys*, 22(4), 617–647.

Shin-Yi, C., Rashad, I., & Grossman, M. (2008). Fast-food restaurant advertising on television and its influence on childhood obesity. *Journal of Law and Economics*, 51(4), 599–618.

World Bank. (2006). *Where is the wealth of nations?: Measuring capital for the 21st century.* Washington, DC: World Bank.

Yanovski, S. Z., & Walsh, B. T. (2003). Binge eating disorder and obesity in 2003: Could treating an eating disorder have a positive effect on the obesity epidemic? *International Journal of Eating Disorders*, 34(S1), S117–S20.

Zagorsky, J. L., ed. (1997). *NLSY79 Users' Guide 1997*. Columbus: Center for Human Resource Research, Ohio State University.

Zagorsky, J. L. (2004). Is obesity as dangerous to your wealth as to your health? *Research on Aging*, 26(1), 130–152.

Zagorsky, J. L. (2005). Health and wealth. The late-20th century obesity epidemic in the US. *Economics and Human Biology*, 3(2), 296–313.

CHAPTER 27

FAMILY ECONOMICS AND OBESITY

SVEN E. WILSON

27.1 INTRODUCTION

THE field of health economics has, at least since Arrow's seminal 1963 article, operated under the assumption that health is both fundamental to human welfare and fundamentally different from most other goods that trade in markets. Health is an investment good because people can devote economic resources to improving it, yet it is profoundly different from most goods—it is nontransferable, multidimensional, only partially observable, and highly unpredictable.

Economics brings powerful concepts to the study of human health. Two in particular stand out. First is the notion that promotion of health is associated with opportunity costs, which are the foregone opportunities associated with health-promoting actions by consumers and providers, including the costs of medical care, the time spent on health-promoting activities such as exercise, and the reduction in utility associated with health promotion, such as the displeasure incurred by foregoing favorite foods.

The second concept, directly related to the first, is that of capital investment. Beginning with the work of Mushkin (1962) and Becker (1964), the concept of health capital was extended from the study of education to health. Grossman (1972) formalized these concepts into a model of health capital investment in which individuals use time and medical care as inputs into a health production function, and the stock of health capital (which depreciates at an increasing rate) determines the time available for work and is a direct input into the consumer's utility function. In the Grossman framework, health can be improved at will through investment, and life span is chosen by the optimizing agent who dies when the health capital stock is allowed to dip below the minimum level necessary to maintain life.

Obviously, salient aspects of human health are left out of this basic model. The psychology of appetite and willpower are not addressed. Furthermore, uncertainty is ubiquitous in real-life health behavior, as is irreversibility. Individuals must accept that many health conditions and disabilities are irreversible and cannot be improved regardless of the resources invested. Unplanned death is, of course, the ultimate irreversibility.

In recent decades, obesity has gone from a little-studied backwater of human health to the forefront of the nation's public health agenda. And, even as great strides have been made to reduce smoking—the most important behavioral risk factor around the globe—an epidemic of obesity has occurred in the developed world.[1] This epidemic stands in stark contrast to the normal narrative of economic development, in which more prosperous countries have populations that live longer and are in significantly better health (Preston, 1975). Thus, obesity is a crucial topic of study to economists not only because of concerns over public health, but also because of the critical paradox the obesity epidemic poses to our understanding of economic development.

27.2 The Health Capital of Families

In addition to expanding (and redefining) human capital theory, Gary Becker is the founder of family economics, which studies why relationships form and dissolve and what function they play in human societies as a primary consuming unit made up of several individuals. At the core of his study of the allocation of time within households (1965) is the concept of a household producing goods and services that enter into the utility functions of household members.

The two most salient points of connection between health capital theory and family economics are (1) that health capital is produced in a family context, and, therefore, the health status depends critically on family-related risk factors; and (2) that the formation, structure, and duration of families are determined in part by human health. These connections are true of health in general, but obesity proves an illuminating case study because body shape and size are central components of attractiveness, and, therefore, the study of obesity is inseparably connected to the study of human relationships. Indeed, obesity demands not only a new brand of health economics, but a new brand of *family economics* as well.

27.2.1 The Household's Production of Health

In Grossman's model, the consumer's demand for health determines the demand for medical care and the investment of time. The opportunity cost of time is, of course, the wage rate that the individual can earn. In a broader household production framework, the opportunity cost of health investment is the foregone production of household "commodities," things like meals, entertainment, sex, children, recreation, housing, home decor, and all the other things that the household uses to produce utility-generating commodities.

In the production model, therefore, household welfare is produced not only by investing in the human capital to produce higher wages (as well as longer and healthier lives), but also through making the household more efficient. Single-person households are at a distinct disadvantage because many household commodities are more efficiently produced by multiperson households. We can think of the household as a small economy. There are gains from specialization and exchange within the household and from decreasing per capita costs associated with many commodities, such as lower per person housing, utility, and meal costs. Furthermore, the direct benefits of love and companionship associated with marriage and children are obtained by forming unions and creating families.

In short, marriage provides a mechanism to significantly augment the household production technology, which results in an increased production of goods that produce welfare, including health and longevity. Families based on long-term commitments will have even greater incentives to invest in health since the prospects of future gains in the utility raise the return on current investment—another way of saying that forward-looking people in committed relationships have more to live for than do singles.

Family members also promote health by providing care directly. Parsons (1977) referred to a family as the "informal health service organization" (p. 711). In addition to nursing care, this informal care may include providing information and monitoring activities such as medication taking. Waite and Gallagher (2000) refer to the virtues of the "nagging" spouse. Single people living alone often lack ready access to family-provided informal care (although in later life single people may have children who serve as caregivers).

This theory predicts a positive association between marriage and health, which has been a consistent empirical finding going back for several decades (Holt-Lunstad, Birmingham, & Jones, 2008; Koball, Moiduddin, Hendersion, Goesling, & Besculides, 2010; Liu & Umberson, 2008; Wood, Goesling, & Avellar, 2007). The studies include a wide array of health outcomes, with the relationship between marital status and mortality being an especially prominent focus of the literature (Fu & Goldman, 1996; Liu, 2009; Manzoli, Villari, Pironi, & Boccia, 2007; Rendell, Weden, Favreault, & Waldron, 2011; Ross, Morowsky, & Goldsteen, 1990). The problem of endogenous selection into marriage remains a significant challenge for work in this area. Longitudinal studies (see the review by Wilson & Oswald, 2005) limit the endogeneity problem because researchers can control for observable health variables either before or at the time of marriage. Unobservables related to both health and marriage, however, remain a source of endogeneity in longitudinal studies.

Of course, families shape child health in profound ways as well. Indeed, parents provide children not only with a genetic endowment but with an environment that shapes health outcomes, and parental decisions regarding diet and other activities form the foundation of a child's health. The role of socioeconomic status (SES) and parental education have played a dominant role in this literature (Bornstein & Bradley, 2012; Bradley & Corwyn, 2002; Goodman, 1999).

27.2.2 The Case of Obesity

Much of the social scientific work on health developed without particular attention to obesity because it wasn't until fairly recent decades that obesity was seen as a widespread public health concern. Persistent increases in obesity (Komlos & Brabec, 2011; Ogden, Carroll, & Curtin, 2006) have brought the obesity problem center stage.

From a demographic perspective, obesity is made more difficult to study on account of the long lag between weight gain and the incidence of disease. High body mass is a risk factor for important diseases such diabetes, cardiovascular disease, and cancer, but typically those diseases present themselves long after adult weight gain has occurred. Thus, important demographic data affecting the onset of obesity occur in early and mid-adulthood, whereas the chronic conditions resulting from the disease usually occur in later life. The same is true for mortality. Few datasets track the same individuals over many decades, so a life course perspective on the interaction between obesity and health requires fitting different pieces of evidence together.

The incidence of obesity with respect to age is changing as adolescent obesity increases and as median age at marriage increases. These forces together mean that the percentage of single young adults who are obese or overweight has increased in recent decades. This has potentially serious implications for the functioning of marriage markets because physical attractiveness is an important determinant of partner selection (Belot & Fidrmuc, 2010; Buss, Shackelford, Kirkpatrick, & Larsen, 2001), and body shape plays an important role in ratings of physical attractiveness, especially for women (Carmalt, Cawley, Joyner, & Sobal, 2008; Conley & Glauber, 2007; Fu & Goldman, 1996; Maisey, Vale, Cornelissen, & Toveé, 1999; Singh & Young, 1995; Tovée, Reinhardt, Emery, & Cornelissen, 1998).

Obesity is thus separated from many other important risk factors, such as hypertension, hyperlipidemia, or genetic disease markers, because obesity is readily observable in the marriage market. Scholars have long tried to determine the impact of mate selection on the empirical association between health and marriage, and nowhere is this more challenging than in the case of obesity because obesity influences attractiveness and is also an indicator of health and health history.

The familial roots of obesity extend powerfully to the case of childhood obesity as well. Increasing assortative mating affects the distribution of genetic endowments received by children, and, perhaps more powerfully, parents play the primary role in shaping the diet and time use of young children. Theories abound as to why childhood obesity has increased so much, but it is hard to imagine a scenario in which parental behavior (perhaps in response to changing market incentives) has not played a foundational role. Of course, from very young ages, children are the objects of advertising by a powerful food industry, which was made even more effective with the advent of television (Komlos & Brabec, 2011). Food makers face strong profit incentives that end up promoting childhood obesity.

Obesity poses more than one paradox for economic theory. Even as the cross-sectional relationship between body mass index (BMI) and SES is strongly negative, wealthy nations are becoming steadily heavier. This is much like the happiness paradox, in which income is positively related to happiness within a society, but societies do not become happier as national income increases. Another paradox is that even though marriage is associated with longer life and a host of positive health benefits, numerous studies indicate that marriage actually promotes weight gain.

The fundamental life patterns—aspects like diet, physical activity, smoking, and emotional well-being—that determine body mass are the same patterns that constitute our social lives. Thus, an economics that can understand the changing patterns of body weight has to pertain, at its core, to family economics. The tools that economics brings to bear on health and on the family should be a fruitful marriage of ideas.

27.3 Marital Unions

27.3.1 Union Formation

Body weight is an important component of relationship formation starting early in life. And, from early ages, significant gender differences exist with respect to BMI (Feingold & Mazzella, 1998; Furnham, Badmin, & Sneade, 2002). Halpern et al. (Halpern, King, Oslak, & Udry, 2005) find that for each one point increase in BMI, the probability of adolescent females being in a romantic relationship decreases by 6%. Furthermore, they find that girls in nonsexual romantic relationships have an increased likelihood of dieting. Pearce et al. (Pearce, Boergers, & Prinstein, 2002) find similar patterns for adolescent girls but no such pattern for boys.

The general finding that men place greater importance on physical attractiveness when searching for mates (Buss, 1994; Fisman, Iyengar, Kamenica, & Simonson, 2006; Hitsch, Hortascu, & Ariely, 2010 extends to the case of obesity, as noted earlier. Data on reported preferences confirm gender-based differences in mate selection based on body weight. For example, Chen and Brown (2005) found in a study of college students that men are more likely to rate the attractiveness of potential sexual partner using obesity as a criterion than are women. Indeed, the authors note that obese women were less desirable than those with significant physical disability or with sexually transmitted diseases.

Body weight has been shown empirically to affect transition into marriage in a highly gendered fashion. Averett et al. (Averett, Sikora, & Argys, 2008) show that among a cohort of younger adults, thinner women are more likely to enter into a relationship than are heavier women, and Conley and Glauber (2007) find a similar pattern in a sample of somewhat older women. Obese women, when they do marry, are more likely to marry men with lower earnings (Averett & Korenman, 1996). In later life (after age 50), BMI has a positive effect on entrance into marriage for men, but a negative effect for women (Wilson, 2012).

In the economic model of marriage formation, individuals bring a bundle of characteristics to the marriage market. The empirical regularity of assortative mating,[2] in which characteristics such as education or attractiveness have a positive correlation between partners, has been observed by scholars going back a century and is one of the strongest regularities in social science. Sociologists have emphasized the importance of social class, segmentation, and networks that lead to people finding mates who tend to have similar educational levels, religious backgrounds, political views, and many other characteristics.

Instead of concentrating on exogenous social structure, the economic approach views people as utility maximizing agents who seek the best possible match in the competitive market. As is the case with exchange theory, individuals may trade a high value in one characteristic (say attractiveness) to compensate for a low value in another (such as earning potential). Stevens et al. (Stevens, Owens, & Schaefer, 1990) conclude that there isn't trade across characteristics; instead, similar characteristics simply sort positively. But more recent work by Carmalt et al. (2008) find evidence that education and body weight are being exchanged for both men and women, although positive sorting on the same traits was still dominant. They find that obese individuals are less likely to have attractive partners, with this disadvantage being greater for women than for men and greater for white women than for black women.

The economic model pioneered by Becker provides a simple economic model to explain the basics of the long-observed assortative mating in marriage markets. In Becker's framework, people participating in the marriage market are seeking to maximize their share of the commodities produced by the household. Thus, it is how the traits of partners interact with one another in the production process that determines their value. In other words, personal traits have match-specific value in addition to generic value in the market. Traits that are complements raise household production.[3] Thus, classical musical lovers or tennis players gain value from matching with people with similar traits because of this complementarity. A trait such as income, on other hand, can be substituted across partners (since it is the pooled income of the household that determines what market goods can be purchased). Becker's model predicts that substitutable traits will tend to be negatively sorted because high-income people use their income to buy desirable traits such as attractiveness. However, as Becker noted, because income is so tightly tied to education, the substitutability of income may be masked because education is highly complementary in household production for reasons beyond its ability to generate income. Social networks dominated by occupation and education background and marriage markets segmented by social class reinforce the strong tendency for SES to be strongly positively correlated because people often seek mates within a particular segment of the general population.

In the marriage market, people tend to end up with a mate who has a level of physical attractiveness similar to their own (Feingold, 1988; Stevens et al., 1990). Since preference for attractive partners is ubiquitous, positive sorting on the dimension of attractiveness is hardly surprising. But whether attractiveness is *complementary* in household production with respect to Becker's framework is a question that has not been addressed by family economists. Such a complementarity would mean not only that attractiveness was valued in a partner, which is obvious, but also that the attractiveness of one's partner increases the productive value of one's own level of attractiveness.[4]

27.3.2 Body Weight Across Marital States and Transitions

The empirical relationship between body mass and marital status is somewhat mixed, although studies tend to find that entrance into marriage is associated with weight gain and exit from marriage with weight loss, holding other attributes constant (Eng, Kawachi, Fitzmaurice, & Rimm, 2005; Kahn & Williamson, 1990; Klein, 2011; Lee et al., 2005; Shafer, 2010; Sobal, Rauschenbach, & Frongillo, 2003; The & Gordon-Larsen, 2009; Umberson, Wortman, & Kessler, 1992; Wilson, 2012). The cross-sectional relationship studies find that married people are heavier than single people (Sobal, Hanson, & Frongillo, 2009).

Thus, obesity is a significant outlier to the positive relationship between marriage and health found in the scholarly literature. This poses a significant challenge to the idea that marriage facilitates the investment in health. Some have argued (Averett et al., 2008; Sobal et al., 2003) that various "social obligations" of marriage induce frequent eating and a higher consumption of calorie-dense foods. But it is not obvious why these attendant obligations should be stronger than other investment incentives.

The role that body shape plays in romantic attractiveness may also affect the relationship between marriage and BMI. Marriage (at least happy marriage) reduces the incentive to maintain a body weight that has market value, and, therefore, the weight gain may have more to do with a reduction in market pressure than with health. Similarly, marital dissolution (or the threat thereof[5]) reverses those incentives, and those seeking new partners have incentive to lose weight.

An alternative psychological view (Umberson, Liu, & Powers, 2009), however, is that marital crisis causes stress, which can lead to weight loss. The crisis model is consistent with short-term effects of marital transitions on BMI; however, as Wilson (2012) points out, the crisis model cannot account for the *persistence* of marriage–BMI correlations. Furthermore, the psychological literature is unclear whether crisis should, on balance, be associated with weight gain or weight loss.[6]

27.3.3 Spousal Concordance in Body Weight

Marriage market forces result in a strong interspousal correlation in body weight, which is supported by evidence from numerous studies across countries (Brown, Hole, & Roberts, 2010; Hebebrand et al., 2000; Jacobson, Torgerson, Sjostrom, & Couchard, 2007; Meyler, Stimpson, & Peek, 2007; Monden, 2007; Oreffice & Quintana-Domeque, 2010; Speakman, Djafarian, & Stewart, 2007). The literature is divided, however, on the question of whether spousal concordance is due entirely to sorting in the market (Klein, 2011; Knuiman, Divitini, Bartholomew, & Welborn, 1996; Silventoinen, Kaprio, Lahelma, Viken, & Rose, 2003) or whether a shared environment and behavior contributes to the correlation (The & Gordon-Larsen, 2009).

There are essentially three factors that can contribute to spousal concordance in BMI: (1) sorting on BMI in the marriage market, (2) sorting on factors related to BMI, and (3) spouses growing more similar over time because of shared behaviors and a shared environment. One piece of evidence indicating that spousal concordance on BMI is not merely incidental is the relative lack of spousal concordance between health-related factors less salient in the market than BMI. For instance, the spousal correlations in cardiovascular risk factors for BMI are much lower than for BMI or smoking (Di Castelnuovo, Quacquaruccio, Donati, de Gaetano, & Iacoviello, 2008; Inoue, Sawada, Suge, Nao, & Igarashi, 1996), and the correlation is insignificant for cancer (Friedman & Quesenberry, 1999). Thus, marriage market outcomes are likely influenced by sorting directly on BMI.

The third factor (increasing similarity over time or assimilation) is integral to the idea of household-based production of health, but it has the least supporting evidence, probably because of the high data requirements necessary to establish such a finding. Some evidence, though, does exist. The and Gordon-Larsen (2012) find that partner concordance for obesity-related behaviors is high, suggesting that coordination of behavior plays some role. Jeffery and Rick (2002) estimate that the changes in spouses' weight over a 2-year period is significantly correlated, and Wilson (2012) finds the same co-movement in body weight over several successive waves of the Health and Retirement Study, a study of older adults.

27.3.4 Marital Conflict

Extensive research has shown the negative impact of high-conflict marriages on a variety of health outcomes. Kiecolt-Glaser and Newton (2001) conclude that women's physiological changes following marital conflict show greater persistence than men's. Additionally, Umberson et al. (Umberson, Williams, Powers, Liu, & Needham, 2006) show that the effects of marital strain are *cumulative* over the life course and that the negative aspects of marriage are more consequential at later ages.[7]

Although marital conflict has a negative impact on a variety of health indicators (Holt-Lunstad et al., 2008), the effect of conflict on BMI is not clear. One recent study (Whisman & Uebelacker, 2011), however, indicates that poor "marital adjustment" among men raises the risk of metabolic syndrome (of which obesity is a prominent indicator) among their wives.

27.4 Children

27.4.1 The Economics of Child Investment

An early important model of fertility (Willis, 1974) applied Becker's concept of household production to include both the demand for children and the quality of children. In this economic framework, parents choose the number and quality of children so as to maximize family utility given the constraints of the production function and the family income. Higher income families have more resources to put toward having children, but they also have greater opportunity costs because raising children is time-intensive. Michael (1974) noted that the negative correlation between parents' education and number of children is one of the most frequently observed regularities related to human fertility. Typically, the higher income created by education (as well as, perhaps, more effective fertility control practices) leads parents to invest more in increasingly fewer children.

27.4.2 Obesity and Technological Change

Economists looking for an explanation of the obesity epidemic have focused on the impact of technological change and the resulting effects on market prices (Cawley, 2006; Philipson & Posner, 1999, 2008). Lakdawalla and Philipson (2009) attribute 40% of the rise in BMI at the time of their study to lower food prices (including the time costs of preparing food). Cutler, Glaeser, and Shapiro (2003) point to the role that technological change has had on decreasing the relative price of processed foods compared to whole foods. Cawley (2006) notes that there is some degree of uncertainty related to changes in the price of certain types of foods relative to others but that energy-dense foods (high in sugars and fats) have become less expensive relative to other foods.

Because the preparation of food is time-intensive, changes in the value of time for family members will affect the choice of when, where, and what to eat. One crucial change in the family's allocation of time has been the increase in maternal employment generated by rising economic opportunities for women. Cawley and Liu (2007) note that mothers with children under age 18 increased their labor force participation rate from 47% to 71% between 1975 and 2005. When work outside the home increases, the value of time inside the home increases, and the price of producing time-intensive household commodities (such as healthy meals) increases as well. Studies in both the United States and the United Kingdom have found that rising maternal employment has had a statistically significant positive effect on child obesity (Anderson, Butcher, & Levine, 2003; Courtemanche, 2009; von Hinke Kessler Scholder, 2008). Cawley (2011) notes that time use data suggest that increased hours of TV viewing by children and decreases in the time spent by mothers in shopping, preparing, and eating food with their children may account for the maternal employment effect, although mechanisms are not entirely clear.

Technology and market forces have also induced changes in physical activity. Rising market wages increase the opportunity cost of all home production activities that are time-intensive, including exercise. And, as Philipson and Posner (2008) note, exercise has also gotten more expensive because work at home and in the market has become less physically demanding. Recent research shows the importance not only of physical inactivity but of extensive sedentary behavior (sitting), which is significantly associated with metabolic syndrome (Edwardson et al., 2012). Before labor-saving conveniences were common, people burned a large amount of calories in the course of their normal workday activities. Indeed, for most of history, getting enough calories was the fundamental human problem. Children, no longer required to assist with manual labor, also lead much more sedentary lives, and the introduction of television, personal computers, and video games further induces children to spend more time in physical inactivity. And given that so few jobs require physical strength or fitness these days, human capital investment in children is not likely to include significant attention to physical development.

Higher childhood BMI is often seen as bad because of the negative health consequences, but basic economic theory is unambiguous that falling prices (and, hence, rising real income) will increase welfare. Therefore, in the canonical economic model with no externalities, even if falling food prices cause a shift toward the consumption of fattening foods, total welfare will increase. This is essentially the point made by Lakdawalla, Philipson, and Bhattacharya (2005) who argue that obesity is merely a "side effect of progress" (253), one that occurs when people rationally and efficiently respond to the lower prices caused by technological growth.

The canonical model, however, is surely inapplicable in the case of obesity. Families—especially children—are subject to a variety of external forces such as peer effects, manipulative advertising, government food subsidies, and significant lack of information. In the case of obesity, the negative externalities are likely to outweigh the simple reallocation of the budget due to price changes.

The crucial questions, then, are whether market failures exist to the extent that rising obesity can be interpreted as a social ill and whether policy actions can correct those failures. This question is especially pressing for the case of children, whose body weight is largely a function of their genes, opportunities, and home environment—all shaped by their parents and all subject to considerable external pressure and influence.

27.4.3 Market Failures

The most obvious market failure related to food consumption is uninformed demand. The demand for fattening foods may have increased because consumers are often poorly informed about the food they consume (through poor labeling, misleading advertising, or lack of education). Research on the effect of product labeling through the Nutrition Labeling and Education Act (NLEA) of 1990 and other efforts to inform consumers on their food choices of has shown inconclusive results (Cawley, 2011). Furthermore, dietary science is a rapidly expanding field whose results do not always translate well into policy or public education. For example, some argue convincingly that the rise of the obesity epidemic corresponds with widespread government advocacy of low-fat diets and the corresponding increase in the consumption of diets high in sugars. Because fat became an obsession of nutrition advocates beginning in the 1960s, per capita consumption of dietary fat has fallen considerably, but obesity has skyrocketed. Even though the beneficial value of dietary fat in most of its forms has been largely redeemed among researchers of metabolic syndrome (the source of most obesity), public knowledge lags behind.[8] Recent mass market books (Lustig, 2012; Taubes, 2008; Teicholz, 2014) attempting to educate the public about the science related to diet and obesity may help improve public knowledge in the future.

Uninformed demand is particularly complex when it comes to the case of children. As children grow older, they gain more autonomy over their dietary choices. But the obesity epidemic is occurring at very young ages as well, where we expect children to have relatively little direct control over their diets. Of course, since the advent of television, children have been subject to the direct effects of powerful and effective advertising. We can think of direct marketing to children, who often lack the emotional and intellectual capacities to resist such efforts, as a market failure. Parents who try to promote healthier diets often face the prospect of unhappy children who have been manipulated by media.

Because parental behaviors remain a powerful determinant of child diets, the question of childhood obesity is at the core of family economics: namely, the question of how parents make decisions on behalf of their children and of how much autonomy children have available to make their own decisions. But because of the influence of external forces, this is not just about family behavior but also includes the welfare consequences of uninformed demand.

Obese individuals impose significant externalities in the health care system. Finkelstein et al. (Finkelstein, Ruhm, & Kosa, 2005) estimated that, in 2008, obesity-related illnesses cost Medicare $19.7 billion and Medicaid $8 billion. The costs of obesity imposed by children is relatively small because children, as a group and including obese children, have relatively low health care costs. But at least a portion of the externalities imposed on the health care system by obesity are the result of parental actions in childhood. A large share of the costs, of course, are attributable to organized interests directly promoting poor diets among children.

Similarly, when schools allow children access to unhealthy foods through vending machines in exchange for compensation by the food industry, they are imposing externalities on future generations. Children who are allowed to become obese through parental actions have costs imposed on them for decades to come.

Of course, children eventually become adolescents who gain significant control over their diets and who often care an enormous amount about their body weight, which also can have negative health consequences. Cawley, Markowitz, and Tauras (2004) note, for instance, that being overweight leads to a significant increase in smoking initiation among adolescent girls. Indeed, weight-related body image contributes to eating disorders and other psychological problems among adolescents, particularly girls. At the same time that one group of scholars is concerned about rising rates of obesity among adolescents and what to do about it, another group is concerned about poor body image and excessive dieting. Thus, public policy faces the challenge of trying to fight childhood obesity without promoting negative body image. This is one of the trickier challenges faced by both parents and policy-makers, especially in a hypersexualized popular culture saturated with unrealistic and mostly unattainable ideals of beauty.

Public policy has done relatively little to address the externalities that parents, schools, and society are imposing on the future lives of their children through obesity. Taxing foods that lead to weight gain or subsidizing activities, such as sports or recreation, that lead to more exercise are both viable options. But because children do not have significant control over household production decisions, they might not gain as much as policy-makers hope from such efforts if their parents counteract the effects of these taxes and subsidies through reallocation of goods and services within the household.

27.4.4 Genetics and Obesity

It is obvious from both simple life observation and numerous studies that obesity is a highly heritable trait. Indeed, the concordance in parental obesity is a powerful and easily identified risk factor for obesity in children (Jacobson et al., 2007). Correlations between twins and between parents and children are strong (Maes, Neale, & Eaves, 1997; Schousboe et al., 2004), thus indicating a strong genetic basis for obesity, yet adoption studies indicate that family environment also has a substantial impact on childhood obesity (Silventoinen et al., 2003). Furthermore, the heritability question is far from settled because the search for specific genetic markers has been elusive, and only a small fraction of the variance in obesity can be attributed to yet uncovered molecular genetic factors (Flier, 2004; Gesta, Tseng, & Kahn, 2007; Hebebrand, Volckmar, Knol, & Hinney, 2010; Speliotes et al., 2010).

Even though obesity is strongly heritable, it was not thought until relatively recently that evolutionary change in the human genome could have played much of a role in the recent increase in obesity prevalence because the genome evolves slowly over many generations. The exploding field of epigenetics, however, has changed that view. The epigenetic environment determines when and how genes are expressed, resulting in different phenotypes. The epigenetic environment can change quickly, and changes in that environment can have effects for decades to come. Barker (1997) hypothesized that the intrauterine environment could affect disease in later life, and epigenetic research has provided a foundation for those findings. Changes in maternal diet, in particular, can affect not only obesity in children, but can possibly influence the tendency to obesity in the next generation as well (Wang et al., 2012).

27.5 Conclusion and Future Directions

Family economists study why families form and the choices they make. Yet family economists have paid scant attention to the question of health, and health economists have largely ignored families. Studies around the globe (Spogard & James, 1999) show that what people most care about are their families and their health. Economists would surely be well-served by thinking about these foundational human concerns because, as I have argued here, there are so many theoretical and empirical connection points between the obesity epidemic and the family.

The case of obesity is worthy of more attention not only because of its prominence as a public health concern but also because body appearance is a central component of physical attractiveness and, therefore, helps drives marriage market and labor market outcomes over the life cycle. Obesity is a health risk for both males and females, but obesity has a special role in the area of women's health and welfare that deserves more attention. Overweight and obese women face negative consequences in the marriage market, which can have long-term effects on their health.

Obesity is also a compelling topic to study because of the intriguing social patterns associated with it. The negative relationship between SES and health is one of the most universal and widely studied topics in the social sciences,[9] and obesity is characterized by a unique and fascinating set of patterns. Not only does the direction of the effect reverse sign in moving from developing to developed economies, but, in the developed world, there is a significant inverse association between body mass and SES for women but no such relationship for men (McLaren, 2007; Sobal & Stunkard, 1989). A compelling question for additional study is to identify the role that marriage market forces play in these relationships.[10]

In important ways, the marriage market influences both health outcomes and economic outcomes. Hebebrand et al. (2000) hypothesized that the obesity epidemic is due in part to assortative mating. The timing of the obesity epidemic also coincides with the delay in age at marriage that occurred since the 1960s. As marriage age occurs later and the onset of obesity occurs earlier, it becomes easier to ascertain a prospective partner's likelihood of becoming obese (Speakman et al., 2007). Just as wealth transfers between generations are strongly influenced by family relationships, those same strong relationships may be driving health outcomes in the next generation as well.

To a large extent, the modern public health agenda is driven by a desire to reduce social disparities. The role that families play—their resources, their collective knowledge, their decision-making process, their internal bonds, and their place in larger social networks—will be essential for understanding how those disparities form and how they can be alleviated.

Notes

1. Recent evidence from the United States indicates that obesity has leveled off for both children and adults. Ogden et al. (Ogden, Carroll, Kit, & Flegal, 2014) use the National Health and Nutrition Examination Survey to show that there was not a significant increase in obesity between 2003–04 and 2009–10.
2. Assortative mating, sometimes referred to as *endogamy* or *homogamy*, is the tendency of like to match with like.
3. Formally, traits are complementary when the cross-partial derivative of household production with respect to the level of the trait for each partner is greater than zero.

4. Of course, psychological theories addressing the strong correlation in attractiveness between mates has a long history, going back to Walster et al. (Walster, Aronson, Abrahams, & Rottman, 1966).
5. Lundborg, Nystedt, and Lindgren (2007) provide evidence from Europe that married individuals have lower body weight in markets where divorce risk is high.
6. For instance, depression, which is likely to result from divorce, is significantly associated with weight gain (Blaine, 2008).
7. Umberson and Williams (2005) show that even though the impact of poor marital quality is roughly the same for men and women, women experience lower levels of marital quality, which translates into a sustained disadvantage for the health of women over the life course compared to married men.
8. And, of course, the food industry (with its powerful lobbying arm) is heavily invested in the widespread persistence of low-cost, highly processed foods.
9. The literature is vast. See Glymour, Avendano, and Kawachi (2014) for a recent review.
10. Averett and Korenman (1999) find, for instance, that the negative effect of obesity on socioeconomic status works through marriage.

References

Anderson, P. M., Butcher, K. F., & Levine, P. B. (2003). Maternal employment and overweight children. *Journal of Health Economics*, *22*, 477–504.

Arrow, K. (1963). Uncertainty and the welfare economics of medical care. *American Economic Review*, *53*, 941–973.

Averett, S., & Korenman, S. (1996). The economic reality of the beauty myth. *Journal of Human Resources*, *31*, 304–330.

Averett, S., & Korenman, S. (1999). Black-white differences in social and economic consequences of obesity. *International Journal of Obesity and Related Metabolic Disorders*, *23*, 166–173.

Averett, S., Sikora, A., & Argys, L. M. (2008). For better or worse: Relationship status and body mass index. *Economics and Human Biology*, *6*, 330–349.

Barker, D. J. P. (1997). Maternal nutrition, fetal nutrition, & disease in later life. *Nutrition*, *13*, 807–813.

Becker, G. S. (1964). *Human capital: A theoretical analysis with special reference to education*. New York: National Bureau for Economic Research.

Becker, G. S. (1965). A theory of the allocation of time. *Economic Journal*, *75*, 493–517.

Belot, M., & Fidrmuc, J. (2010). Anthropometry of love: Height and gender asymmetries in interethnic marriages. *Economics & Human Biology*, *8*, 361–372.

Blaine, B. (2008). Does depression cause obesity? A meta-analysis of longitudinal studies of depression and weight control. *Journal of Health Psychology*, *13*, 1190–1197.

Bornstein, M. H., & Bradley, R. H. (2012). *Socioeconomic status, parenting, and child development*. New York: Routledge.

Bradley, R. H., & Corwyn, R. F. (2002). Socioeconomic status and child development. *Annual Review of Psychology*, *53*, 371–399.

Brown, H., Hole, A. R., & Roberts, J. (2010). *Going the same weigh: Spousal correlations in obesity in the UK*. Sheffield Economic Research Paper Series No. 2010012. University of Sheffield, UK.

Buss, D. M. (1994). The strategies of human mating, *American Scientist, 82*, 238–249.
Buss, D. M., Shackelford, T. K., Kirkpatrick, L. A., & Larsen, R. J. (2001). A half century of mate preferences: The cultural evolution of values. *Journal of Marriage and Family, 63*, 491–503.
Carmalt, J. H., Cawley, J., Joyner, J., & Sobal, J. (2008). Body weight and matching with a physically attractive romantic partner. *Journal of Marriage and Family, 70*, 1287–1296.
Cawley, J. (2006). Markets and childhood obesity. *Future of Children, 16*, 69–88.
Cawley, J. (2011). The economics of obesity. In J. Cawley (Ed.), *The Oxford handbook of the social science of obesity*. New York: Oxford University Press, 120-147.
Cawley, J., & Liu, F. (2007). *Mechanisms for the association between maternal employment and child cognitive development* (NBER Working Paper 13609). New York: National Bureau of Economic Research.
Cawley, J., Markowitz, S., & Tauras, J. (2004). Lighting up and slimming down: The effects of body weight and cigarette prices on adolescent smoking initiation. *Journal of Health Economics, 23*, 293–311.
Chen, E. Y., & Brown, M. (2005). Obesity stigma in sexual relationships: *Obesity Research, 13*, 1393–1397.
Conley, D., & Glauber, D. (2007). Gender, body mass, and socioeconomic status: New evidence from the PSID. *Advances in Health Economics and Health Services Research, 17*, 253–275.
Courtemanche, C. (2009). Longer hours and larger waistlines? The relationship between work hours and obesity. *Forum for Health Economics and Policy, 12*, Article 2.
Cutler, D. M., Glaeser, E. L., & Shapiro, J. M. (2003). Why have Americans become more obese? *Journal of Economic Perspectives, 17*(3), 93–118.
Di Castelnuovo, A., Quacquaruccio, G., Donati, M. B., de Gaetano, G., & Iacoviello, L. (2008). Spousal concordance for major coronary risk factors: A systematic review and meta-analysis Augusto. *American Journal of Epidemiology, 169*, 1–8.
Edwardson, C. L., Gorely, T., Davies, M. J., Gray, L. J., Khunti, K., Wilmot, E. G., . . . Biddle, S. J. (2012). Association of sedentary behaviour with metabolic syndrome: A meta-analysis. *PLoS ONE, 7*(4), E34916.
Eng, P. M., Kawachi, I., Fitzmaurice, G., & Rimm, E. B. (2005). Effects of marital transitions on changes in dietary and other health behaviours in U.S. male health professionals. *Journal of Epidemiology & Community Health, 59*, 56–62.
Feingold, A. (1988). Matching for attractiveness in romantic partners and same-sex friends: A meta-analysis and theoretical critique. *Psychological Bulletin, 104*, 226–235.
Feingold, A., & Mazzella, R. (1998). Gender differences in body image are increasing. *Psychological Science, 98*, 190.
Finkelstein, E. A., Ruhm, C. J., & Kosa, K. M. (2005). Economic causes and consequences of obesity. *Annual Review of Public Health, 26*, 239–257.
Fisman, R., Iyengar, S. S., Kamenica, E., & Simonson, I. (2006). Gender differences in mate selection: Evidence from a speed dating experiment. *Quarterly Journal of Economics, 121*, 673–697.
Flier, J. S. (2004). Obesity wars: Molecular progress confronts an expanding epidemic. *Cell, 116*, 337–350.
Friedman, G. D., & Quesenberry, C. P., Jr. (1999). Spousal concordance for cancer incidence: A cohort study. *Cancer, 86*, 2413–2419.
Fu, H., & Goldman, N. (1996). Incorporating health into models of marriage choice: Demographic and sociological perspectives. *Journal of Marriage and the Family, 58*, 740–758.

Furnham, A., Badmin, N., & Sneade, I. (2002). Body image dissatisfaction: Gender differences in eating attitudes, self-esteem, & reasons for exercise. *Journal of Psychology, 136*, 581–596.

Gesta, S., Tseng, Y., & Kahn, C. R. (2007). Developmental origin of fat: Tracking obesity to its source. *Cell, 131*, 242–256.

Glymour, M. M., Avendano, M., & Kawachi, I. (2014). Socioeconomic status and health. In L. F. Berkman, T. D. Cabot, & M. M. Glymour (Eds.), *Social epidemiology* (pp. 76–94). New York: Oxford University Press.

Goodman, E. (1999). The role of socioeconomic status gradients in explaining differences in US adolescents' health. *American Journal of Public Health, 89*, 1522–1528.

Grossman, M. (1972). On the concept of health capital and the demand for health. *Journal of Political Economy, 80*, 223–255.

Halpern, C. T., King, R. B., Oslak, S. G., & Udry, J. R. (2005). Body mass index, dieting, romance, & sexual activity in adolescent girls: Relationships over time. *Journal of Research on Adolescence, 15*, 535–559.

Hebebrand J., Volckmar, A., Knol, N., & Hinney, A. (2010). Chipping away the missing heritability: Giant steps forward in the molecular elucidation of obesity—but still lots to go. *Obesity Facts, 3*, 294–303.

Hebebrand, J., Wulftange, H., Georg, T., Ziegler, T., Hinney, A., Barth, N., . . . Remschmidt, H. (2000). Epidemic obesity: Are genetic factors involved via increases rates of assortative mating? *International Journal of Obesity and Related Metabolic Disorders, 24*, 345–353.

Hitsch, G. J., Hortascu, A., & Ariely, D. (2010). Matching and sorting in online dating. *American Economic Review, 100*, 130–163.

Holt-Lunstad, J., Birmingham, W., & Jones, B. Q. (2008). Is there something unique about marriage? The relative impact of marital status, relationship quality, and network social support on ambulatory blood pressure and Mental Health. *Annals of Behavioral Medicine, 35*, 239–244.

Inoue, K., Sawada, T., Suge, H., Nao, Y., & Igarashi, M. (1996). Spouse concordance of obesity, blood pressures, & serum risk factors for atherosclerosis. *Journal of Human Hypertension, 10*, 455–459.

Jacobson, P., Torgerson, J. S., Sjostrom, L., & Couchard, C. (2007). Spouse resemblance in body mass index: Effects on adult obesity prevalence in the offspring generation. *American Journal of Epidemiology, 165*, 101–108.

Jeffery, R. W., & Rick, A. M. (2002). Cross-sectional and longitudinal associations between body mass index and marriage-related factors. *Obesity Research, 10*, 809–815.

Kahn, H. S., & Williamson, D. F. (1990). The contributions of income, education and changing marital status to weight change among U.S. men. *International Journal of Obesity, 14*, 1057–1068.

Kiecolt-Glaser, J. K., & Newton, T. L. (2001). Marriage and health: His and hers. *Psychological Bulletin, 127*, 472–503.

Klein, T. (2011). Relationship status, marriage market, and body weight. *Cologne Journal of Sociology and Social Psychology, 63*, 459–479.

Koball, H. L., Moiduddin, E., Hendersion, J., Goesling, B., & Besculides, M. (2010). What do we know about the link between marriage and health? *Journal of Family Issues, 20*, 1–22.

Komlos, J., & Brabec, M. (2011). The trend of BMI values of US adults by deciles, birth cohorts 1882–1986 stratified by gender and ethnicity. *Economics & Human Biology, 9*, 234–250.

Knuiman, M., Divitini, M., Bartholomew, H., & Welborn, T. (1996). Spouse correlations in cardiovascular risk factors and the effect of marriage duration. *American Journal of Epidemiology, 143*, 48–53.

Lakdawalla, D., & Philipson, T. (2009). The growth of obesity and technological change. *Economics & Human Biology*, *7*, 283–293.

Lakdawalla, D., Philipson, T., & Bhattacharya, J. (2005). Welfare-enhancing technological change and the growth of obesity. *American Economic Review*, *95*, 253–257.

Lee, S., Cho, E., Grodstein, F., Kawachi, I., Hu, F. B., & Colditz, G. A. (2005). Effects of marital transitions on changes in dietary and other health behaviors in U.S. women. *International Journal of Epidemiology*, *34*, 69–78.

Liu, H. (2009). Till death do us part: Marital status and U.S. mortality trends, 1986–2000. *Journal of Marriage and Family*, *51*, 1158–1173.

Liu, H., & Umberson, D.J. (2008). The times they are a changin': Marital status and health differentials from 1972–2003. *Journal of Health and Social Behavior*, *49*, 239–253.

Lundborg, P., Nystedt, P., & Lindgren, B. (2007). Divorce risks and investment in attractive body mass among married Europeans. *Journal of Biosocial Science*, *39*, 531–544.

Lustig, R. H. (2012). *Fat chance: Beating the odds against sugar, processed food, obesity, and disease*. New York: Hudson Street Press.

Maes, H. H., Neale, M. C., & Eaves, L. J. (1997). Genetic and environmental factors in relative body weight and human adiposity. *Behavioral Genetics*, *27*, 325–351.

Maisey, D. S., Vale, E. L. E., Cornelissen, P. L., & Tovée, M. J. (1999). Characteristics of male attractiveness for women. *Lancet*, *353*, 1500.

Manzoli, L., Villari, P., Pironi, M., & Boccia, A. (2007). Marital status and mortality in the elderly: A systematic review and meta-analysis. *Social Science Medicine*, *64*, 77–94.

McLaren, L. (2007). Socioeconomic status and obesity. *Epidemiologic Reviews*, *29*, 29–48.

Meyler, E., Stimpson, J., & Peek, M. (2007). Health within couples: A systematic review. *Social Science & Medicine*, *64*, 2297–2310.

Michael, R. T. (1974). Education and the derived demand for children. In T. W. Schultz (Ed.), *Economics of the family: Marriage, children, and human capital* (pp. 120–159). Chicago: National Bureau of Economic Research.

Monden, C. (2007). Partners in health? Exploring resemblance in health between partners in married and cohabiting couples. *Sociology of Health & Illness*, *29*, 391–411.

Mushkin, S. J. (1962). Health as an investment. *Journal of Political Economy*, *70*(Suppl.), 129–157.

Ogden, C. L., Carroll, M. D., & Curtin, L. R. (2006). Prevalence of overweight and obesity in the United States, 1999-2004. *Journal of the American Medical Association*, *295*, 1549–1555.

Ogden, C. L., Carroll, M. D., Kit, B. K., & Flegal, K. M. (2014). Prevalence of childhood and adult obesity in the United States, 2011–2012. *Journal of the American Medical Association*, *311*(8), 806–814.

Oreffice, S., & Quintana-Domeque, C. (2010). Anthropometry and socioeconomics among couples: Evidence in the United States. *Economics and Human Biology*, *8*, 373–384.

Parsons, D.O. (1977). Health, family structure, & labor supply. *American Economic Review*, *67*, 703–712.

Pearce, M. J., Boergers, J., & Prinstein, M. J. (2002). Adolescent obesity, overt and relational peer victimization, & romantic relationships. *Obesity Research*, *10*, 386–393.

Philipson, T., & Posner, R. (2008). *Is the obesity epidemic a public health problem? A decade of research on the economics of obesity* (NBER Working Paper No. 14010). New York: National Bureau of Economic Research.

Philipson, T. K., & Posner, R. A. (1999). *The long-run growth in obesity as a function of technological change* (NBER Working Paper No. 7423). New York: National Bureau of Economic Research.

Preston, S. H. (1975). The changing relation between mortality and level of economic development. *Population Studies, 29*, 231–248.

Rendell, M. S., Weden, M. M., Favreault, M. M., & Waldron, H. H. (2011). The protective effect of marriage for survival: A review and update. *Demography, 48*, 81–506.

Ross, C. E., Mirowksy, J., & Goldsteen, K. (1990). The impact of the family on health: The decade in review. *Journal of Marriage and Family, 52*, 1059–1078.

Schousboe, K., Visscher, P. M., Erbas, B., Kyvik, K. O., Hopper, J. L., Henriksen, J. E., . . . Sørensen, T. I. A. (2004). Twin study of genetic and environmental influences on adult body size, shape, & composition. *International Journal of Obesity, 28*, 39–48.

Shafer, E. F. (2010). The effect of marriage on weight gain and propensity to become obese in the African American community. *Journal of Family Issues, 31*, 1166–1182.

Silventoinen, K., Kaprio, J., Lahelma, E., Viken, R. J., & Rose, R. J. (2003). Assortative mating by body height and BMi: Finnish twins and their spouses. *American Journal of Human Biology, 15*, 620–627.

Singh, D., & Young, R. K. (1995). Body weight, waist-to-hip ratio, breasts and hips: Role in judgments of female attractiveness and desirability for relationships. *Ethology and Sociobiology, 16*, 483–507.

Sobal, J., Hanson, K. L., & Frongillo, E. A. (2009). Gender, ethnicity, marital status, & body weight in the United States. *Obesity, 17*, 2223–2231.

Sobal, J., Rauschenbach, B., & Frongillo, E. (2003). Marital status changes and body weight changes: A U.S. longitudinal analysis. *Social Science & Medicine, 56*, 1543–1546.

Sobal J., & Stunkard, A. J. (1989). Socioeconomic status and obesity: A review of the literature. *Psychological Bulletin, 105*, 260–275.

Speakman, J. R., Djafarian, K., & Stewart, J. (2007). Assortative mating for obesity. *American Journal of Clinical Nutrition, 86*, 316–323.

Speliotes, E. K., Willer, C. J., Berndt, S. I., Monda, K. L. Thorleigsson, G. Jackson, A. U, . . . Loos, R. J. (2010). Association analyses of 249,796 individuals reveal 18 new loci associated with body mass index. *Nature Genetics, 42*, 937–948.

Spogard, R., & James, M. (1999). Governance and democracy—the people's view: A global opinion poll. *Gallup International*. http://www.peace.ca/gallupmillenniumsurvey.htm

Stevens, G., Owens, D., & Schaefer, E. C. (1990). Education and attractiveness in marriage choices. *Social Psychology Quarterly, 53*, 62–70.

Taubes, G. (2008). *Good calories, bad calories: Fats, carbs, and the controversial science of diet and health*. New York: Anchor Books.

Teicholz, N. (2014). *The big fat surprise*. New York: Simon & Schuster.

The, N. S., & Gordon-Larsen, P. (2009). Entry into romantic partnership is associated with obesity. *Obesity, 17*, 1441–1447.

Tovée, M. J., Reinhardt, S., Emery, J. L., & Cornelissen, P. L. (1998). Optimum body-mass index and maximum sexual attractiveness. *Lancet, 352*, 548.

Umberson, D., Liu, H., & Powers, D. (2009). Marital status, marital transitions, & body weight. *Journal of Health and Social Behavior, 50*, 327–343.

Umberson, D., & Williams, K. (2005). Marital quality, health and aging: Gender equity? *Journals of Gerontology, 60*, S109–S113.

Umberson, D., Williams, K., Powers, D. A., Liu, H., & Needham, B. (2006). You make me sick: Marital quality and health over the life course. *Journal of Health and Social Behavior, 47*, 1–16.

Umberson, D., Wortman, C. B., & Kessler, R. C. (1992). Widowhood and depression: Explaining gender differences in vulnerability. *Journal of Health and Social Behavior, 33*, 10–24.

Von Hinke Kessler Scholder, S. (2008). Maternal employment and overweight children: Does timing matter? *Health Economics, 17*, 889–906.

Walster, E., Aronson, V., Abrahams, D., & Rottman, I. (1966). Importance of physical attractiveness in dating behavior. *Journal of Personality and Social Psychology, 4*, 508–516.

Waite, L., & Gallagher, M. (2000). *The case for marriage: Why married people are happier, healthier and better off financially*. New York: Doubleday.

Wang, J., Wu, Z., Li, D., Li, N., Dindot, S. V., Satterfield, M. C., . . . Wu, G. (2012). Nutrition, epigenetics, & metabolic syndrome. *Antioxidants & Redox Signaling, 17*, 282–301.

Whisman, M. A., & Uebelacker, L. A. (2011). A longitudinal investigation of marital adjustment as a risk factor for metabolic syndrome. *Health Psychology, 31*, 80–86.

Willis, R. (1974). Economic theory of fertility behavior. In T. W. Schultz (Ed.), *Economics of the family: Marriage, children, and human capital* (pp. 25–75). Chicago: National Bureau of Economic Research.

Wilson, C. M., & Oswald, A. J. (2005). *How does marriage affect physical and psychological health? A survey of the longitudinal evidence* (IZA Discussion Paper Series, No. 1619). Bonn, DE: IZA.

Wilson, S. E. (2012). Marriage, gender, & obesity in later life. *Economics and Human Biology, 10*, 329–332.

Wood, R. G., Goesling, B., & Avellar, S. (2007). *The effects of marriage on health: A synthesis of recent research evidence.* Princeton, NJ: Mathematica Policy Research.

CHAPTER 28

OBESITY AND WELFARE REGIMES

AVNER OFFER

28.1 Approaches to Obesity

In the marketing imagination, affluence is associated with slimness, youth, and freedom. In contrast, the reality of Western societies since the 1970s is overweight, aging, and debt. Large body form used to signal higher social standing in poor societies but is generally regarded as unsightly and unhealthy in wealthy ones. It is also very common. The standard measure of body weight controlled for height is the body mass index (BMI = weight in kg/height in m^2). Conventionally, the range 20–25 is regarded as normal, 25–30 as overweight, and 30 plus as obese. By the end of the 20th century, the incidence of obesity (thus defined) was about 30% in North America, and around 20% in Western Europe, with Australasia in between (Ng et al., 2014). Obesity has been identified as a top public health issue by the World Health Organization (WHO, 2000), together with mental disorder, another affliction of affluence with which it shares some attributes (Offer, 2006, pp. 347–356).

Social concern about obesity is indicated by its academic and policy salience: a recent study was able to collect 1,769 surveys of body weight since 1989 across the globe that were usable for meta-analysis (Ng et al., 2014). Most of the vast academic literature is biomedical. This research effort has been to no avail as far as remedies are concerned. No society has been able to reduce the prevalence of obesity since the 1980s. Knowledge of obesity is now immense but is not of the kind that can provide reliable interventions to halt and control it. In the humanities, there is some discussion about the experience of obesity, and the social sciences provide narrative and analytical insights into behavior and political economy (e.g., Wisman & Capehart, 2010). Most social science contributions, however, take the form of statistical analysis of surveys previously undertaken by governments or collected for other academic purposes, usually adding some contextual variables. With covariance as the main form of research, it is important to find observables that vary with the incidence of obesity.

The most obvious one to investigate is income, and this reveals one of the dynamics of the problem. As a stylized fact, in poor countries, the rich are fat; in rich countries, the poor are fat, and the proportion of overweight and obese people has increased steadily over time since the 1970s (McLaren, 2007; Sobal & Stunkard, 1989). Body weight is a social signal of capacity for control. In poor countries, only the rich can afford to be fat, and body weight signifies social status. In rich countries, food is abundant, and self-control is the scarce factor: its possession is signaled by slimness. There is an income gradient in body weight, with higher earners having lower body weights, with differences among countries and between the genders; but, over time, whole societies, rich and poor, men and women, have risen steadily in average body weight. A suggestive finding about the signaling function of body form is that the negative association between obesity and income in affluent societies is only found clearly among women, for whom presumably more is at stake in this regard in mating and employment competitions (Devaux & Sassi, 2013; Ljungvall & Gerdtham, 2010; Ljungvall & Zimmerman, 2012; McLaren, 2007; Offer, 2001). Although levels of obesity differ by socioeconomic status and gender, that they are trending upward for all groups makes obesity an encompassing epidemic. That suggests a driver that affects societies as a whole, rather than particular individuals.

Economics is driven by the assumption of "methodological individualism"; that is, that aggregate social outcomes are determined by individual choices. In the postwar period, calorie cost has come down, and the cost of physical activity has risen. Manual work has declined, people drive more and walk less, and they need to pay for a gym or drive out of town in order to exercise. Preprocessed food—in the supermarket, at McDonald's, or in a restaurant—has become more tasty. Rational consumers, faced with these changing costs, have chosen to put on weight and are better off overall as a result. Obesity can be seen as a reasonable adaptation (Cutler, Glaeser, & Shapiro, 2003; Lakdawalla, Philipson, & Bhattacharya, 2005; Philipson & Posner, 2003). From this point of view, obesity is an increase in welfare and a new benign equilibrium. It has to be said that this conclusion hardly requires the analysis that precedes it—it begins with the premise that consumers only choose what is good for them. The intellectual challenge is merely to get the facts to fit the premise.

Obesity can also result from the breakdown of "rationality." In the economic theory of consumer behavior, this concept implies that consumers are the best judges of their welfare and that they pursue their self-interest consistently and optimally over time. But, in the case of body weight, consumers make eating and exercise choices that they subsequently come to regret. This suggests that the theory of consumption in economics may not be correct and that people might find it difficult to reconcile conflicting objectives, especially if the payoffs occur at different times. In this case, the gratifications of eating are inconsistent with the longer term objective of looking good. This line of inquiry has been developed in behavioral economics, which investigates actual choice behavior and is particularly interested in divergence from normative rational choice. It tends to attribute such "bounded rationality" by consumers to the failure of actual consumers to live up to the omniscience and consistency over time that is assumed in microeconomic theory.

Choice can fail. Most weight gain arises from eating more, not from reducing physical activity (Bleich, Cutler, Murray, & Adams, 2008). People spend money and time on reversing the consequences of their eating decisions by means of dieting, exercise, and medical treatment for obesity and its consequences (the latter was about 9% of medical expenditure in the United States in 1998). Altogether, what may be termed the money "regret costs" of eating and drinking came to about 15% of the outlays on food and alcohol in the United States at the end of the 20th century (Offer, 2006, pp. 164–165). This inconsistency of preferences over time is myopic. People diverge from formal rationality norms by having inconsistent objectives at different time ranges (e.g., pizza now and a slim body later). When later becomes now, pizza wins out again. In standard decision theory, the future is discounted by the value of time (expressed as a percentage decline per unit of time; i.e., the "discount rate"). This is consistent because any delay is fully compensated by its value. In contrast, "time-inconsistency" has been modeled formally (as "hyperbolic discounting") by assuming that value is inversely related to the passage of time. This values the present highly by showing a steep discount initially and a shallow one later (Offer, 2006, pp. 42–47 and ch. 7). Willpower is undermined by the flow of novelty. Affluence is a sequence of new and cheaper forms of arousal, experiences, and opportunities. One of these novelties has been the rise of palatable, energy-rich, and cheap fast food, which in the aggregate can be regarded as a "fast-food shock." Faced with this challenge to their willpower, consumers are further pressured by intensive marketing and advertising (Zimmerman, 2011). Consumer self-possession is a threat to corporate profits and has been under incessant attack. Increased availability of cheap palatable food is regarded as the top driver of obesity, but that shifts the question to the differential availability of such food in different countries. It is reasonable to regard the packaged fast-food system as an effective and cheap way to deliver calories to a low-income workforce: its palatability induces cravings, and low-quality ingredients keep down costs and also provide high markups. Healthy food is not available in low-income neighborhoods, and the poor cannot afford it. This fast-food availability has imparted a malign short-term bias to choice (Drewnowski, 2012; Schlosser, 2001): "Higher obesity rates in poor neighborhoods may be the toxic consequence of economic insecurity" (Drewnowski, 2012, p. 95). That is how hardwired psychology and a stressful environment undermine the well-being of consumers and induce them toward obesity (Offer, 2001, 2006, chs. 3–4, 7). From this point of view, obesity represents a breakdown of self-control in response to an external "insult" (the medical term for physical or mental injury).

Myopia can be overcome by prior commitment. In food consumption, for example, this might be a rule of "no eating between meals" (Offer, 2006, ch. 3). The fast-food shock, however, can overwhelm existing commitment devices. Commitment is costly. Think of those sessions in the gym. The better-off have more resources, both financial and cognitive, to invest in precommitment. They also have more to lose from succumbing to obesity.

Consumers do not face a market alone. Another feature of postwar affluence is the rise of government. During the postwar years, government expenditure has increased between two- and threefold and is typically between 30% and 60% of gross domestic product (GDP). Two-thirds and more of this spending is devoted to the three big items of social welfare: education, health, and social insurance. The overall growth of government expenditure stopped in the 1980s, and the level stabilized at that point, but welfare expenditures continue to rise everywhere, reaching an average of about 30% of GDP in the core countries of the Organization for Economic Cooperation and Development (OECD). It is striking that the rise of obesity has coincided with a hiatus of growth in government expenditure. Another approach then, and the one that is followed here, is that the distinctive socioeconomic environment faced by individuals is not free markets, but regulated ones.

All affluent societies have welfare states, but some are more generous than others. Welfare states provide individuals with education and health care, and they protect them from uncertainty and insecurity by means of social insurance. Welfare states extend these benefits, particularly health care, as a universal entitlement that overrides the inability to pay. If the stress of economic competition generates obesity, then welfare states protect against that stress and are therefore likely to have lower levels of obesity than more market-friendly ones in which health care and other social protections have to be paid for directly. That is the hypothesis that we investigate.

More specifically, the hypothesis is this: overeating is a response to stress, a form of self-medication by means of food. Affluent societies differ in the amount of stress they induce. Market-liberal societies with weak welfare states expose people to more uncertainty than do welfare states. Hence, we can expect to find higher levels of overweight and obesity in market-liberal societies, and especially in English-speaking ones. A variant of this argument attributes the sources of stress not to uncertainty but to the experience of subordination under inequality. The two are to some extent interdependent, but it is possible to try to separate them statistically. Research has established a prima facie case that is consistent with the hypothesis (Offer, Pechey, & Ulijaszek, 2010). Another issue canvassed is that, in liberal societies, marketing is less regulated, and corporations have more freedom to influence governments and manipulate consumers. The present survey will consider the original argument and the extent to which subsequent work has confirmed it or otherwise.

28.2 The Original Study

Welfare regimes fall into distinct categories. Esping-Andersen (1990) distinguished among "three worlds of welfare capitalism": liberal, conservative, and social democratic. The last category was identified primarily with the Scandinavian countries, with high welfare spending and individual entitlement. The second category was made up of most countries in the core of Western Europe, where welfare expenditure also tended to be high but was often conditional on family status. The third category constituted mostly English-speaking countries, with a low commitment to welfare and a stronger belief in markets and consumer discretion. We call this latter type of regime "market-liberal." Up to the 1970s, all affluent countries were building up welfare entitlements and outlays. A clear divergence began in the 1980s. This is captured by inequality levels, which began to rise sharply in the United Kingdom and the United States in the 1980s, while the trend among affluent European societies was, if anything, slightly downward (Piketty, 2014, pp. 316–321). Unemployment also rose sharply at that point in market-liberal societies, and deindustrialization intensified. That is also the point in time when obesity began to take off.

Evidence for stress as a spur to overeating comes initially from the field of animal behavior. When animals in the wild experience food uncertainty, they tend to put on weight. This is also observed in animals in captivity. Humans are also animals, and the assumption is that similar biological mechanisms affect humans as well. The actual mechanism is assumed to be a link between insecurity and the triggers of appetite (Smith, 2009, 2012). There is also direct evidence of a causal link between stress and obesity among humans (Block, He, Zaslavsky, Ding, & Ayanian, 2009; Sapolsky, 2004). Welfare regimes are an attribute of society, but obesity is an attribute of individuals. What is the mechanism that transmits society-level changes into attributes of individuals? We have highlighted stress as the mediator, but what kind of stress, and how does it work? There are two social mechanisms, both of which are explored here. The first is the stress of economic insecurity, which can reach life-threatening intensity. An alternative mechanism is the stress of subordination, which is generated by inequality. Both forms of stress have intensified in market-liberal societies since the 1980s.

These hypotheses were investigated by Offer et al. (2010). This study made use of 96 body weight surveys undertaken in 11 countries, including four English-speaking "market-liberal societies" (Australia, Canada, the United Kingdom, the United States), and seven European countries (Finland, France, Italy, Norway, Spain, Sweden) between 1994 and 2004. The surveys were all conducted over a short period of time (1–2 years), most were nationally representative, although a few covered large regional samples. Both genders were covered, although not in all surveys, and the coverage was mostly of adults with different minimum and maximum ages.

If overeating is a response to stress, then the prevalence of obesity should reflect stress levels in society. The hypothesis, then, is that obesity prevalence should vary with economic insecurity and that this stressor can be captured statistically at the national level. Accordingly, the surveys were analyzed in a pooled ecological regression (in which the units are not individuals but populations) using ordinary least squares (OLS) regressions. The dependent variable was percentage obesity prevalence.

Two stress variables were used in different models. One was a composite variable incorporating four indices: security from unemployment, illness, single-parent poverty, and poverty in old age (Osberg, 2009). Another composite stress variable, used in a second model, was of stress related to work (International Labour Office, 2004). The independent variables in both models were (1) whether weight was measured or self-reported, (2) whether a society was English-speaking market-liberal or not, (3) a time variable, (4) economic security, and (5) economic equality (the latter represented by two different variables, one of them called "Inverse_Gini," using the Gini coefficient, which measures inequality). Separate estimates were made for men, women, and market-liberal countries. Fast-food availability was proxied by means of the price of MacDonald's Big Mac Hamburger as reported annually in the *Economist* magazine.

The method of analysis is OLS. The precise model used and other technical details are elaborated in the journal article (Offer et al., 2010). Selected findings are reported in Tables 28.1, 28.2, and 28.3 herein. Their general thrust can also be followed by nontechnical readers: in each table, a numbered variable at the top of a column (the dependent variable) is statistically explained by an array of variables listed vertically on the left-hand side (the independent variables). The relative strength of the explanation is expressed by the beta statistics for each variable. These are comparable with each other: the higher the beta, the more powerful the variable. If the sign is negative, then the variable's impact is negative. The main coefficients (in the same row as the label) are also informative, and their meaning is indicated in Section 3. Stars indicate statistical significance. Double starred variables are reliable, single-starred are less reliable, and non-starred results can be ignored. The constant is of no relevance. R^2 measures what fraction of the variance in the dependent variable can be explained. The levels observed (0.7–0.8) are high. The number of observations varies among countries, and countries also differ in population, but each country is given the same weight. The dependent variable is percentage prevalence of obesity (TOTAL_OBESE). Obesity is defined as BMI equal to or greater than 30.

In the descriptive statistics (not shown here), market-liberal (English-speaking) countries have a significantly higher mean obesity prevalence (25.5:19.7%). The United States is in a class of its own with a prevalence of 29.5. The different columns (each representing a separate statistical model) in Table 28.1 all explain a high proportion of the variability, with an R^2 of 0.7–0.8 and higher. When the explanatory power of the variables is normalized (i.e., expressed on the equivalent "beta" scale), then the ranking of the significant variables by strength of effect is economic security first, then self-reporting (which reduces weight), and market-liberal (all controlled for the passage of time), with only slight differences for male, female, and total samples. Inequality, which has a strong effect in bivariate correlations with obesity prevalence, is not statistically significant in models with a larger number of variables. Table 28.2 shows that fast food (proxied by the price of MacDonald's Big Mac hamburger product, which is the same in all countries) has a strong explanatory power in models that exclude insecurity and market-liberal variables but becomes insignificant when these variables are restored. In other words, the market liberalism that gives rise to cheap fast food is sufficient to explain its effect all by itself.

The most powerful influence uncovered on levels of obesity prevalence is economic insecurity This effect remains even after controlling for a market-liberal (or English-speaking) welfare regime, which has a strong, significant, and positive effect in most regressions. The bottom line is that the economic insecurity hypothesis of obesity is intuitively plausible and is confirmed in this study.

Table 28.1 Obesity and economic security and/or equality

	(1)	(2)	(3)	(4)	(5)	(6)
VARIABLES	total_obese	male_obese	female_obese	total_obese	male_obese	female_obese
MEASURED	9.093**	7.965**	9.643**	9.144**	7.836**	9.497**
t-statistic	(6.849)	(9.761)	(8.993)	(6.833)	(9.629)	(8.625)
beta	0.646	0.670	0.687	0.650	0.659	0.676
MARKET_LIB	4.106**	3.101**	2.120	3.598*	2.672**	1.859
t-statistic	(2.667)	(2.745)	(1.316)	(2.511)	(2.642)	(1.292)
beta	0.327	0.271	0.157	0.286	0.234	0.138
TIME	0.477**	0.539**	0.465**	0.523**	0.559**	0.460**
t-statistic	(4.133)	(4.796)	(3.349)	(4.494)	(5.215)	(3.110)
beta	0.222	0.279	0.204	0.243	0.290	0.202
ECON_SECURITY	0.279**	−0.262**	−0.262**	−0.266**	−0.244**	−0.248**
t-statistic	(−8.995)	(−7.857)	(−6.904)	(−8.623)	(−8.500)	(−7.235)
beta	−0.718	−0.742	−0.630	−0.685	−0.692	−0.595
ECON_EQUALITY	0.0726**	0.0434	0.0124			
t-statistic	(2.872)	(1.376)	(0.291)			
beta	0.261	0.170	0.0412			
INVERSE_GINI				0.0528*	0.0226	−0.00304
t-statistic				(2.575)	(0.867)	(−0.0859)
beta				0.201	0.0946	−0.0108
CONSTANT	22.29**	22.95**	25.14**	22.92**	23.17**	25.12**
t-statistic	(6.935)	(10.55)	(8.185)	(7.444)	(10.94)	(8.653)
Observations	88	88	88	88	88	88
Adjusted R^2	0.824	0.779	0.730	0.821	0.775	0.729

Robust *t*-statistics in parentheses.

** $p < .01$, * $p < .05$.

Table 28.2 The impact of the fast-food shock

	(1)	(2)	(3)	(4)	(5)
VARIABLES	total_obese (market-liberal)	total_obese (non–market-liberal)	total_obese	total_obese (market-liberal)	total_obese
MEASURED	7.357**	10.03**	8.761**	6.256**	9.246**
t-statistic	(10.50)	(5.268)	(7.247)	(5.237)	(7.663)
beta	0.761	0.740	0.652	0.647	0.688
MARKET_LIB					3.867**
t-statistic					(3.137)
beta					0.311
TIME	0.743**	0.276	−0.318	0.387*	0.576**
t-statistic	(7.804)	(1.520)	(−1.839)	(2.065)	(3.790)
beta	0.464	0.167	−0.149	0.242	0.270
ECON_SECURITY	−0.194**	−0.192			−0.279**
t-statistic	(−10.11)	(−1.863)			(−8.153)
beta	−0.741	−0.207			−0.749
INVERSE_GINI					0.0648**
t-statistic					(2.961)
beta					0.230
BIG_MAC			−0.0821**	−0.0668**	0.0100
t-statistic			(−4.944)	(−3.193)	(0.722)
beta			−0.424	−0.393	0.0518
CONSTANT	22.85**	21.77**	22.71**	19.51**	21.83**
t-statistic	(17.50)	(2.951)	(8.870)	(7.841)	(7.724)
Observations	47	41	81	47	81
Adjusted R^2	0.852	0.699	0.601	0.563	0.811

Robust *t*-statistics in parentheses.

** $p < .01$, * $p < .05$.

It is possible to decompose the economic security variable into its components (Offer et al., 2010, table 4). These are financial security in old age, security from unemployment, security in single-parenthood, and security from ill-health. The first three are indices that combine the chance of being in the affected category, multiplied by an index of the strength of social protection. The fourth, security from ill-health, is an index of private medical expenses expressed as a percentage of disposable income. Rather unexpectedly, this variable, which proxies the risk of incurring private medical costs, has the strongest effect on obesity and is the only one that is statistically significant. On reflection, this is plausible. The risk of high medical spending is lumpy and volatile; it gives rise to financial, employment, and psychological stress and, in some instances, to sustained physical pain and discomfort. In the United States, medical costs were implicated in most personal bankruptcies, which constituted a greater hazard than heart disease or divorce (Himmelstein, Thorne, Warren, & Woolhandler, 2009; Warren & Tyagi, 2003, pp. 6, 193–194, n7). The Osberg security index we used in Table 28.1 focuses on conditions of dependency and expectations of social support. It is a powerful variable, but when broken down to its components (Offer et al., 2010, table 4, p. 303) almost all the work is done by just one of them: namely, the uncertainty arising from having to pay for health care out of personal income. This highlights an elevated risk of obesity for individuals with uncertain access to health care, especially in the United States.

At work, unionization and income security are associated with lower obesity (Table 28.3). ILO_Security is a measure of insecurity produced by the International Labour Organization (ILO). When included in regressions (not shown here) with the Osberg economic security variable, ILO_Security remains statistically significant but drops down to the bottom of the ranking of variables by power. This is not decisive because the economic security variable has a greater resolution: annual observations versus a single observation for security at work. On the other hand, annual change is controlled for in the case of economic security by a time variable, so that both security variables capture levels, not trends. In Table 28.3, the variables listed above ILO_Security are its constituents. Of these constituents, worker representation (i.e., unionization) and income security have the expected negative sign—obesity falls as they increase. Representation (an aspect of employment security) is a particularly strong determinant. But these two variables are partially offset by skill security, which is also strong but has a positive sign (i.e., obesity increases when the labor force is more skilled). One way of interpreting this finding is that "representative security" stands for the ability of workers to bargain collectively and skill security (or individual human capital) for their ability to bargain individually. The skill variable measures the general rise of educational and training levels. The accumulation of personal human capital may have inclined workers toward more individualistic forms of bargaining (Offer, 2008). But this security may be delusive, and it provides little respite from the rising anxieties of market competition (Ehrenreich, 2006; Hacker, 2008; Newman, 1988; Offer, 2006). As workplace security declined throughout our period, the general rise in educational levels that has taken place in the most advanced societies was paradoxically accompanied by insecurity and its corollary, obesity. In this case, the accumulation

Table 28.3 **Alternative specifications of economic security**

VARIABLES	(1) total_obese	(2) total_obese	(3) total_obese (market–liberal)	(4) total_obese	(5) total_obese
MEASURED	7.716**	8.424**	5.687**	8.050**	7.881**
t-statistic	(5.493)	(7.017)	(8.616)	(6.005)	(6.144)
beta	0.548	0.599	0.588	0.572	0.560
TIME	0.458**	0.385*	0.729**	0.391**	0.408**
t-statistic	(3.382)	(2.405)	(7.489)	(3.448)	(4.064)
beta	0.213	0.179	0.455	0.182	0.190
MARKET_LIB	4.112**				
t-statistic	(3.006)				
beta	0.327				
LABOUR_ SECURITY				−0.0606	
t-statistic				(−0.430)	
beta				−0.0843	
EMPLOYMENT_ SECURITY				0.00396	
t-statistic				(0.0528)	
beta				0.00906	
JOB_SECURITY				0.0271	
t-statistic				(0.422)	
beta				0.0388	
SKILL_SECURITY				0.881**	0.768**
t-statistic				(5.087)	(7.126)
beta				0.723	0.631
WORK_SECURITY				0.0397	
t-statistic				(0.335)	
beta				0.0663	
REPRESENTATION_ SECURITY				−0.306**	−0.279**

Table 25.1 Contniued

	(1)	(2)	(3)	(4)	(5)
t-statistic				(−4.072)	(−11.64)
beta				−0.749	−0.683
INCOME_ SECURITY				−0.400**	−0.360**
t-statistic				(−2.817)	(−5.210)
beta				−0.437	−0.393
ILO_SECURITY	−0.0943	−0.195**	−0.399**		
t-statistic	(−1.938)	(−5.275)	(−8.037)		
beta	−0.188	−0.387	−0.593		
CONSTANT	15.20**	24.95**	40.28**	−5.922	−1.649
t-statistic	(3.355)	(7.832)	(11.98)	(−0.977)	(−0.406)
Observations	88	88	47	88	88
Adjusted R^2	0.692	0.623	0.810	0.797	0.800

Robust *t*-statistics in parentheses.
** $p < .01$, * $p < .05$.

of human capital appears to act in an opposite direction to worker representation. One tentative interpretation is that, taken in the aggregate, the security provided by human capital encourages workers to abandon unionization and labor market protections, but that individual bargaining power is often delusive. It is the resulting insecurity that we associate here with obesity, especially for those with lower human capital. Alternatively, and perhaps more plausibly, the rise of obesity in higher human capital countries does not indicate that it is higher skilled persons who are becoming more obese. The shift to individual bargaining will have benefited those who have bargaining power while worsening the position of the rest. Hence, it may not be the brain workers who suffer from obesity in these countries but, disproportionately, the manual workers who have been left behind and who have lost their bargaining power. This is indicated in the decline of real manual wages in the United States since the 1970s (Kearney, Hershbein, & Jácome, 2015).

That is not to say, for example, that trade unionists have lower obesity prevalence or that households that suffer medical adversity are prone to weight gain. The surveys tell us nothing about individuals—it could well be that the general climate of insecurity is what affects individuals and not all of them in the same way. The actual mechanisms suggested here for obesity growth are psychological. They are not detectable in the aggregate results of surveys. But they are consistent with the hypothesis that insecurity of competitive market societies is conducive to obesity.

It has been argued that market-liberal countries have much higher levels of passive transportation (mostly driving) and that this needs to be taken into account. In 2000, Europeans walked more than twice as far as United States residents and cycled almost five times as much (Bassett, Pucher, Buehler, Thompson, & Crouter, 2008). The data are not good enough to integrate in quantitative analysis, but the preference for private transport appears to be an attribute of market-liberal regimes. The United States, Australia, and New Zealand began as settler societies and have generous land endowments per person (that itself might be a determinant of market liberalism). The "market-liberal" variable captures the distinctive attributes of these countries and thus captures this difference in locomotion choices as well. Even after controlling for insecurity and the food shock (which are higher in market-liberal countries), "market-liberal" remains a significant and powerful determinant of the level of obesity.

This chapter is a snapshot of obesity in advanced countries at the end of the 20th century and allows some preliminary conclusions. Market-liberal countries stand out as having high levels of obesity and higher rates of obesity growth. The time variable is more powerful in market-liberal countries, suggesting a more intense fast-food shock. The United States in particular is an outlier, ranking highest on both levels and rates of growth of obesity, but market-liberal distinctiveness remains even when the United States is left out. One reason is market freedoms: fast-food prices, as proxied by the Big Mac variable, are considerably lower in market-liberal countries due to lower levels of taxation and the lower wages that prevail in these countries (confirmed in De Vogli, Kouvonen, & Gimeno, 2011; De Vogli, Kouvonen, Elovainio, & Marmot, 2014). In other words, the "fast-food shock," which is invoked in explanation of obesity, has worked more strongly in market-liberal countries.

Inequality is another explanatory contender. In multivariable analysis, equality is dominated by security. But that does not settle the matter: insecurity may be a consequence of inequality, and the measure of inequality used may not be the best one. In bivariate analysis, higher equality is inversely related to obesity prevalence, and that is also the case for unemployment protection, which likewise has the "wrong" sign in the multivariate model. That frequently occurs when two independent variables are highly correlated with each other. When they are both inserted into a regression, one of them can acquire the wrong sign and magnitude due to this multicollinearity.

The original study was essentially cross-sectional, covering a single decade, but it raises a historical question. If welfare regimes are such a critical determinant of obesity prevalence, where do such regimes themselves come from? The United States clustered at the high end, and the Scandinavian countries clustered at the low end. The market-liberal countries in our sample all shared English as a common language. Norway and Sweden, at the low end of obesity and high end of security, both use variants of the same language and share a common culture and religion, in addition to having similar welfare regimes. This suggests that welfare regimes have historical and cultural roots and that the search for causes needs to venture into the past; that a disposition for excess or moderation, for risk-taking or security, may be rooted in the respective cultures. On the other hand, culture may not be destiny. Social pathologies can respond to experience and learning and can moderate seemingly of their own accord. Out of several examples that could be chosen, smoking rose to majority use in the first half of the 20th century and has declined ever since, not least in response to government action. The trajectory of obesity in the United States and the United Kingdom also appears to have flattened in the past few years (Ng et al., 2014).

28.3 Replication and Further Investigation

The hypothesis has generated extensions and replications, which are reviewed in this section. The initial article was followed by an edited book (Offer, Pechey, & Ulijaszek, 2012) that contained anticipations, extrapolations, and some criticism, together with a version of the original study. It provides more probative and indirect support. Among several striking contributions, one confirmed that subordination is a source of stress that covaries with obesity (Bell, Atsi-Selmi, & Marmot, 2012). An independent role for sleep deprivation was typical of hectic competitive societies (Whybrow, 2012). The link with inequality was restated by the original authors (Pickett & Wilkinson, 2012). Two articles explored the early temporal emergence of obesity in the United States (Komlos & Brabec, 2012) and Denmark (Sørensen, Rokholm, & Ajslev, 2012), both of which indicate anticipations well in advance of the obesity eruption of the 1980s, but with uncertain bearing on the welfare regime hypothesis.

Among the several relevant studies that followed, there is one skeptical comment that dismisses the findings outright (Kenworthy, 2012). It takes inequality and insecurity as single cause of obesity prevalence and finds inequality wanting on various statistical grounds, an argument that is not contested here. It makes heavy weather of the difference between self-reported and measured weight, but this is controlled for in the original model. A valid criticism is that the inequality measures used were derived from household surveys, which cut off the top of the income distribution, and that wealth inequality is not measured. A more accurate representation of inequality could well have given it a bigger role. With regard to insecurity, it is confirmed that English-speaking countries form a distinctive cluster. The essay (a blog) is critical of the insecurity measures, but, in fact, several were provided, further decomposed to their constituent elements, so this objection is not well-founded. Evidence for insecurity from mental health incidence is dismissed on grounds that the historical timing is not right, but visual examination of the graphs in a subsequent publication does suggest that most of the increase occurred after 1980 (Twenge et al., 2010). Kenworthy (2012) shows that between two data points (1988–94 and 2005–08), obesity among low-income adult women in the United States (by far the most obese group) rose less than among high- and middle-income women (at much lower absolute levels of obesity prevalence) and takes this as a disconfirmation of the insecurity hypothesis. This is far from compelling, since it is likely that low-income women would have been highly stressed already at the start of the period. A recent survey lists 19 studies that establish a link between maternal stress and child obesity (Gundersen, Mahatmya, Garasky, & Lohman, 2011), and others have followed since.

The initial spur for the insecurity hypothesis came from Smith (2009), who pointed out that insecurity was associated with weight gain for animals both in the wild and in captivity. He followed up with a longitudinal study of US individuals that showed body weight rising in environments of insecurity, unemployment, income volatility, and poor access to safety nets (Smith, Stoddard, & Barnes, 2009). People put on weight in response to stress, whether associated with subordinate status (Marmot, 2004), work insecurity (Hannerz, Albertsen, Nilesen, Tuchsen, & Burr, 2004), or financial insecurity (Gerace & George, 1996). In the United States, high levels of obesity are associated locally with high levels of food insecurity. The US Department of Agriculture stopped using the word "hunger" in its reports and uses "food insecurity" instead (Dolnick, 2010), and the prevalence of overweight is high among food-insecure children (Eisenmann, Gundersen, Lohman, Garasky, & Stewart, 2011). A recent study of the United States since 1986 deploys individual-level data on body weight and demographic data (including stratification and employment characteristics) in a panel that also includes group-level variables for unemployment, inequality, and a new "Economic Security Index." In this study, the insecurity index variable is statistically very significant and also substantively effective for most (but not all) demographic groups, thus increasing confidence in the insecurity hypothesis. This result is preliminary but is authorized for citation (Smith, Stillman, & Craig, 2013).

One manifestation of stress is mental disorder, of which there has been an upward shift since the 1980s. The United States is an upward outlier in this respect (Offer, 2006, ch. 14; Twenge et al., 2010). A commercial report claims that more than a quarter of American women were using mental health medication in 2010, up from 21% in 2001 (Medco Health Solutions, 2011). Financial hardship is another source of stress. Two studies have found a link between financial hardship and obesity. A cross-sectional study in Germany carried out in 2006 has found that "Over-indebtedness was associated with an increased prevalence of overweight and obesity that was not explained by traditional definitions of socioeconomic status" (Münster, Ruger, Ochsmann, Letzel, & Toschke, 2009), whereas an American longitudinal study found evidence that "having trouble paying bills may be a cause of obesity for women" (Averett & Smith, 2014). In the original regressions (Offer et al., 2010, pp. 303–304), among the determinants of economic insecurity, the proportion of medical expenses paid for privately was found to be the most powerful. This suggests that the insecurities associated with lack of access to health care can loom very large. Almost two-thirds of all personal bankruptcies in the United States were associated with medical costs. The jeopardy was dual: economic immiseration, combined with denial of health care. The private medical care system in the United States exposed its customers to loss of livelihood and health and threatened their very existence (Offer, 2012). Things do not get much more stressful than that. The number of personal bankruptcies in a single year was more than 1 million, representing 2.7 million people (i.e., almost 1% of the population). Insurance was no protection: fewer than one-quarter of the bankrupts were uninsured (Himmelstein et al., 2009).

The hypothesis that inequality is the source of stress (rather than insecurity) has been pursued further in two investigations that compared regions within the United Kingdom. One of them found no evidence that inequality is a determinant of obesity prevalence (Zala, 2013). Another found that both insecurity and inequality are associated with the geographical patterning of adult obesity rates across England (Ulijaszek, 2014). The first was undertaken under the auspices of the right-wing think-tank the Institute of Economic Affairs and published in its journal, the other by a member of our original team, which is inclined in the opposite direction; in both cases, the result is consistent with one's prior expectations in that respect.

The economic crisis of 2008 might seem to provide a natural experiment because it involved a considerable rise in unemployment, and the austerity policies which followed have undermined social protections. The rise in obesity was moderating somewhat before the crisis in 2008. The time that has passed since 2008 is relatively short, and the transmission mechanisms from economic crisis to personal weight gain are not transparent. The Health Survey for England publishes an annual survey that currently runs up to 2013 (Great Britain, Health and Social Care Information Centre, HSE2013-Adult-trend-tbls.xls, table 4, 2014). Obesity prevalence had increased steeply from 1993 to about 2000 and moderated thereafter, with larger variability after 2008. There was a dip in 2009 and a remarkable spike in 2010 of four percentage points for men (from 22.1 to 26.2) and 2.2 for women (to 26.1). That was the peak year. Thereafter, male prevalence levels fell and then resumed at a higher rate of growth than previously, whereas female prevalence actually declined. Although not conclusive, these observations are not inconsistent with the insecurity hypothesis. Comprehensive international comparisons have been reported recently in *The Lancet*. These indicate that obesity continues to increase everywhere. In developed countries, the rates of increase were highest between 1992 and 2002 and began to moderate thereafter (Ng et al., 2014, p. 775). Visual observation suggests an uptick in child overweight and obesity after 2008.

Two studies have explored the welfare regime approach to insecurity further. Both of them take large international samples at the aggregate level and included a market-liberal indicator among their independent variables, an "economic freedom index" devised by a market-liberal think-tank to measure conformity with its norms. One of these studies follows 31 high- and medium-income countries between 1980 and 2008. Most countries have five observations during this period, while some have fewer. The weight variable is mean BMI, and two models are estimated: one for rate of change, the other for levels. In both these models, there are controls for income, education, and female labor force participation. The modeling is quite elaborate, but the results are clear. In both models, "the aggregate economic freedom index consistently results in a positive and significant relationship" (Ljungvall, 2013, p. 12). The index is made up of five components. When it is unbundled, only two out of the five components are significant, and the main driver is regulation—or rather lack of it. Regulation applies both to the marketing of food and to working conditions: low regulation means more direct exposure to market forces, both in fast-food consumption and in labor market insecurities. A second statistically significant determinant is "sound money"; in the policy context of the period 1980–2008, this is associated with anti-inflation policy, in which price stability ranked as a higher policy priority than did full employment. Workers in countries with "sounder" money were more exposed to employment insecurity, other things kept equal. This study provides strong confirmation of the welfare regime hypothesis.

Another investigation draws a link between the fast-food exposure and the rise of BMI. The link between fast-food outlet density and obesity was already shown by Chou, Grossman, and Saffer (2004) in the American Midwest, where obesity is high. This time, the scope of the study was 25 high-income member countries of the OECD between 1999 and 2008. The question was to find the determinants of this density, and, for this purpose, the same economic freedom index variable was included (De Vogli et al., 2014). This model combined fast-food restaurant density and the economic freedom index, together with a basket of confounding variables. Once again, the result was a strong and significant coefficient for economic freedom as a covariant of obesity.

It is possible to approach the hypothesis from the other end. Using American survey data, a study shows that long-term satisfaction with life overall (the Aristotelian concept of "eudomaneia") is associated with lower BMI (Yemiscigil, 2013). If we assume that eudomaneia and economic insecurity are not consistent with each other, then this also provides indirect support. To conclude, then, the evidence is suggestive but not yet conclusive. The association of insecurity and obesity does not provide any immediate policy handle. If valid, it may be taken as further evidence for the social desirability of particular welfare regimes. The incidence of obesity alone, massive as it is, is unlikely to sway adherents or opponents of particular welfare regimes. But it provides some insights into the attributes of these regimes. It suggests that the economic benefits of flexible and open markets, such as they are, may be offset by costs to personal and public health that are rarely taken into account. The controlled market economies (those we have defined here as not being "market liberal") all support successful and affluent societies. They also appear to perform better on this important dimension of personal and public health.

28.4 Conclusion

The welfare regime hypothesis argues that obesity can be thought of as a response to stress and that stress is generated by market competition, and, more specifically, by the uncertainty that market competition gives rise to. This was confirmed in society-level comparisons of 11 developed countries in the period 1994–2004 (Offer et al., 2010). That study found that with the full set of independent variables, inequality had no independent effect and that fast-food availability as a variable was a good proxy for the welfare regime (i.e., that fast food was cheaper and less regulated in market-liberal regimes). Obesity prevalence rose rapidly during this period. The United State had by far the highest obesity prevalence, but the same patterns were also found when it was excluded from the analysis. Decomposing the sources of uncertainty, the strongest effects were attributable to insecurity of health coverage, lack of representation at work, and (unexpectedly) the prevalence of higher skill levels.

The welfare regime hypothesis of obesity in developed countries has now been confronted with evidence in research designs that did not set out to replicate it directly. On the whole, the hypothesis has done well. Three additional studies have identified a link between market stresses (debt, generalized insecurity, low income) and obesity, whereas one has found that high life satisfaction is associated with lower obesity. Two studies in Britain have reached conflicting conclusions about causation from generalized inequality (a social phenomenon) to the prevalence obesity. The most direct confirmation has come from two multicountry panel studies in which the economic freedom index, a measure of market-liberal penetration, was used as one of the independent variables: these studies (both statistically rigorous, with large samples and with different research designs) have established this as a strong and significant determinant of mean BMI (which is highly correlated with obesity prevalence). The financial crisis of 2008 may be regarded as a natural experiment in which a worsening of economic conditions might be expected to be followed by a rise in obesity prevalence. Obesity prevalence, although still rising, had moderated its increase at the beginning of the 2000s. The pattern in Britain, which has good annual health surveys, is not inconsistent with this interpretation, as is (perhaps) the pattern of child obesity internationally. No such result can be detected in graphics that aggregate the results from almost 200 countries. That in itself is not conclusive: the resolution of these data is coarse, they include countries in various stages of development, the aggregation methods are open to criticism, and they are not presented numerically with diagnostic statistics. Furthermore, the mechanisms and the time lags between shocks and obesity rises have yet to be studied.

Taking these results as a whole, 4 years of additional research provide support for the hypothesis. But it should not be taken to be a linear law-like relation. Obesity impinges on virtually all societies, at all levels of development, and at all levels of marketization. As in the case of previous public health epidemics like smoking and heart disease, it is likely that societies may begin to mitigate its prevalence by means of a learning process that involves public awareness, regulation, commercial strategies, and individual behavioral adaptation, and they will find ways to slow down and eventually reverse the prevalence of obesity. This is slow because it is resisted by those who profit from making and marketing the commodities that result in obesity. An example of both progress and frustration is the tax on saturated fats introduced in Denmark in 2011 and repealed under popular and vested interest pressure a year later (Euractiv, 2015).

References

Averett, S. L., & Smith, J. K. (2014). Financial hardship and obesity. *Economics & Human Biology*, *15*, 201–212.

Bassett, D. R., Jr., Pucher, J., Buehler, R., Thompson, D. L., & Crouter, S. E. (2008). Walking, cycling, and obesity rates in Europe, North America, and Australia. *Journal of Physical Activity and Health*, *5*(6), 795–814.

Bell, R., Aitsi-Selmi, A., & Marmot, M. (2012). Subordination, stress, and obesity. In A. Offer, R. Pechey, & S. J. Ulijaszek (Eds.), *Insecurity, inequality, and obesity in affluent societies* (pp. 105–128). Oxford, England: Oxford University Press (for the British Academy).

Bleich, S., Cutler, D., Murray, C., & Adams, A. (2008). Why is the developed world obese? *Annual Review of Public Health*, *29*, 273–295.

Block, J. P., He, Y. L., Zaslavsky, A. M., Ding, L., & Ayanian, J. Z. (2009). Psychosocial stress and change in weight among US adults. *American Journal of Epidemiology* *170*(2), 181-192.

Chou, S. Y., Grossman, M., & Saffer, H. (2004). An economic analysis of adult obesity: Results from the Behavioral Risk Factor Surveillance System. *Journal of Health Economics*, *23*(3), 565–587.

Cutler, D. M., Glaeser, E. L., & Shapiro, J. M. (2003). Why have Americans become more obese? *Journal of Economic Perspectives*, *17*(3), 93–118.

De Vogli, R., & Kouvonen, A., & Gimeno, D. (2011). 'Globesization,' Ecological evidence on the relationship between fast food outlets and obesity among 26 advanced economies. *Critical Public Health*, *21*(4), 395–402.

De Vogli, R., Kouvonen, A., Elovainio, M., & Marmot, M. (2014). Economic globalization, inequality and body mass index: A Cross-national analysis of 127 countries. *Critical Public Health*, *24*(1), 7–21.

Devaux, M., & Sassi, F. (2013). Social inequalities in obesity and overweight in 11 OECD countries. *European Journal of Public Health*, *23*(3), 464–469.

Dolnick, S. (2010, March 13). The obesity-hunger paradox. *New York Times*, http://www.nytimes.com/2010/03/14/nyregion/14hunger.html?hpw. Accessed 14 March 2010.

Drewnowski, A. (2012). The economics of food choice behavior: Why poverty and obesity are linked. In A. Drewnowski & B. J. Rolls (Eds.), *Obesity treatment and prevention: New directions* (pp. 95–112). Karger: Nestlé Nutrition Institute.

Ehrenreich, B. (2006). *Bait and switch: The futile pursuit of the corporate dream*. London: Granta.

Eisenmann, J. C., Gundersen, C., Lohman, B. J., Garasky, S., & Stewart, S. D. (2011). Is food insecurity related to overweight and obesity in children and adolescents? A summary of studies, 1995–2009. *Obesity Reviews*, *12*(501), E73–E83.

Esping-Andersen, G. (1990). *The three worlds of welfare capitalism*. Cambridge, England: Polity.

Euractiv. (2015). *Commission opens Inquiry into Danish "fat tax"*. Retrieved from http://www.euractiv.com/sections/health-consumers/commission-opens-inquiry- danish-fat-tax-311890

Gerace, T. A., & George, V. A. (1996). Predictors of weight increases over 7 years in fire fighters and paramedics. *Preventive Medicine*, *25*(5), 593–600.

Great Britain, Health and Social Care Information Centre. (2014). *Health survey for England—2013, Trend tables [NS]*. Retrieved from http://www.hscic.gov.uk/catalogue/PUB16077, Accessed 2 April 2015.

Gundersen, C., Mahatmya, D., Garasky, S., & Lohman, B. (2011). Linking psychosocial stressors and childhood obesity. *Obesity Reviews, 12*(501), E54–E63.

Hacker, J. S. (2008). *The great risk shift, The new economic Insecurity and the decline of the American dream.* New York: Oxford University Press.

Hannerz, H., Albertsen, K., Nielsen, M. L., Tuchsen, F., & Burr, H. (2004). Occupational factors and 5-year weight change among men in a Danish national cohort. *Health Psychology, 23*(3), 283–288.

Himmelstein, D. U., Thorne, D., Warren, E., & Woolhandler, S. (2009). Medical bankruptcy in the United States, 2007: Results of a national study. *American Journal of Medicine, 122*(8), 741–746.

International Labour Office. (2004). *Economic security for a better world.* Geneva: Author.

Kearney, M. S., Hershbein, B., & Jácome, E. (2015). *Profiles of change, Employment, earnings, and occupations from 1990–2013.* Washington, DC: Brookings Institution/The Hamilton Project. Retrieved from http://hamiltonproject.org/files/downloads_and_links/worker_profiles_changes_earnings_occupations_1990-2013_FINAL.pdf

Kenworthy, L. (2012). Is rising obesity a product of income inequality and economic insecurity? Retrieved, from http://lanekenworthy.net/2012/06/10/is-rising-obesity-a-product-of-income-inequality-and-economic-insecurity/, Accessed 2 April 2015.

Komlos, J., & Brabec, M. (2012). The transition to post-industrial BMI values in the United States. In A. Offer, R. Pechey, S. J. Ulijaszek (Eds.), *Insecurity, inequality, and obesity in affluent societies* (pp. 141–159). Oxford, England: Oxford University Press (for the British Academy).

Lakdawalla, D., Philipson, T., & Bhattachrya, J. (2005). Welfare-enhancing technological change and the growth of obesity. *American Economic Review, 95*(2), 253–257.

Ljungvall, A. (2013). *The freer the fatter? A panel study of the relationship between body-mass index and economic freedom* (Department of Economics Working Paper No. 2013:23). Lund, SE: Lund University.

Ljungvall, A., & Gerdtham, U. (2010). More equal but heavier: A longitudinal analysis of income-related obesity inequalities in an adult Swedish cohort. *Social Science & Medicine, 70*(2), 221–231.

Ljungvall, A., & Zimmerman, F. J. (2012). Bigger bodies, Long-term trends and disparities in obesity and body-mass index among US adults, 1960-2008. *Social Science & Medicine, 75*(1), 109–119.

Marmot, M. G. (2004). *Status syndrome, How your social standing directly affects your health and life expectancy.* London, England: Bloomsbury.

McLaren, L. (2007). Socioeconomic status and obesity. *Epidemiologic Reviews, 29*, 29–48.

Medco Health Solutions, Inc. (2011). *America's state of mind.* http://apps.who.int/medicinedocs/documents/s19032en/s19032en.pdf. Accessed 20 July 2015.

Münster, E., Ruger, H., Ochsmann, E., Letzel, S., & Toschke, A. M. (2009). Over-indebtedness as a marker of socioeconomic status and its association with obesity: A cross-sectional study. *BMC Public Health, 9*, 286. doi:10.1186/1471-2458-9-286. http://www.biomedcentral.com/1471-2458/9/286

Newman, K. S. (1988). *Falling from grace: The experience of downward mobility in the American middle class.* New York: Free Press.

Ng, M., Fleming, T., Robinson, M., Thomson, B., Graetz, N., & Gakidou, E. (2014). Global, regional, and national prevalence of overweight and obesity in children and adults during

1980-2013: A systematic analysis for the global burden of disease study 2013. *Lancet, 384*, 766–781.

Offer, A. (2001). Body weight and self-control in the United States and Britain since the 1950s. *Social History of Medicine, 14*(1), 79–106.

Offer, A. (2006). *The challenge of affluence: Self-control and well-being in the United States and Britain Since 1950*. Oxford, England: Oxford University Press.

Offer, A. (2008). British manual workers: From producers to consumers, c. 1950–2000. *Contemporary British History, 22*(4), 537–571.

Offer, A. (2012). A warrant for pain: *Caveat emptor* vs. the duty of care in the American medical system c. 1970–2010. *Real-World Economics Review, 61*, 85–99.

Offer, A., Pechey, R., & Ulijaszek, S. (2010). Obesity under affluence varies by welfare regimes: The effect of fast food, insecurity, and inequality. *Economics and Human Biology, 8*(3), 297–308.

Offer, A., Pechey, R., & Ulijaszek, S. (Eds.). (2012). *Insecurity, inequality, and obesity in affluent societies*. Oxford, England: Oxford University Press (for the British Academy).

Osberg, L. (2009). *Measuring economic security and insecure times: New perspectives, new events, and the index of economic well-being* (CSLS Research Report No. 2009-12). Ottawa, ON: Centre for the Study of Living Standards.

Philipson, T. J., & Posner, R. A. (2003). The long-run growth in obesity as a function of technological change. *Perspectives in Biology and Medicine, 46*(Suppl.), S87–S107.

Pickett, K. E., & Wilkinson, R. G. (2012). Income inequality and psychosocial pathways to obesity. In A. Offer, R. Pechey, & S. J. Ulijascek (Eds.), *Insecurity, inequality, and obesity in affluent societies* (pp. 179–198). Oxford, England: Oxford University Press (for the British Academy).

Piketty, T. (2014). *Capital in the twenty-first century*. Cambridge, MA: Harvard University Press.

Sapolsky, R. M. (2004). Social status and health in humans and other animals. *Annual Review of Anthropology 33*, 393-418.

Schlosser, E. (2001). *Fast food nation: What the all-American meal is doing to the world.* London: Allen Lane, Penguin.

Smith, T. (2009). Reconciling psychology with economics—Obesity, behavioral biology, and rational overeating. *Journal of Bioeconomics, 11*, 249–282.

Smith, T. (2012). Behavioural biology and obesity. In A. Offer, R. Pechey, & S. J. Ulijascek (Eds.), *Insecurity, inequality, and obesity in affluent societies* (pp. 69–81). Oxford, England: Oxford University Press (for the British Academy).

Smith, T. G., Stoddard, C., & Barnes, M. G. (2009). Why the poor get fat: Weight gain and economic insecurity. *Forum for Health Economics & Policy, 12* (article 5).

Smith, T. G., Stillman, S., & Craig, S. (2013). *The US obesity epidemic: New evidence from the economic security index.* Presented at the Agricultural and Applied Economics Annual Meeting, Washington, DC.

Sobal, J., & Stunkard, A. J. (1989). Socioeconomic-status and obesity—A review of the literature. *Psychological Bulletin, 105*(2), 260–275.

Sørensen, T. I. A., Rokholm, B., & Ajslev, T. A. (2012). The history of the obesity epidemic in Denmark. In A. Offer, R. Pechey, & S. J. Ulijascek (Eds.), *Insecurity, inequality, and obesity in affluent societies* (pp. 161–178). Oxford, England: Oxford University Press (for the British Academy).

Twenge, J. M., Gentile, B., DeWall, C. N., Ma, D., Lacefield, K., & Schurtz, D. R (2010). Birth cohort increases in psychopathology among young Americans, 1938–2007: A cross-temporal meta-analysis of the MMPI. *Clinical Psychology Review, 30*(2), 145–154.

Ulijaszek, S. J. (2014). Do adult obesity rates in England vary by insecurity as well as by inequality? An ecological cross-sectional study. *BMJ Open*, *4*(5). e004430. doi:10.1136/bmjopen-2013-004430.

Warren, E., & Tyagi, A. W. (2003). *The two-income trap: Why families went broke when mothers went to work*. New York: Basic Books.

Whybrow, P. (2012). Time urgency, sleep loss, and obesity. In A. Offer, R. Pechey, & S. J. Ulijascek (Eds.), *Insecurity, inequality, and obesity in affluent societies* (pp. 129–140). Oxford, England: Oxford University Press (for the British Academy).

Wisman, J. D., & Capehart, K. W. (2010). Creative destruction, economic insecurity, stress, and epidemic obesity. *American Journal of Economics and Sociology*, *69*(3), 936–982.

World Health Organization (WHO). (2000). *Obesity, preventing and managing the global Epidemic* (Who Technical Report Series 894). Geneva: Author.

Yemiscigil, A. (2013). *Are we hungry for meaning? The link between obesity and eudaimonic well-being*. Master's thesis, University of Warwick, Coventry, UK.

Zala, D. (2013). Challenging the spirit level: Is there really a relationship between inequality and obesity? *Economic Affairs*, *33*(2), 232–245.

Zimmerman, F. J. (2011). Using marketing muscle to sell fat: The rise of obesity in the modern economy. *Annual Review of Public Health*, *32*, 285–306.

CHAPTER 29

CHILDREN'S ANTHROPOMETRICS AND LATER DISEASE INCIDENCE

KARRI SILVENTOINEN

29.1 Introduction

Childhood is an important phase of life for the formation of the health risk profile in adulthood. Addressing poor health conditions and inculcating good health habits in childhood can play an important role in the prevention of adult diseases. Identifying factors in childhood affecting further health offers measures to improve population health. Inexpensive health interventions, for example through lunches and physical exercise education, are feasible in schools and kindergarten. Many of the health habits affecting further risk of diseases are formed in childhood, and childhood is considered an important period of life for the prevention of obesity in adulthood (Baird et al., 2005). Poor childhood living conditions, such as inadequate nutrition, may also affect future health risks.

Because the childhood environment is difficult to measure directly, anthropometric measures in childhood and adulthood give important information on the material environment as it reflects childhood nutrition and other environmental conditions. When undernutrition is prevalent in a population, short stature indicates poor childhood nutrition, which leads also to poorer health and general frailty. This can be seen even in modern societies indicated in Figure 29.1. The height difference between children who grew up in the two Koreas reaches an apex at age 7, when North Korean children were, on average, about 10 cm shorter than South Korean children at the same age (Schwekendiek, 2009). Those North Korean children experienced severe famine in the mid-1990s (Haggard & Noland, 2007), and thus the shorter stature indicates severe undernutrition.

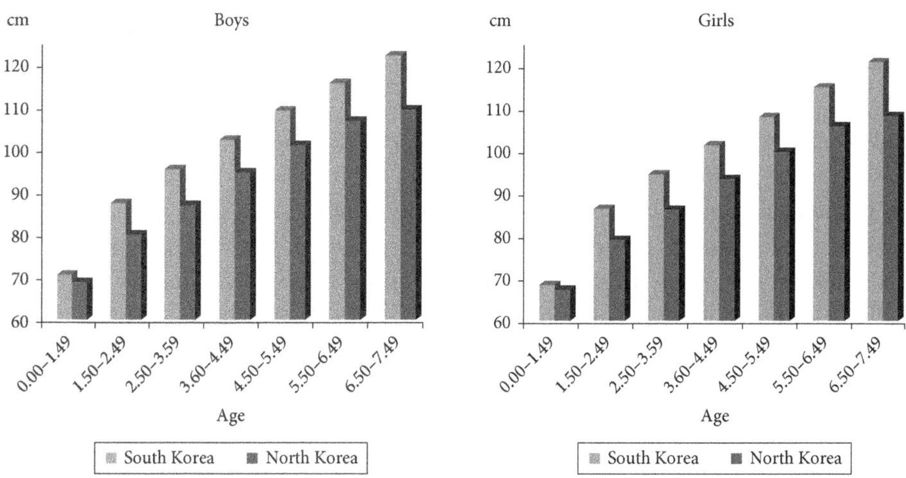

FIGURE 29.1 Height in South and North Korean children from birth until 7 years of age in 2002/2003.

Source: Schwekendiek (2009).

Within wealthy societies, there are no groups suffering severe undernutrition. However, the dark side of this beneficial development is increased overnutrition leading to the increasing prevalence of obesity. Severe childhood obesity may predispose to type 2 diabetes (T2D) starting already in adolescence (Sinha et al., 2002), but even slight overweight in childhood is hazardous to health because overweight children have a high probability of becoming obese adults (Baird et al., 2005). Obesity in adulthood is one of the main risk factors of many chronic diseases, such as coronary heart disease (CHD) and T2D (Haslam & James, 2005). Thus, body mass index (BMI, kg/m^2) has replaced height as the most important childhood anthropometric indicator of further health problems in industrialized societies.

Abnormal growth patterns in height can indicate immediate health problems as well as problems in the material conditions at home. Many chronic diseases have deep roots in childhood and thus emphasize the importance of optimal living conditions for children for the further health of a population (Lozano et al., 2012). Most studies on childhood anthropometrics have examined metabolic diseases, especially CHD but also stroke and T2D. These diseases have important public health value because stroke and CHD are the leading causes of death in industrialized countries, and they are also increasingly important causes of death in many developing countries; T2D incidence has also strongly increased around the world in the past two decades, and it is not only an important cause of death by itself but also increases strongly the risk of CHD (Lozano et al., 2012). In this chapter, the associations between cross-sectional anthropometric measures and risk of metabolic diseases are first discussed. After that, results on the role of developmental trajectories in childhood in the formation of the disease risk are shown.

29.2 Cross-Sectional Measures

Studies using cross-sectional anthropometric measures and information on later disease incidence provide considerable insights into the role of childhood body morphology in the formation of future disease risk. In most of these studies, the baseline data are collected for reasons other than scientific purposes and decades later merged with data on chronic diseases. This sets certain limitations for research, and, in most of the studies, only the most basic anthropometric measures are available. However, in spite of these limitations, these studies give evidence on how body morphology at a certain age predicts health risks in adulthood. They are thus important when studying the role of childhood nutrition and other environmental factors in the formation of the risk profile for metabolic diseases later in life.

29.2.1 Birthweight

Birthweight is the most important indicator of fetal nutrition and other environmental conditions in the uterus, since only rarely are direct measures on fetal growth available. Birthweight is a more widely used indicator than birth length in epidemiological studies needing large sample sizes because it is much easier to measure reliably. Low birthweight can be caused by intrauterine growth restrictions, prematurity, or mother's use of toxins such as alcohol, drugs, or cigarettes (Valero De Bernabe et al., 2004). Thus, birthweight can refer to actual weight at birth, or it can be calculated according to the baby's gestational age. However, most epidemiological studies have focused only on absolute birthweight. This is at least partly because a follow-up period of several decades is needed to study chronic diseases, and reliable information on gestational age is not always available in these old baseline datasets.

The association between low birthweight and increased risk of cardiovascular diseases (CVD) has been known for decades. One of the first researchers to pay attention to this association was a British epidemiologist, David Barker, who found that weight at 1 year of age was inversely associated with increased CHD mortality in the United Kingdom (Barker, Winter, Osmond, Margetts, & Simmonds, 1989). These observations contributed to his theory of biological programming, which suggests that children exposed to undernutrition in the uterus but experiencing good nutrition later in life are especially predisposed to metabolic diseases in adulthood (Barker, 1998). The association between birthweight and increased risk of CVD and its main physiological risk factors, such as hypertension, are well-demonstrated in several longitudinal studies. In a large meta-analysis of nearly 200,000 participants, an inverse association was found between birthweight and systolic blood pressure in adulthood (Gamborg et al., 2007). Low birthweight has also been found to be consistently associated with higher CHD incidence in a review of 23 studies; in the pooled meta-analyses, low birthweight was found to be associated with 20% higher incidence of CHD (Wang et al., 2014). For stroke, the studies are rarer, but there is clear evidence that low birthweight also increases the risk of stroke (Lawlor, Ronalds, Clark, Smith, & Leon, 2005). An association has also been found between birthweight and T2D. In a meta-analysis of 31 studies, increase in birthweight by 1 kg was associated with a 25% decreased risk of T2D (Whincup et al., 2008). Epidemiological studies thus suggest that low birthweight is consistently associated with a higher risk for all metabolic diseases.

When considering the physiological background of these associations, it is important to note that a number of factors affect fetal growth and future disease risk in addition to fetal nutrition. The study of twins offers an interesting opportunity to test the causal associations. It is well known that twin pregnancies are characterized by lower birthweight compared to singleton pregnancies (Buckler & Green, 2004), which should thus predispose them to a higher risk of future metabolic diseases. However, previous studies have shown that both CVD (Oberg et al., 2012) and T2D risks (Petersen, Nielsen, Beck-Nielsen, & Christensen, 2011) are similar in twins and singletons. This shows that the low birthweight in twins is not a similar factor for future risk of these diseases as it is in singletons. There are two possible explanations for this discrepancy between twin and low-birthweight singleton pregnancies when predicting the risk of metabolic diseases in adulthood. First, it is possible that, in singletons, the association between low birthweight and further disease risk is affected by confounding factors, such as the low socioeconomic position of mother and maternal smoking, both of which are associated with lower birthweight (Valero De Bernabe et al., 2004). These factors may directly or indirectly increase the newborn's lifetime risk of metabolic diseases. Second, the developmental trajectories of fetus in twin pregnancies differ both from normal and low-birthweight singleton pregnancies (Muhlhausler, Hancock, Bloomfield, & Harding, 2011). So, it is possible that intrauterine environmental factors associated with restricted fetal growth patterns in singleton pregnancies predispose to further metabolic diseases, but the same does not apply to the factors affecting lower birthweight in twin pregnancies.

The latter hypothesis is supported by a study showing that in dizygotic (DZ) co-twins discordant for birthweight, the lighter twin showed a higher risk of CVD (Öberg, Cnattingius, Sandin, Lichetenstein, & Iliadou, 2011). Because co-twins share the same postnatal environment, this result suggests that the association is caused by fetal environmental factors. Prenatal environment may differ between co-twins because of vascular differences that are common both in monozygotic (MZ) and DZ twins. Thus, it is possible that the same factors, such as intrauterine nutrition, affecting low birthweight in singleton pregnancies also affect twin pregnancies, creating differences in birthweight between co-twins and affecting CVD risk in adulthood. These factors can be independent of the factors affecting the generally lower birthweight of twins and that are not associated with further CVD risk.

This hypothesis is supported by epidemiological evidence based on the cohorts born during and after the Dutch Hunger Winter. In the years 1943–1945, the Netherlands suffered a severe famine, which ended immediately when Allied forces liberated the area.

Those persons who were exposed to the famine in early gestation had a higher risk of CHD later in life; the prevalence of CHD was three times higher among those exposed to undernutrition in early gestation than in those who were not exposed prenatally. This difference was not explained by gestational age, socioeconomic factors, or smoking (Roseboom et al., 2000). There is also evidence of vascular endothelial dysfunction, increased aortic stiffness, and thicker aortic-intima media in low-birthweight children, all predisposing them to a higher risk of CVD in adulthood (Norman, 2008). Thus, there is clear evidence that fetal growth restriction measured as lower birthweight and caused by, for example, poor fetal nutrition predisposes the individual to changes in vascular function and later in life increased risk of CVD.

29.2.2 Height

Height has a special role among anthropometric indicators because it is easy to measure and does not change in adulthood except for slight shrinking in old age. Height has been the most commonly measured anthropometric trait, and there is a vast body of scientific literature on biological, socioeconomic, and health-related factors associated with height (Komlos, 1998). Inadequate nutrition, especially the lack of protein, affects growth velocity. Poor nutrition during the period of very rapid growth in the first 2 years of life also affects adult stature (Sinclair, 1989). If living conditions later improve, catch-up growth may compensate for the delay in growth but does not necessarily eliminate it. This was demonstrated in a review of studies on international adoptions, which found rapid but not totally complete recovery of the gap in height in 2 years after adoption as compared to the reference population (van Ijzendoorn, Bakermans-Krananburg, & Juffer, 2007). Furthermore, catch-up growth does not necessarily eliminate the increased disease risks related to shorter stature in early childhood. Socioeconomic differences in height can be found even in modern affluent societies, suggesting that not only severe malnutrition but otherwise inadequate diet or other material living conditions in childhood can affect growth and consequently stature in adulthood (Silventoinen, 2003). Thus, adult height can be used as an indicator of nutritional status in childhood in modern industrialized societies. Height is more widely available than birthweight in large epidemiological datasets, and thus the associations between height and chronic diseases have attracted a lot of scientific interest in epidemiological studies.

The association between height and CHD risk has been widely studied; the first study showing this association was published in 1951 (Gertler, Gatn, & White, 1951). A meta-analysis of 52 studies found that short height was systematically associated with higher risk of CHD, and, in the shortest category, CHD risk was about 50% higher than in the tallest category (Paajanen, Oksala, Kuukasjarvi, & Karhunen, 2010). Most of the studies were conducted in Caucasian populations, but a similar association was also found in a large study of the South Korean population (Song, Smith, & Sung, 2003). This suggests that the association between height and CHD risk is similar in East Asian populations notwithstanding their shorter mean stature as compared to Caucasian populations. The studies on the association between height and stroke are rarer. However, there is still clear evidence that short stature increases the risk of stroke both in East Asian (Song et al., 2003) and Caucasian populations. In a large Swedish study, this association did not differ according to the type of stroke (i.e., intracerebral hemorrhage, subarachnoid hemorrhage, or intracerebral infarction), and one standard deviation (*SD*) increase in height was associated with an approximate 10% decreased risk of these diseases (Silventoinen, Magnusson, Tynelius, Batty, & Rasmussen, 2009).

Studies on height in childhood and CHD risk are rarer because suitable datasets with adequate sample size and follow-up time are not widely available. However, this association is likely because height in childhood is an important predictor of height in adulthood. This issue was examined in a study of Swedish boys undergoing longitudinal measures from birth until 18 years of age. Because the study participants were twins, it was possible to decompose the trait correlation into genetic correlation and a correlation of environmental factors specific for each twin. Figure 29.2 presents the results of this study (panel A). The correlation of height at 1 year of age was 0.52 with adult height. The correlation increased when the children grew older; at 4 years of age, it was 0.74; from 12 to 15 years of age, the correlation was somewhat lower (probably as an effect of puberty because the start of the pubertal growth peak varies between children independently of the final stature; Silventoinen et al., 2008).

Taking into account the close association between height in childhood and final adult height, it is not surprising that in a large Danish study height at 7 years of age was inversely associated with incidence of CHD in adulthood so that taller boys and girls had lower incidence of CHD because the hazard ratios are less than 1 (Figure 29.3). However, the association became weaker from 7 to 9 year of age insofar as the hazard ratios were increasing: at 7 years of age, a 1 *SD* increase in height was associated with a 9% lower CHD risk in boys and with a 12% lower risk in girls, whereas at 13 years of age,

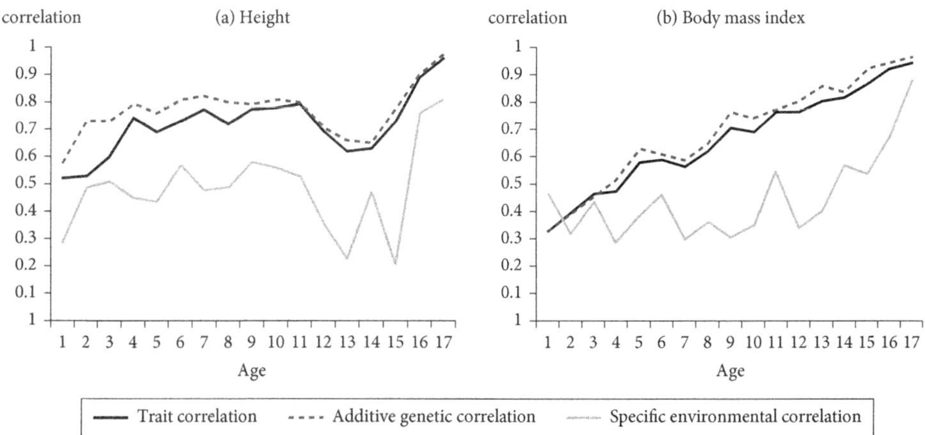

FIGURE 29.2 Trait correlations and additive genetic and specific environmental correlations of height and body mass index from 1 to 17 years of age with 18 years of age in Swedish twin boys.

Source: Silventoinen et al. (2007, 2008).

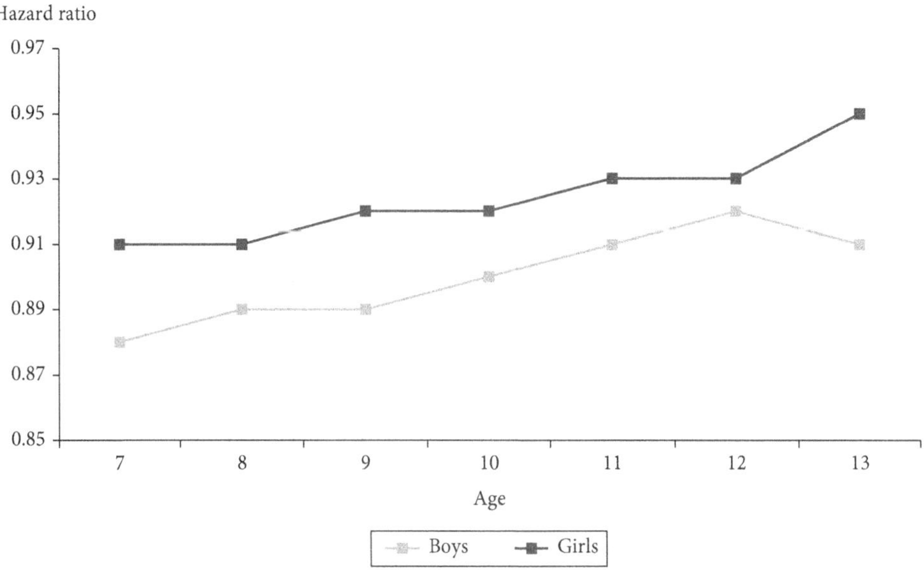

FIGURE 29.3 Hazard ratios for CHD incidence in adulthood per 1 unit increase in *z*-scores of height from 7 to 13 years of age in Danish children.

Source: Silventoinen, Baker, et al. (2012).

the risk decreased to only 5% and 9%, respectively (Silventoinen, Baker, & Sørensen, 2012). These results suggest that stature in childhood may be a better predictor of future disease risk than adult height because catch-up growth in later childhood may be associated with increased CHD risk. The greater heterogeneity of CHD risk among tall people in late childhood and in adulthood may be because this group includes both those who have been tall throughout childhood as compared to their peers and thus have low CHD risk, as well as those who have experienced rapid growth later in childhood and thus have a higher CHD risk. This underlines that adult height measures cannot fully replace measures in childhood when collecting information on childhood environment and emphasizes the importance of collecting height measures at different phases of the growth period.

There is also evidence that short stature in adulthood is a risk factor of T2D even though there are far fewer studies on this topic than on the association between height and CHD. A review of nine studies found that height was inversely associated with T2D risk in women; in men, the association in the pooled analysis was about the same as in women but because of larger confidence intervals it slightly failed to be statistically significant (Janghorbani, Momeni, & Dehghani, 2012). These results are not surprising because T2D and CVD share many of the same metabolic risk factors. This suggests that short stature is widely associated with an adverse metabolic profile, leading to metabolic diseases in adult life. Studies on the association between height in childhood and T2D in adulthood are rare. Nonetheless, the close association between height in childhood and adulthood suggests that short children have increased risk for T2D in adulthood.

Studies combining longitudinal measures of height in childhood to T2D incidence data in adulthood are, however, needed to analyze whether this association will change over childhood (as found for CHD risk).

As in the case of birthweight, it is not clear which factors are behind the association between height and metabolic diseases. Sometimes height is regarded purely as an indicator of childhood nutrition, and thus this association is interpreted to show that suboptimal nutrition in early childhood predisposes to further metabolic abnormalities (Barker, 1998). However, height is also associated with many other factors, such as socioeconomic position, that may also explain this association (Silventoinen, 2003). This issue was studied in a large study utilizing Nordic twin cohorts. The pooled analyses found that in twin pairs discordant for height the shorter co-twin had a higher probability of death from CHD than the taller co-twin (Silventoinen et al., 2006). Also in a large Swedish study, the associations of height with stroke and CHD were not explained by socioeconomic factors (Silventoinen et al., 2009). These results suggest that the association of height with adult CVD risk is not caused at least totally by social background or other postnatal environmental factors affecting height and further CVD risk, but is also affected by fetal environmental factors.

29.2.3 Relative Weight

Obesity is currently one of the most important public health problems, not only in affluent societies but increasingly in developing countries (Komlos & Baur, 2004). Obesity and overweight strongly increase the risk of many chronic disease, including CVD and T2D (Haslam & James, 2005). Childhood obesity is rapidly increasing in many countries, and severe obesity in childhood can lead to impaired glucose tolerance or even T2D beginning in adolescence (Sinha et al., 2002). However, the most important health consequence of childhood overweight is that it is strongly associated with obesity in adulthood. Thus, relative weight in childhood is one of the key indicators of later health. It is well known that weight loss in adulthood is difficult, and thus the prevention of overweight in childhood is crucial. There is an important role for the prevention of childhood overweight in the prevention of adult obesity, especially because the school environment offers a unique opportunity for health interventions.

Birthweight has been found to be associated with overweight risk in adulthood. A meta-analysis found that of 66 high-quality studies, 59 showed a linear association between birthweight and overweight risk in adulthood (Schellong, Schulz, Harder, & Plagemann, 2012). This association can be caused by fetal nutrition, but also because of genetic factors. Only four studies reported a U-shaped association between birthweight and adult BMI, and, in general, low birthweight was associated with a lower risk of overweight in adulthood. These results emphasize that the same anthropometric factor can affect future health risks through different physiological pathways. For example, it is possible that genetic factors explain the linear association between birthweight and adult obesity but environmental factors explain the inverse association between birthweight and risk of metabolic diseases. More studies are needed to disentangle these different physiological pathways.

The association between current BMI and BMI in adulthood becomes stronger as children grow older. A Swedish longitudinal twin study found that the correlation between BMI at 1 year of age with BMI at 18 years of age was 0.32 (Figure 29.1, panel B); this correlation increased during aging, and the correlation of BMI at 9 years of age was 0.69 with BMI at 18 years of age (Silventoinen et al., 2007). Genetic correlations also were high, suggesting that largely the same set of genes affects relative weight from early childhood to adulthood. Similar results on the important role of genetic factors in the tracking of BMI over childhood have also been found in other twin studies, but the follow-up periods in these other studies ended before adulthood (Silventoinen & Kaprio, 2009). The genes affecting BMI can modify metabolism, but it is likely that most of them are more related to behavioral factors such as eating styles predisposing to obesity (Faith, Carnell, & Kral, 2014). Thus, relative weight in childhood indicates further risk of obesity and the increased risk of subsequent metabolic diseases. However, the development of obesity can also be avoided by lifestyle changes because a major part of the genes predisposing to obesity probably act through behavior.

Taking into account that adult BMI is one of the most important risk factors of CVD, and the strong relationship between childhood and adult BMI, BMI in childhood also predicts future risk of metabolic diseases. This was demonstrated in a large Danish study finding that BMI from 7 to 13 years of age was linearly associated with the risk of CHD in adulthood. The association also became stronger over this age period: at 7 years of age, one unit increase of BMI increased the CHD risk by 9%, and this association increased to 20% at 13 years of age (Baker, Olsen, & Sørensen, 2007). These results are consistent with the increasing correlation of BMI during the course of childhood with BMI in adulthood (Silventoinen et al., 2007). It is also noteworthy that the association between childhood BMI and risk of CHD was linear; thus, not only overweight children but also children with average BMI had increased risk to develop CHD as compared to lean children (Baker et al., 2007). These results clearly suggest that even mild overweight in childhood predisposes to CVD later in life and thus underline the need for early interventions to prevent overweight.

29.2.4 Other Anthropometric Measures

Height and weight are the most widely measured anthropometric indicators in childhood, but other indicators have also sometimes been used (e.g., head circumference, chest circumference, and leg length). The use of these anthropometric indicators can be important because they have different sensitivity periods and thus can give additional information on the role of environmental factors at different phases of physical development as compared to height and weight measures. However, a problem in epidemiological studies is that they need long follow-up times, and there is a lack of studies with both detailed anthropometric measures and sufficient sample size to study the associations between measures and future health risks. Thus, much less is known about how these other anthropometric indicators are associated with future health—as compared with height and weight—especially when using childhood measures that need follow-up times of several decades.

After height and weight, head circumference is the most widely measured anthropometric indicator in newborns and young children. The main reason for this interest is that enlarged head circumference can indicate hydrocephalus, a potentially fatal but treatable condition in which cerebrospinal fluid accumulates in the ventricles of the brain (Zahl & Wester, 2008). The nonpathological variation of head circumference is linearly associated with cognitive performance (Heinonen et al., 2008), and abnormal growth patterns can also indicate increased risk of autism (Hazlett et al., 2005). However, there is a lack of epidemiological studies indicating whether head circumference may be associated with metabolic or other chronic physical diseases in adulthood. A review of studies of internationally adopted children found rapid catch-up growth in height and weight but relatively small catch-up growth in head circumference even when these children had remarkable smaller head circumferences as compared to the reference population (van Ijzendoorn et al., 2007). This suggests that head circumference may be more sensitive to fetal conditions and is affected less by postnatal environment than is height. Thus, epidemiological studies on the associations between head circumference and risk of metabolic diseases are warranted and may give evidence on the role of fetal nutrition in the risk of these diseases.

Chest circumference of newborns has sometimes been used, especially in developing countries, because it has been found to be the most precise indicator of birthweight and so is a good proxy indicator where measuring birthweight is not feasible (e.g., because of lack of scales) (Goto, 2011). This conclusion was supported by a Japanese twin study that found chest circumference was highly correlated with birthweight and that a substantial part of this correlation was caused by environmental factors affecting both traits (Silventoinen, Kaprio, Dunkel, & Yokoyama, 2012). In industrialized countries, measuring chest circumference is rare, and there are no previous studies of whether it is associated with risk of adult diseases. As in the case of head circumference, such studies are warranted because they may give new evidence on the role of early nutrition in the risk of adult diseases.

In contrast to head and chest circumferences, leg length—both in childhood and adulthood—has attracted a lot of scientific interest in epidemiology. As in the case of height, the advantage of leg length is that it does not change in adulthood, and thus adult measures can be used as an indicator of childhood environmental conditions. During the very rapid growth period of the first 2 years of life, legs grow relatively more quickly than do other parts of body (Sinclair, 1989). Thus, it is attractive to speculate that leg length would better capture differences in early nutrition as compared to stature. In a large Chinese study, leg length was inversely associated with CVD mortality in women but not in men. However, in women the association was also weaker than for height (Wang et al., 2011). Similar results were also found in a UK study finding that height was a better predictor of CHD incidence than was leg length (Ferrie, Langenberg, Shipley, &

Marmot, 2006). On the other hand, in a study of UK 14-year-old children, leg length was a better predictor of CHD mortality than was height (Gunnell et al., 1998). There is also evidence that not only short leg length but also a small leg length-to-height ratio is associated with increased risk of T2D (Asao et al., 2006; Conway et al., 2012; Johnston et al., 2013). Thus, there is consistent evidence that leg length is inversely associated with a risk of metabolic diseases, and it may have additional value when combined with total height in predicting T2D. However, more original research and a systematic meta-analysis are needed to study which of the components of height is the best predictor of further risk of metabolic diseases. Also, more detailed studies on children with sufficiently long follow-up time and measures on leg length and other components of height would be useful to determine how they are associated with further disease risks.

29.3 Longitudinal Measures

It is very possible that growth trajectories over childhood are more important factors affecting future health risks than is body morphology at a certain age. These trajectories are not captured by the cross-sectional studies discussed earlier. For example, the theory of biological programming suggests that poor nutrition in fetal life predisposes to further risk of metabolic diseases, especially if it is associated with a good postnatal environment (Barker, 1998). This theory would thus predict that especially rapid catch-up growth over childhood would be associated with increased risk of metabolic diseases because it indicates a large improvement in nutrition from pre- to postnatal life. Longitudinal studies that can capture the relationships between growth trajectories and future health risks are thus important because they can give more information on environmental changes. The challenge, however, is that the prolonged periods of time between childhood and adult health outcomes means that such studies are rarer than studies using only cross-sectional measures.

Evidence on the association between catch-up growth and increased risk of CVD was found in a Finnish study. This study found that people with hypertension at 63 years of age had lower birthweight and showed catch-up growth in height and weight until 11 years of age when compared to men and women with normal blood pressure (Eriksson, Forsen, Kajantie, Osmond, & Barker, 2007). In this same cohort, it was also found that CHD incidence was higher in women who had short birth length and who had experienced catch-up growth until 7 years of age (Forsen, Eriksson, Tuomilehto, Osmond, & Barker, 1999). These results seem to support the hypothesis that early catch-up growth associated with low birthweight and short birth length is associated with a higher incidence of CVD in adulthood. However, even in these studies, it is difficult to separate the effect of low birthweight and further catch-up growth. As discussed earlier in this chapter, birthweight by itself is associated with the risk of metabolic diseases, and it is natural that (at least in modern societies with good infant nutrition) low-birthweight babies experience catch-up growth. Further studies are needed to separate the effects of low birthweight and further catch-up growth on the risk of metabolic diseases.

Catch-up growth in mid-childhood may also be associated with future CVD risk. In a Danish study, rapid growth between 7 and 9 years of age was associated with increased CHD incidence in adulthood (Silventoinen, Baker, et al., 2012). These results show that even at the time of the slow growth of mid-childhood, growth is associated with CHD risk. However, the strongest association was found between rapid growth from 9 to 11 years in girls and 11 to 13 years in boys. This suggests that especially rapid growth at the onset of puberty, probably indicating an early start of puberty, is associated with higher CHD risk. This result is consistent with previous studies finding that early puberty is associated with several risk factors of CHD, including hypertension (Hardy, Kuh, Whincup, & Wadsworth, 2006) and adverse lipid profile (Feng et al., 2008). In this Danish study, the association between height in childhood and further CHD risk was, however, not modified by birthweight (Silventoinen, Baker, et al., 2012); this study did not find evidence that catch-up growth from infancy to mid-childhood was important for CHD risk.

Thus, there is some evidence that those children who grow more quickly than their peers have a higher risk of CHD in adulthood even when the results are not fully consistent. However, these results should be treated with caution because so few epidemiological studies use longitudinal anthropometric measures, compared to those studies using cross-sectional measures. All these previous studies are based on Nordic populations and represent only two epidemiological cohorts. Replications in other datasets collected in other populations with different environmental exposures are thus warranted. The role of catch-up growth in infancy as an independent risk factor of CHD especially needs more research.

29.4 CONCLUSION

In this chapter, the role of different anthropometric indicators in the formation of risk for metabolic diseases was discussed. Childhood physical development is sensitive to environmental factors, especially nutrition, and thus it has attracted scientific interest because anthropometric measures are convenient proxy measures of childhood environmental conditions. Birthweight and birth length are affected by the fetal environment, whereas height also reflects environmental conditions over the growth period. Thus, the associations between low birthweight and short stature with increased risk of CHD, stroke, and T2D suggest that environmental factors during the growth period predisposes to metabolic abnormalities. Overweight in childhood is a strong predictor of obesity in adulthood, and even children with slight overweight have increased risk of CHD in adulthood as compared to lean children. All these associations demonstrate the importance of early life in the formation of the metabolic risk profile affecting health decades later.

In spite of intensive research, there are still important gaps in knowledge when considering the associations between childhood anthropometrics and future disease risk. Epidemiological studies need long follow-up time and thus usually have to rely on datasets collected for other than research purposes. Height and weight have been part of the health check-up protocol for decades in many countries and can thus be used in epidemiological studies, but much less is known about other anthropometric measures, especially in children. Because the growth velocity of body parts varies at different phases of childhood, it is possible that they also capture different environmental variation. Thus, use of different anthropometric indicators, such as head or chest circumference, may give additional information on the susceptibility periods for future disease risks. So far, leg length is the only anthropometric measure widely used in epidemiological studies in addition to height and weight. There is evidence that leg length can give additional information compared to height when predicting T2D risk, but for CHD the results are somewhat inconsistent. However, these results suggest that the use of other anthropometric indicators is warranted in further epidemiological studies.

Another area of research where relatively little is known is the association of developmental trajectories with further disease risks. Only a few large datasets include longitudinal anthropometric measures over childhood and information on disease incidence in adulthood; studies so far suggest that rapid growth from infancy to the onset of puberty is associated with increased risk of CHD. However, it is still unclear how much of this association is related to low birthweight or early onset of puberty, which are both associated with increased risk of metabolic diseases. These studies are important because they can give more information on the poorly understood physiological pathways between childhood anthropometrics and future disease incidence.

The third large gap in our knowledge concerns the associations between childhood anthropometrics and chronic diseases other than metabolic diseases. For example, it is known that tall stature is a risk factor of different cancers, both in men and women; thus, the associations of height with risk of cancer is opposite to the risk of metabolic diseases (Wiren et al., 2014). It is noteworthy that height is associated with an increased risk of very different types of cancers, such as melanoma and colon cancer, which otherwise have different environmental risk factors. These associations suggest that physical development in childhood is also important for future cancer risk, but very little is known about the physiological pathways behind these associations. Thus, this area warrants further research, preferably using longitudinal measures of physical development in childhood.

In conclusion, epidemiological studies have shown that low birthweight, short stature, and short leg length are associated with increased risk of CVD and T2D. Stature and leg length can also be measured in adulthood, but measures in childhood are more sensitive to environmental conditions and give better estimates for future disease risk. These associations suggest that inadequate nutrition in early life predisposes to metabolic abnormalities that lead to increased disease risk decades later. However, in industrialized societies and increasingly also in developing countries, excess nutrition has replaced undernutrition as a major risk factor for future health. Subsequently, relative weight has replaced stature as the most important anthropometric indicator of future risk of metabolic diseases. All these associations, however, demonstrate the deep roots of adult health in early life and emphasize the need for optimal environments if children are to develop as healthy adults.

References

Asao, K., Kao, W. H., Baptiste-Roberts, K., Bandeen-Roche, K., Erlinger, T. P., & Brancati, F. L. (2006). Short stature and the risk of adiposity, insulin resistance, and type 2 diabetes in middle age: The third National Health and Nutrition Examination Survey (NHANES III), 1988–1994. *Diabetes Care, 29*, 1632–1637.

Baird, J., Fisher, D., Lucas, P., Kleijnen, J., Roberts, H., & Law, C. (2005). Being big or growing fast: Systematic review of size and growth in infancy and later obesity. *British Medical Journal, 331*, doi:10.1136/bmj.38586.411273.EO

Baker, J. L., Olsen, L. W., & Sørensen, T. I. A. (2007). Childhood body-mass index and the risk of coronary heart disease in adulthood. *New England Journal of Medicine, 357*, 2329–2337.

Barker, D. J. P. (1998). *Mothers, babies and health in later life*. Edinburgh, England: Churchill Livingstone.

Barker, D. J., Winter, P. D., Osmond, C., Margetts, B., & Simmonds, S. J. (1989). Weight in infancy and death from ischaemic heart disease. *Lancet, 2*(8663), 577–580.

Buckler, J. M., & Green, M. (2004). A comparison of the early growth of twins and singletons. *Annals of Human Biology, 31*, 311–332.

Conway, B. N., Shu, X. O., Zhang, X., Xiang, Y. B., Cai, H., Li, H., ... Zheng, W. (2012). Age at menarche, the leg length to sitting height ratio, and risk of diabetes in middle-aged and elderly Chinese men and women. *PloS One, 7*, e30625.

Eriksson, J. G., Forsen, T. J., Kajantie, E., Osmond, C., & Barker, D. J. (2007). Childhood growth and hypertension in later life. *Hypertension, 49*, 1415–1421.

Faith, M. S., Carnell, S., & Kral, T. V. (2014). Genetics of food intake self-regulation in childhood: Literature review and research opportunities. *Human Heredity, 75*, 80–89.

Feng, Y., Hong, X., Wilker, E., Li, Z., Zhang, W., Jin, D., ... Xu, X. (2008). Effects of age at menarche, reproductive years, and menopause on metabolic risk factors for cardiovascular diseases. *Atherosclerosis, 196*, 590–597.

Ferrie, J. E., Langenberg, C., Shipley, M. J., & Marmot, M. G. (2006). Birth weight, components of height and coronary heart disease: Evidence from the Whitehall II study. *International Journal of Epidemiology, 35*, 1532–1542.

Forsen, T., Eriksson, J. G., Tuomilehto, J., Osmond, C., & Barker, D. J. (1999). Growth in utero and during childhood among women who develop coronary heart disease: Longitudinal study. *British Medical Journal, 319*, 1403–1407.

Gamborg, M., Byberg, L., Rasmussen, F., Andersen, P. K., Baker, J. L., Bengtsson, C., ... Sørensen, T. I. A. (2007). Birth weight and systolic blood pressure in adolescence and adulthood: Meta-regression analysis of sex- and age-specific results from 20 Nordic studies. *American Journal of Epidemiology, 166*, 634–645.

Gertler, M. M., Gatn, S. M., & White, P. D. (1951). Young candidates for coronary heart disease. *Journal of the American Medical Association, 147*, 621–625.

Goto, E. (2011). Meta-analysis: Identification of low birthweight by other anthropometric measurements at birth in developing countries. *Journal of Epidemiology, 21*, 354–362.

Gunnell, D. J., Davey Smith, G., Frankel, S., Nanchahal, K., Braddon, F. E., Pemberton, J., & Peters, T. J. (1998). Childhood leg length and adult mortality: Follow up of the Carnegie (Boyd Orr) Survey of Diet and Health in pre-war Britain. *Journal of Epidemiology and Community Health*, *52*, 142–152.

Haggard, S., & Noland, M. (2007). *Famine in North Korea: Markets, aid, and reform.* New York: Columbia University Press.

Hardy, R., Kuh, D., Whincup, P. H., & Wadsworth, M. E. (2006). Age at puberty and adult blood pressure and body size in a British birth cohort study. *Journal of Hypertension*, *24*, 59–66.

Haslam, D. W., & James, W. P. (2005). Obesity. *Lancet*, *366*, 1197–1209.

Hazlett, H. C., Poe, M., Gerig, G., Smith, R. G., Provenzale, J., Ross, A., . . . Piven, J. (2005). Magnetic resonance imaging and head circumference study of brain size in autism: Birth through age 2 years. *Archives of General Psychiatry*, *62*, 1366–1376.

Heinonen, K., Räikkönen, K., Pesonen, A. K., Kajantie, E., Andersson, S., Eriksson, J. G., . . . Lano, A. (2008). Prenatal and postnatal growth and cognitive abilities at 56 months of age: A longitudinal study of infants born at term. *Pediatrics*, *121*, e1325–e1333.

Janghorbani, M., Momeni, F., & Dehghani, M. (2012). Hip circumference, height and risk of type 2 diabetes: Systematic review and meta-analysis. *Obesity Reviews*, *13*, 1172–1181.

Johnston, L. W., Harris, S. B., Retnakaran, R., Gerstein, H. C., Zinman, B., Hamilton, J., & Hanley, A. J. (2013). Short leg length, a marker of early childhood deprivation, is associated with metabolic disorders underlying type 2 diabetes: The PROMISE cohort study. *Diabetes Care*, *36*, 3599–3606.

Komlos, J. (1998). Shrinking in a growing economy? The mystery of physical stature during the Industrial Revolution. *Journal of Economic History*, *58*, 779–802.

Komlos, J., & Baur, M. (2004). From the tallest to (one of) the fattest: The enigmatic fate of the American population in the 20th century. *Economics and Human Biology*, *2*, 57–74.

Lawlor, D. A., Ronalds, G., Clark, H., Smith, G. D., & Leon, D. A. (2005). Birth weight is inversely associated with incident coronary heart disease and stroke among individuals born in the 1950s: Findings from the Aberdeen Children of the 1950s prospective cohort study. *Circulation*, *112*, 1414–1418.

Lozano, R., Naghavi, M., Foreman, K., Lim, S., Shibuya, K., Aboyans, V., . . . Memish, Z. A. (2012). Global and regional mortality from 235 causes of death for 20 age groups in 1990 and 2010: A systematic analysis for the Global Burden of Disease Study 2010. *Lancet*, *380*, 2095–2128.

Muhlhausler, B. S., Hancock, S. N., Bloomfield, F. H., & Harding, R. (2011). Are twins growth restricted? *Pediatric Research*, *70*, 117–122.

Norman, M. (2008). Low birth weight and the developing vascular tree: A systematic review. *Acta Paediatrica*, *97*, 1165–1172.

Öberg, S., Cnattingius, S., Sandin, S., Lichtenstein, P., & Iliadou, A. N. (2011). Birth weight predicts risk of cardiovascular disease within dizygotic but not monozygotic twin pairs: A large population-based co-twin-control study. *Circulation*, *123*, 2792–2798.

Oberg, S., Cnattingius, S., Sandin, S., Lichtenstein, P., Morley, R., & Iliadou, A. N. (2012). Twinship influence on morbidity and mortality across the lifespan. *International Journal of Epidemiology*, *41*(4), 1002–1009.

Paajanen, T. A., Oksala, N. K., Kuukasjarvi, P., & Karhunen, P. J. (2010). Short stature is associated with coronary heart disease: A systematic review of the literature and a meta-analysis. *European Heart Journal*, *31*, 1802–1809.

Petersen, I., Nielsen, M. M., Beck-Nielsen, H., & Christensen, K. (2011). No evidence of a higher 10 year period prevalence of diabetes among 77,885 twins compared with 215,264 singletons from the Danish birth cohorts 1910–1989. *Diabetologia, 54*, 2016–2024.

Roseboom, T. J., van der Meulen, J. H., Osmond, C., Barker, D. J., Ravelli, A. C., Schroeder-Tanka, J. M., . . . Bleker, O. P. (2000). Coronary heart disease after prenatal exposure to the Dutch famine, 1944–45. *Heart, 84*, 595–598.

Schellong, K., Schulz, S., Harder, T., & Plagemann, A. (2012). Birth weight and long-term overweight risk: Systematic review and a meta-analysis including 643,902 persons from 66 studies and 26 countries globally. *PloS One, 7*, e47776.

Schwekendiek, D. (2009). Height and weight differences between North and South Korea. *Journal of Biosocial Science, 41*, 51–55.

Silventoinen, K. (2003). Determinants of variation in adult body height. *Journal of Biosocial Science, 35*, 263–285.

Silventoinen, K., Baker, J. L., & Sørensen, T. I. A. (2012). Growth in height in childhood and risk of coronary heart disease in adult men and women. *PloS One 7*(1), e30476.

Silventoinen, K., & Kaprio, J. (2009). Genetics of tracking of body mass index from birth to late middle age: Evidence from twin and family studies. *Obesity Facts, 2*, 196–202.

Silventoinen, K., Kaprio, J., Dunkel, L., & Yokoyama, Y. (2012). Genetic and environmental influences on chest circumference during infancy: A longitudinal study of Japanese twins. *Paediatrics and Perinatal Epidemiology, 26*, 553–560.

Silventoinen, K., Magnusson, P. K., Tynelius, P., Batty, G. D., & Rasmussen, F. (2009). Association of body size and muscle strength with incidence of coronary heart disease and cerebrovascular diseases: A population-based cohort study of one million Swedish men. *International Journal of Epidemiology, 38*, 110–118.

Silventoinen, K., Pietiläinen, K. H., Tynelius, P., Sørensen, T. I. A., Kaprio, J., & Rasmussen, F. (2007). Genetic and environmental factors in relative weight from birth to age 18: The Swedish Young Male Twins Study. *International Journal of Obesity, 31*, 615–621.

Silventoinen, K., Pietiläinen, K. H., Tynelius, P., Sørensen, T. I. A., Kaprio, J., & Rasmussen, F. (2008). Genetic regulation of growth from birth to 18 years of age: The Swedish Young Male Twins Study. *American Journal of Human Biology, 20*, 292–298.

Silventoinen, K., Zdravkovic, S., Skytthe, A., McCarron, P., Herskind, A. M., Koskenvuo, M., . . . Kaprio, J. (2006). Association between height and coronary heart disease mortality: A prospective study of 35,000 twin pairs. *American Journal of Epidemiology, 163*(7), 615–621.

Sinclair, D. (1989). *Human growth after birth*. Oxford, England: Oxford University Press.

Sinha, R., Fisch, G., Teague, B., Tamborlane, W. V., Banyas, B., . . . Caprio,S. (2002). Prevalence of impaired glucose tolerance among children and adolescents with marked obesity. *New England Journal of Medicine, 346*, 802–810.

Song, Y. M., Smith, G. D., & Sung, J. (2003). Adult height and cause-specific mortality: A large prospective study of South Korean men. *American Journal of Epidemiology, 158*, 479–485.

Valero De Bernabe, J., Soriano, T., Albaladejo, R., Juarranz, M., Calle, M. E., Martinez, D., & Dominguez-Rojas, V. (2004). Risk factors for low birth weight: A review. *European Journal of Obstetrics, Gynecology, and Reproductive Biology, 116*, 3–15.

van Ijzendoorn, M. H., Bakermans-Kranenburg, M. J., & Juffer, F. (2007). Plasticity of growth in height, weight, and head circumference: Meta-analytic evidence of massive catch-up after international adoption. *Journal of Developmental and Behavioral Pediatrics, 28*, 334–343.

Wang, S. F., Shu, L., Sheng, J., Mu, M., Wang, S., Tao, X. Y., . . . Tao, F. B. (2014). Birth weight and risk of coronary heart disease in adults: A meta-analysis of prospective cohort studies. *Journal of Developmental Origins of Health and Disease*, *5*, 408–419.

Wang, N., Zhang, X., Xiang, Y. B., Yang, G., Li, H. L., Gao, J., . . . Shu, X. O. (2011). Associations of adult height and its components with mortality: A report from cohort studies of 135,000 Chinese women and men. *International Journal of Epidemiology*, *40*, 1715–1726.

Whincup, P. H., Kaye, S. J., Owen, C. G., Huxley, R., Cook, D. G., Anazawa, S., . . . Yarbrough, D. E. (2008), Birth weight and risk of type 2 diabetes: A systematic review. *Journal of the American Medical Association*, *300*, 2886–2897.

Wiren, S., Haggstrom, C., Ulmer, H., Manjer, J., Bjorge, T., Nagel, G., . . . Stattin, P. (2014). Pooled cohort study on height and risk of cancer and cancer death. *Cancer Causes & Control*, *25*, 151–159.

Zahl, S. M., & Wester, K. (2008). Routine measurement of head circumference as a tool for detecting intracranial expansion in infants: What is the gain? A nationwide survey. *Pediatrics*, *121*, e416–e420.

CHAPTER 30

BIRTH WEIGHT AS AN INDICATOR OF HUMAN WELFARE

W. PETER WARD

BIRTH weight is a biometric measure of health and well-being widely used in clinical practice and epidemiological research. As a subject of research inquiry, it reaches back to the 18th century and it continues to the present, yielding a large scientific literature. Newborn weight identifies a primary physiological characteristic of both individual neonates and populations of newborns that serves as a universal health indicator for infants. It also offers insights into maternal and population health more generally.

The frequency distribution of birth weights forms a normal or Gaussian curve with an extended lower tail. Generally, the weights located on the normal curve are of infants born at full term, whereas those on the lower tail usually are growth retarded or premature (Wilcox & Russell, 1983, pp. 314–315). The most commonly reported population measures of weight at birth are the mean and the proportion of low birth weight (LBW) infants—newborns weighing less than 2,500 g. Investigators have tended to select study populations consisting either of all live births or of live, singleton, full-term births, but other definitions have also been used. Consequently, researchers and international agencies have relied increasingly on the percentage of LBW infants when comparing group outcomes (OECD, 2013, pp. 38–39; UNICEF, 2012, pp. 92–95).

The LBW threshold has long been used to identify newborns at higher risk of infant morbidity and mortality. Recently more sharply defined categories—extremely LBW (<1,000 g), very LBW (1,000–1,500 g), and moderately LBW (1,500–2,500 g)—have specified some risk groups more precisely. LBW is associated with preterm delivery or poor growth during pregnancy. Those born too soon have missed the end of the normal gestational cycle; those born too small have experienced growth retardation. In some instances, newborns suffer from both deficits. Like many broad epidemiological measures, LBW has significant limitations. Some premature and growth-retarded newborns weigh more than the 2,500 g benchmark. In addition, some infants are more likely than others to fall below it.

Female newborns tend to weigh slightly less than males, for example, and therefore are likely to be overrepresented in an LBW population. Consequently, the universal applicability of the 2,500 g risk threshold to individual babies and to wider populations is increasingly recognized as arbitrary and insensitive to geographical and sociocultural differences (Juárez, Ploubidis, & Clarke, 2014; United Nations Children's Fund and World Health Organization, 2004; Wilcox, 2001). Nevertheless, it remains a leading population health statistic and a common index of individual newborn health. What it lacks in specificity is offset by its simplicity, its universality, its utility as a public health indicator, and its strong association with vulnerable newborns.

Average birth weight and the incidence of LBW vary widely in the contemporary world. Wealthy western societies generally experience the highest average weights. Surveys in North America and Western Europe report levels ranging between 3,250 g and 3,500 g for full-term singleton neonates (Ananth & Wen, 2002; Blondel & Kermarrec, 2011; Donahue, Kleinman, Gillman, & Oken, 2010). The lowest weights are found in some of the globe's poorest nations, particularly in south Asia, where means between 2,600 g and 2,700 g are common (Metgud, Naik, & Mallapur, 2012; Persson et al., 2012).

Rates of LBW vary widely. Globally, 15% of newborns weighed less than 2,500 g in the early 21st century, ranging from 5% in east Asia, through 7% in Europe, and 8% in the Americas, to 24% in southeast Asia (World Health Organization [WHO], 2012). But considerable variation also occurs within regions. The two most populous Asian countries report strikingly different LBW rates: China 6% and India 30%. Even in wealthy North America, the differences are significant: Canada 6% and the United States 8%.

30.1 The History of Weighing Newborns

Scientific interest in birth weight first appeared in the mid-18th century, when the German physician J. G. Roederer measured a small group of full-term newborns. He determined that the males weighed 6 pounds 12 ounces avoirdupois (3,060 g) on average, the females 6 pounds 5 ounces (2,910 g) (Tanner, 1981, pp. 254–298; Ward, 1993, p. 22). Over the next several decades, scattered reports confirmed his findings. The systematic weighing and measuring of infants immediately after birth began to spread during the early 19th century, for the most part in maternity hospitals, the primary locus of growing medical interest in fetal growth and parturition. By mid-century, it had become a common practice in some leading obstetric clinics in Western Europe and eastern North America. The information gathered was part of a larger body of data collected by the clinics' physician-directors, their motives ranging from simple curiosity about human biology to broad concern for newborn health and mortality.

The Brussels statistician Adolphe Quetelet placed the measurement of newborn weight and length in its modern anthropometric setting during the 1830s, when he published the first age-specific growth charts for boys and girls based on information gathered from the city's foundling hospital and other institutions for the young (Quetelet, 1835, pp. 6–9). The newborn lengths in his series provided a baseline measure from which later growth could be measured. Yet the larger significance of fetal size remained largely unexamined until the second half of the century, when investigators began to identify diagnostic insights embedded in the physical dimensions of newborns. These emphasized birth weight as an index of fetal maturity and routine weighing as a means of monitoring neonatal health (Frankenhäuser, 1859; Odier, 1868; von Hecker, 1866).

At the same time, systematic research began to identify factors associated with variation in size at birth, particularly infant sex, birth order, and maternal age (Duncan, 1864; Pinard, 1878; Veit, 1855, 1856). By the end of the century, weighing and measuring infants at birth had become standard practice in maternity clinics, as well as in private obstetric practice throughout most of the Western world. At that point, birth weight was accepted as the main index of fetal maturity and a major reference point for assessing future physical growth.

30.2 Factors Influencing Fetal Growth

Although a wide range of factors affect the process of fetal growth, most cannot be quantified, and many are not yet fully understood. Thus, the influences on newborn weight are best described in general terms. They fall into five broad categories: genetic, environmental, gestational, socioeconomic, and nutritional.

A mother's genetic makeup and her child's genetic constitution, inherited equally from both parents, both influence birth weight. Although estimates differ, they suggest that maternal and fetal genetic influences explain a third to a half of variation in newborn weight. Maternal height and ethnicity have both been identified with systematic differences in birth weight. The case of height is clear. The babies of taller women tend to be heavier than those of shorter mothers. The broad differences in birth size found in different ethnic and racial groups have also been explained as genetically based, at least in part, but the evidence is not conclusive. There is no firm basis at present for the assumption that ethnic or racial variations in mean birth weight stem from genetic causes. The most obvious fetal genetic association with birth size is neonatal sex; in the developed world today, males weigh about 150 g more than females, the difference narrowing somewhat in poorer nations.

Some environmental factors may also influence newborn weight. The effect of altitude is well established. Fetal growth is reduced among women living at high elevations (Zamudio et al., 2007). The relationship between climate and birth weight, however, remains less clear. Some studies have found seasonal patterns in newborn weight, with the highest means in winter and the lowest in summer (Juárez, 2011, pp. 106–107; Ward, 1993, pp. 116–117). Hypotheses explaining these differences include variations in the availability of nutritional resources and the effects of sunlight and cold on gestational processes—greater exposure to the former increasing and to the latter reducing newborn weight. But the evidence to date has not established firm causal relationships. Recent research also points to the adverse effects of air and noise pollution on birth weight, as well as the benefits of access to urban green spaces (Dadvand et al., 2013; Hystad et al., 2014).

Several characteristics of an individual pregnancy are also associated with birth weight variation. Gestational age—the duration of pregnancy—has a major influence on fetal development and neonatal size. The normal gestational period is 37–41 completed weeks; prematurely born infants generally are smaller than those delivered at term. Also, children born of twin or higher multiple pregnancies are significantly lighter than singletons. Newborn size also varies with parity or birth order; firstborns tend to weigh less than their later-born siblings, and some findings suggest that weights decline again among the later born in families of six or more (Ward, 1993, p. 13). Some evidence also indicates that birth intervals under 18 months and longer than 5 years are related to increased levels of LBW and fetal growth retardation, although intermediate intervals are not. Maternal age, however, has only slight influence, if any, on newborn weight, apart from women at the beginning or the end of their reproductive years; mothers in their teens or 40s are somewhat more likely to bear LBW infants than those in their 20s and 30s.

A woman's health before and during pregnancy affects the growth of her unborn child. Some infectious diseases are associated with lower levels of newborn weight, including malaria, the venereal diseases, and pulmonary infections, particularly tuberculosis (Ward, 2006). In addition, some noninfectious medical conditions are correlated with lower birth weight, among them chronic heart disease and disorders of the blood, circulatory, and renal systems. Diabetes and hypertension are also linked with abnormal birth weights, the former associated with heavier newborns, the latter with lighter, and these conditions may have serious implications for fetal and maternal health. Larger fetal size, commonly defined as weight over 4,500 g, raises the level of risk to both mother and child during pregnancy and delivery. Hypertension is associated with preeclampsia, a toxic condition of pregnancy that may cause death if not treated successfully (Goldstein, 1981; Peters et al., 1983). Smoking, as well as alcohol and addictive drug consumption, all adverse to both maternal and fetal health, are also linked with lower birth weight and the increased possibility of fetal abnormalities.

In addition, numerous socioeconomic factors are associated with systematic differences in newborn weight. Maternal social position is highly correlated with birth size. Variation according to a woman's class or status is found even in communities with low levels of social inequality, with more advantaged mothers bearing heavier children than their less-favored contemporaries (Garn, Shaw, & McCabe, 1977). One study in Sweden, where social differences have long been among the lowest in the developed world, indicated that the full-term singleton newborns of privileged mothers weighed 155 g more than those of underprivileged ones (Ericson, Eriksson, Källén, & Zetterström, 1989). The relationship itself, however, is not causal. Those in the upper levels of most societies commonly share numerous social and economic advantages that directly affect their health and well-being. Class and status are simply markers of other factors that exert these influences. A social gradient of birth weight distributions is found in all contemporary Western societies, fetal size varying with parental socioeconomic status. National social differences tend to vary inversely with levels of social equality, with the smallest found in the most egalitarian communities, the largest in the least equal.

Marital status is also commonly associated with birth weight variation, married women delivering slightly larger newborns than the unmarried (Shah, Zao, & Ali, 2011). Similarly, some evidence suggests that women with adequate prenatal education and medical supervision during pregnancy bear heavier children than do those who lack them, although in this case the association of superior health care with higher social standing may account for much of the difference (Ward, 1993, pp. 15–16).

Understandings of the effects of work on birth weight have varied over time. The first studies, done during the late 19th century, revealed that the children of women who performed heavy physical labor until they gave birth weighed less than those whose mothers rested for a period before delivery (Pinard, 1895, 1899). Since the 1970s, however, studies in developed societies have indicated that working women tend to bear heavier infants than the rest of the population. This result seems to reflect the changed nature of women's work in late industrial and postindustrial societies, for recent evidence from both the developed and the developing world also indicates that hard physical work continues to have an adverse influence on newborn weight (Saurel-Cubizolles & Kaminski, 1986).

The effects of maternal nutrition on fetal size are complex. Although birth weight is commonly accepted as a leading measure of maternal nutritional status, the influence of diet on fetal development is only partly understood. Ethical considerations limit research possibilities because the diets of pregnant women usually cannot be manipulated in order to examine the consequences for their unborn infants. Nevertheless, the evidence to date suggests that the degree of influence varies widely. Birth weight means fell dramatically during severe local famines in Europe over the course of World War II (Antonov, 1947; Stein, 1975), although these deficits disappeared once normal food supplies were restored. Moderate malnutrition, however, is generally associated with much less severe outcomes. Diet intervention studies indicate that undernourished women bear heavier babies when their nutritional condition improves, although adequately nourished women do not. The precise dietary constituents that lead to improved birth weights, however, are not clear. At least one group of researchers has hypothesized the existence of a nutritional threshold below which fetal growth retardation occurs and above which maternal diets may vary without affecting birth weight (Lechtig et al., 1975).

30.3 Trends in Birth Weight

An overview of human physical growth patterns at the end of the 20th century noted that, unlike heights, birth weights have not revealed a secular trend (Cole, 2000). The remark appears premature. Although the study of human stature since the 18th century has flourished in recent years, producing impressive evidence of change over the long term, only a few of the thousands of birth weight studies have been longitudinal. This is a significant oversight because newborn weight is an independent measure of health, one offering particular insights into the experience of women and the newly born, populations that the research on stature generally overlooks. In addition, the studies of birth weight concerned with change over time reveal important regional and temporal differences. Time itself appears to be an important variable because shifting socioeconomic and environmental circumstances are reflected in fetal growth and newborn size. In the United States, birth weight means appear not to have changed much since the mid-19th century and have commonly ranged between 3,400 g and 3,500 g (Costa, 1998). On the other hand, newborn weights in Western Europe and Canada either declined or remained flat during the past four decades of the century, followed by a modest, sustained increase after 1900 (Rosenberg, 1988; Ward, 1993, 2003). In contrast, northern Italy saw an upward trend in mean birth weight from under 2,900 g to more than 3,300 g between 1880 and 1940, rising from among the lowest European levels recorded during the later 19th century to the mid range of continental averages by the outbreak of World War II (Ward, 2006).

Short-term fluctuations in birth weight averages are also common. Among the best known are those that occurred during disruptions associated with warfare. During World War I, newborn weights in Vienna declined sharply as the Austrian economy gradually collapsed, and they fell further as the economic crisis accelerated during the postwar inflationary spiral (Peller & Bass, 1924; Ward, 1993). Children born at the height of the siege of Leningrad (1941–1943) weighed 500–600 g less than normal, whereas those delivered in the Netherlands during the "Hunger Winter" of 1944–45 showed marked, though lesser, reductions (Antonov, 1947; Stein, 1975). Less severe circumstances have also been linked to lower birth weight means, including declines in England, the Netherlands, and northern Italy during the economic depression of the 1930s (Razzell, Spence, & Vines, 2004; Ward, 2003, 2006).

Over the long term, LBW rates have tended to move inversely with birth weight means, one rising and the other falling, in response to the same underlying causal structures. Increases in the proportion of LBW newborns have been particularly evident in the crisis circumstances just noted. However, no secular trend has been evident until the recent past. Between 1980 and 2010, the global LBW rate fell gradually, from 17% to 15% of live births (WHO, 1980, 2012). These reductions were achieved almost entirely in the developing world. In the developed world, LBW rates have increased during this period, notably in Japan (OECD, 2013; Takimoto, Yokoyama, Yoshiike, & Fukuoka, 2005). The growing use of fertility treatments; the increasing reliance on medical interventions during delivery, such as induction and caesarian section; and the rising maternal age of childbearing are all related to recent higher levels of LBW.

30.4 The Significance of Birth Weight

As a measure of human well-being, birth weight is associated with both individual and population health. Much of the early scientific interest in newborn size emerged from a medical concern for the relationship between gestational history and perinatal outcomes, particularly mortality. The recognition that neonatal weight could be used as an index of infant welfare was an important development in obstetric and pediatric medicine. The systematic weighing of children at birth and in the first weeks of life provided clinicians and their patients with a simple way to assess the welfare of newborns during their early, vulnerable moments. The growing acceptance of the concept of LBW and its 2,500 g threshold created a benchmark to identify high-risk infants, and, even though its limitations have been acknowledged, its practical utility remains largely unimpaired. In the developed world, weighing newborns has long been universal, and the practice continues to spread in the developing world, with the identification of high-risk newborns a leading goal.

Globally, LBW newborns are approximately 20 times more likely to die than heavier infants (United Nations Children's Fund and World Health Organization, 2004), although their mortality rates are substantially lower in the developed world. For this reason, weighing newborns systematically, identifying infants exposed to higher morbidity and mortality risk, and understanding the causes of LBW remain primary goals of worldwide prenatal and neonatal health care.

The implications of newborn weight for health beyond infancy have attracted growing interest as well. An early study of male Dutch military recruits born during the hunger winter of 1944–45 revealed no long-term effects of substantial nutritional deprivation on health, stature, or mental performance, apart from a small increase in abnormalities of the central nervous system (Stein, 1975, pp. 229–236). Subsequent studies, however, have identified relationships between LBW and a range of health problems in later life. In an extensive series of papers, David Barker and colleagues have demonstrated an association between LBW and adult illnesses, including hypertension, coronary heart disease, and non-insulin-dependent diabetes (Barker, 1993, 1998; Osmond & Barker, 2000). Other studies have confirmed these associations and offer evidence of links between birth weight and such disparate phenomena as young adult cognitive functioning, reproductive success, cancer, and all-cause adult mortality (dos Santos Silva, De Stavola, & McCormack, 2008; Lummaa, 2003; Rich-Edwards et al., 1997; Risnes et al., 2011; Sørensen et al., 1997). Barker has hypothesized that gestational undernutrition programs patterns in fetal metabolic and structural growth that have lifelong implications for health, predisposing individuals to a range of disease conditions in their later years. But he also has cautioned that birth weight is a crude measure of fetal development and that the pathways linking nutrition to in utero growth are not well understood (Barker, 1998). Critics of the Barker hypothesis note that the effects of fetal malnutrition on health over the long term may occur independently of birth weight and that they may not be evident even in instances of LBW (Lumey, 1998, p. 133). They also caution against the assumption that the relationship between birthweight and later health outcomes is causal, noting that the pathways remain poorly understood and that the concept of LBW is imprecise and uninformative (Wilcox, 2001).

Beyond infancy, birth weight serves as a broad indicator of population health and the health of women in particular. The importance of this fact should not be overlooked. Insights into the social condition of women are often more elusive than those concerning men and, as a small but suggestive number of studies have demonstrated, birth weight offers a means of countering this disadvantage (Rosenberg, 1988; Ward, 1993, 2006). The benefit is particularly important in communities where the inequality of the sexes systematically disadvantages girls and women in relationship to boys and men. To choose one common example, in societies experiencing chronic undernutrition, males often enjoy a nutritional advantage over their feminine relations because they benefit from practices and customs that prefer their needs over those of females.

30.5 Conclusion

As the product of factors whose individual contributions cannot be specified precisely, birth weight is a summary measure, commonly reported with other vital statistics. First employed in this manner during the mid-20th century, it has become one of many indices used to describe health conditions and identify public health problems (Gruenwald, 1968; Mironov, 2007; World Health Organization & Expert Committee on Maternal and Child Health, 1950). WHO, UNICEF, and the World Bank, as well as many national governments, regularly publish national data on birth weight. Historians have deployed it in a similar manner to explore infant and maternal health in earlier times (Rosenberg, 1988; Goldin & Margo, 1989; Ward, 1993). The widespread availability of this information permits comparisons over time and across geographic space.

Yet, despite the many influences on fetal growth and the broad meanings attributed to birth weight, its influence on health outcomes is not entirely clear. Although many associations link LBW with health in infancy and later life, association is not causation. Thus, neonatal weight remains principally a broad index of newborn health, one influenced by a wide range of factors, changes in which may affect well-being over the entire life course.

References

Ananth, C. V., & Wen, S. W. (2002). Trends in fetal growth among singleton gestations in the United States and Canada, 1985 through 1998. *Seminars in Perinatology, 26*, 260–267.

Antonov, A. N. (1947). Children born during the siege of Leningrad in 1942. *Journal of Pediatrics, 30*(3), 250–259.

Barker, D. J. P. (1993). Fetal and infant origins of adult disease: Papers. *British Medical Journal, 311*, 171–174.

Barker, D. J. P. (1998). In utero programming of chronic disease. *Clinical Science, 95*(2), 115–128.

Blondel, B., & Kermarrec, M. (2011). *Enquête nationale périnatale: Les naissances en 2010 et leur évolution depuis 2003*. Paris: Institut national de la santé et de la recherche médicale.

Cole, T. J. (2000). Secular trends in growth. *Proceedings of the Nutrition Society, 59*(2), 317–324.

Costa, D. L. (1998). Unequal at birth: a long-term comparison of income and birth weight. *Journal of Economic History, 58*(4), 987–1009.

Dadvand, P., Parker, J., Bell, M. L., Bonzini, M., Brauer, M., Darrow, L. A., . . . Woodruff, T. J. (2013). Maternal exposure to particulate air pollution and term birth weight: A multi-country evaluation of effect and heterogeneity. *Environmental Health Perspectives, 121*(3), 267–373.

Donahue, S. M. A., Kleinman, K. P., Gillman, M. W., & Oken, E. (2010). Trends in birth weight and gestational length among singleton term births in the United States: 1990–2005. *Obstetrics and Gynecology, 115*(2), 357.

dos Santos Silva, I., De Stavola, B., & McCormack, V. (2008). Birth size and breast cancer risk: Re-analysis of individual participant data from 32 studies. *PLoS One Medicine, 5*, E193.

Duncan, J. M. (1864). On the weight and length of the newly-born child in relation to the mother's age. *Edinburgh Medical Journal, 10*, 497–502.

Ericson, A., Eriksson, M., Källén, B., & Zetterström, R. (1989). Socio-economic variables and pregnancy outcome birthweight in singletons. *Acta Paediatrica, 78*(s360), 48–55.

Frankenhäuser, F. (1859). Über einige verhältnisse, die einfluss auf die stärkere oder schwächere entwickelung der frucht während der schwangerschaft haben. *Monatsschrift für Geburtskunde und Frauenkrankheiten, 13*, 170–179.

Garn, S. M., Shaw, H. A., & McCabe, K. D. (1977). Effects of socioeconomic status and race on weight-defined and gestational prematurity in the United States. In D. Reed (Ed.), *The epidemiology of prematurity* (pp. 127–143). Baltimore: Urban and Schwarzenberg.

Goldin, C., & Margo, R. A. (1989). The poor at birth: Birth weights and infant mortality at Philadelphia's Almshouse Hospital, 1848–1873. *Explorations in Economic History, 26*(3), 360–379.

Goldstein, H. (1981). Factors related to birth weight and perinatal mortality. *British Medical Bulletin, 37*(3), 259–264.

Gruenwald, P. (1968). Fetal growth as an indicator of socioeconomic change. *Public Health Reports, 83*(10), 867–872.

Hystad, P., Davies, H. D., Frank, L., Van Loon, J., Gehring, U., Tamburic, L., & Brauer, M. (2014). Residential greenness and birth outcomes: Evaluating the influence of spatially correlated built-environment factors. *Environmental Health Perspectives, 122*(10), 1095–1102.

Juárez, S. P. (2011). *Qué es lo que importa del peso al nacer: La paradoja epidemiológica en la población inmigrada de la comunidad de Madrid.* PhD thesis, Universidad Complutense de Madrid.

Juárez, S., Ploubidis, G. B., & Clarke, L. (2014). Revisiting the 'low birthweight paradox' using a model-based definition. *Gaceta Sanitaria, 28*(2), 160–162.

Lechtig, A., Yarbrough, C., Delgado, H., Habicht, J. P., Martorell, R., & Klein, R. E. (1975). Influence of maternal nutrition on birth weight. *American Journal of Clinical Nutrition, 28*(11), 1223–1233.

Lumey, L. H. (1998). Reproductive outcomes in women prenatally exposed to undernutrition: A review of findings from the Dutch Famine Birth Cohort. *Proceedings of the Nutrition Society, 57*(1), 129–135.

Lummaa, V. (2003). Early developmental conditions and reproductive success in humans: Downstream effects of prenatal famine, birthweight, and timing of birth. *American Journal of Human Biology, 15*(3), 370–379.

Metgud, C. S., Naik, V. A., & Mallapur, M. D. (2012). Factors affecting birth weight of a newborn–a community based study in rural Karnataka, India. *PloS One, 7*(7), E40040.

Mironov, B. (2007). Birth weight and physical stature in St. Petersburg: Living standards of women in Russia, 1980–2005. *Economics & Human Biology, 5*(1), 123–143.

Odier, L. R. (1868). *Recherches sur la loi d'accroissement des nouveau-nés constaté par le système des pesées régulières et sur les conditions d'un bon allaitement*. Paris: Germer-Baillière.

OECD. (2013). Infant health: Low birth weight. In *Health at a glance 2013: OECD indicators* (pp. 38–39). Paris: Author.

Osmond, C., & Barker, D. J. (2000). Fetal, infant, and childhood growth are predictors of coronary heart disease, diabetes, and hypertension in adult men and women. *Environmental Health Perspectives, 108*(Suppl. 3), 545–553.

Peller, S., & Bass, F. (1924). Die rolle exogener faktoren in der intrauterinen entwicklung des menschen mit besonderer berücksichtigung der kriegs-und nachkriegsverhältnisse. *Archiv für Gynäkologie, 122*(1–2), 208–238.

Persson, L., Arifeen, S., Ekström, E., Rasmussen, K. M., Fronqillo, E. A., Yunus, M., . . . MINIMat Study Team. (2012). Effects of prenatal micronutrient and early food supplementation on maternal hemoglobin, birth weight, and infant mortality among children in Bangladesh: The Minimat Randomized Trial. *Journal of the American Medical Association, 307*(19), 2050–2059.

Peters, T. J., Golding, J., Butler, N. R., Fryer, J. G., Lawrence, C. J., & Chamberlain, G. V. P. (1983). Plus ça change: Predictors of birthweight in two national studies. *British Journal of Obstetrics and Gynaecology, 90*(11), 1040–1045.

Pinard, A. (1878). Foetus. I. Anatomie et physiologie. In *Dictionnaire encyclopédic des sciences médicles* (pp. 452–535). Paris: Masson.

Pinard, A. (1895). Note pour servir à l'histoire de la puériculture intrauterine. *Bulletin de l'Académie de Médecine, 3rd series, 34*, 594–595.

Pinard, A. (1899). *Clinique obstétricale*. Paris: G. Steinheil.

Quetelet, A. (1835). *Sur l'homme et le développement de ses facultés ou essai de physique sociale* (Vol. *II*). Paris: Bachelier.

Razzell, P., Spence, C., & Vines, K. (2004). Poverty, birthweight, and infant weight gain in Hertfordshire, 1923–1939. *International Journal of Epidemiology, 33*(6), 1228–1233.

Rich-Edwards, J. W., Stampfer, M. J., Manson, J. E., Rosner, B., Hankinson, S. E., Colditz, G. A., . . . Willet, W. C. (1997). Birth weight and risk of cardiovascular disease in a cohort of women followed up since 1976. *British Medical Journal, 315*(7015), 396–400.

Risnes, K. R., Vatten, L. J., Baker, J. L., Jameson, K., Sovio, U., Kajantie, E., . . . Bracken, M. B. (2011). Birthweight and mortality in adulthood: A systematic review and meta-analysis. *International Journal of Epidemiology, 40*(3), 647–661.

Rosenberg, M. (1988). Birth weights in three Norwegian cities, 1860–1984: Secular trends and influencing factors. *Annals of Human Biology, 15*(4), 275–288.

Saurel-Cubizolles, M. J., & Kaminski, M. (1986). Work in pregnancy: Its evolving relationship with perinatal outcome (a review). *Social Science & Medicine, 22*(4), 431–442.

Shah, P. S., Zao, J., & Ali, S. (2011). Maternal marital status and birth outcomes: A systematic review and meta-analyses. *Maternal and Child Health Journal, 15*(7), 1097–1109.

Sørensen, H. T., Sabroe, S., Olsen, J., Rothman, K. J., Gillman, M. W., & Fischer, P. (1997). Birth weight and cognitive function in young adult life: Historical cohort study. *British Medical Journal, 315*(7105), 401–403.

Stein, Z. (1975). *Famine and human development: The Dutch Hunger Winter of 1944–1945*. New York: Oxford University Press.

Takimoto, H., Yokoyama, T., Yoshiike, N., & Fukuoka, H. (2005). Increase in low-birth weight infants in Japan and associated risk factors, 1980–2000. *Journal of Obstetrics and Gynaecology Research, 31*(4), 314–322.

Tanner, J. M. (1981). *A history of the study of human growth.* Cambridge, UK: Cambridge University Press.

UNICEF. (2012). *The state of the world's children 2012: Children in an urban world.* New York: United Nations Publications.

United Nations Children's Fund and World Health Organization. (2004). *Low birth-weight: Country, regional and global estimates.* New York: UNICEF.

Veit, G. (1855). Beiträge zur geburtshülflichen Statistik. *Monatsschrift für Geburtskunde und Frauenkrankheiten, 5*, 344–381.

Veit, G. (1856). Beiträge zur geburtshülflichen Statistik. *Monatsschrift für Geburtskunde und Frauenkrankheiten, 6* 101–132.

von Hecker, C. (1866). Über das gewicht des fötus und seiner anhänge in den verschiedenen monaten der schwangerschaft. *Monatsschrift für Geburtskunde und Frauenkrankheiten, 27*, 286–299.

Ward, W. P. (1993). *Birth weight and economic growth: Women's living standards in the industrializing west.* Chicago: University of Chicago Press.

Ward, W. P. (2003). Perinatal mortality in Utrecht, the Netherlands, 1880–1940. *Economics and Human Biology, 1*(3), 379–398.

Ward, W. P. (2006). Women's health, size at birth, and socio-economic change Bologna, Italy, 1880–1940. *Popolazione e Storia, 2*, 85–108.

Wilcox, A. J. (2001). On the importance—and the unimportance—of birthweight. *International Journal of Epidemiology, 30*(6), 1233–1241.

Wilcox, A. J., & Russell, I. T. (1983). Birthweight and perinatal mortality. I. On the frequency distribution of birthweight. *International Journal of Epidemiology, 12*, 314–318.

World Health Organization. (1980). *World Health Statistics 1980.* Geneva: World Health Organization.

World Health Organization. (2012). *World Health Statistics 2012.* Geneva: World Health Organization.

World Health Organization & Expert Committee on Maternal and Child Health. (1950). *Public health aspect of low birth weight.* WHO Technical report series. Author.

Zamudio, S., Postigo, L., Illsley, N. P., Rodriguez, C., Heredia, G., Brimacombe, M., . . . Vargas, E. 2007 Maternal oxygen delivery is not related to altitude-and ancestry-associated differences in human fetal growth. *Journal of Physiology, 582*(2), 883–895.

CHAPTER 31

A POUND OF FLESH

The Use of Birthweight as a Measure of Human Capital Endowment in Economics Research

FLORENCIA TORCHE AND DALTON CONLEY

MOUNTING evidence suggests that exposures during the prenatal period have long-lasting consequences for health and cognition, education, earnings, and other determinants of economic well-being. Pioneered by the fetal origins approach (Barker, 1990, 1995; Barker & Osmond, 1986) and elaborated by theories of early human capital formation (Cunha & Heckman, 2007; Heckman, 2006, 2007), this approach indicates that the prenatal period is among the critical developmental stages of the life course and, moreover, sensitive to the environment, such that even mild shocks can have enduring effects (Almond & Currie, 2011). Some of these effects are immediate and translate into infant mortality and health difficulties (Conley, Strully, & Bennett, 2003) and adversity in childhood (Chatterji, Kim, & Lahiri, 2014*a*, 2014*b*), while others are latent and emerge only in adulthood (Barker, 1990, 1995; Chen & Zhang, 2011) or reverberate through the life course (Dessi, Puddu, Ottonello, & Fanos, 2013).

Birthweight has gained relevance as a measure of prenatal exposures and proxy for health status at the starting gate of life. Birthweight is relatively easy to measure and contains little measurement error, particularly when obtained from vital records. A continuous variable, birthweight is usually recoded as an ordinal variable distinguishing very low birthweight (VLBW; <1,500 g), low birthweight (LBW; <2,500 g), normal weight (2,500–4,000 g), and macrosomia (>4,000 or >5,000 g). Although arbitrary, the lower thresholds LBW and particularly VLBW identify infants who are most at risk for mortality, morbidity, and developmental problems (Eikenes, Lohaugen, Brubakk, Skranes, & Haberg, 2011; Kline, Stein, & Susser, 1989; Madzwamuse, Baumann, Jaekel, Bartmann, & Wolke, 2015), and they are used to target interventions to promote children's well-being in the developed and developing world (e.g., Bale, Stoll, & Lucas, 2003; Brooks-Gunn et al., 1994). Mean birthweight increased in most of the world since the mid-20th century, but it has declined in the United States and other advanced industrial countries in the past two decades. Part of this decline is attributable to the increasing rates of live births of preterm babies due to obstetric interventions, labor induction, and, to a lesser extent, elective cesarean sections; but, for unknown reasons fetal growth has also declined independently of gestational age (Morisaki, Esplin, Varner, Henry, & Oken, 2013; Oken, 2013). Finally, the socio-demographic and racial composition of the neonatal population has shifted such that higher risk groups (such as minorities and low-income households) are more prevalent than they were before (Collins & David, 2009; Heisler, 2012).

Social scientists have deployed birthweight as a sensitive measure that reflects both maternal health care inputs as well as the impacts of stressors and environmental toxicants. Research using causal inference techniques has identified the effect on birthweight of exposure to acute stressors and toxicants such as natural disasters (Currie & Rossin-Slater, 2013; Torche, 2011), war (Mansour & Rees, 2012; Torche & Shwed, 2015), civil conflict (Camacho, 2008) pollution and particulate matter (Currie & Walker, 2011; Currie et al., 2011; Currie & Schwandt, 2014), cigarette smoking (Lien & Evans, 2005), among other exposures. The literature also documents the positive effect of policies intended to improve the nutritional wellbeing the population (Hoynes, Miller, & Simon, 2015; Hoynes, Page, & Stevens, 2011). As the literature becomes more sophisticated, an increasing concern with selection and biological and social mechanisms accounting for the effects of exposure is emerging (Torche & Villarreal, 2014).

Birthweight also has been examined as a measure of endowment at birth that—unlike genotype—can be observed readily by parents who may make investment and resource allocation decisions within the household in an exacerbating (i.e., efficiency maximizing) or compensatory (equalizing) manner in response to the observed endowments of their offspring. Indeed, in theory, differential investment in children by birthweight may be part of the mechanism by which the effects of "a pound of flesh" manifest.

31.1 A Genealogy of Research on the Effect of Birthweight: From Correlations to Natural Experiments

Early medical and epidemiological studies focused on the simple association between birthweight and short-term health outcomes. Abundant evidence demonstrated that LBW babies are more likely to die soon after birth, and, if they survive, they are more likely to experience health and developmental problems (see, e.g., Hack et al., 2002). VLBW babies are most at risk of severe neurosensory and developmental handicaps, but variation in birthweight among babies heavier than 1,500 and even 2,500 g also appears to be relevant (Hack et al., 1995; Wade, Browne, Madigan, Plamondon, & Jenkins, 2014). This literature has been expanded to include outcomes beyond early life and health measures and has attempted to include controls to address the important problem of unobserved heterogeneity (i.e., the fact that birthweight is correlated with biological and social factors including genetic diversity, mother's behavior during pregnancy, and access to social support, among others that may have an independent effect on the outcomes of interest). Research attempting to account for these potential confounders by adding controls in a multivariate model framework has shown a detrimental effect of low birthweight on children's developmental outcomes (Boardman, Powers, Padilla, & Hummer, 2002; Shenkin, Starr, & Deary, 2004) and education (Corman & Chaikind, 1998; Currie & Hyson, 1999; Hack et al., 2002). However, others have found the effect of birthweight to weaken after controls such as mother's education and other indicators of socioeconomic status are included (Richards, Hardy, Kuh, & Wadsworth, 2001; Shenkin et al., 2001), suggesting spuriousness mainly driven by socioeconomic disadvantage.

Given the difficulty in measuring all potential confounders, a second generation of research has used within-family, between-siblings (and sometimes between-cousins) comparisons to assess the effect of birthweight. By comparing birthweight and outcomes within families, this research accounts for any family-specific sources of confounding that do not vary over time or across children (e.g., family norms and some portion of genetic variation, given that siblings share half of their genomes on average). Studies using sibling comparisons show a negative effect of birthweight on outcomes during childhood or early adulthood such as children's cognitive ability (Conley, Pfeiffer, & Velez, 2007; Fletcher, 2011; Lawlor, Bor, O'Callaghan, Williams, & Najman, 2005) and educational attainment (Conley & Bennett, 2000; Fletcher, 2011), as well as on the weight of the next generation (Currie & Moretti, 2007).

Studies based on sibling comparisons do not account for time-varying characteristics of the family, the pregnancy, the upbringing of the child, or for a portion of genetic differences. As a result, they are susceptible to bias if, for example, pregnancies occurred in different economic circumstances or if the mother smoked in one pregnancy but not the other. More recent research uses comparison between twins and other natural experiments to address the remaining sources of confounding. These strategies are claimed to provide a strong test of the causal effect of birthweight. Because twins share the same pregnancy, any characteristic of the mother and pregnancy is equivalent. Furthermore, because monozygotic twins share all their genes, between-twin comparisons of identical twins also account for any source of genetic variation that may be correlated with both birthweight and the outcome of interest.

A small cottage industry on the effect of birthweight on short-, medium-, and long-range outcomes using twin fixed effects exists. Research has shown an effect of between-twins differences in birthweight on short-range outcomes such as infant mortality and scores in the Apgar test, which is given to newborns to evaluate their physical condition (Almond, Chay, & Lee, 2005; Black, Devereux, & Salvanes, 2007; Conley, Strully, & Bennett, 2006; Oreopoulos, Stabile, Walld, & Roos, 2008); on medium-range outcomes such as children's cognitive outcomes (Conley, Pfeiffer, & Velez, 2007; Figlio, Guryan, Karbownik, & Roth, 2013; Newcombe, Milne, Caspi, Poulton, & Moffitt, 2007; Pettersson et al., 2015; Torche & Echevarría, 2011); and on long-range outcomes such as education and labor market outcomes (Behrman & Rosenzweig, 2004; Black et al., 2007; Oreopoulos et al., 2008; Royer, 2009) and even on the birthweight of the next generation (Royer, 2009).

Comparison of birthweight effects based on monozygotic twins fixed effects, on the one hand, and sibling models or cross-family models that merely control for observed covariates, on the other, shows that the effect of birthweight (read: fetal growth per se) on short-run health outcomes such as neonatal and infant mortality is smaller than was initially suspected (Almond et al., 2005; Black et al., 2007; Oreopolous et al., 2008). This decline in the magnitude of parameters suggests that genetic factors play a substantial role in accounting for the effect of birthweight and early mortality and health. The differences may also be due to the fact that twin models factor out gestational age, which itself may significantly contribute to mortality risk over and above weight at birth. In contrast, the effect of birthweight on longer term cognitive, educational, and labor market outcomes captured by twin comparisons seems to be similar or larger in magnitude than effects captured by cross-sectional or siblings models. Most likely these differences have to do with the different parts of the birthweight distribution on which twin and singleton births fall. Namely, since twin birthweights are shifted to the left—where each additional ounce may matter more—it does not seem surprising that the twin difference models yield higher estimates. These differences in the estimates for long-term effects may also be due to exacerbation of differences in parental investment within families in response to differences in endowment perceived at birth by birthweight discordance, an issue we turn to later in this chapter.

Natural experiments, in turn, exploit occurrences allocated at random that affect birthweight to examine its effects on later development. For example, temporal and spatial (i.e., latitudinal) variation in Ramadan-induced fasting among Muslims provides a plausibly random source of birthweight variation (Almond & Mazumder, 2011). That is, because fasting takes place during daylight hours, those further from the equator have either longer (if Ramadan falls during summer months) or shorter (if Ramadan occurs in the winter months) periods without food each day. Exposure to historically specific famines (Lumey, Stein, Kahn, & Romijn, 2009; Schulz, 2010) may provide a natural experiment for the effect of birthweight under the (strong) assumption that no other pathways of influence linking famine exposure to later outcomes is present.

That said, although birthweight may be tempting to use as an instrumental variable for educational attainment or cognitive ability (especially twin or sibling differences in birthweight or birthweight predicted by an exogenous shock), it likely fails the exclusion restriction. For example, some researchers have suggested using birthweight to instrument educational attainment in a wage regression to obtain an unbiased estimate of the returns to schooling (Behrman & Rosenzweig, 2004). However, it is probable that birthweight has direct effects on wages through health, noncognitive ability, or educational achievement (which is poorly proxied by years of schooling or degree attainment). Thus, although reduced-form estimations of the impact of birthweight on any of these outcomes (or others such as parental investment, for instance) are likely to be consistent, using birthweight as an instrument is ill-advised (Angrist, Imbens, & Rubin, 1996; Angrist & Krueger, 2001; Bound & Solon, 1999).

31.2 What Is the Effect Being Identified by Twin Fixed-Effects Models?

Within-twin comparisons and other natural experiments provide perhaps the "cleanest" source of identification for the effect of birthweight by accounting for mother's, pregnancy-specific, and (in the case of monozygotic twins) genetic sources of confounding. The tradeoff is the narrowness of the effect captured. Birthweight has but two proximate determinants: gestational age and intrauterine fetal growth. These determinants have different etiologies and consequences (Hobel, Goldstein, & Barrett, 2008; Paneth, 1995). Twins do not vary in gestational age, so the only source of variation in birthweight in twin comparisons is differences in fetal growth. Within-twin pair comparison is based on the assumption that birthweight discrepancy between twins (particularly monozygotic twins) emerges solely from random differences in access to nutritional intakes resulting, for example, from position in the uterus or umbilical cord attachment to the placenta. (Among monozygotic twins, there are other sources of variation above and beyond genetic differences, such as differences in chorionic or placental architecture if the twins are dichorionic or diplacental—but these, too, are thought to be random, at least after controlling for genotype.) As a result of this assumption of randomness, the effect captured is that of nutritional and oxygen deficits in utero only.

Although it is important to isolate this effect, the main cause of low birthweight in advanced industrial countries is gestational age rather than fetal growth restriction. About 70% of low-weight births in developed countries are preterm but normal-for-gestational age (Falkner, Holzgreve, & Schloo, 1994). The etiology of preterm birth is still not fully clear, and it is increasingly recognized that it is a syndrome with multiple etiologies correlated with sociodemographic, behavioral, and sociodemographic factors, as well as with medical conditions and environmental toxicants (for a review, see Behrman & Butler, 2007). The proximate biological pathways leading to preterm birth include neuroendocrine mechanisms involving the hypothalamic-pituitary-adrenal (HPA) axis (Baibazarova et al., 2013; Dunkel-Schetter, 2011), infection (Whidbey et al., 2015), amniotic inflammation (Combs et al., 2014), and gestational diabetes and/or preeclampsia (Hedderson, Ferrara, & Sacks, 2003; Hegaard, Pedersen, Bruun Nielsen, & Damm, 2007).

Additionally, much has been made of the comparison of birthweight effects estimates in cross-sectional samples versus twin samples. But most of these comparisons do not restrict the measure to fetal growth (accounting for gestational age) in cross-sectional samples. As a result the comparison is not valid because estimates of the birthweight effects in cross-sectional samples are also (and largely in the United States and other advanced industrial countries) driven by variation in gestational age. To compound this problem, when gestational age is accounted for, sometimes it is measured as the simple quotient of birthweight and gestational age (Behrman & Rosenzweig, 2004; Royer, 2009). This quotient is strongly correlated with birthweight because fetal growth is nonlinear and picks up later in the pregnancy. The correct measure is the gestational age- and sex-specific birthweight percentile, sometimes dichotomized to distinguish small for gestational age (SGA) infants with birthweights below the gestational age-specific 10th percentile (Battaglia & Lubchenco, 1967).

Furthermore, twins have their own potential confounders, such as fetal transfusion syndrome, in which one monozygotic twin dominates the flow of nutrients and oxygen from a shared placenta, seriously compromising the health and development of the other (Sakata, Utsu, & Maeda, 2006). This, in itself, is not a problem for the internal validity of the design (i.e., the differences between twins can still be considered a random event), but such dynamics do raise important questions about the external validity or generalizability of twin-based studies (Behrman & Rosenzweig, 2004). One potential way to address this concern is to compare within-twin estimates based on monozygotic pairs (where this transfusion syndrome is a possibility) with those based on same-sex dizygotic pairs (where it is not). Of course, dizygotic pairs add genetic differences to the error term (dizygotic twins, like singleton siblings, share on average half their genomes). However, the placental architecture of dizygotic twins is more similar to that of singleton pregnancies, in which each twin has its own placenta and chorionic sack. (Another possibility is to compare monozygotic twin results from dichorionic and monochorionic sets; however, most studies do not have information about chorionicity.)

Concerns about the generalizability of both monozygotic and dizygotic twin analyses are amplified by questions about the etiology of birthweight for twins compared to singletons and the potential nonlinearity in the effect of birthweight (Behrman & Rosenzweig, 2004). If the smallness of twins results from factors other than twinning—in particular the selectivity of parents who produce twins—or if sharing the uterus alters fetal development (e.g., by fostering lung and brain maturation), then the results may not be extended to singletons. Furthermore, if the effect of birthweight varies across the weight distribution, then differences mostly at the lower end captured by twin-based studies may not extend to differences in birthweight in higher segments of the distribution.

31.3 Mechanisms for the Effect of Birthweight: From Biology to Behavioral Responses

Perhaps the most well-studied mechanism between LBW and negative outcomes is brain abnormality and development. Research has consistently shown that VLBW children in particular have restricted cortical development and lower total brain volume (Bjuland, Lohaugen, Martinussen, & Skranes, 2013; Bjuland, Rimol, Lohaugen, & Skranes, 2014; Ganella et al., 2015; Murray et al., 2014; Skranes et al., 2013). Moreover, even among VLBW children and normal controls with identical total brain volumes, structural abnormalities remain (Taylor et al., 2011). Others find positive associations between birthweight and cognitive function even above the normal threshold, suggesting a linear relationship between cortical development and weight (Wade et al., 2014). Robinson (2013) takes the unique approach of decomposing LBW infants into "symmetric" and "asymmetric" types: the former where all organs grow in unison, and the latter where the brain is "spared" and is not subject to the growth restriction of the fetus more generally. Asymmetric LBW children exhibited similar cognition to their peers in the normal range, suggesting an avenue for future research on the links between birthweight and brain development.

Although these mechanisms focus on direct biological pathways, another potential (yet unproved) mechanism linking LBW and outcomes is the differential treatment by parents, who may invest more resources in vulnerable children to compensate for disadvantage or exacerbate initial adversity by focusing investment on more robust siblings. Findings on whether parents distribute resources based on birthweight are mixed. Datar et al. (Datar, Kilburn, & Loughran, 2010) find that parents reinforce differences in birthweight between siblings, whereas Del Bono et al. (Del Bono, Ermisch, & Francesconi, 2012) find evidence of inequity aversion and disproportionate investment in more vulnerable children, using breastfeeding decisions as a proxy for resource allocation. Other studies find no significant associations between differences in birthweight and parental investments among siblings (Kelly, 2011; Lynch & Brooks, 2013; Royer, 2009).

Parental responses may also account for the socioeconomic heterogeneity of birthweight effects if advantaged parents are more able to compensate for the detrimental effect on LBW and/or disadvantaged parents are more likely to reinforce initial disadvantage (i.e., invest in the higher birthweight child in any way, thus exacerbating the disadvantage of the low-weight child). In this vein, Hsin (2012) and Restrepo (2012) use sibling fixed effects and find that better-educated mothers attempt to compensate for the initial disadvantage of LBW by investing more in the lower weight child, but less-educated mothers do not.

This could potentially reflect material and time constraints in a deprived context, which prevents less-advantaged parents from compensating. Research using measures other than birthweight as proxy for early child ability and instrumental variable or twin fixed effects approaches to address the endogeneity of early ability has found that parents do invest more in robust siblings, but these studies do not address any systematic differences among advantaged or disadvantaged families (Aizer & Cunha, 2012; Frijters, Johnston, & Shah, 2013). Furthermore, very few studies address socioeconomic heterogeneity of parental responses.

31.4 Recent Topics

31.4.1 The Heterogeneity of the Effect of Birthweight

Increasingly, researchers have moved from the aggregate effect of birthweight to variation along multiple dimensions, including levels of birthweight, gestational age, genetic profile, and family socioeconomic status (SES). Some research finds the effect of nutritional and oxygen uterine environment is stronger at lower levels, suggesting "diminishing returns" to marginal increases in birthweight (Almond et al., 2005; Black et al., 2007; Chatterji et al., 2014*a*), although other studies show a close-to-linear association across the birthweight distribution (Behrman & Rosenzweig, 2004; Wade et al., 2014), and still others show a stronger effect above the 2,500 g LBW threshold (Royer, 2009). The same finding emerges across gestational age: the effect of fetal nutrition on infant mortality is substantial among preterm births (<37 weeks) but insignificant among term pregnancies (≥37 weeks) (Conley et al., 2006).

Race is another potential source of heterogeneity. It has long been observed that, in the US context at least, African Americans have a birthweight distribution that is shifted to the left of that for other groups (Spong, Iams, Goldenberg, Hauck, & Willinger, 2011). Even after accounting for standard socioeconomic factors such as age and education level (e.g., 38% of African-American children and youth live in poverty[1]), about three-quarters of black–white differences in LBW are left unexplained (Lhila & Long, 2012). One theory is that black mothers experience social stressors (e.g., discrimination) that affect their health and likelihood of having a LBW child. The "weathering" hypothesis holds that these disadvantages are cumulative, such that older women of color are at higher risk of having LBW children (Geronimus, 1991), and is supported by recent findings (Collins, Rankin, & Hibbs, 2015; Dennis & Mollborn, 2013). Living in minority–majority neighborhoods has also been found to have a protective effect on birthweight for African-American women (Madkour, Harville, & Xie, 2014; Vang & Elo, 2013), which suggests that social support and lower levels of discrimination are possible mediating factors. Other research has noted that African and Caribbean-born black women in the United States have significantly fewer LBW children compared to their US-born peers (Elo, Vang, & Culhane, 2014; Vang & Elo, 2013). The same is observed for Latin-American (particularly Mexican) women compared with their native-born counterparts (Lara, Gamboa, Kahramanian, Morales, & Bautista, 2005). This suggests that cultural factors may play an important role in explaining the stratification of birth outcomes between and among subpopulations (Abdou, Dominguez, & Myers, 2013).

Pertinent to the present discussion is the fact that survival rates for LBW babies also vary by race. The United States has the highest infant mortality rate in the developed world, with 6.6 per 1,000 live births, and infant mortality is more than twice higher among blacks than non-Hispanic whites (Collins & David, 2009; Heisler, 2012). Namely, whereas African Americans suffer from a distribution of birthweight that is shifted to the left of that for whites, the birthweight conditional mortality rates are lower for this population, even if their overall infant mortality rate is higher. LBW is 8% among whites but 16% among blacks,[2] four times as high as in Sweden or Finland.[3] This combination of smaller babies who appear more robust has led some scholars to suggest that African Americans have adapted to disadvantage in the United States (and in African before the epoch of the Middle Passage) by accelerating fetal maturation through genetic selection or continual environmental response in each generation (Geronimus, 1991). This highly speculative "weathering" hypothesis does not have a lot of empirical support, however. Indeed, when gestational age is controlled through the twin difference approach, fetal growth appears to have a larger effect on the survivability of African-American infants as compared to white infants (Conley & Strully, 2012)—meaning that holding gestational maturity constant, the effect of birthweight is bigger for blacks. That said, despite any mortality differences conditional on birthweight (or gestational age) differences, African Americans demonstrate the same negative developmental sequelae for LBW as their white counterparts (Conley et al., 2003).

In terms of socioeconomic variation, some research suggests a gradient, with a stronger effect of birthweight among disadvantaged families and virtually null effect among their advantaged peers (Torche & Echevarría, 2011). By the same token, Almond et al. (Almond, Edlund, & Palme, 2009) show that the negative effect of prenatal exposure to radioactivity following the Chernobyl explosion on cognitive outcomes is concentrated among lower class children. Others, however, find no variation across mother's education (Black et al., 2007; Figlio et al., 2013). Given that all these analyses use a twin fixed-effects approach—except for Almond et al. (2009) who use sibling fixed-effects—the divergence in findings cannot be attributed to dissimilar methodologies. Nor does it appear to emerge from differences in national contexts—socioeconomic variation is found in Chile and Sweden (Almond et al., 2009; Torche & Echevarría, 2011) but is found to be absent in Norway and the state of Florida (Black et al., 2007; Figlio et al., 2013). More research is necessary to understand socioeconomic variation in the effect of birthweight and its determinants, including the potentially important role of stratified parental responses

A recent frontier of stratification is genetic markers. Along the lines of the "differential sensitivity" hypothesis (Belsky, 1997; Belsky & Pluess, 2009; Belsky, 2013), birthweight has no effect on cognition during late adolescence among individuals without genetic variants thought to be associated with plasticity ("dandelions"), but a strong effect among who do have the labile versions of those alleles ("orchids") (Cook & Fletcher, 2015).

Related research focusing on phenotypical variation in child temperament has found that infants prone to distress were particularly susceptible to the effects of negative parenting techniques (Poehlmann et al., 2011) and that sensitive parenting may even close the cognitive gap between low and normal birthweight children (Wolke, Jaekel, Hall, & Baumann, 2013). Work that employs twin fixed effects, however, has found that the interaction between genetic background and environment is largely insignificant in predicting outcomes, thus stressing the need for addressing endogeneity in future research (Conley & Rauscher, 2012).

The gene-environment interaction (G×E) literature is one in which it is particularly important to deploy both monozygotic twins and dizygotic twins. In the case of monozygotic twins—as already discussed—we can know that the birthweight differences are themselves randomly assigned to each twin. However, since identical twins share 100% of their genome, the genetic part of the interaction effect must be estimated off between-pair differences, which themselves may be correlated with unobserved environmental differences, thus biasing the estimate. However, dizygotic twins offer the opportunity to estimate genetic effects through random assignment at conception of parental alleles through within-twin set discordances at particular loci. Of course, the birthweight differences between dizygotic twins—as already discussed—are partly genetic and partly random differences in uterine environment due to implantation position.

The solution, then, is to estimate main genetic effects using dizygotic twins and main birthweight effects using monozygotic twins. The interaction effects can be estimated in both populations as a check. If they converge, then the researcher can be confident as to their consistency. This is the approach used by Conley and Rauscher (2012) with data from the National Longitudinal Survey of Adolescent Health (Add Health). In this study, they treat lower birthweight as an environmental insult that they interact with genotype (the serotonin transporter promoter region copy number variant, to be specific). The results obtain in the opposite direction of prior studies (cf. Caspi et al., 2003), thus highlighting the value of birthweight as an exogenous shock and the importance of such exogeneity in G×E research.

31.4.2 How Big Is Too Big? The Consequences of Fetal Macrosomia

To date, the question about consequences of birthweight largely has been focused on LBW. But the proportion of births that are high-weight or macrosomic (diversely defined as >4,000, >4,500, or >5,000 g) has doubled between 1990 and 2008 in the United States, partly because of increasing obesity, pregnancy weight gain, and gestational diabetes (Fraser & Lawlor, 2014; Leddy, Power, & Schulkin, 2008; Oken, 2013). Fetal macrosomia predicts negative outcomes during delivery and the immediate neonatal period, including prolonged labor, operative deliveries, shoulder dystocia, perinatal asphyxia, and other birth trauma resulting in neonatal unit admission (Santangeli, Sattar, & Huda, 2015; Zhang, Decker, Platt, & Kramer, 2008). Macrosomia is linked not only to high weight but also to a changes in actual body composition, with an increase in hyperinsulinemic birth and increased adipocyte size and number, potentially contributing to childhood and adolescence obesity, type-2 diabetes, and cardiovascular disease (Johnsson, Haglund, Ahlsson, & Gustafsson, 2014; Santangeli et al., 2015; Skilton et al., 2014). An important question is whether high birthweight has an impact on other outcomes, such as cognitive ability and educational attainment, and the mechanisms for such effect. To the best of our knowledge, the current evidence is extremely limited (e.g., Kristensen et al., 2014), and more research using plausible identification strategies is needed to address this question.

31.4.3 Mitigation

Because LBW has a complex etiology that makes prevention and intervention difficult, some researchers have explored ways to mitigate its effects. With respect to physical health, some experimental studies have shown that omega-3 lipid supplementation in infancy has been linked to attenuated cardiovascular problems in LBW children (Skilton, Raitakari, & Celermajer, 2013; Skilton et al., 2014). Exercise and physical activity early in life also appear to be important to cardiovascular and metabolic function in adulthood, whereby active, fit, LBW adults exhibit similar health outcomes to their normal birthweight peers, while associations between birthweight and metabolic syndrome are accentuated in the unfit (Siebel, Carey, & Kingwell, 2012). In terms of cognition, Duncan and Sojourner (2013) use random assignment into childhood intervention programs to show that they are particularly helpful for lower income children and would essentially eliminate income-based cognitive gaps among those with LBW. Although these results are promising, the research on ameliorating the effects of LBW is still limited, requiring more work to confidently draw conclusions.

31.5 Conclusion

In sum, birthweight is an important marker of individual health/human capital endowments at the starting gate of life, one that is shaped by environmental influences and predictive of later development and attainment. The recent social-scientific literature has moved from empirical associations to diverse strategies to assess the causal effects of birthweight. The recent literature is also starting to integrate biological and behavioral perspectives to the understanding of birthweight determinants and outcomes. We expect this topic to be a focus of continued attention in many disciplines because of the increasing availability of birthweight data and the growing recognition that the early life course has long-lasting and significant consequences on attainment and well-being.

Notes

1. http://www.census.gov/hhes/www/poverty/data/historical/people.html table 3.
2. http://www.cdc.gov/nchs/data/nvsr/nvsr62/nvsr62_09.pdf p. 55.
3. http://whqlibdoc.who.int/publications/2004/9280638327.pdf p. 11.

REFERENCES

Abdou, C. M., Dominguez, T. P., & Myers, H. F. (2013). Maternal familism predicts birthweight and asthma symptoms three years later. *Social Science and Medicine, 76*, 28–38.

Aizer, A., & Cunha, F. (2012). *The production of human capital: Endowments, investments and fertility* (Working Paper No. 18429). National Bureau of Economic Research.

Almond, D., Chay, K. Y., & Lee, D. S. (2005). The costs of low birth weight. *Quarterly Journal of Economics, 120*, 1031–1083.

Almond, D., Edlund, L., & Palme, M. (2009). Chernobyl's subclinical legacy: Exposure to radioactive fallout and school outcomes in Sweden. *Quarterly Journal of Economics, 124*(4), 1729–1772.

Almond, D., & Currie, J. (2011). Killing me softly: The fetal origins hypothesis. *Journal of Economic Perspectives, 25*(3), 153-172.

Almond, D., & Mazumder, B. (2011). Health capital and the prenatal environment: The effect of Ramadan observance during pregnancy. *American Economic Journal: Applied Economics, 3*(4), 56–85.

Angrist, J. D., Imbens, G. W., & Rubin, D. B. (1996). Identification of causal effects using instrumental variables. *Journal of the American statistical Association, 91*(434), 444–455.

Angrist, J., & Krueger, A. B. (2001). *Instrumental variables and the search for identification: From supply and demand to natural experiments* (Working Paper No. 8456). National Bureau of Economic Research.

Baibazarova, E., van de Beek, C., Cohen-Kettenis, P. T., Buitelaar, J., Shelton, K. H., & van Goozen, S. M. H. (2013). Influence of prenatal maternal stress, maternal plasma cortisol and cortisol in the amniotic fluid on birth outcomes and child temperament at 3 months. *Psychoneuroendocrinology, 38*, 907–915.

Bale, J. R., Stoll, B. J., & Lucas, A. O. (2003). The problem of low birthweight. In J.R. Bale, B.J. Stoll, & A.O. Lucas (Eds.), *Improving birth outcomes: Meeting the challenge in the developing world* (pp. 205-235). Washington DC: National Academies Press.

Barker, D. J. (1990). The fetal and infant origins of adult disease. *British Medical Journal, 301*, 1111.

Barker, D. J. (1995). Fetal origins of coronary heart disease. *British Medical Journal, 311*, 171.

Barker, D. J., & Osmond, C. (1986). Infant mortality, childhood nutrition, and ischaemic heart disease in England and Wales. *The Lancet, 327*(8489), 1077–1081.

Behrman, R., & Butler, A.S. (Eds). (2007). *Preterm birth: Causes, consequences, and prevention.* Washington, DC: National Academies Press.

Behrman, J. R., & Rosenzweig, M. R. (2004). Returns to birthweight. *The Review of Economics and Statistics, 86*(2), 586–601.

Belsky, J. (1997). Theory testing, effect-size evaluation, and differential susceptibility to rearing influence: The case of mothering and attachment. *Child Development, 68*(4), 598–600.

Belsky, J. (2013). Differential susceptibility to environmental influences. *International Journal of Child Care and Education Policy, 7*, 15–31.

Belsky, J., & Pluess, M. (2009). Beyond diathesis stress: Differential susceptibility to environmental influences. *Psychological Bulletin, 135*(6), 885–908.

Battaglia, F., & Lubchenco, L. (1967). A practical classification of newborn infants by weight and gestation age. *Pediatrics, 71*, 159–170.

Bjuland, K. J., Lohaugen, G. C. C., Martinussen, M., & Skranes, J. (2013). Cortical thickness and cognition in very-low-birth-weight late teenagers. *Early Human Development, 89*, 371–380.

Bjuland, K. J., Rimol, L. M., Lohaugen, G. C. C., & Skranes, J. (2014). Brain volumes and cognitive function in very-low-birth-weight (VLBW) young adults. *European Journal of Pediatric Neurology*, *18*, 578–590.

Black, S., Devereux, P., & Salvanes, K. (2007). From the cradle to the labor market? The effect of birth weight on adult outcomes. *Quarterly Journal of Economics*, *22*, 409–439.

Boardman, J. D., Powers, D. A., Padilla, Y. C., & Hummer, R. A. (2002). Low birth weight, social factors, and developmental outcomes among children in the United States. *Demography*, *39*(2), 353–368.

Bound, J., & Solon, G. (1999). Double trouble: On the value of twins-based estimation of the return to schooling. *Economics of Education Review*, *18*(2), 169–182.

Brooks-Gunn, J., McCarton, C. M., Casey, P. H., McCormik, M. C., Bauer, C. R., Bernbaum, J. C., ... Meinert, C. L. (1994). Early intervention in low-birth-weight premature Infants: Results through age 5 years from the infant health and development program. *Journal of the American Medical Association*, *272*(16), 1257–1262.

Caspi, A., Sugden, K., Moffitt, T. E., Taylor, A., Craig, I. W., Harrington, H., ... Poulton, R. (2003). Influence of life stress on depression: Moderation by a polymorphism in the 5-HTT gene. *Science* *301*(5631), 386-389.

Camacho, A. (2008). Stress and birthweight: evidence from terrorist attacks. *American Economic Review: Papers and Proceedings*, *98*(2), 111-115.

Chatterji, P., Kim, D., & Lahiri, K. (2014*a*). Birth weight and academic achievement in childhood. *Health Economics*, *23*, 1013–1035.

Chatterji, P., Kim, D., & Lahiri, K. (2014*b*). Fetal growth and neurobehavioral outcomes in childhood. *Economics and Human Biology*, *15*, 187–200.

Chen, M., & Zhang, L. (2011). Epigenetic mechanisms in developmental programming of adult disease. *Drug Discovery Today*, *16*, 1007–1018.

Collins, J., & David, R. (2009). Racial disparity in low birth weight and infant mortality. *Clinics in Perinatology*, *36*(1), 63–73.

Collins, J. W., Rankin, K. M., & Hibbs, S. (2015). The maternal age related patterns of infant low birth weight rates among non-Latino Whites and African Americans: The effect of maternal birth weight and neighborhood income. *Maternal and Child Health Journal*, *19*, 739–744.

Combs, C. A., Gravett, M., Garite, T. J., Hickok, D. E., Lapidus, J., Porreco, R., ... ProteoGenix/ Obstetrix Collaborative Research Network. (2014). Amniotic fluid infection, inflammation, and colonization in preterm labor with intact membranes. *American Journal of Obstetrics and Gynecology*, *210*, E1–E15.

Conley, D., & Bennett, N. G. (2000). Is biology destiny? Birth weight and life chances. *American Sociological Review*, *65*(3), 458–467.

Conley, D., Pfeiffer, K. M., & Velez, M. (2007). Explaining sibling differences in achievement and behavioral outcomes: The importance of within—and between—family factors. *Social Science Research*, *36*(3), 1087–1104.

Conley, D., & Rauscher, E. (2012). Genetic interactions with prenatal social environment: Effects on academic and behavioral outcomes. *Journal of Health and Social Behavior*, *54*, 109–127.

Conley, D., Strully, K., & Bennett, N. G. (2003). *A pound of flesh or just proxy? Using twin differences to estimate the effect of birth weight on life chances* (Working Paper No. 9901). National Bureau of Economic Research.

Conley, D., Strully, K. W., & Bennett, N. G. (2006). Twin differences in birth weight: The effects of genotype and prenatal environment on neonatal and post-neonatal mortality. *Economics and Human Biology*, *4*(2), 151–183.

Conley, D., & Strully, K. W. (2012) Birth weight, infant mortality, and race: Twin comparisons and genetic/environmental inputs. *Social Science and Medicine*, *75*, 2446-2454.

Cook, C. J., & Fletcher, J. M. (2015). Understanding heterogeneity in the effects of birth weight on adult cognition and wages. *Journal of Health Economics*, *41*, 107–116.

Corman, H., & Chaikind, S. (1998). The effect of low birthweight on the school performance and behavior of school-aged children. *Economics of Education Review*, *17*(3), 307–316.

Cunha, F., & Heckman, J. (2007). The technology of skill formation *American Economic Review*, *87*, 31–47.

Currie, J., Grenstone, M., & Moretti, E. (2011). Superfund cleanups and infant health. *American Economic Review*, *101*(3), 435–441.

Currie, J., & Hyson, R. (1999). *Is the impact of health shocks cushioned by socioeconomic status? The case of low birthweight* (Working Paper No. 6999). National Bureau of Economic Research.

Currie, J., & Moretti, E. (2007). Biology as destiny? Short and long-run determinants of intergenerational transmission of birth weight. *Journal of Labor Economics*, *25*(2), 231-264.

Currie, J., & Rossin-Slater, M. (2013). Weathering the storm: Hurricanes and birth outcomes. *Journal of Health Economics*, *32*(3), 487–503.

Currie, J., & Schwand, H. (2014). *The 9/11 dust cloud and pregnancy outcomes: A reconsideration* (Working Paper No. 20368). National Bureau of Economic Research.

Currie, J., & Walker, R. (2011). Traffic congestion and infant health: Evidence from E-Z pass. *American Economic Journal: Applied Economics*, *3*, 65–90.

Datar, A., Kilburn, M. R., & Loughran, D. S. (2010). Endowments and parental investments in infancy and early childhood. *Demography*, *47*(1), 145–162.

Del Bono, E., Ermisch, J., & Francesconi, M. (2012). Intrafamily resource allocations: A dynamic structural model of birth weight. *Journal of Labor Economics*, *30*, 657–706.

Dennis, J., & Mollborn, S. (2013). Young maternal age and low birth weight risk: An exploration of racial/ethnic disparities in the birth outcomes of mothers in the United States. *Social Science Journal*, *50*, 625–634.

Dessi, A., Puddu, M., Ottonello, G., & Fanos, V. (2013). Metabolomics and fetal-neonatal nutrition: Between 'not enough' and 'too much.' *Molecules*, *18*, 11724–11732.

Duncan, G. J., & Sojourner, A. J. (2013). Can intensive early childhood intervention programs eliminate income-based cognitive and achievement gaps? *Journal of Human Resources*, *48*, 945–968.

Dunkel-Schetter, C. (2011). Psychological science on pregnancy: Stress processes, biopsychosocial models, and emerging research issues. *Annual Review of Psychology*, *62*, 531–558.

Elo, I. T., Vang, Z., & Culhane, J. F. (2014). Variation in birth outcomes by mother's country of birth among non-Hispanic Black women in the United States. *Maternal and Child Health Journal*, *18*, 2371–2381.

Eikenes, L., Lohaugen, G. C., Brubakk, A. M., Skranes, J., & Haberg, A. K. (2011). Young adults born preterm with very low birth weight demonstrate widespread white matter alterations on brain DTI. *Neuroimage*, *54*, 1774–1785.

Falkner, F., Holzgreve, W., & Schloo, R. H. (1994). Prenatal influences on postnatal growth: Overview and pointers for needed research. *European Journal of Clinical Nutrition*, *48*, S15–S24.

Figlio, D. N., Guryan, J., Karbownik, K., & Roth, J. (2013). *The effects of poor neonatal health on children's cognitive development* (Working Paper No. 18846). National Bureau of Economic Research.

Fletcher, J. M. (2011). The medium term schooling and health effects of low birth weight: Evidence from siblings. *Economics of Education Review*, *30*, 517–527.

Fraser, A., & Lawlor, D. A. (2014). Long-term health outcomes in offspring born to women with diabetes in pregnancy. *Current Diabetes Reports*, *14*, 489.

Frijters, P., Johnston, D. W., & Shah, M. (2013). Intrahousehold resource allocation: Do parents reduce or reinforce child ability gaps? *Demography*, *50*, 2187–2208.

Ganella, E. P., Burnett, A., Cheong, J., Thompson, D., Roberts, G., Wood, S., . . . on behalf of the Victorian Infant Collaborative Study Group. (2015). Abnormalities in orbitofrontal cortex gyrification and mental health outcomes in adolescents born extremely preterm and/or at an extremely low birth weight. *Human Brain Mapping*, *36*, 1138–1150.

Geronimus, A. (1991). The weathering hypothesis and the health of African American women and infants. *Ethnicity and Disease*, *2*(3), 207-221.

Hack, M., Flannery, D. J., Schluchter, M., Cartar, L., Borawski, E., & Klein, N. (2002). Outcomes in young adulthood for very-low-birth-weight infants. *New England Journal of Medicine*, *346*, 149–157.

Hack, M., Wright, L. L., Shankaran, S., Tyson, J. E., Horbar, J. D., Bauer, C. R., & Younes, N. (1995). Very-low-birth-weight outcomes of the National Institute of Child Health and Human Development Neonatal Network, November 1989 to October 1990. *American Journal of Obstetrics and Gynecology*, *172*(2), 457–464.

Heckman, J. J. (2006, June). *The technology and neuroscience of skill formation*. The Conway Institute Lecture, Dublin, Ireland.

Heckman, J. J. (2007). The economics, technology, and neuroscience of human capability formation. *Proceedings of the National Academy of Sciences*, *104*(33), 13250–13255.

Hedderson, M. M., Ferrara, A., & Sacks, D. A. (2003). Gestational diabetes mellitus and lesser degrees of pregnancy hyperglycemia: Association with increased risk of spontaneous preterm birth. *Obstetrics & Gynecology*, *102*(4), 850–856.

Hegaard, H. K., Pedersen, B. K., Bruun Nielsen, B., & Damm, P. (2007). Leisure time physical activity during pregnancy and impact on gestational diabetes mellitus, pre-eclampsia, preterm delivery and birth weight: A review. *Acta Obstetricia et Gynecologica Scandinavica*, *86*(11), 1290–1296.

Heisler, E. (2012). *The U.S. infant mortality rate: International comparisons, underlying factors, and federal programs*. Congressional Research Service April 4, 2012. Retrieved from https://www.fas.org/sgp/crs/misc/R41378.pdf

Hobel, C. J., Goldstein, A., & Barrett, E. S. (2008). Psychosocial stress and pregnancy outcomes. *Clinical Obstetrics and Gynecology*, *51*(2), 333–348.

Hoynes, H., Page, M., & Stevens, A. H. (2011). Can targeted transfers improve birth outcomes? Evidence from the introduction of the WIC program. *Journal of Public Economics*, *95*, 813-827.

Hoynes, H., Miller, D., & Simon, D. (2015). Income, the Earned Income Tax Credit, and infant health, *American Economic Journal: Economic Policy* *7*(1), 172–211.

Hsin, A. (2012). Is biology destiny? Birth weight and differential parental treatment. *Demography*, *49*(4), 1385–1405.

Johnsson, I. W., Haglund, B., Ahlsson, F., & Gustafsson, J. (2014). A high birth weight is associated with increased risk of Type 2 diabetes and obesity. *Pediatric Obesity*, *10*, 77–83.

Kelly, E. (2011). The scourge of Asian Flu: In Utero exposure to pandemic influenza and the development of a cohort of British children. *Journal of Human Resources*, 46(4), 669-694.

Kline, J., Stein, Z., & Susser, M. (1989). *Conception to birth: Epidemiology of prenatal development*. New York: Oxford University Press.

Kristensen, P., Susser, E., Irgens, L. M., Mehlum, I. S., Corbett, K., & Bjerkedal, T. (2014). The association of high birth weight with intelligence in young adulthood: A cohort study of male siblings. *American Journal of Epidemiology*, *180*(9), 876–884.

Lara, M., Gamboa, C., Kahramanian, I., Morales, L., & Bautista, E. (2005). Acculturation and Latino health in the United States: A Review of the Literature and its Sociopolitical Context *Annual Review of Public Health*, *26*, 367–397.

Lawlor, D. A., Bor, W., O'Callaghan, M. J., Williams, G. M., & Najman, J. M. (2005). Intrauterine growth and intelligence within sibling pairs: Findings from the Mater-University Study of Pregnancy and its outcomes. *Journal of Epidemiology and Community Health*, *59*, 279–282.

Leddy, M., Power, M., & Schulkin, J. (2008). The impact of maternal obesity on maternal and fetal health. *Reviews in Obstetrics and Gynecology*, *1*(4), 170–178.

Lhila, A., & Long, S. (2012). What is driving the Black-White difference in low birthweight in the US? *Health Economics*, *21*, 301–315.

Lien, D., & Evans, W. (2005). Estimating the impact of large cigarette tax hikes: The case of maternal smoking and infant birth weight. *The Journal of Human Resources*, *40*(2), 373-392.

Lumey, L. H., Stein, A. D., Kahn, H. S., & Romijn, J. A. (2009). Lipid profiles in middle-aged men and women after famine exposure during gestation: The Dutch Hunger Winter Families Study. *American Journal of Clinical Nutrition*, *89*(6), 1737–1743.

Lynch, J. L., & Brooks, R. (2013). Low birth weight and parental investment: Do parents favor the fittest child? *Journal of Marriage and Family*, *75*, 533–543.

Madkour, A. S., Harville, E. W., & Xie, Y. (2014). Neighborhood disadvantage, racial concentration and the birthweight of infants born to adolescent mothers. *Maternal and Child Health Journal*, *18*, 663–671.

Madzwamuse, S. E., Baumann, N., Jaekel, J., Bartmann, P., & Wolke, D. (2015). Neuro-cognitive performance of very preterm or very low birthweight adults at 26 years. *Journal of Child Psychology and Psychiatry*. doi:10.1111/jcpp.12358

Mansour, H., & Rees, D. (2012). Armed conflict and birth weight: Evidence from the al-Aqsa Intifada. *Journal of Development Economics* 99, 190-199.

Morisaki, N., Esplin, M. S., Varner, M. W., Henry, E., & Oken, E. (2013). Declines in birth weight and fetal growth independent of gestational length. *Obstetrics and Gynecology*, *121*(1), 51–58.

Murray, A. L., Scratch, S. E., Thompson, D. K., Inder, T. E., Doyle, L. W., Anderson, J. F. I., & Anderson, P. J. (2014). Neonatal brain pathology predicts adverse attention and processing speed outcomes in very preterm and/or very low birth weight children. *Neuropsychology*, *28*, 552–562.

Newcombe, R., Milne, B. J., Caspi, A., Poulton, R., & Moffitt, T. E. (2007). Birthweight predicts IQ: Fact or artifact? *Twin Research and Human Genetics*, *10*(4), 581–586.

Oken, E. (2013). Secular trends in birthweight. *Nestlé Nutrition Institute Workshop Series*, *71*,103–114.

Oreopoulos, P., Stabile, M., Walld, R., & Roos, L. L. (2008). Short-, medium-, and long-term consequences of poor infant health: An analysis using siblings and twins. *Journal of Human Resources*, *43*(1), 88–138.

Paneth, N. S. (1995). The problem of low birth weight. *The Future of Children*, *5*(1), 19–34.

Pettersson, E., Sjolander, A., Almqvist, C., Anckarsater, H., D'Onofrio, B. M., Lichtenstein, P., & Larsson, H. (2015). Birth weight as an independent predictor of ADHD symptoms: A within-twin pair analysis. *Journal of Child Psychology and Psychiatry*, *56*, 453–459.

Poehlmann, J., Schwichtenberg, A. J. M., Shlafer, R. J., Hahn, E., Bianchi, J. P., & Warner, R. (2011). Emerging self-regulation in toddlers born preterm or low birth weight: Differential susceptibility to parenting? *Development and Psychopathology*, *23*, 177–193.

Restrepo, B. (2012). *Who compensates and who reinforces? Parental investment responses to child endowment shocks*. Unpublished Manuscript. Retrieved from http://www.mwpweb.eu/BrandonRestrepo/projects_255.html

Richards, M., Hardy, R., Kuh, D., & Wadsworth, M. E. J. (2001). Birth weight and cognitive function in the British 1946 Birth Cohort: Longitudinal population based study. *British Medical Journal*, *322*, 199.

Robinson, J. J. (2013). *Sound body, sound mind? Asymmetric and symmetric fetal growth restriction and human capital development* (Working Paper). University of Alabama at Birminham Retrieved March 29, 2015, from http://papers.ssrn.com/sol3/papers.cfm?abstract_id=1941998

Royer, H. (2009). Separated at birth: US twin estimates of the effects of birth weight. *American Economic Journal: Applied Economics*, *1*(1), 49–85.

Santangeli, L., Sattar, N., & Huda, S. S. (2015). Impact of maternal obesity on perinatal and childhood outcomes. *Obstetrics and Gynecology*, *29*(3), 438–448.

Sakata, M., Utsu, M., & Maeda, K. (2006). Fetal circulation and placental bloodflow in monochorionic twins. *The Ultrasound Review of Obstetrics and Gynecology* *6*(3-4), 35-40.

Schulz, L. C. (2010). The Dutch Hunger Winter and the developmental origins of health and disease. *Proceedings of the National Academy of Sciences*, *107*(39), 16757–16758.

Shenkin, S. D., Starr, J. M., & Deary, I. J. (2004). Birth weight and cognitive ability in childhood: A systematic review. *Psychological Bulletin*, *130*(6), 989–1013.

Shenkin, S. D., Starr, J., Pattie, A., Rush, M. A., Whalley, L. J., & Deary, I. J. (2001). Birth weight and cognitive function at age 11 years: The Scottish Mental Survey 1932. *Archives of Disease in Childhood*, *85*, 189–196.

Siebel, A. L., Carey, A. L., & Kingwell, B. A. (2012). Can exercise training rescue the adverse cardiometabolic effects of low birth weight and prematurity? *Clinical and Experimental Pharmacology and Physiology*, *39*, 944–957.

Skilton, M. R., Raitakari, O. T., & Celermajer, D. S. (2013). High intake of dietary long-chain ω-3 fatty acids is associated with lower blood pressure in children born with low birth weight: NHANES 2003–2008. *Hypertension*, *61*, 972–976.

Skilton, M. R., Siitonen, N., Wurtz, P., Viikari, J. S. A., Juonala, M., Seppala, I., . . . Raitakari, O. T. (2014). High birth weight is associated with obesity and increased carotid wall thickness in young adults: The Cardiovascular Risk in Young Finns Study. *Arteriosclerosis, Thrombosis, and Vascular Biology*, *34*, 1064–1068.

Skranes, J., Lohaugen, G. C. C., Martinussen, M., Haberg, A., Brubakk, A. M., & Dale, A. M. (2013). Cortical surface area and IQ in very-low-birth-weight (VLBW) young adults. *Cortex*, *49*, 2264–2271.

Spong, C. Y., Iams, J., Goldenberg, R., Hauck, F. R., & Willinger, M. (2011). Disparities in perinatal medicine. *Obstetrics & Gynecology*, *117*, 948–955.

Taylor, H. G., Filipek, P. A., Juranek, J., Bangert, B., Minich, N., & Hack, M. (2011). Brain volumes in adolescents with very low birth weight: Effects on brain structure and associations with neuropsychological outcomes. *Developmental Neuropsychological*, *36*, 96–117.

Torche, F. (2011). The effect of maternal stress on birth outcomes: Exploiting a natural experiment. *Demography*, *48*, 1473–1491.

Torche, F., & Echevarría, G. (2011). The effect of birthweight on childhood cognitive development in a middle income country. *International Journal of Epidemiology*, *40*(4), 1008–1018.

Torche, F., & Shwed, U. (2015, Forthcoming). The hidden costs of war: Environmental stress exposure and birth outcomes. *Sociological Science*.

Torche, F., & Villarreal, A. (2014). Prenatal exposure to violence and birth weight in Mexico: Selectivity, exposure, and behavioral responses. *American Sociological Review*, *79*(5), 966–992.

Vang, Z., & Elo, I. (2013). Exploring the health consequences of majority-minority neighborhoods: Minority diversity and birthweight among native-born and foreign-born Blacks. *Social Science and Medicine*, *97*, 56–65.

Wade, M., Browne, D. T., Madigan, S., Plamondon, A., & Jenkins, J. M. (2014). Normal birth weight variation and children's neuropsychological functioning: Links between language, executive functioning, and theory of mind. *Journal of the International Neuropsychological Society*, *20*, 909–919.

Whidbey, C., Vornhagen, J., Gendrin, C., Boldenow, E., Samson, J. M., Doering, K., . . . Rajagopal, L. (2015). A streptococcal lipid toxin induces membrane permeabilization and pyroptosis leading to fetal injury. *EMBO Molecular Medicine*, *7*, 488–505.

Wolke, D., Jaekel, J., Hall, J., & Baumann, N. (2013). Effects of sensitive parenting on the academic resilience of very preterm and very low birthweight adolescents. *Journal of Adolescent Health*, *53*, 642–647.

Zhang, X., Decker, A., Platt, R., & Kramer, M. (2008). How big is too big? The perinatal consequences of fetal macrosomia. *American Journal of Obstetrics and Gynecology*, *198*(5), 517.e1–517.e6.

CHAPTER 32

NEUROECONOMICS

A Flourishing Field

JASON A. AIMONE AND DANIEL HOUSER

32.1 INTRODUCTION

PERHAPS the most complex economic system under study today is also the most widely used: the approximately 3-pound mass of cells that comprise the human brain. The importance of the brain to the social sciences is self-evident. Indeed, most interesting problems in this area involve the decisions of people; yet, until very recently, surprisingly little was known about the neural and biological processes that underlie human decision making. This changed during the previous two decades, which have seen substantial advances in our understanding of brain and behavior. Much of this research can be considered as "neuroeconomics." A defining goal of this still rapidly developing area is to discover and understand the biological foundation of human social and economic decision making.

Interest in the neurological basis of economic decisions has existed for centuries. Adam Smith, for instance, referred to muscle memory in *Wealth of Nations* when arguing for the economic value of specialization.[1] Indeed, Smith's *Theory of Moral Sentiments* (Smith, 1761/1982) was an early and prescient discussion of "theory of mind," one of the more widely studied topics in neuroeconomics. Alfred Marshall, one of the fathers of neoclassical economics, frequently refers to economic agents' "nervous force" and even speculated that the "physiological basis of purely mental work is not yet well understood; but what little we do know of the growth of brain structure seems to indicate that practice in any kind of thinking develops new connections between different parts of the brain"[2] (Marshall, 1920/2011).

Although early writings were largely philosophical, the advent of tools to measure in vivo neural activity gave rise to the current field. The first brain imaging study of two-person economic exchange, a study that arguably marks the beginning of modern neuroeconomics, was produced by Kevin McCabe, Daniel Houser, Lee Ryan, Vernon Smith, and Ted Trouard and published in the *Proceedings of the National Academy of Sciences of the United States of America* (McCabe, Houser, Ryan, Smith, & Trouard, 2001). That study shed light on the neural correlates of theory of mind, which refers to the human ability to form beliefs about other people's desires. Theory of mind has been long understood as key to economic behavior. For example, much of Adam Smith's theory of moral sentiments relies on it crucially. In shedding light on the neural underpinnings of theory of mind, McCabe et al. (2001) provide an important bridge between 18th and 21st century scholarship in economic sciences.

This chapter introduces the major tools, methods, and branches of study of this young but vast field of economics. Our exemplar is the highly studied economic phenomenon of social exchange in environments that require trust. We examine how neuroeconomics is used to shed light on key aspects of decision making in this environment. We demonstrate that the tools of neuroeconomics provide fundamental new insights on economic decision making that are unavailable from the study of empirical data from behavioral experiments alone.

Many economic behaviors and processes can be better understood through the lens of neurofunctioning. Here, we look to the human brain to understand the neurobiological bases of decision processes for two purposes. One is for institution design: we wish to improve models of how agents express their preferences (respond to constraints) in the presence of different institutional environments or as a result of experience. For example, why do the same participants in bubbles experiments make different strategic decisions as they obtain increased exposure to particular market institutions? Understanding this can have important implications for financial policies related to asset price volatility (Dufwenberg, Lindqvist, & Moore, 2005). A second purpose is to better understand the *source* of preferences: why do we want what we want? Understanding the source of preferences is key to understanding preference heterogeneity, a topic that has received substantial attention during the past half-century. For example, it is known that there are important differences between males and females (see, e.g., Croson & Gneezy, 2009 who identify many differences such as in risk preferences), as well as behavioral phenotypes (such as "free-riders" or "conditional cooperators"; see, e.g., Urban & Houser, 2001).

Although the behavioral experiments provide insights on individual and group behavior, it can be challenging using these data to identify the *mechanisms* underlying behavioral differences. Neuroeconomics provides the tools to explore mechanism differences and identify genetic, structural, and functional sources for behavioral differences that lead to heterogeneity in economic choices.

32.2 Neuroeconomics Methods

The diversity of the system underlying human brain function means that understanding it requires input from a host of different scientific disciplines. For example, any exploration of the human brain requires understanding of the anatomical and functional workings of neurons. Thus, the field of biology is critical to measuring and understanding communication between cells that control brain processes. Also, the fields of physics and engineering provide the machinery used to measure neural processes. Functional magnetic imaging (fMRIs) scanners, electroencephalograms (EEGs), and many other types of equipment are widely used in neuroeconomic studies. Statistical and mathematical analytical tools and software help neuroeconomists analyze the data produced by this advanced equipment. With interdisciplinary collaboration, behavioral researchers—economists, psychologists, cognitive neuroscientists, or any of many other specialists—can address their questions of interest in a common language and under the common umbrella of neuroeconomics.

Unfortunately, much research in economics, psychology, and related fields operates simultaneously and largely independently, with little pressure to recognize (even closely related) contributions from other disciplines. Neuroeconomics is perhaps unique in that it originated and has continued as a field with strong multidisciplinary emphasis. Neuroeconomists and neuropsychologists have been required to stay abreast of new findings in each other's disciplines. Co-authors on single papers span disciplinary bounds, as do the reviewers for targeted journal outlets. Although the benefits are clear, the cross-disciplinary nature of the field does lead to occasional methodological tension (which is diminishing over time). For example, deception, which is taboo in economics research, is used in some neuroeconomics experiments that appear in noneconomics journals. Similarly, many experimental economists take for granted that studies they read involve salient rewards for decisions, but this is not a requirement in all disciplines that address neuroeconomics questions.

32.3 Neuroeconomics Tools

Neuroeconomics tools are designed to allow researchers to peer into human brains as they make decisions and produce quantifiable data from these observations. In some cases, these tools allow for exogenous changes in the way a brain functions, thus improving causal inference. Each tool has unique advantages in addressing particular questions. This section discusses several primary tools of neuroeconomics.

32.3.1 Functional Magnetic Resonance Imaging

Studies based on fMRI are common in neuroeconomics. fMRI uses a magnetic field to measure the oxygen content of blood. Because the brain's neurons consume oxygen when active, one can detect variation in the blood oxygenation level-dependent (BOLD) signal in real time and thus draw inferences regarding the relatively more and less active parts of the brain. An fMRI machine can plot the brain's activity (the BOLD signal) on a map of approximately 25,000 3 mm cubes. This is often visualized as a cross-sectional picture of a brain with "brain blobs" indicating the areas that are relatively more active at that point in the decision task.

fMRI is attractive because it is noninvasive. It does not require the injection of chemicals and has no known lasting side effects. Participants in fMRI experiments must sit inside a giant donut-shaped machine that produces the magnetic fields and remain very still.[3]

Neuroeconomists conducting fMRI experiments use the BOLD maps to draw conclusions about economic decision-making processes. For example, Tricomi et al. (2010) observed that the ventral striatum, a brain region often associated with reward, was correlated with inequity aversion. They noted that this area responded differently to equity differences in payments between self and others. Weber et al. (2009) observed that money illusion was connected with the ventromedial prefrontal cortex. Perception differences, such as between looking at skewed or symmetric gambles, can be difficult to notice in behavioral experiments beyond ultimate choices. However, by using fMRI, experimenters can observe how people respond to observing such differences in financial decisions, as in Wu et al. (2011), who observed that the insula responded differently between skewed and symmetric gambles and that the nucleus accumbens responded to whether the skew was negative or positive. Such studies help to provide explanations for otherwise hard-to-explain common behaviors. Wu et al. (2011), for instance, discusses how the neural responses to skewness may provide a clue for why people disproportionately respond to unlikely financial events, purchase lottery tickets, and sometimes are seen overinsuring.

As replication and new studies are conducted, the same brain regions are often found to be involved in similar situations. Over time, robust patterns have been discovered, and the structure, nature, and plausible roles of different brain regions have been identified. This line of research is often called "brain mapping." Brain mapping facilitates the exploration of how and why different environmental, health, cultural, and institutional factors affect the way an individual responds in economic environments. For example, fMRI tools can be used to identify differences in the way the brains of males and females produce social and economic decisions. Often, there are no gender-specific neural differences, as with ventral striatum signal fluctuations with relative income comparisons (Dohmen, Falk, Fliessbach, Sunde, & Weber, 2011); however, gender differences are apparent in other environments, as when evaluating trustworthiness (Riedl, Hubert, & Kenning, 2010). Riedl et al. thought that by using fMRI experiments they might be able to explain why there were observed differences between men and women in online trust and attitudes to information and technology (IT) usage and perception. They found that there was substantial evidence for differences in how male and female brains processed trust perception tasks, in particular difference in the striatum and ventral medial prefrontal cortex. fMRI tools are commonly used in attempts to understand how special populations differ from typical populations in economic decision making. For example, Chiu, Lorenz, et al. (2008) explored how smokers' brains differ from those of nonsmokers in the learning process. They found that previously studied fictive error-related signals, signals of "what might have been" had a different choice been made, were similarly present in both smokers' and nonsmokers' brains. However, they found that such signals, although still present, were uncorrelated with behavior for the smokers unlike for nonsmokers, thus reflecting a gap in the typical reinforcement learning process connected to addiction. Such findings help to guide the development of neural models and theories of behavior by helping to parse out the differences between necessary and sufficient processes for certain behaviors and by guiding the discovery of associated processes that contribute to behavior.

Although fMRI provides good locational accuracy in measuring neural activity during decision making, it is relatively slow in measuring that activity. It takes about 2 seconds to measure "current" activity in brain. Although this can provide a time course of neural activity, measurement occurs much more slowly than the brain processes information. Consider that it takes only about .5 seconds for a baseball to travel from a pitcher's hand to home plate while umpires, batters, and catchers analyze, accurately evaluate, and respond to its trajectory. Many, perhaps even most, neural processes that interest researchers relate to decisions made rapidly or reflexively, such as judgments of risk and value, spontaneous decisions to buy a product in line at the grocery store, or a Wall Street stock trader's adjustments to price changes. This highlights the importance of complementing fMRI techniques with additional tools.

32.3.2 Electroencephalography

EEG is an alternative neural measurement tool that is strong where fMRI is weak and vice-versa. Rather than measuring blood flow, EEG takes advantage of the direct electrical properties of neural activity. Neurons communicate with each other through electrical currents. When large numbers of these neurons communicate systematically at the same time, the electrical potential caused by such communication rises to a point at which the potential can be measured by probes placed on a person's scalp. Whereas BOLD signal detection is relatively slow, EEG probes measure this electrical potential on the scalp relatively rapidly, on the millisecond level. As with fMRI, EEG readers provide a quantitative map showing areas of the brain where neural activity occurs at that point in time. However, because EEG uses electrical properties of the skull, it is relatively imprecise regarding the location within the brain where that activity occurs. Nevertheless, neural activity on the "surface" area of the brain, such as the prefrontal cortex and motor cortex, can be captured fairly precisely because there is little to occupy space between that part of the brain and the scalp sensors. Knoch et al. (2010), for example, used EEG to measure the baseline activity in the right prefrontal cortex and found that this resting cortical activity is strongly predictive of willingness to punish in ultimatum games. Measuring activity in the center of the brain, on the other hand, such as in the ventral striatum (a region that fMRI studies indicate responds to reward and value), is prone to more errors with EEG measurement because there is a great deal of other brain and scalp matter between that region and the sensors. Like fMRI, EEG is also safe and noninvasive, so much so that it has even been used to explore how infants think. fMRI and EEG measurements can be taken concurrently, although there have been few such studies to date. One reason is adverse interactions between the magnetic fields induced by the fMRI and the probes measuring electrical potential in EEG.

32.3.3 Transcranial Magnetic Stimulation

EEG and fMRI complement each other's temporal and location accuracy, but both are suited primarily for passive observation of neural activity. In particular, these methods do not allow for direct manipulation of brain regions, and this limits their use for causal inference. Transcranial magnetic stimulation (TMS), allows researchers either to block or artificially stimulate a region of the brain. TMS takes advantage of the same magnetic and electrical properties of the brain used by EEG and fMRI. When participating in a TMS experiment, an electromagnetic coil is positioned near the subject's head adjacent to the region of the brain to be stimulated or suppressed. By varying the electrical field emanated by the coil, that brain area can be suppressed or stimulated, thus providing researchers with greater ability to identify the causal role that certain areas play in various economic decisions. As with EEG, spatial resolution of TMS is difficult, and, as with fMRI, the temporal resolution is a concern. Nevertheless, TMS provides researchers a useful complementary approach to inference about brain function.

One can think of TMS as creating artificial lesions in the brain. The problems with spatial resolution and reduced ability to explore more central regions of the brain are overcome in studies using participants who have actual lesions in the brain. fMRI studies can identify accurately what structural areas of the brain are damaged or missing in these individuals. Behavioral decision-making studies can then explore differences in choices between individuals without lesions, those with natural or artificial lesions in the regions that previous studies have identified as being related to a decision process, and control individuals with natural or artificial lesions in areas unrelated to areas previously identified as relevant to the decision. Observing similar or different behavior between these groups can help to illustrate whether the regions identified by fMRI, EEG, or TMS studies are necessary regions for certain decision processes. TMS can also be used in conjunction with imaging tools. Although safe, because TMS does (temporarily) change a person's brain function, it is more invasive than fMRI or EEG.

Knoch et al. (2006) used TMS to disrupt/reduce activation in the right or left dorsolateral prefrontal cortex (DLPFC) in order to test whether an increasing DLPFC activation is acting in a causal channel leading one to reject unfair ultimatum game offers, thus fundamentally overriding selfish monetary maximization. They found that acceptance rates for unfair offers did not differ significantly between controls (9.3% acceptance rate) and those with left DLPFC TMS disruption (14.7% acceptance rate), but those with right DLPFC TMS disruption increased acceptance rates significantly to 44.7%. This provided supporting evidence for the causal role of the right DLPFC (but not left) in rejections of unfair offers. Their controls, including computer conditions and fairness evaluations, led the authors to conclude that the DLPFC is causally related to fairness behaviors such as rejections in ultimatum games, but not to fairness-related evaluations. This helps to explain the nature of behavioral changes associated with damage to the right DLPFC.

32.3.4 Chemical Manipulations

Whereas FMRI, EEG, TMS, and lesion studies take a direct approach to exploring the neural roots of economic choice, there are several other indirect routes used in neuroeconomics. Medicines and chemicals were used extensively in the 20th century to modify behavior and study the mechanisms by which these substances work. Many of these substances, such as caffeine and marijuana, are not normally present in the body and artificially change the way the brain functions. Other substances, such as the neuropeptide oxytocin and the hormone cortisol, are naturally occurring in the body but can be artificially manipulated. Recently, research has attempted to explore how economic decisions are governed or impacted by the body's levels of these substances.

Most studies on these types of substances are behavioral in design, with treatments exogenously creating increases or decreases of the levels of these substances. Kandasamy et al. (2014) demonstrate through a double-blind placebo-controlled experiment that cortisol levels (which are related to stress levels), modulated through ingested capsules, can cause changes in financial risk decisions. Whereas temporary increases in cortisol were seen to have no effect on risk choices, chronically elevated levels (over about a week) led people to be significantly more risk averse in their decision making. Studies exploring oxytocin, typically manipulated in placebo-controlled studies using intranasal sprays, also have presented evidence of strong effects of the neuropeptide in decision making. Domes et al. (2007), for example, showed in their study that elevated oxytocin levels improve the ability of participants to infer the mental states of other people. Oxytocin levels are also strongly related to behavior in trust games, which we discuss in more detail later.

Studies on substance influence on neural and economic functioning are not limited to small-scale economic environments. For example, Zak and Fakhar (2006) used survey data from 41 countries to explore the impact of oxytocin and neuroactive hormones on cross-country macroeconomic trust levels. They collected measures for each country on frequency of social interaction, dietary patterns (to reflect the amounts of phytoestrogens in food), temperature, breastfeeding rates, and more in an effort to reflect the typical hormonal conditions of people within each country, and then they explored reported interpersonal trust rates. They concluded that their study showed strong evidence of the macroeconomic effects on generalized trust caused by oxytocin's positive impact on trust.

Technology is improving in ways that allow researchers to measure some neurochemicals within the brain. Recently, researchers have begun to measure dopamine levels in the brain in nearly real time during economic decisions made while patients were undergoing open brain surgery. Kishida et al. (2011) demonstrated the feasibility of such methods by showing that dopamine levels in the brain track market prices. Although this study may suggest a future direction for neuroeconomics research, as well as a path for new discoveries, these neurochemical measurement techniques are limited because they are highly invasive in that they require open brain surgery.

32.3.5 Studies with Nonhuman Populations

Economists have long looked to nonhuman species to see what aspects of behavior are unique to humans, which are likely learned or culturally based, and which are innate across species. For example, in the late 1970s and early 1980s, John Kagel and Ray Battalio extensively studied and tested basic economic theories in nonhuman experimental subjects. As summarized by Kagel (1987), they explored risk preferences, demand curves, poverty, time preferences, and other economic concepts and theories using animals such as rats and pigeons as their participant samples. Researchers including Sarah Brosnan and Franz de Waal have continued this type of exploration by investigating whether monkeys, whose brains are more similar to humans' than those of rats and pigeons, display social preferences such as inequality aversion (Brosnan & de Waal, 2003; for a survey, see Chen & Houser, 2012). Researchers have also studied the economic decision making of bees (Gaeger & Thomson, 2004). Although these studies cannot tell us precisely how the human brain functions, they do tell us that many fundamental economic principles and preferences can be computed absent the advanced higher level neural functions of the human brain. Finally, Kagel (1987) explains how using nonhuman subjects also allows economists to explore questions with exogenous controls that would be unethical in humans (e.g., the impact of extended time periods of poverty).

32.4 Application: Neuroeconomics of Trust and Betrayal

Trust is an important and ubiquitous component of economic interactions ranging from buying products of unknown quality to investing one's retirement funds using the advice of a stockbroker. Economists, psychologists, neuroscientists, and others have studied trust extensively. In neuroeconomics, much of this research involves variants of the trust game introduced by Berg et al. (1995). In this game, a first mover—the investor—can send a portion of his or her monetary endowment to a second mover, the trustee. On being sent, the money is multiplied by, typically, a factor of three, thus reflecting gains from trade. The trustee then has the option to send a portion of this now larger pot of money back to the investor. Any amount sent is considered to reflect trust on the part of the investor because there are no guarantees that the trustee will send back anything. Any amount returned by the trustee is considered reciprocation. Although simple, this game is useful in identifying and studying many facets of human preferences and behavior from theory of mind, to altruism, to betrayal aversion, and many other decision-making factors. Its ubiquity also has led researchers to engage almost every type of neuroeconomics tool to improve our understanding of this economic relationship (for other reviews, see Fehr, Fischbacher, & Kosfeld, 2005; Riel & Javor, 2012).

Laboratory experiments have identified behavioral regularities in the trust game. From the initial Berg et al. (1995) paper onward, researchers have observed that Nash equilibrium (in which purely selfish investors invest nothing and purely selfish trustees return nothing) is uncommon. These behavioral studies have indicated, for example, that partner matching in repeated interaction trust games increases trust rates (59%) compared to stranger matching (32%) (Bohnet & Huck, 2004). Risk preferences, which normally would be expected to influence behavior in all forms of trust games, do not appear to affect investors decisions in a single-shot trust game (e.g., Eckel & Wilson, 2004; Houser, Schunk, & Winter, 2010) but do seem to affect behavior in repeated trust games (Aimone, Ball and King-Kasas 2014a). Croson and Gneezy (2009) show that, across behavioral studies looking at gender differences, male investors tend to trust as much as women and, in many cases, trust significantly more, whereas the opposite holds true for trustee reciprocation.

These behavioral studies, and many more exploring other facets of behavior, are effective at identifying preference types, behavioral biases, and how institutional structures influence decisions. Behavioral studies are more limited in identifying *why* these differences exist in the first place and how they manifest in the underlying decision-making process. For example, in the cases of borderline personality disorder, post-traumatic stress disorder, or autism, behavioral studies alone can detect that such individuals have difficulty in social interactions; left unanswered is why. Identifying the source of these difficulties is critical to developing appropriate medical and/or therapeutic treatments. Neural studies are an effective tool for exploring the sources and mechanisms underlying these behaviorally identified decision-making differences. Once the neural underpinnings of decision making are identified, it becomes possible to begin to understand how institutions, interventions, and other solutions to problems act to change, suppress, or amplify existing neural processes.

Trust studies can be divided into two primary types. The first strives to understand why people fail to conform to economic theory by trusting and reciprocating trust. Trust and reciprocation are dual puzzles because standard game theory predicts that no one would reciprocate in a one-shot trust game because it strictly lowers one's earnings. Likewise, no profit maximizing investor would choose to trust as backwards induction would lead them to the prediction of no reciprocation (and the resulting earnings losses). The second type of trust study investigates the biological basis of conforming to theory by failing to trust or choosing to betray trust. This sort of behavior could reasonably be game theoretic play; however, such behaviors could also arise due to other motivations, which is what this line of research explores. The former approach more closely mirrors the behavioral work on trust and is seen in the earliest neurostudies of trust, whereas neuroeconomic studies of betrayal have appeared only recently. Both types have revealed complex brain processes contributing to an ultimate trust (or betrayal) decision.

32.4.1 Why Trust?

In the first fMRI study of trust (indeed, the first fMRI study of two-person economic exchange), McCabe et al. (2001) found evidence that cooperators, but not non-cooperators, displayed significantly amplified medial prefrontal cortex activity when playing trust games with human counterparts as compared to when they played trust games with computer counterparts. They suggest that their results reflect possible inhibition of immediate rewards allowing for cooperation. King-Casas et al. (2005) approached a repeated investor/trustee relationship slightly differently as a mutual trust game in which they modeled investors' changes of reciprocation rates as their own form of trust associated with expected reciprocity from investors. They found that the caudate nucleus strongly responded to prediction error related to expected reciprocity of investors and that such activity was related to changes in trustee behavior throughout the exchange relationship. In other studies, such as Delgado et al. (2005), the caudate was found to be important in an investor's decision making. This advances the idea that the caudate aids in updating and learning from feedback in repeated trust exchanges. Tomlin et al. (2006) demonstrated that the cingulate cortex was insensitive to such errors and outcomes in trust exchange but specifically responded according to whether the actor of observed information was oneself or one's partner, presumably identifying the agency of newly observed information about a decision so it can be appropriately processed by the brain and thus potentially allowing for "credit" to be appropriately assigned to the correct economic agent.

Using a different presentation of a trust game, in which the fMRI scanned participant could learn about the trustworthiness of his or her partner, Behrens et al. (2008) found that social and reward learning, each occurring in different areas of the anterior cingulate cortex, was "combined" by the brain in the ventral medial prefrontal cortex. These patterns of neural activity led researchers to think of activity observed in the brain not as occurring in isolated, independent regions, but rather as occurring within an integrated network, with components that specialize in different aspects of decision making.

Repeated trust interactions do not only involve responding to past information, but also involve strategic thinking about the potential actions of one's trust partner. Krueger et al. (2007) demonstrated that those in nondefecting trust partnerships engage "mentalizing" regions of the brain—particularly the paracingulate cortex (PcP)—very differently than do trust partnerships that have periods of defections. They found that when initially building their trust relationships, nondefecting groups engaged their PcPs significantly more than did defecting groups and that, in the later rounds, the opposite relationship was seen while trust relationships were maintained.

32.4.2 Why Not Trust?

21.4.2.1 *Special Populations*

We turn next to the second type of study that focuses on why people fail to trust and why people betray another's trust. This approach often involves special populations, where observed behavioral deficits in trust and reciprocation motivate the "why do they behave differently?" question. For example, Koscik and Tranel (2011) suggest that most people's default decision is to trust and that the amygdala provides a needed role of down-regulating that trust. They hypothesize that this can help to explain why those with amygdala damage/lesions display abnormal social behavior. Their study suggests that whereas individuals without amygdala damage reduce trust when betrayed by a trustee, those with amygdala lesions are observed increasing trust after betrayals and separately report overall ratings of trustworthiness that are noticeably greater than those without damage. These results echo those of Adolphs et al. (1998), whose bilateral amygdala lesion patients reported higher levels of trustworthiness for unfamiliar faces than did controls. With respect to trustees, lesion studies have indicated a potential role of the ventral-medial prefrontal cortex (VMPFC). For example, Krajbich et al. (2009) showed that those with VMPFC lesions are less sensitive to guilt as well as less trustworthy than are other trustees.

Many fMRI studies approach the study of disorders and their effects on trust from this perspective as well. Neuroeconomics studies can provide a useful tool in these situations because disorders often are associated with abnormal behavior, but the sources of the abnormal behaviors are unknown. Why, for example, would individuals with generalized social anxiety disorder (GSAD) have difficulty in social environments? Using an fMRI experiment, Sripada et al. (2009) observed that the striatal responses of healthy control investors differed between cooperative and uncooperative partners; on the other hand, those with GSAD showed no such differences. This study helped to narrow the focus to the striatum as a key to behavioral trust abnormalities, rather than other plausible sources like fear or responses to social norms.

Another question may ask why individuals with borderline personality disorder (BPD) have difficulties trusting and forming relationships. With fMRI, we are able to provide evidence on the source of the difficulty and thus guide interventions and treatments. In the case of BPD, King-Casas et al. (2008) used a repeated trust game played in an fMRI to identify that those with BPD lacked the two-way response of the insula to both offers and returns that healthy participants show, which are thought to reflect awareness of own and other's social norm violations.

Autism spectrum disorder (ASD) is likewise associated with difficulties in interpreting social signals, but high-functioning autistics can often carry out social behavior consistent with that of individuals without ASD. Chiu, Kayla, et al. (2008) engaged participants with high-function ASD in a trust game. They found that, behaviorally, those with ASD made decisions no different from controls. Even though observed behavior is similar, their neural data demonstrate that the two groups approach the game very differently on the neural level. Specifically, healthy trustees in a trust game experience high levels of activation in the anterior cingulate cortex when playing a trust game with a human partner as compared to playing a trust game with a known nonhuman partner (a computer), whereas trustees with ASD show no such differentiation. The authors explain how these findings point to a hindered ability to model one's own social intentions, which helps to explain results in other environments where differences exist between those with and without ASD. These results demonstrate that indistinguishable behavior between two groups of interest does not imply that the underlying neural processes are equivalent.

32.4.2.2 *Healthy Populations and the Role of Oxytocin*

A significant part of the neuroeconomics literature investigates why healthy individuals fail to trust. Interesting investigations in this area involve exogenous manipulation of the neuropeptide oxytocin, which has surfaced as an intriguing player in the brain's decision whether to trust. Studies surrounding trust and oxytocin use many different neuroeconomics methods. Working together, these tools help us better to understand the puzzle of economic trust.

Whereas oxytocin has long been thought to influence pair-bonding and as critical for infant–parent bonding, Kosfeld et al. (2005) suggested that it also plays a role in the general decision to trust. More specifically, they suggested that oxytocin modulated betrayal aversion, the aversion to the negative emotions associated with discovery that one's trust was betrayed (see Aimone & Houser, 2013, for a review of this literature). Kosfeld's study showed that when oxytocin was administered intranasally, those with amplified levels of oxytocin in their body showed an increased willingness to trust but no increased expectations of reciprocation, no changes in tolerance for monetary risk, and no changes in willingness to betray trust. As such, a plausible explanation for oxytocin's effect on trust was not so much that it actually increased trust as it reduced barriers to trust and particularly betrayal aversion.

Kirsch et al. (2005) followed up on Kosfeld et al. (2005) by placing participants with placebo or intranasally administered oxytocin into an fMRI scanner to judge fear responses. They identified oxytocin as modulating the amygdala's response to fear thus attributing the Kosfeld trust results as stemming from a decreased amygdala response during the trust exchange. This would be in line with the aforementioned lesion studies on the amygdala (Adolphs et al., 1998; Koscik & Tranel, 2011) that showed that decreased (or absent/lesioned) amygdala response is related to increased trust rates. These ties among oxytocin, the amygdala, and trust were further strengthened by Domes et al. (2007) whose intranasal oxytocin study connected oxytocin administration with improved performance on "Reading the Mind's Eye" tests, related to both amygdala responses and an increased ability to infer the mental states of others. Baumgartner et al. (2008) followed up with another oxytocin fMRI experiment but had participants play both a risk and a trust game while in the scanner. This study completed the ties among oxytocin, trust, and the amygdala by showing that placebo controls relative to oxytocin-administered participants showed a higher elevated amygdala response in the trust game compared to the risk game where the probabilities were identical but there was no social partner.

This line of oxytocin research supports the hypothesis that oxytocin reduces betrayal aversion via reducing amygdalar responses during trust games. However, Lauharatanahirun et al. (2012) demonstrated in their fMRI study that the amygdala was also strongly correlated to how people respond to the source of risk, whether social or nonsocial in origin, in environments absent a counterpart and thus void of betrayal aversion concerns. This study thus indicates that it is unclear from the past studies whether oxytocin was affecting trust relative to risk choices because betrayal aversion is reduced or because the source of uncertainty is changed from a social to a nonsocial source of uncertainty.

Recently, Aimone, Houser, and Weber (2014b) isolated the neural foundations of betrayal aversion in an fMRI study that compared trust decisions to decisions regarding an analogous socially originated risk. They discovered that rather than betrayal aversion relating to amygdala responses, such aversion seems instead to be primarily related to insula responses, thus suggesting that betrayal aversion is related to expected negative emotions or norm violations (both connected to insula activation) rather than fear concerns (connected to amygdala activation). The data reported by Aimone et al. (2014b) suggest that oxytocin might play a role in betrayal aversion as well. Although there have not yet appeared any studies on this issue, future work will surely address this topic.

32.5 Conclusion

This chapter highlighted key methods and results in neuroeconomics. Research in this field has been expanding rapidly, enough to see the emergence of a journal devoted to publishing research in this area.[4] Important neuroeconomics papers have been published connecting economic decisions to emotion and emotion expression (e.g., Xiao & Houser, 2005) and emotion regulation (Heilman, Crisan, Houser, Miclea, Mau & Houser, 2010), as well as describing links between risk tolerance and specific emotions such as anxiety (Miu, Miclea, & Houser, 2008). In view of the many significant findings that have emerged, the excitement seen in the field in the late 1990s continues unabated today. This is surely a case where there is much more to do than has been done, with each new study suggesting half a dozen others.

Genetics and genomics are fields closely related to neuroeconomics but not explored in this chapter. With the decreasing cost of collecting and analyzing portions of the human genome has come an expanding number of studies exploring what economics can learn from the code wrapped up in our own DNA. Studies like that of Lundborg and Stenberg (2010) highlight the many micro- and macroeconomic policy issues of concern that can be aided with molecular genetic studies (see also Set et al., 2014).

Although excitement for neuroeconomics research is high, a variety of methodological criticisms have emerged. For example, a cautionary note was provided by Van Lange et al.'s (2011) study showing that the procedure and act of measuring one's heart rate in a game changed behavior in relation to a baseline where heart rate was not measured. Their study emphasizes the importance of recognizing that the methods of obtaining neural and biological measurements may influence behavior in those games. The challenge is to ensure that any cross-study comparisons among multiple studies take into account the methods of data acquisition and measurement.

Neuroeconomics is a multidisciplinary field that has found research traction in economics, psychology, and neuroscience. We have highlighted contributions to the literature on trust, which matters to economists because of its importance to exchange, to psychologists because of the complex motives underlying trust and betrayal, and to neuroscientists because of the complex neural processes that underlie trust and betrayal decisions. We have described how the early findings are informative in important ways to each of these disciplines. Continued efforts made on uncovering the biological foundation of decision processes hold the promise of informing not only general knowledge but also institutions and policy and thus promoting not only the narrow goal of economic prosperity, but also safety, happiness, and peace.

Notes

1. Smith (1791/1981), book 1, chapter 1, paragraph 6.
2. Marshall (1920/2011), book IV, chapter IX, pp. 166–167.
3. Although most participants have no issues with this, those who are sensitive to noise, suffer from claustrophobia, or who have shrapnel or internal metallic medical devices may be unable to participate in these studies.
4. The *Journal of Neuroscience, Psychology and Economics*, published quarterly by the American Psychological Association since 2011, is the leading journal devoted to highest quality research in neuroeconomics.

References

Adolphs R., Tranel, D., & Damasio, A. R. (1998). The human amygdala in social judgment. *Nature, 395*, 470–474.

Aimone, J. A., Ball, S., & King-Casas, B. (2014a). Anxiety, risk preferences, betrayal aversion, and the growth of interpersonal trust (SSRN Working Paper 2402413). Retrieved from Social Science Research Network website: http://dx.doi.org/10.2139/ssrn.2402413.

Aimone, J. A., & Houser, D. (2013). Harnessing the benefits of betrayal aversion. *Journal of Economic Behavior and Organization 89*, 1–8.

Aimone J. A., Houser, D., & Weber, B. (2014b). Neural signatures of betrayal aversion: An fMRI study of trust. *Proceedings of the Royal Society B, 281*, 20132127.

Baumgartner, T., Heinrichs, M., Vonlanthen, A., Fischbacher, U., & Fehr, E. (2008). Oxytocin shapes the neural circuitry of trust and trust adaptation in humans. *Neuron, 58*, 639–650.

Behrens, T. E. J., Hunt, L. T., Woolrich, M. W., & Rushworth, M. F. S. (2008). Associative learning of social value. *Nature, 456*, 245–250.

Berg, J., Dickhaut, J., & McCabe, K. (1995). Trust, reciprocity, & social history. *Games and Economic Behavior, 10*(1), 122–142.

Bohnet I., & Huck, S. (2004). Repetition and reputation: Implications for trust and trustworthiness when institutions change. *American Economic Review Papers and Proceedings, 94*(2), 362–366.

Brosnan, S. F., & de Waal, F. B. M. (2003). Monkeys reject unequal pay. *Nature, 425*, 297–299.

Chen, J., & Houser, D. (2012). Non-human primate studies inform the foundation of fair and just human institutions. *Social Justice Research, 25*(3), 277–297.

Chiu, P. H., Kayali, M. A., Kishida, K. T., Tomlin, D., Klinger, L., Klinger, M. R., & Montague, P. R. (2008). Self responses along cingulate cortex reveal quantitative neural phenotype for high-functioning autism. *Neuron, 57*, 463–473.

Chiu, P. H., Lohrenz, T. M., & Montague, P. R. (2008). Smokers' brains compute but ignore a fictive error signal in a sequential investment task. *Nature Neuroscience, 11*, 514–520.

Croson, R., & Gneezy, U. (2009). Gender differences in preferences. *Journal of Economic Literature, 47*(2), 448–474.

Delgado, M. R., Frank, R. H., & Phelps, E. A. (2005). Perceptions of moral character modulate the neural systems of reward during the trust game. *Nature Neuroscience, 8*(11), 1611–1618.

Dohmen, T., Falk, A., Fliessbach, K., Sunde, U., & Weber, B. (2011). Relative versus absolute income, joy of winning, and gender: Brain imaging evidence. *Journal of Public Economics, 95*, 279–285.

Domes, G., Heinrichs, M., Michel, A., Berger, C., & Herpertz, S. C. (2007). Oxytocin improves "mind-reading" in humans. *Biological Psychiatry, 61*, 731–733.

Dufwenberg, M., Lindqvist, T., & Moore, E. (2005). Bubbles and experience: An experiment. *American Economic Review, 95*(5), 1731–1737.

Eckel, C. C., & Wilson, R. K. (2004). Is trust a risky decision? *Journal of Economic Behavior & Organization, 55*(4), 447–465.

Fehr, E., Fischbacher, U., & Kosfeld, M. (2005). Neuroeconomic Foundations of Trust and Social Preferences: Initial evidence. *American Economic Review Papers and Proceedings, 95*(2), 346–351.

Gaeger, R. J., & Thomson, J. D. (2004). Does the flower constancy of bumble bees reflect foraging economics? *Ethology, 110*, 793–805.

Heilman, R. M., Crisan, L. G., Houser, D., Miclea, M., Mau, A. C., & Houser, D. (2010). Emotion regulation and decision making under risk and uncertainty. *Emotion, 10*(2), 257–265.

Houser, D., Schunk, D., & Winter, J. (2010). Distinguishing trust from risk: An anatomy of the investment game. *Journal of Economic Behavior and Organization, 74*, 72–81.

Kagel, J. (1987). Economics according to the rats (and pigeons too): What have we learned and what can we hope to learn? In A. E. Roth (Ed.), *Laboratory experimentation in economics* (pp. 155–192). New York: Cambridge University Press.

Kandasamy, N. B., Hardy, L., Page, M., Schaffner, J., Graggaber, A. S., Powlsona, P. C. et al. (2014). Cortisol shifts financial risk preferences. *Proceedings of the National Academy of Sciences.* Advance online publication. doi:10.1073/pnas.1317908111

King-Casas, B., Sharp, C., Lomax-Bream, L., Lohrenz, T., Fonagy, P., & Montague, P. R. (2008). The rupture and repair of cooperation in borderline personality disorder. *Science, 321*, 806–810.

King-Casas, B., Tomlin, D., Anen, C., Camerer, C. F., Quartz, S. R., & Montague, P. R. (2005). Getting to know you: Reputation and trust in a two-person economic exchange. *Science, 308*, 78–83.

Kirsch, P., Esslinger, C., Chen, Q., Mier, D., Lis, S., Siddhanti, S. H., . . . Meyer-Lindenberg, A. (2005). Oxytocin Modulates Neural Circuitry for Social Cognition and Fear in Humans. *The Journal of Neuroscience*, *25*(49), 11489–11493.

Kishida, K. T., Sandberg, S. G., Lohrenz, T., Comair, Y. G., Suez, I., Phillips, P. E. M., & Montague, P. R. (2011). Sub-second dopamine detection in human striatum. *PLoS One*, *6*(8), 1–5 e23291.

Knoch, D., Gianotti, L. R. R., Baumgartner, T., & Fehr, E. (2010). A neural marker of costly punishment behavior. *Psychological Science*, *21*, 337–342.

Knoch, D., Pascual-Leone, A., Meyer, K., Treyer, V., & Fehr, E. (2006). Diminishing reciprocal fairness by disrupting the right prefrontal cortex. *Science*, *314*, 829–832.

Koscik, T. R., & Tranel, D. (2011). The human amygdala is necessary for developing and expressing normal interpersonal trust. *Neuropsychologia*, *49*, 602–611.

Kosfeld, M., Heinrichs, M., Zak, P. J., Fischbacher, U., & Fehr, E. (2005). Oxytocin increases trust in humans. *Nature*, *435*, 673–676.

Krajbich, I., Adolphs, R., Tranel, D., Denburg, N. L., & Camerer. C. F. (2009). Economic games quantify diminished sense of guilt in patients with damage to the prefrontal cortex. *Journal of Neuroscience*, *29*(7), 2188–2192.

Krueger, F., McCabe, K., Moll, J., Kriegeskorte, N., Zahn, R., Strenziok, A., . . . Grafman, J. (2007). Neural correlates of trust. *Proceedings of the National Academy of Sciences*, *104*(50), 20084–20089.

Kurzban, R., & Houser, D. (2001). Individual differences in cooperation in a circular public goods game. *European Journal of Personality*, *15*, S37–S52.

Lauharatanahirun, N., Christopoulos, G. I., & King-Casas, B. (2012). Neural computations underlying social risk sensitivity. *Frontiers in Human Neuroscience*, *6*, 213.

Lundborg, P., & Stenberg, A. (2010). Nature, nurture and socioeconomic policy—What can we learn from molecular genetics? *Economics & Human Biology*, *8*(3), 320–330.

Marshall, A. (1920/2011). *Principles of economics* (8th ed.) [M. Schemmann, Ed.). Thailand: ThaiSunset.

McCabe K., Houser, D., Ryan, L., Smith, V., & Trouard, T. (2001). A functional imaging study of cooperation in two-person reciprocal exchange. *Proceedings of the National Academy of Sciences*, *98*(20), 11832–11835.

Miu, A. C., Miclea, M., & Houser, D. (2008). Anxiety and decision-making: Toward a neuroeconomic perspective. In D. Houser & K. McCabe (Eds.), *Neuroeconomics* (vol. *55–84*). London: Emerald Group Publishing.

Riedl, R., Hubert, M., & Kenning, P. (2010). Are there neural gender differences in online trust? An fMRI study on the perceived trustworthiness of eBay offers. *MIS Quarterly*, *34*(2), 397–428.

Riedl, R., & Javor, A. (2012). The biology of trust: Integrating evidence from genetics, endocrinology, and functional brain imaging. *Journal of Neuroscience, Psychology, and Economics*, *5*(2), 63–91.

Set, E., Saez, I., Zhu, L., Houser, D. E., Myung, N., Zhong, S., . . . Hsu, M. (2014). Dissociable contribution of prefrontal and striatal dopaminergic genes to learning in economic games. *Proceedings of the National Academy of Sciences*, *111*(26), 9615–9620.

Smith, A. (1791/1981). *An inquiry into the nature and causes of the wealth of nations* (vol. *1*). (R. H. Campbell, A. S. Skinner, & W. B. Todd Eds.). Indianapolis, IN: Liberty Fund.

Smith, A. (1761/1982). *The theory of moral sentiments*. (D. D. Raphael & A. L. Macfie, Eds.). Indianapolis, IN: Liberty Fund.

Sripada, C., Angstadt, M., Liberzon, I., McCabe, K., & Phan, K. L. (2009). Functional neuroimaging of mentalizing during the trust game in social anxiety disorder. *Neuroreport, 20*(11), 984–989.

Tomlin D., Kayali, M. A., King-Casas, B., Anen, C., Camerer, C. F., Quartz, S. R., & Montague, P. R. (2006). Agent-specific responses in the cingulate cortex during economic exchanges. *Science, 312*, 1047–1050.

Tricomi, E., Rangel, A., Camerer, C. F., & O'Doherty, J. P. (2010). Neural evidence for inequality-averse social preferences. *Nature, 463*, 1089–1092.

Van Lange, P. A. M., Finkenauer, C., Popma, A., & van Vugt, M. (2011). Electrodes as social glue: Measuring heart rate promotes giving in the trust game. *International Journal of Psychophysiology, 80*, 246–250.

Weber, B., Rangel, A., Wibral, M., & Falk, A. (2009). The medial prefrontal cortex exhibits money illusion. *Proceedings of the National Academy of Science, 106*(13), 5025–5028.

Wu, C. C., Bossaerts, P., & Knutson, B. (2011). The affective impact of financial skewness on neural activity and choice. *PLoS ONE, 6*(2), e16838.

Xiao, E., & Houser, D. (2005). Emotion expression in human punishment behavior. *Proceedings of the National Academy of Sciences, 102*(20), 7398–7401.

Zak, P. J., & Fakhar, A. (2006). Neuroactive hormones and interpersonal trust: International evidence. *Economics & Human Biology, 4*(3), 412–429.

PART IV

REGIONAL STUDIES

CHAPTER 33

THE AFRICAN ENIGMA

The Mystery of Tall African Adults Despite Low National Incomes Revisited

ALEXANDER MORADI AND KALLE HIRVONEN

33.1 The African Enigma

The nexus between income and height underlies much of the economics and human biology literature. Typically, income is positively correlated with the proximate determinants of height—nutrition and health—and thereby height itself. The "antebellum puzzle" is the best-known and a well-researched anomaly: while incomes were growing in antebellum America 1800–60, heights of native-born whites were decreasing (Fogel, Engerman, Floud, Steckel, & Trussell, 1982; Komlos 1987, 1996; Haines, Craig, & Weiss 2003). Cross-country evidence from Africa provides another anomaly. Deaton (2007) observed that adult Africans are tall despite of the very low income levels that prevail in Africa. What is more, African children grow up under a very severe disease environment and poor health, and that is also at odds with the observation of tall adults. This is true for levels as well as trends. Inasmuch as infant mortality rates in sub-Saharan Africa 1950–80 were declining, heights have not been increasing consistently (Akachi & Canning, 2010). Scatter plots display these anomalies (Figure 33.1 and Figure 33.2). Heights of African populations are clustered far above the line of best fit based on data for non-African countries, indicating that Africa significantly deviates from the global patterns of income, mortality, and height.

Bozzoli, Deaton, and Quintana-Domeque (2009) proposed a solution to this puzzle by pointing to the scarring and selection effects of childhood diseases. *Scarring* is the long-term negative effect of diseases on survivors. Those who survive the diseases are, on average, shorter than they would have been if they had not contracted the disease in early childhood. *Selection*, on the other hand, removes the least healthy (shorter) members of the population by mortality, so that the survivors are healthier (taller). In such

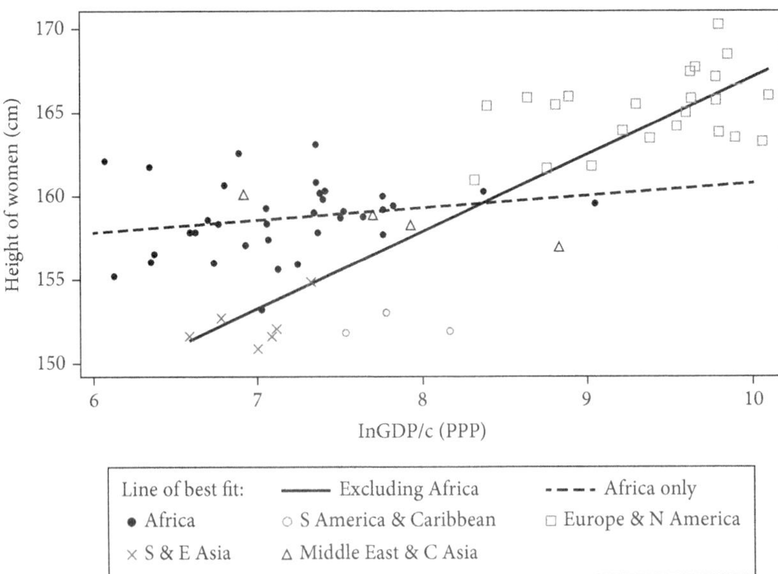

FIGURE 33.1 Tall adult Africans despite low incomes. Each dot represents a country-wide average. Heights of women born 1971–80 were derived from Demographic and Health Surveys and the 2005 Eurobarometer. Gross Domestic Product (GDP) per capita (PPP, 2005 US dollars) from Penn World Tables 8.0 are averaged over 1971–80.

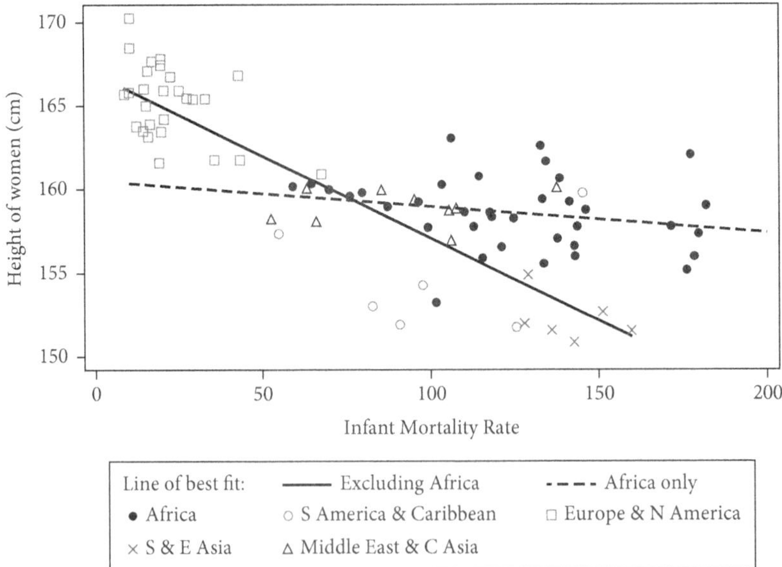

FIGURE 33.2 Tall adult Africans despite high infant mortality rates. Each dot represents a country-wide average. Heights of women born 1971–80 were derived from Demographic and Health Surveys and the 2005 Eurobarometer. Infant mortality rates (number of deaths of children under 1 year old per 1,000 live births) from 2014 World Development Indicators are averaged over 1971–80.

cases, only the surviving (taller) population is included in the sample, whereas those (short) individuals who have passed away are not. Bozzoli, Deaton, and Quintana-Domeque (2009) suggested that, for Africa, precisely because of the high-mortality environment, the selection effect would dominate the scarring effect. The higher mortality risk of shorter than average children is indeed well-documented for Africa (Billewicz & McGregor, 1982; Boerma, Sommerfelt, & Bicego, 1992; Rouanet, 2011). Moradi (2010*b*), however, showed in simulations that the selection effect is too small to account for the observed size of the anomaly in the heights of African adults.

In this chapter, we discuss the income–height nexus for African populations. We begin by narrowing down possible explanations. We find that

- income does correlate positively with height within any one country in Africa; and
- heights of African children do fit into the global income–height pattern.

These two findings let us conclude that the anomaly at the continental level must arise during the period between childhood and adulthood. We present evidence for substantial catch-up growth involving almost the entire population. This catch-up growth leaves the income–height relationship within and between African countries largely intact, but it has the effect of raising the adult height of Africans. We discuss possible reasons for this catch-up growth including genetics, and, above all, better nutrition and health conditions during adolescence.

33.2 Income–Height Nexus at the Microlevel: A Meta-review

One of the most consistent findings in the height literature is a positive relationship between height and socioeconomic status (SES) within a country. Does this positive correlation between income and height at the individual level also hold within African countries?

We conducted a meta-analysis reviewing studies that took individual children or adults as the unit of observation (microlevel studies).[1] The articles differ widely in their methodologies. The choice of model specification, as well as the set of control variables, varies. Some studies use instrumental variable techniques.[2] The more convincing studies use natural experiments or interventions. Here, we do not distinguish between methodologies or quality of analyses. Our aim is only to see whether microstudies find a positive income–height correlation within African populations.[3] Results are summarized in Table 33.1.

The overwhelming majority of studies found a statistically significant and positive correlation between income and height (e.g., Alderman, Hoogeveen, & Rossi, 2006; Cogneau & Jedwab, 2012; Sahn, 1994; Thomas, Lavy, & Strauss, 1996). Only one study,

Table 33.1 Findings of microlevel studies on the height-income relationship in Africa

Height determinant	Income	Assets	Education of mother	Education of father	Urban
Positive effect	18	18	23	5	17
Nonsignificant	1	2	9	2	2
Negative effect	0	1	1	1	0

Total number of articles reviewed is 71. Articles did not necessarily test the impact of all indicators. Studies that analyzed more than one country and tested determinants measured at the microlevel under country fixed-effects specifications are included under microlevel because the identifying variation comes from within country differences. Studies in the meta-review are listed at the end of the chapter.

Kebede (2005) found a correlation that was not statistically significant. While this study did document a significant and positive coefficient in ordinary least squares (OLS) regression, when proxying income with household consumption expenditures, the coefficient turns insignificant in subsequent models that exploit individual fixed or random effects. Such models take a large toll on degrees of freedom. Therefore, finding an insignificant coefficient on a household consumption variable (that is typically considered a proxy for permanent income rather than transient income) is not surprising. Kebede (2005) also attempted to address the endogeneity of income using a not entirely convincing instrumental variable approach, which again led to a positive but insignificant coefficient.[4] This is also expected because instrumental variable methods are well-known for producing larger standard errors than OLS. Overall, we can conclude that income is a robust predictor of attained height in microstudies.

Income is difficult to measure in developing countries and is rarely collected in surveys.[5] A common approach is to use asset indices instead to proxy for household wealth. Components of the asset index frequently include housing quality indicators such as type of toilet facility, source of drinking water, or roof and wall type of the dwelling (five studies); consumer durables such as owning a radio, television, refrigerator (five studies), or both (eight studies); and, to a smaller degree, livestock, land, and agricultural tools (three studies). In Fawzi et al. (Fawzi, Herrera, Nestel, El Amin, & Mohamed, 1998) the level of household wealth was assessed subjectively by the interviewer. Similar to the reviewed studies using income, a positive correlation between wealth and height is documented in the overwhelming majority of cases: 18 out of 22 studies find a statistically significant and positive relationship between height and assets. In two studies, the coefficient on the asset variable was not statistically different from zero. Using a sample of 888 children from the Soweto neighborhood in Johannesburg, South Africa, Sheppard et al. (Sheppard, Norris, Pettifor, Cameron, &

Griffiths, 2009) regressed height-for-age (HAZ) scores on individual asset categories (TV, car, education, access to health care). Although the coefficients of untreated variables were positive but insignificant, after collapsing them into different asset indices, they found 4 out of 7 indices positively and significantly associated with HAZ scores. Mamabolo et al. (2005) used data for 162 children from Limpopo province in South Africa and found no statistically significant association between housing type (brick vs. other) and stunting probability at age 3 years. Only Pierre-Louis et al. (Pierre-Louis, Sanjur, Nesheim, Bowman, & Mohammed, 2007) found a negative correlation between children's HAZ scores and household per capita livestock assets in Mali, but the sample was small (N = 49) and nonrepresentative.

Education often serves as a proxy of SES. In Africa, a wage premium is typically associated with secondary schooling and higher (Schultz 1999, 2003). Hence, education is likely to be positively correlated with wage income. In addition, many analysts expect significant benefits beyond monetary channels, for example, through better child care. Most studies tested the correlation with mother's education (26 studies), father's education (one study), or education of both parents (seven studies). Although the correlations for education are less clear-cut than for assets or income, the meta-review largely agrees with Alderman and Headey (2014) in that there is a positive association between education of parents and children's physical development (generally only with secondary education) and that maternal education yields larger returns than does paternal education.

Finally, a significant number of studies highlighted the urban–rural dichotomy in living standards. Urban wages are, on average, higher, and city dwellers typically have better access to health care. A large majority of studies found that living in cities is associated with a significant height advantage (e.g., see Paciorek, Stevens, Finucane, & Ezzati, 2013).[6]

From this meta-review, we conclude that the puzzle does not exist at the microlevel. Income and proxies of income, wealth, and SES are positively correlated with heights. The puzzle is therefore at the macrolevel, originating from studies that compare countries and populations to each other.

33.3 Income–Height Relationship: From Children to Adults

The African Enigma has not been identified in studies of child malnutrition (Klasen, 2008). Figure 33.3 shows that the income–height puzzle does not exist in child anthropometry: African children aged 0–5 years are shorter than their counterparts from other regions, as indicated by lower HAZ scores, in line with the lower incomes prevailing in Africa.[7] In contrast to the case of adults in Figure 33.1, considering the African countries only results in a nearly identical line of best fit. Hence, the same height–income pattern in children holds when considering African countries only.

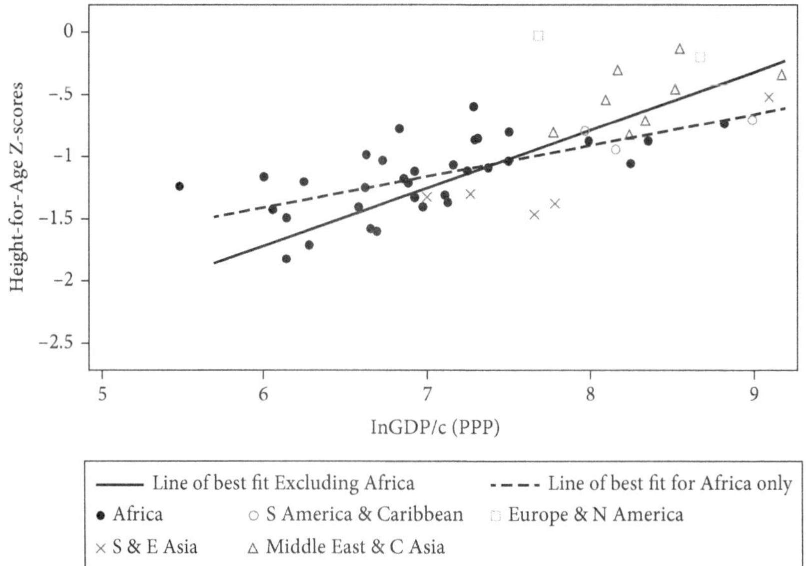

FIGURE 33.3 Height–income relationship in children (0–5 years). See Figure 33.1.

Data from Demographic and Health Surveys conducted around 2005 only. No data for European countries.

African children fit the global height–income relationship, but African adults do not. This may suggest that the anomaly in the height–income relationship in African adults originates after early childhood. We explore this idea further by showing the HAZ scores and income levels prevailing around birth for both adults and children in one graph. We connect the child–adult outcomes for each country by a line indicating the movement in GDP/c and HAZ. Figure 33.4 shows these values for African countries. First, for all but one country, HAZ scores of women exceed those of children. Second, as indicated by the overwhelmingly north-south direction of the lines, this is despite the fact that incomes have not changed much between 1970–80 and 2000–05. Hence, the higher HAZ scores of adult women cannot be explained by higher incomes at birth. This pattern does not exist in other regions of the world. Figure 33.5 shows non-African countries. Here, as indicated by the predominantly southwest-northeast direction of the lines, incomes and HAZ scores both improved when moving from the adult cohort to the child cohort. The slope of the lines fit very much the cross-sectional pattern: there is only one income–height relationship that holds in the cross-section and over the birth/age cohorts. This is not the case in African countries. Figure 33.4 rather indicates that there are *two* income–height relationships for African countries: one for adult women and one for children. Figures 33.6 and 33.7 further confirm this interpretation.

Figure 33.6 compares the HAZ–income relationship between African children and adults.[8] We excluded the Sahel countries (Burkina Faso, Chad, Mali, Niger, Senegal) when computing the line of best fit. Sahel countries are outliers insofar as adult women are extraordinarily tall despite of low incomes prevailing around the time of their birth.[9] Moradi (2012) argued that in the Sahel countries GDP per capita in the 1970s did not

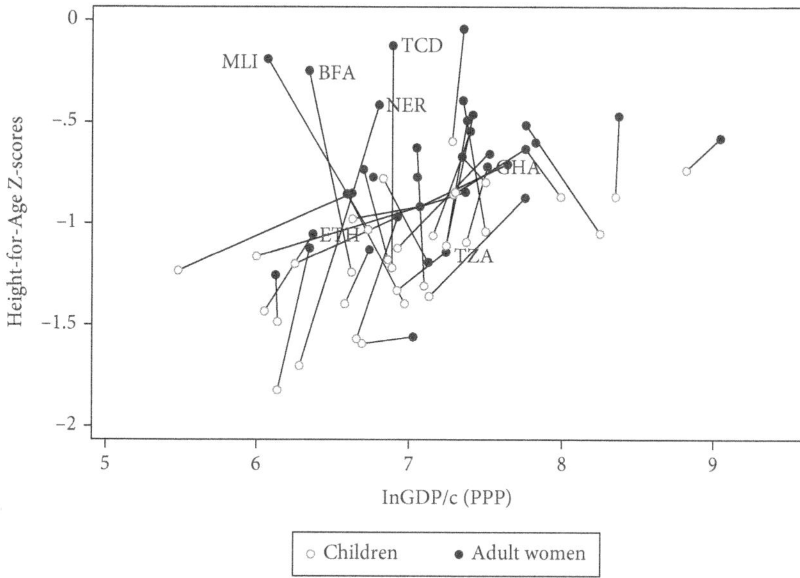

FIGURE 33.4 Correlation between height of children and women and gross domestic product (GDP) per capita (PPP) at birth: African countries. The graph shows HAZ scores of children born 2000–05, HAZ scores of women born 1971–80, and their respective GDP per capita at birth. The HAZ score of women is connected to the HAZ score of children of the same country. Hence, vertical lines from bottom (children) to top (women) indicate higher HAZ scores for adults despite of the same GDP per capita. MLI, Mali; BFA, Burkina Faso; NER, Niger; TCD, Chad; TZA, Tanzania; GHA, Ghana; and ETH, Ethiopia.

reflect nutritional intakes. The Sahel countries are beyond the fringe of trypanosomiasis endemic areas. Cattle holdings per capita are high compared to the African countries in the tropical forests, and cattle provide protein in the form of milk and meat and are associated with better HAZ scores of children and adults (Hoddinott, Headey, & Dereje, 2015; Moradi & Baten, 2005).[10] The 1970s saw droughts and famines, and nutrition deteriorated to levels more in line with the low GDP per capita. As a consequence, the outlier status of Sahel countries disappears in children born in 2000–05 (Moradi, 2012). Figure 33.6 confirms the pattern of two income–height relationships for African countries. The regression lines for children and adults are almost parallel, but the child data lie well below the adult data. Figure 33.7 shows that such differences do not exist in data from non-African countries. Thus, if income remained constant over time, we would still find that short children become tall adults in Africa. In other words, African children catch up after early childhood. For any income level, African adults lie on a 0.5–0.6 standard deviation higher HAZ curve than do African children. In adult heights 0.5 HAZ scores corresponds to about 3.4–4.1 cm.

Multivariate regression analysis confirms this finding. We regressed HAZ scores on GDP per capita, the infant mortality rate (IMR), and an Africa dummy. The latter indicates the size of the African Enigma: by how much are African populations taller

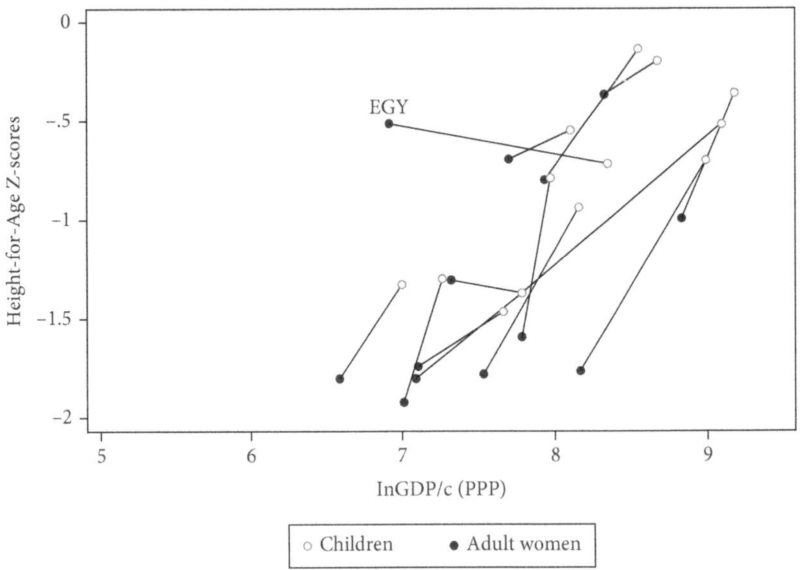

FIGURE 33.5 Correlation between height of children and women and gross domestic product (GDP) per capita (PPP) at birth: non-African countries. The graph shows HAZ scores of children born 2000–05, HAZ scores of women born 1971–80, and their respective GDP per capita at birth. Diagonal lines from top (children) to bottom (women) indicate higher HAZ scores and GDP per capita at birth for children as compared to adults. EGY, Egypt.

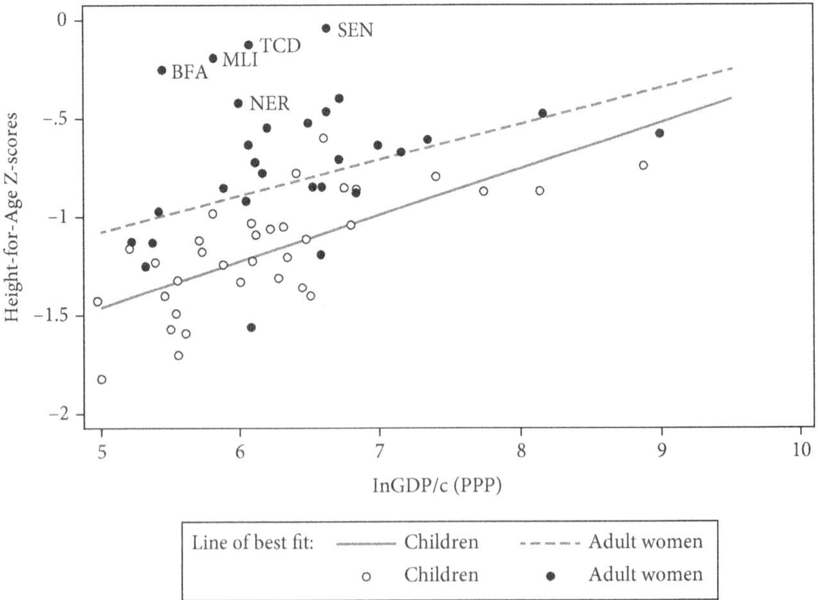

FIGURE 33.6 Height income nexus in children (0–5 years) and adult women: African countries. Line of best fit excludes Sahel states (Burkina Faso, Chad, Mali, Niger, and Senegal).

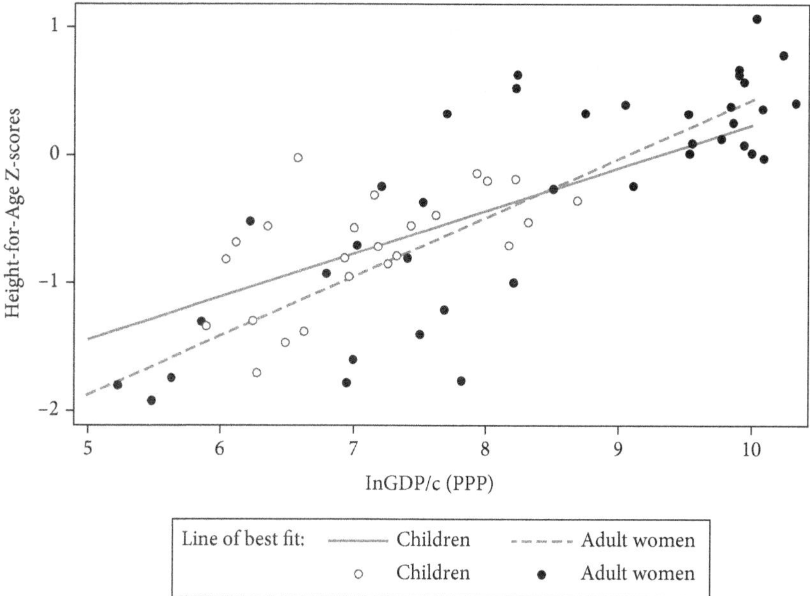

FIGURE 33.7 Height income nexus in children (0–5 years) and adult women: non-African countries. Each dot represents a country-wide average. Heights of women born 1971–80 were derived from Demographic and Health Surveys and the 2005 Eurobarometer. Heights of children born ca. 2005 from DHS only. Gross Domestic Product (GDP) per capita (PPP, 2005 US dollars) from Penn World Tables 8.0 are averaged over birth years.

given their income and mortality rates. Column 1 of Table 33.2 shows the estimates for children based on the Demographic and Health Survey (DHS) data for developing and emerging countries. The coefficient on national income is highly significant and positive, whereas the IMR coefficient is negative but insignificant. Note that income and infant mortality rates are collinear: the correlation coefficient equals −0.6 in the children's sample and −0.9 in the adults' sample.[11] The Africa dummy coefficient, however, is close to zero and insignificant, thus indicating that the HAZ scores of African children correspond well with their low incomes and high mortality rates. Column 2 of Table 33.2 shows the estimates for adults based on DHS for developing or emerging countries and Eurobarometer data for countries of the Organization for Economic Cooperation and Development (OECD). The coefficients for income and IMR do not change much, but the coefficient on the Africa dummy variable does. African adults are, on average, 0.52 HAZ scores taller than one would expect from their income and IMR. Column 3 of Table 33.2 shows the estimates of the pooled regression. The slope parameters for GDP per capita and IMR are stable across generations. Interestingly, after controlling for national income and infant mortality rate, adults seem to have generally somewhat higher HAZ scores in general than do children (by 0.22 HAZ) but not significantly so at the 5% level. Most importantly, relative to their national income and IMR, African child populations are not taller than others (the Africa dummy variable is only 0.02). The

Table 33.2 Multivariate regression analysis of the height–income relationship at the macrolevel

	Children	Adults	Pooled	Pooled: DHS only
	(1)	(2)	(3)	(4)
ln GDP per capita	0.24***	0.22***	0.24***	0.18***
	(5.03)	(3.01)	(5.25)	(4.13)
Infant mortality rate	-0.004	-0.007***	-0.006***	-0.003*
	(-1.38)	(-2.68)	(-3.47)	(-1.74)
Adults			0.22*	-0.21
			(1.79)	(-1.19)
Africa dummy	-0.08	0.52***	0.02	-0.16
	(-0.59)	(3.22)	(0.16)	(-1.49)
Africa × Adults			0.48***	0.80***
			(3.35)	(4.63)
Data source	DHS	DHS + Eurobarometer	DHS + Eurobarometer	DHS
R^2-adjusted	0.56	0.61	0.66	0.43
Number of observations	58	69	127	100

See Figure 33.1. Ordinary least squares (OLS) estimator. All regressions include a constant; robust t-statistics in parentheses. Significance denoted at *** p<0.01, ** p<0.05, * p<0.1.

height anomaly only exists in African adults who are taller. Overall, Africans adults have higher HAZ scores than do African children by 0.7 HAZ units (0.48 + 0.22). This is in line with African children experiencing considerable catch-up growth after early childhood. Column 4 restricts the data to countries for which we have data on both child and adult heights. Dropping the OECD countries from the adult sample renders the coefficient on the adult dummy insignificant. The coefficient on the Africa–adult interaction term remains highly significant, and the overall magnitude of the difference is similar to the one obtained in Column 3. According to Column 4, African adults are on average 0.6 HAZ units (−0.16 + 0.80) taller than African children.

At what age does this catch-up growth occur? The analysis is made difficult by the fact that most household surveys in developing countries, including DHS, do not collect anthropometric data for children older than 5 years. The few surveys that do contain anthropometric data for a representative sample of all ages support the view that African children's growth catches up considerably during puberty. Figure 33.8 shows

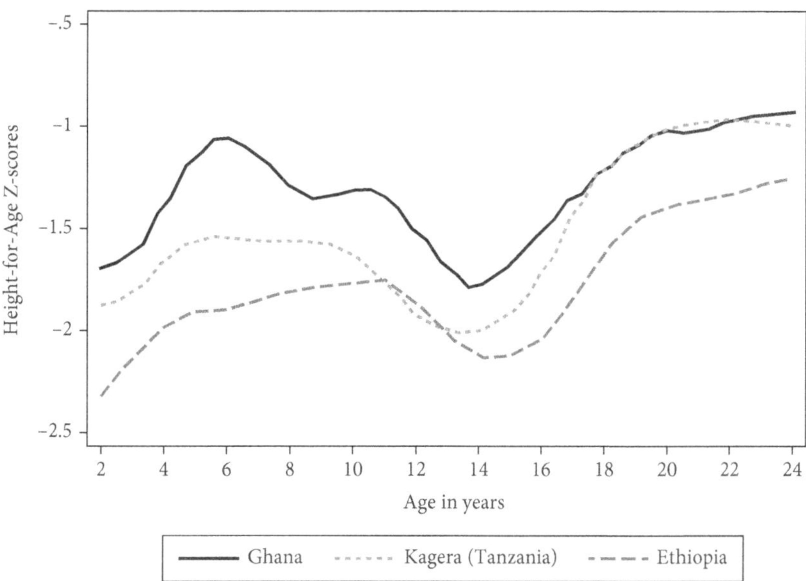

FIGURE 33.8 Catch-up growth in Ghana, Tanzania, and Ethiopia: age 2–24 years, males and females. Kernel-weighted local polynomial regression. HAZ based on CDC-2000 growth standard. All data sets are longitudinal and contain more than one height observations per individual. The data for Ghana is based on the Ghana Living Standard Measurement Study surveys 1988/1989 (total number of height observations; N = 25,349). The data for Kagera (Tanzania) is based on Kagera Health and Development Survey 1991/94 (N = 14,228). Using the information from the follow-up surveys administered 10–16 years later, individuals who did not survive their 18th birthday were removed from the sample. The data for Ethiopia are based on Ethiopia Rural Household Survey 1995–97 (N = 23,340). The 95% confidence intervals (not reported) are small, around 0.1 HAZ.

growth curves for three datasets. In Figure 33.8, the HAZ scores of Ethiopian and Tanzanian children remain relatively stable in children aged 5–10 years. HAZ scores then decrease at ages of around 12–14 years.[12] This decrease is due to the fact that at this age the reference population enters the adolescent growth spurt, and their growth velocity significantly increases, whereas the growth velocity of the study populations remain stable because the growth spurt is delayed in malnourished and stunted populations (Eveleth & Tanner, 1990). However, when Ethiopian and Tanzanian teenagers enter puberty, they experience remarkable catch-up growth, leading them to a HAZ score of attained adult height that exceeds the one before puberty by approximately 0.5 units—roughly the same size as we found in Table 33.2. Ghanaian children, although starting from a higher level, also recover from prepubertal growth faltering during puberty.[13]

We assumed that the observed patterns in the growth curves of Figure 33.8 are mainly due to age effects. In other words, we assumed that children follow the same HAZ–age trajectory as they become older. However, since the underlying data are cross-sectional, a valid objection to this assumption is that the HAZ differences at

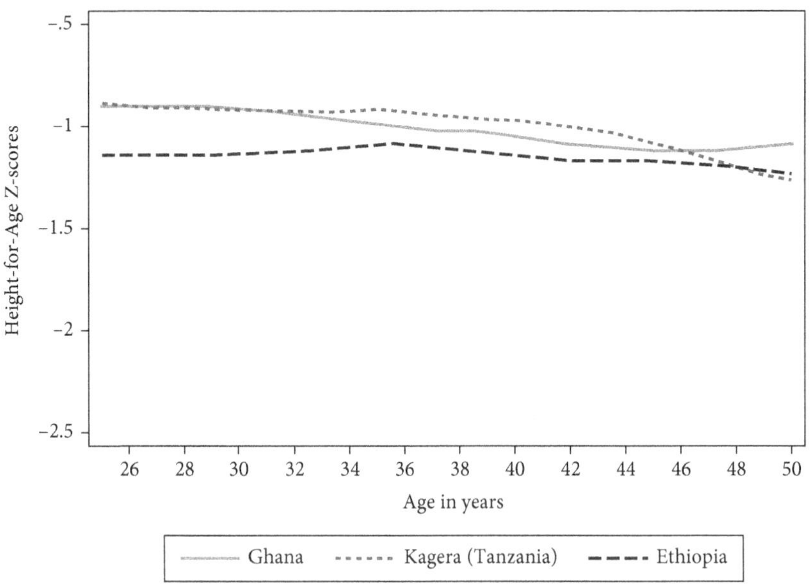

FIGURE 33.9 Catch-up growth in Ghana, Tanzania, and Ethiopia: age 25–50 years, males and females. See Figure 33.8.

certain ages could reflect birth cohort effects as well: children's heights could differ because they were born under different economic conditions. This is unlikely to be the case, though. The income data do not support the notion that economic conditions improved substantially just when these children were adolescent. In fact Tanzanian GDP per capita stagnated between 1973 and 1980 (the birth period of those Tanzanians aged 13–20 years in the sample), and Ethiopian GDP per capita was only $100 higher in 1976–80 compared to 1991–96 (the birth periods of those aged 16–20 and 0–5, respectively).[14] Moreover, in Figure 33.9, we do not observe similar substantial variation in adult heights: HAZ curves between 25 and 50 years of age are stable compared to Figure 33.8. Figure 33.9 also confirms the lack of upward secular trend in adult heights in African countries.

Longitudinal studies that follow children from early childhood to adulthood enable us to eliminate the role of the birth cohort effects. Evidence from three such longitudinal studies confirms our previous results. Coly et al. (2006) tracked 2,900 Senegalese children for two decades and documented nearly complete catch-up growth in puberty. Prentice et al. (2013) provided similar evidence for Gambia, exploiting longitudinal data of 160 children aged 8–24 years and finding nearly complete catch-up growth that occurred in puberty. Using 19-year tracking data from the Kagera region in Tanzania, Hirvonen (2014) found that the mean HAZ score in the cohort of 540 children improved from −1.86 in early childhood to −1.20 in adulthood; cross-sectional evidence then suggested that most of this catch-up growth took place in puberty. Finally, economic historians have documented similar growth patterns among African Americans (Komlos, 1992; Steckel, 1987).

33.4 Possible Explanations for the African Enigma

We have argued that the explanation for tall African adults lies in catch-up growth. But what triggers this catch-up growth? Evidence is limited. Using a longitudinal survey from Tanzania, Hirvonen (2014) observed that the HAZ distribution of the *whole* adolescent population shifts upward. With almost universal catch-up growth, even cohort studies are unable to shed light on the determinants of catch-up growth. This is because, if the whole population catches up, then there is limited variation in catch-up growth between individuals. Therefore, individual-level differences cannot account for the larger universal experience.[15] This then also suggests that "something" at the national (or population) level is causing the catch-up growth. Therefore, the explanation of this finding must remain for future researchers to explore.

We cannot rule out the genetic argument. Although a large fraction of height differences between individuals can be explained by genetics (Silventoinen, 2003), it is typically assumed that populations of different ethnic backgrounds have the same genetic potential throughout the growing years. In other words, it is expected that populations growing up under the same nutrition and health conditions attain the same mean height.[16] A large number of studies have documented how well-nourished and healthy children from different ethnic backgrounds attain very similar mean heights (Bhandari, Bahl, Taneja, de Onis, & Bhan, 2002; Habicht, Martorel, Yarbroug, Malina, & Klein, 1974; WHO Multicentre Growth Reference Study Group & de Onis, 2006).[17] Therefore, for genetics to explain tall African adults, its impact must be somehow switched on during puberty. Pradhan, Sahn, and Younger (2003, p. 277), for example, allude to this when they justify the use of children's height as a health indicator but "reject the use of heights of adults because of genetic variability" although without providing any evidence or citation for this presumption.[18] Overall, the genetics of the African population has not been explored sufficiently and is a topic for further research.

We can nevertheless provide "soft evidence" against genetics as an explanation using data for African Americans. It can be assumed that African Americans share approximately the same genetic pool as modern-day Africans but are exposed to a very different disease and socioeconomic environment (Eltis, 1982). In Figure 33.10, we use data from the latest available National Health and Nutrition Examination Survey (NHANES) round and construct HAZ scores for African Americans. The HAZ curve is relatively flat, hovering around the zero line and thus implying that the growth curve of an average African-American child approximately follows the growth trajectory of the median child in the American reference population. This suggests that environmental factors are more likely candidates to explain the catch-up growth rather than genetics. Steckel (1987, 2000), for example, found considerable catch-up growth among African-American slaves in 1820–60 when they came of working age, and slave owners markedly improved their diet to maintain the slaves' labor productivity. Moradi (2010*a*) found that economic growth measured around age of puberty strongly predicts final attained

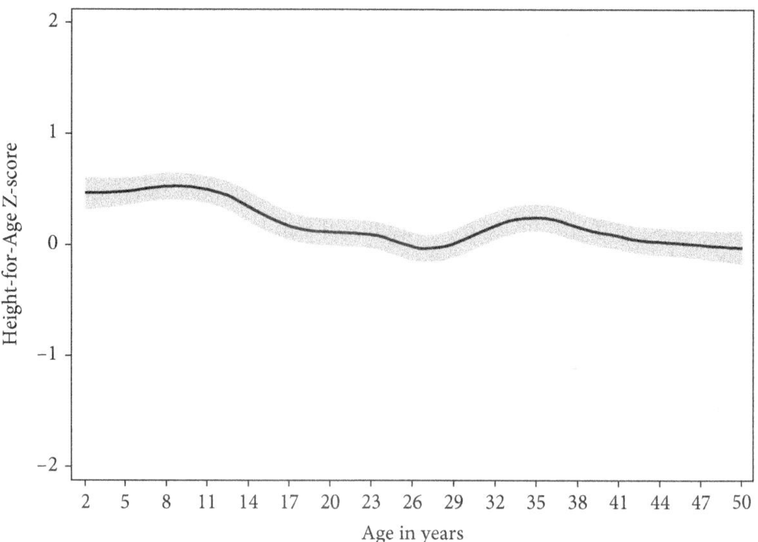

FIGURE 33.10 HAZ of African Americans 2012. HAZ based on CDC-2000 growth standard. Data drawn from NHANES 2011–12. Kernel-weighted local polynomial regression.

height of African women: the birth cohorts born in the 1970s were so much affected by the economic crisis of the 1980s (the lost decade) that they attained a height shorter than 1960 birth cohorts even though conditions at birth were similar or better. In a similar vein, Akresh et al. (Akresh, Bhalotra, Leone, & Osili, 2012) found adult height of women of ethnic groups exposed to the Nigerian Civil War at age 13–16 years to be more affected than women exposed to the war at younger ages.

Moradi (2010*b*) put forward two hypotheses that did not have a genetic basis. First, the incidence of diseases is much less severe during puberty compared to early childhood. Age-specific mortality rates underline this. Most of the deaths are concentrated in infancy and childhood, not among adolescents. This can be due to a less harsh age-specific morbidity as well as to acquired immunity at puberty. Better health conditions then translate into considerable catch-up growth when children go through the adolescent growth spurt. Second, puberty is also the age when adolescents start to contribute more to the household income. This may improve their intrahousehold bargaining power, thus leading to increased food shares within the household, or it can supplement their food portions from their own income. Although plausible, there is no strong evidence for these hypotheses as of yet.

33.5 More Research Is Needed on African Heights

Is catch-up growth that results in an adult height anomaly of 3 or 4 cm substantial enough to merit attention? In most countries, we observe a secular trend in adult height

(Cole, 2003). In the United States and Western Europe between 1880 and 1980, the secular trend in mean male heights reached about 0.9 cm per decade (Baten & Blum, 2012; Costa & Steckel, 1997). During the same period, Latin American and East Asian heights increased by about 0.4 cm and 0.5 cm per decade, respectively (Baten & Blum, 2012). Hence, a 3–4 cm difference would correspond to an improvement in nutrition and health status of about four to eight decades. We therefore think this height anomaly is substantial enough to merit further attention.

Heights have been shown to correlate with earnings, productivity, cognitive abilities, educational outcomes, and lower morbidity and mortality in later life (e.g., Steckel, 2009). Most studies that investigate adult outcomes such as wages or cognitive test scores use adult height and, to a lesser degree, height of children, but not both.[19] Indeed, if HAZ scores are more or less stable from childhood to adulthood, it will be difficult to distinguish between the two, and the approach is justified. The important implication of the African Enigma is that this is not the case for African countries. The damage during early childhood—as reflected in stunted height—is partly reversed during puberty. It may well be that adult height rather than childhood height is more important for certain outcomes (such as physical strength, labor productivity, and earnings). Putting the entire focus on childhood may therefore be misleading. This calls for future research. In particular, emphasis should be given to a better understanding of what happens to Africans during puberty and how the experience during this specific period affects later outcomes.

Notes

1. We searched three databases for articles published before June 20, 2014: PubMed, Scopus, and Web of Science. To restrict the search to height in African countries, we used "Height" and "Africa*" as keywords that both had to be mentioned at least once anywhere in the title, abstract, or body text of the article. The asterisk refers to a wildcard: it considers all words that start with "Africa"; e.g., Africa, African, Africans. In addition, we used the three keywords "Income," "Socioeconomic" and "Wealth," of which at least one had to be mentioned in the article. The search led to the identification of 876 distinct articles. After a first screening of title and abstract, we excluded 768 articles that did not study the height–income relationship or did not use data from the African continent. Out of 108 articles, 20 were not accessible and 11 did not study or report height–income or height–wealth associations. Six articles studied mean heights at the country (macro) level. This left us with 71 articles for the final review. They are listed at the end of this chapter.
2. We are very critical about the use of instrumental variable regressions in the height literature. Although in theory using instruments is a sound way to account for endogeneity, in practice, it is very difficult for any instrument to pass the exclusion restriction for height, a variable that is demonstrably influenced by so many channels.
3. We did not distinguish between child and adult populations because findings did not appear to differ between the two groups.
4. Kebede (2005) instruments household expenditures with per capita land size cultivated by the household and the size of land owned by the parents of spouses. This strategy is valid only if land sizes do not exert an independent impact on children's HAZ (other than

through household incomes). This is unlikely to be the case because, for example, larger land holdings also allow the cultivation of a wider range of food products that may in turn contribute positively to children's diet diversity and, in turn, to their HAZ.

5. Measurement problems also exist for GDP per capita estimates of African countries (Jerven, 2013). Note, however, that African countries would only fit into the international income–height relationship as indicated by the regression line in Figure 33.1 if GDP per capita were around $5,000–10,000. This is highly implausible.
6. The urban "dividend" is largely a 20th-century phenomenon. Pre-20th century urban dwellers in Europe, for example, were found to be shorter than their rural counterparts.
7. Height-for-age z-scores measure the distance to the median height of a healthy and well-nourished reference population of equal sex and age in terms of standard deviations of that same reference population. For instance, a HAZ score of −2 indicates that the child (population) is two standard deviations shorter than the median child (population) of the reference population. Median and standard deviation vary by age and gender. We used the US 2000 NCHS/CDC as a reference population because it allows the calculation of HAZ scores from birth to 20 years of age and is constructed using the same reference throughout the entire growth period (Kuczmarski et al., 2002). Height-for-age *z*-scores were calculated using the zanthro command in Stata 13.
8. The data are based on adult women and on children who are less than 5 years of age. The observed patterns are not due to gender differences in early childhood: using data for female children produces a nearly identical graph.
9. The mean heights of women are as follows: Burkina Faso (161.7 cm), Chad (162.5), Mali (162.1), Niger (160.6), and Senegal (163.1). Overall, women in the five Sahel countries are about 0.7 HAZ scores (4.7 cm) taller than African populations with the same GDP/c.
10. The significant height advantage of African pastoral populations is in line with this observation (Little, 1989; Little, Gray, & Campbell, 2001). Even though poor in income terms, their diets are high in proteins; for example, the protein intakes of Kenyan Maasai and Senegalese Fulani were reported to exceed 200% of recommended daily intakes (Benefice, Chevassus-Agnes, & Barral, 1984; Nestel, 1986). Caloric intakes, in contrast, are low.
11. The higher correlation in adults is due to the inclusion of developed countries in the adult sample.
12. "Our results do not change when using "Height-for-age difference" as a measure of catch-up growth as recently suggested by Leroy et al. (2015)."
13. There are gender differences in the growth trajectories not shown in Figure 33.8: girls begin their pubertal growth spurt earlier. In Tanzania and Ghana, the gender difference in catch-up growth between age 2–5 years and 20–24 years is negligible, whereas in Ethiopia girls catch up more than boys, by about 0.31 HAZ. The average HAZ score of adult women in the African DHS surveys is −0.72.
14. Because Ethiopia was very poor—GDP per capita was only $600 in the 1976–80 period—$100 implies a rather large difference in relative terms of 20 percentage points. But, again, this variation in GDP per capita is small compared to the variation experienced in the 1950–80 period, when the survey's adults aged 25–50 years grew up, see Figure 33.9.
15. Econometrically speaking, catch-up growth would then be included in the constant.
16. There is a long-lasting debate on whether height differences across populations are due to genetics or other factors (diets, environment, and income); see in particular the "small but healthy" debate by Seckler (1982, 1984), Messer (1986), and Beaton (1989); for a more recent

version of the genetics debate, see Panagariya (2013); Coffey, Deaton, Dreze, Tarozzi, and Spears (2013), and Gillespie (2013).

17. Adoption studies from non-African countries also support this view (Graham & Adrianzen, 1971; Winick, Meyer, & Harris, 1975).
18. In height regressions, genetics is picked up by the residual that captures height differences that cannot be explained by environmental conditions. The Africa dummy can be claimed to be genetics, but it can also represent environmental conditions at puberty, which are rather similar across African countries and that previous models have omitted so far.
19. We are not aware of a single study that disentangles the two.

References

Akachi, Y., & Canning, D. (2010). Health trends in Sub-Saharan Africa: Conflicting evidence from infant mortality rates and adult heights. *Economics & Human Biology, 8*(2), 273–288.

Akresh, R., Bhalotra, S., Leone, M., & Osili, U. O. (2012). War and stature: Growing up during the Nigerian Civil War. *American Economic Review, 102*(3), 273–277.

Alderman, H., & Headey, D. D. (2014). *The nutritional returns to parental education* (IFPRI Discussion Paper 01379). Washington, DC: International Food Policy Research Institute.

Alderman, H., Hoogeveen, H., & Rossi, M. (2006). Reducing child malnutrition in Tanzania: Combined effects of income growth and program interventions. *Economics & Human Biology, 4*(1), 1–23.

Baten, J., & Blum, M. (2012). Growing tall but unequal: New findings and new background evidence on anthropometric welfare in 156 countries, 1810–1989. *Economic History of Developing Regions, 27*(Supplement 1), S66–S85.

Beaton, G. H. (1989). Small but healthy? Are we asking the right question? *Human Organization, 48*(1), 30–39.

Benefice, E., Chevassus-Agnes, S., & Barral, H. (1984). Nutritional situation and seasonal variations for pastoralist populations of the Sahel (Senegalese Ferlo). *Ecology of Food and Nutrition, 14*(3), 229–247.

Bhandari, N., Bahl, R., Taneja, S., de Onis, M., & Bhan, M. K. (2002). Growth performance of affluent Indian children is similar to that in developed countries. *Bulletin of the World Health Organization, 80*(3), 189–195.

Billewicz, W. Z., & McGregor, I. A. (1982). A birth-to-maturity longitudinal study of heights and weights in two West African (Gambian) villages 1951–1975. *Annals of Human Biology, 9*(4), 309–320.

Boerma, J. T., Sommerfelt, A. E., & Bicego, G. T. (1992). Child anthropometry in cross-sectional surveys in developing countries: An assessment of the survivor bias. *American Journal of Epidemiology, 135*(4), 438–449.

Bozzoli, C., Deaton, A., & Quintana-Domeque, C. (2009). Adult height and childhood disease. *Demography, 46*(4), 647–669.

Coffey, D., Deaton, A., Dreze, J., Tarozzi, A., & Spears, D. (2013). Stunting among children. *Economic and Political Weekly, 48*(34), 68–69.

Cogneau, D., & Jedwab, R. (2012). Commodity price shocks and child outcomes: The 1990 cocoa crisis in Côte d'Ivoire. *Economic Development and Cultural Change, 60*(3), 507–534.

Cole, T. J. (2003). The secular trend in human physical growth: A biological view. *Economics & Human Biology, 1*(2), 161.

Coly, A. N., Milet, J., Diallo, A., Ndiaye, T., Benefice, E., Simondon, F., . . . Simondon K. B. (2006). Preschool stunting, adolescent migration, catch-up growth, and adult height in young Senegalese men and women of rural origin. *Journal of Nutrition, 136*(9), 2412–2420.
Costa, D. L., & Steckel, R. H. (1997). Long term trends in health, welfare and economic growth in the United States. In R. H. Steckel & R. Floud (Eds.), *Health and welfare during industrialization* (pp. 47–89). Chicago: University of Chicago Press.
Deaton, A. (2007). Height, health, & development. *Proceedings of the National Academy of Sciences of the United States of America, 104*(33), 13232–13237.
Eltis, D. (1982). Nutritional trends in Africa and the Americas: Heights of Africans, 1819–1839. *Journal of Interdisciplinary History, 12*(3), 453–475.
Eveleth, P. B., & Tanner, J. M. (1990). *Worldwide variation in human growth* (2nd ed.). Cambridge, UK: Cambridge University Press.
Fawzi, W. W., Herrera, M. G., Nestel, P., El Amin, A., & Mohamed, K. A. (1998). A longitudinal study of prolonged breastfeeding in relation to child undernutrition. *International Journal of Epidemiology, 27*(2), 255–260.
Fogel, R. W., Engerman, S. L., Floud, R., Steckel, R. H., & Trussell, J. (1982). *Changes in American and British stature since the mid-eighteenth century: A preliminary report on the usefulness of data on height* (NBER Working Paper No. 0890). Cambridge, MA: National Bureau of Economic Research.
Gillespie, S. (2013). Myths and realities of child nutrition. *Economic and Political Weekly, 48*(34), 64–67.
Graham, George G., & B. Adrianzen. (1971). Growth, inheritance and environment. *Pediatric Research*, 5, 691–697.
Habicht, J. P., Martorel R., Yarbroug C., Malina R. M., & Klein, R. E. (1974). Height and weight standards for preschool-children—how relevant are ethnic differences in growth potential. *Lancet, 1*(7858), 611–614.
Haines, M. R., Craig, L. A., & Weiss, T. (2003). The short and the dead: Nutrition, mortality, & the "Antebellum Puzzle" in the United States. *Journal of Economic History, 63*(2), 382–412.
Hirvonen, K. (2014). Measuring catch-up growth in malnourished populations. *Annals of Human Biology, 41*(1), 67–75.
Hoddinott, J., Headey, D., & Dereje, M. (2015). Cows, missing milk markets and nutrition in rural Ethiopia. *Journal of Development Studies.*
Jerven, M. (2013). *Poor numbers: How we are misled by African development statistics and what to do about it.* Ithaca, NY: Cornell Studies in Political Economy.
Kebede, B. (2005). Genetic endowments, parental and child health in rural Ethiopia. *Scottish Journal of Political Economy, 52*(2), 194–221.
Klasen, S. (2008). Poverty, undernutrition, & child mortality: Some inter-regional puzzles and their implications for research and policy. *Journal of Economic Inequality, 6*(1), 89–115.
Komlos, J. (1987). The height and weight of West Point cadets: Dietary change in Antebellum America. *Journal of Economic History, 47*(4), 897–927.
Komlos, J. (1992). Toward an anthropometric history of African-Americans: The case of the Free Blacks in antebellum Maryland. In C. Goldin & H. Rockoff (Eds.), *Strategic factors in nineteenth century American Economic History: A volume to honor Robert W. Fogel* (pp. 297–329). Chicago: University of Chicago Press.
Komlos, J. (1996). Anomalies in economic history: Toward a resolution of the Antebellum Puzzle. *Journal of Economic History, 56*(1), 202–214.

Kuczmarski, R. J., Ogden, C. L., Guo, S. S., Grummer-Strawn, L. M., Flegal, K. M., Mei, Z., et al. (2002). 2000 CDC growth charts for the United States: Methods and development. *Vital and Health Statistics, 11*(246), 1–190.

Little, M. A. (1989). Human biology of African pastoralists. *American Journal of Physical Anthropology, 32*(S10), 215–247.

Little, M. A., Gray, S. J., & Campbell, B. C. (2001). Milk consumption in African pastoral peoples. In I. DeGarine & V. DeGarine (Eds.), *Drinking: Anthropological approaches* (pp. 66–86). New York: Berghahn Books.

Mamabolo, R. L., Alberts, M., Steyn, N. P., Delemarre-van de Waal, H. A., & Levitt, N. S. (2005). Prevalence and determinants of stunting and overweight in 3-year-old black South African children residing in the central region of Limpopo Province, South Africa. *Public Health Nutrition, 8*(5), 501–508.

Messer, E. (1986). The small but healthy hypothesis: Historical, political, & ecological influences on nutritional standards. *Human Ecology, 14*(1), 57–75.

Moradi, A. (2010*a*). Nutritional status and economic development in sub-Saharan Africa, 1950–1980. *Economics & Human Biology, 8*(1), 16–29.

Moradi, A. (2010*b*). *Selective mortality or growth after childhood? What really is key to understand the puzzlingly tall adult heights in sub-Saharan Africa* (CSAE Working Paper No. 2010-17). Oxford, UK: Centre for the Studies of African Economies.

Moradi, A. (2012). Climate, height and economic development in sub-Saharan Africa. *Journal of Anthropological Sciences Forum, 90*, 1–4.

Moradi, A., & Baten, J. (2005). Inequality in sub-Saharan Africa: New data and new insights from anthropometric estimates. *World Development, 33*(8), 1233–1265.

Nestel, P. (1986). A society in transition: Developmental and seasonal influences on the nutrition of Maasai women and children. *Food & Nutrition Bulletin, 8*(1), 2–18.

Paciorek, C. J., Stevens, G. A., Finucane, M. M., & Ezzati, M. (2013). Children's height and weight in rural and urban populations in low-income and middle-income countries: A systematic analysis of population-representative data. *Lancet Global Health, 1*(5), e300–e309.

Panagariya, A. (2013). Does India really suffer from worse child malnutrition than sub-Saharan Africa? *Economic & Political Weekly, 48*(18), 98–111.

Pierre-Louis, J. N., Sanjur, D., Nesheim, M. C., Bowman, D. D., & Mohammed, H. O. (2007). Maternal income-generating activities, child care, & child nutrition in Mali. *Food Nutrition Bulletin, 28*(1), 67–75.

Pradhan, M., Sahn, D. E., & Younger, S. D. (2003). Decomposing world health inequality. *Journal of Health Economics, 22*(2), 271–293.

Prentice, A. M., Ward, K. A., Goldberg, G. R., Jarjou, L. M., Moore, S. E., Fulford, A. J., & Prentice, A. (2013). Critical windows for nutritional interventions against stunting. *American Journal of Clinical Nutrition, 97*(5), 911–918.

Rouanet, L. (2011). *The double African paradox: What does selective mortality tell us?* (PSE Working Paper). Paris: Paris School of Economics.

Sahn, D. E. (1994). The contribution of income to improved nutrition in Côte d'Ivoire. *Journal of African Economies, 3*(1), 29–61.

Schultz, T. P. (1999). Health and schooling investment in Africa. *Journal of Economic Perspectives, 13*(3), 67–88.

Schultz, T. P. (2003). Wage rentals for reproducible human capital: Evidence from Ghana and the Ivory Coast. *Economics & Human Biology, 1*(3), 331–366.

Seckler, D. (1982). Small but healthy: A basic hypothesis in the theory, measurement and policy of malnutrition. In P. V. Sukhatme (Ed.), *Newer concepts in nutrition and their implications for policy* (pp. 127–137). Pune, India: Maharashtra Association for the Cultivation of Science.

Seckler, D. (1984). The 'small but healthy?' hypothesis: A reply to critics. *Economic and Political Weekly*, *19*(44), 1886–1888.

Sheppard, Z. A., Norris, S. A., Pettifor, J. M., Cameron, N., & Griffiths, P. L. (2009). Approaches for assessing the role of household socioeconomic status on child anthropometric measures in urban South Africa. *American Journal of Human Biology*, *21*(1), 48–54.

Silventoinen, K. (2003). Determinants of variation in adult body height. *Journal of Biosocial Science*, *35*, 263–285.

Steckel, R. H. (1987). Growth depression and recovery: The remarkable case of American slaves. *Annals of Human Biology*, *14*(2), 111–132.

Steckel, R. H. (2000). Diets versus diseases in the anthropometrics of slave children: A reply. *Journal of Economic History*, *60*(1), 247–259.

Steckel, R. H. (2009). Heights and human welfare: Recent developments and new directions. *Explorations in Economic History*, *46*(1), 1–23.

Thomas, D., Lavy, V., & Strauss, J. (1996). Public policy and anthropometric outcomes in the Côte d'Ivoire. *Journal of Public Economics*, *61*(2), 155–192.

WHO Multicentre Growth Reference Study Group, & de Onis, M. (2006). Assessment of differences in linear growth among populations in the WHO Multicentre Growth Reference Study. *Acta Paediatrica*, *95*(S450), 56–65.

Winick, M., Meyer, K. K., & Harris, R. C. (1975). Malnutrition and environmental enrichment by early adoption. *Science*, *190*(4220), 1173–1175.

Bibliography for the Meta Review

Addo, O. Y., Stein, A. D., Fall, C. H., Gigante, D. P., Guntupalli, A. M., et al. (2013). Maternal height and child growth patterns. *Journal of Pediatrics*, *163*(2), 549–554.

Alderman, H., Hoddinott, J., & Kinsey, B. (2006). Long term consequences of early childhood malnutrition. *Oxford Economic Papers*, *58*(3), 450–474.

Alderman, H., Hoogeveen, H., & Rossi, M. (2006). Reducing child malnutrition in Tanzania—Combined effects of income growth and program interventions. *Economics & Human Biology*, *4*(1), 1–23.

Arimond, M., & Ruel, M. T. (2004). Dietary diversity is associated with child nutritional status: Evidence from 11 demographic and health surveys. *Journal of Nutrition*, *134*(10), 2579–2585.

Beegle, K., De Weerdt, J., & Dercon, S. (2009). The intergenerational impact of the African orphans crisis: A cohort study from an HIV/AIDS affected area. *International Journal of Epidemiology*, *38*(2), 561–568.

Black, M. M., & Krishnakumar, K. (1999). Predicting longitudinal growth curves of height and weight using ecological factors for children with and without early growth deficiency. *Journal of Nutrition*, *129*(2), 539S–543S.

Bouzitou, G. D. N., Fayomi, B., & Delisle, H. (2005). Child malnutrition and maternal overweight in same households in poor urban areas of Benin. *Cahiers Sante*, *15*(4), 263–270.

Burchi, F. (2010). Child nutrition in Mozambique in 2003: The role of mother's schooling and nutrition knowledge. *Economics & Human Biology*, *8*(3), 331–345.

Burchi, F. (2012). Whose education affects a child's nutritional status? From parents' to household's education. *Demographic Research*, *27*, 681–703.

Burgard, S. (2002). Does race matter? Children's height in Brazil and South Africa. *Demography*, *39*(4), 763–790.

Cameron, N., De Wet, T., Ellison, G. T., & Bogin, B. (1998). Growth in height and weight of South African urban infants from birth to five years: The birth to ten study. *American Journal of Human Biology*, *10*(4), 495–504.

Chopra, M. (2003). Risk factors for undernutrition of young children in a rural area of South Africa. *Public Health Nutrition*, *6*(7), 645–652.

Cogneau, D., & Jedwab, R. (2012). Commodity price shocks and child outcomes: The 1990 cocoa crisis in Cote d'Ivoire. *Economic Development and Cultural Change*, *60*(3), 507–534.

Custodio, E., Descalzo, M. A., Roche, J., Molina, L., Sánchez, I., Lwanga, M., et al. (2010). The economic and nutrition transition in Equatorial Guinea coincided with a double burden of over-and under nutrition. *Economics and Human Biology*, *8*(1), 80–87.

Custodio, E., Descalzo, M. Á., Roche, J., Sánchez, I., Molina, L., Lwanga, M., et al. (2008). Nutritional status and its correlates in Equatorial Guinean preschool children: Results from a nationally representative survey. *Food and Nutrition Bulletin*, *29*(1), 49–58.

Dannhauser, A., Bester, C., Joubert, G., Badenhorst, P., Slabber, M., Badenhorst, A., et al. (2000). Nutritional status of preschool children in informal settlement areas near Bloemfontein, South Africa. *Public Health Nutrition*, *3*(3), 303–312.

Delpeuch, F., Traissac, P., Martin-Prével, Y., Massamba, J. P., & Maire, B. (2000). Economic crisis and malnutrition: Socioeconomic determinants of anthropometric status of preschool children and their mothers in an African urban area. *Public Health Nutrition*, *3*(1), 39–47.

Deolalikar, A. B. (1996). Child nutritional status and child growth in Kenya: Socioeconomic determinants. *Journal of International Development*, *8*(3), 375–393.

Espo, M., Kulmala, T., Maleta, K., Cullinan, T., Salin, M. L., & Ashorn, P. (2002). Determinants of linear growth and predictors of severe stunting during infancy in rural Malawi. *Acta Paediatrica*, *91*(12), 1364–1370.

Fawzi, W. W., Herrera, M. G., Nestel, P., Amin, A. E., & Mohamed, K. A. (1998). A longitudinal study of prolonged breastfeeding in relation to child undernutrition. *International Journal of Epidemiology*, *27*(2), 255–260.

Fink, G., Sudfeld, C. R., Danaei, G., Ezzati, M., & Fawzi, W. W. (2014). Scaling-up access to family planning may improve linear growth and child development in low and middle income countries. *PLoS One*, *9*(7), e102391.

Friedman, J. F., Kwena, A. M., Mrel, L. B., Kariuki, S. K., Terlouw, D. J. Phillips-Howard, P. A., et al. (2005). Malaria and nutritional status among pre-school children: Results from cross-sectional surveys in western Kenya. *American Journal of Tropical Medicine and Hygiene*, *73*(4), 698–704.

Goduka, I. N., Poole, D. A., & Aotakiphenice, L. (1992). A comparative-study of Black South-African children from 3 different contexts. *Child Development*, *63*(3), 509–525.

Groenewold, W. G., & Tilahun, M. (1990). Anthropometric indicators of nutritional status, socioeconomic factors and mortality in hospitalized children in Addis Ababa. *Journal of Biosocial Science*, *22*(3), 373–379.

Haddad, L., & Hoddinott, J. (1994). Women's income and boy-girl anthropometric status in the Cote d'Ivoire. *World Development*, *22*(4), 543–553.

Hadley, C., Belachew, T., Lindstrom, D., & Tessema, F. (2011). The shape of things to come? Household dependency ratio and adolescent nutritional status in rural and urban Ethiopia. *American Journal of Physical Anthropology*, *144*(4), 643–652.

Handa, S., Simler, K. R., & Harrower, S. (2004). Human capital, household welfare, & children's schooling in Mozambique. *Research Report of the International Food Policy Research Institute*, *134*, 1–85.

Hartwig, R., & Grimm, M. (2012). An assessment of the effects of the 2002 food crisis on children's health in Malawi. *Journal of African Economies*, *21*(1), 124–165.

Henneberg, M., Harrison, G. A., & Brush, G. (1998). The small child: Anthropometric and physical performance characteristics of short-for-age children growing in good and in poor socio-economic conditions. *European Journal of Clinical Nutrition*, *52*(4), 286–291.

Hoddinott, J., & Kinsey, B. (2001). Child growth in the time of drought. *Oxford Bulletin of Economics and Statistics*, *63*(4), 409–436.

Kabubo-Mariara, J., Ndenge, G. K., & Mwabu, D. K. (2009). Determinants of children's nutritional status in Kenya: Evidence from demographic and health surveys. *Journal of African Economies*, *18*(3), 363–387.

Kebede, B. (2005). Genetic endowments, parental and child health in rural Ethiopia. *Scottish Journal of Political Economy*, *52*(2), 194–221.

Kedir, A. B. (2013). Schooling, BMI, height and wages: Panel evidence on men and women. *Economic Issues*, *18*(2), 1–18.

Kennedy, G., Nantel, G., Brouwer, I. D., & Kok, F. J. (2006). Does living in an urban environment confer advantages for childhood nutritional status? Analysis of disparities in nutritional status by wealth and residence in Angola, Central African Republic and Senegal. *Public Health Nutrition*, *9*(2), 187–193.

Lavy, V. (1996). Quality of health care, survival and health outcomes in Ghana. *Journal of Health Economics*, *15*(3), 333–357.

Leroy, J. L., Ruel, M. T., Habicht, J.-P., & Frongillo, E. A. (2015). Using Height-for-Age Difference instead of Height-for-Age Z-scores for the meaningful measurement of catch-up growth in Children under 5 years of age. In D. Sahn (Ed.), *The Fight against Hunger & Malnutrition: The Role of Food, Agriculture, and Targeted Policies* (pp. 19–35). Oxford: Oxford University Press.

Madhavan, S., & Townsend, N. (2007). The social context of children's nutritional status in rural South Africa. *Scandinavian journal of Public Health. Supplement*, *69*, 107–117.

Mamabolo, R. L., Alberts, A., Levitt, N. S., Delemarre-van de Waal, H. A., & Steyn, N. P. (2007). Association between insulin-like growth factor-1, insulin-like growth factorbinding protein-1 and leptin levels with nutritional status in 1–3-year-old children, residing in the central region of Limpopo Province, South Africa. *British Journal of Nutrition*, *98*(4), 762–769.

Mamabolo, R. L., Alberts, M., Mbenyane, G. X., Steyn, N. P., Nthangeni, N. G., Delemarre-van De Waal, H. A., & Levitt, N. S. (2004). Feeding practices and growth of infants from birth to 12 months in the central region of the Limpopo Province of South Africa. *Nutrition*, *20*(3), 327–333.

Mamabolo, R. L., Alberts, M., Steyn, N. P., Delemarre-van de Waal, H. A., & Levitt, N. S. (2005). Prevalence and determinants of stunting and overweight in 3-year-old black South African children residing in the Central Region of Limpopo Province, South Africa. *Public Health Nutrition*, *8*(5), 501–508.

Margo, G., Baroni, Y., Brindley, M., Green, R., & Metz, J. (1976). Protein energy malnutrition in Coloured children in Western Township, Johannesburg. II. Prevalence and severity. *South African Medical Journal*, *50*(32), 1241–1245.

Martin-Prevel, Y., Traissac, P., Delpeuch, F., & Maire, B. (2001). Decreased attendance at routine health activities mediates deterioration in nutritional status of young African children under worsening socioeconomic conditions. *International Journal of Epidemiology, 30*(3), 493–500.

Maxwell, D., Levin, C., & Csete, J. (1998). Does urban agriculture help prevent malnutrition? Evidence from Kampala. *Food Policy, 23*(5), 411–424.

Molteno, C. D., Hollingshead, J., Moodie, A. D., Bradshaw, D., Willoughby, W., Bowie, M. D., & Smallman, L. A. (1991). Growth of preschool coloured children in Cape Town. *South African Medical Journal, 79*(11), 670–676.

Mwadime, R. K. N., Omwega, A. M., Kielmann, N., & Korte, R. (1996). Predictors of nutritional status among participants in a rice irrigation scheme in Kenya. *Ecology of Food and Nutrition, 35*(4), 263–274.

Onyango, A. W., Esrey, A. S., & Kramer, M. S. (1999). Continued breastfeeding and child growth in the second year of life: A prospective cohort study in western Kenya. *Lancet, 354*(9195), 2041–2045.

Outes, I., & Porter, C. (2013). Catching up from early nutritional deficits? Evidence from rural Ethiopia. *Economics and Human Biology, 11*(2), 148–163.

Paciorek, C. J., Stevens, G. A., Finucane, M. M., Ezzati, M., Barquera, S., Bhutta, Z., et al. (2013). Children's height and weight in rural and urban populations in low-income and middle-income countries: A systematic analysis of population-representative data. *Lancet Global Health, 1*(5), e300–e309.

Padonou, G., Le Port, A., Cottrell, G., Guerra, J., Choudat, I., Rachas, A., et al. (2014). Factors associated with growth patterns from birth to 18 months in a Beninese cohort of children. *Acta Tropica, 135*, 1–9.

Pawloski, L. R. (2002). Growth and development of adolescent girls from the Segou region of Mali (West Africa). *American Journal of Physical Anthropology, 117*(4), 364–372.

Pelletier, D. L., Low, J. W., Johnson, F. C., & Msukwa, L. A. (1994). Child anthropometry and mortality in Malawi: Testing for effect modification by age and length of follow-up and confounding by socioeconomic factors. *Journal of Nutrition, 124*(10 Suppl.), 2082S–2105S.

Pierre-Louis, J. N., Sanjur, D., Nesheim, M. C., Bowman, D. D., & Mohammed, H. O. (2007). Maternal income-generating activities, child care, and child nutrition in Mali. *Food and Nutrition Bulletin, 28*(1), 67–75.

Pongou, R., Ezzati, M., & Salomon, J. A. (2006). Household and community socioeconomic and environmental determinants of child nutritional status in Cameroon. *BMC Public Health, 6*. doi: 10.1186/1471-2458-6-98

Psaki, S. R., Seidman, J. C., Miller, M., Gottlieb, M., Bhutta, Z. A., Ahmed, T., et al. (2014). Measuring socioeconomic status in multicountry studies: Results from the eight-country MAL-ED study. *Population Health Metrics, 12*(1).

Ramphele, M. A., Heap, M., & Trollip, D. K. (1995). A survey of the physical health status of pupils aged 10–14 years in Standards 3–5 at three schools in New Crossroads, near Cape Town in the Western Cape. *South African Medical Journal, 85*(10), 1007–1012.

Ruel, M. T., Levin, C. E., Armar-Klemesu, M., Maxwell, D., & Morris, S. S. (1999). Good care practices can mitigate the negative effects of poverty and low maternal schooling on children's nutritional status: Evidence from Accra. *World Development, 27*(11), 1993–2009.

Sahn, D. E. (1994). The contribution of income to improved nutrition in Cote d'Ivoire. *Journal of African Economies, 3*(1), 29–61.

Sahn, D. E., & Alderman, H. (1997). On the determinants of nutrition in Mozambique: The importance of age-specific effects. *World Development*, *25*(4), 577–588.

Sawadogo, P. S., Martin-Prevel, Y., Savy, M., Kameli, Y., Traissac, P., Traore, A. S., & Delpeuch, F. (2006). An infant band child feeding index is associated with the nutritional status of 6-to 23-month-old children in rural Burkina Faso. *Journal of Nutrition*, *136*(3), 656–663.

Seid, A. K. (2013). Health and nutritional status of children in Ethiopia: Do maternal characteristics matter? *Journal of Biosocial Science*, *45*(2), 187–204.

Sheppard, Z. A., Norris, S. A., Pettifor, J. M., Cameron, N., & Griffiths, P. L. (2009). Approaches for assessing the role of household socioeconomic status on child anthropometric measures in urban South Africa. *American Journal of Human Biology*, *21*(1), 48–54.

Subramanian, S. V., Özaltin, E., & Finlay, J. E. (2011). Height of nations: A socioeconomic analysis of cohort differences and patterns among women in 54 low–to middle-income countries. *PLoS One*, *6*(4).

Thomas, D., Lavy, V., & Strauss, J. (1996). Public policy and anthropometric outcomes in the Cote D'Ivoire. *Journal of Public Economics*, *61*(2), 155–192.

Timæus, I. M. (2012). Stunting and obesity in childhood: A reassessment using longitudinal data from South Africa. *International Journal of Epidemiology*, *41*(3), 764–772.

VanderJagt, D. J., Waymire, L., Obadofin, M. O., Marjon, N., & Glew, R. H. (2009). A cross-sectional study of the growth characteristics of Nigerian infants from birth to 2 years of age. *Journal of Tropical Pediatrics*, *55*(6), 356–362.

Vella, V., Tomkins, A., Borghesi, A., Migliori, G. B., Adriko, B. C., & Crevatin, E. (1992). Determinants of child nutrition and mortality in north-west Uganda. *Bulletin of the World Health Organization*, *70*(5), 637–643.

Victora, C. G., Adair, L., Fall, C., Hallal, P. C., Martorell, R., Richter, L., et al. (2008). Maternal and child undernutrition: Consequences for adult health and human capital. *Lancet*, *371*(9609), 340–357.

Victora, C. G., Vaughan, J. P., Martines, J. C., & Barcelos, L. B. (1984). Is prolonged breast-feeding associated with malnutrition? *American Journal of Clinical Nutrition*, *39*(2), 307–314.

Walker, A. R. P., Walker, B. F., Jones, J., & Kadwa, M. (1989). Growth of South African Indian schoolchildren in different social classes. *Journal of the Royal Society of Health*, *109*(2), 54–56.

Walsh, C. M., Dannhauser, A., & Joubert, G. (2002). The impact of a nutrition education programme on the anthropometric nutritional status of low-income children in South Africa. *Public Health Nutrition*, *5*(1), 3–9.

Wamani, H., Åstrøm, A. N., Peterson, S., Tumwine, J. K., & Tylleskär, T. (2007). Boys are more stunted than girls in sub-Saharan Africa: A meta-analysis of 16 demographic and health surveys. *BMC Pediatrics*, *7*.

Westcott, G. M., & Stott, R. A. P. (1977). The extent and causes of malnutrition in children in the Tsolo district of Transkei. *South African Medical Journal*, *52*(24), 963–968.

CHAPTER 34

EAST ASIA ON THE RISE

The Anthropometric History of China, Japan, and Korea

DANIEL JONG SCHWEKENDIEK

34.1 Introduction

The body mass index (BMI), weight, and, physical stature of populations are reliable indicators of biological living standards because these physical measurements reflect the quantity and quality of food consumed less energy requirements used to fight diseases and maintain bodily functions. Since the 1970s, the United Nations World Health Organization has employed stature and weight measurements of preschool children worldwide as indicators of human welfare (Waterlow, Buzina, Keller, Lane, Nichaman & Tanner, 1977). Steckel (2009) reports that during the period 1995–2008 there were four times as many height-related articles published in social science journals as there were in the period 1997–94, suggesting that anthropometrics have become a widely accepted biosocial indicator, along the same lines as those of life expectancy and infant mortality. Similarly, anthropometric history has now become a popular topic at international conferences such as the World Economic History Congresses, as well as at the meetings of the Economic History Association and the Social Science History Association (Schwekendiek, 2013, p. 40).

Although most studies in anthropometric history have focused on Europeans and Americans, East Asian countries are of great interest as well, not only because of their economic success but also because one-fifth of the world's population lives in this dynamic region. The aim of this chapter is to provide an overview of published studies that focus on the anthropometric history of the three core populations of East Asia: those of China, Japan, and Korea. The latter includes both the Democratic People's Republic of Korea (hereafter North Korea) and the Republic of Korea (referred to as South Korea).

It should be noted that this review focuses on studies in which the anthropometric values were actually measured. Thus, a few studies based on self-reported anthropometric data are excluded (e.g., see Shay, 1994, p. 182, for a sample of self-reported height of 155 Japanese men). Also excluded are osteometric studies in which skeletal remains were measured to reconstruct anthropometric measurements.[1]

34.2 East Asia on the Rise

In general, research has established a clear relationship between gross domestic product (GDP) per capita and mean human body measurements. Brinkman, Drukker, & Slot (1997) find a negative relationship between GDP per capita and stunting (correlation coefficient = −0.62) among preschool children living in today's developing countries. About 55% of the total variance in stunting is explained by GDP per capita alone. In a similar vein, Baten and Blum (2012, p. S77) report a significant correlation between mean height of adults and (log) GDP per capita from 1810 to 1989 in 156 countries (correlation coefficient = +0.64).

As a rule, there is a positive linear relationship between anthropometric measurements and economic growth; however, there are notable exceptions in which, at least in the short run, there is a U-shaped relationship. The decline in human stature despite remarkable economic growth in 19th-century Europe is commonly known as the "early-industrial-growth puzzle" (Komlos, 1998) and the one in the United States as the "antebellum puzzle" (Margo & Steckel, 1983). The solution to these puzzles are found in those socioeconomic developments that accompanied the Industrial Revolution, chiefly the negative impact of urbanization, accelerated population growth, and lagging agricultural productivity (Komlos, 2012).

In the case of East Asia, let us consider the evolution of GDP per capita in China, Japan, and Korea. Between 1500 and 1700, income per capita in China and Japan was not far behind that in Western Europe (Table 34.1). With the Industrial Revolution, which began in Great Britain in the late 18th century and within a few decades had spread to continental Europe, the income gap between the East and the West widened dramatically.

However, thanks to "big-push" industrialization policies (Allen, 2011) initiated by strong developmental states and, at times, by authoritarian rulers in Japan and South Korea, the gap closed (Table 34.1). Indeed, by 2010, the mean income of Japanese (21,900international dollars) and South Koreans (21,700 international dollars) was almost equal to that of their counterparts in Western Europe (21,800 international dollars). This is not very surprising, since Japan had become the "first-mover" of industrialization in East Asia and South Korea the fastest "follower," not only in Asia but worldwide (Maddison, 2001, p. 148). In contrast, in terms of contemporary income per capita, both China (8,000 international dollars) and North Korea (1,100 international dollars) continue to lag far behind Western Europe, despite the fact that they, too,

Table 34.1 Gross domestic product (GDP) per capita in East Asia and the world, 1500–2010

	Selected Regions and Countries					
Year	World	Western Europe	China	South Korea	North Korea	Japan
1500	600	800	600			500
1600	600	900	600			500
1700	600	1,000	600			600
1820	700	1,200	600			700
1870	900	2,100	500			700
1913	1,500	3,700	600			1,400
1950	2,100	5,000	400	800	800	1,900
2010	7,800	21,800	8,000	21,700	1,100	21,900

Western Europe is represented by Austria, Belgium, Denmark, Finland, France, Germany, Italy, Netherlands, Norway, Sweden, Switzerland, and the United Kingdom. Data for North Korea as of 2010 refer to 2008. Data pertain to rounded GDP per capita in 1990 international dollars.

Source: Maddison (2003), pp. 184, 262; Maddison (2001), p. 306; all data for 2010 from the Maddison Project website.

introduced massive industrialization programs. On the other hand, the economies of both countries have been controlled by socialist governments that delayed the liberalization practiced by Japan and South Korea.

GDP per capita has been estimated for almost all world regions and from ancient to present times (Maddison, 2001, 2003). A much more difficult task is to summarize the long-term anthropometric history of East Asia. On account of differing analytic methods and obvious selection biases, reported results vary. The next sections introduce important studies of the anthropometric history of the aforementioned East Asian nations.

34.3 Anthropometric Trends in East Asia Until World War II

Pre-modern studies featuring anthropometric measurements with large sample sizes are difficult to come by. Anthropometric data on females in pre-modern times are even rarer. In Europe and America, the most common historical sources used in anthropometric history were military rosters (Baten, 1999; Floud, Fogel, Harris, & Hong, 2011; Haines, 1998; Komlos, 1987; Schoch, Staub, & Pfister, 2012; Schuster, 2005). Indeed, as Western nations engaged in extensive warfare with each other, conscription of all eligible males was enforced by the state. Needless to say, physical measurements were systematically taken from the recruits for their biometric identification (to track deserters) or simply to assess their physical prowess on the battlefield. In East Asia, a "world war" had not occurred until the Imjin War (1592–98), which resulted in by far the largest military mobilization in China, Korea, and Japan in pre-modern times (Hawley, 2005). Not surprisingly, the earliest systematic height data based on large sample sizes comes from militia recruits measured during this war (Lewis, Jun, & Schwekendiek, 2013). The heights of Korean militia recruits, representing the vast majority of the population (commoners and non-free "slaves" but not nobles), was collected from the Imjin War to the late 18th century; however, decimal units of the Korean "foot" disappeared after the mid-18th century (probably as a result of a long period of peace), thus making statistical comparisons meaningless thereafter (Lewis, Jun, & Schwekendiek, 2013). Interestingly, whereas height data on pre-modern Korean recruits were collected for almost three centuries, Chinese military rosters comparable to those found in Korea have not been discovered. Morgan (1998, p. 29) indicates that the earliest anthropometric data on militia and regular recruits in China probably stem from the 1930s, although it is strongly doubted that these records have survived. In pre-modern Japan, military service was hereditary; there was no recruitment procedure, and no physical measurements were recorded (Lewis, Jun, & Schwekendiek, 2013, p. 263). In fact, because military conscription was enacted in Japan as late as 1873 (Shay, 1994, p. 180), the anthropometric history of Japan does not start in earnest until the 19th century. In light of this fact, the Korean militia rosters appear to be unique for East Asia.

Analyzing the heights of male Korean militia recruits who were born between the late 16th and the early 18th centuries, Lewis, Jun, & Schwekendiek) (2013, p. 261) conclude that mean height was about 164–166 cm, indicating that French recruits born between the mid-17th and the mid-18th centuries were not taller than Koreans at that time (Komlos, Hau, & Bourguinat, 2003). This finding suggests that the "great divergence" between East and West possibly did not occur until the advent of the Industrial Revolution in Europe. Further research is needed to clarify this issue.

As a by-product of industrialization, the West also drastically upgraded its military technology, launching an era of high imperialism. The Opium Wars (1839–42 and 1856–60) led to the opening of China, and US gunboat diplomacy led to the opening of Japan in 1853. Japan quickly adapted to industrialization, upgraded its military, and took formal control over Taiwan (1895–1945) and Korea (1910–45) as a new imperial power after having defeated major rivals in the region in the First Sino-Japanese War (1894–95) and Russo-Japanese War (1904–05). Several anthropometric surveys were conducted in East Asia during the era of high imperialism. Japan implemented some systematic anthropometric surveys in its main colonies, Taiwan and Korea, most of which were conducted for health and sanitation reasons (Kimura, 1993; Olds, 2003) or for biometric identification reasons on account of the numerous independence fighters incarcerated in local political prisons (Choi & Schwekendiek, 2009).

In Japan itself, the confrontation with Western imperial powers led to major military reforms. In 1873, conscription of all 20-year-old males was enacted. For this purpose, physical checkups of the recruits were conducted and their heights recorded; beginning in 1926, their weights were added to the data (Bassino, 2006, p. 67). Height data of Japanese conscripts have been analyzed extensively (Bassino, 2006; Honda, 1997, pp. 267–269; Mosk, 1996, pp. 96–100; Shay, 1994). The height of Japanese conscripts increased from about 156 cm in 1892 to about 160 cm in 1937, corresponding to an increase of about 1 cm per decade (Shay, 1994, p. 183). Nevertheless, Japanese men in 1937 were still 3–8 cm shorter than men in Great Britain, Norway, Sweden, and Hungary at that time (Honda, 1997, pp. 267–268). Also, men living near big towns were shorter.

The opening of China facilitated not only immigration but also mass emigration, mostly from South China, to the New World. Data were therefore recorded in destinations such as the United States (Carson, 2006, 2007), Canada (Ward, 2013), and Australia (Morgan, 2009). In addition to this, Chinese labor migrants were also measured in regions such as Indonesia and Surinam (Baten & Hira, 2008). The mean height of Chinese adults born between the 1820s and the 1860s and imprisoned in the American West ranged from 163 to 165 cm (Carson, 2007, p. 175). That of Chinese men born between 1810 and 1880 and incarcerated in Australia was estimated at 163–164 cm (Morgan, 2009).

Analyzing the average height of male Chinese contract workers measured in Surinam and Indonesia, Baten and Hira (2008) find a stagnant trend in cohorts born between 1830 and 1864: about 161–164 cm in Surinam and 161–163 cm in Indonesia. Chinese in America and Australia were slightly taller because they were from better-off families (since migrants or their kin had to own some land as security for passage), whereas Chinese contract workers in Surinam and Indonesia were shorter because they were generally poor (Baten & Hira, 2008, p. 219). This pair of height estimates (penniless Chinese contract workers migrating to Surinam and Indonesia vs. richer, land-owning Chinese migrating to Australia and the United States) therefore mark the somewhat lower and somewhat upper bounds of the Chinese-emigrant height range (Baten & Hira, 2008).

Ward (2013) believes that the Chinese measured in Canada "represented the broad middle strata." The mean stature of Chinese men who were measured for taxation reasons upon their arrival in Canada ranged from 163 to 164 cm from the 1850s to the 1880s (Ward, 2013, p. 500). Their mean height was indeed somewhat in between those of richer emigrants to Australia and the United States and poorer emigrants to Surinam and Indonesia.

Finally, there is a rare instance of a study that draws on height data recorded inside China: those of men born during the period 1880–1930 and working in state-run enterprises, chiefly the Chinese National Railways and the Post and Telegraph Administration (Morgan, 2004). The data differ from the migrant ones in another respect as well. Workers also came from different regions, not only from South China. These employees were deemed to be of a somewhat higher socioeconomic class on account of their education and their employment in government posts. Their mean height was about 166–168 cm, and between 1900 and 1929 featured a slight upward trend, ranging from 0.2 cm in North China to 1.3 cm in East China (Morgan, 2004, p. 210). Another study, based on student health data in the late 20th century (Morgan, 2000, p. 39), finds extreme regional disparities in China, with a height gap of up to 10 cm across regions. Note that this gap is corroborated in a later section of this chapter (Table 34.2).

As for Korea in the late 19th century, the average height of men born between 1890 and 1916 increased from about 164 to about 166 cm (Choi & Schwekendiek, 2009). These data are derived from the prison records of political convicts during the period of Japanese colonial rule (1910–45); they came from every social strata and every region of the peninsula. In a similar vein, Gill (1998) analyzes height data of Koreans who were employed by the Korean Medical Health Insurance Corporation. Because they were government employees (mostly working as teachers in public schools), they were considered to be members of the upper middle class. Gill (1998) finds that the average height of men born between 1920 and 1945 (the end of colonial period) increased from 167 to 168 cm, thus corroborating Kimura (1993) as well as Choi and Schwekendiek (2009), who conclude that biological living conditions did not decline under Japanese rule.[2] Whereas almost

Table 34.2 Rural–urban differences in stunting, wasting and underweight of preschool children in the world around 2000

	Rural–Urban Height for Age Stunting Ratios		Rural–Urban Weight for Height Wasting Ratios		Rural–Urban Weight for Age Underweight Ratios	
Rank	Country	Ratio	Country	Ratio	Country	Ratio
1	China	696.6	South Africa	213.6	China	460.0
2	Peru	300.0	Kenya	212.5	Peru	368.8
3	Dominican Rep.	277.8	Zimbabwe	208.1	Serbia & Monten.	281.8
4	Mexico	273.3	Nicaragua	207.7	Georgia	264.7
5	Brazil	243.6	Honduras	185.7	Morocco	245.8
Mean	World (93 nations)	160.6	World (94 nations)	121.4	World (95 nations)	160.6

Data pertain to preschool-aged children measured around the year 2000 in random national surveys. "Rural–urban height for age stunting ratio" defined as 100 × (percentage of rural stunting/percentage of urban stunting); "rural–urban weight for height wasting ratio" defined as 100 × (percentage of rural wasting /percentage of urban wasting); "rural–urban weight for age underweight ratio" defined as 100 × (percentage of rural underweight/percentage of urban underweight); with "stunting," "wasting," and "underweight" following standard definitions of the United Nations World Health Organization.
Source: Adapted from Guntupalli and Schwekendiek (2009).

all anthropometric studies of China prior to World War II are based on measurements of immigrants to the New World, such data are absent in the case of Korea. As Japan gradually took control of Korea in the late 19th century, it halted Korean migration to the New World early because Koreans were recruited by Westerners as strikebreakers against Japanese (and also Chinese) labor migrants (Takaki, 1998). The Japanese also feared that Korean immigrants would become active in the independence movement from overseas. There are, therefore, no anthropometric studies of 19th-century Korean immigrants to the New World.

34.4 Anthropometric Trends in East Asia After World War II

Anthropometric data on East Asians after World War II stem from two sources: industry-related and education-related government agencies. Large, nationally representative anthropometric surveys were carried out in order to adapt consumer products to the local market: for instance, car seats and clothing (Pak, 2004; Schwekendiek & Pak, 2009). Like Western governments, East Asia ones started to routinely measure students in schools (Kim, Oh, Lee, Choi, Choe & Yoon, 2008; Morgan, 2000; Mosk, 1996). Since the end of World War II, school-enrollment rates in China, Japan, and Korea have been high, so these school surveys can be considered a good proxy for the total population. The chief drawback of both of these types of surveys is that access to raw data is limited or completely denied to external scholars—on account of data-protection issues. As a result, research on the anthropometric history of modern China (Morgan, 2000), Japan (Mosk, 1996), South Korea (Schwekendiek & Jun, 2010), and the two Koreas in comparative perspective (Pak, 2004, 2010; Pak, Schwekendiek, & Kim, 2011; Schwekendiek, 2009; Schwekendiek & Pak, 2009) has not included in-depth analysis based on raw data but has been limited to analyzing reported group values.

The recent anthropometric history of East Asia, as derived from these two types of data sources, is summarized in Tables 34.3 to 34.5. It should be noted that although data for Japan and the two Koreas were stratified only by gender and measurement year, it is common to stratify Chinese data by rural–urban residence as well (Li, Zong, Zhang, & Zhu, 2011; Morgan, 2000) on account of the fact that the country is the most populous nation on earth and, more importantly, because it currently represents the most extreme outlier in rural–urban stunting (as well as underweight) rates (Table 34.2). Rural–urban stunting gaps were found to be statistically insignificant in other East Asian nations, such as market-oriented South Korea (Schwekendiek, 2014) and socialist North Korea (Schwekendiek, 2008*a*, 2008*b*). The vast rural–urban gaps in China are a result of the household registration system (*hokou*), which effectively prevents migration into the cities (Chan & Zhang, 1999), in combination with extreme socioeconomic differences across regions (Morgan, 1998).

Table 34.3 Height, weight, and body mass index (BMI) of 6-year-old children in East Asia, 1985–2005

Country:	China (urban)		China (suburban)		China (rural)		South Korea (national)		North Korea (national)	Japan (national)	
Year	1985	2005	1985	2005	1985	2005	1985	2005	2005	1985	2005
Males											
Height	116.2	120.0	111.8	117.4	109.9	113.5	113.9	117.0	109.3	116.4	116.6
Weight	19.8	22.5	18.3	20.8	17.9	19.1	19.7	22.4	17.6	21.2	21.6
BMI	14.7	15.6	14.7	15.1	14.8	14.8	15.2	16.4	14.7	15.6	15.9
Females											
Height	115.5	118.9	111.3	116.5	109.1	112.5	113.4	116.0	108.1	115.7	115.8
Weight	19.1	21.6	17.9	20.1	17.4	18.4	19.1	21.5	16.9	20.7	21.1
BMI	14.3	15.2	14.5	14.8	14.6	14.5	14.9	16.0	14.5	15.5	15.7

Height in cm, weight in kg, BMI in units. BMI was calculated based on mean height and weight. The Chinese data for age 6-years-old group in the data table of the originally published study were obviously subsequently mislabeled as "age 6~7"; in fact, all children were "under 7 years of age" in the surveys. Data for South Korea as of 1985 refer to 1984, and data for North Korea as of 2005 refer to 2002. Also, North Korean children were in fact 6.50 to 6.99 years of age.

Source: Li, Zong, Zhang, & Zhu (2011), pp. 4–6; Ministry of Education, Culture, Sports, Science and Technology of Japan (2012), pp. 134–137; Kim, Oh, Lee, Choi, Choe, & Yoon (2008), pp. 232–233; Schwekendiek (2009), p. 53.

Comparative data of 6-year-old children from China, South Korea, North Korea, and Japan are available for the period 1985 to 2005 (except for data on North Korea, which are limited to 2005) (Table 34.3). The effect of genes on height and weight in these age groups is assumed to be small (Habicht, Martorell, Yarbrough, Malina, & Klein, 1974). Body measurements of preschool children in China have dramatically increased in rural, suburban, and urban areas. However, as of 2005, the rural–urban divide (Table 34.2) is still clearly evident, with rural children in China being closer to those in underdeveloped North Korea. Conversely, the measurements of their peers in urban China even surpass the national average of children living in the neighboring Organisation for Economic Co-operation and Development (OECD) countries of South Korea and Japan as of 2005 (Table 34.3). This suggests that members of the Chinese upper class, who commonly reside in the most urbanized areas of the country, have enjoyed biological living standards comparable to those of their peers in developed countries. Moreover, in 1985, the average heights and weights of South Korean children were inferior to those of their Japanese peers. However, by 2005, the ranking was reversed. Less surprising is the fact that, of all of the groups under consideration, North Korean children consistently had the lowest anthropometric values.

Analyzing height, weight, and BMI of 17-year-old adolescents in East Asia has the drawback that these measurements are complicated by catch-up growth (Table 34.4), since final height is not reached even in the best-nourished societies among girls until the age of 18 and mostly later among boys. Nonetheless, Table 34.4 offers insights into the long-term anthropometric trend in modern East Asia. However, the Chinese data cover only 16 cities.[3] Needless to say, since these are China's largest and most prosperous cities, these data are not representative of the whole population. Heights in 1955 in China, Japan, and South Korea (as of 1965) were very similar. However, by 2005, the heights and weights of South Korean and Chinese urban adolescents were remarkably greater than those of their Japanese peers whereas, at the back of the pack—not surprisingly—were the North Koreans, whose heights and weights roughly correspond to the anthropometric measurements of the other countries in East Asia in the 1950s (Table 34.4), indicating that North Koreans lag five decades behind the rest of the region in this respect.

The height of the adult populations (Table 34.5) corroborates the anthropometric rankings of preschool children and that of adolescents (Tables 34.3 and 34.4).[4] South Koreans are at the top of the group, while North Koreans are at the bottom. One of the most perplexing findings is that, in 2005, Japanese were relatively short in this group (Table 34.3 to 34.5) despite ranking economically as high as South Koreans (Table 34.1). In a similar vein, Baten and Blum (2012, p. 76) conclude that "Japanese values are exceptional in that they are marked by lower height than expected from GDP." Although genetic differences cannot be ruled out, Shay (1994, p. 182) offers a more plausible explanation. Because an individual's final genotype size is a function not only of genetics but also of the size of the mother, it takes many generations to reach the maximal height. Because in pre-modern Japan average height was considerably inferior to average height in Korea and China, it follows that it takes more time in Japan than in China and South Korea to reach a maximal height. For illustration, whereas Chinese men born in the early 19th century were on average already 161–164 cm tall (Baten & Hira, 2008; Morgan, 2009), and Korean men born in the 1890s were on average 164 cm tall (Choi &

Table 34.4 Height, weight and body mass index (BMI) of 17-year-old adolescents in East Asia, 1955–2005

Country:	China (major cities)				South Korea (national)					North Korea (refugees)	Japan (national)					
Year	1955	1985	1995	2005	1965	1975	1985	1995	2005	2005	1955	1965	1975	1985	1995	2005
Males																
Height	165.1	170.3	171.4	172.8	165.9	166.4	168.3	172.2	173.1	163.7	163.4	166.8	168.8	170.2	170.8	170.8
Weight	51.2	56.3	59.6	62.4	54.5	55.8	58.2	63.2	68.7		54.5	57.5	59.2	61.5	63.0	63.8
BMI	18.8	19.4	20.3	20.9	19.8	20.2	20.5	21.3	22.9		20.4	20.7	20.8	21.2	21.6	21.9
Females																
Height	155.3	158.8	160.3	161.3	155.5	156.3	156.6	160.4	160.2	153.7	153.2	154.8	156.3	157.6	158.0	158.0
Weight	47.5	49.4	51.9	54.1	49.6	50.6	51.8	54.6	56.0		49.8	51.2	52.2	52.8	53.3	53.7
BMI	19.7	19.6	20.2	20.8	20.5	20.7	21.1	21.2	21.8		21.2	21.4	21.4	21.3	21.4	21.5

Height in cm, weight in kg, BMI in units. BMI was calculated based on mean height and weight (except for China, where weight was calculated based on mean height and BMI). Data for China as of 1955 refer to the 1950s. Data for South Korea as of 1985 refer to 1984 and as of 1995 to 1997. Data for North Korea as of 2005 refer to refugees measured upon their arrival in South Korea from 1995 to 2007. Also, the North Korean age group of 17 refers to the age group of 17.50 to 18.49. Weight and BMI data of North Koreans were reported but excluded herein because the refugees spent on average 2 years in transit countries where their weight and BMI (but to a lesser extent height) started to recover.

Source: Ministry of Education, Culture, Sports, Science and Technology of Japan (2012), pp. 134–137; Kim, Oh, Lee, Choi, Choe, & Yoon (2008), pp. 232–233; Pak (2010), p. 388; Ji and Chen (2008), p. 533.

Table 34.5 Height, weight, and body mass index (BMI) of adults in East Asia around 2000

Country:	China (national)	South Korea (national)	North Korea (refugees)	Japan (national)
Year:	1988	2000	1997-2007	1994
Age:	18-60	18-59	20-69	18-59
Males				
Height	167.8	170.7	163.5-166.6	169.0
Weight	59.0	66.0		65.5
BMI	21.0	22.7		22.9
Females				
Height	157.0	158.8	151.7-155.6	156.9
Weight	52.0	53.5		52.2
BMI	21.1	21.2		21.2

Height in cm, weight in kg, BMI in units, age in years. BMI was calculated based on mean height and weight. Year refers to the year of the published report. Data for North Korea refer to refugees measured upon their arrival in South Korea from 1997 to 2007.

Source: Lin, Wang, & Wang (2004), p. 174; Pak, Schwekendiek, & Kim. (2011), p. 147.

Schwekendiek, 2009, p. 260), Japanese men measured in the late 19th century were on average only 156 cm tall (Shay, 1994, p. 201). Indeed, when Imperial Japan began to take control of East Asia, the oppressed peoples called the foreign rulers "island dwarfs."

Another likely reason that Chinese and Korean heights (and thus weight and BMI) have increased more than those of the Japanese is that their diet has been more Westernized. China and South Korea rigorously enforced milk supplement programs in schools over the past few decades.[5] The fact that South Koreans are taller than all other East Asians is likely due to the fact that the traditional diet has been supplemented with high-protein Western meat and dairy products (Schwekendiek & Jun, 2010). Indeed, previous research suggests that, historically, access to animal proteins, particularly milk, has had a significant positive impact on physical growth (Baten & Murray, 2000; Blum, 2013). At the same time, differences in cooking techniques probably account for the fact that Chinese weight (and thus BMI) rates have recently increased while those in South Korea have remained relatively low (Lee, Popkin, & Kim, 2002). Additionally, the low weight (and thus BMI) of the Japanese (Mosk, 1996, p. 31) and South Korean populations (Schwekendiek, Yeo, & Ulijaszek, 2013, p. 144) are probably a result of dieting, in order to increase one's chances in the highly competitive job and marriage markets (Table 34.6).

Table 34.6 Protein, calorie, and fat consumption in East Asia, 1979–2004

	Calorie (kcal/person/day)			Protein (g/person/day)			Fat (g/person/day)		
Country	1979–81	1989–91	2000–02	1979–81	1989–91	2000–02	1979–81	1989–91	2000–02
China	2,330	2,680	2,960	55	65	82	33	53	87
North Korea	2,280	2,440	2,140	73	80	62	37	47	34
South Korea	2,990	3,020	3,060	83	82	88	37	57	76
Japan	2,710	2,820	2,780	87	95	92	69	80	86

Source: FAO (2004), pp. 189–192.

Whereas calorie consumption in China (2,960 kcal) at the turn of this century was almost equal to that in South Korea (3,060 kcal), in Japan it has been considerably lower (2,780 kcal) (Table 34.6). This is perhaps partly due to the fact that portions are very small in Japan. The contemporary South Korean diet is almost as rich in protein (88 g) as the Japanese diet (92 g), but the South Korean diet has less fat (76 g) than the Chinese (87 g) and Japanese (86 g) diets while providing a generous amount of calories. Needless to say, North Koreans consumed fewer calories (2,140 kcal), proteins (62 g), and fat (34 g) than did any other East Asian population.

34.5 Conclusion

East Asian anthropometrics have improved dramatically over the past few decades. This positive trend is similar to that found in many other countries at the start of their industrialization drive (Hauspie, Vercauteren, & Susanne, 1996). Although the biological standards of living of Chinese living in major cities and urban areas are on a par with those of OECD countries in the region, most notably Japan and South Korea, China's rural population lags far behind. In fact, China represents the world's largest outlier in rural–urban stunting gaps (Table 34.2). However, as of 2005, their anthropometric status is superior to that of their socialist counterparts in North Korea (Table 34.3)—no surprise, since the latter's economic performance is the worst in East Asia (Table 34.1). Because South Koreans are on average taller than other East Asians and are catching up with Americans (Schwekendiek & Jun, 2010, p. 164), these differences between the two Koreas cannot be explained by genetic predispositions.[6] Japan's anthropometrics, on the other hand, have not matched its increasing economic power. However, the fact that the quantity and quality of food intake in Japan differs from that found in the rest of East Asia indicates that differences in food culture, along with intergenerational factors, may account for these variations.

Until now, the vast body of the anthropometric literature dealing with East Asia has focused on the task of estimating baseline height trends or assessing socioeconomic differences in anthropometrics. However, recent studies have begun to expand this field by combining numeracy (as a proxy for education) with anthropometrics (Baten, Ma, Morgan, & Wang, 2010). Other specialized studies have looked at the impact of early-life experience (proxied by the month of birth) on adult heights in China (Zhang, 2011) and North Korea (Schwekendiek, Pak, & Kim, 2009). Given the global importance of the East Asian region, many more anthropometric studies are sure to come.

Acknowledgments

This research was supported by the National Research Foundation of the Republic of Korea (NRF-2007-361-AL0014).

Notes

1. For a recent review of ancient Japanese and Korean osteometric data, see Shin et al. (Shin, Oh, Kim, & Hwang, 2012, p. 438). Among other notable studies providing indirect anthropometric assessments of East Asians is one based on clay statues excavated in China (Komlos, 2003) and one based on human corpses recovered in Korea (Kim & Park, 2011).
2. Height in colonial Korea (1910–45) and in colonial Taiwan (1895–1945) did not decline during Japanese rule. On the contrary, height of colonial Taiwanese and colonial Koreans slightly increased by 1–2 cm (Olds, 2003, Choi & Schwekendiek, 2009), suggesting that living conditions might have improved despite harsh foreign occupation.
3. The 16 cities are Beijing, Tianjin, Shenyang, Changchun, Harbin, Shanghai, Nanjing, Hangzhou, Hefei, Nanchang, Jinan, Wuhan, Changsha, Guangzhou, Chengdu, and Xian.
4. Most of the data on adults include individuals up to 59 years of age. As height (and thus weight and BMI) tends to diminish drastically after the age of 50, one should take these data with a grain of salt.
5. For instance, in South Korea schoolchildren were even beaten by their teachers if they refused to drink milk.
6. Eighteen-year-old males from the United States were 10.5 cm taller than their peers from South Korea in the 1980s. However, they were only 3.9 cm taller by the 2000s (Schwekendiek & Jun, 2010, p. 164).

References

Allen, R. (2011). Global economic history. Oxford, UK: Oxford University Press.

Bassino, J. -P. (2006). Inequality in Japan (1892–1941): Physical stature, income, and health. *Economics and Human Biology, 4*, 62–88.

Baten, J. (1999). *Ernährung und wirtschaftliche Entwicklung in Bayern, 1730–1880*. Stuttgart, DE: Steiner.

Baten, J., & Blum, M. (2012). Growing tall but unequal: New findings and new background evidence on anthropometric welfare in 156 countries, 1810–1989. *Economic History of Developing Regions, 27*, 66–85.

Baten, J., & Hira, S. (2008). Anthropometric trends in southern China, 1830–1864. *Australian Economic History Review, 48*, 209–226.

Baten, J., Ma, D., Morgan, S., & Wang, Q. (2010). Evolution of living standards and human capital in China in the 18-20th centuries: Evidences from real wages, age-heaping, and anthropometrics. *Explorations in Economic History, 47*, 347–359.

Baten, J., & Murray, J. (2000). Heights of men and women in 19th-century Bavaria: Economic, nutritional, and disease influences. *Explorations in Economic History, 37*, 351–369.

Blum, M. (2013). Cultural and genetic influences on the "biological standard of living". *Historical Methods, 46*, 19–30.

Brinkman, H. -J., Drukker, J., & Slot, B. (1997). *GDP per capita and the biological standard of living in contemporary developing countries* (Research Memorandum GD-35). Groningen Growth and Development Centre. Retrieved October 27, 2014, from http://www.ggdc.net/publications/memorandum/gd35.pdf

Carson, S. (2006). The biological living conditions of nineteenth-century Chinese males in America. *Journal of Interdisciplinary History, 37*, 201–217.

Carson, S. (2007). Statures of 19th century Chinese males in America. *Annals of Human Biology*, *34*, 173–182.

Chan, K. W., & Zhang, L. (1999). The Hukou system and rural–urban migration in China: Processes and changes. *China Quarterly*, *160*, 818–855.

Choi, S. -J., & Schwekendiek, D. (2009). The biological standard of living in colonial Korea, 1910–1945. *Economics and Human Biology*, *7*, 259–264.

FAO. (2004). *FAO statistical yearbook 2004*. Rome: Food and Agricultural Organization.

Floud, R., Fogel, R. W., Harris, B., & Hong, S. C. (2011). The changing body: Health, nutrition, and human development in the western world since 1700. Cambridge, UK: Cambridge University Press.

Gill, I. (1998). Stature, consumption, and the standard of living in colonial Korea. In J. Komlos & J. Baten (Eds.), *The biological standard of living in comparative perspective* (pp. 122–138). Stuttgart, DE: Steiner.

Guntupalli, A., & Schwekendiek, D. (2009). Is it better to live in rural or urban areas? A worldwide study on child health. In S. Quintero (Ed.), *Child welfare issues and perspectives* (pp. 77–96). New York: Nova.

Habicht, J. -P, Martorell, R., Yarbrough, C., Malina, R., & Klein, R. (1974). Height and weight standards for preschool children. How relevant are ethnic differences in growth potential? *Lancet*, *1*, 611–614.

Haines, M. (1998). Health, height, nutrition, and mortality: Evidence on the "Antebellum Puzzle" from Union Army recruits for New York State and the United States. In J. Komlos & J. Baten (Eds.), *The biological standard of living in comparative perspectives* (pp. 155–180). Stuttgart, DE: Steiner.

Hauspie, R. C., Vercauteren, M., & Susanne, C. (1996). Secular changes in growth. *Hormone Research*, *45*, 8–17.

Hawley, S. (2005). *The Imjin War: Japan's sixteenth-century invasion of Korea and attempt to conquer China*. Seoul: The Royal Asiatic Society Korea Branch; Berkeley, CA: Institute of East Asian Studies Berkeley.

Honda, G. (1997). Differential structure, differential health: Industrialization in Japan, 1868–1940. In R. Steckel & R. Floud (Eds.), Health and welfare during industrialization (pp. 251–284). Chicago and London: University of Chicago.

Ji, C. -Y., & Chen, T. -J. (2008). Secular changes in stature and body mass index for Chinese youth in sixteen major cities, 1950s–2005. *American Journal of Human Biology*, *20*, 530–537.

Kim, D., & Park, H. (2011). Measuring living standards from the lowest: Height of the male Hangryu deceased in colonial Korea. *Explorations in Economic History*, *48*, 590–599.

Kim, J. -Y., Oh, I. -H., Lee, E. -Y., Choi, K. -S., Choe, B. -K., Yoon, T. -Y. (2008). Anthropometric changes in children and adolescents from 1965 to 2005 in Korea. *American Journal of Physical Anthropology*, *136*, 230–236.

Kimura, M. (1993). Standards of living in colonial Korea: Did the masses become worse off or better off under Japanese rule? *Journal of Economic History*, *53*, 629–652.

Komlos, J. (1987). The height and weight of West Point cadets: Dietary change in antebellum America. *Journal of Economic History*, *47*, 897–927.

Komlos, J. (1998). Shrinking in a growing economy? The mystery of physical stature during the industrial revolution. *Economic History*, *58*, 779–802.

Komlos, J. (2003). The size of the Chinese terra-cotta warriors—3rd century B.C. *Antiquity*, Project Gallery, No. 296, June 2003. Retrieved October 27, 2014, from http://antiquity.ac.uk/projgall/296.html.

Komlos, J. (2012). A three-decade history of the Antebellum Puzzle: Explaining the shrinking of the U.S. population at the onset of modern economic growth. *Journal of the Historical Society, 12*, 395–445.

Komlos, J., Hau, M. H., & Bourguinat, N. (2003). An anthropometric history of early-modern France, 1666–1766. *European Review of Economic History, 7*, 159–189.

Lee, M. -J., Popkin, B., & Kim, S. (2002). The unique aspects of the nutrition transition in South Korea: The retention of healthful elements in their traditional diet. *Public Health Nutrition, 5*, 197–203.

Lewis, J. B., Jun, S. H., & Schwekendiek, D. (2013). Toward an anthropometric history of Chosŏn Dynasty Korea, sixteenth to eighteenth century. *Journal of the Historical Society, 13*, 239–270.

Li, H., Zong, X., Zhang, J., & Zhu, Z. (2011). Physical growth of children in urban, suburban and rural mainland China: A study of 20 years change. *Biomedical and Environmental Sciences, 24*, 1–11.

Lin, Y. -C., Wang, M. -J. J., & Wang, E. M. (2004). The comparisons of anthropometric characteristics among four peoples in East Asia. *Applied Ergonomics, 35*, 173–178.

Maddison, A. (2001). *The world economy. A millennial perspective.* Paris: OECD.

Maddison, A. (2003). *The world economy: Historical statistics.* Paris: OECD.

Margo, R., & Steckel, R. (1983). Heights of native born northern whites during the antebellum period. *Journal of Economic History, 43*, 167–174.

Ministry of Education, Culture, Sports, Science and Technology of Japan. (2012). *Physical education and sports.* Tokyo: MEXT. Retrieved October 27, 2014, from http://www.mext.go.jp/english/statistics/1302984.htm

Morgan, S. (1998). Biological indicators of change in the standard of living in China. In J. Komlos & J. Baten (Eds.), *The biological standard of living in comparative perspective* (pp. 7–34). Stuttgart, DE: Franz Steiner.

Morgan, S. (2000). Richer and taller: Stature and living standards in China, 1979–1995. *China Journal, 44*, 1–39.

Morgan, S. (2004). Economic growth and the biological standard of living in China, 1880–1930. *Economics and Human Biology, 2*, 197–218.

Morgan, S. (2009). Stature and economic development in south China, 1810–1880. *Explorations in Economic History, 46*, 53–69.

Mosk, C. (1996). Making health work: Human growth in modern Japan. Berkeley: University of California Press.

Olds, K. (2003). The biological standard of living in Taiwan under Japanese occupation. *Economics and Human Biology, 1*, 187–206.

Pak, S. (2004). The biological standard of living in the two Koreas. *Economics and Human Biology, 2*, 511–521.

Pak, S. (2010). The growth status of North Korean refugee children and adolescents from 6 to 19 years of age. *Economics and Human Biology, 8*, 385–395.

Pak, S., Schwekendiek, D., & Kim, H. K. (2011). Height and living standards in North Korea, 1930s–1980s. *Economic History Review, 64*, 142–158.

Schoch, T., Staub, K., & Pfister, C. (2012). Social inequality and the biological standard of living: An anthropometric analysis of Swiss conscription data, 1875–1950. *Economics and Human Biology, 10*, 154–173.

Schuster, K. (2005). *Wirtschaftliche entwicklung, sozialstruktur und biologischer lebensstandard in München und dem südlichen Bayern im 19.* Jahrhundert. St. Katharinen: Scripta Mercaturae Verlag.

Schwekendiek, D. (2008*a*). Determinants of well-being in North Korea: Evidence from the post-famine period. *Economics and Human Biology, 6*, 446–454.

Schwekendiek, D. (2008*b*). The North Korean standard of living during the famine. *Social Science and Medicine, 66*, 596–608.

Schwekendiek, D. (2009). Height and weight differences between South and North Korea. *Journal of Biosocial Science, 41*, 51–57.

Schwekendiek, D. (2013). An interview with John Komlos. *Newsletter of the Cliometric Society, 28*, 38–44.

Schwekendiek, D. (2014). *The Saemaul Undong in Biosocial Retrospect and Prospect.* Paper presented at the 2014 UN Public Service Forum, Seoul, South Korea, June 23–26.

Schwekendiek, D., & Jun, S. -H. (2010). From the poorest to the tallest in East-Asia: The secular trend in height of South Koreans. *Korea Journal, 50*, 151–175.

Schwekendiek, D., & Pak, S. (2009). Recent growth of children in the two Koreas: A meta-analysis. *Economics and Human Biology, 7*, 109–112.

Schwekendiek, D., Pak, S., & Kim, H. K. (2009). Variations in the birth-season effects on height attainment in the two Koreas. *Annals of Human Biology, 36*, 421–430.

Schwekendiek, D., Yeo, M., & Ulijaszek, S. (2013). On slimming pills, growth hormones and plastic surgery: The socioeconomic value of the body in South Korea. In C. Banwell, S. Ulijaszek, & J. Dixon (Eds.), *When culture impacts health* (pp. 141–153). London, Waltham and San Diego: Academic Press.

Shay, T. (1994). The level of living in Japan, 1885–1938: New evidence. In J. Komlos (Ed.). *Stature, living standards, and economic development: Essays in anthropometric history* (pp. 173–201). Chicago: University of Chicago.

Shin, D. H., Oh, C. S., Kim, Y. -S., & Hwang, Y. -I. (2012). Ancient-to-modern secular changes in Korean stature. *American Journal of Physical Anthropology, 147*, 433–442.

Steckel, R. (2009). Heights and human welfare: Recent developments and new directions. *Explorations in Economic History, 46*, 1–23.

Takaki, R. (1998). Strangers from a different shore: A history of Asian Americans. Boston: Little, Brown and Company.

Ward, P. (2013). Stature, migration and human welfare in South China, 1850–1930. *Economics and Human Biology, 11*, 488–501.

Waterlow, J., Buzina, R., Keller, W., Lane, J., Nichaman, M., & Tanner, J. (1977). The presentation and use of height and weight data for comparing the nutritional status of groups of children under the age of 10 years. *Bulletin of the World Health Organization, 55*, 489–498.

Zhang, W. (2011). Month of birth, socioeconomic background and height in rural Chinese men. *Journal of Biosocial Science, 43*, 641–656.

CHAPTER 35

ECONOMICS AND HUMAN BIOLOGY IN LATIN AMERICA

MORAMAY LÓPEZ-ALONSO

SCHOLARSHIP in the field of economics and human biology focusing on Latin America has evolved around three main themes: the relationship between living standards and economic conditions over the very long run, dating back to the pre-Columbian era; how changes in biological standard of living enhance our understanding of how they were affected by economic development in comparison with other regions of the world; and the comprehension of interactions between health and nutrition indicators and economic performance among different groups in the contemporary period. Anthropometric methods that use height and body mass are one way of looking at the evolution of living standards and income distribution. Height can be used as a proxy of well-being because the final height of an adult is achieved through the interaction of several variables, all related to income (Cuff, 2005; Sokoloff, 1995). These interactions make height a multidimensional measure of well-being because it assesses the effects of nutrition, health, education, and income on living standards. The logic is as follows: if people during their childhood have good nutrition, adequate clothing, reasonable shelter, and receive some schooling, they are more likely to grow taller than those who, despite having the same genetic endowment, grow up under less favorable conditions (Steckel, 1995, 1998). Not having one or several of these inputs puts an individual at a disadvantage in developing to his or her optimum. Thus, in a given society, people from richer income strata should be taller than people from poorer income strata. Two additional points give relevance to height as a measure of living standards and inequality. First, in premonetized societies, the use of stature is one valid way to measure living standards. In the case of agrarian societies, height provides us with an easy way to draw comparisons at the international level and over time, as economies experience the transformation of productive processes. Also, in recent years, as the study of inequality has gained momentum, developmental economists and economic historians have begun to consider anthropometric measures as a proxy of inequality (Baten & Carson, 2010; Bértola, de la Escosura, & Williamson, 2010).

35.1 Pre-Columbian Era

The first pillar of this scholarship explores the evolution of living conditions in Latin American populations during the pre-Columbian era. These studies are being conducted by paleodemographers, physical anthropologists who specialize in bioarchaeology, as well as geographers, epidemiologists, human biologists, and other specialists in the natural sciences (Steckel & Rose, 2002). There are two advantages to studying Latin America in a long-run perspective. First, it was the cradle of three major ancient civilizations: the Inca in the Andes and the Maya and the Mexica in Mesoamerica. Given the extant evidence and tools to analyze it, this research agenda has centered on developing paleoenvironmental reconstructions to recreate the living conditions of ancient settlements and their evolution over time (i.e., the reasons that allowed for their emergence, flourishing, and eventual demise). Second, researchers can take advantage of the natural experiment created by the fact that the Western Hemisphere was to a great extent isolated from the rest of the world until 1492.

As the natural sciences in fields such as dendrochronology and palynology develop more methods and tools to study the past, it will become possible to expand studies on regions that had smaller and less complex human settlements for which more traditional sources, such as written records or large archaeological sites, are not available. For now, there are more studies on the Maya civilization, hence there is more evidence available on this group. One objective of this line of study is to link findings from the past with the living conditions of contemporary indigenous population, a population that is transitioning into new forms of living and working, as we shall see in the section that examines the contemporary period. Still needed are more studies that link the 16th century to the 18th century, and the new tools available should bridge the lacunae of traditional sources. Although the Spanish Crown was exceptionally good at creating administrative documents, and the volume of documents on the 18th century tends to be much larger than in the previous two centuries, there was much more written on regions that were wealthier and at the core of the colonies than on the peripheral and frontier zones. Brazil, which yields a different historiography because it was a colony of Portugal and later became an empire on it own, remains understudied; most of the extant knowledge on this country comes from archaeological studies (Neves et al., 2004; Araujo, Neves & Piló, 2004; Neves, Bernardo, & Okumura, 2007).

Some of the most representative studies devoted to the pre-Columbian era examine the regions at the core of the ancient civilizations, especially those that left written records. Scholars have addressed how past civilizations were organized, how their economies worked, and the living conditions of their peoples (de Lourdes Márquez, 1984, Márquez Morfin, 2010; Storey, 1992). In particular, studies have been devoted to the Maya and groups living in the Central Valley of Mexico, such as those in the settlement of Teotihuacán (Márquez et al., 1997; McCaa et al., 2002). One of their main findings concerns the secular decline in height among the Maya. People living during the

Pre-Classic period (2000 B.C.–250 A.D.) were taller than present-day Maya, who are known to be a population short in stature, and their decline in stature was due to "biological adaptation to the environment, change of activities, dietary variations, population fluctuations, and excessive work burdens," which led to increasingly precarious living conditions for most of the population during the Classic period (A.D. 250–900; Márquez et al. quoted in Whittington et al., 1997, p. 60). As the modes of production gained complexity and more people began to labor in nonagricultural-related activities, food may not have been distributed equitably. This hypothesis is consistent with the prevalence of high frequencies of nutritional diseases such as anemia and scurvy, as evidenced by lesions on Pre-Hispanic skeletal remains (cribra orbitalia, spongy hyperostosis, enamel hypoplasia). This line of research and hypothesis coincide with the thesis of Cohen and Armelagos that hunter-gatherers, because of their social organization, daily activities, and nutrition, enjoyed better health than agriculturalists (Cohen, Armelagos, & Wenner-Glen Foundation, 1984; Cohen & Armelagos, 2013). We can then assert that, in terms of biological standards of living, there has been a gradual deterioration during the transition from hunter-gatherers, to agricultural societies, to nonagricultural societies in which there is a more complex division of labor. This has led to increased differentiation and inequality. Civilization has not been all-conducive to improving the health of human populations.

Other studies look at the biological encounter between the Old and New Worlds after 1492. This scholarship has contributed to a better understanding of the extent to which biology was a determinant of the colonization process (Crosby, 1972), proving that germs were a more powerful killer than guns (Diamond, 2005). This emphasis on biological factors is contrary to the traditional historiography that asserted that the Spaniards had killed the Indians on purpose. New evidence shows that the decimation of the indigenous population was not mainly due to Spanish conquistadors' intent to commit mass killings of Indians but rather due to the Indians lack of immunity to newly introduced diseases. The oldest and most important debate on this topic is over the size of the population of the Central Valley of Mexico on the eve of the Conquest (Cook & Borah, 1979) and the extent of the killer epidemics of the 16th century that followed (Cook & Borah, 1979; Gibson, 1964). As new sources are discovered and new analytical tools fashioned, more becomes known about this tragic natural experiment in history. There is not yet a consensus on the size of the population of the Central Valley of Mexico, other than the fact that it had the largest human settlement in the Western Hemisphere prior to the arrival of Spaniards (5–20 million people) and that it had a sophisticated political and economic organization. We do, however, have a better understanding of how people lived in that region on the eve of the Conquest (Livi-Bacci, 2006; McCaa, 2000). New research has refined the hypothesis on the causes and the dimensions of the demographic collapse: the epidemics came in waves, and not all pathogens behind the demographic catastrophe of the 16th century were foreign. New evidence that uses documents produced in the native languages as well as advances in the field of paleodemography and paleopathology suggest that the killer germs comprised both local and foreign strains of disease. Nutritional variations in the region as a result of bad crops and warfare debilitated the population, thus increasing the likelihood of the incidence and spread of epidemics (Brooks, 1993; Marr & Kiracofe, 2000; McCaa, 1995; Warinner, Robles García, Spores & Tuross, 2012).

Going beyond the specific study of the demographic collapse of the 16th century, the use of new methodologies sheds light on the influence of environmental change on the biological standards of living of populations, thus providing a broader perspective encompassing long-term processes. For example, we are beginning to understand how the introduction of new animal species brought from Europe, such as horses and pigs, affected the ecosystems of the New World and the livelihoods of its dwellers (e.g., severe erosion generated in Central Mexico due to the introduction of sheep; Crosby, 1972, 1994; Melville, 1994). Studies of tree rings, which indicate variations in rainfall, and of indigenous sources that cover the pre-Columbian era, the Conquest, and the post-Conquest period give insight into environmental variations and their impact on the biological standards of living of settlers, both indigenous and Spanish. Food shortages caused malnutrition, which created a breeding ground for epidemic and nutrition-related diseases (Acuña-Soto et al., 2002; Therrell et al., 2004, 2006). Environmental degradation began before 1492, and the encounter of the two worlds exacerbated this process.

35.2 Economic Development

The second pillar of scholarship consists of studies that are normally grounded in the field of economic history. The pioneering works of historical anthropometry looked at the cases of Europe and the United States; however, in the past two decades, this methodology has been adopted to study populations in Latin America.

The literature that examines the synergies between economics and human biology from an economic historical perspective has taken shape over the past two decades. We now have a long-term comprehensive view of certain countries such as Argentina, Colombia, and Mexico. Historiography on other countries remains impressionistic but promises much potential for further studies, as in the cases of Brazil and Peru. Many sources remain to be explored for those countries that are still virgin ground to researchers. The findings so far show that a fuller understanding of the sometimes contrasting trajectories between economic performance and biological well-being, in part reflecting inequalities, can shed light on the causes of why Latin America fell behind from the 18th century to the 20th century. In many countries, periods of economic expansion were not conducive to an improvement in the biological standards of living of the population. Industrialization does not appear to have had a strong impact on human welfare for the population at large but export-led growth did. More scholarship is needed to assess from an economic historical perspective the importance on biological well-being of education and public health initiatives during the transition from the pre-industrial era to the industrialized one and to evaluate if there was ever a significant urban penalty in the region or how the epidemiological transition was experienced in different countries. The region was and remains plagued by inequalities, but we need to comprehend better the differing nature of inequality across countries. As economic historians of Latin America continue to explore the roots of underdevelopment in the region, there is fertile ground to expand studies on this topic.

Geographic location and the common experience of being or having been colonies of the same monarchies are the criteria used to define Latin America. Nonetheless, there are profound differences across the region, and these correlate with differences in economic performance trajectories.[1] Secular trends of height in Latin American populations have been used to evaluate the evolution of biological standards of living for the population in periods of sustained economic growth, export-led growth, industrialization, and during sudden crisis, such as revolutions. It has also been possible to assess, with the use of heights, the extent of inequality in living standards across social classes. As we mentioned at the beginning of this chapter, heights can be used as a proxy of well-being because the final height of an adult is the result of the interactions of several variables, all related to income. These interactions make it a multidimensional measure of well being because height assesses the effects of nutrition, health, education, and income on living standards. Analogous to studies in other parts of the world that utilize records of physical stature to examine the biological standards of living, Latin American studies have complemented and contrasted their specific findings with those obtained with other, more conventional indicators, such as demographic or price and wage data. It is important to work with all indicators to examine why there are episodes in which anthropometric measures do not follow the same trends as traditional indicators because this can provide a useful guide for the design of public policies geared toward decreasing inequality.

Latin America is especially interesting because the region fell behind in economic growth and development vis-à-vis other continents (Haber, 1997). The region began to lag in economic development as the colonial era came to an end despite the fact that some of these former colonies had produced enormous riches for their metropoles to pay for wars and conspicuous consumption. The region was marked by inequalities then and remains so to this day. After gaining independence (post-1821), Latin American nations endeavored to emulate the economic models of the United States and Western European countries, with a focus on industrialization. Hopes and expectations were based on Latin America's perceived comparative advantages of space, natural resource endowments, and, in some cases, abundance of labor. Such hopes were not fulfilled: the region's economies did not grow steadily, there were economic booms followed by crises, and some sectors flourished (e.g., export agriculture products) while others languished (e.g., textile production for domestic markets). Overall, the region lagged behind the North Atlantic world.

For three reasons, the study of biological standards of living covering the 18th to the 20th centuries sheds light on the success or failure of policies of public and private groups that aimed to attain sustained economic growth and thus affected the livelihoods and living conditions of the region's people. First, the national governments of this region lacked the resources to produce high-quality comprehensive statistics that spanned the entire period (as was the case for the United States and Western Europe). Hence, the quality of the data for the indicators traditionally used to measure living standards, such as prices and wages, or even general demographic data, is not nearly as good as it is for Western Europe or the United States for periods prior to the mid-20th century. Identifying biological living standards and their changes can therefore serve as an alternative measurement. Second, because Latin America is renowned for extreme inequalities, even if wealth were created, it would not have been distributed in an equitable way. Indicators of biological standards of living can be used to evaluate how unequal was the actual impact of any economic growth on the various populations of the different countries and how this evolved over time. Third, the determination of biological living standards can be applied to assess the effect of long-term processes encompassing industrialization, epidemiological transitions, and mortality revolutions, which affected different populations differently within countries and within regions.

One additional reason to examine biological standards of living relates to the diversity of the region: historical anthropometry can produce a clearer picture of how similar political-economic development programs and policies yielded different outcomes in living standards. One major point that becomes evident from the scholarship on this topic is that there tends to be an absence of synchronicity between economic performance and the evolution of biological well-being. Countries experience economic growth while inequality prevails, and they fail to improve the living standards of their populations.

Mexico has been extensively studied. New Spain at the end of the 18th century was the richest colony of the Spanish empire, yet, by the third decade of the 19th century it was an impoverished, indebted new nation. This impoverishment was due to the excessive taxation imposed by the metropole during the last decade of the 18th century and the cost of the War of Independence during the first decades of the 19th century. Historiography on the 18th century that focuses on living standards has concentrated on its evolution and its links to inequality and on defining their determinant. Initial studies concluded that there was a great decline in the population's biological standards of living that began with cohorts born in the 1730s and extended into the first decades of the 19th century due to "increasing hardship in acquiring food staples and harsher climatic conditions" (Challú, 2009, 2010). This was especially true for the rural people of Central Mexico who became wage laborers. This decline in living standards is consistent with the hypothesis advanced by Coatsworth (1978) that the roots of Mexican underdevelopment should be traced to the 19th century and the last decades of the colonial era. However, more recent works argue that New Spain was not as unequal a region as once claimed, and, moreover, that compared to the rest of the world, the decline in living standards experienced during this period was not as steep or as dramatic (Dobado-González & García-Montero, 2010, 2014). New data sources are being explored that will enable us to delve deeper into the evolution of the biological standards of living standards of this time period and their connections to agricultural disasters and wealth produced by silver mining (Grajales-Porras & López-Alonso, 2011).

A long-term study on the evolution of living standards in Mexico from 1850 to 1950 shows that there was economic growth with persistent inequality that at times improved and at other times deteriorated. During this time period, the years of good economic performance did not translate into improved stature, and, contrary to the argument of traditional historiography of that time period, the Mexican Revolution (1910–20) and its progressive institutional changes were not conducive to better biological standards of living. There are disparities across regions and across social classes: Mexicans from the north were taller than their counterparts in the central and southern regions, and people with higher incomes were taller than those in the lower income strata. The average stature of well-to-do Mexicans increased over time whereas that of the lower classes declined and stagnated, except for a short a period of recovery and increase in stature. These findings are consistent with the regional disparities in economic growth and with persistent inequality that other economic indicators suggest. Actually, it is not until the launching of a welfare state and its policies in 1937 that we observe an improvement in the biological standard of living for the population. These studies show that height can be used as a proxy of wealth distribution and as a tool to analyze the relative success of social policies geared toward reducing poverty and improving the biological and social well-being of the population at large (López-Alonso & Porras-Condey, 2003, López-Alonso 2007, 2012). Studies that look at the evolution of biological standards of living after 1950 show that, although the stature of the Mexican population as a whole improved, there disparities continued across regions and social classes (López-Alonso & Vélez-Grajales, 2015). The quality of both economic and biological data for the post-1950 era comes from national statistics that permit more accurate estimations of the evolution of stature and its correlation with other social development variables.

Biological evidence also indicate that, at least since the 19th century, Mexicans from the north tended to be better off than their counterparts in the south, but, compared to their neighbors in the southwestern United States, they did not do so well: both Mexican Americans and Americans in the U.S. southwest were taller than Mexicans (Carson, 2005, 2007, 2009). The differences in stature and body mass index may be explained by people growing up in the southwestern United States having had better nutrition and less exposure to disease than their Mexican counterparts. A possible confounding factor is self-selection of Mexican migrants to the United States in the 1920s and 1930s because these migrants were taller than the Mexican national average (Kosack & Ward, 2014).

Argentina provides an interesting case because of the variation in its economic conditions. During the 19th and early 20th centuries, it experienced a substantial commodity boom that led to spectacular economic expansion. As an export economy, it suffered dearly from the two world wars and the Great Depression. Significantly, the evolution of biological standards of living did not go in the same direction as economic performance. During the golden era of export-led growth, there was a decline in net nutrition, as evidenced by a decline in stature; in contrast, biological standards of living improved and Argentines grew taller during the period known as the "Great Delay," the time between the two world wars and characterized by economic downturn. This downturn did not affect the price of food, and, at the same time, the government invested in education and health. There was a decline in height for cohorts born and growing up in the post-World War II period coinciding with the rise of the Peronist redistributionist political party. This party's policies were geared toward the creation of a voting clientele, not necessarily toward improving the living standards of the population at large. In Argentina, too, there were persistent social and regional differences in biological standards of living. Argentines from Buenos Aires and its surroundings were taller than their counterparts in the provinces of the Northwest (Santiago del Estero, Tucumán, Catamarca, Salta, and Jujuy) (Salvatore, 2004a, 2004b, 2004c, 2007, 2009, Salvatore et al. 2010).

Colombia provides especially good data on biological measures for the post-1870 period because the country's national identity cards contain information on height; in addition, passport records have been utilized. Studies of Colombia find a secular increase in population height, with significant regional and intrapersonal convergence in height, although there were class disparities, with the upper income strata of the population measuring taller (Meisel & Vega, 2007*a*,*b*). There are also differences between ethnic groups: for instance, Afro-Colombian men and women were the tallest ethnic group. Indigenous Colombians, who were a shorter group compared to the rest, were more likely than other ethnic groups to experience an increase in biological well-being as a consequence of an improvement in their socioeconomic status, thereby reducing the average stature gap between them and the rest of the population (Acosta & Meisel, 2013). This suggests that indigenous people were able to catch up with the rest of the population. Colombia's economy had neither the episodes of spectacular export-led growth that Argentina experienced or the terrible crises experienced by Mexico in the mid-19th century due to civil wars and foreign interventions, and this explains why, in Colombia, the evolution of its biological standards of living did not follow trends that contrasted with those of its cycles of economic growth.

Studies of Brazil cover specific regions during shorter time periods. Preliminary work on the biological standards of living of Brazilian slaves and African slaves brought to Brazil during the last three decades of the slave trade (1830–60) suggest that there was a decline in the height of Brazilian-born slaves and that there was an urban penalty for Rio de Janeiro dwellers with respect to their rural counterparts (Frank, 2006). This suggests that Brazilian-born slaves had a lower standard of living than other slave populations in the Americas (e.g., those in the English-speaking North Atlantic colonies) and that Rio de Janeiro had many of the same public health issues that many other cities faced in the first half of the 19th century. The Rio Grande do Sul experienced economic expansion and a large inflow of immigrants from Europe between 1880 and 1914. Immigrants' children were tall for world standards of the time (about 166.7 cm for males), and there were no significant differences between the heights of European immigrants and their children; instead of a secular increase in height during that time period, there was stagnation and even a slight decrease (Monasterio, 2013). This indicates that, although this in-migration of Europeans was for economic reasons, it was not one in which people were undernourished: the conditions they experienced in Brazil were not necessarily better than those in their homelands, at least not during the first three decades of the migration wave. A study of the 20th century draws a comparison in heights between the richest and the poorest quintiles of the population for the decades 1940–80 and finds sharp differences, suggesting that, despite per capita increases in income, there was no equivalent improvement in the material conditions of life (Monasterio et al., 2010). Interestingly, a new study covering the 1950–80 period finds that income, not disease, appears to be the main correlate of Brazilian population heights in the second half of the 20th century, with the wealthier population being taller (De Oliveira & Quintana-Domeque, 2014).

Further evidence of the relationship between income and height comes from a recent study of 20th-century Guatemala based on preliminary data showing that heights of rural indigenous people, who are also the poorest strata of the population, increased only by 3 cm during the century—indeed, 20th-century Guatemalans were only as tall as their pre-Columbian counterparts. This is the result of adverse economic and social conditions that preclude children from developing under optimal health and nutritional conditions (Ríos, 2009). That general economic growth does not bring equal benefits is indicated by a study from Peru during the first decades of the national era (1820–80). This was a time of economic prosperity due to the substantial profits generated by guano exports. The study shows that the stature of men and women from the laboring classes stagnated throughout the period, indicating that the benefits of economic prosperity did not reach lower strata of the population (Twrdek & Manzel, 2010).

That different sectors benefitted unequally from changing economic conditions is clear from a comparative study of Argentina, Brazil, and Peru during the late 19th and early 20th centuries. Although each of the countries experienced export-led growth during this period that fostered economic development, only farmers' and landowners' welfare improved, and only Brazilians experienced a substantial nutritional improvement (Baten, Pelger, & Twrdek, 2009). Biological indicators provide insights into the relationships among trade, inequality, and trade policies in seven Latin American countries during the second half of the 20th century. This is a period in which most Latin American economies transitioned from a closed economy based on an import substitution industrialization model to a free trade model. The authors found that greater inequality, measured by anthropometric indicators, tended to favor the "closing" of the economy: that is, policy-makers in an economy characterized by more inequality did not favor trade liberalization (Baltzer & Baten, 2008).

35.3 The Contemporary Period

The third pillar of scholarship is linked to public policy research and analysis geared toward understanding the efficacy of public health initiatives oriented to improving the livelihood of marginalized communities and to understanding the efficacy of poverty alleviation programs that allocate resources to improving health and nutrition. Studies of the contemporary period are the result of multidisciplinary collaborative efforts conducted by development economists working both in academic and international organizations focused on human health and development matters. The topics that receive greatest attention are those related to obesity and child development, living conditions, indigenous groups, and migration patterns. Other studies examine the biological welfare of low-income strata of the population vis-à-vis the adoption of certain policies that are aimed at improving their living conditions or the challenges they may face in the future (e.g., climate change).

One focus has been on the causes and repercussions of the alarming spread of the obesity epidemic in entire countries and within certain groups in different countries. The rise of obesity is the result of an epidemiological trap, in which several countries are slow to catch up with the provision of health and educational services while they are simultaneously being flooded by industrialized foodstuffs of low price, low nutritional value, and high caloric content.[2] As a public health problem, obesity has touched some societies more than others; in Latin America, the percentage of obese people is increasing very rapidly. Development economists and policy-makers are looking into the causes, consequences, and evolution of this epidemic in the region.

The rapid morphological change in humans that results from environmental changes is evident in children who migrated into the United States over the past 25 years: they have grown taller than their counterparts who stayed in their homeland. Studies of children migrating from Guatemala and Mexico or of the first generation born in the United States yield both interesting success stories in height increase and cautionary tales in weight gain. The increase in stature is correlated to an increase in access to health care and clean water, higher caloric intake, and higher protein intake. For Mexican American children it is also correlated to a larger gain in maternal height. Guatemalan children who migrated into the United States are much taller (10 cm) and have longer legs than their counterparts in Guatemala (Smith, Bogin, Varela-Silva, & Loucky, 2003; Bogin & Rios, 2003; Bogin, Varela & Ríos 2007; Delajara & Rodríguez-Segura, 2010). The rapid increase in stature shows the magnitude of improvement that can be expected in biological standards of living by providing better health, public infrastructure, and protein intake.

On the other hand, these migrating children who grew taller also grew heavier, to obese levels. Migration into the United States in recent years is also accompanied by the adoption of unhealthy lifestyles patterns, such as diets dense in energy, little regular physical activity, and much leisure time spent in front of a television or computer monitor. These patterns have made this group more prone to overweight and obesity and eventually will lead to stunting with respect to other US population groups (Markowitz & Cosminsky, 2005; Van Hook, Baker, Altman, & Frisco, 2012). These findings are useful for understanding the different implications of migration in the contemporary period and assessing the potential effects of radical changes in disease and nutrition environments not only for groups of Latin Americans migrating into the United States (where they become "Hispanics"). but also for informing policy-makers on the potential outcomes of policies geared toward changing the nutrition and health environments of a given community.

Obesity is an epidemic in the United States that is more common among Hispanic populations, and Mexico seems to be suffering from the same disease, with obesity and diabetes growing there at alarming rates. The effects of migratory patterns on biological standards of living could assist in understanding the spread of this epidemic in Mexico. Some researchers have found patterns of stunted children growing into overweight adults. These patterns have been found among people in the Yucatán Peninsula, where tourism-based economic development has transformed social and economic conditions (Leatherman, Goodman, & Stillman, 2010); similar patterns also have been found in neighboring communities in Guatemala. Recent studies show a correlation between maternal overweight and child stunting; this has been defined as a *malnutrition duality* that results from economic inequality (Lee, Houser, Must, de Fulladolsa, & Bermudez, 2010, 2012). These patterns need to be detected so that they can be corrected with well-designed social policies.

The potential effects on biological well-being of changing lifestyle patterns have been investigated in other societies in transition, such as hunter-gatherer to agriculturalist, agriculturalist to industrialist, industrialist to post-industrialist, and rural to urban. This is the case in some indigenous communities that are changing the basis of their livelihoods. Research teams in the Andean regions of Bolivia and parts of Argentina have made interesting findings. In Bolivia, there is a high prevalence of health problems and malnutrition that is the result of cultural and physical determinants of child nutrition, such as cultural beliefs that relate to dietary habits that may deprive children of certain nutrients (e.g., not feeding them fruits or meats at different stages of growth) as well as to mother's characteristics, household assets, and access to public services (Morales, Aguilar, & Calzadilla, 2004). Focusing more narrowly on the specific characteristics of different Bolivian groups, studies show that among the Tsimane's, a foraging-farming society of native Amazonians in Bolivia, community variables (inequality, social capital) explain little of the variance in anthropometric indices of nutritional status, but individual-level variables (schooling, wealth) are positively correlated with nutritional status (Zeng, Eisenberg, et al., 2013; Zeng, Unudrragada, et al., 2013). In these cases, having an education or owning land of better quality will translate into better standards of living. Dietary quality, access to foraging technology, and traditional knowledge of medicinal plants are related to better anthropometric indices (Godoy, Reyes-García, Vadez, Leonard, Huanca & Bauchet, 2005). Also among the Tsimane's, height premiums and stunting penalties are not common (Godoy, Magvanjav, Nyberg, Eisenberg, McDade, Leonard, Reyes-García, Huanca, Tanner and Gravlee, 2010), but there is also no accuracy of perceived parental height among these people (Patel, Godoy, Seyfried, Reyes-García, Huanca, Leonard, McDade & Tanner, 2007). Thus, for this particular society, being tall or short has no relevance for economic advancement or for receiving preferential treatment, as is common in other groups; it also appears that the perceptions of individual statures within the community do not always correspond to actual measurements. These findings go against the common assumptions on stature and its relevance that many anthropometric studies have shown. This provides an interesting finding in itself, but how it relates to biological standards of living remains to be determined by further analysis. Among the indigenous peoples of northern Argentina (the Toba and the Wichí), there has been a transition from hunter-gatherer economies to more sedentary occupations and engagement with temporary wage labor and local political positions. The result is higher rates of obesity for those who have achieved better political positions and socioeconomic status (Valeggia, Burke, & Fernandez-Duque, 2010).

Child development is of special interest, and studies show that for those groups with limited access to sanitation and education, investment in these services can improve human development indicators. Brazil reduced infant mortality over the past 30 years (Alves & Belluzzo, 2004), but not all regions are affected in the same way, and welfare disparities are more acute in poorer regions (Skoufias & Katayama, 2009). In Brazil, differences are seen in nutritional outcomes between white and black children in addition to the disparities generated by household income, parental education, and other socioeconomic attributes when using anthropometric measures such as the height of children aged 6–60 months (Reis, 2012). In rural Colombia, similar patterns of health and anthropometric measurement improvements among children have been identified as a result of local governments investing in sanitation and parental education (Attanasio, Gomez, Rojas, & Vera-Hernández, 2004). In Mexico, recent studies have found that maternal cognitive and education levels, quality of health, and nutrition all have a positive correlation with children's height (Reyes, Chavez, Little, & Malina, 2010; Rubalcava & Teruel, 2004). Similar studies have yielded corresponding patterns for Peru (Valdivia, 2004), Guatemala (Sweeney, Davenport, & Grace, 2013), Honduras, and Nicaragua (David, Moncada & Ordonez, 2004). Studies on Argentina show that prenatal care helps prevent low birthweights and preterm birth (Wehby, Murray, Castilla Lopez-Camelo, & Ohsfeldt, 2009). For the region in general, a positive correlation has been found between height and later-life cognitive function (Maurer, 2010).

Although welfare and health policies can have beneficial results, social and political events can also produce negative impacts on the biological standards of living of the population, as in the case of stress during *La Violencia* in Colombia. A study that examined secular changes in mean age at menarche among women born between 1941 and 1989 reports that trends indicate more violence tended to increase the age at menarche. These results could suggest a potential impact on maturation of psychosocial stress in childhood due to exposure to a generalized atmosphere of violence and fear (Villamor, Chavarro, & Caro, 2009).

Other forms of stress have been found to impact the welfare of different populations. These stresses can be social, economic, or environmental, and they can affect children as much as adults. Environmental hazards such as tropical storms can have negative influences on the living standards of individuals who experienced them at sensitive stages in their lives. A study of Puerto Rico that examined the effects of the tropical storms of 1928 and 1932 on the health of individuals shows that individuals in the womb or in early infancy who lived through either of the two tropical storms were more likely to have a diagnosis of hypertension, high cholesterol, and diabetes in adulthood and also tended to have less formal schooling (Sotomayor, 2013). Knowing that climate change will cause more of these environmental hazards, policy analysts are warning governments that populations at risk, such as marginalized communities in southeastern Mexico, are being put at even higher risk and that this could further deteriorate their living standards and reduce the height of their children. Social policies like *Progresa*, designed to alleviate poverty through cash transfers and increasing health and education services, should be geared to prevent this (Skoufias & Vinha, 2012; Skoufias, Vinha & Cornoy, 2011). Other environmental effects will be harder to control but are worth knowing about, such as the fact that altitude reduces birthweight, and the effects of altitude are larger for infants with low fetal health endowments (Wehby, Castilla, & Lopez-Camelo, 2010).

Social and economic factors can have varying effects. Land ownership is considered an important variable to improve living standards. Still, current research findings yield contrasting results. For instance, in Uruguay, secure property rights to land are conducive to better health for those who possess them (Gandelman, 2010). In contrast, in Peru, urban land titling leads to a possibility of increased prevalence of obesity among children (Vogl, 2007). This line of research deserves further study to provide a better understanding of land ownership in relation to living standards.

35.4 Conclusion

In recent years, the study of inequality in Latin America has gained momentum. Developmental economists and policy-makers who study the region are aware of the need to understand the historical origins of social developmental challenges that the region faces today because these problems are better understood through a long-term perspective. They are aware that the region is diverse, that there is a lack of reliable data of more traditional indicators for many countries, and that the natural sciences are creating tools and generating data that are useful to assess these challenges and the efficacy of programs aiming to alleviate them. Hence, it should be possible to establish a fruitful dialogue between the past and the present on economic and human biology topics. This chapter synthesized what has been done and what remains as a pending assignment to continue this dialogue.

For the pre-Columbian period, many aspects of human life remain to be analyzed as the natural sciences fashion better techniques to assist archaeologists, palynologists, paleopathologists, paleodemographers, bioarchaeologists, and dendrochronologists in their endeavors to recreate the living conditions of people far back in time. Such projects can illuminate the advantages and disadvantages of the constant process of human social development and organization. They also can be a way to better understand the interactions between human populations and their environments so as to improve the quality of contemporary life in sustainable ways.

More studies covering the 18th to 20th centuries need to be done to get a better sense of the different experiences of evolving biological standards of living across countries. At this point, we only have a clear picture for a very few countries; many studies present only impressionistic information, and this is not sufficient to assess the region as a whole. The findings of these studies will shed light on our understanding of the present, and a solid knowledge of historical context can provide the clue to why certain results appear to be counterintuitive at first glance. Also, the interaction between economics and human biology are better understood when analyzed through a long-term perspective.

For the contemporary period, better information can lead to better public policy recommendations. Some historiographical findings are still preliminary, but they are laying the groundwork for further, more in-depth studies, especially in how to utilize research findings from human biology in public policy design. Obesity and all the health-related problems attendant to it appear to be a major challenge for the region in the contemporary period. This challenge becomes more complex in the face of other problems that lead people to fall into the "epidemiological trap," and these problems demand solutions, such as providing adequate access to health care, sanitation, and education to all segments of society, particularly children, but also their parents. All of this involves the reduction of inequality in living standards across regions and social classes. Other challenges include containing, insofar as it is possible to do so, environmental stressors and facilitating the adoption of contemporary lifestyles by traditional societies without this process being harmful to their health. Modern modes of living and eating (e.g., sedentary occupations and higher caloric intake) are not healthier for those groups transitioning from a more traditional lifestyle, and this leads some to conclude that, at least in terms of biological standards of living, a transition to modern life is not positive. However, to date, the relevance and robustness of the findings of these anthropometric studies for different aspects of the health and living standards of various populations—either as complements or alternatives to conventional studies of income derived from wage and price data—surely invites us to expand these research projects to other countries in the region and to continue to study their past as embodied in the records of human biology and their economic well-being.

Notes

1. This scholarship has been mainly published in academic journals; entire issues have been devoted to the topic of living standards in Latin America (*Economics and Human Biology*, 2004, 2010; *Journal of Iberian and Latin American Economic History*, 2010). There are also compilations (Salvatore, Coatsworth, & Challú, 2010) and monographs published on the topic (Meisel & Vega, 2007a; López-Alonso, 2012).
2. Entire issues of *Economics and Human Biology* have been devoted to this topic (2004 2[3]; 2010 *8*[2]).

References

Acosta, K., & Meisel, A. (2013). Anthropometric measurements by ethnicity in Colombia, 1965–1990. *Economics & Human Biology*, *11*(4), 416–425. doi: 10.1016/j.ehb.2013.03.006

Acuña-Soto, R., David W. Stahle, Malcolm. K., Cleaveland, and Matthew, D. Therrell (2002). Megadrought and megadeath in 16th century Mexico. *Emerging Infectious Diseases*, *8*(4), 360–362. doi: 10.3201/eid0804.010175

Alves, D., & Belluzzo, W. (2004). Infant mortality and child health in Brazil. *Economics & Human Biology* (Special Issue on Child Health in Latin America), *2*(3), 391–410. doi: 10.1016/j.chb.2004.10.004

Araujo, A. G. M., Neves, W. A., & Piló, L. B. (2004). Vegetation changes and megafaunal extinction in South America: Comments on de Vivo and Carmignotto (2004). *Journal of Biogeography, 31*(12), 2039–2040.

Attanasio, O., Gomez, L. C., Rojas, A. G., & Vera-Hernández, M. (2004). Child health in rural Colombia: Determinants and policy interventions. *Economics & Human Biology* (Special Issue on Child Health in Latin America), *2*(3), 411–438. doi: 10.1016/j.ehb.2004.10.005

Baltzer, M., & Baten, J. (2008). Height, trade, & inequality in the Latin American periphery, 1950–2000. *Economics & Human Biology, 6*(2), 191–203. doi: 10.1016/j.ehb.2007.11.002

Baten, J., & Carson, S. (2010). Latin American anthropometrics, past and present—an overview. *Economics & Human Biology* (Special Issue Section: Latin American Anthropometrics), *8*(2), 141–144. doi: 10.1016/j.ehb.2010.05.011

Baten, J., Pelger, I., & Twrdek, L. (2009). The anthropometric history of Argentina, Brazil and Peru during the 19th and early 20th century. *Economics & Human Biology, 7*(3), 319–333. doi: 10.1016/j.ehb.2009.04.003

Bértola, L., de la Escosura, L. P., & Williamson, J. G. (2010), Latin American inequality in the long run. *Revista de Historia Económica (Second Series), 28*(Special Issue 02), 219–226. doi: 10.1017/S0212610910000054

Bogin, B., & Rios, L. (2003, September). Rapid morphological change in living humans: Implications for modern human origins. *Comparative Biochemistry and Physiology Part A: Molecular & Integrative Physiology, 136*(1), 71–84. doi: 10.1016/S1095-6433(02)00294-5

Bogin, B., Varela Silva, M. I., & Rios, L. (2007). "Life History Trade-Offs in Human Growth: Adaptation or Pathology?" *American Journal of Human Biology 19* (5), 631–642. doi:10.1002/ajhb.20666

Brooks, F. J. (1993). Revising the conquest of Mexico: Smallpox, sources, & populations. *Journal of Interdisciplinary History, 24*(1), 1.

Carson, S. A. (2005). The biological standard of living in 19th century Mexico and in the American West. *Economics & Human Biology, 3*(3), 405–419. doi: 10.1016/j.ehb.2005.05.002

Carson, S. A. (2007). Mexican body mass index values in the late-19th-century American West. *Economics & Human Biology, 5*(1), 37–47. doi: 10.1016/j.ehb.2006.06.003

Carson, S. A. (2009). Racial differences in body mass indices of men imprisoned in 19th century Texas. *Economics & Human Biology, 7*(1), 121–127. doi: 10.1016/j.ehb.2009.01.005

Challú, Amílcar E. (2009). "Agrlculture Crisis and Biological Well-Being in Mexico, 1730–1835." *Historia Agraria, 47*, 21–44.

Challú, Amílcar E. (2010). "Living Standards and the Great Decline : Biological Well-Being in Mexico, 1730–1840." In *Living Standards in Latin American History: Heights, Welfare & Development, 1750-2000*, First., 23–68. Cambridge, MA: David Rockefeller Center for Latin American Studies/Harvard University Press.

Coatsworth, J. H. (1978). Obstacles to economic growth in nineteenth-century Mexico. *American Historical Review, 83*(1), 80–100. doi: 10.2307/1865903

Cohen, M. N., & Armelagos, G. J. (2013). *Paleopathology at the origins of agriculture*. University Press of Florida, Gainesville, FL.

Cohen, M. N., Armelagos, G. J., & Wenner-Gren Foundation for Anthropological Research, & State University of New York College at Plattsburgh. (1984). *Paleopathology at the origins of agriculture*. Orlando, FL: Academic Press.

Cook, S. F., & Borah, W. W. (1979). *Essays in population history: Mexico and the Caribbean.* Berkeley: University of California Press.

Crosby, A. W. (1972). *The Columbian exchange: Biological and cultural consequences of 1492 (foreword by Otto von Mering).* Westport, CT: Greenwood.

Crosby, A. W. (1994). *Germs, seeds & animals: Studies in ecological history.* Routledge.

Cuff, T. (2005). The Hidden Cost of Economic Development: The Biological Standard of Living in Antebellum Pennsylvania. Burlington, VT: Ashgate.

David, V., Moncada, M., & Ordonez, F. (2004). Private and public determinants of child nutrition in Nicaragua and western Honduras. *Economics & Human Biology* (Special Issue on Child Health in Latin America), *2*(3), 457–488. doi: 10.1016/j.ehb.2004.10.006

Delajara, M., & Rodríguez-Segura, M. (2010). Why are Mexican American boys so much taller now? *Economics & Human Biology* (Special Issue Section: Latin American Anthropometrics), *8*(2), 212–222. doi: 10.1016/j.ehb.2010.05.007

de Lourdes Márquez Morfin, R. M. (1984). *Sociedad colonial y enfermedad: Un ensayo de osteopatologia.* Escuela Nacional de Antropologia e Historia, 1984.

de Oliveira, V. H., & Quintana-Domeque, C. (2014). Early-life environment and adult stature in Brazil: An analysis for cohorts born between 1950 and 1980. *Economics & Human Biology, 15*, 67–80. doi: 10.1016/j.ehb.2014.07.001

Diamond, J. M. (2005). *Guns, germs, & steel: The fates of human societies.* New York & London: W.W. Norton.

Dobado-González, R., & García-Montero, H. (2010). Colonial origins of inequality in Hispanic America? Some reflections based on new empirical evidence. *Revista de Historia Económica, 28*(02), 253–277.

Dobado-González, R., & García-Montero, H. (2014). Neither so low nor so short: Wages and heights in Bourbon Spanish America from an international comparative perspective. *Journal of Latin American Studies, 46*(02), 291–321. doi: 10.1017/S0022216X14000054

Frank, Z. (2006, January). Stature in nineteenth-century Rio de Janeiro: Preliminary evidence from prison records. *Revista de Historia Económica (Second Series), 24*(03), 465–489. doi: 10.1017/S0212610900000604

Gandelman, N. (2010, July). Property rights and chronic diseases: Evidence from a natural experiment in Montevideo, Uruguay 1990–2006. *Economics & Human Biology* (Special Issue Section: Latin American Anthropometrics), *8*(2), 159–167. doi: 10.1016/j.ehb.2010.05.005

Gibson, C. (1964). *The Aztecs under Spanish rule: A history of the Indians of the Valley of Mexico, 1519–1810.* Stanford, CA: Stanford University Press.

Godoy, R., Magvanjav, O., Nyberg, C., Eisenberg, D. T. A., McDade, T. W., Leonard, W. R., . . . Gravlee, C. (2010). Why no adult stunting penalty or height premium? Estimates from native Amazonians in Bolivia. *Economics & Human Biology, 8*(1), 88–99. doi: 10.1016/j.ehb.2009.08.002

Godoy, R., Reyes-García, V. Vadez, V., Leonard, W. R., Huanca, T., & Bauchet, J. (2005). Human capital, wealth, & nutrition in the Bolivian Amazon. *Economics & Human Biology, 3*(1), 139–162. doi: 10.1016/j.ehb.2005.01.001

Grajales-Porras, A., & López-Alonso, M. (2011). Physical stature of men in eighteenth century Mexico: Evidence from Puebla. *Economics & Human Biology, 9*(3), 265–271. doi: 10.1016/j.ehb.2011.02.002

Haber, S. H. (1997). *How Latin America fell behind: Essays on the economic histories of Brazil and Mexico, 1800–1914.* Stanford, CA: Stanford University Press.

Kosack, E., & Ward, Z. (2014). Who crossed the border? Self-selection of Mexican migrants in the early twentieth century. *Journal of Economic History, 74*(04), 1015–1044. doi: 10.1017/S0022050714000849

Leatherman, T. L., Goodman, A. H., & Stillman, T. (2010). Changes in stature, weight, & nutritional status with tourism-based economic development in the Yucatan. *Economics & Human Biology* (Special Issue Section: Latin American Anthropometrics), *8*(2), 153–158. doi: 10.1016/j.ehb.2010.05.008

Lee, J., Houser, R. F., Must, A., de Fulladolsa, P. P., & Bermudez, O. I. (2010). Disentangling nutritional factors and household characteristics related to child stunting and maternal overweight in Guatemala. *Economics & Human Biology* (Special Issue Section: Latin American Anthropometrics), *8*(2), 188–196. doi: 10.1016/j.ehb.2010.05.014

Lee, J., Houser, R. F., Must, A., de Fulladolsa, P. P., & Bermudez, O. I. (2012). Socioeconomic disparities and the familial coexistence of child stunting and maternal overweight in Guatemala. *Economics & Human Biology, 10*(3), 232–241. doi: 10.1016/j.ehb.2011.08.002

Livi-Bacci, M. (2006). The depopulation of Hispanic America after the conquest. *Population and Development Review, 32*(2), 199–232. doi: 10.1111/j.1728-4457.2006.00116.x

López-Alonso, M. (2007). Growth with inequality: Living standards in Mexico, 1850–1950. *Journal of Latin American Studies, 39*(01), 81–105. doi: 10.1017/S0022216X06002045

López-Alonso, M. (2012). *Measuring up: A history of living standards in Mexico, 1850–1950.* Stanford, CA: Stanford University Press.

López-Alonso, M., & Condey, R. P. (2003). The ups and downs of Mexican economic growth: The biological standard of living and inequality, 1870–1950. *Economics & Human Biology, 1*(2), 169–186. doi: 10.1016/S1570-677X(03)00039-X

López-Alonso, Moramay, and Roberto Vélez-Grajales. (2015). "Measuring Inequality in Living Standards with Anthropometric Indicators: The Case of Mexico 1850–1986." *Journal of Human Development & Capabilities, 16*(3), 374–396. doi:10.1080/19452829.2015.1044820.

Markowitz, D. L., & Cosminsky, S. (2005). Overweight and stunting in migrant Hispanic children in the USA. *Economics & Human Biology* (Socio-economic correlates of overweight and obesity), 3(2), 215–240. doi: 10.1016/j.ehb.2005.05.005

Márquez Morfin, L. (2010). *Colecciones esqueleticas humanas en Mexico: Excavacion catalogacion y aspectos normativos.* Tlalpan, DF, Mexico City: Conaculta/Inah.

Márquez, Lourdes, and Del Angel, Andrés. (1997). "Height Among Prehispanic Maya of the Yucatán Peninsula: A Reconsideration." In *Bones of the Maya: Studies of Ancient Skeletons,* (pp. 51–61). University of Alabama Press.

Marr, J. S, & Kiracofe, J. B. (2000). Was the Huey Cocoliztli a haemorrhagic fever? *Medical History, 44*(03), 341–362. doi: 10.1017/S0025727300066746

Maurer, J. (2010, July). Height, education and later-life cognition in Latin America and the Caribbean. *Economics & Human Biology* (Special Issue Section: Latin American Anthropometrics), *8*(2), 168–176. doi: 10.1016/j.ehb.2010.05.013

McCaa, R. (1995, Winter). Spanish and Nahuatl views on smallpox and demographic catastrophe in Mexico. *Journal of Interdisciplinary History, 25*(3), 397.

McCaa, R. (2000). The Peopling of Mexico from Origins to Revolution. In M. Haines, R., & R. H Stickle (Eds.), *The Population History of North America* (pp. 241–304). Cambridge, MA: Cambridge University Press.

McCaa, Robert, Marquez Morfin, Lourdes, Storey, Rebecca, and Del Angel, Andrés. (2002). Health and Nutrition in Prehispanic Mesoamerica. In *The Backbone of History: Health and Nutrition in the Western Hemisphere* (pp. 307–338). Cambridge, MA: Cambridge University Press.

Meisel, A., & Vega, M. (2007*a*). *La calidad de vida biológica en Colombia. Antropometría histórica 1870–2003*. Cartagena. Banco de la República (banco central de Colombia), http://www.banrep.gov.co/es/node/16587

Meisel, A., & Vega, M. (2007*b*). The biological standard of living (and its convergence) in Colombia, 1870–2003: A tropical success story. *Economics & Human Biology*, 5(1), 100–122. doi: 10.1016/j.ehb.2006.10.004

Melville, E. G. K. (1994). *A plague of sheep: Environmental consequences of the conquest of Mexico*. Cambridge, UK/New York: Cambridge University Press.

Monasterio, L. M. (2013). Estatura e inmigración en el sur de Brasil (1889–1914). *América Latina En La Historia Económica, 21*(1), 115–133.

Monasterio, Leonardo M., Nogueról, L. P., and Shikida, C. D. (2010). "Growth and Inequalities of Height in Brazil, 1939-1981." In *Living Standards in Latin American History: Heights, Welfare & Development, 1750-2000*. Cambridge, MA: David Rockefeller Center for Latin American Studies/Harvard University Press.

Morales, R., Aguilar, A. M., & Calzadilla, A. (2004). Geography and culture matter for malnutrition in Bolivia. *Economics & Human Biology* (Special Issue on Child Health in Latin America), *2*(3), 373–389. doi: 10.1016/j.ehb.2004.10.007

Neves, W. A., Bernardo, D. V., & Okumura, M. M. M. (2007). A origem do homem Americano vista a partir da América do sul: Uma ou duas migrações? *Revista de Antropologia, 50*(1), 9–44.

Neves, W. A., Gonzáalez-José, R., Hubbe, M., Kipnis, R., Araujo, A. G. M., & Blasi, O. (2004). Early Holocene human skeletal remains from Cerca Grande, Lagoa Santa, Central Brazil, and the origins of the first Americans. *World Archaeology, 36*(4), 479–501.

Patel, A. M., Godoy, R. A., Seyfried, C., Reyes-García, V., Huanca, T., Leonard, W. R., . . . Tanner, S. (2007). On the accuracy of perceived parental height in a native Amazonian society. *Economics & Human Biology*, 5(1), 165–178. doi: 10.1016/j.ehb.2006.10.005

Reis, M. (2012). Differences in nutritional outcomes between Brazilian white and black children. *Economics & Human Biology, 10*(2), 174–188. doi: 10.1016/j.ehb.2011.12.001

Reyes, M. E. P., Chavez, G. B., Little. B. B., & Malina, R. M. (2010). Community well-being and growth status of indigenous school children in rural Oaxaca, Southern Mexico. *Economics & Human Biology* (Special Issue Section: Latin American Anthropometrics), *8*(2), 177–187. doi: 10.1016/j.ehb.2010.05.009

Ríos, L. (2009) "Guatemala: Una Revisión de Las Fuentes Antropométricas Disponibles." *Historia Agraria 47*, 217–238.

Rubalcava, L. N., & Teruel, G. M. (2004). The role of maternal cognitive ability on child health. *Economics & Human Biology* (Special Issue on Child Health in Latin America), *2*(3), 439–455. doi: 10.1016/j.ehb.2004.10.009

Salvatore, R. D. (2004*a*). Stature decline and recovery in a food-rich export economy: Argentina 1900–1934. *Explorations in Economic History, 41*(3), 233–255. doi: 10.1016/j.eeh.2003.12.002

Salvatore, R. D. (2004*b*). Stature, nutrition, and regional convergence. *Social Science History, 28*(2), 297–324.

Salvatore, R. D. (2004*c*). Stature, nutrition, and regional convergence: The Argentine Northwest in the first half of the twentieth century. *Social Science History, 28*(2), 297–324.

Salvatore, R. D. (2007). Heights, nutrition, & well-being in Argentina, ca. 1850–1950. Preliminary results. *Revista de Historia Económica (Second Series)*, 25(01), 53–85. doi: 10.1017/S0212610900000057

Salvatore, R. D. (2009). Stature growth in industrializing Argentina: The Buenos Aires industrial belt 1916–1950. *Explorations in Economic History* (Special Issue on Heights and Human Welfare Special Issue on Heights and Human Welfare), *46*(1), 70–92. doi: 10.1016/j.eeh.2008.02.002

Salvatore, R. D., Coatsworth, J. H., & Challú, A. E. (2010). *Living standards in Latin American history: Height, welfare, & development, 1750–2000*. Cambridge, MA, Harvard University Press.

Skoufias, E., & Katayama, R. (2009). Sources of welfare disparities across and within regions of Brazil: Evidence from the 2002–03 Household Budget Survey. Policy Research Working Paper Series. Geneva: World Bank. https://ideas.repec.org/p/wbk/wbrwps/4803.html

Skoufias, E., & Vinha, K. (2012). Climate variability and child height in rural Mexico. *Economics & Human Biology*, *10*(1/January 2012): 54–73. doi: 10.1016/j.ehb.2011.06.001

Skoufias, E., Vinha, K., & Conroy, H. V. (2011). The impacts of climate variability on welfare in rural Mexico. Policy Research Working Paper Series. Geneva: World Bank. https://ideas.repec.org/p/wbk/wbrwps/5555.html

Smith, P. K., Bogin, B., Varela-Silva, M. I., & Loucky, J. (2003). Economic and anthropological assessments of the health of children in Maya immigrant families in the US. *Economics & Human Biology*, *1*(2), 145–160. doi: 10.1016/S1570-677X(02)00032-1

Sokoloff, K. L. (1995). "The Heights of Americans in Three Centuries: Some Economic and Demographic Implications." In *Biological Standard of Living in Three Continents: Further Explorations in Anthropometric History*, (pp. 133–150). Boulder, CO: Westview Press.

Sotomayor, O. (2013, July). Fetal and infant origins of diabetes and ill health: Evidence from Puerto Rico's 1928 and 1932 hurricanes. *Economics & Human Biology*, *11*(3), 281–293. doi: 10.1016/j.ehb.2012.02.009

Steckel, R. H. (1995). "Stature and the Standard of Living." *Journal of Economic Literature*, 33(4), 1903–1940.

Steckel, R. H. (1998). "Strategic Ideas in the Rise of the New Anthropometric History and Their Implications for Interdisciplinary Research." *The Journal of Economic History*, *58*(3), 803–821. doi:10.1017/S0022050700021173

Steckel, R. H., & Rose, J. C. (2002). *The backbone of history: Health and nutrition in the western hemisphere*. Cambridge, UK/New York: Cambridge University Press.

Storey, R. (1992). *Life and death in the ancient city of Teotihuacan: A modern paleodemographic synthesis*. Tuscaloosa, Alabama: University of Alabama Press.

Sweeney, S., Davenport, F., & Grace, K. (2013). Combining insights from quantile and ordinal regression: Child malnutrition in Guatemala. *Economics & Human Biology*, *11*(2), 164–177. doi: 10.1016/j.ehb.2012.06.001

Therrell, M. D., Stahle, D. W., & Acuña-Soto, R. (2004, September 1). Aztec Drought and the 'Curse of One Rabbit.' *Bulletin of the American Meteorological Society*, 85(9), 1263–1272. doi: 10.1175/BAMS-85-9-1263

Therrell, M. D., Stahle, D. W., Villanueva-Diaz, J., Cornejo-Oviedo, E. H., & Cleaveland, M. K. (2006). Tree-ring reconstructed maize yield in central Mexico: 1474–2001. *Climatic Change*, *74*(4), 493–504. doi: 10.1007/s10584-006-6865-z

Twrdek, L., & Manzel, K. (2010). The seed of abundance and misery: Peruvian living standards from the early Republican Period to the end of the Guano Era (1820–1880). *Economics &*

Human Biology (Special Issue Section: Latin American Anthropometrics), *8*(2), 145–152. doi: 10.1016/j.ehb.2010.05.012

Valdivia, M. (2004). Poverty, health infrastructure and the nutrition of Peruvian children. *Economics & Human Biology* (Special Issue on Child Health in Latin America), *2*(3), 489–510. doi: 10.1016/j.ehb.2004.10.008

Valeggia, C. R., Burke, K. M., & Fernandez-Duque, E. (2010). Nutritional status and socioeconomic change among Toba and Wichí populations of the Argentinean Chaco. *Economics & Human Biology, 8*(1), 100–110. doi: 10.1016/j.ehb.2009.11.001

Van Hook, J., Baker, E., Altman, C. E., & Frisco, M. L. (2012). Canaries in a coalmine: Immigration and overweight among Mexican-origin children in the US and Mexico. *Social Science & Medicine, 74*(2), 125–134. doi: 10.1016/j.socscimed.2011.10.007

Villamor, E., Chavarro, J. E., & Caro, L. E. (2009, July). Growing up under generalized violence: An ecological study of homicide rates and secular trends in age at menarche in Colombia, 1940s–1980s. *Economics & Human Biology, 7*(2), 238–245. doi: 10.1016/j.ehb.2009.03.002

Vogl, T. S. (2007, July). Urban land rights and child nutritional status in Peru, 2004. *Economics & Human Biology, 5*(2), 302–321. doi: 10.1016/j.ehb.2007.01.001

Warinner, C., Robles García, N., Spores, R., & Tuross, N. (2012). Disease, demography, and diet in early colonial New Spain: Investigation of sixteenth-century Mixtec cemetery at Teposcolula Yucundaa. *Latin American Antiquity, 23*(4), 467–489.

Wehby, G. L., Castilla, E. E., & Lopez-Camelo, J. (2010). The impact of altitude on infant health in South America. *Economics & Human Biology* (Special Issue Section: Latin American Anthropometrics), *8*(2), 197–211. doi: 10.1016/j.ehb.2010.04.002

Wehby, G. L., Murray, J. C., Castilla, E. E., López-Camelo, J. S., & Ohsfeldt, R. L. (2009). Prenatal care demand and its effects on birth outcomes by birth defect status in Argentina. *Economics & Human Biology, 7*(1), 84–95. doi: 10.1016/j.ehb.2008.10.001

Whittington, Stephen L., David M. Reed, and Society for American Archaeology. Meeting (1994 : Anaheim, Calif.). (1997). *Bones of the Maya: Studies of Ancient Skeletons*. Tuscaloosa, Alabama: University of Alabama Press.

Zeng, W., Eisenberg, D. T. A., Jovel, K. R., Undurraga, E. A., Nyberg, C., Tanner, S., . . . Godoy, R. (2013). Adult obesity: Panel study from native Amazonians. *Economics & Human Biology, 11*(2), 227–235. doi: 10.1016/j.ehb.2012.01.005

Zeng, W., Undurraga, E. A., Nyberg, C., Eisenberg, D. T. A., Parida, S., Zycherman, A., . . . Godoy, R. (2013). Sibling composition during childhood and adult blood pressure among native Amazonians in Bolivia. *Economics & Human Biology, 11*(3), 391–400. doi: 10.1016/j.ehb.2012.08.002

CHAPTER 36

RACIAL DIFFERENCES IN HEALTH IN THE UNITED STATES

A Long-Run Perspective

LEAH PLATT BOUSTAN AND ROBERT A. MARGO

36.1 Introduction

The United States has a long and ongoing history of racial inequality. Labor economists and economic historians have documented the secular evolution of racial differences in income, wealth, and education over the late 19th and 20th centuries.[1] Our chapter follows in this tradition by describing long-term trends in racial differences in health.

Like other economists, we view health as a component of human capital that can contribute directly to a person's well-being. Better health is also an input into the production of income. A healthy person can provide more labor and earn more income if she desires, and health and other forms of human capital, such as schooling, may complement each other.[2] Health is a function of inherited characteristics (genetics) and environmental conditions experienced throughout the life cycle. These environmental factors include income and wealth, which can be used to purchase commodities that create better health—better diet, shelter, clothing, access to medical care—and local public goods, such as clean water.

We begin our chapter with a short review of contemporary racial differences in health, setting the stage for our discussion of long-term health trends. Throughout the chapter, we focus on standard measures of health—namely, life expectancy and infant mortality—but we also consider data on specific diseases and chronic conditions.

Comments from Dora Costa, Michael Haines, and John Komlos are gratefully acknowledged.

Our basic conclusion is that African Americans experienced substantial improvements in average health during the 20th century, both in absolute terms and in comparison with whites. These absolute and relative gains in health for African Americans occurred steadily over time against a backdrop of improving health for whites. Investments in public health infrastructure in cities, disease eradication campaigns in the South, and decreases in racial discrimination in access to medical care all played roles in reducing the racial gap in health outcomes over time, but the most important causal factors may have been narrowing racial differences in education and incomes. Despite the long-term improvements in black health, significant racial gaps in infant mortality, life expectancy, and other outcomes persist in the contemporary United States and remain a pressing problem for policy makers and health care providers.

36.2 Racial Disparities in Health and Their Long-Term Evolution

36.2.1 Contemporary Racial Disparities in Health

We begin our discussion of contemporary racial differences in health by focusing on life expectation at various ages (Table 36.1).[3] In 2011, life expectancy at birth (age 0) for African Americans was 75.3 years, compared with 79 years for whites. Conditional on surviving the first year of life, the racial gap in life expectation (black–white) declines as people age. For example, at age 1, the racial gap in life expectation in favor of whites is 3.2 years, compared with 3.7 years at birth. By age 40, the gap in life expectation falls to 2.6 years in favor of whites, and, by age 70, the gap is less than 1 year. However, if the gap is measured in relative terms (black/white), the pattern over the life cycle is more complex. The black/white ratio of life expectation is approximately constant at about 0.95 (95%) from birth to age 20, but declines slowly through middle age, reaching 0.93 at age 60. At older ages, the racial difference in life expectation gap narrows sharply and eventually reverses sign, implying a black/white ratio greater than 1.

The age patterns observed in Table 36.1 suggest that racial disparities in health begin very early in life. Consistent with this observation, the black infant mortality rate currently is twice as high as the white infant mortality rate (1,058 vs. 516 deaths per 100,000 live births). Such early disparities are a key factor in the emergence of chronic conditions later in life that, in turn, produce higher levels of adult mortality for middle-aged blacks and those nearing retirement.[4] The subsequent narrowing and eventual reversal of the racial gap at advanced ages likely reflects the impact of selective attrition. That is, persons who survive to old age likely have a genetic predisposition to longer life or an unusual healthy lifestyle; because of the higher mortality rates faced by blacks at younger and middle ages, these forces of selective attrition may be greater in the black population, causing those who survive to advanced ages to be unusually hardy relative to whites.

Table 36.1 Life expectancy at various ages by race, 2011.

Age	White	Black	Black–White	Black/White
0	79	75.3	−3.7	0.95
1	78.4	75.2	−3.2	0.96
10	69.5	66.4	−3.1	0.96
20	59.7	56.6	−3.1	0.95
40	40.7	38.1	−2.6	0.94
60	23.2	21.5	−1.7	0.93
70	15.5	14.7	−0.8	0.95
80	9	9.1	0.1	1.01
90	4.5	5.1	0.6	1.13

Source: computed from National Center for Health Statistics (2013, Table 7).

In an accounting sense, higher rates of black mortality can be due either to a higher prevalence of particular medical conditions or to a lower probability of survival, conditional on contracting a specific disease. Overall, the distribution of causes of death today is remarkably similar by race (Figure 36.1).[5] That said, it is difficult to get accurate data on racial disparities in the prevalence of disease because individuals typically need to be in contact with the medical establishment in order to receive a diagnosis. If access to medical care varies by race, self-reported health conditions may be biased. Survival rates conditional on having a particular disease are easier to observe and do seem to vary by race. Cancer is an important example. For the most recent period for which data are available (2004–10), black cancer patients are about 10% less likely to survive than are white patients (Table 36.2). Blacks may be less likely to survive a cancer diagnosis either because they receive their diagnosis at a later stage in the disease or because they are less likely to have access to high-quality treatment at a given stage of the disease. Differences in medical treatment, in turn, may be attributable to racial differences in health insurance coverage (blacks are more likely to be uninsured) or ability to pay (blacks have lower income levels).

36.2.2 Historical Data on Health by Race: Issues of Data Comparability

The remainder of this section places current racial disparities into a long-run perspective by presenting historical trends on health for blacks and whites. Before doing so, this subsection describes the available historical data on health outcomes for the

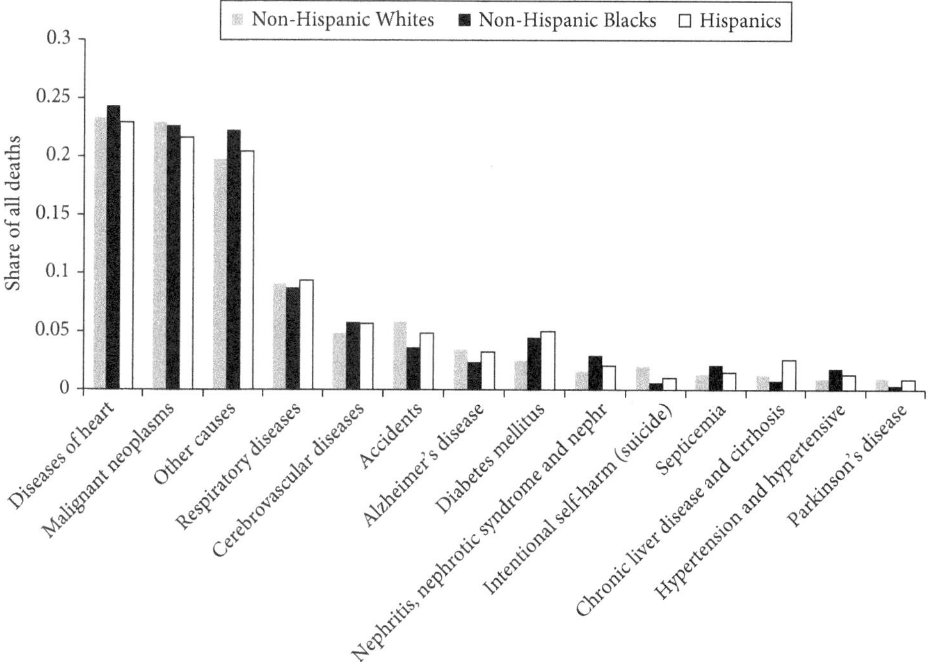

FIGURE 36.1 Causes of death by race, 2011.

Source: computed from National Center for Health Statistics (2013).

Table 36.2 Survival rates conditional on cancer diagnosis by race

	1974–1976	1980–1982	1989–1994	2004–2010
White	50	52	62	66.7
Black	39	40	47	59.7
Black/White	0.78	0.77	0.76	0.90

Sources: 1974–1994 values from Landis et al. (1999). 2004–2010 values from Howlader et al. (2013).

United States, along with concerns about data comparability over time. Our discussion begins with historical mortality data and then proceeds to health outcomes among the living.

In the contemporary United States, "vital events"—births and deaths—are recorded by public officials at the time of their occurrence. The Census Bureau also tracks the age structure of the population by conducting annual surveys, supplemented by full population counts in the decennial census years. With this information, it is possible to estimate changes in population on an annual basis and, in particular, to produce reliable annual estimates of age-specific death rates and complete life tables both for the overall population and for various subgroups.

The first state to implement a system of vital registration was Massachusetts in the 1850s. Other states followed, but sufficient information to construct national life tables using a subset of states was only available by 1900 (Glover, 1921). By 1933, all states met government standards to be incorporated into the official Birth Registration Area (BRA) and Death Registration Area (DRA). Yet under-reporting was still a problem in some states. By 1950, the records were considered sufficiently complete to be reliable. With regard to age structure, shortly after World War II, the Census Bureau began to routinely collect the Current Population Survey, a moderate-sized sample that tracks population on a monthly basis, and, in 2001, the American Community Survey, a much larger random sample began to be collected on an annual basis.

For the years before the official birth and death registries began, estimates of life expectancy can be inferred from the age structure of the population in decennial censuses. In particular, demographers combine information on changes in the age structure between successive censuses with data on net migration to estimate 10-year survival rates for various age groups.[6] These survival rates are then matched to standard model life tables in order to compute life expectancy at birth or other ages.[7] The earliest census for which such calculations are feasible for either race is 1850. Using these methods, trends in white life expectation can be measured (fairly) reliably from the middle of the 19th century to the present. Yet the statistical situation for blacks is far less sanguine. Although there are estimates of black life tables prior to 1900, their quality is questionable due to measurement problems in the underlying census data on age.

We believe that both approaches used to produce historical estimates of life expectation—death records from the selected states incorporated into the DRA and census survival rate methods—are severely biased when applied to the black population. In particular, estimates of black life expectancy circa 1900 are likely too low, thereby overstating the degree of improvement in black health that took place in the first half of the 20th century.

Using data from the DRA states, Glover (1921) estimated that black life expectation at birth was 33 years in 1900–02. Based on this estimate, it would appear that black life expectation at birth increased by 42 years since 1900, more than doubling from 1900 to the present. Even at the time, the Census Bureau recognized that the infant mortality experience of blacks in the DRA states was not likely to be representative of the national black population (US Bureau of the Census, 1918). Most DRA states in 1900 were in the North, and blacks resident in these states were predominantly urban. Circa 1900, there was a substantial urban penalty in infant mortality (Condran & Cummins, 1980; Haines, 2001; Preston & Haines, 1991). The Census Bureau believed that infant mortality in the rural South, where the vast majority of African Americans lived in 1900, was considerably lower than for blacks in the DRA states.[8] Correcting for this bias could easily produce a higher estimate of black life expectation at birth in the early 20th century.

To evaluate this concern, demographers applied the census survivorship technique discussed earlier to the black age structure data in the late 19th- and early 20th-century censuses (Demeny & Gingrich 1967; Meeker 1976). These calculations again yielded estimates of black life expectation at birth in the vicinity of 33 years, similar to Glover's. Because these calculations were based on the national black age structure, rather than data from the DRA states alone, they seemed to validate Glover's original figure. However, census survivorship estimates are generated from Census counts of individuals between the ages of 5 and 40 (see footnote 6). Yet black mortality rates at these prime ages were relatively high in the late 19th century, whereas infant and child mortality was correspondingly low. Thus, in fitting the high prime-age mortality to model life tables, blacks were assumed to have a low level of life expectation at birth.

In considering the evidence, we believe that estimates of black life expectancy based on either DRA states or on census survival methods are understated circa 1900. Instead, we are convinced by Preston and Haines (1991), who re-estimate black life expectancy from census data on child mortality by race in 1900 and 1910. In these years, the census asked adult women to report both their number of children ever born and their number of surviving children (as of the census date). Ages of children still present in the household are also known. Preston and Haines use this data to produce estimates of "q(A)," or the cumulative probability of death prior to age A. Preston and Haines then fit these estimates to model life tables to recover life expectancy.[9]

After extensive data analysis Preston and Haines consider their most reliable estimates to be q(3), q(5), and q(10). For whites, these estimates differ relatively little from Glover's but, for blacks, the differences are substantial. Consider q(5), the cumulative probability of death before age 5. Glover's estimate for blacks is 0.338—that is, approximately 34% of black children born at the turn of the 20th century died before reaching their fifth birthday. Preston and Haines' preferred estimate is 0.255, considerably lower than Glover's.[10] Preston and Haines' best estimate of black life expectation at birth is 41.8 years circa 1900, almost *nine years* higher than the estimate based on the census survival method. The major source of discrepancy between the two estimates is the fact that blacks had lower child mortality circa 1900 than one would expect given the relatively high rates of adult mortality in that year.[11]

Beyond mortality data, it is also useful to have information on morbidity, both chronic and acute, among the living. Although there are numerous modern sources of data on health outcomes among the living, their historical counterparts are few. Questions on certain types of disabilities—for example, blindness—were asked of the population from 1850–80 (in 1850–60, for slaves as well as free persons). The 1880 census also included questions on whether the individual was sick on the day of enumeration "so as to be unable to attend to ordinary business or duties" or whether the individual was "maimed, crippled, bedridden, or otherwise disabled." Reported rates of sickness and disability in 1880 were low (around 2% of the population), suggesting that the true prevalence of these conditions was under-reported. If taken at face value, the Census measure suggests little difference in sickness and disability by race; 1.7% of prime-age blacks (16–64 years old) report being sick or disabled in 1880, compared to 1.8% of whites. In the 2000 Census, prime-age blacks are substantially more likely than prime-age whites to report having "a lasting physical or mental health condition that causes difficulty working" (17% vs. 11%).

36.2.3 Long-Run Trends in Life Expectation at Birth by Race

Keeping the issues of data comparability in mind, Figure 36.2 graphs several time series of life expectation at birth by race compiled from available sources. The "white—PH" and "black—PH" series combine estimates from Preston and Haines (1991) and Haines (2001) for 1900 and 1910 with national vital statistics data from 1940 to the present for whites and from 1970 to the present for blacks.[12]

We believe that the two PH series provide the best currently available information about long-run trends in life expectancy by race in the US. For comparison, we also illustrate two series from the (shifting set of) states incorporated into the DRA. The "white—DRA" series runs from 1900 to 1939 and thereafter is identical with the national "white—PH" series. The "non-white" series pertains to selected DRA states before 1940 and thereafter reports the standard national series for non-whites. These series have been used widely by economic historians and demographers in prior work.

The dominant message of Figure 36.2 is the strong upward trend in life expectation at birth for both races. Between 1900 and 1950, life expectation at birth for whites increased by 19.5 years, before increasing by another 10 years between 1950 and 2011. Approximately two-thirds of the rise in white life expectancy since 1900 occurred during the first half of the 20th century. Blacks also experienced notable improvements in life expectation, but the extent of this improvement depends on the data series in question. According to the PH series, black life expectancy increased by 18 years from 1900 to 1950, and then again by around 16 years from 1950 to 2011, suggesting that the increase in black life expectation occurred in equal measure in the first half and second half of the 20th century.[13] The pace of improvement in life expectancy varied substantially across time periods for both races (Table 36.3).[14] For whites, the largest improvements in life expectancy occurred between 1900 and 1940, a period associated with improvements in sanitation and public health in urban areas. For blacks, instead, the largest improvement in life expectancy occurred between 1940 and 1960. Both races experienced large increases in life expectancy between 1970 and 1980. Figure 36.2 also suggests that the annual fluctuations in mortality were much larger before 1940 for both races. Although some of these fluctuations reflect biases due to changing coverage of the DRA states and other sources of incomplete data, others are real events. The most obvious example is the 1918 flu epidemic, which greatly lowered life expectation at birth in the immediate short run.

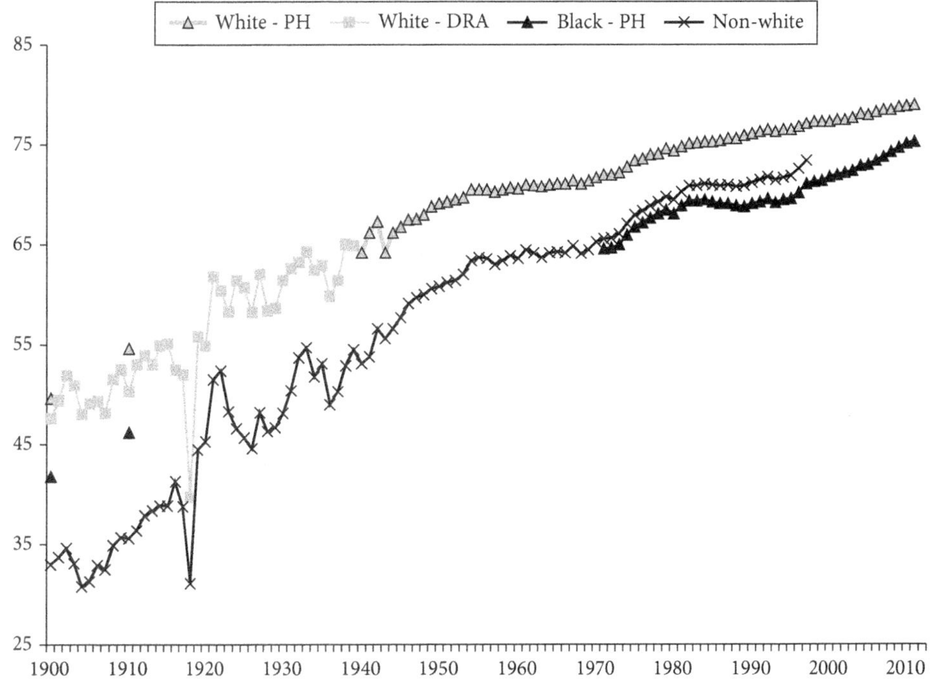

FIGURE 36.2 Life expectancy by race, 1900–2011.

Sources: "white-PH" and "black-PH" values in 1900 and 1910 from Preston and Haines (1991, Table 2.5). All other values are from Haines (2006) (1900–1997) and National Center for Health Statistics (2013).

36.2.4 Long-Run Trends in Infant Mortality by Race

There have been enormous declines in infant mortality for both races since 1920 (Figure 36.3). White infant mortality rates fell from 82 per 1,000 live births in 1920 to 5 per 1,000 live births in 2011. Over the same period, black infant mortality rates fell from 135 per 1,000 live births to 12 per 1,000 live births. As with overall life expectancy, there were steeper improvements in infant mortality before 1950 than afterward.

Interpreting the evolution of black–white differences in infant mortality over time is sensitive to choice of measure. In absolute terms, the racial gap in infant mortality declined from 53 deaths per 1,000 live births in 1920 to 7 deaths per 1,000 live births in 2011. Yet, in relative terms, the racial gap in infant mortality rates has worsened over time. In 1920, the black infant mortality rate was 64% higher than the white rate, whereas today the black infant mortality rate is now 140% higher than the white rate.

The second panel of Table 36.3 presents average annual reductions in infant deaths per 1,000 live births by race over selected periods. For both races, the largest declines in infant mortality occurred between 1925 and 1945. For whites, the pace of improvement in infant mortality then declines monotonically over the century. In contrast, there is a noticeable uptick in improvements in black infant mortality rates from 1965 to 1980, a period directly after the passage of Civil Rights legislation that resulted in, among

Table 36.3 Improvements in life expectancy and infant mortality by period and race

Average Annual Additions to Life Expectancy (in Years)		
	White	Black
1900–40	0.39	0.28
1940–60	0.28	0.50
1960–70	0.09	0.11
1970–80	0.29	0.44
1980–2010	0.14	0.22
Average Annual Reductions in Infant Deaths per 1,000 Live Births		
	White	Black
1920–45	1.65	2.58
1945–65	0.68	0.73
1965–80	0.69	1.36
1980–2010	0.18	0.25

Notes: Calculated from three-year moving averages of data series presented in Figures 36.2 and 36.3. Life expectancy calculations are based on the Preston and Haines series.

other things, the desegregation of southern hospitals. These patterns are consistent with Collins and Thomasson (2004), who analyze state-level infant mortality rates by race between 1920 and 1970. Even after controlling for race-specific income and education levels, they find that infant mortality declined most sharply between 1920 and 1950 and that the pace of improvement leveled off thereafter.

Another common measure of health early in life is birth weight. Costa (2004*b*) examined nearly 2,000 births that took place to predominately working-class mothers at the Johns Hopkins hospital in Baltimore, Maryland, in the first three decades of the 20th century. In comparing this sample to modern data from the National Maternal and Infant Health Survey (from 1988), she finds that the birth weights of both black and white babies have remained remarkably constant over the century.[15] However, in each period, black infants weighed around 10% less than white infants. Lower black birth weights can be explained, in part, by higher black rates of prematurity. Premature infants tend to weigh less than infants who are born at full term, and black babies were

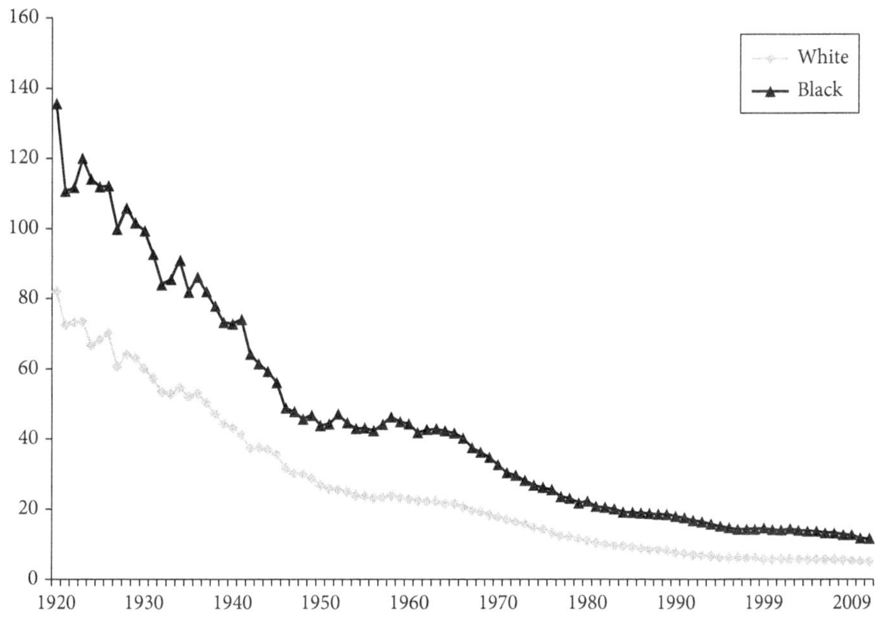

FIGURE 36.3 Infant mortality rates per 1,000 live births by race, 1920–2011.

Sources: 1920–1997 from Haines (2006); 1998–2011 from National Center for Health Statistics (2013).

more than twice as likely as white babies to be born preterm (13% vs. 7% in the Johns Hopkins sample).[16]

36.2.5 Causes of Death and Chronic Conditions

Understanding the roots of improvement in life expectancy is aided by examining long-run trends in causes of death and the prevalence of chronic conditions. A useful source of historical information on these patterns is the study of the health status of Union Army veterans undertaken at the Center for Population Economics (CPE) at the University of Chicago.[17] Extensive health information on Civil War veterans was collected in the late 19th and early 20th centuries as part of their process of applying for a federal pension. This information has been retrieved by the CPE and augmented by linking individuals to census data. Samples have been produced for both white (the Union Army or UA sample) and black soldiers (the United States Colored Troops or USCT sample).

Data on chronic conditions is based on a surgeon's examination conducted as part of the pension application process. Cause of death is typically gleaned from death certificates sent to the pension office by deceased relatives (e.g., widows) seeking to prove eligibility for further benefits. Figure 36.4 shows racial differences in causes of death for men ages 60–74 in the UA and USCT samples circa 1910. As in the more recent data

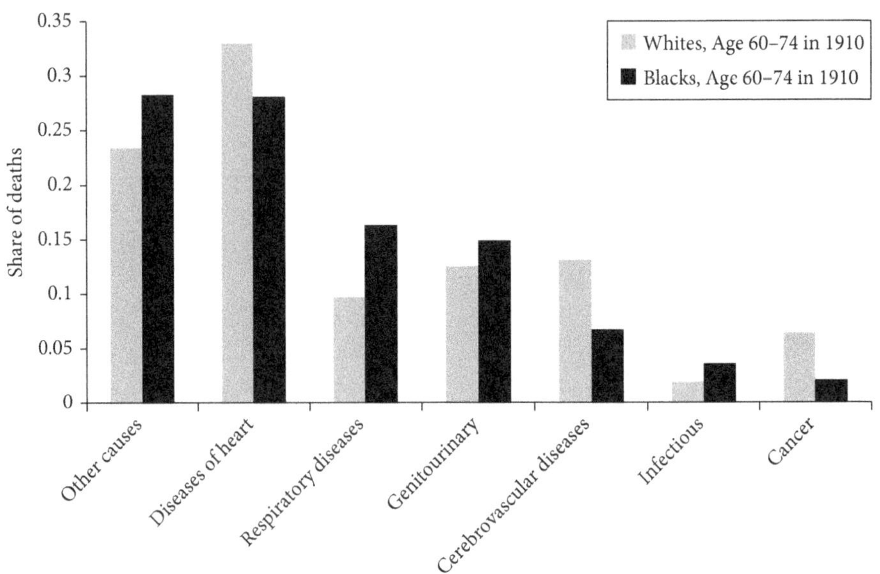

FIGURE 36.4 Causes of death, Union Army sample, Men aged 60–74 in 1910.

Source: computed from Costa, Helmchen, and Wilson (2007), Table 3. Data include whites and blacks in the Union Army data in the birth cohorts of 1836–1850.

(Figure 36.1), the causes of death by race were similar in the early 20th century. The two largest categories—diseases of the heart and other causes—account for 56% of deaths for both groups, although whites are five percentage points more likely to die from heart disease and blacks are five percentage points more likely to be in the "other" category. Among the less common conditions, blacks were more likely than whites to die of infectious and respiratory diseases or of genitourinary disease (including syphilis) and were less likely to die of cerebrovascular disease (strokes) or cancer (on this point, see also Costa, 2005).

The UA and USCT samples also provide evidence on the prevalence of chronic conditions in the early 20th century. Figure 36.5 compares the relative prevalence of each condition by race in 1910 and in the 1990s. In 1910, doctors examining Union Army veterans were more likely to report that black patients had five of the eight chronic conditions: joint and back pains ("musculoskeletal problems" associated with manual labor), irregular pulse and arteriosclerosis (signs of heart disease), and decreased breath sounds (sign of respiratory problems). Whites were more likely to have "adventitious sounds"—"added" sounds such as crackles and wheezes when breathing. Blacks and whites had similar rates of heart murmurs and valvular heart disease.

By the 1990s, the prevalence of chronic conditions had declined for both blacks and whites, but the black–white prevalence ratios were again at or above 1 for nearly all conditions, indicating higher rates of disease in the black population.[18] Furthermore, for five conditions, the racial gap in prevalence rose over time. The most notable case is arteriosclerosis, for which the black–white ratio increased from 1.7 in 1910 to 2.6 in the 1990s. The one exception to this pattern is back problems, the prevalence of which

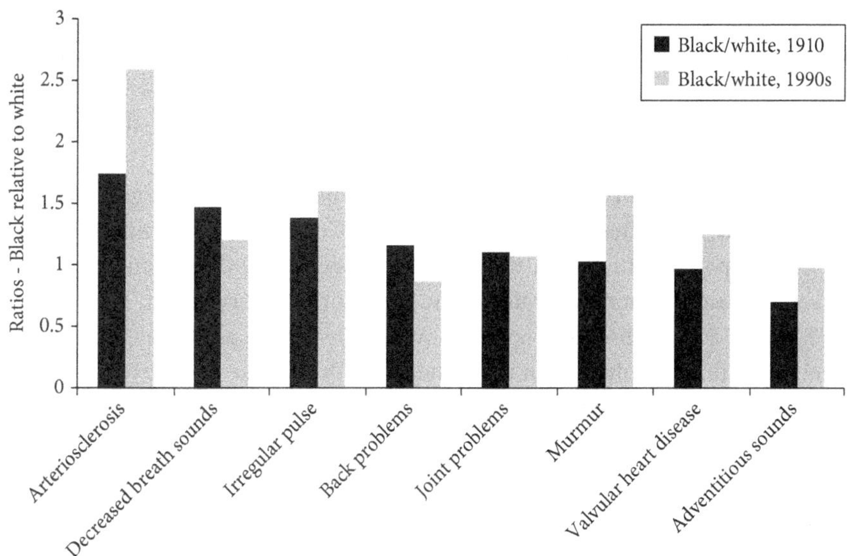

FIGURE 36.5 Black–white ratios of chronic condition prevalence over time. Men aged 60–74, circa 1910 and circa 1990.

Source: computed from Costa, Helmchen, and Wilson (2007), Table 2. Data for 1910 include whites and blacks in the Union Army data in the birth cohorts of 1836–1850; data from 1990s from the National Health and Nutritional Examination Surveys. We report data from 1999–2004 when available; in other years, we report data from 1988–94. Prevalence rates are physician-reported, with the exception of heart murmurs and valvular heart disease.

declined over time for both groups but at a slower rate in the white population, leading to slightly higher rates of back problems among whites by the 1990s.

Costa (2004*a*) compares soldiers in the Union Army by race on a series of anthropometric measures, including height and body mass index (BMI). In general, height is positively correlated with health and BMI is negatively associated with health, at least at higher levels. For men in their late 20s, black soldiers were 1.5 centimeters shorter than white soldiers, were slightly heavier than white soldiers, but also exhibited less central body fat. On net, this anthropometric evidence does not provide particularly strong evidence of ill health for blacks in the mid-19th century. Military data from 1988 attests to general growth in BMI over the 20th century; a similar racial gap in BMI is also apparent in the modern data.

36.3 Historical Explanations for Improvements in Black Life Expectancy

In this section, we consider a number of potential causes for the improvements in black life expectancy during the 20th century, including investments in public health and sanitation in cities, improvements in the disease environment in the South, migration from the South to the North, improvements in black income and education, and so-called Great Society programs of the 1960s, including the racial desegregation of hospitals. We organize these explanations into three time periods: 1900–40; 1940–60 and 1965–85. After 1985, the pace of improvements in black life expectancy slowed, although notable improvements in black life expectation did occur in the 2000s.

In 1900, there was a substantial urban mortality penalty, due in large part to higher rates of infectious and water-borne disease in cities (Condran & Cummins, 1980; Haines, 2001).[19] Municipal investments in clean water and sewerage infrastructure resulted in a large decline in urban mortality rates in the early 20th century (Alsan & Goldin, 2014; Cutler & Miller, 2005). Troesken (2004) convincingly demonstrates that black residents benefited from these public health investments, both because the networked structure of sewer pipes made it difficult to exclude black neighborhoods and because black urban dwellers lived in (relatively) unsegregated neighborhoods circa 1910.

Investments in disease eradication in the South were important in explaining overall increases in black life expectancy in the early 20th century. Given its climate and high rates of poverty, the South was beset by a series of tropical diseases at the time including yellow fever, malaria, pellagra, and hookworm.[20] Aided by private philanthropy, southern areas reduced disease rates from 1900 to 1940. Bleakley (2007) studied the efforts of the Rockefeller Sanitary Commission to eradicate hookworm in southern counties. Surveys conducted by the Rockefeller Commission discovered that, in 1910, 40% of southern children were infected by hookworm. The Commission combined immediate treatment for infected individuals with a public health campaign emphasizing the importance of hygiene and prevention. As a result, infection rates were cut in half over the next 10 years. Bleakley shows that children in treated cohorts enjoyed improved literacy rates and adult earnings.

The Rockefeller Foundation was also involved with malaria control in the South (Humphreys, 2001; Stapleton, 2004). Reduction in malaria transmission was primarily achieved by draining wetlands to eliminate mosquitoes and their breeding grounds. Malaria became rare in southern cities by 1900 but was still prevalent in the countryside. Therefore, migration from rural areas to southern cities and particularly to the North contributed to declines in malaria rates. Barreca, Fishback, and Kantor (2012) demonstrate that migration during the 1930s in response to the Agricultural Adjustment Act of 1933 tended to shift population from high-malaria to low-malaria environments. Kitchens (2013) describes a countertrend, whereby the Tennessee Valley Authority dams built in the 1930s created pools of standing water, thereby increasing malaria prevalence. Yet, despite the TVA-driven rise in malaria, overall malaria rates in the US South had fallen substantially by 1940.

More than 40% of the southern black population migrated out of the South between 1915 and 1970, typically to large industrial cities. These migrants left behind the poor disease environment of the South and moved to cities with new public investments in clean water and sewerage. Yet, despite reductions in the urban health penalty in the early 20th century, it is not clear that moving to a city generated a net improvement in health. Black migrants lived in dense, segregated neighborhoods close to industrial sites that, through exposure to pollution, may have contributed to deaths from heart disease, cancer, and other causes.

Two recent papers suggest that black migration to urban areas worsened health conditions. Black et al. (2015) use Medicare records to assess the effect of migration on black mortality rates. The Medicare system keeps detailed records on a recipient's place of birth, thus allowing the authors to instrument for migration using proximity to a train line during childhood. They find that moving to the North reduced longevity—for example, increasing the likelihood of dying between the ages of 65 and 70 by around five percentage points. Eriksson and Niemesh (2014) document higher infant mortality rates of black migrant households compared to households that remained in the South, even after controlling for a series of family background characteristics.

Taken together, blacks benefited from improvements in health conditions in both the rural South (due to disease eradication) and the urban North (due to public health improvements). Yet there was also a substantial net migration to urban areas, which continued to be associated with a health penalty. We conclude that reductions in place-specific mortality from 1900 to 1940 were partially offset by migration to a less-healthy environment.

The pace of improvement in black health increased over the next 20 years, with black life expectancy increasing by 10 years from 1940 to 1960. This period corresponds to an era of rapid racial convergence in income (Donohue & Heckman, 1991; Smith & Welch, 1989). Black–white earnings convergence was due, in part, to relative increases in black educational attainment, which began in earnest in the birth cohort of 1910, members of which would have entered the labor market circa 1930 (Aaronson & Mazumder, 2011; Collins & Margo, 2006; Margo, 1990).

A large literature in epidemiology documents a negative gradient between income (or education) and mortality (Backlund, Sorlie, & Johnson, 1996, 1999; Sorlie, Rogot, Anderson, Johnson, & Backlund, 1992). On this topic, economists have conducted a series of studies on the relationship between education and mortality by exploiting variation in compulsory schooling laws across states and over time (Lleras-Muney, 2005; Mazumder, 2008; Oreopoulos & Page, 2006). We use estimates from this literature to gauge the share of improvement in black health outcomes from 1940 to 1960 that can be explained by growth in black incomes and education.

Existing estimates suggest that increases in black earnings and educational attainment can explain a large portion of the reduction in black mortality rates from 1940 to 1960. Age-adjusted death rates per 100,000 in the black population fell from 1,500 to 1,000 over this period, a decline of 33% (Haines, 2006). At the same time, median black earnings increased by around $8,000 (in 2000 dollars). According to Backlund, Sorlie, and Johnson (1999), an earnings increase of this magnitude would be associated with a 10% reduction in the relative risk of mortality, which can account for around one-third of the decline in black mortality over this period. Furthermore, black educational attainment also increased substantially, rising from a median of 6 years of schooling for prime-age adults (18–65) in 1940 to a median of 8 years of schooling by 1960. Lleras-Muney (2005) estimates that an additional year of schooling is associated with a 1.7–3.7 percentage point reduction in the probability of dying over the next 10 years, on a base of around 10% (or a 17–37% decline). Even her lower bound implies that improvements in black education can explain all of the improvements in black mortality over this period.

Blacks entering the labor market circa 1940 can be characterized not only by their relative increases in years of educational attainment, but also by improvements in the average quality of the school that they attended, as measured by pupil–teacher ratios, the length of the school term, or per-pupil expenditures (Card & Krueger, 1992; Margo, 1990). Frisvold and Golberstein (2011) find modest evidence that improvements in school quality contributed further to black health improvements, particularly in self-rated health.

Black infant mortality rates experienced a notable decline from 1965 to 1980. These years coincided with key civil rights legislation ending the segregation of hospitals in the South. Almond, Chay, and Greenstone (2006) document that, before this period, 40% of black births in the rural South occurred outside of hospitals, compared to 4% of white births. The Civil Rights Act of 1964 forbade institutions receiving federal funding from discriminating on the basis of race. The establishment of Medicare in 1965 provided a large potential stream of federal dollars, which encouraged hospitals in the South to desegregate. Almond and co-authors demonstrate that the rapid desegregation of hospitals in 1965 encouraged black births to take place in hospitals, thereby contributing to reductions in black infant mortality.

Other Great Society programs of the 1960s may have contributed to general improvements in black life expectancy. Goodman-Bacon (2015) shows that the introduction of Medicaid reduced black infant and child mortality in the 1960s and 1970s. The impact of the introduction of Medicaid is large enough, according to Goodman-Bacon, to account for about 15% of the narrowing racial gap in child mortality between the mid-1960s and 1980.[21] Bailey & Goodman-Bacon (2015) show that the Community Health Centers program, which began in 1965 and continues to the present, significantly reduced mortality among poor adults aged 50 and over relative to the non-poor. Unlike Medicare or Medicaid, which provides subsidies to purchase private care, the CHC program directly delivers primary care to individuals. Although Bailey and Goodman-Bacon's data do not permit them to directly examine the impact of the CHC program on racial differences in mortality, CHCs almost certainly did reduce the racial gap given that the geographic diffusion disproportionately favored counties with a (much) higher than average share of the black population (Bailey & Goodman-Bacon 2015, p. 1067).

36.4 Conclusion and Suggestions for Further Research

This chapter has examined long-run trends in racial differences in health. Our discussion concentrated heavily on mortality trends, which have the most complete historical records and therefore have received the most attention from social scientists, but we have also surveyed the available evidence on chronic conditions and disabilities.

Our most basic conclusion is that racial disparities in health have narrowed substantially over the course of the 20th century. It is easier to list the factors behind the long-term narrowing of racial differences in health than to conclusively measure and rank their relative importance. Blacks benefited from public health improvements in the early 20th century and later from policy interventions in the 1960s that expanded health care. Yet much of the improvement in black health outcomes, in our view, should probably be ascribed to increases in household incomes and education—particularly the latter, since some historical pathways to higher incomes, such as migration from the rural South to the North, appear to be associated with worsening health outcomes, at least in the short run. At the same time, there remain in the United States today medically and economically significant gaps in health outcomes by race—black health status continues to lag behind white health status. Although further improvements in access to medical care (e.g., through increased insurance coverage from the Affordable Care Act) may help to narrow the remaining gaps, racial differences in income and education continue to loom large in the contemporary United States. Our findings suggest that further improvements in the relative health of African Americans will likely necessitate improvements in relative incomes and education.

Although the historical trend in black mortality rates is clear, as is the basic contours of a historical explanation for the trend, much research remains to be done. In particular, the exact timing and location of changes in black mortality from the late 19th century to World War II requires further illumination. Further work is also needed to clarify the specific mechanisms behind the long-term decline in black mortality and other health outcomes.

Notes

1. This extensive literature includes Higgs (1982), Smith (1984), Margo (1984, 1990), Smith and Welch (1989), Donohue and Heckman (1991), and Collins and Margo (2006, 2011).
2. On these points, see Deaton (2003); Currie (2009); and Bleakley, Costa, and Lleras-Muney (2014).
3. There is an enormous literature on racial differences in health. For brief introductions see Smedley, Stith, and Nelson (2009); Peterson et al. (1997); Bach, Cramer, Warren, and Begg (1999); and Barnato, Lucas, Staiger, Wennberg, and Chandra (2005).
4. The relationship between health conditions in utero and later-life disease was first proposed by David Barker and his co-authors (Barker, Osmond, Golding, Kuh, & Wadsworth 1989; Barker, Osmond Winter, Margetts, & Simmonds, 1989). Currie and Almond (2011) survey the literature in economics testing the "Barker hypothesis." Preston, Hill, and Drevenstedt (1998) show that some childhood conditions, including having literate parents and being co-resident with both parents, are associated with longevity for African Americans.
5. A higher proportion of blacks do succumb to heart disease, but a somewhat smaller fraction die from cancer, the two largest killers. Among less common conditions, blacks are

more likely to die from complications from diabetes and hypertension but are less likely to commit suicide, die in accidents, or succumb to Alzheimer's disease. However, as noted in the text, these racial differences are small relative to the overall average.

6. Survival rates are usually not calculated for persons under age 5 or over age 40 in the base year because of concerns over underenumeration (under age 5) or age misreporting (over age 50). Because the survival estimates do not cover the full range of ages, the data alone cannot be used to provide a full life table and must instead be matched to model life tables to generate life expectation estimates.
7. A model life table is the average of a set of country-specific life tables that are known to be based on accurate data. Model life tables are grouped into "systems" thought to represent similar overall mortality conditions. The most commonly used Princeton tables are grouped into four such systems—North, South, East, and West—representing different regions of the world. They are then further categorized by mortality level.
8. Less than 5% of the black population lived in the DRA states in 1900; see Preston and Haines (1991, p. 50). In contrast, nearly 30% of the white population lived in a DRA state in this year, and the white urbanization rate did not differ much between covered and noncovered states.
9. In particular, Preston and Haines calculate the proportion of children surviving to the census date by age for women in a given age range or in a given range of marital duration. Alternatively, they propose a method that uses as a starting point a model life table to get an initial set of q(A)s and then iterates backward from the age structure of surviving children to produce a final set of q(A)s that match the total number of children ever born and surviving, along with their ages.
10. Preston and Haines' estimate of q(5) for whites is 0.161 circa 1900, only slight lower than Glover's estimate (0.177). See Preston and Haines (1991, pp. 58–59) for comparisons between Glover's estimate of q(5) for blacks and various foreign countries ca. 1900. Glover's estimate implies that black child mortality circa 1900 substantially exceeded levels throughout Europe, but the Preston and Haines estimate of 0.255 is very similar to q(5) estimates for Germany, France, Italy, and Belgium (although still higher than Great Britain, Australia, and New Zealand).
11. To compare their estimate with Glover's, Preston and Haines use their methods to estimate black child mortality for the DRA states in 1900. Their estimates in these states closely resemble Glover's, further confirming that the DRA states were not representative of the national average.
12. 1970 is the first year in which vital statistics were reported separately for blacks, as opposed to all non-whites. Ninety-eight percent of the non-white population was African American in 1900. This share had fallen to 90% by 1970.
13. We do not have a separate estimate for black life expectancy in 1950. If we assume that the ratio of black to non-white life expectation is constant between 1950 and 1970, we can compute that black life expectation was 59.7 years in 1950 (ratio of black to non-white = 0.98). The DRA series, which likely understates black life expectancy in 1900 and 1910, instead suggests much larger improvements for blacks between 1900 and 1950 (28 years). According to the DRA series, the absolute gap in life expectation declined from 15 years in 1900 to 4 years in 2011, whereas the Preston-Haines series shows a much more muted decline (from 9 years to 4 years).
14. Periods were selected to correspond to particular eras in African-American economic history, but also to reflect noticeable differences in the pace of improvement in life expectancy over time.

15. The infants born at Johns Hopkins may have weighed less than the national average circa 1910, given the health penalty likely present in a big city like Baltimore and the selection of more complicated births into hospitals at the time.
16. Costa (2004*b*) speculates that a large portion of the racial gap in prematurity in the early 20th century can be explained by high rates of untreated syphilis in the black population at the time. Today's gap is more difficult to explain, but may be due to differences in teen pregnancy rates.
17. The project was originally directed by the late Robert Fogel and is currently directed by Dora Costa, Department of Economics, UCLA.
18. Costa (2000) studies the potential causes of the decline in chronic conditions for white men over the 20th century. She documents that around 30% of the decline can be attributed to a shift from manual to white-collar occupations. Another 20% is due to a reduction in exposure to infectious disease.
19. Costa (2005) documents that the urban penalty was substantially larger for blacks than for whites in the late 19th century, perhaps because black households did not have the income necessary to protect themselves against disease (e.g., through adequate nutrition).
20. Humphreys (2009) discusses the campaigns to investigate and eliminate each disease in the South.
21. On the other hand, Finkelstein and McKnight (2008) find no effect of the introduction of Medicare either on overall mortality or on mortality of non-whites in the late 1960s; they speculate that hospitals could do little to treat chronic conditions at the time, which are the principal cause of elderly mortality.

References

Aaronson, D., & Mazumder, B. (2011). The impact of the Rosenwald Schools on black achievement. *Journal of Political Economy, 119*, 821–888.

Almond, D., Chay, K., & Greenstone, M. (2006). Civil rights, the war on poverty, & black-white convergence in infant mortality in the rural south and Mississippi (Working Paper 07-04). Department of Economics, Massachusetts Institute of Technology.

Alsan, M., & Goldin, C. (2014). Watersheds and infant mortality: Massachusetts, 1880-1915. Department of Economics, Harvard University, unpublished manuscript.

Bach, P., Cramer, L., Warren, J., & Begg, C. (1999). Racial differences in the treatment of early-stage lung cancer. *New England Journal of Medicine, 341*(16), 1198–1205.

Backlund, E., Sorlie, P. D., & Johnson, N. J. (1996). The shape of the relationship between income and mortality in the United States: Evidence from the National Longitudinal Mortality Survey. *Annals of Epidemiology, 6*, 12–20.

Backlund, E., Sorlie, P. D., & Johnson, N. J. (1999). A comparison of the relationships of education and income with mortality: The National Longitudinal Mortality Study. *Social Science & Medicine, 49*(10), 1373–1384.

Bailey, M. J., & Goodman-Bacon, A. (2015). The war on poverty's experiment in public medicine: Community health centers and the mortality of older Americans. *American Economic Review, 105*(3), 1067–1104.

Barker, D. J., Osmond, C., Golding, J., Kuh, D., & Wadsworth, M. E. (1989). Growth in utero, blood pressure in childhood and adult life, and mortality from cardiovascular disease. *British Medical Journal, 298*(6673), 564.

Barker, D. J., Osmond, C., Winter, P. D., Margetts, B., & Simmonds, S. J. (1989). Weight in infancy and death from ischaemic heart disease. *Lancet, 334*(8663), 577–580.

Barnato, A. E., Lucas, F. L., Staiger, D., Wennberg, D. E., & Chandra, A. (2005). Hospital-level racial disparities in acute myocardial infarction treatment and outcomes. *Medical Care, 43*(4), 308.

Barreca, A., Fishback, P., & Kantor, S. (2012). Agricultural policy, migration, and malaria in the 1930s United States. *Explorations in Economic History, 49*, 381–398.

Black, D. A., Sanders, S. G., Taylor, E. J., & Taylor, L. J. (2015). The impact of the Great Migration on the mortality of African-Americans: Evidence from the Deep South. *American Economic Review, 105*(2), 477–503.

Bleakley, H. (2007). Disease and development: Evidence from hookworm eradication in the American South. *Quarterly Journal of Economics, 122*, 73–117.

Bleakley, H., Costa, D., & Lleras-Muney, A. (2014). Health, education, & income in the United States, 1820-2000. In L. Boustan, C. Frydman, & R. A. Margo (Eds.), *Human capital in history: The American record* (pp. 121–160). Chicago: University of Chicago Press.

Card, D., & Krueger, A. (1992). School quality and Black-White relative earnings: A direct assessment. *Quarterly Journal of Economics, 1007*, 151–200.

Collins, W., & Margo, R. A. (2006). Historical perspectives on racial differences in schooling in the United States. In E. Hanushek & F. Welch (Eds.), *Handbook on the economics of education* (vol. *1*, pp. 107–154). Amsterdam: North Holland.

Collins, W., & Margo, R. A. (2011). Race and home ownership from the end of the Civil War to the present. *American Economic Review: Papers and Proceedings, 101*, 355–359.

Collins, W. J., & Thomasson, M. A. (2004). The declining contribution of socioeconomic disparities to the racial gap in infant mortality rates, 1920–1970. *Southern Economic Journal, 70*(4), 746–776.

Condran, G. A., & Cummins, E. (1980). Mortality differential between rural and urban states in the northern United States, 1890-1900. *Journal of Historical Geography, 6*, 174–202.

Costa, D. L. (2000). Understanding the twentieth-century decline in chronic conditions among older men. *Demography, 37*(1), 53–72.

Costa, D. L. (2004*a*). The measure of man and older age mortality: Evidence from the Gould sample. *Journal of Economic History, 64*(1), 1–23.

Costa, D. L. (2004*b*). Race and pregnancy outcomes in the twentieth century: A long-term comparison. *Journal of Economic History, 64*(4), 1056–1086.

Costa, D. L. (2005). Race and older-age mortality: Evidence from Union Army Veterans. National Bureau of Economic Research Working Paper No. 10902, Cambridge MA.

Costa, D. L., Helmchen, L. A., & Wilson, S. (2007). Race, infection, & arteriosclerorosis in the past. *Proceedings of the National Academy of Sciences of the United States, 104*, 13219–13224.

Currie, J. (2009). Healthy, wealthy, and wise? Socioeconomic status, poor health in childhood, and human capital development. *Journal of Economic Literature, 47*, 87–122.

Currie, J., & Almond, D. (2011). Human capital development before age five. In O. Ashenfelter & D. Card (Eds.), *Handbook of labor economics* (vol. *4*, pp. 1315–1486). Amsterdam: North Holland.

Cutler, D. M., & Miller, G. (2005). The role of public health improvements in health advances: The twentieth century United States. *Demography, 42*, 1–22.

Deaton, A. (2003). Health, inequality, and economic development." *Journal of Economic Literature, 41*, 113–158.

Demeny, P., & Gingrich, P. (1967). A reconsideration of Negro-White mortality differentials in the United States. *Demography, 4*, 820–837.

Donohue, J. J., & Heckman, J. (1991). Continuous versus episodic change: The impact of civil rights policy on the economic status of Blacks. *Journal of Economic Literature, 29*, 1603–1643.

Eriksson, K., & Niemesh, G. (2014). The impact of migration in infant health: Evidence from the Great Migration." Department of Economics, Miami University, unpublished manuscript.

Finkelstein, A., & McKnight, R. (2008). What did Medicare do? The initial impact of Medicare on mortality and out-of-pocket medical spending. *Journal of Public Economics, 92*, 1644–1668.

Frisvold, D., & Golberstein, E. (2011). School quality and the education-health relationship: Evidence from Blacks in segregated schools. *Journal of Health Economics, 30*, 1232–1245.

Glover, J. W. (1921). *United States life tables, 1890, 1901, 1910, & 1901–1910*. Washington, DC: Government Printing Office.

Goodman-Bacon, A. (2015). Public insurance and mortality: Evidence from Medicaid implementation. School of Public Health, University of California, Berkeley, unpublished manuscript.

Haines, M. R. (2001). The urban mortality transition in the United States, 1800-1940 (NBER Historical Working Paper No. 134). Cambridge, MA.

Haines, M. R. (2006). Vital statistics. In S. B. Carter, S. S. Gartner, M. R. Haines, A. L. Olmstead, R. Sutch, & G. Wright (Eds.), *Historical statistics of the United States: Millennial Edition, Volume I: Population* (pp. 381–390). Cambridge, UK: Cambridge University Press.

Higgs, R. (1982). Accumulation of property by southern Blacks before World War I. *American Economic Review, 72*, 725–737.

Howlader N., Noone, A. M., Krapcho, M., Garshell, J., Miller, D., Altekruse, S. F., . . . Cronin, K. A. (Eds.). (2013). *SEER cancer statistics review, 1975–2011*. Bethesda, MD: National Cancer Institute.

Humphreys, M. (2001). *Malaria: Poverty, race, and public health in the United States*. Baltimore: Johns Hopkins University Press.

Humphreys, M. (2009). How four once common diseases were eliminated from the American South. *Health Affairs, 28*, 1734–1744.

Kitchens, C. (2013). The effects of the Works Progress Administration's anti-malaria programs in Georgia 1932–1947. Department of Economics, University of Mississippi, unpublished manuscript.

Landis, S. H., Murray, T., Bolden, S., & Wingo, P. A. (1999). Cancer statistics, 1999. *CA: A Cancer Journal for Clinicians, 49*(1), 8–31.

Lleras-Muney, A. (2005). The relationship between education and adult mortality in the United States. *Review of Economic Studies, 72*, 189–221.

Margo, R. A. (1984). Accumulation of property by southern Blacks before World War I: Comment and further evidence. *American Economic Review, 74*, 768–776.

Margo, R. A. (1990). *Race and schooling in the South, 1880–1950: An economic history*. Chicago: University of Chicago Press.

Mazumder, B. (2008). Does education improve health: A reexamination of the evidence from compulsory schooling laws. *Economic Perspectives, 33*(2), 2–17.

Meeker, E. (1976). Mortality trends of southern Blacks, 1850-1910: Some preliminary findings. *Explorations in Economic History, 13*, 13–42.

National Center for Health Statistics. (2013). Deaths: Final data for 2011. *National Vital Statistics Reports* 63.3. Hyattsville, MD: National Center for Health Statistics.

Oreopoulos, P., & Page, M. E. (2006). The intergenerational effects of compulsory schooling. *Journal of Labor Economics, 24*, 729–760.

Peterson, E. D., Shaw, L., DeLong, E., Pryor, D., Califf, R., & Mark, D. (1997). Racial variation in the use of coronary-revascularization procedures—Are the differences real? Do they matter? *New England Journal of Medicine, 336*, 480–486.

Preston, S. H., & Haines, M. R. (1991). *Fatal years: Child mortality in late nineteenth century America*. Princeton, NJ: Princeton University Press.

Preston, S. H., Hill, M. E., & Drevenstedt, G. L. (1998). Childhood conditions that predict survival to advanced ages among African Americans. *Social Science and Medicine, 47*(9), 231–246.

Smedley, B. D., Stith, A. Y., & Nelson, A. R. (Eds.). (2009). *Unequal treatment: Confronting racial and ethnic disparities in health care*. Washington DC: National Academies Press.

Smith, J. (1984). Race and human capital. *American Economic Review, 74*, 685–698.

Smith, J., & Welch, F. (1989). Black economic progress after Myrdal. *Journal of Economic Literature, 27*, 519–564.

Sorlie, P., Rogot, E. Anderson, R., Johnson, N. J., & Backlund, E. (1992). Black–white differences by family income. *Lancet, 340*, 346–350.

Stapleton, D. H. (2004). Lessons of history? Anti-malaria strategies of the International Health Board and the Rockefeller Foundation from the 1920s to the era of DDT. *Public Health Reports, 119*(2), 206–215.

Troesken, W. (2004). *Water, race, and disease*. Cambridge, MA: MIT Press.

US Bureau of the Census. (1918). *Negro population, 1790-1918*. Washington, DC: Government Printing Office.

CHAPTER 37

ANTEBELLUM PUZZLE

The Decline in Heights at the Onset of Modern Economic Growth

LEE A. CRAIG

37.1 Modern Economic Growth: An Introduction

Adam Smith often receives credit for raising the issue of what generated the "wealth of nations," but, even before Smith, moral philosophers (the term "economist" had yet to be conjured) and other writers struggled with the definition of aggregate economic wealth and what caused or retarded its growth. A related debate revolved around how the definition and measurement of wealth reflected the broader well-being of a nation's citizens—that is, its living standard. Smith's seminal contributions notwithstanding, these issues had been discussed for nearly a century before he formalized them in *Wealth of Nations*. In the late 17th century, Pierre le Pesant, Sieur de Boisguillebert, a member of the minor French nobility, made the connection between a nation's wealth and the volume of its economic transactions, which he in turn tied to the circulation of money. This proved to be a clever insight, one that would ultimately yield the expenditures side of the national income and product accounts, of which the product of prices and quantities exchanged form the foundation.

Boisguillebert was born in 1646, two years before the Peace of Westphalia ended the Thirty Years War and led to the formation of modern nation states. The Peace essentially formed European states out of the hereditary fiefs that had demarcated Western civilization since the decline of Rome twelve centuries earlier. To inquire about a nation's wealth or its economic growth before the concept of a nation had been conceived would have been truly prescient. The characters of Shakespeare's *Hamlet*, first performed more than a decade before the onset of the Thirty Years War, use the words "Norway" and "Poland" to denote kings not nation states. Boisguillebert thought explicitly about nations and their wealth in a way that Shakespeare and his audiences, just a generation earlier, would have been hard pressed to conceive.

In the 18th century, English writers took up the same question with which Boisguillebert wrestled. A few years before Smith published his *Wealth of Nations*, Arthur Young, a farmer by trade, published a tract on the relative productivity of agriculture in England, Ireland, and France. Because of agriculture's size relative to other sectors of the economy at the time, it was typically viewed as representative of overall economic performance (a view much in vogue in French intellectual circles between Boisguillebert's day and Smith's).[1] Young collected farm-level data over a 40-year period, and from those records he concluded that, overall, English agriculture was more productive than that of either Ireland or France, and thus, England was a wealthier nation (Young, 1771, vol. 4). He also speculated on the allocation of income among land, labor, and capital. This aggregation of firm-level output into a national total (the microfoundations of macroeconomics, as it would subsequently be called), with reference to the allocation of income among the factors of production, provided the underpinning for what became the income approach to the national income and product accounts.

For his part, Smith, while recognizing the importance of exchange (like Boisguillebert) and production (like Young), focused on consumption as the key indicator of a nation's capacity to create wealth for its citizens. He described consumption as "the sole end and purpose of all production" (Smith, 1976, vol. 2, p. 179). Smith's insight, his capacity for elaboration on important points, and his often colorful digressions (which together caused his masterpiece to run well past a thousand pages), yielded an eminence that eluded Boisguillebert and Young. Still, more than a century and a half passed before economists, working from the intellectual foundations of these 17th- and 18th-century thinkers, formally constructed the national income and product accounts that systemized measures such as real gross domestic product (GDP) and national income, and that, in their per capita forms, came to represent the standard of living for much of the economics profession and policy makers more generally.

Simon Kuznets, arguably the most important figure in the history of national income accounting, coined the expression "modern economic growth" to describe situations in which the growth rate of real GDP, or national income, exceeded the population growth rate by enough—and for long enough—that periodic downturns would not disrupt the long-run increase in the standard of living (Kuznets, 1966). By this definition, modern economic growth did not characterize the economies of Western civilization before, at the earliest, the late 18th century (Clark, 2007).[2] By the middle of the 19th century, however, the phenomenon was well-established in the United States, Great Britain, and much of continental Europe. For many scholars who study the era, the 18th century represents a period of transition from an age of no growth to modern economic growth, with industrialization as a key—perhaps *the* key—component of that transition (see, e.g., Komlos, 1989, 2000).

Whereas prior to 1700 the long-run annual compounded growth of real GDP per capita was essentially zero, from the end of the Napoleonic Wars, annual growth rates in the range of 1–2% have been common. Thus, the standard of living—again, conventionally defined as real GDP per capita—has been doubling once or twice per generation since the early 19th century, and the pace of growth accelerated over time, slowing only in recent decades. For example, in the United States, between 1790 and 1860, real GDP per capita increased by 1.3% per annum; between 1860 and 1910, the figure was 1.6%; and, until recently, it was roughly 2.0% (Williamson, 2013).

With the perspective of more than a century of modern economic growth, Kuznets recognized that there existed a number of potential social problems that accompanied the process. He referred to these as "negative results" (1973, p. 257) and suggested an increase in income inequality as one of the more prominent features of modern economic growth. Although Kuznets's negative results did not show up in the long-run trends in national income, real GDP, or mean wages, scholars subsequently identified stagnation and, in some cases, actual downturns in a number of biological indicators, including mean adult stature, body mass indices, infant mortality, and the expectation of life. Of these biological measures, stature is arguably the most valuable indicator of what has become known as the "biological standard of living." Thus, anthropometricians, the scholars who study the biological standard of living, have come to question uncritical praise for the economic marvel of modern economic growth.

Given that the income elasticities of medical care and food, broadly defined, are positive, as is that for education (which could be expected to yield more mentally and less physically taxing employment), it follows that the higher incomes generated by modern economic growth should have yielded better biological outcomes, and thus the trend in the biological standard of living should have mirrored trends in the more conventional measures, such as real GDP per capita. This is especially the case in a country like the United States, with such an abundance of natural resources. As noted earlier, from the founding of the republic to the Civil War, US real GDP per capita grew at a rate in excess of 1% per annum. Compared to Western civilization's experience over the previous 20 centuries or so, this was a tremendous achievement, especially at a time when population growth was considerable; however, during that same 70-year period, both the expectation of life and mean adult stature declined substantially (Haines, Craig, & Weiss, 2003, Figure 37.1), suggesting an erosion in the biological standard living at exactly the time modern economic growth set in. This, then, is the "antebellum puzzle."[3] Only much later in the century, after 1890, did the biological standard living begin to trace the conventional measures.

The puzzle results from the fact that the logic of what works well for an individual (i.e., a higher income generates better health outcomes) fails in the aggregate (i.e., economies that produce rising incomes per capita do not necessarily generate taller, healthier, longer-lived populations). This is because the distribution of income might well become skewed in a way that yields a positive trend in the conventional economic measures but a negative trend in the biological indicators, as Kuznets suspected. Indeed, once we factor in Kuznets's "negative results," including an increase in inequality, which he largely associated with industrialization, there is no mathematical or otherwise theoretical reasoning that would lead one to unambiguously conclude that the trend in the biological standard of living *should* have the same sign as the trend in income or GDP per capita.

The rapid expansion of the industrial sector, largely concentrated in urban areas, highlighted the difficulties of providing nourishment for the urban masses. Of course, that does not matter for the conventional measures of the standard of living: GDP per capita increases, and the allocation of income across and within the factors of production is immaterial, but it matters crucially for the biological standard of living.

In what follows in this chapter, I review in detail the evidence that supports the presence of an antebellum puzzle in the United States and a number of other Western countries that experienced similar puzzles during the same decades in which the phenomenon appeared in the United States. I then turn to explanations of the puzzle, focusing on the social, demographic (i.e., urbanization), and economic changes that caused it. Broadly speaking, it can be said that modernization—which included industrialization, urbanization, and the transportation revolution—caused the antebellum puzzle, but, more specifically, the cause was an increase in inequality and a decrease in the consumption of net nutrients, which resulted from industrialization and the other changes that accompanied the transition from agricultural to industrial economies.

37.2 Evidence

Progress in the biological standard of living ultimately revolves around improvement in net nutritional status, which is the difference between gross nutritional consumption and the energy demands placed on the body as it meets basic metabolic needs, engages in work, and/or battles disease. A positive net nutritional status will stimulate biological growth, holding other factors constant; conversely, a negative net nutritional status will retard growth. The consumption of net nutrients determines whether a person achieves his or her genetically programmed height potential, and the adult stature of an individual serves as an "indicator of net nutritional status over the growth years" (Cuff, 2005, p. 10). Thus, adult stature reflects the biological standard of living enjoyed by an individual during his or her growth years, and, for individuals, income is positively correlated with nutrition and health (Sunder & Woitek, 2005). Historically, as well as today, the rich have always and everywhere been taller than the poor.

Similarly, for the population as a whole, mean adult stature provides information on the biological standard of living for society as a whole; however, at the aggregate level, as noted in the Introduction, the positive correlation between income and health can break down. If the overall gains in income are enjoyed by a small enough proportion of the population, then the traditional economic measures of the standard of living will increase, while the biological measures experienced by the remainder of the population might well deteriorate. Thus, stature reflects the distribution of economic output as manifested through the consumption of nutrients, which in turn reflects the essence of Adam Smith's original conception of the wealth of a nation and its living standard. The time spent at work and the intensity of that effort, as well as working and living conditions and health, determine the body's demand for nutrients. The traditional measures of economic growth—mean values of income and GDP per capita or even wages—do not reflect either the distribution of income or the distribution of the consumption of nutrients or the physical costs associated with the work that determines the size and composition of GDP. Nor do they reflect the living conditions of the workers and their families or the diseases they battle. More physically challenging occupations, as well as those that demand constant or more intense effort, might yield higher wages and incomes while at the same time increasing the energy demands placed on the body, thus leaving fewer nutrients for growth. It follows that the changes brought about by industrialization and urbanization had different impacts on the trends in stature (and the biological standard of living more generally) than they had on the traditional measures of economic well-being. In short, overall, a nation can get wealthier in a Smithian sense (i.e., as measured by GDP or income per capita) while its citizens experience a decrease in the (net) consumption of nutrients and hence an erosion in the biological standard of living.

In addition to work, disease imposes nutritional demands on the body, and disease spread more easily after the transportation revolution dramatically lowered travel costs[4]; it also spread more easily in urban and industrial environments than in rural ones, all of which contributed to an erosion of the biological standard of living. As workers crowded into cities to work in the factories created by industrialization, they received higher mean incomes than they had on the farm, but the germ theory of disease was only mastered in the late 19th century, and both private and public health suffered as the public infrastructure of clean water and sewer systems lagged industrialization and urbanization (Troesken, 2004). As a result, the consumption of net nutrients declined for much of the population, and urbanization and mortality were strongly correlated. Consequently, the adult population became shorter. Figure 37.1 shows that, for the United States, while real output per capita grew by 1.4% per annum from 1820 to 1860, mean adult stature declined by roughly 1 inch (1.5%) over the same period.[5]

Country-by-country studies reveal declines in stature during industrialization as it spread across much of the Western world, and, like the United States, these occurred during periods in which the traditional economic indicators suggest robust growth in the standard of living. Sweden experienced a decline in mean adult male stature of 0.12 inches between 1830 and 1840 (Sandberg & Steckel, 1997); during the same period, the average annual compounded rate of growth of real GDP per capita was 0.42%.[6] In the region of the Netherlands that ultimately became Belgium, stature declined by 0.75 inches between 1810 and 1830, while per capita output expanded by 0.40% per annum. In the Netherlands itself, height declined by 0.97 inches between 1830 and 1860, while per capita output grew by 1.56% per annum (Drukker & Tassenaar, 1997). In Great Britain, mean height declined by more than an inch between 1810 and 1850 (Floud & Harris, 1997), a period during which real output expanded by 1.69% per annum.

Taken together, the data in Figure 37.1 for the United States, and the experience of many other Western countries during the early and mid-19th century, reflect a puzzle when considered in light of the logic of the positive height–income correlation that applies to individuals: Richer individuals have, by definition, higher living standards

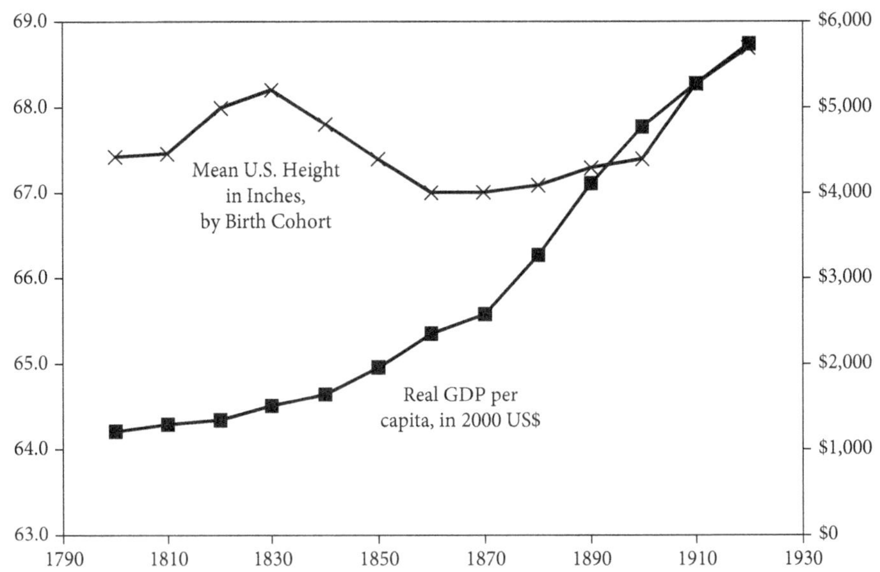

FIGURE 37.1 The Antebellum Puzzle.

Sources: Fogel (1986), NHANES as reported in Komlos (2010), Steckel (2006), and Zehetmayer (2011).

(conventionally measured) and typically enjoy a better biological standard of living; they are taller, live longer, and so forth. But during the early decades of industrialization, that relationship broke down at the aggregate level, and the breakdown occurred in the consumption of net nutrients. The positive relationship was reestablished near the end of the 19th century with the widespread use of refrigeration, public health measures, and improvements in agricultural productivity, which, in turn, were due to mechanization and technological change.

Scholarly discourse on the reduction in net nutrients that yielded the antebellum puzzle often sounds anodyne, but it is important to recognize the harm done to the millions of individuals who experienced it. To take the example of the United States, how much food would an individual need to forego during his growth years in order to suppress his adult height by, say, one-quarter of an inch? In other words, how much less net nutrition did someone born in 1860 consume than someone in 1820 or 1920? Employing a sample of 19th-century US military recruits, Haines et al. (2003) estimate that an additional 20 grams of protein per day (the equivalent of six slices of whole wheat bread or 3 ounces of pork) from birth to adulthood would have generated, roughly, an additional one-quarter of an inch in adult stature.[7] In other words, giving up the protein equivalent of a meal a day would only represent one-third of the peak-to-trough decline in heights in Figure 37.1.[8]

Of course, the decline in the gross consumption of nutrients was not the only cause of the decrease in mean adult stature; the intensity of industrial work and the increase in the incidence of disease in urban areas also played a role by increasing the nutritional demands placed on the body. The other factor is that, on average, people were smaller at the time. As Komlos notes, humans possess an "evolutionary advantage" in that they have the capacity to "adapt to the availability of nourishment" (2012, p. 4). Floud et al. (Floud, Fogel, Harris, & Hong, 2011) show that, during industrialization, humans adjusted their size to the availability of nutrients; that is to say, they got smaller in response to their relative deprivation. This does not mean that the adjustment was without pain; as Craig emphasizes, for these populations "being smaller also meant being weaker, sicker and more likely to die earlier" (2015 p. 7). So the puzzle was more than an academic curiosity; spread over decades, it contributed to a brutish life for millions.

37.3 Explanations

Some of the possible causes of the antebellum puzzle have been mentioned briefly already, but, typically, a more comprehensive list would include (1) immigration, which changed the ethnic composition of the population; (2) an increase in hours and/or the intensification of work resulting from industrialization; (3) transportation improvements, which lowered transport costs and expanded the disease nexus; (4) urbanization, which exposed a larger share of the population to the disease nexus and increased the share of the population living in unsanitary conditions; (5) an increase in income inequality; and (6) declining food consumption accompanied by an increase in the relative price of food.[9]

Of these, **immigration** is arguably the least persuasive. It is logical to conclude that a change in the composition of the population might well lead to a change in mean adult stature and thus be a likely candidate to explain the negative trend in the biological standard of living during the early and mid-19th century, at least in the United States. The argument is that as poorer and less healthy migrants are added to the population (think of the Irish in the US case), subsequent measures of the biological standard of living, especially stature, will naturally erode. However, as Komlos notes, "the decline in stature started at a time when the share of immigrants in the population was still very low [and] . . . the decline in stature was pervasive across all regions of the United States but immigration was not" (1987, p. 908). Furthermore, several studies documenting the puzzle focus on the trend in stature of large but homogenous subpopulations, such as native-born white males of northern European descent (e.g., Haines et al., 2003), which eliminates immigration (and genetics) from the set of potential explanations of the phenomenon. Immigration may have arithmetically contributed to a decrease in mean adult stature in the United States, but it cannot explain the antebellum puzzle.[10]

Because adult stature depends on the consumption of net nutrients, **the intensification of effort at work** would be expected to negatively impact the biological standard of living. Accounts of the changing nature of work during the Industrial Revolution suggest that the migration of labor from farm (and artisanal shop) to factory may have resulted in a reduction in net nutrition. As Marx observed:

> The immoderate lengthening of the working day, produced by machinery in the hands of capital, leads to a reaction on the part of society.... On the basis of such a [now lengthened] day, the intensity of labor was [also] increased. Thus ... the lengthening of the working day went hand in hand with increasing intensity of factory labor. (1932 [1867–1883], pp. 115–116)

While such arguments evoke the immiseration of the proletariat (to borrow Marxist language), there are two problems with them as an explanation of the puzzle. First, as originally noted by Fogel (1986), in the United States, rural populations experienced the largest decline in heights during the antebellum era. The industrial mills might have been dark and satanic, but those who stayed on the farm also experienced the antebellum puzzle. Second, despite Marx's detailed account of life in the factory and his theories which were based upon such accounts, it is not altogether clear that industrialization unambiguously increased the intensity of labor for the mass of workers. After all, as Marx himself emphasized, the substitution of machines for animate power, often supplied by humans, was one of the striking characteristics of industrialization (Mokyr, 2013).

Without the germ theory of disease, **transportation improvements** and **urbanization** should have eroded the biological standard of living by expanding the disease nexus, thus exposing individuals who otherwise would have not been exposed to that nexus. The transportation revolution initially included improved roads and an extension of the canal network; toward the middle of the 19th century, entire railroad systems emerged, with major east-west "trunk" lines connecting the rural hinterlands with eastern seaboard cities and ports. Later still, ocean shipping was transformed by the addition of steam-driven engines and steel-hauled vessels. All of these changes possessed the potential for expanding disease, which in turn reduced the absorption of nutrients (holding other factors constant, of course). At first glance, empirical evidence tends to be supportive. In a sample of Union Army recruits, Haines et al. (2003, p. 402) found that soldiers who grew up in a county through which a navigable waterway ran were, on average, one-half inch shorter than those who grew up in counties without such access. As for urbanization, Fogel (1986) argues that the migration from farm to city accounted for roughly 20% of the decline in mean stature during the antebellum era. In support of this argument, Haines et al. found that, among Union Army recruits, those born in urban counties were, on average, an inch shorter than those born in rural counties (2003, p. 406).

Komlos challenges this disease-nexus interpretation of the impact of urbanization and transportation by highlighting, as, ironically, Fogel had earlier, the "conundrum of the [simultaneous] decline in rural heights. After all, farmers should have benefited from their propinquity to nutrients" (Komlos, 2012, p. 407). So, the transportation revolution and urbanization most likely led to the erosion in the biological standard of living, but they do not explain the antebellum puzzle.

Indeed, Komlos argues that both played a role in the puzzle through their impacts on **inequality** and, ultimately, **food consumption**. He notes that transportation improvements "enabled farmers to [more profitably] export their food surpluses," and urbanization led to "disparities in food consumption stemming from increasing income inequality" in urban-industrial areas relative to rural areas (2012, pp. 441, 443), just as Kuznets suspected. Furthermore, evidence on relative wages and the distribution of income and wealth suggests that inequality increased substantially during the antebellum period; that process continued for some time after the Civil War, a period during which the trend in mean adult stature continued to stagnate. For example, the ratio of the wages of professional workers relative to blue-collar workers increased by roughly one-third between 1810 and 1860 (Lindert & Williamson, 1980, p. 69). As the early years of industrialization, centered on the artisanal shop, gave way to large industrial operations, a development referred to as "de-skilling," which further drove down the wages of blue-collar workers relative to white-collar workers, appeared. The process only began to subside later in the century, following which US heights began their long-run ascent, thus ending the antebellum puzzle (Katz & Margo, 2014, p. 42). As Katz and Margo note, "in nineteenth-century manufacturing, technical change reduced the relative demand for artisans in favor of machines operated by less skilled workers, and in that sense, [industrialization] certainly was de-skilling" (2014, p. 48). In addition, the Gini coefficient for income increased from 0.44 to 0.51 between 1774 and 1860 (Lindert & Williamson, 2012, pp. 35–36), and the share of wealth owned by the richest 10% increased from 58% to 70% between 1810 and 1870 (Piketty, 2014, p. 348).

Of course, a change in the distribution of income and wealth would not *necessarily* lead to a worsening of the biological standard of living. If, for example, real wages, income, and wealth were increasing at a sufficient rate overall, or if public policies of sufficient rigor were in place to redistribute the increase in incomes from the higher to the lower end of the distribution, then it is possible that the biological standard of living (in some absolute sense) could increase, while the standard of living among the poor increased absolutely but decreased only in relation to that of the rich. However, this was not the case in the 19th-century United States, nor was it the case throughout much of the Western world. In the United States, per capita incomes grew at more than 1% per annum between 1800 and 1860, inequality increased, and there was little in the way of a government-supplied safety net or income redistribution at the time. The biological standard of living for much, probably even most, of the population declined absolutely.[11]

Komlos summarizes the importance of the increase in inequality as an explanatory factor by noting that "in every single data set examined we do find that wealthier parents have taller children, everything else being equal" (2012, p. 396). So, incomes increased during the 19th century, and those further up the socioeconomic ladder became taller. But the distribution of income became more unequal, and those further down the ladder—the majority—got shorter; thus, mean stature declined as mean income increased. Overall, then, increasing inequality contributed to a decline in the biological standard of living for the mass of the US population during the onset of modern economic growth, thus creating the antebellum puzzle.

The availability of food—gross nutrition—served as the direct means through which increasing inequality led to an erosion of the biological standard of living. Although

Fogel et al. (1983, pp. 473–474) initially raised the question concerning the role of nutritional intake in causing the puzzle, they dismissed it as an unlikely candidate. After all, productivity in the agricultural sector was increasing dramatically by historical standards (Craig & Weiss, 2000).[12] However, Komlos, in his landmark study of West Point cadets, revisited nutritional intake as a causal factor. After largely rejecting immigration, the intensification of work, transportation improvements, and urbanization, he argued that it was in fact a reduction in the per capita consumption of calories and protein that best explains the timing of the puzzle (1987, pp. 908–991). He showed that, between 1839 and 1869, per capita daily calorie consumption declined by 2–4%, while per capita protein consumption declined by 8–10% (p. 909). Importantly, these declines were marked by a substitution of grains (heavy in carbohydrates) for meat (heavy in protein) in the diets of the middle and lower classes, and, overall, the per capita consumption of meat fell by roughly one-third (p. 913). Supporting the role of nutrition as a cause of the puzzle, Haines et al. found that Union Army recruits born in counties that produced an additional 70 grams of protein per capita per day—that is, heavily agricultural counties—were one- to two-tenths of an inch taller than other recruits.

Komlos and Coclanis (1997) argue that the reduction in transport costs, accompanied by an increase in the demand for food in the growing urban areas, led to an acceleration of the commercialization of agriculture. These changes coincided with (and indeed may have played a role in) changes in the relative prices of nutrients, which caused households to substitute into carbohydrates and away from meats. Furthermore, in the absence of mechanical refrigeration, foods consumed by the rapidly expanding urban population were less dense in nutrients as result of spoilage than were those consumed by rural populations (Craig, Goodwin, & Grennes, 2004); on average, this, too, would have driven down mean stature.

To summarize, although the relative importance of inequality and consumption as causal factors has not gone unchallenged (see, e.g., Gallman, 1996), it is now widely accepted that the US economy became more unequal and much of the US population experienced a decline in nutritional intake during the period and that these factors arguably caused the antebellum puzzle (Komlos, 2012).

37.4 Conclusion

Despite the early 19th-century onset of modern economic growth, as conventionally measured by the increase in real GDP and income per capita and wages, the United States and several other Western countries experienced a downturn in the biological standard of living. This phenomenon is known as the "antebellum puzzle" because the downturn began in the decades before the US Civil War. A number of potential explanations for the puzzle have been offered in the literature, including immigration, an increase in hours and/or the intensification of work resulting from industrialization, and transportation improvements and urbanization, which expanded the disease nexus. Whereas industrialization, the transportation revolution, and urbanization all contributed to the puzzle, they did so primarily through their impact on the increase in inequality that marked the era. It was, in fact, the increase in inequality, which appeared in wealth, income, and wages, that in turn contributed to a reduction in the consumption of net nutrients, which caused the decline in stature and the biological standard of living.

The study of the antebellum puzzle has important implications for understanding the dynamics of economic development and, more specifically, the negative externalities generated by the onset of modern economic growth. The conventional measures of the standard of living omit or otherwise overlook the impacts of industrialization on the biological development of the children who experienced it. Modern economic growth generated a larger quantity of goods and services, both in the aggregate and on a per person basis, an observation reflected in GDP and income measures. However, the fruits of that bounty were unequally distributed from the beginning of industrialization and became more so over time. As a result, the biological standard of living, on average and probably for most of the inhabitants of Western civilization, deteriorated for two generations following the onset of the Industrial Revolution. Amid a growing abundance, mean adult stature, which is determined by net nutrition during one's growth years, declined, as did the expectation of life. This is the antebellum puzzle, which, despite its name, continued into the postbellum era.

Notes

1. See the discussion in Schumpeter (1954, pp. 229–230).
2. This claim has not gone unchallenged. For example, Voth (2008) provides evidence that pre-modern growth rates of the standard of living were probably greater than zero, although still below those achieved following the onset of industrialization.
3. The adjective "antebellum" comes from the decades preceding the US Civil War. The expression was first coined by Komlos (1996).
4. For example, the cost of road travel decreased by 50%, and that of ocean travel fell by 95% between 1815 and 1860 (Taylor, 1960, appendix A).
5. Fogel and Costa (1997) refer to the long-run increase in stature and the overall improvement in the biological standard of living that mark an end to the antebellum puzzle period as the onset of the "techno-physio evolution."
6. Real output per capita figures for the European countries mentioned here are from Bolt and van Zanden (2013).
7. Protein is a crucial nutrient for *Homo sapiens'* growth (Baten & Murray, 2000).
8. The wheat and pork protein equivalents are from Craig and Hammond (2013).
9. This list is comparable, but not identical, to those found in Haines et al. (2003) and Komlos (2012).
10. It is also worth noting that the stature of passport applicants, which disproportionately included upper income groups, did not decline during this period (Sunder, 2007).
11. Sunder (2007, 2011) shows an increase in the inequality of the distribution of heights between the rich and the poor.

12. Craig and Weiss note that the increase in agricultural output was partly caused by an increase in hours at work, which would have contributed to the erosion of rural living standards highlighted by Komlos.

References

Baten, J., & Murray, J. E. (2000). Heights of men and women in 19th-century Bavaria: Economic, nutritional, and disease influences). *Explorations in Economic History*, *37*(4), 351–369.

Bolt, J., & van Zanden, J. L. (2013). *The first update of the Maddison Project: Re-estimating growth before 1820* (Maddison Project Working Paper No. 4), http://www.ggdc.net/maddison/maddison-project/publications/wp4.pdf.

Clark, G. (2007). *A farewell to alms: A brief economic history of the world*. Princeton, NJ: Princeton University.

Craig, L. A. (2015). Nutrition, the biological standard of living, and cliometrics. In C. Diebolt & M. Haupert (Eds.), *Handbook of cliometrics*. New York: Springer.

Craig, L. A., & Hammond, R. (2013). Nutrition and signaling in slave markets: A new look at a puzzle within the Antebellum Puzzle. *Cliometrica*, *7*(2), 189–206.

Craig, L. A., Goodwin, B., & Grennes, T. (2004). The effect of mechanical refrigeration on nutrition in the United States. *Social Science History*, *28*(3), 325–336.

Craig, L. A., & Weiss, T. (2000). Hours at work and total factor productivity growth in 19th-century U.S. agriculture. *Advances in Agricultural Economic History*, *1*(1), 1–30.

Cuff, T. (2005). *The hidden cost of economic development: The biological standard of living in antebellum Pennsylvania*. Aldershot, UK: Ashgate.

Drukker, J. W., & Tassenaar, V. (1997). Paradoxes of modernization and material well-being in the Netherlands during the nineteenth century. In R. H. Steckel & R. Floud (Eds.), *Health and welfare during Industrialization* (pp. 331–378). Chicago: University of Chicago.

Floud, R., Fogel, R. W., Harris, B., & Hong, S. C. (2011). *The changing body: Health, nutrition, and human development in the western world since 1700*. Cambridge, UK: Cambridge University.

Floud, R., & Harris, B. (1997). Health, height and welfare: Britain 1700–1980. In R. H. Steckel & R. Floud (Eds.), *Health and welfare during industrialization* (pp. 91–126). Chicago: University of Chicago.

Fogel, R. (1986). Nutrition and the decline in mortality since 1700. In S. Engerman & R. Gallman (Eds.), *Long-term factors in American economic growth*. Chicago: University of Chicago.

Fogel, R., & Costa, D. (1997). A theory of the technophysio evolution, with some implications for forecasting population, health care costs, and pension costs. *Demography*, *34*(1), 49–66.

Fogel, R. W., Engerman, S. L., Floud, R., Friedman, G., Margo, R. A., Sokoloff, L. et al. (1983). Secular Changes in American and British Stature and Nutrition. *Journal of Interdisciplinary History*, *14*(2), 445–481.

Gallman, R. (1996). Dietary change in antebellum America. *Journal of Economic History*, *56*(1), 193–201.

Haines, M. R., Craig, L. A., & Weiss, T. (2003). The short and the dead: Nutrition, mortality, and the "Antebellum Puzzle" in the United States. *Journal of Economic History*, *63*(2), 385–416.

Katz, L., & Margo, R. (2014). Technical change and the relative demand for skilled labor: The United States in historical perspective. In L. P. Boustan, C. Frydman, & R. A. Margo (Eds.), *Human capital in history* (pp. 15–58). Chicago: University of Chicago.

Komlos, J. (1987). The height and weight of West Point cadets: Dietary change in antebellum America. *Journal of Economic History, 47*(4), 897–927.

Komlos, J. (1989). Thinking about the Industrial Revolution. *Journal of European Economic History, 18*, 191–206.

Komlos, J. (1996). Anomalies in economic history: Toward a resolution of the "Antebellum Puzzle." *Journal of Economic History, 56*(1), 202–214.

Komlos, J. (2000). The Industrial Revolution as the escape from the Malthusian Trap. *Journal of European Economic History, 29*(2–3), 307–331.

Komlos, J. (2010). The recent decline in the height of African-American women. *Economics and Human Biology, 8*(1), 58–66.

Komlos, J. (2011). *The postbellum continuation of the Antebellum Puzzle: Stature in the United States, 1847–1894*. Unpublished manuscript.

Komlos, J. (2012). A three-decade history of the Antebellum Puzzle: Explaining the shrinking of the U.S. population at the onset of modern economic growth. *Journal of the Historical Society, 12*(4), 395–445.

Komlos, J., & Coclanis, P. (1997). On the "puzzling" antebellum cycle of the biological standard of living: The case of Georgia. *Explorations in Economic History, 34*(4), 433–459.

Kuznets, S. (1966). *Modern economic growth: Rate, structure and spread.* New Haven, CT: Yale University.

Kuznets, S. (1973). Modern economic growth: Findings and reflections. *American Economic Review, 63*(3), 247–258.

Lindert, P. H., & Williamson, J. G. (1980). *American inequality: A macroeconomic history.* New York: Academic.

Lindert, P. H., & Williamson, J. G. (2012). *American incomes, 1774–1860* (NBER Working Paper No. 18396). Cambridge, MA: National Bureau of Economic Research.

Marx, K. (1932 [1867–1883]). *Capital* (Max Eastman, Ed.). New York: Modern Library.

Mokyr, J. (2013). *The enlightened economy: An economic history of Britain, 1700–1850*. New Haven, CT: Yale University Press.

Piketty, T. (2014). *Capital in the twenty-first century* (A. Goldhammer, Ed.). Cambridge, MA: Belknap.

Sandberg, L. G., & Steckel, R. H. (1997). Was industrialization hazardous to your health? Not in Sweden! In R. H. Stickel & R. Floud (Eds.), Health and welfare during industrialization (pp. 127–160). Chicago: University of Chicago.

Schumpeter, J. A. (1954). *History of economic analysis*. New York: Oxford University Press.

Smith, A. (1976). *An inquiry into the nature and causes of the wealth of nations.* Chicago: University of Chicago.

Steckel, R. (2006). Physcial Well-Being. In S. B. Carter, S. S. Gartner, M. R. Haines, A. L. Olmstead, R. Sutch, and G. Wright (Eds.), *Historical Statistics of the United State: Millenial Edition*, Vol. 2 (pp. 582–585). New York: Cambridge University Press.

Sunder, M. (2007). *Passports and economic development: An anthropometric history of the U.S. elite in the nineteenth century*. PhD dissertation, University of Munich.

Sunder, M. (2011). Upward and onward: High-society American women eluded the Antebellum Puzzle. *Economics and Human Biology, 9*(2), 65–171.

Sunder, M., & Woitek, U. (2005). Boom, bust, and the human body: Further evidence on the relationship between height and business cycles. *Economics and Human Biology*, *3*(3), 450–466.

Taylor, G. R. (1960). *The transportation revolution, 1815–1860*. New York: Holt Rinehart.

Troesken, W. (2004). *Water, race, and disease*. Cambridge, MA: Massachusetts Institute of Technology.

Voth, H. -J. (2008). Clark's intellectual sudoku. *European Review of Economic History*, *12*(2), 149–155.

Williamson, S. H. (2013). The annual real GDP for the United States, 1790–2012. Retrieved January 20, 2014, from http://www.measuringworth.com/usgdp/

Young, A. (1771). *The farmer's tour through the east of England* (Vol. 4.) London.

Zehetmayer, M. (2011). The continuation of the antebellum puzzle: Stature in the US, 1847–1894. *European Review of Economic History*, *15*(3), 313–327.

CHAPTER 38

THE ANTHROPOMETRIC HISTORY OF THE MEDITERRANEAN WORLD

BRIAN A'HEARN

38.1 Introduction

THE Mediterranean has held an enduring fascination for historians, certainly since Braudel (1949) articulated his vision of a region where enduring features of climate and geography imposed a common framework on seemingly divergent peoples and places. In the same tradition, Horden and Purcell (2000, 2006) see the Mediterranean over the very long run as a collection of local microecologies that share an unpredictable climate that makes primary production risky and that are fragmented by topography but connected by the sea. Economic historians recognize commonalities across southern Europe including low and irregular rainfall, rugged terrain, a lack of coal, and poor access (outside Iberia) to the markets of the Atlantic and North Sea (A'Hearn, 2014). Common characteristics generated common economic outcomes including livestock-poor, low-productivity agriculture, small internal markets, low wages, and high energy costs. New techniques and products adopted in northwest Europe were ill-suited to this environment, leaving the region isolated from the main currents of technical change (Allen, 2009). The economies of the region were also linked by markets. Grain markets were well-integrated from 1500 or earlier, at least for coastal cities (as well-integrated as London and Amsterdam, for comparison; Bateman, 2010). Further commonalities included low literacy, a polarized distribution of land, religious institutions resistant to change, and ineffective governments lacking both effective central control and effective constraints on the executive (Burke, 2012; Dincecco, 2009).

Southern Europe is defined here as the north rim of the Mediterranean, stretching from Portugal to Turkey.[1] If these lands constituted either an integrated regional economy or a collection of similar local economies, the proof ought to show up in the historical record of average heights. Beyond the general level and trend of economic development, there are specific features of the Mediterranean world that ought to have affected height, such as climate-related protein scarcity and other dietary deficiencies (e.g., pellagra-inducing niacin deficiency caused by diets consisting almost exclusively of maize, a New World grain that thrived in the Mediterranean climate) and conditions conducive to endemic diseases such as malaria. A joint reading of the evidence on height and the economy should illuminate both and offer some insight into whether southern Europe is a meaningful analytical category or just a convenient geographic expression.

38.2 European Statures, North and South

Southern Europeans are known for their short stature. In the 21st century, German girls are a perceptible 3.4 cm taller than Italian girls by age 15 according to the growth charts. The advantage of Dutch girls is even greater at 5.7 cm (Cacciari et al., 2006; Rosario, Schienkiewitz, & Neuhauser, 2011; Schönbeck et al., 2013).

Figure 38.1 displays estimates of mean height for adult men born in the late 20th century in 28 European countries. The figures are taken primarily from the Baten and Blum (2012) dataset, a compilation of estimates from a wide range of sources adjusted for distortions resulting from age at measurement, within-country birth region, self-reporting of height, indirect estimation based on female heights, and similar factors.[2] The figures refer to men born in the 1980s. If we define southern Europe in terms of latitude or proximity to the Mediterranean, it is clear that the countries of the region fall into two groups. Turkey, Portugal, Italy, and Spain are among—indeed they almost define—Europe's shortest nations. But the Balkan countries of the former Yugoslavia are well above average. Only Greece lies near the middle of the overall distribution.

38.3 Health, Wealth, and Height in Contemporary Europe

Heights are often taken as an indirect indicator of prosperity, and Figure 38.2 confirms a positive correlation between stature and gross domestic product (GDP) per capita in late 20th-century Europe. Equally clear is the exceptional position of the southern European countries. Italy, Portugal, and Turkey have heights well below similarly prosperous economies. Spain, too, lies below the prediction of a simple regression. At the same time, Serbia and the amalgam of former Yugoslav states on the Adriatic (labeled "Med-Yugo") are extremely tall for their level of development.[3] The range of variation around the regression line is considerable.

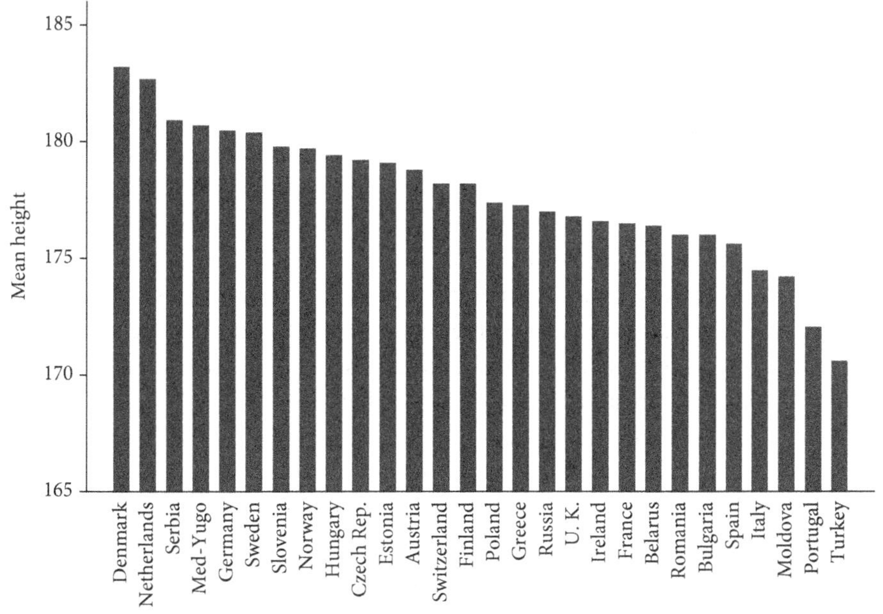

FIGURE 38.1 Adult male height, generation of the 1980s.

Sources: See text and footnote 1.

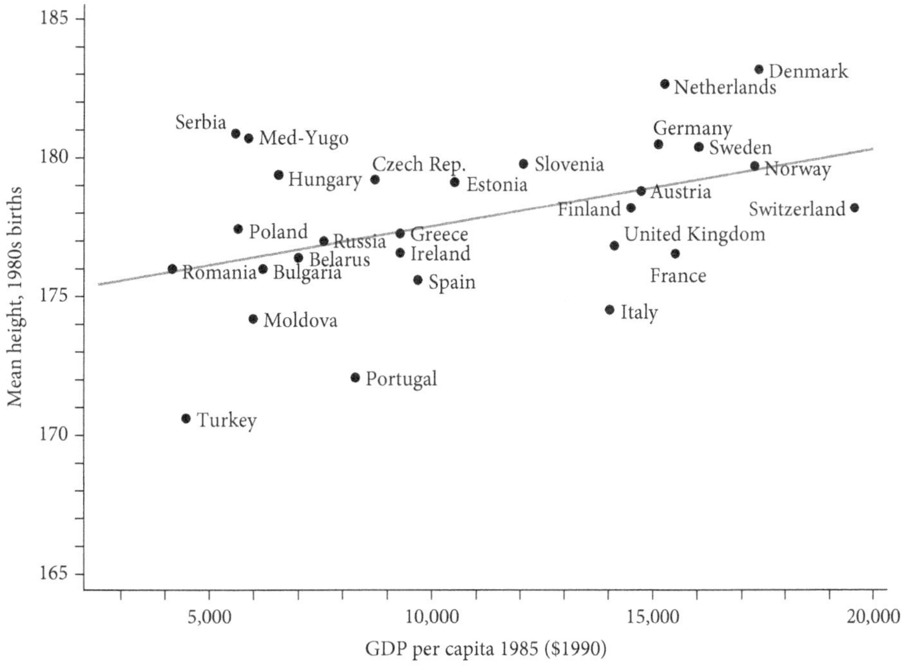

FIGURE 38.2 Gross domestic product (GDP) per capita and mean heights in the 1980s.

Note: The line represents the predicted values of a regression estimated by ordinary least squares.

Sources: Height, Figure 38.1; GDP, Table 38.2.

Inequality might explain some of these discrepancies because increased resources cannot much improve the already-optimal health of the wealthy, whereas a matching decrease for the poor can seriously aggravate their circumstances. Table 38.1 presents estimates of inequality drawn from World Bank development indicators. The Gini index values generally refer to expenditure per adult-equivalent household member and have been averaged from all available estimates for the 1980–89 period.[4]

Turkey emerges as an outlier in these data, being both poor and highly unequal. And if we can take at face value the estimates for the socialist economies, they suggest relatively poor but equal societies, which may have worked to the advantage of health in the Yugoslav states. The cases of Italy and Iberia are rather less clear, however. Inequality was greater than in the egalitarian Nordic countries, but about the same as in the UK, Switzerland, France, or Ireland, all of which had taller men.

Late 20th-century Europe is not the right proving ground for hypotheses about the determinants of height. The sample is too small to have any confidence that measurement errors are not influential. More importantly, the sample is too homogeneous for there to be sufficient—and sufficiently independent—variation in the explanatory variables to permit accurate estimation of their effects. But multiple regression is still a useful way of summarizing patterns in the data and assessing partial correlations. If we regress mean height on GDP per capita and the Gini Index, we find the expected positive and negative relationships, respectively. And we can account for some southern European distinctiveness. In particular, the outlier Turkey's "height deficit" relative to the sample mean is well-predicted by its poverty and inequality. (Compare the Actual and Model 1, "wealth" columns in Table 38.2.) Spain also fits the overall pattern fairly well. But the deficits of Italy and Portugal are *not* well accounted for. And *none* of former Yugoslav states' surplus is "explained"; they are in fact predicted to be below average. As discussed later, genetic factors almost certainly play a role here.

Of course, wealth contributes to height only indirectly, by enabling a society to "buy" living conditions conducive to good health: a nutritious diet, a disease-free environment, a well-heated home, sufficient time for rest and recuperation from labor, access to health care, and so on. A direct examination of these variables should shed further light on the factors behind short statures in southern Europe. Two measures we can consider are life expectancy at birth and protein in the diet.

Longevity ought to correlate well with mean height to the extent that both are measures of overall health. Figure 38.3 shows that the data for 1980s Europe match this expectation. As was the case for GDP, though, the southern European countries are mostly outliers: the Iberians, Italians, and Turks are all surprisingly short, the former Yugoslavs are surprisingly tall. Turkey is an influential outlier. If it is excluded, the slope of the regression line is almost halved and the explanatory power of the regression is minimal. This evidence, then, does not suggest that southern Europe faced more difficult epidemiological conditions that might have reduced health (and height) at any level of development, at any level of expenditure on public health infrastructure or private health care. Turkey excepted, the southern Europeans have the same life expectancy as their taller northern counterparts.

Table 38.1 Adult male height and its determinants, 1980s generation

	Mean Height	GDP per capita	Gini Index	Life expectancy	Protein	
					Animal	Total
Austria	178.8	14,752	23.0	73.1	62	96
Belarus	176.4	7,001	22.8	70.2	52	104
Bulgaria	176.0	6,226	23.4	71.3	47	106
Czech Republic	179.2	8,743	19.4	70.7	58	100
Denmark	183.2	17,384	26.8	74.5	55	88
Estonia	179.1	10,529	23.0	69.3	52	104
Finland	178.2	14,522	22.2	74.3	60	94
France	176.5	15,530	35.7	74.7	76	114
Germany	180.5	15,140	28.6	73.7	60	96
Greece	177.3	9,316	33.4	74.5	54	108
Hungary	179.4	6,557	23.0	69.1	57	103
Ireland	176.6	9,306	36.5	73.1	69	111
Italy	174.5	14,096	33.3	74.8	55	105
Med.-Yugoslavia	180.7	5,894	23.2	70.8	40	105
Moldova	174.2	6,004	24.1	65.1	52	104
Netherlands	182.7	15,283	28.0	76.1	67	99
Norway	179.7	17,320	24.7	75.9	64	101
Poland	177.4	5,660	25.9	71.0	55	103
Portugal	172.1	8,306	31.6	72.3	38	80
Romania	176.0	4,159	23.3	69.7	42	93
Russia (USSR)	177.0	7,569	23.8	67.5	52	104
Serbia	180.9	5,588	23.2	70.2	40	105
Slovenia	179.8	12,110	23.6	71.2	40	105
Spain	175.6	9,722	34.5	76.0	57	99
Sweden	180.4	16,049	23.5	76.3	66	97
Switzerland	178.2	19,586	36.6	76.1	64	98

(*Continued*)

Table 38.1 Contniued

	Mean Height	GDP per capita	Gini Index	Life expectancy	Protein	
					Animal	Total
Turkey	170.6	4,485	43.6	60.2	27	102
United Kingdom	176.8	14,165	28.5	74.1	53	89

Notes: Common national average protein availability reported for former Soviet, Yugoslav, and Czechoslovak states. Russian Gini index refers to the entire USSR. GDP per capita for the former Soviet, Yugoslav, and Czechoslovak states based on individual 1990 relatives scaled to the 1985 national level. Mediterranean-Yugoslavia figures are a 1985 population-weighted average of Bosnia-Herzegovina, Croatia, Macedonia, and Montenegro.

Sources: Gini index average of 1980s estimates, World Bank Development Indicators, Portugal and UK from *Chartbook of Economic Inequality*. Protein availability 1980–85 average, Food and Agriculture Organization food balance sheets. GDP per capita in 1985, Maddison (2010). Life expectancy at birth (male and female) 1980–85 average, World Bank Development Indicators.

Turning now to diet, it has been convincingly demonstrated that the availability of cheap animal proteins (such as milk), which are the most complete source of essential amino acids required by the body, is positively associated with height (Baten, 1999; Baten & Blum 2012; Baten & Murray, 2000). Animal protein might be scarce on southern European tables due to poverty, culinary traditions, or a higher relative price. Table 38.1 presents the Food and Agriculture Organization (FAO) estimates of protein availability in grams per capita per day, averaged over the years 1980–85. The levels are not accurate representations of actual consumption (the lowest totals easily exceed recommended daily allowances for adult males), but the relative values may be meaningful. They indicate that only Portugal, perhaps, had anything approaching a protein scarcity. But the differences in *animal* protein availability are greater. The Southern European countries are at or below average, and the deficiency is severe in the case of Turkey. At the other extreme, the tall Nordic and Central-European countries, along with the Netherlands, all have average or better animal protein values. Yet the correspondence between height and protein is anything but deterministic or linear. And the ex-Yugoslav countries constitute the usual exception: scarce animal protein but very tall statures.

Multiple regression is again useful, even in a small and homogeneous sample, for assessing patterns in the data. Regressing height on life expectancy and the availability of animal protein, we find a strong partial correlation with the former and only a weak and insignificant association with the latter. And although we might have expected superior explanatory power from these directly health-related variables, in fact, the regression R^2 is less than half that of a regression involving wealth and inequality. Furthermore, southern European height deviations are less well accounted for (Model 2, "health" Table 38.2). Half the Turkish (and essentially none of the Italian or Iberian) height deficits are predicted, thus reflecting the simple fact that these countries were healthy but short. The tall statures of the Slavic countries on the Adriatic are not explained either: all

Table 38.2 Actual and predicted height deviations from the European average (cm)

	Actual	Model 1 "wealth"	Model 2 "health"	Model 3 all
Turkey	−7.2	−7.0	−4.4	−7.9
Portugal	−5.7	−2.1	−0.4	−1.9
Moldova	−3.6	−0.6	−2.1	−1.1
Italy	−3.3	−0.7	0.9	−0.6
Spain	−2.2	−2.5	1.3	−1.8
Bulgaria	−1.8	−0.4	−0.4	−0.1
Romania	−1.8	−1.0	−1.1	−0.9
Belarus	−1.4	0.1	−0.6	0.1
France	−1.3	−0.9	1.5	−0.7
Ireland	−1.2	−3.3	0.8	−2.7
United Kingdom	−1.0	0.8	0.6	0.7
Russia	−0.8	0.0	−1.4	−0.3
Greece	−0.5		0.8	
Poland	−0.4	−1.3	−0.3	−1.0
Finland	0.4	2.8	0.9	2.7
Switzerland	0.4	0.2	1.6	0.1
Austria	1.0	2.6	0.6	2.4
Estonia	1.3	1.2	−0.9	0.9
Czech Republic	1.4	1.7	−0.3	1.7
Hungary	1.6	−0.1	−0.8	−0.1
Norway	1.9	3.0	1.5	2.9
Slovenia	2.0	1.5	−0.7	1.2
Sweden	2.6	2.9	1.7	3.0
Germany	2.7	1.1	0.7	1.0
Med–Yugo	2.9	−0.4	−0.8	−0.3
Serbia	3.1	−0.5	−1.0	−0.4
Netherlands	4.9	1.3	1.7	1.5
Denmark	5.4	2.4	0.8	2.1

Note: The table reports actual deviations of mean height from the sample average, along with the deviations predicted by regressions of height on gross domestic product (GDP) per capita and the Gini index (Model 1, "wealth"), life expectancy at birth and protein availability (Model 2, "health"), and all four variables (Model 3).

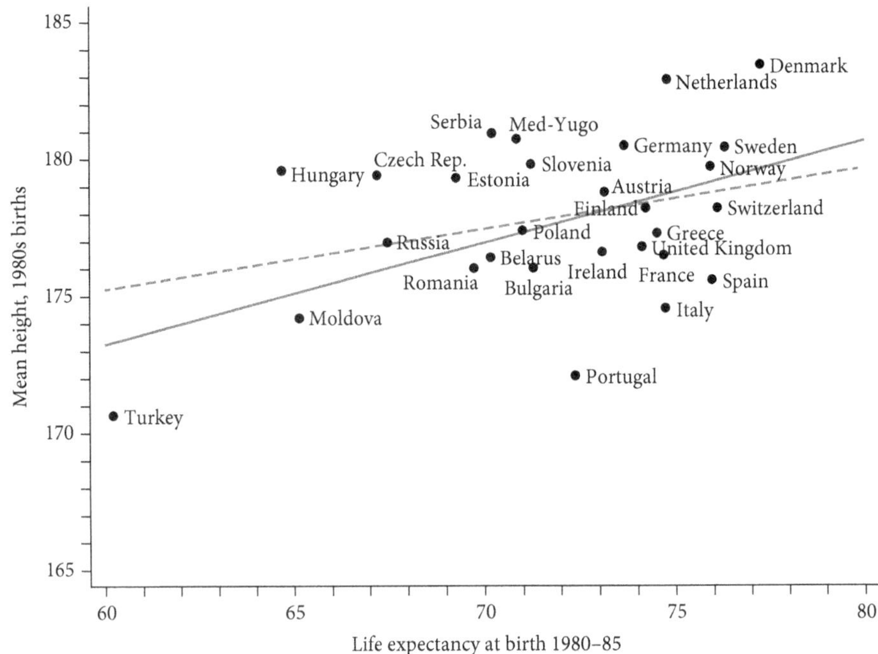

FIGURE 38.3 Height and life expectancy, 1980s births.

Sources: Height, Figure 38.1; life expectancy, Table 38.1.

Note: Lines of best fit estimated by ordinary least squares; dashed line excludes Turkey.

three are predicted to be *shorter* than average. If we include both the "wealth" and the "health" variables in the regression, the latter add little explanatory power and change predicted height values rather little (Model 3 in Table 38.2). The figure in Appendix 4 plots the bivariate relationships of all four variables with height.

Two reactions to this exercise are possible. A "positive" interpretation is that heights accurately reflect a country's living conditions, which are best captured by economic measures. Much of South Europe's height deficit—outside the Balkans, of course—can be explained in this way, and further research ought to focus on better health measures that might explain the rest. Perhaps malaria affects height but not longevity and is independent of diet, for example. A "negative" interpretation is that the correlation with economic variables (themselves poorly measured, at least for eastern Europe) may be misleading and that height differences also depend on more than just current living conditions. There might be intergenerational transmission of health status, for example. Or there might be genetic differences.

38.4 Genetic Influences on Height

It has long been known that European populations are genetically distinct. Early studies in the tradition of classical genetics worked backward from observable traits (phenotypes) to inferences about the underlying genetics.[5] A familiar example involves blood groups. The inheritance patterns of blood types A, B, O, and AB suggested that the trait was determined by a single gene with three variants, or alleles, of which A and B are (co-)dominant and O recessive. From the distribution of phenotypes, allele frequencies could then be calculated. Finally, the joint distribution of allele frequencies for a number of genetic markers (mostly related to proteins, antibodies, and enzymes in blood) could be used to compare populations—by calculating indices of genetic dissimilarity, for example.

In such analyses, systematic differences between northern and southern Europe were found. Using principal components to summarize variation across many alleles, Cavalli-Sforza et al. (Cavalli-Sforza, Menozzi, & Piazza, 1994) found that populations neatly diverged along a North-South axis. An analysis of genetic distance based on the same data indicated that the Italians and Iberians formed a cluster, being less distant from each other than from other populations. The western Scandinavians, the Scots and Irish, or the German-speaking populations of central Europe each formed similar clusters. Interestingly, considerable variation was revealed *within* the Mediterranean: although recognizably southern by their genetic signature, the Sardinians, the Greeks, and the Yugoslavs were (after the Lapps) the three populations in Europe most unique, most dissimilar to all others including each other. In general, genetic distance was found to correlate well with geographic and linguistic distance, both between and within nations.

The technological advances of recent years mean that modern population genetics can proceed from direct knowledge of the DNA sequence. The advent of high-throughput genotyping allows us to identify millions of genetic variants at the level of individual base pairs.[6] The most common form of variation is the substitution, at a particular location on a particular chromosome, of a single nucleotide compared with the human reference genome: a *single-nucleotide polymorphism* (SNP). Generally, an SNP involves only two alleles: G might be the reference, T the alternative, for example.[7]

The lessons of classical population genetics are confirmed by the new methods. A recent study considered data from more than 3,000 Europeans, genotyped at more than half a million SNPs (Novembre et al., 2008).[8] The two principal components best able to summarize variation across this huge set of loci correlate tightly with latitude and longitude, respectively. The gist of the analysis is in its title: "Genes Mirror Geography Within Europe." Meanwhile, variation at loci on the Y chromosome (inherited strictly from the paternal line) and in mitochondrial DNA (maternal) has become a basis for successful commercial testing services used by genealogy enthusiasts to identify their geographic origins. Of course, this does not establish a genetic basis for differences in mean height. It is at best suggestive that some groups with unusual stature compared to their neighbors, such as the short Sardinians or the tall Yugoslavs, are also genetically distinct from them. The same is true of correlations between mean height and the national proportions of different clades identified by common Y-chromosome alleles (Grasgruber, Cacek, Kalina, & Sebera, 2014).[9]

Stature is obviously inherited at the individual level, and studies of twins and siblings consistently indicate that roughly 80% of the variability in individual height is genetic in origin (McEvoy & Visscher, 2009). Classical genetics made little progress in understanding this complex, highly polygenic trait, but high-throughput genotyping has changed the game. Genome-wide association (GWA) studies are based on data from individuals whose alleles at large numbers of SNPs have been identified. A GWA study seeks statistical correlations between SNP alleles and phenotypical traits like height. A 2010 study considered nearly 295,000 SNPs statistically associated with height, finding them jointly capable of explaining about half of its variance (Yang et al., 2010). A *biological*, rather than merely statistical, connection with height was established by Allen et al. (2010), who showed that variants associated with height clustered in loci in or near genes with known links to growth or skeletal development.

It bears emphasis that GWA studies control for ancestry to avoid spurious correlations such as that which might emerge between height and the SNPs for blondeness due to their coincidence in Scandinavia (a whimsical but not unrealistic example). Height-associated SNPs display a correlation with stature both between *and within* populations. Importantly, this means that GWA procedures do not confound genetic differences with environmental differences.

But is there any systematic variation across populations in allele frequencies in these height-associated SNPs? Turchin et al. (2012) answer "yes." Comparing northern and southern European populations, they find systematically higher frequencies of the "tall" alleles in the North. Contrasting US residents of North-European ancestry with Spaniards, for example, the authors find a higher frequency in the first group for 85 of 139 SNPs, or 61%. I pursue the same type of investigation on the basis of a 2014 meta-analysis of GWA studies involving 250,000 individuals.[10] Wood et al. (2014) identify 697 SNPs in 423 different loci with both a strong statistical association and a plausible biological connection to height. Allele frequencies for these height-related SNPs can be retrieved from the 1,000 Genomes Project database, a catalogue of fully sequenced genomes from (more than) a thousand individuals in several populations.[11] I examine a subset of 102 of the 697 height-related SNPs with good support for a biological causal effect on height.[12] Table 38.3 summarizes the cross-population comparisons.

The European data underlying Table 38.3 are from four samples of roughly 100 individuals each: Finns, British (England and Scotland), Italians (Tuscany), and Spaniards. It is worth noting that none of these are cases of extreme national average heights. The North-South differences in the first row of Table 38.3 are based on simple averages of the Finnish and British and the Italian and Spanish allele frequencies, respectively.[13] Column 1 shows that, on average, tall alleles are more frequent in northern Europe, but only slightly: about 1.6%. The underlying positive and negative variations are larger, averaging about 5 points in absolute magnitude (Column 2). Differences for a few SNPs are large: as big as +15 percentage points (Column 3). For reference, Table 38.3 also reports intercontinental differences in Rows 2–5, which are much larger. Though quite small on average, the intra-European differences of Row 1 do systematically favor the North. For 64 of 102 SNPs (63%), the tall allele frequency was greater in the North (Column 4).[14]

It may be going too far to claim all this proves that genetic differences make an important contribution to observed mean stature differences. The number of SNPs statistically associated with height is enormous—more than 9,000 if a threshold p-value of

Table 38.3 Population differences in "tall" allele frequencies, 102 single-nucleotide polymorphisms (SNPs; in percentage points)

	Mean difference	Mean absolute difference	Largest difference	Percentage strictly positive
North–South Europe	+1.6	4.8	+14.5	63
Europe–Africa	+3.3	18.0	−56.0	59
Europe–E. Asia	+1.3	15.2	+47.0	49
Europe–S. Asia	+1.3	10.4	−29.0	59
Europe–Native American	+1.2	7.6	−25.0	56

Note: The table reports summary statistics on the differences, in percentage points, between the frequency of the tall allele in samples from the first and second populations in the leftmost column.

.005 is adopted, but the true number may be much larger, since the 9,000 together explain only 29% of the heritable component of height (Wood et al., 2014). Individual effects are generally tiny, and we have no clear idea of the interactions between the genes that the SNPs identify. Epigenetic variation, induced by environmental conditions and transmitted across generations, may also play a role in determining height (Simeone & Alberti, 2014). What *has* been established, beyond doubt, is that between North and South there are systematic differences in allele frequencies right across the genome and specifically in genes causing height. It would be an unlikely coincidence that these differences should happen exactly to cancel out, and the evidence suggests that, on balance, they favor the North.

38.5 Southern European Heights in Long-Run Perspective

For four southern European countries, long-run historical height series can be constructed that run from the 18th to the late 20th century. These are northern Italy, southern France, Spain, and Portugal. Also displayed are the shorter series available for Croatia, Greece, and Turkey. The estimates are in all cases based on measured, not self-reported, heights and are drawn from military records (and hence refer to conscription-aged males). The only exception is the early Turkish numbers.

The estimates for the 18th century are based on relatively scarce individual-level data from military archives and suffer from familiar problems induced by the unsystematic nature of recruiting operations at the time. These include minimum height requirements,

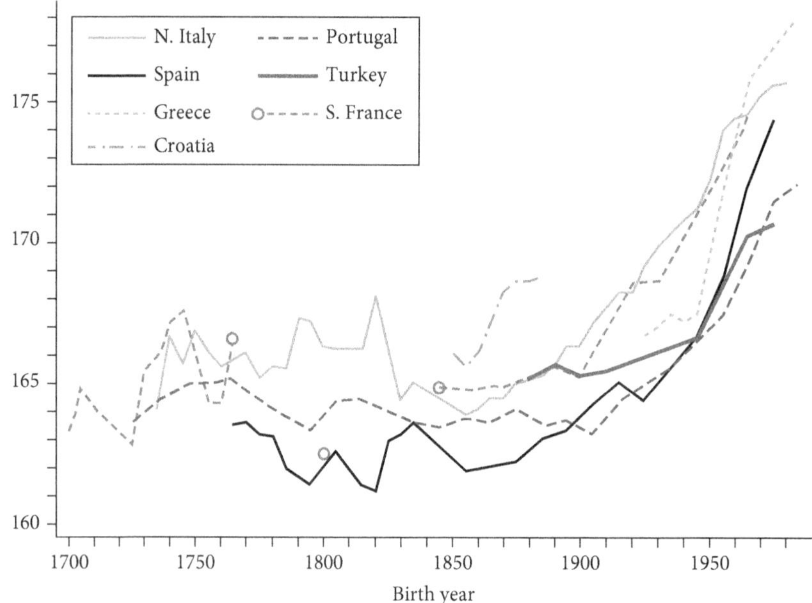

FIGURE 38.4 Adult male stature in southern Europe over the long run (cm).

Sources: See appendix.

heaped and rounded measurement, and nonrandom selection into the sample. The volatility of the early estimates, which we might otherwise interpret as reflecting vulnerability to economic, climatic, or epidemiological shocks, is probably just as much a product of the vagaries of the data and the inadequacies of our statistical methods.

In later years, systematic conscription was introduced yielding more abundant and representative archival data, as well as published statistics on the distribution of height. The Croatian, Greek, and Turkish figures date from this later era, but we have systematic conscription records only for Croatia and for Greece, for birth years 1927–45. Otherwise, we have to rely on smaller scale studies of enlisted soldiers. The late 19th- and early 20th-century Turkish heights are the only case in which we rely on nonmilitary data: a large-scale, nationwide study of 1937 in which more than 35,000 men of all ages were measured. Appendix 1 discusses the sources and methods underlying Figure 38.4 in more detail.

38.6 Declines, Recoveries, and Secular Stagnation: 1700–1850

From the early 18th through the mid-19th centuries, the general impression is of heights fluctuating around a low and stagnant—perhaps even declining—trend. Levels appear strikingly low in comparison to heights attained in the late 20th century, but were not so by the standards of the day. Table 38.4 puts them into comparative perspective for births of the 1780s, a period for which we have estimates for a number of countries. It is interesting that the range spanned for 1780s births, from 161.1 to 166.8 cm, is much narrower than the range for 1980s births in Figure 38.1 (170.6–183.2 cm). In part, that is merely a reflection of the larger sample in the late 20th century, but in part it also reflects the fact that in the earlier period the living conditions and diets of ordinary people *everywhere* were so poor as to stunt their physical development uniformly. In any case, southern

Table 38.4 Mean height estimates for birth cohorts around the 1780s

Country	Age	Birth years	Mean height
Württemberg	24+	1780s	166.8
Sweden	21+	1780s	166.6
Bavaria	21	1780s	166.2
England	20–23	1780s	166.1
North Italy 2	**21**	**1780s**	**165.9**
Saxony	21	1780s	165.9
North Italy 1	**20**	**1780s**	**165.6**
South France 1	**21**	**1760s**	**165.4**
Poland (Galicia)	21	1780s	165.2
Netherlands	20	1795–1804	164.5
Hungary	21	1780s	164.1
Center Italy	**20**	**1780s**	**164.0**
Portugal	**24–50**	**1780s**	**163.8**
France	20–21	1784–92	163.7
Belgium	21	1790s	163.7
Lower Austria	21	1780s	163.5
Moravia	21	1780s	163.3
Spain	**21**	**1780s**	**162.6**
Bohemia	21	1780s	162.5
South France 2	**20**	**1799–1806**	**162.5**
Russia	23 +	1780s	161.1

Notes: North Italy 1, Center Italy, South France 1 and 2, Portugal, and Spain: see Appendix 1. Russia: Mironov (2012), p. 43; all others: A'Hearn (2006).

European heights look rather average from a comparative perspective. Only Spain is clearly near the bottom end of the somewhat compressed distribution.

The other possible exception to this moderately favorable comparison with the rest of Europe is southern France circa 1800. This isolated observation also contributes to an impression of a common downward trend in heights in the late 18th and/or early 19th centuries. As described in the Appendix, the French height data for this period are problematic. Can we trust the estimate?

Throughout France, the generation born around 1800 experienced hardship, being born in the aftermath of the turbulent revolutionary period and growing up during the constant warfare of the Napoleonic period. But things were particularly bad in the South. The region, here defined to include both the Mediterranean and part of the Atlantic coast, had been heavily involved in France's 18th-century trade boom, which came to an untimely end when markets in St. Domingue, Spain, and the Spanish colonies were cut off. Bordeaux had grass growing in the streets, so idle was the town in these years, according to the British consul (Crouzet, 1964). In Languedoc, the export-oriented woolen industry collapsed. Meanwhile, the small owner-occupied and share-tenant farms characteristic of the region were hit by the loss of manpower to the army. Finally, parts of the Mediterranean South, especially Marseille, had long been provisioned from North Africa and the Levant by sea—France lacking a fully integrated national market—and this trade was interrupted by wartime hostilities. The Avignon real wage series in Figure 38.5 reaches an extremely low level in this period. Heights in southern France fall from a centimeter above the national mean in the mid-18th century at least half a centimeter below it in this period. Unusual events, then, characterize this isolated observation, but these are events that we would expect to put pressure on living standards.

Beyond this one episode of coincident economic and biological hardship, what can we learn from a joint reading of the evidence on height and economic variables? Figures 38.5 and 38.6 plot long-run estimates of real wages and real GDP per capita for southern Europe. The real wage estimates are Allen's (2001) welfare ratios: annual earnings at the observed daily wage rate, assuming 250 days of work, expressed in terms of the requirements of a family of four for a respectable life. They refer to an unskilled urban construction laborer. The two exceptions are Istanbul, which is drawn from Özumcur and Pamuk (2002), and Avignon, which is a new estimate described in Appendix 2.[15] The GDP per capita series are recent estimates drawn from several sources, as described in Appendix 3. It is worth emphasizing that the GDP per capita estimates are not independent of the wage and price data used to construct real wages because agricultural output is estimated indirectly from agricultural price movements, assuming a demand function shifted by income as proxied by wages.

Considering the 18th century, the GDP and height evidence aligns rather well. Within southern Europe, both heights and GDP per capita were ranked in the same order: Italy, Portugal, Spain. In a broader comparison, too, stature and economic output were largely in accord. North Italy's respectable mean heights corresponded to a GDP level exceeded only by the Netherlands in the early 18th century. (Britain overtook

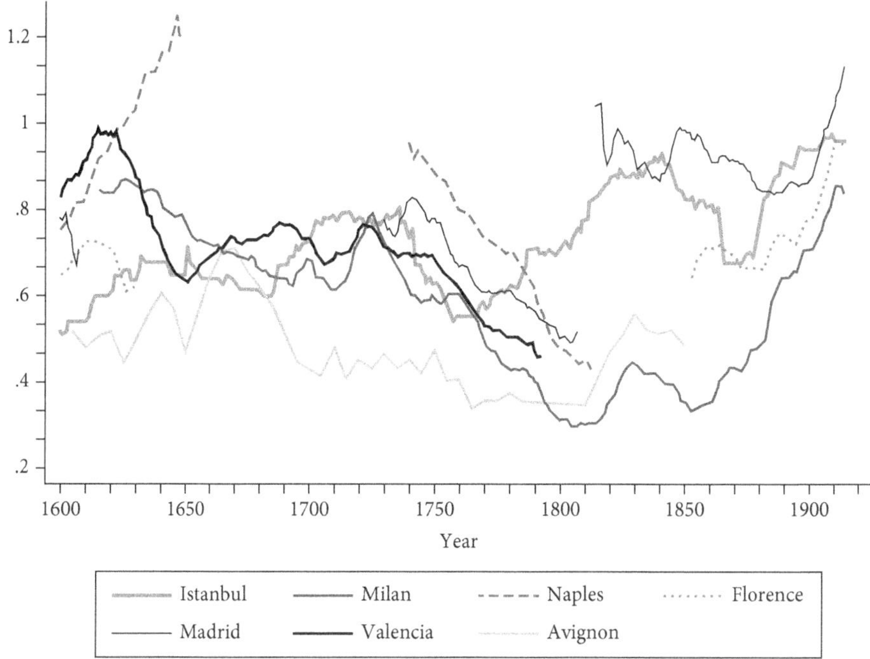

FIGURE 38.5 Real wages in southern European cities.

Notes: Real wages expressed as the purchasing power of 250 days' work in terms of the consumption needs of a family of four. Fifteen-year centered (Istanbul 30) moving averages plotted.

Sources: Istanbul, Özmucur and Pamuk (2002); Avignon, see Appendix 2; all others, Allen (2001).

northern Italy only somewhat later.) At the other extreme, Spanish heights were unusually low in the 18th century, as was GDP; Spanish output per head was the lowest of eight available estimates (adding Belgium, Sweden, and Germany to the countries already mentioned). Unfortunately, we lack comparable estimates for southern France. Isolated guesses for France as a whole suggest that it lagged behind Britain with a GDP per capita level about average for the continent. As for *changes* in stature and GDP over time, these align less neatly, but neither are there important conflicts. In North Italy and in Portugal, the trend in GDP was clearly negative.[16] Spanish GDP was slowly growing, but from a low level.

Real wages do not align neatly with either GDP per capita estimates or height data. By the beginning of the 18th century, Allen's (2001) European great divergence between the northwest and the rest was already in evidence. Real wages in London, Amsterdam, and Antwerp were comfortably above a "respectable" standard, while in other cities they were clearly below it. Low wages in Valencia or Madrid are no surprise, given estimates of Spanish mean height and GDP. But Milan's very low wages clash with both the anthropometric and GDP evidence. Avignon real wages are lower still—as low as any observed in Allen's dataset for all of Europe—but heights in Southern France were quite respectable in mid-century. Nor do Portuguese real wages fit the other evidence: Palma and Reis (2014) estimate Lisbon real wages to be even higher than in London.

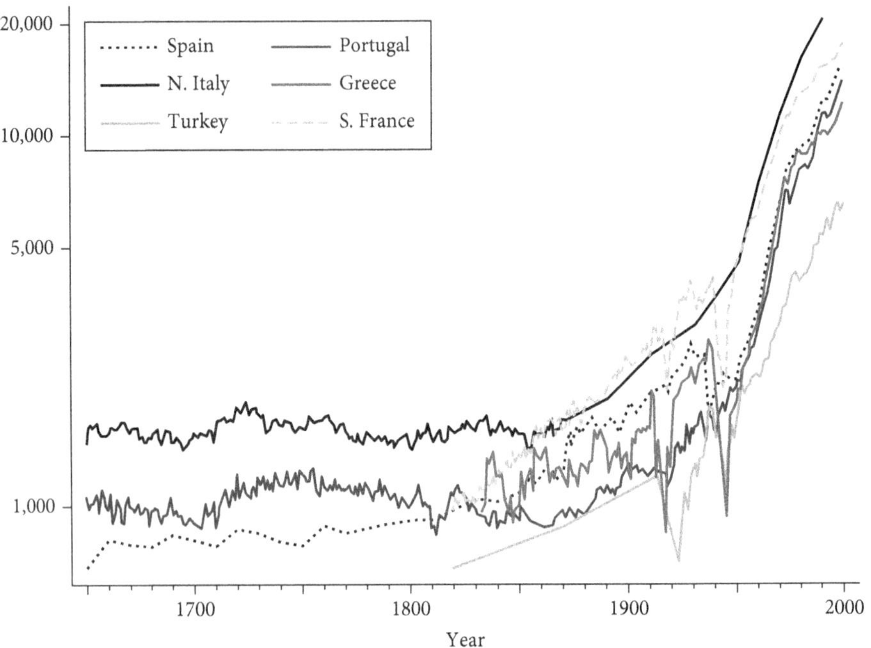

FIGURE 38.6 Real gross domestic product (GDP) per capita estimates, southern Europe.

Sources: See Appendix 3.

If the level of real wages is surprisingly low (judged by heights), so, too, is their downward *trend* surprisingly steep. The most dramatic case is Milan, where the fall is from levels of around 0.7 in the early decades of the century to values below 0.4 by its end. But a similar decline is observed in Valencia, Madrid, Naples, and (somewhat earlier) Avignon. The fall in heights in Spain and Portugal was nothing like as precipitous, and northern Italy did not experience a sustained fall in statures until the 19th century.

A reconciliation between the three indicators is possible if annual days of work per household were increasing over the century. If families substituted market work for leisure or home production they could, to some extent, maintain incomes and protect living standards. To the extent that they were living near the subsistence minimum, this adjustment would have been inescapable. Just such an increase in labor supply has been hypothesized for all three of the north Italian, Spanish, and Portuguese cases (Alvarez-Nogal & Prados de la Escosura, 2012; Malanima, 2011; Palma & Reis, 2014).

Considering the 19th century, as late as 1850 not much had changed; at best, the decline of the late ancien régime had been made good. Southern European heights remained below mid-18th century peaks, stagnant, and in the same rank order. The same generalization holds for GDP per capita, although there are some uncertain signs of growth, from a low level, in Turkey, Spain, and Greece. Only in southern France was a robust, sustained economic expansion under way, one allowing it to catch north Italy by mid-century. The situation with regard to wages is less clear due to gaps in coverage. But in the cases of Milan and Avignon, which we can follow without interruption, wages staged only a partial recovery and remained very low. The situation was apparently different at the other end of the Mediterranean, where Istanbul, having parted company with the western Mediterranean at some point in the 1770s, maintained a fairly high level relative to its own past (although still below what could be considered comfortable).

38.7 Up and Up: 1850–1980

The general impression of the period after 1850 in Figures 38.4 and 38.6 is of heights and GDP both trending up at an accelerating pace, more or less synchronously, while maintaining the same country rankings. But a closer look reveals interesting variations of timing and pace, as we shall see. As for real wages, the data become more abundant in this period, and we can turn to a new source, the revised Williamson (1995) dataset. (For details, see Appendix 2.) The southern European wages plotted in Figure 38.7 refer to

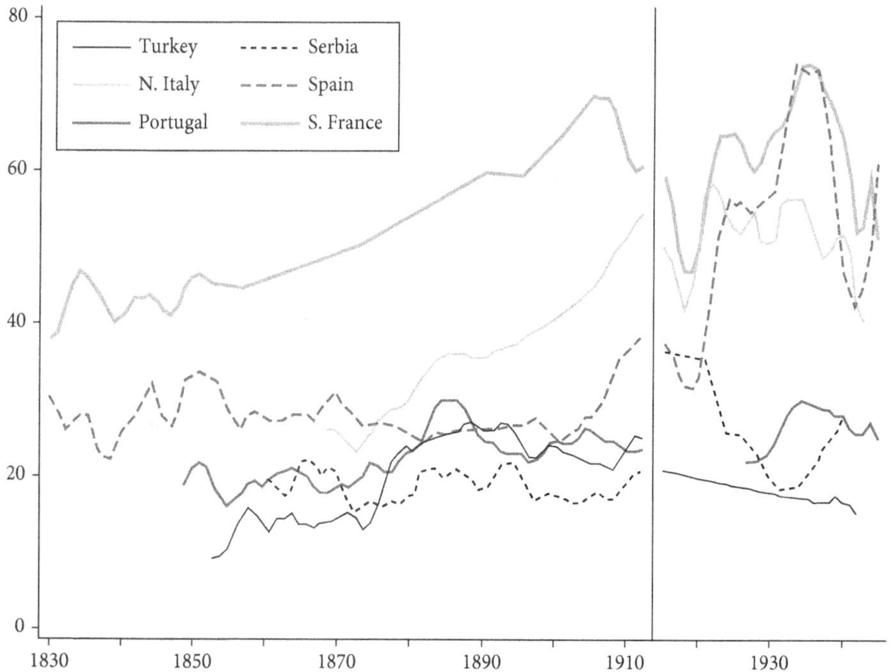

FIGURE 38.7 Real wages in southern Europe, 1850–1945.

Notes: Left panel, Britain in 1905 = 100; right panel, Britain in 1927 = 100. Three-year centered moving averages plotted.

Source: See Appendix 2.

unskilled urban construction laborers. In the left panel, wages are expressed relative to Britain in 1905; in the right panel, relative to the British level of 1927.

Two cases that seem well-paired are northern Italy and southern France. GDP per capita trends and levels were very similar and lay well above the nearest followers. Over the 60 years, from 1870 to 1930, for example, the two maintained a 30% lead over Spain on average. And mean heights in the two neighbors were the tallest in southern Europe—excepting Croatia, of course—until the very end of the period, following similar trajectories. Wages both higher and more steadily growing than elsewhere complete the picture, although the substantial margin in wages favoring the Midi does not fit with the other elements. The similarity of these two regions is interesting, given the dissimilar roles they played in their respective national economies. The north of Italy was the home of modern industry in the country and its most prosperous region. The south of France, although possessed of dynamic industrial centers like Marseille alongside its depopulating internal areas, was instead a lagging part of the French economy, on balance.

Of the Iberian economies, Spain was initially the more dynamic. It forged ahead of a stagnating Portugal in the late 19th century, accumulating a GDP per capita advantage that exceeded 50% throughout much of the early 20th century. Starting from low levels, mean heights, too, overtook the Portuguese by 1900. But Spain let this advantage slip. The Depression, civil war, and the early Franco years crippled the economy. Over the four decades from 1909–13 to 1946–50, GDP per head rose by only 10%; between the peak of 1927 and 1954, there was no improvement at all. Over the same period, Portugal progressed rapidly, closing most of the GDP gap.

Interestingly, the stature of Spanish conscripts born in this difficult period improved steadily—indeed at an accelerating pace.[17] Between 1910 and 1950, the increase was 3.1 cm. A mirror image of this disconnect between economic development and biological well-being is found in Portugal from the 1860s to the early 1900s: while GDP per capita grew by some 35%, heights were stagnant at the same levels that had prevailed a hundred years earlier. And while Portugal's economic performance roughly matched Spain's after the mid-1930s (maintaining a GDP per capita ratio of roughly 90%), heights fell behind. Real wages again have a noisy relationship with the other variables. Before World War II, they are low and stagnant in both countries except for an improbable jump in Spain coinciding with the period of social disruption beginning in the late 1920s.[18] In the postwar decades (not plotted), however, they diverge in the same way as do heights; starting from about 1965, Spanish wages grow to be more than twice Portuguese by the 1980s.

Our knowledge of the eastern Mediterranean economies is less complete. What they appear to have in common are surprising statures. In the case of Croatia, the surprise is extremely tall statures—among the tallest in Europe—at a time when real wages (in neighboring Serbia) were among the continent's lowest and GDP per capita was falling behind Turkey (Maddison-Project, 2013). In the late 19th as in the late 20th century, heights on the Adriatic were inexplicably tall. In Turkey's case, too, the surprise is the initially high level of mean heights at a time when it was one of the poorest countries by either GDP or real wages.[19] Only in the post 1945 era, when overtaken by Spain and Portugal, did Turkey come to have the smallest statures in Europe. It is interesting that the acceleration in heights, however short-lived, preceded the real acceleration in Turkey's economic growth, which takes place in the 1960s. In the case of Greece, what is surprising is the speed and duration of growth in mean stature after 1945. Starting from an already respectable level, mean heights rise by 10.5 cm from mid-1940s to mid-1980s births. By the end of the period, Greek heights clearly exceeded those of southern France or northern Italy, despite the economic gap relative to them not having been closed.

38.8 Conclusion

A line drawn at about 1850 is useful in distinguishing two periods in the history of heights and economic development in southern Europe. Up to this point, levels and trends in height appear to have tracked well the evolution of the economy—perhaps better than real wage estimates. Both heights and GDP per capita stagnated over the long run from the late 17th to the mid-19th century. And it is not implausible to identify a common cycle around that trend, upward until some point in the first half of the 18th century then downward into the early 19th century. The relative rankings of height and income also matched reasonably well, both within southern Europe and in a broader European context.

Interpreting the evidence on real wages is trickier. Low levels to 1850 (Figure 38.5) are certainly consistent with low and stagnant heights and incomes. The same is true of downward trends in wages over much of the 18th century, which appears to have been common across a number of southern European economies, at least in the western Mediterranean. Yet that fall is much more extreme than what is observed for heights or GDP per capita. And the within-south ranking, particularly for Portugal and Istanbul, is inconsistent with height and income estimates.

The evidence on stature in this period thus supports the conjectures of Malanima (2011) and others about increases in days worked per year in Italy and Iberia and the related argument that urban day-wages are a poor guide to living standards in agricultural economies characterized by seasonal underemployment. It is consistent with the notion of a Mediterranean economy distinct from other regions of the European periphery (Reis, 2000) but fails to provide decisive new evidence due to the small sample size. We have continuous series for just three economies, and they do not include the outliers identifiable in broader modern samples.

If heights are perhaps a reasonable proxy for economic development before 1850, afterward their value is probably in providing insight into particular aspects of public health or the relative well-being of children. Mean heights in southern Europe today are not fully explained by either economic variables or rough measures of health, such as life expectancy, with the former Yugoslav countries perhaps the egregious anomaly (as they were in the late 19th century). Some convergence in statures might have been expected as all southern European countries achieved certain absolute levels of income, diet, and public health, but there is none evident in the data. It is quite likely that genetic differences play a role here.

The historical record since 1850 throws up several cases of a "disconnect" between trends in the economy and in stature. Subtle examples in the height record are the sharp acceleration in south France after 1900, the stagnation of Portugal in the late 19th century, the takeoff in Turkey before the acceleration of economic growth, and Greek "super-growth" after World War II. A bigger discrepancy is the rapid improvement in mean heights in Spain across the economically and socially traumatic decades of the mid-20th century. Something similar is observed in south Italy. Between 1911 and 1951, it fell increasingly far behind the north economically, with per capita output growing just 17% as against 80% in the north. But heights rose faster in the *Mezzogiorno*: by 5.3 cm compared with 4.8 cm in the north (A'Hearn & Vecchi, in press; Brunetti, Felice, & Vecchi, in press).

An intriguing possibility is that this improvement in height is related to the eradication of malaria, the incidence of which had been much greater in Italy's southern regions. In the 1880s, malaria mortality rates were as high as 15–20 per thousand in Basilicata, Calabria, Lazio, and Sardinia. By the 1930s, public health measures such as land reclamation in swampy areas and the distribution of quinine had dramatically reduced mortality, but morbidity remained a serious concern until the arrival of DDT with American occupying forces during World War II. Within a few years, the disease had been eradicated, and the generation born around 1950 grew up in a malaria-free world (Atella, Francisci, & Vecchi, 2011; Percoco, 2013). This would be one case of what Steckel (2009) has called a "public health revolution," which loosened the links among urbanization (negative), wealth (positive), and stature.

Returning to the question posed in the introduction about the existence of a Mediterranean economy, the height evidence up to the mid-19th century is clearly supportive but scant. Since then, it is abundant but inconclusive.

Acknowledgments

Thanks for generously sharing data go to Nuno Palma and Jaime Reis; Jean-Pierre Dormois and Jean-Pascal Bassino; Laurent Heyberger, Jeff Williamson, and Kevin O'Rourke; and John Komlos. Thanks for comments and advice to Tim Cheng and Deb Oxley.

APPENDIX 1

HISTORICAL HEIGHT ESTIMATES

North Italy

The estimates for birth years 1735–1839 are new, based on a significant expansion of the Habsburg Army dataset described in A'Hearn (2003). Sample sizes are now on the order of 500–1,000 for most birth quinquennia, except for 1800–19. Maximum likelihood estimation based on a truncated normal distribution is employed again here, this time without imposing either a predetermined error variance or a dummy variable for the earliest recruiting regime. These changes result in a lower level and a flatter profile for heights relative to the 2003 article. A smaller change regards birthplace controls: the present estimates omit city size and substitute regional for provincial dummies. "North Italy" is a weighted average of Piemonte, Lombardia, and Veneto using 1861 regional population figures. (In the case of Veneto, this population is "backcast" from 1871.)

Birth years 1855–1910 are drawn from A'Hearn and Vecchi (in press) and are based on annually published provincial height distributions for all men of draft age, corrected for the inclusion of re-examined conscripts from previous drafts and for age at measurement (standardized to 20 years). Numbers are on the order of 100,000 per 5-year birth cohort. The North Italy and Rest-of-Italy figures are obtained by aggregating the underlying provincial distributions. Finally, mean heights for birth years 1918–80 are drawn directly from the 2011 edition of the *Sommario di statistiche storiche* (Table 38.4.16.1). The North Italy and Rest-of-Italy aggregates are obtained as population-weighted averages of the published regional figures in SSS, linearly interpolating population between decennial censuses.

The estimate for central Italy in Table 38.4 is from Coppola (2013) and refers to a four-region average for a rural-born agricultural laborer aged 20, born in the 1780s. The "North Italy 2" estimate in Table 38.4 is from A'Hearn (2006).

South France

South is defined as the modern regions of Provence-Alpes-Cote d'Azur, Languedoc-Roussillon, Midi-Pyrenees, and Aquitaine; Corsica is excluded.

For the ancien régime period, mean heights are estimated from individual data collected and analyzed by Komlos (2003), by truncated maximum likelihood assuming a Normal distribution. Results are sensitive to choices regarding truncation points and the standard deviation of heights. I follow Komlos in imposing a minimum of 62 French inches throughout (even when the distribution for an enlistment period suggests a lower cutoff might be appropriate) and restricting the standard deviation to 6.86 cm rather than estimating it from the data. Other choices tend to produce taller mean statures. 61.75 inches is the truncation point used in the likelihood function to account for rounding to the nearest half-inch. In addition to dummies for birth decade, age at the time of measurement is the only other control included in the model. The estimates refer to soldiers aged 21.

Because interest here centers on the South and on the 18th century, some differences are introduced relative to the analysis of Komlos (2003). Separate estimates of the trend in heights in the South were not significantly different from the trend in the rest of France (either meaningfully or statistically) but were imprecisely estimated and volatile. Accordingly, I estimated a model using the entire sample with a common trend and a

South dummy to capture any difference in levels. I restricted the sample to 18th-century births. Finally, again to maximize sample size, I analyze soldiers of all ages together (with age controls).

The estimate of 162.46 cm for 1799–1806 births in Figure 38.4 and Table 38.4 ("South France 2") is based on département-level data reported in Aron, Dumont, and Le Roy Ladurie (1972). The data are problematic and deserve a fuller discussion. On this, see also Weir (1997), Heyberger (2014), Bassino and Dormois (2009), or Duclos, Leblanc, and Sahn (2011). The original sources report height frequencies (in whole French inches) among conscripts above the minimum requirement of 4'11", a calculated mean for this truncated sample (in centimeters), and the number of conscripts exempted from service due to insufficient stature. The figure used here is a compromise (simple average) of two calculations. The first converts the published truncated mean to an estimate of the population mean, assuming a Gaussian distribution with a standard deviation of 6.86 cm. The second calculates the sample mean from the published distribution, assuming all conscripts had the exact height describing their interval (e.g., 61 inches) and imputing to those exempted for short stature a height of 57 inches. On average, the second method yields somewhat higher estimates. Both measures are aggregated up from départements using as weights the number examined in the class of 1829 (taken from Heyberger 2005). The estimate for all of France ca. 1790 in Table 38.4 is from Weir (1997) and is an estimate of the national median.

The estimate for the class of 1848 is based on individual-level data kindly provided by Laurent Heyberger for the southern départements in his sample. As described by Heyberger (2014), these observations are drawn from original conscription lists and cover all examined conscripts, including those failing to reach the minimum requirement. I report a simple average.

The estimates at decade intervals from 1860 to 1940 are from Chamla (1964), who drew samples of individual heights from the conscription lists (like Heyberger, including all individuals above and below the minimum) in all départements. Département means were aggregated using Chamla's sample sizes as weights. (If Chamla reported 110 heights and that these were a 1/20 sample from the conscription lists, the weight is 20 × 110 = 2,200.)

The final estimate, for births 1966–71, is based on a large sample of recruits (92,000 in the South) measured in 1988–89 when they were 18 to 22 years old, as reported by Pineau (1993). An average of southern département means was calculated using as means the number of observations. The South is 0.6 cm shorter than the remainder of the country in these data.

Portugal

The Portuguese series is drawn from Stolz, Baten, and Reis (2013). The estimates are based on data similar to those for North Italy, analyzed using similar techniques. Sample sizes are initially small, but from the 1830s onward number several thousand per birth decade. The estimates refer to a nationwide average for a soldier aged 24–50. The most recent statistics (from birth year 1966 on) are based on the entire population of draft-eligible young men, measured at age 18. The mid-20th century is covered by random samples of conscripts from Southern Portugal. The switch from measurement at age 20 to age 18 with the draft of 1960 (hence birth year 1940) could impart a small downward bias to the series from that point on.

Spain (Central/Mediterranean)

The early Spanish estimates (births 1768–1836) are drawn from Garcia-Montero (2014) and refer to a conscript aged 21 from central Spain (Madrid and Toledo province). From 1790 births onward, the data are of poor quality in the sense that for few individuals are both age and a numerical measure of height available. Regarding height, the information is typically limited to whether or not the conscript satisfied the minimum height requirement (MHR). On the basis of generally small samples, the author calculates the share of conscripts meeting the MHR, then estimates mean height assuming a normal distribution with a standard deviation of 6.86 cm, given the known MHR. I have calculated 5-year birth cohort averages to 1786 and 10-year averages for the more sparsely covered period 1790–1836.

The estimates from 1850 onward are taken from Maria-Dolores and Martinez-Carrion (2011). For birth years 1837–1948, the authors rely on a large sample of individual-level height measurements for conscripts at known ages between 19 and 21, not subject to a MHR. The data come from Spain's southeast Mediterranean coast (Andalusia, Murcia, and the Valencia region). In this period, heights in this area were roughly equal to the national average. For birth years after 1948, the authors rely on published statistics giving the share of all men of conscription age in different height categories.

Greece

Mean heights for each year's draft class were published for birth years 1927–45 and are reported in Sapounaki-Dracaki (1998), from which source I have calculated 5-year birth cohort averages. Estimates for three later periods (late '40s, late '60s, and the 1980s) are taken from small-sample studies of serving Greek military personnel. These are reported in Papadimitriou et al. (2008).

Turkey

The estimates for Turkish men in recent decades are drawn from three studies of moderately sized samples of serving soldiers. Kayis and Özok (1991) calculated the mean height of 5,109 soldiers aged 20–26, born in the mid 1960s. Özer (2008) reports the findings of Emekli and Kir regarding 1,865 conscripts aged 20 born in the late 1940s, and 1,159 conscripts aged 19 or more in 1977, respectively.

Turkey is the only case in which I rely on nonmilitary data, exploiting the extraordinary national anthropometric survey undertaken by Afet Inan in 1937. More than 35,000 men of all ages were measured. I rely on the mean heights by age group as reported by Özer (2008). A 1963 NATO study by Hertzberg et al. and reported by Özer is not considered here due to its focus on pilots and aircrews, whose heights were clearly above average.

Croatia

The Croatian estimates are taken from Komlos (2007) and are based on large samples of individual measurements of conscripts for the Austro-Hungarian army in Zagreb and Zara. There is no truncation problem, but age at measurement changed over the period in a way that could be only imperfectly controlled for. This should not be responsible for the upward trend observed.

APPENDIX 2

REAL WAGES

1700–1850

For most cities, the real wages are welfare ratios drawn from Allen (2001). As described in the text, the series for Istanbul is taken from Özumcur and Pamuk (2002) and converted to a welfare ratio on the basis of Pamuk (2005).

The series for Avignon is really a "grain wage" (liters of grain purchasable with a day's wage) masquerading as a welfare ratio. For Strasbourg, where both are available, movements in the two are highly correlated.

The wage data are for unskilled workers in Avignon, taken from Rosenthal (1992). Avignon was not a major city, and, in this sense, the comparison with other cities in Allen's dataset is problematic. It is the only southern French city for which wage data extending into the 19th century could be found. Rosenthal's figures in livres (or francs) were converted to silver using Allen's conversion ratios.

Wheat price data for various French cities including Avignon are taken from the Allen and Unger commodity price database. Price levels differed across southern French markets in the 18th century, but all price series move closely together. (A partial exception is Marseille, which imported wheat from the Levant and North Africa.) Compared with Strasbourg, Avignon has both high wages and high prices in the 18th century.

Most southern French price series end with the Revolution, but there is a long time series available for Toulouse (downloadable from EH.net, contributed by Roehner). In the 18th century, the correlation of Toulouse and Avignon prices is 0.82. These prices were converted to silver and the grain wage for Avignon computed.

The last step was to relate this to Allen's welfare ratios, which are based on a broader basket of consumption goods. Grain wages in Strasbourg and Avignon share a similar trend and are not too far apart in the 18th century. In 1745 (and at one or two other points), they are exactly equal. Strasbourg's welfare ratio in the years around 1745 was 0.53, so this is the value to which the Avignon grain wage index is anchored.

1850–1980

The real wage series in Figure 38.7 are generally taken from Williamson's (1995) dataset, as updated in O'Rourke and Williamson (1998). Wages for Serbia and Turkey are from Williamson (1998, appendix), benchmarked relative to British levels using GDP per capita in 1913 (from Maddison, 2013) as described in Williamson (2000).

National real wage indices for the period up to 1913 are expressed relative to Britain based on a careful purchasing power parity conversion of wage rates for comparable occupations in the 1905–13 period, when detailed information is available. The series in Figure 38.7, left panel, are all expressed relative to the real wage in Britain in 1905. A similar exercise for 1927 pegs national indices to Britain for the transwar period. Comparisons across World War I are not undertaken due to significant changes in relative prices. The series in Figure 38.7, right panel, are expressed relative to the real wage in Britain in 1927.

In general, the real wage series refer to unskilled urban construction laborers, but there are exceptions relevant for southern Europe. In particular, French real wages are an average for nonfarm workers; Italian wages are for industrial workers (primarily in the north); Spanish wages after 1899 are for unskilled textile workers; and Turkish wages after 1913 are primarily for industrial workers. This could affect the trends in these series, which could reflect, for example, evolving skill premia in industry. The *levels* of the real wage series should not be distorted, given the accurate benchmarking exercise described earlier.

The national index for France is converted to a southern France basis using data from Bassino and Dormois (2006), kindly supplied by the authors. Dormois and Bassino calculate "welfare ratios" in the style of Allen (2001) for individual départements in 1853, 1857, 1874, 1891, 1896, 1901, and 1906. I calculate simple averages for the southern départements and for France as a whole. I use the south-to-France ratios (1.04, 1.04, 0.99, 0.95, 0.90, 0.93, 0.92) to adjust Williamson's national real wage series, assuming constant ratios of 1.04 prior to 1853 and 0.92 after 1906.

APPENDIX 3

REAL GDP PER CAPITA

All series are expressed in 1990 dollars, converted at purchasing power parity (ppp) exchange rates.

North Italy

A postunification (post-1871, more accurately) series for the Center-North is derived as follows. The national GDP per capita series in euros in Brunetti, Felice, and Vecchi (in press) is converted first to lire (at 1936 lire/euro), then to nominal 1990 dollars (at the ppp rate of 1,384 lire/dollar), then to constant 1990 dollars (using the Brunetti et al. real GDP per capita series rebased to 1990 = 1).

Brunetti et al. report separate estimates of real GDP pc for the Center-North in selected years (the first is 1871), which I convert to index values relative to the national average. These are multiplied by the real 1990 ppp dollar national series to yield the post-1861 estimates plotted in Figure 38.6.

Malanima's (2011) long-run annual real GDP per capita series for the Center-North, 1310–1913, is then tied to the Vecchi-derived series in 1871.

Portugal

The estimates for 1530–1850 are from Palma and Reis (2014), kindly provided by the authors. These are linked to the Maddison-Project (2013) estimates in 1850.

Spain

The series to 1850 (1285–1855) is from Alvarez-Nogal and Prados de la Escosura (2012), kindly furnished by the authors. The figures are decade averages. This series is linked in 1850 to the Maddison-Project (2013) series.

Greece

This series, 1833–2008, is taken entirely from the Maddison-Project (2013). It incorporates the latest estimates by Kostelenos et al. going back to 1833.

Turkey

From 1923, real GDP per capita is from Maddison-Project (2013). Earlier figures for 1820, 1870, and 1913 are from Pamuk (2006).

South France

The data in Combes et al. (Combes, Lafourcade, Thisse, & Toutain, 2011) indicate that gross value added per inhabitant in the départements of the South, as defined here, was 85.1% of the French national figure in 1860 and 87.8% in 1930. Eurostat regional data indicate that the corresponding figure for 2000 was 87.6%. The series presented here is Maddison's estimates (2013) for France, multiplied by 0.86. This cannot be too far off for the long-run trend from 1860 to 1930 and again to 2000, but will miss region-specific shocks like the one described in the text for the Revolutionary and Napoleonic periods. It may also be misleading for 1820–60.

Other Countries

Sources for other countries mentioned in the text but not plotted in Figure 38.6 are as follows: Belgium: Buyst (2011); Sweden: Edvinsson (2011); Britain: Broadberry, Campbell, Klein, Overton, and van Leuwen (2011); Germany: Pfister (2011); Netherlands: van Zanden and van Leeuwen (2012).

APPENDIX 4

Appendix Figure: bivariate correlations with mean height in late 20th century Europe.

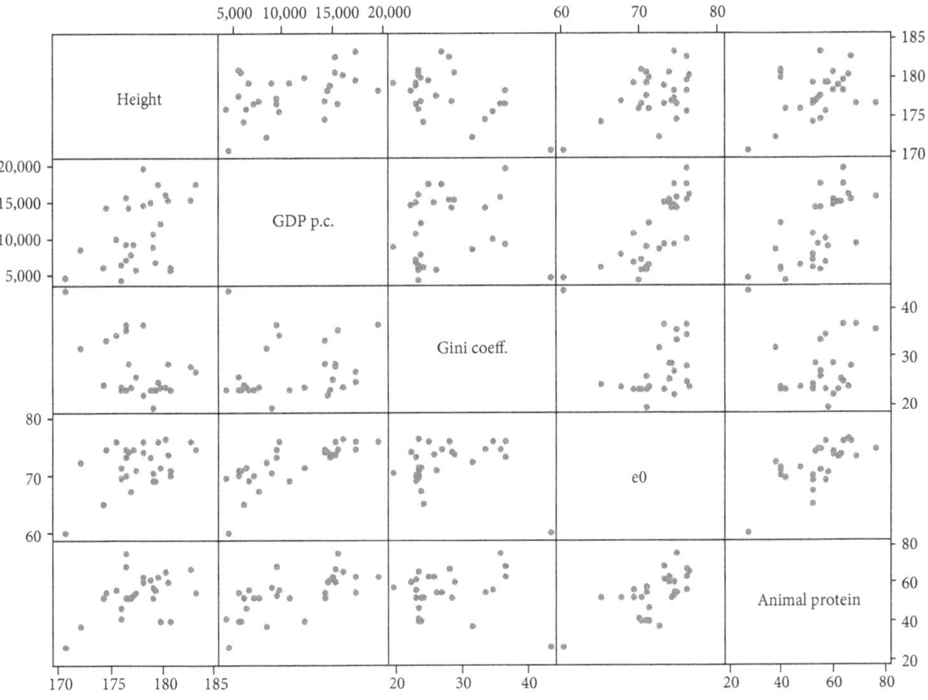

Note: Each panel of the chart is a bivariate scatterplot of a wealth (gross domestic product per capita, Gini index) or health (life expectancy at birth, animal protein availability) variable in the 1980s against the mean height of men born in that decade, with the markers representing countries. The lower triangle of panels is a mirror image of the upper.

Sources: See text and appendices

Notes

1. By excluding North Africa and the Levant, this definition betrays the vision of Braudel and other Mediterraneanists, but the absence of long-run historical evidence on stature, wages, and GDP per capita for these economies leaves little choice in the matter.
2. Baten and Blum's figures for the Czech Republic and Hungary have been "projected forward" to the 1980s assuming a continuation of earlier growth rates (and checking for

plausibility against other estimates). When drawing from other sources, only estimates based on samples of at least 1,000 individuals were used. The estimate for Turkey is taken from a study of conscripts born in the late 1970s, reported in Özer (2008). Estimates for Bulgaria, Romania, Serbia, Slovenia, and Switzerland were taken from Grasgruber et al. (2014). From the same source was constructed a 1985 population-weighted average for the former Yugoslav states Bosnia-Herzegovina, Croatia, Macedonia, and Montenegro, which together reached the threshold of 1,000.

3. For reference, if the United States were included in Figure 38.2, it would lie below the regression line, just beyond the right margin, with 1985 GDP per capita of $20,700 and mean height a bit below Switzerland. Were attention restricted to white men, mean height would be about 0.5 cm above Switzerland.
4. Cross-country comparisons of the Gini index are problematic because it is sensitive to differences in underlying data, definitions, and method, as well as to the form of the distribution. "Adult-equivalent" is a simplification. To reflect economies possible in a large household, equivalence scales give additional adults a weight close to that of children. The estimates for Portugal and the United Kingdom refer to disposable income rather than expenditure and are from the Chartbook of Inequality.
5. This section draws throughout on Cavalli-Sforza et al. (1994).
6. Recall that DNA is like a helical ladder in which the rungs are bonds between the compounds adenine (A), cytosine (C), guanine (G), and thymine (T). G pairs with C, A with T. A nucleotide combines one of these four with a sugar and a phosphate. *Allele* in this context no longer refers to phenotypes such as blood group, but to alternative nucleotides in the same location.
7. Because humans inherit one chromosome each from their mother and father, we could observe any of the homozygous reference GG, heterozygous GT, and the homozygous alternative TT genotypes.
8. A subset of these individuals (1,387) and SNPs (197,146) were used in the analysis described here.
9. Here, *allele* refers not to an individual SNP but to a pattern of variants that occur together over a stretch of DNA.
10. The individuals were all European or of European ancestry. It is possible that the SNPs explaining height variation within Europe do not explain variation between Europe and other parts of the world.
11. www.1000genomes.org.
12. The sample includes SNPs in loci in or near genes that were identified both in previous studies and by the analysis of Wood et al. as having a plausible biological link to height, as set out in their supplementary table 9. All SNPs in these loci, even if "at the wrong end" of the locus and closer to a different gene, were included. There is some overlap between the SNPs considered here and those studied by Turchin et al. (2012).
13. This obscures some variation within North and South, and the Finns are known to be genetic outliers. But none of the four country-to-country comparisons yields a picture different from the one in Table 38.3.
14. This would be an unlikely sampling outcome if the true differences were equally likely to be positive or negative. Discarding the four ties, the probability of 64 or more "successes" in 98 draws is only 0.0016.
15. The real wage estimates in Özmucur and Pamuk (2002) were converted to welfare ratios on the basis of Pamuk (2005).

16. The north Italian case deserves further discussion. Earlier estimates by A'Hearn (2003) indicated a higher level and an earlier fall in mean heights. This better matched GDP and real wage trends. But those height estimates were based on a more prescriptive econometric specification, one fixing the standard deviation of heights and including an early recruiting regime dummy, that is no longer justifiable with the larger sample now available. But the issue is not entirely settled. Coppola's (2013) recent estimates based on the armies of the Papal State match A'Hearn (2003) in showing a clear late 18th-century decline.
17. The "hiccup" in the Spanish mean height series between 1915 and 1925 could reflect hardship experienced in the years immediately prior to measurement in the difficult 1930s and '40s. It remains surprising that men born in those years thrived.
18. The switch from decline to growth in Spanish real wages beginning about 1900 has to be treated with suspicion because it coincides with a switch in the sources from Madrid construction laborers to Barcelona textile workers.
19. It is worth remembering that the Turkish height estimates for the late 19th and early 20th centuries refer to adult civilians of all ages, rather than conscripts aged 20.

References

A'Hearn, B. (2003). Anthropometric evidence on living standards in northern Italy, 1730–1860. *Journal of Economic History*, 63(2), 351–381.

A'Hearn, B. (2006). Remapping Italy's Path to the 19th century: Anthropometric signposts. *Journal of European Economic History*, 35(2), 349–392.

A'Hearn, B. (2014). The British industrial revolution in a European Mirror. In J. R. Floud, J. Humphries, & P. Johnson (Eds.), *The Cambridge economic history of modern Britain* (Vol. 1, pp. 1–52). Cambridge, England: Cambridge University Press.

A'Hearn, B., & Vecchi, G. (in press). Height. In G. Vecchi (Ed.), *For better and for worse: Italian living standards, 1861–2011*. Oxford, England: Oxford University Press.

Allen, R. (2001). The great divergence in European wages and prices from the Middle Ages to the First World War. *Explorations in Economic History*, 38, 411–447.

Allen, R. (2009). *The British Industrial Revolution in global perspective.* Cambridge, England: Cambridge University Press.

Allen, H., Estrada, K., Lettre, G., Berndt, S., Weedon, M., Rivadeneira, F., . . . Hirschhorn, J. N. (2010). Hundreds of variants clustered in genomic loci and biological pathways affect human height. *Nature*, 467, 832–838.

Alvarez-Nogal, C., & Prados de la Escosura, L. (2012). The rise and fall of Spain, 1270–1850. *Economic History Review*, 66(1), 1–37.

Aron, J.-P., Dumont, P., & Le Roy Ladurie, E. (1972). *Anthropologie du conscrit français d'après les comptes numériques et sommaires du recrutement de l'armée1819-26*. Paris: Mouton.

Atella, V., Francisci, S., & Vecchi, G. (2011). Salute. In G. Vecchi (Ed.), *In ricchezza e povertà. Il benessere degli italiani dall'Unità a oggi* (pp. 73–129). Bologna: Il Mulino.

Bassino, J.-P., & Dormois, J.-P. (2006). *Were French Republicans serious about equality? Convergence in real wages, literacy, and the biological standard of living in France 1845–1913*. Unpublished manuscript.

Bassino, J.-P., & Dormois, J.-P. (2009). Comment tenir compte des erreurs de mesure dans l'estimation de la stature des conscrits français? *Histoire, économie et société*, 28(1), 97–122.

Bateman, V. (2010). Market integration in the Mediterranean: 1500-1900. Unpublished manuscript, Gonville and Caius College, University of Cambridge.

Baten, J. (1999). *Ernährung und wirtschaftliche entwicklung in Bayern (1730–1880)*. Stuttgart: Franz Steiner Verlag.

Baten, J., & Blum, M. (2012). Growing tall but unequal: New findings and background evidence on anthropometric welfare in 156 countries, 1810–1989. *Economic History of Developing Regions*, *27*(Suppl. 1), S66–S85.

Baten, J., & Murray, J. (2000). Heights of men and women in nineteenth century Bavaria: Economic, nutritional, and disease influences. *Explorations in Economic History*, *37*, 351–369.

Braudel, F. (1972). *The Mediterranean and the Mediterranean world in the age of Phillip II*. London: William Collins Sons. (First published in French, 1949).

Broadberry, S., Campbell, B., Klein, A., Overton, M., & van Leuwen, B. (2011). British economic growth, 1270–1870: An output-based approach. Unpublished manuscript.

Brunetti, A., Felice, E., & Vecchi, G. (in press). Income. In G. Vecchi (Ed.), *For better and for worse: Italian living standards, 1861–2011*. Oxford, England: Oxford University Press.

Burke, E. (2012). Toward a comparative history of the Modern Mediterranean, 1750–1919. *Journal of World History*, *23*(4), 907–939.

Buyst, E. (2011, March). *Towards estimates of long term growth in the southern low countries ca. 1500–1846*. Paper presented at the Conference on Quantifying Long Run Economic Development, Venice, Italy.

Cacciari, E., Milani, S., Balsamo, A., Spada, E., Bona, G., Cavallo, L., . . . Cicognani, A. (2006). Italian cross-sectional growth charts for height, weight and BMI (2 to 20 yr). *Journal of Endocrinological Investigation*, *29*, 581–593.

Cavalli-Sforza, L., Menozzi, P., & Piazza, A. (1994). *The history and geography of human genes*. Princeton, NJ: Princeton University Press.

Chamla, M.-C. (1964). L'accroissement de la stature en France de 1800 à 1960: Comparaison avec les pays d'Europe occidentale. *Bulletins et Mémoires de la Société d'anthropologie de Paris*, *6*, 201–278.

Combes, P.-F., Lafourcade, M., Thisse, J.-F., & Toutain, J.-C. (2011). The rise and fall of spatial inequalities in France: A long-run perspective. *Explorations in Economic History*, *48*, 243–271.

Coppola, M. (2013). The biological standard of living and mortality in Central Italy at the beginning of the 19th century. *Economics and Human Biology*, *11*, 453–464.

Crouzet, F. (1964). Wars, blockade, and economic change in Europe, 1792–1815. *Journal of Economic History*, *24*(4), 567–588.

Dincecco, M. (2009). Fiscal centralization, limited government, and public revenues in Europe, 1650–1913. *Journal of Economic History*, *69*(1), 48–103.

Duclos, J.-Y., Leblanc, J., & Sahn, D. (2011). Comparing population distributions from bin-aggregated sample data: An application to historical height data from France. *Economics and Human Biology*, *9*, 419–437.

Edvinsson, R. (2011). New estimates of Swedish GDP by activity 1665–2010. *Stockholm Papers in Economic History*, *12*, 1-62.

Food and Agriculture Organization (FAO) of the United Nations. *FAOSTAT* online database. Retrieved January, 2015, from faostat.fao.org/site/354/default.aspx

Garcia-Montero, H. (2014). *Estatura y niveles de vida en la España interior, 1765–1840*. PhD dissertation, Universidad Complutense de Madrid.

Grasgruber, P., Cacek, J., Kalina, T., & Sebera, M. (2014). The role of nutrition and genetics as key determinants of the positive height trend. *Economics and Human Biology*, *15*, 81–100.

Heyberger, L. (2005). *Santé et developpement économique en France au XIX siècle: Essai d'histoire anthropométrique*. Paris: Harmattan.

Heyberger, L. (2014). Received wisdom versus reality: Height, nutrition, and urbanization in mid-nineteenth-century France. *Cliometrica*, *8*(1), 115–140.

Horden, P., & Purcell, N. (2000). *The corrupting sea: A study of Mediterranean History*. Oxford, England: Blackwell.

Horden, P., & Purcell, N. (2006). The Mediterranean and 'the New Thalassology', *American Historical Review*, *111*(3), 722–740.

Kayis, B., & Özok, A. (1991). The anthropometry of Turkish army men. *Applied Ergonomics*, *22*(1), 49–54.

Komlos, J. (2003). An anthropometric history of early-modern France. *European Review of Economic History*, *7*, 159-189.

Komlos, J. (2007). Anthropometric evidence on economic growth, biological well-being and regional convergence in the Habsburg Monarchy, c. 1850–1910. *Cliometrica*, *1*, 211-237.

Maddison, A. (2010). *Statistics on world population, GDP and per capita GDP, 1–2008 AD*. Retrieved from www.ggdc.net/maddison/oriindex.htm, 2010 version.

Maddison-Project. (2013). Retrieved from http://www.ggdc.net/maddison/maddison-project/home.htm, 2013 version.

Malanima, P. (2011). The long decline of a leading economy: GDP in central and northern Italy, 1300–1913. *European Review of Economic History*, *15*, 169–219.

Maria-Dolores, R., & Martinez-Carrion, J. (2011). The relationship between height and economic development in Spain, 1850–1958. *Economics and Human Biology*, *9*, 30–44.

McEvoy, B., & Visscher, P. (2009). Genetics of human height. *Economics and Human Biology*, *7*, 294–306.

Mironov, B. (2012). *The standard of living and revolutions in Russia, 1700–1917*. Abingdon, England: Routledge.

Novembre, J., Johnson, T., Bryc, K., Kutalic, Z., Boyko, A., Auton, A., . . . Bustamante, C. D. (2008). Genes mirror geography within Europe. *Nature*, *456*, 98–103.

O'Rourke, K., & Williamson, J. (1998). Around the European periphery 1870–1913: Globalization, schooling, and growth. *European Review of Economic History*, *1*, 153–190.

Özer, B. (2008). Secular trend in body height and weight of Turkish adults. *Anthropological Science*, *116*(3), 191–199.

Özmucur, S., & Pamuk, S. (2002). Real wages and standards of living in the Ottoman Empire, 1489-1914. *Journal of Economic History*, *62*, 293-321.

Palma, N., & Reis, J. (2014). *Portuguese demography and economic growth, 1500–1850*. Unpublished manuscript.

Pamuk, S. (2005). Urban real wages around the eastern Mediterranean in comparative perspective, 1100–2000. *Research in Economic History*, *23*, 209–228.

Pamuk, S. (2006). Estimating economic growth in the Middle East since 1820. *Journal of Economic History*, *66*(3), 809–828.

Papadimitriou, A., Fytanidis, G., Douros, K., Papadimitriou, D. T., Nicolaidou, P., & Fretzayas, A. (2008). Greek young men grow taller. *Acta Paediatrica*, *97*, 1105–1107.

Percoco, M. (2013). The fight against disease: Malaria and economic development in Italian regions. *Economic Geography*, *89*(2), 105–125.

Pfister, U. (2011, March). *Economic growth in Germany, 1500–1850*. Paper presented at the Conference on Quantifying Long Run Economic Development, Venice, Italy.

Pineau, J.-C. (1993). La stature en France depuis un siècle: Évolution générale et régionale. *Bulletins et Mémoires de la Société d'anthropologie de Paris*, 5(1–2), 257–268.

Reis, J. (2000). How poor was the European periphery before 1850? The Mediterranean vs. Scandinavia. In J. Williamson & S. Pamuk (Eds.), *The Mediterranean response to globalization before 1950* (pp. 17–44). London, England: Routledge.

Rosario, A., Schienkiewitz, A., & Neuhauser, H. (2011). German height references for children aged 0 to under 18 years compared to WHO and CDC growth charts. *Annals of Human Biology*, 38(2), 121–130.

Rosenthal, J.-L. (1992). *The fruits of revolution. property rights, litigation, and French agriculture, 1700–1860*. Cambridge, UK: Cambridge University Press.

Sapounaki-Dracaki, L. (1998). Height and nutritional status in Greece. In J. Komlos & J. Baten (Eds.), *The biological standard of living in comparative perspective* (pp. 408–412). Stuttgart: Franz Steiner Verlag.

Schönbeck, Y., Talma, H., van Dommelen, P., Bakker, B., Buitendijk, S., HiraSing, R., & van Buuren, S. (2013). The world's tallest nation has stopped growing taller: The height of Dutch children from 1955 to 2009. *Pediatric Research*, 73(3), 371–377.

Simeone, P., & Alberti, S. (2014). Epigenetic heredity of human height. *Physiological Reports*, 2(6), e12047.

Steckel, R. (2009). Heights and human welfare: Recent developments and new directions. *Explorations in Economic History*, 46, 1–23.

Stolz, Y., Baten, J., & Reis, J. (2013). Portuguese living standards, 1720–1980, in European comparison: Heights, income, and human capital. *Economic History Review*, 66(2), 545–578.

Turchin, M., Chiang, C., Palmer, C., Sankararaman, S., Reich, D., Genetic Investigation of Anthropometric Traits Consortium, & Hirschhorn, J. N. (2012). Evidence of widespread selection on standing variation in Europe at height-associated SNPs. *Nature Genetics*, 44(9), 1015–1019.

van Zanden, J.-L., & van Leeuwen, B. (2012). Persistent but not consistent: The growth of national income in Holland 1347–1807. *Explorations in Economic History*, 49, 119–130.

Weir, D. (1997). Economic welfare and physical well-being in France, 1750–1990. In R. Steckel & R. Floud (Eds.), *Health and welfare during industrialization* (pp. 161–200). Chicago: University of Chicago Press.

Williamson, J. (1995). The evolution of global labor markets since 1830: Background evidence and hypotheses. *Explorations in Economic History*, 32, 141–196.

Williamson, J. (1998). *Real wages and relative factor prices in the Third World 1820–1940: The Mediterranean Basin* (Discussion Paper No. 1842). Harvard Institute of Economic Research.

Williamson, J. (2000). Real wages and relative factor prices around the Mediterranean, 1500–1940. In J. Williamson & S. Pamuk (Eds.), *The Mediterranean response to globalization before 1950* (pp. 45–75). London, England: Routledge.

Wood, A., Esko, T., Yang, J., Vedantam, S., Pers, T., Gustafsson, S., . . . Frayling, T. M. (2014). Defining the role of common variation in the genomic and biological architecture of adult human height. *Nature Genetics*, 46(11), 1173–1186.

Yang, J., Benyamin, B., McEvoy, B., Gordon, S., Henders, A., Nyholt, D., . . . Visscher, P. M. (2010). Common SNPs explain a large proportion of heritability for human height. *Nature Genetics*, 42(7), 565–569.

Index

Abadie, A. 123, 126
Abrevaya, J. 342
Acemoglu, D. 420
Activity-based measures 465
Actual choice behavior 584–585
Adda, J. 342, 356n11
Adhikari, A. 204
Adiponectin 134–135
Adolescent growth spurt
  deprivation 230–233, 231f, 232f
  nutritional requirements 37, 38f
Adolphs, R. 660
Adrianzen, B. 434
Affluence
  HAZ, factory children 232–233, 232f
  health risks 236
  height, female 228
  market imagination 583
  neighborhoods, poor children 256
  obesity 236, 443
  overweight, urban 302
  psychosomatic symptoms, adolescent 254
  societal 585–587
  weight, body 583
African enigma 669–685
  environmental factors 681–682, 682f
  explanations 681–682, 682f
  future research 682–683
  genetics 681, 682f, 684–685nn16–18
  income–height relationship 673–680 (*See also* Income–height relationship, African enigma)
  scarring *vs.* selection 669–671
  tall adults
    infant mortality, high 669, 670f
    low incomes 669, 670f
Age
  biological 268
  bone 268–269
  gestational 624
  gestational, birthweight 636–637
  obesity 567
  obesity, wealth 551–554, 554f
Aging population 454
Agricultural techniques, height 283
Agricultural transition, Neolithic, height 277–278, 278f
Agüero, J. M. 63
A'Hearn, B. 784–785, 793n16
Aimone, J. A. 662
Aizer, A. 342
Akaike Information Criterion 128n9
Akee, R. 324–325
Akresh, R. 62–63, 682
Alderman, H. 406, 407–409, 408t, 411, 413, 414, 417, 673
Alecke, B. 212
Allele 792n9
Allen, R. 79, 774, 778, 779
Allison, P. D. 554
Almond, D. 58, 60, 62, 424n1, 425n6, 640, 744
Always-takers 116
Amygdala 660, 661–662
Anderson, M. 117, 164
Anderson, T. 115
Angrist, J. 111, 115, 116
Animal donation programs 447
Antebellum puzzle 42–43, 43f, 282, 669, 694, 751–762
  definition 753
  economic development dynamics 761
  economic growth, modern 751–754
  evidence 754–757, 756f
  food consumption 758–760
  immigration 757
  income inequality 758–760

Antebellum puzzle (*Cont.*)
transportation improvements and urbanization 758, 760
work effort intensification 757–758
Anthropometrics, East Asia 693–706
fundamentals 693
GDP and economic growth 694
overview, 1500-2010 694–695, 695t
trends, post–World War II 699–705
adolescents, 1955-2005 701, 702t
adults, 2000 701–703, 703t
children, 1985-2005 700t, 701
data sources 699
data stratification 699
protein, calorie, and fat consumption 703–705, 704t
trends, pre–World War II 695–699
China, emigrants and contract workers 697
China, militia recruits 696
Japan, high imperialism era 696–697
Japan, militia recruits 696–697
Korea, late 1800s 698–699
Korea, militia recruits 696, 698–699
rural–urban differences, 2000 698, 698t, 699
Anthropometrics, indicators 71–72. *See also specific types*
archaeology 90
economic development 456
Anthropometrics, indicators, children 604
BMI, overnutrition 605
height, nutrition 604, 605f
Anthropometrics, indicators, children and later disease 604–617
birthweight 606–608
metabolic diseases 614
catch-up growth
cardiovascular disease 614, 615
coronary heart disease 615
chest circumference 613
cross-sectional measures 606–614
growth trajectories 614
head circumference 613
health risks 604–605, 605f
height 608–611, 609f, 610f
leg length 613–614
longitudinal measures 614–615
weight, relative 611–612
Anthropometrics, Mediterranean history 765–793, 775t, 792nn7–12
1700-1850 767f, 776–781, 777t, 779f, 780f
1850-1980 781–783, 781f
GDP per capita, by country 790–791
genetics 772–775, 775t (*See also* Genetics, Mediterranean)
health, weight, and height, contemporary 766–772, 767f, 769t–771t, 772f
height
bivariate correlations, late 20th century 791f
determinants and, adult males 767f, 768, 769t–770t
GDP per capita, 1980s 766, 767f
historical estimates, by country 784–788
life expectancy, 1980s births 768, 772f
predicted deviations, by model 768–772, 771t
historical study 765
Northern Europe
height 766
height, GDP 767f
Southern Europe 765–766
height 766, 767f
height, GDP 766, 767f
height, long-run 775–776, 776f
wages, real
1700-1850 788–789
1850-1980 789
Anttila-Hughes, J. K. 61
Apgar test, birthweight 634
Apicella, C. L. 341–342
Appetite, growth 270
Arceo-Gomez, E. O. 62
Archeology
anthropometry 90
height trajectory, Europe, 8th century BCE to 18th century CE 73, 74t, 92–93nn10–14
Argentina 713, 721
economic development 716–717
indigenous people 721
Armelagos, G. J. 277, 712

Arora, R. 514
Arps, S. 200
Ashraf, Q. H. 420
Asset index 672
Assortative mating 567, 568–569, 576, 576n2
  obesity 567, 568–569, 576, 576n2
Atella, V. 319–320, 525t
Attenuation bias 113, 127n3
Auld, M. C. 161–162, 328
Au, N. 547, 553
Autism spectrum disorder (ASD) 660–661
Auxology 37, 266. *See also* Growth and maturation
Average treatment effect (ATE) 110–111
Average treatment effect among treated (ATT) 110–111
Averett, S. 525t, 568, 577n10

The Backbone of History: Health and Nutrition in the Western Hemisphere 46
Backlund, E. 743
Baetschmann, G. 509
Baez, J. E. 63
Bailey, M. J. 744
Baird, S. 56
Bakermans-Kranenburg, M. J. 352–353
Bangladesh Rural Advancement Committee (BRAC) 447
Barbaresco, S. 121
Barker, D. J. 134, 340, 410, 574, 606, 627, 745n4
Barker hypothesis 134, 233, 236, 627, 745n4
Barreca, A. I. 60, 61, 742
Barrett, R. 78
Barro, R. 419
Baten, J. 71, 76, 93n18, 179–180, 184–186, 227, 279–280, 279f, 282–284, 287f, 288–293, 290f, 694, 697, 766, 791–792nn2
Baum, C., II 111, 113, 319, 321, 327, 330n1, 525t, 539
Baumgartner, T. 661
Becker, G. S. 564, 565, 569
Behavioral endocrinology 338–339. *See also* Biological time-varying markers
Behavioral Risk Factor Surveillance System (BRFSS)
  food prices and BMI 162–163
  income inequality
    cardiovascular disease 490
    weight status 490–491
Behavior regulation, biological time-varying markers 338
Behrens, T. E. J. 659
Behrman, J. 17, 17t, 407–409, 408t, 409, 411, 413, 417, 424n1, 525t
Bengal Famine (1944) 57
Bennett, D. 59–60
Berg, J. 657–658
Betrayal aversion, oxytocin 661–662
Beydoun, M. A. 329
Bhalotra, S. 236–237
Bhattacharya, J. 320, 538–539, 573
Bhutta, Z. A. 20, 406–407, 409–410, 412
Biddle, J. E. 503
Biggs, B. 251
Binge eating, undereating and 444
Biological age 268
Biological health risks, economic development 454–479. *See also specific types*
  activity-based measures 465
  aging population 454
  anthropometric measures 456
  biomarkers 455–456
  blood-based markers 466–475 (*See also* Blood-based markers)
  body mass index 458–461
  causal models 466–467
  cholesterol, total 469–470, 471f, 478–479n3
  C-reactive protein 473–475, 474f
  data 456–457, 457f
  doubly labeled water 466, 478n2
  glycosylated hemoglobin 470–473, 471f
  height and weight 458–459
  hypertension 461–464, 463f
  noncommunicable diseases 454–455
  nutrient (food) intake measures 465–466
  overweight
    economic prosperity 461
    education 459–461, 460f
    percent 459, 460f
  physical health measures 455
  physical performance measures 456
  self-reports 455

Biological measures, well-being 32–49
frontiers 47–48
health *vs.* income 33–34
height
long-term trends 42–44, 43f
nutritional status 37–41, 38f, 40f
life tables 34–36
morbidity 36–37
Native Americans 44–45
skeletal remains 45–47, 71–72
slaves, American 41–42
Biological programming 606
Biological standard of living (BLS) 71, 292n1, 753, 755
antebellum puzzle 755–756, 756f (*See also* Antebellum puzzle)
anthropometric indicators 71–72
height, environmental factors 71
Middle Ages 72
skeletal remains 45–47, 71–72
Biological standard of living (BLS), Europe 70–99
8th century BCE to 18th century CE 82–89 (*See also* Height trajectory, Europe, 8th century BCE to 18th century CE)
anthropometry with archaeology 90
bones 72–73, 91–92nn5–9
cattle plague 78
cattle share 77, 78, 93n19, 94n27
climate change 75–77, 93nn16–18
cultivation and three-field crop rotation 78
diet quality and quantity 75
epidemics and war/persecution 80, 95n32
fundamentals 70–72
gender inequality 81–82, 96nn42–44
gene-culture co-evolution 94n25
grain 77, 80–81
height, archeological remains, new estimates 73, 74t, 92–93nn10–14
land per capita 78–79, 95nn28–30
legumes, eggs, fish bones 93–94n21
medical care and sanitary conditions 81, 96nn38–41
method and data 72–82
milk and dairy products 77–78, 93–94nn20–26
Roman impact 80–81, 95–96nn33–37
urbanization rate 79, 95n31
Biological time-invariant markers 343–354
definition 337–338
gene–environment interactions 349–354 (*See also* Gene–environment interaction (G×E))
gene–gene interactions 353–354
genetic markers 344–348 (*See also* Genetic markers)
Biological time-varying markers 338–343
behavior regulation 338
definition 337, 338
hormones 341–343
measures 338–339
menstrual cycle 339–340
proxies
2D:4D ratio 340, 343, 355–356n6
fatness 340–341
imaging 341
Biomarkers 337–355. *See also* Blood-based markers; *specific types*
biological time-invariant 337–338, 343–354
biological time-varying 337, 338–343
definitions 337–338
economic development 455–456
future research 354–355
validity 355n1
Biroli, P. 350–351
Birth, human capital endowment 632–642
Birthweight
blood pressure, systolic 606
classification 632
cross-sectional *vs.* twin samples 636–637
determinants 636
environmental factors 623–624
female *vs.* male 622
frequency distribution 621
genetics 623
gestational age 624, 636–637
heavy, diabetes 624
historical use 621
increases, 20th century 632–633
marital status 625
maternal height and ethnicity 623
maternal nutrition 625
maternal social position 624–625

measurement 632
overweight, adult 611–612
parity 624
population health 627–628
public health problems 621–622, 627–628
stressors and toxicants 633
women's health 627–628
Birthweight, growth faltering first 1000 days
identical twin controls 16–17, 17t
longitudinal associations 15, 16t
synthetic cohorts, estimate linking across life cycle 18, 19t
Birthweight, human capital endowment 632–642
confounders 634
differential sensitivity hypothesis 640
effects
heterogeneity 639–641
mechanisms 637–638
exclusion restriction 635
gene–environment interaction 641
genetic factors 635
increases, 20th century 632–633
macrosomia, fetal 641–642
measurement and classification 632
mitigation 642
prenatal exposures 632
race 639–640
Ramadan-induced fasting 635
research, history 633–635
sibling comparison studies 634–635
socioeconomics 640
stressors and toxicants 633
twin fixed-effects models 636–637
twin fixed-effects research 634–635
weathering hypothesis 639–640
Birthweight, human welfare 621–630
fetal growth 623–625
historical use 622–623
significance 626–628
trends 625–626
Birthweight, low 407–411
avoiding, economic value 407–409, 408t
brain effect 637–638
cardiovascular disease 606–608
categories 621
cognitive function 638
consequences, adult 410, 425n6
coronary heart disease 606–607
definition 441
diabetes type 2, 607
female *vs.* male 622
global 622
hypertension 624
infant mortality 627, 633
later disease 606–608
limitations 621–622
metabolic diseases 614
noncommunicable diseases 409, 411
prevention 409–410, 425n5
productivity cost 407–409, 408t
stroke 607
stunting 410
symmetric and asymmetric types 638
threshold 621
well-being, significance 626–628
Bishai, D. 527t
Black, D. A. 743
Black Death 59
Black, R. E. 425n8
Blanchflower, D. G. 533t
Bleakley, H. 742
Blisard, N. 328
Bliss, C. 415
Blood-based markers 466–475. *See also* Biomarkers
causal models 466–467
cholesterol, total 469–470, 471f, 478–479n3
collection methods 467–468
cost decline 467
C-reactive protein 473–475, 474f
glycosylated hemoglobin 470–473, 471f
Blood groups, Mediterranean 772–774
Blood pressure
high (*See* Hypertension)
measurement, field 461–462, 478n1
systolic, birthweight 606
Blum, M. 184, 186, 282, 287f, 293, 694, 766, 791–792n2
BMI-for-age curves, global trends 297
Boas, Franz 44, 287–288
Böckerman, P. 512, 516

Body mass index (BMI) 133–146. *See also* Weight, body
20th century trend 145
applications 296
Barker hypothesis 134
biological family member 537
calculation 157, 296, 448n3, 561n1, 583
calories 133–134
childhood, metabolic disease 612
children, later disease 611–612
classification system 135, 436–437, 583
definition 133, 536
economic prosperity 461
energy gap 144
vs. fat 134–135, 157–158, 193, 536–537
fat *vs.* fat-free mass problems 340–341, 536–537
formula 267
future directions 144–145
GDP increase and 544, 544f
genetics 532t, 537
glycosylated hemoglobin 476, 477f
health 135–136
healthy (WHO) 311n1
income inequality 490–491
increase, 20th century U.S. 485
inflammation 477, 477f
insulin and insulin resistance 134
interpreting 133
marriage 570
measurement 135, 436–437
normal curves 267
obesity prevalence 296
percent hypertensive 475f, 476
productivity 417
reliability 193
selection 144
standard deviation score 268, 269–270
thrifty-gene hypothesis 134, 145n2, 236
total cholesterol 476, 477f
U.S. history 136–138, 137t, 138f, 146n4
weight *vs.* 193
well-nourished population 133, 145n1
Body mass index (BMI), global trends 296–311
BMI-for-age curves 297
children and adolescents 297
data sources 298
definition 297
distribution 304–305
fat mass, subcutaneous 305–306
health impact 306–307
malnutrition
childhood, health outcomes 309–310
prevalence 438, 438f
prevalence, preschool children 298–299
mean BMI 303
morbidity and mortality risk 296
obesogenic environments 310
overweight and obesity 299, 301–309 (*See also* Overweight and obesity, global trends)
pattern, general 302–303
reference distribution 297
reference population 297
time trends 301–302
waist circumference 305–306
Body mass index (BMI), U.S. factors over time 138–141, 139f–141f, 146n5
men 139–140, 139f, 140f
occupations 142, 142t, 144
residence 143, 143t, 144
women 141, 141f
Body size change, secular, global 284–286, 285f, 287f
Body weight. *See* Body mass index (BMI); Weight, body
Bogen, B. 321
Bogin, B. 215
Böhm, A. 284
Boisguillebert, Sieur de, Pierre Le Pesant 751, 752
Boix, C. 182, 278–279
Bolivia 720–721. *See also* Tsimane'
Bone age 268–269
Bones 45
skeletal remains, biological standard of living 72–73, 91–92nn5–9
Borderline personality disorder 660
Bossavie, L. 416
Bouis, H. E. 417
Bounded rationality 584–585
Bozoyan, C. 526t, 537

Bozzoli, C. 669–671
Brabec, M. 139, 301, 306
Brain mapping 653
Braudel, F. 765
Bray, B. E. 186, 284, 285f, 508
Brazil 711, 713, 717–718, 721
Breast milk 216
Brewer, G. 514
Brinkman, H.-J. 694
Brock, W. A. 156
Bröder, A. 339
Brosnan, S. 657
Brown, A. 71
Brown, M. 568
Brunello, G. 319, 320–321, 526t
Bruner, E. 422
Bubonic plague 59
Bundervoet, R. 63
Bundorf, M. K. 320, 538–539
Burgess, R. 61–62
Burkhauser, R. 340–341, 536
Burundi civil war 63

Caballero, B. 441, 443–444
Cabieses Valdes, B. 422
Cai, T. 351
Caliendo, M. 322
Caloric intake, East Asias, post–World War II 703–705, 704t
Cancer survival, U.S. racial differences 732, 733t
Candidate genes 344–345, 347
Cardiovascular disease
  catch-up growth 614, 615
  low birthweight 606–608
  risk factors, income inequality 490
Carmalt, J. H. 569
Carpenter, J. 345
Carrieri, V. 514
Carson, S. A. 144
Cartes Velásquez, R. 200
Case, A. 59, 417, 502, 503, 513
Caspi, A. 349, 351
Catch-up growth 22–27, 38, 210
  adult disease risk 608
  African enigma 678–680, 679f, 680f, 684nn12–15
  cardiovascular disease 614, 615
  coronary heart disease 615
  diets after 2 years 28n11
  height-for-age z-scores 22–24
  implications
    cognitive achievement 24–25
    determinants of growth patterns 25
  individual patterns 24
  life cycle framework 11–14, 12f
  literature, limitations 26–27
  migrants 288
  patterns across ages 22–23
  regression estimates 23–24
  slaves, American 210, 212–215, 213t–214t
Cattle plague
  biological standard of living 78
  height trajectory, Europe, 8th century BCE to 18th century CE 87t, 88
Cattle share
  biological standard of living 77, 78, 93n19, 94n27
  height trajectory, Europe, 8th century BCE to 18th century CE 87, 87t, 94nn23–24, 97–98n52
  height trajectory, Europe, Common Era beginning-1800 279–280, 279f
Causal effect, variation among persons 127
Cavalli-Sforza, L. 773
Cawley, J. 111, 115, 167, 170, 319, 323, 324–326, 330n3, 340–341, 447, 526t–527t, 535, 536, 537, 572, 574
Central-Western Europe 93n12
Cesarini, J. D. 345
Chabris, C. F. 347, 357n18
Chadwick, E. 415
Chang, V. W. 490–491
Charles, K. 126
Charness, G. 167
Chay, K. 744
Cheese, hard 93n20
Chen, E. Y. 568
Chen, Y. 339
Chest circumference, children, later disease 613
Chiang, C. F. 59–60
Childbearing slaves, American 221–223
Child Growth Standards, WHO 297

Children (childhood)
anthropometrics, and later disease 604–617 (*See also* Anthropometrics, indicators, children and later disease)
definition 245–246
early 245–246
health and health habits, on adult disease 604
investment, economics 571–572
mother's height, health 236–237
nutrition investment, subsequent human capital 412–415
Children's growth, female 228–233, 229f, 231f–232f
1960s Britain, velocity 228–229, 229f
deprivation 230–233, 231f, 232f
height-for-age z-scores 230
WHO standards 229–230, 229f
Children's health, socioeconomic inequality 244–259
childhood 245–246
GDP 247
health and well-being 246
importance 244
income inequality
high-income countries 248–251, 249f, 250f
low- and middle-income countries 251–252
inequality 246
key concept definitions 245–246
literature review 246–248, 247f
pathways
epigenetics and chronic stress 257
family life and relationship 254–255
material and psychosocial 253–254
status differentiation 255–257
patterns 248
policy implications 258
poverty 245
social gradients 252–253
UN Convention on the Rights of Children 244
Children's obesity, family economics 571–575
child investment 571–572
genetics 575
market failures 573–575
technological change 572–573
China, anthropometrics 693–706. *See also* Anthropometrics, East Asia
China, anthropometrics, post–World War II 699–705
adolescents, 1955-2005 701, 702t
adults, 2000 701–703, 703t
children, 1985-2005 700t, 701
data sources 699
data stratification 699
protein, calorie, and fat consumption 703–705, 704t
China, anthropometrics, pre–World War II 697–698
emigrants and contract workers 697
militia recruits 696
Chingos, M. 126
Chiu, P. N. 660–661
Choi, S.-J. 698–699
Cholesterol, HDL 478–479n3
Cholesterol, total
body mass index 476, 477f
economic development 469–470, 471f, 478–479n3
Chou, S. 117, 162–163, 174, 598
Christakis, N. 144, 172–173, 490–491
Chronic conditions, U.S. racial differences 739–741, 741f
Chu, P. H. 653
Cigarettes, obesity 173–175
Cinnirella, F. 284, 505, 516
Clark, R. 247
Climate
biological standard of living 75–77, 93nn16–18
height trajectory, Europe, 8th century BCE to 18th century CE 87t, 89
Coates, J. M. 340
Coatsworth, J. H. 715
Coclanis, P. 760
Coefficient of variation (CV) 293n5
height inequality 288–290, 290f, 293n5
Cohen-Cole, E. 173
Cohen, M. N. 277, 712
Coimbra, C. E. A. 200
Colchero, M. 201, 527t
Cole, T. J. 284, 437

Collins, W. 738
Colman, G. 113–114
Colombia 717, 721
Coly, A. N. 680
Community
  growth faltering, first 1000 days 20–21, 21t
  native population weight 201
Compensatory growth. *See* Catch-up growth
Complementary traits, marital unions and obesity 569–570, 576n3
Compliers 116
Concavity-induced income effect 489
Conformity 156
Conley, D. 346, 351, 357n23, 527t, 535, 539, 568, 641
Connelly, L. B. 328
Constant-effect instrumental variable model 114–115
Constitutional delay of growth and puberty (CDGP) 269, 270, 271–272
Consumer behavior theory 584
Conti, G. 352
Coppola, M. 793n16
Cornaglia, F. 342, 356n11
Cornelissen, T. 513
Coronary heart disease
  birthweight, low 606–607
  catch-up growth 615
  height 608–609
  height, childhood 609–610, 609f, 610f
  obesity, childhood 605
Cortisol 135, 341–343
  behavioral endocrinology 338
  risk and decision making 656
Cosmetic discrimination 318, 320
Costa-Barbosa, F. A. 271
Costa, D. 135, 761n5, 738, 740–741, 740f, 741f, 747nn16–19
Costa-Font, J. 329
Cotinine 338, 341, 342, 356n9, 356n11
Counterfactual outcome 110
Courtemanche, C. 121, 124, 174–175
Cox, L. A. 267
Craig, L. A. 757, 762n12
C-reactive protein (CRP) 473–475, 474f
Cribra orbitalia 91n6
Crisis, human biology 52–65. *See also* Disasters, natural
  aggregate 54
  conceptual issues 53–54
  definition 53
  environmental 61–62
  epidemics 59–60
  famines 57–58
  focus 53
  levels 53–54
  natural disasters 60–61
  recessions 54–57
  wars 62–63
Croatia
  height
    historical estimates 788
    long-run 775–776, 776f
Crookston, B. T. 24
Croson, R. 658
Cross-price elasticity 153–154
Cuff, T. 139–140
Cultivation, biological standard of living 78
Cultural norms, obesity 443
Cunha, F. 406, 424n1
Currie, A. 168
Currie, J. 324, 424n1
Curtin, S. 168–169
Cutler, D. M. 165, 572

Dairy products. *See* Cattle share; Milk
Datar, A. 638
Dating, accurate 92n11
Dave, D. 113–114, 126
Davila, A. 533t, 536
Death. *See* Mortality (death)
Deaton, A. 514, 669–671
Deb, P. 125
DeCicca, P. 126
Defiers 116, 127n5
Dehejia, R. H. 55–56
Del Bono, E. 638
Delgado, M. R. 659
Demand
  food 158–159
  food, uninformed consumption 573–574
  growth faltering, first 1000 days 13–14
  nutritional

Demand (*Cont.*)
disease 755
work 755
Demment, M. M. 327
Demographic transition 35
Neolithic 277–279
Dendrochronology 711
DeNeve, J.-E. 345
Denny, K. 514
Deolalikar, A. 63, 417
de Paola, M. 514
Depression
post-partum 411–412
weight gain 577n6
Dercon, S. 58
Deschenes, O. 61
Developmental programming, metabolism and body weight 308
De Waal, F. 657
D'Hombres, B. 319, 320–321, 526t
Diabetes
birthweight, heavy 624
gestational 134, 145n2
Diabetes mellitus type 2
birthweight, low 607
height
adult 610
childhood 610–611
obesity and overweight risk 307
obesity, childhood 605
Diamond, A. 123
Dieffenbach, S. 440
Diet. *See also* Food; *specific foods*
change, native population weight 201
height, adult male, 1980s
Europe 769t–770t, 770
on poverty–obesity link 327–328
quality and quantity 75 (*See also specific topics*)
Diez-Roux, A. V. 490
Difference-in-differences (DDD) 120–123, 121t, 128nn11–12
Differential sensitivity hypothesis, birthweight and human capital 640
Ding, W. 323, 345–346, 350, 353–354, 357n22
Diocletian's price edict 91n3
Disasters, natural 60–62. *See also* Crisis, human biology
Discount rate 585
assumed, on future productivity 408–409
Discrimination, obese 318
cosmetic 318, 320
job promotion 318, 321
statistical 318, 320–321
Discrimination, short people 515–516
Disease. *See also specific types*
childhood anthropometric indicators 604–617 (*See also* Anthropometrics, indicators, children and later disease)
noncommunicable 454–455
nutritional demands 755
Dizygotic twin fixed-effects (MZ-FE) 28n3
DNA, structure 792n6
Doak, C. M. 439–440
Domes, G. 656, 661
Dominance, tall people 515
Donaldson, D. 62
Dopamine 656–657
Dorsolateral prefrontal cortex (DLPFC), left 655–656
Doubly labeled water 466, 478n2
Down syndrome, growth and maturation 272
Dreber, A. 340
Drewnowski, A. 328
Dried blood spots (DBS) 467–468
Drukker, J. 694
Duncan, G. J. 642
Durlauf, S. N. 156
Dutch famine (1944-1945) 57
Dynamic complementarities 406

Early childhood 245–246
Early-industrial-growth puzzle 694
Eaves, L. J. 358n32
Echevarria, G. 410
Eckhardt, C. L. 28n11
Ecological effect, obesity and income inequality 488–490
Econometrics 109–128
attenuation bias 113, 127n3
average treatment effect 110–111
average treatment effect among treated 110–111

causal effect, variation among persons 127
counterfactual outcome 110
difference-in-differences 120–123, 121t, 128nn11–12
first-differencing *vs.* mean-differencing 112–113, 127n1
fundamentals 109–111
heterogeneous treatment effects 123–126
instrumental variables 114–118, 127–128nn4–8
just-identified system 115, 127n4
monotonicity assumption 117, 127–128n7
panel data and fixed effects 111–114
regression discontinuity design 118–120, 128nn9–10
selection bias 110, 127
self-selection problem 109, 110
stable unit treatment value assumption 110
strict exogeneity 112–113, 127n2
treatment effect 110
2SLS estimator 115, 127n7
variation, key independent variables 127
Economic equality 589t–590t
Economic freedom index 597–598
Economic growth, modern
biological standard of living 753
definition 752
history 751–754
Kuznets on 752–753
negative results 753
Economic insecurity hypothesis of obesity 588–591, 589t–590t
Economic Security Index 596
Economic security/insecurity 588–591, 589t–590t
Educational attainment
height 413
global 284
inequality 179–180
wages 513, 514
obesity 323, 443
overweight 459–461, 460f
Edwards, R. D. 247
Eggs 93–94n21
Eisenberg, N. 349
Eisenegger, C. 342
Electroencephalography (EEG) 654–655
Elgar, F. J. 253, 256
Employment and obesity 322–323. *See also* Wages
discrimination, Sweden 522
males *vs.* females 522
Employment security 592t
Endocrine disorders 273–274
Endocrinology, behavioral 338–339. *See also* Biological time-varying markers
Endogamy. *See* Assortative mating
Endogenous stratification 126
Energy gap 144
Engerman, S. L. 219
Environmental crises 61–62
Environmental factors
African enigma 681–682, 682f
birthweight 623–624
height 71
Epidemics 59–60
biological standard of living 80, 95n32
Epidemiological trap 723
Epigenetics, chronic stress and child health 257
Eriksson, K. 743
Eritrean-Ethiopian conflict (1998-2000) 63
Esping-Andersen, G. 586
Ethiopia famine (1984) 58
Ethnicity. *See* Race and ethnicity
Eudomaneia 598
Europe. *See also specific countries and topics; specific topics*
anthropometric history 765–793 (*See also* Anthropometrics, Mediterranean history)
Central-Western 93n12
Mediterranean 93n12
Europe, Northern
height 766
height and GDP 767f
Europe, Southern 765–766
1700-1850
height and GDP per capita 777t, 778–779
real GDP 778, 780–781, 780f
real wages 778–780, 779f
height 766, 767f
GDP 766, 767f
, long-run 775–776, 776f

Eveleth, P. B. 39–40, 40f, 222
Exchange theory, obesity and marriage 569
Exclusion restriction 115, 118, 537
 birthweight and human capital 635
Exercise
 , bodyweight 154, 155–156
 obesity 166–167
Exogeneity, strict 112–113, 127n2
Extreme weather 61–62
Ezzati, M. 157

Fahr, R. 527t, 538
Fakhar, A. 656
Familial short stature 271
Family economics 565
 informal health service organization 566
 obesity 564–577 (*See also* Obesity and family economics)
Family health capital 565–568
 household's production of health 565–566
 obesity 567–568
Family life, children's health 254–255
Famines 57–58
Fast-food exposure 598
Fast-food shock 585
Fat, body
 vs. body mass index 134–135, 157–158, 193, 536–537
 proxies 340–341
 stress and stress hormones 134–135
 subcutaneous mass, global trends 305–306
 wages 158
Fat consumption, East Asia, post–World War II 703–705, 704t
Fawzi, W. W. 672
Fehr, E. 341
Females
 birthweight 622
 children's growth 228–233 (*See also* Children's growth, female)
 employment and obesity 522
 health, birthweight 627–628
 height 226–238 (*See also* Height, female)
 obesity and wages 522, 524, 525t–533t, 535–536
Fertility, natural disasters 61
Fetal growth, mother's height 235–237
Fetal origins hypothesis 410–411
 obesity 443–444
 principles 443–444
Fetal programming, metabolism and body weight 308
Finite mixture models (FMM) 124–125
Finkelstein, A. 574, 747n21
Finlay, J. E. 61
First-differencing 112–113, 127n1
First-stage regression equation 114
Fishback, P. 742
Fish bones 93–94n21
Fixed-effects estimator 330n1
Fixed-effects methods 111–114
Fletcher, J. M. 173, 323, 346, 351, 354
Floud, R. 40, 234–235, 755, 757
Fogel, R. 4, 35–36, 136, 219, 234, 419, 425n12, 446, 758, 760, 761n5
Folate deficiency, pre-conception 411
Fonda, S. J. 548, 553
Fontaine, K. R. 326
Food. *See also specific types*
 demand 158–159
Food assistance programs 330–331n4
Food consumption
 antebellum puzzle 758–760
 biological health risks 465–466
 market failures 573–575
 uninformed demand 573–574
Food diaries 465–466
Food industry, obesity epidemic 577n8
Food insecurity 596
 undernutrition 441
Food intake
 measures 465–466
 prices and income 152, 153
Food prices
 , bodyweight 152, 153–154
 compensating behavior 154
 composite index 160
 data sources 160
 food intake 152, 153
Food prices, obesity 158–165
 adults 162–164
 body weight status 164
 children 161–162

endogeneity and measurement issues 158–165
measurement challenges 159–161
socioeconomic status 165
Food processing technology, self-control 165–166
Food recalls 465–466
Ford, W. 111, 113, 319, 321, 330n1, 525t, 539
Forest fires 62
Fowler, J. 144, 172–173, 345
Frakes, M. 174
France
1700-1850 777t, 778–781, 779f, 780f
1850-1980 781f, 782
height, long-run 775, 776f
France, South
GDP per capita 790
height, historical estimates 785–786
Fraunholz, U. 184
Friedlaender, J. S. 204
Friedman, J. 56
Frisvold, D. 744
Functional magnetic resonance imaging (fMRI) 652–654

Gallagher, M. 566
Gao, W. 506–507
Garcia, J. 507, 528t, 538
Garcia Villar, J. 169
Garfinkel, L. 152–153
Garnsey, P. 95n35
Garrett, J. L. 440
Gelman, A. 119
G*E modifications 353
Gender inequality
biological standard of living 81–82, 96nn42–44
hidden penalties 235–236
Gene-culture co-evolution 94n25
Gene–environment interaction (G×E) 349–354
aggregate macroenvironmental conditions 350, 358n34
birthweight, human capital endowment 641
definition 353
early life environments 349
environmental factor timing 351
gene*cohort effects 350
genetic variation
life cycle 352
within-family 351–352, 358n35
heterogeneity of effects 352–353
modeling G*E effects 350–351
selection bias 349–350, 358n29
Gene–gene interactions 353–354
Generalized social anxiety disorder (GSAD) 660
Genetic disorders, growth and maturation 273–274
Genetic lottery 346–347
Genetic markers 344–348
best practices 347
candidate genes 344–345
candidate genes, literature conflicts 347
early research 344
exogenous variation and comorbidity 345, 356n13
genetic lottery 346–347
genetic polymorphisms 344
plausibility 346
polygenic scores 348
population stratification 346
risk allele count 346
single-nucleotide polymorphisms 344
single-nucleotide polymorphisms, Mediterranean 773–775, 775t, 792nn7–12
SSGAC research 347–348
Genetic polymorphisms 344. *See also* Single-nucleotide polymorphisms (SNPs)
Genetics 662
African enigma 681, 682f, 684–685nn16–18
birthweight 623, 635
growth and maturation 270–271
height 210–211
European trajectory, 8th century BCE to 18th century CE 89, 99nn58–59
global 281–282
obesity, childhood 575
short stature 271

Genetics, Mediterranean 772–775
  blood groups 772
  genome-wide association studies 774
  single-nucleotide polymorphisms 773–775, 775t, 792nn7–12
Genocide 63
Genome-wide association (GWA) studies
  growth and maturation 271
  Mediterranean 774
Genomic-relatedness-matrix restricted maximum likelihood (GREML) 358n27
Genomics 662
Genovese, E. D. 221
Georgiadis, A. 24–25
Gerdtham, U.-G. 55
G*E responses 353
Gertler, P. 414
Gestational age 624
  birthweight 624, 636–637
Gestational diabetes 134, 145n2
Ghrelin 135
Gilaie-Dotan, S. 341
Gill, I. 698
Gill, J. 329
Gini coefficients, height inequality 289–290, 291t, 293n7
Gini Index 768, 792n3
  height, adult male, 1980s Europe 768, 769t–770t
Glaeser, E. L. 165, 572
Glauber, D. 568
Glauber, R. 527t, 535, 539
Global methods 119
Global perspectives 276–293. *See also specific topics*
  agricultural and demographic transition, Neolithic 277–278, 278f
  body size change, secular 284–286, 285f, 287f
  early developments 277–280, 278f, 279f
  fundamentals 276–277
  genetics 281–282
  height inequality 288–292, 290f, 291t, 293n7
  industrialization 282–283
  labor market bias 281
  market integration 282–283
  migration 287–288
  sample selectivity 280–281
Glover, J. W. 734, 735, 746n10
Gluckman, P. 411
Glycosylated hemoglobin (HbA1c)
  body mass index 476, 477f
  economic development 470–473, 471f
Gneezy, U. 167, 658
Golberstein, E. 744
Goldberger, A. S. 344, 356n14
Goldman, D. 163
Goodman-Bacon, A. 744
Gordon-Larsen, P. 571
Gørgens, T. 57–58
Grabka, M. M. 527t
Grain 77, 80–81
Granados, J. A. 55
Grasgruber, P. 99n59, 284–286
Great Famine (China, 1959-1961) 57–58, 64n7
Greece
  1850-1980 783
  GDP per capita 790
  height
    historical estimates 787
    long-run 775–776, 776f
Greenstone, M. 744
Gregory, C. 116, 528t, 537
Grépin, K. A. 59
Greve, J. 320, 528t, 535, 538
Gross domestic product (GDP) per capita 33. *See also specific topics*
  children's health 247
  economic growth and anthropometrics 694
  France, South 790
  Greece 790
  height, adult male, 1980s Europe 767f, 768, 769t–770t
  infant mortality 56
  Italy, North 790
  life expectancy at birth 456, 457f
  other countries 791
  Portugal 790
  Spain 790
  stunting 694
  Turkey 790
  world, body mass index and 544, 544f

world, increases 544
Grossman, M. 117, 162–163, 350–351, 564, 565–566, 598
Gross national income (GNI) 548
Growth and maturation 266–274. *See also specific measures*
appetite 270
auxology 266
biological age 268
body mass index 267
bone age 268–269
constitutional delay of growth and puberty 269, 270, 271–272
Down syndrome 272
endocrine and genetic disorders 273–274
genetics 270–271
diminished growth, causes 272–273
potential, adult height 267–269
short stature 271
genome-wide association studies 271
growth chart 273–274
growth reference 267
growth standard 267
intrauterine growth restriction 272
Laron syndrome 273
leg growth 293n4
medications on 273
mid-parental height 268
monitoring, infants, children, and adolescents 269–270
normal pattern 266
normal pattern, deviations 266–267
pathological 273
Prader-Willi syndrome 272–273
proportionate *vs.* disproportionate 267
target height 267–268, 270
trajectory 268–269
variants 270–272
Growth chart 273–274
Growth faltering, first 1000 days 9–22, 25–28
demand relations 13–14
epidemiology 9, 10f
input determinants 12–13, 12f
life cycle framework 11–14, 12f
literature, limitations 26–27
outcomes and irreversible damage 9–11, 10f, 12f
production functions 11–12, 12f
subsequent life cycle outcomes, growth determinants
household and community 20–21, 21t
nutritional interventions, other 21t, 22
nutritional supplements, protein-dense 21–22
subsequent life stage outcomes, direct estimates 14–20
birthweights, identical twin controls 16–17, 17t
birthweights, synthetic cohorts, estimate linking across life cycle 18, 19t
instrumental variable estimates, HAZ or stunting at 24 months, adult life cycle stages 18–20, 19t
longitudinal associations, birthweights 15, 16t
longitudinal associations, growth faltering and later life outcomes 15, 16t
simplifying assumptions 14
Growth reference 267
Growth standard 267
Gruber, J. 174
Guatemala 718, 719, 720, 721
Guntupalli, A. M. 288
Guo, G. 351
Guo, M. H. 270–271
Gustafsson, P. E. 327

Haas, J. D. 327
Haddad, L. J. 417
Hahn, J. 115, 127n5
Haines, M. R. 735, 736, 736f, 739f, 746nn10–11, 756, 758, 760
Hainmueller, J. 123
Hajat, A. 547
Hajnal, J. 221–222
Halpern, C. T. 568
Hamermesh, D. S. 503, 507
Hammarström, A. 327
Han, E. 319, 320, 322, 323, 330n4, 527t, 529t, 532t, 535, 538, 540n2
Hansen, B. E. 350
Happiness 48
height, wages and 514
Happiness paradox 568

Hardy, R. 327
Härkönen, J. 530t
Hatemi, P. K. 352
Hatton, T. J. 186, 284, 285f, 508
Haushofer, J. 341
Hausman, J. 115, 127n5
Hausman-Taylor estimator 507
Hausman test 118
Hawkesworth, S. 409
Hayden, G. F. 267, 269
HDL cholesterol 478–479n3
Head circumference, children, later disease 613
Headey, D. D. 673
Health. *See also specific topics*
  definition 246
  as health capital 730
  height
    female 233–235, 234f
    wages 513
  household production 565–566
  outcomes *vs.* health behaviors 357n22
  risks (*See* Biological health risks, economic development; *specific types*)
  status, psychosocial factors 486
Health behaviors, *vs.* health outcomes 357n22
Health capital 730
Health capital, family 565–568
  household's production of health 565–566
  obesity 567–568
Health inequality
  economic and natural shocks 423–424
  nutrition 420–424
Health insecurity 591
Health promotion opportunity costs, family economics 564
Heaver, R. 446
Hebebrand, J. 576
Heckman, J. 10, 10f, 349, 352, 406, 424n1, 517
Height. *See also specific topics*
  antebellum, long-term trends 42–44, 43f, 282
  biological standard of living 754
  biology 210
  black-white height gap 508
  coronary heart disease 608–609
  Croatia 788
  cross-country work, problems 420–421
  diabetes type 2 610
  economic development 458–459
  economic dimension 501
  economic output distribution 754
  endogeneity 28n7
  environmental factors 71
  France, South 785–786
  genes 210–211
  genetic potential 267–269
  Greece 787
  growth finalization 92n7
  health and 210
  Imperium Romanum 71–72, 91nn4–5
  income 39–41, 40f
  Italy, North 784–785
  malnutrition 39
  mid-parental 268
  native populations, adult 195t–196t, 201–204 (*See also* Native populations, adult height)
  nutritional status 37–41, 38f, 40f
    boys, GDP 40, 40f
    boys, growth velocity, good conditions 37–38, 38f
  nutrition investment 415–418
  Portugal 786–787
  productivity 415–418
  schooling 413
  self-confidence and leadership 515
  slaves 210–224 (*See also* Slaves, American, heights)
  Spain 787
  stroke 609
  target 267–268, 270
  Turkey 787–788
Height-by-age patterns, American slaves 212–218, 213t–214t
Height, childhood
  coronary heart disease 609–610, 609f, 610f
  diabetes type 2 610–611
  later disease 608–611, 609f, 610f
Height, female 226–238
  affluence on 228
  average, long-term 227
  Barker hypothesis 233, 236

child growth 228–233, 229f, 231f–232f (*See also* Children's growth, female)
child health 236–237
fetal growth and newborn length 235–237
health 233–235, 234f
hidden penalties, gender inequality 235–236
importance 226
maternal, birthweight 623
studies, early 226–228
technophysio evolution 233–234
thrifty-gene hypothesis 236
Height-for-age *z*-scores (HAZ) 230
24 months, adult life cycle stage outcomes 18–20, 19t
Africa 673, 674f, 684n7
calculation 238n1
catch-up growth 22–24
cognitive achievement 24–25
definition 684n7
FTD growth faltering and later life outcomes 15, 16t
Height inequality 179–189
birth cohort 179
coefficient of variation 288–290, 290f, 293n5
distributions 180–183, 181f, 181t, 182f
ethnic groups 185–186
Gini coefficients 289–290, 291t, 293n7
global 288–292, 290f, 291t, 293n7
as human and health capital proxy 179
institutional and political differences 188
macroeconomics 183–185, 183f
marriage success 180
productivity, adult 180
public goods provision 179
regional differences 186–187
schooling 179–180
selection mechanisms 180
social class and birth cohort, Germany 180–182, 181f, 181t
social differences 185
urban *vs.* rural differences 187
Height trajectory, Europe, 8th century BCE to 18th century CE 82–89
archeological remains 73, 74t, 92–93nn10–14
archeological remains, new estimates 73, 74t, 92–93nn10–14
cattle plague 87t, 88
cattle share 87, 87t, 94nn23–24, 97–98n52
climatic temperature 87t, 89
counterbalancing effects 89
data sources and methods 82–85, 83f, 96–97nn45–50
genetic factors 89, 99nn58–59
lactose intolerance 77–78, 89, 94n66
land per capita 87t, 88, 98–99n56
method and data 72–82
plague 87t, 88
Roman impact 87t, 88, 98n54
three-field rotation 87t, 89, 99n57
urbanization rate 87–88, 87t, 98n53
war/persecution 87t, 89
Height, wages and 501–517
age effects 509, 510t–511t
ambiguous causality 513–514
causes 501–502
discrimination, short people 515–516
dominance, interpersonal, tall people 515
education 513
fundamentals 501–502
future studies 517
happiness 514
height premium, basic estimates 508–509, 510t–511t
industries, differences 516
men *vs.* women 509–512, 510t–511t, 512f
methodological aspects 506–507
modeling and theoretical considerations 502–505, 506f
nutrition and health 513
open questions 517
physical capacity 513
regional differences and long-run developments 507–508
wage-height equation 502–503
four-equation model extension 504–505
Sohn and Hübler modification 503
Thomas and Strauss extension 503
Vogl extension 503
weight 514–515
Heineck, G. 507
HemoCue photometer 468

Henderson, R. M. 135
Herrmann, M. 339
Heston, A. 40
Heterogeneous treatment effects 123–126
 endogenous stratification 126
 finite mixture models 124–125
 intent-to-treat-type effect 126
 quantile regression model 124, 125
 selection bias 125–126
Hiermeyer, M. 284
Hira, S. 697
Hirvonen, K. 680, 681
Historical Statistics of the United States 37
A History of the Study of Human Growth 37
HIV/AIDS epidemic 59–60
Hoddinott, J. 18–20, 21, 28n2, 409, 413
Hofferth, S. L. 168–169
Hoffman, M. 340
Hohmann, N. 339
Homogamy. *See* Assortative mating
Hopfensitz, A. 501–502
Horden, P. 765
Hormone-market stress hypothesis 135, 145–146n3
Hormones. *See also specific types*
 biological time-varying markers 341–343
Horrell, S. 230, 232–233
Horton, S. 411
Household. *See also* Family
 economics 566
 environment, on poverty–obesity link 329
Household income inequality (HII) index 490
House, J. S. 486
Houser, D. 662
Houweling, T. A. 258
Hryshko, D. 501
Hsiang, S. M. 61
Hsin, A. 638
Huang, W. 507
Huang, Y. 284
Hübler, O. 503, 506, 507
Huizink, A. 342
Human capital. *See also specific topics*
 childhood nutrition investment 412–415
 weight, native populations 200–201
Hyperbolic discounting 585
Hypertension
 birthweight, low 624
 economic development 461–464, 463f
 measurement, field 461–462, 478n1
Hypertensive, percent, body mass index 475f, 476
Hypothalamic-pituitary-adrenal (HPA) axis, stress 487

Ichino, A. 339
Ill-health insecurity 591
Imbens, G. 109, 116, 119
Imperium Romanum 71–72, 91nn3–4
Income 544–545. *See also specific topics*
 vs. biological measures 33–34
 distribution, health and mortality 485–486
 effects 55–56
 height 39–41, 40f
 measurement, developing countries 672, 684n5
 obesity 584
 overweight and obesity 443 (*See also* Obesity; Overweight and obesity)
 trends, long-run 152
 wealth and 545
 weight, body 156–157
 weight, body, and food intake 152
Income–height relationship, African enigma 673–680
 catch-up growth 678–680, 679f, 680f, 684nn12–15
 children 673–674, 674f
 microlevel 671–673, 672t
 women and children
  vs. GDP per capita, African countries 674, 675f
  vs. GDP per capita, non-African countries 674, 675f
  multivariate regression 675–678, 678t, 684n11
  non-African countries 675, 677f
  without Sahel countries 674–675, 676f, 684nn8–10
Income inequality
 antebellum puzzle 758–760
 body mass index, U.S. 490
 cardiovascular disease 490

health and mortality 486
obesity 485–498, 490–491 (*See also* Obesity and income inequality)
sedentary lifestyle 490
weight status 490–491
Income inequality, child health
family life and relationships 254–255
high-income countries 248–251, 249f, 250f
low- and middle-income countries 251–252
social gradients 252–253
Income, obesity 167–171
adult 169–170
causal effects 170–171
children 168–169
endogeneity and measurement issues 167–168
income insecurity 591
Indian Ocean Tsunami (Indonesia, 2004) 61
Individualism, methodological 584
Industrialization, on height
declines 755–757, 756f
global 282–283
Inequality. *See also specific types*
definition 246
gender 81–82, 96nn42–44, 235–236
height 179–189 (*See also* Height inequality)
income (*See* Income inequality)
socioeconomic, children's health 244–259 (*See also* Children's health, socioeconomic inequality)
Inequality traps 422–423
Infant mortality. *See* Mortality, infant
Inflammation
body mass index 477, 477f
economic development 473–475, 474f
Inflammation markers
body mass index 477, 477f
C-reactive protein 468, 473–475, 474f
obesity epidemic 475
Influenza pandemic (1918) 60, 65n10
Institutions, height inequality 188
Instrumental variables. *See also specific variables*
econometrics 114–118, 127–128nn4–8
regressions 671, 683n2
Insulin 134
Insulin resistance 134
Intake, nutrient. *See also specific types*
age of menarche 418, 425n13
productivity 417–418
Integrated Child Development Services (ICDS) 447
Intent-to-treat-type effect 126
Intrauterine growth restriction (IUGR) 272
Iodine fortification, maternal 411
Iron deficiency, productivity 418
Iron supplementation, infant and maternal mortality 411
Italy
1700-1850 777t, 778–780, 779f, 780f
height, long-run 775, 776f
Italy, North
1850-1980 781f, 782
GDP per capita 790
height, historical estimates 784–785
Izquierdo, C. 197

Japan, anthropometrics 693–706. *See also* Anthropometrics, East Asia
Japan, anthropometrics, post-World War II 699–705
adolescents, 1955-2005 701, 702t
adults, 2000 701–703, 703t
children, 1985-2005 700t, 701
data sources 699
data stratification 699
protein, calorie, and fat consumption 703–705, 704t
Japan, anthropometrics, pre-World War II 696–697
high imperialism era 696–697
militia recruits 696–697
Jayachandran, S. 62
Jee, H. 135–136
Jeffrey, R. W. 571
Job promotion discrimination 318, 321
Job security 592t
Johansson, E. 321, 530t, 537
Johar, M. 530t–531t, 535, 537–538
Johnson, M. J. 743
Johnson, S. 420
Johnston, D. W. 547, 553
Jolliffe, D. 328

Jones, R. 95n29
Just-identified system 115, 127n4

Kaestner, R. 117
Kagel, J. 657
Kahn, H. S. 490
Kalemli-Ozcan, S. 59
Kandasamy, N. 343, 656
Kantor, S. 742
Katan, M. B. 345
Katayama, H. 530t–531t, 535, 537–538
Katz, L. 759
Kawachi, I. 488–489
Kayla, M. A. 660–661
Kebede, B. 672, 683–684n4
Kelly, I. 126
Kendler, K. S. 358n32
Kenworthy, L. 595–596
Kerr, D. A. 202
Khanam, R. 328
Kiecolt-Glaser, J. K. 571
Kimura, M. 698
King-Casas, B. 659, 660
King, M. H. 39
Kinsey, W. 409
Kirsch, P. 661
Kishida, K. T. 656–657
Kitchens, C. 742
Knaul, F. M. 418, 425n14
Knoch, D. 654, 655
Kochanska, G. 349
Koepke, N. 71, 76, 82, 93n18, 227, 279–280, 279f
Kolsteren, P. W. V. J. 198
Komlos, J. 40, 139, 182, 182f, 186, 188, 212, 282–283, 292n1, 301, 306, 321, 508, 757–760, 785
Köpke, N. 186
Korea, anthropometric history 693–706. *See also* Anthropometrics, East Asia
Korea, anthropometrics, pre-World War II 696, 698–699
  late 1800s 698–699
  militia recruits 696, 698–699
Korenman, S. 525t, 577n10
Kortt, M. 531t
Koscik, T. R. 660
Kosfeld, M. 661
Koszegi, B. 174
Koupil, I. 328–329
Krajbich, I. 660
Kristof, N. 339
Kriwy, P. 188, 508
Krueger, F. 659
Kudmatsu, M. 61
Kuh, D. 327
Kuhnen, C. M. 345
Kuhn, P. 504
Kunst, A. E. 258
Kuznets, S. 752–753, 759

Lab-on-a-chip devices 48
Labor market
  height bias, global 281
  obesity and earnings 318–321
Labor security 592t
Lactose intolerance, height 77–78, 89, 94n66
LaFave, D. 416
Lakdawalla, D. 159, 164, 166, 169, 171, 572, 573
Land per capita
  biological standard of living 78–79, 95nn28–30
  height trajectory, Europe, 8th century BCE to 18th century CE 87t, 88, 98–99n56
Laron syndrome 273
Latin America 710–723. *See also specific countries*
  contemporary 718–722
  economic development 713–718
    Argentina 716–717
    Brazil 717–718
    Colombia 717
    Guatemala 718
    Mexico 715–716
  epidemics and demographic collapse, 16th century 712–713
  inequality studies 710
  obesity, Hispanic immigrants to U.S. 719–720
  pre-Columbian era 711–713
  themes and logic 710
Lauderdale, B. E. 508
Lauharatanahirun, N. 662
Lawton, E. L. 267

Leadership, tall people 515
Lee, S. 353
Lee, W.-S. 322, 515
Lee, Y. K. 446
Left dorsolateral prefrontal cortex (DLPFC) 655–656
Leg growth 293n4
Leg length, children, later disease 613–614
Legumes 93–94n21
Lehrer, S. F. 323, 346, 351, 353, 354
Leibenstein, H. A. 415
Leibtag, C. S. 328
Leigh, A. 531t
Lemieux, T. 119
Leptin 135
Lew, E. A. 152–153
Lhila, A. 117
Life cycle framework, growth faltering, first 1000 days 11–14, 12f
Life expectancy at birth 35, 91n6
  GDP per capita 456, 457f
  height, adult male, 1980s Europe 768, 769t–770t, 772f
Life expectancy at birth, U.S. racial differences
  2011 731, 732t
  blacks
    1900-1902, data issues 734–735
    improvement 741–744
  long-run trends 736, 737f, 738t
Life expectancy improvement, U.S. blacks 741–744
  disease eradication, in South 742
  earnings and educational attainment 743–744
  Great Society programs 742, 744
  income and mortality 742
  infant mortality 744
  malaria control 742
  migration out of South 742–743
  urban mortality penalty 742
Life satisfaction equation 505
Life tables 34–36
  cohort 34
  period 34–35
Lillard, D. R. 527t
Limited information maximum likelihood (LIML) 115
Lin, C.-Y.C. 61
Lindeboom, M. 322–323
Lindgren, B. 577n5
Lindqvist, E. 516
Linnemayr, S. 414
Liu, F. 572
Liu, H. 441–442
Lleras-Muney, A. 55–56, 743–744
Llobrera, J. 328
Local average treatment effect (LATE) 117
Logan, E. S. 327
Lorenz, T. M. 653
Low birthweight. *See* Birthweight, low
Lucas, A. M. 60
Lumey, L. H. 284
Lundborg, P. 322–323, 513, 531t, 535, 539, 577n5, 662
Lusk, J. 328
Lutter, C. K. 414

Macroeconomics. *See also specific topics*
  height inequality 183–185, 183f
Macrosimulation models, nutrition investment 419–420
Macrosomia, fetal 641–642
Maddison, A. 35
Maestripieri, D. 340, 341–342
Majumder, A. 532t, 535
Malani, A. 59–60
Malanima, P. 783
Malina, R. M. 203
Malnutrition. *See also* Nutrition; Undernutrition
  age at menarche 222
  height 39
  obesity with (*See* Malnutrition, double burden)
  policy implications 445–446
Malnutrition, childhood. *See also specific topics*
  health outcomes 309–310
  prevalence 438, 438f
  prevalence, preschool 298–299
Malnutrition, double burden 434–448
  causes 435–436
  challenges 436
  consequences 435–436

Malnutrition, double burden (*Cont.*)
  definition 434
  determinants
    overnutrition 442–444
    undernutrition 441–442
  epidemiology 435
  household 435, 440
  individual 435, 437
  measuring 436–437
  policy implications 445–448
  population/group level 435
  prevalence 437–440, 438f, 439f, 448n1
  rise 444–445
  synonyms 434
  United States 435
Malnutrition duality 720
Malthusian trap 98n56
Malthus, T. 59
Mamabolo, R. L. 673
Manning, J. T. 340
Manski, C. 352
Margo, R. 418, 759
Marital status, birthweight 625
Market failures, childhood obesity 573–575
Market integration
  heights, global 282–283
  native populations, adult weight 201
Market liberal countries 586–588, 589t–591t, 594
Market proximity, native population weight 201
Markowitz, S. 574
Marmot, M. 422
Marriage
  body mass index 570
  success, height inequality 180
Marriage, obesity 323–324, 568–571
  assortative mating 567, 568–569, 576, 576n2
  complementary traits 569–570, 576n3
  conflict 571
  formation 568–570, 576n2
  socioeconomic status 577n10
  spousal concordance by weight 570–571
Martínez-Carrión, J.-M. 187
Martin, H. 157
Martorell, R. 9–10, 435
Marx, Karl 758
Material pathways, children's health 253–254
Maternal factors
  on birthweight
    height and ethnicity 623
    nutrition 625
    social position 624–625
  on poverty–obesity link 328
Mating, assortative 567, 568–569, 576, 576n2
Matsa, D. 117, 164
Maya civilization 711–713
Mazumdar, D. 415
Mazzocchi, M. 547
McCabe, K. 651, 659
McEnvoy, B. P. 282
McEvedy, C. 95n29
McKeown, T. 35–36
McKnight, R. 747n21
McLaren, L. 318, 328, 488
McLean, R. A. 318, 531t, 536
Mean-differencing 112–113, 127n1
Measurement error 113
Meat
  height, adult male, 1980s
      Europe 769t–770t, 770
  slave diets 218–220, 220t
Medical care 81, 96nn38–41
Medications, growth and maturation 273
Mediterranean. *See also specific topics*
  anthropometric history 765–793 (*See also* Anthropometrics, Mediterranean history)
  Europe 93n12
Menarche, age at
  malnutrition 222
  nutrient intake 418, 425n13
  slaves, childbearing and 221–223
Mendelian randomization 25, 346, 357nn20
Meng, X. 58
Menstrual cycle 339–340
Mental disorders, stress 596–597
Metabolic diseases. *See also* Diabetes mellitus type 2
  birthweight, children 614
Metabolism and body weight, fetal/developmental programming 308
Methodological individualism 584
Mexico 721

economic development, 1850-1950 715–716
Meyerhoefer, C. D. 328, 330–331n4
Michael, R. T. 572
Microcredit 446–447
Mid-parental height (MPH) 268
Migliano, A. B. 202–203
Migration
catch-up growth 288
on diet 93n13
war-induced 63
Milanovic, B. 96n41
Milk and dairy products
biological standard of living 77–78, 93–94nn20–26, 93nn20
height, adult male, 1980s Europe 769t–770t, 770
production, proximity to 279–280, 279f
Milk, breast 216
Mind, theory of 650
neural correlates 651
Mirrlees, J. A. 415
Mobile examination center (MEC) 467
Mobley, L. R. 488
Mocan, N. H. 524, 532t
Model life table 746n7
Moffitt, T. E. 349
Monotonicity assumption 117, 127–128n7
Monozygotic twin fixed-effects (MZ-FE), first 1000 days growth, and subsequent life stage outcomes 16–17, 17t
Montgomery, P. 339
Moon, M. 318, 531t, 536
Moradi, A. 184, 288–292, 674–675, 681–682
Moran, J. 170, 324–326, 330n3
Morbidity 36–37
BMI, global trends 296
Moreno-Lázaro, J. 187
Moretti, E. 61
Morgan, S. 696
Morretti, E. 339
Morris, S. 322, 532t
Mortality (death)
child, undernutrition 425n2
heat 61
natural disasters 61
obesity 135
probabilities 35
racial differences, U.S. causes 732, 733f, 739–740, 740f
revealed behavior assumption for cost of 408
slaves, American 216–217, 216t
weight, body 152–153
Mortality, infant
birthweight, low 627
forest fires 62
GDP per capita 56
prehistoric 91n4
racial differences, U.S. 737–739, 738t, 739f
weather, extreme 61–62
Mortality transition 35
"Moving to Opportunity" program 256–257
Mumme, C. 289, 290f, 292
Mummert, A. 277–278, 278f
Mumme, U. 179–180, 184–185
Murasko, J. E. 330n4
Murray, J. 135
Mushkin, S. J. 564

Nanosensory systems 48
Nanotechnology 48
Nash equilibrium 658
Näsi, M. 530t
National Income and Product Account (NIPA) 548
Native populations, adult
data sources 193
definition 193
globalization and development 192
nutrition transition 192
Native populations, adult height 201–204
age estimates 202
analysis 202–203
data (reporting) errors 202
findings 203–204
importance 201
trends, by country 195t–196t
Native populations, adult weight 193–201
ambiguous results 197–198
body mass index 193
community 201
market integration and dietary change 201
nutrition transition 193–197
vs. rest of population 198–200, 199t

Native populations, adult weight (*Cont.*)
  trends, by country 195t–196t
  wealth, human capital, and socioeconomic status 200–201
Native populations, U.S., biological well-being 44–45
Natural disasters
  fertility 60
  mortality 60
Natural wealth 549
Navarrete Briones, C. 200
Negative results 753
Neolithic era 71
Net nutritional status. *See* Biological standard of living (BLS)
Net worth 545. *See also* Wealth
Neumayer, E. 61
Neuroeconomics 650–663
  brain mapping 653
  chemical manipulations 656–657
  definition 650
  electroencephalography 654–655
  functional magnetic resonance imaging 652–654
  fundamentals 650–651
  institutional design 651
  methods 651–652
  nonhuman studies 657
  preferences, source 651
  transcranial magnetic stimulation 655–656
Neuroeconomics, trust and betrayal 657–662
  healthy populations and oxytocin 661–662
  principles and studies 657–659
  special populations 660–661
  why not trust? 660–662
  why trust? 659
Never-takers 116
Newborn length, mother's height 235–237
Newton, T. L. 571
Nghiem, H. S. 328
Niemesh, G. 743
Nigerian Civil War 62–63
Nobles, J. 61
Noncommunicable diseases 454–455
North Korea, anthropometrics, post–World War II 699–705
  adolescents, 1955-2005 701, 702t
  adults, 2000 701–703, 703t
  children, 1985-2005 700t, 701
  data sources 699
  data stratification 699
  protein, calorie, and fat consumption 703–705, 704t
Norton, E. C. 319, 320, 322, 323, 330n4, 527t, 529t, 530t, 532t, 535, 537
Nuclear weapons testing, prenatal exposure 65n12
Nutrient intake. *See also specific nutrients*
  height 418
  iron 418
  measures 465–466
Nutrition. *See also* Undernutrition
  adolescent growth spurt requirements 37, 38f
  height, wages and 513
  lack (*See* Malnutrition; *specific types and consequences*)
  maternal, birthweight 625
  net (*See* Biological standard of living (BLS))
Nutritional demands
  disease 755
  work 755
Nutritional status
  height 37–41, 38f, 40f
  net (*See* Biological standard of living (BLS))
Nutritional supplements, growth faltering, first 1000 days
  other 21t, 22
  protein-dense 21–22
Nutrition investment 405–426
  birthweight, low 407–411 (*See also* Birthweight, low)
  childhood, subsequent human capital 412–415
  depression, post-partum 411–412
  dynamic complementarities 406
  fetal origins hypothesis 410–411
  folate 411
  health inequality 420–424
  illness reduction 407
  inequality traps 422–423
  infant and child mortality 407

iodine 411
iron 411
macroeconomic and cross-country evidence 419–424
Fogel's work 419, 425n12
health inequity 420–424
identification and causal inference 419–420
macrosimulation models 419–420
productivity 405, 424n1
height 415–418
iron deficiency 418
nutrient intake 417–418
self-productivity 406
weight 417
skills, cognitive and noncognitive 407
stunting, age patterns 412–413
value of a statistical life 408, 425n4
Nutrition transition
native populations 192
native populations, adult weight 193–197
overnutrition 442–443
Nystedt, P. 531t, 577n5

Obesity 157–175. *See also* Body mass index (BMI); Overweight and obesity; *specific topics*
age and 567
age and, wealth 551–554, 554f
assortative mating 567, 568–569, 576, 576n2
calories 133–134
causes and consequences, estimation strategies 109–128 (*See also* Econometrics)
cigarette consumption 173–175
costs, direct and indirect 521
definition 157, 437
economic issue 152
epidemic 565, 576n1
epidemic, food industry 577n8
exercise 166–167
food prices 158–165 (*See also* Food prices, obesity)
food processing technology, and self-control 165–166
fundamentals 133–135
genetics and BMI 532t, 537
health 135–136, 144
Hispanic immigrants to U.S. 719–720
identification 536–537
income 167–171 (*See also* Income, obesity)
income insecurity, unionization 591
insulin and insulin resistance 134
with malnutrition (*See* Malnutrition, double burden)
marital states and transitions 570
measurement 135, 157–158, 437
prevalence 296, 492, 521
adult 438, 439f
developed countries 317
global 442
productivity 538
rationality, breakdown 584–585
risks 296
smoking initiation, adolescents 574
social interactions 171–173
social science 583–584
socioeconomic status, marriage 577n10
stress 587–588
trends, economic reasons 543
trends, noneconomic reasons 543
Obesity and employment
discrimination, Sweden 522
males *vs.* females 522
Obesity and family economics 564–577
assortative mating 567, 568–569, 576, 576n2
children 571–575 (*See also* Children's obesity, family economics)
family economics 565
future directions 575–576
health capital of families 565–568
health promotion opportunity costs 564
marital unions 568–571 (*See also* Marriage, obesity)
Obesity and income inequality 485–498, 490–491
concavity-induced income effect 489
empirical findings, OECD countries 491–497 (*See also* Obesity and income inequality, OECD countries)
empirical findings, United States 490–491
pathways
ecological effect 488–490
policy 489

Obesity and income inequality (*Cont.*)
social cohesion (capital) 488–489
stress 486–488, 487f
structural 488
relative income hypothesis 486
Obesity and income inequality, OECD countries 491–497
data 492, 493t
Gini index
2002-2010 493, 495f
2010 492, 494f
linear regressions
of changes, by gender, 2002-2010 495–496, 497t
by gender 493–494, 496t
obesity prevalence 492
Pickett's study 491
positive correlations 491
Su's study 491–492
variation, by country and over time 492
Obesity and poverty, developed countries 317–331
bidirectional causality 318
obesity on poverty 318–324
discrimination 318
educational attainment 323
employment 322–323
labor market earnings 318–321
marriage 323–324
wage discrimination 321
poverty on obesity 324–329
dietary patterns and body weight perceptions 327–328
household environment 329
income shocks and SES variation 324–327
maternal factors 328
prevalence 317
Obesity and wages 521–540
body mass index
biological family member 537
genetics and 532t, 537
discrimination 525t, 527t–531t, 538–539
empirical model and results 523–524, 525t–534t, 535
empirical *vs.* causal relationship 522
employment discrimination, Sweden 522
explanations 522–523
face 535
females 522, 524, 525t–533t, 535
fixed effects 524, 525t–527t, 529t–534t, 535, 537, 540n2
gender differences, explanation 531t, 533t, 535–536
instrumental variables 524, 525t–534t, 535, 536, 540n2
instrumental variables, endogeneity 530t, 537
labor supply and demand 523
males 522, 524, 525t–534t, 535–536
obesity identification 536–537
"portly banker" effect 536
prejudice or preferences 523
productivity 538
relationship *vs.* causality 523–524
unobserved heterogeneity and simultaneity 524
wage distribution 530t–531t, 537–538
weight measures 536–537 (*See also* Body mass index (BMI))
Obesity and wealth 543–561
BMI increase
GDP 544, 544f
reasons 543
country-level data, theoretical issues 546–547
cross-national relationship 548–552 (*See also* Wealth, weight and, national-level)
income 544–545
literature review 547–548
person/individual-level data, theoretical issues 544–546
person/individual-level relationship 551–560
10-year age group 551–554, 554f
descriptive statistics 556, 557t
gender 554–556, 555f
males *vs.* female 556–560, 558t, 559t
net worth as DV; weight and BMI as IV 556–560, 558t
statistical validity 554–556, 555f
weight and BMI as DV; net worth as IV 556–560, 559t

wealth (net worth) 545
Obesity and welfare regimes 583–599
actual choice behavior and bounded rationality 584–585
as adaptation, reasonable 584
consumer behavior theory 584
discount rate 585
economic equality 589t–590t
economic freedom index 597–598
economic security/insecurity 588–591, 589t–590t
employment security 592t
eudomaneia 598
fast-food exposure 598
fast-food shock 585
food insecurity 596
government expenditure 586
ill-health insecurity 591
income studies 584
job security 592t
knowledge of obesity 584
labor security 592t
market liberal countries 586–588, 589t–591t, 594
methodological individualism 584
regret costs of eating and drinking 585
representation security 591–593, 592t
skill security 592t
social science 583–584
sound money 598
stress 587–588
stress and mental disorders 596–597
studies, original 586–595, 589t–590t, 592t–593t
studies, replication and further investigation 595–598
Sweden 594
time-inconsistency and hyperbolic discounting 585
unionization and income insecurity 591
United States 594
welfare states 586
work security 591, 592t
Obesity, childhood
on adult health 605
causes 567
Obesity, discrimination
cosmetic 318, 320
job promotion 318, 321
statistical 318, 320–321
Obesity research
randomization 109
self-selection problem 109, 110
Obesogenic environments 310
Occupational classification system 146n4
Offer, A. 7, 587
Olson, C. M. 327
Organization for Economic Cooperation and Development (OECD) countries 485, 498n1
obesity and income inequality 485–498 (*See also* Obesity and income inequality, OECD countries)
Osberg security index 591
Osmani, S. 235–236
Osmond, C. 410
Oster, E. 339
Overnutrition. *See also* Body mass index (BMI); Obesity; Overweight and obesity
definition 485
determinants 442–444
with malnutrition (*See* Malnutrition, double burden)
prenatal, on adult obesity risk 308
Overpopulation 95n28
Overweight. *See also* Obesity
adult, birthweight 611–612
economic prosperity 461
education 459–461, 460f
percent 459, 460f
smoking initiation, adolescents 574
Overweight and obesity
definition and measurement 437
income 443
social stigma 317
Overweight and obesity, childhood 299
health outcomes 309–310
prevalence 438, 438f
Overweight and obesity, global trends 301–309
childhood 299
fat mass, subcutaneous 305–306
health impact 306–307

Overweight and obesity, global trends (*Cont.*)
health impact, cross-generational 307–309
intrauterine and early postnatal risk factors 307–308
morbidity and mortality risk 296
pattern, general 302–303
prevalence 296, 300
reasons, economic 543
reasons, noneconomic 543
time trends 301–302
waist circumference 305–306
Oxley, D. 230, 232–233
Oxytocin
amygdala, and trust 661–662
betrayal aversion 661–662
trust 656
trust, healthy populations 661–662
Özumcur, S. 778

Pace, N. 319–320
Pagan, J. A. 533t, 536
Page, L. B. 204
Pak, S. 188
Palma, N. 779
Palynology 711
Pamuk, S. 778
Panel data
definition 111
fixed effects 111–114
Panel Study of Income Dynamics (PSID) 547
Paracingulate cortex (PcP) 659
Paradoxical malnutrition. *See* Malnutrition, double burden
Parallel trends assumption 121
Paraponaris, A. 322
Parity, maternal, birthweight 624
Parsons, D. O. 566
Patel, A. M. 202
Paxson, C. 59, 417, 502, 503, 513
Pearce, M. J. 568
Pearson, M. 339–340, 355n4
Pérez-Cueto, F. J. A. 198
Performance measures, physical 456
Perkins, J. M. 185
Persecution. *See* War/persecution
Persico, N. 503–504, 509, 512, 514
Persson, M. 327
Peru 713, 718, 721, 722
Pfeifer, C. 513
Philipson, T. 159, 164, 166, 169, 171, 572
Physical capacity, height, wages and 513
Physical health measures 455
Physical performance measures 456
Pickett, K. E. 249–251, 249f, 250f, 256, 422, 486, 491, 498
Pierre-Louis, J. N. 673
Piopiunik, M. 284
Piperata, B. 197, 204
Pischke, J. S. 111, 115
Plague
bubonic 59
height trajectory, Europe, 8th century BCE to 18th century CE 87t, 88
Pleiotrophy 357n23
Plümper, T. 61
Point-of-care monitors 468
Policy pathway, obesity and income inequality 489
Politics, height inequality 188
Pollution 62
Polygenic scores 348
Population stratification 346
Portable monitors 468
Porte, C. 58
"Portly banker" effect 536
Portugal
1700-1850 777t, 778–780, 779f, 780f
1850-1980 781f, 782
GDP per capita 790
height
historical estimates 786–787
long-run 775, 776f
Posner, R. A. 572
Post-partum depression 411–412
Poverty
definition, Sen's 421
undernutrition 442
Poverty, obesity on, developed countries 318–324
discrimination 318
educational attainment 323
employment 322–323
labor market earnings 318–321
marriage 323–324

wage discrimination 321
Poverty, on obesity 324–329
dietary patterns and body weight perceptions 327–328
household environment 329
income shocks and SES variation 324–327
maternal factors 328
Powell, L. M. 161–162, 320, 323, 328, 530t
Prader-Willi syndrome 272–273
Pradhan, M. 681
Pre-Columbian era, Latin America 711–713
Preece-Baines model 222
Prehistory 97n51
Prenatal exposures, birthweight 632
Prentice, A. M. 22, 410, 680
Preston, S. H. 735, 736, 736f, 746nn10–11
Preterm birth, etiology 636
Price, J. A. 167
Prices
food (*See* Food prices)
trends, long-run 152
Produced wealth 549
Productivity
body mass index 417
height 415–418
height inequality 180
iron deficiency 418
nutrition investment 405, 415–418, 424n1
obesity 538
self-productivity 406
Productivity, future
assumed discount rate 408–409
effect size 409
literatures, translations between 409
Programming
biological 606
fetal/developmental, metabolism and body weight 308
PROGRESA 447, 722
Proportional spillovers 156
Protein 761nn7–8
animal, male adult height, 1980s Europe 769t–770t, 770
anthropometrics, East Asia post–World War II 703–705, 704t
growth velocity 608
proximity, on production 279–280, 279f
Psychosocial factors
children's health 253–254
health status and socioeconomic status 486
Puberty
adolescent growth spurt 37, 38f, 230–233, 231f, 232f
timing and tempo 269
Pudrovska, T. 327
Puerto Rico 721
Purcell, N. 765
Puzzello, L. 342

Qaim, M. 440
Qian, N. 58
Qi, Y. 121
Quality-adjusted life years (QALY) 36
Quantile regression (QR) model 124, 125
Quetelet, A. 623
Quintana-Domeque, C. 169, 187, 507, 508, 528t, 538, 669–671

Race and ethnicity
birthweight and human capital 639–640
height inequality 185–186
maternal, birthweight 623
Race, United States 730–747
cancer survival 732, 733t
chronic conditions 739–741, 741f
contemporary disparities, health 731–732, 732t, 733f, 733t
death, causes 732, 733f, 739–740, 740f
environmental factors 730
future research 744–745
historical data, comparability issues 732–736
infant mortality, long-run trends 737–739, 738t, 739f
life expectancies at birth, 2011 731, 732t
life expectancies at birth, long-run trends 736, 737f, 738t
life expectancy improvement, blacks
disease eradication in South 742
earnings and educational attainment 743–744
Great Society programs 742, 744
income and mortality 742
infant mortality 744

Race, United States (*Cont.*)
malaria control 742
migration out of South 742–743
urban mortality penalty 742
racial inequality history 730
Ramadan-induced fasting, birthweight and human capital 635
Ranasinghe, P. 282, 508
Random-effects model 127n2
Randomized controlled trial (RCT) 109
Räsänen, P. 530t
Rashad, I. 167
Rates of return, American slaves 218–221, 220t
Rationality, breakdown, obesity 584–585
Rauscher, E. 351, 641
Rawlings, S. B. 236–237
Recessions, human biology and 54–57
Rees, D. I. 319, 533t, 535
Rees, R. 223
Refugees 63
Register, C. A. 533t
Regression discontinuity design (RDD) 118–120, 128nn9–10
Regret costs, eating and drinking 585
Reif, J. 156
Reis, J. 779
Relationships, children's health 254–255
Relative income hypothesis 486
Remittances, obesity 443
Representation security 591–593, 592t
Restrepto, B. 638
Revealed behavior assumption, cost of mortality 408
Rhoads, J. G. 204
Richman, A. 327
Rick, A. M. 571
Rietveld, C. A. 348, 358n30, 514
Riley, C. 35, 514
Rivera, J. A. 411
Robinson, J. J. 638
Rockoff, J. 339
Roederer, J. G. 622
Roemling, C. 440
Roettger, M. 351
Rogol, A. D. 267, 269, 270
Roman Empire. *See Imperium Romanum*
Roman impact
biological standard of living 80–81, 95–96nn33–37
height trajectory, Europe, 8th century BCE to 18th century CE 87t, 88, 98n54
Rooth, D. 531t
Roseboom, T. J. 57
Rose, J. 47, 71
Rosenbluth, F. 182, 278–279
Rosenquist, J. N. 349, 350, 352, 353
Rosenzweig, M. R. 17, 17t, 20, 525t
Rossin-Slater, M. 324
Rossiter, P. 78
Rubin, D. 109
Rubin, H. 115
Ruel, M. 406, 440
Ruhm, C. 55, 116, 327, 528t, 537
Rural location, height inequality 187
Rural–urban differences, East Asia anthropometrics, 2000 698, 698t, 699
Rutter, M. 349
Rwandan genocide (1994) 63

Sabia, J. J. 319, 533t, 535
Saffer, H. 117, 162–163, 598
Sahn, D. E. 417, 681
Saliba, B. 322
Sample selectivity, heights, global 280–281
Sanitary conditions 81, 96nn38–41
Sargent, J. D. 533t
Satisfaction function 505
Saudino, K .J. 358n32
Savage, M. O. 267
Scarring, African enigma 669–671
Schady, N. 56
Schanzenbach, D. 118–119
Schick, A. 504
Schipper, B. C. 339–340, 355n4
Schooling. *See* Educational attainment
Schott, W. 25
Schroeter, C. 328
Schultz, T. P. 506
Schwekendiek, D. 188, 698–699
Sedentary lifestyle
income inequality, U.S. 490
obesity 443
Selection, African enigma 669–671
Selection bias 110, 125–126, 127

gene-environment interactions 349–350, 358n29
Self-confidence, tall people 515
Self-control, food processing technology 165–166
Self-productivity 406
Self-reports 455
Self-selection problem 109, 110
Sen, A. 57, 235–236, 421
Serbia, 1850-1980 781f, 782
Settle, J. E. 351
Severe adult respiratory syndrome (SARS) epidemic 59–60
Sex hormones 341–343
Shaikh, A. 353
Shanahan, M. J. 351
Shapiro, J. M. 165, 572
Shekar, M. 446
Sheppard, Z. A. 672–673
Shimokawa, S. 534t
Short-and-plump syndrome. *See* Malnutrition, double burden
Short stature
  discrimination 515–516
  familial 271
  undernutrition, childhood 604, 605f
Sibling comparison studies, birthweight and human capital 634–635
Simeonova, E. 324
Simon, K. 170, 324–326, 330n3
Single-nucleotide polymorphisms (SNPs) 344
  Mediterraneans 773–775, 775t, 792nn7–12
Singulate mean 221–222
Skeletal remains
  biological well-being 45–47, 71–72
  height 72–73, 91–92nn5–9
Skill security 592t
Skinfold thickness, global trends 305–306
Slaves, American, biological well-being 41–42
Slaves, American, heights 210–224
  age at menarche and childbearing 221–223
  biology 210
  catch-up growth 210, 212–215, 213t–214t
  child 212–217, 213t–214t
  data sources 211–212, 212t
  future research 223–224
  genes 210–211
  height-by-age patterns 212–218, 213t–214t
  mortality rates 216–217, 216t
  rates of return 218–221, 220t
Slot, B. 694
Smith, A. 415, 650, 751, 752
Smith, P. K. 321, 435
Smith, T. 596
Smoking initiation, overweight adolescents 574
Smyth, R. 506–507
Sobal, J. 317–318
Social class. *See* Socioeconomic status (SES)
Social cohesion (capital) pathway, obesity and income inequality 488–489
Social interactions
  endogenous 171–172
  obesity 171–173
  weight, body 155–156
Social science, obesity 583–584
Social Security Benefits Notch 325–326, 330n3
Socioeconomic status (SES)
  birthweight and human capital 640
  children's health 244–259 (*See also* Children's health, socioeconomic inequality)
  diet 93n13
  food prices and obesity 165
  height inequality 180–182, 181f, 181t, 185
  maternal, birthweight 624–625
  obesity, via marriage 577n10
  psychosocial factors 486
  weight, native populations 200–201
Socioemotional skills 425n3
Sohn, K. 503, 515, 516
Sojourner, A. J. 642
Sorlie, P. D. 743
Sosa-Rubi, S. 201
Sound money 598
South Korea, anthropometrics, post–World War II 699–705
  adolescents, 1955-2005 701, 702t
  adults, 2000 701–703, 703t
  children, 1985-2005 700t, 701
  data sources 699
  data stratification 699
  protein, calorie, and fat consumption 703–705, 704t

Spain
1700-1850 777t, 778–780, 779f, 780f
1850-1980 781f, 782
GDP per capita 790
height
historical estimates 787
long-run 775, 776f
Spears, D. 513
Specter, S. E. 328
Spousal concordance, by weight 570–571
Sripada, C. 660
Stable unit treatment value assumption (SUTVA) 110
Staiger, D. 115
Standard deviation score (SDS)
BMI 268, 269–270
Standard deviation scores (SDS) 230
Standardized Occupational Classification system 146n4
Standard of living, biological. *See* Biological standard of living (BLS)
Statistical discrimination 318, 320–321
Stature. *See* Height
Status differentiation, children's health 255–257
Stearns, S. C. 319, 320, 322, 529t
Steckel, R. H. 3–4, 40, 47, 71, 186, 210, 213t–214t, 215, 216, 216t, 227, 418, 504, 508, 681, 693
Stein, A. D. 440
Stenberg, A. 662
Stereotype threat 256
Stern, N. 415
Stevens, A. H. 55
Stevens, G. 569
Stewart, H. 328
Stimulation, child, cognitive improvements 414–415
Stock, J. 115, 202–203
Stoddard, P. 193, 198, 201
Strauss, J. 417, 503, 513
Stress
chronic, epigenetics and child health 257
chronic, obesity 487–488, 487f
deprivation and health consequences 422
fat accumulation 134–135
health 486–487
hypothalamic-pituitary-adrenal axis 487
mental disorders 596–597
obesity 587–588
obesity and income inequality 486–488, 487f
Stress hormones 135, 145–146n3. *See also specific types*
fat accumulation 134–135
Stressors, birthweight 633
Strict exogeneity 112–113, 127n2
Stroke
birthweight, low 607
height 609
obesity, childhood 605
Structural pathway, obesity and income inequality 488
Stunkard, A. J. 317–318
Stunting
at 24 months, adult life cycle stage outcomes 18–20, 19t
birthweight, low 410
childhood, prevalence 438, 438f
definition and measurement 437
development consequences 414
GDP 694
interventions, preventive 414
nutrition
age patterns 412–413
childhood undernutrition 604, 605f
Subramanian, S. V. 488–489
Substitution effects 55–56
Su, D. 491
Summers, R. 40
Sunder, M. 761nn10–11
Supplemental Nutrition Assistance Program 330–331n4

Takaishi, M. 228, 229f
Tall adults, African enigma
infant mortality, high 669, 670f
low incomes 669, 670f
Tall adults, interpersonal dominance 515
Tanner, J. M. 37, 39–40, 40f, 215, 222, 228, 229f
Tao, H.-L. 515
Target height (TH) 267–268, 270
Taubman, P. 344
Tauras, J. 574

Technological change, childhood obesity 572–573
Technophysio evolution, female 233–234
Tekin, E. 158, 524, 532t, 534t, 536, 537
Telomere length, childhood social disadvantage 257
Temperature, height trajectory, 8th century BCE to 18th century CE Europe 87t, 89
Teotihuacán, pre-Columbian 711–712
Testosterone 341–343, 356n12
  2D:4D ratio 340, 343, 355–356n6
  behavioral endocrinology 338
The, N. S. 571
Theory of mind 650, 651
Thermal inversion 62, 65n11
Thomas, D. 416, 503, 513
Thomasson, M. A. 738
Thompson, O. 351, 358n35
Three-field crop rotation
  biological standard of living 78
  height trajectory, Europe, 8th century BCE to 18th century CE 87t, 89, 99n57
Thrifty-gene hypothesis 134, 145n2, 236
Thronton, R. 339
Time-inconsistency 585
Time-varying biomarkers 338
  biological (*See* Biological time-varying markers)
Tobias, P. V. 203
Toivanen, P. 328–329
Tomlin, D. 659
Torche, F. 410
Total cholesterol, body mass index 476, 477f
Toxicants, birthweight 633
Traill, W. B. 547
Tranel, D. 660
Transcranial magnetic stimulation (TMS) 655–656
Transportation improvements, antebellum puzzle 758, 760
Treatment effect 110
  average 110–111
  average, among treated 110–111
  heterogeneous 123–126
Treiman, D. J. 187
Tricomi, E. 653
Troesken, W. 742
Trust and betrayal, neuroeconomics 657–662
  oxytocin, healthy populations 661–662
  principles and studies 657–659
  special populations 660–661
  why not trust? 660–662
  why trust? 659
Trust game 657–658
Trust, oxytocin 656, 661–662
Trust studies, types 658–659
Tsimane' 193, 195t, 197, 198, 200, 200t, 202, 204, 720
Tulchinsky, T. 81
Turan, B. 59
Turchin, M. 774
Turkey
  1850-1980 781f, 782–783
  GDP per capita 790
  height
    historical estimates 787–788
    long-run 775–776, 776f
Twin fixed-effects (FE)
  birthweight and human capital
    models 636–637
    research 634–635
  dizygotic 28n3
  monozygotic, first 1000 days, subsequent life outcomes 16–17, 17t
2D:4D ratio 340, 343, 355–356n6
2SLS estimator 115, 127n7, 395
  reverse 127n7
Tyner, W. 328
Type 2 diabetes. *See* Diabetes mellitus type 2

Ulijaszek, S. J. 202
Umberson, D. 571, 577n7
Undernutrition
  determinants 441–442
  growth paths 1, 2f
  intervention effects 446–447
  policy implications 445–446
  prenatal, adult obesity risk 308
Underweight, childhood
  definition and measurement 437
  health outcomes 309–310
  prevalence 438, 438f
  prevalence, preschool 298–299

UNICEF index of child well-being, rich countries 249–251, 249f, 250f
Uninformed demand, food consumption 573–574
Unionization, income insecurity, obesity 591
United States. *See also specific topics*
race 730–747 (*See also* Race, United States)
Urban dividend 673, 684n6
Urbanization
antebellum puzzle 758, 760
biological standard of living 79, 95n31
height
European trajectory, 8th century BCE to 18th century CE 87–88, 87t, 98n53
global 282, 283–284
inequality 187
obesity 443
Uruguay 722

Vainiomäki, J. 512, 516
Value of a statistical life (VSL) 408, 425n4
van der Klaauw, B. 322–323
Van Ijzendoorn, M. H. 352–353
Van Lange, P. A. M. 662–663
van Poppel, F. 284
Van Zanden, J. L. 184, 290
Varavikova, E. 81
Variation, key independent variables 127
Vecchi, G. 785
Ventelou, B. 322
Ventral-medial prefrontal cortex (VMPFC) 660
Victora, C. G. 10, 15, 16t, 413
Villermé, Louis R. 3–4
Visscher, P. M. 282
Vogl, T. 416–417, 503
Voigtländer, N. 59
Volland, B. 491
von Hinke Kessler Scholder, S. 514
Voth, H.-J. 59, 761n2
Vuri, D. 319–320

Waaler, H. T. 135, 233, 234f, 458
Wada, R. 158, 534t, 536, 537
Wadsworth, M. 327
Wage-height equation 502–505
basic equation 502–503
four-equation model extension 504–505
Sohn and Hübler modification 503
Thomas and Strauss extension 503
Vogl extension 503
Wages
body fat 158
Europe, real
1700-1850 788–789
1850-1980 789
obesity 521–540 (*See also* Obesity and wages)
discrimination 321
Waist circumference, global trends 305–306
Waite, L. 566
Wang, Y. 304, 329, 488
Ward, P. 697
War/persecution 62–63
biological standard of living 80, 95n32
height trajectory, Europe, 8th century BCE to 18th century CE 87t, 89
Water, doubly labeled 466, 478n2
Weak instruments 115
Wealth
country-level 546
definition 545
functions 545
income and 545
produced *vs.* natural 549
weight 543–561 (*See also* Obesity and wealth)
causality direction 545–546
native populations 200–201
Wealth, weight and, national-level 548–552. *See also* Obesity and wealth
BMI
by country, 2000 549, 550f
top and bottom five countries 549, 549t
BMI change
by country 1995-2005 550, 551t
by country, absolute *vs.* percent change 550–551, 552t
data 548–549, 549t, 550f
produced *vs.* natural wealth 549
Weather, extreme 61–62
Weathering hypothesis, birthweight and human capital 639–640
Weber, B. 653, 662

Wehby, G. 116, 124, 357n24
Weight, body 152–175. *See also* Body mass index (BMI)
  body mass index *vs.* 193
  children, later disease 611–612
  depression, gain in 577n6
  economic development 458–459
  exercising 154, 155–156
  fetal/developmental programming 308
  food prices and obesity 164
  ideal, preferences, health, and 155
  income 156–157
  marital states and transitions 570
  measures 536–537
  mortality 152–153
  native populations, adult 192–201 (*See also* Native populations, adult weight)
  nutrition investment 415–418
  obesity 157–175 (*See also* Obesity)
  perceptions, on poverty–obesity link 328
  prices and income 152, 153
  prices, food 153–154
  social interactions 155–156
  spousal concordance by 570–571
Weight-for-age *z*-scores (WAZ), FTD growth faltering and later life outcomes 15, 16t
Weil, D. N. 420
Weinberger, C. 504
Weiss, T. 762n12
Welfare capitalism, three worlds 586–587
Well-being. *See also specific types*
  aggregate (national) 32–33
  biological measures 32–49 (*See also* Biological measures, well-being)
  biological measures *vs.* income 33–34
  components 32, 33f
  definition 32, 246
  happiness 48
  individual 32
Wells, N. M. 327
West, M. 126
Whitehouse, R. H. 228, 229f
WHO Child Growth Standards 297
Wilde, P. E. 328
Wilkinson, R. G. 249–251, 249f, 250f, 256, 422, 486
Williams, D. R. 486, 533t
Williams, K. 577n7
Williamson, J. 781
Wilson, J. D. 154, 486
Wilson, S. E. 570, 571
Wing, E. 71
Winter, J. 284, 516
Wolbring, T. 526t, 537
Women. *See* Females
Wood, A. 774–775
Wooldridge, J. 112
Work
  effort intensification, antebellum puzzle 757–758
  nutritional demands 755
  security 591, 592t
Worldwide Variation in Human Growth 37
Wranik, T. 501–502
Wright, J. 115
Wu, C. C. 653

Xu, X. 117

Yang, M. 330–331n4
Yogo, M. 115
Young, A. 59, 420, 426n16, 752
Younger, S. D. 681
Yu, I. T. 342

Zagorsky, J. L. 547–548, 553, 560
Zak, P. J. 356n12, 656
Zehetmayer, M. 187, 283
Zethraeus, N. 342
Zhang, J. 17, 20
Zhang, Q. 488
Zhao, Z. 117